The Zohar

by
Rav Shimon bar Yochai
From The Book of Avraham

with
The Sulam Commentary

by
Rav Yehuda Ashlag

The First Ever Unabridged
English Translation with Commentary

Published by
The Kabbalah Centre International Inc.
Dean Rav S. P. Berg Shlita

Edited and Compiled by
Rabbi Michael Berg

Published by
The Kabbalah Centre International Inc.

155 E. 48th St., New York, NY 10017
1062 S. Robertson Blvd., Los Angeles, CA 90035

Director Rav Berg

First Printing 2001
Revised Edition 2003

Printed in USA

ISBN: 1-57189-077-7

With appreciation and gratitude
for providing my Soul this opportunity,
I gladly dedicate,
with endless desire and thankfulness,
the wisdom of Kabbalah.

In loving memory of beloved parents

Bernice Diamond

and

Stuart Sidney Borovay

May their souls rest with eternal peace
and tranquillity in the Light.

Their second loving son,

Jon Darryl Borovay

להורי האהובים
שזכרם יהיה חקוק לנצח בעץ החיים.
כולי אהבה והערכה על ההזדמנות שניתנה לי
להיות חלק בהפצת לימוד הקבלה והזהר בעולם.
שנזכה לגאולה השלמה בקרוב
במהרה בימינו אמן סלה.

לעילוי נשמת
אבי
שמעון בן גורג'
אימי
ברינה בת שמואל
ת.נ.צ.ב.ה.

מנדבת בנם האוהב
יונה בן שמעון
שיזכה לבת זוגו האמיתית בקרוב

APPLYING THE POWER OF THE ZOHAR

The Zohar is a book of great mystical power and wisdom. It is Universally recognized as the definitive work on the Kabbalah – and it is also so Much more.

The Zohar is a wellspring of spiritual energy, a fountainhead of metaphysical power that not only reveals and explains, but literally brings blessing, protection, and well-being into the lives of all those who read or peruse its sacred texts. All that is required is worthy desire, the certainty of a trusting heart, and an open and receptive mind. Unlike other books, including the great spiritual texts of other traditions, The Zohar is written in a kind of code, through which metaphors, parables, and cryptic language at first conceal but ultimately reveal the forces of creation.

As electrical current is concealed in wire and cable before disclosing itself as an illuminated light bulb, the spiritual Light of the Creator is wrapped in allegory and symbolism throughout the Aramaic text of the Zohar. And while many books contain information and knowledge, the Zohar both expresses and embodies spiritual Light. The very letters on its pages have the power to bring spiritual wisdom and positive energy into every area of our lives.

As we visually scan the Aramaic texts and study the accompanying insights that appear in English, spiritual power is summoned from above – and worlds tremble as Light is sent forth in response.

It's primary purpose is not only to help us acquire wisdom, but to draw Light from the Upper Worlds and to bring sanctification into our lives. Indeed, the book itself is the most powerful of all tools for cleansing the soul and connecting to the Light of the Creator. As you open these pages, therefore, do not make understanding in the conventional sense your primary goal.

Although you may not have a knowledge of Aramaic, look first at the Aramaic text before reading the English. Do not be discouraged by difficulties with comprehension. Instead, open your heart to the spiritual transformation the Zohar is offering you.

Ultimately, the Zohar is an instrument for refining the individual soul – for removing darkness from the earth – and for bringing well being and blessing to our fellow man.

Its purpose is not only to make us intellectually wise, but to make us spiritually pure.

Torah

Also known as the Five Books of Moses, the Torah is considered to be the physical body of learning, whereas the Zohar is the internal soul. The literal stories of the Torah conceal countless hidden secrets.` The Zohar is the Light that illuminates all of the Torah's sublime mysteries.

Beresheet	Genesis
Shemot	Exodus
Vayikra	Leviticus
Bemidbar	Numbers
Devarim	Deuteronomy

Prophets

Amos	Amos
Chagai	Haggai
Chavakuk	Habakkuk
Hoshea	Hosea
Malachi	Malachi
Melachim	Kings
Michah	Micah
Nachum	Nahum
Ovadyah	Obadiah
Shmuel	Samuel
Shoftim	Judges
Tzefanyah	Zephaniah
Yechezkel	Ezekiel
Yehoshua	Joshua
Yeshayah	Isaiah
Yirmeyah	Jeremiah
Yoel	Joel
Yonah	Jonah
Zecharyah	Zechariah

Writings

Daniel	Daniel
Divrei Hayamim	Chronicles
Eicha	Lamentations
Ester	Esther
Ezra	Ezra
Nechemiah	Nehemiah
Iyov	Job
Kohelet	Ecclesiastes
Mishlei	Proverbs
Rut	Ruth

Sir Hashirim	Songs of Songs
Tehilim	Psalms

The Ten Sfirot – Emanations

To conceal the blinding *Light* of the Upper World, and thus create a tiny point into which our universe would be born, ten *curtains* were fabricated. These ten *curtains* are called Ten Sfirot. Each successive Sfirah further reduces the emanation of *Light*, gradually dimming its brilliance to a level almost devoid of *Light* – our physical world known as *Malchut*. The only remnant of Light remaining in this darkened universe is a *pilot light* which sustains our existence. This Light is the life force of a human being and the force that gives birth to stars, sustains suns and sets everything from swirling galaxies to busy ant hills in motion. Moreover, the Ten Sfirot act like a prism, refracting the Light into many *colors* giving rise to the diversity of life and matter in our world.

The Ten Sfirot are as follows:

Keter	Crown
Chochmah	Wisdom
Binah	Understanding
Da'at	Knowledge
Zeir Anpin	Small Face,
	(includes the next six Sfirot):
Chesed	Mercy (Chassadim - plural)
Gvurah	Judgment (Gvurot - Plural)
Tiferet	Splendor
Netzach	Victory (Eternity)
Hod	Glory
Yesod	Foundation
Malchut	Kingdom

The Partzufim - Spiritual forms

One complete structure of the Ten Sfirot creates a *Partzuf* or Spiritual Form. Together, these forces are the building blocks of all reality. As water and sand combine to create cement, the Ten Sfirot combine to produce a Spiritual Form *[Partzuf]*. Each of the Spiritual Forms below are therefore composed of one set of Ten Sfirot.

These Spiritual Forms are called:

Atik	Ancient
Atik Yomin	Ancient of Days
Atika Kadisha	Holy Ancient
Atik of Atikin	Anceint of Ancients
Aba	Father
Arich Anpin	Long Face
Ima	Mother
Nukva	Female
Tevunah	Intelligence
Yisrael Saba	Israel Grandfather
Zachar	Male

These names are not meant to be understood literally. Each represents a unique spiritual force and building block, producing a substructure and foundation for all the worlds make up reality.

The Five Worlds

All of the above Spiritual Forms *[Partzufim]* create one spiritual world. There are Five Worlds in total that compose all reality, therefore, five sets of the above Spiritual Forms are required.

Our physical world corresponds to the world of: Asiyah – Action

Adam Kadmon	Primordial Man
Atzilut	Emanation
Briyah	Creation
Yetzirah	Formation
Asiyah	Action

The Five Levels of the soul

Nefesh	First, Lowest level of Soul
Ruach	Second level of Soul
Neshamah	Third level of Soul
Chayah	Fourth level of Soul
Yechidah	Highest, fifth level of Soul

Names of God

As a single ray of white sunlight contains the seven colors of the spectrum, the one Light of the Creator embodies many diverse spiritual forces. These different forces are called *Names of God*. Each Name denotes a specific attribute and spiritual power. The Hebrew letters that compose these Names are the interface by which these varied Forces act upon our physical world. The most common Name of God is the Tetragrammaton (the four letters, *Yud Hei Vav Hei* יהוה.) Because of the enormous power that the Tetragrammaton transmits, we do not utter it aloud. When speaking of the Tetragrammaton, we use the term *Hashem* which means, *The Name*.

Adonai, El, Elohim, Hashem, Shadai, Eheyeh, Tzevaot, Yud Hei Vav Hei

People

Er	The son of Noach
Rabbi Elazar	The son of Rabbi Shimon bar Yochai
Rabbi Shimon bar Yochai	Author of the Zohar
Shem, Cham, Yefet	Noach's children
Shet	Seth
Ya'akov	Jacob
Yishai	Jesse (King David's father)
Yitzchak	Isaac
Yosef	Joseph
Yitro	Jethro
Yehuda	Judah

Angels

Angels are distinct energy components, part of a vast communication network running through the upper worlds. Each unique Angel is responsible for transmitting various forces of influence into our physical universe.

Adriel, Ahinael, Dumah (name of Angel in charge of the dead), Gabriel, Kadshiel, Kedumiel, Metatron, Michael, Rachmiel,

Glossary of Hebrew words

Raphael, Tahariel, Uriel

Nations

Nations actually represent the inner attributes and character traits of our individual self. The nation of Amalek refers to the doubt and uncertainty that dwells within us when we face hardship and obstacles. Moab represents the dual nature of man. Nefilim refers to the sparks of Light that we have defiled through our impure actions, and to the negative forces that lurk within the human soul as a result of our own wrongful deeds.

Amalek, Moab, Nefilim

General

Aba	Father
	Refers to the male principle and positive force in our universe. Correlates to the proton in an atom.
Arvit	The Evening prayer
Chayot	Animals
Chupah	Canopy (wedding ceremony)
Et	The
Avadon	Hell
Gehenom	Hell
Sheol	Hell
	The place a soul goes for purification upon leaving this world.
Ima	Mother
	The female principle and minus force in our universe. Correlates to the electron in an atom.
Kiddush	Blessing over the wine
Klipah	Shell (negativity)
Klipot	Shells (Plural)
Kriat Sh'ma	The Reading of the Sh'ma
Mashiach	Messiah
Minchah	The Afternoon prayer
Mishnah	Study
Mochin	Brain, Spiritual levels of Light
Moed	A designated time or holiday
Negev	The south of Israel
Nukva	Female

Partzuf	Face
Shacharit	The Morning prayer
Shamayim	Heavens (sky)
Shechinah	The Divine presence, The female aspect of the Creator
Tefilin	Phylacteries
The Dinur river	The river of fire
Tzadik	Righteous person
Zion	Another name for Jerusalem
Yisrael	The land of Israel
	The nation of Israel or an individual Israelite
Zohar	Splendor

The Hebrew vowels

Chirik אֱ, Cholam אוֹ אֹ, Kamatz אָ, Patach אַ, Segol אֶ, Sh'va אְ, Shuruk אוּ אֻ, Tzere אֵ.

The Twelve Tribes

Asher, Dan, Ephraim, Gad, Issachar, Judah, Levi, Menasheh, Naphtali, Reuben, Shimon, Zebulun

Jewish Holidays

Rosh Hashanah	The Jewish New Year
Yom Kippur	Day of Atonement
Sukkot	Holiday of the Booths
Shmini Atzeret	The day of Convocation
Simchat Torah	Holiday on which we dance with the Torah
Pesach	Passover
Shavout	Holiday of the Weeks

כרך ב

בראשית ב׳, נח

Vol. II

Beresheet B, Noach

A Prayer from The Ari

Ruler of the universe, and Master of all masters, The Father of mercy and forgiveness, we thank You, our God and the God of our fathers, by bowing down and kneeling, that You brought us closer to Your Torah and Your holy work, and You enable us to take part in the secrets of Your holy Torah. How worthy are we that You grant us with such big favor, that is the reason we plead before You, that You will forgive and acquit all our sins, and that they should not bring separation between You and us.

And may it be your will before You, our God and the God of our fathers, that You will awaken and prepare our hearts to love and revere You, and may You listen to our utterances, and open our closed heart to the hidden studies of Your Torah, and may our study be pleasant before Your Place of Honor, as the aroma of sweet incense, and may You emanate to us Light from the source of our soul to all of our being. And, may the sparks of your holy servants, through which you revealed Your wisdom to the world, shine.

May their merit and the merit of their fathers, and the merit of their Torah, and holiness, support us so we shall not stumble through our study. And by their merit enlighten our eyes in our learning as it stated by King David, The Sweet Singer of Israel: "Open my eyes, so that I will see wonders from Your Torah" (Tehilim 119:18). Because from His mouth God gives wisdom and understanding.

"May the utterances of my mouth and the thoughts of my heart find favor before You, God, my Strength and my Redeemer" (Tehilim 19:15).

Beresheet B

Beginners Paragraphs

Names of the articles

1. The Seven Chambers of the Garden of Eden

The following sections of the holy Zohar explore the metaphysical structure of all reality.

The Zohar is not just another book that provides information. As we scan these Aramaic words and sentences, they convey mystical knowledge, profound spiritual influence, and positive energy into all areas of our lives. The Zohar is a life-enriching instrument that conveys the very same spiritual Light that it describes in its pages. The act of looking at and learning from the Zohar allows us to assimilate the energy that is present in each and every letter. Quite simply, the words on these pages bring Light to places of darkness.

There are seven chambers in the Garden of Eden – that is, seven levels or frequencies of spiritual energy. These seven chambers correspond to seven Sfirot, or dimensions.

Though there are ten Sfirot in all, and these comprise all reality, they are divided into two groups – the Upper Three [*Keter, Chochmah* and *Binah*] and the Lower Seven [*Chesed, Gevurah, Tiferet, Netzach, Hod, Yesod* and *Malchut*].

Generally, the Upper Three have no real influence or sway over our physical world. They are above and beyond the boundaries of our cosmic neighborhood.

The Lower Seven, however, directly affect our world. More than that, they are like a *holographic projector* that projects the Light of The Creator into a three dimensional *hologram* that we perceive as our universe.

Because there are seven Light sources, it's not surprising that the number seven appears again and again:
· Seven notes of music.
· Seven colors of the spectrum.
· Seven seas.
· Seven continents.

‫1. אֲמַר רְבִּי שִׁמְעוֹן הָא תָּנֵינָן, דְּכַד בְּרָא קַדְשָׁא בְּרִיךְ הוּא עָלְמָא,‬
‫גָּלֵיף בְּגִילוּפֵי דְּרָזָא דִמְהֵימְנוּתָא, גּוֹ טְהִירִין, בְּרָזִין עִלָּאִין, וְגָלֵיף‬
‫לְעֵילָּא, וְגָלֵיף לְתַתָּא, וְכֹלָּא בְּרָזָא חָדָא, וַעֲבֵיד עָלְמָא תַּתָּאָה, בְּגַוְונָא‬
‫דְּעָלְמָא עִלָּאָה, וְדָא קָאֵים לָקֳבֵיל דָּא, לְמֶהֱוֵי כֹּלָּא חַד, בְּיִחוּדָא חָדָא,‬
‫וּבְגִין כָּךְ קַדְשָׁא בְּרִיךְ הוּא גָּלֵיף גְּלִיפֵי דְאַתְוָון עֵילָּא וְתַתָּא, וּבְהוּ בְּרָא‬
‫עָלְמִין.‬

1. Rabbi Shimon said: As we have already learned, when the Holy One, blessed be He, created the world, He made inscriptions in the secret of Faith, NAMELY OF MALCHUT, within the lights of the higher secrets, THAT IS, HE ELEVATED MALCHUT TO BINAH. HENCE HE MADE THE SAME INSCRIPTIONS THAT WAS IN MALCHUT ON THE HIGHER SFIROT OF BINAH. THIS IS THE SECRET OF COMBINING THE QUALITIES OF THE MERCY OF BINAH AND THE JUDGMENT OF MALCHUT SHAPED BY THE ONE WHO EMANATED THEM FOR THE PURPOSE OF STRUCTURING THE WORLD. He engraved above, IN BINAH, and He engraved, IN MALCHUT. He established all of this at the same time, MEANING THAT BOTH INSCRIPTIONS HAVE THE SAME FORM, THAT OF BINAH. And He made the lower world, MALCHUT, in the likeness of the upper world, BINAH. And He made one the exact reflection of the other, so that they can be elevated and thus united as one. That is why the Holy One, blessed be He, established the laws of the upper and lower letters of the alphabet, with which He created the worlds.

‫2. וְתָא חֲזֵי כְּגַוְונָא דַּעֲבַד קַדְשָׁא בְּרִיךְ הוּא עָלְמָא, הָכֵי נָמֵי בְּרָא לֵיהּ‬
‫לְאָדָם קַדְמָאָה. פָּתַח וַאֲמַר וְהֵמָּה כְּאָדָם עָבְרוּ בְרִית וְגוֹ', דְּהָא קַדְשָׁא‬
‫בְּרִיךְ הוּא אַעֲטַר לֵיהּ בְּעִטְרִין עִלָּאִין, וּבְרָא לֵיהּ בְּשִׁית סִטְרִין דְּעָלְמָא,‬
‫לְמֶהֱוֵי שְׁלִים בְּכֹלָּא, וְכֹלָּא זָעָאן וְדָחֲלָן מִקַּמֵּיהּ, דְּהָא כַּד אִתְבְּרֵי אָדָם,‬
‫אִתְבְּרֵי בְּדִיּוֹקְנָא עִלָּאָה, וַהֲווֹ מִסְתַּכְּלָן בְּהַהוּא דִּיּוֹקְנָא, וְזָעָאן וְדָחֲלָן‬
‫מִקַּמֵּיהּ.‬

2. Come and see, that in the same manner the Holy One, blessed be He, created the world, WHICH IS TO SAY BY INCLUDING THE QUALITY OF THE

MERCY OF BINAH, AS EXPLAINED ABOVE, He also created THE SOUL OF the first man, ADAM, AND IT RECEIVED THE SAME QUALITY OF MERCY WITH WHICH THE WORLD, MALCHUT, WAS CREATED. SUBSEQUENTLY, HE WAS ALSO ABLE TO ATTAIN THE LEVEL OF THE UPPER EMANATIONS OF BINAH AS WELL AS MALCHUT, AS THE ZOHAR EXPLAINS TO US. He opened up the discussion and said, "but they, like Adam, have transgressed the covenant" (Hoshea 6:7), because the Holy One, blessed be He, crowned Adam with the supernal crowns OF THE MOCHIN OF THE FIRST THREE SFIROT. He also created him with the six directions of the world, NAMELY WITH THE MOCHIN OF THE SIX EXTREMITIES, so that he would be complete in everything. And all THE CREATURES trembled before Adam and feared him because when he was created it was in the supernal form. All the creatures looked at that form and were reverent and fearful of him.

3. וּלְבָתַר אָעִיל לֵיהּ קֻדְשָׁא בְּרִיךְ הוּא בְּגִנְתָּא דְעֵדֶן, לְאִתְעַדְּנָא תַּמָּן בְּעִדּוּנִין עִלָּאִין, וַהֲווֹ מַלְאָכִין עִלָּאִין סַחֲרִין לֵיהּ, וּמְשַׁמְּשִׁין קַמֵּיהּ, וְרָזִין דְּמָרֵיהוֹן הֲווֹ אוֹדְעִין לֵיהּ. תָּא חֲזֵי, בְּשַׁעֲתָא דְאָעִיל לֵיהּ קֻדְשָׁא בְּרִיךְ הוּא לְגִנְתָּא דְעֵדֶן, הֲוָה חָמֵי וְאִסְתַּכַּל מִתַּמָּן, כָּל רָזִין עִלָּאִין, וְכָל חָכְמְתָא, בְּגִין לְמִנְדַע וּלְאִסְתַּכְּלָא בִּיקָרָא דְמָרֵיהּ.

3. Subsequently, the Holy One, blessed be He, brought Adam into the Garden of Eden to enjoy its supernal delights. He was encircled by holy angels, who served him and informed him of the secrets of their Master. Come and behold: When the Holy One, blessed be He, brought Adam into the Garden of Eden, Adam saw and observed all the higher secrets and wisdom, so that he was able to observe and understand the splendors of his Master. ADAM HAD ACCESS TO ALL THAT, BECAUSE HE WAS CREATED IN THE SUPERNAL FORM OF BINAH.

4. שִׁבְעָה הֵיכָלִין מְדוֹרִין אִינּוּן לְעֵילָּא, דְּאִינּוּן רָזָא דִּמְהֵימְנוּתָא עִלָּאָה, וְשִׁבְעָה הֵיכָלִין אִינּוּן לְתַתָּא כְּגַוְונָא דִלְעֵילָּא, וְאִינּוּן שִׁית כְּגַוְונָא עִלָּאָה, וְחַד טָמִיר וְגָנִיז אִיהוּ לְעֵילָּא. וְכָל אִלֵּין אִינּוּן בְּרָזָא עִלָּאָה, בְּגִין דְּכָל הָנֵי הֵיכָלִין, אִית בְּהוּ כְּגַוְונָא דִלְעֵילָּא, וְאִית בְּהוּ כְּגַוְונָא דִלְתַתָּא, לְמֶהֱוֵי כָּלִיל בְּדִיּוֹקְנָא דְרָזָא דִלְעֵילָּא, וּבְדִיּוֹקְנָא דְרָזָא דִלְתַתָּא, וּבְהוֹ הֲוָה דִּיּוּרֵיהּ דְּאָדָם.

1. The Seven Chambers of the Garden of Eden

4. There are seven chambers and seven levels above, which are the secrets of supernal Faith, NAMELY BINAH. And there are seven chambers below, IN MALCHUT, similar to those above, IN BINAH. Six of these chambers are just as they are above, CORRESPONDING TO THE SIX SFIROT OF ZEIR ANPIN, but one CHAMBER, CORRESPONDING TO BINAH, IS hidden and concealed. And all THE CHAMBERS OF MALCHUT, AND EVEN THE LOWER SIX, are part of the holy secret, AND THUS THEY ARE IN THE SHAPE OF BINAH. This is because each of the chambers has some of the likeness of above and some of the likeness of below, so that it is included in the form of the supernal secret OF BINAH as well as in the form of the lower secret OF MALCHUT. Adam resides in these chambers.

ה. וּלְבָתַר דְּאִתְתְּרַךְ מִגִּנְתָּא דְעֵדֶן, אַתְקִין לוֹן קֻדְשָׁא בְּרִיךְ הוּא לְנִשְׁמַתְהוֹן דְּצַדִּיקַיָּא, לְאִשְׁתַּעְשְׁעָא בְּהוּ. כִּדְקָא חָזֵי, מִזִּיוָא דִּיקָרָא עִלָּאָה. וְכָל חַד וְחַד, אִתְתְּקַן כְּגַוְונָא דִּלְעֵילָא, וּכְגַוְונָא דִּלְתַתָּא, כְּמָה דְּאוֹקִימְנָא.

5. And after the expulsion OF ADAM from the Garden of Eden, the Holy One, blessed be He, prepared THE CHAMBERS for the souls of the righteous, to reward them with the blissful splendors of His celestial precious light. And each one OF THOSE CHAMBERS was prepared in the semblance of the supernal shape OF BINAH and the lower shape OF MALCHUT, as we have already explained.

2. First chamber: Yesod

The Zohar explains that, in the first chamber, the souls of the converts enter and stand to behold the Divine Splendor. Three times a day they are illuminated by Divine Light.

6. הֵיכָלָא קַדְמָאָה, אֲתַר דְּאִיהוּ מִתְתַּקַּן לְתַתָּא, לְמֶחֱוֵי כְּגַוְונָא דִּלְעֵילָּא, וְהָא אִתְעֲרוּ חַבְרַיָּיא, נְמוּסֵי דְּגִנְתָּא דְעֵדֶן, כְּמָה דְּאִיהוּ בְּרָזָא עִלָּאָה. וְלָא שָׁלְטָא בֵּיהּ עֵינָא, בַּר נִשְׁמַתְהוֹן דְּצַדִּיקַיָּיא, לְמֶחֱוֵי גְּלִיפָן לְעֵילָא וְתַתָּא, וּלְאִסְתַּכְּלָא מִתַּמָּן, בְּרָזָא דְמָרֵיהוֹן, וּבְעִנּוּגָא דִּלְעֵילָּא.

6. The first chamber below was created in the likeness of that which is above, THAT IS THE SFIRAH OF YESOD WITHIN MALCHUT – SET IN ITS PLACE BELOW TO CORRESPOND TO BINAH. It has already been explained that a law of the Garden of Eden states that ALL ITS ASPECTS ARE EXACTLY THE SAME as those in the divine secret OF BINAH, ALTHOUGH THE ASPECT OF MALCHUT OF THE ATTRIBUTE OF JUDGMENT IS NOT NOTICEABLE THERE. It is not visible to the eye, BECAUSE THE ESSENCE OF MALCHUT IS STORED DEEP WITHIN, AND THUS CANNOT BE SEEN. THE ATTRIBUTE OF MERCY CAN BE SEEN, but only by the souls of the righteous. Such souls are engraved on above and below. REACHING COMPLETION FROM BOTH BINAH AND MALCHUT, THEY ARE ABLE TO ATTAIN THE ESSENCE OF MALCHUT. FURTHERMORE, THROUGH MALCHUT, they are able to behold the secret of their Master and to enjoy divine bliss.

7. וְאִלֵּין אִינּוּן צַדִּיקַיָּא, דְּלָא אַחְלְפוּ יְקָרָא דְמָרֵיהוֹן, בְּגִין דַּחֲלָא אָחֳרָא. כְּתִיב אֵשֶׁת חַיִל עֲטֶרֶת בַּעְלָהּ, רָזָא דִּמְהֵימְנוּתָא, לְאִתְדַּבְּקָא בַּר נָשׁ בְּמָרֵיהּ, וּלְדַחֲלָא מִנֵּיהּ תָּדִיר, וְלָא יִסְטֵי לִימִינָא וּשְׂמָאלָא, וְהָא אוֹקִימְנָא, דְּלָא יִהַךְ בַּר נָשׁ, בָּתַר דַּחֲלָא אָחֳרָא, דְּאִקְרֵי אֵשֶׁת זְנוּנִים, וּבְגִין כָּךְ כְּתִיב לִשְׁמָרְךָ מֵאִשָּׁה זָרָה מִנָּכְרִיָּה אֲמָרֶיהָ הֶחֱלִיקָה.

7. Those WHO REACH MALCHUT WITHIN THE CHAMBERS are the righteous people, who have not betrayed their Master for other Elohim. THEY ATTAIN MALCHUT AS IS IMPLIED BY THE SECRET MEANING OF THE PHRASE "a

virtuous woman is the crown of her husband" (Mishlei 12:4). The secret of Faith – NAMELY MALCHUT – is that whoever attains it should cleave to his Master, always be in awe of Him, and never stray to the left or to the right. As we have explained, one must not follow other deities – which are termed 'a sinful woman'. This is the reason for the verse, "That they may shield you from a foreign woman, from the stranger who flatters with her words" (Mishlei 7:5). AND NO ONE MERITS ANY OF THIS EXCEPT THROUGH MALCHUT. HENCE THE STATURE OF THOSE RIGHTEOUS WHO DO MERIT IT IS VERY HIGH. AND YOU SHOULD KNOW THAT THE ONLY ATTAINABLE CHAMBERS ARE THE SIX OF ZEIR ANPIN; THE SEVENTH IS UNATTAINABLE. THE CHAMBERS, TOGETHER WITH ZEIR ANPIN, ARE CONSIDERED THE TEN SFIROT. REMEMBER THAT THE FIRST CHAMBER OF YESOD ALSO INCLUDES MALCHUT, AND THE LAST CHAMBER OF BINAH ALSO INCLUDES THE THREE TOP SFIROT: KETER, CHOCHMAH AND BINAH.

8. הֵיכָלָא דָא, קָאֵים בְּדִיוֹקְנָא דְרָזָא עִלָּאָה, בְּגִין דְּכַד נִשְׁמָתִין דְּצַדִּיקַיָּא נָפְקֵי מֵהַאי עָלְמָא, עָאלִין גּוֹ אִלֵּין הֵיכָלִין, דִּי בְּגִנְתָּא דְעֵדֶן דִּלְתַתָּא, וְתַמָּן יָתְבִין כָּל חַד וְחַד, כָּל הַהוּא זִמְנָא דְּאִצְטְרִיכָא נִשְׁמָתָא לְמֵיתַב תַּמָּן.

8. This chamber is fixed in the secret of the divine form, WHICH IS BINAH, because when the souls of the righteous leave this world, WHEN THEY DEPART TO THEIR OWN WORLD, they enter those chambers of the lower Garden of Eden. And each one remains there for as long as it is necessary for the soul to be there.

9. וּבְכָל הֵיכָלָא וְהֵיכָלָא, אִית דִּיּוֹקְנִין, כְּגַוְונָא דִלְעֵילָא. וּדִיּוֹקְנִין כְּגַוְונָא דִלְתַתָּא, וְתַמָּן אִתְלַבְּשַׁת נִשְׁמָתָא בִּלְבוּשִׁין כְּגַוְונָא דְּהַאי עָלְמָא, וְאִתְעַדְנַת תַּמָּן כָּל הַהוּא זִמְנָא דְּאִצְטְרִיכַת, עַד דְּמָטוּ זִמְנָא לְסַלְקָא לְאֲתַר עִלָּאָה כְּמָה דְאִצְטְרִיךְ. וּמִגּוֹ הַהוּא מָאנָא דְּאִתְלַבְּשַׁת בֵּיהּ, חָמָאת דִּיּוֹקְנִין עִלָּאִין, לְאִסְתַּכְּלָא בִּיקָרָא דְּמָרֵיהוֹן.

9. In each and every chamber OF THE LOWER GARDEN OF EDEN there are figures in the supernal form OF BINAH, and there are figures in the lower form OF MALCHUT. CONSEQUENTLY, EVEN IF THE SOUL IS NOT ENTIRELY PURIFIED OF BODILY QUALITIES, IT CAN ENTER AND BE THERE IN THE SHAPE OF MALCHUT, WHICH IS CONNECTED WITH THE PHYSICAL NATURE. THE SOUL, WHICH IS THE ASPECT OF BINAH, CAN ALSO ENTER AND, AS EXPLAINED, BE CONNECTED TO BINAH. And therein, IN THE LOWER GARDEN OF EDEN, the soul is clothed with garments similar to those worn in the physical world, and it enjoys all the time it needs there. IT ENJOYS THE BLISS OF SUPERNAL LIGHT, IN ORDER TO BE ENTIRELY CLEANSED OF THE FILTH OF ITS PHYSICAL NATURE, until such a time as it can be elevated to its divine home. THIS MEANS THAT UNTIL ALL THE IMPRINTS OF THE PHYSICAL BODY THAT WERE ATTACHED TO THE SOUL IN THIS WORLD DISSIPATE, IT CANNOT BE ELEVATED TO ITS PLACE IN THE SUPERNAL GARDEN OF EDEN, AS IT NEEDS TO BE – FOR EACH SOUL IS FROM BINAH AND MUST RETURN TO ITS SOURCE, WHICH IS THE UPPER GARDEN OF EDEN. And with the new form or clothing that THE SOUL NOW wears, it is able to see divine entities FROM BINAH, and can thus glimpse the glory of its Master. THIS CLOTHING IS SIMILAR TO WORLDLY GARMENTS, BUT IT ALSO CONTAINS SUPERNAL FORMS FROM BINAH, AND THEREFORE, THROUGH ITS FORM, THE SOUL CAN STRIVE TO SEE THE DIVINE LIGHTS OF BINAH, AND BEHOLD THE GLORY OF ITS MASTER.

10. בְּהַאי הֵיכָלָא, אִית נְהוֹרִין עָלָּאִין, לְאִסְתַּכְּלָא, וְנִשְׁמַתְהוֹן דְּאִינּוּן גִּיּוֹרִין דְּאִתְגַּיְּירוּ, קַיְימִין תַּמָּן, וְעָאלִין תַּמָּן, לְאִסְתַּכְּלָא בִּיקָרָא עִלָּאָה, וּמִתְלַבְּשָׁן תַּמָּן בִּלְבוּשָׁא חָדָא דִּנְהוֹרָא, דְּנָהֵיר וְלָא נָהֵיר. וְהַהוּא הֵיכָלָא מַקְפָא מֵאֶבֶן טָבָא וְדַהֲבָא.

10. This chamber has visible supernal lights, and the souls of the converts enter and stand there to behold the divine splendor. Here they are clad in one luminous garment, that shines and yet also shines not. WITH THE LIGHTS IN THIS CHAMBER, THE RIGHTEOUS ARE ABLE TO SEE AND ENDOW THE SOULS OF THE CONVERTS, ENABLING THEM TO ENTER INSIDE AND RECEIVE THE DIVINE SPLENDOR – AFTER THEY HAVE BEEN DRESSED IN A LUMINOUS GARMENT, THAT BOTH SHINES AND DOES NOT SHINE. THE LIGHTS HAVE TWO FUNCTIONS, WHICH ARE THE SAME: TO SHINE UPON THE WORTHY, AND NOT TO SHINE UPON – IN OTHER

WORDS, TO LEAVE IN DARKNESS — THE UNWORTHY. THE CLOTHING BRINGS THEM JOY, BECAUSE THEY MERIT IT AND ARE FIT TO RECEIVE IT. This chamber is lined with precious stones and gold.

11. וְתַמָּן אִיהוּ פִּתְחָא חָדָא. דְּנָחֵית לָקֳבֵל פִּתְחָא דְּגֵיהִנֹּם, מִתַּמָּן מִסְתַּכְּלָן בְּכָל אִינוּן חַיָּיבֵי, דְּלָא עָאלוּ בִּבְרִית קַיָּימָא קַדִּישָׁא, וְאִתְתָּרְכוּ בְּאִינוּן מַלְאֲכֵי חַבָּלָה, דְּטָרְדֵי לוֹן בְּנוּרָא דְּדָלֵיק, וְאִינוּן חָמָאן וְחָדָאן עַל דְּאִתְגַּיָּירוּ.

11. There is an opening that leads down to the gates of Gehenom. From there, THE CONVERTS look at all the evil, THE IDOL WORSHIPERS, THOSE WHO HAVE NOT CONVERTED AND THUS have not entered the holy covenant. They are chased away by the angels of destruction with fire, and the converts see this, rejoicing that they have converted AND ARE THUS SPARED SUCH A HARSH PUNISHMENT.

12. וּתְלַת זִמְנִין בְּיוֹמָא, נָהֲרִין מִגּוֹ נְהִירוּ עִלָּאָה, וּמִשְׁתַּעְשְׁעָן תַּמָּן, וְעֵילָא מִנְּהוֹן, עוֹבַדְיָה וְאוּנְקְלוֹס גִּיוֹרָא, וּשְׁאָר גִּיוֹרִין דְּאִתְגַּיָּירוּ, כְּגַוְונָא דָא לְעֵילָא, כַּד זָכָאן לְסַלְּקָא נִשְׁמַתְהוֹן לְאִתְעַטְּרָא תַּמָּן.

12. And three times a day they are illuminated by divine light, taking delight in there, IN THE LIGHTS OF THE THREE TOP SFIROT, WHICH ARE DRAWN INTO THIS CHAMBER. Above them reside Ovadyah the convert and Onkelus the convert, and the other SIMILARLY IMPORTANT converts. And, as has been explained REGARDING THIS CHAMBER IN THE LOWER GARDEN OF EDEN, SO TOO IN THE LOWER CHAMBER OF THE UPPER GARDEN OF EDEN, the souls ascend when they can and are adorned, AFTER RESIDING FOR A SUFFICIENT TIME IN THE LOWER GARDEN OF EDEN.

3. Second chamber: Hod

The second chamber is located within the first. The opening to this chamber can be found in our world, deep within the caves of the Patriarchs in Machpelah, Hebron, in the Land of Israel. In this chamber reside the souls who met with adversity and endured hardship in the physical world. Throughout their ordeals, they retained their certainty and Faith in The Creator. These souls understood the purpose of human existence as achieving spiritual growth, and therefore they thanked the Ancient and Holy One for sending them genuine opportunities for attaining that purpose.

13. הֵיכָלָא תִּנְיָינָא, הֵיכָלָא דָא, קַיְימָא לְגוֹ מֵהַאי הֵיכָלָא קַדְמָאָה וְהַאי פִּתְחָא אִיהוּ סָמִיךְ לְגוֹ מְעַרְתָּא דַאֲבָהָן, וְהַאי הֵיכָלָא נָהִיר מִקַּדְמָאָה, הָכָא אִית כָּל אֲבָנִין יַקִּירִין דִּמַקְפָן לֵיהּ.

13. The second chamber is within the first. The opening of this chamber is from within the cave of the Patriarchs, and it is lit by the first chamber. All manner of precious stones surround it.

14. בְּגוֹ דְּהַאי הֵיכָלָא, אִית נְהִירוּ חַד, כָּלִיל מִכָּל גְּוֵונִין, וְאִיהוּ נָהִיר מֵעֵילָא לְתַתָּא. בְּהַאי הֵיכָלָא קַיְימִין אִינּוּן, דְּסָבְלוּ יִסּוּרִין וּמַרְעִין בְּהַאי עָלְמָא, בְּגִין לְאִתְתַּקְּנָא, וַהֲווֹ מוֹדָן וּמְשַׁבְּחָן לְמָרֵיהוֹן כָּל יוֹמָא, וְלָא הֲווֹ מְבַטְּלִין צְלוֹתַיְיהוּ לְעָלְמִין.

14. Within this chamber, there is one light that includes all the colors, THAT IS, THE FOUR COLORS OF CHOCHMAH, BINAH, TIFERET AND MALCHUT, which shine downward from above. In this chamber are found all those who, so as to be made whole BY PERFECT REPENTANCE, suffered illnesses and misfortunes in this world, and who thanked and praised their Master every day, and never once stopped their prayers. THEREFORE THEY ATTAINED ADMITTANCE TO THE CHAMBER OF HOD IN THE GARDEN OF EDEN.

15. לְגוֹ מֵהַאי הֵיכָלָא, קַיְימִין כָּל אִינּוּן, דִּמְקַדְּשִׁין בְּכָל חֵילָא שְׁמָא דְּמָרֵיהוֹן, וַאֲתִיבוּ אָמֵן יְהֵא שְׁמֵיהּ רַבָּא מְבָרֵךְ בְּכָל חֵילָא, וְאִלֵּין אִינּוּן קַיְימִין לְגוֹ, בְּגוֹ הַאי הֵיכָלָא, וְהַהוּא נְהוֹרָא דְּכָלִיל כָּל גְּוֵונִין נָהִיר לוֹן.

מֵהַהוּא נְהִירוּ קַיְּימִין וְהָמָאן נְהוֹרִין אָחֳרָנִין, דְּאִתְאַחֲדָן וְלָא אִתְאַחֲדָן בְּגַוְוַיְיהוּ. וְעֵילָא מִנְּהוֹן מָשִׁיחַ, דְּאִיהוּ עָאל וְקָאֵים בֵּינַיְיהוּ, וְנָחֵית לוֹן.

15. And within this chamber reside all the righteous people who sanctify with all their might the name of their Master, and answer, with all their might, "Amen, may the great name be blessed." THIS THIRD ASPECT OF THE CHAMBER CONTAINS THE THREE TOP SFIROT, TO WHICH THE ABOVE MENTIONED RIGHTEOUS MERIT ADMISSION. They reside in the innermost recesses of the chamber. And the light THAT RESIDES WITHIN CHESED, GVURAH AND TIFERET OF THIS CHAMBER includes all of the colors, CHOCHMAH, BINAH, TIFERET AND MALCHUT. THIS LIGHT shines on them – THAT IS, ON THE RIGHTEOUS IN THE TOP THREE SFIROT OF THE CHAMBER. And by the strength of this light THAT THEY RECEIVE FROM CHESED, GVURAH AND TIFERET OF THE CHAMBER, they can stand and see other lights – BUT THE MAGNITUDE OF THESE OTHER LIGHTS DOES NOT ALLOW THEM TO BE SEEN FULLY. IT IS AS IF THEY CONNECT, YET ALSO DO NOT CONNECT WITH THE LIGHTS. Above THE RIGHTEOUS, stands the Messiah, who enters, walks among them, and draws down that light SO THAT THEY CAN ATTAIN IT FULLY.

4. Third chamber: Netzach

This chamber receives all those souls who have suffered more severe misfortunes and tragedies than the souls who reside in the second chamber. A second kind of soul dwelling in this chamber are the children whose lives where cut short. These young souls died before their time and therefore did not sin. The third type of soul who merits a place in this chamber are those who constantly felt pain and cried over the destruction of the Temples. These souls endured the suffering of the entire world during their existence.

16. אִיהוּ נָטִיל מֵהַאי הֵיכָלָא, וְעָאל בְּהֵיכָלָא תְּלִיתָאָה, וְתַמָּן כָּל אִנּוּן בְּנֵי מַרְעִין וּכְאֵבִין יַתִּיר, וְכָל אִינּוּן דַּרְדְּקֵי דְּבֵי רַבָּן דְּלָא אַשְׁלִימוּ יוֹמִין, וְכָל אִינּוּן דַּעֲצֵבִין עַל חָרוּב בֵּי מַקְדְּשָׁא וַהֲווֹ אוֹשְׁדִין דִּמְעִין, כָּלְּהוֹן קַיְּימִין בְּהַהוּא הֵיכָלָא, וְאִיהוּ מְנַחֵם לוֹן.

16. MESSIAH leaves the SECOND chamber and enters the third. Here are found all those who suffered, FOR THE PURPOSE OF BEING MADE WHOLE, more severe illnesses and greater misfortunes THAN THOSE IN THE SECOND CHAMBER. THIS IS WHY THEY HAVE MERITED A PLACE IN THE THIRD CHAMBER. AND THIS IS THE FIRST TYPE OF SOUL FOUND IN THE CHAMBER. THE SECOND TYPE OF SOUL IN THIS CHAMBER IS THAT OF children who did not live their full lives, WHO DIED BEFORE THEIR TIME, AND THUS DID NOT SIN. SUCH PURE SOULS ASCEND AS *MAYIN NUKVIN* (FEMALE WATERS), AND ATTRACT THE LIGHTS OF THE SECOND CHAMBER. THE THIRD TYPE OF SOUL IN THE CHAMBER IS THAT OF those who mourn the destruction of the Temple and who shed tears, THEREBY DRAWING DOWN THE LIGHTS OF THE TOP THREE SFIROT INTO THIS CHAMBER. All THREE TYPES OF RIGHTEOUS SOULS reside in this chamber AND MESSIAH consoles them, WHICH MEANS THAT HE BESTOWS ON THEM THEIR LIGHTS.

5. Fourth chamber: Tiferet

In this chamber are found the mourners of Zion and Jerusalem. Just as a child can feel the pain of parents who suffer over their children's misdeeds, these souls feel the pain of The Creator. Souls who were slain and executed for their unwavering belief in God are also among this group. The Messiah, the Zohar reveals, wears a garment upon which are inscribed the names of all martyrs.

17. וּנְטֵיל מֵהַאי הֵיכָלָא, וְעָאל בְּהֵיכָלָא רְבִיעָאָה, וְתַמָּן כָּל אִינוּן אֲבֵלֵי צִיּוֹן וִירוּשְׁלֵם, וְכָל אִינוּן קְטוֹלֵי דִּשְׁאָר עַמִּין עכו״ם וְאִיהוּ שָׁרֵי וּבָכֵי, וּכְדֵין כָּל אִינוּן נְשִׂיאִין דְּזַרְעָא דְּדָוִד, כֻּלְּהוּ אֲחִידָן בֵּיהּ, וּמְנַחֲמִין לֵיהּ.

17. He leaves the third and enters the fourth chamber, BECAUSE AFTER BEING COMPLETED WITH ALL THE LIGHTS OF THE THIRD CHAMBER, HE CAN NOW ENTER THE CHAMBER OF TIFERET. In this chamber are all of the mourners of Zion and Jerusalem and all of those murdered by idolatrous nations. And WHEN MESSIAH SEES THEM he breaks down in tears and cries. Then all the princes descended from David hold him and comfort him.

18. שָׁאֲרֵי תִּנְיָינוּת וּבָכֵי, עַד דְּקָלָא נָפֵיק, וּמִתְאַחֵד בְּהַהוּא קָלָא, וְסָלֵיק לְעֵילָּא, וְאִשְׁתָּהֵי תַּמָּן עַד רֵישׁ יַרְחָא. וְכַד נָחֵית נָחֲתִין עִמֵּיהּ כַּמָּה נְהוֹרִין וְזִיוִין, מְנַהֲרִין לְכָל אִינוּן הֵיכָלִין, וְאַסְוָותָא וּנְהוֹרָא לְכָל אִינוּן קְטוֹלִין, וּבְנֵי מַרְעִין וּמַכְאוֹבִין דְּסָבִילוּ עִמֵּיהּ דְּמָשִׁיחַ.

18. MESSIAH starts crying again till a supernal voice emerges and mixes with the Voice OF MESSIAH and HIS VOICE rises up. And it is delayed there until the beginning of the month, when it descends FROM BINAH. THEN it brings down many lights and emanations that shine upon all the chambers. It also brings remedy and light to those killed BY THE IDOLATROUS NATIONS OF THE WORLD and those ailing and with pains who suffer with Messiah SO AS TO BRING FORTH THE REDEMPTION.

19. וּכְדֵין פּוּרְפִּירָא לָבֵישׁ, וְתַמָּן חֲקִיקִין וּרְשִׁימִין כָּל אִינוּן קְטוֹלֵי

דִּשְׁאַר עַמִּין עכו״ם בְּהַהוּא פּוּרְפִּירָא, וְסָלִיק הַהוּא פּוּרְפִּירָא לְעֵילָא,
וְאִתְחַקַּק תַּמָּן גּוֹ פּוּרְפִּירָא עִלָּאָה דְּמַלְכָּא, וְקֻדְשָׁא בְּרִיךְ הוּא זַמִּין
לְאַלְבָּשָׁא הַהוּא פּוּרְפִּירָא וּלְמֵידַן עַמִּין, דִּכְתִיב יָדִין בַּגּוֹיִם מָלֵא גְוִיּוֹת.
עַד דִּי אֲתָא וְנָחֵים לוֹן, וְנָחֲתִין עִמֵּיהּ נְהוֹרִין וְעִדּוּנִין, לְאִתְעַדְּנָא,
וְכַמָּה מַלְאָכִין וּרְתִיכִין עִמֵּיהּ, כָּל חַד וְחַד בְּמַלְבּוּשָׁא, לְאִתְלַבְּשָׁא בְּהוּ
כָּל אִינּוּן נִשְׁמָתִין דְּקַטּוֹלִין, וְתַמָּן מִתְעַדְּנִין כָּל הַהוּא זִמְנָא דְּאִיהוּ
סָלִיק וְנָחֵית.

19. Then MESSIAH puts on the ROYAL purple garment (called *Purfira*), on which the names of all those killed by the idolatrous nations of the world are inscribed and listed. This purple garment OF MESSIAH ascends TO BINAH and is engraved upon the supernal royal garment of the King, WHICH IS ZEIR ANPIN THAT CLOTHES BINAH. THERE, THOSE KILLED BY OTHER NATIONS AND LISTED ON MESSIAH'S GARMENT ARE INSCRIBED ONTO THE SUPERNAL GARMENT, ALONG WITH ALL OTHERS LISTED ABOVE, AND DIVINE LIGHT IS DRAWN BY THEM TO THIS CHAMBER. The Holy One, blessed be He, will one day clothe Himself with this royal garment OF MESSIAH and judge the nations of the world, as it is written: "He shall judge the heathen and He shall fill the places with dead bodies" (Tehilim 110:6). Until MESSIAH descends and returns FROM THE PLACE OF UNION, bringing lights and bliss down with him for the pleasure and consolation of the souls. And many angels and Chariots DESCEND WITH MESSIAH, each carrying a garment for the souls of those killed by THE IDOLATROUS nations. There these souls experience divine bliss while Messiah ascends and descends.

20. לְגוֹ מֵהַאי הֵיכָלָא, קַיְימָא גּוֹ דַּרְגָּא עִלָּאָה, אִינּוּן עֲשָׂרָה רַבְרְבִין
מְמַנָּן, רַבִּי עֲקִיבָא וְחַבְרוֹי, וְכֻלְּהוּ סַלְקֵי בְּסָלִיקוּ, גּוֹ אַסְפַּקְלַרְיָאה
דִּלְעֵילָא, וְנָהֲרִין בְּזִיו יְקָרָא עִלָּאָה, עֲלַיְיהוּ כְּתִיב עַיִן לֹא רָאָתָה
אֱלֹקִים זוּלָתְךָ יַעֲשֶׂה לִמְחַכֵּה לוֹ.

20. On a high level inside this chamber stand the ten appointed ministers, who are Rabbi Akiva and his friends. They all go up through the upper mirror – WHICH IS THE SECRET OF THE LUMINOUS MIRROR – and shine with supernal, glorious splendor. Of them it is written: "Neither has the eye seen, that Elohim, beside You, should do such a thing for him that waits for Him" (Yeshayah 64:4).

6. Fifth chamber: Gvurah

The souls who have made complete repentance reside in the fifth chamber. At its entrance stands *King Menasheh*, the King of Judah, who committed terrible sins throughout his life. Nevertheless, the King atoned for his wrongdoings and his repentance was accepted by The Creator.

‫21. בְּהֵיכָלָא חֲמִישָׁאָה, קַיְימִין כָּל אִינוּן מָארֵיהוֹן דִּתְיוּבְתָּא שְׁלֵימְתָּא,‬
‫דְּתָבוּ מֵחֲטָאֵיהוֹן וְאִתְנַחֲמוּ בְּהוּ, וְנַפְקַת נִשְׁמַתַיְיהוּ בְּדַכְיוּ, וְכָל אִינוּן‬
‫דְּקַדִּישׁוּ שְׁמָא דְּמָרֵיהוֹן, וְקַבִּילוּ עֲלַיְיהוּ מוֹתָא, וּבְתַרְעָא דְּהַאי הֵיכָלָא,‬
‫קָאִים מְנַשֶּׁה מֶלֶךְ יְהוּדָה, דְּקַבֵּיל לֵיהּ קֻדְשָׁא בְּרִיךְ הוּא בִּתְיוּבְתָּא‬
‫שְׁלֵימְתָּא, וַחֲתַר לֵיהּ חֲתִירָא לְקַבְּלָא לֵיהּ.‬

21. Within the fifth chamber reside all those whose repentance is complete – those who have repudiated their wrong deeds and have been consoled for them. THIS MEANS THAT THEY HAVE REPENTED THROUGH LOVE. THEN THEIR WICKEDNESS IS TRANSFORMED INTO VIRTUE AND THEY ARE CONSOLED FOR ALL THEIR SINS BECAUSE THEY HAVE RECEIVED MERIT FOR REPENTING THEM. Their souls leave them purified. In this chamber also RESIDE those who have sanctified their Master's name and have taken upon themselves self-sacrifice FOR HIS HONOR, BLESSED BE HE. And at the entrance to the chamber stands Menasheh, the King of Judah, who has entirely repented his sins and whose repentance the Holy One, blessed be He, accepted. The Holy One, blessed be He, created a recess for his sake UNDERNEATH THE THRONE OF GLORY, to receive him. THAT IS, HE CONCEALED HIM AS IF UNDERGROUND FROM THE EYES OF THE PROSECUTORS SO THAT THEY WOULD NOT ASK FOR JUDGMENT OF HIM.

‫22. וּלְגוֹ מֵהַאי הֵיכָלָא, קַיְימִין, כָּל אִינוּן מָארֵיהוֹן דִּתְיוּבְתָּא תַּקִּיפָא,‬
‫דְּנִשְׁמַתְהוֹן נָפְקַת, בְּשַׁעֲתָא דְּאִתְמַרְמְרוּ עַל עוֹבָדֵיהוֹן, וְאִלֵּין מִתְעַדְּנִין‬
‫בְּעֵדוּנָא עִלָּאָה, בְּכָל יוֹמָא וְיוֹמָא. וּתְלַת זִמְנִין בְּיוֹמָא, נְהִירוּ עָאל‬
‫בְּהַהוּא הֵיכָלָא, דְּמִתְעַדְּנִין בֵּיה כָּל חַד וְחַד כִּדְקָא חָזֵי לֵיהּ. וְכָל חַד‬
‫נְכַוָה, מִנְּהִירוּ דְּחוּפָּה דְּחַבְרֵיה, בֵּין לְתַתָּא בֵּין לְעֵילָּא.‬

22. And within this chamber reside all those, whose repentance is immense, who GAINED SO MUCH POWER THROUGH THEIR REPENTANCE OF MISDEEDS IN LIFE that their souls left through disgust at their own evil actions. They delight in the supernal Eden each and every day. Three times a day the light enters this chamber in which the souls experience bliss, each to the extent that it deserves. THESE THREE TIMES CORRESPOND TO THE THREE COLUMNS TO WHICH THE LIGHTS OF THE THREE TOP SFIROT ARE DRAWN. And each is burned by the light of the canopy of his neighbor, be it in the upper CHAMBERS or the lower. THIS MEANS THAT THE LEVELS OF THE RIGHTEOUS ARE NOT EAQUAL NEITHER IN THE UPPER CHAMBERS NOR THE LOWER. EACH HAS A CANOPY OF HIS OWN THAT NO OTHER CAN TOUCH WITHOUT BEING BURNED.

23. הַאי הֵיכָלָא קַיְימָא, עַל אִינוּן הֵיכְלֵי תַּתָּאֵי, וַאֲפִלוּ צַדִּיקִים גְּמוּרִין לָא יָכְלִין לְאַעֲלָאָה בְּגוֹ הַאי הֵיכָלָא, וּלְמֵיקַם בֵּיה, וְהַאי אִיהוּ דַרְגָּא עִלָאָה עַל כֹּלָּא, בַּר דַרְגָּא דַּחֲסִידֵי דְּאִיהוּ דַרְגָּא עִלָאָה עַל כֹּלָּא.

23. This chamber stands above all the lower chambers, and even the truly righteous in the lower chambers cannot enter or reach it. This CHAMBER, WHICH IS GVURAH, is at a higher level than all other CHAMBERS. Only the level of the righteous, WHO RESIDE IN THE CHAMBER OF CHESED, is a higher level than all the rest, EVEN HIGHER THAN THE CHAMBER OF GVURAH.

7. Sixth chamber: Chesed

This is the chamber of the righteous who say, *What is mine is yours and what is yours is yours*. The truly righteous share everything they possess, desiring and keeping nothing for themselves. This sixth chamber is loftier than all the rest and governs over all others.

‫24. הַאי הֵיכָלָא שְׁתִיתָאָה: הֵיכָלָא דָא הֵיכָלָא דַּחֲסִידֵי, הֵיכָלָא דָא,‬
‫הֵיכָלָא עִלָּאָה עַל כֹּלָּא, וְהַאי הוּא הֵיכָלָא דְּקַיְּימָא עַל כֹּלָּא. הֵיכָלָא‬
‫דִּימִינָא, לֵית מָאן דְּיָקִים בֵּיהּ, אֶלָּא אִינוּן חֲסִידִים קַדִּישִׁין, וְכָל אִינוּן‬
‫דִּמְרַחֲמֵי לְמָרֵיהוֹן בִּרְחִימוּ סַגִּי. וּלְפִתְחָא דְּהַאי הֵיכָלָא, קַיְּימָא כָּל‬
‫אִינוּן דִּמְיַחֲדֵי יִחוּדָא דְּמָרֵיהוֹן בְּכָל יוֹמָא וְאִלֵּין עָאלִין בְּהַאי הֵיכָלָא,‬
‫וּזְמִינִין לְסַלְּקָא בְּקַדְמֵיתָא.‬

24. The sixth chamber is the chamber of the righteous. IT IS FOR THOSE WHOSE CHARACTER IS TO SAY, "WHAT IS MINE IS YOURS AND WHAT IS YOURS IS YOURS." THIS MEANS THAT THEY SHARE, BUT DO NOT RECEIVE ANYTHING FOR THEMSELVES. This is a loftier chamber than the rest, and governs them all. THUS, ONE CANNOT REACH THIS CHAMBER IF ONE HAS NOT PASSED THROUGH ALL OF THE LOWER LEVELS. It is a right-hand chamber BECAUSE THE LEVEL OF CHESED IS CONSIDERED TO BE THE RIGHT COLUMN, and it cannot be attained BY ANYONE except the holy righteous souls and all those who greatly love their Master. At the entrance of this chamber are those who proclaim their Master's unity each day. THESE ARE THE ONES WHO DRAW DOWN THE REVELATION OF HIS UNITY, BLESSED BE HE, FROM THE BLESSED ENDLESS LIGHT TO THE SFIROT AND ALL THE WORLDS. And they are the first to ascend from there to higher chambers, MEANING THEY ARE THE FIRST OF THE RIGHTEOUS IN THAT CHAMBER TO ASCEND.

‫25. וְעֵילָּא מֵהַאי פִּתְחָא אַבְרָהָם, יָמִינָא דְּקֻדְשָׁא בְּרִיךְ הוּא, וּלְפִתְחָא‬
‫אָחֳרָא קַיְּימָא יִצְחָק, דְּאִתְעֲקַד עַל גַּבֵּי מַדְבְּחָא, וַהֲוָה קָרְבָּנָא שְׁלִים‬
‫קַמֵּיהּ דְּקֻדְשָׁא בְּרִיךְ הוּא. וּלְפִתְחָא אָחֳרָא לְגוֹ, קַיְּימָא יַעֲקֹב שְׁלֵימָא,‬
‫וּתְרֵיסַר שִׁבְטִין סַחֲרָנֵיהּ, וּשְׁכִינְתָּא עַל רֵישַׁיְיהוּ.‬

25. Above this entrance, WHERE THE LIGHTS OF NETZACH, HOD AND YESOD ARE, stands Abraham to the right of the Holy One, blessed be He. THAT IS, HE STANDS ON THE SIDE OF CHESED. And at another entrance is Isaac, who was bound upon the altar and was an unblemished sacrifice before the Holy One, blessed be He, AND REPRESENTS GVURAH. And at another entrance stands Jacob, a perfect man, surrounded by twelve tribal heads who have the Shechinah over their heads. THEY CORRESPOND TO THE LIGHTS OF CHESED, GVURAH AND TIFERET OF THIS CHAMBER, AS ABRAHAM, ISAAC AND JACOB ARE THE EMBODIMENTS OF CHESED, GVURAH AND TIFERET, AS WE KNOW.

26. וְכַד יִשְׂרָאֵל בְּעָקוּ אִתְּעָרוּ תְּלַת אַבָּהָן, וּמִתְעָרֵי לָה לִשְׁכִינְתָּא לְאַגָּנָא עֲלַיְיהוּ, וּכְדֵין אִיהִי סַלְקָא וְאִתְעַטְּרָא לְעֵילָא, וְאַגָּנָא עֲלַיְיהוּ דְיִשְׂרָאֵל. וּכְמָה דְאִית הֵיכָלִין לְתַתָּא בְּגִנְתָּא דְעֵדֶן, הָכֵי נָמֵי לְעֵילָא אִית הֵיכָלִין מְתַקְּנָן, דְּאִינּוּן רָזָא דִמְהֵימְנוּתָא.

26. And when Yisrael are in a time of trouble, the three Patriarchs awaken and arouse the Shechinah to protect Yisrael. Consequently, THE SHECHINAH ascends and after being crowned – RECEIVING THE THREE TOP SFIROT, CALLED CROWNS – protects Yisrael. BUT SHE CANNOT PROTECT YISRAEL UNTIL THE PATRIARCHS ARE AWAKENED AND SHE RECEIVES THE CROWNS OF THE TOP THREE SFIROT. Just as chambers are found in the lower Garden of Eden, corrected chambers can be found in the supernal GARDEN OF EDEN. These constructed chambers contain the secret of Faith, NAMELY MALCHUT. FOR MALCHUT, UPON HER COMPLETION, IS CALLED 'FAITH' AND EACH CHAMBER IS AN ASPECT OF MALCHUT.

8. Seventh chamber: Binah

This is the most hidden of all the chambers. All the others are connected to and crowned by this one. It is not a dwelling of souls, but a chamber to which they ascend on the way to their respective places.

Most of the turbulence and turmoil of life occurs within the darkness that is created from an absence of spiritual Light. As we scan the letters that tell the secrets of the seventh chambers, the verses bring the all-embracing Light of The Creator into our lives.

27. וְכָל הָנֵי הֵיכָלִין, כֻּלְּהוּ מִתְקַשְּׁרָן וּמִתְעַטְּרָן בְּחַד הֵיכָלָא דְּאִיהוּ הֵיכָלָא שְׁבִיעָאָה, וְהַאי הֵיכָלָא אִיהוּ גָּנִיז וְסָתִים מִכָּל שְׁאָר הֵיכָלִין. בְּאֶמְצָעִיתָא דְּהַאי הֵיכָלָא קָאֵים חַד עַמּוּדָא, דְּאִיהוּ בִּגְוָונִין סַגִּיאִין: יָרוֹק, חִוָּור, סוּמָק, אוּכָם. וְכַד נִשְׁמָתִין סָלְקִין, אִינוּן עָאלִין גּוֹ הַאי הֵיכָלָא, מָאן דְּאִתְחֲזֵי לְהַאי גַּוֶון סָלִיק בֵּיהּ, וּמָאן דְּאִתְחֲזֵי לְהַאי גַּוֶון סָלִיק בֵּיהּ. כָּל חַד וְחַד כִּדְקָא חֲזֵי לֵיהּ.

27. And all those chambers are connected to and crowned by one chamber, which is the seventh chamber. This chamber is more hidden and concealed than all the others. In the middle of this chamber stands a pillar of the colors green, white, red, and black. And when the souls NEED TO ascend TO A HIGHER LEVEL, they enter THE PILLAR THAT STANDS WITHIN this chamber. And whoever is suitable for one color OF THE PILLAR rises through it, and whoever is suitable for another color rises through it. Each and every SOUL ascends through the color most suitable to it.

28. וְאָלֵין שִׁית הֵיכָלִין אִינוּן לְמָדוֹרָא כִּדְאֲמָרָן, וּשְׁבִיעָאָה לָאו אִיהוּ לְמָדוֹרָא. וְשִׁית, כֹּלָּא בְּרָזָא דְּשִׁית, וְעַל דָּא כְּתִיב בָּרָא שִׁית. שִׁית דַּרְגִּין לְעֵילָא, שִׁית דַּרְגִּין לְתַתָּא, וְכֹלָּא רָזָא חָדָא.

28. The first six chambers are the dwellings OF THE SOULS, as we have said. This seventh CHAMBER, however, is not a dwelling place OF THE SOULS; IT IS ONLY A PLACE WHERE THE SOULS ASCEND THROUGH THE PILLAR CONTAINED THEREIN. And all six CHAMBERS are in the secret of

six. And the fact that it is written: "Bara Sheet," BERESHEET ("IN THE BEGINNING) BEING AN ABBRVIATION OF THE WORDS *BARA* (ENG. 'CREATED') AND *SHEET* (ENG. 'SIX'), TEACHES US THAT THERE ARE six levels above WITHIN BINAH ITSELF, and six levels below. THESE ARE CHESED, GVURAH, TIFERET, NETZACH, HOD AND YESOD OF ZEIR ANPIN AND FEMALE PRINCIPLE. THESE LEVELS ARE CALLED THE SIX DAYS OF THE WEEK, and all are part of the same secret. THIS MEANS THAT WE CAN ONLY COMPREHEND THE SIX SFIROT OF THE LOWER LEVELS AND NOT THOSE OF THE TOP THREE SFIROT.

9. Beresheet, Bara Sheet

The Zohar speaks about the relationship between the Sfirot *Binah* and *Malchut,* or our world. That relationship is the key to the mystery of the word *Beresheet*, meaning *In the Beginning.*

The first part of the word *Beresheet* is *Bara*, which pertains to the Sfirot of *Binah*, the Repository of all spiritual Energy. The second part of the word *Beresheet* is *sheet*, which is *Malchut*, our physical reality. *Malchut* is the vessel through which we, as individuals, receive our Light from Binah.

Bara and *Sheet* are called the two *Hei's* ה. These two *Hei's* are part of the *Tetragrammaton*, the Name of God that is spelled out as *Yud, Hei, Vav, Hei* יהוה.

The Names of God are powerful energy forces, and the *Tetragrammaton* יהוה is one of the strongest *Names of God* in existence.

The First *Hei* in the *Tetragrammaton* pertains to the Sfirah of *Binah,* the Repository of Light.

The *Vov* embodies the realm of *Zeir Anpin*, which enfolds and includes six *Sfirot* within it. The *Vov* is the conduit through which the Light *stored* in *Binah* flows into our physical world. Our world, *Malchut*, is signified by the lower *Hei.*
Rabbi Abba reveals a secret concealed inside the word *Beresheet*, which means, *In the Beginning.*
Within the word we can find two words, *Bara* and *Sheet*, which mean, *He created six.* The six refers to the six Sfirot, or dimensions, compacted within *Zeir Anpin.*

Hence, the purpose of this passage is to connect the reader and our entire world to the upper world (*Zeir Anpin*) so that Light and blessings flow to us endlessly. This divine energy flows to us now.

29. תָּא חֲזֵי, בְּרֵאשִׁית, רַבִּי יְהוּדָה אָמַר, תְּרֵין בָּתִּין הֲוֹו, בַּיִת רִאשׁוֹן

וּבֵית שֵׁנִי, דָּא עִלָּאָה וְדָא תַּתָּאָה, תְּרֵין הֵהֵי"ן אִינּוּן, דָּא עִלָּאָה וְדָא
תַּתָּאָה, וְכֻלְּהוּ חַד, ב' עִלָּאָה פְּתָחָא תַּרְעִין לְכָל סִטְרָא, דְּהָכֵי הוּא
דְּכָלִיל דָּא בְּדָא. רֵאשִׁית. כְּדֵין הוּא רֵאשִׁית לְאַעֲלָא בְּחוּשְׁבְּנָא
דְּבִנְיָנָא, רַבִּי יִצְחָק אָמַר לְמִנְיָנָא.

29. Come and behold: Beresheet ("In the beginning"), Rabbi Yehuda said, there were two Temples, the first and the second. The first was supernal, CORRESPONDING TO BINAH, and the second was lower, CORRESPONDING TO MALCHUT. There are also two *Hei's* IN THE NAME YUD HEI VAV HEI, a supernal *Hei*, RELATING TO BINAH and a lower *HEI*, RELATING TO MALCHUT, and all is one. THIS MEANS THAT THE FIRST AND SECOND TEMPLES ARE ONE WITH THE UPPER *HEI* AND LOWER *HEI*, WHICH ARE BINAH AND MALCHUT. The supernal Bet OF BERESHEET IS THE FIRST TEMPLE, WHICH IS BINAH. IT opens the gates to all directions, because they are truly included within one another. The word "Beginning" INDICATES THAT BINAH is the first to be counted as part of the structure, COMPOSED OF ZEIR ANPIN AND THE FEMALE PRINCIPLE, THAT IS CALLED THE STRUCTURE OF THE WORLD. THIS MEANS THAT BINAH IS CONSIDERED THE FIRST TO DRAW THE MOCHIN TO ZEIR ANPIN AND THE FEMALE PRINCIPLE AND TO THE WORLDS – BRIYAH, YETZIRAH AND ASIYAH. THIS ALLUDES TO THE WORDS "IN THE BEGINNING (BERESHEET)" OF TORAH. BET (HEB. *IN*) REFERS TO THE UPPER TEMPLE, BINAH. "THE BEGINNING" INDICATES THAT IT WAS FIRST TO DRAW THE MOCHIN TO THE WORLDS. Rabbi Yitzchak says THAT BINAH COMES FIRST in the counting.

30. אָמַר רַבִּי אֶלְעָזָר, בְּרֵאשִׁית דָּא כְּלָלָא, דְּיוּקְנָא דְּכָל דְּיוּקְנִין כְּלִילָן
בֵּיהּ, דָּא רָזָא דִכְתִיב הוּא מַרְאֵה דְּמוּת כְּבוֹד ה', חֵיזוּ דְּאִתְחֲזוּן בֵּיהּ
שִׁית אַחֲרָנִין, וְדָא הוּא בְּרֵאשִׁית בָּרָא שִׁית. תָּא חֲזֵי, כַּד עָאלִין בְּהַאי
חֵיזוּ שִׁית גְּוָונִין, הִיא אַתְקִינַת גַּרְמָא לְאַחֲזָאָה לוֹן וּלְמִפְעַל בְּהוּ
אוּמָנוּתָא דְּעָלְמָא, וְאִי תֵימָא דְּהַאי אוּמָנוּתָא דְּעָלְמָא, מִדַּרְגָּא דָּא
הוּא, כְּתִיב בָּרָא שִׁית, שְׁבָחָא דְּשִׁית אִיהוּ, דְּעָבְדֵי אוּמָנוּתָא בְּהַאי.

30. Rabbi Elazar says THE WORD Beresheet IN TORAH is a collective word.

THIS MEANS THAT MALCHUT, WHICH IS THE SECRET OF "THE FACE OF MAN," embraces all forms of REALITY. This is the secret of the verse, "This was the appearance of the likeness of the glory of Hashem" (Yechezkel 1:28). In this appearance, six other LEVELS are discernible. THUS, Beresheet is AN ABBRVIATION FOR bara sheet, BECAUSE THROUGH THE ASCENSION OF MALCHUT TO BINAH, SIX DIRECTIONS ARE FORMED IN BINAH. Come and see: When the six directions OF BINAH enter this MALCHUT, she makes herself ready to reflect them. SHE DRAWS THE SPIRITUAL LIGHTS OF CHOCHMAH FOR THE SAKE OF THEIR REVELATION. THROUGH THE SPIRITUAL LIGHTS OF CHOCHMAH, SHE ENGAGES IN ALL THE WORLDLY WORKMANSHIP. AND THIS WORKMANSHIP IS THE SPIRITUAL LIGHT OF THE ILLUMINATION OF CHOCHMAH, FROM WHICH SPRANG THE REALITY OF THE SIX WEEKDAYS. It is because the workmanship of the world, NAMELY THE SPIRITUAL LIGHT OF CHOCHMAH, comes from the level OF MALCHUT, that it is written bara sheet (He created six). THIS SIGNIFIES THAT credit for the workmanship is attributed to the six ASPECTS OF BINAH, as they perform their craftsmanship in the level OF MALCHUT.

31. רַבִּי יוֹסֵי פָּתַח הַנִּצָּנִים נִרְאוּ בָאָרֶץ, עֵת הַזָּמִיר הִגִּיעַ, וְקוֹל הַתּוֹר נִשְׁמַע בְּאַרְצֵנוּ, הַנִּצָּנִים: דָּא הוּא רָזָא דְּשִׁית דַּרְגִּין. נִרְאוּ בָאָרֶץ בְּגִין דְּאִינּוּן דְּיוֹקְנִין לְאִתְחֲזָאָה בְּהַאי דַּרְגָּא. עֵת הַזָּמִיר הִגִּיעַ: דְּהָא כְּדֵין מְשַׁבַּח וּמְהַדַּר, כְּמָה דְאַתְּ אָמַר לְמַעַן יְזַמֶּרְךָ כָבוֹד וְלֹא יִדֹּם, וּבְגִין כָּךְ אִקְרֵי מִזְמוֹר, כְּמָה דִּתְנִינָן דִּכְתִיב מִזְמוֹר לְדָוִד, דְּשָׁאָרַת עֲלֵיהּ שְׁכִינְתָּא בְּרֵישָׁא, וְדָא הוּא עֵת הַזָּמִיר הִגִּיעַ. רַבִּי חִיָּיא אָמַר, דְּהָא כְּדֵין מָטָא זִמְנָא לְשַׁבְּחָא.

31. Rabbi Yosi quotes, "The flowers appear on the earth, the time of the singing bird has come and the voice of the turtle dove is heard in our land" (Shir Hashirim 11:12). "The flowers" allude to the six levels: CHESED, GVURAH, TIFERET, NETZACH, HOD AND YESOD. In the phrase, they "appear on the earth," EARTH ALLUDES TO MALCHUT. The "flowers" are forms that are not revealed at any level other THAN MALCHUT. "The time of the singing bird has come" SIGNIFIES THAT WHEN THE SHECHINAH, CALLED SONG, IS INSPIRED WITH THE SPIRITUAL LIGHT OF CHOCHMAH, then is the time for praise and glorification, as is written: "So that he may sing your praise and not be silent" (Tehilim 30:13). MALCHUT is therefore

called 'song,' as we have learned from the words, "a song for David"
(Tehilim 3:1) AND NOT "DAVID'S SONG" (TEHILIM 24:1). THIS
INDICATES that first David was inspired by the Shechinah. This is WHY IT IS
SAID THAT "the time of the singing bird has come." FIRST THE SHECHINAH
(CALLED "SONG") REACHED HIM; ONLY THEN DID HE START SINGING
AND PRAISING. Rabbi Chiya said THAT THE TIME OF SONG HAS COME;
THIS should be understood literally as "the time of praise has come,"
MEANING THAT AFTER RECEIVING THE SPIRITUAL LIGHT, IT IS TIME FOR
PRAISE. HE DISAGREED THAT THE SHECHINAH OF HASHEM IS CALLED
"SONG."

32. רְבִּי אַבָּא אֲמַר, עָלְמָא עִלָּאָה סָתִים, וְכָל מִלּוֹי סְתִימִין, בְּגִין
דְּקַיְימָא בְּרָזָא עִלָּאָה, יוֹמָא דְּכָל יוֹמִין, וְכַד בְּרָא וְאַפֵּיק, אַפֵּיק אִלֵּין
שִׁית, וּבְגִין דְּאִיהוּ סָתִים, דְּכָל מִלּוֹי סְתִימִין, אֲמַר בְּרֵאשִׁית, בָּרָא שִׁית
יוֹמִין עִלָּאִין, וְלָא אֲמַר מַאן בָּרָא לְהוֹן, בְּגִין דְּאִיהוּ עָלְמָא עִלָּאָה
סְתִימָא.

32. Rabbi Aba says that the upper world, BINAH, is shrouded in mystery, as
is everything that pertain to it, because it exists in the upper secret, THE
THREE TOP SFIROT OF BINAH, which is a day THAT EMBRACES all days.
And when ARICH ANPIN created and produced BINAH WITH A THOUGHT,
He produced it on THE LOWER six OF BINAH AND NOT THE UPPER THREE
SFIROT. And because ARICH ANPIN is mysterious and His actions are
incomprehensible, it is written in THE SCRIPTURE, "Beresheet," MEANING
"He created six (bara sheet)." THIS HINTS AT THOSE SIX supernal days, but
does not specify who created them. THE SIX DAYS ALLUDED TO IN
BERESHEET belong to an incomprehensible and concealed world.

33. וּלְבָתַר גָּלֵי וְאֲמַר עֲבִידְתָּא תַּתָּאָה, וַאֲמַר מַאן בָּרָא לֵיהּ, בְּגִין
דְּאִיהוּ עָלְמָא דְּקַיְימָא בְּאִתְגַּלְּיָיא, וַאֲמַר בָּרָא אֱלֹקִים אֶת הַשָּׁמַיִם וְאֶת
הָאָרֶץ, וְלָא כְּתִיב בָּרָא סָתִים, בָּרָא אֶת הַשָּׁמַיִם, בְּגִין דְּאִיהוּ עָלְמָא
בְּאִתְגַּלְּיָיא, וַאֲמַר בָּרָא אֱלֹקִים, אֱלֹקִים וַדַּאי שְׁמָא בְּאִתְגַּלְּיָיא, קַדְמָאָה
בִּסְתִימָא דְּאִיהוּ עִלָּאָה, תַּתָּאָה בְּאִתְגַּלְּיָיא. לְמֶהֱוֵי תָּדִיר עוֹבָדָא

דְּקוּדְשָׁא בְּרִיךְ הוּא סָתִים וְגַלְיָא. וְרָזָא דִשְׁמָא קַדִּישָׁא הָכֵי הוּא סָתִים וְגַלְיָא.

33. Later, he revealed The Creator of the lower actopm, NAMELY, THE MALE AND FEMALE PRINCIPLES, because it is a world that stands revealed. He said, "Elohim created the heaven and the earth" (Beresheet 1:1), ALLUDING TO THE MALE AND FEMALE PRINCIPLES. Consequently it is not written vaguely, WITHOUT REFERENCE TO THE CREATOR, that is, just "created the heaven AND THE EARTH," because it is a world of revelation. Thus, it says, "Elohim created." Elohim DID certainly CREATE THEM, as IT IS a revealed name. The first WORLD, BINAH, is concealed, because it is the supernal WORLD. The lower WORLD OF THE MALE AND FEMALE PRINCIPLES is revealed, because the workings of the Holy One, blessed be He, are always both concealed and revealed. So is the secret of the Holy Name concealed and revealed. THE YUD-HEI OF THE NAME YUD HEI VAV HEI ARE CONCEALED, BECAUSE WE HAVE NO COMPREHENSION OF THE THREE TOP SFIROT; VAV-HEI ARE REVEALED BECAUSE THEY ALLUDE TO THE MALE AND FEMALE PRINCIPLES, WHICH ARE COMPREHENSIBLE.

34. אֶת הַשָּׁמַיִם, לְאַסְגָּאָה שָׁמַיִם תַּתָּאֵי לְתַתָּא, וְאֶת הָאָרֶץ לְאַכְלָלָא אֶרֶץ דִּלְתַתָּא, וּלְאַסְגָּאָה כָּל עוֹבָדָהָא כְּגַוְונָא דִלְעֵילָא.

34. THE PARTICLE *Et* (Heb. 'the') WHEN PLACED BEFORE THE WORD "heaven" IN THE SCRIPTURE, includes the lower heaven below; when placed BEFORE THE WORD "earth," however, it also includes in it the earth below, adding the idea that everything done IN THE LOWER EARTH is similar to the upper pattern above.

10. Seven dwellings of the upper and lower earth

The spiritual and physical worlds are each divided into seven.
These are a reflection of the seven Sfirot, or dimensions.

35. וְהָאָרֶץ הָיְתָה תֹהוּ וָבֹהוּ כִּדְקָאֲמָרָן, וְהָאָרֶץ דָּא אֶרֶץ עִלָּאָה,
דְּלֵית לָהּ נְהוֹרָא מִגַּרְמָהּ. הָיְתָה: בְּקַדְמֵיתָא כְּבָר הֲוַת, כִּדְקָא יָאוֹת,
וְהַשְׁתָּא תֹהוּ, וָבֹהוּ, וְחֹשֶׁךְ. הָיְתָה דַּיְיקָא, לְבָתַר אַזְעֵירַת גַּרְמָהּ
וְאַזְעֵירַת נְהוֹרָא. תֹהוּ, וָבֹהוּ, וְחֹשֶׁךְ, וְרוּחַ: אַרְבַּע יְסוֹדֵי עָלְמָא
דְּאִשְׁתַּכְלָלוּ בָּהּ.

35. THE WORDS, "and the earth was without form and void" (Beresheet 1:2)
have already been explained. MOREOVER, the earth is the upper earth, THE
FEMALE PRINCIPLE OF ZEIR ANPIN, which has no light of its own. "Was"
INDICATES that it was originally in its ordered state, but now it has become
formless, void, and dark. THE SCRIPTURE EMPLOYS the word "was"
precisely TO DRAW OUR ATTENTION TO THE FACT THAT IT WAS
COMPLETE. Later, it diminished itself and its light, AND IN IT THERE CAME
ABOUT formlessness, void, darkness, and wind – these being the four
worldly elements that were built into the EARTH.

11. Seven dwellings of the lower earth

The physical realm includes seven compartments, or worlds. These are called, *Eretz, Adamah, Gey, Neshiyah, Tziyah, Arka, Tevel*. Our physical earth corresponds to *Tevel*. When Rabbi Yossi inquires as to the nature of world called *Tziyah*, Rabbi Abba replies that this realm is the location of Hell.

The world of *Nesheyah*, the Zohar explains, is called *oblivion*. It is totally forgotten, for it is without any form.

36. דָּבָר אַחֵר, וְאֵת הָאָרֶץ כִּדְקָאֲמָרָן, לְאַסְגָּאָה אַרְעָא דִלְתַתָּא, דְּאִיהִי אִתְעֲבִידַת בְּכַמָּה מְדוֹרִין, כֹּלָּא כְּגַוְונָא עִלָּאָה, וְדָא הוּא, וְהָאָרֶץ הָיְתָה תֹהוּ וָבֹהוּ וְחֹשֶׁךְ וְרוּחַ. אִלֵּין אִינּוּן מְדוֹרֵי אַרְעָא: אֶרֶץ, אֲדָמָה, גֵּיא, נְשִׁיָּה, צִיָּה, אַרְקָא, תֵּבֵל. וְגָדוֹל שֶׁבְּכוּלָם תֵּבֵל, דִּכְתִיב וְהוּא יִשְׁפֹּט תֵּבֵל בְּצֶדֶק.

36. Another explanation of "and the earth" is that the words include the lower earth, which was made of compartments as was the upper EARTH. And this is WHAT IS MEANT BY, "and the earth was without form and void; and darkness... And the wind..." And the compartments of the earth are called *eretz* (earth), *adamah* (soil), *gey* (valley), *neshiyah* (oblivion), *tziyah* (dryness), *arka* (ground), and *tevel* (world). The major level of earth is *Tevel*, about which it is written: "And He will judge the world (Heb. *tevel*) in righteousness" (Tehilim 9:8). THIS IS NOT SAID ABOUT ANY OTHER LEVEL OF EARTH, AND THUS WE INFER THAT IT IS THE MOST IMPORTANT.

37. אָמַר רְבִּי יוֹסֵי, מָאן הוּא צִיָּה, אָמַר לֵהּ דָּא הוּא אֲתָר דְּגֵיהִנֹּם, כד"א צִיָּה וְצַלְמָוֶת. וְרָזָא דָּא כְּתִיב, וְחֹשֶׁךְ עַל פְּנֵי תְהוֹם, דָּא רָזָא אֲתָר דְּגֵיהִנֹּם, דָּא הוּא צִיָּה, אֲתָר דְּמַלְאַךְ הַמָּוֶת, כִּדְקָאֲמָרָן, דְּאִיהוּ מַחְשִׁיךְ אַנְפַּיְיהוּ דִּבְרִיְּיתָא, וְדָא הוּא אֲתָר דְּחֹשֶׁךְ עִלָּאָה.

37. Rabbi Yosi asks: What is THE NATURE OF THIS EARTH THAT IS CALLED *Tziyah*? RABBI ABA said to him: This is the location of Gehenom, as is said "a land of drought" (Heb. *tziyah*) and "the shadow of death" (Yirmeyah 2:6). AND AS "THE SHADOW OF DEATH" IS THE PLACE OF

GEHENOM, SO IS *TZIYAH*. This is the secret of the words "and darkness on the face of the deep (Heb. *tziyah*)" (Beresheet 1:2), alluding to the place of Gehenom. This is the wilderness, the place of the Angel of Death, of whom it says, that he darkens the faces of all creatures. This is also the place of the upper darkness REFERRED TO IN THE WORDS "AND THE EARTH…"

38. תֹּהוּ דָּא נְשִׁיָה, דְּלָא אִתְחֲזְיָיא בָּה חֵיזוּ כְּלָל, עַד דְּאִתְנְשֵׁי מִכֹּלָּא. וְעַל דָּא אִתְקְרֵי נְשִׁיָה. וָבֹהוּ דָּא אַרְקָא אֲתַר דְּלָא אִתְנְשֵׁי. ר' חִיָּיא אָמַר דָּא גַיא. וְרוּחַ אֱלֹקִים מְרַחֶפֶת דָּא לָקֳבֵל תֵּבֵל דְּאִתְּזָן מֵרוּחַ אֱלֹקִים, וְכֹלָּא כְּחַד הוּא.

38. "Formlessness" is the earth called *neshiyah* (oblivion). IT IS SO CALLED, BECAUSE it has no appearance so that it is completely forgotten. It is therefore called oblivion. "Void" is *arka* (ground), a place that cannot be forgotten. Rabbi Chiya DISAGREES AND says, "this earth called Gey (valley) IS VOID, NOT *ARKA* (GROUND)." And the words, "a wind (also: 'spirit') of Elohim hovers," allude to the EARTH CALLED Tevel (world), which feeds from the spirit of Elohim, NAMELY FROM THE SPIRIT OF BINAH CALLED ELOHIM. They are all parts of the same level.

12. Seven dwellings of the upper earth

Just as there are seven compartments in the lower earth, there are also compartments in the supernal realms. They are arranged on top of one another in parallel dimensions, beyond the range of human perception.

39. כְּגַוְונָא דָא, אִית לְאֶרֶץ עִלָּאָה, שִׁבְעָה מְדוֹרִין אִינוּן לְעֵילָּא, דַּרְגָּא עַל דַּרְגָּא, וּבְכֻלְּהוֹ מְדוֹרִין מַלְאֲכֵי עִלָּאֵי אִלֵּין עַל אִלֵּין. הָכֵי נָמֵי לְתַתָּא, וְכֹלָּא אָחִיד דָּא בְּדָא לְמֶהֱוֵי כֹּלָּא חַד. שִׁבְעָה מְדוֹרִין אִינוּן לְעֵילָּא, וְהָא אֶרֶץ עִלָּאָה אֲחִידַת לוֹן, וְכֻלְּהוֹ קַיְימִין בָּהּ, וּבְכָלְּהוֹן קַיְימָא תּוּשְׁבַּחְתָּא דְּקֻדְשָׁא בְּרִיךְ הוּא. דַּרְגִּין פְּרִישָׁן דָּא מִן דָּא. וְאַתְרִין פְּרִישָׁן דָּא מִן דָּא.

39. Similarly, there are seven compartments in the supernal earth, MALCHUT OF THE WORLD OF ATZILUT, WHICH IS AN ASPECT OF THE EARTH IN MALCHUT OF THE WORLD OF ATZILUT, SIMILAR TO THAT OF THE LOWER EARTH, DISCUSSED ABOVE AS MALCHUT OF ASIYAH. There are seven compartments above, IN MALCHUT, arranged one level on top of another. And in all those compartments reside supernal angels, one above the other, ACCORDING TO THEIR LEVEL. Similarly, there are angels below IN THE SEVEN LEVELS OF THE EARTH OF ASIYAH, and they all cling to one another so that they can be one. There are seven compartments above, IN THE WORLD OF ATZILUT, and the supernal earth, MALCHUT, includes them, and they reside in her. And they encompass the praise of the Holy One, blessed be He. NEVERTHELESS, the levels and their locations differ from one another.

13. First compartment: Yesod

Yesod is a realm of darkness where evil and negative entities reside. By our own wrongful actions, we create the evil entities who wreak havoc and cause suffering in our lives.

40. מָדוֹרָא קַדְמָאָה, לְתַתָּא, הוּא אֲתַר בֵּי חָשׁוּךְ דְּלָא נָהֵיר, וְהוּא מִתְתַּקַן לְמָדוֹרֵי רוּחֵי וְקַסְטִירֵי וְעָלְעוּלֵי תַּקִיפִין דְּלָא אִתְחַזְיָין, וְלָא אִית בֵּיה נְהוֹרָא, וְלָא חֲשׁוֹכָא, וְלָא דְיוֹקְנָא כְּלַל. וְתַמָּן לָא יָדְעִין בֵּיה יְדִיעָא כְּלַל, דְּלָאו בֵּיה צוּרָה גוֹ כְּלַל כּוּרְסָיָיא.

40. The first compartment below, THE LOWER COMPARTMENT OF YESOD, WHICH IS SEQUENTIALLY THE FIRST FROM BELOW, is a place of darkness and does not illuminate anything. It is constructed for the dwellings of spirits, administrators of judgment, and forceful, stormy spirits. THESE KLIPOT are invisible and have no light or darkness, or any shape at all. EACH IS STRONGER THAN THE OTHER, BEGINNING WITH THE FIRST OF THE FOUR KLIPOT. IN THAT PLACE, they are not evident, because they have no shape at all. THIS COMPARTMENT CORRESPONDS TO FORMLESSNESS, AS NO ONE KNOWS OF THE EXISTENCE OF THOSE KLIPOT.

41. וְעַל הַהוּא אֲתַר מְמַנָּא חַד מַלְאָכָא טַהֲרִיאֵל שְׁמֵיה, וְעִמֵּיה שִׁבְעִין מְמַנָּן מְעוֹפְפִין וְאִתְמַחוּן מַזִּיקֵי שְׁבִיבִין, וְלָא קַיָּימִין, וְלָא אִתְחַזּוּן, וְלָא מִשְׁתַּכְּחֵי. וְכַד אָתֵי צַפְרָא כֻּלְּהוּ מִתְחַדְּשָׁן וְלָא קַיְּימֵי, כַּד מָטָאן לְגַבֵּי הַהוּא אֲתַר, אָבְדִין וְלָא מִשְׁתַּכְּחִין, וְעָאלִין בְּחַד נוּקְבָּא דִתְהוֹמָא. וְלָא אִתְחַזּוּן, כַּד אִתְרְמִישׁ לֵילְיָא אִתְמַחוּן מֵאִינּוּן שְׁבִיבִין עַד דְּמָטֵי צַפְרָא.

41. This place has a governing angel named Tahariel, who is accompanied by seventy flying ministers. They are overcome by the blasts of lapping flames above them. SOME are destroyed AND SOME SURVIVE – but these are not seen. SOME ARE VISIBLE, BUT UPON CLOSER EXAMINATION are not really there. When morning comes they are all restored. Yet they are not sustained in existence, because when they reach this place they are dissipated and cannot be found, because they go into a hole in the abyss and disappear. When nighttime comes, they are again wiped out by the flames of fire until morning comes.

14. Second compartment: Hod

This realm contains more Light than the other realms discussed
thus far. The angels who interact with people by virtue of our
actions reside in this compartment. These angels serve to connect
our actions and the Upper Worlds. When we perform positive
actions, the Upper Worlds reflect positive influences back to us
through the medium of the angels. The same process occurs with
all our negative actions.

42. מָדוֹרָא תִנְיָינָא: הוּא אֲתַר דְּנָהֵיר יַתִּיר, וְאִיהוּ חָשׁוּךְ, אֲבָל לָא
חָשׁוּךְ כְּהַהוּא קַדְמָאָה, וְהוּא מִתַתְּקַן לְמָדוֹרֵי מַלְאָכִין עִלָּאִין, דִּי מְמַנָּן
עַל עוֹבָדֵיהוֹן דִּבְנֵי נָשָׁא, וּלְמִסְטֵי לְהוֹן בְּהַהוּא אֹרַח בִּישָׁא דְּאִינּוּן
אָזְלִין. וְהַהוּא אֲתַר אִתְחֲזֵי יַתִּיר מִן קַדְמָאָה, וְאִלֵּין מַלְאָכִין אִית לְהוֹן
קָרְבָא עִם בְּנֵי נָשָׁא, וּמִתְזָנָן מֵרֵיחָא וּבוּסְמָא דְּלַתַתָּא, לְסַלְקָא
בְּתוֹעַלְתָּא, וּלְאַנְהָרָא יַתִּיר.

42. The second compartment is a place of greater enlightenment. It still is
dark, but not as dark as the first. It is reserved as the domain of the upper
angels. THERE ARE NO KLIPOT HERE. THESE ANGELS are responsible for
the actions of people. THEY HELP THEM ACCOMPLISH GOOD DEEDS and
also lead them astray into the evil path they tread. THAT IS, THEY GIVE
STRENGTH ALSO TO THOSE WHO WALK ON EVIL PATHS. NEVERTHELESS,
THEY ARE HOLY ANGELS AND NOT, HEAVEN FORBID, KLIPOT. This place
is more evident than the first COMPARTMENT, BECAUSE THE FORMER
PLACE IS, IN EFFECT, FORMLESS. THE SECOND, ON THE OTHER HAND,
IS REGARDED AS VOID, AS IT IS WRITTEN IN THE SCRIPTURES, AND IS
MORE VISIBLE. These angels are more closely related to humans, MEANING
THAT THEY APPEAR TO PEOPLE IN THEIR OWN SHAPE. They are nourished
by the subtle odors and perfumes that humans emanate from below, and
because of the opportunities they receive they are able to ascend in order to
receive – and therefore give – more light.

43. וַעֲלַיְיהוּ חַד מְמַנָּא קְדוּמִיאָ"ל שְׁמֵיהּ, וְאִלֵּין פָּתְחִין שִׁירָתָא
וּמִשְׁתַּכְּכֵי, וְאָזְלִין לוֹן, וְלָא אִתְחֲזוּן, עַד דְּיִשְׂרָאֵל לְתַתָּא פָּתְחֵי וְאָמְרֵי

שִׁירָתָא, כְּדֵין קַיְימָן בְּדוּכְתַּיְיהוּ, וְאִתְחַזָּן נְהִירִין יַתִּיר, תְּלַת זִמְנִין בְּיוֹמָא מְקַדְּשֵׁי קְדוּשְׁתָּא. וְכַד יִשְׂרָאֵל עָסְקֵי בְּאוֹרַיְיתָא, כֻּלְהוֹן טָאסִין וְסָהֲדֵי סָהֲדוּתָא לְעֵילָא, וְקוּדְשָׁא בְּרִיךְ הוּא חַיֵּיס עֲלַיְיהוּ.

43. They are governed by one minister named Kedumiel, WHO IS FROM THE SIDE OF CHESED, HENCE 'EL,' AND HIS FUNCTION IS TO PROTECT THEM FROM THE FORCES OF JUDGMENT IN THE THIRD COMPARTMENT. These ANGELS UNDER TAHRIEL start singing, then are quieted and driven away – BECAUSE SONG STRENGTHENS THE FORCE OF THE LEFT COLUMN. THIS AWAKENS THE FORCES OF JUDGMENT IN THE THIRD CHAMBER. AFTER THEIR SONG IS INTERRUPTED AND THEY ARE DRIVEN AWAY, they do not appear again until the nation of Yisrael below IN THIS WORLD starts singing. Then they return to their places, RESUME THEIR SONG, and are seen glowing brighter. Three times a day they sing with holiness. And when Yisrael are busy with Torah, all THE ANGELS OF THIS COMPARTMENT take wing and give testimony above; and the Holy One, blessed be He, has compassion for them.

15. Third compartment: Netzach

The energy and intelligence of Judgment dwell in the third compartment. Negative angels of destruction who reside here are the conduits by which judgments befall us.

44. מָדוֹרָא תְּלִיתָאָה: הוּא אֲתַר דִּשְׁבִיבִין וְקֹטוֹרִין, וְתַמָּן נְגִידוּ דִּנְהַר דִּינוּר, דְּנָגִיד וְנָפֵיק, וְאִיהוּ בֵּי מוֹקְדָא דְּנַפְשַׁיְיהוּ דְּרַשִׁיעַיָּיא, דְּמִתַּמָּן נַחֲתִית אֶשָׁא עַל רֵישַׁיְיהוּ דְּרַשִׁיעַיָּיא, וְתַמָּן מַלְאֲכֵי חַבָּלָה דְּטָרְדֵי לְהוּ.

44. The third compartment OF THE SEVEN IN THE UPPER EARTH is a place of tongues of fire and rising smoke. There, the streams of the River of Fire (*Nahar Dinur*) gush forth, BECAUSE THIS IS THE SOURCE OF THE RIVER OF FIRE. It is a crematorium the souls of the evil, the place where fire comes down upon the heads of the wicked – THOSE WHO DWELL UNDERNEATH, IN GEHENOM. And there reside also the angels of destruction, whose task it is to crush the souls that dwell IN GEHENOM.

45. וְתַמָּן אִשְׁתַּכַּח דְּלֵטוֹרַיָּיא דְּלַיְיהוּ דְּיִשְׂרָאֵל לְזִמְנִין, וּלְאַסְטָאָה לוֹן. בַּר בְּזִמְנָא דְּנָסְבֵי אַסְוָותָא לְדַחֲיָיא לֵיהּ, וְחַד מְמַנָּא עֲלַיְיהוּ מִסִּטְרָא דִּשְׂמָאלָא. כֻּלְּהוּ מִסִּטְרָא דְּחֹשֶׁךְ, כְּמָה דְּאַתְּ אָמֵר וְחֹשֶׁךְ עַל פְּנֵי תְהוֹם, וּסְמָאֵ"ל חַיָּיבָא אִשְׁתְּכַח תַּמָּן.

45. There can be found sometimes slanderers, who speak evil of Yisrael and who lead them away FROM THE PATH OF GOOD, BUT THEY CAN DO YISRAEL NO HARM if Yisrael take precautions to keep them away. They are governed by one minister from the left side. All THE ANGELS THERE are from the side of darkness, as it says, "and darkness on the face of the deep." And the evil angel Samael resides in this compartment.

16. Fourth compartment: Tiferet

The fourth compartment is a place of positive energy and Light.
The angels who inhabit this realm are responsible for the acts of
mercy that appear in our lives. These angels also bring about the
salvation that is merited when people repent and transform.

46. מָדוֹרָא רְבִיעָאָה: הוּא אֲתַר דְּנָהֵיר, וְתַמָּן הוּא נְהִירוּ לְמַלְאֲכֵי
עִלָּאֵי, דִּי בִסְטַר יָמִינָא. וּפָתְחוּ שִׁירָתָא וְסַיְּימֵי, וְלָא אָזְלִין לְאַעְבְּרָא
כַּהֲנֵי קַדְמָאֵי, דְּפָתְחִין שִׁירָתָא וּמִתּוֹקְדָן וּמִתְעַבְּרָן בְּנוּר דָּלֵיק, וְתָבִין
וּמִתְחַדְּשִׁין כְּמִלְּקַדְמִין, וְהָנֵי קַיְּימִין בְּדוּכְתַּיְיהוּ וְלָא מִתְעַבְּרָן. וְהָנֵי
מַלְאֲכֵי דְרַחֲמֵי דְּלָא מִשַׁנְּיָין לְעָלְמִין.

46. The fourth compartment, TIFERET, is a place from which light emanates
to the supernal angels of the right. They start singing, and then abruptly end
their song. However, they are not destroyed for their singing, as are those in
the first COMPARTMENT – who start singing and then are scorched by being
sucked down into burning fire, only to be restored again in the morning, as
before. The ANGELS IN HERE are preserved and are not destroyed – they are
the angels of mercy, who never change. BECAUSE THEY ARE OF THE
ASPECT OF MERCY, WHICH DRAWS FROM THE SIDE OF CHESED, THEY
ARE UNAFFECTED BY THE JUDGMENT DRAWN DOWN BY SINGING – AND
THUS THEY CAN FINISH THEIR SONG.

47. וַעֲלַיְיהוּ כְּתִיב עוֹשֶׂה מַלְאָכָיו רוּחוֹת וְגוֹ'. וְאִלֵּין עָבְדִין
שְׁלִיחוּתַיְיהוּ בְּעָלְמָא, וְלָא אִתְחַזוּן לִבְנֵי נָשָׁא בַּר בְּחֶזְוָוא, אוֹ בִּסְטְרָא
אַחֲרָא בְּסַכְלְתָנוּ סַגֵּי. וְחַד מַלְאָכָא מְמַנָּא עֲלַיְיהוּ פָּדָא"ל שְׁמֵיהּ. וּבֵיהּ
פְּתִיחִין מִפְתְּחָן דְּרַחֲמֵי, לְאִינּוּן דְּתַיְיבִין לְגַבֵּיהּ דְּמָארֵיהוֹן, וּפָתְחִין
תַּרְעִין לְאַעְבְּרָא צְלוֹתְהוֹן וּבָעוּתְהוֹן.

47. About THOSE ANGELS it is said, "He makes His angels as spirits"
(Tehilim 104:4). They perform their mission in the world without being
seen by humans, and can only be seen through visions and by other means,
such as intense meditations. One angel governs them and his name is

Padael. THIS NAME IS A COMBINATION OF THE WORDS PADA EL, MEANING 'EL HAS REDEEMED.' ALL THOSE WHO ELEVATE MAYIN NUKVIN (FEMALE WATERS) TO THIS COMPARTMENT THROUGH THEIR GOOD DEEDS RECEIVE THE ILLUMINATION OF CHASSADIM FROM THIS ANGEL, AND EVEN IF THEY HAVE BEEN SENTENCED TO DEATH, THEY ARE REDEEMED AND DO NOT DIE. HENCE THE ANGEL IS NAMED PADAEL. In this CHAMBER, the keys to the gates of mercy are accessible to those who have repented to their Master. These keys open the gates through which their prayers enter – AND ARE THUS ANSWERED.

17. Fifth compartment: Gvurah

This compartment embodies more Light than the courth compartment. Angels of both mercy and judgment reside here. These Angels are likened to Generals of the Upper Worlds, while the angels in the prior compartments are compared to foot soldiers. This realm is primarily one of Judgment. But if our actions in the physical warrant it, we can sweeten judgment through the Angels of mercy who dwell here.

The concept of sweetening judgment can be understood this way: A child misbehaves and the parent reacts with great anger. The parent then spanks the child and harshly scolds him. According to Kabbalah, there is no aspect of mercy included in the actions of the parent. The punishment is pure judgment, rooted in the anger of the parent. But the parent could also restrain himself at the moment anger erupts. He could shut down his reactive nature and release all his negative feelings. Yet the parent still realizes, out of love and concern for the child, that a punishment is called for. Therefore with pure love in his heart, and in complete control of his actions, he reprimands the child. This is still judgment, but it is judgment sweetened with mercy.

48. מְדוֹרָא חֲמִישָׁאָה: הוּא מְדוֹרָא דְּנָהֵיר בִּנְהִירוּ יַתִּיר מִכָּלְּהוּ קַדְמָאֵי, וְאִית בֵּיהּ מַלְאָכִין מִנְהוֹן אֶשָּׁא, וּמִנְהוֹן מַיָּא. לְזִמְנִין אִשְׁתְּכָחוּ בְּרַחֲמֵי, וּלְזִמְנִין אִשְׁתְּכָחוּ בְּדִינָא. אִלֵּין בְּסִטְרָא דָּא, וְאִלֵּין בְּסִטְרָא דָּא, לְזִמְנִין נָהֲרִין אִלֵּין, וְחַשְׁכִין אִלֵּין, וְאִלֵּין מְמַנָּן לְזַמְּרָא לְמָארֵיהוֹן, אִלֵּין בְּפַלְגוּת לֵילְיָא, וְאִלֵּין כַּד סָלֵיק נְהוֹרָא. וְחַד מְמַנָּא עֲלוֹהִי קַדְשִׁיאֵ"ל שְׁמֵיהּ.

48. The fifth compartment is the one in which light shines more brightly than it does in any of the preceding ones. In it are angels, some – ONES WHO REPRESENT JUDGMENT – are fiery angels. Others – ONES REPRESENTING MERCY – are watery angels. Sometimes Mercy is prominent, WHEN THE WATERY ANGELS ARE DOMINANT, and sometimes Judgment is prominent, WHEN THE FIERY ANGELS ARE DOMINANT. Those OF WATER are on the RIGHT side, and those OF FIRE are on the LEFT side. Occasionally, some of these angels glow, while the others are in darkness. Both groups of angels oversee the chanting to their Master, some – ANGELS OF JUDGMENT – at midnight, and others – ANGELS OF MERCY – at dawn. And one minister governs them both; he is called Kadshiel. HIS DUTY IS TO DRAW DOWN HOLINESS (HEB. KDUSHAH) TO THE LOWER WORLDS.

49. כַּד אִתְפְּלַג לֵילְיָא, וְאִתְּעַר רוּחַ צָפוֹן וְקֻדְשָׁא בְּרִיךְ הוּא אָתֵי לְאִשְׁתַּעְשְׁעָא עִם צַדִּיקַיָּיא בְּגִנְתָּא דְעֵדֶן, כְּדֵין רוּחַ צָפוֹן אַקִּישׁ, וּמָטָא לְאִינוּן דִּמְמַנָּן בְּפַלְגוּת לֵילְיָא, לְזַמְּרָא, וְכֻלְּהוֹ מְזַמְּרִין וּפָתְחִין שִׁירָתָא. וְכַד אָתֵי צַפְרָא וּמִתְחַבַּר קַדְרוּתָא דְצַפְרָא בִּנְהוֹרָא, כְּדֵין כֻּלְּהוֹ אָחֳרָנִין אָמְרִין שִׁירָתָא, וְכָל כֹּכְבֵי רְקִיעָא וְכָל שְׁאָר מַלְאָכִין מְסַיְּיעִין לוֹן, כְּמָה דִּכְתִיב בְּרָן יַחַד כֹּכְבֵי בֹקֶר וַיָּרִיעוּ כָּל בְּנֵי אֱלֹקִים, עַד דְּיִשְׂרָאֵל נַטְלֵי שִׁירָתָא וְתוּשְׁבַּחְתָּא אֲבַתְרַיְיהוּ.

49. At midnight, the northern wind arises, and the Holy One, blessed be He, comes to the Garden of Eden to rejoice with the righteous. And this northern wind OF BINAH knocks and reaches those ministers in charge of chanting at midnight. They all sing and begin to chant, THUS ENABLING THE LOWER BEINGS TO SING. When the deep darkness JUST BEFORE DAWN joins with the light of the morning, all the other angels – THE WATER ANGELS ON THE RIGHT – sing. And all the stars in the firmament help them, along with the angels OF FIRE FROM THE LEFT SIDE. BECAUSE SINGING IS OF THE LEFT ASPECT, THEY NEED THE HELP OF THE LEFT COLUMN ANGELS IN ORDER TO SING, as is written: "The morning stars sang together and the sons of Elohim shouted for joy" (Iyov 38:7). BECAUSE ALL THE ANGELS SING IN THE MORNING, until Yisrael below open with singing and praises after them. BECAUSE THOSE ANGELS ARE MORE ELEVATED THAN YISRAEL, YISRAEL RECEIVE STRENGTH FROM THEM TO SING.

18. Sixth compartment: Chesed

While Gvurah, the compartment directly below, personifies Judgment, Chesed is a realm of pure Mercy. The angels residing here are responsible for delivering spiritual influences of mercy into our lives. We bring these angels into motion whenever we show mercy toward others. Everyday acts of sharing and kindness, without any expectations in return, are examples of mercy in this sense.

50. מָדוֹרָא שְׁתִיתָאָה: הוּא, מָדוֹרָא עִלָּאָה קָרֵיב לְמַלְכוּ שְׁמַיָא. וּבֵיהּ אַרְבִּין, וְנַהֲרִין, וְנַחֲלִין, דְּמִתְפַּלְּגִין מִן יַמָּא, וְכַמָּה נוּנִין אִינּוּן, דִּמְרַחֲשָׁן לְאַרְבַּע סִטְרֵי עָלְמָא, וְעֵילָא מִנְהוֹן סָרְכִין מִמַנָּן, וְחַד מְמַנָּא עֲלַיְיהוּ וְאוֹרִיאֵל שְׁמֵיהּ, וְהוּא מְמַנָּא עַל כָּל אִלֵּין תַּתָּאִין.

50. The sixth compartment is very close to the kingdom of heaven, THAT IS, THE INNER MALCHUT. In it are ships and rivers and streams that branch off and leave the sea, WHICH IS MALCHUT. Many are the fish – ALLUDING TO THE ANGELS – that, governed by their ministers, swarm IN THE RIVERS AND STREAMS to the four winds of the world. One minister, called Uriel, is in charge of all the lower ANGELS IN THIS COMPARTMENT. HE IS RESPONSIBLE FOR ALL THE ANGELS FROM THE WESTERN SIDE.

51. וְכֻלְּהוּ נַטְלֵי בְּשַׁעֲתֵי וְרִגְעֵי כַּד נַטְלֵי אַרְבֵּי לְסִטְרָא דָא וּלְסִטְרָא דָא, כַּד נַטְלֵי אַרְבֵּי לִסְטַר דָּרוֹם מְמַנָּא דְקַיְימָא עֲלַיְיהוּ, לְהַהוּא סִטְרָא, הוּא מִיכָאֵל דְּאָתָא מִימִינָא. וְכַד נַטְלֵי אַרְבֵּי לִסְטַר צָפוֹן, מְמַנָּא דְקַיְימָא עֲלַיְיהוּ לְהַהוּא סִטְרָא, הוּא גַּבְרִיאֵל דְּאָתֵי מִסִּטְרָא דִשְׂמָאלָא. וְכַד נַטְלֵי אַרְבֵּי לִסְטַר מִזְרָח הָא תַּמָּן אִיהוּ מְמַנָּא, דְּקַיְימָא עֲלַיְיהוּ, לְהַהוּא סִטְרָא רְפָאֵל שְׁמֵיהּ, וְהוּא לִימִינָא. וְכַד נַטְלֵי אַרְבֵּי לִסְטַר מַעֲרָב, מְמַנָּא דְקַיְימָא עֲלַיְיהוּ, לְהַהוּא סִטְרָא, הוּא אוֹרִיאֵל וְאִיהוּ לְבַתְרָאָה.

51. At those hours and moments when the ships sail, ALL THESE ANGELS TRAVEL WITH THEM in one direction and another – IN THOSE DIRECTIONS

TOWARD WHICH THE SHIPS SAIL. When the ships sail southward, the minister governing them is Michael, who is drawn from the Right COLUMN, WHICH IS CHESED. And when the ships sail northward, the minister governing them is Gabriel, who is drawn from the left side WHICH IS GVURAH. THE FOUR DIRECTIONS, SOUTH, NORTH, EAST AND WEST ARE CHOCHMAH, BINAH, TIFERET AND MALCHUT. AND FROM THE PERSPECTIVE OF THE SIX LOWER SFIROT, THEY ARE CHESED, GVURAH, TIFERET AND MALCHUT. And when the ships are eastbound, the minister governing them on that side is Raphael, who is to the right, THAT IS ON THE SIDE OF THE CHASSADIM. And when the ships are westbound, the minister governing them is Uriel, who is the last, WEST BEING THE LAST OF ALL FOUR DIRECTIONS.

19. Seventh compartment: Binah

The seventh compartment corresponds to Binah, the repository and source of all Light. This realm radiates the brightest Light and fulfillment.

52. מָדוֹרָא שְׁבִיעָאָה: הוּא מָדוֹרָא עִלָּאָה עַל כֹּלָּא. וְתַמָּן לָא אִשְׁתַּכְּחוּ בַּר נִשְׁמָתְהוֹן דְּצַדִּיקַיָּיא דְּתַמָּן מִתְעַדְּנִין בְּהַהוּא זִיהֲרָא עִלָּאָה, וּמִתְעַדְּנִין בְּעִדּוּנִין וְתַפְנוּקִין עִלָּאִין, וְתַמָּן לָא אִשְׁתַּכְּחוּ בַּר אִינוּן זַכָּאִין, וְגִנְזֵי שָׁלוֹם בְּרָכָה וּנְדָבָה, כֹּלָּא הוּא כְּגַוְונָא עִלָּאָה, וְהָא אֲמָרוּ חַבְרַיָּיא.

52. The seventh compartment is the highest, and there, only the souls of the righteous can be found. There, the souls rejoice, nourished by דופקרמשך bliss and splendor. And there, none are to be found, except the righteous. THIS MEANS THAT NO ANGELS RESIDE THERE. There can be found treasures of peace, blessings, and charity. And everything there reflects the higher, NAMELY BINAH, as the friends have explained.

53. כְּדֵין הוּא לְאָרֶץ דִּלְתַתָּא, בְּשִׁבְעָה מָדוֹרִין, וְכֻלְּהוּ כְּגַוְונָא דִּלְעֵילָא. וּבְכֻלְּהוּ אִית זִינִין כְּחֵיזוּ בְּנֵי נָשָׁא, וְכֻלְּהוּ מוֹדָן וּמְשַׁבְּחָן לְקֻדְשָׁא בְּרִיךְ הוּא, וְלֵית מָאן דְּיָדַע יְקָרֵיהּ, כְּאִינוּן דְּאִינוּן בְּמָדוֹרָא עִלָּאָה, וְאִלֵּין חָזָאן יְקָרֵיהּ כִּדְקָא יָאוֹת, לְמִפְלַח לֵיהּ, וּלְשַׁבְּחָא לֵיהּ, וּלְאִשְׁתְּמוֹדַע יְקָרֵיהּ.

53. The same can be found in the seven compartments of the lower land, which are all similar to the SEVEN COMPARTMENTS above. THUS, THE SEVEN COMPARTMENTS OF ASIYAH BELOW ARE EQUAL IN ALL RESPECTS TO THE SEVEN COMPARTMENTS OF MALCHUT OF THE WORLD OF ATZILUT ABOVE. And in all OF THE SEVEN COMPARTMENTS BELOW, there are ANGELS in the shape of humans, CLAD LIKE PEOPLE IN THE CLOTHING OF THE PHYSICAL WORLD. THE DIFFERENCE BETWEEN ABOVE AND BELOW IS THAT ABOVE ONLY IN THE SECOND COMPARTMENT CAN THERE BE FOUND ANGELS WHO ARE RELATED TO HUMANS. BUT FROM THE FOURTH COMPARTMENT UPWARD THERE CANNOT BE ANY RELATION

BETWEEN ANGELS AND HUMANS, SAVE THAT ACHIEVED THROUGH VISIONS AND INTENSE MEDITATION. IN THE LOWER WORLDS, HOWEVER, THE ANGELS ARE ALLOWED TO APPEAR IN HUMAN FORM. They all are grateful and praise the Holy One, blessed be He. Yet none can perceive His BLESSED glory, as can those in the supernal realms. They behold His glory most appropriately, so as to worship, praise, and acknowledge His greatness.

54. וְעָלְמָא דָא עִלָּאָה, דְּאִיהוּ תֵּבֵל, לָא קַיְימָא בְּקִיּוּמֵיהּ, אֶלָּא בְּגִינֵיהוֹן דְּצַדִּיקַיָּיא, דְּאִינוּן גּוּפִין קַדִּישִׁין. כְּגַוְונָא דִלְעֵילָּא לָא קַיְימָא הַהוּא מָדוֹרָא שְׁבִיעָאָה, אֶלָּא לְנִשְׁמַתְהוֹן דְּצַדִּיקַיָּיא, הָכֵי נָמֵי הַאי מָדוֹרָא שְׁבִיעָאָה לְתַתָּא, לָא קַיְימָא אֶלָּא לְגוּפֵיהוֹן דְּצַדִּיקַיָּיא, לְמֶהֱוֵי כֹּלָּא חַד דָּא כְּגַוְונָא דְּדָא.

54. This supernal world, called *Tevel*, exists only for the sake of the righteous, who are holy bodies, WHO ARE FOUND IN THIS WORLD. FOR THEM, THIS WORLD (*TEVEL*) WAS CREATED, AND FOR THEIR SAKE IT CONTINUES TO EXIST. Similar to the upper COMPARTMENTS OF THE SUPERNAL WORLD, this seventh compartment below exists only for the souls of the righteous. Also IN THE COMPARTMENTS OF THE LOWER EARTH, the lower seventh compartment, *TEVEL*, exists only for the bodies of the righteous. One WORLD is similar to the other – much like a reflection of the other. THE SEVEN COMPARTMENTS OF THE LOWER WORLDS ARE A REFLECTION OF, AND ARE DRAWN FROM, THE SEVEN SUPERNAL COMPARTMENTS. EVERY ASPECT ABOVE HAS ITS COUNTERPART BELOW. AS THE SOULS OF PEOPLE ALONE CAN BE FOUND IN THE SUPERNAL SEVENTH COMPARTMENT, SO IN THE LOWER SEVENTH, CALLED *TEVEL* – ONE OF THE SEVEN PHYSICAL WORLDS – CAN BE FOUND ONLY THE BODIES OF RIGHTEOUS PEOPLE. ALTHOUGH ALL THE OTHER KINDS OF CREATURES AND WICKED PEOPLE CAN ALSO BE FOUND THERE, THEY ARE THERE ONLY TO SERVE THE BODIES OF THE RIGHTEOUS, BECAUSE THE WORLD WAS CREATED AND IS MAINTAINED FOR THE SAKE OF THE RIGHTEOUS. AS IS WRITTEN: "THEY HAVE BEEN CREATED TO SERVE ME AND I TO SERVE MY CREATOR."

20. The seven chambers of the upper worlds

The Zohar explains that the preceding seven compartments are the building blocks and foundation for another, still higher level of chambers.

First chamber: Yesod

This realm is the domain of the angel who dispenses great mercy to all those souls who convert and follow the true path of The Creator.

55. תָּא חֲזֵי אָמַר רָבִּי שִׁמְעוֹן ז' מָדוֹרִין אִינוּן דְּקָאֲמָרָן, וּבְגוֹ אִינוּן אִית ז' הֵיכָלִין, מֵאִינוּן רָזֵי מְהֵימְנוּתָא, לָקֳבֵל ז' רְקִיעִין עִלָּאִין, וּבְכָל הֵיכָלָא וְהֵיכָלָא אִית רוּחִין עִלָּאִין. הֵיכָלָא קַדְמָאָה: הָכָא אִית רוּחָא, דְּאִתְמַמְּנוּ עַל נִשְׁמָתְהוֹן דְּגֵּרִין דְּאִתְגַּיָּירוּ, וְרַחֲמִיאֵ"ל שְׁמֵיהּ, וְאִיהוּ נָטִיל לוֹן וְאִתְהַנּוּן מִזִּיו יְקָרָא דִלְעֵילָא.

55. Rabbi Shimon said, Come and behold: These seven compartments OF THE UPPER WORLDS, about which we have spoken, contain seven chambers based on the secrets of Faith, WHICH IS MALCHUT OF THE WORLD OF ATZILUT. These correspond to the seven firmaments. In each and every chamber there are supernal spirits, WHO ARE THE ANGELS RESPONSIBLE FOR THOSE CHAMBERS. The first chamber, WHEN COUNTING FROM BELOW, IS CALLED YESOD AND has a spirit who is in charge of the souls of the converted. His name is Rachmiel, BECAUSE HE EXTENDS MERCY (HEB. RACHAMIM) TO THOSE SOULS. Through him, they delight in the radiance of divine glory.

21. Second chamber: Hod

This realm is the domain of the angel *Ahinael*, who teaches uneducated children the spiritual wisdom of the Torah.

‎56. הֵיכָלָא תִּנְיָינָא: אִית רוּחָא חֲדָא אֲהִינָא"ל שְׁמֵיה, וְדָא קַיְימָא עַל כָּל אִינּוּן נִשְׁמָתִין דְּרַבְיֵי, דְּלָא זָכוּ בְּהַאי עָלְמָא לְמִלְעֵי בְּאוֹרַיְיתָא, וְאִיהוּ קַיְימָא עֲלַיְיהוּ וְאוֹלִיף לוֹן.

56. The second chamber, CALLED HOD, has one spirit named Ahinael. He is in charge of the souls of children who did not merit learning Torah in their lives IN THIS WORLD. He is in charge of them and teaches them TORAH.

22. Third chamber: Netzach

The Angel called *Adrahinael* occupies this chamber. *Adrahinael* helps purify all those people who desired to repent for their wrongdoings, but died before they could compete their full repentance.

57. הֵיכָלָא תְּלִיתָאָה: בְּהַאי אִית רוּחָא חָדָא אֲדְרָהִינָא"ל שְׁמֵיהּ, וְאִיהוּ קַיְּימָא עַל נִשְׁמַתְהוֹן דְּאִינּוּן דְּאַהַדְרוּ בִּתְיוּבְתָּא, וְלָא אַהַדְרוּ, כְּגוֹן דַּחֲשִׁיבוּ וְעַד לָא אַהַדְרוּ בְּהוּ מִיתוּ אִלֵּין טָרְדִין לוֹן בַּגֵּיהִנֹּם וּלְבָתַר עָאלִין לוֹן לְהַאי רוּחָא מְמַנָּא, וְנָטִיל לוֹן, וְחָמְדָן לְאִתְהַנָּאָה מִזִּיו יְקָרָא דְּמָארֵיהוֹן, וְלָא אִתְהַנּוּן. וְאִלֵּין אִקְרוּן בְּנֵי בָשָׂר, וַעֲלַיְיהוּ כְּתִיב וְהָיָה מִדֵּי חֹדֶשׁ בְּחָדְשׁוֹ וּמִדֵּי שַׁבָּת בְּשַׁבַּתּוֹ יָבֹא כָל בָּשָׂר לְהִשְׁתַּחֲווֹת לְפָנַי אָמַר ה'.

57. The third chamber, CALLED NETZACH, has one spirit named Adrahinael. He is in charge of the souls of those who INTENDED repentance, but who have not REPENTED, because they died before they could repent THEIR ACTIONS. THUS, THEIR MINISTERING ANGEL IS CALLED ADRAHINAEL, FROM THE ARAMAIC WORD *HADRINA*, MEANING 'CONTRITION' OR 'REPENTANCE.' These souls are punished in Gehenom, and are then delivered to this spirit, who is in charge, and he receives them. They desire to enjoy their Master's precious glory, but cannot, EXCEPT ON SHABBAT AND THE NEW MOON. Those SOULS are called 'offspring of flesh', as is written: "And it shall come to pass, that on every new moon, and every Shabbat, all flesh shall come to worship before Me, said Hashem" (Yeshayah 66:23). THE REASON THESE SOULS ARE CALLED THE OFFSPRING OF FLESH IS THAT THE TEN SFIROT HAVE MANY NAMES, OF WHICH CHESED, GVURAH AND TIFERET ARE CALLED 'BRAIN, BONE, AND SINEW,' AND NETZACH AND HOD ARE CALLED 'FLESH AND SKIN.' THUS THE SOULS OF THE THIRD CHAMBER OF NETZACH ARE CALLED ALL FLESH, AS NETZACH IS FLESH.

23. Fourth chamber: Tiferet

The Angel *Gadrihael* inhabits this fourth chamber. *Gadrihael* assists souls who were murdered during physical existence in their transition to a place near The Creator. He also assists in executing judgment upon those who commit the act of murder.

58. הֵיכָלָא רְבִיעָאָה: הָכָא קַיְימָא חַד רוּחָא גְּדְרִיהָא"ל שְׁמֵיה, דָא קַיְימָא עַל כָּל אִינּוּן נִשְׁמָתִין דְּקְטוֹלֵי דִּשְׁאָר עַמִּין לְעָאֲלָא לוֹן, גּוֹ פּוּרְפִּרָא דְמַלְכָּא, וְאִתְרְשִׁימוּ תַּמָּן, עַד יוֹמָא דְיִנְקוֹם לוֹן קֻדְשָׁא בְּרִיךְ הוּא דִּכְתִיב יָדִין בַּגּוֹיִם מָלֵא גְוִיּוֹת מָחַץ רֹאשׁ עַל אֶרֶץ רַבָּה.

58. The fourth chamber IS TIFERET. In charge stands the spirit of Gadrihael. THIS ANGEL IS in charge of preparing the souls of those killed by the nations of the world for IMPRINTING ON the King's royal garment. They stay imprinted there until the day when the Holy One, blessed be He, avenges them, as it is written: "He judges among the nations; their land is full of dead bodies; He shall shatter heads over many countries" (Tehilim 110:6). BECAUSE THE HOLY ONE, BLESSED BE HE, RESIDES AMONG THE SOULS OF THE MURDERED.

24. Fifth chamber : Gvurah

All those souls who emanate from the spiritual lineage of the Left
Column – with its energy of judgment, anger, and volatility –
are ruled over by the Angel *Adiriel*, who inhabits the fifth chamber
of Gvurah.

59. הֵיכָלָא חֲמִישָׁאָה: הָכָא קַיְימָא חַד רוּחָא, דְּאִקְרֵי אֲדִירִיאֵ"ל וְדָא
קַיְימָא עַל כָּל אִלֵּין נִשְׁמָתִין, דְּאִתְקַיְימוּ בְּהַהוּא סְטְרָא.

59. The fifth chamber IS CALLED GVURAH. In charge is a spirit named
Adiriel. He stands in charge of the souls who are accomplished from the
aspect of the LEFT side. THE NAME ADIRIEL IS FORMED FROM THE
WORDS *ADIR* AND *EL. ADIR* MEANS MIGHTY, AS HE IS IN CHARGE OVER
THE CHAMBER OF GVURAH (MIGHT).

25. Sixth chamber: Chesed

The greatest of souls are worthy to reside in this, the sixth chamber of Chesed.

וְאִלֵּין אִינּוּן לְעֵילָּא מִכָּלְהוּ, דִּי בִּמְדוֹרָא דָּא, עִלָּאָה עַל כֹּלָּא וּמִיכָאֵל רַב מְמָנָא עַל כָּלְהוּ קַיְימָא בֵּיהּ, וְכַמָה אֶלֶף וְרִבְבָן, כָּלְהוּ קַיְימִין תְּחוֹתֵיהּ בְּהַהוּא סִטְרָא, וְתַמָּן מִתְעַדְּנִין אִינּוּן נִשְׁמָתִין דַּחֲסִידֵי, בְּהַהוּא נְהוֹרָא עִלָּאָה דְּנַגְדָּא מֵעָלְמָא דְּאָתֵי.

The loftiest of all SOULS are found in this loftiest compartment of all. The archangel OF ALL ANGELS, Michael, rules over this CHAMBER, NAMELY THE CHAMBER OF CHESED. Thousands and tens of thousands OF ANGELS reside under his rule on the side OF CHESED. There the souls of the pious delight in the supernal light that is drawn therein from the World to Come. THE LIGHT IS DRAWN FROM BINAH, AS BINAH IS CALLED, THE WORLD TO COME. BUT SINCE THE SEVENTH CHAMBER OF BINAH HAS NO GOVERNING ANGELS, IT IS NOT DISCUSSED AT ALL.

26. The seven chambers of Aba and Ima of Briyah

All prayers must travel within a specific spiritual network in order to reach their intended destination. The Zohar outlines this metaphysical structure so that we may access this realm simply by learning this section. The descriptions and explanations that follow provide the reader with an opportunity to access the spiritual network in such a way that prayers will be answered.

The Chambers of *Abba* [Father] and *Ima* [Mother] pertain to the principles of male and female energy that are built into the fabric of our physical universe. The proton and electron – the *minus* and *plus* charges in electricity, as well as in man and woman – are all branches extending out from this singular spiritual seed.

60. תָּא חֲזֵי אָמַר רָבִּי שִׁמְעוֹן מַאן הוּא דְּיָדַע לְסַדְּרָא צְלוֹתָא דְּמָרֵיהּ כְּמֹשֶׁה, בְּשַׁעֲתָא דְּאִצְטְרִיךְ לֵיהּ, לְסַדְּרָא צְלוֹתֵיהּ בַּאֲרִיכוּת סֵדֶר, וּבְשַׁעֲתָא דְּאִצְטְרִיךְ לֵיהּ לְקַצְרָא הָכֵי נָמֵי. אָמַר רָבִּי שִׁמְעוֹן הָא אַשְׁכַּחְנָא בְּסִפְרֵי קַדְמָאֵי, סְדוּרָא דְּרָזֵי דְּרָזִין, בְּקִשּׁוּרָא חֲדָא, זִמְנִין דְּאִצְטְרִיךְ לְסַדְּרָא צְלוֹתֵיהּ כְּדְקָא יָאוֹת, וּלְקַשְּׁרָא קְשָׁרִין, לְבַסּוּמֵי לְמָארֵיהּ כְּדְקָא יָאוֹת, וּלְמִנְדַּע לְיַחֲדָא יְחוּדָא שְׁלֵימָתָא, לְמִקְרַע רְקִיעִין, וּלְאַפְתְּחָא תַּרְעִין וּפִתְחִין דְּלָא יְהֵא מָאן דְּיִמְחֵי בִּידֵיהּ.

60. Come and behold, Rabbi Shimon said: Who knows how to arrange a prayer to his Master, as did Moses, who knew how to lengthen and shorten his prayer as necessary. Rabbi Shimon said: I found written in ancient books the order of connecting THE GRADES – the inner secrets – into one unit, SO THAT THEY, UNITED, WILL PROJECT LIGHT TO THE LOWER WORLDS. Sometimes it is required to arrange a prayer as to entice and soothe the Master to make the proper unifications, penetrate firmaments, and open gates and passages. One must arrange his prayers so that no one will stop him, NAMELY, THAT THE PROSECUTORS WILL NOT DISTURB HIM.

61. זַכָּאִין אִינוּן צַדִּיקַיָּא, דְּאִנּוּן יָדְעֵי לְמִפְתֵּי לְמָארֵיהוֹן, וּלְבַטּוּלֵי גְּזֵרִין, וּלְאַשְׁרָאָה שְׁכִינְתָּא בְּעָלְמָא, וּלְנַחֲתָא בִּרְכָאן, וּלְמֶעֱדֵּי מָארֵיהוֹן דְּדִינִין דְּלָא יִשְׁלְטוּן בְּעָלְמָא. קָם רָבִּי שִׁמְעוֹן וַאֲמַר, מִי יְמַלֵּל גְּבוּרוֹת

ה' וגו', מַאן יְגַלֵּי עַפְרָא מֵעֵינָךְ אַבְרָהָם חֲסִידָא, יָמִינָא דְקֻדְשָׁא בְּרִיךְ הוּא, דְּגַלֵּי לָךְ רָזָא דְּרָזִין, וְשָׁרִיאַת צְלוֹתִין בְּעָלְמָא, וְאִתְגַּלְּיָין לָךְ הֵיכְלֵי דְמַלְכָּא עִלָּאָה.

61. Blessed are the righteous who know how to appease their Master, cancel decrees, and cause the Shechinah to rest upon the world. They know how to draw down blessings and prevent the administrators of judgment from prevailing in the world. Rabbi Shimon rose and said: "Who can utter the mighty acts of Hashem?" (Tehilim 106:2). Who can remove the dust from your eyes, pious Abraham, the right hand of the Holy One, blessed be He? He revealed to you the ultimate of secrets and the beginning of prayer in the world (AS ABRAHAM INSTITUTED THE MORNING PRAYER), AS WELL AS the chambers of the supernal King.

62. שִׁבְעָה הֵיכָלִין קַדִּישִׁין אִינוּן, וְאִינוּן קַיָּימִין בְּתַרְעִין בְּקִיּוּמָא, וּבְכָל חַד וְחַד עָאל צְלוֹתָא דְיִחוּדָא, דְּמַאן דְּיָדַע לְבַסּוּמֵי לְמָארֵיהּ, וּלְיַחֲדָא יְחוּדָא בִּשְׁלִימוּ, דְּיָדַע לְאָעֲלָא בְּכֻלְּהוּ, וּלְקַשְּׁרָא קִשְׁרִין אִלֵּין בְּאִלֵּין, רוּחָא בְּרוּחָא, רוּחָא תַּתָּאָה בְּרוּחָא עִלָּאָה, כְּתִיב ה' בַּצַּר פְּקָדוּךָ צָקוּן לַחַשׁ מוּסָרְךָ לָמוֹ.

62. There are seven holy chambers and they have well guarded gates, MEANING THAT ALL THE ADMINISTRATORS OF JUDGMENT HAVE BEEN REMOVED FROM THEM AND THEY OPEN ONLY TO THOSE WORTHY OF ENTERING. And into each and every CHAMBER the prayers of unity enter. For of he who knows how to appease his Master, make complete unification, make his way into those chambers, and connect THE CHAMBERS among themselves – spirit with spirit, LOWER SPIRIT WITH A HIGHER SPIRIT – it is said, "Hashem, in trouble have they visited You, they poured out a prayer when the chastening was upon them" (Yeshayah 26:16).

27. The First chamber of Yesod and Malchut:
Livnat Hasapir (Sapphire stone)

This chamber is our connection with the Upper Worlds, from which we draw spiritual Light through our prayers. Without the connection known as the first chamber, we cannot access the Upper Realms.

The term *Sapphire* refers to a spirit called *Sapir*.
The word *stone* refers to the moon. The mystery of this connection is found within the Hebrew word for *stone*, which is *Livnat* לבנת.

Livnat is rooted in the Hebrew word for *moon*, or *Levanah* לבנה. Kabbalah teaches that the moon has no Light of its own. Therefore it represents the physical world, which is signified by the stone.

The Sapphire gemstone glitters and reflects Light, which is illustrative of the Upper Worlds that emanate the Light of The Creator. The *stone* and the *Sapphire* are the physical expressions of these two worlds. The First Chamber is the portal and interface by which we join our world – the stone – to the upper world – the Sapphire – where the spirit *Sapir* dwells. In this way, the spiritual Light is able to enter our lives.

63. הֵיכָלָא קַדְמָאָה: כְּתִיב וְתַחַת רַגְלָיו כְּמַעֲשֵׂה לִבְנַת הַסַּפִּיר, וּכְעֶצֶם הַשָּׁמַיִם לָטֹהַר. רָזָא דְרָזִין, רוּחַ דְּאִקְרֵי סְפִּירָא כְּסַפִּירוּ דְּאֶבֶן טָבָא, נָצִיץ לִתְרֵין סִטְרִין, נְהוֹרָא חַד סָלִיק וְנָחֵית, וְהַהוּא נְהוֹרָא חִוָּור, נָצִיץ לְכָל סְטַר: עֵילָא וְתַתָּא וּלְאַרְבַּע סִטְרֵי עָלְמָא, נְהוֹרֵיה תַּלְיָין סָתִים וְגַלְיָיא.

63. The first chamber, CALLED THE CHAMBER OF YESOD AND MALCHUT, IS THE FIRST FROM BELOW. ABOUT it is written: "and there was under His feet a kind of paved work sapphire stone, and as it were the embodiment of the heaven for clearness" (Shemot 24:10). Here is the secret of secrets: in this chamber, there is a spirit called Sapir (sapphire), who shines as does the precious stone called sapphire. It glitters in two directions, NAMELY CHESED AND GVURAH. One light, THE LIGHT OF CHESED, goes up AS RETURNING LIGHT and goes down AS DIRECT LIGHT. This light is white, shining in every direction, upward, downward, and to all four directions of

the world, ALL SIX EXTREMITIES OF ZEIR ANPIN. Its light is suspended sometimes, hidden yet revealed. THAT IS, IT IS SOMETIMES SUSPENDED WITHOUT DECIDING ON ANY DIRECTION.

64. מִנְהוֹרָא דָא מִתְפָּרְשִׁין ד׳ נְהוֹרִין, לד׳ סְטְרִין, וְכֻלְּהוּ נְהוֹרִין חַד נְהוֹרָא, כְּבוֹצִינָא דְּשַׁרְגָּא דְּדָלֵיק, וְנָצִיץ נְהוֹרִין לְחֵיזוּ דְעַיְינִין דִּבְנֵי נָשָׁא, וְאִינוּן נְהוֹרִין דְּשַׁרְגָּא, סָלְקִין וְנַחְתִּין אַזְלִין וְתַיְיבִין, מִגּוֹ הַהוּא אֶשָׁא דְנְהוֹרָא דְּשַׁרְגָּא דְּדָלֵיק, וְכֻלְּהוּ חַד נְהוֹרָא, הָכֵי נָמֵי אִלֵּין. וּנְצִיצִין כֻּלְּהוּ נְהוֹרִין, כְּחֵיזוּ דִנְחָשָׁא בְּטִישָׁא בְּסוּמְקָא, כְּמָה דְאִתְּמַר, וְנוֹצְצִים כְּעֵין נְחֹשֶׁת קָלָל. דָּא הוּא לְיְמִינָא.

64. From the light OF CHESED, four lights branch out to four sides. THE SECOND LIGHT IS THE LIGHT OF GVURAH OF THE SPIRIT SAPIR. THE FIRST LIGHT, CHESED, SHINES IN SIX DIRECTIONS AND THE SECOND, GVURAH, IN FOUR. THIS IS BECAUSE THE TWO LIGHTS ARE THE MALE AND THE FEMALE ASPECTS OF THE SPIRIT SAPIR; THE FIRST LIGHT REPRESENTS CHOCHMAH, BINAH, DAAT, CHESED, GVURAH AND TIFERET, WHILE THE SECOND REPRESENTS NETZACH, HOD, YESOD AND MALCHUT. All these lights are as one, as the light of a candle that glitters to the eyes of onlookers. The light rays of the candle go up and down, leave and return from the fire of the burning candle. And all are one light. So are the four lights. They glitter like the red color of burnished brass, as it is written: "And they sparkled like the color of burnished brass" (Yechezkel 1:7). All this is to the right, BECAUSE, IN SPITE OF THE FACT THAT THE RED LIGHT OF THE LIGHTS OF SAPIR ILLUMINATES TO THE LEFT SIDE, IT NEVERTHELESS STANDS TO THE RIGHT OF THE CHAMBER.

65. לִשְׂמָאלָא, אִית רוּחָא דְּאִקְרֵי לְבָנָה, וְדָא אִתְכְּלִיל בְּרוּחָא קַדְמָאָה, וְעָאל דָּא בְּדָא, נְהוֹרֵיה סוּמָק וְחִוָּור כַּחֲדָא, בְּגִין דְּנָפְקָא מֵאִינוּן נְהוֹרִין קַדְמָאִין. כַּד אָתוּ נְהוֹרִין דְּדָא, מָטוּ בִּנְהוֹרִין קַדְמָאִין וְאִתְכְּלִילוּ בֵּיה, וְאִינוּן חַד, וְאִתְחֲזוּן נְהוֹרֵי קַדְמָאֵי בִּלְחוֹדַיְיהוּ. וְלָא אִתְגַּלְיָין אִינוּן אַחֲרָנִין, וְלָא אִתְיְדְעוּ דְּעָאלוּ בְּגַוַויְיהוּ, וְאִתְטַמְרוּ בֵּיה. כד״א וְלָא וְלָא נוֹדַע כִּי בָאוּ אֶל קִרְבֶּנָה וגו׳ וְדָא הוּא רוּחָא בְּרוּחָא דְּאִינוּן חַד, נְהוֹרִין

27. The First chamber of Yesod and Malchut:
Livnat Hasapir (Sapphire stone)

בִּנְהוֹרִין דְּאִינוּן חַד. וְהָכָא אִינוּן תְּרֵין רְקִיעִין תַּתָּאִין מֵאִינוּן רְקִיעִין דְּאִקְרוּן שְׁמֵי הַשָּׁמַיִם.

65. To the left OF THE CHAMBER, there is a spirit named *Levanah* (Moon), which is included in and mingles with the first spirit, CALLED SAPIR. The light FROM THIS SPIRIT is simultaneously red and white because it originates from these TWO first lights OF THE SPIRIT SAPIR, WHICH ARE ALSO RED AND WHITE – YET HERE THEY ARE ONE. And when the lights OF THE SPIRIT LEVANAH reach the first lights OF SPIRIT SAPIR and intermingle with them and become one, only the first lights become evident. The other lights OF THE SPIRIT CALLED LEVANAH, are not revealed and are indistinguishable when they enter, as it is written: "and it could not be known that they had entered there" (Beresheet 41:21). This is the intermingling of spirit with spirit to be one and of lights with lights to become one. In this CHAMBER, two lower firmaments shine, and they are called the heaven of heavens.

66. מִתְּרֵין רוּחִין אִלֵּין מְנַצְצָן, אִתְבְּרִיאוּ אִינוּן אוֹפַנִּין, דְּאִינוּן קַדִּישִׁין, דְּדִינַיְיהוּ כְּדִינָא דְּחֵיוֹת, כִּדְכְתִיב מַרְאֵה הָאוֹפַנִּים וּמַעֲשֵׂיהֶם וְגו', וְדָא הוּא דִכְתִיב, וּדְמוּת הַחַיּוֹת מַרְאֵיהֶן כְּגַחֲלֵי אֵשׁ בּוֹעֲרוֹת כְּמַרְאֵה הַלַּפִּידִים. הִיא מִתְהַלֶּכֶת בֵּין הַחַיּוֹת, מָאן הִיא, דָּא רוּחָא קַדִּישָׁא, אֲתָר דְּנַפְקוּ מִנֵּיהּ, וְאִיהִי נָהִיר לוֹן, דִּכְתִיב וְנֹגַהּ לָאֵשׁ, וּמִן הָאֵשׁ יוֹצֵא בָרָק.

66. From the glittering of those two spirits, the holy Ofanim were created. They are treated the same way as are the living creatures, as it is written: "The appearance of the Ofanim (wheels) and their work" (Yechezkel 1:16). THIS IS AS MENTIONED IN THE QUOTATION, "WHEN THOSE MOVED, THESE MOVED; AND WHEN THOSE STOOD STILL, THESE STOOD STILL; AND WHEN THOSE WERE LIFTED UP FROM THE EARTH, THE OFANIM (WHEELS) WERE LIFTED UP ALONG WITH THEM" (IBID. 20). And OF THE OFANIM (WHEELS) it is written: "As for the likeness of the living creatures and their appearance, it was like burning coals of fire, which burn like torches. It flashed up and down among the living creatures" (Ibid. 13). EVEN THOUGH THEY ARE CALLED LIVING CREATURES, THEY ARE

-56-

NEVERTHELESS OFANIM THAT ARE CALLED LIVING CREATURES BECAUSE THEY ARE TREATED THE SAME AS LIVING CREATURES. HE ASKS: To whom DOES THE SCRIPTURE REFER TO AS "it" IN THE VERSE, "IT FLASHED UP AND DOWN AMONG THE LIVING CREATURES?" AND HE ANSWERS: THE REFERENCE IS MADE TO the holy spirit LEVANAH, which is where they originated. And it shines upon them, as the scriptures continue: "And the fire was bright and out of the fire went forth lightning" (Ibid. 13). THE HOLY SPIRIT LEVANAH IS MALCHUT, CALLED BRIGHTNESS, OF WHICH THE SCRIPTURE SAYS, "AND THE FIRE WAS BRIGHT AND OUT OF THE FIRE WENT FORTH LIGHTNING." IT IS THEREFORE SAID OF ITS THAT SINCE IT FLASHED UP AND DOWN AMONG THE LIVING CREATURES, "THEIR APPEARANCE WAS LIKE BURNING COALS OF FIRE." SHE IS THE ASPECT OF BRIGHTNESS FROM WHICH FIRE AND LIGHTNING ARE DRAWN.

67. כַּד אִתְכְּלִיל רוּחָא בְּרוּחָא, נָפֵיק מִנַּיְיהוּ, נְהִירוּ דְּחַד חֵיוְתָא רַמְיָא עַל ד' אוֹפַנִּין, וְהָא דְּיוֹקְנָא דִילֵיהּ כְּאַרְיֵה, שַׁלִּיט עַל אֶלֶף וּתְלַת מְאָה רִבּוֹא דְּאוֹפַנִּין אָחֳרָנִין, גַּדְפָּהָא דְּנִשְׁרָא, הַאי אִתְמַנָּא עַל אִינּוּן אוֹפַנִּים, בְּד' גַּלְגָּלִים, נָטְלִין כָּל חַד וְחַד, מֵאִינּוּן אַרְבַּע, בְּכָל גַּלְגַּלָּא וְגַלְגַּלָּא תְּלַת סַמְכִין וְאִינּוּן תְּרֵיסַר סָמְכִין בְּד' גַּלְגָּלִין, רוּחָא דָּא שָׁלְטָא עַל כֹּלָּא, מֵהָכָא נָפְקוּ, וְדָא רוּחָא קַיְּימָא לְכֻלְּהוּ, מִינָה אִתְזָנוּ.

67. And when one spirit is included in the other – THAT IS THE SPIRIT SAPIR IN THE SPIRIT LEVANAH – the light of one living creatures comes out of them and spreads over four Ofanim. The shape of this living creatures is that of a lion, NAMELY OF CHESED, WHICH IS WHITE. This living creatures rules over thirteen million other Ofanim. The wings of this living creatures are those of an eagle. THE NUMBER OF OFANIM IS THIRTEEN MILLION because each of the four OFANIM travels on four wheels, each of which has three supports. In all, there are twelve supports for the four wheels ON WHICH EACH OFAN TRAVELS. The spirit SAPIR controls them all because they originate from it. This spirit sustains them all, NAMELY THOSE WHEELS AND SUPPORTS, and through it they receive nourishment. HENCE IT IS COUNTED WITH THEM AS A THIRTEENTH.

68. אִלֵּין ד' אוֹפַנִּים, ד' אַנְפִּין לְכָל חַד וְחַד, וְכָל אִינּוּן אַנְפִּין,

27. The First chamber of Yesod and Malchut:
Livnat Hasapir (Sapphire stone)

אִסְתַּכְּיָין לְאַרְבַּע סִטְרִין דְּהַהוּא חֵיוָתָא דְּקַיְימָא עֲלַיְיהוּ. כַּד נַטְלִין אִלֵּין אַרְבַּע תְּחוֹת הַהוּא חֵיוָתָא, עָאלוּ דָּא בְּדָא, וּמְשַׁלְּבָן דָּא בְּדָא. כְּדְ"א מַקְבִּילוֹת הַלּוּלָאוֹת אִשָּׁה אֶל אֲחוֹתָהּ, לְאִתְכְּלָלָא חֲדָא בְּחֲדָא וּלְאֲעָלָא דָּא בְּדָא. כַּד נַטְלִין אִינוּן גַּלְגַּלִּין, אִשְׁתְּמַע קָל נְעִימוּתָא, בְּכָל אִינוּן חֵילִין דִּלְתַתָּא לְזִינַיְיהוּ.

68. Those four Ofanim have four faces each, and all four face toward the four sides of the living creatures set over them. And when the four Ofanim travel under that living creatures, they penetrate and cling to one another, ARE INCLUDED EACH WITHIN THE OTHER, AND RECEIVE SUPPORT FROM EACH OTHER. This is alluded to by: "The loops may correspond one to the other" (Shemot 26:5). Each is within the other and each interpenetrates the other. When the wheels travel, a tender sound is heard among all the lower hosts. THAT IS, THEIR PLEASANT SUSTENANCE REACHES ALL THE LOWER HOSTS.

69. תְּחוֹת הֵיכָלָא דָּא, מִתְפָּרְשִׁין חֵילִין לְבַר, לְכַמָּה סִטְרִין דִּרְקִיעִין דִּלְתַתָּא, עַד דִּמְטוֹ לְכֹכְבָא דְּשַׁבְּתַאי, כֻּלְּהוּ אִסְתַּכְּיָין לְהֵיכָלָא דָּא מִתַּמָּן אִתְחְזְנוּ כָּל אִלֵּין דִּי בְּהֵיכָלָא דָּא, כֻּלְּהוּ אִסְתְּכוּ לְהַהוּא רוּחָא, דִּכְתִיב אֶל אֲשֶׁר יִהְיֶה שָּׁמָּה הָרוּחַ לָלֶכֶת יֵלֵכוּ לֹא יִסַּבּוּ בְּלֶכְתָּן, וְדָא הוּא הֵיכָלָא דְּאִקְרֵי לִבְנַת הַסַּפִּיר.

69. Below this chamber, the hosts spread out to radiate in many directions in the lower firmaments, THROUGH WHICH MATTERS CONCERNING THE LEADING OF THE LOWER WORLD CHANGE. This continues until a planet called *Shabtai* (Saturn) is reached IN THE SECOND FIRMAMENT OF THE WORLD OF ASIYAH. ALL SEVEN PLANETS ARE LOCATED IN THE WORLD OF ASIYAH, AND THEY ARE CALLED *SHABTAI* (SATURN), *TZEDEK* (JUPITER), *MA'ADIM* (MARS), *NOGAH* (VENUS), *COCHAV* (MERCURY), AND *LEVANAH* (MOON). THROUGH THESE PLANETS, EVERY CHANGE COMES TO THE WORLD. THE FIRST PLANET, SHABTAI, FEEDS FROM THE LOWEST OF THE SEVEN CHAMBERS OF THE WORLD OF BRIYAH, AND THE REST OF THE PLANETS FROM THE OTHER CHAMBERS. All THE LOWER WORLDS look toward this chamber FOR THEIR SUSTENANCE. From this chamber all those present are fed and look forward TO RECEIVING SUSTENANCE AND STRENGTH FROM THE SPIRIT OF SAPIR, as it is written: "wherever the spirit was minded to go, they went; they turned not when they went" (Yechezkel 1:12). This chamber is called *Livnat Hasapir* BECAUSE OF THE TWO SPIRITS CONTAINED THEREIN, SAPIR AND LEVANAH.

70. רוּחָא דָא דְּכָלֵיל רוּחָא אָחֶרָא תִּנְיָינָא, סַלְקָא וְנַחְתָּא נְהוֹרֵיהּ, דְּלָא שְׁכִיךְ לְעָלְמִין, כְּנוּרָא דְּשִׁמְשָׁא גּוֹ מַיָא, לֵית מָאן דְּקָאִים עֲלֵיהּ, בַּר רְעוּתֵיהּ דְּבַר נָשׁ זַכָּאָה, בְּהַהוּא צְלוֹתָא, דְּעָאלַת בְּהַהוּא הֵיכָלָא, וְסַלְקָא לְקַשְׁרָא קִשְׁרִין בִּשְׁלִימוּ, בְּשֵׁרוּתָא דְּרוּחַ דָּא כְּדְקָא חָזֵי. כְּדֵין נְהוֹרָא אִתְעַטַּף בֵּיהּ, וְחָדֵי בָהּ וְסַלְקָא עִמָּהּ לְאִתְקַשְׁרָא בְּקִשּׁוּרָא דְּהֵיכָלָא תִּנְיָינָא, לְאִתְכַּלְּלָא רוּחָא דְּכָלֵיל בְּרוּחָא אָחֳרָא עִלָּאָה דַּעֲלֵיהּ.

70. The spirit SAPIR includes the spirit LEVANAH within it and has light that goes up and comes down. Its light never stops shining, as the light of the sun within the water. And nothing other than the desire of a righteous man through his prayer that goes into that chamber can conceive THAT SPIRIT. That prayer elevates so as to connect perfectly – THAT IS, MAKE UNIFICATIONS under the influence of this spirit – as is appropriate. Then THE SPIRIT is enveloped with light and is happy with THE PRAYER, and goes up with it to the second chamber to connect with its unity. This spirit, WHICH INCLUDES WITHIN IT THE SPIRIT LEVANAH, can now mix with a higher spirit IN THE SECOND CHAMBER.

71. וְרוּחָא דָא דְּכָלֵיל, כָּלֵיל בֵּיהּ הַהִיא חֵיוָותָא, וְכָל אִינּוּן אוֹפַנִּין וְגַלְגַּלִּין, וְאִתְאַחֲדָן בֵּיהּ, כְּגַוְונָא דְּאִתְאַחֲדָא אֶשָׁא בְּמַיָא, וּמַיָא בְּאֶשָׁא, דָּרוֹם בְּצָפוֹן, צָפוֹן בְּדָרוֹם, מִזְרָח בְּמַעֲרָב, וּמַעֲרָב בְּמִזְרָח, הָכֵי אִתְאַחֲדָן כֻּלְּהוּ דָּא בְּדָא, וְאִתְקַשְׁרָן דָּא בְּדָא. הַהוּא רוּחָא סַלְקָא לְאִתְקַשְׁרָא, וְהַהִיא חֵיוָתָא אִסְתַּכְּיָיא לְעֵילָּא, לְגַבֵּי הֵיכָלָא תִּנְיָינָא וְאִסְתַּכְּיָין דָּא בְּדָא.

71. This HIGHER spirit, WHICH NOW INCLUDES THE SECOND SPIRIT THAT

27. The First chamber of Yesod and Malchut:
Livnat Hasapir (Sapphire stone)

WENT UP TO THE SECOND CHAMBER AS IT TRAVELS UPWARD, ALSO includes within it all the living creatures, Ofanim, and wheels. They grasp onto it, as does water to fire and fire to water AND AS THE FOUR WINDS GRASP ONTO EACH OTHER, south onto north, north onto south, east onto west, and west onto east. They all link with each other and hold onto each other – LIVING CREATURES, OFANIM, AND TWO SPIRITS – WITH THE SPIRIT OF THE SECOND CHAMBER. This spirit goes up to connect WITH THE SPIRIT OF THE SECOND CHAMBER, and the living creatures, INCLUDED IN THE SPIRIT also looks up toward the second chamber TO RECEIVE ITS SUSTENANCE. They look toward each other AND THE SECOND CHAMBER, AND ALL THEREIN LOOK TOWARD THOSE OF THE LOWER CHAMBER, THAT HAVE COME UP TO IT, SO IT MAY BE COMPLETED BY THEM.

72. בְּאֶמְצָעִיתָא דְהֵיכָלָא דָא, נָעִיץ חַד עַמּוּדָא, דְּסַלְקָא עַד אֶמְצָעִיתָא דְהֵיכָלָא אָחֲרָא, וְאִיהוּ נָקִיב וְנָעִיץ מִתַּתָּא לְעֵילָא, לְאִתְדַּבְּקָא רוּחָא בְּרוּחָא, וְכֵן עַד לְעֵילָא מִכֻּלְהוּ, לְמֶהֱוֵי כֻּלְהוּ רוּחָא חֲדָא, כד"א וְרוּחַ אֶחָד לַכֹּל.

72. In the center of this chamber stands a pillar that reaches the middle of a higher chamber. It pierces THE ROOFS OF ALL THE SEVEN CHAMBERS AND STANDS ERECT WITHIN THEM from bottom to top. This enables the spirits to bond to each other and to elevate FROM ALL THESE CHAMBERS, SO THAT THEY NOW UNITE and become one spirit, as it is written: "They all have one spirit" (Kohelet 3:19).

28. The second chamber: Hod

This chamber is filled with pure white light which remains in a state of potential until the interface of the first chamber acts upon it through our positive actions and prayers. This white light then shines through the first chamber. As it fulfills all our desires, the one light suddenly becomes many. A wonderful illustration of this process is visible in nature, when a ray of sunlight strikes a gemstone and refracts into the seven colors of the rainbow.

73. הֵיכָלָא תִּנְיָינָא: כְּתִיב וּכְעֶצֶם הַשָּׁמַיִם לָטוֹהַר, הָכָא אִיהוּ הַהוּא רוּחָא דְּאִקְרֵי זֹהַר, וְקַיְימָא בְּחִוּוְרְתָּא תָּדִיר, דְּלָא אִתְעָרְבוּ גְּווֹנוֹי בְּאַחֲרָא, וְאִיהוּ עֶצֶם דְּלָא אִשְׁתַּנֵּי לְעָלְמִין. דָּא לָאו אִיהוּ בְּאִתְגַּלְיָא הָכֵי, לְאִתְנַצְצָא כְּאַחֲרָא, דָּא קַשֵּׁי לְאִתְגַּלְיָא. כִּסְתִּימוּ דְּעֵינָא, דְּכַד מִתְגַּלְגְּלָא אִזְדַּהַר, וְנָצֵיץ בְּגִלְגּוּלָא, וְדָא אוּף הָכֵי, בְּגִין דְּכַד הַהוּא רוּחָא קַדְמָאָה סָלְקָא, מְגַלְגֵּל בְּגִלְגּוּלָא, וְגָלֵי לֵיהּ, וְאִתְקַשַּׁר בַּהֲדֵיהּ, בְּקִשּׁוּרָא דְּחִוּוְרְתָּא דְּעֵינָא גּוֹ גָּוָון אַחֲרָא דְּאִיהוּ דַּקִּיק מִנֵּיהּ דְּשָׁאֲרֵי עֲלוֹי.

73. It is said that the second chamber is "the embodiment (Heb. *etzem*) of heaven for clearness" (Shemot 24:10). Here can be found a spirit named Zohar (Eng. 'splendor'), which is always in white, THE COLOR OF THE ILLUMINATION OF CHASSADIM, CALLED WHITE. It cannot mix with any other color. This is called Etzem and never changes. The glittering of this SPIRIT is not so revealed as that of the others. It is harder to distinguish, BECAUSE ALL ITS COLORS ARE INCLUDED IN THE WHITE. This is similar to the hidden part of the eye, THE BLACK PART, WHEREIN LIES THE ABILITY TO SEE. When it rolls, it glitters and glows. The same applies TO THIS SPIRIT: IT CANNOT SHINE UNLESS IT ROLLS AND IT DOES NOT LINGER UPON ANY ONE OF ITS SIDES. THE SPIRIT ROLLS THEM ALL AND THEY GLITTER UNTIL IT REACHES THE WHITE THEREIN. IT STANDS THERE, HAVING EXPOSED IN THE MEANWHILE ITS FOUR SIDES. For when the first spirit, *LIVNAT HASAPIR* elevates TO THIS SPIRIT, it revolves it so as to reveal ITS FULL EMANATIONS, and it THUS RECEIVES ALL ITS FOUR ASPECTS. THE FIRST SPIRIT connects with the SECOND as through the white in the eye, MEANING THAT AFTER RECEIVING ITS FOUR COLORS IT

IS ATTACHED SOLELY TO THE WHITE. This is done through a much fainter color that is shed upon this spirit, THROUGH THE EMANATION OF THE SPIRIT IN THE THIRD CHAMBER OF NETZACH THAT SHINES WITH WHITE LIGHT FROM THE SPIRIT OF THE SECOND CHAMBER. IT IS SO FAINT THAT NO COLOR IS DISTINGUISHABLE IN IT.

74. מִתְגַּלְגְּלָא רוּחָא דָא, מִגּוֹ רוּחָא דִלְתַתָּא, נְהוֹרָא דִלְתַתָּא אַסְחַר לְגַלְגְּלָא נְהוֹרָא דָא וְאִתְנְהֵיר, וְלָא יָכֵיל לְאִתְנַהֲרָא עַד דַּאֲחֵיד תַּתָּאָה בֵּיהּ וְאִתְקַשַׁר בַּהֲדֵיהּ, וּכְדֵין אַנְהֵיר וְאָחֵיד בִּנְהוֹרָא דִלְתַתָּא, דְּהוּא כָּלִיל, וְלָא אִשְׁתַּנֵי כְּלָל, אֶלָּא אִתְגַּלְיָא בְּגִינֵיהּ, בְּגִלְגּוּלָא דִילֵיהּ.

74. This spirit is empowered to rotate when the lower spirit OF LIVNAT HASAPIR RISES TO IT, because the lower light rotates the light of this spirit, and then it shines. This SPIRIT cannot shine until the lower SPIRIT connects with it. Then it shines, connected with the light of the lower SPIRIT that it now contains. ALL ITS ILLUMINATION IS ATTACHED TO THE LOWER SPIRIT AND NOT TO ITSELF. THIS IS because it does not change AND ITS EMANATION REMAINS WHITE, but reveals itself through that rotation only for the sake of THE LOWER SPIRIT.

75. וְכַד נְהוֹרָא דָא מִתְגַּלְגְּלָא, נָטֵיל נְהוֹרָא אָחֳרָא לְסְטַר שְׂמָאלָא, וְאִתְגַּלְגְּלָא בַּהֲדֵיהּ, וְאִסְתַּחַר עִמֵּיהּ, וְרָזָא דָא כְּתִיב חַמּוּקֵי יְרֵכַיִךְ כְּמוֹ חֲלָאִים מַעֲשֵׂה יְדֵי אָמָּן. זַכָּאָה אִיהוּ מָאן דְּיָדַע לְגַלָּאָה נְהוֹרִין.

75. When this light revolves, another light travels to the left, revolving and circling with it. This is the inner meaning of the verse: "the joints of your thighs are like jewels, the handiwork of a crowning craftsman" (Shir Hashirim 7:2). NETZACH AND HOD ARE CALLED THIGHS AND THEIR LIGHTS ARE DIFFICULT TO REVEAL, THEY ARE ALWAYS HIDDEN, EXCEPT WHEN THE LOWER SPIRIT ASCENDS THAT ROLLS IT. THUS, THEY ARE CALLED THE JOINTS OF THIGHS THAT ARE ALWAYS CONCEALED. Happy is he who knows how to reveal the lights OF THIS CHAMBER AND ELEVATE THE SPIRIT OF THE LOWER CHAMBER THAT ROLLS AND REVEALS THE LIGHTS THEREIN.

76. רוּחָא אָחֳרָא אִתְכְּלִיל בַּהֲדֵיהּ וְאִסְתַּחַר וְנָהֵיר סַחֲרָנֵיהּ, בִּגְוָון תְּכֵלָא וְחִוָּור, הַהוּא חִוָּור אִתְקְשַׁר בְּחִוָּור דָּא, וְהַהוּא תְּכֵלָא אִתְקְשַׁר בְּסוּמָקָא דִנְהוֹרָא תַּתָּאָה, דִּלְסְטַר שְׂמָאלָא, וְאִתְכְּלִילוּ דָּא בְּדָא, וַהֲווֹ חַד, וְאִקְרוּן עֶצֶם הַשָּׁמַיִם, וְכָל מַה דִּלְתַתָּא, וְהַהוּא הֵיכָלָא דִלְתַתָּא, כֹּלָא אִתְכְּלֵיל הָכָא, וּבְגִין דְּכֹלָא אִתְכְּלֵיל הָכָא, אִתְקְרֵי עֶצֶם הַשָּׁמַיִם.

76. Another spirit is contained within it, revolving and shining around it in blue and white. As there are two spirits in the first chamber, SAPIR AND LEVANAH, MALE AND FEMALE, SO THERE ARE TWO SPIRITS IN THE SECOND CHAMBER. THE MALE IS NAMED ZOHAR AND THE FEMALE IS CALLED ETZEM. The white OF THE SPIRIT joins with the white of ETZEM, and the blue OF THE SPIRIT joins with the red OF LEVANAH, located to the left side OF THE FIRST CHAMBER. They embrace each other, become one, and are thus called etzem hashamayim (the embodiment of heaven). All that exists below THIS CHAMBER, IN BRIYAH, YETZIRAH AND ASIYAH, along with all that exists in the lower chamber YESOD, is contained within THE CHAMBER CALLED HOD. And because they are all contained IN THIS CHAMBER, it is called the embodiment of heaven. IT EMBODIES THE WHOLE EXISTENCE.

77. מִכְּלָלָא דִּנְהוֹרִין אִלֵּין אִתְבְּרִיאוּ אִינוּן שְׂרָפִים, דְּשִׁית גַּדְפִין, כד"א שְׂרָפִים עוֹמְדִים מִמַּעַל לוֹ שֵׁשׁ כְּנָפַיִם שֵׁשׁ כְּנָפַיִם לְאֶחָד, כֻּלְּהוּ בְּשֵׁשׁ, בְּגִין דְּכֻלְּהוּ מֵעֶצֶם הַשָּׁמַיִם. אִלֵּין אִינוּן דְּאוֹקִידוּ לְאִינוּן דְּלָא חַיְישֵׁי עַל יְקָרָא דְמָארֵיהוֹן, וְרָזָא דְאִשְׁתַּמֵּשׁ בְּתַגָּא חֲלָף. מָאן דְּקָארֵי וְתָנֵי שִׁית סִדְרֵי מִשְׁנָה, דָּא הוּא מָאן דְּיָדַע לְסַדְרָא וּלְקַשְׁרָא קְשׁוּרָא יִחוּדָא דְמָארֵיהּ, כְּדְקָא יָאוֹת, אִלֵּין אִינוּן דִּמְקַדְּשִׁין שְׁמָא קַדִּישָׁא דְמָארֵיהוֹן בְּכָל יוֹמָא תָּדִיר.

77. From the totality of those lights, THROUGH THEIR JOINING, the Seraphim were created. Each has six wings, as is written: "Above it stood the Seraphim, each one had six wings" (Yeshayah 6:2). They all have six WINGS, because they originated from THIS CHAMBER CALLED etzem hashamayim. These Seraphim burn (Heb. sorphim) all those who do not revere their Master's glory, THAT IS, THOSE WHO DEAL WITH THE THREE

TOP SFIROT, and it is said that he who exploits the crown of Torah shall fade away, BECAUSE THE SERAPHIM BURN HIM. And whoever reads and learns the Six Orders of the Mishnah knows how to arrange and connect with his Master's unity, as is fitting. It is he who knows how to sanctify his Master's Holy Name each day always.

78. כַּד מִתְגַּלְגְּלִין נְהוֹרִין, נָפַק מִנַּיְיהוּ נְהִירוּ דְּחַד חֵיוָתָא, דְּאִיהִי קַיְימָא וְרַמְיָא, עַל ד' חֵיוָון, שַׁלִּיטִין עַל קַמָּאי, דִּכְלִילוּ לוֹן בְּגַוְויְיהוּ, וּבְאִלֵּין כַּד נַטְלִין אִתְכַּפְיָין שְׂרָפִים תַּתָּאֵי, נְחָשִׁים דְּנָפְקֵי מִגּוֹ הַהוּא נָחָשׁ שָׂרָף, דְּגָרֵים מוֹתָא לְכָל עָלְמָא.

78. And when those lights revolve, they emit the light of one living creatures WHICH IS BORN AND stands spanning four living creatures. Those latter control the former, NAMELY THE SERAPHIM, because they contain the Seraphim within them. BECAUSE THE LIVING CREATURES ARE EXTRUDED FROM THE REVOLVING LIGHT, THEY ARE VERY WELL-BALANCED AND CAN CONTROL THE SERAPHIM AND MITIEGATE THE JUDGMENT AND FIRE IN THEM. When the living creatures travel, BY FORCE OF THE REVELATION OF THE REVOLVING LIGHT, the lower Seraphim are vanquished AND RENDERED HARMLESS. Those are the serpents that evolve from and are born of the venomous (Heb. *saraph*) serpent that caused death to all people of the world, THE PRIMORDIAL SERPENT.

79. אִלֵּין חֵיוָון אַנְפֵּי נֶשֶׁר, מִסְתַּכְּלָן לְגַבֵּי הַהוּא חֵיוָתָא, נִשְׁרָא עִלָּאָה דַּעֲלַיְיהוּ, כד"א דֶּרֶךְ הַנֶּשֶׁר בַּשָּׁמָיִם, רוּחָא דָּא שָׁלְטָא עַל כֹּלָּא, הַהִיא חֵיוָתָא דְּרַמְיָא עַל כֻּלְּהוּ אִסְתַּכְּיָיא לְעֵילָּא, וְכָלְהוּ לְגַבֵּיה.

79. Those living creatures are FROM the face of an eagle and look upon this higher living creatures above them, which is the supernal eagle, TO RECEIVE THEIR SUSTENANCE. It is written: "the way of an eagle in the air (Heb. *shamayim*)" (Mishlei 30:19). THIS ALLUDES TO THE LIVING CREATURES, WHICH IS AN EAGLE, WHICH RESIDES IN THE CHAMBER OF ETZEM HASHAMAYIM. This spirit NAMED *SHAMAYIM* (HEAVENS) controls all, AT THE TIME OF THE REVOLVING OF LIGHT. BUT IF THE SPIRIT OF ETZEM WAS IN CONTROL, THEN THE FACE OF THE LIVING CREATURES

WOULD BE THAT OF A LION, AS IS THE LIVING CREATURES IN THE FIRST CHAMBER, WHICH IS WHITE, HAVING THE LIGHT OF CHASSADIM. BUT BECAUSE THE PREDOMINANT SPIRIT IS THAT OF SHAMAYIM WHO IS WHITE AND BLUE, CHESED AND GVURAH, THE LIVING CREATURES BORN TO THE LIGHT OF THE ROTATION HAS THE FACE OF AN EAGLE, AN ADMIXTURE OF CHESED AND GVURAH. FOR THE IMAGE OF CHESED IS A LION, AND THE IMAGE OF GVURAH IS AN OX. The living creatures that spans over the four living creatures looks upward TOWARDS THE SPIRIT NAMED SHAMAYIM and the living creatures look upon that SUPERNAL LIVING CREATURES FOR THEIR SUSTENANCE.

80. כֻּלְּהוּ כַּד נָטְלִין מִזְדַּעְזְעִין כַּמָּה חַיָּילִין, מִנְּהוֹן נְהִירִין מִנְּהוֹן מִתְתַּבְּרֵי מִקְּיוּמֵיהוֹן, וְאוֹקִידוּן לוֹן בְּנוּרָא, וְאַתְיָין וּמִתְחַדְּשָׁן כְּמִלְּקַדְּמִין, כֻּלְּהוּ עָאלִין תְּחוֹת הַהוּא חֵיוָתָא, מִסְתַּתְּרִין תְּחוֹת גַּדְפָהָא, לְאַכְלְלָא לוֹן לְעֵילָא.

80. When those living creatures travel, AS WHEN THE REVOLVING LIGHT SHINES IN THEM, many hosts are shaken. Some shine because of them, and some exist no longer. The radiance OF THE LIVING CREATURES burns them with fire and later they are restored. All THE LOWER HOSTS slide under this supernal living creatures and find refuge under its wings so as to be included in it above.

81. אִינוּן ד' חֵיוָון סָלְקִין כַּד רוּחָא אִזְדְּהַר בְּגוֹ הַהוּא חֵיוָותָא. אַרְבַּע גַּלְגַּלִין לְכָל חַד וְחַד, גַּלְגַּלָּא חֲדָא אִסְתְּכֵי לִסְטַר מִזְרָח, תְּלַת סָמְכִין נָטְלִין לֵיהּ, וְאִסְתַּכְּיָין לְאֶמְצָעִיתָא. וְגַלְגַּלָּא חֲדָא אִסְתְּכֵי לִסְטַר מַעֲרָב, וּתְלַת סָמְכִין נָטְלִין לֵיהּ וְאִסְתַּכְּיָין לְאֶמְצָעִיתָא. וְגַלְגַּלָּא חֲדָא אִסְתְּכֵי לִסְטַר דָּרוֹם וּתְלַת סָמְכִין נָטְלִין לֵיהּ וְאִסְתַּכְּיָין לְאֶמְצָעִיתָא. וְגַלְגַּלָּא אָחֳרָא אִסְתְּכֵי לִסְטַר צָפוֹן וּתְלַת סָמְכִין נָטְלִין לֵיהּ וְאִסְתַּכְּיָין לְאֶמְצָעִיתָא. וְכֻלְּהוּ סָמְכִין תְּרֵיסָר, נָטְלִין מִגּוֹ אֶמְצָעִיתָא. וְהַהוּא אֶמְצָעִיתָא סָגִיר וּפָתַח. וְכָל גַּלְגַּלָּא וְגַלְגַּלָּא כַּד נָטְלָא קָלָא אִשְׁתְּמַע בְּכֻלְּהוּ רְקִיעִין.

81. These four living creatures rise when the spirit ETZEM HASHAMAYIM shines within the SUPERNAL living creatures. Each and every living creatures has four wheels. One wheel points east and three pedestals support it; all face THE LIVING CREATURES THAT IS IN the center OF THE FOUR WHEELS. One faces west and also has three pedestals that face TOWARD THE LIVING CREATURES IN the center, and the same is true for the wheels of the south and north. The movement of all twelve pedestals OF EACH LIVING CREATURES is controlled by THE LIVING CREATURES IN the middle OF THEIR WHEELS AND IS NOT TO ANY OF THE SIDES OF THE WHEELS THEY SUPPORT. The living creatures in the middle closes up and opens, MEANING, CONTROLLING ALL BY STOPPING AND REALINSG THE EMANATIONS OF LIGHT. While traveling, each wheel can be clearly heard throughout the firmaments.

82. אֵלֵין אַרְבַּע חֵיוָון כֻּלְּהוּ מִתְלַבְּשָׁן דָּא בְּדָא, וְעָאלִין אִינוּן אוֹפַנִּים דִּלְתַתָּא, בְּגוֹ אֵלֵין חֵיוָון דִּלְעֵילָא, כְּלִילָן אֵלֵין בְּאֵלֵין, רוּחָא דָא דְּאִתְכְּלֵיל בְּאִינוּן רוּחִין, מְלַהֲטָא וְסָלְקָא לְאִתְאַחֲדָא לְעֵילָא. וּלְאִתְקַשְּׁרָא בִּרְעוּתָא דְּבַר נָשׁ זַכָּאָה, בְּהַהִיא צְלוֹתָא דְּצַלֵּי, דְּכַד סָלְקָא וְעָאלַת בְּהַהוּא הֵיכָלָא נָטִיל כֹּלָּא, וְכָלְּהוּ נַטְלִין בַּהֲדָהּ, וְאִתְכְּלִילוּ דָא בְּדָא, עַד דְּאִתְכְּלִילוּ בְּהַהוּא רוּחָא. וְהַהוּא רוּחָא נָטְלָא בִּרְעוּתָא דְּקִשּׁוּרָא דְּיִחוּדָא דִּצְלוֹתָא דִּמְיַחֲדָא כֹּלָּא, עַד דְּמָטוּ כֻּלְּהוּ לְהֵיכָלָא תְּלִיתָאָה, כְּלִילָן דָּא בְּדָא כְּדְקַדְמָאי, אֶשָּׁא בְּמַיָּא, וּמַיָּא בְּאֶשָּׁא, רוּחָא בְּעַפְרָא וְעַפְרָא בְּרוּחָא, מִזְרָח בְּמַעֲרָב, מַעֲרָב בְּמִזְרָח, צָפוֹן בְּדָרוֹם, דָּרוֹם בְּצָפוֹן. וְהָכִי הָנֵי כֻּלְּהוּ מִתְקַשְּׁרָן דָּא בְּדָא, וּמִתְאַחֲדָן דָּא בְּדָא, וּמִשְׁתַּלְּבָן דָּא עִם דָּא, וְכֵן כַּמָּה חַיָּילִין וּמַשִׁרְיָין דְּאִתְאַחֲדוּ לְתַתָּא וְאִתְעָרְבוּ בְּאִינוּן תַּתָּאֵי עַד דְּמָטוּ לְכֹכָבָא דְּצֶדֶק, וְתַמָּן כַּמָּה מְמַנָּן עַל עָלְמָא.

82. The four living creatures interlink, and the Ofanim below IN THE FIRST CHAMBER penetrate the living creatures of THE SECOND CHAMBER above, which are included within one another. This spirit, which is included within the spirits BELOW IN THE FIRST CHAMBER, glows and ascends to THE THIRD CHAMBER above. There it connects with the desire of a righteous man while reciting his prayer. When a prayer goes up and enters the

SECOND chamber, it elevates all IN EXISTENCE IN BOTH THE FIRST AND SECOND CHAMBERS with it and all intermix until they are included in this spirit. This spirit now travels, empowered by the desire of the unification of the prayer. The prayer unifies all until they reach the third chamber and mix with it as the first ones. They mix as fire with water and water with fire, air with earth, earth with air, east with west, west with east, north with south, and south with north. Similarly those here intermingle and intertwine. And many hosts and camps descend, mix, and shine upon those lower ANGELS until they glow upon the planet called *Tzedek* (Jupiter). On Jupiter, many of the governing ministers of the world stay, WHO RECEIVE THIS RADIANCE, AND SUSTAIN THE WORLD.

83. וְכַד רוּחָא דָא דְּאִתְכְּלִיל מִכָּלְּהוּ, וְכָלְהוּ כְּלִילָן בֵּיהּ, סָלֵיק וְאִתְאַחַד וְעָאל בְּגוֹ הֵיכָלָא תְּלִיתָאָה, עַד דְּאִתְאַחַד בְּרוּחָא דְתַמָּן, בְּגוֹ הַהוּא עַמוּדָא דְקָאֵים בְּאֶמְצָעִיתָא, וּכְדֵין כֹּלָּא אִשְׁתְּלֵים עַד הָכָא, כִּדְקָא יָאוֹת. וְכָלְהוּ רוּחָא חֲדָא, כָּלֵיל מִכֹּלָא, וּשְׁלִים מִכֹּלָּא, כד"א וְרוּחַ אֶחָד לַכֹּל, הָכָא הַכְרָעָה לְאִתְדַּבְּקָא בְּמָארֵיהּ.

83. And when this spirit, containing and contained by all THOSE LOWER THAN IT rises, enters the third chamber and connects with the spirit inside the pillar that stands erect in the middle OF THE CHAMBER, then all is complete as it should be until this point. All become as if one spirit that contains all and is complemented by all as was stated before "and they all have one spirit" (Kohelet 3:19). Here is the secret of 'bowing in order to reach full cleavage with his Master.'

29. The third chamber: Netzach

This chamber holds Light in its purest form – Light that is unseen and not yet manifest. Sunlight in the vacuum of space is the clearest illustration of this Kabbalistic truth. Because they lack a physical object to reflect and reveal the Light, the photons of sunlight remain imperceptible to the naked eye. This is why darkness surrounds the earth even though the sun's rays are continually streaming. Sunlight only illuminates when it strikes the physical atmosphere.

84. הֵיכָלָא תְּלִיתָאָה: הֵיכָלָא דָא, אִיהוּ הֵיכָלָא, דְּהַהוּא רוּחָא דְּאִקְרֵי נֹגַהּ, רוּחָא דָא, אִיהוּ דַכְיָיא, בָּרִיר מִכֻּלְּהוּ, לֵית לֵיהּ גַּוְון דְּאִתְחֲזֵי בֵּיהּ, לָאו חִוָּור, וְלָאו יָרוֹק, וְלָאו אוּכָם, וְלָא סוּמָק. וּבְגִין כָּךְ אִקְרֵי טֹהַר, דַּכְיָיא, בְּרִירָא מִכָּל אִלֵּין תַּתָּאִין, וְאַף עַל גַּב דְּאִיהוּ דַכְיָיא מִכֹּלָּא, לָא אִתְחֲזֵי, עַד דְּאִלֵּין תַּתָּאֵי מִתְגַּלְגְּלָן וַאֲחִידָן בֵּיהּ, וְעָאלִין בְּגַוֵּיהּ. כֵּיוָן דְּעָאלִין בְּגַוֵּיהּ, כְּדֵין אַחֲזֵי נְהוֹרֵיהּ, וְלָא גַּוְון חַד מִכֻּלְּהוּ.

84. The third chamber contains the spirit called *Nogah* (brightness), the purest and cleanest of all THE LOWER SPIRITS. No color is distinguishable therein, neither white nor green nor black nor red. Thus, it is called *Tohar* (purity), being purer and cleaner than all those lower than it. But although it is purer than all the others, ITS EMANATION is not visible until the lower SPIRITS OF THE SECOND CHAMBER rotate WITH THE LIGHT, cling to it, and penetrate it. After the lower beings enter it, it shows its light and does not retain any of the colors OF THE LOWER SPIRITS THAT HAVE ENTERED IT.

85. כַּד אִשְׁתְּלַם הַאי רוּחָא, מִכֻּלְּהוּ תַּתָּאֵי, אָפִיק מִנֵּיהּ נְהוֹרָא, דְּכָלִיל בִּתְלַת נְהוֹרִין. אִינּוּן תְּרֵין נְהוֹרִין, סָלְקִין וְנָחֲתִין וְנָצְצִין. בְּהַהוּא נִצוֹצָא אִתְחֲזוּן עֶשְׂרִין וּתְרֵין נְהוֹרִין, מְשַׁנְיָין דָּא מִן דָּא, וְכֻלְּהוּ חַד נְהוֹרָא, וְעָאלִין בְּגוֹ הַהוּא חַד נְהוֹרָא, וְהַהוּא נְהוֹרָא כָּלִיל לוֹן.

85. When this spirit is completed by the lower beings THAT HAVE GONE UP TO IT, it emanates from within it one light composed of three lights, THOSE OF THE CHAMBERS, NETZACH, HOD AND YESOD. Two of those lights,

THOSE OF THE LOWER CHAMBERS HOD AND YESOD, go up, come down, and glitter, BUT THE HIGHER LIGHT OF NETZACH GOES UP AND DOES NOT COME DOWN. And within this glitter there can be seen 22 different lights that become one light. THE LIGHTS THAT HAVE BECOME ONE go up and enter the SUPERNAL light OF THE CHAMBER OF NETZACH and that light contains them.

86. וְלָא נָהִיר, בַּר בְּזִמְנָא דְּאִלֵּין נְהוֹרִין דִּלְתַּתָּא סַלְקִין, וְהַהוּא רְעוּתָא דִּצְלוֹתָא נָטִיל לְכָלְּהוּ, כְּדֵין הַהוּא נְהוֹרָא נָפֵיק מִגּוֹ הַהוּא רוּחָא, אִתְנְהֵיר הַהוּא נְהוֹרָא, וְאַפֵּיק אִלֵּין תְּרֵין נְהוֹרִין, נָצְצִין, וְאִתְחֲזוּן כְּחוּשְׁבַּן כ"ב אַתְוָון דְּאוֹרַיְיתָא. לְבָתַר מִתְהַדְּרִין וּכְלִילָן בְּהַהוּא נְהוֹרָא.

86. THE SPIRIT IN THIS CHAMBER does not shine except when the lower lights OF THE LOWER CHAMBERS elevate to it and the desire in the prayer OF THE RIGHTEOUS supports them all. Then the light MENTIONED EARLIER is born from within the spirit, and from it emanate two glittering lights, which appear as the number of the 22 letters of Torah. These lights then reunite with the light THAT BROUGHT THEM FORTH.

87. כָּל אִינּוּן נְהוֹרִין תַּתָּאֵי, כֻּלְּהוֹן כְּלִילָן בְּהָנֵי נְהוֹרִין, וְכָלְּהוֹ בִּנְהוֹרָא דָּא. הַאי נְהוֹרָא אִיהוּ כָּלֵיל בְּגוֹ הַהוּא רוּחָא, וְהַהוּא רוּחָא, קַיְּימָא בְּהֵיכָלָא תְּלִיתָאָה דָּא, וְלָא קָאִים לְאִתְיַשְּׁבָא, אֶלָּא בְּגוֹ הֵיכָלָא רְבִיעָאָה, דְּתֵיאוּבְתֵּיה לְסַלְקָא לְגַוֵּיה.

87. These lower lights are all included in the 22 lights, as well as in the one light THAT GAVE BIRTH TO THOSE 22 LIGHTS. This light is included in this spirit TO WHICH THEY GAVE BIRTH. This spirit stands in this third chamber. And it does not rest until it reaches the fourth chamber, TIFERET, unto which it desires to ascend.

88. אִלֵּין נְהוֹרִין דְּנָפְקוּ מִגּוֹ הַהוּא רוּחָא, כַּד מְנַצְצִין, מִתְחַבְּרָן כָּלְּהוֹ נְהוֹרִין דְּנָצְצָן, בְּשַׁעֲתָא דְּנָפְקֵי מִגּוֹ הַהוּא נְהוֹרָא חָדָא, וְדָחֲקִין לְאִתְנַצְּצָא, נָפְקֵי מִנַּיְיהוּ חַד חֵיוָתָא קַדִּישָׁא רַבְרְבָא, דְּיוֹקְנָהָא כְּחֵיזוּ

דְּכָל אִינוּן שְׁאָר חֵיוָתָא, דְּיוֹקְנָא דְּאַרְיֵה וּדְיוֹקְנָא דְּנֶשֶׁר כְּלִילָן כַּחֲדָא, וְאִתְעֲבִידוּ בָּהּ חַד דְּיוֹקְנָא מִנַּיְיהוּ.

88. The lights that emanate from that spirit join together as one when they glitter. When THE TWO LIGHTS OF THE CHAMBERS OF HOD AND YESOD extend from the one light OF NETZACH, they press, so as to glow, REFLECT THE RETURNING LIGHT, AND ENCASE THE DIRECT LIGHT BEING DRAWN DOWN. From those two lights a holy and great living creatures is born. The figure of this living creatures is similar to that of the rest of the living creatures FROM THE FIRST AND SECOND CHAMBERS, FROM WHICH CAME THE TWO LIGHTS THAT GAVE BIRTH TO THIS LIVING CREATURES. THIS LIVING CREATURES HAS the face of a lion FROM THE FIRST CHAMBER and the face of an eagle FROM THE SECOND. These faces are combined and formed into one shape. THIS MEANS THAT BOTH THE FACE OF THE LION AND THE FACE OF THE EAGLE COMBINE TOGETHER TO FORM THE FACE OF THIS ONE LIVING CREATURES. THERE IS NO DEFINITE FACE EVIDENT IN THE LIVING CREATURES TO REMIND US OF THE CHAMBER OF NETZACH, BECAUSE THERE IS NO DEFINITE COLOR WITHIN THIS SPIRIT. NO SHAPE CAN BE DISTINGUISHED IN IT, BECAUSE THE LIGHT OF NETZACH DOES NOT HAVE TO TRAVEL WITH THE TWO LIGHTS IN ORDER TO SHINE.

89. תְּחוֹת הַאי חֵיוָתָא, אִית ד' אוֹפַנִּין עִלָּאִין, כְּחֵיזוּ דְּתַרְשִׁישׁ, מְרַקְמָן בִּכְלִילוּ דְּכָל גְּווֹנִין. וְשִׁית מְאָה אֶלֶף רִבּוֹא, כֻּלְּהוֹ בְּגַוַוְיהוּ, וְאִלֵּין ד' אוֹפַנִּים בִּתְמַנְיָא גַּדְפִין כָּלְּהוֹ. וְכֻלְּהוֹ נָפְקִין מִגּוֹ נְהִירוּ דְּהַהוּא חֵיוָתָא, דְּשָׁלְטָא עֲלַיְיהוּ, בְּשַׁעֲתָא דְּנָצִיץ הַהוּא נְהוֹרָא, מִפְּקָא חַיָּילִין חַיָּילִין אִלֵּין.

89. Beneath this living creatures, there are four supernal Ofanim, having the appearance of chrysolite, embroidered with four colors: RED, WHITE, GREEN, AND BLACK. They include six billion lights. Each of the four Ofanim has eight wings and the aspects of these Ofanim emanate from the light of the living creatures that controls them FROM ABOVE. And when the light OF THE LIVING CREATURES shines, THAT IS, WHEN THE REVOLVING LIGHT SHINES IN THEM, all these hosts come out.

90. וְאִלֵּין ד' דִּתְחוֹתָה קַיְימִין בַּד' סִטְרִין דְּעָלְמָא, בַּד' אַנְפִּין כָּל חַד

וְחַד, תְּרֵין אַנְפִּין מִסְתַּכְּלָן לְגַבֵּי הַהוּא חֵיוָתָא, וּתְרֵין אַנְפִּין מְחַפְּיָין בְּגַדְפַיְיהוּ, מֵאִינוּן נְהוֹרִין דְּנָצְצָן דְּלָא יָכְלִין לְאִסְתַּכְּלָא.

90. And these four OFANIM underneath THE LIVING CREATURES face the four winds of the world – EAST, WEST, NORTH AND SOUTH. Each one has four faces. With two faces they look toward the living creatures ABOVE THEM. They conceal the other two faces with their wings to protect them from the brightness of the lights shining upon them which they cannot withstand.

91. בְּכָל זִמְנָא דְּנַטְלֵי אִלֵּין, בְּד' גַּלְגְּלִין וּתְרֵיסַר סַמְכִין כְּקַדְמָאֵי, אִתְעֲבֵיד מֵהַהוּא זֵיעָא דִּלְהוֹן, כַּמָּה חַיָּילִין וּמַשְׁרְיָין, דְּכֻלְּהוּ מְשַׁבְּחִין וּמְזַמְּרֵי דְּלָא מִשְׁתַּכְּכֵי לְעָלְמִין, וּלְאִלֵּין לֵית לוֹן שִׁעוּרָא.

91. And whenever these OFANIM travel, it is as the first ones travel. Each travels on four wheels and twelve supports, SIMILAR TO THE MANNER OF THOSE OF THE CHAMBER OF YESOD. WHENEVER THE REVOLVING LIGHT SHINES WITHIN THEM, many hosts and camps are made from their sweat. They all sing songs of praise and never stop doing so. These hosts are innumerable.

92. אַרְבַּע פִּתְחִין אִית לְהֵיכָלָא דָּא, לְאַרְבַּע סִטְרִין דְּעָלְמָא, עֲשַׂר מְמַנָּן בְּכָל פִּתְחָא וּפִתְחָא, וּבְזִמְנָא דְּכֻלְּהוּ דִּי בְּגוֹ הֵיכָלִין דִּלְתַתָּא, וְאִינּוּן הֵיכָלִין סָלְקִין בִּרְעוּ דִּצְלוֹתָא דַּכְיָיא, כֻּלְּהוּ פִּתְחִין פִּתְחִין, עַד דִּכְלִילָן כֻּלְּהוּ, אִלֵּין בְּאִלֵּין, וּמְשַׁלְבִין אִלֵּין בְּאִלֵּין, וְעָאלִין כֻּלְּהוּ, מְמַנָּן גּוֹ מְמַנָּן, מַשְׁרְיָין גּוֹ מַשְׁרְיָין, אוֹפַנִּים בְּחַיּוֹת, וְחַיּוֹת בְּאוֹפַנִּים בְּאִלֵּין אוֹפַנִּים, נְהוֹרִין בִּנְהוֹרִין רוּחָא בְּרוּחָא, עַד דְּעָאלוּ בְּרוּחָא דָּא.

92. There are four portals to this chamber, and they face the four winds of the world. There are ten ministers in charge of each portal. And because of the desire of pure prayer, those who are present in the lower chambers, YESOD AND HOD, and the chambers themselves elevate TO THIS CHAMBER, and all THE MINISTERS create openings IN THIS CHAMBER for them. One becomes included in the other, and one is entangled in the other,

AND ALL CONGREGATE EACH WITHIN THE OTHER. Ministers congregate with each other, hosts with each other, Ofanim congregate within living creatures, and living creatures congregate with Ofanim, and in those Ofanim, lights mix with other lights – THAT IS, REVEALED FACES MIX WITH CONCEALED FACES, and spirit mixes with spirit until all are included within the spirit OF THIS CHAMBER.

93. בְּהֵיכָלָא דָא, אִית דּוּכְתָּא חָדָא, כְּחֵיזוּ דְּדַהֲבָא דְּנָצִיץ, וְתַמָּן גְּנִיזִין כַּמָּה חַיָּילִין וּמַשְׁרְיָין, דְּלָא סַלְקִין וְלָא מִתְעַטְּרִין לְעֵילָא, אֶלָּא, בְּשַׁעֲתָא דְּכָל אִלֵּין קַשְׁרִין קְשִׁירָן, וְהֵיכָל נָטֵיל לְאִתְעַטְּרָא, כֻּלְּהוֹן נָפְקִין מַלְיָין בְּדִינָא, וְאִקְרוּן מָארֵי תְּרֵיסִין שְׁלִיחָן בְּעָלְמָא, מִגּוֹ מָארֵי דִינִין דִּי בְּהֵיכָלָא רְבִיעָאָה, בְּהַאי דּוּכְתָּא תַּלְיָין, בְּאַרְבַּע סִטְרִין, שִׁית מְאָה אֶלֶף רִבְוָון מְגִינִים דְּדַהֲבָא לְכָל סְטַר וּסְטַר, וְכֵן לְתַתָּא מִנַּיְיהוּ שׁוּרִין מְקָפָן וְאִינּוּן שִׁתִּין.

93. In this chamber there is a place which looks like glittering gold. THIS IS THE PLACE WHERE ALL THE MITIGATED JUDGMENTS CALLED 'GOLD' COLLECT, AND THE RADIANCE OF THEIR REFLECTED LIGHT IS CALLED 'GLITTER.' In this chamber, many hosts and armies of angels are kept. These angels do not ascend. They are not adorned IN THE UPPER CHAMBERS, WHERE THEY COULD RECEIVE THE LIGHT OF THE TOP THREE SFIROT CALLED 'CROWNS' OR 'ADORNMENTS.' THESE ANGELS ALWAYS STAY IN THEIR PLACES IN THIS CHAMBER until all the levels interconnect – THAT IS, UNTIL THEY ARE INCLUDED WITHIN AND UNITE WITH ONE ANOTHER. Then this chamber, NETZACH, moves to be adorned BY THE TOP THREE SFIROT. Then THE ANGELS leave their places, filled with judgment TOWARD THE PROSECUTORS OF YISRAEL. HENCE YISRAEL CAN RECEIVE THE SUSTENANCE OF THE TOP THREE SFIROT WITHOUT FEAR OF INTERVENTION FROM OUTSIDERS. THOSE ANGELS are called protectors, BECAUSE THEY PROTECT YISRAEL. They are emissaries to the administrators of justice who reside in the fourth chamber. THEY ARE COMMISSIONED TO JUDGE THE ACTIONS OF THE LOWER LEVELS ON THE SIDE OF EITHER MERIT OR DEMERIT. AND AFTER YISRAEL IS ACQUITTED BY THE COURT, IT IS PASSED ON TO THESE EMISSARIES FOR PROTECTION. Suspended from the four sides of this place are six billion guardians of the gold in every direction. Below them are sixty GUARDIANS

OF GOLD, surrounding them in rows.

94. וְכָל הָנֵי מְגִּנִים, כֻּלְהוּ מַגִּיחִין קְרָבִין סְיָיפִין וְרוֹמְחִין לְבַר, בְּכָל אִינּוּן שְׁלִיחֵי דִּינִין דְּעָלְמָא, עַד דְּמָטוּ דַּרְגִּין בְּדַרְגִּין לְכֹכָבָא דְּמַאדִים, וּכְדֵין הֵיכָלָא סַלְקָא וְאִתְעַטְּרַת בְּהַהוּא רוּחָא בְּכָל אִינּוּן חַיָילִין, וְאִשְׁתְּאָר הַהוּא דוּכְתָּא בְּאַתְרֵיה, וְהַהוּא דוּכְתָּא אִקְרֵי תָּא הָרָצִים, אִינּוּן שְׁלִיחִין מְרַהֲטֵי לְאַשְׁלָמָא דִינִין וּפֻרְעָנִין בְּכָל סִטְרֵי עָלְמָא.

94. All those guardians do battle with the emissaries of judgment in the world outside THE CHAMBER using swords and spears, AND BURNING THEM. THEY BURN THEM until THE LIGHT OF all levels, in the lower levels, reaches the planet *Ma'adim* (Mars), FROM WHERE THE ACTIONS REACH THIS WORLD. And then the chamber elevates TO THE FOURTH CHAMBER, where it is adorned by the spirit and the hosts therein. This place, TOGETHER WITH ITS PROTECTORS AND ITS GUARDIANS OF GOLD, remains where it is, AND DOES NOT ELEVATE WITH THE CHAMBER. This place is called the couriers' compartment, because the emissaries therein run to finalize the judgments and punishments TO THE ENEMIES OF YISRAEL in every direction on earth. THEY RUN AND MAKE HASTE TO FULFILL THEIR ERRANDS, BECAUSE THEY MAY ONLY DESTROY THE TORMENTORS AND PROTECT YISRAEL WHILE THE CHAMBER IS ELEVATING TO THE HIGHER CHAMBER. AT OTHER TIMES, THEY ARE LOCKED IN AND CANNOT LEAVE.

95. כַּד סָלְקָא צְלוֹתָא נָטִיל כָּל הָנֵי נְהוֹרִין וּמַשִּׁרְיָין וְקָשַׁר קִשְׁרִין וְאִתְכְּלִילוּ כֻּלְהוּ כַּחֲדָא, עַד דְּאִתְקְשַׁר רוּחָא בְּרוּחָא וְאִינּוּן חַד, וְעָאלוּ גּוֹ הַהוּא עַמּוּדָא לְאִתְכְּלָלָא בְּרוּחָא דְהֵיכָלָא רְבִיעָאָה. זַכָּאָה חוּלָקֵיה מַאן דְּיָדַע רָזָא דְמָארֵיה וְאָרֵים דִּגְלֵיה בַּאֲתַר דְּאִצְטְרִיךְ.

95. With the ascension of prayer, all the lights and hosts travel, connect, and intertwine to form a unity until the spirit OF THE LOWER CHAMBER adheres to the spirit OF THE HIGHER CHAMBER, and they become one. They enter the CENTRAL pillar OF THE CHAMBER and elevate through it to be included in the spirit of the fourth chamber ABOVE THEM. Joyful is he who knows the secret of his Master and raises his banner where he ought to.

‎96. וְתָא חֲזֵי כֹּלָּא אִצְטְרִיךְ דָּא לְדָא, וְדָא לְדָא, לְאַשְׁלְמָא דָּא עִם דָּא וּלְהִתְנְהַרָא דָּא בְּדָא, עַד דְּסָלֵיק כֹּלָּא לַאֲתַר דְּאִצְטְרִיךְ שְׁלִימוּ. מִתַּתָּא בְּקַדְמֵיתָא וּמִלְּעֵילָא לְבָתַר, וּכְדֵין אִיהוּ שְׁלִימוּ בְּכָל סִטְרִין וְאִשְׁתְּלֵים כֹּלָּא כִּדְקָא יָאוּת.

96. Come and behold: All THE LEVELS must complement each other and be lit one by the other, until they all elevate to that place that needs perfection. They elevate first from below TO COMPLEMENT THIS SUPERNAL PLACE and then descend TO COMPLEMENT THE LOWER LEVELS. Hence, perfection prevails in all directions, and all are made whole as it should be.

‎97. מָאן דְּיָדַע רָזִין אִלֵּין וְעָבֵיד שְׁלִימוּ, דָּא אִיהוּ מִתְדַּבֵּק בְּמָארֵיהּ וּבַטֵּיל כָּל גְּזֵרִין קַשְׁיִן, וְאִיהוּ אַעֲטַר לְמָארֵיהּ וּמָשֵׁיךְ בִּרְכָאן עַל עָלְמָא, וְדָא אִיהוּ בַּר נָשׁ דְּאִקְרֵי צַדִּיקָא עַמּוּדָא דְעָלְמָא, וּצְלוֹתֵיהּ לָא אַהֲדַר רֵיקַנְיָיא, וְחוּלָקֵיהּ בְּעָלְמָא דְּאָתֵי וְאִיהוּ בְּחוּשְׁבַּן בְּנֵי מְהֵימְנוּתָא.

97. He who knows these secrets and brings about such perfection, adheres to his Master and cancels all terrible decrees. He crowns his Master, BY DRAWING LIGHT FROM THE TOP THREE SFIROT DOWN TO ZEIR ANPIN and brings blessings to the world. Such a man is called 'righteous, pillar of the world,' BECAUSE THE WHOLE WORLD IS PRESERVED AND SUSTAINED FOR HIS SAKE. His prayer is never returned unanswered. His rightful place is in the World to Come, and he is counted among the faithful IN THE WORLD.

‎98. תָּא חֲזֵי כָּל הָנֵי הֵיכָלִין, וְכָל הָנֵי חֵיוָתָא וְכָל הָנֵי חַיָלִין וְכָל הָנֵי נְהוֹרִין וְכָל הָנֵי רוּחִין, כֻּלְהוּ אִצְטְרִיכוּ דָּא לְדָא בְּגִין לְאִשְׁתַּלְמָא מִתַּתָּא וּלְאַשְׁתַּלְּמָא לְבָתַר מִלְּעֵילָא. אִלֵּין הֵיכָלִין אִינוּן מִתְדַּבְּקִין דָּא בְּדָא.

98. Come and behold these chambers. Living creatures, hosts, lights, and spirits all need each other so that THE UPPER LEVELS can be completed BY THE ELEVATION OF *MAYIN NUKVIN* (FEMALE WATERS), and so that, consequently, THE LOWER WORLDS can be completed BY DRAWING *MAYIN*

DUCHRIN (MALE WATERS) from above. These chambers cling to one another.

99. וְכֻלְהוּ כְּגַוְונִין דְּעֵינָא מִתְדַּבְּקִין דָּא עִם דָּא, כָּל מַה דִּי בְּגַוְוייהוּ, אִינּוּן כְּהַהוּא חֵיזוּ דְּמִתְחַזְיָא בִּסְתִימוּ, כַּד מִתְגַּלְגְּלָא עֵינָא, וְאִתְחֲזֵי הַהוּא זָהֲרָא נָצֵיץ. וְהַהוּא מַה דְּלָא אִתְחֲזֵי בְּהַהוּא גִּלְגוּלָא, אִיהוּ הַהוּא רוּחָא דְּשַׁלְטָא עַל כֹּלָּא. וּבְגִין כָּךְ קַיְימָא דָּא בְּדָא, דַּרְגִּין עַל דַּרְגִּין עַד דְּאִתְעַטַּר כֹּלָּא כִּדְקָא יָאוּת.

99. They all cling to one another like the colors of the eye. And all that is included within them is like the sight seen through the hidden part OF THE EYE, when the eye rolls FROM ONE SIDE TO THE OTHER. Then can be seen the glittering splendor, which cannot be detected during this rolling of the spirit that governs all THAT IS IN THIS CHAMBER. That is why they stand, one level upon the other – THAT IS, EACH LEVEL DEPENDS ON THE OTHERV – until all are adorned appropriately.

100. וְתָא חֲזֵי, אִלְמָלֵא כָּל אִינּוּן גַּוְונִין דְּעֵינָא, דְּאִתְחַזְיָין כַּד אַסְתִּים עֵינָא וְאִתְגַּלְגְּלָא בְּגִלְגּוּלָא, לָא אִתְחַזּוּן אִינּוּן גַּוְונִין דְּזָהֲרָן, וְאִלְמָלֵא אִינּוּן גַּוְונִין, לָא אִתְדַּבַּק הַהוּא דְּסָתִים דְּשַׁלְטָא עֲלַייהוּ. אִשְׁתְּכַח דְּכֹלָּא תַּלְיָיא דָּא בְּדָא, וְאִתְקַשַּׁר דָּא בְּדָא.

100. Come and behold: If it were not for those colors in the eye, as seen when the eye is shut and rolling, those shining colors would not be seen. And if it were not for these SHINING colors, the hidden part OF THE EYE that governs all would not be functional for sight. Everything depends upon everything else and connects with everything else.

101. כַּד אִתְכְּלֵיל כֹּלָּא כַּחֲדָא בְּהֵיכָלָא תְּלִיתָאָה, וּרְעוּתָא דִּצְלוֹתָא סַלְקָא לְאִתְעַטְּרָא בְּהֵיכָלָא רְבִיעָאָה, כְּדֵין כֹּלָּא חַד, וּרְעוּתָא חֲדָא, וְקִישׁוּרָא חֲדָא. הָכָא הַשְׁתַּחֲוָאָה לְאִתְרַצָּאָה בְּמָארֵיהּ.

-75-

101. When they are all contained as one in the third chamber, and the desire of prayer elevates them to be crowned in the fourth chamber, then all become one – one desire and one connection. This is the aspect of bowing down, of finding favor with one's Master.

30. The fourth chamber: Gvurah

This chamber represents the intelligence and will that directs and determines where Light will manifest in our physical world.

102. הֵיכָלָא רְבִיעָאָה: הֵיכָלָא דָא אִיהוּ מְשַׁנְיָא מִכָּלְהוּ, אַרְבַּע הֵיכָלִין לְדָא, דָא לְגוֹ מִן דָא, וְכָלְהוּ חַד הֵיכָלָא, הָכָא אִיהוּ רוּחָא, דְּאִקְרֵי זְכוּת, בַּאֲתַר דָא מִתְהַפֵּךְ זְכוּת דְּכָל בְּנֵי עָלְמָא, רוּחָא דָא נָטִיל כֹּלָא.

102. The fourth chamber: This chamber is different from all other chambers. It contains four chambers one within the other, yet all are one chamber. The spirit who inhabits this chamber is named *Zechut* (merit), because here all the liabilities of people are transformed into merits. Zechut takes all, AND HE WHO ATTAINS IT CAN FIND GOOD FAVOR FOR HIMSELF AND THE WHOLE WORLD.

103. מִנֵּיהּ נָפְקוּ שַׁבְעִין נְהוֹרִין, כָּלְהוּ מְנַצְצָן, וְכָלְהוּ בְּעִגּוּלָא, דְּלָא מִתְפַּשְּׁטֵי כְּאִלֵּין אָחֳרָנִין, מִתְדַּבְּקִין דָּא בְּדָא, וּנְהִירִין דָּא בְּדָא אֲחִידָן דָּא בְּדָא. כָּל זַכְיָין דְּעָלְמָא, קַמֵּי אִלֵּין נְהוֹרִין קַיְימִין. מִכָּלְהוּ נָפְקֵי תְּרֵין נְהוֹרִין שְׁקוּלִין כַּחֲדָא, דְּקַיְימֵי קַמַּיְיהוּ תְּדִירָא.

103. From this spirit, ZECHUT, seventy lights radiate. They all glitter simultaneously, shining in circles, not spreading out TO SHINE DOWNWARD like other LIGHTS. THOSE LIGHTS cling to one another and shine within each other BECAUSE THEY HAVE SIMLIARITY OF FORM. THEY SHINE WITHIN EACH OTHER BECAUSE THEY MINGLE TO SHINE AS ONE. THEY CLING TO EACH OTHER BECAUSE THEY NEED EACH OTHER TO SHINE. IF ONE IS MISSING, NONE CAN SHINE. All the merits of the world are before those lights. THIS MEANS THAT THROUGH THEIR LIGHT, IT IS SEEN HOW THE FAULTS OF THE WORLD ARE TURNED INTO MERITS. From the totality OF THOSE SEVENTY LIGHTS, two lights emanate, are counted as one, and stand before them always.

104. לָקֳבֵל אִלֵּין, אִינוּן שַׁבְעִין רַבְרְבָן מְמַנָּן לְבַר, דְּסַחֲרִין כָּל אַרְבַּע הֵיכָלִין. שַׁבְעִין נְהוֹרִין אִלֵּין, וּתְרֵי נְהוֹרִין דְּקַיְימִין קַמַּיְיהוּ, כָּלְהוּ

פְּנִימָאִין, גּוֹ לְגוֹ, וְרָזָא דָא דִּכְתִיב בְּטִנֵךְ עֲרֵמַת חִטִּים סוּגָה בַּשׁוֹשַׁנִּים.

104. Corresponding to those SEVENTY LIGHTS, there are seventy ADMINISTERS OF JUDGMENT IN THE WORLD. THEY encircle these four chambers FROM THE OUTSIDE, but those seventy lights and those two lights that stand before them are innermost. This is the inner meaning of, "your belly is a heap of wheat surrounded by lilies" (Shir Hashirim 7:3). "YOUR BELLY" ALLUDES TO THE INNERMOST, BECAUSE THE BOWELS ARE INSIDE THE BODY. *CHITIM* (ENG. 'WHEAT') ALLUDES TO *CHATAIM* (ENG. 'SINS'), NAMELY THE FAULTS THAT ARE TURNED INTO MERITS BY MEANS OF THE SAID SEVENTY TWO LIGHTS, WHICH ARE IN THE INNERMOST PART OF THE FOUR CHAMBERS. IT THEREFORE SAYS OF THEM "YOUR BELLY IS A HEAP OF WHEAT." THESE ARE SURROUNDED BY LILIES, WHICH ALLUDE TO THE JUDGES WHO ARE THE APPOINTED MINISTERS, RESPONSIBLE FOR ALL THE JUDGMENTS IN THE WORLD. THE SEVENTY MINISTERS CORRESPOND TO THE SEVENTY TWO LIGHTS. THIS IS BECAUSE ALL PUNISHMENT COMES FROM THE SEVENTY MINISTERS, BUT THEY ARE NOT FREE TO PUNISH, EXCEPT SO AS TO SERVE THE SEVENTY LIGHTS IN THEIR PREPARATION OF THE LOWER BEINGS FOR RECEIVING THEIR MAJESTIC REVELATION.

105. לְקַמֵּי נְהוֹרִין אִלֵּין עָאלִין כָּל זְכוּ, וְכָל עוֹבָדִין דְּעָלְמָא, לְאִתְדָּנָא תְּרֵין נְהוֹרִין אִלֵּין, אִינוּן סָהֲדֵי סָהֲדוּתָא, בְּגִין דְּאִית שִׁבְעָה עֵינֵי ה' דִּמְשַׁטְּטֵי בְּכָל אַרְעָא, כָּל מַה דְּאִתְעֲבֵיד בְּעָלְמָא אִתְרְשִׁים בְּהַהוּא עוֹבָדָא מַמָּשׁ, וְהַהוּא זְכוּתָא מַמָּשׁ, וְקָיְימֵי בְּקִיּוּמַיְיהוּ, וְאִלֵּין תְּרֵין נְהוֹרִין חָמָאן בְּהוּ, וּמִסְתַּכְּלָן, וְסָהֲדֵי קַמֵּי אִלֵּין ע' נְהוֹרִין. אִלֵּין ע' גָּזְרֵי גְּזֵרִין, וְדַיְינֵי דִּינִין, הֵן לְטַב הֵן לְבִישׁ, וְהָכָא אִיהוּ אֲתָר דִּזְכוּתָא.

105. Before the SEVENTY lights stand all the merits and actions of the people to be judged. THE SEVENTY LIGHTS ARE THE SECRET OF THE SUPERNAL COURTHOUSE, WHICH JUDGES PEOPLE. The two lights STANDING BEFORE THEM give evidence OF PEOPLE'S ACTIONS. Because, as is written: "Those seven are the eyes of Hashem; they roam around the earth" (Zecharyah 4:10). 'EYES' ALLUDE TO SUPERVISION. THERE ARE SEVEN ATTRIBUTES OF CHESED, GVURAH, TIFERET, NETZACH, HOD,

YESOD AND MALCHUT TO MAKE PEOPLE BEFITTING TO RECEIVE THE
SUPERNAL PLEASURE AND DELIGHT. Therefore, the image of all that
transpires in the world (GOOD OR BAD) is imprinted by the very deed and
the very merit, and they are preserved and upheld FOR ETERNITY. THIS
MEANS THAT NO DEED IS LOST IN THE WORLD, BE IT GOOD OR EVIL.
EACH ACTION IS RECORDED IN ITS MANNER, AS IS QUOTED, "THE SEVEN
EYES OF HASHEM." The two lights watch and see each action and give
evidence before the seventy lights, WHICH ARE THE UPPER COURTHOUSE.
AFTER HEARING THEM OUT, the seventy LIGHTS pass judgment and issue
decrees for good or for bad. This chamber is a place of merit. The judgment
mentioned above is not revealed here, but in the abundance that flows from
the seventy lights that reaches down. There is revealed the bad, but here, in
this chamber, there is only merit.

106. רוּחָא דָא, בֵּיה אִתְרְשִׁימוּ, אַתְוָון תְּלַת דְּאִינּוּן יה"ו דְּכַד אִלֵּין
אַתְוָון מִתְדַּבְּקָן בְּהַאי אֲתַר, בְּאִתְדַּבְּקוּתָא דִּדְכוּרָא וְנוּקְבָא, כְּדֵין
אִתְרְשִׁימוּ בֵּיה, וְלָא אִתְעֲדוּן מִתַּמָּן. לְבָתַר נָפַק חַד נְהוֹרָא, נָהֵיר
לְאַרְבַּע סְטְרִין, הַאי נְהוֹרָא אַפִּיק תְּלַת אָחֳרָנִין, דְּאִינּוּן תְּלַת בָּתֵּי
דִינָא, דְּדַיְיִנִין דִּינִין אָחֳרָנִין, בְּמִלִּין דְּעָלְמָא, בְּעוֹתְרָא בְּמִסְכְּנוּ,
בְּמַרְעִין בִּשְׁלִימוּ, בְּכָל אִינּוּן שְׁאָר מִלִּין, דְּעָלְמָא אַתְדָּן בְּהוּ. חַד
הֵיכָלָא, לְאִינּוּן ע' קַדְמָאֵי לְגוֹ, תְּלָתָא לְאִלֵּין תְּלָתָא אָחֳרָנִין.

106. IN THIS CHAMBER, the spirit ZECHUT has imprinted the three letters
Yud-Hei-Vav. When the letters YUD-HEI-VAV cling to the place,
MALCHUT REFERRED TO AS PLACE AND DESIGNATED BY THE LOWER *Hei*
as the mating of male and female, THEN THE LETTERS are imprinted on
THE SPIRIT and do not depart from there. Then another ray of light extends
and radiates in four directions. This light also extends three other LIGHTS,
NAMELY CHOCHMAH, BINAH AND TIFERET, which are the three courthouses
where judgements are passed in world affairs AND NONCRIMINAL
TRANSGRESSIONS. Here, judgments are passed regarding richness and
poverty, illnesses and health, and other worldly affairs. One chamber is set
aside for the first seventy LIGHTS and is the innermost OF THE FOUR
CHAMBERS OF THE FOURTH CHAMBER. There are three OUTER
CHAMBERS for the three other COURT ASSEMBLIES.

107. סָלְקָא הַאי רוּחָא, וְכָלִיל כָּל אִינוּן דִּלְתַתָּא, וְאַפֵּיק חַד חֵיוָותָא קַדִּישָׁא מִתְלַהֲטָא, וְעַיְינִין לָהּ, כְּעַיְנֵי אֵינָשָׁא, לְאַשְׁגָּחָא בְּאֶלֶף אַלְפִין וְרִבּוֹא רִבְוָון חַיָּילִין, מָארֵיהוֹן דְּדִינָא, כֻּלְּהוּ נָטְלִין פִּתְקִין, וּפַתְחִין וְסַגְרִין בְּעָלְמָא, וְאַשְׁלִימוּ דִינָא.

107. Zechut elevates and, containing all the lower LIGHTS AND THE OTHER THREE LIGHTS, produces one fiery holy living creatures. It has eyes, similar to those of humans, to supervise the thousands upon thousands and tens of thousands armies of administrators of justice. The latter take the verdicts FROM THE COURT and by opening or closing CHANNELS OF SUSTENANCE carry out sentences to the world.

108. תְּחוֹת הַאי חֵיוָתָא, ד' שְׂרָפִים, מְלַהֲטָן, כֻּלְּהוּ כְּחִזּוּר וְשׁוֹשַׁן, וּשְׁבִיבֵי דְּאֶשָּׁא סָלְקִין. ע"ב גַּלְגַּלִין לְכָל חַד, מְלַהֲטָן בְּאֶשָּׁא. כַּד נָטְלִין אִתְעֲבֵיד נָהָר חָד דִּי נוּרָא. אֶלֶף אַלְפִין מְשַׁמְּשִׁין לְהַהוּא נוּרָא, מִתַּמָּן נָפְקֵי כַּמָּה חַיָּילִין, כַּד גַּלְגַּלִין נָטְלִין, כַּמָּה אִינוּן רִבּוֹא רִבְוָון דְּיקוּמוּן מִנַּיְיהוּ, בְּגוֹ הַהוּא נוּרָא. תְּחוֹת הֵיכָלָא תִּנְיָינָא, נָפְקֵי חַיָּילִין דִּמְזַמְּרִין, וְאַתְיָין לְקָרְבָא הָכָא, וְאִתּוֹקְדוּן כֻּלְּהוּ.

108. Below this living creatures four Seraphim glow as buds on flowers, and sparks of fire erupt from them. Each has seventy two wheels that are burning with fire. When they travel, they leave behind a river of fire. Thousands upon thousands OF OFANIM unite with that fire, and from these THOUSANDS OF THOUSANDS many armies emerge. When the wheels travel, myriads upon myriads are born and stand in the fire. Below the second chamber, angels sing, try to come close, and are burned.

109. כָּל אִינוּן מְמַנָּן דְּעָלְמָא דְּאִתְמַנּוּן לְשַׁלְטָאָה, מֵהָכָא נָפֵיק דִּינְהוֹן לְשַׁלְטָאָה, מִגּוֹ הַהוּא רוּחָא דְּאִתְרְשִׁים בִּתְלַת אַתְוָון, וּמֵהָכָא מַעֲבְרִין קִיּוּמַיְיהוּ מֵעָלְמָא, וְאִתְדָּנוּ בְּהַאי נוּרָא דְּנָגִיד וְנָפֵיק. כֹּלָּא אִתְמְסַר בְּהַאי הֵיכָלָא, בְּגִין דְּאִתְרְשִׁימוּ בִּתְלַת אַתְוָון הָכָא, הַאי רוּחָא, אִתְכְּלִיל בְּהוֹ. הַהוּא חֵיוָותָא, אַפֵּיק חַיָּילִין וּמַשְׁרְיָין, דְּלֵית לְהוֹן חוּשְׁבְּנָא.

109. The ministers who are charged with managing the world receive their appointment from here. THE APPOINTMENT COMES from the spirit ZECHUT, who has been branded with the three letters YUD-HEI-VAV. From here they are removed from the world and sentenced by this fire that extends FROM THE DINUR RIVER. Sentencing is delivered from this chamber because it has been branded with the three letters YUD-HEI-VAV, within which the spirit is enclosed. This living creatures brings forth innumerable armies and hosts.

ס110. כָּל דִּינִין דְּעָלְמָא, מֵהַאי הֵיכָלָא נָפְקֵי, הֵן לְטַב הֵן לְבִיש, בַּר תְּלַת: בְּנֵי, חַיֵּי וּמְזוֹנֵי. דְּלָא אִתְיְיהַב רְשׁוּ בַּאֲתַר דָּא, דְּהָא בְּהַהוּא נָהָר עִלָּאָה, דְּכָל נְהוֹרִין נַגְדִין מִנֵּיהּ, קַיְימָא מִלָּה. בְּאֶמְצָעִיתָא דְּהֵיכָלָא דָא, הוּא אֲתַר מְתַקְּנָא לְקַבֵּל רוּחָא דִּלְעֵילָּא, בְּגוֹ רוּחָא דָא, וְדָא סָלְקָא בְּהוּ.

110. All the judgments of the world, whether good or bad, come from this chamber, except for those three pertaining to children, longevity and sustenance. No permission is given to judge these here. They depend on that supernal River CALLED DIKNA (BEARD) OF ARICH ANPIN, OR SUPERNAL MAZAL (DESTINY), from which the lights OF CHILDREN, LONGEVITY AND SUSTENANCE extend. And everything depends on it alone. From the middle of this chamber there is one specific location where the supernal spirit OF THE FIFTH CHAMBER is received by the spirit. This location ascends through them.

ס111. תְּרֵין עֲשַׂר פַּתְחִין אִינּוּן לְהֵיכָלָא דָא. בְּכָל פִּתְחָא וּפִתְחָא כָּל אִינּוּן סָרְכִין וּמְמַנָּן, דְּאִינּוּן מַכְרְזֵי לְאוֹדָעָא לְתַתָּא, כָּל אִינּוּן דִּינִין דִּזְמִינִין לְנַחֲתָא לְתַתָּא, כְּמָא דְאַתְּ אָמֵר קָרֵא בְחַיִל, וְכֵן אוֹמֵר גּוֹדוּ אִילָנָא וגו'.

111. This chamber has twelve portals. At each portal can be found those officials and ministers who notify below of the judgments that are to be brought down. As is written:, "He cried aloud, and said thus, hew down the tree, and cut off its branches" (Daniel 4:11). ALL THE ANNOUNCEMENTS COME FROM HERE.

‏112. וּמִגּוֹ כָּרוֹזֵי אִלֵּין, נָטְלֵי מִלָּה כָּל מָארֵיהוֹן דְּגַדְפִּין, עַד דְּאוֹדְעֵי מִלָּה לָרָקִיעַ דְּחַמָּה, וּמִתַּמָּן כַּד נָפֵיק שִׁמְשָׁא, נָפֵיק מִלָּה, וְאִתְשַׁטְיָיא בְּעָלְמָא, עַד דְּמָטֵי לְהַהוּא חִוְיָא דִּרְקִיעָא, דְּכָל כֹּכְבֵי דִּרְקִיעָא גְּלִידוּ בֵּיהּ, דְּאִיהוּ בְּאֶמְצָעִיתָא דִּרְקִיעָא.‏

112. And those announcements OF THE OFFICIALS AND MINISTERS are received by the winged ones until the firmament of *Chamah* (sun) is notified. And when the sun shines UPON THE EARTH, the announcements are released FROM THE SUN, and roam the world until they reach the serpent of the firmament. All the planets of the firmament are frozen within the sun, which stands in the middle of the firmament.

‏113. וְשַׁמְעִין מִלָּה, וְנַקְטִין לָהּ אִינּוּן סָרְכִין דִּתְחוֹת, וְאִינּוּן דִּמְמַנָּן עַל הַהוּא חִוְיָא, וּמִתַּמָּן אִתְפָּשַׁט לְעָלְמָא, וַאֲפִילוּ רוּחִין וְשֵׁדִין, וַאֲפִילוּ עוֹפֵי שְׁמַיָא, מוֹדְעֵי לֵיהּ בְּעָלְמָא כָּרוֹזִין. תָּבִין וְסָתְמִין פִּתְחִין. לָא סָלְקָא רוּחָא בְּרוּחָא, עַד דְּכָלְהוּ רוּחִין תַּתָּאֵי כָּלְהוּ חַד, בַּהֲדֵי הַאי רוּחָא, וְכָלְהוּ אִתְכְּלִילָן וְעָאלִין דָּא בְּדָא, עַד דְּאִתְעֲבֵיד כֹּלָּא חַד.‏

113. The officials below and those in charge over the serpent hear that. COME AND SEE: IN THE MIDDLE OF THE FIRMAMENT THERE IS ASSEMBLED A BRIGHT TRAIL, WHICH IS THE SERPENT OF THE FIRMAMENT. ALL THE HARDLY NOTICEABLE STARS ARE HEAPED TOGETHER IN IT. IT IS CALLED THE MILKY WAY BY ASTRONOMERS BECAUSE THE CONCENTRATION OF STARS LOOKS LIKE MILK. THOSE STARS ARE IN CHARGE OF THE SECRETIVE ACTIONS OF THE INHABITANTS OF THE WORLD. THE SERPENT IN THE FIRMAMENT IN WHICH ALL THE STARS ARE FROZEN REFERS TO THE MILKY WAY, IN WHICH ALL THE STARS ARE FROZEN AND DO NOT MOVE. FROM THOSE IN CHARGE OVER THE SERPENT IN THE FIRMAMENT AN ANNOUNCEMENT IS MADE AND spread in the world. Even spirits, demons, and birds of the sky relay those announcements to the world. WHEN THE VERDICTS HAVE BEEN CARRIED OUT, the ministers again close the portals. The spirit here does not go up to the HIGHER SPIRIT OF THE FIFTH CHAMBER UNTIL all the spirits in the lower CHAMBERS become one with this spirit here. All THE SPIRITS are embraced within each other until they

become one. THEN THE SPIRIT HERE RISES UP WITH THEM TO THE FIFTH CHAMBER AND IS EMBRACED BY THE SPIRIT THEREIN.

114. בַּר נָשׁ כַּד אִיהוּ בְּבֵי מַרְעֵיהּ, הָכָא אִתְדָּן, הֵן לְחַיִּים, הֵן לַמָוֶת, חַיִּין תַּלְיָיא לְעֵילָא, אִי אִתְדָּן הָכָא לְחַיִּים, יַהֲבֵי חַיִּין מִלְעֵילָא, וְאִי לָא, לָא יַהֲבִין. זַכָּאָה חוּלְקֵיהּ מַאן דְּאִתְדְּבַק בְּמָארֵיהּ, וְיֵעוּל וְנָפֵיק. הָכָא קִידָה בְּאַנְפִּין בְּאַרְעָא, לְאִתְגַּבְּרָא עַל דִּינָא, עַל הַאי הֵיכָלָא אִתְּמַר אֵל אֱמוּנָה וְאֵין עָוֶל וגו'.

114. When a man lies in his sickbed, he is sentenced either to life or to death. Life depends UPON THE SUPERNAL RIVER above AND NOT UPON THE CHAMBER ZECHUT. Indeed, if one is sentenced to life, one is given life from the upper RIVER CALLED MAZAL; if MAZAL does not grant one life, one does not live. Joyful is the portion of he who adheres to his Master and can enter and leave THIS CHAMBER AS HE WISHES. Here, IN THIS CHAMBER, a prostration is practiced where his face touches the ground so as to subdue the judgment. Of this chamber it is written: "El of truth and without iniquity" (Devarim 32:4).

31. The fifth chamber: Chesed

This is the highest chamber, for it is composed of pure love. Whenever Love is generated and made manifest in our physical world, it becomes a vessel. This vessel then awakens the Light of this chamber. It begins flowing through the entire system and into our own realm.

115. הֵיכָלָא חֲמִישָׁאָה, הֵיכָלָא דָא, הֵיכָלָא דְּבִרְקָא זָהִיר, דְּאִיהוּ רוּחָא דְּמַזְהִיר נָהִיר לְאִינּוּן תַּתָּאֵי, רוּחָא דָא אִיהוּ כָּלִיל, וּפָתַח וּסְגֵיר, נָהִיר וְנָצִיץ לְכָל סִטְרִין. מִנְּצִיצוּ דָא, נָהִיר חַד נְהוֹרָא כְּעֵין אַרְגְּוָונָא, נְהוֹרָא דָא, כָּלִיל כָּל גְּווֹנִין דְּנָהֲרִין נְהוֹרָא חִוָּור, וְאוּכָם, סוּמָק, וְיָרוֹק. אִתְכְּלִילָן אִלֵּין בְּאִלֵּין, אִתְרְקִים חִוָּור בְּסוּמָק, אוּכָם בְּיָרוֹק, לְבָתַר חִוָּור בְּאוּכָם, וְאִתְעֲבֵיד חַד חֵיוָותָא מְרֻקְמָא, וְאִתְכְּלֵיל בָּה, יָרוֹק וְסוּמָק, דְּיוֹקְנָהָא כִּדְיוֹקְנָא דְּבַר נָשׁ, דְּכָלִיל כָּל דִּיוֹקְנִין.

115. The fifth chamber is the chamber illuminated by lightning. A spirit NAMED *BARAK* (LIGHTNING) dwells here, shining and illuminating the lower beings. Barak comprehends, opens and closes, and shines in every direction. From this shining extends a ray of light with a purple appearance, but it actually contains the colors, white, black, red and green. The colors mix with each other – the white is embroidered with the red, the black with the green, and the white with the black. From them a living creatures is embroidered containing ALL THE COLORS, BUT MAINLY green and red. It has the face of a man and includes all shapes.

116. מִינָּהּ נָפְקוּ ד' סָמְכִין דְּאִינּוּן חֵיוָון רַבְרְבָן, עַל אִלֵּין דִּלְתַתָּא, חַד אִקְרֵי אוֹפָן, דְּאִיהוּ תְּרֵין, בְּגִין דְּכַד אִתְחֲזֵי הַאי, אִתְגְּנְהֵיר אָחֳרָא בְּגַוֵּויהּ, דָּבֵיק דָּא בְּדָא, עָאל דָּא בְּדָא, לְבָתַר עָאל אָחֳרָא דָּא בְּדָא, וְאִתְחֲזוּן ד' רֵישִׁין, לְד' סִטְרִין דְּעָלְמָא, וְכֻלְּהוּ חַד גּוּפָא, וְאִלֵּין אִינּוּן דִּכְתִיב בְּהוֹ כַּאֲשֶׁר יִהְיֶה הָאוֹפָן בְּתוֹךְ הָאוֹפָן, וְכֻלְּהוּ אִלֵּין קְשׁוּרִין דָּא בְּדָא, כְּחֵיזוּ דְּחֵיוָון עִלָּאִין, דְּלָא מִתְפָּרְשִׁין לְעָלְמִין, הַאי חֵיוָותָא. דְּאַרְבַּע גְּווֹנִין מְרֻקְמָן, אֲחִידָן אִלֵּין בְּאִלֵּין לְד' סִטְרִין. מֵהָכָא, כַּד נָטְלָא חֵיוָותָא דָא, נָטְלָא לִתְרֵין סִטְרִין.

116. From this living creatures, four pedestals are produced which are larger living creatures than those below. One is called Ofan, WHICH IS MALCHUT ALONE, and is two. THEY CLING TO EACH OTHER, because when one is observed, the other shines within it. They adhere to and penetrate one another. ONE GOES INSIDE THE FIRST, and they are perceived as the four heads of the four winds of the world. Yet all four are one body as is written: "*Ofan* (a wheel) in the middle of a wheel" (Yechezkel 1:16). All FOUR DIRECTIONS are connected with each other, as is the case with the upper living creatures OF THIS LIVING CREATURES, they never separate. The four colors embroidered IN THE LIVING CREATURES embrace each other and are drawn toward the four directions. Because of this, it appears that when the living creatures travels, it travels to two directions, BINAH AND MALCHUT, THE EMBODIMENTS OF THE FOUR DIRECTIONS.

117. הַאי רוּחָא דִּבְרָקָא, אִתְכְּלִיל בִּתְרֵין רוּחִין, רוּחָא דָּא דִּבְרָקָא, אָפֵיק חַד חֵיוָתָא וְכָל אִינּוּן נְהוֹרִין. רוּחָא אָחֲרָא אִתְנְהֵיר מִנֵּיהּ, דְּאִקְרֵי רוּחָא מְלַהֲטָא.

117. The spirit of Barak is composed of two spirits. First, the spirit of lightning, which produces the living creatures DESCRIBED ABOVE, WHICH CONTAINS all those mentioned lights. A second spirit, called the blazing spirit, extends from Barak and shines.

118. נָהֲרִין מִנֵּיהּ תְּרֵין נְהוֹרִין דְּאִינּוּן אַרְבַּע. וְאִלֵּין נְהוֹרִין מִתְהַפְּכִין בִּגְווֹנִין, וְהָכָא אִיהוּ לַהַט הַחֶרֶב הַמִּתְהַפֶּכֶת, אִלֵּין אִינּוּן נְהוֹרִין דְּמִתְהַפְּכָן שִׁנָּנָא דְחַרְבָּא. וְאִילוּ קַיְימֵי עַל הֵיכָלָא דִּלְתַתָּא, בְּגִין דְּהַאי לַהַט הַחֶרֶב, קַיְימָא עַל אִינּוּן ע' נְהוֹרִין דְּבֵי דִּינָא מֵהָכָא, כָּל אִינּוּן דַּיְינִין דְּדַיְינֵי דִּינָא, חַרְבָּא תַּלְיָיא עַל רֵישַׁיְיהוּ מִלְעֵילָא.

118. From this BLAZING SPIRIT extend two lights that are really four DIRECTIONS, AS DISCUSSED ABOVE. These lights, which are constantly changing their appearance, are called: "the bright blade of a revolving sword" (Beresheet 3:24). These lights change and turn into the edge of a sword. These LIGHTS stand above THE LIGHTS IN the lower chamber, CALLED THE CHAMBER OF MERIT (*ZECHUT*). The blade of the sword is situated above the seventy lights of the court assembly IN THE CHAMBER

OF MERIT. From this we learn that a sword is hung above the heads of the judges.

119. הַאי לַהַט הַחֶרֶב, דְּאִלֵּין אִינּוּן נְהוֹרִין דִּלְסְטַר שְׂמָאלָא, אַפִּיקוּ חַד חֵיוָתָא אָחֳרָא, דְּקַיְימָא עַל ד', דְּלָא קַיְימֵי בְּקִיּוּמַיְיהוּ, תְּרֵי מִימִינָא, וּתְרֵי מִשְׂמָאלָא, כַּד רוּחָא דְּחֵיוָתָא הַאי עָאל בְּאלֵין, נָצִיץ מִנַּיְיהוּ תְּרֵי נִיצוֹצִין מְלַהֲטָן, וְנָפְקֵי מֵהַאי הֵיכָלָא לְבַר, וּמִתְהַפְּכֵי תָּדִיר. אִלֵּין נִיצוֹצִין מְלַהֲטָן, לִזְמְנִין נוּקְבֵי, לִזְמְנִין גּוּבְרֵי, לִזְמְנִין רוּחִין, לִזְמְנִין עִירִין קַדִּישִׁין.

119. The bright blade of the sword, which is the lights of the left side, produces another living creatures that stands above four OFANIM who are unstable. THEY CANNOT RADIATE OUTWARD, BUT JUST TWINKLE, BECAUSE they are two to the right and two to the left. And when the spirit of this living creatures enters the FOUR UNSTABLE ONES, WHEN IT TRAVELS ON ITS FOUR OFANIM, two blazing sparks come out of them. The sparks leave this chamber and constantly change. They are sometimes female and sometimes male. Sometimes they are spirits and sometimes they are holy angels.

120. מ"ט בְּגִין דְּכַד אִתְכְּלִיל הַאי חֵיוָתָא בְּחֵיוָתָא קַדְמָאָה, מִגּוֹ תְּקִיפוּ דְּאִתְכְּלִילָן דָּא בְּדָא, נָפְקָא חַד נִצוֹצָא מְלַהֲטָא תָּדִיר, דְּלָא אִתְדְּעַךְ לְעָלְמִין, וְשָׁאטָא וְאָזְלָא אֲבַתְרַיְיהוּ דְּאִינּוּן תְּרֵין נִיצוֹצִין.

120. Why? Because when this living creatures was embraced by the first living creatures, WHICH CAME OUT OF BARAK, the strength of the entwinement created an eternal spark that never extinguishes. This SPARK roams after the two sparks described above.

121. וְהַשְׁתָּא אִינּוּן גּוּבְרִין, וְעַבְדִין שְׁלִיחוּתָא בְּעָלְמָא, וְעַד לָא מְסַיְימֵי מִתְדַּעֲכֵי, וְהַהוּא נִיצוֹצָא בָּטַשׁ בְּהוּ, וְנָהִיר לוֹן, וְאִתְחַדְּשׁוּן כְּמִלְּקַדְמִין, וְאִינּוּן נוּקְבֵי, וְאָזְלֵי וְשָׁאטָן, וְעַד לָא מְסַיְימֵי מִתְדַּעֲכֵי, וְהַאי נִיצוֹצָא בָּטַשׁ בְּהוּ, וְנָהִיר לוֹן, וְאִתְהַדְּרָן כְּמִלְּקַדְמִין, בְּגִין דְּהַהוּא

נִיצוֹצָא כָּלִיל מִכֹּלָא, כָּלִיל מד׳ גְוָונִין, וּבְגִין דָא אִינוּן מִתְהַפְּכִין לְכָל הַנֵי גְוָונֵי.

121. Now they are males, and they perform their mission in the world, but are extinguished before they are finished. Then the spark strikes them, shines upon them, and renews them as before. Now, they are females, BECAUSE THEY RECEIVE FROM THE SPARK THE EMANATION OF MALCHUT, WHICH IS CONSIDERED FEMALE, and they go out and float around. Before they end their mission, they are extinguished. WHEN THEY RADIATE FROM THE RIGHT, THEY ARE CALLED SPIRITS AND THEY ROAM. BUT WHEN THEY TOUCH UPON THE LEFT, THEY ARE CALLED ANGELS AND ARE EXTINGUISHED. But the spark then strikes and shines upon them AGAIN, and they are renewed as before. AND SO IT IS EVERY TIME THEY ARE EXTINGUISHED. For this spark comprises THEM all, and consists of the four appearances. Thus, those TWO SPARKS THAT RECEIVE FROM HIM change continuously into the four appearances, MALES, FEMALES, SPIRITS, AND ANGELS.

122. רוּחָא דָא, אִתְכְּלִיל בְּרוּחָא אָחֳרָא, כִּדְקָאֲמָרָן, וְאִתְחֲזוּן תְּרֵין כַּחֲדָא, וְלָא כְּאַחֳרָנִין קַדְמָאִין, דְּכַד אִתְכְּלִיל דָּא בְּדָא, לָא אִתְחֲזֵי בַּר חַד, וְהָכָא אִתְחֲזוּן תְּרֵין, וְקַיְמֵי בַּחֲבִיבוּתָא, כְּלִילָן מִכָּלְּהוּ תַּתָּאֵי, וְאַף עַל גַּב דְּאִינוּן תְּרֵין, אִינוּן חַד. כַּד אִתְפְּשַׁט, רוּחָא בְּרוּחָא, וְאִתְחֲזוּן בַּחֲבִיבוּתָא, כְּלִילָן מִכָּלְּהוּ תַּתָּאֵי, דָא הוּא רָזָא, דִּכְתִיב שְׁנֵי שָׁדַיִךְ כִּשְׁנֵי עֳפָרִים תְּאוֹמֵי צְבִיָּה הָרוֹעִים בַּשּׁוֹשַׁנִּים.

122. This LOWER spirit is included in the other HIGHER SPIRIT, as we said, and both appear as one. Unlike the first ones, which when included, one with the other, appear as one, these are distinguishable. They coexist in love and are composed of all the lower CHAMBERS. Although they appear as two SPIRITS, they are one. And when one spirit expands within the other, they lovingly include all the lower SPIRITS, as it is written: "Your two breasts are like two young roes who are twins and feed among the lilies" (Shir Hashirim 4:5).

123. וְכַד תְּרֵין רוּחִין מִתְפַּשְׁטָן, דָא בְּדָא בַּחֲבִיבוּתָא, כְּדֵין אִתְהַדָּר

הַאי הֵיכָלָא, וְאִקְרֵי הֵיכַל אַהֲבָה, הֵיכָלָא דִּרְחִימוּתָא, הֵיכָלָא דָא,
קָאֵים תָּדִיר בְּקִיּוּמֵיהּ, אִתְגְּנֵיז בְּרָזָא דְרָזִין, לְמַאן דְּאִצְטְרִיךְ לְאִתְדַּבְּקָא
בֵּיהּ. וְהָכָא כְּתִיב אֶתֵּן אֶת דּוֹדַי לָךְ.

123. When those two spirits expand and lovingly fill each other, this chamber again becomes the chamber of *Ahavah* (Love). The chamber of love is always stable and hidden from all within the innermost secrets, except those who seek to cling to it. This is as written: "there I will give you my love" (Shir Hashirim 7:12).

124. לְבָתַר כַּד נָהֲרִין, תְּרֵין רוּחִין דְּאִינוּן חַד, נָפְקֵי כַּמָּה חַיָּילִין,
לְכַמָּה סִטְרִין, אַלְפִין וְרִבְווֹן דְּלֵית לוֹן שִׁעוּרָא, מִנְהוֹן אִקְרוֹן דּוּדָאִים,
מִנְהוֹן גְּפָנִים, מִנְהוֹן רִמּוֹנִים, עַד דְּמָטוּ כַּמָּה חַיָּילִין לְבַר, עַד הַהוּא
כֹּכָבָא דְּאִקְרֵי נֹגַהּ, וְכֻלְּהוּ בַּחֲבִיבוּ דְּלָא מִתְפָּרְשִׁין לְעָלְמִין, בְּהָכָא
כְּתִיב אִם יִתֵּן אִישׁ אֶת כָּל הוֹן בֵּיתוֹ בָּאַהֲבָה בּוֹז יָבוּזוּ לוֹ. הָכָא
הִשְׁתַּחֲוָאָה וּפְרִישׁוּ דִּידִין לְאִתְדַּבְּקָא בִּרְחִימוּ דְּמָארֵיהּ.

124. Later, when the two spirits that are one shine, innumerable thousands and tens of thousands of different hosts emerge from them. Some are called mandrakes, ACCORDING TO THE SECRET MEANING OF "THE MANDRAKES GIVE A FRAGRANCE" (IBID. 14); some are called vines, ACCORDING TO THE SECRET MEANING OF "LET US SEE IF THE VINE HAS FLOWERED" (IBID. 13); and others are called pomegranates, AS IS THE SECRET OF "AND THE POMEGRANATES BUD FORTH." Until some of the hosts outside THE CHAMBER reach the planet *Nogah* (Venus). AND FROM THIS PLANET, THE LOWER PLANETS DRAW DOWN SUSTENANCE. AFTER THE INTERMIXING OF THOSE SPIRITS, they are bound by love and never separate. This is as it is written: "If a man would give all the substance of his house for love, it would be utterly ridiculed" (Shir Hashirim 8:7). Here, one bows one's head and spreads one's hands to cleave to his Master's love.

32. The sixth chamber: Tiferet

Herein lies the source of all desires. *Desire* is the vital component and engine which draws the Light. Without *desire*, the Light remains in a state of potential. Actions alone are not enough to arouse and draw in Light. According to Kabbalah, every action must be coupled with an active desire to receive the Light. Desires can be either positive or negative. A negative desire for Light arouses the energy, but it will be utilized for evil purposes. Just as electrical current can be applied for both positive and destructive means, our intent and desire determines how Light will be revealed in our world.

125. הֵיכָלָא שְׁתִיתָאָה: הָכָא הוּא רוּחָא דְּאִקְרֵי חוּט הַשָּׁנִי רָזָא דִּכְתִיב כְּחוּט הַשָּׁנִי שִׂפְתוֹתַיִךְ, הַאי הֵיכָלָא אִקְרֵי הֵיכַל הָרָצוֹן, הָכָא רוּחָא דְּאִיהוּ רַעֲוָא, דְּכָל הָנֵי רוּחִין תַּתָּאִין רָהֲטִין אֲבַתְרֵיהּ, לְאִתְדַּבְּקָא בֵּיהּ, בִּנְשִׁיקָה בִּרְחִימוּתָא.

125. The sixth chamber is called the chamber of *Ratzon* (desire). Here dwells the spirit called *Chut Hashani* (thread of scarlet), about which it is written: "your lips are like a thread of scarlet" (Shir Hashirim 4:3). All the lower spirits chase the spirit Ratzon in an effort to catch it and cleave to it with a loving kiss.

126. הַאי רוּחָא אִתְכְּלִיל בְּשִׁית, וְקָיְימָא בְּשִׁית, אִתְכְּלִיל בְּשִׁית דִּלְתַתָּא בַּהֲדֵיהּ, וְקָיְימָא בְּשִׁית עִלָּאִין, וּבְגִין כָּךְ, הַאי רוּחָא אַפִּיק תְּרֵיסַר נְהוֹרִין, כְּלִילָן כָּלְהוּ מִתַּתָּא וּמִלְעֵילָא, הָנֵי תְּרֵיסַר נְהוֹרִין, אִינוּן חָדוֹן לְסַלְּקָא לְעֵילָא, וּלְקַבְּלָא כָּל אִינוּן דִּלְתַתָּא.

126. This spirit consists of six, and is sustained by six. It comprises the six chambers below it and is sustained by six above it. This spirit, therefore, produces twelve lights. EACH LIGHT includes all the upper and the lower six. These twelve lights are happy to elevate higher, as well as to receive all that are below.

127. הֵיכָלָא דָּא, דְּאִיהוּ רָצוֹן, רַעֲוָא דְּכֹלָּא, מָאן דְּקָשַׁר קִשְׁרִין, וְסָלִיק

לוֹן הָכָא, דָא הוּא דְאַפֵּיק רָצוֹן מֵה' בַּחֲבִיבוּתָא. בְּגוֹ הֵיכְלָא דָא,
אִתְכְּנֵישׁ מֹשֶׁה, בִּרְחִימוּ דְנָשֵׁיק נְשִׁיקֵי רְחִימוּתָא, הַאי הוּא הֵיכְלָא
דְמֹשֶׁה, רוּחָא דָא, רוּחָא דִרְחִימוּתָא, רוּחָא דִיחוּדָא, דְאַמְשִׁיךְ רְחִימוּ
לְכָל סִטְרִין.

127. This is the chamber of Ratzon, being the overall desire. And he who forms connections, THAT IS, UNIFIES and elevates THE LOWER CHAMBERS up to this chamber, draws good will (desire) from Hashem, with love. Into this chamber, Moses was gathered TO HIS PEOPLE with love. He was kissed with the kiss of love, AS IS WRITTEN: "AND MOSES, THE SERVANT OF HASHEM, DIED HERE IN THE LAND OF MOAB, ACCORDING TO THE WORD (LIT. 'MOUTH') OF HASHEM" (DEVARIM 34:5). THIS IS THE SECRET MEANING OF THE KISS OF LOVE. This is called the chamber of Moses. This spirit is the spirit of love, the spirit of unison. It draws love to every part, AND THE TWELVE LIGHTS WITHIN THE SPIRIT RISE AND GLOW.

128. אִינוּן תְּרֵיסַר נְהוֹרִין, סַלְקִין וְלַהֲטִין, מִנְּצִיצוּ דִּלְהוֹן נָפְקֵי, אַרְבַּע
חֵיוָון קַדִּישִׁין, רְחִימֵי דְאַהֲבָה, אִלֵּין אִקְרוּן חַיּוֹת גְּדוֹלוֹת, לְאִתְחַבְּרָא
אִינוּן זוּטֵי, לְאִתְכְּלָלָא בְּהוֹ דִכְתִיב חַיּוֹת קְטַנּוֹת עִם גְּדוֹלוֹת.

128. And the twelve lights OF THE SPIRIT rise and glow. From their shining, four holy living creatures are produced. These living creatures, which are the true manifestations of love, are called the "great living creatures (Heb. *chayot*)." They embrace the smaller living creatures and contain them, as is said: "both small and great beasts (Heb. *chayot*)" (Tehilim 104:25).

129. אִלֵּין אֲחִידָן דָא בְּדָא, לְד' סִטְרִין, כְּאֶגוֹזָא דְמִתְחַבְּרָא לְד'
סִטְרִין, וּבְגִין כָּךְ אִקְרֵי הֵיכְלָא דָא גִּנַּת אֱגוֹז, דִכְתִיב אֶל גִּנַּת אֱגוֹז
יָרַדְתִּי, מַאי אֶל גִּנַּת אֱגוֹז, בְּגִינֵיה דְגִנַּת אֱגוֹז, יָרַדְתִּי, דְאִיהוּ הֵיכְלָא
דִרְחִימוּ, לְאִתְדַּבְּקָא דְכוּרָא בְּנוּקְבָא.

129. THE GREAT LIVING CREATURES contain one another in all four directions, just as the four segments of a walnut are included IN THE FRUIT ITSELF. THIS MEANS THAT EACH OF THE FOUR HAS FOUR PARTS IN IT.

Hence, this chamber is called the garden of walnuts, as it is written: "I went down into the garden of walnuts" (Shir Hashirim 6:11). What is ment by the garden of walnuts? IT MEANS, I went down to the chamber of Ahavah, to unite the male and the female.

130. אִלֵּין אַרְבַּע, מִתְפָּרְשָׁן לִתְרֵיסַר, תְּלַת תְּלַת לְכָל סְטַר, כָּל אִינוּן תַּתָּאֵי כְּלִילָן בְּהוּ, וּבְהוּ קַיְימִין רוּחִין בְּרוּחִין, נְהוֹרִין בִּנְהוֹרִין, כָּלְּהוּ אִלֵּין בְּאִלֵּין, עַד דְּאִתְעֲבִידוּ חַד, וּכְדֵין הַאי רוּחָא דְּכָלִיל מִכָּלְּהוּ, סָלְקָא לְאִתְעַטְּרָא בְּרוּחָא דִלְעֵילָא, הַהוּא דְּאִקְרֵי שָׁמַיִם, וְזַמִּין לֵיהּ, לְאִתְחַבְּרָא בַּהֲדֵיהּ, כֵּיוָן דְּאִתְקְשָׁרוּ כָּלְּהוּ דִלְתַתָּא בַּהֲדֵיהּ, אָמַר יִשָּׁקֵנִי מִנְּשִׁיקוֹת פִּיהוּ, וּכְדֵין אִיהוּ חֶדְוָה לְאִתְקַשְּׁרָא רוּחָא בְּרוּחָא, וּלְאִשְׁתַּלְּמָא דָּא בְּדָא, כְּדֵין אִיהוּ שְׁלִימוּ בְּחִבּוּרָא חֲדָא.

130. Those four GREAT LIVING CREATURES are divided into twelve, three for each side OF THE FOUR SIDES, and all of the lower CHAMBERS are contained within them. THE TWELVE LIGHTS INCLUDE SIX FROM THE CHAMBER ITSELF AND SIX FROM THE LOWER CHAMBERS, WHICH HAVE ELEVATED. THE SAME EFFECT IS PRODUCED IN THE LIVING CREATURES: THE SIX LIGHTS OF THE CHAMBER PRODUCE FOUR GREAT LIVING CREATURES, NAMELY CHOCHMAH, BINAH, TIFERET AND MALCHUT. EACH ONE OF THE FOUR GREAT LIVING CREATURES HAS FOUR SIDES. HENCE, THERE ARE SIXTEEN LIGHTS. AND THE SIX LIGHTS EMANATING FROM THE LOWER CHAMBERS PRODUCE THE TWELVE SMALL LIVING CREATURES. EACH OF THESE LIVING CREATURES CONTAINS ONLY THREE ASPECTS. And within THESE SMALL LIVING CREATURES, spirits are contained in spirits and lights within lights. All are contained within the other, until they become one. And then, AFTER ALL THE LOWER BEINGS UNITE, the spirit includes them all. IT THUS ENCOMPASSES THE TWELVE LIGHTS, WHICH IN TURN ARE INCLUDED WITHIN THE FOUR GREAT AND TWELVE SMALL LIVING CREATURES, AND THE TWELVE SMALL LIVING CREATURES INCLUDE ALL THE LOWER BEINGS, AS PREVIOUSLY EXPLAINED. THE SPIRIT rises WITH THEM to be adorned by the higher spirit called *Shamayim* (heaven), WHICH IS THE SECRET OF ZEIR ANPIN OF ATZILUT, AS ZEIR ANPIN IS THE SECRET OF THE RUACH OF ATZILUT AND IS CALLED 'HEAVEN.' It invites it to be united with it. And when all those from below are attached to it, it says, "Let him kiss me with the kisses of his mouth" (Shir Hashirim 1:1). Then there is the joy of uniting a spirit with a spirit. THAT IS, THE SPIRIT OF DESIRE, WHICH INCLUDES ALL THE LOWER BEINGS, JOINS WITH THE SPIRIT OF ATZILUT, WHICH IS THE SECRET OF ZEIR ANPIN CALLED 'HEAVEN,' to complement each other. This union results in perfection. BY UNITING ALL OF THE LOWER CHAMBERS, THE SPIRIT BECOMES WHOLE, BOTH WITH CHASSADIM AND CHOCHMAH.

131. כֵּיוָן דְּהַאי רוּחָא אִתְחַבַּר בַּהֲדֵיהּ, וְאִשְׁתְּלִים דָּא בְּדָא, וְאִתְנְהִירוּ דָּא בְּדָא בְּכָל שְׁלִימוּ, כִּדְקָא חָזֵי, בְּהַאי רְעוּתָא דְצַלֵּי ב"נ זַכָּאָה, דְּסָלִיק כּוֹלָּא כִּדְקָא חָזֵי, עַד הַהוּא אֲתַר לְחַבְּרָא רְחִימוּ דָא בְּדָא, כְּדֵין כָּל אִינוּן הֵיכָלִין, וְכָל אִינּוּן רוּחִין דְּאִתְכְּלִילוּ בְּהַאי, כָּל חַד וְחַד מֵאִינוּן רוּחִין וְהֵיכָלִין, דְּאִינּוּן בִּכְלָלָא דִשְׁמַיִם, כָּל חַד וְחַד נָטִיל הַהוּא הֵיכָלָא, וְהַהוּא רוּחָא דְּאִתְחֲזֵי לֵיהּ, לְאִתְחַבְּרָא בַּהֲדֵיהּ, וּלְאִשְׁתַּלְּמָא בַּהֲדֵיהּ, כִּדְקָא יָאוּת. בְּגִין דְּהַהוּא רוּחָא שְׁתִיתָאָה דְּאִקְרֵי רָצוֹן, סָלִיק לוֹן לְגַבַּיְיהוּ, בְּהַהוּא יִחוּדָא.

131. The spirit OF RATZON connects with THE SPIRIT OF ATZILUT, CALLED SHAMAYIN, and each complements the other WITH THE EMANATIONS OF CHOCHMAH. They are lit by each other THROUGH THE LIGHT OF CHASSADIM, and perfection ensues. All of this happens when the desire of a righteous man reciting his prayers elevates all OF THE CHAMBERS OF BRIYAH to this place IN THE WORLD OF ATZILUT, for the sake of lovingly joining them together. ALL THIS IS DONE THROUGH THE DESIRE OF A RIGHTEOUS MEN, WHO PRAYED AND RAISED ALL THE CHAMBER OF BRIYAH TO THAT PLACE FOR UNION BY A KISS, TO JOIN THEM WITH MUTUAL LOVE. Then each of the spirits, all of the chambers that are contained within THE SPIRIT CALLED RATZON (DESIRE), and each and every spirit or chamber contained in ZEIR ANPIN OF ATZILUT, CALLED Shamayim, pick the chamber and spirit most suitable for it to connect with and to be complemented by. Through this unification, the sixth spirit, called Ratzon, elevates all OF THE LIGHTS AND SPIRITS IN THE CHAMBERS OF BRIYAH TO THE LIGHTS AND SPIRITS IN ZEIR ANPIN OF ATZILUT.

132. וְהָכֵי אִתְחַבְּרָן: שָׁמַיִם דְּאִיהִי רוּחָא קַדִּישָׁא לְעֵילָא, נָטִיל הֵיכָלָא

דָּא, רוּחָא דָא דְּאִקְרֵי רָצוֹן, לְאִתְנַשְּׁקָא דָּא בְּדָא, לְאִתְחַבְּרָא דָּא בְּדָא,
לְאִשְׁתַּלְּמָא דָּא בְּדָא, וְרָזָא דָּא וַיִּשַּׁק יַעֲקֹב לְרָחֵל וְגוֹ'.

132. Thus connect EVERY ASPECT OF ZEIR ANPIN WITH EVERY
CORRESPONDING ASPECT OF THE CHAMBERS. Shamayim, NAMELY ZEIR
ANPIN, or the supernal holy spirit therein, receives the UPPER chamber and
the upper spirit called Ratzon, so that they can kiss, connect with, and
complement each other. This is the concealed meaning of "and Jacob kissed
Rachel" (Beresheet 29:11). JACOB IS THE SECRET OF ZEIR ANPIN, AND
RACHEL IS THE FEMALE PRINCIPLE CONTAINING ALL OF THE CHAMBERS
THAT ELEVATED TO ATZILUT.

133. אַבְרָהָם, דְּאִיהוּ יָמִינָא לְעֵילָּא, נָטִיל רוּחָא דְּאִקְרֵי אַהֲבָה,
לְאִתְקַשְּׁרָא דָּא בְּדָא לְאִתְחַבְּרָא דָּא בְּדָא, לְמֶהֱוֵי חַד, וְסִימָנָיךְ, הִנֵּה
נָא יָדַעְתִּי כִּי אִשָּׁה יְפַת מַרְאֶה אָתְּ, וְשַׁפִּירוּ דְּאִתְּתָא בְּאִינּוּן שָׁדַיִם.

133. Hence, Abraham, who is the Right COLUMN OF ZEIR ANPIN; THAT IS,
CHESED, takes this spirit, called Ahavah (love), and causes them to connect
and embrace each other. This is evident in the words, "I know that you are a
beautiful woman" (Beresheet 12:11). And the beauty of a woman lies in her
breasts, NAMELY IN THE FIFTH CHAMBER SIGNIFYING BREASTS.

134. יִצְחָק, דְּאִיהוּ שְׂמָאלָא, נָטִיל הַהוּא הֵיכָלָא דְּבֵי דִינָא, דְּכָל דִּינִין
מִתְעָרִין מִתַּמָּן, רוּחָא דְּאִקְרֵי זְכוּתָא, לְאִתְחַבְּרָא דָּא בְּדָא,
וּלְאִשְׁתַּלְּמָא דָּא בְּדָא, לְמֶהֱוֵי כֹּלָּא חַד כְּדְקָא יָאוּת. שְׁאָר נְבִיאִים
נָטְלִין תְּרֵין הֵיכָלִין, תְּרֵין רוּחִין, נוֹגַהּ וְזֹהַר בְּרָזָא דִּכְתִיב חֲמוּקֵי יְרֵכַיִךְ
וְגוֹ' לְאִתְקַשְּׁרָא אִלֵּין בְּאִלֵּין לְמֶהֱוֵי חַד.

134. Isaac, who is the Left COLUMN OF ZEIR ANPIN; THAT IS, GVURAH,
takes the chamber of the courthouse, WHICH IS THE FOURTH CHAMBER,
from where come all the judgments, and joins it with Zechut. They connect
with and complete each other, and they are one, as should be. The other
prophets BESIDE MOSES, NAMELY NETZACH AND HOD OF ZEIR ANPIN,
receive the two chambers containing the two spirits of *Nogah* (brightness)

and *Zohar* (splendor), as it is written: "the joints of your thighs are like jewels" (Shir Hashirim 7:1), BECAUSE THE TWO CHAMBERS ARE CONTAINED IN NETZACH AND HOD OF THE FEMALE PRINCIPLE AND ARE LIKE THIGHS, WHICH connect with each other to be one.

135. יוֹסֵף הַצַּדִּיק, עַמּוּדָא דְעָלְמָא, נָטֵיל הֵיכְלָא דְסַפִּיר, רוּחָא דְאִקְרֵי לִבְנַת הַסַּפִּיר, וְאַף עַל גַּב דִּכְתִיב וְתַחַת רַגְלָיו, בְּגִין יְקָרָא דְמַלְכָּא, וְהָכֵי הוּא וַדַּאי. וּלְבָתַר עַמּוּדָא דָא נָטֵיל יַתִּיר, דְּאִיהוּ רָזָא דְרָזִין, בַּאֲתַר דְּהֵיכְלָא שְׁבִיעָאָה. עַד הָכָא מִתְחַבְּרָן דַּרְגִּין, וּמִתְחַבְּרָן דָּא בְּדָא, לְאִשְׁתַּלְּמָא דָּא עִם דָּא, לְמֶהֱוֵי כֻּלְהוּ חַד, כֹּלָּא כִּדְקָא חֲזֵי. וּכְדֵין ה' הוּא הָאֱלֹקִים וְגוֹ'. זַכָּאָה חוּלָקֵיהּ בְּעָלְמָא דֵין, וּבְעָלְמָא דְאָתֵי, מָאן דְּיָדַע לְקַשְּׁרָא לוֹן, וּלְאִתְדַּבְּקָא בְּמָארֵיהּ.

135. Joseph the righteous, the pillar of the world, NAMELY YESOD OF ZEIR ANPIN, takes the chamber of Sapir and the spirit called Livnat Hasapir. Because it is written: "And beneath His feet as if it were a paved work of sapphire stone (Heb. *Livnat Hasapir*)" (Shemot 24:10), ONE MIGHT THINK THAT LIVNAT HASAPIR IS BENEATH YESOD OF ZEIR ANPIN, BEYOND HIS GRADE. Nevertheless, "beneath his feet" was said for the honor of the King, but it certainly is YESOD OF ZEIR ANPIN THAT TAKES THE CHAMBER OF LIVNAT HASAPIR. Furthermore, this pillar, NAMELY YESOD OF ZEIR ANPIN, takes more. This is a highly secret matter TO EXPOUND ON, because HE TAKES in the seventh chamber. Now the levels OF ZEIR ANPIN are linked WITH THE LEVELS OF THE CHAMBERS, and the two complete one another until they become one. All is as it should be, and hence "Hashem is Elohim" (I Melachim 18:39). THAT IS, ZEIR ANPIN, WHICH IS CALLED YUD HEI VAV HEI, BECOMES ONE WITH THE FEMALE PRINCIPLE, CALLED ELOHIM, IN SUCH A WAY THAT YUD HEI VAV HEI IS ELOHIM. Joyous is the portion in this world and the next of he who knows how to link them and cleave to his Master.

136. הָכָא הַכְרָעָה וְהִשְׁתַּחֲוָאָה, וְקִידָה, וּפְרִישׁוּ דְּכַפִּין, וּנְפִילָה דְאַפִּין. לְאַמְשָׁכָא רְעוּתָא דְרוּחָא עִלָּאָה, נִשְׁמָתָא דְּכָל נִשְׁמָתִין, דְּאִיהוּ תַּלְיָא לְעֵילָּא עַד אֵין סוֹף, דְּמִנֵּיהּ נָפְקֵי נְהִירוּ וּבִרְכָאן לְאַשְׁלָמָא כֹּלָּא מִלְּעֵילָּא כִּדְקָא יָאוּת. וּלְמֶהֱוֵי כֹּלָּא בִּשְׁלִימוּ, מִתַּתָּא וּמִלְּעֵילָּא, וְכָל

אַנְפִּין נְהִירִין בְּכָל סִטְרִין כְּדְקָא יָאוּת. כְּדֵין כָּל גִּזְרֵי דִינִין מִתְבַּטְּלִין,
וְכָל רְעוּתָא אִתְעֲבֵיד לְעֵילָא וְתַתָּא. וְעַל דָּא כְּתִיב וַיֹּאמֶר לִי עַבְדִּי
אַתָּה יִשְׂרָאֵל אֲשֶׁר בְּךָ אֶתְפָּאָר. וּכְתִיב אַשְׁרֵי הָעָם שֶׁכָּכָה לּוֹ, אַשְׁרֵי
הָעָם שֶׁה' אֱלֹקָיו.

136. Here, IN THE CHAMBER OF RATZON, the bowing, prostration, spreading of open hands, and genuflection ARE PRACTICED. WHAT IS PRACTICED IN THE LOWER CHAMBERS IS PRACTICED HERE, BUT THE LOWERING OF THE FACE IS ADDED HERE. THE LOWERING OF THE FACE IS PRACTICED ONLY IN THIS CHAMBER, BECAUSE ALL OF THE LOWER CHAMBERS ARE CONTAINED HERE. THIS IS NECESSARY to draw on the good will of the supernal spirit, NAMELY THE TOP THREE SFIROT OF ZEIR ANPIN. The soul of all souls, suspended above IN SUPERNAL ABA AND IMA so that it draws from the Endless Light, DRAWS ON IT BY THE UNION BY A KISS. From the ENDLESS LIGHT above come lights and blessings to complement all appropriately. THIS IS THE NECESSARY means through which all can be completed from above BY THE LIGHT OF CHASSADIM and from below BY THE LIGHT OF CHOCHMAH. After this completion, all the faces shine suitably. AND BECAUSE OF THE LIGHT OF CHOCHMAH, all judgments are annulled. And BECAUSE OF THE LIGHT OF CHASSADIM, good will fills above and below. Hence, it is written: "And He said to me, you are My servant, O Yisrael, in whom I will be glorified" (Yeshayah 49:3) and "Happy is the people that this is its lot, Happy is the people, whose Elohim is Hashem" (Tehilim 144:15).

33. Seventh chamber: *Kodesh Kodashim* (Holy of Holies)

This realm is defined as the source of all sources. We must enter into this highest realm in order to ignite and activate all the complex processes that occur in the previous chambers. This realm is symbolized by the ancient Temple of Jerusalem, and specifically in the chamber known as the Holy of Holies. Though the physical Temple no longer stands, our daily prayers are metaphysically structured to lead us into the spiritual essence of the Holy of Holies.

These seven chambers complete the structure and framework that form the Upper Worlds.

137. הֵיכָלָא שְׁבִיעָאָה: הֵיכָלָא דָא, לָאו בֵּיהּ דִּיוֹקְנָא מַמָּשׁ, כֹּלָּא אִיהוּ בִּסְתִימוּ. גּוֹ רָזָא דְרָזִין, פְּרוּכְתָּא דִּפְרִיסָא. קַיְימִין כֻּלְּהוּ הֵיכָלִין, דְּלָא לְאִתְחֲזָאָה תְּרֵין כְּרוּבִים. לְגוֹ מִן דָּא קַיְימָא כַּפּוּרְתָּא, דִּיוֹקְנָא דְּקֹדֶשׁ קוּדְשִׁין, בְּגִין כָּךְ הֵיכָלָא דָא אִקְרֵי קֹדֶשׁ הַקֳּדָשִׁים. הַאי קֹדֶשׁ הַקֳּדָשִׁים, אֲתַר מִתְתַּקְּנָא, לְהַהוּא נִשְׁמָתָא עִלָּאָה, כְּלָלָא דְכֹלָּא, עָלְמָא דְּאָתֵי לְגַבֵּי הַאי עִלָּאֵי.

137. The seventh chamber has no real shape. Everything in it is concealed, deep within the innermost of mysteries of the closed *parochet* (curtain). Here, all of the chambers exist, so as to conceal two cherubim, A MALE AND A FEMALE. ALL THE LOWER CHAMBERS ARE ELEVATED TO BE CONTAINED IN THIS CURTAIN, SO THAT THEY COVER THE MALE AND THE FEMALE WHILE THEY MATE; HENCE THE CHAMBERS ARE ABLE TO ASCEND. THIS CURTAIN SEPARATES THE SIX CHAMBERS WHICH ARE HOLIES AND THE SEVENTH CHAMBER, WHICH IS HOLIES OF HOLIES. Beyond THE CURTAIN can be found the *caporet* (cover of the ark), which is the image of Holy of Holies, BECAUSE THIS CHAMBER IS THE PLACE OF UNION. Therefore, it is called the Holy of Holies, a place designated to receive the supernal soul, which is the totality of all the worlds. This is the World to Come of the supernal beings.

138. דְּהָא כַּד מִתְחַבְּרָן, כֻּלְּהוּ רוּחֵי דָא בְּדָא, וְאִשְׁתַּלִימוּ דָא עִם דָּא, כִּדְקָא חָזֵי, כְּדֵין אִתְּעַר רוּחָא עִלָּאָה נִשְׁמָתָא דְכֹלָּא, לְגַבֵּי עֵילָא,

סְתִימָא דְּכָל סְתִימִין, לְאִתְעָרָא עַל כֹּלָּא, לְאַנְהָרָא לוֹן מֵעֵילָא לְתַתָּא, וּלְאַשְׁלָמָא לוֹן לְאַדְלְקָא בּוֹצִינִין.

138. When all the spirits OF THE CHAMBERS have joined with and completed each other, a supernal spirit, the soul of all, rises toward the supreme who is the most concealed, NAMELY ARICH ANPIN, to bring sustenance down to all, to shine on them from above WITH THE LIGHT OF THE RIGHT COLUMN, and to complete them and light the candles WITH THE LIGHT OF THE LEFT COLUMN.

139. וְכַד כֹּלָּא בִּשְׁלִימוּ, בִּנְהִירוּ דְּכֹלָּא, וְנָחֵית נְהִירוּ עִלָּאָה, כְּדֵין הַאי הֵיכָלָא שְׁבִיעָאָה, אִיהוּ הֵיכָלָא סְתִימָאָה, בִּסְתִימוּ דְּכֹלָּא, לְקַבְּלָא הַהוּא קֹדֶשׁ הַקֳּדָשִׁים, נְהִירוּ דְּנָחִית, וּלְאִתְמַלְיָא מִתַּמָּן, כְּנוּקְבָא דְּמִתְעַבְּרָא מִן דְּכוּרָא, וְאִתְמַלְיָיא, וְלָא אִתְמַלְיָיא אֶלָּא מֵהַאי הֵיכָלָא, דְּמִתְתַּקְּנָא לְקַבְּלָא הַהוּא נְהִירוּ עִלָּאָה, וְרָזָא דָא, הֵיכָלָא שְׁבִיעָאָה, אִיהוּ אֲתַר דְּחִבּוּרָא דְּזִוּוּגָא, לְאִתְחַבְּרָא שְׁבִיעָאָה בִּשְׁבִיעָאָה, לְמֶהֱוֵי כֹּלָּא חַד שְׁלִימוּ, כִּדְקָא חֲזֵי.

139. When all are perfected by the light THAT SHINES on all, and the supernal light descends, the seventh chamber, which is concealed with utmost concealment, receives the Holy of Holies, which is the descending supernal light. The light fills the seventh chamber, as a woman who conceives from a male is filled BY HIM. The chamber is designed FOR CONCEALMENT FROM ALL, so that it may receive the supernal light. NAMELY IF THE CONCEALMENT WAS NOT SET THERE, IT WOULD NOT HAVE BEEN ABLE TO RECEIVE THE SUPERNAL LIGHT. This is the secret of the seventh chamber, which is the place of the connection made during union. The union links the seventh with the seventh, so that all is one unity, as is appropriate.

140. וּמַאן דְּיָדַע לְקַשְּׁרָא יְחוּדָא דָּא, זַכָּאָה חוּלָקֵיהּ, רְחִים לְעֵילָא, רְחִים לְתַתָּא, קֻדְשָׁא בְּרִיךְ הוּא גָּזֵיר וְאִיהוּ מְבַטֵּל. סָלְקָא דַּעְתִּין, דְּאִיהוּ מְקַטְרְגָא בְּמָארֵיהּ, לָאו הָכִי, אֶלָּא בְּגִין דְּכַד אִיהוּ קָשִׁיר קְשִׁירִין, וְיָדַע לְיַחֲדָא יְחוּדָא, וְכָל אַנְפִּין נְהִירִין, וְכָל שְׁלִימוּ אִשְׁתְּכַח,

וְכֹלָּא אִתְבָּרְכָא כִּדְקָא יָאוֹת, כָּל דִּינִין מִתְעַבְּרִין וּמִתְבַּטְּלִין, וְלָא
אִשְׁתְּכַח דִּינָא בְּעָלְמָא. זַכָּאָה חוּלְקֵיהּ בְּעָלְמָא דֵין, וּבְעָלְמָא דְאָתֵי,
דָּא הוּא לְתַתָּא דִּכְתִיב בֵּיהּ וְצַדִּיק יְסוֹד עוֹלָם, דָּא הוּא קִיּוּמָא
דְעָלְמָא, בְּכָל יוֹמָא קָארֵי עֲלוֹי כָּרוֹזָא וְאַתָּה תָּגִיל בַּה׳ בִּקְדוֹשׁ יִשְׂרָאֵל
תִּתְהַלָּל.

140. Joyful is the portion of he who knows to connect with this unification. He is beloved above and below. The Holy One, blessed be He, decrees and he (that man) nullifies. He asks: How is it conceivable that a righteous man criticizes his Master's will? How is it possible that he cancels out the desire of the Holy One, blessed be He? And he answers: This is only possible when a righteous man forms links and knows how to make unifications, so that all faces shine, all is complete, and everything is wholly blessed. Then all judgments are abolished and none can be found in this world. Joyful is such a man's lot in this world and the next. All that has been said about the righteous man refers to his actions below, in this world. Hence it is written of him: "the righteous is the foundation of the world" (Mishlei 10:25), as he is the subsistence of the world. And each day a declaration is made about him: "And you shall rejoice in Hashem and shall glory in the Holy One of Yisrael" (Yeshayah 41:16).

141. כְּגַוְונָא דָּא קַרְבָּנָא סָלְקָא תְּנָנָא, וּמִסְתַּפְּקִין כָּל חַד וְחַד, כִּדְקָחֲזֵי
לֵיהּ, וְכַהֲנֵי בִּרְעוּתָא, וְלֵוָאֵי בְּבַסִימוּ דְּשִׁירָתָא, דָּא אִתְכְּלִיל בְּדָא,
וְעָיְילֵי הֵיכְלָא בְּהֵיכְלָא, רוּחָא בְּרוּחָא, עַד דְּמִתְחַבְּרָן בְּדוּכְתַּיְיהוּ
כִּדְקָא חָזֵי לֵיהּ, שַׁיְיפָא בְּשַׁיְיפָא, וְאִשְׁתְּלִימוּ דָּא בְּדָא, וְאִתְיַיחֲדוּ דָּא
בְּדָא, עַד דְּאִנּוּן חַד. וְנַהֲרִין דָּא בְּדָא.

141. Sacrifices achieve an effect similar TO THAT OF A RIGHTEOUS MAN'S PRAYER. The smoke OF THE SACRIFICE goes up and provides to each and every CHAMBER what is needed, as is becoming. The priests, by their desire TO BRING GRATIFICATION TO THE SUPERNAL, and the Levites, by their chanting DURING THE OFFERING OF SACRIFICES, become unified with each other. THE LEVITES ARE UNIFIED WITH THE PRIESTS AND THE PRIESTS WITH THE LEVITES. THIS IS BECAUSE THE PRIESTS CHANNEL THE RIGHT COLUMN AND THE LEVITES CHANNEL THE LEFT.

COMPLETION CANNOT OCCUR WHEN ONE IS WITHOUT THE OTHER. One chamber penetrates the other, and one spirit the other, until they all rest in their proper places, as is suitiable. One organ is within the other and one complements the other. The elements merge, until they become one BY THE UNION BY A KISS and shine within each other BY EMBRACING.

142. כְּדֵין נִשְׁמָתָא עִלָּאָה דְּכֹלָּא, אַתְיָא מִלְעֵילָא, וְנָהֵיר לוֹן, וַהֲווֹ נְהִירִין כָּלְּהוֹ בּוֹצִינִין בִּשְׁלִימוּ, כְּדְקָא חָזֵי, עַד דְּהַהוּא נְהוֹרָא עִלָּאָה אִתְּעַר, וְכֹלָּא אָעֵיל לְגַבֵּי קֹדֶשׁ הַקֳּדָשִׁים, וְאִתְבָּרְכָא וְאִתְמַלְיָא כְּבֵירָא דְּמַיִין נָבְעִין, וְלָא פָּסְקִין, וְכֻלְּהוֹ מִתְבָּרְכָאן לְעֵילָא וְתַתָּא.

142. Consequently, this most supernal soul descends and shines on them, and all the candles, OR SFIROT, are becomingly lit in all their perfection, until this supernal light is aroused and all the chambers enter the Holy of Holies, WHICH IS THE SEVENTH CHAMBER. THIS IS WHAT IS INDICATED BY THE INNER MEANING OF 'THE UNION OF SEVENTH WITH SEVENTH'. THE SEVENTH CHAMBER is blessed and filled like a well of spring water that never ceases to flow, and all the upper and lower CHAMBERS are blessed.

143. הָכָא רָזָא דְּרָזִין, הַהוּא דְּלָא אִתְיְידַע, וְלָא אָעֵיל בְּחוּשְׁבְּנָא, רְעוּתָא דְּלָא אִתְפַּס לְעָלְמִין, בָּסִים לְגוֹ לְגוֹ בְּגַוַויְיהוּ, וְלָא אִתְיְידַע הַהוּא רְעוּתָא, וְלָא אִתְפַּס לְמִנְדַע, וּכְדֵין כֹּלָּא רְעוּתָא חָדָא, עַד א״ס, וְכֹלָּא אִיהוּ בִּשְׁלִימוּ, מִתַּתָּא וּמִלְעֵילָא, וּמִגּוֹ לְגוֹ. עַד דְּאִתְעֲבֵיד כֹּלָּא חַד.

143. The innermost of secrets is THE LIGHT that cannot be conceived or be taken into account AMONG THE TEN SFIROT. It is a will that can never be grasped. THIS LIGHT REFERS TO THE LIGHT OF YECHIDAH, BECAUSE THE TEN SFIROT BEGIN FROM CHOCHMAH, BINAH, DA'AT, CHESED, GVURAH, TIFERET, NETZACH, HOD, YESOD AND MALCHUT. The light of Yechidah is mitigated deep within the Sfirot, and its desire cannot be conceived, NOT EVEN BY THOUGHT directed at knowing it. Thus, all THE LEVELS up to the Endless Light, BLESSED BE HE, unite into one, and everything is perfected from above, below, and within.

144. הַאי רְעוּתָא, לָא אָעֵיל לְגוֹ, אַף עַל גַּב דְּלָא אִתְיְידַע, עַד דְּכֹלָּא
אַשְׁתְּלֵים, וְאִתְנְהֵיר בְּקַדְמֵיתָא בְּכֻלְּהוּ סִטְרִין, כְּדֵין בָּסִים הַהוּא
רְעוּתָא, וְלָא אִתְּפַס לְגוֹ בְּגוֹ בִּסְתִימוּ, וּכְדֵין זַכָּאָה חוּלָקֵיהּ מָאן
דְּיִתְדַּבַּק בְּמָארֵיהּ, בְּהַהִיא שַׁעֲתָא. זַכָּאָה אִיהוּ לְעֵילָא, זַכָּאָה אִיהוּ
לְתַתָּא, עֲלֵיהּ כְּתִיב יִשְׂמַח אָבִיךָ וְאִמֶּךָ וְתָגֵל יוֹלַדְתֶּךָ.

144. This will, THE LIGHT OF YECHIDAH, is not encased IN THE INNER PART OF THE LEVELS. Nevertheless, it stays within them unobserved, until they reach completion and radiate with every aspect, BOTH THE LIGHT OF CHOCHMAH AND THE LIGHT OF CHASSADIM, AS BEFORE. Hence, this will that can not be grasped, is mitigated, and is ENCASED AND concealed deep within the inner parts. At that time, joyful is the portion of he who can cleave to his Master. He is complete above and below. Of him it is written: "Your father and mother will be glad and she who gave birth to you shall rejoice" (Mishlei 23:25).

145. תָּא חֲזֵי, כֵּיוָן דְּכֻלְּהוֹן אִשְׁתַּלִּימוּ דָּא בְּדָא, וְאִתְקַשְׁרוּ דָּא בְּדָא,
בְּקִשּׁוּרָא חֲדָא, וְנִשְׁמָתָא עִלָּאָה נָהֵיר לוֹן מִסִּטְרָא דִּלְעֵילָא, וְכֹלָּא
נְהוֹרִין אִינוּן בּוֹצִינָא חֲדָא, בִּשְׁלִימוּ, כְּדֵין רְעוּתָא חֲדָא דְּמַחֲשָׁבָה
אִתְּפַס, נְהִירוּ דְּלָא אִתְּפַס וְלָא אִתְיְידַע, בַּר הַהוּא רְעוּ דְּמַחֲשָׁבָה
תָּפִיס, וְלָא יָדַע מַה תָּפִיס, אֶלָּא דְּאִתְנְהֵיר וְאִתְבַּסַּם, הַהוּא רְעוּ
דְּמַחֲשָׁבָה, וְאִתְמַלְיָא כֹּלָּא, וְאִשְׁתְּלֵים כֹּלָּא, וְאִתְנְהֵיר וְאִתְבַּסַּם כֹּלָּא,
כְּדְקָא יָאוּת. וְעַל דָּא כְּתִיב אַשְׁרֵי הָעָם שֶׁכָּכָה לוֹ וְגוֹ'.

145. Come and behold: Because they have been completed by each other and bind each other in oneness, and because the supernal soul, NAMELY BINAH, shines on them from above, all the lights become one perfect candle. Then, this light that cannot be grasped or observed, is grasped by a desire of the mind. Yet, this will of the mind, CALLED THE LIGHT OF CHAYAH, THAT ENCASES THE LIGHT OF YECHIDAH, still does not know what it has grasped. THIS IS BECAUSE THE LIGHT RADIATES WITHIN IT IN A CONCEALED MANNER. Still, THE WILL OF THE MIND shines because of, and is soothed by it, as it contains it. All THE LEVELS are filled WITH ITS LIGHT. All reach completion and all shine because of it and are suitably

appeased. Hence, it is written "Happy are the people that this is their lot" (Tehilim 144:15).

146. מָאן דְּזָכֵי לְאִתְדַּבְּקָא בְּמָארֵיהּ, כְּהַאי גַּוְונָא, יָרִית עָלְמִין כָּלְהוּ, רְחִימָא לְעֵילָּא, רְחִימָא לְתַתָּא, צְלוֹתֵיהּ לָא אֲהַדְרָא רֵיקַנְיָא, דָּא אִתְחֲטֵי קַמֵּי מָארֵיהּ, כִּבְרָא קַמֵּי אֲבוֹי, וְעָבֵיד לֵיהּ רְעוּתָא בְּכָל מַה דְּאִצְטְרִיךְ, וְאֵימְתֵיהּ שַׁלִּיט עַל כָּל בִּרְיָין, אִיהוּ גָּזֵיר וְקֻדְשָׁא בְּרִיךְ הוּא עָבֵיד. עֲלֵיהּ כְּתִיב וְתִגְזַר אֹמֶר וְיָקָם לָךְ וְעַל דְּרָכֶיךָ נָגַהּ אוֹר.

146. And he who merits being attached to his Master in this manner inherits all the worlds. He is beloved above and below. His prayer never returns unanswered. He purifies himself before his Master as a son who satisfies all of his father's wishes, giving him all that he requires. The fear of him is upon all creation and whatever he decrees, the Holy One, blessed be He, fulfills. Of him it is written: "You shall decree and it shall be established unto you, and the light shall shine upon your ways" (Iyov 22:28).

34. "Let there be light"

An unprepared Vessel can be spiritually dangerous and destructive. Similarly, if acid is poured into a paper cup, the cup is not designed to receive the acid and it dissolves. Preparing the vessel of your being is the first step that must be taken before you even activate your desire to draw in spiritual Light.

Perusing the Hebrew letters from this segment of the Zohar prepares our Vessel so that we can receive and safely contain the awesome Light of The Creator.

147. וַיֹּאמֶר אֱלֹקִים יְהִי אוֹר וַיְהִי אוֹר. אָמַר רָבִּי יִצְחָק מִכָּאן דַּעֲקָרָן קֻדְשָׁא בְּרִיךְ הוּא לְהָנֵי נְטִיעָן, וְשָׁתֵיל לוֹן, מַשְׁמַע דִּכְתִיב יְהִי. ר' יְהוּדָה אוֹמֵר, אוֹר שֶׁכְּבָר הָיָה, תְּנַן מַשְׁמַע דִּכְתִיב וַיְהִי אוֹר, וְהָיָה לָא כְּתִיב, אֶלָּא וַיְהִי. וְכַד אִסְתַּכַּל קֻדְשָׁא בְּרִיךְ הוּא בְּאִינוּן דָּרִין דְּרַשִׁיעַיָּיא. גָּנֵיז לֵיהּ לְצַדִּיקַיָּיא, הה"ד אוֹר זָרוּעַ לַצַּדִּיק וּלְיִשְׁרֵי לֵב שִׂמְחָה, וְהָא אִתְּמַר וַיֹּאמֶר אֱלֹקִים יְהִי אוֹר הה"ד מִי הֵעִיר מִמִּזְרָח וְגוֹ'.

147. "And Elohim said, 'Let there be light;' and there was light" (Beresheet 1:3). Rabbi Yitzchak said that we learn from these words that the Holy One, blessed be He, uprooted these plants and replanted them elsewhere. Hence the expression, "there was." Rabbi Yehuda said, that this implies that light had already existed. This is indicated in, "there was." It was not written, "there became light," but "there was light." And when the Holy One, blessed be He, viewed the generations of the wicked, WHO ARE NOT WORTHY OF THE LIGHT, He stored it for the righteous. This is mentioned in the verse "light is sown for the righteous and gladness for those upright in hearts" (Tehilim 97:11). Thus it is written: "And Elohim said, 'Let there be light'," as is written: "Who raised up one from the east..." (Yeshayah 41:2).

148. וַיַּרְא אֱלֹהִים אֶת הָאוֹר כִּי טוֹב, מַאי רָאָה אָמַר רָבִּי חִיָּיא כִּדְקָאָמְרָן, חָמָא בְּעוֹבָדַיְיהוּ דְּרַשִׁיעַיָּיא וְגָנֵיז לֵיהּ. ר' אַבָּא אָמַר וַיַּרְא אֱלֹקִים אֶת הָאוֹר כִּי טוֹב לִגְנוֹז אוֹתוֹ. וַיַּרְא אֱלֹקִים אֶת הָאוֹר, דְּסָלֵיק

נְהוֹרֵיהּ מִסְיָיפֵי עָלְמָא עַד סְיָיפֵי עָלְמָא, וְכִי טוֹב הוּא לְאַגְנָזָא לֵיהּ דְּלָא יְהֱנוּן מִנֵּיהּ חַיָּיבֵי עָלְמָא.

148. "And Elohim saw the light, that it was good" (Beresheet 1:4). What did He see? Rabbi Chiya said that this implies that He foresaw the actions of the wicked and stored the light, as we said before. Rabbi Aba DISAGREES, AND says, "And Elohim saw the light, that it was good," to store it away. THAT IS, HE DID NOT LOOK AT THE ACTIONS OF THE WICKED, BUT SAW THE MAGNIFICENCE OF THE LIGHT ITSELF, AND DECIDED THAT IT WAS GOOD FOR IT TO BE CONCEALED AND NOT REVEALED TO THE WORLD. "And Elohim saw the light." He saw its radiance beaming from one end of the world to the other, and He saw that it was better to store it, so that sinners might not benefit from it.

149. אָמַר רַבִּי שִׁמְעוֹן, וַיַּרְא אֱלֹקִים אֶת הָאוֹר כִּי טוֹב, דְּלָא יִשְׁתְּכַח בֵּיהּ רִתְחָא, כְּתִיב הָכָא כִּי טוֹב, וּכְתִיב הָתָם כִּי טוֹב בְּעֵינֵי ה' לְבָרֵךְ אֶת יִשְׂרָאֵל, וְסוֹפָא דִּקְרָא וַיַּבְדֵּל אֱלֹקִים בֵּין הָאוֹר וּבֵין הַחֹשֶׁךְ, וּבְגִין כָּךְ לָא אִשְׁתְּכַח בֵּיהּ רִתְחָא, וְאַף עַל גַּב דְּשִׁתֵּף לוֹן קוּדְשָׁא בְּרִיךְ הוּא כַּחֲדָא.

149. Rabbi Shimon said "And Elohim saw the light, that it was good." THIS MEANS THAT HE DECIDED THAT no anger or judgment would be found in it. Similarly, it was said IN CONNECTION TO BILAAM, "That it was good in the eyes of Hashem to bless Yisrael" (Bemidbar 24:1), SO THAT A CURSE WILL NOT BEFALL YISRAEL. This is proven by the end of the verse, "And Elohim divided the light from the darkness" (Beresheet 1:4), to prevent wrath AND JUDGMENT. And even though the Holy One, blessed be He, afterward combined LIGHT AND DARKNESS as one, NEVERTHELESS THERE WAS NO FURTHER CONFLICT AND ANGER.

150. תָּא חֲזֵי, נְהִירוּ עִלָּאָה, לְמֶהֱוֵי נָהֵיר הַאי אוֹר, וּמֵהַהוּא נְהִירוּ, חֲדוּ לְכֹלָּא בֵּיהּ, וְהוּא יָמִינָא לְאִתְעַטְּרָא גּוּלְפוֹי גְּלִיפִין בַּהֲדֵיהּ, וְהָא אִתְּמַר כְּתִיב מָה רַב טוּבְךָ אֲשֶׁר צָפַנְתָּ לִּירֵאֶיךָ פָּעַלְתָּ לַחוֹסִים בָּךְ, מָה

רַב טוּבְךָ, דָּא אוֹר קַדְמָאָה דְּגָנֵיז קוּדְשָׁא בְּרִיךְ הוּא לִירֵאָיךָ, לַצַּדִּיקִים,
לְאָנוּן דַּחֲלֵי חַטָּאָה כִּדְקָאֲמָרָן.

150. Come and behold: The supernal radiance, BINAH, should continue to radiate, and through its radiance, it should bring gladness to all. This is THE POSITION OF the right, which was crowned with the right to make engravings OF THE LEFT. It is written: "How great is Your goodness, which You have laid upon those who fear You and which You have wrought for they who trust in You" (Tehilim 31:20). "How great is Your goodness" alludes to the primordial light that the Holy One, blessed be He, stored away. "They who fear You" alludes to the righteous who fear sin, and as we said, ONLY THEY SHOULD ENJOY THE LIGHT.

35. "And there was evening and there was morning"

True spiritual power is achieved through the existence of both Light and Darkness. Spiritual transformation requires darkness so that there is something tangible to transform, and Light is actually generated during this stage of transformation.

A simple candle can provide us with analogies to help enrich our understanding of the need for darkness. A tiny candle has no significance or worth when flickering against the backdrop of a brilliant sunlit day. But even a massive darkened arena responds to the lighting of one candle. In that setting, the candlelight assumes great importance and value. Moreover, it is the dark burning wick that gives rise to the candle's bright flickering flame. It is for reasons like these that darkness came into existence. Intently browsing the text of Hebrew letters, together with the knowledge gained by reading this section, delivers streams of shining Light into areas of darkness that may be present in our lives.

151. וַיְהִי עֶרֶב וַיְהִי בֹקֶר יוֹם אֶחָד, וַיְהִי עֶרֶב מִסְּטְרָא דְחֹשֶׁךְ, וַיְהִי בֹקֶר, מִסְּטְרָא דְאוֹר, וּמִגּוֹ דְּאִנּוּן מִשְׁתַּתְּפֵי כַּחֲדָא, כְּתִיב יוֹם אֶחָד, רַבִּי יְהוּדָה אָמַר, מַאי טַעֲמָא, בְּכָל יוֹמָא וְיוֹמָא כְּתִיב, וַיְהִי עֶרֶב וַיְהִי בֹקֶר. לְמִנְדַּע, דְּהָא לֵית יוֹם, בְּלָא לַיְלָה, וְלֵית לַיְלָה בְּלָא יוֹם, וְלָא אִבְעוּן לְאִתְפָּרְשָׁא.

151. "And there was evening and there was morning, one day" (Beresheet 1:5) "And there was evening," WAS DRAWN from the side of darkness, NAMELY THE NUKVA. "And there was morning," WAS DRAWN from the side of light, NAMELY ZEIR ANPIN. And since ZEIR ANPIN AND NUKVA join together as one, it is written of them, "one day." THIS INDICATES THAT EVENING AND MORNING ARE LIKE ONE BODY, AND BOTH MAKE THE DAY. Rabbi Yehuda asks: IF THE THE SCRIPTURE HAS ALREADY STATED THAT "THERE WAS EVENING AND THERE WAS MORNING" MEANS THE MATING OF ZEIR ANPIN AND HIS NUKVA, why then are the words "and there was evening and there was morning" repeated each day? HE ANSWERS THAT it is to acknowledge that there cannot be day without night, nor night without day, and that they are inseparable.

152. אָמַר רַבִּי יוֹסֵי, הַהוּא יוֹם דְּנָפַק אוֹר קַדְמָאָה, אִתְפְּשַׁט בְּכֻלְּהוּ

יוֹמֵי, דִּכְתִיב בְּכָלְהוֹ יוֹם. אֲמַר רַבִּי אֶלְעָזָר, מַשְׁמַע דִּכְתִיב בְּכָלְהוֹ בֹּקֶר,
וְלָאו בֹּקֶר אֶלָּא מִסִּטְרָא דְּאוֹר קַדְמָאָה. רָבִּי שִׁמְעוֹן אֲמַר, יוֹמָא
קַדְמָאָה, אָזֵיל עִם כָּלְהוֹ, וְכָלְהוֹ בֵּיהּ, בְּגִין לְאַחֲזָאָה דְּלָאו בְּהוֹ פְּרוֹדָא,
וְכֹלָּא חַד.

152. Rabbi Yosi said that the day from which the primal light emerged extended into all the other days OF CREATION, as the word "day" is repeated in them all. Rabbi Elazar said that we learn this FROM THE FACT that the name morning was used in them all, because morning only relates to the primal light. THAT IS, MORNING MEANS THE FIRST REVELATION OF LIGHT. Rabbi Shimon said that the first day accompanies all THE OTHERS, and that all are contained in THE FIRST. This shows that there is no fragmentation between them, and that all are one.

36. "Let there be light"

The power of these verses from the Zohar literally makes the Light manifest in our lives.

153. וַיֹּאמֶר אֱלֹקִים יְהִי אוֹר, יְהִי, אִתְפַּשְׁטוּתָא דְּהַאי אוֹר לְתַתָּא, וְאִלֵּין אִינוּן מַלְאָכִין דְּאִתְבְּרִיאוּ בְּיוֹמָא קַדְמָאָה, אִית לוֹן קִיוּמָא, לְאִתְקַיְּימָא לְסְטַר יָמִינָא. וַיַּרְא אֱלֹקִים אֶת הָאוֹר כִּי טוֹב, אֶת לְאִתְכְּלָלָא אִסְפַּקְלַרְיָאָה דְּלָא נָהֲרָא עִם אִסְפַּקְלַרְיָאָה דְּנָהֲרָא דְּאִתְּמַר כִּי טוֹב, אָמַר רָבִּי אֶלְעָזָר, אֶת לְאִתְכְּלָלָא וּלְאַסְגָּאָה כָּלְהוּ מַלְאָכִין דְּאַתְיָין מִסְּטְרָא דְּאוֹר דָּא, וְכָלְהוֹן נָהֲרִין כְּקַדְמֵיתָא בְּקִיוּמָא שְׁלִים.

153. "And Elohim said, 'Let there be light'" (Beresheet 1:3), ALLUDES TO the spreading of light downward. These are the angels that were created on the first day, and who subsist on the right side, BECAUSE THE FIRST DAY, CHESED, IS CONSIDERED TO PERTAIN TO THE RIGHT SIDE. HENCE, THE ANGELS DRAWN FROM IT PERTAIN TO THE RIGHT. In the quotation, "And Elohim saw the light, that it was good" (Ibid. 4), the particle *Et* (the) joins the opaque mirror THAT IS MALCHUT, with the shining mirror THAT IS ZEIR ANPIN. This is the union that was pronounced, "good." Rabbi Elazar said that the particle *Et* (the) includes all the angels who come from the side of the light OF CHESED, and that they all shine as wholly as the first LIGHT, AS IT IS SAID OF THEM, "AND IT WAS GOOD."

37. "Let there be a firmament"

The light of sun requires reflection off a physical object in order to illuminate. This is the secret of the word *Firmament*. To create resistance and a circuit of energy, a burning light bulb requires a filament. Man requires a metaphysical filament – the firmament – to create resistance against the Left Column energy of our desire to receive, which is our Evil Inclination. This firmament or filament is our free will to resist the negative urges and desires of the ego. When we apply this resistance, we create a metaphysical circuit that generates spiritual Light.

154. יְהִי רָקִיעַ בְּתוֹךְ הַמַּיִם, אָמַר רַבִּי יְהוּדָה בְּהַאי אִתְפְּרָשׁוּ, מַיִין עִלָּאִין מִמַּיִין תַּתָּאִין. רָקִיעַ: פְּשִׁיטוּתָא דְּמַיִין, וְהָא אִתְּמַר, וִיהִי מַבְדִּיל, בֵּין מַיִין עִלָּאִין לְתַתָּאִין.

154. "Let there be a firmament in the midst of the water" (Beresheet 1:6). Rabbi Yehuda said that these words indicate that the upper water was separated from the lower water and that a "firmament" means the spreading of water. Hence, he continues, the words "and let it divide water from water," mean let there be a division between the upper and lower waters.

155. וַיַּעַשׂ אֱלֹקִים אֶת הָרָקִיעַ, דַּעֲבֵיד בֵּיה עֲבִידְתָּא, בְּסַגִּיאוּ עִלָּאָה, וַיְהִי רָקִיעַ לָא כְּתִיב, אֶלָּא וַיַּעַשׂ, דְּאַסְגֵּי לֵיה, בְּרִבּוּ סַגִּיא.

155. "And Elohim made the firmament" (Ibid. 7). THE WORDS "AND ELOHIM MADE" INDICATE THAT He acted by supernal greatness. It was not said 'there was a firmament,' but that He "made the firmament," indicating that He invested it with greatness.

156. אָמַר רַבִּי יִצְחָק, בַּשֵּׁנִי אִתְבְּרֵי גֵּיהִנֹּם, לְחַיָּיבֵי עָלְמָא, בַּשֵּׁנִי אִתְבְּרֵי מַחֲלוֹקֶת, בַּשֵּׁנִי לָא אִשְׁתְּלִים בֵּיה עֲבִידְתָּא, וּבְגִין כָּךְ לָא כְּתִיב בֵּיה כִּי טוֹב, עַד דְּאָתָא יוֹם תְּלִיתָאָה, וְאִשְׁתְּלֵים בֵּיה עֲבִידְתָּא, בְּגִין כָּךְ כִּי טוֹב תְּרֵי זִמְנֵי, חַד עַל אַשְׁלָמוּת עֲבִידְתָּא דְּיוֹם שֵׁנִי, וְחַד לְגַרְמֵיה. בְּיוֹם תְּלִיתָאֵי אִתְתַּקָּן יוֹם שֵׁנִי, וְאִתְפְּרַשׁ בֵּיה מַחֲלוֹקֶת, וּבֵיה

אִשְׁתְּלִימוּ רַחֲמֵי עַל חַיָּיבֵי גֵּיהִנֹּם, בְּיוֹמָא תְּלִיתָאָה מִשְׁתַּכְּכִין שְׁבִיבִין דְּגֵיהִנֹּם, בְּגִינֵי כָּךְ אִתְכְּלֵיל בֵּיהּ יוֹם שֵׁנִי, וְאִשְׁתְּלֵים בֵּיהּ.

156. Rabbi Yitzchak said that in the second DAY Gehenom was created for the wicked of the world. On the second DAY, conflict was created. The work was not finished on the second DAY, BUT ON THE THIRD. Thus the words "and it was good" were not used in conjunction with the second day. They were used only when the third day came, and the work was accomplished. Hence, "and it was good" was said twice, once for finishing the work started on the second day and once in reference to the third day's work. On the third day, the second day was corrected, and the conflict was settled FOR THE SAKE OF REVEALING THE RADIANCE OF BOTH. On the third day, mercy was extended to EXEMPT all of the sinners in Gehenom FROM PUNISHMENT. On the third day, the flames of Gehenom were moderated, OR COOLED, SO THAT THEY DID NOT SCORCH ANYMORE. Hence the second day was included in the third and completed by it.

157. ר' חִיָּיא הֲוָה יָתֵיב קַמֵּיהּ דְּרָבִּי שִׁמְעוֹן, אָמַר לוֹ הַאי אוֹר בְּיוֹם רִאשׁוֹן, וְחֹשֶׁךְ בְּיוֹם שֵׁנִי, וְאִתְפְּרָשׁוּ מַיָּא, וּמַחְלוֹקֶת הֲוָה בֵּיהּ, אַמַּאי לָא אִשְׁתְּלֵים בְּיוֹם רִאשׁוֹן, דְּהַאי יְמִינָא כָּלֵיל לִשְׂמָאלָא, אָמַר לוֹ עַל דָּא הֲוָה מַחְלוֹקֶת, וּתְלִיתָאָה בָּעֵי לְמֵיעַל בֵּינַיְיהוּ, לְאַכְרָעָא וּלְאַסְגָּאָה בְּהוּ שְׁלָם.

157. Rabbi Chiya, who was sitting in front of Rabbi Shimon, asked him why if the light emerged on the first day and if darkness, the separation of waters, and discord occurred on the second, was all not perfected by THE ILLUMINATION OF the first day, when the right embraced the left? BECAUSE THE LIGHT OF THE RIGHT, CONSIDERED THE ROOT OF THE SECOND DAY, HAD ALREADY EMERGED ON THE FIRST DAY, WHY WAS THE SECOND DAY MADE IN NEED OF THE THIRD DAY'S CORRECTION? RABBI CHIYA FURTHER POINTED OUT THAT THROUGH THE SECOND DAY'S CORRECTION BY THE THIRD DAY, ITS OWN RADIANCE WAS REDUCED, SUCH THAT IT COULD NOT SHINE DOWNWARD. IF THE SECOND DAY HAD BEEN CORRECTED BY THE FIRST DAY, THEN IT WOULD HAVE MAINTAINED ITS ESSENCE, AND NOT HAVE REDUCED ITSELF. RABBI SHIMON said that this was the reason for the conflict. Actually, THE FIRST

DAY WANTED TO CORRECT THE DEFICIENCY OF THE SECOND, AS THE ROOT WANTS TO CORRECT THE BRANCH. BUT THE SECOND DAY WOULD NOT ACCEPT ANY CONTROL BY THE FIRST DAY AND DISSENTED. Hence, it was necessary for the third day to intervene, settle the conflict between them, and restore peace.

38. "Let the earth bring forth grass"

The Zohar explains that the first *Five Days of Creation* do not deal
with real time, but rather with spiritual phases. During these *Five
Days* all the forces and entities of creation were maintained in a
state of potential. The *Sixth day of Creation* refers to their physical
manifestation, and the start of their physical existence.

Here, through the spiritual influences that emanate from each and
every letter, the Zohar provides us with an opportunity to manifest
and express the potential Light in our lives.

158. תַּדְשֵׁא הָאָרֶץ דֶּשֶׁא אִתְחַבְּרוּתָא דְּמַיִין עִלָּאִין בְּתַתָּאִין, לְמֶעְבַּד
פֵּירִין, מַיִין עִלָּאִין, וְעַבְדֵי אִיבִין, וְתַתָּאֵי קָרָאן לוֹן לְעִלָּאִין, כְּנוּקְבָּא
לְגַבֵּי דְכוּרָא, בְּגִין דְּמַיִין עִלָּאִין דְּכוּרִין, וְתַתָּאֵי נוּקְבִין.

158. "Let the earth bring forth grass" (Beresheet 1:11), indicates the union
of the upper waters with the lower waters to bear fruit. The upper produce
fruit and the lower call upon the upper TO RECEIVE FROM THEM THE FRUIT
THEY ARE TO BEAR IN THE WORLD. This is as the female calls upon the
male TO CONCEIVE FROM HIM AND BRING FORTH OFFSPRING TO THE
WORLD. This is because the upper waters are male, and the lower WATERS
are female.

159. רַבִּי שִׁמְעוֹן אָמַר, כָּל דָּא הוּא לְעֵילָא, וְהוּא לְתַתָּא, אָמַר רַבִּי
יוֹסֵי אִי הָכֵי אֱלֹקִים דְּקָא אָמְרָן מַאי אֱלֹקִים, אֱלֹקִים חַיִּים לְעֵילָא, וְאִי
תֵימָא לְתַתָּא אֱלֹקִים סְתָם. אֶלָּא לְתַתָּא אִיהוּ תּוֹלְדוֹת כְּמָה דְאַתְּ אָמֵר,
אֵלֶּה תוֹלְדוֹת הַשָּׁמַיִם וְהָאָרֶץ בְּהִבָּרְאָם, וְאָמְרִינָן בְּה' בְּרָאָם, וְהַהוּא
לְעֵילָא, אֲבָהָן דְּכֹלָּא הוּא, אִיהִי עֲבִידְתָּא, וְעַל דָּא אַרְעָא עָבְדַת
תּוֹלְדוֹת, דְּהָא הִיא מִתְעַבְּרָא כְּנוּקְבָּא מִן דְּכוּרָא.

159. Rabbi Shimon explains FURTHER that what is true for above is true for
below. Rabbi Yosi said that if this be so, then what does "Elohim" mean IN
THE PASSAGE, "AND ELOHIM SAID, 'LET THE EARTH PUT FORTH
GRASS.'" What is THE NAME "Elohim" in the verse? It is the living Elohim
above, NAMELY BINAH, AS REFERRED TO BY ALL 32 MENTIONS OF THE
NAME ELOHIM IN THE WORKS OF CREATION. Are we to accept that THE

NAME ELOHIM below is a plain Elohim? THIS, HE SAID, IS CONTRARY TO WHAT WAS EXPLAINED EARLIER (THAT IS, THAT ALL 32 ELOHIM IN THE WORKS OF CREATION ARE THE NAMES OF BINAH, WHICH IS A LIVING ELOHIM). RABBI YOSI REPLIED: Not so, the offspring are below. He quotes: "These are the generations of the heavens and earth when they were created (Heb. *Behibar'am*)" (Beresheet 2:4). As has already been explained, they were created by the letter Hei (Heb. *behei bra'am)*, THE LAST HEI OF YUD HEI VAV HEI, FROM WHERE COME ALL THE OFFSPRING. AND one above are the Patriarchs of all LEVELS. Consequently, the earth bears fruit by being made pregnant as a female by a male.

160. ר' אֶלְעָזָר אָמַר, כָּל חֵילִין הֲווֹ בְּאַרְעָא, וְלָא אַפִּיקַת חֵילָהָא, וְאִינּוּן תּוֹלְדוֹתֵיהָ, עַד יוֹם הַשְּׁשִׁי, דִּכְתִיב תּוֹצֵא הָאָרֶץ נֶפֶשׁ חַיָּה, וְאִי תֵימָא וְהָא כְתִיב וַתּוֹצֵא הָאָרֶץ דֶּשֶׁא, אֶלָּא אֲפִּיקַת תִּקּוּן חֵילָהָא לְאִתְיַישְׁבָא כִּדְקָא יָאוֹת, וְכֹלָּא הֲוָה גָּנִיז בֵּהּ עַד דְּאִצְטְרִיךְ, דְּהָא בְּקַדְמֵיתָא כְּתִיב צַדְיָיא וְרֵיקַנְיָא כְּתַרְגּוּמוֹ, וּלְבָתַר אִתְתַּקְּנַת, וְאִתְיַישְׁבַת וְקַבֵּילַת זַרְעָא, וּדְשָׁאִין וְעִשְׂבִּין וְאִילָנִין כִּדְקָא יָאוֹת, וְאַפִּיקַת לוֹן לְבָתַר. וּמְאוֹרוֹת הָכֵי נָמֵי לָא שִׁמְשׁוּ נְהוֹרָא דִּלְהוֹן עַד דְּאִצְטְרִיךְ.

160. Rabbi Elazar then said that all the forces were latent in the earth, WHICH IS MALCHUT, but she did not fulfill her potential for bringing forth offspring, until the sixth day. This is as it is written: "let the earth bring forth living creatures" (Beresheet 1:24). Where it is written: "the earth brought forth grass," DOES NOT MEAN THAT THE GRASS EMERGED IN ACTUALITY. IT MEANS ONLY THAT it did not activate its forces UNTIL THE SIXTH DAY. All remained stored until the time came TO RELEASE THE FORCES, NAMELY ON THE SIXTH DAY. For at first it is written: "IT WAS WITHOU FORM AND VOID," MEANING *desolate* and *empty* in the Aramaic translation. THAT IS, IT WAS A DESERT. Then, ON THE THIRD DAY, it was suitably furnished with seeds, grass, plants, and trees. Finally, it put them forth ON THE SIXTH DAY. Similarly, the luminary bodies did not emit their light until it was needed.

39. "Luminaries" with defective spelling

In these verses, we are given the ability to remove curses, all forms
of negativity, and all forms of deprivation from our lives.

161. יְהִי מְאֹרֹת בִּרְקִיעַ הַשָּׁמַיִם, לְאַכְלָלָא חִוְיָא בִישָׁא, דְּאַטִּיל זוּהֲמָא,
וַעֲבַד פֵּרוּדָא, דְּלָא מְשַׁמֵּשׁ שִׁמְשָׁא בְּסִיהֲרָא. מְאֵרֹת לְוָוטִין, וְעַל דָּא
גָּרֵים דְּאִתְלַטְיָיא אַרְעָא, דִּכְתִיב אֲרוּרָה הָאֲדָמָה, וּבְגִין כָּךְ מְאֹרֹת כְּתִיב.

161. THE WORDS, "Let there be luminaries (Heb. *me'orot*) in the firmament
of heaven" (Beresheet 1:14) are for the inclusion of the evil serpent, who
befouled and caused the separation between the sun and the moon. As a
result, they are not able to mate. The word *me'orot* IS THEREFORE
SPELLED WITHOUT A VAV so that it means 'curses.' The adjustment to the
spelling IS BECAUSE THE SERPENT caused the earth to be cursed, as is
written: "cursed is the ground for your sake" (Beresheet 3:17). THAT IS,
THE SERPENT WAS THE CAUSE OF THE SIN OF THE TREE OF KNOWLEDGE,
A CONSEQUENCE OF WHICH WAS THAT THE EARTH WAS CURSED. Hence it
is written *me'orot* WITHOUT A VAV, WHICH MEANS CURSES.

162. חַד, יְהִי מְאֹרֹת דָּא סִיהֲרָא, רְקִיעַ הַשָּׁמַיִם דָּא שִׁמְשָׁא, וְתַרְוַויְיהוּ
בִּכְלָלָא חֲדָא, לְאִזְדַּוְּוגָא לְאַנְהָרָא עָלְמִין, לְעֵילָּא וְתַתָּא, מַשְׁמַע
דִּכְתִיב עַל הָאָרֶץ, וְלָא כְתִיב בָּאָרֶץ, דְּמַשְׁמַע לְעֵילָּא וְתַתָּא, חוּשְׁבַּן
דְּכֹלָּא בְּסִיהֲרָא הוּא.

162. "Let there be luminaries" refers to one LUMINARY, AS IT IS SPELLED
WITHOUT THE VAV (CONNOTING SINGULAR LUMINARY). It is the moon.
And THE WORDS, "the firmament of heaven," refer to the sun. THUS, THE
ENTIRE EXPRESSION, "LET THERE BE LUMINARIES IN THE FIRMAMENT
OF HEAVEN," INDICATES THAT both THE SUN AND MOON CHEST OF ZEIR
ANPIN and below. It is written "on the earth," and not "in the earth," to
indicate RADIANCE above and below, AND TO TEACH US THAT all
calculations are done according to the moon.

163. רַבִּי שִׁמְעוֹן אָמַר, גִּימַטְרִיָאוֹת וְחֻשְׁבַּן תְּקוּפוֹת וְעִבּוּרִין, כֹּלָּא
הוּא בְּסִיהֲרָא, דְּהָא לְעֵילָּא לָאו אִיהוּ. אָמַר לוֹ ר' אֶלְעָזָר, וְלָא, וְהָא

כַּמָה חוּשְׁבְּנִין וְשִׁיעוּרִין קָעָבְדֵי חַבְרַיָיא. אָמַר לוֹ, לָאו הָכֵי, אֶלָּא
חוּשְׁבְּנָא קַיְימָא בְּסִיהֲרָא, וּמִתַּמָן יֵעוֹל בַּר נָשׁ לְמִנְדַּע לְעֵילָא, אָמַר לוֹ
וְהָא כְּתִיב וְהָיוּ לְאוֹתוֹת וּלְמוֹעֲדִים. אָמַר לוֹ, לְאָתֵת כְּתִיב, חָסֵר. אָמַר
לוֹ הָא כְּתִיב וְהָיוּ. אָמַר לוֹ הַוְיָין כֻּלְּהוֹן דִּיהֲווֹן בֵּיהּ כְּאִסְקוּפָא דָּא,
דְּאִתְמַלְיָא מִכֹּלָא, אֲבָל חוּשְׁבְּנָא דְּכֹלָּא בְּסִיהֲרָא הוּא.

163. Rabbi Shimon said that numerical measurements, determination of periods, and intercalary calculations are all made according to the moon, because above THE MOON, THIS MATING cannot be found TO RADIATE THE *MOCHIN* OF NUMERICAL CALCULATIONS. Rabbi Elazar said to him, however, this is not so, AS THERE ARE THE MOCHIN OF CALCULATIONS AND MEASUREMENT ABOVE THE MOON, for many calculations and measurements are made by our friends. But RABBI SHIMON explained that this is not what he meant. The MOCHIN OF calculation are made in the moon AND NOT IN ANY OTHER LEVEL, yet from this BASIS a man may proceed further and grasp CALCULATIONS IN higher LEVELS. INDEED, FROM THERE A MAN MAY ALSO PROCEED TO ATTAIN THE MOCHIN OF CALCULATIONS FROM LEVELS BEYOND THE MOON. RABBI ELAZAR said to him: Yet it is written: "Let them be for signs (Heb. *otot*), and for seasons, and for days, and years" (Beresheet 1:14). THIS USE OF THE PLURAL INDICATES THAT THE MOCHIN OF CALCULATION IS REVEALED BOTH IN THE MOON AND EVEN IN THE SUN, WHICH IS ZEIR ANPIN. RABBI SHIMON said to him: *Otot* is spelled without *Vav,* INDICATING THE SINGULARITY OF THE MOON AND EXCLUDING THE SUN. RABBI ELAZAR said: It is written: "Let them be," INDICATING PLURALITY, THUS INCLUDING THE SUN. RABBI SHIMON said: THIS IS NOT SAID ABOUT THE SUN AND MOON, BUT ABOUT THE PHASES OF THE MOCHIN. They were all within THE MOON, WHICH IS like a boat, filled with everything, but calculating them all is done only according to the moon, NOT THE SUN.

164. תָּא חֲזֵי, נְקוּדָה חַד אִית, וּמִתַּמָן שֵׁירוּתָא לְמִמְנֵי, דְּהָא מַה דִּלְגוֹ
דְּהַהִיא נְקוּדָה, לָא אִתְיְדַע, וְלָא אִתְיְיהַב לְמִמְנֵי, וְאִית נְקוּדָה לְעֵילָא
סְתִים, דְּלָא אִתְגַּלְיָא כְּלַל, וְלָא אִתְיְדַע, וּמִתַּמָן שֵׁירוּתָא לְמִמְנֵי, כָּל
סְתִים וְעוּמְקָא, הָכֵי נָמֵי אִית נְקוּדָה לְתַתָּא דְּאִתְגַּלְיָא, וּמִתַּמָן הוּא

שֵׁרוּתָא לְכָל חוּשְׁבְּנָא, וּלְכָל מִנְיָן, וְעַל דָּא, הָכָא הוּא אֲתַר לְכָל
תְּקוּפוֹת, וְגִימַטְרִיָאוֹת, וְעִבּוּרִין, וְזִמְנִין, וְחַגֵּי, וְשַׁבַּתֵּי. וְיִשְׂרָאֵל דְּדָבְקֵי
בְּקֻדְשָׁא בְּרִיךְ הוּא עָבְדֵי חוּשְׁבַּן לְסִיהֲרָא, וְאִנּוּן דָּבְקִין בֵּיהּ, וְסָלְקִין
לֵיהּ לְעֵילָא, דִּכְתִיב וְאַתֶּם הַדְּבֵקִים בַּה׳ אֱלֹקֵיכֶם וגו׳.

164. Come and see: There is one point, which is the beginning of reckoning and account. THAT IS, ARICH ANPIN, CALLED BEGINNING. That which is within, THAT IS, AND BEYOND ARICH ANPIN is completely unknowable. There is one point above, where all is hidden, unrevealed, and unknown. IT IS BINAH OF ARICH ANPIN. From there start the reckoning AND THE REVELATION of all that is hidden and deep, NAMELY THE SEVEN LOWER SFIROT OF BINAH OF ARICH ANPIN. There is also a point below, NAMELY THE NUKVA OF ZEIR ANPIN, which is the starting point OF THE REVELATION of all calculations and numbers. Consequently, it is the place from where THE MOCHIN RADIATE UPON all numerical measurements, determinations of seasons, intercalary days, festivals, holy days, and Shabbatot. And Yisrael who cleave to the Holy One, blessed be He, reckon by the moon, AS THE SAGES HAVE SAID "YISRAEL RECKON BY THE MOON AND THE NATIONS OF THE WORLD BY THE SUN." They cleave to it and ascend it TO CLOTHE THE SUPERNAL BINAH, as it is written: "But you that did cleave of Hashem your Elohim are alive every one of you this day" (Devarim 4:4).

40. "Let the water swarm abundantly"

The *Swarms* refer to the numerous angels that continually interact with humanity. The power to remove negative angels and their influences from our lives derives from the sacred letters. At the same time, we gain the power to connect ourselves to the positive influences of the good angels that populate the upper spiritual atmospheres.

165. יִשְׁרְצוּ הַמַּיִם שֶׁרֶץ נֶפֶשׁ חַיָּה, אָמַר רַבִּי אֶלְעָזָר, הָא אוֹקְמוּהָ, דְּאִינוּן מַיִין רְחִישׁוּ וְאוֹלִידוּ כְּגַוְונָא דִּלְעֵילָא, וְהָא אִתְּמָר. וְעוֹף יְעוֹפֵף עַל הָאָרֶץ, יָעוּף מִבָּעֵי לֵיהּ, מַהוּ יְעוֹפֵף.

165. "Let the water swarm abundantly with moving creatures that have life" (Beresheet 1:20). Rabbi Elazar said: We have already explained that the LOWER waters teemed and gave birth like the upper WATERS, MEANING THAT THE LOWER WATERS GAVE BIRTH TO WHAT THEY RECEIVED FROM ABOVE. It is said, "birds to fly over the earth." Why, he then inquired, use the word *yeofef* (to fly), instead of the simple *yauf*?

166. אָמַר רַבִּי שִׁמְעוֹן רָזָא הוּא, וְעוֹף הָא מִיכָאֵל, דִּכְתִיב וַיָּעָף אֵלַי אֶחָד מִן הַשְּׂרָפִים. יְעוֹפֵף הָא גַּבְרִיאֵל, דִּכְתִיב וְהָאִישׁ גַּבְרִיאֵל אֲשֶׁר רָאִיתִי בֶחָזוֹן בַּתְּחִלָּה מֻעָף בִּיעָף. עַל הָאָרֶץ, הָא אֵלִיָּהוּ, דְּאִשְׁתְּכַח תָּדִיר בְּאַרְעָא, וְלָא מִסִּטְרָא דְּאַבָּא וְאִמָּא אִשְׁתְּכַח, דְּאִיהוּ בַּד' טָאסִין, דִּכְתִיב וְרוּחַ ה' יִשָּׂאֲךָ עַל אֲשֶׁר לֹא אֵדָע, וְרוּחַ ה' חַד, יִשָּׂאֲךָ תְּרֵין, עַל אֲשֶׁר תְּלַת, לֹא אֵדַע אַרְבַּע.

166. Rabbi Shimon said: This is a secret, BECAUSE IT ALLUDES TO THE CREATION OF ANGELS. 'Bird' refers to Michael, of whom it is written: "And one of the Seraphim flew to me" (Yeshayah 6:6), "ONE OF THE SERAPHIM" REFERS TO MICHAEL. To fly (*yeofef*) is said about Gabriel, as it is written: "the man Gabriel, whom I had seen in the vision at the who is continuously upon the earth. beginning, approached close to me in swift flight" (Daniel 9:21). It is Elijah ELIJAH is not connected to the side of Aba and Ima because he FLIES with four wings as it is written: "And the spirit of Hashem shall carry you where I know not" (I Melachim 18:12). The "spirit

of Hashem" indicates one wing, and "carry you" the second WING. "Where" the third, and "I know not" the fourth. THUS, HE FLIES WITH FOUR WINGS.

167. עַל פְּנֵי, דָּא מַלְאַךְ הַמָּוֶת, דְּהוּא אַחְשִׁיךְ פְּנֵי עָלְמָא, וּכְתִיב בֵּיהּ וְחֹשֶׁךְ עַל פְּנֵי תְהוֹם, רְקִיעַ הַשָּׁמַיִם, כִּדְאֲמָרָן, עוֹלֶה וּמַסְטִין וכו'. אֲמַר רַבִּי אַבָּא, וְהָא מַלְאַךְ הַמָּוֶת בַּשֵּׁנִי אִתְבְּרֵי, אֶלָּא, עַל הָאָרֶץ, דָּא רְפָאֵל, דְּאִיהוּ מְמָנָא לְאַסְוָוֹתָא דְּאַרְעָא, דִּבְגִינֵיהּ אִתְרַפִּיאַת אַרְעָא, וְקַיְּים בַּר נָשׁ עֲלָהּ, וְרָפֵי לְכָל חֵילֵיהּ, עַל פְּנֵי רְקִיעַ הַשָּׁמַיִם דָּא אוֹרִיאֵל. וְכֹלָּא הוּא בַּקְּרָא.

167. The words "upon the face" allude to THE CREATION OF the Angel of Death, because he darkens the face of the world. It is as written of him: "and darkness upon the face of the deep" (Beresheet 1:1). The words, "the open firmament of heaven," mean, as is written, that THE ANGEL OF DEATH goes up to heaven and accuses. HE IS THE SATAN, HE IS THE EVIL INCLINATION, HE IS THE ANGEL OF DEATH. HE IS CALLED THE ANGEL OF DEATH, BECAUSE AFTER HE ACCUSES, HE TAKES THE ACCUSED'S SOUL. IT IS THEREFORE WRITTEN OF HIM, "UPON THE FACE OF THE FIRMAMENT OF HEAVEN" (IBID. 20), BECAUSE IT IS HIS WAY TO ACCUSE IN THE FIRMAMENT OF HEAVEN. Rabbi Aba said: But the Angel of Death was created on the second day! HOW CAN YOU SAY THAT "THE OPEN FIRMAMENT OF HEAVEN" IS CONNECTED TO HIS CREATION WHEN, AS WAS STATED, IT IS CONNECTED TO THE FIFTH DAY? But "above the earth" refers to the angel Raphael, who is in charge of healing the earth. Through Raphael, the earth is healed and becomes inhabitable for man. He is the healer to the powers OF THE EARTH. AND BECAUSE THE HEALING OF THE EARTH COMES FROM HIM, HIS CREATION IS INDICATED IN THE WORDS "ABOVE THE EARTH," WHILE the words "upon the face of the firmament of heaven" refer to THE CREATION OF THE ANGEL Uriel. And all THE FOUR ANGELS, THE CARRIERS OF THE CHARIOT, are ALLUDED TO in this verse.

168. וּבְגִין כָּךְ, כְּתִיב בַּתְרֵיהּ, וַיִּבְרָא אֱלֹקִים אֶת הַתַּנִּינִם הַגְּדוֹלִים, אֲמַר רַבִּי אֶלְעָזָר אִלֵּין אִינוּן שַׁבְעִין מְמָנָן רַבְרְבָן, עַל שַׁבְעִין עַמִּין, וּבְגִין כָּךְ אִתְבְּרִיאוּ כֻּלְּהוּ, לְמֶהֱוֵי שַׁלִּיטָאן עַל אַרְעָא.

168. The text proceeds, "And Elohim created the great crocodiles" (Beresheet 1:21). Rabbi Elazar said: Those are the seventy ministers OF THE UPPER WORLDS, in charge of the seventy nations, created for the purpose of controlling the earth. THUS THEY ARE CALLED "THE GREAT," INSTEAD OF "THAT MOVED," TO TEACH US THAT THEY WERE CREATED TO BE IN CHARGE.

169. וְאֵת כָּל נֶפֶשׁ הַחַיָּה הָרוֹמֶשֶׂת, אִלֵּין אִינּוּן יִשְׂרָאֵל, דְּאִינּוּן נֶפֶשׁ וַדַּאי דְּהַהוּא חַיָּה, וְאִקְרוּן גּוֹי אֶחָד בָּאָרֶץ. אֲשֶׁר שָׁרְצוּ הַמַּיִם לְמִינֵיהֶם, דְּאִינּוּן מִשְׁתַּדְלִין בְּאוֹרַיְיתָא. וְאֵת כָּל עוֹף כָּנָף לְמִינֵהוּ, אִלֵּין צַדִּיקַיָּיא דִּבְהוֹן, וּבְגִין כָּךְ אִינּוּן נֶפֶשׁ חַיָּה. ד"א וְאֵת כָּל עוֹף כָּנָף כִּדְקָא אִתְּמַר, אִלֵּין אִינּוּן שְׁלוּחֵי עָלְמָא.

169. The words: "And every living creature (Heb. *Nefesh living chayah*) that moves" (Beresheet 1:21) refer to THE CREATION OF THE NEFESH OF Yisrael, who are surely the Nefesh of Chayah, WHICH IS THE NUKVA OF ZEIR ANPIN. THIS IS CERTAIN, BECAUSE THE ENTIRETY OF THE WORLD OF ATZILUT IS CONSIDERED THE LIGHT OF CHAYAH. They are therefore called "one nation in the earth" (II Shmuel 7:23). THE WORDS: "which the waters brought forth abundantly after their kind" (Beresheet 1:21) REFER TO those who occupy themselves with Torah. 'WATER' ALWAYS ALLUDES TO TORAH, AND WHOEVER OCCUPIES HIMSELF WITH HER MERITS THE NEFESH OF CHAYAH. AND HE WHO DOES NOT OCCUPY HIMSELF ALWAYS WITH TORAH DOES NOT HAVE A HOLY NEFESH. THE WORDS: "And every winged bird after its kind" (Beresheet 1:21) ALLUDE TO the righteous among them, AMONG THOSE WHO OCCUPY THEMSELVES WITH TORAH, and for this reason, FOR BEING RIGHTEOUS, they merit the Nefesh of Chayah. According to another interpretation, the words, "every winged bird," refer to the angels, worldly messengers, of whom we have already spoken.

170. אָמַר רַבִּי אַבָּא, נֶפֶשׁ חַיָּה אִינּוּן יִשְׂרָאֵל, בְּגִין דְּאִינּוּן בְּנֵי דְּקֻדְשָׁא בְּרִיךְ הוּא וְנִשְׁמַתְהוֹן קַדִּישִׁין מִנֵּיהּ אַתְיָין. נַפְשָׁאן דִּשְׁאָר עַמִּין עעכו"ם מֵאָן אֲתָר הוּא, אָמַר רַבִּי אֶלְעָזָר, מֵאִינּוּן סִטְרֵי שְׂמָאלָא,

-118-

דְּמְסָאֲבֵי לוֹן, אִית לוֹן נִשְׁמָתִין, וּבְגִין כָּךְ כָּלְּהוּ מְסָאֲבִין, וּמְסָאֲבִין לְמָאן דְּקָרִיב בַּהֲדַיְיהוּ.

170. Rabbi Aba said that the words, "living Nefesh" refer to Yisrael, because they are children of the Holy One, blessed be He, from whom their holy souls originate. HE ASKS: From where do the souls of idolatrous nations originate? Rabbi Elazar said: Their souls come from the forces of the left, which defile them. Therefore, they are all impure and convey impurity to those who come close to them.

171. וַיֹּאמֶר אֱלֹקִים תּוֹצֵא הָאָרֶץ נֶפֶשׁ חַיָּה וגו', כָּלְּהוֹן שְׁאָר חֵיוָון אָחֳרָנִין כָּל חַד וְחַד כְּפוּם זִינֵיהּ, וְאָמַר רָבִּי אֶלְעָזָר, הַאי מְסַיֵּיעַ לְמַה דַּאֲמָרָן, נֶפֶשׁ חַיָּה אִלֵּין יִשְׂרָאֵל, דְּאִינוּן נֶפֶשׁ חַיָּה קַדִּישָׁא עִלָּאָה. בְּהֵמָה וָרֶמֶשׂ וְחַיְתוֹ אֶרֶץ, אִלֵּין שְׁאָר עַמִּין עכו"ם, דְּלָאו אִינוּן נֶפֶשׁ חַיָּה, אֶלָּא כִּדְקָאֲמָרָן.

171. "And Elohim said, 'Let the earth bring forth living creatures...'" (Beresheet 1:24). These words refer to the rest of the Chayot, APART FROM YISRAEL, each and every one receives according to its kind. Rabbi Elazar added, This supports our statement that "living Nefesh" refers to Yisrael, who are holy supernal living souls. The words "Cattle, and creeping things, and beasts of the earth" (Beresheet 1:24) refer to the idolatrous nations, which are not living souls. Rather, they are, as we have said, DRAWN FROM THE FORCES OF THE LEFT, WHICH DEFILE THEM.

41. "Let us make man"

The body of man is a reflection of Upper World forces. Every act we perform in our lower world initiates a corresponding spiritual action in the Upper Worlds. The magnitude of each action, however, is concealed from us. The simple physical hand movement of reaching into one's pocket to draw a few coins for charity arouses little effect in our physical environment. In the realm of the spirit, however, this act moves mountains. Scanning through the Aramaic text is another such action. It generates unimaginable positive energy for the reader, and for the world.

172. "נַעֲשֶׂה אָדָם בְּצַלְמֵנוּ כִּדְמוּתֵנוּ", דְּאִתְכְּלֵיל בְּשִׁית סִטְרִין, כָּלִיל מִכֹּלָּא, כְּגַוְונָא דִלְעֵילָא, בְּשַׁיְיפֵי מְתַקְּנָן, בְּרָזָא דְּחָכְמְתָא, כְּדְקָא יָאוּת, כֹּלָּא תִּקּוּנָא עִלָּאָה. נַעֲשֶׂה אָדָם, רָזָא דְּכַר וְנוּקְבָא, כֹּלָּא בְּחָכְמְתָא קַדִּישָׁא עִלָּאָה. בְּצַלְמֵנוּ כִּדְמוּתֵנוּ, לְאִשְׁתַּכְלְלָא דָּא בְּדָא, לְמֶהֱוֵי הוּא יְחִידָאי בְּעָלְמָא, שַׁלִּיט עַל כֹּלָּא.

172. The words "Let us make man in our image, after our likeness" (Beresheet 1:26) indicate that MAN was composed of the six directions that comprise all, THAT IS, CHOCHMAH AND CHASSADIM, after the supernal image. Limbs are structured according to secret wisdom, according to the supernal structure. The words, "Let us make man," refer to the secret of male and female, made according to the holy supernal wisdom. ALL WAS DONE SO THAT MAN COULD RECEIVE SUPERNAL AND HOLY CHOCHMAH. AND SINCE CHOCHMAH CAN ONLY BE DRAWN THROUGH THE NUKVA, MAN WAS CREATED MALE AND FEMALE. IN THE VERSE, "In our image and in our likeness," IN WHICH *IMAGE* IS THE MOCHIM OF MALE AND *LIKENESS* IS THE MOCHIM OF FEMALE, they will construct each other, making MAN unique in the world and fit to rule over everything .

42. "And Elohim saw everything that He made"

When God created us, He saw the final outcome of His intention to bestow infinite fulfillment upon the Vessel for all eternity. The Creator actually saw the result even in the original thought, because He is above any concept of time. He perceives the end in the beginning. We, however, who are under the influence of time, find ourselves in a process of transformation that eventually paves the way for infinite fulfillment.

This section of the Zohar connects us to The Creator's original thought of creation. We can accelerate the process of change and connect ourselves to Light that is destined to be ours when we achieve our final correction.

173. וַיַּרְא אֱלֹקִים אֶת כָּל אֲשֶׁר עָשָׂה, וְהִנֵּה טוֹב מְאֹד, הָכָא אִתְתַּקַּן, מַה דְּלָא אִתְּמָר כִּי טוֹב בַּשֵּׁנִי, בְּגִין דְּאִתְבְּרֵי בֵּיהּ מוֹתָא, וְהָכָא אִתְּמָר וְהִנֵּה טוֹב מְאֹד. וְאַזְלָא כְּמָה דְּאָמְרֵי חַבְרַיָּא, וְהִנֵּה טוֹב מְאֹד זֶה מָוֶת.

173. "And Elohim saw everything that He had made, and, behold, it was very good" (Beresheet 1:31). These words correct the omission of the words, "it was good," in the second day. These words were omitted on the second day, because on it, death was created. Now, the words, "it was very good" are used. The friends have explained that "it was very good" refers to death. BECAUSE THIS IS SO, IT WAS FITTING TO USE "IT WAS GOOD" ON THE SECOND DAY, THE DAY ON WHICH DEATH WAS CREATED. BUT THE WORDS WERE NOT USED UNTIL THE SIXTH DAY, WHEN IT WAS REVEALED THAT DEATH IS VERY GOOD.

174. וַיַּרְא אֱלֹקִים אֶת כָּל אֲשֶׁר עָשָׂה, וְהִנֵּה טוֹב מְאֹד, וְכִי לָא חָמָא לֵיהּ קוֹדֶם, אֶלָּא כֹּלָּא חָמָא לֵיהּ קֻדְשָׁא בְּרִיךְ הוּא, וּמַאן דַּאֲמַר אֶת כָּל, לְאַסְגָּאָה כָּל דָּרִין דְּיֵיתוּן לְבָתַר כֵּן, וְכֵן כָּל מַה דְּיִתְחַדֵּשׁ בְּעָלְמָא, בְּכָל דָּרָא וְדָרָא, עַד לָא יֵיתוּן לְעָלְמָא. אֲשֶׁר עָשָׂה דָּא כָּל עוֹבָדִין דִּבְרֵאשִׁית, דְּתַמָּן אִתְבְּרֵי יְסוֹדָא וְעִקָּרָא לְכָל מַה דְּיֵיתֵי וְיִתְחַדֵּשׁ בְּעָלְמָא לְבָתַר כֵּן. וּבְגִין כָּךְ חָמָא לֵיהּ קֻדְשָׁא בְּרִיךְ הוּא, עַד לָא הֲוָה, וְשַׁוֵּי כֹּלָּא בְּעוֹבָדָא דִּבְרֵאשִׁית.

174. "And Elohim saw everything that He made and behold, it was very good." HE ASKS: Did He not see that before? THE WORDS "AND ELOHIM SAW" GIVE THE IMPRESSION THAT HE ONLY SAW AFTER HE HAD CREATED. HE EXPLAINS: The Holy One, blessed be He, saw all – THE THINGS THAT HAD BEEN MADE AND THOSE YET TO BE MADE. And some commented that the particle *Et* before the word "everything" indicates that He saw all the generations to be and all that was to happen in the world in each generation, before those generations even came to existence. THE WORDS, "which He had made," ALLUDE TO all the works of Creation RECOUNTED IN BERESHEET. There, the foundation and root of all that was to be and will subsequently come to pass in the world, was established. Hence, the Holy One, blessed be He, foresaw all and placed all in the works of Creation.

175. יוֹם הַשִּׁשִּׁי מַאי שְׁנָא בְּכָלְהוּ יוֹמֵי דְּלָא אִתְּמַר בְּהוּ הֵ"א, אֶלָּא הָכָא כַּד אִשְׁתַּכְלֵל עָלְמָא, אִתְחַבְּרַת נוּקְבָא בִּדְכוּרָא, בְּחִבּוּרָא חַד, ה' בַּשִּׁשִּׁי לְמֶהֱוֵי כֹּלָּא חַד. וַיְכֻלּוּ אִשְׁתַּכְלְלוּ כֹּלָּא חַד, אִשְׁתַּכְלְלוּ מִכֹּלָּא, וְאִשְׁתַּלִימוּ בְּכֹלָּא.

175. The unique aspect of the words, "the sixth day," is the letter *Hei* (Heb. 'the'). The *Hei* was used in reference to no day EXCEPT THE SIXTH. FOR THE FORMULA IS NOT 'THE FIRST DAY', 'THE SECOND DAY', AND SO ON, BUT RATHER "ONE DAY," "A SECOND DAY," AND SO ON. This is because now the world was finished. WHICH IS ZEIR ANPIN AND NUKVA, WHO WERE COMBINED AT THE END OF THE WORKS OF CREATION, as the female was united with the male into one unit, *Hei* with "sixth," to be completely one. "Thus the heavens and earth were finished" indicates that the unification OF THE MALE AND FEMALE was complete in every detail. THE WORKS OF CREATION were completed in every way and were fully equipped with everything.

43. "Thus the heavens and the earth were finished"

The spiritual intention of this passage is to help us recognize that
the Torah is not a book about morals, values, and ethics. The
Torah is the actual channel and portal by which we connect to the
Light of The Creator. This awareness gives us the ability to
activate the Torah's spiritual powers. When we study the Torah, it
becomes a vehicle by which we literally elevate into the Upper
Worlds.

176. וַיְכֻלּוּ הַשָּׁמַיִם וְהָאָרֶץ וְכָל צְבָאָם, רַבִּי אֶלְעָזָר פָּתַח, מָה רַב
טוּבְךָ אֲשֶׁר צָפַנְתָּ לִירֵאֶיךָ פָּעַלְתָּ לַחוֹסִים בָּךְ נֶגֶד בְּנֵי אָדָם, תָּא חֲזֵי
קוּדְשָׁא בְּרִיךְ הוּא בָּרָא לְבַר נָשׁ בְּעָלְמָא, וְאַתְקֵין לֵיהּ לְמֶהֱוֵי שְׁלִים
בְּפוּלְחָנֵיהּ, וּלְאִתְתַּקְּנָא אָרְחוֹי, בְּגִין דְּיִזְכֵּי לִנְהוֹרָא עִלָּאָה, דְּגָנִיז
קוּדְשָׁא בְּרִיךְ הוּא לְצַדִּיקַיָּיא, כד"א לֹא רָאָתָה אֱלֹהִים זוּלָתְךָ
יַעֲשֶׂה לִמְחַכֵּה לוֹ.

176. "Thus the heavens and the earth were finished, and all their hosts"
(Beresheet 2:1). Rabbi Elazar quoted, "How great is Your goodness which
You have laid out for those who fear You. You have wrought for them who
put their trust in You, before the sons of men" (Tehilim 31:20). Come and
behold: The Holy One, blessed be He, created man in the world. He gave
him the abilities to perfect himself in His service and to correct his ways so
as to merit the supernal light that the Holy One, blessed be He, saved for the
righteous. This is, as it is written: "neither has the eye seen, that Elohim,
besides You" (Yeshayah 64:3) ALLUDING TO THE STORED LIGHT. The
words, "should do such a thing for him that waits for Him," REFER TO THE
RIGHTEOUS.

177. וּבַמֶּה יִזְכֵּי לֵיהּ לְבַר נָשׁ לְהַהוּא נְהוֹרָא, בְּאוֹרַיְיתָא. דְּכָל מַאן
דְּאִשְׁתַּדַּל בְּאוֹרַיְיתָא בְּכָל יוֹמָא, יִזְכֵּי לְמֶהֱוֵי לֵיהּ חוּלָקָא בְּעָלְמָא
דְּאָתֵי, וְיִתְחֲשַׁב לֵיהּ כְּאִלּוּ בָּאנֵי עָלְמִין, דְּהָא בְּאוֹרַיְיתָא אִתְבְּנֵי עָלְמָא
וְאִשְׁתַּכְלַל, הה"ד ה' בְּחָכְמָה יָסַד אֶרֶץ כּוֹנֵן שָׁמַיִם בִּתְבוּנָה, וּכְתִיב
וָאֶהְיֶה אֶצְלוֹ אָמוֹן וָאֶהְיֶה שַׁעֲשׁוּעִים יוֹם יוֹם, וְכָל דְּאִשְׁתַּדַּל בָּהּ,
שַׁכְלִיל עָלְמִין, וְקַיֵּים לֵיהּ, בְּרוּחָא חֲזֵי, וְתָא חֲזֵי, בְּרוּחָא עֲבִיד קוּדְשָׁא בְּרִיךְ הוּא

עָלְמָא, וּבְרוּחָא מִתְקַיְּימָא, רוּחָא דְּאִינוּן דְּלָעָאן בְּאוֹרַיְיתָא, וְכָל שֶׁכֵּן רוּחָא דְּהֶבֶל דְּרַבְיֵי דְּבֵי רַב.

177. And how can one merit this STORED light? THE ANSWER IS, only through CONSTANT OCCUPATION WITH Torah. He who occupies himself with Torah every day merits a place in the World to Come, and it is considered as if he had built worlds. Through Torah, the world was built and completed. Thus, the words, "Hashem founded the earth with wisdom, He established the heavens with understanding" (Mishlei 3:19), REFER TO THE WISDOM AND UNDERSTANDING FOUND IN TORAH. And it is also written, "And I was by Him, as a nurseling (Heb. *amon*); and I was daily His delight" (Mishlei 8:30), WHICH MEANS THAT TORAH WAS HIS CRAFTSMANSHIP (HEB. *UMANUT*) IN CREATING THE WORLD. Thus, whoever is occupied IN TORAH completes and preserves the worlds. Come and behold: The Holy One, blessed be He, made the world by a breath and by a breath it is preserved. IT IS PRESERVED BY the breath of the mouths of those who study Torah. It is preserved even more by the breath of the children in the houses of learning, BECAUSE THE WORLD IS PRESERVED BY IT.

178. מָה רַב טוּבְךָ, דָּא טוּבָא דְּאִתְגְּנִיז. לִירֵאֶיךָ, לְאִינוּן דַּחֲלֵי חַטָּאָה. פָּעַלְתָּ לַחוֹסִים בָּךְ, מַאי פָּעַלְתָּ, דָּא עוֹבָדָא דִּבְרֵאשִׁית. רַבִּי אַבָּא אָמַר, דָּא גַּן עֵדֶן, דְּהָא בְּאוּמָנוּתָא עָבִיד לֵיהּ קֻדְשָׁא בְּרִיךְ הוּא בְּאַרְעָא, כְּגַוְונָא דִּלְעֵילָא. לְאִתְתַּקְפָא בֵּיהּ צַדִּיקַיָּיא, הה"ד פָּעַלְתָּ לַחוֹסִים בָּךְ נֶגֶד בְּנֵי אָדָם, דְּהָא הוּא נֶגֶד אָדָם וְאַחֲרָא נֶגֶד עֶלְאִין קַדִּישִׁין. אָמַר רָבִּי שִׁמְעוֹן גַּן עֵדֶן לְעֵילָא וְנֶגֶד בְּנֵי אָדָם הֲוֵי, לְאִתְכַּנְּשָׁא בֵּיהּ צַדִּיקַיָּיא דְּעַבְדֵי רְעוּתָא דְּמָארֵיהוֹן.

178. FURTHERMORE, "How great is Your goodness" refers to the hidden good, OR THE STORED LIGHT. "Those who fear You" relates to those who fear wrongdoing – THOSE WHO OCCUPY THEMSELVES CONSTANTLY WITH TORAH – FOR WHOM THE LIGHT WAS STORED. "You have wrought for them who trust in You." HE ASKS: What is the meaning of "wrought," AND HE RESPONDS THAT it refers to the works of Creation. THE WHOLE OF CREATION DID NOT COME ABOUT, AND COULD NOT BE MAINTAINED, IF

NOT FOR THOSE WHO STUDY TORAH, THOSE WHO CAN DRAW, THROUGH THEIR LEARNING, UPON THE STORED LIGHT. Rabbi Aba said: THE WORD "WROUGHT" refers to the Garden of Eden, which the Holy One, blessed be He, crafted on earth in the image of the supernal Garden of Eden for the righteous to reinforce themselves. The words are "wrought for them who put their trust in You, which You had laid out for those who fear You before the sons of men," because THE LOWER GARDEN OF EDEN is for humans and the other one – THE SUPERNAL GARDEN OF EDEN – is only for supernal holy beings – NOT FOR PEOPLE. Rabbi Shimon said: THE WORD "WROUGHT" REFERS TO the supernal Garden of Eden, but even so, it is for the "sons of men." For there gather the righteous, who do the will of their Master. ALTHOUGH THE UPPER GARDEN OF EDEN IS NOT FOR HUMANS, THE RIGHTEOUS IN THE LOWER GARDEN OF EDEN RISE THROUGH THE AIR INTO THE UPPER GARDEN OF EDEN. EVEN THOUGH THE RIGHTEOUS MUST DESCEND AND RETURN TO THEIR PLACES, THE UPPER GARDEN IS STILL CONSIDERED FOR PEOPLE.

179. וַיְכֻלּוּ, דְּכָלוּ עוֹבָדִין דִּלְעֵילָא וְעוֹבָדִין דִּלְתַתָּא, הַשָּׁמַיִם וְהָאָרֶץ, לְעֵילָא וְתַתָּא. רַבִּי שִׁמְעוֹן אָמַר עוֹבָדָא וְאוּמָנוּתָא דְּאוֹרַיְיתָא שֶׁבִּכְתָב, וְעוֹבָדָא וְאוּמָנוּתָא דְּתוֹרָה שֶׁבְּעַל פֶּה. וְכָל צְבָאָם, אִלֵּין פְּרָטֵי דְּאוֹרַיְיתָא, אַפִּין דְּאוֹרַיְיתָא, שִׁבְעִים פָּנִים לַתּוֹרָה. וַיְכֻלּוּ, דְּאִתְקַיְימוּ וְאִשְׁתַּכְלְלוּ דָּא בְּדָא, שָׁמַיִם וָאָרֶץ פְּרָט וּכְלָל, וְכָל צְבָאָם רָזֵי דְּאוֹרַיְיתָא, דַּכְיָאן דְּאוֹרַיְיתָא מְסָאֲבָן דְּאוֹרַיְיתָא.

179. "were finished" indicates that all the work that was to be done, both above and below, was finished, for "the heavens and the earth" represent above and below. THE WORD "HEAVENS" ALLUDES TO THE HIGHER WORLDS ABOVE, AND EARTH ALLUDES TO THE LOWER WORLDS BELOW. Rabbi Shimon said: THE WORD "HEAVENS" ALLUDES TO THE COMPLETION OF the works and craftsmanship of the Written Torah, THAT IS, THE STRUCTURE OF ZEIR ANPIN, WHICH IS CALLED "THE WRITTEN TORAH." And THE WORD "EARTH" REFERS TO THE COMPLETION OF the works and craftsmanship of the Oral Torah, THAT IS, THE STRUCTURE OF THE NUKVA CALLED "ORAL TORAH." THE WORD "WORKS" REFERS TO THE SIX EXTREMITIES OF ZEIR ANPIN AND "CRAFTS" REFERS TO THE TOP THREE SFIROT. "All their hosts" refers to the details of Torah, the

seventy alternative aspects of Torah, WHICH ARE THE DETAILS OF THE STRUCTURE OF ZEIR ANPIN, CALLED "TORAH." "THUS THE HEAVENS AND EARTH were finished" MEANS that both ZEIR ANPIN AND THE NUKVA, CALLED HEAVEN AND EARTH, can coexist and complement each other. The heavens and the earth are particular and general. "And all their hosts" are the SECRETS of Torah and the rules of cleanliness and uncleanness in Torah.

44. "And Elohim ended by the seventh day"

The Power of Blessing is the final necessary stage for any endeavor. *Blessing* assures that positive energy remains constant and consistent.

Focused visual connection with the Zohar's text arouses and imbues the Power of Blessing into our lives, especially in the areas of greatest need.

180. וַיְכַל אֱלֹקִים בַּיּוֹם הַשְּׁבִיעִי, דָּא תּוֹרָה שֶׁבְּעַל פֶּה, דְּאִיהוּ יוֹם שְׁבִיעִי, וּבֵיהּ אִשְׁתַּכְלֵל עָלְמָא, דְּאִיהוּ קִיּוּמָא דְּכֹלָּא. מְלַאכְתּוֹ אֲשֶׁר עָשָׂה, וְלֹא כָּל מְלַאכְתּוֹ, דְּהָא תּוֹרָה שֶׁבִּכְתָב, אַפֵּיק כֹּלָּא, בְּתוֹקְפָּא דִּכְתַב דְּנָפַק מֵחָכְמְתָא.

180. "And Elohim ended by the seventh day" (Beresheet 2:2), alludes to the Oral Torah, NAMELY MALCHUT, the seventh day. ZEIR ANPIN CONTAINS SIX DAYS AND THE NUKVA, WHICH IS MALCHUT, IS THE SEVENTH. On the seventh day, the world was completed, and all was preserved. It is written: "His work which He had done," and not 'all His work,' because the Written Torah, WHICH IS ZEIR ANPIN, created the world through the power of written words, which are MOCHIN extended from Chochmah. HENCE, THE WORK WAS FINISHED ON THE SEVENTH DAY, WHICH IS MALCHUT, THE NUKVA OF ZEIR ANPIN.

181. תְּלַת זְמְנִין הָכָא בַּיּוֹם הַשְּׁבִיעִי, וַיְכַל אֱלֹקִים בַּיּוֹם הַשְּׁבִיעִי, וַיִּשְׁבּוֹת בַּיּוֹם הַשְּׁבִיעִי וַיְבָרֶךְ אֱלֹקִים אֶת יוֹם הַשְּׁבִיעִי, הָא תְּלַת, וַיְכַל אֱלֹקִים, בַּיּוֹם הַשְּׁבִיעִי, דָּא תּוֹרָה שֶׁבְּעַל פֶּה, דְּעִם יוֹם הַשְּׁבִיעִי דָּא, אִשְׁתַּכְלֵל עָלְמָא כִּדְקָא אֲמָרָן.

181. The seventh day was mentioned three times in the text, "And Elohim ended by the seventh day...and He rested on the seventh day... and Elohim blessed the seventh day." "And Elohim ended by the seventh day" refers to the Oral Torah, WHICH IS MALCHUT, THE NUKVA OF ZEIR ANPIN. For by means of the seventh day, the world was finished and completed, as we have said.

182. וַיִּשְׁבּוֹת בַּיּוֹם הַשְּׁבִיעִי, דָּא יְסוֹדָא דְעָלְמָא, בְּסִפְרָא דְרַב יֵיבָא סָבָא דָּא יוֹבְלָא, וְעַל כָּךְ כְּתִיב הָכָא מִכָּל מְלַאכְתּוֹ, דְּכֹלָּא נָפֵיק מִנֵּיהּ. וַאֲנָן, דָּא יְסוֹדָא כִּדְקָאָמְרָן דְּהָא נַיְיחָא בֵּיהּ הֲוָה, יַתִּיר מִכֹּלָּא.

182. "And He rested on the seventh day" refers to the foundation of the world. In the book of Rav Yeba Saba, it is written THAT "HE RESTED…" refers to the Jubilee, NAMELY THE ILLUMINATION OF THE LEFT SIDE OF BINAH. Hence, it is written: "from all of His work," because all originates from this. And we say that "AND HE RESTED" alludes to Yesod, not to the Jubilee, because there is more rest in it than in everything else. THAT IS, REST IN THE ILLUMINATION OF YESOD IS MORE REVEALED THAN THE REST IN THE ILLUMINATION OF THE JUBILEE.

183. וַיְבָרֶךְ אֱלֹקִים אֶת יוֹם הַשְּׁבִיעִי, דָּא כֹּהֵן גָּדוֹל, דִּמְבָרֵךְ לְכֹלָּא, וְהוּא נָטֵיל בְּרֵישָׁא, דְּתָנָן כֹּהֵן נוֹטֵל בָּרֹאשׁ, וּבִרְכָאן בֵּיהּ שַׁרְיָין לְבָרְכָא. וְאִקְרֵי שְׁבִיעִי. רַבִּי יֵיסָא סָבָא אָמַר, הָנֵי תְּרֵי, חַד בִּיסוֹדָא דְעָלְמָא אִיהוּ, וְחַד בְּעַמּוּדָא דְּאֶמְצָעִיתָא.

183. "And Elohim blessed the seventh day" refers to the High Priest, who blesses all and takes the first share. As we have learned, the priest takes the first share OF ALL FEASTS, and he is blessed. Hence, he can bless OTHERS, and is called the seventh. Rabbi Yesa Saba said that "AND…ENDED" refers to the Yesod (Foundation) of the world, AND "BLESSED" to the central pillar, WHICH IS TIFERET.

184. וְכֵן וַיְקַדֵּשׁ אוֹתוֹ, לְמַאן, לְהַהוּא אֲתַר, דְּאַת קַיְּימָא, בֵּיהּ שַׁרְיָא, כד"א וְהִרְאַנִי אוֹתוֹ וְאֶת נָוֵהוּ, וּבְהַאי אֲתַר שַׁרְיָין כָּל קְדוּשִׁין לְעֵילָּא, וְנַפְקֵי מִנֵּיהּ לִכְנֶסֶת יִשְׂרָאֵל, לְמֵיהַב לָהּ תַּפְנוּקָא, לֶחֶם פָּנָג, וְאַזְלָא הָא כְּמָה דִכְתִיב מֵאָשֵׁר שְׁמֵנָה לַחְמוֹ וְהוּא יִתֵּן מַעֲדַנֵּי מֶלֶךְ. מֵאָשֵׁר, דָּא קַיָּים שְׁלִים, שְׁמֵנָה לַחְמוֹ, דַּהֲוָה לֶחֶם עֹנִי, אִתְהַדַּר לְמֶהֱוֵי לֶחֶם פָּנָג. וְהוּא יִתֵּן מַעֲדַנֵּי מֶלֶךְ, מַאן מֶלֶךְ דָּא כְּנֶסֶת יִשְׂרָאֵל, הוּא יָהֵיב כָּל תַּפְנוּקִין דְּעָלְמִין, וְכָל קְדוּשִׁין דְּנָפְקִין מִלְּעֵילָּא מֵהַאי אֲתַר נָפְקִין. וְעַל דָּא וַיְקַדֵּשׁ אוֹתוֹ, הַהוּא אֵת קַיְּימָא.

184. RABBI SHIMON SAID THAT "and sanctified it" (Beresheet 2:3) also REFERS TO YESOD, BECAUSE IT SAYS "AND SANCTIFIED IT" WITHOUT SAYING what HE SANCTIFIED. THIS PHRASE IS UNLIKE THE PREVIOUS PASSAGES "AND ELOHIM BLESSED," "AND HE RESTED," because it refers to the place where the sign of the covenant is fixed, NAMELY YESOD. THE WORD *OTO* (IT) CAN BE INTERPRETED AS THE PLACE OF THE SIGN (HEB. *OT*) OF THE COVENANT, NAMELY YESOD, because it is written: "and show me both it (Heb. *oto*) and His habitation" (II Shmuel 15:25). "OTO" REFERS TO YESOD, AND "HIS HABITATION" REFERS TO MALCHUT. This place, YESOD, is the dwelling of all supernal sanctities, the place from which the Nukva descends upon the Congregation of Yisrael to bestow upon her luxuries and the bread of joy. This is in accordance with the verse, "From Asher his bread shall be fat, and he shall yield the dainties of the king" (Beresheet 49:20). "From Asher" alludes to the perfect covenant. "His bread shall be fat," indicates that BEFORE THE CORRECTION OF YESOD, it was bread of shame, but now, AFTER THE CORRECTION, it has become the bread of joy. In the words, "And he shall yield the dainties of the king," "the king" refers to the Congregation of Yisrael, WHICH IS THE NUKVA OF ZEIR ANPIN, to whom YESOD gives all the luxuries of the world. And all the sanctities that emerge from above originate from this place. Hence, "and sanctified it (*oto*)" – the very sign (*ot*) of the covenant, THE YESOD.

45. "Which Elohim created and performed"

When the Sabbath was brought forth into Creation, it greatly diminished the influence of the created negative forces. In our world, this same power is given to us through the Sabbath. Learning this section helps us weaken the negative forces in our daily existence.

185. כִּי בוֹ שָׁבַת, בֵּיהּ נַיְיחָא דְכֹלָּא, דְעֶלָּאִין וְתַתָּאִין, בֵּיהּ שַׁבַּתָּא לְנַיְיחָא, אֲשֶׁר בָּרָא אֱלֹקִים מִכְּלָלָא דִזָכוֹר נַפְקָא שָׁמוֹר, לְאַתְקָנָא עֲבִידְתָּא דְעָלְמָא. לַעֲשׂוֹת, דָּא אוֹמָנָא דְעָלְמָא, לְמֶעְבַּד עֲבִידְתָּא דְּכֹלָּא.

185. "For on it He rested" indicates that in it, NAMELY WITHIN YESOD, there is rest for all, the upper and lower. In it is the Shabbat, for rest. "Which Elohim created" indicates that from "remember," "keep" had come forth, to finalize the manufacturing of the world. "performed" is the craftsmanship of the world; "and performed" alludes to the completed work, A DOING THAT PERFECTS EVERYTHING.

186. תּוּ, פָּרֵישׁ ר' שִׁמְעוֹן מִלָּה וַאֲמַר, כְּתִיב שׁוֹמֵר הַבְּרִית וְהַחֶסֶד, שׁוֹמֵר, דָּא כְּנֶסֶת יִשְׂרָאֵל, הַבְּרִית, דָּא יְסוֹדָא דְעָלְמָא, וְהַחֶסֶד דָּא אַבְרָהָם, דִּכְנֶסֶת יִשְׂרָאֵל הִיא שׁוֹמֵר הַבְּרִית וְהַחֶסֶד, וְאִקְרֵי שׁוֹמֵר יִשְׂרָאֵל, דָּא הוּא נָטִיר פִּתְחָא דְכֹלָּא, בֵּיהּ תַּלְיָין כָּל עֲבִידָן דְעָלְמָא וַדַּאי. אֲשֶׁר בָּרָא אֱלֹקִים לַעֲשׂוֹת, לְשַׁכְלָלָא לְאַתְקָנָא כֹּלָּא, כָּל יוֹמָא וְיוֹמָא, וּלְאַפָּקָא רוּחִין וְנִשְׁמָתִין וַאֲפִלּוּ רוּחִין וְשֵׁדִין.

186. Rabbi Shimon further elucidated THE SENTENCE, "WHICH ELOHIM CREATED AND PERFOORMED," WITH THE WORDS, "who keeps the covenant and the truth (Heb. *Chesed*)" (Devarim 7:9). He explained that "who keeps" refers to the Congregation of Yisrael, WHICH IS MALCHUT. "The covenant" is the foundation of the world, WHICH IS YESOD OF ZEIR ANPIN, and Chesed is Abraham, WHO IS CHESED OF ZEIR ANPIN. Because the Congregation of Yisrael, MALCHUT, is the keeper of the covenant and Chesed, MEANING IT IS THE KEEPER OF CHESED AND OF

YESOD OF ZEIR ANPIN. MALCHUT is called the Protector of Yisrael, BECAUSE ZEIR ANPIN IS CALLED YISRAEL AND MALCHUT PROTECTS HIS SFIROT. It protects the gateway to all THE SFIROT OF ZEIR ANPIN, YESOD BEING HIS LOWEST SFIRAH AND CHESED HIS UPPERMOST. AND BECAUSE MALCHUT PROTECTS THEM, IT IS VIEWED AS THE PROTECTOR OF ALL HIS SFIROT, FROM YESOD UP TO CHESED. Upon it depends the functioning of the world, BECAUSE IT PROTECTS ZEIR ANPIN FROM ANY INTEREFERENCE FROM OUTSIDE FORCES BY MEANS OF THE NEGATIVE PRECEPTS. SIMILARLY, ALL CORRECTIONS AND DEEDS DEPEND ON IT, BY MEANS OF THE POSITIVE PRECEPTS. Hence, "that Elohim created and performed," corrects and finalizes each and every day OF THE SIX DAYS OF CREATION, WHICH ARE THE SIX SFIROT OF ZEIR ANPIN. These words give birth to Holy spirits and souls; even evil spirits and demons ARE INCLUDED IN THE PHRASE, "WHICH ELOHIM CREATED AND PERFORMED."

187. וְאִי תֵימָא דְּלָאו אִינוּן תִּקּוּנָא דְעָלְמָא, לָאו הָכֵי, דְּהָא אִינוּן לְתִקּוּנָא דְעָלְמָא הֲווֹ, וּלְאַלְקָאָה בְּהוּ לְחַיָּיבֵי עָלְמָא, דְּאִנּוּן אָזְלִין לְקִבְלַיְיהוּ לְאוֹכָחָא לְהוּ, וּמַאי דַּאֲזִיל לִשְׂמָאלָא, אִתְאַחִיד בְּסִטְרָא שְׂמָאלָא לְקִבְלַיְיהוּ, בְּגִינֵי כָךְ לְתִקּוּנָא הֲווֹ. תָּא חֲזֵי מַה כְּתִיב בִּשְׁלֹמֹה וְהוֹכַחְתִּיו בְּשֵׁבֶט אֲנָשִׁים וּבְנִגְעֵי בְּנֵי אָדָם מַאן נִגְעֵי בְּנֵי אָדָם אֵלֵין אִינוּן מַזִּיקִין.

187. And it is not true that EVIL SPIRITS AND DEMONS play no role in correcting the world. Even they were created for the correction of the world—to slap the hands of the wicked of the world and admonish them, so they will follow correct paths. Whoever veers to the left side will find himself adhering to THE DEMONS AND EVIL SPIRITS OF the left side, who will punish him. In this way, THE DEMONS AND EVIL SPIRITS help correct THE WORLD. Come and see what was written about Solomon: "I will chasten him with the rod of men and with the plagues of the children of men" (II Shmuel 7:14). Those "plagues of the children of men" are the harmful pests WHO ARE THE DEMONS AND EVIL SPIRITS. BECAUSE THEY WERE CREATED TO PUNISH TRANSGRESSORS, PEOPLE FEAR THEM AND KEEP AWAY FROM SINS.

188. תָּא חֲזֵי, בְּשַׁעֲתָא דְּאִתְבְּרִיאוּ, אִתְקַדַּשׁ יוֹמָא, וְאִשְׁתָּאֲרוּ רוּחָא

בְּלָא גוּפָא, וְאִלֵּין אִינוּן בָּרְיָין דְּלָא אִשְׁתַּכְלָלוּ, וּמִסְטַר שְׂמָאלָא אִינוּן זוּהֲמָא דְּדַהֲבָא, וְעַל דָּא, בְּגִין דְּלָא אִשְׁתַּכְלָלוּ וְאִינוּן פְּגִימִין, שְׁמָא קַדִּישָׁא לָא שַׁרְיָא בְּהוֹ, וְלָא אִתְדַּבְּקוּ בֵּיה, וּדְחִילוּ דִלְהוֹן מִשְּׁמָא קַדִּישָׁא אִיהוּ, וְזָעִין וְדַחֲלִין מִנֵּיה, וּשְׁמָא קַדִּישָׁא לָא שַׁרְיָא בַּאֲתַר פָּגִים.

188. Come and behold: At the time THE DEMONS AND EVIL SPIRITS were being created, the day, SHABBAT, was being sanctified. The demons and evil spirits were left without bodies, BECAUSE HE DID NOT HAVE THE TIME TO MAKE THEM BODIES. They are creatures who were not finalized, come from the left, and are considered the refuse of gold. Thus, because they were not finished and remained defective, the Holy Name cannot rest upon them, and they cannot cleave to it. They are terrified of the Holy Name and sweat with fear upon its mention. THEREFORE, THEY CANNOT CLEAVE TO IT. Furthermore, the Holy Name cannot dwell in an imperfect place.

189. וְתָא חֲזֵי, הַאי ב" נ דְּאִתְפְּגִים דְּלָא שָׁבַק בַּר בְּהַאי עָלְמָא, כַּד נָפַק מִנֵּיה, לָא אִתְדְּבַק בִּשְׁמָא קַדִּישָׁא, וְלָא עָאלִין לֵיה בְּפַרְגּוֹדָא, בְּגִין דְּאִיהוּ פָּגִים וְלָא אִשְׁתְּלִים, וְאִילָנָא דְּאִתְעַקַּר, בָּעֵיא נְטִיעָא זִמְנָא אָחֳרָא, בְּגִין דִּשְׁמָא קַדִּישָׁא אִשְׁתְּלִים בְּכָל סִטְרִין, וּפְגִימוּ לָא אִתְדְּבַק בֵּיה לְעָלְמִין.

189. Come and behold: A man who is imperfect because he does not leave a son behind him when he departs from THIS WORLD cannot cleave to the Holy Name and will not be allowed beyond the curtain OF THE HOLY ONE, BLESSED BE HE, because he is defective and was not completed. And a tree that was uprooted, THAT IS, A MAN WHO DIES WITHOUT A CHILD, has to be replanted, BY BEING REINCARNATED INTO THIS WORLD a second time, because the Holy Name is perfect in all aspects. The defective man cannot therefore cleave to Him, BECAUSE SPIRITUAL CLEAVING IS A MATTER OF SIMILARITY OF FORM, AND THE DEFECTIVE ARE AS FAR AS EAST IS TO WEST FROM THE PERFECT.

190. וְתָא חֲזֵי, הָנֵי בָּרְיָין, פְּגִימִין אִינוּן, מֵעֵילָא וּמִתַּתָּא, וּבְגִינֵי כָךְ לָא

מִתְדַּבְּקָן לְעֵילָא, וְלָא מִתְדַּבְּקָן לְתַתָּא, וְאִלֵּין דִּכְתִיב בְּהוֹ אֲשֶׁר בָּרָא
אֱלֹקִים לַעֲשׂוֹת, דְּלָא אִשְׁתַּלִּימוּ עֵילָא וְתַתָּא. וְאִי תֵימָא הָא רוּחִין
אִינוּן, אֲמַאי לָאו אִשְׁתַּלִּימוּ לְעֵילָא, אֶלָּא כֵּיוָן דְּלָא אִשְׁתַּלִּימוּ לְתַתָּא
בְּאַרְעָא, לָא אִשְׁתַּלִּימוּ לְעֵילָא, וְכֻלְּהוּ מִסְּטַר שְׂמָאלָא קָא אַתְיָין,
וּמִתְכַּסְיָין מֵעֵינָא דִּבְנֵי נָשָׁא, וְקַיְימֵי לְקִבְלַיְיהוּ לְאַבְאָשָׁא לוֹן. תְּלַת
לוֹן כְּמַלְאֲכֵי הַשָּׁרֵת, וּתְלַת לוֹן כִּבְנֵי נָשָׁא, וְהָא אוּקְמוּהָ.

190. Come and behold: Those creatures, NAMELY THE DEMONS AND EVIL SPIRITS, are defective above and below. Thus, they cannot join the upper, ON THE SIDE OF BINAH, or the lower, ON THE SIDE OF MALCHUT. Of them, it was written, "that Elohim created and performed," WHICH MEANS HE CREATED CREATURES THAT NEED CORRECTING AND FINISHING. These creatures were not completed above or below, NEITHER FROM THE SIDE OF BINAH NOR FROM THE SIDE OF MALCHUT. But if they are BODILESS spirits, why are they not completed above FROM THE SIDE OF BINAH? Because THE SPIRITS were not perfected below on earth, BY RECEIVING A BODY, they cannot be completed above, IN THE LIGHTS. BECAUSE THEY CAME FROM THE ASPECT OF MALCHUT, THEY NEED TO BE CLOTHED IN BODIES. AND SINCE THEY HAVE NO BODIES, THEIR SPIRITS ARE DEFECTIVE AS WELL, AND THEY CANNOT BE CORRECTED FROM ABOVE, IN BINAH. They all come from the left side and are invisible to the human eye. They stand in opposition to people so that they can harm them. They have three of the characteristics of the ministering angels and three features in common with people. As has been explained, THEY HAVE WINGS, FLY FROM ONE END OF THE WORLD TO THE OTHER, AND FORETELL THE FUTURE AS DO THE MINISTERING ANGELS. THEY EAT, DRINK, PROCREATE, AND DIE LIKE PEOPLE.

191. בָּתַר דְּאִתְבְּרִיאוּ רוּחִין, אִשְׁתָּאֲרוּ אִינוּן רוּחִין, בָּתַר רֵחַיָּיא
דְּנוּקְבָּא דִּתְהוֹמָא רַבָּא, לֵילְיָא דְּשַׁבַּתָּא וְיוֹמָא דְּשַׁבַּתָּא, כֵּיוָן דִּנְפַק
קְדוּשְׁתָּא דְּיוֹמָא, וְלָא אִשְׁתַּלִּימוּ, נָפְקוּ לְעָלְמָא, וְשַׁטְאָן לְכָל סִטְרִין,
וּבָעְיָא עָלְמָא לְאִתְנַטְרָא מִנַּיְיהוּ. דְּהָא כְּדֵין כָּל סְטַר שְׂמָאלָא אִתְעַר,
וְאֶשָּׁא דְּגֵיהִנָּם מְלַהֲטָא, וְכָל אִינוּן דִּבְסְטַר שְׂמָאלָא, אָזְלִין וְשַׁטְאָן
בְּעָלְמָא, וּבָעָאן לְאִתְלַבְּשָׁא בְּגוּפָא, וְלָא יָכְלִין, כְּדֵין בָּעֵינָא

לְאִסְתַּמְּרָא מִנַּיְיהוּ וְאַתְקִינוּ שִׁיר דִּפְגָעִים, בְּכָל שַׁעֲתָא דִּדְחִילוּ דִּלְהוֹן שַׁרְיָא בְּעָלְמָא.

191. After their creation, these spirits are left behind the millstones of the chasm of the great abyss. When the sanctity of the Shabbat day has passed – AFTER THE SHABBAT – these incomplete SPIRITS come into the world and fly around in all directions. People should beware of them. Then, once again, the entire left side reawakens and the flames of Gehenom blaze. All WHO COME from the left side float around the world; they want to clothe themselves with bodies, but they are unable to do so. At this time, people must protect themselves against them. Thus, the sages prescribed the saying of the "Hymn for afflictions" (Tehilim 91), whenever one fears them in the world.

46. The Tabernacle of Peace

A protective shield of Light surrounds our world during the Sabbath. We can awaken this protective field of energy and draw it into our lives during all seven days of the week.

192. תָּא חֲזֵי כַּד אִתְקַדַּשׁ יוֹמָא בְּמַעֲלֵי שַׁבַּתָּא, סוּכַּת שָׁלוֹם שַׁרְיָא, וְאִתְפְּרִיסַת בְּעָלְמָא, מָאן סוּכַּת שָׁלוֹם, דָּא שַׁבַּתָּא, וְכָל רוּחִין וְעִלְעוּלִין וְשֵׁדִין, וְכָל סִטְרָא דִּמְסָאֲבֵי כֻּלְּהוּ טְמִירִין, וְעָאלִין בְּעֵינָא דְּרֵיחַיָּיא דְּנוּקְבָּא דִּתְהוֹמָא רַבָּא, דְּהָא כֵּיוָן דְּאִתְעַר קְדוּשָׁתָא עַל עָלְמָא, רוּחַ מְסָאֲבָא לָא אִתְעַר בַּהֲדֵיהּ, וְדָא עָרִיק מִקַּמֵּיהּ דְּדָא.

192. Come and behold: When the day is sanctified on the evening of Shabbat, a Tabernacle of Peace descends and settles on the world. HE ASKS: What is this Tabernacle of Peace? AND HE ANSWERS: It is the Shabbat. On Shabbat, all the evil spirits, stormy spirits, demons, and the defiled hide behind the millstone of the chasm of the great abyss. For when the sanctity spreads over the world, the spirit of defilement does not waken; one runs from the other. HOLINESS SHUNS THE UNCLEAN, AND THE UNCLEAN SHUNS HOLINESS.

193. וּכְדֵין עָלְמָא בִּנְטִירוּ עִלָּאָה. וְלָא בָּעֵינָן לְצַלָּאָה עַל נְטִירוּ, כְּגוֹן שׁוֹמֵר אֶת עַמּוֹ יִשְׂרָאֵל לָעַד אָמֵן, דְּהָא דָּא בְּיוֹמָא דְּחוֹל אִתְתַּקַּן, דְּעָלְמָא בָּעְיָא נְטִירוּ, אֲבָל בְּשַׁבָּת, סוּכַּת שָׁלוֹם אִתְפְּרִיסָא עַל עָלְמָא, וְאִתְנְטֵיר בְּכָל סִטְרִין, וַאֲפִילוּ חַיָּיבֵי גֵּיהִנֹּם נְטִירִין אִינּוּן, וְכֹלָּא בִּשְׁלָמָא אִשְׁתַּכְחוּ, עִלָּאִין וְתַתָּאִין, וּבְגִין כָּךְ בִּקְדוּשָׁא דְּיוֹמָא מְבָרְכִינָן הַפּוֹרֵס סֻכַּת שָׁלוֹם עָלֵינוּ וְעַל כָּל עַמּוֹ יִשְׂרָאֵל וְעַל יְרוּשָׁלָם.

193. Thus, ON SHABBAT, the world is under supernal protection. As a result, there is no need to pray for protection, as when one says, "who protects His people, Yisrael, forever, Amen." This blessing was prescribed for weekdays, when the world needs protection, but on Shabbat, a Tabernacle of Peace is spread over the world and protects it from all directions. Even the sinners of Gehenom are preserved, and all remain in peace, both the upper and lower. Hence, upon sanctifying the day, we say,

"He who spreads the tabernacle of peace over us and over all His people Yisrael and over Jerusalem," INSTEAD OF "HE WHO PROTECTS HIS PEOPLE YISRAEL," AS ON WEEKDAYS.

194. אַמַּאי עַל יְרוּשְׁלָם, אֶלָּא דָא הִיא מְדוֹרָא דְּהַהִיא סֻכָּה, וּבָעֵינָא לְזַמְּנָא לְהַהִיא סֻכָּה, דְּאִתְפְּרָסַת עֲלָנָא, וּלְמֵשְׁרָא עִמָּנָא, וּלְמֶהֱוֵי עֲלָנָא כְּאִמָּא דְּשַׁרְיָיא עַל בְּנִין, וּבְג"ד לָא דָּחֲלִין מִכָּל סִטְרִין, וְעַל דָּא הַפּוֹרֵס סֻכַּת שָׁלוֹם עָלֵינוּ.

194. YET, HE ASKS: Why over Jerusalem? AND HE ANSWERS: Because it is the abode of this tabernacle. It behooves one to PRAY AND summon the Tabernacle OF PEACE, so that it will be spread upon us, dwell with us, and be to us like a mother protecting her children. One, therefore, fears nothing ON SHABBAT from any side OF THE WORLD. Therefore, one says, "who spreads the tabernacle of peace over us," AND THERE IS NO NEED TO SAY "WHO PROTECTS HIS PEOPLE, YISRAEL, FOREVER, AMEN."

195. תָּא חֲזֵי, בְּשַׁעֲתָא דְּיִשְׂרָאֵל מְבָרְכִין וּמְזַמְּנִין לְהַאי סֻכַּת שָׁלוֹם, אוּשְׁפִּיזָא קַדִּישָׁא, וְאַמְרֵי הַפּוֹרֵס סֻכַּת שָׁלוֹם, כְּדֵין קְדֻשְׁתָא עִלָּאָה נַחְתָּא, וּפְרִיסַת גַּדְפָהָא עֲלַיְיהוּ דְּיִשְׂרָאֵל, וּמְכַסְיָא לוֹן כְּאִמָּא עַל בְּנִין, וְכָל זִינִין בִּישִׁין, אִתְכַּנִּישׁוּ מֵעָלְמָא, וְיָתְבֵי יִשְׂרָאֵל תְּחוֹת קְדֻשְׁתָא דְּמָארֵיהוֹן, וּכְדֵין דָּא סֻכַּת שָׁלוֹם, יָהִיב נִשְׁמָתִין חַדְתִּין לִבְנָהָא, מַאי טַעֲמָא בְּגִין דְּבֵיהּ נִשְׁמָתִין שַׁרְיָין, וּמִנֵּיהּ נָפְקִין וְכֵיוָן דְּשַׁרְיָא, וּפְרִיסַת גַּדְפָהָא עַל בְּנָהָא, אֲרִיקַת נִשְׁמָתִין חַדְתִּין לְכָל חַד וְחַד.

195. Come and behold: When Yisrael bless and call the Tabernacle of Peace, the 'Holy Guest' – WHICH ONLY APPEARS ON SHABBAT AND IS AN INFREQUENT GUEST – they say, "He who spreads the Tabernacle of Peace." Then the supernal sanctity comes down, spreads its wings over Yisrael, and covers them as a mother covers her children. And all evil leaves the world, and Yisrael remain under the holiness of their Master. Consequently, this Tabernacle of Peace gives new souls to its children. HE ASKS: what is the reason IT GIVES NEW SOULS TO YISRAEL? AND HE ANSWERS that souls dwell in and issue from it, BECAUSE IT IS BINAH. And because THIS

TABERNACLE OF PEACE dwells upon and spreads its wings over its children, it sheds new souls upon each and every one of them.

196. תּוּ, אָמַר רַבִּי שִׁמְעוֹן, עַל דָּא תָּנֵינָן שַׁבָּת, דּוּגְמָא דְּעָלְמָא דְּאָתֵי אִיהוּ, הָכֵי הוּא וַדַּאי, וְעַל דָּא, שְׁמִיטָה וְיוֹבֵל, דּוּגְמָא דָּא בְּדָא, וְשַׁבָּת וְעָלְמָא דְּאָתֵי הָכֵי הוּא, וְהַהוּא תּוֹסֶפֶת דְּנִשְׁמָתָא, מֵרָזָא דְּזָכוֹר קָא אַתְיָא, עַל הַאי סֻכַּת שָׁלוֹם, דְּנָטִיל מֵעָלְמָא דְּאָתֵי, וְדָא תּוֹסֶפֶת יַהֲבַת לְעַמָּא קַדִּישָׁא, וּבְהַהוּא תּוֹסֶפֶת, חָדָאן, וְיִתְנְשֵׁי מִנַּיְיהוּ כָּל מִלִּין דְּחוֹל, וְכָל צַעֲרִין, וְכָל עָאקִין, כְּד"א, בְּיוֹם הָנִיחַ ה' לְךָ מֵעָצְבְּךָ וּמֵרָגְזֶךָ וּמִן הָעֲבֹדָה הַקָּשָׁה וְגו'.

196. Rabbi Shimon says further that this is the reason why we have learned that Shabbat is similar to the World to Come, and this is true. Just as the Sabbatical Year and Jubilee are equal to one another, so are Shabbat and the World to Come. LIKE THE SABBATICAL YEAR, SHABBAT IS MALCHUT; LIKE JUBILEE, THE WORLD TO COME IS BINAH. AND SINCE WE LEARNED THAT SHABBAT AND THE WORLD TO COME ARE EQUAL TO EACH OTHER, THEN THE SABBATICAL YEAR AND JUBILEE ARE EQUAL TO ONE ANOTHER. The extra soul THAT THE TABERNACLE OF PEACE BESTOWS UPON ITS CHILDREN comes from the secret of "remember'" ZEIR ANPIN, to the Tabernacle of Peace that extends from the World to Come. THE TABERNACLE OF PEACE RECEIVES the additional SOULS FROM ZEIR ANPIN and gives them to the Holy Nation. The people are elated with the addition, and all worldly matters, sorrows, and evil are forgotten. Thus, it is written: "On the day that Hashem shall give you rest from sorrow and from your troubles" (Yeshayah 14:3) INDICATING THE TIME WHEN THE ADDITIONAL SOULS ARE RECEIVED FROM THE TABERNACLE OF PEACE.

197. וּבְלֵילְיָא דְּשַׁבְּתָּא, בָּעֵי ב"נ לְאַטְעֲמָא מִכֹּלָּא, בְּגִין לְאַחֲזָאָה, דְּהַאי סֻכַּת שָׁלוֹם, מִכֹּלָּא אִתְכְּלִילַת, וּבִלְבַד דְּלָא יַפְגִּים, מֵיכְלָא חֲדָא לְיוֹמָא, וְאִית דְּאָמְרֵי תְּרֵין, לִתְרֵין סְעוּדָתֵי אַחֲרָנִין דְּיוֹמָא, וְשַׁפִּיר, וְכָל שֶׁכֵּן אִי סָלִיק יַתִּיר לְיוֹמָא, וְיָכֵיל לְמִטְעַם מִמֵּיכְלִין אַחֲרָנִין, וּלְזַעֵירֵי בִּתְרֵי תַבְשִׁילִין סַגְיָא, וְאוֹקְמוּהָ חַבְרַיָּא.

197. On the evening of Shabbat, one should taste of all THE FOOD HE HAS, to show that this Tabernacle of Peace embraces all THREE COLUMNS OF BINAH. This is as long as nothing is lacking from the Shabbat day meal, BECAUSE THE HONOR OF THE DAY IS GREATER THAN THAT OF THE NIGHT. Others say further that ONE SHOULD BEWARE THAT NOTHING IS LACKING from the two meals of the day, and it is well TO BE VERY CAREFUL WITH THAT. And it is needless to say that if one has more than two MEALS on SHABBAT day, he can still taste of all the foods ON THE EVE OF SHABBAT, as long as two dishes remain for the day of Shabbat. This was fully expounded upon.

198. נֵר שֶׁל שַׁבָּת, לִנְשֵׁי עַמָּא קַדִּישָׁא אִתְיְיהֵיבַת לְאַדְלָקָא, וְחַבְרַיָּיא הָא אֲמָרוּ, דְּאִיהִי כִּבְּתָה בּוֹצִינָא דְעָלְמָא, וְאַחֲשִׁיכַת לֵיהּ כוּ' וְשַׁפִּיר. אֲבָל רָזָא דְמִלָּה, הַאי סֻכַּת שָׁלוֹם מַטְרוֹנִיתָא דְעָלְמָא הִיא, וְנִשְׁמָתִין דְּאִינּוּן בּוֹצִינָא עִלָּאָה, בָּהּ שַׁרְיָין, וְעַל דָּא מַטְרוֹנִיתָא בַּעְיָא לְאַדְלָקָא, דְּהָא בְּדוּכְתָּהָא אִתְאַחֲדַת וַעֲבָדַת עוֹבָדָא.

198. The Shabbat candles were given to the wives of the holy people to light, and the friends have given a reason for that. They explained that when Eve extinguished the candle of the world BY CAUSING ADAM TO EAT OF THE FRUIT OF THE TREE OF KNOWLEDGE, she brought DEATH AND darkness to the world. THUS, BY LIGHTING THE SHABBAT CANDLES, WOMEN SET TO RIGHT THAT WHICH EVE, THE FIRST WOMAN, DID, and this is good. Nevertheless, a deeper interpretation is that the Tabernacle of Peace THAT SHINES ON SHABBAT is the Mother of the world, and the souls, which are supernal candles, reside within her. Thus, a mother, OR A WOMAN, should light the candles. By doing so, she stands in the stead OF THE SUPERNAL MOTHER OF CHILDREN, THE TABERNACLE OF PEACE. BECAUSE she does so, THE UPPER MOTHER OF CHILDREN BESTOWS HOLY SOULS UPON HER CHILDREN, WHICH IS THE SECRET OF THE SUPERNAL SPIRITUAL CANDLES.

199. וְאִתְּתָא בַּעְיָא בְּחֶדְוָה דְלִבָּה וּרְעוּתָא, לְאַדְלָקָא בּוֹצִינָא דְשַׁבָּת, דְּהָא יְקָרָא עִלָּאָה הִיא לָהּ, וְזָכוּ רַב לְגַרְמָה, לְמִזְכֵּי לִבְנִין קַדִּישִׁין, דְּיהוֹן בּוֹצִינָא דְעָלְמָא, בְּאוֹרַיְיתָא, וּבְדַחֲלְתָּא, וְיַסְגּוֹן שְׁלָמָא בְּאַרְעָא,

וִיהֵיבַת לְבַעֲלָה אוֹרְכָּא דְחַיִּין, בְּגִין כָּךְ בַּעֲיָא לְאִזְדַּהֲרָא בָּהּ.

199. FOR THIS REASON, a woman should light the candles of Shabbat with a joyful heart and great concentration, because the supernal glory is hers. It is a great merit to herself to beget, IN LIGHTING THE CANDLES, holy sons who are the shining candles of Torah and piety, and who will bring peace to the world. By lighting the candles, she also gives her husband long life. Hence, she should be very careful with THE LIGHTING OF THE CANDLES, AND SHOULD DO SO WITH GREAT CONCENTRATION.

200. תָּא חֲזֵי, שַׁבָּת, לֵילְיָא וְיוֹמָא, זָכוֹר וְשָׁמוֹר, אִיהוּ כַּחֲדָא, וְעַל דָּא כְּתִיב זָכוֹר אֶת יוֹם הַשַּׁבָּת לְקַדְּשׁוֹ, וּכְתִיב שָׁמוֹר אֶת יוֹם הַשַּׁבָּת, זָכוֹר לִדְכוּרָא שָׁמוֹר לְנוּקְבָא, וְכֹלָּא חַד. זַכָּאִין אִינּוּן יִשְׂרָאֵל, חוּלָקֵיהּ דְּקֻדְשָׁא בְּרִיךְ הוּא, עַדְבֵיהּ וְאַחֲסַנְתֵּיהּ, עֲלַיְיהוּ כְּתִיב אַשְׁרֵי הָעָם שֶׁכָּכָה לוֹ, אַשְׁרֵי הָעָם שֶׁה' אֱלֹקָיו.

200. Come and behold: The evening and day of Shabbat combine "Remember" and "Keep." IN THE FIRST TABLETS, it was written, "Remember the Shabbat" (Shemot 20:8) and IN THE SECOND TABLETS, it was written, "Keep the Shabbat" (Devarim 5:12). BECAUSE "Remember" is the male PRESENCE OF ZEIR ANPIN and "Keep" is the female PRESENCE, OR THE NUKVA, OF ZEIR ANPIN, when "Remember" joins "Keep," all is one. Joyful are the people of Yisrael, who are the lot of the Holy One, blessed be He, His destiny and His inheritance. Of them, it is written: "Happy is the people that this is its lot. Happy is the people, whose Elohim is Hashem" (Tehilim 144:15).

47. "And Hashem Elohim built the rib"

This section helps every human being attract their true soulmates. Moreover, the letters and words of the Zohar help existing marriages rekindle the flames of passion and spiritual enlightenment.

201. וַיִּבֶן ה' אֱלֹקִים אֶת הַצֵּלָע אֲשֶׁר לָקַח מִן הָאָדָם וגו', אָמַר רָבִּי שִׁמְעוֹן כְּתִיב אֱלֹקִים הֵבִין דַּרְכָּהּ וְהוּא יָדַע אֶת מְקוֹמָהּ. הַאי קְרָא גְוֹונִין סַגִּיאִין אִית בֵּיהּ, אֶלָּא מַהוּ אֱלֹקִים הֵבִין דַּרְכָּהּ, כד"א וַיִּבֶן ה' אֱלֹקִים אֶת הַצֵּלָע, דָּא תּוֹרָה שֶׁבְּע"פ, דְּאִית בָּהּ דֶּרֶךְ, כְּד"א הַנּוֹתֵן בַּיָּם דֶּרֶךְ, בְּגִינֵי כָּךְ אֱלֹקִים הֵבִין דַּרְכָּהּ.

201. "And of the side, which Hashem Elohim had taken from the man, He made" (Beresheet 2:22). Rabbi Shimon says: It is written, "Elohim understood her ways and He knew her place" (Iyov 28:23). There are many ways of looking at it, but what is the principal way of interpreting "Elohim understood (Heb. *hevin*) her ways?" It is similar to "the side... He made (Heb. *vayiven*)," SIDE meaning the Oral Torah, WHICH IS MALCHUT, in which there is a path, as it is written, that "makes a way in the sea" (Yeshayah 43:16). THE SEA IS MALCHUT, AND IN IT HE MADE A PATH. Hence "And Elohim understood her ways."

202. וְהוּא יָדַע אֶת מְקוֹמָהּ, מָאן מְקוֹמָהּ, דָּא תּוֹרָה שֶׁבִּכְתָב, דְּאִית בָּהּ דַּעַת. ה' אֱלֹקִים, שֵׁם מָלֵא, לְאַתְקָנָא לָהּ בְּכֹלָּא, וְעַל דָּא אִתְקְרִיאַת חָכְמָה, וְאִתְקְרִיאַת בִּינָה, בְּגִין דַּהֲוָה בְּשֵׁם מָלֵא, ה' אֱלֹקִים, בְּכֹלָּא בִּשְׁלִימוּ בִּתְרֵי שְׁמָהָן.

202. "And He knew her place." HE ASKS: What is "her place?" AND HE ANSWERS: It is the Written Torah, NAMELY ZEIR ANPIN. The Written Torah, WHICH IS THE SECRET OF THE UPPER ZEIR ANPIN AND OF THE NUKVA FROM THE CHEST UPWARD, has knowledge. Hashem Elohim is a complete name to correct MALCHUT in everything. Hence, THE MOCHIN OF THE NUKVA, OR MALCHUT, are called Chochmah and Binah, because they are created, with the full perfection, in the two names YUD HEI VAV HEI AND ELOHIM, WITH YUD HEI VAV HEI CORRESPONDING TO CHOCHMAH

AND ELOHIM TO BINAH. HENCE "ELOHIM UNDERSTOOD HER WAYS" RELATES TO THE EMANATION OF CHOCHMAH THAT COMES THROUGH BINAH, AND THIS EMANATION IS CALLED ELOHIM. "AND HE KNEW HER PLACE" IS DA'AT, THE LIGHT OF CHASSADIM AND THE SECRET OF YUD HEI VAV HEI, DRAWN FROM ABA THROUGH ZEIR ANPIN.

203. אֶת הַצֵּלָע, דָּא אַסְפַּקְלַרְיָאה דְּלָא נָהֲרָא, כְּד״א וּבְצַלְעִי שָׂמְחוּ וְנֶאֱסָפוּ. אֲשֶׁר לָקַח מִן הָאָדָם, בְּגִין דְּהָא מִתּוֹרָה שֶׁבִּכְתָב נָפְקַת. לְאִשָּׁה, לְאִתְקַשְּׁרָא בִּשְׂלַהוֹבָא דִסְטַר שְׂמָאלָא, דְּהָא אוֹרַיְיתָא מִסְּטְרָא דִגְבוּרָה אִתְיְהֵיבַת. לְאִשָּׁה, לְמֶהֱוֵי אֵשׁ ה׳ קָטִיר כַּחֲדָא.

203. "The side (Heb. tzela)" is the mirror that does not shine – MALCHUT. As it is written: "But when I stumble (Heb. tzal'I) they rejoice and gather, they assembled together" (Tehilim 35:15). THE WORD INDICATES THE OPAQUE GLASS, WHICH NEEDS CORRECTING. THE WORDS, "THE SIDE which Hashem Elohim had taken from the man," MEAN THAT HE TOOK MALCHUT OUT OF THE WRITTEN TORAH, WHICH IS ZEIR ANPIN, because She originates in MALCHUT OF the Written Torah. "to the woman" indicates her connection with the flames of the left side. Torah, NAMELY ZEIR ANPIN, was given from the side of Gvurah, WHICH IS RELATED TO THE NUKVA. The word for woman (ishah) IS AN ABBREVIATION OF esh, meaning fire OR THE SIDE OF GVURAH, and Hei, INDICATING (THE HEI,) THE NUKVA to which the fire OF GVURAH is connected.

204. וַיְבִאֶהָ אֶל הָאָדָם, בְּגִין דְּלָא בַּעֲיָא לְאִשְׁתַּכְּחָא בִּלְחוֹדָהָא, אֶלָּא לְאִתְכְּלָלָא וּלְאִתְחַבְּרָא בַּתּוֹרָה שֶׁבִּכְתָב, כֵּיוָן דְּאִתְחַבְּרַת בַּהֲדֵיהּ, הוּא יָזוּן לָהּ, וִיתַקֵּן לָהּ, וְיִתֵּן לָהּ מַה דְּאִצְטְרִיךְ, הַיְינוּ דִכְתִיב, וְאֶת הָאָרֶץ, וְהָא אוֹקִימְנָא.

204. "And He brought her to to the" because it is not fitting FOR THE NUKVA to exist alone; she is included within and cleaves to the Written Torah, ZEIR ANPIN. And when THE NUKVA has united WITH ZEIR ANPIN, he feeds and prepares for her and bestows upon her all that she needs. Hence, it is written "and the earth" (Beresheet 1:1), IN WHICH THE VAV (AND) IN "AND THE EARTH" ALLUDES TO ZEIR ANPIN, WHICH BESTOWS

AN ABUNDANCE UPON HER, CALLED "FOOD," as we have already explained.

205. מִכָּאן אוֹלִיפְנָא, מָאן דְּאַנְסִיב בְּרַתֵּיהּ, עַד לָא תֵיעוֹל לְבַעֲלָה, אֲבוּהָ וְאִמָּהּ מְתַקְּנִין לָהּ, וְיָהֲבִין לָהּ כָּל מַה דְּאִצְטְרִיךְ, כֵּיוָן דְּאִתְחַבְּרַת בְּבַעֲלָה, הוּא יָזוּן לָהּ, וְהוּא יִתֵּן לָהּ מַה דְּבָעְיָא. תָּא חֲזֵי, בְּקַדְמֵיתָא כְּתִיב, וַיִּבֶן ה' אֱלֹקִים אֶת הַצֵּלָע, דְּאַבָּא וְאִמָּא אַתְקִינוּ לָהּ, וּלְבָתַר, וַיְבִאֶהָ אֶל הָאָדָם, לְאִתְקַשְּׁרָא בֹּלָא כַּחֲדָא, וּלְאִתְחַבְּרָא חַד בְּחַד, וְהוּא יָהֵיב לָהּ מַה דְּאִצְטְרִיךְ.

205. Here we learn that the mother and father must supply all the needs of a daughter before she is wed. After she has been joined with her husband, it is for him to feed and give her what she requires. Come and behold: It is first written, "And of the side which Hashem Elohim had taken from the man' He made," that is, that mother and father have prepared for her. Then, it is written: "He brought her to the man," so they could join together and cleave to one another. Then, it is for HER HUSBAND to give her what she requires.

206. דָּבָר אַחֵר, אֱלֹקִים הֵבִין הֲבִין דַּרְכָּהּ, כַּד בְּרַתָּא בְּבֵי אִמָּא, הִיא אִסְתַּכְּלָא בְּכָל יוֹמָא, בְּכָל מַה דְּבַעֲיָא בְּרַתָּה, דִּכְתִיב אֱלֹקִים הֵבִין דַּרְכָּהּ, כֵּיוָן דְּחַבְרַת לָהּ בְּבַעֲלָה הוּא יָהֵיב לָהּ כָּל מַה דְּבַעֲיָא, וִיתַקֵּן עוֹבָדָהָא, הֲדָא הוּא דִכְתִיב, וְהוּא יָדַע אֶת מְקוֹמָה.

206. Another interpretation of the verse, "Elohim understood her ways," is that when the daughter is in her mother's home, her mother cares for all her needs every day. Hence, Elohim, THE MOTHER, understood the ways OF THE NUKVA. When her husband marries her, he gives her what she wants and satisfies her needs. Thus, it is said that He, NAMELY THE HUSBAND, "knew her place," MEANING THAT THE HUSBAND CARES FOR THE WIFE ONCE SHE IS MARRIED TO HIM.

48. "And Hashem Elohim formed the man"

Man is born into this world with an Evil Inclination built into his nature. True transformation of character occurs through the assistance and spiritual power of a soulmate. This relationship gives us inner strength and willpower to complete our transformation.

207. כְּתִיב וַיִּיצֶר ה' אֱלֹקִים אֶת הָאָדָם. הָכָא אִשְׁתַּכְלֵל בְּכֹלָּא, בִּימִינָא וּבִשְׂמָאלָא, וְהָא אוֹקִימְנָא דְּאִתְכְּלִיל בְּיֵצֶר הַטּוֹב, אֲבָל וַיִּיצֶר ה' אֱלֹקִים, בְּיֵצֶר טוֹב וּבְיֵצֶר רָע, אַמַּאי, אֶלָּא יֵצֶר טוֹב לֵיה לְגַרְמֵיה, יֵצֶר הָרָע, לְאִתְעָרָא לְגַבֵּי נוּקְבֵי. רָזָא דְמִלָּה, מִכָּאן אוֹלִיפְנָא דְּצָפוֹן אִתְעַר תָּדִיר לְגַבֵּי נוּקְבָא, וְאִתְקַשַּׁר בַּהֲדָהּ, וּבְגִין כָּךְ אִתְקְרִיאַת אִשָּׁה.

207. It is written: "Hashem Elohim formed (Heb. *vayyitzer*) the man" (Beresheet 2:7). *VAYYITZER* IS SPELLED WITH TWO YUD'S TO HINT THAT here man was completely formed, with both right and left. As we have explained, he was created with only the Good Inclination, NOT WITH THE EVIL INCLINATION. But LATER with "And Hashem Elohim formed," THE EVIL INCLINATION IS ALSO INCLUDED IN HIM. THIS IS THE HIDDEN REASON FOR THE TWO YUD'S – ONE ALLUDES TO the Good Inclination, THE OTHER TO the Evil Inclination. HE ASKS: WHY WAS HE GIVEN TWO INCLINATIONS? AND HE RESPONDS: The reason is that he was given the good for himself and the evil to awaken his desire for the woman. The secret meaning of this is that the North, WHICH IS THE LEFT SIDE, always wakes toward the female and cleaves to her. Hence, she is called *Ishah*, WHICH IS AN ABBREVIATION OF THE FIRE (HEB. *ESH*) OF *HEI*, WHICH IS FEMALE. FOR THE NUKVA IS BUILT BY, AND EMERGES FROM THE LEFT SIDE.

208. וְתָא חֲזֵי יֵצֶר טוֹב וְיֵצֶר הָרָע, בְּגִין דְּאִתְיַיהֲבַת נוּקְבָא בֵּינַיְיהוּ וְאִתְקַשְּׁרָא בַּהֲדַיְיהוּ, וְלָא מִתְקַשְּׁרָא עַד דְּיֵצֶר הָרָע אִתְעַר לְגַבָּהּ. וּמִתְקַשְּׁרָן דָּא בְּדָא, וְכֵיוָן דְּמִתְקַשְּׁרָן דָּא בְּדָא, כְּדֵין אִתְעַר יֵצֶר טוֹב, דְּאִיהוּ חֶדְוָה, וְאַיְיתֵי לָהּ לְגַבֵּיה.

208. Come and behold: The Good and Evil inclinations WERE GIVEN TO MAN because the female was placed between the two Inclinations, connected to both. Yet, she cannot be placed between them until the Evil

Inclination awakens within her and the two inclinations connect. After they are connected, the Good Inclination, which is joy, rouses itself and draws THE NUKVA to itself.

209. אֶת הָאָדָם, הָא אוֹקִימְנָא. אֲבָל דְּכַר וְנוּקְבָא כַּחֲדָא, מִתְפָּרְשָׁן לְמֶהֱוֵי אַפִּין בְּאַפִּין. מַה כְּתִיב עָפָר מִן הָאֲדָמָה. הַשְׁתָּא קַיְימָא לְאַתְקְנָא. תָּא חֲזֵי, אִתְּתָא כַּד אִתְחַבְּרַת בְּבַעֲלָה, אִתְקְרִיאַת עַל שֵׁם בַּעֲלָה, אִישׁ אִשָּׁה, צַדִּיק צֶדֶק, אִיהוּ עוֹפֶר, וְאִיהִי עָפָר, אִיהוּ צְבִי וְאִיהִי צְבִיָּה, צְבִי הִיא לְכָל הָאֲרָצוֹת.

209. We have already explained "the man," yet MAN WAS ALSO COMPRISED of both male and female aspects, unable to separate and face each other. The words "dust from the earth" indicate that now he is about to be made ready, THAT IS, NOW THE TWO ASPECTS WILL SEPARATE AND FACE EACH OTHER. Come and behold: When a woman is wed to her husband, she is called by her husband's name, man – woman, righteous – righteousness. He is a young deer (Heb. *ofer*), she is dust (Heb. *afar*); he is a deer, and she a gazelle (Heb. *tzviyah*).

49. "Baal and Asherah"

These two words refer to two aspects of idol worship. *Idol Worshipping* refers not only to bowing down before statues and icons. *Idol worshipping* includes any material possession or external situation that controls our emotions and behavior or that motivates us in any way. When any of these influences determine our degree of contentment and joy in life, then we have surrendered control and severed our connection to the Light, the true source of all fulfillment. Often, our negative tendencies lead us to become worshippers of wealth, or disciples of our own egos.

We can remove the power and allure of the "idols" that control us by meditating upon the Hebrew passages.

210. כְּתִיב לֹא תִטַּע לְךָ אֲשֵׁרָה כָּל עֵץ אֵצֶל מִזְבַּח ה' אֱלֹהֶיךָ אֲשֶׁר תַּעֲשֶׂה לָּךְ. אֵצֶל מִזְבַּח, וְכִי לְעֵילָא מִנֵּיהּ, אוֹ בַּאֲתָר אָחֳרָא מָאן שַׁרְיֵיהּ, אֶלָּא הָא אוֹקִימְנָא, אֲשֶׁר, דָּא בַּעֲלָה, דְּאִתְּתָא אִתְקְרִיאַת עַל שׁוּם בַּעֲלָה, אֲשֵׁרָה, וְעַל דָּא כְּתִיב לַבַּעַל וְלָאֲשֵׁרָה, בְּגִין כָּךְ כְּתִיב לֹא תִטַּע לְךָ אֲשֵׁרָה כָּל עֵץ אֵצֶל מִזְבַּח ה' אֱלֹקֶיךָ, לָקֳבֵל אֲתָר דְּהַהוּא מִזְבַּח ה', דְּהָא מִזְבַּח ה' אִיהוּ קַיְּימָא עַל דָּא, וְעַל דָּא לָקַבְלָה, לֹא תִטַּע לְךָ אֲשֵׁרָה אָחֳרָא.

210. It is written: "You shall not plant an *asherah* (grove) of any tree near the altar of Hashem your Elohim, which (Heb. *asher*) you shall make" (Devarim 16:21). ARE WE TO UNDERSTAND FROM THE WORDS "near the altar" THAT ONLY NEAR AN ALTAR IT IS NOT PERMITTED TO PLANT A GROVE? If so, then who permitted planting a grove anywhere else, or above the altar? But, as we have explained, Asher is the name of the husband and his wife is called after him, Asherah. Thus, the words "for the Baal and Asherah" (II Melachim 23:4) INDICATE THE SIDE CORRESPONDING TO ZEIR ANPIN AND NUKVA OF HOLINESS; THE SIDE WHERE BAAL (ENG. HUSBAND) CORRESPONDS TO ZEIR ANPIN, AND ASHERAH CORRESPONDS TO THE NUKVA. Hence, WE UNDERSTAND THE QUESTION OF WHY it says, "You shall not plant an asherah of any tree near the altar of Hashem your Elohim." IN THE WORDS, "NEAR THE ALTAR," "NEAR" IS LIKE "INSTEAD OF." THE VERSE MEANS "YOU SHALL NOT PLANT AN ASHERAH" OF IDOLATRY in the place of Hashem your Elohim because the altar of Hashem is situated upon it, THAT IS, ABOUT TO ANNUL THE KLIPAH OF ASHERAH, AS WAS SAID BEFORE. Thus, do not plant another Asherah OF IDOLATRY by the altar.

211. תָּא חֲזֵי, בְּכָל אֲתַר, כָּל אִינוּן פָּלְחֵי שִׁמְשָׁא, אִקְרוּן עוֹבְדִין לַבַּעַל, וְאִינוּן דְּפָלְחִין לְסִיהֲרָא אִיקְרוּן עוֹבְדֵי אֲשֵׁרָה, וְעַל דָּא, לַבַּעַל וְלָאֲשֵׁרָה, וַאֲשֵׁרָה אִתְקְרֵי עַל שׁוּם בַּעֲלָהּ אָשֵׁר. אִי הָכֵי אַמַּאי אִתְעֲבַר שְׁמָא דָא, אֶלָּא אֲשֵׁרָה עַל שׁוּם דִּכְתִיב בְּאָשְׁרֵי כִּי אִשְּׁרוּנִי בָנוֹת, וְהוּא דְּלָא אַשְׁרוּהָ שְׁאָר עַמִּין, וְקַיְּימָא אַחֲרָא תְּחוֹתָהּ, וְלָא עוֹד, אֶלָּא דִּכְתִיב כָּל מְכַבְּדֶיהָ הִזִּילוּהָ וּבְגִין כָּךְ אִתְעֲבַר שְׁמָא דָא, וּבְגִין דְּלָא יִתְתַּקְּפוּן אִינוּן דְּעָבְדֵי שְׁאָר עַמִּין עעכו"ם, וְקָרֵינָן מִזְבֵּחַ, דְּאִיהוּ מֵאֲדָמָה, דִּכְתִיב מִזְבַּח אֲדָמָה וגו', בְּגִינֵי כָּךְ עָפָר מִן הָאֲדָמָה.

211. Come and behold: All those who worship the sun are always referred to as the worshippers of Baal, and those who worship the moon are called worshippers of Asherah. Hence, the above passage "for the Baal and Asherah" REFERS TO BAAL, WHO IS THE SUN AND IS MALE, AND THE ASHERAH, WHO IS THE MOON AND IS FEMALE. She is called Asherah after her husband Asher. But, if she is called Asherah after her husband Asher, why is THE NUKVA not called ASHERAH anymore? ALTHOUGH THE NUKVA OF PURITY IS NO LONGER CALLED SO, she was called Asherah in the past after the passage: "Happy (Heb. *oshri*) am I, for the girls will call me blessed" (Beresheet 30:13). SHE WAS CALLED SO BY THOSE WHO PRAISED AND AKNOWLEDGED HER. AND, IT IS WRITTEN OF HER: "BEAUTIFUL OF ALL SITES, THE JOY OF THE WHOLE EARTH" (TEHILIM 48:3). But the other nations did not acknowledge her, erected AN ASHERAH OF IDOL WORSHIP in her stead, and moreover BELITTLED HER, as it is written: "All that honored her despised her" (Eichah 1:8). And hence, the name Asherah was taken away from her BECAUSE THEY STOPPED ACKNOWLEDGING HER. And to prevent the other idolatrous nations from gaining strength, she is called an altar, which is made of earth. This is as written: "An altar of earth YOU SHALL MAKE FOR ME" (Shemot 20:24). Hence, it is said OF ADAM: "AND HASHEM ELOHIM MADE ADAM FROM the dust of the earth" (Beresheet 2:7), WHERE DUST IS MALCHUT AND EARTH IS BINAH. THUS, THROUGH THIS SWEETENING OF DUST WITH EARTH, HE MERITED RECEIVING THE MOCHIN OF NESHAMAH OF LIFE.

212. וַיִּפַּח בְּאַפָּיו נִשְׁמַת חַיִּים, אִתְכְּלִיל נִשְׁמַת חַיִּים בְּהַהוּא עָפָר כְּנוּקְבָא דְּמִתְעַבְּרָא מִן דְּכוּרָא דְּהָא מִתְחַבְּרָן, וְאִתְמַלְיָא הַאי עָפָר מִכֹּלָּא, וּמַאי אִיהוּ רוּחִין וְנִשְׁמָתִין. וַיְהִי הָאָדָם לְנֶפֶשׁ חַיָּה, הַשְׁתָּא אִתְתַּקַּן וְקַיַּים אָדָם לְאַתְקָנָא וּלְמֵיזַן לְנֶפֶשׁ חַיָּה.

212. AFTER THE DUST WAS SWEETENED WITH EARTH, IT IS WRITTEN: "and breathed in his nostrils the breath (Heb. *Neshamah*) of Life" (Ibid.). As the soul of life was breathed into the dust, THE BODY OF ADAM WAS SOOTHED, like a woman conceiving from a man. Through this process, SOUL AND BODY become joined. BECAUSE THE LIGHT OF BINAH IS CALLED NESHAMAH AND BECAUSE THE BODY IS SWEETENED TO BECOME AN ADEQUATE VESSEL FOR BINAH, LIGHT AND VESSEL EMBRACE EACH OTHER. This dust, WHICH IS THE BODY, becomes filled with EMANATIONS OF LIGHT. HE ASKS: What are THOSE LIGHTS? AND HE SAYS: THEY ARE the Ruach and Neshamah. It is written that then "and man became a living soul (Heb. *Nefesh*)" (Ibid.), WHICH MEANS THAT he was now complete IN BODY AND SOUL and could now correct and sustain the living Nefesh THAT WAS HIS WIFE.

213. וַיִּבֶן ה' אֱלֹהִים, אוּף הָכֵי נָמֵי בְּשֵׁם מָלֵא, דְּהָא אַבָּא וְאִמָּא אַתְקִינוּ לָהּ, עַד לָא אָתַת לְבַעֲלָהּ. אֶת הַצֵּלָע, כד"א שְׁחוֹרָה אֲנִי וְנָאוָה בְּנוֹת יְרוּשָׁלָם, אַסְפַּקְלַרְיָאה דְּלָא נָהֲרָא, אֲבָל אַבָּא וְאִמָּא אַתְקִינוּ לָהּ, לְאִתְפַּיְיסָא בַּעֲלָהּ בַּהֲדָהּ.

213. "And of the side, which Hashem Elohim... He made" Here also, IN THE BUILDING OF THE SIDE, the full name is used, AS IT WAS USED IN "AND HASHEM ELOHIM MADE MAN." Because her father and mother corrected her before the woman came to her husband's home, ZEIR ANPIN, HENCE A FULL NAME IS MENTIONED, AS HASHEM IS ABA AND ELOHIM IS IMA. "The side" is described in the verse, "I am black, but comely, O daughters of Jerusalem" (Shir Hashirim 1:5), MEANING IT WAS FASHIONED AFTER THE SECRET OF the mirror that does not shine. Later, her father and mother prepare her, so that her husband world reconcile to her. THIS IS WHAT IS MEANT BY, "HE BROUGHT HER THE MAN."

50. Soothing and asking permission

The Zohar discloses the importance of treating one's wife with the utmost love, honor, and respect. A man must make every attempt towards elevating his wife to the highest level. Here the Zohar is not simply emphasizing the need for moral and ethical behavior between a man and wife. Rather, the Zohar is revealing supernal secrets. The woman corresponds to the Sfirot of *Malchut*. She is the vessel, and is therefore responsible for manifesting Light for the entire family. Accordingly, the male must prepare and build the vessel if he hopes to maximize the spiritual Light to be received. The husband's actions arouse the Light in the Upper Worlds, while the wife manifests the Light in our world.

In pursuing their own religious goals, some men relegate their wives to a secondary position. Herein lies the difference between a religious mindset and a genuinely spiritual one. Spiritually, a man can never grow and develop without elevating his wife to her rightful place. From these passages, we draw the consciousness and inspiration to strive for this kind of marriage.

‏214. וַיְבִאֶהָ אֶל הָאָדָם, מֵהָכָא אוֹלִיפְנָא דְּבָעֵאן אַבָּא וְאִמָּא דְּכַלָּה, לְאַעֲלָה בִּרְשׁוּתֵיה דְּחָתָן, כד"א אֶת בִּתִּי נָתַתִּי לָאִישׁ הַזֶּה וגו', מִכָּאן וָאֵילָךְ בַּעֲלָה יֵיתֵי לְגַבָּה, דְּהָא בֵּיתָא דִּילָהּ הוּא, דִּכְתִיב וַיָּבֹא אֵלֶיהָ, וַיָּבֹא גַם אֶל רָחֵל, בְּקַדְמֵיתָא וַיְבִאֶהָ אֶל הָאָדָם, דְּעַד הָכָא אִית לְאַבָּא וּלְאִמָּא לְמֶעֱבַד, לְבָתַר אִיהוּ יֵיתֵי לְגַבָּה, וְכָל בֵּיתָא דִּילָהּ הוּא, וְיִטּוֹל רְשׁוּת מִינָהּ.

214. "And He brought her to the man" (Beresheet 2:22). From this we learn that it is incumbent on the father and mother of the bride to transfer her to the charge of her bridegroom, as we read: "My daughter I have given to this man" (Devarim 22:16). Henceforward, the husband is to come to the wife, because the house is hers and not his. IT BEHOOVES HIM, THEREFORE, TO COME TO HER, as it is written: "And he went in to her" (Beresheet 29:23) and "And he went in also to Rachel" (Ibid. 30). In the beginning, it is written "and He brought her to the man" because not until the mother and father prepare her TO RECEIVE THE LIGHT OF CHASSADIM FROM ZEIR ANPIN will ZEIR ANPIN come to her. All the whole house is THE FEMALE'S. And he has to have her permission BEFORE MATING.

215. וְעַל דָּא אִתְעָרְנָא, דִּכְתִיב וַיִּפְגַּע בַּמָּקוֹם וַיָּלֶן שָׁם, דְּנָטִיל רְשׁוּ בְּקַדְמֵיתָא, מִכָּאן אוֹלִיפְנָא, דְּמַאן דְּמִתְחַבֵּר בְּאִנְתְּתֵיהּ, בָּעֵי לְמִפְגַּע לָהּ, וּלְבַסְּמָא לָהּ בְּמִלִּין, וְאִי לָאו לָא יָבִית לְגַבָּהּ בְּגִין דִּיהֵא רְעוּתָא דִּלְהוֹן כַּחֲדָא בִּדְלָא אֲנִיסוּ.

215. And upon this we commented, "and he lighted on a certain place, and tarried there" (Beresheet 28:11), meaning that he asked permission first. From this we learn that he who wants to mate with his wife must soothe her first and soften her with sweet talk. Failing to do so, he shall not sleep with her, because their desire must be mutual and without coercion.

216. וַיָּלֶן שָׁם כִּי בָא הַשֶּׁמֶשׁ, לְאַחֲזָאָה, דַּאֲסִיר לֵיהּ לְבַר נָשׁ, לְשַׁמְּשָׁא עַרְסֵיהּ בִּימָמָא. וַיִּקַּח מֵאַבְנֵי הַמָּקוֹם וַיָּשֶׂם מְרַאֲשׁוֹתָיו, הָכָא אוֹלִיפְנָא, דַּאֲפִילּוּ יְהוֹן לְמַלְכָּא עַרְסֵי דְּדַהֲבָא, וּלְבוּשֵׁי יְקָר לְמֵיבַת בְּהוֹ, וּמַטְרוֹנִיתָא תַּתְקִין לֵיהּ עַרְסָא, מִתְתַּקַּן בְּאַבְנִין, יִשְׁבּוֹק דִּילֵיהּ, וְיָבֵית בְּמָה דְּאִיהִי תַּתְקִין, דִּכְתִיב וַיִּשְׁכַּב בַּמָּקוֹם הַהוּא.

216. "And tarried there all night, because the sun was set" comes to teach that sexual intercourse is forbidden during the day. "And he took of the stones of that place" (Ibid.). We have learned that even if a king has beds of gold and glorious bed gowns to sleep in, yet the matron prepared for him a bed of stones, he should leave his own and use what she has prepared, as it is written: "and lay down in this place," NAMELY ON THAT BED OF STONES.

217. תָּא חֲזֵי, מַה כְּתִיב הָכָא, וַיֹּאמֶר הָאָדָם זֹאת הַפַּעַם וְגוֹ', הָא בְּסִימוּ דְּמִלִּין, לְאַמְשָׁכָא עִמָּהּ חֲבִיבוּתָא, וּלְאַמְשָׁכָא לָהּ לִרְעוּתֵיהּ, לְאִתְעָרָא עִמָּהּ רְחִימוּתָא, חָמֵי כַּמָּה בְּסִימִין אִינּוּן מִלִּין, כַּמָּה מִלֵּי דִּרְחִימוּתָא אִינּוּן, עֶצֶם מֵעֲצָמַי וּבָשָׂר מִבְּשָׂרִי, בְּגִין לְאַחֲזָאָה לָהּ דְּאִינּוּן חַד, וְלָא אִית פֵּרוּדָא בֵּינַיְיהוּ בְּכֹלָּא.

217. Come and behold: It is written: "And the man said, This is now" (Beresheet 2:23). These are loving words, spoken to win a woman's

affections, draw her closer to him, and arouse love within her. See how tender and how love enticing are the words, "A bone of my bones and flesh of my flesh" (Ibid.). They show her that the two are one and inseparable.

218. הַשְׁתָּא שָׁרֵי לְשַׁבָּחָא לָה, לְזֹאת יִקָּרֵא אִשָּׁה, דָּא הִיא דְּלָא יִשְׁתַּכַּח כַּוְותָה, דָּא הִיא יְקָרָא דְּבֵיתָא, כֻּלְּהוֹן נָשִׁין גַּבָּה כְּקוֹפָא בִּפְנֵי בְּנֵי נָשָׁא, אֲבָל לְזֹאת יִקָּרֵא אִשָּׁה, שְׁלִימוּ דְּכֹלָּא, לְזֹאת וְלָא לְאַחֲרָא, כֹּלָּא הוּא מָלֵי רְחִימוּתָא, כְּמָא דְאַתְּ אָמֵר רַבּוֹת בָּנוֹת עָשׂוּ חָיִל וְאַתְּ עָלִית עַל כֻּלָּנָה.

218. And then he should praise her saying, "She shall be called woman" (Ibid.), WHICH MEANS she is peerless and the pride of the house. Other women, compared to her, are as apes before men. "She shall be called woman," perfect in every regard, she and no other. All those are loving words, similar to those in the verse, "Many daughters have done virtuously, but you excel them all" (Mishlei 31:29).

219. עַל כֵּן יַעֲזָב אִישׁ אֶת אָבִיו וְאֶת אִמּוֹ וְדָבַק בְּאִשְׁתּוֹ וְהָיוּ לְבָשָׂר אֶחָד כֹּלָּא לְאַמְשָׁכָא לָה בִּרְחִימוּ, וּלְאִתְדַּבְּקָא בַּהֲדָה, כֵּיוָן דְּאִתְעַר לְגַבָּהּ כָּל מִלִּין אִלֵּין, מַה כְּתִיב, וְהַנָּחָשׁ הָיָה עָרוּם וְגוֹ', הָא אִתְּעַר יֵצֶר הָרָע לְאַחֲדָא בָּהּ, בְּגִין לְקַשְּׁרָא לָהּ בְּתֵיאוּבְתָּא דְגוּפָא, וּלְאַתְעָרָא לְגַבָּהּ מִלִּין אָחֳרָנִין דְּיֵצֶר הָרָע אִתְעַנַּג בְּהוֹ.

219. "This is why a man leaves his father and his mother and cleaves to his wife, and they become one flesh" (Beresheet 2:24). This is to draw her to him with affection and to cleave to her. Because he was aroused toward her with those words, it is written: "And the serpent was cunning" (Beresheet 3:1). The Evil Inclination was awakened to embrace her, connect her with physical desires, and arouse her to other things in which the Evil Inclination delights.

220. עַד לְבָתַר מַה כְּתִיב, וַתֵּרֶא הָאִשָּׁה כִּי טוֹב הָעֵץ לְמַאֲכָל, וְכִי תַאֲוָה הוּא לָעֵינַיִם, וַתִּקַּח מִפִּרְיוֹ וַתֹּאכַל. קַבִּילַת לֵיהּ בִּרְעוּתָא, וַתִּתֵּן

גַּם לְאִישָׁהּ עִמָּהּ, הָא כְּדֵין הִיא אִתְעָרָא לְגַבֵּיהּ בְּתֵיאוּבְתָּא לְאִתְעָרָא
לֵיהּ רְעוּתָא וּרְחִימוּ, דָּא מִלָּה לְאַחֲזָאָה עוֹבָדָא לִבְנֵי נָשָׁא כְּגַוְונָא
דִּלְעֵילָּא.

220. Eventually, "the woman saw that the tree was good for food, and that it was a delight to the eyes, and she took of the fruit, and did eat" (Ibid. 6). She received THE EVIL INCLINATION willingly AND LUSTFULLY. "And gave also to her husband with her," because she was lustfully aroused and wanted to win her husband's love and affection. These passages explain the process to people, as it occurs above BETWEEN THE UPPER MALE AND FEMALE. ALTHOUGH THE SCRIPTURE TALKS OF ADAM AND EVE BELOW, IT NEVERTHELESS ALLUDES PRINCIPALLY TO THE SUPERNAL MALE AND FEMALE. AND PEOPLE SHOULD ATTUNE THEIR ACTIONS TO THEIRS.

221. אָמַר רַבִּי אֶלְעָזָר, אִי הָכֵי, בְּמַאי נוֹקִים לֵיהּ לְעֵילָּא, יֵצֶר הָרָע
דְּאָחִיד בָּהּ בְּנוּקְבָא. אָמַר לֵיהּ, הָא אִתְעָרָא, אִלֵּין לְעֵילָּא וְאִלֵּין
לְתַתָּא, יֵצֶר טוֹב וְיֵצֶר רָע, יֵצֶר טוֹב מִיָּמִינָא, וְיֵצֶר רָע מִשְׂמָאלָא,
וּשְׂמָאלָא לְעֵילָּא, אָחִיד בְּנוּקְבָא, לְקַשְּׁרָא לָהּ כַּחֲדָא בְּגוּפָא, כד"א
שְׂמֹאלוֹ תַּחַת לְרֹאשִׁי וְגו', וְעַל דָּא, מִלִּין אִתְפָּרְשָׁן לְעֵילָּא וְתַתָּא, עַד
הָכָא, מִכָּאן וּלְהָלְאָה מִלִּין בְּזוּטְרָא דְּזִיפְתָּא לִזְעֵירֵיהּ דְּטִינָקִין לְפָרְשָׁא
מִלָּה. וְהָא אִתְעָרוּ בֵּיהּ חַבְרַיָּיא.

221. Rabbi Elazar said: If it be so, THAT THE SCRIPTURE TALKS OF THE SUPERNAL MALE AND FEMALE, how do we account for the Evil Inclination overtaking the female, BECAUSE IT IS INCONCEIVABLE THAT THE EVIL INCLINATION CAN AFFECT THE SUPERNAL FEMALE. He said to him: I HAVE ALREADY EXPLAINED, some things pertain to the upper realms and others to the lower, MEANING THOSE HAPPENINGS IN THE UPPER APPLY TO THE LOWER, WHICH ARE THEIR BRANCHES. EVERYTHING IN THE LOWER HAS A ROOT IN THE UPPER, FROM WHENCE IT IS DRAWN AND GROWS. HENCE the Good and Evil Inclinations ARE DRAWN FROM THEIR UPPER ROOTS, the good from the right and the evil from the left. The supernal left, THE UPPER LEFT COLUMN FROM WHICH THE EVIL INCLINATION IS DRAWN, embraces the body, or the female, to join with it as one. As it is written: "His left hand is under my head" (Shir Hashirim 2:6). Hence, the

scripture was explained both in terms of the upper MALE AND FEMALE, and of the lower, ADAM AND EVE. From this point on, the account is smeared slightly with tar, WHICH MEANS THAT IT IS EASY TO UNDERSTAND HOW THE LOWER RELATES TO THE UPPER, and even the smallest child can elucidate on this matter. And the friends have discussed it.

51. He who goes on a journey

No matter how high we climb spiritually, we are always beholden to our wives, for it is through their essence that we receive all our Light. The woman is the direct manifestation of God's presence, or *Shechina*, in our world.

Rabbi Akiva, the great and holy master of the eminent sage Rabbi Shimon, once told his students "All that is yours and all that is mine is hers." He was indicating the indispensable role a woman plays in a man's spiritual work.

222. רָבִּי שִׁמְעוֹן הֲוָה אָזֵיל לִטְבֶרְיָה, וַהֲווֹ עִמֵּיהּ ר' יוֹסֵי וְרַבִּי יְהוּדָה וְר' חִיָּיא, אַדְּהֲכֵי חָמוּ לֵיהּ לְרַבִּי פִּנְחָס דַּהֲוָה אָתֵי, כֵּיוָן דְּאִתְחַבָּרוּ כַּחֲדָא, נַחֲתוּ וְיָתְבוּ תְּחוֹת אִילָנָא חַד, מֵאִילָנֵי טוּרָא, אָמַר רַבִּי פִּנְחָס, הָא יָתֵיבְנָא, מֵאִלֵּין מִלֵּי מַעַלְיָיתָא דְּאַתְּ אָמַר בְּכָל יוֹמָא בְּעֵינָא לְמִשְׁמַע.

222. Rabbi Shimon was going to Tiberias, accompanied by Rabbi Yosi, Rabbi Yehuda and Rabbi Chiya. On the way, they saw Rabbi Pinchas coming toward them. When they met, they dismounted FROM THEIR DONKEYS and sat under one of the trees on the mountain. Rabbi Pinchas said: Now that we are seated, MEANING NOW THAT WE ARE PREPARED TO LEARN TORAH, I would like to hear of the good teachings you expound every day.

223. פְּתַח רַבִּי שִׁמְעוֹן וְאָמַר, וַיֵּלֶךְ לְמַסָּעָיו מִנֶּגֶב וְעַד בֵּית אֵל עַד הַמָּקוֹם אֲשֶׁר הָיָה שָׁם אָהֳלֹה בַּתְּחִלָּה בֵּין בֵּית אֵל וּבֵין הָעָי. וַיֵּלֶךְ לְמַסָּעָיו, לְמַסָּעוֹ מִבָּעֵי לֵיהּ, מַאי לְמַסָּעָיו, אֶלָּא תְּרֵין מַטְלָנִין אִינּוּן, חַד דִּידֵיהּ, וְחַד דִּשְׁכִינְתָּא, דְּהָא כָּל בַּר נָשׁ בָּעֵי לְאִשְׁתַּכְּחָא דְּכַר וְנוּקְבָּא, בְּגִין לְאַתְקָפָא מְהֵימְנוּתָא, וּכְדֵין שְׁכִינְתָּא לָא אִתְפָּרְשָׁא מִנֵּיהּ לְעָלְמִין.

223. Rabbi Shimon then opened a discourse by saying, "And he went on his journeys from the Negev..." (Beresheet 13:3). It says "journeys" IN THE PLURAL, where it should have said "journey," IN THE SINGULAR. Why did the scripture say "journeys" IN THE PLURAL? Because there were two journeys, one his own, and the second that of the Shechinah. The dual journey indicates that everyone should be male and female, so that his faith may be strong and the Shechinah may never depart from him.

224. וְאִי תֵימָא, מָאן דְּנָפֵיק לְאוֹרְחָא, דְּלָא אִשְׁתְּכַח דְּכַר וְנוּקְבָא, שְׁכִינְתָּא אִתְפָּרְשָׁא מִנֵּיהּ, תָּא חֲזֵי, הַאי מַאן דְּנָפֵיק לְאָרְחָא, יְסַדֵּר צְלוֹתָא קַמֵּי קֻדְשָׁא בְּרִיךְ הוּא, בְּגִין לְאַמְשְׁכָא עֲלֵיהּ שְׁכִינְתָּא דְּמָרֵיהּ עַד לָא יִפּוֹק לְאָרְחָא, בְּזִמְנָא דְּאִשְׁתְּכַח דְּכַר וְנוּקְבָא. כֵּיוָן דְּסַדֵּר צְלוֹתֵיהּ וְשַׁבְחֵיהּ, וּשְׁכִינְתָּא שַׁרְיָיא עֲלֵיהּ, יִפּוֹק, דְּהָא שְׁכִינְתָּא אִזְדַּוְוגַת בַּהֲדֵיהּ, בְּגִין דְּיִשְׁתְּכַח דְּכַר וְנוּקְבָא, דְּכַר וְנוּקְבָא בְּמָתָא, דְּכַר וְנוּקְבָא בְּחַקְלָא, הה״ד צֶדֶק לְפָנָיו יְהַלֵּךְ וְיָשֵׂם לְדֶרֶךְ פְּעָמָיו.

224. And you may ask if the sojourner is not both male and female, will the Shechinah then leave him? Come and behold: He who goes on a journey should pray to the Holy One, blessed be He, BEFORE HE LEAVES, so as to draw upon himself his Master's Shechinah, when still at home and still both male and female. And when he prayed and praised, and the Shechinah rests upon him, then he can go on his way. Now that the Shechinah is with him, he can be male and female both in the city, THAT IS, AT HOME and in the field, ON HIS JOURNEY, BECAUSE THE SHECHINAH IS JOINED TO HIM. This is the meaning of, "Righteousness shall go before him," WITH RIGHTEOUSNESS REPRESENTING THE SHECHINAH, "and then he shall place his footsteps on the way" (Tehilim 85:14).

225. תָּא חֲזֵי, כָּל זִמְנָא דְּבַר נָשׁ אִתְעַכַּב בְּאוֹרְחָא, בָּעֵי לְנַטְרָא עוֹבָדוֹי, בְּגִין דְּזִוּוּגָא עִלָּאָה לָא יִתְפָּרַשׁ מִנֵּיהּ, וְיִשְׁתְּכַח פָּגִים בְּלָא דְּכַר וְנוּקְבָא, בְּמָתָא אִצְטְרִיךְ כַּד נוּקְבֵיהּ עֲמֵיהּ, כ״שׁ הָכָא דְּזִוּוּגָא עִלָּאָה אִתְקַשְּׁרַת בֵּיהּ, וְלָא עוֹד, אֶלָּא דְּהָא זִוּוּגָא עִלָּאָה נָטֵיר לֵיהּ בְּאָרְחָא, וְלָא מִתְפָּרְשָׁא מִנֵּיהּ, עַד דְּיִתוֹב לְבֵיתֵיהּ.

225. Come and behold: As long as a man is traveling, he should beware of sinning, so that the supernal mate, NAMELY THE SHECHINAH, will not desert him, causing him to become defective, that is, not composed of male and female. Just as he guards his actions in the city, when his wife is with him, he should do so all the more on the road, when the supernal mate, NAMELY THE SHECHINAH, is attached to him. Furthermore, because the supernal mate, NAMELY THE SHECHINAH protects him on the road and does not depart from him until he returns to his home, HE SHOULD, THEREFORE, WATCH HIS ACTIONS AT HOME TOO, SO THAT THE SHECHINAH DOES NOT DESERT HIM.

226. בְּשַׁעֲתָא דְעָאל לְבֵיתֵיהּ, בָּעָא לְחַדְתָּא דְּבֵיתְהוּ, בְּגִין דִּדְבֵיתְהוּ גַּרְמָא לֵיהּ, הַהוּא זִוּוּגָא עִלָּאָה, כֵּיוָן דְּאָתָא לְגַבָּהּ, בָּעֵי לְחַדְתָּא לָהּ, בְּגִין תְּרֵין גַּוְונֵי, חַד בְּגִין חֶדְוָתָא דְּהַהִיא זִוּוּגָא, חֶדְוָתָא דְּמִצְוָה הִיא, וְחֶדְוָתָא דְּמִצְוָה, חֶדְוָתָא דִשְׁכִינְתָּא אִיהוּ.

226. When he returns home, he should please his wife, because it is she who procured the supernal mate for him. BY RECITING A PRAYER FOR THE JOURNEY WHILE STILL AT HOME WITH HIS WIFE, HE MERITED THE SUPERNAL MATING ON THE JOURNEY. THUS HIS WIFE BROUGHT ABOUT HIS SUPERNAL MATING ON THE WAY, NAMELY THE INSPIRATION OF THE SHECHINAH. And when he comes to her, he should please her for two reasons. First, because of the joy of mating, as this mating is the joy of a precept, and because rejoicing in a precept is the joy of the Shechinah.

227. וְלָא עוֹד אֶלָּא דְּאַסְגֵּי שָׁלוֹם סְתָם, הה"ד וְיָדַעְתָּ כִּי שָׁלוֹם אָהֳלֶךָ וּפָקַדְתָּ נָוְךָ וְלֹא תֶחֱטָא. וְכִי אִי לָא פָּקִיד לְאִתְּתֵיהּ, חֲטָא אִיהוּ, הָכֵי הוּא וַדַּאי, בְּגִין דְּגָרַע יְקָר זִוּוּגָא עִלָּאָה, דְּאִזְדַּוְּוגַת בֵּיהּ וּדְבֵיתְהוּ גַּרְמָא לֵיהּ.

227. Furthermore, he increases peace at home, as it is written: "You shall know that your tent is at peace and you shall visit your habitation and not sin" (Iyov 5:24). HE ASKS: If he does not mate with his wife, is that a sin? ACCORDING TO THE WORDS, "AND YOU SHALL VISIT YOUR HABITATION AND NOT SIN?" AND HE SAYS: Evidently so, IT IS A SIN. He has diminished the glory of the supernal mating, NAMELY THE SHECHINAH, who has mated with him on the way because of the actions of his wife. AND IF HE IS UNGRATEFUL TO HER, HE THUS REVEALS HIS OPINION THAT THE SUPERNAL COMPANION WAS NOT SO IMPORTANT TO HIM AND HENCE

DEROGATES HER HONOR.

228. וְחַד דְּאִי מִתְעַבְּרָא אִתְּתֵיהּ, זִוּוּגָא עִלָּאָה אֲרִיקַת בָּהּ, נִשְׁמָתָא קַדִּישָׁא, דְּהַאי בְּרִית אִקְרֵי בְּרִית דְּקֻדְשָׁא בְּרִיךְ הוּא, וְעַל דָּא בָּעֵי לְכַוְּונָא, בְּחֶדְוָותָא דָא כְּמָה דְבָעֵי בְּחֶדְוָותָא דְשַׁבָּת, דְּאִיהוּ זִוּוּגָא דַחֲכִימִין, וְעַל דָּא, וְיָדַעְתָּ כִּי שָׁלוֹם אָהֳלֶךָ, דְּהָא שְׁכִינְתָּא אַתְיָא עִמָּךְ, וְשַׁרְיָא בְּבֵיתָךְ, וְעַל דָּא וּפָקַדְתָּ נָוְךָ וְלֹא תֶחֱטָא, מַאי וְלֹא תֶחֱטָא, לְשַׁמְּשָׁא קַמֵּי שְׁכִינְתָּא, חֶדְוָותָא דְמִצְוָה.

228. The second REASON WHY HE SHOULD GLADDEN HIS WIFE is that if his wife conceives in consequence of this mating, the supernal mating endows her with a holy soul. For this covenant OF THE SUPERNAL MATE THAT ENDOWS THE HOLY SOUL is the covenant of the Holy One, blessed be He. BY THIS MATING WITH HIS WIFE, HE CAUSES THE MATING OF THE HOLY ONE, BLESSED BE HE, WITH HIS SHECHINAH. It behooves one, then, to concentrate on that joy, as one should concentrate on mating on Shabbat, which is the sages' mating, THAT IS, THE HOLINESS OF THE MATING WHEN ONE RETURNS FROM A JOURNEY EQUALS THE HOLINESS OF THE MATING ON SHABBAT EVE. Hence, the quotation, "you shall know that your tent is at peace" indicates that you will know the Shechinah is with you and has settled on your home. Hence, "…and you shall visit your habitation and not sin," means that you should not sin by refraining from intercourse before the Shechinah, which is the joy in a precept, NAMELY ONE MUST NOT PREVENT THE UNION OF THE HOLY ONE, BLESSED BE HE, WITH HIS SHECHINAH, THROUGH WHICH A SOUL CAN BE ENDOWED. THIS IS A GREAT SIN.

229. כְּגַוְונָא דָא, תַּלְמִידֵי חֲכָמִים, דְּמִתְפָּרְשָׁן מִנְשַׁיְיהוּ, כָּל אִינוּן יוֹמִין דְּשַׁבַּתָּא, בְּגִין לְאִתְעַסְּקָא בְּאוֹרַיְיתָא, זִוּוּגָא עִלָּאָה אִזְדַּוְּוג בְּהוּ, וְלָא מִתְפָּרְשָׁא מִנַּיְיהוּ, בְּגִין דְּיִשְׁתְּכַח דְּכַר וְנוּקְבָא. כֵּיוָן דְּעָאל שַׁבָּת, בָּעְיָין תַּלְמִידֵי חֲכָמִים, לְחַדְתָּא לִדְבֵיתְהוּ, בְּגִין יְקַר זִוּוּגָא עִלָּאָה, וּלְכַוְּונָא לִבַּיְיהוּ, בִּרְעוּתָא דְּמָארֵיהוֹן כְּמָה דְאִתְּמָר.

229. Similarly, the great scholars abstain from their wives all weekdays, so

as not to be distracted from their full occupation with Torah. The supernal mate consorts with them, and THE SHECHINAH does not leave them, so that they remain male and female. And when Shabbat comes, these scholars have to please their wives for the honor of the supernal mate, as we have explained, CAUSING THE SUPERNAL MATE TO ENDOW THEM WITH HOLY SOULS. They should meditate on their Master's desire.

230. כְּגַוְונָא דָא, הַאי מַאן דְּאִתְּתֵיה בְּיוֹמֵי מְסָאֲבוּ דִילָה, וְנָטִיר לָה כִּדְקָא יָאוֹת, כָּל אִינוּן יוֹמִין, זוּוּגָא עִלָּאָה אִזְדַּוּוג בַּהֲדֵיה, דְּיִשְׁתְּכַח דְּכַר וְנוּקְבָּא, כֵּיוָן דְּאִתְדַּכְיַאת אִתְּתֵיה, בָּעֵי לְחַדְתָּא לָה, חֶדְוָה דְמִצְוָה, חֶדְוָה עִלָּאָה, וְכֻלְהוּ טַעֲמֵי דְּקָא אֲמָרָן בְּחַד דַּרְגָּא סָלְקִין. סְתָמָא דְמִלָּה כָּל אִינוּן בְּנֵי מְהֵימְנוּתָא, בָּעֲיִין לְכַוְונָא, לִבָּא וּרְעוּתָא בְּהַאי.

230. Similarly, the supernal mate joins with a man whose wife is on her unclean days and who dutifully abides by the laws of family purity all those days, so that he remains male and female. And when his wife is purified, he is obligated to rejoice with her, with the joy in a precept, the joy of the supernal. All the reasons we have discussed reach the same conclusion: the main objective is that the faithful must concentrate in their heart and wishes on.

231. וְאִי תֵּימָא, אִי הָכֵי, שְׁבָחָא הוּא דְּבַר נָשׁ, כַּד נָפֵיק לְאָרְחָא, יַתִּיר מִן בֵּיתֵיה, בְּגִין זוּוגָא עִלָּאָה דְּאִזְדַּוּוגַת בַּהֲדֵיה. תָּא חֲזֵי, בְּזִמְנָא דְּבַר נָשׁ הוּא בְּבֵיתֵיה, עִקָּרָא דְּבֵיתָא דְּבֵיתְהוּ, בְּגִין דִּשְׁכִינְתָּא לָא אִתְעַדֵּי מִן בֵּיתָא, בְּגִין דְּבֵיתְהוּ, כְּמָה דְּתָנִינָן, דִּכְתִיב וַיְבִיאֶהָ יִצְחָק הָאֹהֱלָה שָׂרָה אִמּוֹ, דִּשְׁרַגָּא אִתְדְּלָקַת, מַאי טַעְמָא, בְּגִין דִּשְׁכִינְתָּא אָתַת לְבֵיתָא.

231. One may say that a man is more praiseworthy while journeying than when he is at home, because the supernal mate embraces him WHILE HE IS ON HIS WAY. Come and behold: When a man is at home, the foundation of the house is the wife, because of whom the Shechinah does not leave the house. As we have learned, it is written that when "He brought her to the tent of his mother Sarah" (Beresheet 24:67), the candle was rekindled, AS IT WAS WHEN SARAH, HIS MOTHER, WAS ALIVE. That is because the

Shechinah came to the house FOR HIS WIFE'S MERIT. THE SHECHINAH, THEREFORE, DWELLS IN THE HOUSE BECAUSE OF THE WIFE'S MERIT.

232. רָזָא דְּמִלָּה, אִמָּא עִלָּאָה לָא אִשְׁתַּכְּחַת גַּבֵּי דְכוּרָא, אֶלָּא בְּזִמְנָא דְּאִתְתַּקְּנַת בֵּיתָא, וְאִתְחַבְּרוּ דְּכַר וְנוּקְבָא, כְּדֵין אִמָּא עִלָּאָה, אֲרִיקַת בִּרְכָאן, לְבָרְכֵי לוֹן. כְּגַוְונָא דָא אִמָּא תַּתָּאָה, לָא אִשְׁתַּכְּחַת לְגַבֵּי דְכוּרָא, אֶלָּא בְּזִמְנָא דְּאִתְתַּקְּנַת בֵּיתָא, וְאָתֵי דְּכַר לְגַבָּהּ דְּנוּקְבֵיהּ, וְאִתְחַבְּרוּ כַּחֲדָא, כְּדֵין אִמָּא תַּתָּאָה, אֲרִיקַת בִּרְכָאן לְבָרְכָא לוֹן.

232. The concealed reason behind this is that the supernal Ima, BINAH, does not coexist with the male, NAMELY ZEIR ANPIN, until the house has been prepared and both male and female – NAMELY ZEIR ANPIN AND NUKVA – have been joined. Then the supernal Ima brings blessings upon them both. Similarly, the lower Ima – NAMELY THE SHECHINAH – cannot be found with the male – NAMELY MAN BELOW – except when the house has been prepared, the male comes unto the female, and they join together as one. Consequently, the lower Ima, THE SHECHINAH, brings upon them a wealth of blessings.

233. וְעַל דָּא בִּתְרֵי נוּקְבִין, אִתְעַטַּר דְּכוּרָא בְּבֵיתֵיהּ, כְּגַוְונָא דִּלְעֵילָא. וְהַיְינוּ רָזָא דִּכְתִיב, עַד תַּאֲוַת גִּבְעוֹת עוֹלָם, הַאי עַל דָּא, תֵּיאוּבְתָּא דְּגִבְעוֹת עוֹלָם בֵּיהּ, נוּקְבָא עִלָּאָה, לְאַתְקְנָא לֵיהּ, וּלְאַעֲטָרָא לֵיהּ, וּלְבָרְכָא לֵיהּ. נוּקְבָא תַּתָּאָה, לְאִתְחַבְּרָא בֵּיהּ, וּלְאִתְזְנָא מִנֵּיהּ.

233. Hence, a man is crowned with two females in his home similar to the supernal ZEIR ANPIN, as the secret of the words: "to (Heb. *ad*) the utmost bound (also "desire')of the everlasting hills" (Beresheet 49:26). *Ad* IN THE VERSE "TO THE UTMOST DESIRE," IS THE MOCHIN OF THE SUPERNAL GARDEN OF EDEN. In it are the desires of the everlasting hills, WHICH ARE THE TWO FEMALES. The supernal female, BINAH, desires to correct and crown THE MALE, WITH THE MOCHIN OF THE THREE SFIROT and to bless him WITH CHASSADIM. The lower female DESIRES to embrace THE MALE and to be fed by him WITH THE MOCHIN OF *AD*, BECAUSE OF WHICH THE SUPERNAL MOTHER, BINAH, DESIRES TO ENDOW HIM WITH THESE MOCHIN. HENCE THE MALE IS CROWNED BY THE TWO FEMALES. FOR

WERE IT NOT FOR THE LOWER FEMALE'S NEED FOR THE MOCHIN OF AD, THE SUPERNAL MOTHER WOULD NOT HAVE ENDOWED THE MALE WITH THEM, BECAUSE THE MALE DOES NOT NEED THEM. HE NEEDS ONLY CONCEALED CHASSADIM.

234. וּכְגַוְונָא דָא לְתַתָּא, כַּד דְּכוּרָא אִנְסִיב, תָּאוַת גִּבְעוֹת עוֹלָם לְגַבֵּיהּ, וְאִתְעֲטַר בִּתְרֵי נוּקְבֵי, חַד עִלָּאָה וְחַד תַּתָּאָה, עִלָּאָה לְאַרְקָא עֲלֵיהּ בִּרְכָאן, תַּתָּאָה לְאִתְּזְנָא מִנֵּיהּ, וּלְאִתְחַבְּרָא בַּהֲדֵיהּ, וּבְ"ּנ בְּבֵיתֵיהּ, תָּאוַת גִּבְעוֹת עוֹלָם לְגַבֵּיהּ, וְאִתְעֲטַר בְּהוּ.

234. That WHICH HAS BEEN EXPLAINED ABOUT THE UPPER MALE, ALSO applies to the lower male, THAT IS MAN IN THIS WORLD. When he marries a woman, he receives the desires of the everlasting hills. He is crowned by two females, CALLED THE EVERLASTING HILLS. One is supernal, NAMELY THE SHECHINAH, and one lower, NAMELY HIS WIFE. The supernal is to pour blessings upon him, and the lower, his wife, should be fed by him and joined with him.

235. כַּד נָפֵיק בְּאָרְחָא, לָאו הָכֵי, אִימָּא עִלָּאָה אִתְחַבְּרַת בַּהֲדֵיהּ, וְתַתָּאָה אִשְׁתְּאָרַת. כַּד תָּב לְבֵיתֵיהּ, בָּעֵי לְאִתְעַטְּרָא בִּתְרֵי נוּקְבֵי כִּדְקָאֲמָרָן. אָמַר ר' פִּנְחָס אֲפִילוּ בִּקְלִיפֵּי סַנְפּוֹרֵי קַטְרָא לָא פָּתְחֵי עֲטְרָא קַמָּךְ.

235. But when he journeys, it is not so, THAT IS, HE IS NOT CROWNED BY THE TWO FEMALES, but solely by the supernal Ima, NAMELY THE SHECHINAH, who cleaves to him upon his sojourning. The lower, HIS WIFE, stays AT HOME. And when he returns home, he crowns himself again with two females, as we have said. HENCE, HE WHO STAYS AT HOME IS MORE DIGNIFIED THAN HE WHO TRAVELS. Rabbi Pinchas said to Rabbi Shimon: Even in SIMPLE MATTERS OF the scales and fins of a fish, no one will open his mouth to brag before you. THAT IS, RABBI PINCHAS WAS SO AMAZED AT THE DEPTH OF RABBI SHIMON'S INTERPRETATION THAT HE SAID, EVEN ON SIMPLE MATTERS OF DECIDING WHETHER A FISH IS KOSHER FOR EATING OR NOT, NO ONE WILL DARE TO EXPOUND BEFORE YOU.

52. Voice and speech

A deeply hidden secret pertains to the spiritual powers of the mouth. As letters and words arouse the very forces that they describe, the mouth animates the spiritual forces that it speaks. Positive words generate positive angels, while negative speech produces negative angels. The good and bad events in our lives are merely the net effect of the angelic influences created through the power of speech. The Evil Inclination works to blind us from this spiritual truth. Having succumbed to the uncertainty and doubt implanted within us by our negative tendencies, most of us disregard the words that come out of our mouths. Yet Kabbalah teaches that it is far more important to consider what comes out of the mouth than what goes into it. It is fitting that, through the power of the Zohar's words, we can draw Light to help us use our speech in a positive manner.

236. אָמַר רָבִּי שִׁמְעוֹן, כְּגַוְונָא דָא אוֹרַיְיתָא קָאֵים בֵּין תְּרֵי בָּתִּים, כְּמָה דִּכְתִיב לִשְׁנֵי בָתֵּי יִשְׂרָאֵל וגו'. חַד סְתִימָא עִלָּאָה, וְחַד אִתְגַּלְיָא יַתִּיר, עִלָּאָה, קוֹל גָּדוֹל, דִּכְתִיב קוֹל גָּדוֹל וְלֹא יָסָף.

236. Rabbi Shimon said: similarly, Torah, THAT IS, ZEIR ANPIN, is situated between two houses – BETWEEN TWO FEMALES. FOR IMA IS CALLED "HOUSE," as in "For both houses of Yisrael" (Yeshayah 8:14). One is upper and sealed – THE SUPERNAL IMA, BINAH; the other is more revealed. The supernal, SEALED one is the great voice referred to in: "A great voice which was not heard again" (Devarim 5:19).

237. וְהַאי קוֹל פְּנִימָאָה אִיהוּ, דְּלָא אִשְׁתְּמַע, וְלָא אִתְגַּלְיָא, וְדָא הוּא, כַּד נָבִיעַ בֵּי גָרוֹן, אַפִּיק ה' בַּחֲשַׁאי, וּנְבִיעַ תָּדִיר וְלָא פָּסַק, וְאִיהוּ דַּקָּה פְּנִימָאָה, דְּלָא אִשְׁתְּמַע לְעָלְמִין.

237. This is an inner voice that cannot be heard or revealed. IT IS NOT HEARD IN THE FORM OF A VOICE AND NOT REVEALED IN SPEECH. It is produced when the palate is connected to the larynx to produce Hei in a SOUNDLESS whisper. This is perpetually produced; it never ceases. It is a very thin inner voice that can never be heard.

238. וּמֵהָכָא נָפְקָא אוֹרַיְיתָא, דְּאִיהוּ קוֹל יַעֲקֹב, וְהַאי אִשְׁתְּמַע, דְּנָפְקָא מֵהַהִיא דְּלָא אִשְׁתְּמַע, וּלְבָתַר אִתְאֲחִיד דִּבּוּר בַּהֲדֵיהּ, וְנָפַק לְבַר, מֵחֵילֵיהּ וּמִתַּקְפֵּיהּ, וְקוֹל דְּיַעֲקֹב דְּאִיהוּ אוֹרַיְיתָא, אָחִיד בֵּין תְּרֵי נִקְבֵי, אָחִיד בְּהַאי פְּנִימָאָה דְּלָא אִשְׁתְּמַע, וְאָחִיד בְּהַאי דִּלְבַר דְּאִשְׁתְּמַע.

238. From this voice, FROM ABA AND IMA, THE GREAT VOICE, Torah, called "the voice of Jacob," NAMELY ZEIR ANPIN, originates. This audible VOICE comes from THE VOICE THAT IS not heard, NAMELY ABA AND IMA. Subsequently, speech is linked to the inner voice. Speech comes AND IS HEARD through the strength and initiative OF JACOB'S VOICE. The voice of Jacob, called Torah, THAT IS, ZEIR ANPIN, is embraced between two females. It is then linked to the inaudible inner VOICE, NAMELY IMA, and to the audible external one, NAMELY THE NUKVA.

239. תְּרֵין אִינוּן דְּלָא אִשְׁתְּמַעוּ, וּתְרֵין אִינוּן דְּאִשְׁתְּמַעוּ. תְּרֵין דְּלָא אִשְׁתְּמַעוּ, דָּא הוּא חָכְמָה עִלָּאָה סְתִימָאָה, דְּקָיְימָא בְּמַחֲשָׁבָה, דְּלָא אִתְגַּלְיָא וְלָא אִשְׁתְּמַע. לְבָתַר נָפְקָא וְאִתְגַּלְיָא זְעֵיר בַּחֲשַׁאי, דְּלָא אִשְׁתְּמַע, הַהוּא דְּאִקְרֵי קוֹל גָּדוֹל, דְּהוּא דַק וְנָפֵיק בַּחֲשַׁאי.

239. There are two inaudible VOICES, CALLED CONCEALED CHASSADIM, and two other VOICES that are audible EXTERNALLY. IN THEM – IN THE CHASSADIM – THESE VOICES ARE REVEALED BY THE RADIANCE OF CHOCHMAH. HE EXPLAINS, the two inaudible voices are the supernal and concealed Chochmah, NAMELY ARICH ANPIN, CLOTHED by thought, AND THE SUPERNAL ABA, heard neither in speech nor IN THE ASPECT OF voice. First, it is revealed slightly by an inaudible whisper, AS IN THE ISSUING OF THE LETTER *Hei*, called the great voice. The great voice is a faint sound emitted secretly, AND IT IS THE SUPERNAL IMA. THOSE ARE THE TWO INAUDIBLE VOICES, ABA AND IMA.

240. תְּרֵין אִינוּן דְּאִשְׁתְּמַעוּ, אִינוּן דְּנָפְקֵי מֵהָכָא, קוֹל דְּיַעֲקֹב, וְדִבּוּר דְּאִתְאֲחִיד בַּהֲדֵיהּ. הַאי קוֹל גָּדוֹל, דְּאִיהוּ בַּחֲשַׁאי וְלָא אִשְׁתְּמַע, אִיהִי בֵּית לַחָכְמָה עִלָּאָה, וְכָל נוּקְבָא בֵּית אִקְרֵי, וְהַאי דִּבּוּר בַּתְרָאָה, אִיהוּ

בַּיִת לְקוֹל דְּיַעֲקֹב, דְּאִיהוּ אוֹרַיְיתָא. וְעַל דָּא אוֹרַיְיתָא שַׁרְיָא בְּבֵי"ת,
בֵּי"ת רֵאשִׁית.

240. The two audible voices are emitted from here, PRODUCED BY THE TWO INAUDIBLE ONES. THOSE ARE the voice of Jacob, NAMELY ZEIR ANPIN, and the speech that cleaves to it, WHICH IS THE NUKVA OF ZEIR ANPIN. The great voice, BINAH, is whispered and not heard. It is a house (Heb. *bayit*) for the supernal Chochmah, WHICH IS ABA. Because each female is called "House," BINAH IS CALLED "HOUSE." Speech, WHICH IS THE NUKVA OF ZEIR ANPIN, is the house (*Bayit*) for the Voice of Jacob, which is Torah, OR ZEIR ANPIN. Hence Torah starts with the letter *Bet* or Beresheet (in Hebrew, both *bayit* and the letter Bet are spelled in the same way).

241. פְּתַח וְאָמַר, בְּרֵאשִׁית בָּרָא אֱלֹקִים, הַיְינוּ דִּכְתִיב וַיִּבֶן ה' אֱלֹקִים אֶת הַצֵּלָע. אֶת הַשָּׁמַיִם, הַיְינוּ דִּכְתִיב וַיְבִיאֶהָ אֶל הָאָדָם. וְאֶת הָאָרֶץ, כד"א וְעֶצֶם מֵעֲצָמִי, וַדַּאי הַאי אִיהִי אֶרֶץ הַחַיִּים.

241. RABBI SHIMON said that the words "In the beginning Elohim created" correspond to "the side, which Hashem Elohim... had made." THE STRUCTURING OF THE NUKVA BY ABA AND IMA IS INSINUATED HERE. The words "the heaven" CORRESPOND TO THE SECRET OF THE GREAT MALE AND FEMALE IN the words, "and brought her to the man." Likewise, "and the earth" corresponds to "bone of my bones," THE SECRET OF THE SMALLER MALE AND FEMALE. THE SMALL NUKVA, ALLUDED TO IN "AND THE EARTH" is called "the land of the living."

53. "Hashem said to my master"

The Zohar describes the metaphysical process by which the negative *desire to receive for the self alone* is transformed into the *desire to receive for the sake of sharing*. This transformation opens the way to the final redemption, which will be achieved by the 7th millennium. We can hasten this process through our efforts in reading this section.

242. תּוּ, פְּתַח ר' שִׁמְעוֹן וַאֲמַר נְאֻם ה' לַאדֹנִי שֵׁב לִימִינִי עַד אָשִׁית אוֹיְבֶיךָ הֲדֹם לְרַגְלֶיךָ. נְאֻם ה' לַאדֹנִי, דַּרְגָּא עִלָּאָה, לְדַרְגָּא תַּתָּאָה קָאָמַר, שֵׁב לִימִינִי, לְאִתְקַשְּׁרָא מַעֲרָבִית בִּדְרוֹמִית, שְׂמָאלָא בִּיָמִינָא, בְּגִין לְתַבְּרָא חֵילֵיהוֹן, דִּשְׁאָר עַמִּין עכו"ם. נְאֻם ה' לַאדֹנִי, נְאֻם ה', דָּא יַעֲקֹב. לַאדֹנִי, דָּא אֲרוֹן הַבְּרִית אֲדוֹן כָּל הָאָרֶץ.

242. Rabbi Shimon further said, "Hashem said to my master, Sit at My right hand till I have made your enemies as your footstools" (Tehilim 110:1). "Hashem said to my master," this MEANS THAT the upper level, ZEIR ANPIN, says to the lower level, THE NUKVA, "Sit at My right," so as to link west, THE NUKVA, with the south, CHESED OF ZEIR ANPIN, and the left, THE NUKVA with the right, ZEIR ANPIN. These linkages break the power of the idolatrous nations. THE QUOTATION CONTINUES, "TILL I HAVE MADE YOUR ENEMIES AS YOUR FOOTSTOOLS" BECAUSE "Hashem said" is Jacob, ZEIR ANPIN, AND "to my master," is "the ark of the covenant of the Master of all the earth" (Yehoshua 3:11), NAMELY THE NUKVA.

243. דָּבָר אַחֵר נְאֻם ה', דָּא יוֹבְלָא. לַאדֹנִי, דָּא שְׁמִיטָה. דִּכְתִיב בָּהּ אָהַבְתִּי אֶת אֲדֹנִי. שֵׁב לִימִינִי, דְּהָא יְמִינָא בְּיוֹבְלָא שָׁרְיָא, וּשְׁמִיטָה בָּעֵי לְאִתְקַשְּׁרָא בִּיָמִינָא.

243. An alternative explanation is that "Hashem says" is the Jubilee, WHICH IS BINAH, and "to my master" is the Sabbatical Year, THE NUKVA, of whom it is said, "I love my master" (Shemot 21:5). JUBILEE SAYS TO THE SABATICAL YEAR, "Sit at My right," because the right, WHICH IS CHASSADIM, exists in Jubilee, NAMELY BINAH and the Sabbatical Year, WHICH IS THE NUKVA, must link with the right, AS WE HAVE EXPLAINED.

244. תָּא חֲזֵי, שְׁמִיטָה דָא, לָא אִתְקְשַׁר בְּקִיּוּמָא שְׁלִים, בִּימִינָא
וּבִשְׂמָאלָא, מִיּוֹמָא דְּאִשְׁתַּכְּחַת, כַּד בָּעְיָא לְאִתְקַשְּׁרָא, אוֹשִׁיט דְּרוֹעָא
שְׂמָאלָא לְקַבְּלָהּ, וּבָרָא עָלְמָא דֵין, וּבְגִין דְּהוּא מִסִּטְרָא דִשְׂמָאלָא,
לֵית בֵּיהּ קִיּוּמָא, עַד זִמְנָא דְּאֶלֶף שְׁבִיעָאָה, דִּבְהַהוּא יוֹמָא לְחוֹד,
אִתְקְשַׁר כְּדֵין בִּימִינָא, וּכְדֵין תֶּהֱוֵי בֵּין יְמִינָא וּשְׂמָאלָא, בְּקִיּוּמָא
שְׁלִים, וְיִשְׁתַּכְּחוּן שָׁמַיִם חֲדָשִׁים, וְאֶרֶץ חֲדָשָׁה, וּכְדֵין לָא תַעֲדֵי מִתַּמָּן
לְעָלְמִין.

244. Come and behold: The Sabbatical Year, NAMELY THE NUKVA, was not
thoroughly connected to right and left ever since it existed. And when THE
NUKVA wants to link WITH THE RIGHT AND THE LEFT, ZEIR ANPIN spreads
out His left arm toward her and creates this world. THAT IS, THE LEFT
ASPECT OF THE NUKVA, CALLED "THIS WORLD." And since it is now only
the aspect of the left, she has no stable existence, THAT IS, NO COMPLETE
MOCHIN. THIS WAS THE STATE OF AFFAIRS FOR THE SIX THOUSAND
YEARS before the seventh millennium. At the inception of the seventh
millennium – and only on that day – THE NUKVA links with the right,
NAMELY CHASSADIM. Then THE NUKVA is embraced completely between
right and left, THAT IS, WITH FULL MOCHIN, and a new heaven and earth
will come into being. She will never be removed from there, BECAUSE SHE
WILL BE BALANCED BETWEEN RIGHT AND LEFT FOREVER.

245. אִי הָכֵי בְּמַאי נוֹקִים שֵׁב לִימִינִי, אֶלָּא עַד זִמְנָא יְדִיעָא, דִּכְתִיב
עַד אָשִׁית אוֹיְבֶיךָ הֲדֹם לְרַגְלֶיךָ, וְלָא תָדִיר. אֲבָל בְּהַהוּא זִמְנָא, לָא
תַעֲדֵי מִתַּמָּן לְעָלְמִין, דִּכְתִיב כִּי יָמִין וּשְׂמֹאל תִּפְרוֹצִי, לְמֶהֱוֵי כֹּלָּא
חַד.

245. HE RAISES A DIFFICULTY: If what you say is correct, AND ONLY IN
THE SEVENTH MILLENNIUM WILL THE NUKVA LINK WITH THE RIGHT, how
do we explain that "Sit at My right" WHICH MEANS DURING THE SIX
THOUSAND YEARS AND NOT NECESSARILY AT THE ADVENT OF THE
SEVENTH MILLENNIUM. AND HE EXPLAINS, THE VERSE "SIT AT MY
RIGHT" applies to a specified time period. It says "till I make your enemies
to be your footstools," which is not forever. But at that time, IN THE

SEVENTH MILLENNIUM, she will never be removed, as it is written of her "You shall spread to the right and to the left" (Yeshayah 54:3). That is, SHE WILL COMPRISE IN HERSELF THE RIGHT COLUMN AND THE LEFT COLUMN, and all will be one WITHIN HER.

246. תָּא חֲזֵי, אֶת הַשָּׁמַיִם, דָּא שְׁכִינְתָּא עִלָּאָה. וְאֶת הָאָרֶץ, דָּא שְׁכִינְתָּא דִלְתַתָּא, בְּאִתְחַבְּרוּתָא דִּדְכַר וְנוּקְבָא כַּחֲדָא. וְהָא אִתְּמַר כְּמָה דְאִתְעָרוּ בֵּיה חַבְרַיָּיא עַד כְּעָן.

246. Come and behold: The words "the heaven" (Beresheet 1:1) allude to the upper Shechinah, NAMELY THE NUKVA FROM THE CHEST UPWARD, and the words "and the earth" (Ibid.) allude to the lower Shechinah, THE NUKVA FROM THE CHEST DOWNWARD OF ZEIR ANPIN. They are joined together as male and female. All this has been explained by the friends.

54. The Rising Flame

A glowing ember or lit candle holds many supernal secrets concerning the revelation of spiritual Light. By learning this section, we awaken these wondrous forces of Light in our own lives.

247. בָּעוֹ לְמֵיזַל, קָמוּ, אָמַר רָבִּי שִׁמְעוֹן, מִלָּה הָכָא גַּבָּן, פָּתַח רָבִּי שִׁמְעוֹן וְאָמַר, תְּרֵי קְרָאֵי כְּתִיבֵי, כִּי ה' אֱלֹקֶיךָ אֵשׁ אוֹכְלָה הוּא. וּכְתִיב הָתָם וְאַתֶּם הַדְּבֵקִים בַּה' אֱלֹקֵיכֶם חַיִּים כֻּלְּכֶם הַיּוֹם. הָנֵי קְרָאֵי אוֹקִימְנָא לְהוּ, בְּכַמָּה אֲתַר, וְאִתְעָרוּ בְּהוּ חַבְרַיָּיא. תָּא חֲזֵי, כִּי ה' אֱלֹקֶיךָ אֵשׁ אוֹכְלָה הוּא, הָא אִתְּמַר, מִלָּה דָא, בְּגוֹ חַבְרַיָּיא, דְּאִית אֶשָׁא אָכְלָא אֶשָׁא, וְאָכִיל לָהּ וְשֵׁצֵי לָהּ, בְּגִין דְּאִית אֶשָׁא תַּקִּיפָא מֵאֶשָׁא, וְאוֹקְמוּהָ.

247. When they rose to leave, Rabbi Shimon said: We have something with us, MEANING THAT HE HAD ONE MORE THING TO TELL THEM. Rabbi Shimon then said: Two passages are written. One says, "Because Hashem your Elohim is a consuming fire" (Devarim 4:24), SIGNIFYING THAT IT IS IMPOSSIBLE TO CLEAVE TO HIM, AS IT IS IMPOSSIBLE TO CLEAVE TO FIRE. The other says, "But you that did cleave of Hashem your Elohim are all alive every one of you this day" (Devarim 4:4), SIGNIFYING THAT IT IS POSSIBLE TO CLEAVE TO HIM. These SEEMINGLY CONFLICTING passages have been explained repeatedly by the friends who have tackled them. But come and behold: the verse, "Because Hashem your Elohim is a consuming fire." The friends have discussed that there is a fire that consumes and destroys even fire. Thus, there is a fire that is stronger than NORMAL fire, and that has been explained.

248. אֲבָל תָּא חֲזֵי, מָאן דְּבָעֵי לְמִנְדַּע חָכְמְתָא דְּיִחוּדָא קַדִּישָׁא, יִסְתַּכַּל בְּשַׁלְהוֹבָא דְּסַלְקָא מִגּוֹ גַּחֶלְתָּא, אוֹ מִגּוֹ בּוֹצִינָא דְּדָלֵיק, דְּהָא שַׁלְהוֹבָא לָא סַלְקָא אֶלָּא כַּד אִתְאַחִיד בְּמִלָּה גַּסָּה.

248. But, come and behold: one who wants to learn the wisdom of holy unification must examine the flames arising from a glowing ember or lit candle, because the flames only rise if coming from a coarse object.

249. תָּא חֲזֵי, בְּשַׁלְהוֹבָא דְסָלְקָא, אִית תְּרֵין נְהוֹרִין, חַד נְהוֹרָא חִוְורָא, דְּנָהֵיר, וְחַד נְהוֹרָא דְּאִתְאֲחֵיד בָּהּ, אוּכְמָא אוֹ תְּכְלָא. הַהוּא נְהוֹרָא חִוְורָא אִיהוּ לְעֵילָא, וְסָלְקָא בְּאוֹרַח מִישׁוֹר. וּתְחוֹתֵיהּ, הַהוּא נְהוֹרָא תִּכְלָא אוֹ אוּכְמָא, דְּאִיהוּ כָּרְסַיָא לְהַהוּא חִוְורָא.

249. Come and see: In the rising flame there are two lights. One is a white and luminous light; the other is a blue or black light to which the white light is linked. The white shining light is higher and direct. Underneath it is the blue or black light, which serves as a pedestal for the white.

250. וְהַהוּא נְהוֹרָא חִוְורָא, שָׁארֵי עֲלוֹיֵהּ, וְאִתְאֲחִידוּ דָא בְּדָא, לְמֶהֱוֵי כֹּלָּא חַד, וְהַהוּא נְהוֹרָא אוּכְמָא, אוֹ גַּוָון תִּכְלָא, דְּאִיהוּ לְתַתָּא, הוּא כָּרְסַיָא דִיקָר, לְהַהוּא חִוְורָא. וְעַל דָּא רָזָא דִתְכֶלְתָּא.

250. This shining white light spreads over THE BLUE, and the two lights unite to become one. And this black light, or the blue tint underneath it, serves as a Throne of Glory for the white light. Hence, its appearance is the secret of blue. IT IS THE ASPECT OF THE THRONE OF GLORY, WHICH RESEMBLES BLUE, AS IS GENERALLY KNOWN.

251. וְהַאי כָּרְסַיָא תִּכְלָא אוּכְמָא, אִתְאֲחַד בְּמִלָּה אָחֳרָא לְאִתְדַּלְּקָא, דְּהוּא מִתַּתָּא, וְהַהוּא אִתְעַר לֵיהּ, לְאִתְאַחֲדָא בִּנְהוֹרָא חִוְורָא.

251. This throne of black or bluish light links to something underneath it, so it has something on which to burn. This thing compels it to cling to the white light.

252. וְדָא תִּכְלָא אוּכְמָא, לְזִמְנִין אִתְהֲדַר סוּמָקָא, וְהַהוּא נְהוֹרָא חִוְורָא דַּעֲלֵיהּ, לָא אִשְׁתַּנֵּי לְעָלְמִין, דְּהָא חִוְורָא הוּא תָּדִיר. אֲבָל הַאי תִּכְלָא אִשְׁתַּנֵּי לִגְוָונִין אִלֵּין, לְזִמְנִין תִּכְלָא אוֹ אוּכְמָא, וּלְזִמְנִין סוּמָקָא.

252. The black and blue LIGHT sometimes turns red again. Yet the white light above it never changes; it is always white. But the blue changes. It is sometimes blue or black, sometimes red.

253. וְהַאי אִתְאֲחֵיד לִתְרֵין סִטְרִין, אִתְאֲחֵיד לְעֵילָא, בְּהַהוּא נְהוֹרָא חִוָורָא. אִתְאֲחֵיד לְתַתָּא, בְּהַהוּא מִלָּה דִּתְחוֹתוֹי, דְּמִתַּקְּנָא בֵּיה לְאַנְהָרָא וּלְאִתְאַחֲדָא בֵּיה.

253. This BLUE LIGHT links in two directions. It connects to the white light above it and to the COARSE object underneath it, NAMELY THE WICK. The wick is designated as the place to which the light may connect and from which it radiates. THE WICK SERVES AS THE POINT AT WHICH THE BLUE LIGHT CONNECTS WITH THE SHINING WHITE LIGHT.

254. וְדָא אָכְלָא תָּדִיר, וְשֵׁצֵי לְהַהוּא מִלָּה דְּשַׁוְיָין לֵיה, דְּהָא בְּכָל מַה דְּאִתְדַּבַּק בֵּיה לְתַתָּא, וְשַׁרְיָא עֲלוֹי הַהוּא נְהוֹרָא תִּכְלָא, שֵׁצֵי לֵיה, וְאָכֵיל לֵיה, בְּגִין דְּאוֹרְחוֹי הוּא לְשֵׁיצָאָה, וּלְמֶהֱוֵי אָכֵיל, דְּהָא בֵּיה תַּלְיָא שֵׁצוּ דְכֹלָּא, מוֹתָא דְכֹלָּא, וּבְגִינֵי כָךְ אִיהִי אָכֵיל, כָּל מַה דְּאִתְדַּבַּק בֵּיה לְתַתָּא.

254. The BLUE LIGHT OF THE CANDLE always consumes and destroys the COARSE object prepared for it, NAMELY THE WICK, because the blue light consumes and burns all that it comes into contact with underneath it. And because its nature is to consume and scorch, it is the source of the destruction and death of all. THE BLUE LIGHT IS THE SECRET OF THE NUKVA, OR THE TREE OF KNOWLEDGE, FROM WHICH DEATH AND DESTRUCTION ORIGINATE. It therefore consumes whatever it links to below.

255. וְהַהוּא נְהוֹרָא חִוָורָא דְּשַׁרְיָא עֲלוֹי, לָא אָכֵיל וְלָא שֵׁצֵי לְעָלְמִין, וְלָא אִשְׁתַּנֵּי נְהוֹרֵיה. וְעַל דָּא אָמַר מֹשֶׁה, כִּי ה' אֱלֹקֶיךָ אֵשׁ אוֹכְלָה הוּא, אוֹכְלָה וַדַּאי, אָכֵיל וְשֵׁצֵי כָּל מַה דְּשַׁרְיָא תְּחוֹתוֹי. וְעַל דָּא אָמַר ה' אֱלֹהֶיךָ, וְלָא אֱלֹקֵינוּ, בְּגִין דְּמֹשֶׁה, בְּהַהוּא נְהוֹרָא חִוָּורָא דִּלְעֵילָא הֲוָה, דְּלָא שֵׁצֵי וְלָא אָכֵיל.

255. The white light that prevails on THE BLUE LIGHT never consumes or destroys, and it never changes color. IT IS THE LIGHT OF CHASSADIM, WHICH NEVER CHANGES OR BECOMES COARSE AND WHICH IS FREE FROM JUDGMENT. THEREFORE, IT DOES NOT DESTROY OR CHANGE. That is why Moses said, "For Hashem your Elohim is a consuming fire." It is because fire consumes and destroys all that is underneath it that MOSES said, "your Elohim" and not "our Elohim." Moses was A CHARIOT FOR the supernal white light that neither burns nor destroys, AND WHICH CANNOT BE TOUCHED BY JUDGMENTS.

256. תָּא חֲזֵי, לֵית לֵיהּ אִתְּעֲרוּתָא, לְאִתְדַּלְּקָא הַאי נְהוֹרָא תִּכְלָא, לְאִתְאַחֲדָא בִּנְהוֹרָא חִוְּורָא, אֶלָּא עַל יְדֵי יִשְׂרָאֵל, דְּאִינּוּן מִתְדַּבְּקָן בֵּיהּ תְּחוֹתוֹי.

256. Come and see: This blue light cannot awaken, kindle, or link to the white light without Yisrael connecting to it from underneath. THIS IS THE SAME AS THE LINKING OF THE WICK TO THE BLUE LIGHT.

257. וְתָא חֲזֵי, אַף עַל גַּב דְּאוֹרְחֵיהּ דְּהַאי נְהוֹרָא תִּכְלָא אוּכְמָא, לְשֵׁיצָאָה כָּל מַה דְּאִתְדַּבַּק בֵּיהּ תְּחוֹתוֹי, יִשְׂרָאֵל מִתְדַּבְּקָן בֵּיהּ תְּחוֹתוֹי, וְקַיְימִין בְּקִיּוּמָא, הֲדָא הוּא דִכְתִיב וְאַתֶּם הַדְּבֵקִים בַּה' אֱלֹקֵיכֶם חַיִּים. בַּה' אֱלֹקֵיכֶם, וְלָא אֱלֹקֵינוּ, בְּהַהוּא נְהוֹרָא תִּכְלָא אוּכְמָא, דְּאָכֵיל וְשֵׁיצֵי, כָּל מַה דְּאִתְדַּבַּק בֵּיהּ תְּחוֹתֵיהּ, וְאַתּוּן מִתְדַּבְּקָן בֵּיהּ וְקַיְימֵי, דִּכְתִיב חַיִּים כֻּלְּכֶם הַיּוֹם.

257. Come and behold: Although it is the nature of this blue – black light to destroy all that contacts it from beneath, Yisrael still cleave to it from beneath and survive. This is written: "But you that did cleave of Hashem your Elohim are all alive every one of you this day." It is written: "of Hashem your Elohim," WHICH IS THE NUKVA, and not, "our Elohim," WHICH WOULD ALLUDE TO ZEIR ANPIN, FOR WHOM MOSES WAS A CHARIOT. HE SAID TO THEM, YOU CLEAVE to the blue and black light that burns and destroys all, but nevertheless you survive, as it is written: "are all alive every one of you this day," BECAUSE THIS BLUE LIGHT DID NOT BURN YOU.

258. וְעַל נְהוֹרָא חִוָּורָא, שַׁרְיָיא לְעֵילָא נְהוֹרָא סְתִימָא דְּאַקִּיף לֵיהּ. וְרָזָא עִלָּאָה הָכָא. וְכֹלָּא תִשְׁכַּח בְּשַׁלְהוֹבָא דְּסָלֵיק, וְחָכְמְתִין דְּעֶלְיוֹנִין בֵּיהּ. אָתָא רַבִּי פִּנְחָס וּנְשָׁקֵיהּ, אָמַר בְּרִיךְ רַחֲמָנָא דְּאִיעֲרַעְנָא הָכָא, אָזְלוּ עִמֵּיהּ דְּרַבִּי פִּנְחָס תְּלַת מִילִין.

258. A concealed light envelops this white light. It is a supernal secret THAT THIS LIGHT REFERS TO THE SUPERNAL LIGHT THAT CLOTHES ZEIR ANPIN, WHICH IS THE WHITE LIGHT. THIS LIGHT CANNOT BE CONCEIVED OR UNDERSTOOD. Everything, INCLUDING THE BLUE, WHITE, AND CONCEALED, SURROUNDING LIGHT, can be found in the rising flame of a candle. And all great wisdoms are insinuated therein. Rabbi Pinchas approached and kissed him saying: Blessed be the Merciful One, who led me to meet you here. They accompanied Rabbi Pinchas for three miles.

259. אֲהַדְרוּ רַבִּי שִׁמְעוֹן וְחַבְרַיָּיא. אָמַר רַבִּי שִׁמְעוֹן הָא דַּאֲמָרָן רָזָא דְחָכְמְתָא אִיהוּ בְּיִחוּדָא קַדִּישָׁא, דִּבְגִין כָּךְ ה"א בַּתְרָאָה דִּשְׁמָא קַדִּישָׁא, אִיהוּ נְהוֹרָא תְּכֵלָּא אוּכְמָא, דְּאִתְאַחִיד בֵּיה"ו, דְּהוּא נְהוֹרָא חִוָּורָא דְּנָהֵיר.

259. When Rabbi Shimon and the friends returned, AFTER ESCORTING RABBI PINCHAS, Rabbi Shimon said: What we said is the secret of wisdom of sacred unification. Consequently, the last Hei of the Holy Name, THE NUKVA, is the blue and black light that links to THE LETTERS Yud-Hei-Vav, NAMELY ZEIR ANPIN, the bright white light.

260. תָּא חֲזֵי, לִזְמְנִין הַאי נְהוֹרָא תְּכֵלָּא ד', וּלְזִמְנִין ה', אֶלָּא בְּזִמְנָא דְּלָא מִתְדַּבְּקָן בֵּיהּ יִשְׂרָאֵל לְתַתָּא, לְאַדְלְקָא לֵיהּ, לְאִתְאַחֲדָא בִּנְהוֹרָא חִוָּורָא, אִיהוּ ד'. וּלְזִמְנָא דְּמִתְעָרֵי לֵיהּ, לְאִתְחַבְּרָא עִם נְהוֹרָא חִוָּורָא, כְּדֵין אִקְרֵי ה'.

260. Come and behold: sometimes the blue light is the letter *Dalet* and sometimes *Hei*. When Yisrael does not connect to it from below, so as to kindle it and connect it to the white light, it is *Dalet*. And when Yisrael

awakens her, BY ELEVATING THE MAYIN NUKVIN (FEMALE WATERS), to connect her with the white light, then it is called *Hei.*

261. מְנָלָן, דִּכְתִיב כִּי יִהְיֶה נַעֲרָה בְתוּלָה, נַעַר כְּתִיב, בְּלָא ה', מ"ט בְּגִין דְּלָא אִתְחַבְּרַת בִּדְכוּרָא, וּבְכָל אֲתַר דְּלָא אִשְׁתַּכְּחוּ דְּכַר וְנוּקְבָא, ה"א לָא אִשְׁתְּכַח, וְסָלְקָא מִתַּמָּן, וְאִשְׁתָּאַר ד'.

261. Whence do we know this? From the words, "If a girl (*na'ara*) is a virgin" (Devarim 22:23), "na'ara" is spelled without a letter *Hei.* What is the reason for this? It is because she has not been linked to a male. And wherever male and female are separate, the letter *Hei* cannot be found. NA'ARA IS THEREFORE SPELLED WITHOUT THE *HEI,* and THE *HEI* ascends, while THE NUKVA stays AS THE LETTER *Dalet,* WHICH ALLUDES TO POVERTY.

262. דְּהָא אִיהִי כָּל זִמְנָא דְּאִתְחַבַּר בִּנְהוֹרָא חִוָּורָא דְּנָהֵיר, אִקְרֵי ה'. דְּהָא כְּדֵין כֹּלָּא אִתְחַבַּר כַּחֲדָא, אִיהִי אִתְדַּבְּקַת בִּנְהוֹרָא חִוָּורָא, וְיִשְׂרָאֵל מִתְדַּבְּקָן בָּהּ, וְקַיְימָא תְּחוֹתָהּ, לְאַדְלָקָא לָהּ, וּכְדֵין כֹּלָּא חַד.

262. Because whenever the blue and black light connect to this bright white light, it is called *Hei,* indicating unity. THE NUKVA cleaves to the white light, and Yisrael cling to her and stand underneath her to kindle her. THROUGH THE FEMALE WATER (MAYIN NUKVIN), THEY RISE TO HER, and unity is found. YISRAEL, BY BRINGING UP THE FEMALE WATER TO HER, KINDLE THE NUKVA AND CAUSES HER TO CLEAVE TO AND JOIN ZEIR ANPIN. WERE IT NOT FOR THE FEMALE WATER, THE NUKVA WOULD NOT HAVE JOINED ZEIR ANPIN. THUS, THEY TOO ARE ATTACHED TO ZEIR ANPIN. THIS IS BECAUSE WHATEVER ONE EFFECTS IN THE UPPER REALMS, HE ALSO MERITS BELOW. HENCE, THE HOLY ONE, THE SHECHINAH, AND YISRAEL BECOME ONE.

263. וְדָא הוּא רָזָא דְּקָרְבָּנָא, דִּתְנָנָא דְּסָלֵיק, אַתְעַר לֵיהּ, לְהַאי נְהוֹרָא תְּכֵלָא לְאַדְלָקָא, וְכַד אִתְדְּלַק, אִתְחַבַּר בִּנְהוֹרָא חִוָּורָא, וּשְׁרַגָּא דָּלֵיק בְּיִחוּדָא חַד.

263. This is the inner purpose of the sacrifice. The smoke rises and kindles the blue light. When it is lit, it links to the white light and then to the candle, MEANING THAT THE SHECHINAH alights in unity. AND WHEN SHE CLEAVES TO THE WHITE LIGHT AND THE SMOKE, THE THREE BECOME ONE.

264. וּבְגִין דְּאָרְחֵיהּ דְּהַאי נְהוֹרָא תְּכֶלָא לְשֵׁיצָאָה, וּלְמֶהֱוֵי אָכֵיל כָּל מַה דְּאִתְדַּבַּק בֵּיהּ תְּחוֹתֵיהּ, כַּד רַעֲוָא אִשְׁתַּכַּח, וּשְׁרַגָּא דָּלֵיק בְּחִבּוּרָא חַד, כְּדֵין כְּתִיב וַתִּפֹּל אֵשׁ ה' וַתֹּאכַל אֶת הָעוֹלָה וְגוֹ'. וּכְדֵין אִתְיְיְדַע, דְּהַהִיא שְׁרַגָּא דָּלֵיק בְּחִבּוּרָא חַד, וְקִשּׁוּרָא חַד. נְהוֹרָא תְּכֶלָא אִתְדַּבַּק בִּנְהוֹרָא חִוְּרָא, וְאִיהוּ חַד. אָכֵיל תְּחוֹתֵיהּ תַּרְבִּין וְעָלָוָון, דְּמַשְׁמַע דְּהָא לָא אָכֵיל תְּחוֹתֵיהּ, אֶלָּא בְּזִמְנָא דְּאִיהוּ סָלֵיק, וְכֹלָּא אִתְקְשַׁר וְאִתְחַבַּר בִּנְהוֹרָא חִוְּרָא, וּכְדֵין שְׁלָמָא דְּעָלְמִין כֻּלְּהוּ, וְכֹלָּא אִתְקְשַׁר בְּיִחוּדָא חַד.

264. The nature of the blue light is to burn and consume all that it contacts from below. When THE SACRIFICE is pleasing and the candle burns in unity, it is written "the fire of Hashem fell, and consumed the burnt offering" (I Melachim 18:38). WHEN ALL HAS BEEN BURNED COMPLETELY, it is known that the candle, WHICH IS THE SHECHINAH, is burning in complete unity, and the blue light, WHICH IS THE NUKVA, has united with the white light, WHICH IS ZEIR ANPIN, and THE TWO have become one. FURTHERMORE, THE BLUE LIGHT BURNS AND consumes the fats and burnt offerings, meaning that it does not burn and consume from beneath, except when it is elevating FOR THE WHITE LIGHT. THIS INDICATES THAT all, INCLUDING THE SMOKE AND THE BLUE LIGHT, link to the white light. Hence, peace is made in all the worlds and all is embraced in unity.

265. וּלְבָתַר דְּסַיֵּים לְשֵׁיצָאָה תְּחוֹתֵיהּ, הַאי נְהוֹרָא תְּכֶלָא. מִתְדַּבְּקָן בֵּיהּ תְּחוֹתֵיהּ, כַּהֲנֵי וְלֵיוָאֵי וְיִשְׂרָאֵל. אִלֵּין בְּחֶדְוָה דְּשִׁיר, וְאִלֵּין בִּרְעוּתָא דְּלִבָּא, וְאִלֵּין בִּצְלוֹתָא. וּשְׁרַגָּא דָּלֵיק עֲלַיְיהוּ, וְאִתְדַּבְּקוּ נְהוֹרִין כְּחַד, וּנְהִירִין עָלְמִין, וּמִתְבָּרְכִין עִלָּאִין וְתַתָּאִין.

265. And when this blue light is through burning and consuming all that is underneath, all the priests and Levites and Yisrael come and cleave onto it. THE LEVITES cleave with the joy of singing; THE PRIESTS with the meditation of their hearts; and YISRAEL with prayer. And the candle, NAMELY THE SHECHINAH, burns and shines upon them. All the lights unify, the worlds glow, and all above and below are blessed.

266. וּכְדֵין וְאַתֶּם הַדְּבֵקִים בַּה' אֱלֹקֵיכֶם חַיִּים כֻּלְּכֶם הַיּוֹם. וְאַתֶּם, אַתֶּם מִבָּעֵי לֵיה, אֶלָּא ו' לְאוֹסְפָא, עַל תַּרְבִּין וְעֶלָוֹון, דְּאִינּוּן מִתְדַּבְּקִין בֵּיה, וְאָכְלִין וְשָׁצָאן. וְאַתּוּן מִתְדַּבְּקָן בֵּיה, בְּהַהוּא נְהוֹרָא תְּכֶלָא אוּכְמָא דְּאָכְלָא, וְאַתּוּן קַיְּימִין, הֲדָא הוּא דִכְתִיב חַיִּים כֻּלְּכֶם הַיּוֹם.

266. Hence the words, "But you that did cleave of Hashem your Elohim are all alive every one of you this day" (Devarim 4:4), APPLY TO YISRAEL. HE ASKS: THE PASSAGE SAYS, "But (Heb. *ve*, Vav) you": Should it not be just "you?" HE ANSWERS, *Vav* shows Yisrael's virtue to that of the offerings and fat, because when the offerings and fat connect to THE BLUE LIGHT, they are consumed and burned. But you cleave to this blue – black light that burns and consumes, yet are alive. THIS VIRTUE IS ALLUDED TO BY THE *VAV* IN "But you...are all alive every one of you this day."

267. כָּל גְּווֹנִין טָבִין לְחֶלְמָא, בַּר מִתְכֶלָא, דְּאִיהוּ אָכֵיל וְשֵׁצֵי תָּדִיר, וְאִיהוּ אִילָנָא דְּבֵיה מוֹתָא, וְשַׁרְיָא עַל עָלְמָא תַּתָּאָה, וּבְגִין דְּכֹלָא שַׁרְיָא תְּחוֹתֵיה, אִיהוּ אָכֵיל וְשֵׁצֵי.

267. In a dream, all colors, except for blue, are a good sign. Blue always destroys and consumes. It is the tree where death is found. IT IS THE NUKVA, WHICH IS CALLED THE TREE OF KNOWLEDGE. It reigns over the lower world, WHICH IS THIS WORLD, and it consumes and destroys everything that exists underneath it.

268. וְאִי תֵימָא, הָכֵי נָמֵי שַׁרְיָא, בִּשְׁמַיָא לְעֵילָא, וְכַמָּה חַיָּלִין אִינּוּן לְעֵילָא, וְכֻלְּהוּ קַיְּימֵי. תָּא חֲזֵי, כָּל אִינּוּן דִּלְעֵילָא בְּהַהוּא נְהוֹרָא תְּכֶלָא אִתְכַּלְּלָן. אֲבָל תַּתָּאֵי לָאו הָכֵי, דְּאִינּוּן מִלָּה גַּסָּה, עָלְמָא דְּקַיְּימָא וְשַׁרְיָא עֲלֵיה, וּבְגִין כָּך אָכֵיל וְשֵׁצֵי לוֹן, וְלֵית לָה מִלָּה אָחֳרָא

לְתַתָּא בְּעָלְמָא, דְּלָא אִשְׁתְּצֵי, בְּגִין דִּנְהוֹרָא תְּכְלָא שֵׁצֵי, לְכָל מַה דְּקַיְימָא עֲלֵיהּ.

268. THE NUKVA OF ZEIR ANPIN is found in the upper heavens, NAMELY THE WORLD OF ATZILUT, and there are many upper hosts IN THE WORLDS OF BRIYAH, YETZIRAH, AND ASIYAH. Yet they live and subsist. SO HOW IS IT, ONE MIGHT ASK, THAT YOU SAY THAT THE BLUE LIGHT, WHICH IS THE NUKVA OF ZEIR ANPIN, CONSUMES ALL THAT IS UNDERNEATH? Come and behold: all the upper HOSTS IN THE WORLDS OF BRIYAH, YETZIRA AND ASIYAH, WHICH ARE HIGHER WORLDS THAN THIS, are included in the blue light itself – NOT UNDERNEATH IT. Yet the lower beings OF THIS WORLD are not INCLUDED IN THE BLUE LIGHT ITSELF, because they are the coarse objects by which the world is supported. THE WORLD LINKS TO THE LOWER BEINGS AND SUBSISTS ON THEM, JUST AS THE WICK OF A CANDLE. WITHOUT IT, THE WORLD WOULD NOT EXIST. Hence, the blue light consumes and destroys them and there can be nothing down here in this world that is not destroyed, because the blue light destroys all that is underneath it.

55. "By forty-five colors of light"

As white sunlight refracts into the seven colors of the spectrum, the Light of The Creator also refracts into colors that produce the diversity of Creation. The Zohar describes the refraction of the supernal Light, and the birth of the countless colors that we experience as joy, bliss, and happiness upon performing a positive spiritual action. Through these passages, we gain a profound connection to all the colors of Light. Our reading literally ignites the extraordinary eruption of color in the Upper Worlds so that all the grades of Light begin to radiate in our souls.

269. בְּאַרְבְּעִין וְחָמֵשׁ גַּוְונֵי זִינֵי נְהוֹרִין, אִתְפְּלֵיג עָלְמָא, שַׁבְעָה מִתְפַּלְּגִין, לְשַׁבְעָה תְּהוֹמִין. כָּל חַד בָּטַשׁ בִּתְהוֹמָא דִילֵיהּ, וַאֲבָנִין מִתְגַּלְגְּלִין בְּגוֹ תְּהוֹמָא. וְעָיֵיל הַהוּא נְהוֹרָא, בְּאִינּוּן אֲבָנִין, וּנְקַב לוֹן, וּמַיָּא נָפְקוּ בְּהוּ, וְשַׁקְעִין כָּל חַד וְחַד, עַל תְּהוֹמָא, וְחַפְיָיא לִתְרֵין סִטְרִין.

269. The world, THE NUKVA OF ZEIR ANPIN, is differentiated by forty-five colors and types of lights. Seven SFIROT divide into seven chasms, each plumbing its own abyss, NAMELY MALCHUT. And stones turn within the abyss, MEANING THAT THEY OVERTURN SO AS TO SHINE DOWNWARD. And the light penetrates and pierces the stones, creating holes through which water flows and is poured into and covers both sides of OF ITS ABYSS.

270. נָפְקוּ מַיָּא בְּאִינּוּן נוּקְבִין, וְעָאל נְהוֹרָא וּבָטַשׁ לְאַרְבַּע סִטְרֵי תְּהוֹמָא, מִתְגַּלְגְּלָא נְהוֹרָא בַּחֲבֶרְתָּהּ, וְאִעָרְעוּ בְּחַד. וּפַלְגִין מַיִין.

270. As the water exits through the holes IN THE STONES, SUPERNAL light OF THE ENDLESS WORLD shines through them and strikes the four sides of the abyss. Each light OF THE FOUR SIDES includes all others AT THE TIME OF STRIKING. They join as one, and the water FROM ZEIR ANPIN splits WITHIN IT.

271. וַאֲחִידָן כָּל אִינּוּן שַׁבְעָה בְּשַׁבְעָה תְּהוֹמֵי, וְכָרְאן בַּחֲשׁוֹכֵי תְּהוֹמָא. וַחֲשׁוֹכֵי אִינּוּן אִתְעָרְבֵי בְּהוֹן, וְסַלְקִין מַיָּא וְנַחֲתִין, וּמִתְגַּלְגְּלִין בְּאִינּוּן

נְהוֹרִין, וְאִתְעָרְבוּ כַּחֲדָא. נְהוֹרִין, וַחֲשׁוֹכִין, וּמַיִין. וְאִתְעֲבִידוּ מִנַּיְיהוּ
נְהוֹרִין דְּלָא אִתְחַזְיָאן, חֲשׁוֹכָאן.

271. The seven SFIROT OF ZEIR ANPIN cling to their seven chasms, OR MALCHUTS, BECAUSE EACH SFIRAH CONTAINS SEVEN SFIROT ONE OF WHICH IS ALSO MALCHUT. They dig in that dark abyss, where darknesses mix with ALL THE SFIROT OF THE NUKVA, And water rises UPWARD FROM BELOW. THAT IS, THE LIGHT OF CHASSADIM, CALLED 'WATER,' WHICH IS THE SECRET OF THE RIGHT COLUMN, FIRST SHINES UPWARD FROM BELOW. And then CHASSADIM fall back down TO THE LEFT COLUMN and links with the lights OF THE LEFT, THE LIGHT OF CHOCHMAH THAT IS DARK. And they all mix together – lights, darknesses, and water – and from them are made dark, invisible lights.

272. בָּטַשׁ כָּל חַד בְּחַבְרֵיהּ, וּמִתְפַּלְּגִין לְשַׁבְעִין וְחָמֵשׁ צִנּוֹרֵי תְּהוֹמָא, וּבְהוּ נָגְדָן מַיָּא. כָּל צִנּוֹרָא וְצִנּוֹרָא סָלִיק בְּקָלֵיהּ, וְאִזְדַּעְזְעָן תְּהוֹמִין, וְכַד הַהוּא קָלָא אִשְׁתְּמַע, כָּל תְּהוֹמָא קָרֵי לְחַבְרֵיהּ וַאֲמַר, פְּלִיג מֵימָךְ וְאֵעוֹל בָּךְ. הֲדָא הוּא דִּכְתִיב תְּהוֹם אֶל תְּהוֹם קוֹרֵא לְקוֹל צִנּוֹרֶיךָ.

272. When each OF THE SEVEN CHASMS OF ZEIR ANPIN has struck its companion, ITS CORRESPONDING ASPECT IN THE ABYSS OF THE NUKVA, they split into 75 channels of the abyss, through which water – MEANING LIGHTS – is channeled. Each pipe raises its voice and the chasms OF THE RECEPTOR are shaken. When the voices are heard, each abyss calls to its companion, "split your waters so, that I can enter within you." As is written: "Deep calls to deep, at the noise of your Your cataracts" (Tehilim 42:8).

273. תְּחוֹת אִלֵּין, תְּלַת מְאָה וְשִׁתִּין וַחֲמִשָּׁה גִּידִין, מִנְּהוֹן חִוָּורִין, מִנְּהוֹן אוּכְמִין, מִנְּהוֹן סוּמָקִין, אִתְכְּלִילוּ דָּא בְּדָא, וְאִתְעֲבִידוּ גַּוַּון חָד. אִינּוּן גִּידִין אִתְרְקִימוּ בְּשַׁבַע עֶשְׂרֵה רְשָׁוָות. וְכָל חַד, רֶשֶׁת גִּידִין אִקְרֵי, אִתְרְקִימוּ דָּא בְּדָא, וְנַחֲתִין בְּשִׁפּוּלֵי תְּהוֹמֵי. תְּחוֹת אִלֵּין, תְּרֵין רִשְׁתִּין קַיְימִין, כְּחֵיזוּ דְּפַרְזְלָא, וּתְרֵין רִשְׁתִּין אַחֲרָנִין כְּחֵיזוּ דִּנְחָשָׁא.

273. Beneath the 75 CHANNELS extend 365 sinews. Some are white, some are black, and some are red. They mix with each other, become included

-176-

within each other, and turn into one color. The 365 sinews are enmeshed in seventeen nets, each of which is called a network of sinews. Enmeshed within each other, they descend to the end of the abyss BECAUSE THEY TOOK ON THE ASPECT OF YESOD, WHICH TERMINATES THE STRUCTURE OF THE LEVEL. Underneath THE SEVENTEEN NETS ARE FOUR MORE. Two nets resemble iron, and two resemble copper.

274. תְּרֵין כָּרְסָוָון קַיְימֵי עֲלַיְיהוּ, חַד מִיָּמִינָא, וְחַד מִשְּׂמָאלָא, כָּל אִינוּן רְשָׁתִין מִתְחַבְּרָן כַּחֲדָא, וּמַיִין נָחֲתִין מֵאִינוּן צִנּוֹרִין, וְעָאלִין בְּאִלֵּין רְשָׁתִין. אִינוּן תְּרֵין כָּרְסָוָון, חַד כָּרְסְיָיא דִּרְקִיעָא אוּכְמָא, וְחַד כָּרְסְיָיא דִּרְקִיעָא סַסְגּוֹנָא.

274. Two pedestals stand OVER ALL THESE ASPECTS, one to the right and one to the left. All the nets join to be one, and the water, WHICH IS THE LIGHTS, flows down the channels and enters the nets. THE CHANNELS, THE NETS, AND ALL THEIR LIGHTS ARE INCLUDED WITHIN these two pedestals. One pedestal is made of the black firmament; the other is made of a firmament that is the color of a badger, WHICH IS REDDISH.

275. אִלֵּין תְּרֵין כָּרְסָוָון, כַּד אִינוּן סָלְקִין, סָלְקִין בְּהַהוּא כָּרְסְיָיא דִּרְקִיעָא אוּכְמָא, וְכַד נָחֲתִין, נָחֲתִין בְּהַהוּא כָּרְסְיָיא דִּרְקִיעָא סַסְגּוֹנָא.

275. When THE LIGHTS rise, THAT IS, WHEN THEY RADIATE UPWARD, they elevate through the pedestal of the black firmament THAT SHINES UPWARD. And when they descend, they do so through the firmament of the badger color THAT SHINES DOWNWARD.

276. אִלֵּין תְּרֵין כָּרְסָוָון, חַד מִיָּמִינָא, וְחַד מִשְּׂמָאלָא. וְהַהוּא כָּרְסְיָיא דִּרְקִיעָא אוּכְמָא, מִיָּמִינָא. וְהַהוּא כָּרְסְיָיא דִּרְקִיעָא סַסְגּוֹנָא, מִשְּׂמָאלָא. כַּד סָלְקִין בְּכָרְסְיָיא דִּרְקִיעָא אוּכְמָא, מָאִיךְ כָּרְסְיָיא דִּרְקִיעָא שְׂמָאלָא, וְנָחֲתִין בֵּיהּ.

276. One of the pedestals is to the right; the other is to the left. The right pedestal is on the black firmament; the left one on the firmament of the badger color. And when THE LIGHTS go up through the pedestal of the

black firmament, the pedestal of the left firmament goes down against it, AND THE LIGHTS go down through it.

277. מִתְגַּלְגְּלִין כָּרְסַוָון, חַד בְּחַד. נָקְטִין כָּל אִינוּן רְשָׁתִּין בְּגַוַוייהוּ, וְעָאלִין לוֹן, בִּשְׁפּוּלָא דִתְהוֹמָא תַּתָּאָה, קָאִים חַד כָּרְסְיָיא, וְסָלֵיק לְעֵילָא מִכָּל אִינוּן תְּהוֹמֵי, וְקָאִים כָּרְסְיָיא אָחֳרָא, לְתַתָּא דְּכָל תְּהוֹמֵי. בֵּין תְּרֵין כָּרְסַוָון אִלֵּין, מִתְגַּלְגְּלִין כָּל אִינוּן תְּהוֹמֵי, וְכָל אִינוּן צִנּוֹרִין אִתְנְעֲצוּ בֵּין תְּרֵין כָּרְסַוָון אִלֵּין.

277. Each pedestal is embraced within the other. Within them, they contain all the nets, and they lure the lights to the very end of the lower abyss. One pedestal rises and elevates above all the chasms. The second remains at the bottom of the chasms. Between them, the chasms revolve and become perfected. As the chasms revolve, the channels are inserted between the two pedestals.

278. שַׁבְעִין וְחָמֵשׁ צִנּוֹרִין אִינוּן, שִׁבְעָה, אִינוּן עִלָּאֵי דְּכֹלָּא, וְכָל אִינוּן אָחֳרָנִין אֲחִידָן בְּהוּ. וְכֻלְּהוּ נְעִיצֵי בְּגַלְגְּלוֹי דְּהַאי כָּרְסְיָיא, בְּסִטְרָא דָא וּנְעִיצִין בְּגַלְגְּלוֹי דְּהַאי כָּרְסְיָיא, בְּסִטְרָא דָא.

278. There is a total of 75 pipes, YET of them, THE SEVEN ABYSSES OF ZEIR ANPIN are superior. They are above the others, which cling to them. The 75 PIPES are inserted in the wheels of the pedestals of the RIGHT and LEFT sides.

279. בְּהוֹן מַיִין סָלְקִין וְנַחֲתִין, אִינוּן דְּנַחֲתִין כָּרָאן בִּתְהוֹמֵי, וּבְקָעֵי לוֹן. אִינוּן דְּסָלְקִין עָאלִין, בְּאִינוּן נוּקְבֵי אַבְנִין, וְסָלְקִין וּמַלְיָין לְשֶׁבַע יַמִּין, עַד כָּאן שִׁבְעָה גַּוְונֵי נְהוֹרִין בְּרָזָא עִלָּאָה.

279. Through THE SEVEN CHASMS OF ZEIR ANPIN, WHICH ARE THE MOST SUPERNAL CHASMS, water, ALLUDING TO LIGHTS, flows up and down. Those that flow down – dig into the chasms and pierce them. These rising lights enter the holes that are pierced in the stones, rise, and then fill

up the seven seas. Thus, WE HAVE EXPLAINED the seven kinds of lights THAT EMANATE from the supernal secret.

280. שִׁבְעָה נְהוֹרִין אָחֲרָנִין, מִתְפַּלְּגִין לְשִׁבְעָה יַמִּים. וְיַמָּא חַד כָּלִיל לוֹן, הַהוּא יַמָּא חָד, אִיהוּ יַמָּא עִלָּאָה, דְּכָלְהוּ שְׁבַע יַמִּין כְּלִילָן בֵּיהּ.

280. Seven other lights divide into seven seas, and one sea includes them all. This one sea is the supernal sea that includes all the other seven seas.

281. שִׁבְעָה נְהוֹרִין אִלֵּין, עָאלִין לְגוֹ הַהוּא יַמָּא, וּמָחָאן לֵיהּ לְיַמָּא, לְשִׁבְעָה סִטְרִין. וְכָל סִטְרָא וְסִטְרָא אִתְפְּלַג לְשִׁבְעָה נַחֲלִין. כִּדְכְתִיב וְהִכָּהוּ לְשִׁבְעָה נְחָלִים וְגו', וְכָל נַחֲלָא וְנַחֲלָא אִתְפְּלַג לְשִׁבְעָה נַהֲרִין. וְכָל נַהֲרָא וְנַהֲרָא אִתְפְּלַג לְשִׁבְעָה אָרְחִין. וְכָל אוֹרְחָא וְאוֹרְחָא אִתְפְּלַג לְשִׁבְעָה שְׁבִילִין. וְכָל מֵימוֹי דְּיַמָּא כֻּלְּהוֹן עָאלִין לְגַוַּויְיהוּ.

281. The seven lights go into the sea – REFERRING TO THIS ONE SUPERNAL LIGHT THAT INCLUDES SEVEN – and strike it. As a result, THIS SEA has seven sides. Each side splits into seven streams, as it is written: "And he shall smite it into seven streams" (Yeshayah 11:15). Each stream then splits into seven rivers, each river splits into seven routes, and each route into seven lanes. And all the waters of the seas flow through them.

282. שִׁבְעָה נְהוֹרִין סָלְקִין וְנַחֲתִין לְשִׁבְעָה סִטְרִין, שִׁבְעָה נְהוֹרִין עִלָּאִין, עָאלִין לְגוֹ יַמָּא. שִׁתָּא אִינוּן, וּמֵחַד עִלָּאָה נָפְקֵי. כְּמָה דְּנָטִיל יַמָּא, הָכֵי פָּלִיג מֵימוֹי לְכָל אִינוּן יַמִּין, לְכָל אִינוּן נְהָרִין.

282. Seven lights ascend and descend in seven directions. Seven supernal lights enter the LOWER sea OF THE SEVEN UPPER SEAS. Nevertheless, they are only six, INSTEAD OF SEVEN, and originate from the supernal one. TOGETHER, THEY ARE CONSIDERED AS SEVEN. And in the same manner that the sea receives, it divides its waters into the other seas and waters.

283. חַד תַּנִּינָא לְתַתָּא, בְּסִטְרָא שְׂמָאלָא, שָׁאט בְּכָל אִינוּן נְהָרִין. אָתֵי בְּסִטַר, קַשְׁקְשׁוֹי כֻּלְּהוֹן תַּקִּיפִין כְּפַרְזְלָא. וּמָטֵי לְשָׁאֲבָא, וְשָׁאִיב אַתְרָה.

וְכָל אִינּוּן נְהוֹרִין אִתְחַשְׁכָּן קַמֵּיהּ, פּוּמֵיהּ וְלִישָׁנֵיהּ מְלַהֲטָא אֶשָׁא חָדוּד לִישָׁנֵיהּ, כְּחַרְבָּא תַּקִּיפָא.

283. There is a serpent below, from the left side, that swims in all the rivers. It comes to the side – THE LEFT SIDE, BECAUSE IT CAN ONLY DRAW SUSTENANCE FROM THE LEFT SIDE OF THE RIVERS. Its scales are strong like iron, REFERRING TO ITS JUDGMENTS, WHICH ARE VERY STRONG. It draws sustenance FROM THE SINS OF LOWER BEINGS and invades the place. All lights in the rivers are thus darkened before the serpent. Its mouth and tongue are blazing fires, its tongue as sharp and tough as a sword – MEANING THAT HIS JUDGMENTS ARE VERY SEVERE, AND THERE IS NO SALVATION FROM HIM.

284. עַד דְּמָטֵי לְמֵיעַל לְמַקְדְּשָׁא, גּוֹ יַמָּא. וּכְדֵין סָאֵיב מַקְדְּשָׁא, וְאִתְחַשְׁכָּן נְהוֹרִין. וּנְהוֹרִין עִלָּאִין סַלְקִין מִן יַמָּא, כְּדֵין יַמָּא מִתְפַּלְגִין מֵימוֹי, בְּסְטַר שְׂמָאלָא, וְיַמָּא קָאֲפֵי, וְלָא נָגְדִין מֵימוֹי.

284. When THE SERPENT enters the temple in the sea, WHICH IS MALCHUT, the temple is defiled, and its lights are extinguished. Thus, the supernal lights, THE LIGHTS OF THE TOP THREE SFIROT, leave the sea. Then, the waters of the sea split and go to the left side. The sea then freezes, and its waters do not flow.

285. וְעַל דָּא רָזָא דְמִלָּה, כְּמָה דִכְתִיב, וְהַנָּחָשׁ הָיָה עָרוּם מִכָּל חַיַּת הַשָּׂדֶה אֲשֶׁר עָשָׂה ה' אֱלֹקִים. רָזָא דְחִוְיָא בִישָׁא, נָחִית מֵעֵילָא לְתַתָּא, וְהוּא שָׁאט עַל אַפֵּי מַיִין מְרִירָן, וְנָחִית לְאַפְתֵּי לְתַתָּא, עַד דְּיִפְּלוּן גּוֹ רִשְׁתּוֹי.

285. This explains the hidden meaning of: "now the serpent was craftier than all the beasts" (Beresheet 3:1). The secret is that the wicked serpent descends from the upper to the lower. IT DRAWS THE LIGHTS OF THE LEFT DOWNWARD, and it swims upon the bitter water. Thus, it went down to ensnare EVE INTO EATING FRUIT FROM THE TREE OF KNOWLEDGE. IT DRAWS THE LIGHTS OF THE LEFT DOWN and ensnares them in his net.

286. הַאי חִוְיָא הִיא מוֹתָא דְעָלְמָא. וְהוּא עָאל בְּמֵעוֹי דְסָתִים דְּבַר נָשׁ, הוּא לִסְטַר שְׂמָאלָא, וְאִית חִוְיָא אַתְרָא דְחַיֵּי, בִּסְטַר יָמִינָא, תַּרְוַויְיהוּ אָזְלֵי עִמֵּיה דְּבַר נָשׁ. כְּמָה דְאוּקְמוּהָ.

286. This serpent is death in the world, BECAUSE IT ENTICED EVE WITH THE TREE OF KNOWLEDGE AND THUS BROUGHT DEATH TO THE WORLD. It penetrates the closed intestine of man – the appendix, which is to the left – FROM WHICH IT DRAWS SUSTENANCE. Another serpent, which brings life, is located in the right side, WHICH IS THE GOOD INCLINATION – THE ONE THAT BRINGS LIFE TO MAN. Both sides – THE GOOD AND EVIL INCLINATIONS – accompany man, as has already been explained.

287 (א). מִכָּל חַיַּת הַשָּׂדֶה, דְּהָא כָּל שְׁאָר חֵיוָן דְּחַקְלָא, לֵית בְּהוּ חַכִּים לְאַבְאָשָׁא כְּהַאי, בְּגִין דְּאִיהוּ זוּהֲמָא דְּדַהֲבָא. וַוי לְמַאן דְּאִתְמְשִׁיךְ אֲבַתְרֵיה. דְּאִיהוּ גָרֵים לֵיה מוֹתָא, וּלְכָל דְּאַתְיָין אֲבַתְרֵיה, וְהָא אוּקְמוּהָ.

287 (A). "…than all the beasts of the field" (Ibid.). WE LEARN FROM THESE WORDS THAT OF ALL THE BEASTS OF THE FIELD, THE KLIPOT, there is none that causes harm as the serpent does, because he is the dross of gold. Woe to him, ALLUDING TO ADAM, who was seduced by the serpent. He brought death upon himself and all who came after him. All of this has been explained already.

287 (ב). אָדָם, אִתְמְשִׁיךְ אֲבַתְרֵיה לְתַתָּא, וְנָחֵית לְמִנְדַּע, בְּכָל מַה דִלְתַתָּא, כְּמָה דִּנְחֵית הָכֵי אִתְמְשִׁיךְ רְעוּתֵיה, וְאָרְחוֹי אֲבַתְרַיְיהוּ, עַד דִּמְטִין לְהַאי חִוְיָא, וְחָמוּ תֵּיאוּבְתֵּיה דְעָלְמָא, וְשָׁטוּ אוֹרְחוֹי בַּאֲתַר דָּא. כְּדֵין קָם וְאִתְמְשִׁיךְ אִיהוּ אֲבַתְרַיְיהוּ דְּאָדָם וְאִתְּתֵיה, וְאִתְדַּבַּק בְּהוֹ, וְגָרֵים לְהוּ מוֹתָא, וּבְכָל דָּרֵי דְּאָתוּ אֲבַתְרֵיה. עַד דִּמְטוּ יִשְׂרָאֵל, לְטוּרָא דְסִינַי, לָא פָּסַק זוּהֲמָא דִילֵיה מֵעָלְמָא, וְהָא אִתְּמַר.

287 (B). Adam was drawn downward after THE SERPENT. He went down to learn of all that is below. As he went down FOR THE PURPOSE OF DRAWING LIGHT FROM ABOVE DOWNWARDS, his desires and his ways were drawn after THE KLIPOT. THIS DRAWING DOWNWARD OF THE LIGHT OF UNION IS THE SECRET OF THE PROHIBITION OF THE TREE OF KNOWLEDGE. SINCE HE INTENDED TO DRAW THE LIGHT DOWNWARD, HE CLEAVED IMMEDIATELY TO THE KLIPOT, EVEN THOUGH HE HAD NOT YET ACTUALLY DRAWN ANY LIGHT. They went down to the serpent and saw the desire of the world. And his ways were swayed to this place OF MALCHUT, WHICH IS THE SECRET OF EATING OF THE TREE OF KNOWLEDGE. Then THE SERPENT was drawn after Adam and his wife. It cleaved onto them WITH ITS FILTH, bringing death to them and all subsequent generations. Its venom did not cease to exist in the world, until Yisrael stood at Mount Sinai. This has already been stated.

56. "They heard...walking in the garden"

When Adam and Eve sinned, they disconnected themselves from The Creator. The secret to reestablishing our own connection can be found in the spiritual concepts of *close* and *distance*. Closeness refers to two entities that possess similarity of form and resemblance of nature. It is our difference of nature – our negative aspect of receiving in contrast to The Creator's positive aspect of sharing – that causes the separation. The rays of Light that resonate from the mystic shapes of the Hebrew letters awaken the sharing nature in our souls. We achieve greater similarity of form with The Creator, which in turns generates greater unity.

288. כֵּיוָן דְּחָטוּ, וְאִתְדַּבְּקוּ בְּאִילָנָא דְּשַׁרְיָא בֵּיהּ מוֹתָא לְתַתָּא. מַה כְּתִיב, וַיִּשְׁמְעוּ אֶת קוֹל ה' אֱלֹקִים מִתְהַלֵּךְ בַּגָּן. מְהַלֵּךְ אֵין כְּתִיב כָּאן, אֶלָּא מִתְהַלֵּךְ תָּא חֲזֵי, עַד לָא חָטָא אָדָם, הֲוָה סָלִיק וְקָאֵים בְּחָכְמָה דִּנְהִירוּ עִלָּאָה. וְלָא הֲוָה מִתְפְּרַשׁ מֵאִילָנָא דְחַיֵּי. כֵּיוָן דְּאַסְגֵּי תֵּיאוּבְתָּא לְמִנְדַּע, וּלְנַחֲתָא לְתַתָּא, אִתְמְשַׁךְ אֲבַתְרַיְיהוּ, עַד דְּאִתְפְּרַשׁ מֵאִילָנָא דְחַיֵּי, וְיָדַע רָע וְשָׁבַק טוֹב, וְעַל דָּא כְּתִיב כִּי לֹא אֵל חָפֵץ רֶשַׁע אַתָּה לֹא יְגוּרְךָ רָע. מַאן דְּאִתְמְשַׁךְ בָּתַר רָע, לֵית לֵיהּ דִּירָה, עִם אִילָנָא דְחַיֵּי.

288. And because they sinned and attached themselves to the tree where death dwells below, it is written: "And they heard the voice of Hashem Elohim walking (Heb. *mit'halech*) in the garden" (Beresheet 3:8). Note that the word is not *mehalech* (walking), WHICH WOULD INDICATE THE MALE GENDER, but *mit'halech,* WHICH INDICATES THE FEMININE GENDER. FOR THE ADDITIONAL LETTER TAV INDICATES THE FEMININE GENDER. Come and behold: Before he sinned, Adam was continually ascending TO HIGHER LEVELS, had access to celestial wisdom, and was never disconnected from the Tree of Life. But he was drawn after the lights and parted from the Tree of Life, descending AND DRAWING DOWN LIGHT FROM ABOVE because of his increasing desire for knowledge. He discovered evil and left good. Thus, it is written: "For You are not El that has pleasure in wickedness, neither shall evil dwell with You" (Tehilim 5:5), because he who is drawn after evil has no dwelling with the Tree of Life.

289. וְעַד לָא חָטָאוּ, הֲווֹ שָׁמְעִין קָלָא מִלְעֵילָא, וַהֲווֹ יָדְעֵי חָכְמְתָא עִלָאָה, וְקַיְּימֵי בְּקִיּוּמָא דְזִיהֲרָא עִלָאָה, וְלָא דָחֲלֵי. כֵּיוָן דְּחָטָאוּ, אֲפִילוּ קָלָא דִלְתַתָּא, לָא הֲוֵי יָכְלִין לְמֵיקַם בֵּיה.

289. And as long as they did not sin, they could hear the divine voice, partake of supernal wisdom, exist within THE MOCHIN OF the holy radiance, and have no fear. But, once they sinned, they could no longer withstand it.

290. כְּגַוְונָא דָא, עַד לָא חָבוּ יִשְׂרָאֵל, בְּשַׁעֲתָא דְקָיְימוּ יִשְׂרָאֵל עַל טוּרָא דְסִינַי, אִתְעֲבַר מִנַּיְיהוּ זוּהֲמָא, דְּהַאי חִוְיָא, דְּהָא כְּדֵין בָּטוּל יֵצֶר הָרָע הֲוָה מֵעָלְמָא, וְדָחוּ לֵיה מִנַּיְיהוּ. וּכְדֵין אִתְאֲחִידוּ בְּאִילָנָא דְחַיֵּי, וְסָלְקוּ לְעֵילָא, וְלָא נָחֲתוּ לְתַתָּא.

290. Similarly, as long as Yisrael did not sin, from the time they stood at Mount Sinai, the filth of this serpent was removed from them. There was a total annulment of the Evil Inclination in the world when Yisrael rejected the serpent. They clung to the Tree of Life, elevated, and did not go down. THIS MEANS THAT THEY ELEVATED THE LIGHT OF THE LEFT FROM BELOW AND DID NOT DRAW ANY LIGHT DOWNWARD. WHICH IS THE ASPECT OF THE TREE OF LIFE.

291. כְּדֵין הֲווֹ יָדְעִין וְחָמָאן אִסְפַּקְלַרְיָאן עִלָאִין, וְאִתְנְהָרִין עֵינַיְיהוּ, וְחָדָאן לְמִנְדַּע וּלְמִשְׁמַע, וּכְדֵין חָגַר לוֹן קֻדְשָׁא בְּרִיךְ הוּא חֲגוֹרִין דְּאַתְוָון דִּשְׁמֵיה קַדִּישָׁא, דְּלָא יֵיכוֹל לְשַׁלְטָאָה עֲלַיְיהוּ, הַאי חִוְיָא, וְלָא יְסָאַב לוֹן כְּקַדְמֵיתָא.

291. Then they knew and saw the holy mirrors. Their eyes were lit and they were happy to know and to hear. Hence, the Holy One, blessed be He, wrapped them with cords made of letters from His Holy Name, so that the serpent could not control them and would not defile them, as before. THIS IS THE SECRET OF THE ORNAMENTS THAT THEY RECEIVED ON MOUNT HOREB.

292. כֵּיוָן דְּחָטְאוּ בָּעֵגֶל, אִתְעֲבַר מִנַּיְיהוּ כָּל אִינּוּן דַּרְגִּין, וּנְהוֹרִין עִלָּאִין, וְאִתְעֲבָרוּ מִנַּיְיהוּ אִינּוּן חֲגִירוּ מְזַיְינִין, דְּאִתְעַטָּרוּ מִשְׁמָא עִלָּאָה קַדִּישָׁא, וְאַמְשִׁיכוּ עֲלַיְיהוּ חִוְיָא בִּישָׁא, כְּמִלְּקַדְּמִין, וְגָרְמוּ מוֹתָא, לְכָל עַלְמָא.

292. And because they sinned with the Calf, all those supernal levels and lights were taken away from them. And all the armed cords, ornamented with the Holy Name, were retrieved. They drew upon them the evil serpent as before and caused death to all the world.

293. וּלְבָתַר מַה כְּתִיב וַיַּרְא אַהֲרֹן וְכָל בְּנֵי יִשְׂרָאֵל אֶת מֹשֶׁה וְהִנֵּה קָרַן עוֹר פָּנָיו וַיִּירְאוּ מִגֶּשֶׁת אֵלָיו. תָּא חֲזֵי, מַה כְּתִיב בְּקַדְמֵיתָא, וַיַּרְא יִשְׂרָאֵל אֶת הַיָּד הַגְּדוֹלָה. וְכֻלְּהוּ חָמָאן זָהֲרִין עִלָּאִין, וּמִתְנַהֲרִין בְּאַסְפַּקְלַרְיָא דְּנָהֲרָא, דִּכְתִיב וְכָל הָעָם רוֹאִים אֶת הַקּוֹלוֹת, וְעַל יַמָּא הֲווֹ חָמָאן וְלָא דָּחֲלִין, דִּכְתִיב זֶה אֵלִי וְאַנְוֵהוּ, לְבָתַר דְּחָטוּ פְּנֵי הַסַּרְסוּר לָא הֲווֹ יָכְלִין לְמֶחֱמֵי, דִּכְתִיב וַיִּירְאוּ מִגֶּשֶׁת אֵלָיו.

293. Subsequently, it is written: "And when Aaron and all the children of Yisrael saw Moses, behold, the skin of his face shone, and they were afraid to come near him" (Shemot 34:30). Come and behold: it is written before, "And Yisrael saw the great hand" (Shemot 14:31). Before, they all saw the divine lights and were enlightened by the shining mirror, WHICH IS ZEIR ANPIN. As it is written: "And all the people saw the voices" (Shemot 20:18). And also upon the sea they saw yet were not afraid, as indicated by the words: "He is my El, and I shall praise Him" (Shemot 15:2). But, after they sinned, they could not withstand the sight of even the mediator, MOSES, as it was written "and they were afraid to come near him."

57. "And the children of Yisrael stripped themselves of their ornaments from Mount Horeb"

The Revelation of Light on Mount Sinai was so great that it extinguished all darkness, including death. When the Israelites sinned by building the Golden Calf, they mirrored Adam's original sin and disconnected from the Light. Death was reborn. Reading this section helps replenish the original volume of Light that existed on Sinai, and arouses the forces of immortality.

294. תָּא חֲזֵי, מַה כְּתִיב בְּהוֹ, וַיִּתְנַצְּלוּ בְּנֵי יִשְׂרָאֵל אֶת עֶדְיָם מֵהַר חוֹרֵב. דְּאִתְעֲבַר מִנַּיְיהוּ אִינוּן מִזַיְינָן, דְּאִתְחַגָּרוּ בְּהוֹן בְּטוּרָא דְסִינַי. בְּגִין דְּלָא יִשְׁלוֹט בְּהוֹ הַהוּא חִוְיָא בִישָׁא, כֵּיוָן דְּאִתְעֲבַר מִנַּיְיהוּ, מַה כְּתִיב וּמֹשֶׁה יִקַּח אֶת הָאֹהֶל וְנָטָה לוֹ מִחוּץ לַמַּחֲנֶה הַרְחֵק מִן הַמַּחֲנֶה.

294. Come and behold: it is written of YISRAEL, "And the children of Yisrael stripped themselves of their ornaments from Mount Horeb" (Shemot 33:5). They were stripped of the ornaments that they received at Mount Sinai, the ornaments intended to prevent the wicked serpent from controlling them. When their ornaments were taken away, it is written: "And Moses took the Tent, and pitched it outside the camp, afar off from the camp" (Ibid. 7).

295. אָמַר רַבִּי אֶלְעָזָר, מַאי הַאי קְרָא, לְגַבֵּי הַאי, אֶלָּא, כֵּיוָן דְּיָדַע מֹשֶׁה דְּאִתְעֲבָרוּ מִנַּיְיהוּ דְיִשְׂרָאֵל אִינוּן זַיְינִין עִלָּאִין, אָמַר, הָא וַדַּאי מִכָּאן וּלְהָלְאָה חִוְיָא בִישָׁא יֵיתֵי לְדַיְירָא בֵּינַיְיהוּ, וְאִי יָקוּם מַקְדְּשָׁא הָכָא בֵּינַיְיהוּ, יִסְתְּאָב. מִיָּד וּמֹשֶׁה יִקַּח אֶת הָאֹהֶל וְנָטָה לוֹ מִחוּץ לַמַּחֲנֶה הַרְחֵק מִן הַמַּחֲנֶה. בְּגִין דְּחָמָא מֹשֶׁה, דְּהָא כְּדֵין יִשְׁלוֹט חִוְיָא בִישָׁא, מַה דְּלָא הֲוָה מִקַּדְמַת דְּנָא.

295. Rabbi Elazar asks: What connection is there between this verse and THE STRIPPING OF THE ORNAMENTS? AND HE ANSWERS: Because Moses knew that supernal protection was stripped from them, WHEN THEY TOOK OFF THEIR ORNAMENTS, it was clear that from now on the wicked serpent would reside among them. If the Temple was erected there, it would be

defiled. Immediately then, "And Moses took the Tent, and pitch it outside the camp, afar off from the camp," because he saw that the wicked serpent would control them, unlike before.

296. וְקָרָא לוֹ אֹהֶל מוֹעֵד, וְכִי לָא הֲוָה בְּקַדְמֵיתָא אֹהֶל מוֹעֵד. אֶלָּא, בְּקַדְמֵיתָא אֹהֶל סְתָם, הַשְׁתָּא אֹהֶל מוֹעֵד. מַאי מוֹעֵד, ר' אֶלְעָזָר אֲמַר לְטַב וְרַבִּי אַבָּא אֲמַר לְבִישׁ. ר' אֶלְעָזָר אֲמַר לְטַב: מַה מוֹעֵד דְּאִיהוּ יוֹם חֶדְוָה, דְּסִיהֲרָא דְּאִתּוֹסְפָא בֵּיהּ קְדוּשָׁה, לָא שָׁלְטָא בֵּיהּ פְּגִימוּתָא. אוֹף הָכָא, קָרָא לַהּ, בִּשְׁמָא דָא, לְאַחֲזָאָה דְּהָא אִתְרְחִיק אֹהֶל מִבֵּינַיְיהוּ, וְלָא אִתְפְּגִים. וְעַל דָּא וְקָרָא לוֹ אֹהֶל מוֹעֵד כְּתִיב.

296. "And he called it the Tent of Meeting (Heb. *moed*)" (Ibid.). HE ASKS: Was it not called the Tent of Meeting before? AND HE ANSWERS: Before then, it was called only a tent, but now it was called it the Tent of Meeting. What is the meaning of *moed* (appointment)? Rabbi Elazar said: For MERIT AND good. Rabbi Aba said: For DISCREDIT AND evil. Rabbi Elazar explains that it was for good, because *moed* means a festive day, which is the happiness of the moon, WHICH IS THE SHECHINAH. Because of the Shechinah's added sanctity, no defects mar Her ON THAT DAY. Hence, he called THE SHECHINAH by the name *MOED*, to show that the Tent, WHICH ALLUDES TO THE SHECHINAH, had alienated Herself from them at the time OF THE SIN OF THE CALF, and thus was not made defective. Hence it was written: "…and he called it the Tent of Meeting."

297. וְרַבִּי אַבָּא אֲמַר לְבִישׁ: דְּהָא בְּקַדְמֵיתָא הֲוָה אֹהֶל סְתָם, כד"א אֹהֶל בַּל יִצְעָן בַּל יִסַּע יְתֵדוֹתָיו לָנֶצַח. וְהַשְׁתָּא אֹהֶל מוֹעֵד. בְּקַדְמֵיתָא, לְמֶיהַב חַיִּין אֲרוּכִין לְעָלְמִין, דְּלָא יִשְׁלוֹט בְּהוֹ מוֹתָא. מִכָּאן וּלְהָלְאָה אֹהֶל מוֹעֵד, כד"א וּבֵית מוֹעֵד לְכָל חַי, הַשְׁתָּא אִתְיְיהִיב בֵּיהּ זִמְנָא וְחַיִּין קְצוּבִין לְעָלְמָא, בְּקַדְמֵיתָא לָא אִתְפְּגִים, וְהַשְׁתָּא אִתְפְּגִים. בְּקַדְמֵיתָא, חַבְרוּתָא וְזִוּוּגָא דְּסִיהֲרָא בְּשִׁמְשָׁא דְּלָא יַעֲדוּן. הַשְׁתָּא, אֹהֶל מוֹעֵד זִוּוּגָא דִּלְהוֹן מִזְּמַן לִזְמַן, וּבְגִינֵי כָּךְ, וְקָרָא לוֹ אֹהֶל מוֹעֵד, מַה דְּלָא הֲוָה קוֹדֶם.

57. "And the children of Yisrael stripped themselves of their ornaments from Mount Horeb"

297. Rabbi Aba said: IT WAS CALLED *MOED* SO AS to show unworthiness. AFTER THE GIVING OF TORAH, THE SHECHINAH was a mere tent, as it is written: "a tent that shall not be taken down; its pegs shall not be removed for ever" (Yeshayah 33:20), AND IT WAS CONTINUOUSLY ILLUMINATED. But now, AFTER THE SIN OF THE GOLDEN CALF, it was called the Tent of Meeting, BECAUSE IT WAS ONLY ILLUMINATED FROM TIME TO TIME. Before, it gave long life to the world, and death was powerless. AFTER THE GIVING OF TORAH, THERE WAS FREEDOM FROM THE ANGEL OF DEATH. But, after THE SIN OF THE CALF, THE SHECHINAH became the Tent of Meeting (also: 'appointment'), as it is written: "the house appointed (Heb. *moed*) to all living" (Iyov 30:23). Now it is governed by time, and life is limited in the world. Earlier, BEFORE THE SIN OF THE CALF, THE TENT was not faulty, but now it was rendered defective BY THE SIN OF THE CALF. Before, that mating between the sun and the moon – BETWEEN MALE AND FEMALE – was continuous. Now it is the Tent of Meeting, because their mating is only periodic, BECAUSE THEIR MATING CEASES WHEN THE SERPENT COMES CLOSE. Hence, it was now called the Tent of Meeting, WHICH MEANS THAT UNION OCCURRED ONLY PERIODICALLY.

298. רַבִּי שִׁמְעוֹן הֲוָה יָתֵיב לֵילְיָא חַד וְלָעֵי בְּאוֹרַיְיתָא, וַהֲווֹ יַתְבֵי קַמֵּיהּ רַבִּי יְהוּדָה, וְרַבִּי יִצְחָק, וְרַבִּי יוֹסֵי. אָמַר רַבִּי יְהוּדָה, הָא כְּתִיב וַיִּתְנַצְּלוּ בְּנֵי יִשְׂרָאֵל אֶת עֶדְיָם מֵהַר חוֹרֵב, וְקָאַמְרִינָן דְּגָרְמוּ מוֹתָא עֲלַיְיהוּ, מֵהַהוּא זִמְנָא וּלְעֵילָא, וְשַׁלִּיט בְּהוּ הַהוּא חִוְיָא בִּישָׁא, דְּאַעֲדוּ לֵיהּ מִנַּיְיהוּ בְּקַדְמֵיתָא. יִשְׂרָאֵל תֵּינַח. יְהוֹשֻׁעַ דְּלָא חָטָא אַעֲדֵי מִנֵּיהּ הַהוּא זַיְינָא עִלָּאָה דְּקַבֵּל עִמְּהוֹן בְּטוּרָא דְסִינַי אוֹ לָא.

298. Rabbi Shimon stayed up one night and was busy with Torah. Before him sat Rabbi Yehuda, Rabbi Yitzchak and Rabbi Yosi. Rabbi Yehuda said: It is written: "And the children of Yisrael stripped themselves of ornaments from Mount Horeb" and we explained, that in so doing, they brought death upon themselves and all future generations. And the serpent governed them, although they had earlier removed it from their midst, AS IT WAS SAID THAT THEY HAD FREEDOM FROM THE ANGEL OF DEATH. HE THEN ASKS: This applies to Yisrael, because they sinned, but what about Joshua who did not sin? HE ASKS: Did he also separate from that supernal ornament that he had received with Yisrael on Mount Sinai, or not?

299. אִי תֵּימָא דְּלָא אַעֲדֵי מִנֵּיהּ, אִי הָכֵי אַמַּאי מִית כִּשְׁאָר בְּנֵי נָשָׁא. אִי תֵּימָא דְּאִתְעֲדֵי מִנֵּיהּ, אַמַּאי. וְהָא לָא חָטָא, דְּהָא אִיהוּ עִם מֹשֶׁה הֲוָה, בְּשַׁעֲתָא דְּחָבוּ יִשְׂרָאֵל. וְאִי תֵּימָא דְּלָא קַבֵּיל הַהוּא עִטְרָא בְּטוּרָא דְּסִינַי, כְּמָה דְּקַבִּילוּ יִשְׂרָאֵל, אַמַּאי.

299. If it was not taken away from him, then why did he die like any other man? And if it was taken away from him, then why? He did not sin, having been with Moses at the time that Yisrael sinned. And if you say that JOSHUA was not crowned at Mount Sinai with the rest of Yisrael, then why? WHY WAS JOSHUA DIFFERENT FROM THE REST OF YISRAEL?

300. פְּתַח וַאֲמַר, כִּי צַדִּיק ה' צְדָקוֹת אָהֵב יָשָׁר יֶחֱזוּ פָנֵימוֹ. הַאי קְרָא אֲמָרוּ בֵּיהּ חַבְרַיָּיא מַאי דְּקָאֲמָרוּ. אֲבָל כִּי צַדִּיק ה', צַדִּיק הוּא, וּשְׁמֵיהּ צַדִּיק וּבְגִינֵי כָּךְ, צְדָקוֹת אָהֵב.

300. He said, "For Hashem is righteous and loves righteousness, and the upright behold His face" (Tehilim 11:7). And the friends have commented on this verse that Hashem, NAMELY ZEIR ANPIN, is righteous, and His name, NAMELY THE NUKVA OF ZEIR ANPIN, is righteous. For that reason He loves righteousness, THAT IS, HE LOVES THE UNION OF THE RIGHTEOUS (HEB. TZADIK) AND RIGHTEOUSNESS (HEB. TZEDEK) TO BESTOW CHARITY (HEB. TZEDAKAH).

301. יָשָׁר: אִיהוּ יָשָׁר כד״א צַדִּיק וְיָשָׁר. וְעַל דָּא, יֶחֱזוּ פָנֵימוֹ, כָּל בְּנֵי עָלְמָא, וִיתַקְנוּ אָרְחַיְיהוּ, לְמֵיהַךְ בְּאֹרַח מֵישָׁר, כִּדְקָא יָאוּת. תָּא חֲזֵי, כַּד דָּאִין קוּדְשָׁא בְּרִיךְ הוּא עָלְמָא, לָא דָן לֵיהּ אֶלָּא לְפוּם רוּבָּן דִּבְנֵי נָשָׁא.

301. He is also upright as is said, "righteous and upright." Thus, all the people of the world "behold His face," BLESSED BE HE, improving their ways and following the right path. FOR EVENTUALLY ALL THE WORLD WILL FOLLOW THAT PATH ANYWAY. Come and see: ACCORDING TO THIS, when

the Holy One, blessed be He, judges the world, He does so according to the majority of people.

302. וְתָא חֲזֵי, כַּד חָב אָדָם בְּאִילָנָא דַּאֲכַל מִנֵּיהּ, גָּרַם לְהַהוּא אִילָנָא, דְּשָׁרֵי בֵּיהּ מוֹתָא לְכָל עָלְמָא. וְגָרִים פְּגִימוּ לְאַפְרָשָׁא אִתְּתָא מִבַּעֲלָהּ. וְקָאִים חוֹבָה דִּפְגִימוּ דָא בְּסִיהֲרָא, עַד דְּקָיְימוּ יִשְׂרָאֵל בְּטוּרָא דְסִינַי. כֵּיוָן דְּקָיְימוּ יִשְׂרָאֵל בְּטוּרָא דְסִינַי, אִתְעֲבַר הַהוּא פְּגִימוּ דְּסִיהֲרָא, וְקָיְימָא לְאַנְהָרָא תָּדִיר.

302. Come and behold: When Adam sinned by eating of the tree, he brought death to the whole world. He caused a defect that separated a woman from her husband, NAMELY THE NUKVA FROM ZEIR ANPIN. This sin, or defect, was imprinted upon the moon, WHICH IS THE NUKVA, until the time when Yisrael stood at Mount Sinai. When they were at Mount Sinai, the defect was wiped out from the moon, which was enabled to shine forever. THAT IS, AFTER THE DEFECT OF THE SIN OF THE TREE OF KNOWLEDGE WAS REMOVED, SHE RETURNED TO MATE WITH ZEIR ANPIN IN A NEVERENDING UNION. THUS, SHE FOREVER SHINES WITHOUT DIMINUTION AND THEY OBTAINED THE SECRET OF FREEDOM FROM THE ANGEL OF DEATH AT THAT TIME.

303. כֵּיוָן דְּחָבוּ יִשְׂרָאֵל בַּעֲגְלָא, תָּבַת כְּמִלְּקַדְמִין סִיהֲרָא לְאִתְפַּגְּמָא, וְשָׁלְטָא חִוְיָא בִישָׁא, וְאָחִיד בָּהּ, וּמָשִׁיךְ לָהּ לְגַבֵּיהּ. וְכַד יָדַע מֹשֶׁה דְּחָבוּ יִשְׂרָאֵל, וְאִתְעֲבַר מִנַּיְיהוּ אִינּוּן זַיְינִין קַדִּישִׁין עִלָּאִין, יָדַע וַדַּאי דְּהָא חִוְיָא אָחִיד בָּהּ בְּסִיהֲרָא, לְאַמְשָׁכָא לָהּ לְגַבֵּיהּ, וְאִתְפַּגְּמַת, כְּדֵין אַפִּיק לָהּ לְבַר.

303. When Yisrael sinned with the calf, the moon became defective as it was before THE GIVING OF THE TORAH. The evil serpent regained control over her, held her, and drew her to him. When Moses realized that Yisrael had sinned and that the holy supernal ornaments had been taken away from them, he knew with certainty that the serpent had control over the moon, WHICH IS THE NUKVA. He knew that it was drawing her to it and that she was becoming defective. That is when he isolated her. THAT IS WHAT IS

MEANT BY, "AND MOSES TOOK THE TENT, AND PITCH IT OUTSIDE THE CAMP." THE TENT IS THE SHECHINAH, AS MENTIONED ABOVE.

304. וְכֵיוָן דְּקַיְימָא לְאִתְפַּגְמָא, אַף עַל גַּב דִּיהוֹשֻׁעַ קָאֵים בְּעִטְרָא דְזַיְינִין דִּילֵיהּ כֵּיוָן דִּפְגִימוּ שַׁרְיָא בָּהּ, וְאִתְהַדְרַת כְּמָה דְּאִתְפַּגְימַת בְּחוֹבָא דְאָדָם, לָא יָכִיל בַּ"נ לְאִתְקַיְימָא בַּר מֹשֶׁה, דַּהֲוָה שַׁלִּיט בָּהּ, וּמוֹתֵיהּ הֲוָה בְּסִטְרָא אָחֳרָא עִלָּאָה. וְעַל דָּא, לָא הֲוָה רְשׁוּ בָּהּ, לְקַיְימָא לִיהוֹשֻׁעַ תָּדִיר, וְלָא לְאָחֳרָא, וְעַל כָּךְ, אֹהֶל מוֹעֵד קָרֵי לֵיהּ, אֹהֶל דְּהָא שַׁרְיָא בֵּיהּ, זְמַן קָצִיב לְכָל עָלְמָא.

304. She was blemished and defective, having reverted to her state, as after the sin of Adam. Therefore, although Joshua was still adorned and crowned with ornaments, no man can live forever anymore. The only exception to this rule was Moses, who had control over her, and whose supernal death WAS CALLED THE KISS OF DEATH OF ZEIR ANPIN. THIS IS AS WRITTEN, "SO MOSES, THE SERVANT OF HASHEM DIED ACCORDING TO THE WORD OF HASHEM" (DEVARIM 34:5), BECAUSE MOSES WAS THE SUSTAINER OF THE NUKVA, AND NOT HER RECIPIENT, AS WERE THE REST OF THE PEOPLE. HENCE THE FAULT IN THE NUKVA HAD NO EFFECT ON HIM. THE NUKVA did not have permission to keep Joshua, nor anyone else, alive forever. Hence, it was called the Tent of Appointment, NAMELY A TENT that has a time limitation for the whole world, MEANING THAT EVERYONE HAD TO DIE.

305. וְעַל דָּא רָזָא דְמִלָּה, אִית יָמִינָא לְעֵילָא, וְאִית יָמִינָא לְתַתָּא. אִית שְׂמָאלָא לְעֵילָא, וְאִית שְׂמָאלָא לְתַתָּא. אִית יָמִינָא לְעֵילָא, בִּקְדוּשָׁה עִלָּאָה. וְאִית יָמִינָא לְתַתָּא, דְּאִיהוּ בְּסִטְרָא אָחֳרָא.

305. The inner meaning of all this is that there is right above as there is right below. There ALSO is left above and below. HE CONTINUES BY SAYING THAT there is a right in the supernal holiness – NAMELY MALE AND FEMALE. And there is a right below on the Other Side – NAMELY THE KLIPOT.

306. אִית שְׂמָאלָא לְעֵילָא, בִּקְדוּשָׁה עִלָּאָה, לְאִתְעָרָא רְחִימוּתָא, לְאִתְקַשְּׁרָא סִיהֲרָא בַּאֲתַר קַדִּישָׁא לְעֵילָא לְאִתְנַהֲרָא. וְאִית שְׂמָאלָא

57. "And the children of Yisrael stripped themselves of their ornaments from Mount Horeb"

לְתַתָּא, דְּאַפְרֵישׁ רְחִימוּתָא דִּלְעֵילָא, וְאַפְרֵישׁ לָהּ מִלְאַנְהָרָא בְּשִׁמְשָׁא, וּלְאִתְקָרְבָא בַּהֲדֵיהּ. וְדָא הוּא סִטְרָא דְּחִוְיָא בִּישָׁא.

306. There is a left above in supernal holiness that arouses love, so that the moon can connect to a holy place above, and shine FROM THERE. BECAUSE WHEN ZEIR ANPIN IS CHANNELING THE LIGHT OF THE LEFT TO THE NUKVA, SHE IS CONSOLED BY HIM AND PERMITS HIM TO MATE AND GIVE HER LIGHT. There is a left SIDE below, ON THE OTHER SIDE. It disrupts the supernal love, blocking the moon, WHICH IS THE NUKVA, from shining by the sun, WHICH IS ZEIR ANPIN, and from coming close to him AND MATING WITH HIM. This is the aspect of the evil serpent.

307. דְּכַד שְׂמָאלָא דָּא דִלְתַתָּא אִתְּעֲרַת, כְּדֵין מָשִׁיךְ לָהּ לְסִיהֲרָא, וְאַפְרֵישׁ לָהּ מִלְעֵילָא, וְאִתְחֲשַׁךְ נְהוֹרָאָהּ, וְאִתְדַּבְּקַת בְּחִוְיָא בִּישָׁא. וּכְדֵין שְׁאִיבַת מוֹתָא לְתַתָּא לְכֹלָּא, וְאִתְדַּבְּקַת בְּחִוְיָא וְאִתְרַחֲקַת מֵאִילָנָא דְּחַיֵּי.

307. And when this lower left, THE SERPENT, is aroused, it draws the moon, THE NUKVA OF ZEIR ANPIN, TOWARD IT and separates her from above, FROM ZEIR ANPIN. Her radiance darkens, and she cleaves to the evil serpent and draws death to the whole world. For she links with the serpent and alienates herself from the Tree of Life, THAT IS ZEIR ANPIN. HENCE, HER CONNECTION WITH THE TREE OF LIFE IS NOT CONTINUOUS, BUT PERIODIC, AND THE LIFE SHE GETS FROM HIM IS ALSO PERIODIC.

308. וְעַל דָּא גְּרִים מוֹתָא לְכָל עָלְמָא, וְדָא הוּא, דִּכְדֵין אִסְתְּאָבַת מַקְדְּשָׁא, עַד זְמַן קָצִיב, דְּאִתְקָנַת סִיהֲרָא וְתָבַת לְאַנְהָרָא, וְדָא הוּא אֹהֶל מוֹעֵד. וְעַל דָּא, יְהוֹשֻׁעַ לָא מִית, אֶלָּא בְּעֵיטָא שֶׁל נָחָשׁ דָּא דְּקָרֵיב וּפָגִים מַשְׁכְּנָא, כִּדְקַדְמֵיתָא.

308. When the Temple, WHICH IS THE NUKVA, was defiled, death was caused to the world for the period of time until the moon, WHICH IS THE NUKVA, is corrected and resumes her radiance. She is now called the Tent of Meeting, WHICH INDICATES A LIMITED PERIOD OF TIME, BECAUSE

HER UNION WAS DISRUPTED BY THE PROXIMITY OF THE SERPENT. Hence, Joshua died only because of the serpent, which came close to and caused the Tabernacle, THE NUKVA, to be blemished, as in the beginning – AS BEFORE THE GIVING OF TORAH.

309. וְדָא הוּא רָזָא, דִּכְתִיב וִיהוֹשֻׁעַ בֶּן נוּן נַעַר לֹא יָמִישׁ מִתּוֹךְ הָאֹהֶל. דְּאַף עַל גַּב דְּאִיהוּ נַעַר לְתַתָּא, לְקַבְּלָא נְהוֹרָא, לֹא יָמִישׁ מִתּוֹךְ הָאֹהֶל. כְּמָה דְּאִתְפְּגִים דָּא, הָכֵי נָמֵי אִתְפְּגִים דָּא. אַף עַל גַּב דְּזַיְינָא קַדִּישָׁא הֲוָה לֵיהּ, כֵּיוָן דְּאִתְפְּגִים סִיהֲרָא, הָכֵי הוּא וַדַּאי, לָא אִשְׁתְּזֵיב בִּלְחוֹדוֹי מִנֵּיהּ, מֵהַהוּא גַּוְונָא מַמָּשׁ.

309. This is the inner meaning of, "but his servant Joshua, the son of Nun, a young man, did not depart out of the Tent" (Shemot 33:11). Even though he was a young man below, he received light FROM THE NUKVA BECAUSE HIS CAPACITY WAS AUGMENTED TO BE CONSIDERED LIKE THE ANGEL METATRON. METATRON IS CALLED A YOUNG MAN BELOW ATZILUT. Nevertheless, he "did not depart out of the Tent" (Ibid.), WHICH ALSO MEANS THAT HE WAS NO BETTER THAN THE TENT ITSELF, THE NUKVA. As THE TENT was deformed, so was JOSHUA. And although he still had the holy ornaments, when the moon became defective Joshua could not escape alone from that very defect. THIS MEANS THAT THE SAME DEFECT, WHICH WAS CAUSED BY THE SIN OF YISRAEL, AFFECTED BOTH THE MOON AND JOSHUA.

310. תָּא חֲזֵי, כְּגַוְונָא דָא כֵּיוָן דְּחָב אָדָם, נָטַל קוּדְשָׁא בְּרִיךְ הוּא מִנֵּיהּ אִינוּן זַיְינֵי אַתְוָון, נְהִירִין קַדִּישִׁין, דְּאַעֲטַר לֵיהּ קוּדְשָׁא בְּרִיךְ הוּא. וּכְדֵין דָּחֲלוּ, וְיָדְעוּ דְּהָא אִתְפְּשַׁטוּ מִנַּיְיהוּ, הה"ד וַיֵּדְעוּ כִּי עֵרוּמִים הֵם. בְּקַדְמֵיתָא הֲווֹ מִתְלַבְּשָׁן בְּאִינוּן כִּתְרֵי יְקָר מִזַיְינִין, דְּאִינוּן חִירוּ מִכֹּלָּא. כֵּיוָן דְּחָבוּ, אִתְפְּשַׁטוּ מִנַּיְיהוּ. וּכְדֵין יָדַע, דְּהָא מוֹתָא קָרֵי לוֹן, וְיָדְעוּ דְּאִתְפְּשִׁיטוּ מֵחֵירוּ דְּכֹלָּא, וְגָרְמוּ מוֹתָא לוֹן וּלְכָל עָלְמָא.

310. Come and behold: Similarly, when Adam sinned WITH THE TREE OF KNOWLEDGE, the Holy One, blessed be He, took away his ornaments – the luminous and sacred letters with which He had crowned him, NAMELY THE

57. "And the children of Yisrael stripped themselves of their ornaments from Mount Horeb"

LETTERS THAT FORM THE HOLY NAME. Hence, they saw and knew the meaning of removing their ornaments, as it is written: "They knew that they were naked" (Beresheet 3:7). Beforehand, they were clothed with precious, armed crowns, which gave them freedom from all. After sinning, those PRECIOUS CROWNS were taken from them. They knew then that death called for them, that they were stripped of that freedom from all, and that they had brought death upon themselves and the world.

58. "And they sewed fig leaves together"

Here the totality of spiritual wisdom is conveyed through the metaphor of a seed. The unfolding of this wisdom is personified through the metaphor of a grown Tree – that is, the Tree of Life and Tree of Knowledge. The evil intention to utilize this wisdom for negative purposes is conveyed through the symbol of the fig leaf. *Adam and Eve wearing fig leaves* denotes their dabbling in the dark side of wisdom. These verses can help prevent ourselves from falling into the negativity.

311. וַיִּתְפְּרוּ עֲלֵה תְאֵנָה. הָא אוֹקִימְנָא, דְּאוֹלִיפוּ כָּל זַיְינֵי חֲרָשִׁין וְקוֹסְמִין, וַאֲחִידוּ בְּהַאי דִלְתַתָּא. כְּמָה דְּאִתְּמָר. וְהַהִיא שַׁעֲתָא אִתְגְּרַע זְקִיפוּ וְקוֹמָה דְּאָדָם מֵאָה אַמִּין. וּכְדֵין אִתְעֲבֵיד פְּרוּדָא, וְקָאִים אָדָם בְּדִינָא, וְאִתְלַטְיָא אַרְעָא. וְהָא אוֹקִימְנָא.

311. "And they sewed fig leaves together" (Beresheet 3:7). From these words, we learn that they learned all types of magical spells and sorcery and that they cleaved onto the lower one, WHICH IS THE OTHER SIDE, as was explained. Consequently, the height of Adam was reduced to 100 cubits, and a separation BETWEEN ZEIR ANPIN AND THE NUKVA was effected. Now, Adam lived under Judgment, and the earth was cursed, as has been explained.

59. "So He drove out the man"

Our lives are the sum of our decisions and the paths we've chosen to walk. The moment we choose a path, we immediately invite the totality of spiritual forces associated with that path into our life. We are thrust into a whole new world.

According to the Kabbalist, all possible paths exist in parallel universes. We switch universes at the moment we choose a path, as if we'd walked out of one movie to enter another movie that's far more enjoyable. The power to choose which "movie" of life we experience resides in our choices and spiritual actions.

We are now receiving the spiritual enlightenment to always know the right path. By so doing, we envelope ourselves in all things positive.

312. וַיְגָרֶשׁ אֶת הָאָדָם, אָמַר רַבִּי אֶלְעָזָר לָא יִדַעְנָא מָאן עָבֵיד תֵּרוּכִין לְמָאן, אִי קֻדְשָׁא בְּרִיךְ הוּא עָבַד תֵּרוּכִין לְאָדָם, אִי לָא. אֲבָל מִלָּה אִתְהַפִּיךְ, וַיְגָרֶשׁ אֶת, אֶת דַיְיקָא. וּמָאן גֵּרַשׁ אֶת, הָאָדָם. הָאָדָם וַדַּאי גֵּרַשׁ אֶת.

312. "So He drove out the man" (Beresheet 3:24). Rabbi Elazar asks: Who drove whom out? Could it have been the Holy One, blessed be He, who expelled Adam? BECAUSE IT WAS NOT WRITTEN THAT HASHEM DROVE MAN OUT, JUST "HE DROVE OUT THE MAN." The particle ET ('THE') BEFORE "THE MAN" is reversed. IT SHOULD HAVE BEEN, 'man drove out Et.' IN THE WORDS "DROVE OUT ET," THE PARTICLE ET CLEARLY INDICATES THE SHECHINAH. Adam certainly did drive out Et, BUT THE WORDS ARE REVERSED.

313. וּבְגִין דָּא כְּתִיב, וַיְשַׁלְחֵהוּ ה' אֱלֹהִים מִגַּן עֵדֶן, אַמַאי וַיְשַׁלְחֵהוּ, בְּגִין דְּגֵרַשׁ אָדָם אֶת, כִּדְקָאֲמָרָן. וַיִּשְׁכֵּן: אִיהוּ אַשְׁרֵי לוֹן בַּאֲתַר דָּא, דְּאִיהוּ גָּרֵים, וְסָתִים אוֹרְחִין וּשְׁבִילִין, וְאַשְׁרֵי דִּינִין עַל עָלְמָא, וְאַמְשִׁיךְ לְוָוטִין, מֵהַהוּא יוֹמָא וּלְעֵילָא.

313. Hence, it was written before: "therefore Hashem sent him out of the Garden of Eden" (Ibid. 23). Why was it written that He sent him out?

Because Adam expelled *Et,* WHICH IS THE SHECHINAH, as we have said. THEREFORE "HASHEM SENT HIM OUT OF THE GARDEN OF EDEN." IT IS THEN WRITTEN, JUST "And He placed" (Ibid. 24), instead of, 'and Hashem placed.' This is because it was Adam who placed THE CHERUBS at this place, because he has brought about the blocking of the SUPERNAL paths and ways. SUSTENANCE WAS WITHHELD, Judgment was brought upon the world, and curses have been upon the world ever since.

314. וְאֶת לַהַט הַחֶרֶב הַמִּתְהַפֶּכֶת. כָּל אִינוּן דִּשְׁרָיָין בְּקוֹזְפֵי דִינִין עַל עָלְמָא, דְּמִתְהַפְּכִין לְגַוְונִין סַגִּיאִין, בְּגִין לְאִתְפָּרְעָא מֵעָלְמָא. לְזִמְנִין גּוּבְרִין, לְזִמְנִין נָשִׁין, לְזִמְנִין אֶשָּׁא מְלַהֲטָא, וּלְזִמְנִין רוּחִין, דְּלֵית מָאן דְּקָאֵים בְּהוּ. וְכָל דָּא, לִשְׁמוֹר אֶת דֶּרֶךְ עֵץ הַחַיִּים, דְּלָא יוֹסִיפוּן לְאַבְאָשָׁא כְּקַדְמֵיתָא.

314. "And the bright blade of a revolving sword" (Ibid.) refer to those who effect Judgments in the world. THEY KEEP LEAPING FROM ONE SHAPE TO ANOTHER AND FROM ONE MANIFESTATION TO ANOTHER. They keep changing into many shapes, so as to make the world pay its dues. Sometimes they manifest as men; other times as women. At times they are scorching fires, and at times they are spirits. And no one can control them. All this is "to guard the way of the Tree of Life" (Ibid.) to prevent them from doing harm as they did before.

315. לַהַט הַחֶרֶב. אִינוּן דִּמְלַהֲטָאן אֶשָּׁא וְקוֹסְטִירֵי עַל רָאשֵׁיהוֹן דְּרַשִׁיעַיָּא וְחַיָּיבַיָּא, וּמִתְהַפְּכִין גַּוְונִין לְכַמָּה זַיְינִין, לְפוּם אָרְחַיְיהוּ דִּבְנֵי נָשָׁא. וְעַל דָּא לַהַט, כְּמָא דְאַתְּ אָמֵר וְלַהֵט אוֹתָם הַיּוֹם הַבָּא וְגו'. וְהָא אִתְּמָר.

315. "The bright blade of a revolving" are all those who blaze fire and severe punishment upon the heads of the wicked and the sinners. The shapes change themselves into several kinds of judgments, according to the actions of the humans. They are CALLED bright, as it is written: "and the day that is coming shall burn them up" (Malachi 3:19).

316. הַחֶרֶב: דָּא חֶרֶב לַה'. כד"א חֶרֶב לַה' מָלְאָה דָם וְגו'. אָמַר רַבִּי

יְהוּדָה, לַהַט הַחֶרֶב, כָּל אִינּוּן קַסְטְרִין דִּלְתַתָּא, דְּמִתְהַפְּכִין מִדִּיוֹקְנָא לְדִיוֹקָנָא, כֻּלְּהוֹן מְמַנָּן עַל עָלְמָא לְאַבְאָשָׁא, וּלְאַסְטָאָה לוֹן לְחַיָּיבֵי עָלְמָא, דְּעָבְרִין עַל פִּקוּדֵי דְמָארֵיהוֹן.

316. THEY ARE CALLED "swords," which is "the sword of Hashem" as it is written: "The sword of Hashem is filled with blood" (Yeshayah 34:6). Rabbi Yehuda said that the flames of the sword are the avengers below, IN THIS WORLD, who change from one shape to another. They are given charge of harming and accusing the wicked, who transgress their Master's commands.

317. תָּא חֲזֵי, כֵּיוָן דְּחָב אָדָם, אַמְשִׁיךְ עֲלֵיהּ כַּמָּה זַיְינִין בִּישִׁין, וְכַמָּה גַּרְדִינֵי נְמוּסִין, וְדָחִיל מִכֻּלְּהוֹ, וְלָא יָכִיל לְקַיְימָא עֲלַיְיהוּ. שְׁלֹמֹה יָדַע חָכְמְתָא עִלָּאָה, וְשַׁוִּוי לֵיהּ קֻדְשָׁא בְּרִיךְ הוּא עִטְרָא דְמַלְכוּתָא, וַהֲווֹ דָחֲלֵי מִנֵּיהּ כָּל עָלְמָא. כֵּיוָן דְּחָב אַמְשִׁיךְ עֲלֵיהּ כַּמָּה זַיְינִין בִּישִׁין, וְכַמָּה גַּרְדִינֵי נְמוּסִין וְדָחִיל מִכֻּלְּהוֹ, וּכְדֵין יָכִילוּ לְאַבְאָשָׁא לֵיהּ, וּמַה דַּהֲוָה בִּידֵיהּ נְטָלוּ מִנֵּיהּ.

317. Come and see: Once man sinned, he drew upon himself a number of evil spirits and judges and judgments of which he was terrified and could not subdue. Solomon was versed in supernal wisdom and the Holy One, blessed be He, crowned him with royalty. Hence, all the people of the world feared him. But when he sinned, he drew upon himself many harmful and punitive agents and weavers of judgments, NAMELY JUDGMENT MONGERS, and he feared them all. They were able to harm him, and all that he had they took away from him.

318. וְעַל דָּא בַּמֶּה דְּאָזֵיל ב"נ, וּבְהַהוּא אָרְחָא דְּאִתְדַּבַּק בֵּיהּ, הָכִי מָשִׁיךְ עֲלֵיהּ, חֵילָא מְמַנָּא, דְּאָזֵיל לְקִבְלֵיהּ. כָּךְ אָדָם הֲוָה מָשִׁיךְ עֲלֵיהּ חֵילָא אָחֳרָא מְסָאַב דְּסָאֵיב לֵיהּ וּלְכָל בְּנֵי עָלְמָא.

318. Hence, by his actions, and according to the path he chooses, man draws upon himself emissaries that go towards him. Adam, BY HIS SIN, drew upon

himself another defiled force and that force defiled him and all mankind after him.

319. תָּא חֲזֵי כַּד חָב אָדָם, מָשִׁיךְ עֲלֵיהּ חֵילָא מְסָאֲבָא, וְסָאִיב לֵיהּ וּלְכָל בְּנֵי עָלְמָא, וְהַאי הוּא חִוְיָא בִּישָׁא, דְּאִיהוּ מְסָאַב וְסָאִיב עָלְמָא. דְּתָנִינָן כַּד אָפֵיק נִשְׁמָתִין מִבְּנֵי נָשָׁא, אִשְׁתָּאַר מִנֵּיהּ גּוּפָא מְסָאָב, וְסָאִיב בֵּיתָא, וְסָאִיב לְכָל אִינּוּן דְּמִקָרְבִין בֵּיהּ. הֲדָא הוּא דִּכְתִיב הַנּוֹגֵעַ בְּמֵת וְגוֹ'.

319. Come and behold: When Adam sinned, he drew upon himself the force of defilement, and he defiled himself and all the people in the world. This is the evil serpent who is unclean and defiled the world. As we have learned, when THE ANGEL OF DEATH removes the soul of a person, what is left is an unclean body that defiles the house and all those who approach it. Hence, "He that touches the dead body..." (Bemidbar 19:11), BECAUSE DEATH COMES FROM THE DEFILED EVIL SERPENT.

320. וְעַל דָּא, כֵּיוָן דְּאִיהוּ נָטִיל נִשְׁמָתָא, וְסָאִיב גּוּפָא, כְּדֵין אִתְיְיהֵיב רְשׁוּ, לְכָל אִינּוּן סִטְרֵי מְסָאֲבָן לְשַׁרְיָא עֲלוֹי. דְּהָא הַהוּא גּוּפָא אִסְתָּאַב, מִסִּטְרָא דְּהַהוּא חִוְיָא בִּישָׁא, דְּשַׁרְיָא עֲלוֹי. וְעַל דָּא, בְּכָל אֲתָר דְּהַהוּא חִוְיָא בִּישָׁא שָׁארֵי מְסָאַב לֵיהּ, וְאִסְתָּאַב.

320. For this reason, when THE ANGEL OF DEATH has taken the soul and has defiled the body, permission is granted for all sorts of defilement to settle on that body. The body has been defiled by the side of the evil serpent that has taken possession of it, BECAUSE DEATH COMES FROM IT. Hence, wherever that evil serpent dwells is made unclean.

321. וְתָא חֲזֵי, כָּל בְּנֵי עָלְמָא בְּשַׁעֲתָא דְּנַיְימֵי עַל עַרְסַיְיהוּ בְּלֵילְיָא, וְלֵילְיָא פָּרֵישׂ גַּדְפָהָא עַל כָּל בְּנֵי עָלְמָא, טַעֲמֵי טַעֲמָא דְּמוֹתָא, וּמִגּוֹ דְּטַעֲמֵי טַעֲמָא דְּמוֹתָא, הַאי רוּחָא מְסָאֲבָא שַׁטְיָא עַל עָלְמָא, וְסָאִיב עָלְמָא וְשַׁרְיָא עַל יְדוֹי דְּבַר נָשׁ וְאִסְתָּאַב.

321. Come and behold: When people sleep on their beds at night, and when

night spreads its wings upon the world, they taste the taste of death. Because they do, the spirit of defilement roams around the world and defiles it. It settles upon a man's hands, and he is made unclean.

322. וְכַד אִתְּעַר, וְאִתְהַדָּר לֵיהּ נִשְׁמָתֵיהּ, בְּכָל מַה דְיִקְרַב בִּידוֹי, כֻּלְּהוּ מְסָאֲבֵי, בְּגִין דְשַׁרְיָא עֲלַיְיהוּ רוּחַ מְסָאֲבָא, וְעַל דָא לָא יִסַּב ב״נ מָנוֹי לְאַלְבָּשָׁא, מִמַּאן דְלָא נָטִיל יְדוֹי, דְהָא אַמְשִׁיךְ עֲלֵיהּ הַהוּא רוּחַ מְסָאֲבָא, וְאִסְתָּאַב, וְאִית לֵיהּ רְשׁוּ, לְהַאי רוּחַ מְסָאֲבָא, לְשַׁרְיָא בְּכָל אֲתַר, דְאִשְׁתְּכַח רְשִׁימוּ מִסִּטְרֵיהּ.

322. And when he wakes from his sleep, and his soul is returned to him, all that he touches with his hands is made unclean, because the spirit of uncleanliness is upon those. Hence, one should not receive his clothes from the hands of another who has not washed his hands, because in so doing, he will draw upon himself the spirit of defilement and become unclean. This spirit of defilement then receives permission to dwell anywhere that his mark can be found.

323. וְעַל דָא, לָא יִטוֹל יְדוֹי, ב״נ, מִמַּאן דְלָא נָטִיל יְדוֹי. בְּגִין דְאַמְשִׁיךְ עֲלֵיהּ הַהוּא רוּחַ מְסָאֲבָא, וְקַבֵּיל לֵיהּ הַאי דְנָטַל מַיָא מִנֵּיהּ. וְאִית לֵיהּ רְשׁוּ לְשַׁרְיָא עֲלוֹי דְבַר נָשׁ. בְּגִין כָּךְ בָּעֵי בַּר נָשׁ לְאִסְתַּמְּרָא בְּכָל סִטְרוֹי, מִסִּטְרָא דְהַאי חִוְיָא בִּישָׁא, דְלָא יִשְׁלוֹט עֲלוֹי. וְזַמִּין קֻדְשָׁא בְּרִיךְ הוּא לְעָלְמָא דְאָתֵי לְאַעְבְּרָא לֵיהּ מֵעָלְמָא, הה״ד וְאֶת רוּחַ הַטֻּמְאָה אַעֲבִיר מִן הָאָרֶץ. וּכְתִיב בִּלַּע הַמָּוֶת לָנֶצַח וְגוֹ׳.

323. Hence, one should not receive the vessel for washing his hands from another who has not washed his hands already, and has drawn upon himself the spirit of uncleanliness. And the spirit of defilement has permission to settle upon he who receives water from such a person. Hence, one should be very careful in whichever way he turns and beware of the side of the evil serpent, so that it does not gain control of him. In the future, the Holy One, blessed be He, will remove the spirit of uncleanliness from this world and the World to Come. Hence it is written: "I will cause the spirit of uncleanliness to pass out of the earth" (Zecharyah 13:2), and, "He will destroy death forever" (Yeshayah 25:8).

60. "And the man knew"

The path we choose for ourselves is the path that is automatically laid out for our children. This secret is found within the story of Cain murdering his brother Abel. Cain's father, Adam, chose the spiritual path of good and evil. Cain followed in his father's footsteps, becoming vulnerable to the Evil Inclinations that are inherent in this reality. By scanning these passages, we become always mindful of our children when making choices in life, and we draw positive spiritual influences into the lives of our children.

324. וְהָאָדָם יָדַע אֶת חַוָּה אִשְׁתּוֹ וְגוֹ'. רַבִּי אַבָּא פָּתַח מִי יוֹדֵעַ רוּחַ בְּנֵי הָאָדָם הָעוֹלָה הִיא לְמַעְלָה וְרוּחַ הַבְּהֵמָה הַיּוֹרֶדֶת הִיא לְמַטָּה לָאָרֶץ. הַאי קְרָא, כַּמָּה גְוָונִין אִית בֵּיהּ, וְהָכֵי הוּא כָּל מִלּוֹי דְאוֹרַיְיתָא, כַּמָּה גְוָונִין בְּכָל חַד וְחַד, וְכֻלְּהוּ יָאוֹת.

324. "And the man knew Eve his wife" (Beresheet 4:1). Rabbi Aba opened his discourse with, "Who knows whether the spirit of man goes upwards and the spirit of the beast goes downwards to the earth?" (Kohelet 3:21). This verse has many interpretations, and so it is with the words of Torah. Each and every word has many interpretations, and all are true.

325. וְהָכֵי אִינּוּן, וְכָל אוֹרַיְיתָא מִתְפָּרְשָׁא בְּשַׁבְעִין אַנְפִּין, לָקֳבֵיל שַׁבְעִין סִטְרִין, וְשַׁבְעִין אַנְפִּין, וְהָכֵי הוּא בְּכָל מִלָּה וּמִלָּה דְאוֹרַיְיתָא, וְכָל מַאי דְנָפֵיק מִכָּל מִלָּה וּמִלָּה, כַּמָּה גְוָונִין אִתְפָּרְשָׁן מִנֵּיהּ לְכָל סִטְרִין.

325. The entire Torah can be interpreted in seventy different ways, corresponding to the seventy sides and seventy aspects OF ZEIR ANPIN. So, each topic in the Torah, and whatever is derived from each topic, has many interpretations, explained in all directions.

326. תָּא חֲזֵי כַּד ב"נ אָזִיל בְּאֹרַח קְשׁוֹט, הוּא אָזִיל לִימִינָא, וְאַמְשִׁיךְ עֲלֵיהּ, רוּחָא קַדִּישָׁא עִלָּאָה מֵעֵילָא. וְהַאי רוּחַ סָלִיק בִּרְעוּתָא קַדִּישָׁא, לְאִתְאַחֲדָא לְעֵילָא, וּלְאִתְדַּבְּקָא בִּקְדוּשָׁה עִלָּאָה, דְּלָא אִתְעֲדֵי מִנֵּיהּ.

326. Come and behold: When a man follows the path of truth, he keeps to the right and only attracts to himself a holy spirit from above. This spirit serves him as a holy desire to unite with the upper and to cleave onto the supernal sanctity, so that it will never leave him.

327. וְכַד בַּר נָשׁ אָזִיל בְּאוֹרַח בִּישׁ, וְסָטֵי אוֹרְחוֹי, הוּא אַמְשִׁיךְ עֲלֵיהּ רוּחַ מְסָאֲבָא דְּלִסְטַר שְׂמָאלָא, וְסָאִיב לֵיהּ, וְאִסְתָּאַב בֵּיהּ, כד"א וְלֹא תְטַמְּאוּ בָּהֶם וְנִטְמֵתֶם בָּם. אָתָא לְאִסְתָּאֲבָא מְסָאֲבִין לֵיהּ.

327. However, when man walks on a path of evil and veers off the RIGHT path, he draws upon himself from the left side a spirit of uncleanliness. This spirit defiles him, and he becomes unclean because of it. Hence, it is written: "And you shall not make yourselves unclean with them nor be defiled by them" (Vayikra 11:43), because he who defiles himself is led further into defilement.

328. וְתָא חֲזֵי, בְּשַׁעְתָּא דְּבַר נָשׁ אָזִיל בְּאֹרַח קָשׁוֹט, וְאַמְשִׁיךְ עֲלֵיהּ רוּחָא קַדִּישָׁא עִלָּאָה וְאִתְדַּבֵּיק בֵּיהּ, בְּרָא דְּיוֹלִיד וְיִפּוֹק מִנֵּיהּ לְעָלְמָא, הוּא מָשִׁיךְ עֲלֵיהּ קְדוּשָׁה עִלָּאָה, וִיהֵא קַדִּישׁ בִּקְדוּשָׁה דְּמָארֵיהּ, כְּמָה דִּכְתִיב וְהִתְקַדִּשְׁתֶּם וִהְיִיתֶם קְדוֹשִׁים וגו'.

328. Furthermore, come and behold: When a man walks along the path of truth and attracts a spirit of holiness from above to himself and cleaves to it, he also draws a spirit of Holiness from above to the son that is born to him. He will be sanctified with his Master's holiness, as it is written: "you shall therefore sanctify yourselves, and you shall be holy" (Ibid. 44).

329. וְכַד אִיהוּ אָזִיל בְּסִטַר שְׂמָאלָא, וְאַמְשִׁיךְ עֲלֵיהּ רוּחַ מְסָאֲבָא, וְאִתְדַּבֵּק בֵּיהּ, בְּרָא דְּיִפּוֹק מִנֵּיהּ לְעָלְמָא, הוּא אַמְשִׁיךְ עֲלֵיהּ רוּחַ מְסָאֲבוּ, וְיִסְתָּאַב בִּמְסָאֲבוּ דְּהַהוּא סִטְרָא.

329. And when a man follows the left side and draws upon himself a spirit of defilement and cleaves to it, he draws that spirit of uncleanliness to his son, and his son is defiled by that side.

330. וְעַל דָּא כְּתִיב, מִי יוֹדֵעַ רוּחַ בְּנֵי הָאָדָם הָעוֹלָה הִיא לְמַעְלָה. כַּד אִיהוּ בְּאִתְדַּבְּקוּת יְמִינָא, סַלְקָא הִיא לְעֵילָא. וְכַד אִיהוּ בְּאִתְדַּבְּקוּת שְׂמָאלָא, הַהוּא סְטַר שְׂמָאלָא, דְּאִיהוּ רוּחַ מְסָאֲבוּ, נָחִית מֵעֵילָא לְתַתָּא, וְשַׁוֵּי דִּיּוּרֵיהּ בְּבַר נָשׁ, וְלָא אַעֲדֵי מִנֵּיהּ. וּבְרָא דְּאוֹלִיד בְּהַהוּא מְסָאֲבוּ אִיהוּ הֲוֵי בְּרֵיהּ, מֵהַהוּא רוּחַ מְסָאַב, אִיהוּ הַהוּא בְּרָא.

330. This is what is meant by the verse: "who knows the spirit of THE SONS OF man." For when MAN cleaves to the right, THE LIGHT HE DRAWS FROM BELOW ascends UPWARD. And when a man is bound to the left – THE LEFT SIDE – which is the spirit of defilement, he descends AND DRAWS LIGHT downward from above. It resides with that man and never leaves him. The child born to him, while he is so defiled, is considered the child of the unclean spirit.

331. אָדָם אִתְדַּבַּק בְּהַהוּא רוּחַ מְסָאַב, וְאִתְּתֵיהּ אִתְדַּבְּקָא בֵּיהּ בְּקַדְמֵיתָא, וְנַטְלַת וְקַבִּילַת הַהוּא זוּהֲמָא מִנֵּיהּ. אוֹלִיד בַּר, הַאי בְּרָא, בְּרָא דְּרוּחַ מְסָאֲבָא אִיהוּ. וְעַל דָּא, תְּרֵין בְּנִין הֲווֹ, חַד מֵהַהוּא רוּחַ מְסָאַב, וְחַד כַּד תָּב אָדָם בִּתְיוּבְתָּא, וּבְגִינֵי כָּךְ, הַאי מִסִּטְרָא מְסָאֲבָא, וְהַאי מִסִּטְרָא דַכְיָיא.

331. Adam clove to the unclean spirit, THE SERPENT, and his wife, EVE, clung to it first and took and received defilement from it. He begot a son; that son was the son of the impure spirit. Thus, there were two sons: one from the unclean spirit, WHO IS CAIN, and another who was born after Adam had repented, WHO IS ABEL. Hence, one was born of the side of impurity, NAMELY CAIN, and one of the side of purity, NAMELY ABEL.

332. רַבִּי אֶלְעָזָר אָמַר, בְּשַׁעְתָּא דְּאַטִּיל נָחָשׁ הַהוּא זוּהֲמָא בָּהּ בְּחַוָּה, קַבִּילַת לֵיהּ, וְכַד אִשְׁתַּמַּשׁ עִמָּהּ אָדָם, אוֹלִידַת תְּרֵין בְּנִין, חַד מֵהַהוּא סִטְרָא מְסָאֲבָא, וְחַד מִסִּטְרָא דְּאָדָם. וַהֲוֵי דָּמֵי הֶבֶל, בְּדִיּוֹקְנָא דִלְעֵילָא, וְקַיִן בְּדִיּוֹקְנָא דִלְתַתָּא. וּבְגִין כָּךְ אִתְפָּרְשׁוּ אָרְחַיְיהוּ דָּא מִן דָּא.

332. Rabbi Elazar said: When the serpent injected its impurity into Eve, she absorbed it, MEANING THAT SHE WAS MADE PREGNANT BY IT. And when

Adam had intercourse with her, she gave birth to two sons, one from the impure side, AND THAT WAS CAIN, and the other from the side of Adam, AND THAT WAS ABEL. Abel resembled the upper image and Cain the lower. Consequently, their paths parted.

333. וַדַּאי קַיִן, בְּרָא דְרוּחַ מְסָאֲבָא הֲוָה, דְּאִיהוּ חִוְיָא בִּישָׁא הֲוָה. וּבְגִין דְּקַיִן אָתָא מִסִּטְרָא דְמַלְאַךְ הַמָּוֶת, קָטִיל לֵיהּ לַאֲחוּי. וְהוּא בְּסִטְרָא דִילֵיהּ, וּמִנֵּיהּ כָּל מְדוֹרִין בִּישִׁין, וּמַזִּיקִין וְשֵׁדִין וְרוּחִין אַתְיָין לְעָלְמָא.

333. It was evident that Cain was the son of the impure spirit, which is the evil serpent. Because he originated from the side of the Angel of Death, he killed his brother. THEREFORE, THE MURDER OF ABEL IS IDENTICAL TO THE SIN OF EATING FROM THE TREE OF KNOWLEDGE, AND BOTH WERE INCITED BY THE SERPENT. AND, AS IN THE AFFAIR OF THE TREE OF KNOWLEDGE, IN WHICH THE ANGEL OF DEATH GAINED CONTROL OVER THE WHOLE WORLD, HERE TOO HE GAINED CONTROL – TAKING OUT THE SOUL OF ABEL. CAIN comes from the side of the Angel of Death, and all the evil habitations, demons, and harmful spirits come to the world from him.

334. אֲמַר רַבִּי יוֹסֵי, קַיִן קִינָא דִמְדוֹרִין בִּישִׁין, דְּאָתוּ מִסִּטְרָא דִמְסָאֲבָא לְעָלְמָא. וּלְבָתַר אַיְיתִיאוּ קָרְבָּנָא. דָּא אַקְרִיב מִסִּטְרָא דִילֵיהּ, וְדָא אַקְרִיב מִסִּטְרָא דִילֵיהּ. הַהַ"ד וַיְהִי מִקֵּץ יָמִים וַיָּבֵא קַיִן מִפְּרִי הָאֲדָמָה וְגו'. ר' שִׁמְעוֹן אֲמַר, וַיְהִי מִקֵּץ יָמִים, מַאי מִקֵּץ יָמִים, דָּא הוּא קֵץ כָּל בָּשָׂר. וּמָאן אִיהוּ דָּא מַלְאַךְ הַמָּוֶת.

334. Rabbi Yosi said: THE NAME Cain indicates a nest (Heb. *ken*) of the evil habitations that come to the world from the impure side. Afterward, they brought sacrifices, each from his own side. So it is written: "And it came to pass, at the end of days, that Cain brought of the fruit of the earth" (Beresheet 4:3). Rabbi Shimon said: it is written, "at the end of days." What is "the end of days?" It is the End of all Flesh. What is THE END OF ALL FLESH? It is the Angel of Death, INDICATING THAT THE SACRIFICE CAIN BROUGHT WAS FROM THE SIDE OF IMPURITY.

335. וְקַיִן מֵהַהוּא קֵץ יָמִים אַיְיתֵי קָרְבָּנָא, דַּיְיקָא דְּקָאָמַר מִקֵּץ יָמִים, וְלָא אָמַר מִקֵּץ יָמִין. וּבְגִין כָּךְ כָּתוּב בְּדָנִיֵּאל וְאַתָּה לֵךְ לַקֵּץ וְתָנוּחַ וְתַעֲמוֹד לְגוֹרָלְךָ. אָמַר לוֹ לְקֵץ הַיָּמִים אוֹ לְקֵץ הַיָּמִין. אָמַר לוֹ לְקֵץ הַיָּמִין. וְקַיִן מִקֵּץ הַיָּמִים אַיְיתֵי.

335. Cain brought his offering from this "end of days." To be exact, the text uses the word *Yamim* (Days) and not *Yamin* (Right). Hence, it is written of Daniel, "And you go your way till the end and rest, and hence stand at your destiny" (Daniel 12:13). DANIEL asks THE HOLY ONE, BLESSED BE HE, "the end of Yamim or Yamin?" For YAMIM IS AN EVIL KLIPAH. And He replied: "at the end of days (*yamin*)." But Cain brought his offering from the end of *Yamim*, WHICH IS THE SIDE OF THE ANGEL OF DEATH, BECAUSE HE BROUGHT HIS OFFERING FROM HIS SIDE.

336. וַיָּבֵא קַיִן מִפְּרִי הָאֲדָמָה. כד"א וּמִפְּרִי הָעֵץ. אָמַר ר' אֶלְעָזָר, מִפְּרִי הָאֲדָמָה, כד"א אוֹי לְרָשָׁע רָע כִּי גְמוּל יָדָיו וגו'. גְּמוּל יָדָיו. דָּא מַלְאַךְ הַמָּוֶת. יֵעָשֶׂה לּוֹ, דְּאִתְמְשַׁךְ עֲלַיְיהוּ, וְיִתְדַּבַּק בְּהוּ לְקַטְלָא לוֹן וּלְסָאֲבָא לוֹן. וְעַל דָּא קַיִן אַקְרִיב מִסִּטְרָא דִּילֵיהּ.

336. "Cain brought of the fruit of the earth." These words are parallel to "the fruit of the Tree" (Beresheet 3:3). AS THE TREE OF KNOWLEDGE IS A REPRESENTATION OF THE EVIL SERPENT, SO HERE HE BROUGHT HIS OFFERING FROM THE EVIL SERPENT. Rabbi Elazar said, "the fruit of the earth" is similar to "Alas! It shall be ill with the wicked, for according to the deserving of his hands shall be done to him" (Yeshayah 3:11). For "of his hands" refers to the Angel of Death, WHO IS THE DESERVING FRUIT OF THE DEEDS OF THE WICKED. BECAUSE IF IT WAS NOT FOR THE SIN, HE WOULD NOT HAVE COME TO THE WORLD. "Shall be done to him" means that it is drawn to and cleaves to them, killing and defiling them. Hence, THE WORDS "THE FRUIT OF THE EARTH" INDICATE that Cain's offering came from his side, WHICH MEANT IT CAME FROM THE SERPENT AND THE ANGEL OF DEATH.

337. וְהֶבֶל הֵבִיא גַּם הוּא מִבְּכוֹרוֹת. לְאַסְגָּאָה סִטְרָא עִלָּאָה, דְּאַתְיָא מִסְּטַר קְדוּשְׁתָּא. וּבְגִינֵי כָּךְ, וַיִּשַׁע ה' אֶל הֶבֶל וְאֶל מִנְחָתוֹ וְאֶל קַיִן וְאֶל

מִנְחָתוֹ לֹא שָׁעָה. לָא קַבֵּיל לֵיהּ קֻדְשָׁא בְּרִיךְ הוּא. וְעַל דָּא וַיִּחַר לְקַיִן מְאֹד וַיִּפְּלוּ פָּנָיו. דְּהָא לָא אִתְקַבִּילוּ אַנְפּוֹי, אִינּוּן אַנְפִּין דִּסְטַרְוֹי, וְקַבֵּיל לֵיהּ לְהֶבֶל.

337. "And Abel also brought of the firstlings" (Beresheet 4:4). THE FUNCTION OF THE WORD "ALSO" IS to strengthen the upper side, THE PART FROM THE CHEST UPWARD, that is the holy side. That is why "Hashem turned to Abel and his offering," BECAUSE IT WAS FROM THE SIDE OF HOLINESS, "but to Cain and his offering, He did not turn" (Ibid. 6). The Holy One, blessed be He, did not accept CAIN'S SACRIFICE BECAUSE IT WAS FROM THE UNCLEAN SIDE. Hence, "Cain was very angry and his face fell," because his face, meaning that the offering from his side, was not accepted, but Abel's offering was.

338. וּבְגִינֵי כָּךְ כָּתוּב, וַיְהִי בִּהְיוֹתָם בַּשָּׂדֶה. בַּשָּׂדֶה דָּא אִתְּתָא, כְּד"א כִּי בַשָּׂדֶה מְצָאָהּ, וְקַיִן קָנֵי עַל נוּקְבָא יְתֵירָה, דְּאִתְיְלִידַת עִם הֶבֶל. דִּכְתִיב, וַתּוֹסֶף לָלֶדֶת וְהָא אִתְּמַר.

338. Hence, it is written: "And it came to pass when they were in the field" (Ibid. 8). The word, "field," here refers to a woman, as it was in, "For he found her in the field" (Devarim 22:27), IN WHICH "FIELD" ALSO REFERRED TO A WOMAN. BY ANALOGY, THE "FIELD" IN THE FORMER VERSE ALSO ALLUDES TO A WOMEN. Cain was jealous of the additional twin girl born with Abel, as it is written: "And she again bore to his (Heb. *et*) brother (Heb. *et*) Abel" (Beresheet 4:2). THIS DOUBLE USE OF THE PARTICLE *ET* IS A REFERENCE TO THE TWO GIRLS BORN WITH ABEL.

61. "If you do well, shall you not be accepted"

If a person does not constantly elevate himself during his spiritual journey, he actually begins regressing. As if we were standing still on a downward escalator, making no effort forward allows us to be carried backwards. In these passages we receive the Light that will help us always strive for greater heights.

339. הֲלֹא אִם תֵּיטִיב שְׂאֵת, כְּמָה דְּאִתְּמָר. אֲבָל שְׂאֵת, כִּדְאָמַר רַבִּי אַבָּא, שְׂאֵת: תִּסְתַּלַּק לְעֵילָא, וְלָא תֵּיחוֹת לְתַתָּא. אָמַר רַבִּי יוֹסֵי הַאי מִלָּה הַשְׁתָּא אִתְּמַר, וְיָאוּת הוּא. אֲבָל הָכֵי שְׁמַעְנָא, שְׂאֵת: יִסַּלַּק מִינָּךְ, וְיִשְׁבּוֹק לָךְ, אִתְדַּבְּקוּתָא דָּא, דְּרוּחַ מְסָאֲבָא.

339. "If you do well, shall you not be accepted (also: 'raised')" (Beresheet 4:7). These words have already been explained. The word "raised" means, as Rabbi Aba explained, that you will ascend toward the upper rather than descend. THIS MEANS THAT YOU SHOULD RETURN THE LIGHTS FROM BELOW UPWARD AND STOP DRAWING THEM DOWNWARD FROM ABOVE, WHICH WAS HOW ABEL WAS KILLED. Rabbi Yosi said that this explanation, which had just been put forward, WAS NOVEL, but good. But, I have heard that "raised" MEANS, "REMOVAL" AND "PARDON,"AS THE HOLY ONE, BLESSED BE HE, SAID TO HIM, "IF YOU DO WELL, that cleavage to the unclean spirit will be undone, and you shall be forgiven."

340. וְאִי לָא, לַפֶּתַח חַטָּאת רוֹבֵץ. מַאי לַפֶּתַח, דָּא דִּינָא עִלָּאָה, דְּאִיהוּ פִּתְחָא דְּכֹלָּא. כְּד"א פִּתְחוּ לִי שַׁעֲרֵי צֶדֶק. חַטָּאת רוֹבֵץ. הַהוּא סִטְרָא דְּאִתְדַּבְּקַת בֵּיהּ, וְאִתְמַשְׁכַת עֲלָךְ, יְהֵא נָטִיר לָךְ, לְאִתְפַּרְעָא מִנָּךְ, כְּתַרְגּוּמָא.

340. Rabbi Yosi quoted, "and if you do not well, sin crouches at the door" (Ibid.). AND HE THEN ASKS: "which door?" It is the upper Judgment, THE JUDGMENT OF MALCHUT, which is the doorway open to all, as it is written: "open to me the gates of righteousness" (Tehilim 118:19). ACCORDING TO THE ARAMAIC TRANSLATION, the words "sin crouches" MEAN THAT THE HOLY ONE, BLESSED BE HE, SAID TO ADAM, that the side to which you clung and which you have drawn upon yourself lies in wait for you and will exact punishment from you.

62. Cain killed Abel

The Power of Repentance is manifested in the cosmos through the story of Cain's repentance for the murder of his brother. Adam is truly amazed at this unique force and phenomenon when he sees God accept Cain's repentance. The spiritual forces associated with the Hebrew letters that compose this story are the actual instruments by which repentance became a force that we can apply in our world. Our understanding of the importance of repentance is the power by which we activate it in our own lives. Reading these words awakens our desire to repent for our negative actions.

341. אָמַר רְבִּי יִצְחָק, תָּא חֲזֵי, בְּשַׁעֲתָא דְּקָטֵיל קַיִן לְהֶבֶל, לָא הֲוָה יָדַע הֵיךְ יַפִּיק נִשְׁמָתֵיה מִנֵּיה, וַהֲוָה נָשִׁיךְ לֵיה בְּשִׁינֵּיה כְּחִוְיָא. וְהָא אוּקְמוּהָ חַבְרַיָּא. בֵּיה שַׁעֲתָא לַיִיט לֵיה קֻדְשָׁא בְּרִיךְ הוּא, וַהֲוָה אָזִיל לְכָל סִטְרֵי עָלְמָא, וְלָא הֲוָה אֲתַר דִּמְקַבֵּל לֵיה, עַד דְּאַטְפַּח עַל רֵישֵׁיה וְתָב קַמֵּי מָארֵיה. וְקַבִּילַת לֵיה אַרְעָא, בִּמְדוֹרָא לְתַתָּא.

341. Rabbi Yitzchak said, Come and behold: when Cain killed Abel, he did not know how his soul could leave him, THAT IS, THAT BY HIS ACTIONS HE COULD, IN EFFECT, EXTRACT THE SOUL FROM ABEL AND KILL HIM. And he was biting him with his teeth, as a serpent. At that instant, the Holy One, blessed be He, cursed Cain. He wandered in every direction, but no place accepted him until he hit himself upon the head and repented before his Master. Then the earth received him in one of the lower compartments, BECAUSE HIS REPENTANCE WAS NOT COMPLETE AND THEREFORE NOT ACCEPTED IN THIS WORLD.

342. ר' יוֹסֵי אָמַר, אַרְעָא קַבִּילַת לֵיה, לְמֵיהַךְ בָּהּ. דִּכְתִיב, וַיָּשֶׂם ה' לְקַיִן אוֹת. ר' יִצְחָק אָמַר, לָאו הָכִי, אֶלָּא, לְתַתָּא קַבִּילַת לֵיה אַרְעָא, בִּמְדוֹרָא חֲדָא דִּתְחוֹתָהּ. דִּכְתִיב, הֵן גֵּרַשְׁתָּ אוֹתִי הַיּוֹם מֵעַל פְּנֵי הָאֲדָמָה. מֵעַל פְּנֵי הָאֲדָמָה גוֹרֵשׁ, אֲבָל לְתַתָּא לָא גוֹרֵשׁ.

342. Rabbi Yosi said that the earth itself accepted him so that he could walk upon it, as it is written: "Hashem set a sign upon Cain" (Beresheet 4:15). THIS INTERPRETATION IS THAT THE HOLY ONE, BLESSED BE HE,

ACCEPTED CAIN'S REPENTANCE, AND THUS THE EARTH ACCEPTED HIM
AGAIN. According to Rabbi Yitzchak, however, the earth only accepted
Cain to a level beneath it, as it is written: "You have driven me, this day,
from the face of the earth" (Beresheet 4:14). He was driven from the face of
the earth, but not from underneath it. HE WAS TAKEN IN BY THE LOWER
COMPARTMENT UNDERNEATH. THUS, RABBI YITZCHAK DISAGREED
WITH RABBI YOSI'S INTERPRETATION. RABBI YITZCHAK'S POSITION WAS
THAT CAIN WAS ADMITTED TO THE LOWER LEVEL ONLY. WHY?
BECAUSE HIS REPENTENCE WAS INCOMPLETE.

343. וּבְאָן אֲתַר קַבֵּילַת לֵיהּ אַרְעָא, בְּאַרְקָא. וְכָל אִינוּן דְּדַיְירֵי תַּמָּן.
עֲלֵיהוֹן כְּתִיב יֵאבָדוּ מֵאַרְעָא וּמִתְּחוֹת שְׁמַיָּא אֵלֶּה. וְתַמָּן שַׁוֵּי מְדוֹרֵיהּ,
וְהַיְינוּ דִּכְתִיב, וַיֵּשֶׁב בְּאֶרֶץ נוֹד קִדְמַת עֵדֶן.

343. HE ASKS, "And into which place did earth admit him?" AND HE SAYS,
into *Arka*, WHICH IS ONE OF THE SEVEN PHYSICAL LEVELS OF EARTH. Of
all who reside there, it is written: "these shall perish from the earth and from
beneath the heavens" (Yirmeyah 10:11). There, he established his place of
living. This place is referred to in the words: "And he dwelt in the land of
Nod east of Eden" (Beresheet 4:16). THIS ALLUDES TO THE LOWER
COMPARTMENT CALLED 'ARKA.' THIS COMPARTMENT IS ALSO CALLED
"NOD (SWAY)," BECAUSE THE RESIDENTS HAVE TWO HEADS AND SWAY
FROM ONE SIDE OF DARKNESS TO THE OTHER SIDE OF LIGHT.

תוספתא

344. תּוֹסֶפְתָּא כֵּיוָן דַּאֲמַר קַיִן, גָּדוֹל עֲוֹנִי מִנְּשֹׂא. מָחַל לֵיהּ קֻדְשָׁא
בְּרִיךְ הוּא, פַּלְגוּ מֵעוֹנָשֵׁיהּ. בְּגִין דְּגָזַר עֲלֵיהּ בְּקַדְמֵיתָא, וַאֲמַר לֵיהּ, נָע
וְנָד תִּהְיֶה בָאָרֶץ. וְהַשְׁתָּא, אִשְׁתְּאַר בְּנוֹד בִּלְחוֹדוֹי. הֲהָ"ד וַיֵּצֵא קַיִן
מִלִּפְנֵי ה' וְגו'. כְּלוֹמַר, דְּכַד נָפַק מִן קֳדָם ה' הֲוָה, בְּגִין לְמֶהֱוֵי נָד
בְּאַרְעָא, וְלָא נָע.

Tosefta (Addendum)

344. When Cain said, "My punishment is greater than I can bear"
(Beresheet 4:13), MEANING AFTER HE CONFESSED AND REPENTED, the

-209-

Holy One, blessed be He, withdrew one half of his punishment. In the original punishment, He stated: "you shall be a fugitive (Heb. *na*) and a vagabond (Heb. *nad*) on the earth" (Ibid. 12), but now he stayed only in *Nod*. And so it is written: "And Cain when out from the presence of Hashem and dwelt in the land of Nod" (Ibid. 16), meaning that he left the presence of Hashem to be a vagabond, but not a fugitive, on the earth, BECAUSE HALF HIS PUNISHMENT HAD BEEN WITHDRAWN.

345. וְעוֹד אָמְרוּ, כַּד נָפַק קַיִן, מִן קֳדָם ה', אֲמַר לוֹ אָדָם, מָה אִתְעֲבִיד עַל דִּינָךְ. אֲמַר לוֹ קַיִן, אַבָּא, כְּבָר אִתְבַּשְׂרִית, דִּמְחַל לִי קֻדְשָׁא בְּרִיךְ הוּא, בְּנוֹד בִּלְחוֹדוֹי. אֲמַר לוֹ, הֵיאַךְ הוּא. אֲמַר לוֹ, בְּגִין דְּתָבִית, וְאוֹדִית קַמֵּיהּ. אָמַר אָדָם, וְכִי דֵּין הוּא רַב וְתַקִּיף חֵילָא דִתְשׁוּבָה, וַאֲנָא לָא יְדִיעַת. שָׁרָא לְשַׁבָּחָא לְמָרֵיהּ, וּלְאוֹדָאָה לֵיהּ, פָּתַח וַאֲמַר, מִזְמוֹר שִׁיר לְיוֹם הַשַּׁבָּת טוֹב לְהוֹדוֹת לַה'. כְּלוֹמַר, טוֹב לְשַׁבָּחָא וְלַאֲתָבָא וּלְאוֹדָאָה קַמֵּיהּ קֻדְשָׁא בְּרִיךְ הוּא

(ע"כ תוספתא)

345. THE RABBIS further said that when Cain left the presence of Hashem, Adam asked him, my son, what was done with your sentence? Cain replied, 'Father, I was already given the good news that the Holy One, blessed be He, has forgiven me and that I can reside in Nod alone.' Adam then asked him, 'How did you merit that?' and Cain answered, 'Because I repented and confessed before Him.' Adam said, 'The strength of repentance is so great and powerful, and I did not know that.' He began to say praises to his Master and to thank him. He started reciting "A song for the day of Shabbat. It is good to thank Hashem" (Tehilim 92:1). For it is good to praise, repent, and thank before the Holy One, blessed be He.

End of Tosefta (Addendum)

346. וְאָמַר רַבִּי יִצְחָק, מֵהַהִיא שַׁעֲתָא דְּקָטִיל קַיִן לְהֶבֶל, אִתְפְּרַשׁ אָדָם מֵאִתְּתֵיהּ. תְּרֵין רוּחִין נוּקְבִין, הֲווֹ אַתְיָין וּמִזְדַּוְּוגָן עִמֵּיהּ, וְאוֹלֵיד רוּחִין וְשֵׁדִין דְּשָׁאטָן בְּעָלְמָא.

346. Rabbi Yitzchak said that from the time that Cain killed Abel, Adam separated from his wife. Two female spirits used to come and mate with him. And he bore from them spirits and demons that roam around the world. THE REASON THERE WERE TWO SPIRITS IS BECAUSE PROSTITUTION IS A KLIPAH OF THE RIGHT, ON WHICH SIDE THEY ARE MOCKING. YET, EVENTUALLY THE SPIRITS PUNISH PEOPLE AND MAKE THEM SUFFER, WHICH IS THE JURISDICTION OF THE LEFT. HENCE, THERE WERE TWO SPIRITS – ONE WAS A KLIPAH OF THE RIGHT, AND THE OTHER A KLIPAH OF THE LEFT.

347. וְלָא תִּקְשֵׁי לָךְ הַאי, דְּהָא בַּר נָשׁ, כַּד אִיהוּ בְּחֶלְמֵיהּ, אַתְיָין רוּחִין נוּקְבִין וְחַיְיכָן עִמֵּיהּ, וּמִתְחַמְּמָן מִנֵּיהּ, וְאוֹלִידִין לְבָתַר. וְאִלֵּין אִקְרוּן נִגְעֵי בְּנֵי אָדָם. וְלָא מִתְהַפְּכָן, אֶלָּא לִדְיוֹקְנֵי בְּנֵי נָשָׁא וְלֵית לוֹן שַׂעֲרִין בְּרֵישָׁא. וְעַל דָּא כְּתִיב בִּשְׁלֹמֹה, וְהוֹכַחְתִּיו בְּשֵׁבֶט אֲנָשִׁים וּבְנִגְעֵי בְּנֵי אָדָם. וַאֲפִילוּ כְּהַאי גַוְונָא, רוּחִין דְּכוּרִין אַתְיָין לִנְשֵׁי עָלְמָא, וּמִתְעַבְּרָן מִנַּיְיהוּ, וְאוֹלִידָן רוּחִין, וְכֻלְּהוֹן נִגְעֵי בְּנֵי אָדָם אִקְרוּן.

347. This need not be difficult to accept, because even when a man is dreaming, female spirits often come, seduce him, conceive from him, and eventually give birth. THESE OFFSPRING are called the plagues of mankind and take only the shape of humans. They have no hair on their heads, BECAUSE these OFFSPRING COME FROM THE KLIPAH OF THE RIGHT, AND HAIR IS CONNECTED TO THE LEFT. And of these Solomon said, "And I shall chastise them with the whip of men and with the plagues of the sons of men" (II Shmuel 7:4). Similarly, there are male spirits that visit women, IN THEIR DREAMS. Those WOMEN conceive from them, give birth to spirits, and all are called 'the plagues of mankind'.

348. בָּתַר מְאָה וּתְלָתִין שְׁנִין, אִתְלַבַּשׁ אָדָם בְּקִנּוּיָא, וְאִתְחַבַּר בְּאִתְּתֵיהּ, וְאוֹלִיד בַּר, וּקְרָא שְׁמוֹ שֵׁת. רָזָא, דְּסוֹפָא דְּאַתְוָון בְּקִיטְרֵי גְלִיפָן. רַבִּי יְהוּדָה אָמַר, רָזָא דְּרוּחָא דְּאִתְאֲבֵיד, דְּאִתְלַבַּשׁ בְּגוּפָא אָחֳרָא בְּעָלְמָא. הֲדָא הוּא דִכְתִיב כִּי שָׁת לִי אֱלֹקִים זֶרַע אַחֵר תַּחַת הֶבֶל.

348. After 130 years, Adam felt jealousy of his wife, had intercourse with her, and begot a son whom he called Seth (Heb. *shet*, Shin Tav). This is the secret of the ordering of the last TWO LETTERS within the 22 letters of the Hebrew alphabet. THIS IS UNIQUE AND DIFFERENT FROM ALL OTHER SEQUENCES OF THE ALPHABET, WHICH DO NOT END WITH THESE SAME TWO LETTERS, NAMELY SHIN AND TAV. Rabbi Yehuda said that THE NAME SETH SYMBOLIZES the secret of the lost spirit, NAMELY THAT OF ABEL, which was clothed in the earthly body OF SETH. Hence, it is written: "Elohim has replaced (Heb. *shat*) for me another seed instead of Abel" (Beresheet 4:25).

349. וְאָמַר רַבִּי יְהוּדָה, כְּתִיב וַיּוֹלֶד בִּדְמוּתוֹ כְּצַלְמוֹ, מַשְׁמַע דִּבְנִין אָחֳרָנִין לָא הֲווֹ בְּדִיּוֹקְנָא דִילֵיהּ, וְדָא בִּדְמוּתוֹ כְּצַלְמוֹ, בְּתִיקוּנָא דְגוּפָא, וּבְתִיקוּנָא דְנַפְשָׁא, בְּאֹרַח מֵישָׁר. כְּמָה דְאָמַר רַבִּי שִׁמְעוֹן, מִשְּׁמֵיהּ דְּרַב יֵיבָא סָבָא. בְּנִין אָחֳרָנִין, בְּאִתְדַּבְּקוּתָא דְזוּהֲמָא דְנָחָשׁ, וְהַהוּא דְרָכֵיב בֵּיהּ דְּאִיהוּ סָמָאֵ"ל הֲווֹ, וּבְגִינֵי כָּךְ לָא הֲוָה בְּדִיּוֹקְנָא דְאָדָם. וְאִי תֵּימָא, הָא אֲמָרַת, דְּהֶבֶל מִסִּטְרָא אָחֳרָא הֲוָה. הָכֵי הוּא. אֲבָל תַּרְוַויְיהוּ, לָא הֲווֹ בְּדִיּוֹקְנָא דִלְתַּתָּא.

349. Rabbi Yehuda continued by saying, "And he begot in his own likeness after his image" (Beresheet 5:3). This indicates that his other sons, CAIN AND ABEL, were not after his likeness, but Seth was in his own likeness and after his image, both physically and spiritually. As Rabbi Shimon said, in the name of Rav Yeba Saba (the elder), Adam's other sons had been produced in defilement, through attachment to the serpent and its rider, who is Samael. Hence, they bore no resemblance to Adam. Even though Abel, unlike Cain, was from another side OF PURITY AND NOT FROM THE SIDE OF THE SERPENT, neither had the form of Adam. THEY BOTH LACKED THE CENTRAL COLUMN, WHICH IS THE FORM OF ADAM. ABEL WAS FROM THE RIGHT SIDE AND CAIN FROM THE LEFT. HENCE, THEY WERE NOT CREATED IN THE LIKENESS OF ADAM.

350. אָמַר ר' יוֹסֵי, וְהָא כְּתִיב, וְהָאָדָם יָדַע אֶת חַוָּה אִשְׁתּוֹ וַתַּהַר וַתֵּלֶד אֶת קַיִן. וְלָא כְּתִיב וַיּוֹלֶד אֶת קַיִן. וַאֲפִילוּ בְּהֶבֶל לָא כְּתִיב וַיּוֹלֶד, אֶלָּא

וַתּוֹסֶף לָלֶדֶת אֶת אָחִיו אֶת הֶבֶל. וְדָא הוּא רָזָא דְמִלָּה. אֲבָל בְּהַאי מַה כְּתִיב וַיּוֹלֶד בִּדְמוּתוֹ כְּצַלְמוֹ.

350. Rabbi Yosi BRINGS FURTHER PROOF TO STRENGTHEN THE CASE THAT ABEL TOO WAS NOT COMPLETE. HE says: It is written: "And the man knew his wife, Eve, and she conceived, and bore Cain" (Beresheet 4:1), but it is not written that Adam begot Cain. This was not written of Abel either. Instead, it is written: "And she again bore his brother, Abel" (Ibid. 2). And here lies the concealed truth, THAT EVEN ABEL WAS NOT IN THE IMAGE OR LIKENESS OF ADAM. But of Seth it is written: "And he begot in his own likeness, after his image." THUS, HE IS RELATED TO ADAM.

351. רַבִּי שִׁמְעוֹן אָמַר, מֵאָה וּתְלָתִין שְׁנִין, אִתְפְּרַשׁ אָדָם מֵאִתְּתֵיהּ. וְכָל אִינוּן מֵאָה וּתְלָתִין שְׁנִין, הֲוָה אוֹלִיד רוּחִין וְשֵׁדִין בְּעָלְמָא. בְּגִין הַהוּא חֵילָא דְזוּהֲמָא, דַּהֲוָה שָׁאִיב בֵּיהּ. כֵּיוָן דְּחַסִּיל מִנֵּיהּ הַהוּא זוּהֲמָא, תָּב וְקַנֵּי לְאִנְתְּתֵיהּ, וְאוֹלִיד בַּר. כְּדֵין כְּתִיב, וַיּוֹלֶד בִּדְמוּתוֹ כְּצַלְמוֹ.

351. Rabbi Shimon said that for a hundred and thirty years Adam separated from his wife, and during that time he begot in the world spirits and demons from the force of impurity that was sucked from him. And when that impurity was exhausted, he turned and became jealous for his wife and begot a son. It then is written: "...and he begot in his own likeness, after his image."

352. תָּא חֲזֵי, כָּל ב"נ דַּאֲזֵיל לִסְטַר שְׂמָאלָא וְסָאִיב אָרְחוֹי, כָּל רוּחֵי מְסָאֲבֵי, מָשִׁיךְ עַל גַּרְמֵיהּ. וְרוּחַ מְסָאָב אִתְדַּבַּק בֵּיהּ, וְלָא אַעֲדֵי מִנֵּיהּ. וְאִתְדַּבְּקוּתָא דְּהַהוּא רוּחָא מְסָאָב, הֲוֵי בְּהַאי ב"נ, וְלָא בְּאָחֳרָא, וּבְגִינֵי כָּךְ, אִתְדַּבְּקוּתָא דִּלְהוֹן לָאו אִיהוּ, אֶלָּא בְּאִינוּן דְּמִתְדַּבְּקִין בְּהוֹ. זַכָּאִין אִינוּן צַדִּיקַיָּא, דְּאָזְלֵי בְּאֹרַח מֵישָׁר, וְאִינוּן זַכָּאֵי קְשׁוֹט. וּבְנַיְיהוּ זַכָּאִין בְּעָלְמָא. וַעֲלַיְיהוּ כְּתִיב כִּי יְשָׁרִים יִשְׁכְּנוּ אָרֶץ.

352. Come and behold: when a man veers to the left and defiles his ways, he draws upon himself all kinds of impure spirits. And the spirit of defilement clings to him and does not leave him. This spirit only links to the man who drew it – and not to another. Hence, they only cleave to those who cleave to them. Happy are the righteous, who walk in the straight path and who are the truly righteous. Their sons are righteous in the world. Of them it is written: "For the upright shall dwell in the earth" (Mishlei 2:21).

353. אָמַר ר׳ חִיָּיא, מַאי דִּכְתִיב, וַאֲחוֹת תּוּבַל קַיִן נַעֲמָה. מַאי אִירְיָא הָכָא, דְּקָאֲמַר קְרָא דִּשְׁמָהּ נַעֲמָה. אֶלָּא, בְּגִין דְּטָעֲיָין בְּנֵי נָשָׁא אֲבַתְרָהּ, וַאֲפִילוּ רוּחִין וְשֵׁדִין. רַבִּי יִצְחָק אָמַר, אִינּוּן בְּנֵי הָאֱלֹהִים עַזָּא וַעֲזָאֵל, טָעוּ בַּתְרָהּ.

353. Rabbi Chiya quotes, "And the sister of Tuval Cain was Na'amah" (Beresheet 4:22). Why do the scriptures mention her name, Na'amah (Eng. 'pleasant')? It is because people were seduced by her OVERWHELMING BEAUTY AND PLEASANTNESS, and even spirits and demons LUSTED AFTER HER. Rabbi Yitzchak said that the sons of Elohim, Aza, and Azael were seduced by her. BECAUSE OF THOSE SEDUCTIONS, SHE WAS NAMED NA'AMAH.

354. רַבִּי שִׁמְעוֹן אָמַר, אִמָּן שֶׁל שֵׁדִים הֲוַת, דְּמִסִּטְרָא דְּקַיִן נָפְקַת, וְהִיא אִתְמַנַּת עִם לִילִית בְּאַסְכְּרָה דְּרַבְיֵי. אָמַר לֵיהּ רַבִּי אַבָּא, וְהָא אָמַר מַר, דְּהִיא אִתְמַנַּת לְחַיְיכָא בִּבְנֵי נָשָׁא. אָמַר לוֹ, הָכֵי הוּא וַדַּאי, דְּהָא אִיהִי אָתְיַית וְחַיְיכַאת בְּהוֹ בִּבְנֵי נָשָׁא. וְלִזְמְנִין דְּאוֹלֵידַת רוּחִין בְּעָלְמָא מִנַּיְיהוּ. וְעַד כָּאן אִיהִי קַיְּימַת לְחַיְיכָא בְּהוֹ בִּבְנֵי נָשָׁא.

354. Rabbi Shimon said that she was the mother of demons, being of the side of Cain, and that along with Lilit, she is responsible for the epileptic death of babies. Rabbi Aba said to him: But sir, RABBI SHIMON, NA'AMAH was charged with seducing men IN THEIR SLEEP WHILE THEY DREAM, PLACING HER TO THE RIGHT OF THE KLIPOT. KILLING CHILDREN, HOWEVER, IS FROM THE LEFT ASPECT.   HE RESPONDED THAT this is precisely correct, because she seduced men and bore spirits in the world. She still persists in her seductive work in the world. BUT RABBI SHIMON SAID SHE COOPERATES WITH LILIT, AND THE DEATH COMES FROM THE SIDE OF LILIT, NOT THAT OF NA'AMAH.

355. אָמַר לוֹ רַבִּי אַבָּא, וְהָא אִינּוּן מֵתִין כִּבְנֵי נָשָׁא, מַאי טַעְמָא, אִיהִי קַיָּימַת עַד הַשְׁתָּא. אָמַר לוֹ, הָכֵי הוּא. אֲבָל לִילִית וְנַעֲמָה, וְאָגְרַת בַּת מַחֲלַת דְּנָפְקַת מִסִּטְרָא דִּלְהוֹן כֻּלְּהוּ קַיָּימוֹת עַד דִּיבַעֵר קֻדְשָׁא בְּרִיךְ הוּא, רוּחַ מְסָאֲבָא מֵעָלְמָא. דִּכְתִיב וְאֶת רוּחַ הַטֻּמְאָה אַעֲבִיר מִן הָאָרֶץ.

355. Rabbi Aba asks him: But since those demons die like human beings, how can you say that NA'AMAH has survived to this day? He said to him that this is true, THAT DEMONS DIE AS HUMANS DO. Yet Lilit and Na'amah and Agrat, the daughter of Machalat, who originated from their side, will continue to live until the Holy One, blessed be He, burns the spirit of uncleanliness from earth. This is as it is written: "I will cause the unclean spirit to pass out of the land" (Zecharyah 13:2).

356. אֲמַר רַבִּי שִׁמְעוֹן, וַוי לוֹן לִבְנֵי נָשָׁא, אִינּוּן דְּלָא יָדְעִין וְלָא מַשְׁגִּיחִין, וְלָא מִסְתַּכְּלִין, וְכֻלְּהוּ אֲטִימִין, דְּלָא יָדְעִין כַּמָּה מַלְיָיא עָלְמָא מִבִּרְיָין מְשַׁנְיָין, דְּלָא אִתְחֲזוּן, וּמְמַלִּין סְתִימִין, דְּאִלְמָלֵא אִתְיְיהַב רְשׁוּ לְעֵינָא לְמֶחֱזֵי, יִתְמְהוּן בְּנֵי נָשָׁא, הֵיךְ יָכְלִין לְאִתְקַיְימָא בְּעָלְמָא.

356. Rabbi Shimon said: Woe to people, for they are not aware and do not take heed nor search for knowledge. They are all blindfolded and do not know how full the world is with strange and invisible creatures and things. If permission were to be given to the eye to see, people would wonder greatly as to how is it possible to survive in this world.

357. תָּא חֲזֵי, הַאי נַעֲמָה, אִימָּא דְּשֵׁדִין הֲוַת, וּמִסִּטְרָהּ אַתְיָין, כָּל אִינּוּן שֵׁדִין, דְּמִתְחַמְּמָן מִבְּנֵי נָשָׁא, וְנַטְלֵי רוּחַ תִּיאוּבְתָּא מִנַּיְיהוּ, וְחַיְיכַת בְּהוֹן, דְּעָבְדֵי לוֹן בַּעֲלֵי קֶרְיָין. וּבְגִין דְּבַעַל קֶרִי, אָתֵי מִסִּטְרָא דְּרוּחַ מְסָאֲבָא, בָּעֵי לְאַסְחָאָה גַרְמֵיהּ, לְאִתְדַּכָּאָה מִנֵּיהּ, וְהָא אוֹקְמוּהָ חַבְרַיָּיא.

357. Come and behold: this Na'amah is the mother of demons. From her side originate all those demons who sexually arouse men, absorb the spirit of lust from them, seduce them, and eventually cause them to release semen in vain. And since this wastage of semen comes from the side of the spirit of defilement, one has to wash and to purify himself. This the friends have already explained.

63. "This is the book of the generations of Adam"

The power of self-sacrifice and true sharing is awakened in the cosmos through a thoughtful action of sharing by Adam. Reading this story empowers us to put others before ourselves. The Kabbalists believe that the motivation for sharing should never be based upon moral and ethical principles. Instead, the age-old *What's in it for me?* attitude is a far better motivator. The more we give of ourselves, the more the Light The Creator bestows upon us. This is a simple principle to understand, but one that requires extraordinary character to apply.

358. זֶה סֵפֶר תּוֹלְדוֹת אָדָם: לִדְיוֹקְנֵי. אָמַר רָבִּי יִצְחָק, אַחְמֵי קֻדְשָׁא בְּרִיךְ הוּא לְאָדָם, דְּיוֹקְנֵי דְּכָל אִינוּן דָּרִין דְּיֵיתוּן לְעָלְמָא. וְכָל חַכִּימֵי עָלְמָא, וּמַלְכֵי עָלְמָא, דְּזְמִינִין לְקַיְּימָא עֲלַיְיהוּ דְיִשְׂרָאֵל. מָטָא לְמֶחֱמֵי, דָּוִד מַלְכָּא דְיִשְׂרָאֵל. דְּאִתְיְילִיד וּמִית. אָמַר לוֹ, מִשְׁנִין דִּילִי, אוֹזִיף לֵיהּ ע' שְׁנִין. וְגָרְעוּ מֵאָדָם ע' שְׁנִין, וְסָלֵיק לוֹן קוּדְשָׁא בְּרִיךְ הוּא לְדָוִד.

358. In the words, "This is the book of the generations of Adam" (Beresheet 5:1), "GENERATIONS" REFERS to images OF THE SOULS, BECAUSE ALL THE SOULS WHO ORIGINATED FROM ADAM ARE LISTED IN THE BOOK. Rabbi Yitzchak said: The Holy One, blessed be He, revealed to Adam the images OF THE SOULS of all the generations who will come into the world and of all the sages and kings of the world destined to rule over Yisrael. When he saw David, King of Yisrael, who was born and then died BECAUSE HE HAD NO DAYS IN HIS LIFE, he said TO THE HOLY ONE, BLESSED BE HE, 'I will give him seventy years of my life.' Hence seventy years were taken from Adam and the Holy One, blessed be He, gave them to David.

359. וְעַל דָּא שַׁבַּח דָּוִד וַאֲמַר, כִּי שִׂמַּחְתַּנִי ה' בְּפָעֳלֶךָ בְּמַעֲשֵׂי יָדֶיךָ אֲרַנֵּן. מָאן גָּרַם לִי חֶדְוָה בְּעָלְמָא, פָּעֳלֶךָ. דָּא הוּא אָדָם קַדְמָאָה, דְּאִיהוּ פָּעֳלוּ דְּקֻדְשָׁא בְּרִיךְ הוּא, וְלָא פָּעֳלוּ דְּבָשָׂר וָדָם. מַעֲשֵׂה יָדָיו דְּקֻדְשָׁא בְּרִיךְ הוּא וְלָא מִבְּנֵי נָשָׁא. וְעַל דָּא, גָּרְעוּ אִינוּן שַׁבְעִין שְׁנִין מֵאָדָם, מֵאֶלֶף שְׁנִין דַּהֲוָה לֵיהּ לְאִתְקַיְּימָא בְּהוֹ.

359. It was for this that David said the praise, "For You have made me glad, Hashem, by Your actions. I will be joyous in the work of Your hands" (Tehilim 92:5). Who caused me to be happy and live in the world? It was Adam WHO CAUSED ME TO BE HAPPY. He was the handiwork of the Holy One, blessed be He, and not of flesh and blood. HE WAS NOT BORN TO ANY MAN, BECAUSE HE WAS MADE BY THE HOLY ONE, BLESSED BE HE. THUS, those seventy years were deducted from Adam's thousand-year life expectancy.

360. וְאַחְמֵי לֵיהּ קֻדְשָׁא בְּרִיךְ הוּא, כָּל חַכִּימֵי דָּרָא וְדָרָא, עַד דְּמָטָא לְדָרֵיהּ דְּרַבִּי עֲקִיבָא, וְחָמֵי אוֹרַיְיתָא דִּידֵיהּ וְחָדֵי. חָמֵי מִיתָתֵיהּ וַעֲצִיב, פָּתַח וַאֲמַר וְלִי מַה יָּקְרוּ רֵעֶיךָ אֵל מֶה עָצְמוּ רָאשֵׁיהֶם.

360. The Holy One, blessed be He, showed him all the sages of each and every generation until he reached the generation of Rabbi Akiva. He saw his Torah and was happy; he saw his death BY THE HANDS OF THE EVIL KINGDOM and was saddened. ADAM said: "How precious are your thoughts (also: 'companions') to me, El how great is the sum of them" (Tehilim 139:17).

361. זֶה סֵפֶר, סֵפֶר וַדַּאי. וְהָא אוֹקִימְנָא, דְּכַד הֲוָה אָדָם בְּגִנְתָּא דְעֵדֶן, נָחִית לֵיהּ קֻדְשָׁא בְּרִיךְ הוּא סִפְרָא, עַל יְדָא דְרָזִיאַ"ל, מַלְאָכָא קַדִּישָׁא, מְמַנָּא עַל רָזֵי עִלָּאִין קַדִּישִׁין. וּבֵיהּ גְּלִיפִין, גְּלוּפֵי עִלָּאִין, וְחָכְמָה קַדִּישָׁא, וְשַׁבְעִין וּתְרֵין זִינֵי דְחָכְמְתָא, הֲווֹ מִתְפָּרְשָׁן מִנֵּיהּ, לְשִׁית מְאָה וְשַׁבְעִין גְּלִיפִין דְּרָזֵי עִלָּאָה.

361. IT IS WRITTEN: "This is the book OF THE GENERATIONS OF ADAM," and there literally is a book. We have already explained that when Adam was in the Garden of Eden, the Holy One, blessed be He, sent a book down to him with Raziel, the holy angel who is in charge of the supernal sacred secrets (Heb. *razin*). In THE BOOK were supernal inscriptions, holy Chochmah and 72 branches of sacred wisdom. SHE IS BESTOWED on 670 inscriptions of the supernal secrets.

362. בְּאֶמְצָעִיתָא דְּסִפְרָא, גְּלִיפָא דְּחָכְמְתָא, לְמִנְדַּע אֶלֶף וַחֲמֵשׁ מְאָה

מִפְּתְחָן, דְּלָא אִתְמַסְרָן לְעֶלָּאֵי קַדִּישֵׁי. וְכֻלְהוּ אִסְתְּימוּ בֵּיה בְּסִפְרָא, עַד דְּמָטָא לְגַבֵּי דְּאָדָם, הֲווֹ מִתְכַּנְּשֵׁי מַלְאֲכֵי עִלָּאֵי, לְמִנְדַּע וּלְמִשְׁמַע, וַהֲווֹ אָמְרֵי, רוּמָה עַל הַשָּׁמַיִם אֱלֹקִים עַל כָּל הָאָרֶץ כְּבוֹדֶךָ.

362. In the middle of the book, there is an engraving of wisdom. It is prepared to receive the 1,500 keys that were not delivered to the supernal holy beings, FOR THE LAST 6,000 YEARS. All those SECRETS were concealed in the book before it came to the hands of Adam. AND WHEN HE RECEIVED IT, holy angels used to congregate around him, so as to know and hear of them. They used to say: "Be exalted, Elohim, above the heavens. Let Your glory be above the earth" (Tehilim 57:12).

363. בָּה שַׁעֲתָא, אִתְרְמִיז לְגַבֵּיה הדרניא״ל מַלְאָכָא קַדִּישָׁא, וַאֲמַר לֵיה: אָדָם אָדָם, הֲוֵי גָּנִיז יְקָרָא דְּמָארָךְ, דְּלָא אִתְיְיהִיב רְשׁוּתָא לְעֶלָּאֵי, לְמִנְדַּע בִּיקָרָא דְּמָרָךְ, בַּר אַנְתְּ. וַהֲוָה עִמֵּיה טָמִיר וְגָנִיז, הַהוּא סִפְרָא, עַד דְּנָפַק אָדָם מִגִּנְתָּא דְּעֵדֶן.

363. At that point, the holy angel Hadarniel hinted to him and said, "Adam, Adam conceal the glory of your Master, AND DO NOT REVEAL IT TO THE ANGELS, for permission was given you alone, AND NOT EVEN TO THE SUPERNAL ANGELS, to know the glory of your Master." Therefore, he concealed it with him until he left the Garden of Eden.

364. דְּהָא בְּקַדְמֵיתָא, הֲוָה מְעַיֵּין בֵּיה, וּמִשְׁתַּמֵּשׁ כָּל יוֹמָא בְּגִינְזַיָּא דְּמָרֵיה, וְאִתְגַּלְיָין לֵיה רָזִין עִלָּאִין, מַה דְּלָא יָדְעוּ שַׁמָּשֵׁי עִלָּאִין. כֵּיוָן דְּחָטָא, וַעֲבַר עַל פִּקּוּדָא דְּמָארֵיה, פָּרַח הַהוּא סִפְרָא מִנֵּיה. וַהֲוָה אָדָם טָפַח עַל רֵישׁוֹי, וּבָכֵי, וְעָאל בְּמֵי גִיחוֹן עַד קַדְלֵיה, וּמַיָּא עָבְדִין גּוּפֵיה חֲלָדִין חֲלָדִין, וְאִשְׁתַּנֵּי זִיוֵויה.

364. At first, he used to study and use the secrets of his Master daily. Supernal secrets that none of the supernal angels knew were revealed to him. When, however, he transgressed the command of his Master BY EATING OF THE TREE OF KNOWLEDGE, the book flew away from him. Adam used to beat upon his head and weep. He went into the waters of the

River Gichon up to his neck, BECAUSE HE REPENTED AND MORTIFIED HIMSELF, UNTIL his body became wrinkled and porous and his radiance changed.

365. בְּשַׁעֲתָא הַהִיא, רָמַז קֻדְשָׁא בְּרִיךְ הוּא לִרְפָאֵל, וְאָתֵיב לֵיהּ הַהוּא סִפְרָא. וּבֵיהּ הֲוָה מִשְׁתַּדַּל אָדָם, וַאֲנַח לֵיהּ לְשֵׁת בְּרֵיהּ. וְכֵן לְכָל אִינּוּן תּוֹלְדוֹת. עַד דְּמָטָא לְאַבְרָהָם, וּבֵיהּ הֲוָה יָדַע לְאִסְתַּכְּלָא בִּיקָרָא דְּמָארֵיהּ. וְהָא אִתְּמַר. וְכֵן לַחֲנוֹךְ, אִתְיְיהַב לֵיהּ סִפְרָא, וְאִסְתַּכַּל מִנֵּיהּ, בִּיקָרָא עִלָּאָה.

365. At that point, the Holy One, blessed be He, signaled to the angel Raphael to return the book TO ADAM. Adam occupied himself with it. He left it to his son Seth and to all the generations after him until Abraham came along. Abraham knew how to use the book to examine his Master's glory. This has already been explained. This book was also given to Enoch, and through it, he perceived the supernal gory.

64. "Male and female He created them"

Lack of fulfillment and joy in the world is rooted in the disunity between the supernal male and female forces that permeate existence. This is exemplified in the separation between man and woman. Through relations between husband and wife, we can influence and ignite a bonding in the Upper Worlds, provided this is our spiritual intent. Each time this occurs, we remove an aspect of evil from our midst. Relationships that lack this spiritual foundation cannot affect any positive change on either a supernal or a physical level.

The Kabbalists teach us that this lack of spiritual understanding is the primary source for the darkness that governs our world. We can become aware that the quality of a marriage affects the universe, and that there is spiritual meaning and purpose in every union.

366. זָכָר וּנְקֵבָה בְּרָאָם. רַבִּי שִׁמְעוֹן אֲמַר, רָזִין עִלָּאִין, אִתְגַּלְיָין בְּהָנֵי תְּרֵי קְרָאֵי. זָכָר וּנְקֵבָה בְּרָאָם, לְמִנְדַע יְקָרָא עִלָּאָה, רָזָא דִּמְהֵימָנוּתָא, דְּמִגּוֹ רָזָא דְּנָא אִתְבְּרֵי אָדָם.

366. "Male and female He created them" (Beresheet 1:28). Rabbi Shimon said that supernal secrets have been revealed by the two verses, "THIS IS THE BOOK" AND "male and female He created them." THE LATTER VERSE COMES to teach US the supernal glory of the secret of Faith, by which secret man was created. THIS IS THE SECRET OF SUPERNAL ZEIR ANPIN AND THE NUKVA CALLED 'HEAVEN AND EARTH'.

367. תָּא חֲזֵי, בְּרָזָא דְּאִתְבְּרִיאוּ שָׁמַיִם וָאָרֶץ, אִתְבְּרֵי אָדָם. בְּהוּ כְּתִיב, אֵלֶּה תּוֹלְדוֹת הַשָּׁמַיִם וְהָאָרֶץ. בְּאָדָם כְּתִיב, זֶה סֵפֶר תּוֹלְדוֹת אָדָם. בְּהוּ כְּתִיב בְּהִבָּרְאָם, בְּאָדָם כְּתִיב, בְּיוֹם הִבָּרְאָם.

367. Come and see: in the same concealed manner in which heaven and earth were created, SIGNIFYING THE SUPERNAL MALE AND FEMALE, so man was created. Of the heaven and the earth it is written: "These are the generations of the heaven and of the earth" (Beresheet 2:4); of man, "This is the book of the generations of Adam;" of THE HEAVENS AND THE EARTH,

"when they were created;" and of Adam, "in the day when they were created" (Beresheet 5:2). THE TWO ARE EQUAL AS THEY WERE CREATED BY THE SAME PRINCIPLE.

368. זָכָר וּנְקֵבָה בְּרָאָם. מֵהָכָא, כָּל דִּיוֹקְנָא דְּלָא אִשְׁתְּכַח בֵּיהּ, דְּכַר וְנוּקְבָּא, לָאו אִיהוּ דִּיוֹקְנָא עִלָּאָה כְּדְקָא חָזֵי. וּבְרָזָא דְמַתְנִיתִין אוֹקִימְנָא.

368. From the words "male and female He created them" we learn that any figure not comprised of both male and female is not a supernal figure. We have explained this with the secrets of Mishnah.

369. תָּא חֲזֵי, בְּכָל אֲתָר דְּלָא אִשְׁתַּכְּחוּ, דְּכַר וְנוּקְבָּא כַּחֲדָא, קֻדְשָׁא בְּרִיךְ הוּא לָא שָׁוֵי מְדוֹרֵיהּ בְּהַהוּא אֲתָר. וּבִרְכָאן לָא אִשְׁתַּכְּחוּ, אֶלָּא בַּאֲתָר דְּאִשְׁתְּכַח דְּכַר וְנוּקְבָּא. דִּכְתִיב, וַיְבָרֶךְ אוֹתָם וַיִּקְרָא אֶת שְׁמָם אָדָם, בְּיוֹם הִבָּרְאָם, וְלָא כְּתִיב וַיְבָרֶךְ אוֹתוֹ, וַיִּקְרָא אֶת שְׁמוֹ אָדָם, דַּאֲפִילוּ אָדָם, לָא אִקְרֵי, אֶלָּא דְּכַר וְנוּקְבָּא כַּחֲדָא.

369. Come and behold: the Holy One, blessed be He, cannot reside in a place where there are no male and female together. Blessings can be found only in a place where male and female are together. As it is written: "And He blessed them and called their name man (Heb. *Adam*), on the day when they were created" (Ibid.). It was not said that He blessed him and called him man. THIS TEACHES US that he was not even called BY THE NAME OF man, except as a male and female combined.

370. רַבִּי יְהוּדָה אָמַר, מִיּוֹמָא דְּאִתְחָרַב בֵּי מַקְדְּשָׁא, בִּרְכָּאן לָא אִשְׁתַּכְּחוּ בְּעָלְמָא, וְאִתְאֲבִידוּ בְּכָל יוֹמָא. דִּכְתִיב הַצַּדִּיק אָבַד. מַאי אָבַד, אָבַד בִּרְכָּאן דַּהֲווֹ שָׁרְיָין בֵּיהּ, כְּמָה דִּכְתִיב בְּרָכוֹת לְרֹאשׁ צַדִּיק. וּכְתִיב אָבְדָה הָאֱמוּנָה. כְּגַוְונָא דָא כְּתִיב, וַיְבָרֶךְ אוֹתָם, וּכְתִיב וַיְבָרֶךְ אוֹתָם אֱלֹקִים.

370. Rabbi Yehuda said that ever since the destruction of the Temple, there are no blessings on earth and they are lost every day. As it is written: "The righteous perishes" (Yeshayah 57:1). What is the meaning of "perishes?" It is that the blessings that used to dwell in the righteous perished, as in the words, "Blessings are on the head of the righteous" (Mishlei 10:6), and, "Truth has perished" (Yirmeyah 7:28), MEANING THE NUKVA, WHICH RECEIVES BLESSINGS FROM YESOD OF ZEIR ANPIN, THE RIGHTEOUS, WHICH IS THE SECRET OF THE MALE. Similarly, AT THE TIME OF PERFECTION, it is written: "And Elohim blessed them AND CALLED THEIR NAME ADAM," BECAUSE THEY WERE WHOLE.

371. מִשֵּׁת אִתְיַיחֲסוּ כָּל דָּרֵי עָלְמָא וְכָל אִינוּן צַדִּיקֵי קְשׁוֹט, דַּהֲווֹ בְּעָלְמָא. אֲמַר רַבִּי יוֹסֵי, אִלֵּין אַתְוֹון בַּתְרָאִין דַּהֲווֹ בְּאוֹרַיְיתָא, אִשְׁתַּכָּחוּ בָּתַר דַּעֲבַר אָדָם עַל אַתְוֹון דְּאוֹרַיְיתָא כֻּלְּהוּ. וּבְתִיוּבְתֵּיה לְקַמֵּי מָארֵיה, אָחִיד בְּאִלֵּין תְּרֵין. וּמִכְּדֵין, אִתְהַדְּרוּ אַתְוֹון לְמִפְרַע, בְּסֵדֶר תשר"ק.

371. It is to Seth that all the generations of earth and all the truly righteous of the world trace their descent. Rabbi Yosi said that those two final letters of the Torah, SHIN AND TAV, were left intact even after Adam had transgressed against all the letters of the Torah, BECAUSE THE SIN OF THE TREE OF KNOWLEDGE AFFECTED THE WHOLE TORAH. And when he repented before his Master, he cleaved to those two LETTERS, SHIN AND TAV, WHICH HAD REMAINED WHOLE, and, at that point, the original letters returned in the reverse order of Tav, Shin, Resh, Kof, and so on.

372. וּבְגִין כָּךְ, קָרָא לְהַהוּא בְּרָא דְּאִתְיְלֵיד לֵיה, דְּאִיהוּ בִּדְמוּתוֹ כְּצַלְמוֹ, שֵׁת. דְּאִינוּן סִיּוּמָא דְּאַתְוֹון, וְלָא אִתְתַּקְּנוּ אַתְוֹון, עַד דְּקַיְימוּ יִשְׂרָאֵל עַל טוּרָא דְּסִינַי, וּכְדֵין אֲהַדְּרוּ אַתְוֹון עַל תִּקּוּנַיְיהוּ, כְּיוֹמָא דְּאִתְבְּרִיאוּ שָׁמַיִם וָאָרֶץ. וְאִתְבַּסַּם עָלְמָא, וְקַיְימָא עַל קִיּוּמֵיה.

372. He then called the son he begot in his own likeness, after his image, Seth, a name composed of the last two letters of the alpha bet and the only two letters with which he was left. The order of the letters was not fully constructed, THAT IS, PROPERLY ORDERED, until Yisrael stood at Mount Sinai. Then the letters returned to their proper order – the order they had when heaven and earth were created – THE ORDER IN WHICH THEY

APPEARED BEFORE THE SIN OF EATING OF THE TREE OF KNOWLEDGE Then, the world was appeased and more securely established.

373. ר' אַבָּא אָמַר, יוֹמָא דַּעֲבַר אָדָם עַל פְּקוּדָא דְּמָארֵיה, בָּעְיָין שָׁמַיִם וָאָרֶץ, לְאִתְעַקְּרָא מֵאַתְרַיְיהוּ. מ״ט, בְּגִין דְּאִינוּן לָא קַיְימוּ, אֶלָּא עַל בְּרִית דִּכְתִיב אִם לֹא בְרִיתִי יוֹמָם וָלַיְלָה חֻקּוֹת שָׁמַיִם וָאָרֶץ לֹא שָׂמְתִּי. וְאָדָם עָבַר בְּרִית, שֶׁנֶּאֱמַר וְהֵמָּה כְּאָדָם עָבְרוּ בְרִית.

373. Rabbi Aba said that on the day that Adam transgressed his Master's command, heaven and earth wanted to be uprooted from their places. Why? Because they are based only on the covenant, as it is written: "If My covenant be not day and night, it were as if I had not appointed the ordinances of heaven and earth" (Yirmeyah 33:25). Adam broke the covenant, as it is written: "But they like Adam have transgressed the covenant" (Hoshea 6:7). HENCE, THEY LOST THEIR FOUNDATION AND ASKED TO BE UPROOTED.

374. וְאִלְמָלֵא דְּגָלֵי קַמֵּי קֻדְשָׁא בְּרִיךְ הוּא, דִּזְמִינִין יִשְׂרָאֵל לְקַיְימָא עַל טוּרָא דְּסִינַי, לְקַיְימָא הַאי בְּרִית, לָא אִתְקַיַּים עָלְמָא. רַבִּי חִזְקִיָּה אָמַר, כָּל מָאן דְּאוֹדֵי עַל חֲטָאֵיה, קוּדְשָׁא בְּרִיךְ הוּא שָׁבִיק לֵיה, וּמָחִיל עַל חוֹבֵיה.

374. Were it not for the fact that it was clear to the Holy One, blessed be He, that Yisrael would stand at Mount Sinai to keep the covenant, the world would not have survived THE SIN OF EATING OF THE TREE OF KNOWLEDGE. Rabbi Chizkiyah said that the Holy One, blessed be He, forgives and pardons the iniquities of he who confesses his sins. HENCE, CONTRARY TO WHAT RABBI ABA SAID, IT IS BECAUSE ADAM CONFESSED HIS SINS AND REPENTED THAT THE WORLD SURVIVED AND HE DOES NOT WANT TO SAY THAT THE REASON IS, THAT IT WAS CLEAR TO THE HOLY ONE, BLESSED BE HE, THAT YISRAEL WOULD STAND AT MOUNT SINAI.

375. תָּא חֲזֵי, כַּד בָּרָא קֻדְשָׁא בְּרִיךְ הוּא עָלְמָא, עֲבַד הַאי בְּרִית, וְקַיְימָא עֲלֵיה עָלְמָא. מְנָלָן, דִּכְתִיב בָּרָא שִׁית, דָּא בְּרִית דְּעָלְמָא

קָיְמָא עֲלֵיהּ. שִׁית, דְּמִנֵּיהּ, נְגִידִין וְנָפְקֵי בִּרְכָאן לְעָלְמָא, וַעֲלֵיהּ
אִתְבְּרֵי עָלְמָא. וְאָדָם עֲבַר עַל הַאי בְּרִית, וְאַעֲבַר לֵיהּ מֵאַתְרֵיהּ.

375. Come and behold: when the Holy One, blessed be He, created the
world, WHICH IS THE SECRET OF THE NUKVA, He made the covenant,
WHICH IS YESOD OF ZEIR ANPIN. He established the world upon it, AS
THE NUKVA RECEIVES HER SUSTENANCE FROM ZEIR ANPIN. From where
do we know that? From the word 'BERESHEET,' WHICH IS A COMBINATION
OF *bara* (created) and *sheet* (six). *SHEET* IS the covenant upon which the
world rests. This *sheet,* WHICH STANDS FOR YESOD, is the place from
where all blessings are drawn into the world, and by it the world was
created. Adam, BY HIS SIN OF EATING OF THE TREE OF KNOWLEDGE,
broke that covenant and removed it from its place. HENCE, HEAVEN AND
EARTH ASKED TO BE UPROOTED.

376. הַאי בְּרִית, אִתְרְמִיזַת בְּאָת יו״ד, אָת זְעֵירָא, עִקְּרָא וִיסוֹדָא
דְּעָלְמָא. כַּד אוֹלִיד בַּר, אוֹדֵי עַל חֶטְאוֹ, וְקָרָא שְׁמֵיהּ ש״ת, וְלָא אַדְכַּר
בֵּיהּ יו״ד, לְמֶהֱוֵי שִׁית, בְּגִין דַּעֲבַר עֲלֵיהּ. וּבְגִין כָּךְ, קֻדְשָׁא בְּרִיךְ הוּא
מִנֵּיהּ אִשְׁתִּיל עָלְמָא, וְאִתְיַיחֲסוּ כָּל דָּרָא זַכָּאָה דְּעָלְמָא.

376. This covenant is symbolized by the smallest letter, which is Yud,
which is the essence and the foundation of the world. BASED ON IT, THE
WORLD WAS STRUCTURED. And when ADAM bore a son, he confessed his
sin, called him Seth, and did not include the letter Yud in his name. If his
name had included Yud, it would have been *sheet*. Because Adam broke
THE COVENANT, AS WAS SAID EARLIER, "THEY LIKE ADAM HAVE
TRANSGRESSED THE COVENANT," HE NAMED HIS SON SETH, SPELLED
WITHOUT YUD, THEREBY CONFESSING TO HIS SIN. Because HE
CONFESSED HIS SIN, the Holy One, blessed be He, populated the world
from him, and he was made forefather to all the generations of righteous
people in the world. THUS, BECAUSE OF HIS CONFESSION OF HIS SIN,
THE HOLY ONE, BLESSED BE HE, FORGAVE HIM AND THE WORLD
SURVIVED.

377. וְתָא חֲזֵי, כַּד קָיְמוּ יִשְׂרָאֵל עַל טוּרָא דְּסִינַי, עָאל בֵּין תְּרֵין אַתְוָון
אִלֵּין, רָזָא דִּבְרִית, בֵּי״ת. וּמַאן אִיהוּ, בֵּי״ת. וְעָאל בֵּין תְּרֵין אַתְוָון

דְּאִשְׁתְּאָרוּ, וְיָהֵיב לֵיהּ לְיִשְׂרָאֵל. וְכַד עָאל בי״ת, רָזָא דִּבְרִית, בֵּין תְּרֵין
אַתְוָון אִלֵּין, דְּאִינּוּן שי״ן תי״ו, וְאִתְעֲבִידוּ שַׁבָּת, כד״א וְשָׁמְרוּ בְנֵי
יִשְׂרָאֵל אֶת הַשַּׁבָּת לַעֲשׂוֹת אֶת הַשַּׁבָּת לְדוֹרוֹתָם בְּרִית עוֹלָם, כְּמָה
דַּהֲוָה שֵׁירוּתָא דְּעָלְמָא, לְאִתְיַיחֲסוּ בְּהוֹ כָּל דָּרֵי עָלְמָא, מֵאִלֵּין תְּרֵין
אַתְוָון ש״ת. הֲווֹ תַּלְיָין, עַד דְּאִשְׁתַּכְלֵל עָלְמָא, כְּדְקָא יָאוּת, וְעָאל
בֵּינַיְיהוּ בְּרִית קַדִּישָׁא, וְאִשְׁתַּכְלֵל בִּשְׁלִימוּ, וְאִתְעֲבִידוּ שַׁבָּת.

377. Come and behold: when Yisrael stood before Mount Sinai, a letter was inserted between the letters SHIN AND TAV. This was the letter Bet, which is the secret of the covenant (Heb. *brit*). THIS IS THE BET OF BERESHEET. It was inserted between the two letters that remained AFTER THE SIN OF THE TREE OF KNOWLEDGE, NAMELY BETWEEN SHIN AND TAV, AND SHABBAT was given to Yisrael. And when the letter Bet, which is the secret of the covenant, was inserted between the two letters Shin and *Tav*, they became Shabbat, as it is written: "Wherefore the children of Yisrael shall keep the Shabbat, to observe the Shabbat throughout their generations, for a perpetual covenant" (Shemot 31:16), FOR THEY DESERVED TO RECEIVE THE SHABBAT PERPETUALLY FOR ALL THEIR GENERATIONS. As in the beginning of the world, the lineage of all future generations was determined by those two letters. So, BY THE INSERTION OF THE LETTER BET, THOSE TWO LETTERS PERPETUALLY ENLIGHTEN THE GENERATIONS. Shin and Tav were in suspension until the world was adequately completed. THEN, WITH THE GIVING OF THE TORAH, the world was fully completed. Then, the Holy covenant came in between the letters, and they became Shabbat.

378. אָמַר רָבִּי יוֹסֵי, אִלֵּין תְּרֵין אַתְוָון, אִשְׁתַּכְלָלוּ בָּאת בֵּי״ת. וְכַד
אִתְהַדָּר אַתְוָון לְמַפְרֵעַ, מִן יוֹמָא דְּאִתְיְילִיד שֵׁת, אֲהַדְרוּ אַתְוָון בְּכָל
דָּרָא וְדָרָא, עַד דְּמָטֵי יִשְׂרָאֵל לְטוּרָא דְּסִינַי, וְאִתְתַּקָּנוּ.

378. Rabbi Yosi said that because those two letters were fully perfected by the letter *Bet*, THEY ARE NOW ABLE TO RECEIVE DIRECT LIGHT AT THE GIVING OF THE TORAH. THOSE letters began falling into their proper order on the day that Seth was born, NOT RECEIVING LIGHT FROM ABOVE DOWNWARD, BUT DRAWING ONLY FROM BELOW UPWARD. THIS HAS REMAINED THE CASE in each and every generation, SHINING ONLY

UPWARD, WHICH IS THE LIGHT OF NEFESH, until Yisrael reached Mount Sinai. Then, the letters were fully corrected, BECAUSE THE LETTER BET ILLUMINATED THEM FROM ABOVE DOWNWARD, AND THEY BECAME SHABBAT.

379. אָמַר רבי יְהוּדָה, לְתַתָּא אתהדרו, וְכָל דָּרָא וְדָרָא הֲוָה גָּפֵיף עָלְמָא בְּאַתְוָון, וְלָא מתיישבין בְּדוּכְתַּיְיהוּ. כַּד אתייהבת אורייתא לישְׂרָאֵל, אתתקן כֹּלָּא. ר׳ אֶלְעָזָר אוֹמֵר, בְּיוֹמֵי אֱנוֹשׁ, הֲווֹ חכּימין בְּנֵי נָשָׁא, בְּחָכְמָה דְּחַרְשִׁין וְקוֹסְמִין, וּבְחָכְמְתָא לְמֶעְצַר לְחֵילֵי דשְׁמַיָא. וְלָא הֲוָה בַּר נָשׁ מִיּוֹמָא דנָפַק אָדָם מִגִּנְתָּא דְעֵדֶן, וְאַפִּיק עֲמֵיהּ חָכְמְתָא דְּטַרְפֵי אִילָנָא, דְּאִשְׁתַּדַּל בָּהּ, דְּהָא אָדָם וְאִתְּתֵיהּ, וְאִינּוּן דנָפְקוּ מִנֵּיהּ, עַד דְּאָתָא אֱנוֹשׁ, שְׁבִיקוּ לָהּ.

379. Rabbi Yehuda said: They started TO RADIATE again FROM ABOVE downward, WHICH IS THE LIGHT OF RUACH. THUS, HE DISAGREED WITH RABBI YOSI, WHO MAINTAINED THAT THEY ONLY SHONE FROM BELOW UPWARD, WHICH IS THE LIGHT OF NEFESH, BEFORE THE TORAH WAS GIVEN. And in each and every generation BEFORE THE GIVING OF THE TORAH, the world was manipulating those two letters, and they could not settle in their appropriate place. Only when Torah was given to Yisrael was everything established. Rabbi Elazar said that at the time of Enosh, people were skilled in magic and divination and in the wisdom of controlling the heavenly forces, SO THAT THESE FORCES SHOULD NOT HAVE AFFECTED THE WORLD. When Adam left the Garden of Eden and brought out with him the wisdom of the fig leaves (WHICH IS WITCHCRAFT), there was no one to use this knowledge, because Adam, his wife, and all those born from them, until Enosh came, stayed clear of this KNOWLEDGE AND DID NOT USE IT.

380. כַּד אָתָא אֱנוֹשׁ, חָמָא לוֹן, וְחָמָא חָכְמַתְהוֹן מְשַׁנְיָין עִלָּאִין, וְאִשְׁתַּדְּלוּ בְּהוֹן, וְעָבְדִין עֲבִידְתִּין, וְחַרְשִׁין וְקוֹסְמִין, וְאוֹלִיפוּ מִנְּהוֹן, עַד דְּאִתְפַּשְּׁטַת הַהִיא חָכְמְתָא, בְּדָרָא דְּמַבּוּל. וְכֻלְּהוּ הֲווֹ עַבְדֵי עֲבִידְתַּיְיהוּ לְאַבְאָשָׁא.

380. But when Enosh came, he saw those FIG LEAVES that their wisdom contradicts the holy beings, THAT IS, IT DENIES HOLINESS. Then, people once again practiced magic and sorcery, and they shared their knowledge WITH OTHERS. This wisdom spread widely in the generation of the flood, when magic and sorcery were practiced for evil purposes.

381. וַהֲווֹ מִתְתַּקְפֵי לְגַבֵּי נֹחַ, בְּאִינּוּן חָכְמָתָן, וְאָמְרֵי דְּלָא יָכִיל דִּינָא דְּעָלְמָא לְאַשְׁרָאָה עֲלַיְיהוּ, דְּהָא אִינּוּן עָבְדֵי חָכְמָתָא, לְדַחְיָיא לְכָל אִינּוּן מָארֵי דְדִינָא. וּמֵאֱנוֹשׁ שָׁרִיאוּ כֻּלְּהוּ לְאִשְׁתַּדְּלוּ בְּאִלֵּין חָכְמָתָן. הה"ד אָז הוּחַל לִקְרֹא בְּשֵׁם ה'.

381. The people defied Noah with this wisdom WHEN HE WARNED THEM OF THE IMPENDING FLOOD. They said that no punishment could ever be executed upon them, because they could avoid, by use of this knowledge, any execution of judgment. From the time of Enosh onward, everyone began practicing these skills. Thus, it was written: "then men began (Heb. *huchal*) to call on Hashem by name" (Beresheet 4:26). THE WORD *HUCHAL* MEANS THAT THEY MADE A PROFANE (HEB. *CHULIN*) USE OF THE NAME OF HASHEM, THROUGH THE WITCHCRAFT THEY EMPLOYED.

382. ר' יִצְחָק אָמַר, כָּל אִינּוּן זַכָּאִין דַּהֲווֹ בְּהוּ לְבָתַר, בְּהַהוּא דָּרָא, כֻּלְּהוּ הֲווֹ מִשְׁתַּדְּלֵי לְמָחָאָה בְּהוּ, כְּמוֹ יֶרֶד מְתוּשֶׁלַח וַחֲנוֹךְ, וְלָא יָכִילוּ, עַד דְּאִתְפַּשְּׁטוּ חַיָּיבִין, מָרְדֵי בְּמָארֵיהוֹן, וְאָמְרֵי מַה שַׁדַּי כִּי נַעַבְדֶנּוּ.

382. Rabbi Yitzchak said that all those righteous people who lived after that generation OF ENOSH, such as Jared, Methushelach, and Enoch, tried hard to rebuke them, but were unsuccessful. The world became full of sinners who rebelled against their Master saying, "What is Shadai, that we should serve Him?" (Iyov 21:15).

383. וְכִי הַאי טִפְּשׁוּתָא הֲווֹ קָא אָמְרֵי. אֶלָּא, בְּגִין דַּהֲווֹ יָדְעֵי כָּל אִינּוּן חָכְמָתָן, וְכֻלְּהוּ מְמַנָּן דְּעָלְמָא, דְּאִתְפַּקְּדָן עֲלַיְיהוּ, וַהֲווֹ מְרַחֲצָן בְּהוּ. עַד דְּאָתֵיב קוּדְשָׁא בְּרִיךְ הוּא עָלְמָא כְּדְקָא הֲוָה, דְּהָא בְּקַדְמֵיתָא הֲוָה מַיִם בְּמַיִם. וּלְבָתַר אָתֵיב לֵיהּ לְעָלְמָא כִּדְקַדְמֵיתָא, וְלָא אִתְחָרֵיב מִכֹּלָּא,

דְּהָא בְּרַחֲמִין אַשְׁגַּח עֲלַיְיהוּ, דִּכְתִיב ה' לַמַּבּוּל יָשָׁב, וְלָא כְּתִיב אֱלֹקִים.

383. HE ASKS: How could they have been so foolish as to say, "WHAT IS SHADAI, THAT WE SHOULD SERVE HIM?" HE ANSWERS THAT THIS WAS because they had vast wisdom and knew and had faith in the ministers in charge of ruling the world. THEY HAD FAITH IN THEIR WISDOM AND BELIEVED THAT BY MEANS OF OATHS THEY COULD BIND THOSE MINISTERS AND PROTECT THEMSELVES SO THAT NO HARM COULD BEFALL THEM. Then, the Holy One, Blessed be He, restored the world to its original state, THROUGH THE FLOOD OF WATER. IN ITS ORIGINAL STATE, AS ON THE SECOND DAY OF CREATION, the world was water upon water; THIS WAS BEFORE THE DRY LAND WAS CREATED. After THE FLOOD, He again reestablished the world and not everything was destroyed BY THE FLOOD, because He treated them with mercy as indicated by the fact that it is written: "Hashem sat at the flood" (Tehilim 29:10). The word "Hashem" SIGNIFIES THE ATTRIBUTE OF MERCY, whereas the word "Elohim" WOULD HAVE SIGNIFIED JUDGMENT. BECAUSE HE JUDGED THEM WITH MERCY, NOT ALL WAS DESTROYED BY THE FLOOD.

384. בְּיוֹמוֹי דָּאֱנוֹשׁ, אֲפִילוּ יְנוֹקֵי דְּהַהוּא דָּרָא, כֻּלְּהוּ הֲווֹ מַשְׁגִּחָן בְּחָכְמְתָאן עִלָּאִין, וַהֲוֵי מִסְתַּכְּלָן בְּהוּ. אָמַר רְבִּי יֵיסָא, אִי הָכֵי טִפְּשִׁין הֲווֹ, דְּלָא הֲווֹ יָדְעִין דְּזַמִּין קוּדְשָׁא בְּרִיךְ הוּא לְאַיְיתָאָה עֲלַיְיהוּ מֵי טוֹפָנָא, וִימוּתוּן בְּהוּ.

384. In the days of Enosh, even children were acquainted with this supernal wisdom, which they learned AND OBSERVED. Rabbi Yesa said that if this is so, they were stupid, because they did not know that the Holy One, blessed be He, was bound to bring the waters of the flood upon them, and they would die.

385. אָמַר רְבִּי יִצְחָק, מִנְדַּע יָדְעֵי, אֲבָל אָחִידוּ טִפְּשׁוּתָא בְּלִבַּיְיהוּ, דְּאִינוּן הֲווֹ יָדְעֵי הַהוּא מַלְאָכָא דִּמְמַנָּא עַל אֶשָׁא, וְהַהוּא דִּמְמַנָּא עַל מַיָּא, וַהֲווֹ יָדְעִין לְמֶעֱצַר לוֹן, דְּלָא יָכְלִין לְמֶעֱבַּד דִּינָא עֲלַיְיהוּ. וְאִינוּן

לָא הֲווֹ יָדְעִין דְּקוּדְשָׁא בְּרִיךְ הוּא שַׁלִּיט עַל אַרְעָא, וּמִנֵּיהּ יֵיתֵי דִּינָא עַל עָלְמָא.

385. Rabbi Yitzchak said that although they knew, foolishness grabbed hold of their hearts. They thought that by knowing the name of the angel in charge of fire and the angel in charge of the waters, they could prevent them from executing judgment upon them. HENCE, THEY HAD NO FEAR OF PUNISHMENT. But what they did not know was that the Holy One, blessed be He, controlled the earth, and from therein judgment would come upon the world.

386. אֶלָּא הֲווֹ חָמָאן, דְּעָלְמָא אִתְפְּקַד בִּידָא דְּאִינּוּן מְמַנָּן, וּבְהוּ כָּל מִלֵּי עָלְמָא. וּבְגִינֵי כָּךְ, לָא הֲווֹ מִסְתַּכְּלָן בֵּיהּ בְּקֻדְשָׁא בְּרִיךְ הוּא, וְלָא מַשְׁגִּיחִין בַּעֲבִידְתֵּיהּ, עַד דְּאַרְעָא אִתְחַבָּלַת. וְרוּחַ קוּדְשָׁא אַכְרֵיז בְּכָל יוֹמָא, וַאֲמַר יִתַּמּוּ חַטָּאִים מִן הָאָרֶץ וּרְשָׁעִים עוֹד אֵינָם.

386. They only saw that the world was entrusted to those ministers and that all worldy matters depended upon them. Thus, they took no notice of the Holy One, blessed be He, nor did they observe His works until the earth was demolished. And the Holy Spirit proclaimed upon them every day, "let sinners be wiped out of the earth and let the wicked be no more" (Tehilim 104:35).

387. וְאוֹרִיךְ קֻדְשָׁא בְּרִיךְ הוּא לוֹן כָּל הַהוּא זִמְנָא, דְּאִינּוּן זַכָּאִין: יֶרֶד וּמְתוּשֶׁלַח וַחֲנוֹךְ קַיְּימִין בְּעָלְמָא. כֵּיוָן דְּאִסְתַּלָּקוּ מֵעָלְמָא, וּכְדֵין אַנְחֵית קוּדְשָׁא בְּרִיךְ הוּא דִּינָא עֲלַיְיהוּ וְאִתְאֲבִידוּ. כְּמָה דְּאַתְּ אָמֵר וַיִּמָּחוּ מִן הָאָרֶץ.

387. And the Holy One, blessed be He, waited for them while those righteous men, like Jared, Metushelach, and Enoch lived. And when they passed from the world, the Holy One, blessed be He, then released judgment upon the wicked, and they perished, as it is said: "They were blotted out from the earth" (Beresheet 7:23).

65. "And Enoch walked with Elohim"

The following section has the power to instill fear at the sudden prospect of falling into negativity. We become aware of the evil forces that stand ready to sabotage our spiritual efforts at the first sign of an opening.

388. וַיִּתְהַלֵּךְ חֲנוֹךְ אֶת הָאֱלֹקִים וְאֵינֶנּוּ כִּי לָקַח אוֹתוֹ אֱלֹקִים. ר' יוֹסֵי פָּתַח עַד שֶׁהַמֶּלֶךְ בִּמְסִבּוֹ נִרְדִּי נָתַן רֵיחוֹ. הַאי קְרָא אִתְּמַר. אֲבָל תָּא חֲזֵי, כָּךְ אָרְחוֹי דְּקֻדְשָׁא בְּרִיךְ הוּא, בְּשַׁעְתָּא דְּבַר נָשׁ אִתְדַּבַּק בֵּיהּ, וְהוּא אַשְׁרֵי דִּיּוּרֵיהּ עֲלֵיהּ, וְיָדַע דִּלְבָתַר יוֹמִין יִסְרַח, אַקְדִּים וְלָקִיט רֵיחֵיהּ טַב מִנֵּיהּ, וְסָלִיק לֵיהּ מֵעָלְמָא.

388. "And Enoch walked with Elohim, and he was not, for Elohim took him" (Beresheet 5:24). Rabbi Yosi said: "While the king was still feasting, my spikenard sent forth its fragrance" (Shir Hashirim 1:12). This verse has been expounded on, yet come and behold: it is the way of the Holy One, blessed be He, that when a man cleaves to Him, He in turn sets His Shechinah upon the man. And when He knows that this man will sin, He acts preemptively, plucks away his good fragrance, and removes him from the world.

389. הה"ד עַד שֶׁהַמֶּלֶךְ בִּמְסִבּוֹ נִרְדִּי נָתַן רֵיחוֹ. עַד שֶׁהַמֶּלֶךְ: דָּא קֻדְשָׁא בְּרִיךְ הוּא. בִּמְסִבּוֹ: דָּא הַהוּא בַּר נָשׁ דְּאִתְדַּבַּק בֵּיהּ, וְאָזִיל בְּאָרְחוֹי. נִרְדִּי נָתַן רֵיחוֹ: אִינּוּן עוֹבָדִין טָבִין דְּבֵיהּ, דִּבְגִינֵיהוֹן יִסְתַּלַּק מֵעָלְמָא, עַד דְּלָא מָטָא זִמְנֵיהּ.

389. "The king" mentioned above is the Holy One, blessed be He. His feasting is the man who cleaves to Him, and follows in His path. The spikenard that gives fragrance consists of all the man's good deeds, in honor of which he is taken away from this world prematurely. THIS PREVENTS HIM FROM CORRUPTING HIS DEEDS.

390. וְעַל דָּא הֲוָה שְׁלֹמֹה מַלְכָּא אָמַר, יֵשׁ הֶבֶל אֲשֶׁר נַעֲשָׂה עַל הָאָרֶץ אֲשֶׁר יֵשׁ צַדִּיקִים וְגוֹ'. יֵשׁ צַדִּיקִים אֲשֶׁר מַגִּיעַ אֲלֵיהֶם כְּמַעֲשֵׂה

הָרְשָׁעִים, כְּמָה דְאוֹקִימְנָא, דִּבְגִין דְּעוֹבָדֵיהוֹן טָבִין, קֻדְשָׁא בְּרִיךְ הוּא
סָלֵיק לוֹן מֵעָלְמָא, עַד לָא מָטָא זִמְנַיְיהוּ, וְעָבֵיד בְּהוֹן דִּינִין. וְיֵשׁ
רְשָׁעִים אֲשֶׁר מַגִּיעַ אֲלֵיהֶם כְּמַעֲשֵׂה הַצַּדִּיקִים, דְּקֻדְשָׁא בְּרִיךְ הוּא
אוֹרִיךְ לוֹן יוֹמִין, וְאוֹרִיךְ רוּגְזֵיהּ בְּהוּ. וְכָל דָּא, כְּמָה דְאִתְּמַר, אִלֵּין
בְּגִין דְּלָא יִסְרְחוּן, וְאִלֵּין בְּגִין דְּלַהֲדְרוּ לְגַבֵּיהּ, אוֹ בְּגִין דְּיִפּוֹק מִנַּיְיהוּ
בְּנִין דְּמַעֲלֵי.

390. King Solomon said of this, "There is a vanity which is done upon the earth; that there are righteous men, to whom it happens according to the deeds of the wicked" (Kohelet 8:14). There are righteous people who are rewarded as if they were wicked, as we have explained. For because of their good deeds the Holy One, blessed be He, removes them from the world prematurely and inflicts judgment upon them, SO THEY WILL NOT CORRUPT THEIR WAYS. And there are wicked men to whom it happens according to the deeds of the righteous" (Ibid.), for the Holy One, blessed be He, gives them a respite and is patient with them, AS IN THE DAYS OF THE FLOOD. And all this is, as we have explained, so that they should not sin AND CORRUPT THEIR GOOD WAYS. HENCE, THEY RECEIVE JUDGMENT AS IF THEY WERE WICKED, so that they may repent or because good children are expected to come from them, THEREFORE HE WAITS FOR THEM AND HOLDS BACK HIS ANGER; HENCE THEY RECEIVE A REWARD AS IF THEY WERE RIGHTEOUS.

391. תָּא חֲזֵי, חֲנוֹךְ זַכָּאָה הֲוָה, וְקֻדְשָׁא בְּרִיךְ הוּא חָמָא לֵיהּ דְּיִסְרַח
לְבָתַר, וְלָקִיט לֵיהּ עַד לָא יִסְרַח, הה"ד וְלִלְקֹט שׁוֹשַׁנִּים. בְּגִין דְּיַהֲבֵי
רֵיחָא טַב, לָקִיט לוֹן קֻדְשָׁא בְּרִיךְ הוּא עַד לָא יִסְרְחוּ. וְאֵינֶנּוּ כִּי לָקַח
אוֹתוֹ אֱלֹקִים. וְאֵינֶנּוּ: לְאַרְכָא יוֹמִין כִּשְׁאָר בְּנֵי נָשָׁא, דַּהֲווֹ אוֹרְכֵי
יוֹמִין. מ"ט, בְּגִין דְּלָקַח לֵיהּ קֻדְשָׁא בְּרִיךְ הוּא, עַד לָא מָטֵי זִמְנֵיהּ.

391. Come and see: Enoch was a righteous man. The Holy One, blessed be He, saw that he was eventually bound to degenerate and took him before he sinned. This is what is meant by the "to gather lilies" (Shir Hashirim 6:2). THIS MEANS THAT because of their good scent, the Holy One, blessed be He, gathers them before they become corrupt. SIMILAR IS THE VERSE: "and he was not, for Elohim took him." "And he was not" means that he was not to live a long life, as did his contemporaries, because the Holy One, blessed be He, took him away before his time.

392. רָבִּי אֶלְעָזָר אָמַר, חֲנוֹךְ נָטִיל לֵיהּ קֻדְשָׁא בְּרִיךְ הוּא מֵאַרְעָא, וְאַסְקֵיהּ לִשְׁמֵי מְרוֹמִים וְאָמְסַר בִּידֵיהּ כָּל גִּנְזֵי עִלָּאִין. וּמ״ה מַפְתְּחָן סִתְרֵי גְלִיפִין, דִּבְהוּ מִשְׁתַּמְּשֵׁי מַלְאֲכֵי עִלָּאֵי. וְכֻלְּהוּ אִתְמְסָרוּ בִּידֵיהּ. וְהָא אוּקִימְנָא.

392. Rabbi Elazar said that the Holy One, blessed be He, removed Enoch from the earth, elevated him to the highest heavens, and handed him all supernal treasures as well as 45 keys to the concealed engravings used by supernal angels. They were all delivered to him. This has been already explained.

66. "And Hashem saw that the wickedness of man"

When a man wastes the life-force and seed used for procreation, negative forces immediately attach themselves to him. He has destroyed the unborn souls that exist in a state of potential within the seed. Meditating upon these verses removes negative sexual thoughts. Our intense sexual desires are positively channeled towards our spouse, bringing a renewed sense of passion and fire to our relations.

393. וַיַּרְא ה' כִּי רַבָּה רָעַת הָאָדָם בָּאָרֶץ וְכָל יֵצֶר מַחְשְׁבֹת לִבּוֹ, רַבִּי יְהוּדָה פָּתַח, כִּי לֹא אֵל חָפֵץ רֶשַׁע אָתָּה לֹא יְגֻרְךָ רָע. הַאי קְרָא אִתְּמַר וְאוֹקְמוּהָ. אֲבָל תָּא חֲזֵי, מַאן דְּאִתְדַּבַּק בְּיֵצֶר הָרָע וְאִתְמְשִׁיךְ אֲבַתְרֵיהּ, וְיִסְתָּאַב הוּא, וִיסָאֲבוּן לֵיהּ, כְּמָה דְאִתְּמַר.

393. "And Hashem saw that the wickedness of man was great upon the earth, and the impulse of the thoughts of his heart was only evil continually" (Beresheet 6:5). Of the verse, "For You are not El who has pleasure in wickedness; nor shall evil dwell with you" (Tehilim 5:5), Rabbi Yehuda said: This verse has been discussed and explained, yet come and behold: he who cleaves to and is led by the Evil Inclination is defiled and will be led further into defilement, as we have learned.

394. כִּי רַבָּה רָעַת הָאָדָם. כָּל בִּישִׁין הֲווֹ עָבְדֵי, וְלָא אִשְׁתְּלִים חוֹבַיְיהוּ, עַד דַּהֲווֹ אוֹשְׁדִין דָּמִין לְמַגָּנָא עַל אַרְעָא. וּמַאן אִינוּן. דַּהֲווֹ מְחַבְּלִין אָרְחַיְיהוּ עַל אַרְעָא. הה"ד רַק רַע כָּל הַיּוֹם. כְּתִיב הָכָא רַק רַע, וּכְתִיב הָתָם וַיְהִי עֵר בְּכוֹר יְהוּדָה רַע בְּעֵינֵי ה'.

394. "The wickedness of man was great," because men committed all sorts of sins and their guilt was complete when they spilled blood in vain upon the ground. This refers to those who pollute their ways upon the earth, THAT IS, THEY SPILL THEIR SPERM IN VAIN. Thus, it is written: "Only evil (Heb. *ra*) all day." In another place it is written: "And Er, the son of Judah, was evil (Heb. *ra*) in the eyes of Hashem" (Beresheet 38:7), BECAUSE HE SPILLED HIS SEED UPON THE EARTH. THIS INDICATES THAT THE WORD *RA* REFERS TO THE WASTE OF SEED.

395. אָמַר רַבִּי יוֹסֵי, וְכִי רָע לָאו אִיהוּ רָשָׁע. אָמַר לוֹ לָא. רָשָׁע: אֲפִילוּ
אָרִים יְדֵיהּ לְגַבֵּי חַבְרֵיהּ. אַף עַל גַּב דְּלָא עָבִיד לֵיהּ מִידֵי, אִקְרֵי רָשָׁע.
כְּמָה דִכְתִיב וַיֹּאמֶר לָרָשָׁע לָמָּה תַכֶּה רֵעֶךָ. הִכִּיתָ לָא כְּתִיב, אֶלָּא
תַכֶּה.

395. Rabbi Yosi then asked, "Is not evil (ra) the same as wicked (Heb. rasha)?" THAT YOU DETERMINE THAT RA IS USED SOLELY TO INDICATE THOSE WHO WASTE THEIR SEED? RABBI YEHUDA answered: No. Even he who lifts his hand against his friend is called wicked, even if he causes his friend no harm. It is written: "And he said to the wicked, why do you smite your fellow?" (Shemot 2:13), and not 'Why did you smite your fellow?' THE LATTER WOULD HAVE INDICATED THAT HE HAD ALREADY DONE SO. THUS, EVEN THOUGH HE HAD NOT YET HIT HIM, THE SCRIPTURE CALLS HIM WICKED.

396. אֲבָל רַע לָא אִקְרֵי אֶלָּא מַאן דִּמְחַבֵּל אָרְחֵיהּ, וְסָאִיב גַּרְמֵיהּ,
וְסָאִיב אַרְעָא, וְיָהִיב חֵילָא וְתוֹקְפָּא לְרוּחַ מְסָאֲבָא דְּאִקְרֵי רָע. דִּכְתִיב,
רַק רַע כָּל הַיּוֹם. וְלָא עָאל בְּפָלְטְרִין, וְלָא חָמֵי אַפֵּי שְׁכִינְתָּא. בְּגִין
דִּבְהַאי אִסְתַּלַּק שְׁכִינְתָּא מֵעָלְמָא.

396. Yet, only he who corrupts his ways, thereby defiling himself and the earth, gives strength and power to the spirit of defilement called Ra. As it is written: "Only evil all day." Such a person will not enter the palace OF HASHEM, nor gaze upon the face of the Shechinah, because this sin causes the Shechinah to depart from the world.

397. מְנָלָן, מִיַּעֲקֹב. דְּכַד אִסְתַּלַּק שְׁכִינְתָּא מִנֵּיהּ, חָשִׁיב דִּבְנוֹהִי הֲוָה
פִּיסוּל, דִּבְגִינַיְיהוּ אִתְתַּקַּף בְּעָלְמָא רוּחָא מְסָאֲבָא, וְגָרַע נְהוֹרָא מִן
סִיהֲרָא, וּפָגִים לָהּ. וְאִי תֵימָא, אַמַּאי. בְּגִין דְּדָא סָאִיב מַקְדְּשָׁא,
וְאִסְתַּלָּקָא שְׁכִינְתָּא מֵעֲלֹוי דְּיַעֲקֹב. כָּל שֵׁכֶן הַהוּא דִּמְסָאֵב אָרְחֵיהּ,
וְסָאִיב גַּרְמֵיהּ, דְּהוּא אַתְקִיף לֵיהּ לְרוּחָא מְסָאֲבָא, וּבְגִין כָּךְ, כַּד
אִסְתָּאַב, אִקְרֵי רָע.

397. From where DO WE KNOW THAT THE SHECHINAH LEAVES BECAUSE OF THIS SIN? From Jacob. For when the Shechinah left him, he concluded that there was a defect in his sons AS A RESULT OF THEIR INDULGENCE IN THE ABOVE MENTIONED SIN. Because of this sin, he concluded, the spirit of defilement was strengthened in the world and the light of the moon, WHICH IS THE NUKVA OF ZEIR ANPIN, was impaired and rendered defective. FOR THIS REASON, THE SHECHINAH WAS GONE FROM HIM. One might wonder why HE THOUGHT SO. It is because this SIN defiled the Temple, and hence the Shechinah left Jacob, EVEN THOUGH HE HIMSELF DID NOT SIN. One who actually defiles his ways and himself gives all the more strength to the unclean spirit. Consequently, when he is defiled, he is called *ra* (evil).

398. תָּא חֲזֵי, כַּד בַּר נָשׁ אִסְתָּאַב, לָא יִתְפְּקַד מֵעִם קְדָשָׁא בְּרִיךְ הוּא לְטָב. וּבְכָל זִמְנָא אִתְפְּקִיד מֵהַהוּא דְּאִתְקְרֵי רָע, לְבִישׁ. הֲהָ"ד וְשָׂבֵעַ יָלִין בַּל יִפָּקֵד רָע. כַּד אָזֵיל בְּאֹרַח מֵישָׁר, כְּדֵין בַּל יִפָּקֵד רָע. וְעַל דָּא כְּתִיב, רַק רַע כָּל הַיּוֹם. וּכְתִיב לֹא יְגוּרְךָ רָע. וְדָא אִקְרֵי רָע, וְלָא אִקְרֵי רָשָׁע. וּכְתִיב גַּם כִּי אֵלֵךְ בְּגֵיא צַלְמָוֶת לֹא אִירָא רָע כִּי אַתָּה עִמָּדִי.

398. Come and behold: when a man is defiled BY THE ABOVE MENTIONED SIN, he is not remembered by the Holy One, for merit, and he is constantly remembered by THE SPIRIT OF DEFILEMENT, called 'evil', for evil. HENCE, THE SHECHINAH LEAVES HIM AS SOON AS HE IS VISITED BY THE SPIRIT OF DEFILEMENT. Thus, it is said, "he that has it shall abide satisfied; he shall not be visited with evil" (Mishlei 19:23), MEANING THAT he who follows the right path AND DOES NOT FALL PREY TO THE ABOVE MENTIONED SIN "shall not be visited with evil. Thus, it is written: "Only evil all day" and also, "nor shall evil dwell with You" (Tehilim 5:5), and they are called 'evil' and not 'wicked.' Also, it is written: "even though I walk through the valley of the shadow of death, I shall not fear evil, for You are with me" (Tehilim 23:4). THIS IS BECAUSE IT ALSO WORKS THE OTHER WAY: IF THE SHECHINAH IS ACCOMPANYING A MAN, HE NEED NOT FEAR THE SPIRIT OF DEFILEMENT, AS IT IS WRITTEN: "I SHALL NOT FEAR EVIL, FOR YOU ARE WITH ME." JUST AS THE SHECHINAH FLEES DEFILEMENT, SO DEFILEMENT FLEES FROM THE SHECHINAH.

67. "It grieved Him to His heart"

Evil forces lull us into a blinding complacency as they strategically maneuver their way into our consciousness. The Zohar gives us the power to perceive these forces. By removing destructive influences, complacency is replaced by inspiration toward change and spiritual development.

399. וַיִּנָּחֶם ה' כִּי עָשָׂה אֶת הָאָדָם בָּאָרֶץ וַיִּתְעַצֵּב אֶל לִבּוֹ. ר' יוֹסֵי פָּתַח, הוֹי מוֹשְׁכֵי הֶעָוֹן בְּחַבְלֵי הַשָּׁוְא וְכַעֲבוֹת הָעֲגָלָה חַטָּאָה. הוֹי מוֹשְׁכֵי הֶעָוֹן: אִלֵּין בְּנֵי נָשָׁא דְּחָטָאן קַמֵּי מָארֵיהוֹן, בְּכָל יוֹמָא, וְאִתְדָּמָן בְּעֵינַיְיהוּ אִינוּן חוֹבִין, דְּאִינוּן כְּחַבְלֵי הַשָּׁוְא. וְחָשְׁבִין דְּהַהוּא עוֹבָדָא דְּעָבְדִין, וְהַהוּא חוֹבָא דְּעָבְדִין, דְּלָאו אִיהוּ כְלוּם, וְלָא אַשְׁגַּח בְּהוּ קֻדְשָׁא בְּרִיךְ הוּא, עַד דְּעָבְדִין לְהַהוּא חוֹבָא תַּקִּיף וְרַבֵּי, כַּעֲבוֹת הָעֲגָלָה, דְּאִיהוּ תַּקִּיף, דְּלָא יָכִיל לְאִשְׁתְּצָאָה.

399. "And Hashem regretted that He made man on the earth, and it grieved Him to His heart" (Beresheet 6:6). Rabbi Yosi said upon this verse, "Woe to them who draw iniquity with cords of vanity, and sin as it were with cart rope" (Yeshayah 5:18). Those who draw iniquity are the men who sin every day before the Holy One, blessed be He, and they regard their sins as worthless cord because they think that the actions they engage in and their iniquities are of no consequence and that the Holy One, blessed be He, does not watch them. They thus transform all of their sins into one big, powerful sin – as the cart rope which is strong and thick and cannot be destroyed.

400. וְתָא חֲזֵי, כַּד עָבִיד קֻדְשָׁא בְּרִיךְ הוּא דִּינָא בְּחַיָּיבֵי עָלְמָא, אַף עַל גַּב דְּאִינוּן חָטָאן קַמֵּי קֻדְשָׁא בְּרִיךְ הוּא, וְאַרְגִּזִין לֵיהּ כָּל יוֹמָא, לָא בָּעֵי לְאוֹבָדָא לְהוּ מֵעָלְמָא. וְכַד אַשְׁגַּח בְּעוֹבָדֵיהוֹן, אִתְנַחֵם עֲלַיְיהוּ, עַל דְּאִינוּן עוֹבְדֵי יְדוֹי, וְאוֹרִיךְ לוֹן בְּעָלְמָא.

400. Come and behold: when the Holy One, blessed be He, executes judgment upon the wicked of the world, even though they transgress before Him and anger Him all day, He still has no desire to destroy them. And when He reviews their deeds, he is consoled by the fact that they are His handiwork and He has patience with them in this world.

401. וּבְגִין דְּאִינּוּן עוֹבָדֵי יְדוֹי, נָטֵיל נְחָמָה, וְאִתְנַחֵם עֲלַיְיהוּ, וְחַיִּיס עֲלַיְיהוּ. וְכַד בָּעֵי לְמֶעְבַּד בְּהוֹ דִּינָא, כִּבְיָכוֹל עָצִיב. דְּכֵיוָן דְּעוֹבָדֵי יְדוֹי אִינּוּן, עָצִיב עֲלַיְיהוּ. כְּמָה דְּאַתְּ אָמֵר וְדַחֲוָן לָא הַנְעֵל קָדָמוֹהִי.

401. And because they are the work of His hands, He is consoled, gives them respite, and has mercy on them. And when He wants to execute judgment, He is saddened, as it were, because they are the work of His Hands and He is sad because of them, as it is written: "nor were entertainments brought before him" (Daniel 6:19).

402. כְּתִיב הוֹד וְהָדָר לְפָנָיו עוֹז וְחֶדְוָה בִּמְקוֹמוֹ. אָמַר רַבִּי יוֹסֵי, תָּא חֲזֵי, וַיִּתְעַצֵּב אֶל לִבּוֹ כְּתִיב. אֶל לִבּוֹ עָצִיב, וְלָא לַאֲתַר אָחֳרָא. לִבּוֹ כד"א כַּאֲשֶׁר בִּלְבָבִי וּבְנַפְשִׁי יַעֲשֶׂה. רַבִּי יִצְחָק אָמַר, וַיִּנָּחֶם ה', כד"א וַיִּנָּחֶם ה' עַל הָרָעָה אֲשֶׁר דִּבֶּר לַעֲשׂוֹת לְעַמּוֹ.

402. It is written: "Honor and majesty are before Him, strength and joy in His place" (Tehilim 96:6). Rabbi Yosi said, come and behold: it is written: "And it grieved Him to his Heart," INDICATING THAT He was saddened to His heart, and not to another place. The words, "His heart" function here in the same manner as in the verse, "according to that which is in my heart and in my desire" (I Shmuel 2:35). Rabbi Yitzchak said that the words "Hashem regretted" are similar to "And Hashem relented of the evil He thought do to His people" (Shemot 32:14). THUS THE VERSE "AND HASHEM REGRETTED" HAVING MADE MAN TEACHES US THAT HE DID NOT WANT TO PUNISH THEM, AND WHEN THE TIME CAME TO EXECUTE JUDGMENT, HE WAS SADDENED TO HIS HEART.

403. ר' יֵיסָא אָמַר, לְטַב. רַבִּי חִזְקִיָּה אָמַר, לְבִיש. ר' יֵיסָא אָמַר לְטַב: כְּמָה דְּאִתְּמַר, דְּקֻדְשָׁא בְּרִיךְ הוּא נָחִים עַל דְּאִינּוּן עוֹבָדֵי יְדוֹי, וְחַיִּיס עֲלַיְיהוּ. וַיִּתְעַצֵּב: בְּגִין דְּאִינּוּן חָטָאן קַמֵּיה.

403. Rabbi Yesa said, OF THE PASSAGE, "AND HSHEM REGRETTED..." THAT IT WAS SAID for good, but Rabbi Chizkiyah said that it was said for bad. Rabbi Yesa EXPLAINED FURTHER BY saying that it is for good because the Holy One, blessed be He, regretted because those were the work of His hands, and pitied them. THE WORDS "AND HASHEM REGRETTED" TEACH US THAT THE HOLY ONE, BLESSED BE HE, HAD PITY ON MAN BECAUSE HE MADE HIM, AND HE IS HIS HANDIWORK. "And it grieved Him" means that it saddened Him that they had sinned before Him.

404. וְרַבִּי חִזְקִיָּה אָמַר, לְבִישׁ: דְּכַד קֻדְשָׁא בְּרִיךְ הוּא בָּעֵי לְאוֹבָדָא לְחַיָּיבֵי עָלְמָא, נָטִיל נְחוּמִין עֲלַיְיהוּ, וְקַבֵּיל נִיחוּמִין כִּבְיָכוֹל, כְּמַאן דִּמְקַבֵּל נִיחוּמִין עַל מַה דַּאֲבֵיד. כֵּיוָן דְּקַבֵּל נִיחוּמִין, וַדַּאי דִּינָא אִתְעֲבַד, וְלָא תַלְיָא מִלְּתָא בִּתְשׁוּבָה.

404. Rabbi Chizkiyah said: It was all said for demerit, because when the Holy One, blessed be He, wants to destroy the wicked people of the world, He is consoled for their loss, like a person who resigns himself to the loss of something. And once He is comforted, judgment takes its course and repentance is of no avail.

405. אֵימָתַי תַּלְיָא בִּתְשׁוּבָה, עַד לָא קַבֵּיל תַּנְחוּמִין עֲלַיְיהוּ, הָא קַבֵּיל תַּנְחוּמִין עֲלַיְיהוּ, לָא תַלְיָיא מִלְּתָא בִּתְשׁוּבָה כְּלַל. וְדִינָא אִתְעֲבֵיד. וּכְדֵין אוֹסִיף דִּינָא עַל דִּינָא, וְאַתְקִיף לְהַהוּא אֲתָר דְּדִינָא, לְמֶעְבַּד דִּינָא, וְאוֹבִיד לוֹן לְחַיָּיבַיָּא מִן עָלְמָא. וְכֹלָּא בַּקְרָא, דִּכְתִיב וַיִּנָּחֶם ה', קַבֵּל תַּנְחוּמִין. וּלְבָתַר וַיִּתְעַצֵּב אֶל לִבּוֹ. יָהַב תּוּקְפָּא לְדִינָא, לְמֶעְבַּד דִּינָא.

405. So, when is repentance effective? Only up to the point when He is consoled. Once He is consoled, repentance is of no avail and judgment is carried out. THE HOLY ONE, BLESSED BE HE, adds judgment upon Judgment and He gives strength to the place of judgment, so it will carry out the verdict. THE NUKVA CARRIES OUT THE VERDICT, and the sinners are completely destroyed. All this WE SEE in the passages "Hashem regretted " and "He was grieved to His heart." He gave strength to the place of Judgment, so that it could carry out the verdict. THE SECRET OF THE NUKVA IS HIS HEART, WHICH IS THE PLACE OF JUDGMENT. BY

"GRIEVED," IT IS MEANT THAT HE GAVE THE NUKVA EXTRA STRENGTH.

406. רַבִּי חִיָּיא אֲמַר, וַיִּנָּחֶם ה' כִּי עָשָׂה אֶת הָאָדָם בָּאָרֶץ. נָטַל תַּנְחוּמִין וְחֶדְוָה, כַּד עֲבַד קֻדְשָׁא בְּרִיךְ הוּא לְאָדָם בְּאַרְעָא, דְּאִיהוּ כְּגַוְונָא עִלָּאָה, וְכָל מַלְאֲכֵי עִלָּאֵי, מְשַׁבְּחָן לֵיהּ לְקוּדְשָׁא בְּרִיךְ הוּא, כַּד חָמֵי לֵיהּ, בִּדְיוּקְנָא עִלָּאָה. וַאֲמָרוּ וַתְּחַסְּרֵהוּ מְעַט מֵאֱלֹקִים וְכָבוֹד וְהָדָר תַּעֲטְרֵהוּ.

406. Rabbi Chiya said that the verse says "And Hashem regretted (also: 'was consoled') that He had made man," because He received consolation and joy. When the Holy One, blessed be He, created man upon the earth, he was in the supernal image. The angels of heaven praised the Holy One, blessed be He, and when they saw his supernal shape, they said: "You have made him slightly lower than Elohim and have crowned him with glory and honor" (Tehilim 8:6).

407. לְבָתַר, כַּד חָטָא אָדָם, אִתְעֲצֵּב קֻדְשָׁא בְּרִיךְ הוּא עַל דְּחָטָא, דְּיָהַב פִּתְחוֹן פֶּה, לְמַלְאֲכֵי הַשָּׁרֵת, דַּאֲמָרוּ קַמֵּיהּ בְּקַדְמֵיתָא, כַּד בָּעָא לְמִבְרֵי לֵיהּ. מָה אֱנוֹשׁ כִּי תִזְכְּרֶנּוּ וּבֶן אָדָם כִּי תִפְקְדֶנּוּ.

407. Later, when Adam sinned, the Holy One, blessed be He, was saddened, because Adam had now justified what the ministering angels asked Him when He wanted to create man: "What is this man that You are mindful of him and the son of man that You visit him" (Idib. 5). HENCE, THE VERSE "AND HASHEM REGRETTED..." MEANS THAT HE REJOICED AND WAS COMFORTED BY THE ANGELS BEFORE THE SIN, AND "GRIEVED" AFTER THE SIN.

408. אֲמַר רַבִּי יְהוּדָה, וַיִּתְעַצֵּב אֶל לִבּוֹ. בְּגִין דְּבָעֵי לְמֶעְבַּד בְּהוּ דִּינָא, שֶׁנֶּאֱמַר בְּצֵאת לִפְנֵי הֶחָלוּץ וְאוֹמְרִים הוֹדוּ לַה' כִּי לְעוֹלָם חַסְדּוֹ. וַאֲמַר רַבִּי יִצְחָק, אַמַּאי לָא כְּתִיב הָכָא כִּי טוֹב, אֶלָּא, בְּגִין דְּאוֹבִיד עוֹבְדֵי יְדוֹי, קַמַּיְיהוּ דְּיִשְׂרָאֵל.

408. Rabbi Yehuda said that "He was grieved to His heart" because He had to execute judgment upon them, as it is written: "as they went out before the army, and who should say, Give thanks to Hashem, for His steadfast love endures forever" (II Divrei Hayamim 20:21). Rabbi Yitzchak asks why it was not written, 'GIVE THANKS TO HASHEM for He is good'. HE ANSWERED: Because He was destroying the work of His hands for the sake of Yisrael.

409. כְּגַוְונָא דָא, כַּד הֲוֹו יִשְׂרָאֵל עָבְרִין יַמָּא. אָתוּ מַלְאֲכֵי עִלָּאֵי לְמֵימַר שִׁירָה קַמֵּיה קֻדְשָׁא בְּרִיךְ הוּא, בְּהַהוּא לֵילְיָא. אָמַר לוֹ קֻדְשָׁא בְּרִיךְ הוּא, וּמַה עוֹבְדֵי יְדַי טָבְעִין בְּיַמָּא, וְאַתּוּן אָמְרִין שִׁירָה. כְּדֵין וְלֹא קָרַב זֶה אֶל זֶה כָּל הַלַּיְלָה. אוֹף הָכָא, בְּכָל זִמְנִין, דְּאִיבּוּד רַשִּׁיעַיָא אִיהוּ מֵעָלְמָא, כְּדֵין עֲצִיבוּ אִשְׁתְּכַח עֲלַיְיהוּ.

409. Similarly, on the night when Yisrael crossed the sea, the supernal angels came along to sing before the Holy One, blessed be He. He said to them, "behold, the work of My hands are drowning in the sea, and you are singing!" Thus, it is written: "One did not come near the other all night" (Shemot 14:20). The same applies here, for whenever the wicked are taken out of this world, He is greatly saddened.

410. רַבִּי אַבָּא אָמַר, בְּשַׁעֲתָא דְּחָב קַמֵּי קֻדְשָׁא בְּרִיךְ הוּא אָדָם, וְעָבַר עַל פִּקוּדוֹי, כְּדֵין אִשְׁתְּכַח עֲצִיבוּ קַמֵּיה. אָמַר לֵיה קֻדְשָׁא בְּרִיךְ הוּא, אָדָם, וַוי דְּחַלְשַׁת חֵילָא עִלָּאָה. בְּהַאי שַׁעֲתָא אִתְחַשְׁכַת נְהוֹרָא חַד. מִיָּד תָּרִיךְ לֵיה מִגִּנְתָּא דְּעֵדֶן.

410. Rabbi Aba said that The Holy One, blessed be He, was grieved when Adam sinned before Him and transgressed His commands. He said to him, "Adam, woe to you that you have weakened the heavenly power." At that moment one light OF THE NUKVA was extinguished, and forthwith He banished him from the Garden of Eden.

411. אָמַר לֵיה, אֲנָא אַעֲלִית לָךְ לְגִנְתָּא דְעֵדֶן, לְקָרְבָא קָרְבְּנָא, וְאַתְּ פְּגִימַת מַדְבְּחָא, דְּלָא אִתְקְרַב קָרְבְּנָא. מִכָּאן וּלְהָלְאָה, לַעֲבוֹד אֶת הָאֲדָמָה. וְגָזַר עֲלֵיה מִיתָה. וְחָס עֲלֵיה קֻדְשָׁא בְּרִיךְ הוּא, וְגָנִיז לֵיה

בְּשַׁעֲתָא דְּמִית סָמִיךְ לְגִנְתָּא.

411. He said to him, "I placed you in the Garden of Eden to offer sacrifices" – BY UNIFYING THE HOLY ONE, BLESSED BE HE, AND HIS SHECHINAH – and you have impaired the altar, WHICH IS THE NUKVA, so much that offerings cannot be brought to it anymore. Henceforth, GO AWAY AND work the land. And He sentenced him to death. Taking pity on him, however, the Holy One, blessed be He, buried him, when he died, close to the garden, IN THE CAVE OF MACHPELAH, WHERE THE ENTRANCE TO THE GARDEN OF EDEN IS LOCATED.

412. מַה עֲבַד אָדָם, עֲבַד מְעַרְתָּא חֲדָא, וְאִתְטַמַּר בָּהּ, הוּא וְאִתְּתֵיה. מְנָא יָדַע. אֶלָּא, חָמָא חַד נְהוֹרָא דַּקִּיק, עָיֵיל בְּהַהוּא אֲתַר, דְּנָפֵיק מִגִּנְתָּא דְּעֵדֶן, וְתָאב תֵּיאוּבְתֵּיה לְקַבְרֵיה. וְתַמָּן הוּא אֲתַר, סָמִיךְ לְתַרְעָא דְּגִנְתָּא דְּעֵדֶן.

412. Adam made a cave, THE CAVE OF MACHPELAH, and both he and his wife hid in it. How did he know TO CHOOSE THIS PLACE? Because he saw a faint ray of light emanating from the Garden of Eden that reached to the cave. His desire was awakened to be buried there, close to the entrance to the Garden of Eden.

413 תָּא חֲזֵי, לָא אִסְתַּלַּק בַּר נָשׁ מֵעָלְמָא, עַד דְּחָמֵי לֵיה לְאָדָם הָרִאשׁוֹן. שָׁאִיל לֵיה, עַל מַה אָזֵיל מֵעָלְמָא, וְהֵיךְ נָפֵיק. הוּא אֲמַר לֵיה, ווי, דִּבְגִינָךְ נְפַקְנָא מֵעָלְמָא. וְהוּא אֲתֵיב לֵיה, בְּרִי, אֲנָא עֲבָרִית עַל פְּקוּדָא חֲדָא, וְאִתְעֲנָשִׁית בְּגִינָהּ. חָמֵי אַתְּ, כַּמָּה חוֹבִין, וְכַמָּה פְּקוּדִין דְּמָארָךְ עֲבַרְתְּ.

413. Come and behold: no one leaves this world without seeing Adam. Adam asks him for what reason he left this world and how HIS SOUL departed. Each person replies, "Woe to you that because of you I had to die," BECAUSE IT WAS AS A CONSEQUENCE OF THE SIN OF THE TREE OF KNOWLEDGE THAT DEATH WAS DECREED UPON THE WORLD. ADAM then replies, "My son, I have transgressed one commandment, and have been punished because of it. Yet look at yourself. How many sins and how many transgressions on the precepts of your Master have you committed?"

414. אָמַר רַבִּי חִיָּיא, עַד כְּדוּ יוֹמָא, קָאִים אָדָם הָרִאשׁוֹן וְחָזֵי בַּאֲבָהָן, תְּרֵין זִמְנִין בְּיוֹמָא. וְאוֹדֵי עַל חוֹבוֹי, וְאַחְמֵי לוֹן הַהוּא אֲתַר דַּהֲוָה בֵּיה, בִּיקָרָא עִלָּאָה, וְאָזֵיל וְחָמֵי כָּל אִינוּן צַדִּיקַיָּיא, וַחֲסִידֵי דְּנָפְקוּ מְנֵּיה. וְיָרְתוּ לְהַהוּא יְקָרָא עִלָּאָה דִּבְגִנְתָּא דְּעֵדֶן. וַאֲבָהָן כֻּלְּהוֹן, אוֹדָן וְאַמְרִין, מַה יָּקָר חַסְדְּךָ אֱלֹקִים וּבְנֵי אָדָם בְּצֵל כְּנָפֶיךָ יֶחֱסָיוּן.

414. Rabbi Chiya said that until this very day, Adam continues to face the forefathers and confess his sins twice a day. He shows them the very location IN THE GARDEN OF EDEN, where he resided in supernal glory BEFORE HE SINNED. He also goes and looks at all the pious and righteous people among his descendants, who have inherited the supernal glory HE HAD in the Garden of Eden BEFORE HE SINNED. The Patriarchs praise and say, "How precious is Your kindness, Hashem. The children of man (Heb. *Adam*) take refuge under the shadow of Your wings" (Tehilim 36:8).

415. רַבִּי יֵיסָא אָמַר, כֻּלְּהוֹ בְּנֵי עָלְמָא, חָמָאן לֵיה לְאָדָם הָרִאשׁוֹן, בְּשַׁעֲתָא דְּמִסְתַּלְּקֵי מִן עָלְמָא, לְאַחֲזָאָה סַהֲדוּתָא, דִּבְגִין חוֹבוֹי דְּבַר נָשׁ, אִיהוּ אִסְתַּלַּק מֵעָלְמָא, וְלָא בְּגִינֵיה דְּאָדָם. כְּמָה דִּתְנִינָן אֵין מִיתָה בְּלָא חֵטְא.

415. Rabbi Yesa said: THE REASON Adam appears to each person at the moment of their departure from this world is to testify that this person is dying on account of his own sins and not because of those of Adam. As we have learned, there is not death without sin.

416. בַּר אִינוּן תְּלָתָא, דְּאִסְתַּלְּקוּ בְּגִין הַהוּא עֵיטָא דְּנָחָשׁ הַקַּדְמוֹנִי. וְאִלֵּין אִינוּן: עַמְרָם, לֵוִי וּבִנְיָמִין. וְאִית דְּאָמְרֵי, אוֹף נָמֵי יִשַׁי. דְּלָא חָבוּ, וְלָא אִשְׁתְּכַח עֲלַיְיהוּ חוֹבָא דִּימוּתוּן בֵּיה, בַּר דְּאִדְכַּר עֲלַיְיהוּ הַהוּא עֵיטָא דְּנָחָשׁ. כִּדְאֲמְרָן.

416. The only exceptions are the three who had to leave this world because of the prompting of the primal serpent, WHO CONVINCED EVE TO EAT OF THE TREE OF KNOWLEDGE. THEY DID NOT DIE FOR OF THEIR OWN SINS. Those three are Amram, Levi, and Benjamin. Some friends also include Yishai among them. None of them ever sinned and no blemish could be found to explain their deaths except for the prompting of the serpent, as we have said.

417. תָּא חֲזֵי, כָּלְּהוֹן דָּרִין דַּהֲווֹ בְּיוֹמוֹי דְּנֹחַ, כָּלְּהוּ אַפְשִׁיטוּ חוֹבִין, עַל עָלְמָא בְּאִתְגַּלְיָא, לְעֵינֵיהוֹן דְּכֹלָּא. רַבִּי שִׁמְעוֹן, הֲוָה אָזִיל יוֹמָא חַד, בְּפִילֵי דִטְבֶרְיָה. חָמָא בְּנֵי נָשָׁא דַּהֲווֹ מְקַטְרֵי בְּקִיטְרָא דְקַשְׁתָּא בְּקוּלְפָא דְקַנְסִיר. אָמַר, וּמַה חוֹבָא דָא בְּאִתְגַּלְיָא, לְאַרְגָּזָא לְמָרֵיהוֹן. יָהִיב עֵינוֹי בְּהוֹ, וְאִתְרְמִיוּ לְגוֹ יַמָּא, וּמִיתוּ.

417. Come and behold: all the generations contemporary to Noah committed their sins openly, for all to see. Rabbi Shimon was strolling one day near the gates of Tiberias, where he saw some men drawing arrows tightly into their bows and shooting them at earthenware pots. THIS MEANS THAT THEY WERE WASTING THEIR SEED IN VAIN AND IN THE OPEN. He said, 'Why are they committing this sin openly, if not to provoke their Master's anger?' He stared at them and they were thrown into the sea and drowned.

418. תָּא חֲזֵי, כָּל חוֹבָא דְּאִתְעֲבֵיד בְּאִתְגַּלְיָא, דָּחֵי לָהּ לִשְׁכִינְתָּא מֵאַרְעָא, וּסְלֵיקַת דִּיּוּרָהּ מֵעָלְמָא. אִלֵּין הֲווֹ אָזְלִין בְּרֵישָׁא זָקִיף, וְעָבְדֵי חוֹבַיְיהוּ בְּאִתְגַּלְיָא, וְדָחוּ לָהּ לִשְׁכִינְתָּא מֵעָלְמָא, עַד דְּקַדְשָׁא בְּרִיךְ הוּא דָּחָא לוֹן, וְאַעֲבֵיר לוֹן מִנֵּיה. וְעַל דָּא כְּתִיב הֲגוֹ רָשָׁע לִפְנֵי מֶלֶךְ וְגו'. הֲגוֹ סִגִים מִכֶּסֶף וְגו'.

418. Come and behold: any sin that is committed publicly repels the Shechinah from the earth and causes Her to remove Her residence from the world. Those IN THE GENERATION OF THE FLOOD walked defiantly with their heads high, WITHOUT SHAME. They sinned openly and repelled the Shechinah from the world until the Holy One, blessed be He, rejected them and removed them from HIS PRESENCE. As it is written: "Take away the impurity from the silver and there shall come forth a vessel for the smith. Take away the wicked from the presence of the king and his throne shall be established in righteousness" (Mishlei 25:4-5).

68. "My spirit shall not strive with man"

Our world mirrors the Upper World. Actions performed in this physical realm ignite spiritual forces in the worlds above. Reading this section gives us the ability to positively influence and affect the Upper World in ways that benefit our lives.

419. וַיֹּאמֶר ה' לֹא יָדוֹן רוּחִי בָאָדָם לְעוֹלָם בְּשַׁגַּם הוּא בָשָׂר וגו'. אָמַר רַבִּי אֶלְעָזָר תָּא חֲזֵי, כַּד בְּרָא קֻדְשָׁא בְּרִיךְ הוּא עָלְמָא, עֲבַד לְהַאי עָלְמָא, לְאִשְׁתַּמְּשָׁא כְּגַוְונָא דִּלְעֵילָא. וְכַד בְּנֵי עָלְמָא אִינּוּן זַכָּאִין, דְּאַזְלֵי בְּאֹרַח מֵישָׁר, קֻדְשָׁא בְּרִיךְ הוּא אִתְּעַר רוּחָא דְּחַיֵּי דִּלְעֵילָא עַד דְּמָטוֹ, אִינּוּן חַיִּין, לַאֲתַר דְּיַעֲקֹב שַׁרְיָא בֵּיהּ.

419. "And Hashem said, My spirit shall not strive with man forever, for he is also flesh" (Beresheet 6:3). Rabbi Elazar said, Come and behold: when the Holy One, blessed be He, created the world, He made the world, WHICH IS MALCHUT, to be used as the supernal WORLD, WHICH IS BINAH. THIS MEANS THAT ALL THE LIGHTS SHINING IN BINAH SHOULD ALSO SHINE IN MALCHUT, THE SECRET OF THIS WORLD. Now, when people are righteous and follow the correct path, the Holy One, blessed be He, reveals the spirit of life, WHICH ARE THE MOCHIN of above FROM BINAH, until this life reaches the place where Jacob abides, NAMELY ZEIR ANPIN, BECAUSE FROM BINAH THE MOCHIN FLOW THROUGH ZEIR ANPIN.

420. וּמִתַּמָּן נָגְדֵי אִינּוּן חַיִּין, עַד דְּאִתְמְשִׁיךְ הַהוּא רוּחָא, לְהַאי עוֹלָם, דְּדָוִד מַלְכָּא שַׁרְיָא בֵּיהּ. וּמִתַּמָּן נָגְדֵי בִּרְכָאן לְכֻלְּהוּ אִינּוּן תַּתָּאֵי. וְהַהוּא רוּחָא עִלָּאָה, אִתְנְגִיד וְאִתְמְשִׁיךְ לְתַתָּא. וְיַכְלִין לְאִתְקַיְּימָא בְּעָלְמָא.

420. From there, life flows until the spirit OF LIFE reaches this world, THE NUKVA, the place where King David resides. Hence, all the blessings flow to all the lower beings IN BRIYAH, YETZIRAH AND ASIYAH. This supernal spirit spreads downward, enabling the lower beings to maintain their existence.

421. וּבְגִינֵי כָּךְ, לְעוֹלָם חַסְדּוֹ. דָּא הוּא עוֹלָם, דְּדָוִד מַלְכָּא. וּבְגִין כָּךְ

כְּתִיב לְעָלָם בְּלָא וָא"ו. דְּהָא כַּד הַהוּא רוּחָא אִתְנְגִיד לְהַהוּא עוֹלָם.
מִתַּמָּן נָפְקֵי בִּרְכָאן וְחַיִּין לְכֹלָּא, לְאִתְקַיְּמָא. הַשְׁתָּא דְּחָבוּ בְּנֵי נָשָׁא,
אִסְתַּלַּק כֹּלָּא. בְּגִין דְּלָא יִמְטֵי הַהוּא רוּחָא דְּחַיֵּי לְהַאי עוֹלָם,
לְאִתְהַנָּאָה מִנֵּיהּ תַּתָּאֵי, וּלְאִתְקַיְּימָא בֵּיהּ.

421. Hence, IT IS WRITTEN: "His kindness (Heb. *chasdo*) is everlasting (also: 'for the world')" (II Divrei Hayamim 20:21). *CHASDO* IS SPELLED WITH *VAV*. The world is of King David, NAMELY THE NUKVA, NURTURED BY THE *VAV*, THE SPIRIT OF LIFE, WHICH DRAWS LIFE TO IT. Hence, it is written: "MY SPIRIT SHALL NOT STRIVE WITH MAN for the world" without *Vav*, because when that spirit is drawn into the world. Blessings and life are released from it to sustain all. Yet now IN THE GENERATION OF THE FLOOD, when people sinned BY DRAWING LIGHT FROM ABOVE DOWNWARD, DISRUPTING THE CENTRAL COLUMN AND ATTACHING THEMSELVES TO THE LEFT COLUMN, everything left THIS WORLD. Thus, the spirit of life ceased flowing into this world for the pleasure and sustenance of the lower beings. HENCE, *OLAM* IS SPELLED WITHOUT *VAV*, WHICH IS THE CENTRAL COLUMN AND THE SPIRIT OF LIFE, BECAUSE THEY DEFILED IT AND ATTACHED THEMSELVES TO THE LEFT.

422. בְּשַׁגָּם הוּא בָשָׂר. בְּגִין דְּלָא יִתְרַק הַאי רוּחָא לְהַאי עוֹלָם. מ"ט,
דְּלָא לְאַסְגָּאָה נָחָשׁ, תַּתָּאָה דְּדַרְגִּין, דְּיִתְתַּקַּף בֵּיהּ רוּחָא דִּקְדוּשָׁא דְּלָא
יִתְעָרַב בְּרוּחַ מְסָאָב. בְּשַׁגָּם הוּא בָשָׂר, דָּא נָחָשׁ קַדְמָאָה דְּיִתְבָּרַךְ. בְּגִין
כָּךְ הוּא בָשָׂר: כד"א קֵץ כָּל בָּשָׂר בָּא לְפָנַי, וְאָמַר רָבִּי שִׁמְעוֹן, דָּא
מַלְאַךְ הַמָּוֶת. וְהָיוּ יָמָיו מֵאָה וְעֶשְׂרִים שָׁנָה. אוֹרִיכוּ דְּקוֹסְטִירָא
דְּקִיטְרָא.

422. "For he is also flesh." Therefore the spirit OF LIFE will not be drawn into the world. The reason is to prevent the serpent, CALLED 'FLESH,' the lowest of all levels, from increasing in power THROUGH THE SPIRIT OF LIFE. It is also to assure that the Holy Spirit will not have to mix with the spirit of defilement OF THE SERPENT. The verse, "...for he is also flesh," teaches us that the primeval serpent IS ALSO FLESH, AND might also be blessed BY THE SPIRIT OF LIFE. Hence, THE SERPENT is called 'flesh', as it is written: "The End of all Flesh came before Me" (Beresheet 6:13). Rabbi Shimon said that THE PRIMAL SERPENT, CALLED FLESH, is the Angel of Death. The words, "His days will be 120 years" (Beresheet 6:3), means the gift of an attached tower.

69. "The Nefilim were on the earth"

Many negative angels enter our realm and take on human form. We can protect ourselves from these negative angels, as well as from people who connect themselves to the dark forces.

423. הַנְּפִילִים הָיוּ בָאָרֶץ. תָּנֵי רַבִּי יוֹסֵי, אִלֵּין עַזָּא וַעֲזָאֵל. כְּמָה דְּאִתְּמָר, דְּאַפֵּיק לוֹן קֻדְשָׁא בְּרִיךְ הוּא מִקְּדוּשָׁתָא דִּלְעֵילָא. וְאִי תֵימָא וְהֵיךְ יָכְלוּ לְאִתְקַיְּימָא בְּהַאי עָלְמָא. אָמַר רַבִּי חִיָּיא, אִלֵּין הֲווֹ מֵאִינוּן דִּכְתִיב וְעוֹף יְעוֹפֵף עַל הָאָרֶץ. וְהָא אִתְּמָר, דְּאִלֵּין אִתְחֲזוּ לִבְנֵי נָשָׁא, בְּחֵיזוּ דִּלְהוֹן. וְאִי תֵימָא, הֵיךְ יָכְלִין לְאִתְהַפְּכָא. הָא אִתְּמָר דְּאִתְהַפְּכָן לְכַמָּה גְוָונִין. וּבְשַׁעֲתָא דְּנָחֲתֵי אַגְלִימוּ בַּאֲוִירָא דְּעָלְמָא, וְאִתְחֲזוּן כִּבְנֵי נָשָׁא.

423. "The Nefilim were on the earth..." (Beresheet 6:4). Rabbi Yosi taught that those CALLED NEFILIM were Aza and Azael and as we have learned, they were so called because the Holy One, blessed be He, dropped (Heb. hepil) them from the upper sanctity. How, you may well ask, can they subsist in this world? Rabbi Chiya said that they are among those referred to as "Birds which fly upon the earth" (Beresheet 1:20). And these, as we have discussed, appear to men in the form OF HUMAN BEINGS. And how, you may ask, do they transform themselves FROM THE SHAPE OF AN ANGEL TO THAT OF HUMAN BEINGS? As we have learned, they can transform themselves into all kinds OF SHAPES, and when they come down INTO THIS WORLD, they clothe themselves with the garments of earth's atmosphere and take on human form.

424. וְהָנֵי, עַזָּא וַעֲזָאֵל, דְּמָרְדוּ לְעֵילָא, וְאַפִּיל לוֹן קֻדְשָׁא בְּרִיךְ הוּא, וְאַגְלִימוּ בְּאַרְעָא, וְאִתְקַיְּימוּ בֵּיהּ, וְלָא יָכִילוּ לְאִתְפַּשְּׁטָא מִנֵּיהּ. וּלְבָתַר טָעוּ בָּתַר נְשֵׁי עָלְמָא. וְעַד כְּעַן יוֹמָא דָא, אִינוּן קַיְּימֵי וְאוֹלְפֵי חַרְשִׁין לִבְנֵי נָשָׁא. וְאוֹלִידוּ בְּנִין, וְקָרוּ לְהוֹ עֲנָקִים, גִּבָּרִין. וְאִינוּן נְפִילִים, אִקְרוּן בְּנֵי אֱלֹהִים. וְהָא אִתְּמָר.

424. Aza and Azael, who rebelled above, and whom the Holy One, blessed

-249-

be He, caused to fall from heaven, were forced to put on and to live with the garments of the earth. They could not divest themselves of these garments AND COULD NOT RETURN TO THEIR FORMER RESIDENCE WITH THE REST OF THE ANGELS. THEY REMAINED FOREVER ON EARTH. Subsequently, they were seduced by earthly women. They exist to this day, teaching sorcery to people. They begot sons, whom they called 'mighty' and 'giants'. The Nefilim are referred to as "sons of Elohim," as has already been explained.

70. "I shall destroy man"

God always gives ample warning before great judgments and catastrophes brought on by the negative actions of man. Sadly, in most cases we fail to heed the warnings. The Zohar empowers us to see the signs of warning when they appear.

425. וַיֹּאמֶר ה' אֶמְחֶה אֶת הָאָדָם אֲשֶׁר בָּרָאתִי מֵעַל פְּנֵי הָאֲדָמָה. רַבִּי יוֹסֵי פָּתַח, כִּי לֹא מַחְשְׁבוֹתַי מַחְשְׁבוֹתֵיכֶם. תָּא חֲזֵי כַּד בַּר נָשׁ בָּעֵי לְנָקְמָא מֵאָחֳרָא, שָׁתִיק וְלָא אָמַר מִידֵּי, דְּאִילּוּ אוֹדְעֵיהּ, יִסְתַּמַּר, וְלָא יָכִיל לֵיהּ.

425. "And Hashem said, 'I shall destroy man, whom I have created from the face of the earth'" (Beresheet 6:7). Rabbi Yosi quotes, "For My thoughts are not your thoughts" (Yeshayah 55:8). Come and behold: when a man wants to take vengeance on another, he keeps quiet and tells him nothing. Because if he discloses HIS INTENTIONS, his opponent will be on guard and hard to overpower.

426. אֲבָל קֻדְשָׁא בְּרִיךְ הוּא לָאו הָכִי עָבִיד. לָא עָבִיד דִּינָא בְּעָלְמָא, עַד דְּאַכְרִיז וְאוֹדַע לְהוּ, זִמְנָא, תְּרֵין וּתְלָתָא. בְּגִין, דְּלָא אִיתָאי דְּיִמְחֵי בִּידֵיהּ, דְּיֵימָא לֵיהּ מַה עֲבַדְתְּ, וְלָא יִסְתַּמַּר מִנֵּיהּ, וְלָא יָכִיל לְקַיְּימָא קַמֵּיהּ.

426. Yet the Holy One, blessed be He, does not act in this manner. He does not execute judgment on the world before He declares and informs it OF HIS INTENTIONS once, twice, and three times. Then, no one may reproach Him and ask, 'What are You doing?' Nor can one guard against Him or stand up to Him.

427. תָּא חֲזֵי וַיֹּאמֶר ה' אֶמְחֶה אֶת הָאָדָם אֲשֶׁר בָּרָאתִי מֵעַל פְּנֵי הָאֲדָמָה. אוֹדַע לוֹן, עַל יְדָא דְּנֹחַ, וְאַתְרֵי בְּהוֹן כַּמָּה זִמְנִין, וְלָא שָׁמְעֵי. בָּתַר דְּלָא שָׁמְעוּ, אַיְיתֵי עֲלֵיהוֹן דִּינָא, וְאוֹבִיד לוֹן מֵעַל אַפֵּי אַרְעָא.

427. "And Hashem said, 'I shall destroy man, whom I have created from the

face of the earth.'" He announced these words through Noah, and He warned them several times, but they did not listen. Eventually, He executed judgment and exterminated them.

428. תָּא חֲזֵי, מַה כְּתִיב בֵּיהּ בְּנֹחַ, וַיִּקְרָא אֶת שְׁמוֹ נֹחַ לֵאמֹר זֶה יְנַחֲמֵנוּ מִמַּעֲשֵׂנוּ. מְנָא הֲוָה יָדַע. אֶלָּא, בְּשַׁעֲתָא דְּלָיְיט קֻדְשָׁא בְּרִיךְ הוּא עָלְמָא, דִּכְתִּיב, אֲרוּרָה הָאֲדָמָה בַּעֲבוּרֶךָ. אֲמַר אָדָם קַמֵּי קֻדְשָׁא בְּרִיךְ הוּא, רִבּוֹנוֹ שֶׁל עוֹלָם: עַד מָתַי יְהֵא עָלְמָא בְּלַטְיוּתָא. אֲמַר לֵיהּ עַד דְּיִתְיְלִיד לָךְ בֵּן מָהוּל, כְּגַוְונָא דִּילָךְ.

428. Come and behold what was said of Noah: "And he called his name Noah saying, This one shall comfort us (Heb. *yenachamenu*) from our work" (Beresheet 5:29). How did he know THAT HE WOULD COMFORT HIM AS SOON AS HE WAS BORN? It says that when the Holy One, blessed be He, cursed the world, saying, "cursed is the ground for your sake" (Beresheet 3:18). Adam said to Him, "Master of the universe, until when will the world be subject to this curse?" The Holy One, blessed be He, replied, "Until you beget a son who is born circumcised like yourself."

429. וַהֲווֹ מְחַכָּאן, עַד שַׁעֲתָא דְּאִתְיְלִיד נֹחַ. וְכֵיוָן דְּאִתְיְילִיד, חָמָא לֵיהּ גְּזִיר, רָשִׁים בְּאָת קַדִּישָׁא. וְחָמָא שְׁכִינְתָּא מִתְדַּבְּקָא בַּהֲדֵיהּ. כְּדֵין קָרָא שְׁמֵיהּ עַל מָה דְּעָבֵיד לְבָתַר.

429. And they waited until the time when Noah was born. And when he was born, Adam saw that he was circumcised and marked with a sacred sign. And when he saw that the Shechinah embraced the baby, IT THEN BECAME CLEAR TO HIM THAT THE CURSE WOULD BE CANCELED DURING HIS LIFETIME, and so he named him in anticipation of what would transpire.

430. בְּקַדְמֵיתָא, לָא הֲווֹ יָדְעֵי לְמִזְרַע, וּלְמֶחֱצַד, וּלְמֶחֱרָשׁ. וַהֲווֹ עַבְדֵי פּוּלְחָנָא דְּאַרְעָא בִּידַיְיהוּ. כֵּיוָן דְּאָתָא נֹחַ, אַתְקִין אוּמָנוּתָא לְהוֹ, וְכָל מָאנִין דְּצְרִיכִין לְתַקָּנָא אַרְעָא, לְמֶעֱבַד פֵּירִין. הֲדָא הוּא דִכְתִיב זֶה יְנַחֲמֵנוּ מִמַּעֲשֵׂנוּ וּמֵעִצְּבוֹן יָדֵינוּ מִן הָאֲדָמָה. דְּאִיהוּ, אַפִּיק אַרְעָא,

מִמַּה דְּאִתְלַטְיָיא. דַּהֲווֹ זַרְעִין חִטִּין, וְקַצְרִין גּוֹבִין וְדַרְדְּרִין. וּבְגִינֵי כָךְ, כְּתִיב, אִישׁ הָאֲדָמָה.

430. In the beginning, they did not know how to sow, reap, or plow, and they worked the earth with their hands. But Noah came along and manufactured tools needed for working the ground, so that it would bear fruit. Thus, it was written: "this one shall comfort us from our work and from the toil of our hands, because of the ground which Hashem has cursed." Noah liberated the earth from its curse. Before he came, the people used to sow wheat and reap thorns and thistles. Hence, he was called "a husbandman" (Beresheet 9:20).

431. רַבִּי יְהוּדָה אֲמַר, אִישׁ הָאֲדָמָה, כד"א אִישׁ נָעֳמִי. בְּגִין, דְּאִקְרֵי צַדִּיק, וְאַפֵּיק לָהּ לְאַרְעָא, בְּקָרְבָּנָא דְּעָבֵד, מִמַּה דְּאִתְלַטְיָיא. דִּכְתִיב לֹא אוֹסִיף לְקַלֵּל עוֹד אֶת הָאֲדָמָה בַּעֲבוּר הָאָדָם. וּבְגִין דָּא, אִקְרֵי אִישׁ הָאֲדָמָה. וְעַל דָּא קָרָא לֵיהּ שְׁמָא, עַל מַה דְּיֵיתֵי.

431. Rabbi Yehuda said "a husbandman" often means that he was considered the "husband of the ground," as it says, "Naomi's man" (Rut 1:3). This is because he was called righteous, and nullfied the earth's curse by means of the sacrifices he offered. Hence, it is written: "I will curse the ground any more for man's sake" (Beresheet 8:21). For this reason Noah was called "a man of the ground." And hence he was called NOAH (Eng. 'comfort'), because of what would one day occur.

71. "Come, behold the works of Elohim, Who has made desolations in the earth"

71. "Come, behold the works of Elohim, Who has made desolations in the earth"

A person's name establishes a profound link to his soul and essence. The letters that compose a name instill a particular set of attributes that comprise a person's nature. This section of the Zohar helps us strengthen the bond to our name so that we can awaken its positive influences within our soul.

432. רַבִּי יְהוּדָה פָּתַח, לְכוּ חֲזוּ מִפְעֲלוֹת אֱלֹקִים אֲשֶׁר שָׂם שַׁמּוֹת בָּאָרֶץ. הַאי קְרָא אוּקְמוּהָ וְאִתְּמַר. אֲבָל, לְכוּ חֲזוּ וְגוֹ'. דְּאִלּוּ הֲווֹ מִפְעֲלוֹת יוֹד הֵא וָאו הֵא, שָׂם קִיּוּם בָּאָרֶץ, אֲבָל בְּגִין דַּהֲווֹ מִפְעֲלוֹת שְׁמָא דֶאֱלֹקִים, שָׂם שַׁמּוֹת בָּאָרֶץ.

432. Rabbi Yehuda expounded upon the verse: "Come, behold the works of Elohim, who has made desolations in the earth" (Tehilim 46:9). He said that this text has been explained, but if the world would have been created by Yud-Vav-Dalet, Hei-Aleph, Vav-Aleph-Vav, Hei-Aleph, A NAME INDICATIVE OF MERCY, then it would have given earth a firm structure. But since it was created by the works of Elohim, WHICH IS JUDGMENT, a desolation, A WASTELAND, He "has" made desolations in the of earth." IT SEEMS THE ZOHAR HAD A DIFFERENT VERSION, BECAUSE IN OUR SCRIPTURES IT IS WRITTEN, 'THE WORKS OF HASHEM'.

433. אָמַר לוֹ רַבִּי חִיָּיא, הַשְׁתָּא אִתְעָרַת לְהַאי, לָאו אֲנָא הָכֵי אֲמִינָא לֵיהּ, בְּגִין דְּבֵין שְׁמָא דָּא, וּבֵין שְׁמָא דָּא, כֹּלָּא הוּא שְׁבָחָא. אֲבָל, אֲנָא אֲמִינָא לֵיהּ, כְּמָה דְּאִתְעָרוּ חַבְרַיָּיא. דְּשַׁוִּי שְׁמָהָן שֵׁמוֹת בָּאָרֶץ, שֵׁמוֹת מַמָּשׁ.

433. Rabbi Chiya said to him: Although you believe THAT DESOLATIONS (HEB. SHAMOT) SIGNIFIES A WASTELAND (HEB. SHEMAMAH), I see it differently, because both the names YUD HEI VAV HEI AND ELOHIM indicate benevolence. I tend to agree with the friends in saying that he had placed "shemot (Eng. 'names') in the earth." SHEMOT ALLUDES TO ACTUAL NAMES THAT HE PUT IN THE EARTH.

434. ר' יִצְחָק אָמַר, כֹּלָּא הוּא וַאֲפִילוּ מַה דְּאָמַר רָבִּי יְהוּדָה, שַׁפִּיר
קָאָמַר. דְּאִילּוּ יְהֵא עָלְמָא בִּשְׁמָא דְרַחֲמֵי, יִתְקַיַּים עָלְמָא, אֲבָל, בְּגִין
דְּאִתְבְּרֵי עָלְמָא עַל דִּינָא, וְקַיְּימָא עַל דִּינָא, שָׂם שְׁמָוּת בָּאָרֶץ. וְשַׁפִּיר
הוּא, דְּאִלְמָלֵא כָּךְ, לָא יָכִיל עָלְמָא לְאִתְקַיְּימָא, מִקַּמֵּי חוֹבֵיהוֹן דִּבְנֵי
נָשָׁא.

434. Rabbi Yitzchak said that both interpretations are true, and even the one
put forward by Rabbi Yehuda is good. For if the world WAS CREATED with
the name of Mercy, then the world would have been resilient. Yet because
the world was created by Judgment and is founded upon Judgment, He put
Holy Names in the earth TO PROTECT IT, and this is very true, because had
He not done so, the world would not have been able to survive the
consequences of people's sins.

435. תָּא חֲזֵי, נֹחַ כַּד אִתְיְילִיד, קָרוֹן לֵיהּ עַל שְׁמָא דִּנְחָמָה. וְלֶהֱוֵי
שְׁמָא גָרִים. אֲבָל קֻדְשָׁא בְּרִיךְ הוּא לָאו הָכֵי. נֹחַ בְּהִפּוּךְ אַתְוָון, חֵן.
כד"א וְנֹחַ מָצָא חֵן. אָמַר רָבִּי יוֹסֵי, חֵן, הַיְינוּ נֹחַ. בְּצַדִּיקַיָּיא, שְׁמֵיהוֹן
גָּרִים לְטַב. בְּחַיָּיבַיָּא, שְׁמֵיהוֹן גָּרִים לְבִישׁ. בְּנֹחַ, כְּתִיב וְנֹחַ מָצָא חֵן בְּעֵינֵי
ה'. בְּעֵר בְּכוֹר יְהוּדָה, אִתְהַפְּכוּ אַתְוֵוי לְבִישׁ, עֵר רָע. רַע בְּעֵינֵי ה'.

435. Come and behold: when Noah was born, he was given that name,
because it connoted consolation (Heb. nechamah), indicating that he would
bring consolation. Yet, the Holy One, blessed be He, did not agree WITH
THEM. HE BROUGHT THE FLOOD UPON THEM, BECAUSE HE WANTED
THEM TO CORRECT THEIR WAYS AND REPENT. The letters of Noah's name
(Nun and Chet), when written in reverse order, form the word chen, which
means favor. This is as it was written: "Noah found favor in the eyes of
Hashem" (Beresheet 6:8). Rabbi Yosi said that Chen is Noah FOR THEY
ARE SPELLED WITH THE SAME LETTERS. The names of the righteous IN
ANY SEQUENCE cause beneficence. The names of the wicked IN ANY
SEQUENCE cause THEM harm. Of Noah it was said, "Noah found favor
(Heb. chen) in the eyes of Hashem," BECAUSE THE LETTERS WERE
REVERSED FOR GOOD. But of Er, the son of Judah, the letters were
reversed for lack of merit and harm, as it is written: "And Er (Ayin Resh)
was evil (Heb. ra, Resh Ayin) in the eyes of Hashem" (Beresheet 38:7).

71. "Come, behold the works of Elohim, Who has made desolations in the earth"

436. תָּא חֲזֵי, כֵּיוָן דְּאִתְיְילִיד נֹחַ, חָמָא עוֹבָדֵיהוֹן דִּבְנֵי נָשָׁא, דְּאִינּוּן חָטָאן קַמֵּי קֻדְשָׁא בְּרִיךְ הוּא, וַהֲוָה גָּנִיז גַּרְמֵיהּ, וְאִשְׁתַּדַּל בְּפוּלְחָנָא דְּמָארֵיהּ. בְּגִין דְּלָא לְמֵהַךְ בְּאוֹרְחַיְיהוּ. וְכ"ת, בַּמֶּה אִשְׁתַּדַּל. בְּהַהוּא סִפְרָא דְּאָדָם. וְסִפְרָא דַּחֲנוֹךְ. וַהֲוָה אִשְׁתַּדַּל בְּהוֹ לְמִפְלַח לְמָרֵיהּ.

436. Come and behold: when Noah was born, he saw that people were sinning before the Holy One, blessed be He. He used to hide himself so as not to be drawn to their ways and occupied himself with serving his Master. You may well ask, with what did he occupy himself? HE STUDIED the books of Adam and Enoch, and he struggled TO LEARN from those books how to worship his Master.

437. תָּא חֲזֵי, דְּהָכֵי הוּא, דְּהָא נֹחַ, מְנָא הֲוָה יָדַע, לְקָרֵב קָרְבָּנָא לְמָארֵיהּ. אֶלָּא, בְּגִין דְּאַשְׁכַּח חָכְמְתָא, עַל מַה מִּתְקַיֵּים עָלְמָא, וְיָדַע דְּעַל קָרְבָּנָא מִתְקַיֵּים. וְאִלְמָּלֵא קָרְבָּנָא, לָא הֲווֹ קַיְימֵי עִלָּאֵי וְתַתָּאֵי.

437. Come and behold: he indeed STUDIED THE BOOKS OF ADAM AND ENOCH because otherwise, how would Noah have known how to offer sacrifices to his Master? He found wisdom relating to the maintenance of the world IN THE BOOKS OF ADAM AND ENOCH. AND FROM THESE BOOKS, he learned that the world exists for the sake of sacrifices. Were it not for the sacrifices, neither the upper nor lower beings would have existed. HENCE, HE OFFERED A SACRIFICE.

438. רַבִּי שִׁמְעוֹן הֲוָה אָזִיל בְּאָרְחָא, וַהֲווֹ עִמֵּיהּ רַבִּי אֶלְעָזָר בְּרֵיהּ, וְרַבִּי יוֹסֵי, וְרַבִּי חִיָּיא. עַד דַּהֲוָה אָזְלֵי, אָמַר רַבִּי אֶלְעָזָר לַאֲבוּהִי, אָרְחָא מְתַקְּנָא קַמָּן, בָּעֵינָן לְמִשְׁמַע מִלֵּי דְּאוֹרַיְיתָא.

438. Rabbi Shimon was on his way, accompanied by Rabbi Elazar, his son, Rabbi Yosi, and Rabbi Chiya. As they were going, Rabbi Elazar said to his father, "the road is clear before us, and we would like to hear words of Torah."

439. פָּתַח רַבִּי שִׁמְעוֹן וְאָמַר, גַּם בַּדֶּרֶךְ כְּשֶׁהַסָּכָל הוֹלֵךְ לִבּוֹ חָסֵר וְגו'.

כַּד ב"נ בָּעֵי לְאַתְקָנָא אָרְחֵיה קַמֵּי קֻדְשָׁא בְּרִיךְ הוּא. עַד לָא יִפּוֹק לְאָרְחָא, בָּעֵי לְאַמְלָכָא בֵּיה, וּלְצַלֵּי קַמֵּיה עַל אָרְחֵיה. כְּמָה דִּתְנֵינָן, דִּכְתִיב צֶדֶק לְפָנָיו יְהַלֵּךְ וְיָשֵׂם לְדֶרֶךְ פְּעָמָיו. דְּהָא שְׁכִינְתָּא לָא אִתְפָּרְשָׁא מִנֵּיה.

439. Rabbi Shimon began to speak of the words, "Even when a fool walks by the way, his heart fails him" (Kohelet 10:3). When a man wants to make his ways worthy before the Holy One, blessed be He, he should, before he proceeds, consult Him and pray to Him, so that He should ensure his journey. This is as we have learned regarding the verse, "Righteousness shall go before him, and walks in the way of his steps" (Tehilim 85:14), meaning that HE SHOULD PRAY THAT the Shechinah, CALLED 'RIGHTEOUSNESS,' should not part from him. ONLY AFTER HE HAS PRAYED SHOULD HE GO ON HIS WAY.

440. וּמָאן דְּאִיהוּ לָא מְהֵימְנָא בְּמָרֵיה, מַה כְּתִיב בֵּיה, וְגַם בַּדֶּרֶךְ כְּשֶׁהַסָּכָל הוֹלֵךְ לִבּוֹ חָסֵר, מַאן לִבּוֹ, דָּא קֻדְשָׁא בְּרִיךְ הוּא, דְּלָא יְהַךְ עִמֵּיה בְּאָרְחָא, וְגָרַע מִן סִיַּיעְתֵּיה בְּאָרְחֵיה. בְּגִין דְּהַהוּא בַּר נָשׁ, דְּלָא מְהֵימָן בֵּיה בְּמָארֵיה, עַד לָא יִפּוֹק בְּאָרְחָא, לָא בָּעֵי סִיַּעְתָּא דְמָארֵיה.

440. Of he who has no faith in his Master, it is written: "Even when a fool walks on his way, his heart fails him." HE ASKS: What is "his heart?" AND HE REPLIES: IT is the Holy One, blessed be He, WHO CAUSES HIS SHECHINAH TO RESTS IN THE HEART OF THE RIGHTEOUS, THAT does not accompany him on his way. THUS "HIS HEART FAILS HIM" THE INSPIRATION OF THE SHECHINAH and lacks His aid along the way. This is all because this man, who does not believe in his Master, WHO IS CALLED "A FOOL," BECAUSE ONE DOES NOT SIN UNLESS THE SPIRIT OF FOOLISHNESS ATTACHES ITSELF TO HIM, does not seek help from his Master before he starts his journey.

441. וַאֲפִילוּ בְּאָרְחָא, כַּד אִיהוּ אָזִיל, לָא אִשְׁתַּדַּל בְּמִלֵּי דְאוֹרַיְיתָא. וּבְגִינֵי כָךְ, לִבּוֹ חָסֵר, דְּלָא אָזִיל בַּהֲדֵיה דְמָרֵיה, וְלָא אִשְׁתְּכַח בְּאָרְחֵיה. וְאָמַר לַכֹּל סָכָל הוּא. אֲפִילוּ כַּד שָׁמַע מִלָּה דִמְהֵימְנוּתָא

דְּמָארֵיה, הוּא אָמַר, דְּטִפְּשׁוּתָא הוּא, לְאִשְׁתַּדְּלָא בֵּיה.

441. And even when he is on his way, he is not occupied with the study of Torah, and thus "his heart fails him." Because he does not follow his Master, his Master is not on his way. THE VERSE CONTINUES, "And he proclaims to all that he is foolish" (Kohelet 10:3), meaning that even when he hears a word of true faith in his Master, he says that it is foolish to pay attention to it.

442 כְּהַאי דְּשָׁאִילוּ לְבַר נָשׁ, עַל אָת קַיָּימָא, דְּרְשִׁימוּ בְּבִשְׂרֵיה דְּבַר נָשׁ, וַאֲמַר לָאו אִיהוּ מְהֵימְנוּתָא. שָׁמַע רַב יֵיבָא סָבָא, וְאִסְתַּכַּל בֵּיה, וְאִתְעֲבֵיד תְּלָא דְּגַרְמֵי. וַאֲנַן בְּהַאי אוֹרְחָא, בְּסַיְיעַתָּא דְּקֻדְשָׁא בְּרִיךְ הוּא, בָּעִינָן לְמֵימַר מִלֵּי דְאוֹרַיְיתָא.

442. Similarly, there was a man who asked about the sign of the holy covenant imprinted upon the human flesh, and said that it was not an article of Faith. Rabbi Yeba Saba (the elder) heard, looked upon him and transformed him into a pile of bones. And we ARE upon this path with the help of the Holy One, blessed be He. Hence, we should recite words of Torah.

443. פְּתַח וַאֲמַר, הוֹרֵנִי ה' דַּרְכֶּךָ אֲהַלֵּךְ בַּאֲמִתֶּךָ יַחֵד לְבָבִי לְיִרְאָה שְׁמֶךָ. הַאי קְרָא קַשְׁיָא, דְּהָא תָּנִינָן, כֹּלָּא הִיא בִּידָא דְּקֻדְשָׁא בְּרִיךְ הוּא, בַּר לְמֶהֱוֵי זַכָּאָה, אוֹ חַיָּיבָא. וְדָוִד הֵיךְ תָּבַע דָּא מֵעִם קוּדְשָׁא בְּרִיךְ הוּא.

443. He started a discourse by commenting on the verse: "Teach me, Hashem, Your way, I will walk in Your truth. Make my heart single to fear Your name" (Tehilim 86:11). This is a difficult verse, because we learned that everything except becoming a righteous person or becoming wicked is in the hands of the Holy One, blessed be He. AS IT IS WRITTEN: "ALL IS IN THE HANDS OF HEAVEN EXCEPT FOR THE FEAR OF HEAVEN." WHY then did David ask the Holy One, blessed be He, to be given that?"

444. אֶלָּא, דָּוִד הָכֵי קָאֲמַר, הוֹרֵנִי ה' דַּרְכֶּךָ. הַהוּא אֹרַח מֵישׁוֹר,

וּמִתַקְנָא, לְגַלָּאָה עֵינַי, וּלְמִנְדַּע לֵיהּ, וּלְבָתַר, אֲהַלֵּךְ בַּאֲמִתֶּךְ. אֵיהַךְ
בְּאֹרַח קְשׁוֹט, וְלָא אַסְטֵי לְיָמִינָא וְלִשְׂמָאלָא. יַחֵד לְבָבִי. מַאן לְבָבִי.
כד"א צוּר לְבָבִי וְחֶלְקִי. וְכָל דָּא, אֲנָא תָּבַע, לְיִרְאָה אֶת שְׁמֶךָ,
לְאִתְדַּבְּקָא בִּדְחִלְתָּךְ, לְאִסְתַּמְּרָא אֹרְחֵי כְּדְקָא יָאוֹת. לְיִרְאָה שְׁמֶךָ.
אֲתַר חוּלָקִי, דְּבֵיהּ שַׁרְיָא דַחֲלְתָּא לְמִדְחַל.

444. David said, "Teach me Your way." HE ASKED THE HOLY ONE,
BLESSED BE HE, to open his eyes and show him the right path. Then,
"...walk in Your truth." He himself would walk the right path and not waver
to the right or the left. He also said: "Make my heart single." "Heart," as in
"the strength of my heart and my portion" (Tehilim 73:26), MEANING THE
SHECHINAH, CLOTHED BY THE HEART, AND CALLED 'STRENGTH OF
HEART'. FOR HER SAKE HE ASKED, "MAKE MY HEART SINGLE." All this I
entreat, DAVID SAID, in order "to fear your name," to be attached to the fear
of You and properly to keep to the path." "To fear Your name" refers to
David's lot, NAMELY MALCHUT, DAVID'S PORTION, in which fear of Him
dwells. FOR MALCHUT IS THE SECRET OF FEAR, AND IS CALLED 'FEAR,'
AS IS KNOWN.

445. תָּא חֲזֵי, כָּל בַּר נָשׁ, דְּדָחִיל לֵיהּ לְקֻדְשָׁא בְּרִיךְ הוּא, שַׁרְיָא עִמֵּיהּ
מְהֵימְנוּתָא כְּדְקָא יָאוֹת. דְּהָא הַהוּא ב"נ שְׁלִים בְּפוּלְחָנָא דְמָרֵיהּ.
וּמַאן דְּלָא שַׁרְיָא בֵּיהּ דַּחֲלָא דְמָרֵיהּ, לָא שַׁרְיָיא עִמֵּיהּ מְהֵימְנוּתָא.
וְלָאו אִיהוּ כְּדַאי לְמֶהֱוֵי לֵיהּ חוּלָקָא, בְּעָלְמָא דְאָתֵי.

445. Come and behold: Faith dwells with he who fears the Holy One,
blessed be He, for he is wholeheartedly in his Master's service. Yet, Faith is
not with he who does not fear his Master, and he does not deserve to have a
portion in the World to Come.

446. תּוּ, פְּתַח וַאֲמַר, וְאֹרַח צַדִּיקִים כְּאוֹר נֹגַהּ הוֹלֵךְ וָאוֹר, עַד נְכוֹן
הַיּוֹם. זַכָּאִין אִינוּן צַדִּיקַיָא, בְּעָלְמָא דֵין וּבְעָלְמָא דְאָתֵי, דְקֻדְשָׁא בְּרִיךְ
הוּא בָּעֵי בִּיקָרֵיהוֹן. תָּא חֲזֵי, מַה כְּתִיב, וְאֹרַח צַדִּיקִים כְּאוֹר נֹגַהּ, מַאי
כְּאוֹר נֹגַהּ כְּהַהוּא נְהוֹרָא דְנָהִיר, דְּבָרָא קֻדְשָׁא בְּרִיךְ הוּא, בְּעוֹבָדָא

71. "Come, behold the works of Elohim, Who has made desolations in the earth"

דִּבְרֵאשִׁית, הָא הוּא דְּגָנֵיז לוֹן לְצַדִּיקַיָּא לְעָלְמָא דְּאָתֵי. הוֹלֵךְ וָאוֹר,
דְּאִיהוּ סָלִיק בִּנְהוֹרֵיהּ תָּדִיר, וְלָא גָּרַע מִנֵּיהּ.

446. He then opened a discourse on the verse: "But the path of just men is like the glean of sunlight, that shines ever more lightly until the height of noon day" (Mishlei 4:18). Happy are the righteous in this world and in the World to Come, because the Holy One, blessed be He, desires their glory. Come and behold: it is written that "the path of just men is like the glean of sunlight." What is the glean of light? It is like the illuminating light that the Holy One, blessed be He, made during the works of Creation. This is THE LIGHT that He stored away for the righteous in the World to Come. The words, "...that shines ever more brightly," indicate that the righteous person's light is ever increasing and never lacking.

447. אֲבָל, בְּחַיָּיבַיָּא מַה כְּתִיב, דֶּרֶךְ רְשָׁעִים כָּאֲפֵלָה לֹא יָדְעוּ בַּמֶּה
יִכָּשֵׁלוּ. לֹא יָדְעוּ, וְכִי לָא יָדְעִין. אֶלָּא חַיָּיבַיָּא, אָזְלֵי בַּעֲקִימוּ דְּאָרְחָא,
בְּהַאי עָלְמָא, וְלָא בָּעָאן לְאִסְתַּכְּלָא, דְּזַמִּין קֻדְשָׁא בְּרִיךְ הוּא לְמֵידַן
לְהוּ בְּהַהוּא עָלְמָא וּלְאַעֲלָאָה לוֹן, בְּדִינָא דְּגֵיהִנֹּם, וְאִינּוּן צָוְוחִין
וְאָמְרִין וַוי לָן: דְּלָא אוֹרִיכְנָא אוּדְנִין, וְלָא אֲצֵיתְנָא, בְּהַהוּא עָלְמָא.
וּבְכָל יוֹמָא, אָמְרֵי וַוי דָא.

447. Yet, of the wicked it is written: "The way of the wicked is as darkness, they do not know on what they stumble" (Ibid. 19). How is it they do not know WHAT MAKES THEM STUMBLE? The wicked follow a crooked path in this world. They do not want to see that the Holy One, blessed be He, will judge them in the World OF TRUTH and bring them to be judged in Gehenom. IN GEHENOM, they shout, "Woe to us that we did not lend our ears to His commandments while we were in the world," and they repeat this lament each and every day.

448. תָּא חֲזֵי, זַמִּין קֻדְשָׁא בְּרִיךְ הוּא לְאַנְהָרָא לוֹן לְצַדִּיקַיָּא לְעָלְמָא
דְּאָתֵי, וּלְמֵיהַב לוֹן, אֲגַר חוּלָקְהוֹן, אֲתַר דְּעֵינָא לָא שַׁלְטָא, לְמֵיקַם
עֲלֵיהּ. כד"א עַיִן לֹא רָאָתָה אֱלֹקִים זוּלָתְךָ יַעֲשֶׂה לִמְחַכֵּה לוֹ. וּכְתִיב

וְיָצְאוּ וְרָאוּ בְּפִגְרֵי הָאֲנָשִׁים הַפּוֹשְׁעִים בִּי. וּכְתִיב וְעַסוֹתֶם רְשָׁעִים כִּי יִהְיוּ אֵפֶר תַּחַת כַּפּוֹת רַגְלֵיכֶם. זַכָּאִין אִינוּן צַדִּיקַיָּא, בְּעָלְמָא דֵין וּבְעָלְמָא דְאָתֵי. עֲלַיְיהוּ כְּתִיב צַדִּיקִים לְעוֹלָם יִירְשׁוּ אָרֶץ. וּכְתִיב אַךְ צַדִּיקִים יוֹדוּ לִשְׁמֶךָ יֵשְׁבוּ יְשָׁרִים אֶת פָּנֶיךָ.

448. Come and behold: the Holy One, blessed be He, will shine upon the righteous in the World to Come and will give them their destined reward in a place that no eye has ever beheld. It is, as it is written: "neither has the eye seen Elohim, beside You, should do such a thing for him that waits for Him" (Yeshayah 64:3); and: "...and they shall go forth and look upon the carcasses of the men who have transgressed against Me" (Yeshayah 66:24); and also: "And You shall tread down the wicked for they shall be ashes under the soles of your feet" (Malachi 3:21). Joyful are the righteous in this world and the World to Come. Of them it is written: "Righteous; they shall inherit the land forever" (Yeshayah 60:21) and: "Verily, the righteous shall praise Your name, the upright shall dwell in Your presence" (Tehilim 140:14).

בָּרוּךְ ה׳ לְעוֹלָם אָמֵן וְאָמֵן.

Blessed be Hashem forever. Amen and Amen.

Noach

Beginners paragraphs

1-4, 9-11, 13, 14, 17, 19, 20, 24, 28-46, 54-60, 69-72, 74, 77-84, 88-95, 100, 108-111, 115, 117-119, 131, 132, 135, 138, 139, 140, 142, 144, 146, 147, 150-153, 155, 156, 158, 161, 165-169, 175-177, 180, 182-184, 186-189, 191-193, 195-197, 200-202, 205-209, 213-215, 218, 220-222, 225-229, 234, 237, 238, 240, 246-248, 252-256, 257, 258, 260, 261, 268, 273, 275-279, 285, 286, 290, 292-295, 298, 299, 304-307, 312-318, 320-322, 324, 325, 331, 338, 342, 346, 348, 352, 353, 357, 358, 360-364, 366-371, 372-378, 381-383, 385-388,

Names of the Articles

1. Noah and the ark

The Zohar reveals secrets within the literal story of Noah and the Ark. Noah embodies the Sfirot of *Yesod*. The Ark is a metaphor for our world of *Malchut*. The sins of this generation literally separated the *Malchut* from *Yesod*, which was its source of Light. This is the mystery behind the flood's destruction. Any disconnection from Light produces darkness, and from within this darkness chaos and destruction emerge. Reading this section helps bond *Malchut* with *Yesod*. It is comparable to the simple action of throwing a light switch and banishing the darkness in a room. Moreover, by reading these passages we arouse spiritual forces of Light to combat and eradicate the present day negative actions of society that once again are beginning to sever the link between the *Malchut* and *Yesod*.

1. רַבִּי חִיָּיא פָּתַח, וְעַמֵּךְ כֻּלָּם צַדִּיקִים לְעוֹלָם יִירְשׁוּ אֶרֶץ נֵצֶר מַטָּעַי מַעֲשֵׂה יָדַי לְהִתְפָּאֵר, זַכָּאִין אִינוּן יִשְׂרָאֵל, דְּמִשְׁתַּדְּלֵי בְּאוֹרַיְיתָא, וְיָדְעֵי אָרְחִין דְּאוֹרַיְיתָא, דִּבְגִינָה יִזְכּוּן לְעָלְמָא דְּאָתֵי.

1. "These are the generations of Noah..." (Beresheet 6:9). Rabbi Chiya opened the discussion with the verses: "NOAH WAS A RIGHTEOUS MAN...", AND, "Your people also shall be all righteous: they shall inherit the land forever; they shall be the branch of My planting, the work of My hands, that I may be glorified" (Yeshayah 60:21). A WAS RAISED AFTER THE STATEMENT, "THESE ARE THE GENERATIONS OF NOAH," THE TEXT SHOULD HAVE CONTINUED, 'SHEM, HAM, AND JAPHETH.' IT SHOULD NOT HAVE ENDED WITH "NOAH WAS A RIGHTEOUS MAN." HE FURTHER STATED: Happy are Yisrael, who occupy themselves with the Torah and are familiar with its paths, through which they will merit the World to Come.

2. תָּא חֲזֵי, כָּל יִשְׂרָאֵל אִית לוֹן חוּלָקָא לְעָלְמָא דְּאָתֵי, מַאי טַעְמָא, בְּגִין דְּנָטְרִין בְּרִית דְּעָלְמָא אִתְקַיֵּים עֲלֵיהּ, כד"א אִם לֹא בְרִיתִי יוֹמָם וָלַיְלָה חֻקּוֹת שָׁמַיִם וָאָרֶץ לֹא שָׂמְתִּי. וְעַל דָּא, יִשְׂרָאֵל דְּנָטְרֵי בְּרִית, וְקַבִּילוּ לֵיהּ, אִית לוֹן חוּלָקָא בְּעָלְמָא דְּאָתֵי.

2. Come and behold! All Yisrael have a portion in the World to Come. Why

is this so? Because they observe the covenant on which the world is established. This is as it is written in the verse: "If My covenant be not day and night, it were as if I had not appointed the ordinance of heaven and earth" (Yirmeyah 33:25), MEANING THAT YISRAEL KEEP IN HOLINESS THE COVENANT OF CIRCUMCISION BY NEVER DESECRATING IT WITH SPILLING OF SEMEN IN VAIN, OR BY SEXUAL IMMORAL BEHAVIOR. Therefore, Yisrael, who has accepted the covenant and observe it, have a portion in the World to Come.

3. וְלֹא עוֹד, אֶלָּא בְּגִין כָּךְ אִקְרוּן צַדִּיקִים, מִכָּאן אוֹלִיפְנָא, כָּל מָאן דְּנָטִיר הַאי בְּרִית, דְּעָלְמָא אִתְקַיַּים עֲלֵיהּ, אִקְרֵי צַדִּיק. מְנָא לָן מִיּוֹסֵף, בְּגִין דְּנָטַר לֵיהּ לִבְרִית עָלְמָא, זָכָה דְּאִקְרֵי צַדִּיק, וְעַל כָּךְ, וְעַמֵּךְ כֻּלָּם צַדִּיקִים לְעוֹלָם יִירְשׁוּ אָרֶץ.

3. Furthermore, as a result, they are called 'righteous.' We deduce from this that whoever observes the covenant upon which the world is established is called 'righteous.' How do we know this? We know this from Joseph, who observed the everlasting covenant BY NOT MATING WITH HIS MASTER'S WIFE, and was therefore called 'righteous.' And this is why it is written: "Your people also shall be all righteous: they shall inherit the land forever." RABBI CHIYA THUS EXPLAINED THE VERSE, "NOAH WAS A RIGHTEOUS MAN," AS MEANING THAT NOAH OBSERVED THE COVENANT. FOR THIS REASON, HIS OFFSPRING HAVE CONTINUITY. THE VERSE THUS STATES: "THESE ARE THE GENERATIONS OF NOAH. NOAH WAS A RIGHTEOUS MAN;" BECAUSE HIS RIGHTEOUSNESS AND THE CONTINUITY OF HIS CHILDREN ARE CONNECTED.

4. רַבִּי אֶלְעָזָר אָמַר, אֵלֶּה בְּכָל אֲתַר פָּסַל אֶת הָרִאשׁוֹנִים תְּנִינָן וכו', מַה כְּתִיב לְעֵילָא בְּפָרְשָׁתָא דִּבְרֵאשִׁית, וְנָהָר יוֹצֵא מֵעֵדֶן לְהַשְׁקוֹת אֶת הַגָּן וּמִשָּׁם יִפָּרֵד וגו'. הַהוּא נָהָר דְּנַגִּיד וְנָפִיק, וְעַיֵּיל לְגִנְתָּא, וְאַשְׁקֵי לֵיהּ מִשַּׁקְיוּ דִּלְעֵילָא, וְעָבֵיד לֵיהּ נַיְיחָא, וְעָבֵיד אִיבִּין, וְרַבֵּי זַרְעִין, וְהוּא כְּדֵין נַיְיחָא לְכֹלָּא, וְדָא נַיְיחָא לֵיהּ לְגִנְתָּא, וְדָא עָבֵיד נַיְיחָא בֵּיהּ, כד"א כִּי בוֹ שָׁבַת, וּכְתִיב וַיִּשְׁבּוֹת בַּיּוֹם הַשְּׁבִיעִי, וְדָא רָזָא דְּמִלָּה, דָּא עָבֵיד תּוֹלְדוֹת וְלָא אָחֳרָא.

4. Rabbi Elazar said that we have learned that whenever the term "These (Heb. *eleh*)" appears, it always annuls something previously mentioned. Now, it is written in the portion of Beresheet, "And a river went out of Eden to water the garden; and from thence it was parted" (Beresheet 2:10). THIS MEANS THAT this river, WHICH IS YESOD, is drawn and comes out OF EDEN, WHICH IS CHOCHMAH, and enters the garden, WHICH IS MALCHUT, to water it from the supernal waters and bring it pleasure, making it produce fruit and seed. This gives satisfaction to everyone. The garden is pleased WITH ITS FRUIT, which brings pleasure to the river, BECAUSE IT MADE THE FRUIT. As it is written: "Because in it He rested" (Ibid. 3), MEANING "IN THE RIVER," WHICH IS YESOD. And it is also written: "And He rested on the seventh day" (Ibid. 2), MEANING IN THE GARDEN WHICH IS MALCHUT. AS RABBI ELAZAR EXPLAINED, THE WORD "RESTED" IS DERIVED FROM 'REST' AND 'SATISFACTION'. This is the secret of the matter OF THE RIVER THAT COMES OUT OF EDEN – MEANING YESOD, for it produces offspring, and no other SFIRAH CAN PRODUCE ANY FRUIT.

5. תָּא חֲזֵי, כְּגַוְונָא דָא, נֹחַ לְתַתָּא, קְיָימָא קַדִּישָׁא הֲוָה, דּוּגְמָא דִּלְעֵילָא, וְעַ"ד אִקְרֵי אִישׁ הָאֲדָמָה, וְרָזָא אוֹלִיפְנָא, דְּהָא נֹחַ אִצְטְרִיךְ לְתֵיבָה, לְאִתְחַבְּרָא בָּהּ, וּלְקַיָּימָא זַרְעָא דְּכוֹלָּא, דִּכְתִיב לְחַיּוֹת זֶרַע.

5. Come and behold: so it was with Noah below. Noah was the sacred covenant below, as YESOD, OR THE RIVER THAT COMES OUT OF EDEN, is above. And he is called "Man of the earth," BECAUSE THE EARTH REFERS TO MALCHUT AND YESOD IS MALCHUT'S MAN. So now we have learned a secret, that Noah needed the ark, WHICH ALLUDES TO MALCHUT, so he could unite with it and preserve the seed of the whole world. As it is written: "to keep seed alive" (Beresheet 7:3).

6. מָאן תֵּיבָה, דָא אֲרוֹן הַבְּרִית, וְנֹחַ וְתֵיבָה לְתַתָּא, הָכֵי הֲוֹוֹ, כְּדוּגְמָא דִּלְעֵילָא. נֹחַ כְּתִיב בֵּיהּ בְּרִית, דִּכְתִיב וַהֲקִימוֹתִי אֶת בְּרִיתִי אִתָּךְ וְגו', וְעַד דְּאִתְקַיַּים בֵּיהּ בְּרִית, לָא עָיֵיל לְתֵיבוּתָא, דִּכְתִיב וַהֲקִימוֹתִי אֶת בְּרִיתִי אִתָּךְ וּבָאתָ אֶל הַתֵּיבָה, וּכְדֵין הֲוָה תֵּיבָה אֲרוֹן הַבְּרִית.

6. RABBI ELAZAR ASKS: What is the ark? AND HE ANSWERS: It is the ark, WHICH IS MALCHUT, of the covenant AFTER SHE RECEIVES YESOD,

WHICH IS CALLED THE COVENANT WITHIN HER. And Noah and the ark below were like YESOD AND MALCHUT above, BECAUSE the covenant is mentioned in relation to Noah, as it is written: "And I will establish My covenant with you" (Beresheet 6:18). As long as the covenant was not established in Noah, he did not enter the ark, as it is written: "And I will establish my covenant with you; and you shall come into the ark." Only then does the ark become the ark of the covenant, MEANING THAT AFTER THE ARK RECEIVED AND ACCEPTED NOAH THE RIGHTEOUS, WHO IS THE COVENANT, IT BECAME THE ARK OF THE COVENANT.

7. תֵּיבָה וְנֹחַ, כֹּלָּא כְּגַוְונָא דִלְעֵילָּא, וּבְגִין דְּהַאי בְּרִית לְעֵילָּא הוּא עָבִיד תּוֹלְדוֹת, כְּגַוְונָא דָּא נֹחַ, אִיהוּ עָבִיד תּוֹלְדוֹת. בְּגִינֵי כָּךְ אֵלֶּה תּוֹלְדוֹת נֹחַ.

7. So the ark and Noah are completely, as are MALCHUT AND THE COVENANT above. And because the covenant above brings forth offspring, so Noah begets generations. That is why IT IS WRITTEN: "These are the generations of Noah." THIS IS TO TEACH US THAT LIKE THE COVENANT ABOVE, WHICH IS YESOD OF ATZILUT, NOAH BORE EVERLASTING GENERATIONS, BECAUSE HE MERITED THE HOLY COVENANT, AND YESOD OF ATZILUT, WHICH IS CALLED THE COVENANT, RESTS UPON HIM.

8. נֹחַ אִישׁ צַדִּיק, הָכֵי הוּא וַדַּאי, כְּגַוְונָא דִלְעֵילָּא, וְעַל דָּא וְצַדִּיק יְסוֹד עוֹלָם כְּתִיב, וְאַרְעָא עַל דָּא אִתְקָיְימַת, דְּהָא אִיהוּ, עַמּוּדָא דְּעָלְמָא קַיְימָא עֲלֵיהּ. וּמָאן אִיהוּ, דָּא צַדִּיק, וְנֹחַ אִקְרֵי צַדִּיק לְתַתָּא.

8. "Noah was a righteous man." This is assuredly so, for his righteousness corresponds to YESOD above. That is why it is written: "the righteous are the foundation (Heb. Yesod) of the world" (Mishlei 10:25), and the earth, WHICH IS MALCHUT, is established upon him. He is the pillar that upholds the world, WHICH IS MALCHUT. THAT IS WHY HE IS CALLED THE FOUNDATION OF THE WORLD. And what is THIS YESOD? It is the Righteous. Thus, Noah is the righteous below, AMONG THE SOULS. AND HENCE IT IS WRITTEN: "NOAH WAS A RIGHTEOUS MAN" – TO TEACH US THAT THE WORLD IS MAINTAINED BY HIM.

9. וְרָזָא דְכֹלָּא, אֶת הָאֱלֹהִים הִתְהַלֶּךְ נֹחַ דַּיְיקָא, דְּלָא אִתְפְּרַשׁ מִנֵּיהּ לְעָלְמִין, וּלְמֶהֱוֵי הוּא בְּאַרְעָא, כְּגַוְונָא דִלְעֵילָּא, אִישׁ צַדִּיק, יְסוֹדָא דְעָלְמָא, בְּרִית שָׁלוֹם שְׁלָמָא דְעָלְמָא, אִישׁ הָאֲדָמָה וַדַּאי, וְעַל דָּא, וְנֹחַ מָצָא חֵן בְּעֵינֵי ה'.

9. And the secret of all this is revealed in the words, "And Noah walked with Elohim" (Beresheet 6:9), which mean to teach us that he never separated himself from Him, FROM MALCHUT. And he merited being called a righteous man on earth, as did the supernal Yesod, the foundation of the world.' He is the covenant of peace and the peace of the world. Thus, he is called "man of the earth," MEANING THE 'HUSBAND' OF THE EARTH. And that is why the verse is written: "Noah found favor in the eyes of Hashem" (Ibid. 8).

10. תָּמִים הָיָה בְּדוֹרוֹתָיו, מַאי בְּדוֹרוֹתָיו, אֵלֶּין אִינּוּן דְּנָפְקוּ מִנֵּיהּ, הוּא אַשְׁלִים לְכָלְּהוּ, וְהוּא הֲוָה שְׁלִים מִכָּלְּהוּ, תָּמִים הָיָה דְּאִתְיְלִיד מָהוּל, דִּכְתִיב הִתְהַלֵּךְ לְפָנַי וֶהְיֵה תָמִים. בְּדוֹרוֹתָיו, וְלֹא בְּדָרִין דְּעָלְמָא, דְּהָא מִנֵּיהּ נָפְקוּ תוֹלְדוֹת בְּעָלְמָא.

10. RABBI ELAZAR ASKS: What is the meaning of "his generations" IN THE VERSE "perfect in his generations?" AND HE REPLIES THAT they are his descendants, who issued from him, all of whom he perfected THROUGH HIS RIGHTEOUSNESS and by whom he was also perfected. IN OTHER WORDS, THE VERSE "PERFECT IN HIS GENERATIONS" HAS TWO MEANINGS: (A) HIS WHOLENESS PERFECTED ALL THE GENERATIONS THAT DESCENDED FROM HIM, AND (B) HE WAS PERFECTED BY THE GENERATIONS THAT DESCENDED FROM HIM. ANOTHER EXPLANATION IS THAT Perfect MEANS that he was born circumcised. As it is written: "Walk before Me and be perfect" (Beresheet 17:1), MEANING CIRCUMCISED. "In his generations" includes only Noah's descendants and not the generations in the world in general because they descended from him. IN OTHER WORDS, EVEN THOUGH THE VERSE MEANS THAT HE WAS PERFECT IN ALL THE GENERATIONS OF THE WORLD, IT SAYS "HIS GENERATIONS" TO INDICATE THAT ALL THE GENERATIONS OF THE WORLD ARE HIS, AS THEY ALL DESCEND FROM HIM.

11. תָּא חֲזֵי, נֹחַ אִתְחֲזֵי מִיּוֹמָא דְּאִתְבְּרֵי עָלְמָא, לְמֶהֱוֵי בְּתֵיבָה בְּחִבּוּרָא חַד, וּלְמֵיעַל בָּהּ. וְעַד לָא אִתְחַבְּרוּ כַּחֲדָא, לָא הֲוָה עָלְמָא כִּדְקָא יָאוֹת, לְבָתַר מַה כְּתִיב וּמֵאֵלֶּה נָפְצָה כָל הָאָרֶץ, מַהוּ נָפְצָה, כְּמָה דְאַתְּ אָמֵר וּמִשָּׁם יִפָּרֵד, דְּמִתַּמָּן אִשְׁתְּכַח פְּרוּדָא, וְאִתְבַּדְּרוּ תּוֹלְדוֹת לְכָל סִטְרִין.

11. Come and behold: from the day the world was created, Noah was destined to be joined in union with and to enter the ark. And until they were joined as one, the world had not reached a fully stable condition. And as soon as this occurred, it is written: "From these was the whole earth overspread" (Beresheet 9:19). What is meant by "overspread?" These words are analogous to the verse: "and from thence the river parted" (Beresheet 2:10), MEANING THAT SPREADING OUT IS SIMILAR TO THE SUPERNAL ARK, WHICH IS THE SECRET OF THE GARDEN. For from that point in the text onward, we find the separation and diffusion of progeny into all quarters of the world. THIS MEANS THAT AFTER THEY WERE PERFECTED IN THE ARK, THEY WERE ABLE TO COME FORTH AND EXIST IN THE WORLD OF SEPARATION WITHOUT BEING ANNIHILATED, AS WAS THE GENERATION OF THE GREAT FLOOD.

12. וְכֹלָּא חַד, כְּדוּגְמָא חֲדָא, בְּגִינֵי כָךְ, אֵלֶּה תּוֹלְדוֹת נֹחַ, אֵלֶּה וַדַּאי, דְּהָא יְסוֹדָא דְּעָלְמָא אִיהוּ, דְּעָבִיד תּוֹלְדוֹת, לְקַיְּימָא בְּאַרְעָא. אָתָא רִבִּי אַבָּא וּנְשָׁקֵיהּ, אָמַר אַרְיָא בְּחֵילֵיהּ טִינָרָא נָקִיב וְתָבַר. כָּךְ הוּא וַדַּאי. וְתָא חֲזֵי מִשִׁעוּרָא דְּתֵיבוּתָא, אוּף נָמֵי הָכֵי הוּא.

12. And all is one and one is like the other, BECAUSE THE BRANCHES BELOW ARE SIMILAR TO THEIR ROOTS ABOVE. So THE VERSE STATES, "These are the generations of Noah." "These" SURELY ANNULS THAT THE FORMER GENERATIONS THAT DID NOT SURVIVE IN THE WORLD. Only Yesod (the foundation) of the world, WHICH IS NOAH, produced the fruit that still exists in the world. Rabbi Aba approached and kissed RABBI ELAZAR saying, 'The lion in his might has pierced through the rock and broke it asunder,' MEANING THAT IT WAS HARD AS A ROCK FOR HIM TO UNDERSTAND THE INNER MEANING OF THESE VERSES, BUT RABBI ELAZAR REMOVED ALL THE DIFFICULTIES HE HAD IN COMPREHENDING

THE TEXT. All this is certainly true, BECAUSE ALL THAT HAS BEEN SAID ABOUT NOAH AND THE ARK BELOW CORRESPONDS TO THEIR SUPERNAL ROOTS IN THE WORLD OF ATZILUT ABOVE. Even the measurements of the ark correspond to their roots above.

תוספתא

13. לָמָּה נֹחַ נֹחַ תְּרֵי זִמְנֵי, אֶלָּא כָּל צַדִּיק וְצַדִּיק דִּי בְּעָלְמָא אִית לֵיהּ תְּרֵין רוּחִין, רוּחָא חַד בְּעָלְמָא דֵין, וְרוּחָא חַד בְּעָלְמָא דְּאָתֵי וְהָכֵי תִּשְׁכַּח בְּכֻלְּהוּ צַדִּיקֵי, מֹשֶׁה מֹשֶׁה. יַעֲקֹב יַעֲקֹב. אַבְרָהָם אַבְרָהָם. שְׁמוּאֵל שְׁמוּאֵל. שֵׁם שֵׁם. בַּר מִיִּצְחָק דְּלָא כְּתִיב בֵּיהּ, כְּמָה דִכְתִיב בְּהוּ, בְּגִין דְּיִצְחָק בְּשַׁעֲתָא דְּאִתְקְרַב עַל גַּבֵּי מַדְבְּחָא, נָפְקַת נִשְׁמָתֵיהּ דַּהֲוַת בֵּיהּ בְּהַאי עָלְמָא, וְכֵיוָן דְּאִתְּמַר בֵּיהּ בְּאַבְרָהָם בָּרוּךְ מְחַיֵּה הַמֵּתִים, תָּבַת בֵּיהּ נִשְׁמָתֵיהּ דְּעָלְמָא דְּאָתֵי. בְּגִין דָּא תִּשְׁכַּח דְּלָא יִיחֵד קֻדְשָׁא בְּרִיךְ הוּא שְׁמֵיהּ אֶלָּא עַל יִצְחָק, בְּגִין דְּאִתְחֲשַׁב כְּמֵת, וְעַל דָּא רָמַז קְרָא וַאֲמַר הֵן בִּקְדוֹשָׁיו לֹא יַאֲמִין וְגו'.

Tosefta (addendum)

13. RABBI ELAZAR ASKS: Why is "Noah Noah" (Beresheet 6:9) written twice? AND HE ANSWERS: Each and every righteous person in the world has two spirits. One stays in this world, while the other is in the World to Come. And so we find that the Holy One, blessed be He, named all the righteous twice: "Moses, Moses" (Shemot 3:4), "Jacob, Jacob" (Beresheet 46:2), "Abraham, Abraham" (Beresheet 22:11), "Samuel, Samuel" (I Shmuel 3:10) – with the exception of Isaac. He is not named twice because when he approached the altar to be sacrificed, the soul that was within him in this world left him. And because it is said of Abraham, "blessed are You who resurrect the dead" – THAT IS, "LAY NOT YOUR HAND UPON THE LAD" (BERESHEET 22:12), AFTER HE HAD LIFTED HIS HAND, INTENDING TO SLAY HIS CHILD, so only the soul of the World to Come was returned to him. AND THAT IS WHY HE IS NOT NAMED TWICE, 'ISAAC, ISAAC'. And that is why you shall find that the name of the Holy One, blessed be He, was not unified UPON ANY OTHER RIGHTEOUS PERSON DURING HIS LIFETIME.

It was unified only on Isaac, because he was already considered as dead. FOR HE HAD NO SOUL OF THIS WORLD, ONLY THAT OF THE WORLD TO COME. HE WAS LIKE THOSE WHO PASS AWAY FROM THIS WORLD. The verse therefore states: "Behold, He puts no trust in His holy ones" (Iyov 15:15) BECAUSE HE DOES NOT UNIFY HIS NAME ON THE RIGHTEOUS DURING THEIR LIFETIMES.

14. דָּבָר אַחֵר אֵלֶּה תּוֹלְדוֹת, בְּגִין דַּהֲוָה צַדִּיק שַׁבַּח לֵיהּ תְּרֵי זִמְנֵי, תָּמִים הָיָה בְּדוֹרוֹתָיו, אֲבָל בְּדָרִין אַחֲרָנִין אֵינוּ נֶחְשָׁב לִכְלוּם, כְּמוֹ דָרָא דְאַבְרָהָם, וְדָרָא דְמֹשֶׁה וְדָרָא דְּדָוִד. דָּבָר אַחֵר חָמֵי מַאי עָבַד בְּדָרָא דְּכָלְהוּ חַיָּיבִים, קַל וָחוֹמֶר אִלּוּ הָיָה בְּדָרָא דְכוֹלְהוּ צַדִּיקִים.

עַד כָּאן

14. A different explanation given OF THE WORDS "NOAH, NOAH" is that because he was righteous, He praised him twice BY CALLING HIM "NOAH, NOAH." THAT IS, "perfect in his generations," but if he had lived in any other generation, such as that of Abraham or Moses or King David, then he would not have been considered at all. Still another explanation is that if this is what he was able to perform in a generation in which all were wicked, how much more he could have done in a generation in which all were righteous.

(end of the Tosefta)

2. "Come, behold the works"

Noah was given his name because it was a direct reflection of his spiritual character. Noah is derived from the Hebrew word *Nechamah*, נחמה which means *to console*. Noah's spiritual work and destiny was to *console the earth* in the aftermath of the flood and the destruction of the world. This great spiritual mission, expressed through his name, was Noah's connection to the Light of the Creator. Our name, too, is our bridge and link to the Creator. The name is like a strand of *spiritual DNA* that motivates and gives rise to our personal attributes, our inner character, and our mission in life. This section of the Zohar strengthens our name's spiritual function of connecting us to the Light.

15. רַבִּי אֶלְעָזָר פָּתַח, לְכוּ חֲזוּ מִפְעֲלוֹת ה' אֲשֶׁר שָׂם שַׁמּוֹת בָּאָרֶץ, הַאי קְרָא, הָא אִתְּמַר וְאוּקְמוּהָ, אֲבָל לְכוּ חֲזוּ, מַאי חֲזוּ כד"א חֲזוּת קָשָׁה הוּגַּד לִי, בְּעוֹבָדוֹי, דְּקֻדְשָׁא בְּרִיךְ הוּא עָבִיד, אִתְגְּלֵי נְבוּאָה עִלָּאָה לִבְנֵי נָשָׁא. אֲשֶׁר שָׂם שַׁמּוֹת, שֵׁמוֹת וַדַּאי, דְּהָא שְׁמָא גָּרִים לְכֹלָּא.

15. Rabbi Elazar opened his discourse WITH THE VERSES: "THESE ARE THE GENERATIONS OF NOAH" AND "Come, behold the works of Hashem, who has made desolations in the earth" (Tehilim 46:9). AND HE ASKS, "Come, behold (Heb. *chazu*)": what is the meaning of "behold?" AND HE ANSWERS: It is related to the verse, "a grievous vision (Heb. *chazut*) has been declared to me (Yeshayah 21:2). Because by His deeds, the Holy One, blessed be He, reveals his prophecy to man. AND WHEN A PROPHECY IS REVEALED BY PRECEDING GRIEVOUS DEEDS, IT IS CALLED 'A GRIEVOUS VISION.' "Who has made desolations (Heb. *shamot*)" assuredly alludes to names (Heb. *shemot*), for a name is the cause of everything that happens. THIS MEANS THAT WE SHOULD CONSIDER THE NAME OF WHATEVER HAPPENS. FOR THE HOLY ONE, BLESSED BE HE, PUTS THE NAME IN THE MOUTH OF MAN SO HE CAN NAME EVERYTHING ON EARTH. SO THE VERSE IS ACTUALLY CALLING US TO GO AND OBSERVE THE WORKS OF HASHEM THROUGH THE NAMES BY WHICH THEY ARE CALLED BY MAN ON EARTH. BECAUSE THE HOLY ONE, BLESSED BE HE, PUTS NAMES IN THE MOUTH OF MAN AS PROPHECY, BY PRECEDING THEM BY ACTIONS.

16. כְּתִיב וַיִּקְרָא אֶת שְׁמוֹ נֹחַ לֵאמֹר זֶה וגו', אַמַּאי הָכָא לֵאמֹר,

וְאַמַּאי זֶה, אֶלָּא לֵאמֹר, דָּא אִתְּתָא, זֶה, דָּא צַדִּיק, כְּתִיב הָכָא זֶה
יְנַחֲמֵנוּ, וּכְתִיב הָתָם זֶה ה' קִוִּינוּ לוֹ. זַכָּאִין אִינוּן צַדִּיקַיָּא דִּרְשִׁימִין
בִּרְשִׁימוּ דְּגוּשְׁפַנְקָא דְּמַלְכָּא, לְמֶהֱוֵי בִּשְׁמֵיהּ רְשִׁימִין, וְאִיהוּ שָׁוֵי שְׁמָהָן
בְּאַרְעָא כִּדְקָא יָאוֹת.

16. The verse states: "And he called his name Noah, saying: This..." (Beresheet 5:29). RABBI ELAZAR ASKS: Why does the verse read, "saying: This?" AND HE ANSWERS: The word "saying" refers to the Female Principle, WHICH IS MALCHUT, while "This" refers to the Righteous, WHO IS NOAH. AND THE PROOF THAT IS it is written here and elsewhere, "This one shall comfort us" (Ibid.), "This is Hashem; we have waited for Him" (Yeshayah 25:9). AND WE LEARN THROUGH ANALOGOUS MEANING: THE WORD "THIS" REFERS HERE TO HASHEM, WHO IS CALLED RIGHTEOUS, AND THEREFORE THE MEANING OF "THIS" IN ANY OTHER VERSE MEANS RIGHTEOUS AS WELL. HERE, IT REFERS TO NOAH, WHO IS RIGHTEOUS, LIKE HASHEM. LIKEWISE, THE VERSE THAT STATES, "AND HE CALLED HIS NAME NOAH," REFERS TO THE SUPERNAL FEMALE PRINCIPLE OR MALCHUT, WHO CALLED HIM NOAH, FOR THE FEMALE WAS SAYING, "THIS," THAT IS, NOAH "SHALL COMFORT US." Blessed are the righteous who are marked with the imprints of the ring of the King, THE HOLY ONE, BLESSED BE HE, for they are marked with His name. And He has put "names" on earth, MEANING IN MAN'S MOUTH, so that everything can be called by its name correctly.

17. כְּתִיב וַיִּקְרָא אֶת שְׁמוֹ נֹחַ, וּכְתִיב וַיִּקְרָא שְׁמוֹ יַעֲקֹב, אַמַּאי לָא
כְּתִיב אֶת, אֶלָּא הָתָם דַּרְגָּא אַחֲרָא, וְהָכָא דַּרְגָּא אוֹחֲרָא, כִּדְכְתִיב
וָאֶרְאֶה אֶת ה' וָאֶרְאֶה ה' לָא כְּתִיב, אֶלָּא אֶת ה', אוֹף הָכָא בְּנֹחַ,
וַיִּקְרָא אֶת שְׁמוֹ נֹחַ, וַיִּקְרָא שְׁמוֹ יַעֲקֹב דַּרְגָּא דִּילֵיהּ, קֻדְשָׁא בְּרִיךְ הוּא
מַמָּשׁ, קָרָא לֵיהּ יַעֲקֹב, אֲבָל הָכָא אֶת, לְאִתְכְּלָלָא שְׁכִינְתָּא.

17. The verse states: "And he called his name (Heb. *et*) Noah," and it is also written: "And he called his name Jacob" (Beresheet 25:26). Why does it not say *et* IN REGARD TO JACOB, AS WITH NOAH? Because each one refers to a different level. As it is written in the verse: "I saw (*et*) Hashem" (Yeshayah 6:1). It does not say 'I saw Hashem,' but "Et Hashem." THIS INDICATES

THAT THE PARTICLE *ET* (THE) HAS A SPECIFIC MEANING. Here too, it is written of Noah: "And he called his *et* name Noah." As for, "And he called his name Jacob," in reality his level is that of the Holy One, blessed be He, and this is why the particle *et* is not mentioned there. But with Noah, the particle *et* is mentioned so as to connect him with the Shechinah, WHICH IS THE FEMALE PRINCIPLE. BECAUSE THE SHECHINAH IS CALLED *ET*, THE PARTICLE *ET* DOES NOT APPEAR IN JACOB'S NAME. FOR HIS LEVEL IS THAT OF A CHARIOT FOR THE HOLY ONE, BLESSED BE HE, WHILE NOAH, WHO IS THE SECRET OF THE RIGHTEOUS AND IS ALWAYS CONNECTED WITH THE SHECHINAH, HAS THE WORD *ET* PRECEEDING HIS NAME.

3. "A good man lends with a good grace"

We are given the opportunity to enhance our connection to the spiritual dimension of *Yesod*.

18. אֵלֶּה תּוֹלְדוֹת נֹחַ וְגוֹ', רַבִּי יְהוּדָה פָּתַח טוֹב אִישׁ חוֹנֵן וּמַלְוֶה יְכַלְכֵּל דְּבָרָיו בְּמִשְׁפָּט. טוֹב אִישׁ דָּא קוּדְשָׁא בְּרִיךְ הוּא, דְּאִקְרֵי טוֹב כְּמָה דִּכְתִיב טוֹב ה' לַכֹּל, וּכְתִיב ה' אִישׁ מִלְחָמָה, לְהַאי כָּל חוֹנֵן וּמַלְוֶה, לַאֲתַר דְּלֵית לֵיהּ מִדִּילֵיהּ, וְהַהוּא אֲתַר מִנֵּיהּ אִתְּזָן. יְכַלְכֵּל דְּבָרָיו בְּמִשְׁפָּט, דְּהָא הַהוּא דָּבָר לָא אִתְּזָן, אֶלָּא בְּמִשְׁפָּט, כְּמָה דְּאַתְּ אָמֵר צֶדֶק וּמִשְׁפָּט מְכוֹן כִּסְאֶךָ.

18. "These are the generations of Noah" (Beresheet 6:9). Rabbi Yehuda began his discourse on the verse: "A good man lends with a good grace; he conducts his affairs justly" (Tehilim 112:5). He said that "a good man" refers to the Holy One, blessed be He, who is called 'good', as it is written: "Hashem is good to all" (Tehilim 145:9). And it is also stated that "Hashem is a man of war" (Shemot 15:3). He is gracious and lends to "all" which is Yesod. BECAUSE Yud Hei Vav Hei, WHO IS ZEIR ANPIN, BESTOWS AND LENDS HIS ABUNDANCE OF MOCHIN UPON YESOD to the place that has nothing of its own, WHICH IS FEMALE PRINCIPLE. That place, THE FEMALE PRINCIPLE, is nourished by it, YESOD. The words, "he conducts his affairs justly" refer to the fact that THE FEMALE PRINCIPLE is nourished only according to justice, WHICH IS THE MOCHIN OF THE ILLUMINATION OF CHOCHMAH, as it is written: "Righteousness and justice are the foundation of Your throne" (Tehilim 89:15). SO RIGHTEOUSNESS, WHICH IS THE FEMALE PRINCIPLE, IS NOURISHED BY JUSTICE.

19. דָּבָר אַחֵר טוֹב אִישׁ, דָּא צַדִּיק, דִּכְתִיב אִמְרוּ צַדִּיק כִּי טוֹב כִּי פְרִי מַעַלְלֵיהֶם יֹאכֵלוּ. רַבִּי יוֹסֵי אָמַר דָּא נֹחַ, דִּכְתִיב נֹחַ אִישׁ צַדִּיק. רַבִּי יִצְחָק אָמַר דָּא שְׁבָחָא דְּשַׁבָּת, דְּבֵיהּ פָּתַח טוֹב, דִּכְתִיב טוֹב לְהוֹדוֹת לַה'.

19. A different meaning is that "a good man" signifies the righteous. As it is written: "Say to the righteous, that it shall be well with him (or: that he is

good), for they shall eat the fruit of their doings" (Yeshayah 3:10). SO THE
RIGHTEOUS ARE CALLED 'GOOD'. Rabbi Yosi said that "A GOOD MAN"
alludes to Noah, as it is written: "Noah was a righteous man." Rabbi
Yitzchak said that "a good man" alludes to the glory of the Shabbat,
REFERRING TO THE MOCHIN OF THE DAY OF SHABBAT, because the text
begins with the words: "It is a good thing to give thanks to Hashem"
(Tehilim 92:2).

20. רַבִּי חִיָּיא אֲמַר כֹּלָּא חַד וְכֻלְּהוּ מִלָּה חֲדָא אֲמָרוּ, וְדָא עֲבִיד
תּוֹלְדוֹת בְּעָלְמָא, תּוֹלְדוֹת דְּעָלְמָא מָאן אִינּוּן, אִלֵּין נִשְׁמַתְהוֹן
דְּצַדִּיקַיָּא דְּאִינּוּן אִיבָּא דְּעוֹבָדוֹי דְּקוּדְשָׁא בְּרִיךְ הוּא.

20. Rabbi Chiya said: It all amounts to the same thing, and they all said one
thing, that THE RIGHTEOUS produces offspring in the world. HE ALSO
ASKS: Who are the offspring of the world? AND HE ANSWERS: They are the
souls of the righteous, as they are the fruit of the handiwork of the Holy
One, blessed be He.

21. רַבִּי שִׁמְעוֹן אֲמַר, בְּשַׁעֲתָא דְּקֻדְשָׁא בְּרִיךְ הוּא מִתְעַטֵּר בְּעִטְרוֹי,
מִתְעַטֵּר מֵעֵילָא וּמִתַּתָּא, מֵעֵילָא, מֵאֲתַר דַּעֲמִיקָא דְּכֹלָּא, מִתְעַטֵּר
מִתַּתָּא, בַּמֶּה, בְּנִשְׁמַתְהוֹן דְּצַדִּיקַיָּא, כְּדֵין אִתּוֹסַף חַיִּים מֵעֵילָא
וּמִתַּתָּא, וְאִתְכְּלֵל אֲתַר מִקְדְּשָׁא מִכָּל סִטְרִין, וּבֵירָא אִתְמַלְיָא, וְיַמָּא
אַשְׁתְּלִים, וּכְדֵין יָהַב לְכֹלָּא.

21. Rabbi Shimon said: When the Holy One, blessed be He, puts on His
diadems, He crowns himself from above and from below: above, by the
region of absolute depth, WHICH IS ABA AND IMA, and below by the souls
of the righteous. The result is that an increment of life from above and
below embraces the place of sanctuary on all sides, causing the cistern to
become full and the sea to be replenished, thereby providing life to all.

4. "Drink water out of your own cistern"

Our realm of *Malchut* cannot draw in the Light without first arousing desire, and desire is aroused through the building of one's Vessel. According to the Zohar, righteous souls build Vessels through their positive actions and spiritual deeds. This secret is concealed within the story of Noah. The Ark signifies the realm of *Malchut*. Noah represents the righteous souls. We learn that after Noah built and *entered* the Ark he was then able to beget offspring to populate the world. Building and *entering* the Ark is the mystery concerning the awakening of desire in *Malchut*, and the *offspring* of Noah pertain to the Light of the Creator that is revealed in our physical realm. We become righteous souls who awaken the desire of *Malchut* each time we recognize, admit, and thus uproot our own negative traits, transforming them into positive attributes. From this section we receive the ability to act with righteousness, thus arousing the desires of *Malchut*.

22. כְּתִיב שְׁתֵה מַיִם מִבּוֹרֶךָ וְנוֹזְלִים מִתּוֹךְ בְּאֵרֶךָ, אַמַּאי בּוֹרֶךָ בְּקַדְמֵיתָא, וּלְבָתַר בְּאֵרֶךָ, דְּהָא בּוֹר לָא אִקְרֵי אֶלָּא רֵיקַנְיָא דְּלָא נְבִיעַ, בְּאֵר: מַיִין דְּנָבְעִין, אֶלָּא כֹּלָּא אֲתַר חַד הוּא, אֶלָּא אֲתַר דְּמִסְכְּנֵי אֲחִידָן בֵּיה, אִקְרֵי בּוֹר, דְּלֵית לֵיה מִדִּילֵיה, אֶלָּא מַה דְּיַהֲבִין בְּגַוֵּיה, וּמַאן אִיהוּ דלי"ת.

22. It is written: "Drink water out of your own cistern, and running water out of your own well" (Mishlei 5:15). HE ASKS: Why does it say "your own cistern" first and then "your own well," since a cistern is an empty place without water, while a well is a fountain of running water? THEY ARE DIFFERENT FROM EACH OTHER. HE ANSWERS: Both are the same, MEANING THAT BOTH REFER TO THE FEMALE PRINCIPLE. But when the poor are attached to that region, MEANING WHEN THE FEMALE PRINCIPLE IS NOT CONNECTED WITH ZEIR ANPIN, WHO IS HER HUSBAND, SHE IS CONSIDERED TO BE POOR AND is called 'a cistern', with nothing of its own except what is put inside it. This is the letter *Dalet,* OR THE FEMALE PRINCIPLE WHEN SHE IS NOT CONNECTED WITH ZEIR ANPIN.

23. לְבָתַר אִתְעֲבִיד בְּאֵר, דְּאִיהוּ נְבִיעַ, וּמַלְיָא מִכָּל סִטְרִין, וּמַאן אִיהוּ ה"א אִתְמַלְיָא מֵעֵילָא, וּנְבִיעַ מִתַּתָּא, אִתְמַלְיָא מֵעֵילָא כְּמָה דַּאֲמָרָן,

וּנְבִיעַ מִתַּתָּא, מִנִּשְׁמַתְהוֹן דְּצַדִּיקַיָּא.

23. And later, WHEN SHE MATES WITH ZEIR ANPIN, she becomes a well filled from all sides. THIS MEANS THAT SHE IS FILLED FROM THE RIGHT COLUMN OF ZEIR ANPIN AND FROM THE CENTRAL COLUMN FROM THE SOULS OF THE RIGHTEOUS. And what do these signify? It is the letter *Hei*, OR THE FEMALE PRINCIPLE WHEN SHE IS MATING WITH ZEIR ANPIN. SHE IS CALLED *HEI*, when she is being filled from above FROM ZEIR ANPIN and flowing from below from the souls of the righteous.

24. דָּבָר אַחֵר, שְׁתֵה מַיִם מִבּוֹרֶךָ: דָּא דָוִד מַלְכָּא, דִּכְתִיב בֵּיהּ מִי יַשְׁקֵנִי מַיִם מִבּוֹר בֵּית לֶחֶם. וְנוֹזְלִים: דָּא אַבְרָהָם. מִתּוֹךְ: דָּא יַעֲקֹב, דְּאִיהוּ בְּאֶמְצָעִיתָא. בְּאֵרֶךָ: דָּא יִצְחָק, דְּאִקְרֵי בְּאֵר מַיִם חַיִּים. הָא בְּהַאי קְרָא אִשְׁתְּכַח רְתִיכָא קַדִּישָׁא עִלָּאָה מֵאֲבָהָן, וְדָוִד מַלְכָּא אִתְחַבַּר עִמְּהוֹן.

24. A different explanation for the verse, "Drink water out of your own cistern," is that it refers to King David, who wrote: "O that one would give me drink of the water of the cistern of Bethlehem" (II Shmuel 23:15). Here, the words, "running water," refer to Abraham, and "out of (lit. 'from the midst')" refer to Jacob, who is in the center. "FROM THE MIDST" MEANS OUT OF THE CENTER. "Your own well" signifies Isaac, who is called "well of living water." Thus, in this verse, we find a reference to both the sacred Chariot of the Patriarchs, and of King David, who joined them.

25. תִּיאוּבְתָּא דְּנוּקְבָא לְגַבֵּי דְּכוּרָא, לָאו אִיהוּ, אֶלָּא כַּד עָיֵיל רוּחָא בָּהּ, וְאַשְׁדַּת מַיָּא לְקֳבְלָא, מַיִּין עִלָּאִין דְּכוּרִין, כָּךְ כְּנֶסֶת יִשְׂרָאֵל, לָא אִתְעָרַת תִּיאוּבְתָּא לְגַבֵּי קוּדְשָׁא בְּרִיךְ הוּא, אֶלָּא בְּרוּחָא דְּצַדִּיקַיָּא דְּעָאלִין בְּגַוָּוהּ, וּכְדֵין נָבְעִין מַיָּא מִגַּוָּוהּ, לְקֳבְלָא מַיִּין דִּדְכוּרָא וְכֹלָּא אִתְעֲבִיד תִּיאוּבְתָּא חֲדָא, וּצְרוֹרָא חֲדָא, וְקִשּׁוּרָא חֲדָא, וְדָא הוּא רְעֲוָא דְּכֹלָּא, וְטִיּוּלָא דִּמְטַיֵּיל קוּדְשָׁא בְּרִיךְ הוּא בְּנִשְׁמַתְהוֹן דְּצַדִּיקַיָּא.

25. The passion of the female toward the male is only aroused when he puts the spirit into her. And the flow of Mayin Nukvin (Female Waters) ascends to meet Mayin Duchrin (Male Waters) above. And the Congregation of Yisrael, OR MALCHUT, conceives a longing for the Holy One, blessed be He, only when the spirits of the righteous enter her, IN THE SECRET OF THE FEMALE WATERS. And then do waters flow from within her, THAT ILLUMINATE IN HER BY THE POWER OF THE SOULS OF THE RIGHTEOUS, toward the Male Waters, WHICH ARE THE LIGHTS OF THE RIGHT COLUMN. And so, all OF THESE THREE ASPECTS become one passion, one union, and one tie, and this appeases everyone. And it is then that the Holy One, blessed be He, walks among the righteous.

26. תָּא חֲזֵי, כָּל אִינוּן תּוֹלְדוֹת דְּגִנְתָּא דְּעֵדֶן, לָא נָפְקִין מִצַּדִּיק, אֶלָּא כַּד עָיֵיל בְּהַאי תֵּבָה בְּחִבּוּרָא חָדָא, וְכֹלָּא גְּנִיזִין בָּהּ. וּלְבָתַר מִינָהּ נָפְקִין. אוֹף הָכָא נֹחַ אִישׁ צַדִּיק, לָא אַפִּיק תּוֹלְדוֹת לְמִפְרֵי בְּעָלְמָא, עַד דְּעָאל לַתֵּיבָה, וְאִתְכְּנַשׁ כֹּלָּא בָּהּ, וַהֲווֹ גְּנִיזִין בָּהּ, וּלְבָתַר מִנָּהּ נָפְקוּ לְמִפְרֵי בְּעָלְמָא, וּלְאִתְקַיְּימָא בְּאַרְעָא, וְאִלְמָלֵא דְּנָפְקוּ מִגּוֹ תֵּיבָה, לָא אִתְקַיְּימוּ בְּעָלְמָא.

26. Come and behold: all the offspring – THE SOULS – from the Garden of Eden, WHICH IS THE FEMALE PRINCIPLE OF ZEIR ANPIN THAT ENCLOTHES THE SUPERNAL IMA, DO not issue from the Righteous, YESOD OF ZEIR ANPIN, until it enters the ark and becomes one with it. And all THE SOULS THAT SHE RECEIVES FROM THE RIGHTEOUS are hidden there FOR A CERTAIN TIME after which they ARE BORN AND leave it. The same applies here. Noah the righteous man did not beget any offspring to populate the world until he entered the ark and all gathered and were concealed in FOR A CERTAIN TIME, after which, they came out. They emerged from the ark to multiply in the world and to survive on earth. Had they not come from the ark, they would not have endured in the world.

27. וְכֹלָּא כְּגַוְונָא דִּלְעֵילָּא, מִגּוֹ תֵּיבָה נָפְקֵי לְעֵילָּא, מִגּוֹ תֵּיבָה נָפְקֵי לְתַתָּא, דָּא כְּגַוְונָא דָּא וְהָכָא אִתְקַיְּים עָלְמָא וְלָא מִקַּדְמַת דְּנָא, דִּבְגִינֵי כָּךְ כְּתִיב וְנוֹזְלִים מִתּוֹךְ בְּאֵרֶךָ. וּכְתִיב וַיּוֹלֶד נֹחַ שְׁלֹשָׁה בָנִים.

27. All this was DONE according to the divine pattern. For, just as they left the ark, OR THE FEMALE PRINCIPLE above, so they left the ark OF NOAH

below. Only now was the world able to exist permanently but not before. That is why the words, "And running waters out of your well" are related to, "And Noah begot three sons" (Beresheet 6:10).

5. "And the earth was corrupt"

The spiritual lesson revealed through these verses concerns the residue of negativity created by our immoral actions. The forces of negativity, aroused when we sin, remain with us and within the world indefinitely until true repentance is achieved by the wrong doer. This lingering negativity that hovers in our spiritual atmosphere can also influence others if their spiritual intentions are balanced on the narrow edge between good and evil. Should the remnants of a person's negative actions tip another person to the evil side, the original wrong doer must assume a measure of responsibility for the second sinner's actions.

28. וַתִּשָׁחֵת הָאָרֶץ לִפְנֵי הָאֱלֹקִים, אָמַר רַבִּי יְהוּדָה, כֵּיוָן דִּכְתִיב וַתִּשָׁחֵת הָאָרֶץ, אַמַּאי לִפְנֵי הָאֱלֹקִים, אֶלָּא כֵּיוָן דַּעֲבָדוּ חוֹבֵיהוֹן בְּאִתְגַּלְיָא, לְעֵינֵיהוֹן דְּכֹלָּא, בְּדֵין לִפְנֵי הָאֱלֹקִים כְּתִיב.

28. "And the earth was corrupt before Elohim" (Beresheet 6:11). Rabbi Yehuda asked: If it says "And the earth was corrupt," why "before Elohim"? IS IT NOT OBVIOUS? AND HE REPLIED: It is because they performed their sins openly, in front of everyone's eyes. And that is why the verse states, "before Elohim."

29. רַבִּי יוֹסֵי אָמַר, אֲנָא אִפְּכָא אֲמָרִית, וַתִּשָׁחֵת הָאָרֶץ לִפְנֵי הָאֱלֹקִים, בְּקַדְמֵיתָא לִפְנֵי הָאֱלֹקִים, דְּלָא הֲווֹ עָבְדֵי בְּאִתְגַּלְיָיא, לִפְנֵי הָאֱלֹקִים עָבְדוּ, וְלָא לִפְנֵי בְּנֵי נְשָׁא, וּלְבַסּוֹף עָבְדוּ בְּאִתְגַּלְיָא, הה"ד וַתִּמָּלֵא הָאָרֶץ חָמָס, דְּלָא הֲוָה אֲתַר בְּכָל אַרְעָא, דְּלָא הֲוָה בְּאִתְגַּלְיָא, וּבְגִין כָּךְ, בִּתְרֵי גְּווֹנֵי אָמַר קְרָא.

29. Rabbi Yosi said: I believe the opposite. "And the earth was corrupt before Elohim" means that they did not sin openly. They sinned only before Elohim and not before man. But eventually, they also sinned openly. As it is written: "And the earth was filled with violence" (Ibid.), which indicates that there was not a place on earth that did not witness their sins. Therefore, the verse declares that they sinned in two ways, THAT IS, IN HIDING AND IN THE OPEN.

30. אֵלֶה תּוֹלְדוֹת נֹחַ, רַבִּי אַבָּא אָמַר, מִיּוֹמָא דַּעֲבַר אָדָם עַל פְּקוּדָא דְּמָרֵיה, כָּל בְּנֵי עָלְמָא דְּאִתְיְלִידוּ לְבָתַר, אִקְרוּן בְּנֵי הָאָדָם, וְלָא לִשְׁבָחָא אִקְרוּן הָכִי, אֶלָּא כְּמַאן דַּאֲמַר, בְּנוֹי דְּהַהוּא דַּעֲבַר עַל פְּקוּדָא דְּמָרֵיה.

30. "These are the generations of Noah." Rabbi Aba said, From the day that Adam transgressed his Master's command, all succeeding generations were called "sons of Adam." But it was not said to praise him, as much as to say, 'These are the sons of the man who transgressed his Master's command.'

31. כֵּיוָן דְּאָתָא נֹחַ, אִקְרוּן בְּנֵי עָלְמָא עַל שְׁמֵיה דְּנֹחַ, תּוֹלְדוֹת נֹחַ, לִשְׁבָחָא. דְּקָאֵים לוֹן בְּעָלְמָא, וְלָא תּוֹלְדוֹת דְּאָדָם, דְּאַעֲבַר לוֹן מֵעָלְמָא, וְגָרִים מוֹתָא לְכֻלְּהוּ.

31. But after Noah had appeared, all the descendants of mankind are named after him, "the generations of Noah." And this describes Noah's descendents in an honorable sense, because he secured for us permanent existence in the world, in contrast with "the generations of Adam," which describes us in a dishonorable sense, as he caused us to be driven out of this world by bringing death to all.

32. אָמַר לֵיה רַבִּי יוֹסֵי, אִי הָכִי, הָא כְּתִיב לְבָתַר וַיֵּרֶד ה' לִרְאוֹת אֶת הָעִיר וְאֶת הַמִּגְדָּל אֲשֶׁר בָּנוּ בְּנֵי הָאָדָם, בְּנֵי הָאָדָם כְּתִיב, וְלָא כְּתִיב בְּנֵי נֹחַ, אָמַר לֵיה, בְּגִין דְּאָדָם חָטָא קַמֵּי מָרֵיה, טַב לֵיה דְּלָא אִבְרֵי, וְלָא יִכְתּוֹב עֲלֵיה הַאי קְרָא.

32. Rabbi Yosi said to him: If it is really so, we nevertheless see that in a later passage it is written: "Hashem came down to see the city and the tower, which the children of men had built" (Beresheet 11:5). The verse clearly states "the children of Adam" and not "the children of Noah," EVEN THOUGH THEY WERE DESCENDED FROM NOAH. Rabbi Aba replied that because Adam sinned before his Master, THE VERSE INVOKES HIS NAME. And it would have been better for him had he not been created than to be mentioned in the Torah in such a manner.

33. אֶלָא תָּא חֲזֵי, כְּתִיב בֵּן חָכָם יְשַׂמַּח אָב, כַּד בְּרָא טַב, כָּל בְּנֵי עָלְמָא דָּכְרִין לֵיהּ לַאֲבוֹי לְטַב, וְכַד אִיהוּ בִּישׁ, כֹּלָא דָּכְרִין לֵיהּ לַאֲבוֹי לְבִישׁ. אָדָם בְּגִין דְּחָטָא וְעָבַר עַל פְּקוּדָא דְּמָרֵיהּ, כַּד אָתוּ אִינוּן דְּמָרְדוּ בְּמָרֵיהוֹן, מַה כְּתִיב, אֲשֶׁר בָּנוּ בְּנֵי הָאָדָם, בְּנוֹי דְּאָדָם קַדְמָאָה, דְּמָרַד בְּמָרֵיהּ, וַעֲבַר עַל פְּקוּדֵיהּ.

33. Come and behold: it is written: "A wise son makes a glad father" (Mishlei 10:1). When a son is good, then all the people will mention his father's name with praise. But if a son is bad, they will mention his father with reproach. Now because Adam sinned and transgressed his Master's command, when THE TOWER BUILDERS came and rebelled against their Master, what was written about them? "That the children of Adam had built"! These are the children of Adam, the first man who had rebelled against his Master and transgressed His command.

34. וּבְגִינֵי כָךְ, אֵלֶּה תּוֹלְדוֹת נֹחַ, אֵלֶּה וְלָא קַדְמָאֵי, אֵלֶּה דְּנָפְקוּ וְעָאלוּ גוֹ תֵּיבָה וְאַפִּיקוּ תּוֹלְדִין לְעָלְמִין, וְלָא תּוֹלְדוֹת אָדָם דְּנָפַק מִגִּנְתָּא דְעֵדֶן, וְלָא אַפִּיק לוֹן מִתַּמָּן.

34. That is why the verse states that "These are the generations of Noah." These GENERATIONS ARE CONSIDERED TO BE THE DESCENDANTS and not the former ones. Those who came out of the ark and emerged from it ARE THE GENERATIONS. They are not the generations of Adam, who came out of the Garden of Eden and did not beget there, AND ARE THEREFORE NOT DESTINED TO EXIST.

6. If Adam had not sinned, he would not have begotten any offspring

From the time of Adam's sin, the children born into our world retain an aspect of the Evil Inclination within their essence. This section helps prevent this evil presence from occurring in new children. Moreover, these words weaken and remove this negative influence from our children as we meditate upon the pages.

‎35. תָּא חֲזֵי, אִלּוּ אַפִּיק אָדָם תּוֹלְדוֹת, מִגִּנְתָּא דְעֵדֶן, לָא יִשְׁתְּצוּן לְדָרֵי דָרִין, וְלָא אִתְחַשַּׁךְ נְהוֹרָא דְסִיהֲרָא לְעָלְמִין, וְכֻלְּהוּ הֲווֹ קַיְימִין לְעָלְמִין, וַאֲפִילוּ מַלְאֲכֵי עִלָּאֵי, לָא קַיְימֵי קַמַּיְיהוּ, בִּנְהוֹרָא וְזִיוָא וְחָכְמְתָא, כְּמָה דְאַתְּ אָמַר בְּצֶלֶם אֱלֹקִים בָּרָא אוֹתוֹ, אֲבָל כֵּיוָן דִּגְרֵים חֶטְאָה, וּנְפַק אִיהוּ מִגִּנְתָּא דְעֵדֶן, וַעֲבַד תּוֹלְדוֹת לְבַר, לָא אִתְקַיְימוּ.

35. Come and behold: if Adam had brought generations with him from the Garden of Eden, they would have lived for generations. And the light of the moon, WHICH REFERS TO THE LIGHT OF MALCHUT, would have never been darkened. And all would have lived forever; and not even the angels above could have stood before them and borne their light, brilliance and wisdom. As it is written: "In the image of Elohim He created him" (Beresheet 1:27). But because he was the cause of the sin, he had to leave the Garden of Eden and bear children outside. So his generations did not last BECAUSE THEY WERE NOT FIT.

‎36. אָמַר רַבִּי חִזְקִיָּה, וְכִי הֵיךְ יָכְלִין לְמֶעְבַּד תּוֹלְדוֹת תַּמָּן, דְּהָא אִלְמָלֵא לָא אִתְמְשִׁיךְ עֲלֵיהּ יֵצֶר הָרָע וְחָטָא, אִתְקַיַּים אִיהוּ בְּעָלְמָא בִּלְחוֹדוֹי, וְלָא יַעֲבֵיד תּוֹלְדוֹת. כְּגַוְונָא דָא, אִלְמָלֵא דְּחָבוּ יִשְׂרָאֵל בְּעֶגְלָא, וְאַמְשִׁיכוּ עֲלַיְיהוּ יֵצֶר הָרָע, לָא עָבְדוּ תּוֹלְדוֹת לְעָלְמִין, וְלָא יֵיתוּן דָּרִין אָחֳרָנִין לְעָלְמָא.

36. Rabbi Chizkiyah then asked: How could they have begotten offspring there – IN THE GARDEN OF EDEN? Had the Evil Inclination not been drawn down on him and he sinned, he would have dwelled alone in the world and would have not begotten any offspring! The same applies to Yisrael; had they not sinned by the golden calf and drawn upon themselves the Evil Inclination AFTER ACCEPTING THE TORAH, they also would have never borne any offspring, and no new generations would have come into the world. THE MAIN POINT IS THAT THE POWER OF MATING DERIVES MAINLY FROM THE EVIL INCLINATION. SO WITHOUT THE EVIL INCLINATION THERE CAN BE NO OFFSPRING.

37. אֲמַר לֵיהּ אִלְמָלֵא לֹא חָטָא אָדָם, לָא עָבִיד תּוֹלָדוֹת כְּגַוְונָא דָא מִסִּטְרָא דְיֵצֶר הָרָע, אֲבָל עָבִיד תּוֹלָדוֹת מִסִּטְרָא דְרוּחָא קַדִּישָׁא, דְהַשְׁתָּא לָא עָבִיד תּוֹלָדוֹת אֶלָּא מִסִּטְרָא דְיֵצֶר הָרָע, וּבְגִין דְּכָל תּוֹלָדוֹת דִּבְנֵי נָשָׁא, כֻּלְּהוּ מִסִּטְרָא דְיֵצֶר הָרָע, בְּגִין כָּךְ לֵית לוֹן קִיּוּם, וְאִי אֶפְשָׁר לוֹן לְאִתְקַיְּימָא, דְסִטְרָא אָחֳרָא אִתְעָרַב בְּהוּ.

37. He said to him: Had Adam not sinned, he would not have borne offspring from the side of the Evil Inclination, but he would have borne them from the side of the Holy Spirit. But because he produced offspring only from the side of the Evil Inclination, all the offspring of mankind are born from the side of the Evil Inclination. They have no permanent existence therefore, because the Other Side has been mixed with them.

38. אֲבָל אִלְמָלֵא לֹא חָטָא אָדָם, וְלָא אִתְתָּרַךְ מִגִּנְתָּא דְעֵדֶן, הֲוָה עָבִיד תּוֹלָדוֹת מִסִּטְרָא דְרוּחַ קוּדְשָׁא דְקַדִּישִׁין, כְּמַלְאֲכֵי עִלָּאִין קַיְּימִין לְדָרֵי דָרִין כְּגַוְונָא דִלְעֵילָּא, כֵּיוָן דְּחָטָא וְאוֹלִיד בְּנִין לְבַר מִגִּנְתָּא דְעֵדֶן, וְלָא זָכָה לְאַפָּקָא לוֹן מִגִּנְתָּא, לָא אִתְקַיְּימוּ, אֲפִילוּ לְאִשְׁתְּרָשָׁא בְּעָלְמָא דָא, עַד דְּאָתָא נֹחַ דְּאִיהוּ צַדִּיק, וְעָאל בַּתֵּיבָה, וּמִן תֵּיבָה נָפְקוּ כָּל דָרִין דְּעָלְמָא, וּמִתַּמָּן אִתְבַּדְּרוּ לְכָל אַרְבַּע רוּחֵי עָלְמָא.

38. But if Adam had not sinned and had not been driven out of the Garden of Eden, he would have begotten offspring from the side of the Spirit of the holy of holies. And they would have been as the supreme angels, and lived generations upon generations as angels do above. THIS MEANS THAT THERE ARE TWO KINDS OF MATING: ONE IS THE SPIRITUAL MATING OF THE ANGELS; THE SECOND IS THE MATING OF YESOD FOR THE SOULS. THAT NEED FOR THE EVIL INCLINATION RELATES ONLY TO THE MATING OF YESOD AND NOT TO THE SPIRITUAL MATING THAT COMES FROM THE SIDE OF THE HOLY SPIRIT. But because he sinned and begot children

6. If Adam had not sinned, he would not have begotten any offspring

outside the Garden of Eden and he did not merit to beget them in the Garden of Eden, therefore they did not survive even only to take root in this world until Noah came and went into the ark. And from the ark all descending generations of mankind emerged and spread to all four corners of the earth.

7. "And Elohim looked on the earth"

Reading these paragraphs helps purify the earth, which is constantly being corrupted and defiled through both small and large actions of negativity.

39. וַיַּרְא אֱלֹקִים אֶת הָאָרֶץ וְהִנֵּה נִשְׁחָתָה. אַמַּאי נִשְׁחָתָה, בְּגִין כִּי הִשְׁחִית כָּל בָּשָׂר אֶת דַּרְכּוֹ, כְּמָה דְּאִתְּמָר. רַבִּי חִיָּיא פָּתַח קְרָא וַאֲמַר, וַיַּרְא אֱלֹקִים אֶת מַעֲשֵׂיהֶם כִּי שָׁבוּ מִדַּרְכָּם הָרָעָה, תָּא חֲזֵי, בְּשַׁעֲתָא דִּבְנֵי נָשָׁא זַכָּאן, וְנַטְרֵי פִּקּוּדֵי דְאוֹרַיְיתָא, כְּדֵין אַרְעָא אִתְתַּקְפַת, וְכָל חֵידוּ אִשְׁתְּכַחַת בָּה, מַאי טַעֲמָא בְּגִין דִּשְׁכִינְתָּא שַׁרְיָא עַל אַרְעָא, וּכְדֵין כֹּלָּא עִלָּאֵי וְתַתָּאֵי בְּחֶדְוָה.

39. "And Elohim looked on the earth, and, behold, it was corrupt" (Beresheet 6:12). Why was the earth corrupt? CAN IT BE THAT IT DESERVED TO BE PUNISHED? AND HE ANSWERS: YES, "because all flesh had corrupted its way" (Ibid.), as has already been explained. Rabbi Chiya opened the discussion, saying, "And Elohim saw from their deeds that they had repented from their evil way" (Yonah 3:10). Come and behold: when the people are righteous and observe the commandments of the Torah, the earth is invigorated and full of joy. And why is that? Because the Shechinah dwells upon the earth and everyone – both above and below – is joyous.

40. וְכַד בְּנֵי נָשָׁא מְחַבְּלָן אָרְחַיְיהוּ, וְלָא נַטְרֵי פִּקּוּדֵי אוֹרַיְיתָא, וְחָטָאן קַמֵּי מָארֵיהוֹן, וּכְדֵין כִּבְיָכוֹל דַּחֲיָין לָהּ לִשְׁכִינְתָּא מֵעָלְמָא, וְאִשְׁתְּאָרַת אַרְעָא מְחַבְּלָא, דְּהָא שְׁכִינְתָּא אִתְדַּחְיָיא, וְלָא שַׁרְיָא עֲלָהּ, וּכְדֵין אִתְחַבְּלַת, מַאי טַעֲמָא אִתְחַבְּלַת, בְּגִין דְּשַׁרְיָא רוּחָא אָחֳרָא עֲלָהּ דִּמְחַבְּלָא עָלְמָא וְעַל דָּא אַמְרִינָן דְּיִשְׂרָאֵל יָהֲבֵי עוֹז לֵאלֹקִים, דִּמְקַיְימִין עָלְמָא, אֱלֹקִים דָּא שְׁכִינְתָּא, וְאִם חַס וְשָׁלוֹם אִי יִשְׂרָאֵל יִשְׁתַּכְּחוּ חַיָּיבִין, מַה כְּתִיב רוּמָה עַל הַשָּׁמַיִם אֱלֹקִים וגו' מִשּׁוּם דְּרֶשֶׁת הֵכִינוּ לִפְעָמָי. כָּפַף נַפְשִׁי בְּסִבַּת חָמָס וְשִׂנְאַת חִנָּם, כָּרוּ לְפָנַי שׁוּחָה וגו', כְּגַוְונָא דְּדוֹר הַמַּבּוּל, דִּבְגִין חָמָס דַּהֲוַת בֵּינַיְיהוּ, הֲוָה בֵּינַיְיהוּ שִׂנְאָה וּדְבָבוּ.

40. But when people corrupt their ways, do not observe the commandments of the Torah, and sin before its Master, then it is as if they drive the Shechinah out of the world. Then the earth is left corrupt, for the Shechinah is repelled by it and does not dwell on it. Then, the earth is corrupt. And why should the earth be corrupt? Because a different spirit rests upon it, causing the corruption.

41. יָכוֹל אַף דְּאַרְעָא דְיִשְׂרָאֵל כֵּן, וְהָא תָּנֵינָן, אַרְעָא דְיִשְׂרָאֵל לָא שַׁרְיָא עֲלָהּ רוּחָא אָחֳרָא, וְלָא מְמַנָּא אָחֳרָא, בַּר קוּדְשָׁא בְּרִיךְ הוּא בִּלְחוֹדוֹי. תָּא חֲזֵי דְּאַרְעָא דְיִשְׂרָאֵל הָכִי הוּא, דְּלָא שַׁרְיָא עֲלָהּ מְמַנָּא וְלָא שְׁלִיחָא אָחֳרָא, בַּר קוּדְשָׁא בְּרִיךְ הוּא בִּלְחוֹדוֹי. אֲבָל שַׁעֲתָא חֲדָא שַׁרְיָא עֲלָהּ, לְחַבְּלָא בְּנֵי נָשָׁא, מְנָלָן מִדָּוִד, דִּכְתִיב וַיַּרְא דָוִד אֶת מַלְאַךְ ה' וְחַרְבּוֹ שְׁלוּפָה בְּיָדוֹ נְטוּיָה עַל יְרוּשָׁלַיִם, וּכְדֵין אִתְחַבְּלַת אַרְעָא.

41. Can the same be applied to the land of Yisrael as well, THAT IS ANOTHER SPIRIT COULD BE DWELLING THERE? But we have learned that no other spirit rests upon the Land of Yisrael, and there is no other appointed angel beside the Holy One, blessed be He Himself. IF SO, THEN WHY WAS THE LAND OF YISRAEL CORRUPTED? AND HE REPLIES: Come and behold: it is true that no other appointee or messenger dwells in the land of Yisrael, beside the Holy One, blessed be He, Himself, but there is one time that the evil spirit may govern the land in order to destroy people. How do we know about that? From David, as it is written: "And he saw the angel of Hashem standing between the earth and the heavens, with a drawn sword in his hand stretched out over Jerusalem" (I Divrei Hayamim 21:16) and then the land was destroyed.

42. אָמַר רַבִּי אֶלְעָזָר, אֲפִילוּ בְּהַהִיא שַׁעֲתָא, קוּדְשָׁא בְּרִיךְ הוּא הֲוָה, כְּתִיב הָכָא מַלְאַךְ ה', וּכְתִיב הָתָם הַמַּלְאָךְ הַגּוֹאֵל אוֹתִי, וּכְתִיב וַיִּסַּע מַלְאַךְ הָאֱלֹקִים, הֵן לְטַב וְהֵן לְבִישׁ, קוּדְשָׁא בְּרִיךְ הוּא שַׁלִּיט עֲלָהּ, לְטַב: בְּגִין דְּלָא אִתְמַסְרָא תְּחוֹת שְׁאָר מְמַנָּן, וְכָל דַּיְּירֵי עָלְמָא יִכְסְפוּן מִן עוֹבָדַיְיהוּ. לְבִישׁ בְּגִין דְּלָא יֶחֱדוּן אִינּוּן לְשַׁלְטָאָה עֲלָהּ.

42. Rabbi Elazar said: Even in that time, WHEN HE SAW THE ANGEL OF HASHEM STANDING, it was the Holy One, blessed be He. Because what is written here, "the angel of Hashem," is analogous to "The angel who redeemed me" (Beresheet 48:16) and also to "the angel of Elohim" (Shemot 14:19). AND AS THESE VERSES REFER TO THE HOLY ONE, BLESSED BE HE, SO DOES THIS ONE. Be it for the best or the worst, the Holy One, blessed be He, shall always govern this land. For the best – because the land of Yisrael was never passed on to any other supernal governor, AND THE HOLY ONE, BLESSED BE HE, ALONE CAN DO IT GOOD. And all the other inhabitants of the world should be ashamed of their deeds, BECAUSE THEY ARE UNDER MINISTERS. For the worst MEANS THAT ONLY THE HOLY ONE, BLESSED BE HE, RULES OVER THIS LAND to prevent the other ministers from delighting in ruling over it.

43. וְאִי תֵימָא וְהָא כְּתִיב כִּי רָאֲתָה גוֹיִם בָּאוּ מִקְדָּשָׁהּ, וַחֲרִיבוּ בֵּיתָא, וְאִי לָאו שָׁלְטִין אִינוּן מִמַּנָּן, לָא אִתְחָרַב מַקְדְּשָׁא, תָּא חֲזֵי כְּתִיב כִּי אַתָּה עָשִׂיתָ, וּכְתִיב עָשָׂה ה' אֵת אֲשֶׁר זָמָם.

43. And if you will ask is it not written: "For she has seen that the heathen nations invaded her sanctuary" (Eichah 1:10) and destroyed the Temple, WHICH IMPLIES THAT if really no other ministers ruled, then the Temple would not have been destroyed! Come and behold: it is stated, "For you have done" (Ibid. 21) and "Hashem has done that which he devised" (Eichah 2:17). SO YOU CAN SEE THAT IT WAS DONE BY THE HOLY ONE, HIMSELF, BLESSED BE HE, AND NOT BY MINISTERS.

44. תָּא חֲזֵי, כְּתִיב וַיַּרְא אֱלֹקִים אֶת הָאָרֶץ וְהִנֵּה נִשְׁחָתָה. נִשְׁחָתָה וַדַּאי, כְּמָה דְּאִתְּמָר. הָכֵי נָמֵי וַיַּרְא אֱלֹקִים אֶת מַעֲשֵׂיהֶם כִּי שָׁבוּ מִדַּרְכָּם הָרָעָה, דְּהָא כְּדֵין אַרְעָא קָרָאת לְעֵילָא, וְסָלְקָא בִּסְלִיקוּ עִלָּאָה, וּמְקַשְּׁטָא אַנְפָּהָא, כְּנוּקְבָּא דִּמְקַשְּׁטָא לְגַבֵּי דְכוּרָא, הָכֵי נָמֵי אַרְעָא, דְּהָא גְּדֵילַת בְּנִין זַכָּאִין לְמַלְכָּא.

44. Come and behold: it is written: "And Elohim looked on the earth, and, behold, it was corrupt" (Beresheet 6:12). It was surely corrupt. And furthermore, it is also stated: "And Elohim saw their deeds, in that they turned from their evil way" (Yonah 3:10). Because then the earth calls out to the higher, TO ZEIR ANPIN, and rises to an upper grade; it beautified its face, as though it were a woman beautifying herself for a man. In the same manner, the earth pleased the "King," WHO IS ZEIR ANPIN, for it raised righteous children for Him.

45. וְהָכָא דְּלָא תָבוּ דְּרָא דְּטוֹפָנָא, מַה כְּתִיב, וַיַּרְא אֱלֹקִים אֶת הָאָרֶץ וְהִנֵּה נִשְׁחָתָה וגו', כְּאִתְּתָא דְּאִסְתָּאֲבַת וְאַסְתִּירַת אַנְפָּהָא מִבַּעֲלָה, וּבְזִמְנָא דְּאַסְגִּיאוּ חוֹבֵי בְּנֵי נָשָׁא בְּאִתְגַּלְיָא, אַרְעָא שַׁוְיתָא אַנְפָּהָא כְּנוּקְבָא דְּלֵית לָהּ כְּסוּפָא מִכֹּלָּא, כְּמָה דְאַתְּ אָמֵר וְהָאָרֶץ חָנְפָה תַּחַת יוֹשְׁבֶיהָ, וְעַל דָּא וַיַּרְא כִּי נִשְׁחָתָה וַדַּאי, מַאי טַעֲמָא בְּגִין כִּי הִשְׁחִית כָּל בָּשָׂר אֶת דַּרְכּוֹ עַל הָאָרֶץ.

45. While here, what is written about the generation of the Flood that did not repent? "And Elohim looked on the earth, and, behold it was corrupt," like a wife who committed adultery and hides her face from her husband. When the sins of people multiply and they sin openly, the earth becomes brazen like a woman who has no shame. As it is written: "And the earth was defiled under its inhabitants" (Yeshayah 24:5). And so it is said, that He "looked" it was corrupt" assuredly. You may ask, why? Because "all flesh had corrupted its way upon the earth."

8. "Hashem has done that which He devised"

As a parent feels the pain of a child whose iniquities have caused the child great suffering, the Creator feels the pain of all the souls who walk this earth. We should attempt to understand the Creator's love for us, and become inspired to relieve His pain by transforming ourselves. And in the process of doing so, we will relieve our own pain as well.

46. רַבִּי אֶלְעָזָר אֲזַל לְגַבֵּיה דְּרַבִּי יוֹסֵי ב"ר שִׁמְעוֹן בֶּן לָקוֹנְיָא חָמוֹי, כֵּיוָן דְּחָמָא לֵיה, אַתְקִין לֵיה תּוֹפְסִיתָא דְּקוֹמְרָא, בְּמָטוֹן דְּקוֹלְפָא, וְיתִיבוּ. א"ל חָמוֹי, אֶפְשָׁר דְּשָׁמַעְתְּ מֵאָבוּךְ, הַאי דִכְתִיב עָשָׂה ה' אֲשֶׁר זָמַם בִּצַּע אֶמְרָתוֹ אֲשֶׁר צִוָּה מִימֵי קֶדֶם.

46. Rabbi Elazar went over to Rabbi Yosi, the son of Rabbi Shimon, ben Lakunya, his father-in-law. As soon as he saw him, he spread carpets over planks of wood and prepared a canopy under which they both sat. His father-in-law asked him if, by any chance, he had learned from his father the meaning of the verse: "Hashem has done that which He devised; He has performed His word that He commanded in the days of old" (Eichah 2:17).

47. אֲמַר לֵיה הָא אוֹקְמוּהָ חַבְרַיָּא, בִּצַּע אֶמְרָתוֹ דְּבָזַע פּוֹרְפִּירָא דִּילֵיה, אֲשֶׁר צִוָּה מִימֵי קֶדֶם, דְּהָא פּוֹרְפִּירָא פָּקִיד לָה, מֵאִינוּן יוֹמֵי קַדְמָאֵי עִלָּאֵי, וּבְיוֹמָא דְּאִתְחָרֵיב בֵּי מַקְדְּשָׁא, בָּזַע לָה, בְּגִין דְּהַאי פּוֹרְפִּירָא אִיהִי יְקָרָא דִּילֵיה, וְתִיקוּנָא דִּילֵיה, וּבָזַע לֵיה.

47. He answered: Our friends have already explained it. "He has performed His word (also: 'He tore His hem')" means that He ripped His precious cloak; "that He commanded in the days of old" means that this cloak He commanded from the supernal days of old – MEANING FROM THE SFIROT OF THE PARTZUF OF ATIK, CALLED "DAYS OF OLD." On the day the Temple was destroyed, He ripped His cloak, for it is His glory and perfection, NAMELY MALCHUT, WHICH IS CALLED THE GLORY OF HASHEM, AND IT IS HIS PERFECTION BECAUSE THROUGH IT, HE PERFECTS HIMSELF WITH THE MOCHIN OF THE ILLUMINATION OF CHOCHMAH. And He ripped it, MEANS THAT THE FIRST NINE SFIROT

LEFT HER AND ONLY THE TENTH REMAINED.

48. אָמַר לֵיהּ עָשָׂה ה' אֲשֶׁר זָמָם, וְכִי מַלְכָּא חָשִׁיב לְאַבְאָשָׁא לִבְנוֹי, עַד לָא יֵיתוּן לְמֶחְטֵי. אָמַר לֵיהּ, לְמַלְכָּא דַּהֲוָה לֵיהּ, מָאן יְקַר, וּבְכָל יוֹמָא הֲוָה דָּחִיל עֲלֵיהּ, דְּלָא יִתְבַּר, וַהֲוָה מִסְתַּכֵּל בֵּיהּ, וְתַקִּין בְּעֵינוֹי, לְיוֹמִין אָתָא בְּרֵיהּ, וְאַרְגִּיז לֵיהּ לְמַלְכָּא, נָטַל מַלְכָּא הַהוּא מָאן יְקַר, וּתְבַר לֵיהּ, הֲדָא הוּא דִּכְתִיב עָשָׂה ה' אֲשֶׁר זָמָם.

48. He asks, "Hashem has done that which He devised:" Is this the way of a king to devise evil against his children even before they have sinned? And he answers him: It is like a king who had a precious vessel and was constantly afraid that it might one day break. So he used to watch it by keeping it under his eye. One day his son came along and made the king angry. So the king took his precious vessel and smashed it. That is why it says "that which He devised."

49. תָּא חֲזֵי, מִן יוֹמָא דְּאִתְבְּנֵי בֵּי מַקְדְּשָׁא, הֲוָה קֻדְשָׁא בְּרִיךְ הוּא מִסְתַּכֵּל בֵּיהּ, וַחֲבִיב עֲלֵיהּ סַגִּי, וַהֲוָה דָּחִיל עֲלַיְיהוּ דְיִשְׂרָאֵל דִּיחֶטוּן, וְיַחֲרֵב בֵּי מַקְדְּשָׁא, וְכֵן בְּכָל זִמְנָא דַּהֲוָה אָתֵי לְגַבֵּי בֵּי מַקְדְּשָׁא, הֲוָה לָבֵישׁ הַהוּא פּוּרְפִּירָא, לְבָתַר דְּגָרְמוּ חוֹבִין, וְאַרְגִּיזוּ קַמֵּי מַלְכָּא, אִתְחָרַב בֵּי מַקְדְּשָׁא, וּבְזַע הַהִיא פּוּרְפִּירָא, הַיְינוּ דִּכְתִיב עָשָׂה ה' אֲשֶׁר זָמָם בִּצַּע אֶמְרָתוֹ.

49. Come and behold: from the day the Temple was built, the Holy One, blessed be He, used to watch it, because it was very precious to Him. And He used to worry that Yisrael might sin and cause the Temple to be destroyed. So every time He came to the Temple, He wore a precious mantle, MEANING THAT HE MATED WITH MALCHUT. But when Yisrael sinned and made the King furious, the Temple was destroyed and He tore His cloak apart. That is the meaning of "Hashem has done that which He has devised... HE TORE HIS HEM."

50. הַאי אֶמְרָתוֹ, בְּקַדְמֵיתָא יַתְבָא בְּרֹאשׁ אָמִיר, וְהָא אִתְעַטְּרוּ עֲטְרָא

לְרֵישָׁא, וְאִילָן נָאֶה לְפָנָיו, וְאִיהִי מִימֵי קֶדֶם וַדַּאי. וּכְדֵין עֲצִיבוּ קַמֵּיהּ,
בְּבָתֵּי בָּרָאֵי וַדַּאי, וְהֵן אֶרְאֶלָם צָעֲקוּ חוּצָה.

50. "His hem (Heb. *imratto*)" as mentioned here, REFERS TO MALCHUT, which was sitting before on the top of the tree (Heb. *amir*). And the King crowned Himself with it and had before Him a beautiful tree; THE TREE OF THE SOULS BEFORE THEY COME INTO THIS WORLD. BUT NOW, AFTER THE DESTRUCTION OF THE TEMPLE, HE TORE HER, MEANING THAT THE UPPER NINE SFIROT LEFT MALCHUT AND ONLY THE LIGHT OF NEFESH REMAINED THERE. So now, AFTER THE DESTRUCTION, there is sadness before Him all over in the external houses, BUT NOT IN THE INTERNAL ONES. As the verse reads: "Behold, the valiant ones shall cry without" (Yeshayah 33:7), THAT IS, ONLY EXTERNAL ONES.

51. וַיִּקְרָא ה' צְבָאוֹת בַּיּוֹם הַהוּא וגו'. הַיְינוּ בְּזִמְנָא דְּאִתְחָרֵיב בֵּי
מַקְדְּשָׁא, אֲבָל בְּזִמְנָא אָחֳרָא, לֵית חֶדְוָה קַמֵּי קַדְשָׁא בְּרִיךְ הוּא כְּזִמְנָא
דְּאִתְאֲבִידוּ חַיָּיבֵי עָלְמָא, וְאִינוּן דְּאַרְגִּיזוּ קַמֵּיהּ, הה"ד וּבַאֲבוֹד רְשָׁעִים
רִנָּה. וְכֵן בְּכָל דָּרָא וְדָרָא, דְּעָבִיד דִּינָא בְּחַיָּיבֵי עָלְמָא, חֶדְוָה
וְתוּשְׁבַּחְתָּא קַמֵּי קֻדְשָׁא בְּרִיךְ הוּא.

51. "And on that day Hashem Tzva'ot called to weeping, to mourning, to baldness, and to girding with sackcloth" (Yeshayah 22:12). This means that only on that day, when the Temple was destroyed, DID HE CALL FOR WEEPING AND MOURNING. But aside from that day, there is no greater joy for the Holy One blessed be He, than when the wicked of the world, who provoke Him, are removed from this world. As it is written: "And when the wicked perish there is joy" (Mishlei 11:10). So in each generation, when judgment is executed on wicked people, there is joy and songs before the Holy one, blessed be He.

52. וְאִי תֵימָא, הָא תָּנִינָן, דְּלֵית חֶדְוָה קַמֵּי קֻדְשָׁא בְּרִיךְ הוּא, כַּד אִיהוּ
עָבִיד דִּינָא בְּחַיָּיבַיָּא. אֶלָּא תָּא חֲזֵי, בְּשַׁעֲתָא דְּאִתְעֲבֵיד דִּינָא בְּחַיָּיבַיָּא,
חֶדְוָון וְתוּשְׁבְּחָן קַמֵּיהּ, עַל דְּאִתְאֲבִידוּ מֵעָלְמָא, וְהָנֵי מִילֵּי, כַּד מָטָא
הַהוּא זִמְנָא, דְּאוֹרִיךְ לוֹן, וְלָא תָּאבָן לְגַבֵּיהּ מֵחוֹבַיְיהוּ, אֲבָל אִי

אִתְעֲבֵיד בְּהוּ דִּינָא, עַד לָא מָטָא זִמְנַיְיהוּ, דְּלָא אִשְׁתַּלִּים חוֹבַיְיהוּ, כד"א כִּי לֹא שָׁלֵם עֲוֹן הָאֱמֹרִי עַד הֵנָּה, כְּדֵין לֵית חֶדְוָה קַמֵּיה, וּבְאִישׁ קַמֵּיה עַל דְּאִתְאֲבִידוּ.

52. And if you claim that we learned that there is no joy before the Holy One, blessed be He, when He passes His judgment on the sinners, come and behold: when judgment is delivered on the wicked, there is joy and exultation before Him, because they are removed from this world. But, when is there joy? When the time that He has waited for them TO REPENT is over, and they have not returned to Him from sinning. But if judgment is delivered on them before their time has come, and the measure of their sins has not yet been completed, it is, as it is written: "the iniquity of the Emorite is not yet full" (Beresheet 15:16), AND THERE STILL IS A CHANCE THAT THEY MAY REPENT; thus, there is no joy. And there is grief before Him because of their destruction.

53. וְאִי תֵימָא, אִיהוּ, עַד לָא מָטוּ זִמְנַיְיהוּ, אַמַּאי עָבֵיד בְּהוּ דִּינָא. אֶלָּא אִינוּן גָּרְמִין בִּישָׁא לְגַרְמַיְיהוּ, דְּהָא קֻדְשָׁא בְּרִיךְ הוּא לָא עָבֵיד בְּהוּ דִּינָא, עַד לָא מָטָא זִמְנַיְיהוּ, אֶלָּא, בְּגִין דְּמִשְׁתַּתְּפֵי בַּהֲדַיְיהוּ דְּיִשְׂרָאֵל, לְאַבְאָשָׁא לוֹן, וּבְגִין כָּךְ עָבֵיד בְּהוּ דִּינָא, וְאוֹבִיד לוֹן מֵעָלְמָא בְּלָא זִמְנָא, וְדָא הוּא דְּאַבְאִישׁ קַמֵּיה. וּבְגִין כָּךְ אַעֲבַר מִצְרָאֵי בְּיַמָּא, וְאוֹבִיד שַׂנְאֵיהוֹן דְּיִשְׂרָאֵל בִּימֵי יְהוֹשָׁפָט. וְכֵן כֻּלְּהוּ, דְּהָא בְּגִינֵיהוֹן דְּיִשְׂרָאֵל אִתְאֲבִידוּ בְּלָא זִמְנָא.

53. But, you might ask: If their time has not come yet, then why should judgment be delivered on them? Because it is they who inflict the punishment on themselves, as the Holy One, blessed be He, would never punish them before their time has come. Because they associate with Yisrael in an effort to harm them, He passes His Judgment on them and entirely removes them from the world before their time is up. And now there is grief before Him, FOR HE DESTROYED THEM BEFORE THEIR TIME. This is also the reason why He drowned the Egyptians in the sea and destroyed the enemies of Yisrael in the days of Yehoshafat. They were all destroyed before their time because they harmed Yisrael.

54. אֲבָל כַּד אִשְׁתְּלֵים זִמְנָא דְּאוֹרִיךְ לוֹן, וְלָא תָבוּ, כְּדֵין חֶדְוָה
וְתוּשְׁבַּחְתָּא קַמֵּיהּ עַל דְּאִתְאֲבִידוּ מֵעָלְמָא. בַּר בְּזִמְנָא דְּאִתְחָרֵיב בֵּי
מַקְדְּשָׁא, דְּאַף עַל גַּב דְּאִשְׁתְּלֵים זִמְנָא דִּלְהוֹן, דְּאַרְגִּיזוּ קַמֵּיהּ, לָא הֲוָה
חֶדְוָה קַמֵּיהּ, וּמֵהַהוּא זִמְנָא, לָא הֲוָה חֶדְוָה לְעֵילָא וְתַתָּא.

54. So only when the time that He waits for them is completed, and they do not mend their ways, is their destruction a cause for joy and exaltation before Him. The only exception was the time when the Temple was destroyed, because even though their time for angering Him had expired, there was no joy before Him. From that time onward, there has been happiness neither above nor below.

9. "For in another seven days"

Learning the words that compose these powerful verses help us understand the spiritual dangers associated with the wasting of one's sperm. The negative forces in our midst automatically attach themselves to any gateway where the greatest Light can shine. This is *Yesod* in the Upper World, and the sexual organ in the physical world.

The Kabbalist, however, does not consider the vague concepts of morality and codes of right and wrong as motivation for maintaining sexual relations within the spiritual confines of marriage. Rather, it is our own spiritual understanding of the metaphysical forces at work, including the laws of cause and effect, that will provide the impetus. Historically, religious and moral authorities, according to the Kabbalist, have not been granted great influence in regulating sexual relations. Instead, individual people must be empowered with knowledge that can assist them in understanding the consequences of their actions. If they are to be truly motivated, people must recognize the benefits to themselves derived from any particular spiritual action

55. כִּי לְיָמִים עוֹד שִׁבְעָה אָנֹכִי מַמְטִיר עַל הָאָרֶץ אַרְבָּעִים יוֹם וְאַרְבָּעִים לַיְלָה וְגוֹ'. רַבִּי יְהוּדָה אָמַר הָנֵי אַרְבָּעִים יוֹם וְאַרְבָּעִים לַיְלָה, מַאי עֲבִידְתַּיְיהוּ, אֶלָּא, אַרְבָּעִים יוֹם לְאַלְקָאָה חַיָּיבֵי עָלְמָא, וּכְתִיב אַרְבָּעִים יַכֶּנּוּ לֹא יוֹסִיף, לָקֳבֵל אַרְבַּע סִטְרֵי עָלְמָא, לְכָל חַד עֲשָׂרָה, בְּגִין דב"נ מֵאַרְבַּע סִטְרֵי עָלְמָא אִתְבְּרֵי, וְעַל דָּא וּמָחִיתִי אֶת כָּל הַיְקוּם, וְאִצְטְרִיךְ אַרְבָּעִים לְאַלְקָאָה וּלְאִתְמְחֵי עָלְמָא.

55. "For in another seven days, I will cause it to rain upon the earth forty days and forty nights" (Beresheet 7:4). Rabbi Yehuda said: What is the meaning of these forty days and forty nights? These forty days are to strike the wicked of the world, as is written: "forty strikes he may give him, and not exceed" (Devarim 25:3), corresponding to the four winds of the world, WHICH ARE THE SECRET OF CHOCHMAH, BINAH, TIFERET AND MALCHUT, As each one has ten, THERE ARE ALTOGETHER FORTY. For man was created from the four winds of the world. So, the verse continues: "And every living substance that I have made will I destroy from the face of the earth." Forty strikes are needed to destroy the world.

56. רַבִּי יִצְחָק הֲוָה שְׁכִיחַ קַמֵּיהּ דְּרַבִּי שִׁמְעוֹן, אָמַר לוֹ הַאי קְרָא
דִּכְתִיב וַתִּשָּׁחֵת הָאָרֶץ לִפְנֵי הָאֱלֹקִים, אִי בְּנֵי נָשָׁא חָטָאן, אַרְעָא בַּמֶּה.
אָמַר לוֹ, בְּגִין דִּכְתִיב כִּי הִשְׁחִית כָּל בָּשָׂר אֶת דַּרְכּוֹ, כְּמָה דְּאִתְּמַר,
כְּגַוְונָא דָא, וַתִּטְמָא הָאָרֶץ וָאֶפְקוֹד עֲוֹנָה עָלֶיהָ. אֶלָּא בְּנֵי נָשָׁא חָטָאן,
וְאִי תֵימָא אַרְעָא בַּמֶּה, אֶלָּא עִקְּרָא דְּאַרְעָא בְּנֵי נָשָׁא אִינוּן, וְאִינוּן
מְחַבְּלִין אַרְעָא, וְהִיא אִתְחַבְּלַת, וּקְרָא אוֹכַח, דִּכְתִיב וַיַּרְא אֱלֹקִים אֶת
הָאָרֶץ וְהִנֵּה נִשְׁחָתָה כִּי הִשְׁחִית כָּל בָּשָׂר אֶת דַּרְכּוֹ עַל הָאָרֶץ.

56. Rabbi Yitzchak was visiting Rabbi Shimon, and he asked him about the verse that states: "And the earth was corrupt before the Elohim" (Beresheet 6:11). Now, if it was man who sinned and was corrupt, what was the earth's sin? Rabbi Shimon answered, as it is written: "for all flesh had corrupted his way upon the earth" (Ibid.) and, also, "And the land was defiled, therefore I do punish its iniquity upon it" (Vayikra 18:25). So it is mankind that sins. But if you ask what is the sin of the earth, you should know that mankind constitutes the essence of the earth. If mankind corrupts it, it becomes corrupted. This is proven by the verse: "And Elohim looked on the earth, and, beheld it was corrupt, for all flesh had corrupted its way upon the earth."

57. תָּא חֲזֵי, כָּל חֲטָאוֹי דְּבַר נָשׁ, כֻּלְּהוּ חַבְלוּתָא דִּילֵיהּ, תַּלְיָין
בִּתְשׁוּבָה, וְחֶטְאָה דְּאוֹשִׁיד זַרְעָא עַל אַרְעָא, וּמְחַבְּלָא אָרְחֵיהּ, וְאַפִּיק
זַרְעָא עַל אַרְעָא, מְחַבֵּל לֵיהּ, וּמְחַבֵּיל אַרְעָא. וַעֲלֵיהּ כְּתִיב נִכְתָּם
עֲוֹנֵךְ לְפָנַי, וּכְתִיב בֵּיהּ כִּי לֹא אֵל חָפֵץ רֶשַׁע אָתָּה לֹא יְגוּרְךָ רָע, בַּר
בִּתְשׁוּבָה סַגִּי. וּכְתִיב וַיְהִי עֵר בְּכוֹר יְהוּדָה רַע בְּעֵינֵי ה' וַיְמִתֵהוּ ה',
וְהָא אִתְּמַר.

57. Come and behold: all of man's sins and corruption can be atoned for by repentance. But by the sin of spilling his seed on the earth, man corrupts himself and the earth as well. And of such a person, it is written: "The stain of your iniquity is before Me," (Yirmeyah 2:22) and "For You are not an El that has pleasure in wickedness, nor shall evil sojourn with You" (Tehilim 5:5). THIS MEANS THAT A PERSON WHO WASTES HIS SEMEN ON THE EARTH IS CALLED EVIL, AND HE SHALL NOT SOJOURN ANYMORE WITH

THE HOLY ONE, BLESSED BE HE. IN OTHER WORDS, HE SHALL NOT ACCEPT HIS REPENTANCE, except after great penitence. It is also written that "Er, Judah's firstborn, was wicked in the sight of Hashem; and Hashem slew him" (Beresheet 38:7), as was already explained elsewhere.

58. אָמַר לוֹ אַמַאי דְּאִין קָדְשָׁא בְּרִיךְ הוּא עָלְמָא בְּמַיָּא, וְלָא בְּאֶשָּׁא, וְלָא בְּמִלָּה אָחֲרָא. אָמַר לוֹ רָזָא הוּא, דְּהָא אִינּוּן חַבִּילוּ אָרְחַיְיהוּ, בְּגִין דְּמַיִין עִלָּאִין וּמַיִין תַּתָּאִין לָא אִתְחַבָּרוּ דְּכַר וְנוּקְבָא כְּדְקָא יָאוֹת, מַאן אִינּוּן דְּחַבִּילוּ אָרְחַיְיהוּ, כְּגַוְונָא דָּא מַיִין דְּכוּרִין וְנוּקְבֵי. וְעַל דָּא אִתְדְּנוּ בְּמַיָּא, בַּמֶּה דְּאִינּוּן חָבוּ.

58. He asked him: Why did the Holy One, blessed be He, bring His Judgment on the world – NAMELY, THE GENERATION OF THE FLOOD – punishing them with water and not with fire or something else? Rabbi Shimon replied that there is a secret behind this. As they corrupted their ways, the upper waters and the lower waters were unable to join as the male and the female ought. Anyone who corrupts his ways also corrupts the male and female waters. THIS MEANS THAT HE CAUSES A DEFECT IN THE MALE AND FEMALE WATERS, PREVENTING THEM FROM BEING CONNECTED WITH EACH OTHER. So, they were punished by water, just as they had sinned.

59. וּמַיִין הֲווֹ רְתִיחָן וּפָשְׁטוּ מַשְׁכָא מִנַּיְיהוּ, כְּמָה דְּחַבִּילוּ אָרְחַיְיהוּ בְּמַיִין רְתִיחָן, דִּינָא לָקֳבֵל דִּינָא, הה"ד נִבְקְעוּ כָּל מַעְיְינוֹת תְּהוֹם רַבָּה, הָא מַיִין תַּתָּאִין. וַאֲרוּבוֹת הַשָּׁמַיִם נִפְתָּחוּ, דָּא מַיִין עִלָּאִין. מַיִין עִלָּאִין וְתַתָּאִין.

59. These waters were boiling and they skinned them alive, just like they corrupted their ways in boiling water, one Judgment for another, MEANS THAT HE PUNISHED THEM MEASURE FOR MEASURE. "All the fountains of the great deep broke open" (Beresheet 7:11), refers to the lower waters, while "and the windows of heaven were opened" refers to the upper waters. THUS THEY WERE PUNISHED BY both – upper and lower waters.

60. רַבִּי חִיָּיא וְרַבִּי יְהוּדָה, הֲווֹ אַזְלֵי בְּאָרְחָא, וּמָטוֹ לְגַבֵּי טוּרִין רַבְרְבָן,

וְאַשְׁכָּחוּ בֵּינֵי טוּרַיָּא, גַּרְמֵי בְּנֵי נָשָׁא, דַּהֲווֹ מֵאִינּוּן בְּנֵי טוֹפָנָא, וּפָסְעוּ
תְּלַת מְאָה פְּסִיעָן, בְּגַרְמָא חֲדָא. תְּווֹהוּ, אֲמְרוּ, הַיְינוּ דַּאֲמְרוּ חַבְרָנָא,
דְּאִינּוּן לָא הֲווֹ מִסְתָּפֵי מִדִּינָא דְּקֻדְשָׁא בְּרִיךְ הוּא, כְּמָה דִכְתִיב וַיֹּאמְרוּ
לָאֵל סוּר מִמֶּנּוּ וְדַעַת דְּרָכֶיךָ לֹא חָפָצְנוּ. מַה עֲבָדוּ, הֲווֹ סְתִימִין
בְּרַגְלַיְיהוּ, מַבּוּעֵי תְהוֹמָא, וּמַיָּין נָפְקִין רְתִיחָן, וְלָא יָכִילוּ לְמֵיקַם בְּהוֹ,
עַד דַּהֲווֹ נִשְׁמָטִין, וְנָפְלוּ בְּאַרְעָא וּמַיְיתִין.

60. Rabbi Chiya and Rabbi Yehuda were walking on their way. Reaching some great mountains, they found human bones that belonged to the generation of the Flood. They walked alongside one of these bones, which measured three hundred steps. Astonished, they said to each other: This clarifies what our friends have said, that they did not fear the Judgment of the Holy One, blessed be He, as is written: "They said to El, depart from us, for we desire not the knowledge of Your ways" (Iyov 21:14). So what did they do? They clogged the fountains of the deep with their feet. But the waters were too hot, and when they could no longer bear it, they slipped, fell on the ground, and eventually died.

10. "And Noah begot three sons"

We receive assistance in purifying our souls from the Hand of the Creator Himself, who literally removes the soul, cleanses it, renews it from one of the Three Upper Worlds discussed here, and then gently returns it to our being. This process, which occurs as we meditate upon the Zohar, is subtle and unobserved by the human senses.

61. וַיּוֹלֶד נֹחַ שְׁלֹשָׁה בָנִים וגו'. אָמַר רַבִּי חִיָּיא לְרַבִּי יְהוּדָה, תָּא וְאֵימָא לָךְ מִלֵּי דִשְׁמַעְנָא בְּהַאי, מָתָל, לְבַר נָשׁ דְּאָעֵיל לְנוּקְבָא אִיבָּא דִּמְעָהָא בְּזִמְנָא חָדָא, וְנָפְקֵי תְּרֵין אוֹ תְּלָתָא בְּנִין, חַד מִתְפָּרְשָׁא מֵאָחֳרָא, בְּאֹרְחֹוי, בְּעוֹבָדוֹי, דָּא זַכָּאָה, וְדָא חַיָּיבָא, וְדָא בֵּינוֹנִי, אוֹף הָכָא נָמֵי, תְּלַת קִטְרֵי דְרוּחָא אָזְלִין, וְשָׁטָאן, וְאִתְכְּלִילָן בִּתְלַת עָלְמִין.

61. "And Noah begot three sons" (Beresheet 6:10): Rabbi Chiya said to Rabbi Yehuda: Come and let me tell you what I have heard about this. It resembles a situation in which a man mates with his wife once, and then two or three children are born. Each one is different from the other in his ways and character: one is virtuous, one is wicked, and one is average. So there are three strands of the spirit that stretch out, fly, and are included within three worlds: BRIYAH, YETZIRAH AND ASIYAH.

62. תָּא חֲזֵי, נִשְׁמָתָא נָפְקַאת, וְאָעֵיל בֵּין טוּרֵי פְּרוּדָא, וְאִתְחַבַּר רוּחָא בְּנִשְׁמָתָא, נָחֵית לְתַתָּא, אִתְחַבַּר נֶפֶשׁ בְּרוּחַ, וְכֻלְּהוּ אָזְלֵי וּמִתְחַבְּרִין דָּא עִם דָּא, אָמַר רַבִּי יְהוּדָה, נֶפֶשׁ וְרוּחַ כְּלִילָן דָּא עִם דָּא, נִשְׁמָתָא שַׁרְיָא בְּאָרְחוֹי דְּבַר נָשׁ, וְהִיא מְדוֹרָא טְמִירָא דְּלָא אִתְיְידַע אַתְרָהָא.

62. Come and behold: the Neshamah emerges FROM MALE AND FEMALE OF ATZILUT, and it passes through mountains of separation INTO THE WORLDS OF BRIYAH, YETZIRAH AND ASIYAH. There, the Ruach connects to the Neshamah. The Neshamah descends further down toward and the Nefesh, joins the Ruach, and they all connect with each other. Rabbi Yehuda said: The Nefesh and the Ruach are included one with the other WHEN A PERSON IS BORN IN THE WORLD. AND THERE CAN NEVER BE A NEFESH WITHOUT A RUACH. The Neshamah resides in a man's ways,

WHICH MEANS THAT THE NESHAMAH IS NOT BORN WITH THE NEFESH AND RUACH. THEREFORE, HE SHOULD DRAW HIS NESHAMAH DOWN TO HIM BY WALKING THE STRAIGHT AND GOOD PATH. The Neshamah resides in a secret compartment, whose location is unknown. IT IS BORN WITH THE SIX EXTREMITIES, WHICH ARE NEFESH AND RUACH; WHILE THE UPPER THREE SFIROT REMAIN IN THE FEMALE PRINCIPLE OF ATZILUT, HIDDEN FROM THE RESIDENTS OF BRIYAH, YETZIRAH AND ASIYAH.

63. אָתָא בַּר נָשׁ לְאִתְדַּכָּאָה, מְסַיְיעִין לֵיהּ בְּנִשְׁמָתָא קַדִּישָׁא, וְדָכְאן לֵיהּ, וּמְקַדְּשִׁין לֵיהּ, וְאִקְרֵי קָדוֹשׁ. לָא זָכָה, וְלָא אָתֵי לְאִתְדַּכָּאָה, תְּרֵין דַּרְגִּין פְּתִיחִין, דְּאִינוּן נֶפֶשׁ וְרוּחַ בֵּיהּ, נִשְׁמָתָא קַדִּישָׁא לֵית בֵּיהּ. וְלָא עוֹד, אֶלָּא דְּאִי יִסְתָּאַב מְסָאֲבִין לֵיהּ, וְסִיּוּעָא דִּלְעֵילָא אַעֲדִיו מִינֵּיהּ. מִכָּאן וּלְהָלְאָה, כָּל חַד לְפוּם אָרְחֵיהּ.

63. A person who comes to purify himself is aided with a holy Neshamah. He is then purified, sanctified, and called holy. But if he does not merit and does not come to purify himself, then only two grades – Nefesh and Ruach – are open to him; for him, there is no holy Neshamah. Not only that, but if a person comes to defile himself, then he is defiled and loses heavenly support. Therefore, each person is judged according to his ways. THAT IS WHY IF A PERSON REPENTS AND COMES TO PURIFY HIMSELF, HE WILL GET THE SUPPORT AGAIN.

תוספתא

64. קְטוּרֵי רָמָאי דְּקַסְטוֹרֵי דְּהַהוּא סִטְרָא אֲנַן פְּתִיחָן עַיְינִין, פְּתִיחָן אוּדְנִין, כָּל מִן קָלַיָא נָחֵית מֵעֵילָא לְתַתָּא, מִתְבַּר טוּרִין וְטִנָּרִין, מָאן אִינוּן דְּחָמָאן וְלָא חָמָאן, אֲטִימִין אוּדְנִין, סְתִימִין עַיְינִין, לָא חָמָאן וְלָא שָׁמְעִין, לָא יָדְעִין בְּסָכְלְתָנוּ, חַד דְּכְלִילָא בִּתְרֵין בְּגַוַוייהוּ, דְּחַיָּין לֵיהּ לְבַר.

Tosefta (addendum)

64. We are the high ties of the greatest of fortresses. THE TERM 'TIES' REFERS TO THE NEFESH, RUACH AND NESHAMAH, WHICH ARE CALLED

'THREE TIES.' IN OTHER WORDS, OUR NEFESH, RUACH AND NESHAMAH ARE TIED TOGETHER IN THE CENTRAL COLUMN, WHICH IS THE STRONGEST OF ALL THE FORTRESSES. IT IS CAPABLE OF STANDING UP TO THE 'OTHER SIDE.' Therefore, the eyes and the ears are open, MEANING CHOCHMAH AND BINAH, WHO ARE CALLED 'EYES' AND 'EARS.' A voice from the voices descends from above and smashes mountains and rocks, MEANING THAT THE CENTRAL COLUMN, WHICH IS CALLED THE 'VOICE' AND IS DA'AT, INCLUDES THE THREE VOICES OF CHOCHMAH, BINAH AND DA'AT OF DA'AT. BUT ONLY ONE VOICE DESCENDS AND ILLUMINATES FROM ABOVE DOWNWARD AND SMASHES ALL THE STRONG KLIPOT THAT ARE CALLED 'MOUNTAINS' AND 'ROCKS'. BUT THE TWO UPPER VOICES, WHICH ARE CHOCHMAH AND BINAH OF DA'AT, ARE NOT DRAWN DOWN. Those who see, yet do not see, and who have become hard of hearing and have difficulty seeing; who do not see, do not hear, and do not know how to understand the one located and included between the two – they are pushed out.

65. אִינוּן מִתְדַּבְּקָן בֵּיהּ בְּאִינוּן תְּרֵי. חַד אוּמָנָא דְּאוּמָנָא, לָא שַׁרְיָא בְּגַוַוייהוּ, לָא עָאלִין בֵּין סִפְרֵי קַדִּישִׁין, כָּל אִינוּן דְּאוּמָנָא דָּא לָא שַׁרְיָא בְּגַוַוייהוּ, לָא אִכְתְּבוּ בְּסִפְרֵי דְכָרְנָיָיא, אִתְמְחוּן מִסִּפְרָא דְחַיֵּי, כְּמָא דְאַתְּ אָמֵר יִמָּחוּ מִסֵּפֶר חַיִּים וְעִם צַדִּיקִים אַל יִכָּתֵבוּ.

65. They cling to these two – MEANING TO THE TWO COLUMNS OF RIGHT AND LEFT WHICH ARE CHOCHMAH AND BINAH. While the one – the best of craftsmen, WHICH IS THE CENTRAL COLUMN AND THE MASTER CRAFTSMAN, ON WHOM ALL THE MOCHIN DEPEND – does not reside among them, THEREFORE they do not enter among the holy books. Because all those who do not have the craftsman, OR THE CENTRAL COLUMN residing among them are not written in the 'Books of Memories.' THIS MEANS THAT THEY DO NOT RECEIVE THE GREAT MOCHIN OF BINAH, WHICH IS CALLED THE 'BOOK OF MEMORIES', AND THE 'BOOK OF LIFE.' Therefore, they are erased from the 'Book of Life' and have no share in it. As it is written: "Let them be blotted out of the book of the living, and not be written with the righteous" (Tehilim 69:28).

66. וַי לוֹן כַּד יִפְּקוּן מֵהַאי עָלְמָא, וַוי לוֹן, מַאן יִתְבַּע לוֹן, כַּד יִתְמַסְּרוּן

בִּידָא דְדוּמָה, וְיִתּוֹקְדוּן בְּנוּרָא דְּדָלֵיק וְלָא יִפְּקוּן מִנֵּיהּ, בַּר בְּרֵישׁ יַרְחֵי
וְשַׁבַּתֵּי, כד״א וְהָיָה מִדֵּי חֹדֶשׁ בְּחָדְשׁוֹ וּמִדֵּי שַׁבָּת בְּשַׁבַּתּוֹ יָבֹא כָל בָּשָׂר
לְהִשְׁתַּחֲוֹת לְפָנַי אָמַר ה'. לְבָתַר כָּרוֹזָא דְּבִסְטַר צָפוֹן אַכְרֵיז עֲלַיְיהוּ
וְאָמַר   יָשׁוּבוּ רְשָׁעִים לִשְׁאוֹלָה וגו'. כַּמָּה חֲבִילֵי טְרִיקִין אִתְכַּנָּשׁוּ
עֲלַיְיהוּ, בְּאַרְבַּע סִטְרִין אֶשָּׁא מְלַהֲטָא בְּגֵי בֶּן הִנֹּם.

66. Woe to those when they leave this world. Who shall ask about them and plead for them when they are turned over to hands of THE ANGEL Dumah, and are in the burning fire, which they can leave only on the first day of the month and on the days of Shabbat? As it is written: "And it shall come to pass, that every new moon and every Shabbat, shall all flesh come to bow down to the ground before Me, says Hashem" (Yeshayah 66:23). When THE SHABBAT AND THE BEGINNING OF THE MONTH are over, an announcer from the north says, "The wicked shall be turned back to Sheol" (Tehilim 9:18), many angels of destruction then gather and attack them. From four sides, fire is burning in the valley of Ben Hinnom. THEY DO SO TO PUNISH THE WICKED WHO SPOILED THE FOUR ASPECTS OF CHOCHMAH, BINAH, TIFERET AND MALCHUT.

67. תְּלַת זִמְנִין בְּיוֹמָא מִתְפַּקְּדָן, וְלָא עוֹד אֶלָּא בְּזִמְנָא דְיִשְׂרָאֵל אֲתִיבוּ
בְּקוֹל רָם אָמֵן יְהֵא שְׁמֵיהּ רַבָּא מְבָרַךְ, קֻדְשָׁא בְּרִיךְ הוּא אִתְמְלֵי
רַחֲמִין, וְחַיֵּיס עַל כֹּלָּא, וְרָמִיז לְמַלְאָכָא דִּמְמַנָּא עַל תַּרְעֵי דְגֵיהִנֹּם,
סַמְרִיאֵל שְׁמֵיהּ, וּתְלַת מַפְתְּחָן בִּידֵיהּ, וּפָתַח תְּלַת תַּרְעִין דִּבְסְטַר
מַדְבְּרָא, וְחָמָאן נְהוֹרָא דְּהַאי עָלְמָא, אָתָא תְּנָנָא דְנוּרָא, וְסָתִים
אוֹרְחִין.

67. They are visited three times a day DURING THE THREE PERIODS OF MATING BETWEEN ZEIR ANPIN AND THE FEMALE PRINCIPLE. THESE VISITS OCCUR DURING THE THREE PRAYERS OF EACH DAY TO EASE THEIR PUNISHMENT. Not only that, but when Yisrael say aloud, 'Amen, may the great name of Hashem be praised,' during the Kadish, THEN THERE IS UNION IN THE UPPER WORLDS, and the Holy One, blessed be He, is filled with compassion and mercy and forgives all. Then He signals to the angel appointed over the gates of Gehenom, whose name is Samariel and who has three keys with which he opens the three gates to the side of the desert. And then they see the light of this world, AND IMMEDIATELY a fiery smoke comes and conceals the ways OF LIGHT.

68. כְּדֵין תְּלַת מְמַנָּן, דִּתְחוֹת יְדַיְיהוּ תְּלַת מַגְרוֹפִין, מְנַשְׁבָן בִּידַיְיהוּ, וְאָתִיבוּ תְּנָנָא לְאַתְרַיְיהוּ. וְרַוְוחִין לוֹן שַׁעֲתָא וּפַלְגוּת שַׁעֲתָא, וּלְבָתַר תַּיְיבִין לְאֶשָׁיְיהוּ. וְכֵן תְּלַת זִמְנִין בְּיוֹמָא, וּבְכָל זִמְנִין דְּאָמְרֵי יִשְׂרָאֵל אָמֵן יְהֵא שְׁמֵיהּ רַבָּא מְבָרַךְ וכו' אִינוּן רַוְוחִין לוֹן. זַכָּאִין אִינוּן צַדִּיקַיָּיא דְּאוֹרְחֵיהוֹן מְנַהֲרָא בְּהַהוּא עָלְמָא, לְכָל סִטְרִין, כד"א וְאוֹרַח צַדִּיקִים כְּאוֹר נוֹגַהּ הוֹלֵךְ וָאוֹר עַד נְכוֹן הַיּוֹם.

(עַד כָּאן לְשׁוֹן הַתּוֹסֶפְתָּא).

68. Then the three in charge, who have trowels in their hands, use them to fan the smoke and blow it back to its place. Then, they are at ease for an hour and a half, after which they return to the fire. They are also at ease three times a day, as well as each and every time Yisrael answer 'Amen, may the great name of Hashem be praised.' Happy are the righteous whose paths and ways illuminate and shine to all directions in the World to Come. As it is written: "But the path of just men is like the gleam of sunlight that shines ever more brightly until the height of noonday" (Mishlei 4:18).

End of Tosefta

11. The punishment in Gehenom

A positive and healthy fear of sin can inspire us to pursue spiritual development, thereby avoiding the negative repercussions inherent in our world of cause and effect.

69. רְבִּי אַבָּא אֲמַר בְּגֵיהִנֹּם אִית מְדוֹרִין עַל מְדוֹרִין, תִּנְיָינִין תְּלִיתָאִין עַד שֶׁבַע, וְהָא אוֹקְמוּהָ חַבְרַיָּיא. וְזַכָּאִין אִינוּן צַדִּיקַיָּא, דְּאִינוּן מִסְתַּמְּרִין מֵחוֹבֵי חַיָּיבַיָּא, וְלָא אָזְלֵי בְּאָרְחַיְיהוּ, וְלָא מִסְתָּאֲבֵי בְּהוֹ, וְכָל מַאן דְּאִסְתָּאַב, כַּד אָזִיל לְהַהוּא עָלְמָא, נָחִית לַגֵּיהִנֹּם, וְנָחִית עַד מְדוֹרָא תַּתָּאָה.

69. Rabbi Aba said that in Gehenom, there are compartments upon compartments, seconds, thirds, and so on until seven – the friends have already explained this issue. Blessed are the righteous who guard themselves from the sins of the wicked and do not follow in their paths nor defile themselves. For when a person who has become impure dies and passes onto the World of Truth, he goes down into Gehenom. There he descends, until he reaches the lowest compartment.

70. וּתְרֵין מְדוֹרִין אִינוּן, דִּסְמִיכִין דָּא עִם דָּא, שְׁאוֹל וַאֲבַדּוֹן. מַאן דְּנָחִית לִשְׁאוֹל דַּיְינִין לֵיה תַּמָּן, וּמְקַבֵּל עָנְשֵׁיה, וּסְלִיקוּ לֵיה לִמְדוֹרָא אַחֲרָא עִלָּאָה, וְכֵן דַּרְגָּא בָּתַר דַּרְגָּא, עַד דְּאִנּוּן סָלְקִין לֵיה. אֲבָל מָאן דְּנָחִית לַאֲבַדּוֹן, לָא סָלְקִין לֵיה לְעָלְמִין, וּבְגִין כָּךְ אִקְרֵי אֲבַדּוֹן, דְּהָא אָבִיד הוּא מִכֹּלָּא.

70. And there are two compartments close to each other that are called Sheol and Avadon. Whoever reaches Sheol is judged and punished there and is then raised to a different, but higher, compartment. This continues until he is released from there. But those who go down and reach Avadon are never raised from there again. That is why it is called Avadon (Eng. 'perdition'), because they are lost there forever.

71. תָּא חֲזֵי, נֹחַ זַכָּאָה, הֲוָה אַתְרֵי בִּבְנֵי דָרֵיה, וְלָא הֲווֹ שָׁמְעֵי לֵיה, עַד דְּקֻדְשָׁא בְּרִיךְ הוּא אַיְיתֵי עֲלַיְיהוּ דִּינָא דְּגֵיהִנֹּם. מַאי דִּינָא דְּגֵיהִנֹּם,

אֶשָׁא וְתַלְגָּא, מַיָּיא וְאֶשָׁא, דָּא צְנִינָא וְדָא רְתִיחָא. וְכֻלְּהוּ בְּדִינָא דְגֵיהִנֹּם אִתְדָּנוּ, וְאִתְאֲבִידוּ מֵעָלְמָא.

71. Come and behold: Noah the righteous warned the people of his generation, but they did not heed him until the Holy One, blessed be He, brought the punishment of Gehenom upon them. What is the punishment Gehenom? It is fire and snow, water and fire; the first is cold, the other boiling. And all of that generation were sentenced to punishment in Gehenom and lost from the world.

72. וּלְבָתַר, אִתְקַיָּים עָלְמָא כִּדְקָא חָזֵי לֵיהּ, וְעָאל נֹחַ בַּתֵּיבָה, וְאָעִיל בָּהּ כָּל זִינָא וְזִינָא דְּעָלְמָא. וַדַּאי נֹחַ עֵץ עוֹשֶׂה פְּרִי הֲוָה, וְנַפְקוּ מִן תֵּיבָה כָּל זִיְינֵי עָלְמָא, כְּגַוְונָא דִלְעֵילָא.

72. After that punishment, the world was able to exist and function correctly. Noah entered the ark and brought into it all the species of creatures. So, of course, Noah was a fruit tree yielding fruit, MEANING THAT HE WAS YESOD WHO IS CALLED RIGHTEOUS. And then all the species of the world emerged from the ark just as it happened above – MEANING JUST AS IN YESOD AND MALCHUT ABOVE.

73. תָּא חֲזֵי, כַּד הַאי עֵץ עוֹשֶׂה פְּרִי אִתְחַבַּר בְּעֵץ פְּרִי, כָּל אִינּוּן זַיְינִין דִּלְעֵילָא, חֵיוָון רַבְרְבָן וּזְעֵירָן, וְכַמָּה זַיְינִין, וְכָל חַד לְזִינֵיהּ, כד"א חַיּוֹת קְטַנּוֹת עִם גְּדוֹלוֹת. כְּגַוְונָא דָא נֹחַ בַּתֵּיבָה, וְכֻלְּהוּ נָפְקוּ מִן תֵּיבוּתָא, וְאִתְקַיָּים עָלְמָא כְּגַוְונָא דִלְעֵילָא. וּבְגִינֵי כָךְ נֹחַ אִישׁ הָאֲדָמָה אִקְרֵי. נֹחַ אִישׁ צַדִּיק אִקְרֵי, וְהָא אוֹקְמוּהָ.

73. Come and behold: when the fruit tree yielding fruit, YESOD OF ZEIR ANPIN, is joined with the fruit tree, WHICH IS MALCHUT, then all the species of above – great and small living creatures and all their varieties – come forward, each with other members of its species. As it is written: "both small and great beasts" (Tehilim 104:25). So was the case with Noah and the ark. They all emerged from the ark, MEANING THEY ALL WERE CORRECTED WHILE THEY WERE IN THE ARK. IT IS THE SAME WITH THE OFFSPRING ABOVE, WHO RECEIVE THEIR CORRECTION FROM MALCHUT.

And the world existed just as IT DID above. And this is why Noah is called a husbandman, that is the husband of the earth, and "a righteous man," MEANING THAT THE RIGHTEOUS IS JUST AS IS YESOD ABOVE, as has been previously explained.

74. רַבִּי חִיָּיא אֲמַר, תְּלַת מְאָה שְׁנִין, עַד לָא אָתֵי טוֹפָנָא, הֲוָה נֹחַ אַתְרֵי בְּהוֹ, עַל עוֹבָדֵיהוֹן, וְלָא הֲווֹ שָׁמְעִין לֵיה, עַד דְּקֻדְשָׁא בְּרִיךְ הוּא אַשְׁלִים זִמְנָא דְּאוֹרִיךְ לוֹן, וְאִתְאֲבִידוּ מֵעָלְמָא. תָּא חֲזֵי, מַה כְּתִיב לְעֵילָא וַיְהִי כִּי הֵחֵל הָאָדָם לָרוֹב עַל פְּנֵי הָאֲדָמָה, וּבָנוֹת יוּלְדוּ לָהֶם, וַהֲווֹ אָזְלִין עַרְטִילָאִין לְעֵינֵיהוֹן דְּכֹלָּא, מַה כְּתִיב וַיִּרְאוּ בְּנֵי הָאֱלֹקִים אֶת בְּנוֹת הָאָדָם וְגוֹ', וְדָא הֲוָה יְסוֹדָא וְעִקָּרָא לְמֵיגַד בְּחוֹבֵיהוֹן, עַד דְּגָרִים לוֹן לְאִשְׁתְּצָאָה מֵעָלְמָא. וּבְגִין כָּךְ אִתְמַשְׁכָאן בָּתַר יֵצֶר הָרָע, וּבְגִזְעוֹי וְשָׁרְשׁוֹי, וְדָחוּ מְהֵימְנוּתָא קַדִּישָׁא מִבֵּינַיְיהוּ, וְאִסְתָּאֲבוּ, כְּמָה דְּאִתְּמָר. בְּגִין כָּךְ קֵץ כָּל בָּשָׂר בָּא לְפָנַי לַאֲלָפָא קָטֵיגוֹרְיָיא עֲלַיְיהוּ.

74. Rabbi Chiya said: For 300 years before the Great Flood, Noah warned them to change their ways but they did not listen to him until the time when the Holy One, blessed be He, had finished waiting for them to repent. THIS IS AS WRITTEN: "AND HIS DAYS SHALL BE A HUNDRED AND TWENTY YEARS" (BERESHEET 6:3). Then they were lost from the world. Come and behold: IN THE PREVIOUS WEEKLY PORTION, it is written: "And it came to pass, when men began to multiply on the face of the earth, and daughters were born to them" (Ibid. 1), who they went naked in front of everyone. And then, what is written? "And the sons of Elohim saw the daughters of men (Ibid. 2). This was the main cause THAT BROUGHT THEM to continue sinning until it finally caused them to be destroyed. And because of that they followed the Evil Inclination, held fast to its trunk and roots, rejected the holy faith from among themselves, and became defiled. So it is written: "The End of all Flesh is come before Me" (Ibid. 13), to teach that they were guilty.

12. "The End of all Flesh"

When the Angel of Death is given free rein as a result of the
accumulated negative actions of mankind, his power becomes
vastly enlarged. Even innocent souls who inadvertently cross his
path fall victim to his powers of death and destruction.
Nevertheless, Noah was able to find refuge within the Ark. The
Zohar reveals that the Zohar itself is an embodiment of the Ark,
and can therefore provide protection in times of chaos and
destruction.

75. וַיֹּאמֶר אֱלֹקִים אֶל נֹחַ קֵץ כָּל בָּשָׂר בָּא לְפָנַי. רַבִּי יְהוּדָה פְּתַח
הוֹדִיעֵנִי ה' קִצִּי וּמִדַּת יָמַי מָה הִיא אֵדְעָה מֶה חָדֵל אָנִי. אֲמַר דָּוִד קַמֵּי
קֻדְשָׁא בְּרִיךְ הוּא תְּרֵין קִצִּין אִינּוּן, חַד לִימִינָא וְחַד לִשְׂמָאלָא, וְאִינּוּן
תְּרֵין אוֹרְחִין לְמֵהַךְ בְּהוֹ בְּנֵי נָשָׁא לְהַהוּא עָלְמָא. קֵץ לִימִינָא, דִּכְתִיב
לְקֵץ הַיָּמִין, וְקֵץ לִשְׂמָאלָא, דִּכְתִיב קֵץ שָׂם לַחֹשֶׁךְ וּלְכָל תַּכְלִית הוּא
חוֹקֵר אֶבֶן אוֹפֶל וְצַלְמָוֶת. מַאי וּלְכָל תַּכְלִית הוּא חוֹקֵר, מַאן הוּא
חוֹקֵר, אֶלָּא הַהוּא קֵץ לִשְׂמָאלָא דְּמַחְשִׁיךְ אַפֵּיהוֹן דִּבְרִיָּיתָא.

75. "And Elohim said to Noah, 'The End of All Flesh is come before Me'"
(Beresheet 6:13). Rabbi Yehuda related this verse to the one reading,
"Hashem, make me know my end, and the measure of my days, what it is; I
will know how frail I am" (Tehilim 39:5). King David said to the Holy One,
blessed be He: There are two 'ends,' one on the right and one on the left.
And they are two paths for man to walk to the World of Truth. THERE IS an
end to the right, because it is written: "at the end of the days (also: 'right')"
(Daniel 12:13). And THERE ALSO IS an end of the left, as is written: "He
sets an end to darkness, and searches out all perfection; the stones of
darkness and the shadow of death" (Iyov 28:3). What is meant by, "searches
out all perfections"? (also: 'ending'). Who is it that searches? He is none
other than the end WHO IS to the left; HE IS THE SEARCHER who brings
darkness upon the faces of the creatures.

76. קֵץ לִימִינָא, כִּדְקָאֲמָרָן, דִּכְתִיב לְקֵץ הַיָּמִין. אָמַר לוֹ קֻדְשָׁא בְּרִיךְ
הוּא לְדָנִיֵּאל, וְאַתָּה לֵךְ לַקֵּץ וְתָנוּחַ. אָמַר לוֹ מְנוּחָה בְּהַאי עָלְמָא, אוֹ
בְּהַהוּא עָלְמָא, אָמַר לוֹ בְּהַהוּא עָלְמָא, כד"א יָנוּחוּ עַל מִשְׁכְּבוֹתָם.

אָמַר לוֹ בְּזִמְנָא דִיקוּמוּן מֵעַפְרָא, אֵיקוּם בֵּינַיְיהוּ, אוֹ לָאו, אָמַר לוֹ
וְתַעֲמוֹד, אָמַר לוֹ הָא יְדַעְנָא דִּי יְקוּמוּן כִּתּוּת כִּתּוּת, מִנְּהוֹן דְּזַכָּאֵי
קְשׁוֹט, וּמִנְּהוֹן דְּחַיָּיבֵי עָלְמָא, וְלָא יְדַעְנָא עִם מָאן מִנְּהוֹן אֵיקוּם, א״ל
לְגוֹרָלְךָ. אָמַר לֵיהּ, הָא אֲמַרְתְּ וְאַתָּה לֵךְ לַקֵּץ, אִית קֵץ לְיָמִינָא, וְאִית
קֵץ לִשְׂמָאלָא, וְלָא יְדַעְנָא לְאָן קֵץ, לְקֵץ הַיָּמִין, אוֹ לְקֵץ הַיָּמִים. אָמַר
לוֹ לְקֵץ הַיָּמִין.

76. 'The end of the right' is, as we have previously said, "at the end of the right." As the Holy One, blessed be He, said to Daniel: "But go your way till the end be; for you shall rest" (Daniel 12:13). Daniel asked Him: "in this world or in the World of Truth?" He answered him, In the World of Truth! As it is written: "Peace to them that rest in their graves" (Yeshayah 57:2). He asked Him, At the time when they shall rise from the earth – MEANING AT THE TIME OF THE RESURRECTION OF THE DEAD – "shall I rise and be among them or not?" He answered him: "And stand." Daniel continued, "I know that at the time of the resurrection they shall rise in groups. Some of them shall be the righteous, while the others shall be the wicked of the world. But I do not know with whom shall I rise!" He answered him, "for your allotted portion," MEANING AMONG THE RIGHTEOUS. He continued, But You said "go your way till the end be." But there is the 'end of the right' and the 'end of the left,' and I do not know to which one I will go. He answered him, "at the end of the right" (Daniel 12:13).

77. אוֹף הָכָא, דָּוִד אָמַר לוֹ לְקֻדְשָׁא בְּרִיךְ הוּא הוֹדִיעֵנִי ה׳ קִצִּי, מָה
אִיהוּ חוּלַק עַדְבִי, וְלָא נָח דַּעְתֵּיהּ עַד דְּאִתְבַּשַּׂר דְּיֶהֱוֵי לְיָמִינָא, דִּכְתִיב
שֵׁב לִימִינִי. תָּא חֲזֵי אוֹף קֻדְשָׁא בְּרִיךְ הוּא אָמַר לוֹ לְנֹחַ, קֵץ כָּל בָּשָׂר
בָּא לְפָנַי, מָאן אִיהוּ, דָּא קֵץ, דְּאַחְשָׁךְ אַפַּיְיהוּ דִּבְרִיָּיתָא, דְּאִיהוּ קֵץ
כָּל בָּשָׂר.

77. Similarly, David said to the Holy One, blessed be He : "Hashem, make me know my end," what is the portion of my lot. THAT IS, HE WANTED TO KNOW HIS FATE. And he had no rest until he was told, "Sit you at My right hand" (Tehilim 110:1). Come and behold: the Holy one, blessed be He, told Noah as well: "The End of all Flesh is come before Me." Noah asked, "which end"? THE END OF THE RIGHT OR THE END OF THE LEFT?" AND

HE ANSWERS, It is the end that brought darkness upon the faces of the creatures, being the End of all Flesh, WHICH MEANS IT IS THE END OF THE LEFT, WHICH IS THE ANGEL OF DEATH.

78. בָּא לְפָנַי. מִכָּאן אוֹלִיפְנָא, חַיָּיבֵי עָלְמָא מַקְדִּימִין לֵיהּ, וּמָשְׁכָן לֵיהּ עֲלַיְיהוּ, לְאַחְשָׁכָא לוֹן, דְּכֵיוָן דִּיְהֵבִי לֵיהּ רְשׁוּתָא, נָטִיל נִשְׁמָתָא, וְלָא נָטִיל עַד דִּיְהֵבִי לֵיהּ רְשׁוּתָא, וְעַל דָּא בָּא לְפָנַי, לְמֵיטַל רְשׁוּ לְאַחְשָׁכָא אַפַּיְיהוּ דִּבְנֵי עָלְמָא, וּבְגִינֵי כָּךְ, וְהִנְנִי מַשְׁחִיתָם אֶת הָאָרֶץ. וְעַל דָּא, עֲשֵׂה לְךָ תֵּבַת עֲצֵי גוֹפֶר, בְּגִין לְאִשְׁתְּזָבָא, וְלָא יָכִיל לְשַׁלְטָאָה עֲלָךְ.

78. From the words "is come before Me" we learn that wicked people hasten to attract the Angel of Death upon themselves in order to bring darkness upon themselves. Therefore, because they give him permission, he grabs the soul. But he never takes the soul without permission. That is why THE VERSE READS, "is come before Me." THIS MEANS THAT HE COMES BEFORE ME to get permission to bring darkness upon the faces of people of the world. And that is why it is written: "I will destroy them with the earth" (Beresheet 6:13). Because I GAVE HIM PERMISSION: "make an ark of Gopher wood" (Ibid. 14), on which to save yourself so that he should have no power over you.

79. תָּא חֲזֵי תְּנִינָן, בְּזִמְנָא דְּמוֹתָא אִית בְּמָתָא אוֹ בְּעָלְמָא, לָא יִתְחֲזֵי בַּר נָשׁ בְּשׁוּקָא, בְּגִין דְּאִית לֵיהּ רְשׁוּ לִמְחַבְּלָא לְחַבָּלָא כֹּלָּא. בְּגִינֵי כָּךְ אָמַר לוֹ קֻדְשָׁא בְּרִיךְ הוּא, בָּעֵי לָךְ לְאִסְתַּמְּרָא, וְלָא תֶחֱזֵי גַּרְמָךְ, קַמֵּי דִּמְחַבְּלָא, דְּלָא יִשְׁלוֹט עֲלָךְ.

79. Come and behold: We have learned that when there is a plague in a city or in the world, a person should not show himself in the marketplace, because the Angel of Destruction has received permission to destroy everything. This is why the Holy one, blessed be He, told Noah, 'It behooves you to take heed and not show yourself before the Angel of Destruction, so that he may not have power to rule over you.'

80. וְאִי תֵימָא מַאן יָהִיב הָכָא מְחַבְּלָא, דְּהָא מַיִין הֲווֹ וְאִתְגַּבָּרוּ. תָּא חֲזֵי, לֵית לָךְ דִּינָא בְּעָלְמָא, אוֹ כַּד אִתְמַחֵי, אוֹ כַּד אִתְמְסַר עָלְמָא

בְּדִינָא, דְּלָא אִשְׁתְּכַח הַהוּא מְחַבְּלָא, דְּאָזִיל בְּגוֹ אִינּוּן דִּינִין
דְּאִתְעֲבִידוּ בְּעָלְמָא. אוֹף הָכֵי הָכָא, טוֹפָנָא הֲוָה, וּמְחַבְּלָא אָזִיל בְּגוֹ
טוֹפָנָא, וְאִיהוּ אִקְרֵי הָכֵי דְּאִתְכְּלֵיל בִּשְׁמָא דָא. וְעַל דָּא, אֲמַר קֻדְשָׁא
בְּרִיךְ הוּא לְנֹחַ, לְטַמְרָא גַּרְמֵיהּ, וְלָא יִתְחֲזֵי בְּעָלְמָא.

80. But, you might say, who mentioned an Angel of Destruction here? It was only the onrush of the waters THAT BECAME A FLOOD. Now come and behold: Whether the world is stricken, or even when the world is only given over for judgment, the Angel of Destruction is in the middle of all punishment done in the world. Now, here as well, there was the Flood. The Angel of Destruction walked within the Flood, and, as a result, he was called 'THE FLOOD.' Thus, he was included within it. So the Holy One, blessed be He, told Noah to hide himself INSIDE THE ARK and not to show himself to the world.

81. וְאִי תֵּימָא הַאי תֵּיבוּתָא אִתְחֲזֵי בְּגוֹ הַאי עָלְמָא, וּמְחַבְּלָא אָזִיל
בְּגַוְּויהּ. כָּל זִמְנָא דְּלָא יִתְחֲזֵי אַפֵּי דְּב״נ קַמֵּי מְחַבְּלָא, לָא יָכִיל
לְשַׁלְטָאָה עֲלֵיהּ. מְנָלָן מִמִּצְרַיִם, דִּכְתִּיב וְאַתֶּם לֹא תֵצְאוּ אִישׁ מִפֶּתַח
בֵּיתוֹ עַד בֹּקֶר, מַאי טַעְמָא, בְּגִין דְּאִיהוּ אִשְׁתַּכַּח, וְיָכִיל הוּא לְחַבְּלָא,
וְלָא אִצְטְרִיךְ לְאִתְחַזָּאָה   קַמֵּיהּ. בְּגִין כָּךְ הֲוָה גָּנִיז נֹחַ, וְכָל אִינּוּן
דְּעִמֵּיהּ בְּתֵיבוּתָא, וּמְחַבְּלָא לָא יָכִיל לְשַׁלְטָאָה עֲלַיְיהוּ.

81. And you may wonder how the ark survived, even though it was seen in the world through which the Angel of Destruction walked? But, as long as the face of the person is not seen by the Angel of Destruction, he cannot rule over him. And how do we know this? From Egypt. Because the verse reads: "as none of you shall go out of the door of his house until the morning" (Shemot 12: 22). The reason is that the Angel of Destruction was present OUTSIDE and could destroy anyone, and none should be seen before him. This is why Noah and all those who joined him hid within the ark. There, the Angel of Destruction had no power over them.

82. רַבִּי חִיָּיא וְרַבִּי יוֹסֵי הֲווֹ אָזְלֵי בְּאָרְחָא, אַעֲרַע בְּהַנֵי טוּרֵי דְּקַרְדּוֹ,
חָמוּ רְשִׁימִין בְּקִיעִין בְּאָרְחָא, דַּהֲווֹ מִן יוֹמֵי דְּטוֹפָנָא, א״ל רַבִּי חִיָּיא

לְרַ' יוֹסֵי, הַנֵּי בְּקִיעִין דַּהֲווֹ מִיּוֹמוֹי דְּטוֹפָנָא, וְקָדְשָׁא בְּרִיךְ הוּא שָׁבִיק לוֹן לְדָרֵי דָרִין, בְּגִין דְּלָא יִתְמָחֵי חוֹבֵיהוֹן דְּרַשִּׁיעַיָּא קַמֵּיה.

82. Rabbi Chiya and Rabbi Yosi were on their way, when they came upon the mountains of Ararat, where they observed some deep ravines which had been left from the days of the Great Flood. Rabbi Chiya told Rabbi Yosi: These ravines are from the days of the Great Flood, and the Holy One, blessed be He, has left them to stay on throughout all the generations to come, so that the sins of the wicked would not be erased before Him.

83. דְּכָךְ אָרְחוֹי דְּקֻדְשָׁא בְּרִיךְ הוּא, לְזַכָּאִין דְּעָבְדִין רְעוּתֵיה, בָּעֵי דְּיִדְכְּרוּן לְהוֹ לְעֵילָא וְתַתָּא, וְלָא יִתְנְשֵׁי דּוּכְרָנֵיהוֹן לְדָרֵי דָרִין לְטַב. כְּגַוְונָא דָא לְרַשִּׁיעַיָּא דְּלָא עָבְדִין רְעוּתֵיה, בְּגִין דְּלָא יִתְנְשֵׁי חוֹבַיְיהוּ, וּלְאַדְכָּרָא עָנְשַׁיְיהוּ וְדָכְרָנֵיהוֹן לְבִישׁ לְדָרֵי דָרִין. הַיְינוּ דִכְתִיב נִכְתָּם עֲוֹנֵךְ לְפָנַי וגו'.

83. Because it is the way of the Holy One blessed be He. He desires that the righteous who fulfill His will be remembered above as well as below. He desires that their memories not be forgotten through the generations. Likewise, He also desires that the wicked who do not fulfill His will BE REMEMBERED. HE DESIRES that their sins never be forgotten and their punishments and their wicked ways always remembered, as it is written: "The stain of your iniquity is before Me" (Yirmeyah 2:22).

13. "Lift up your voice...poor Anatot!"

Whereas Moses was able to help generate the revelation of Light on Mount Sinai, including the state of immortality, Noah was unable to accomplish the same feat in his time. The Zohar explains that Noah was a force of one, while Moses achieved a critical mass of people through the six hundred thousand souls who stood on Sinai. Awareness and inner motivation to bring about the total removal of evil and chaos from this earth is imbued to the reader through these passages. They awaken a desire to transform our own negative nature, and to share the Light of the Zohar. According to all Kabbalists, the Zohar is the most effective of all instruments for removing the negative inclinations born into the hearts of mankind. When a critical mass of people have embraced its wisdom, we will permanently eradicate all of humanity's pain and suffering.

84. פְּתַח רַבִּי יוֹסֵי וַאֲמַר, צַהֲלִי קוֹלֵךְ בַּת גַּלִּים הַקְשִׁיבִי לַיְשָׁה עֲנִיָּה עֲנָתוֹת. הַאי קְרָא אוּקְמוּהָ חַבְרַיָּא, אֲבָל הַאי קְרָא עַל כְּנֶסֶת יִשְׂרָאֵל אִתְּמַר. צַהֲלִי קוֹלֵךְ בַּת גַּלִּים, בְּרַתֵּיהּ דְּאַבְרָהָם אָבִינוּ. הָכֵי אוּקְמוּהָ, בַּת גַּלִּים כְּדִכְתִיב גַּל נָעוּל. גַּלִּים אִינּוּן נְהוֹרִין דְּמִתְכַּנְּשֵׁי וְאָזְלֵי וְעָאלִין לְגַוָּוה, וּמַלְּיָין לָהּ כְּדִכְתִיב שְׁלָחַיִךְ פַּרְדֵּס רִמּוֹנִים.

84. Rabbi Yosi quoted: "Lift up your voice, oh daughter of Gallim! hearken Laishah! O, poor Anatot!" (Yeshayah 10:30). The friends have already explained this verse, which refers to the Congregation of Yisrael, WHICH IS MALCHUT. So "Lift up your voice, O daughter of Gallim" refers to the daughter of Abraham the Patriarch IN THE SECRET OF 'THE FATHER ESTABLISHES THE DAUGHTER.' AND HE IS CHESED THAT ASCENDED TO CHOCHMAH. AND WHEN THE DAUGHTER HAS THE MOCHIN OF ABA, SHE IS THEN CALLED THE DAUGHTER OF *GALLIM* (Eng. 'springs'), as it is written: "A spring (Heb. *gal*), shut up" (Shir Hashirim 4:12), MEANING THAT MALCHUT IS CALLED '*GAL*' OR 'SPRING' WHEN SHE RECEIVES THE MOCHIN, ABA. THEREFORE, HERE SHE IS ALSO CALLED '*GALLIM*' OR 'SPRINGS,' BECAUSE 'springs' refer to the UPPER lights that gather, enter MALCHUT, and fill her. THE GATHERING OF THESE LIGHTS IS THE SECRET OF THE THREE VOWELS – CHOLAM, SHURUK AND CHIRIK. As has already been quoted: "Your shoots are a garden of pomegranates" (Ibid.

13). So, THE SHOOTS REFER ALSO TO THE UPPER LIGHTS THAT GATHER AND ARE DRAWN INTO MALCHUT, LIKE STREAMS AND RIVERS.

85. הַקְשִׁיבִי לַיְשָׁה. כְּד"א לַיִשׁ אוֹבֵד מִבְּלִי טֶרֶף, לַיִשׁ דָּכָר, לַיְשָׁה נוּקְבָא. אֲמַאי אִקְרֵי לַיִשׁ, אִי מִשּׁוּם דִּכְתִיב לַיִשׁ גִּבּוֹר בַּבְּהֵמָה אוֹ מִשּׁוּם דִּכְתִיב לַיִשׁ אוֹבֵד מִבְּלִי טֶרֶף. אֶלָּא כֹּלָּא אִיהוּ לַיִשׁ: גְּבוּרָה תַּתָּאָה, וּדְאָתֵי מִגְּבוּרָה עִלָּאָה; לַיִשׁ אוֹבֵד מִבְּלִי טֶרֶף, בְּשַׁעְתָּא דְּאִינּוּן נַחֲלִין מִסְתַּלְּקִין וְלָא עָאלִין לְגַוֵּיהּ, כְּדֵין אִתְקְרֵי לַיְשָׁה, דַּאֲבֵידַת מִבְּלִי טֶרֶף, דִּכְתִיב לַיִשׁ אוֹבֵד מִבְּלִי טֶרֶף וּבְנֵי לָבִיא יִתְפָּרָדוּ.

85. "Hearken Laishah:" The word 'Laishah' also appears in the verse, "The lion (Heb. *laish*) perishes for lack of prey" (Iyov 4:11). THIS MEANS IT IS THE OPPOSITE OF THE NAME 'GALLIM,' AS IT REFERS TO THE TIME WHEN MALCHUT, LACKING ABUNDANCE, PERISHES. 'Laish' is the masculine term; 'Laishah' is the feminine. SO WHEN THE TERM 'LAISHAH' APPEARS, IT REFERS TO MALCHUT, WHICH IS THE FEMALE PRINCIPLE. AND HE ASKS, "Why is she called AFTER THE NAME 'laish'? Is it because it is written: 'a lion which is strongest among beasts'? (Mishlei 30:30). DOES THIS SIGNIFY THE LION'S MIGHT, or is it written to remind us that "the lion perishes for lack of prey" – WHICH IS BECAUSE OF LACK OF ABUNDANCE? AND HE ANSWERS: All that is said refers to 'laish.' AT THIS STAGE, MALCHUT IS CALLED the lower Gvurah, as she is drawn down from the upper Gvurah, MEANING FROM THE GVURAH OF BINAH. AND THAT IS WHY SHE IS DESCRIBED AS "A LION WHICH IS STRONGEST AMONG BEASTS." But also, she is "the lion perishes for lack of prey." When these streams, WHICH ARE THE SUPERNAL LIGHTS, depart and do not enter her, then she is called the 'laishah' (lioness), which perishes for lack of prey. As is written: "The lion perishes for lack of prey, and the lion's whelps are scattered abroad" (Iyov 4:11).

86. וּמַה דַּאֲמַר, לַיְשָׁה, הַיְינוּ עֲנִיָּה עֲנָתוֹת, מִסְכֵּנָא דְּמִסְכְּנוּתָא, כְּד"א מִן הַכֹּהֲנִים אֲשֶׁר בַּעֲנָתוֹת, וּכְתִיב עֲנָתֹת לֵךְ עַל שָׂדֶיךָ. מַאי אִירְיָא. אֶלָּא כָּל זִמְנָא דְּדָוִד מַלְכָּא הֲוָה קַיָּים, אִסְתַּלַּק אֶבְיָתָר בְּעוֹתְרָא וּבְכֹלָּא, לְבָתַר א"ל שְׁלֹמֹה עֲנָתֹת לֵךְ עַל שָׂדֶיךָ.

86. And when the verse mentions "Laishah" or "poor Anatot," meaning the poorest of the poor, the meaning is the same as in, "of the priests that were in Anatot" (Yirmeyah 1:1), and "Anatot, to your own fields" (I Melachim 2:26). THESE TERMS OF 'ANATOT' ALWAYS INDICATE POVERTY. HE FURTHER ASKS: What does SOLOMON want to teach us BY THE TERM 'ANATOT?' AND HE ANSWERS: As long as King David was alive, Evyatar became wealthy and prosperous. But after that, WHEN KING DAVID DIED, EVYATAR BECAME POOR. THEN Solomon told him, "Anatot, to your own fields."

87. אַמַּאי קָרֵי לֵיהּ שְׁלֹמֹה הָכִי, אֶלָּא אָמַר לֵיהּ בְּיוֹמָךְ הֲוָה אַבָּא בְּמִסְכֵּנוּ, וְהַשְׁתָּא לֵךְ עַל שָׂדֶיךָ. הַשְׁתָּא אִית לוֹמַר, אַמַּאי אִקְרֵי אֶבְיָתָר עֲנָתוֹת, אִי תֵימָא דַּהֲוָה מִן עֲנָתוֹת, הָא תָּנִינָן דִּכְתִיב וַיִּמָּלֵט בֶּן אֶחָד לַאֲחִימֶלֶךְ בֶּן אֲחִיטוּב וּשְׁמוֹ אֶבְיָתָר, וְהוּא מִנּוֹב הֲוָה, דְּהָא נוֹב עִיר הַכֹּהֲנִים הֲוָה. וְאע"פ דַּאֲמָרוּ דְּהִיא נוֹב הִיא עֲנָתוֹת, וְאַמַּאי אִקְרֵי עֲנָתוֹת, בְּגִין דְּנָחֲתַת לְמִסְכֵּנוּ, וְאִתְאֲבִיד קַרְתָּא עַל יְדָא דְּשָׁאוּל, וְאִתְאֲבִידוּ כָּהֲנֵי. אֶלָּא עֲנָתוֹת כְּפַר הֲוָה, וְלָאו הוּא נוֹב, וְעַל דָּא קָרֵי לֵיהּ אֶבְיָתָר עֲנָתוֹת, בְּגִין דַּאֲמַר וְכִי הִתְעַנִּיתָ בְּכֹל אֲשֶׁר הִתְעַנָּה אָבִי, וּמְקַרְתָּא דְּנוֹב הֲוָה, וְעַל מִסְכְּנוּ דְּדָוִד דַּהֲוָה בְּיוֹמוֹי, אִקְרֵי לֵיהּ הָכִי.

87. HE ASKS: What is the true reason that Solomon called him BY THE NAME ANATOT? WHY SHOULD HE CALL HIM WITH A NAME OF DISGRACE? AND HE ANSWERS: He wanted to tell him, during your days, my father lived in poverty, but now THAT I AM RICH, "to your own fields." FOR A PERSON WHO SERVED DURING THE DAYS OF POVERTY IS NOT FIT TO SERVE DURING THE DAYS OF PROSPERITY. HE FURTHER STATES that we should now explain why Evyatar was called Anatot. Should one assume that it was because he was from Anatot? We have already learned from the verse: "And one of the sons of Achimelech, the son of Achituv, named Evyatar, escaped" (I Shmuel 22:20). And he came from Nov, the city of the priests. We have learned that Nov is also called Anatot and why is it called Anatot – because of the poverty and destitution to which it had been reduced by King Saul through the slaughter of all its priestly inhabitants. Nevertheless, THIS IS NOT THE TRUE REASON FOR THE NAME, BECAUSE Anatot was the name of a village and is not Nov. Rather, King Solomon called Evyatar Anatot, "because you were afflicted (Heb. *hit'anita*) in all that my father was afflicted" (I Melachim 2:26) – and because he also came from the city of Nov. So the true reason is that because King David lived in poverty in his days, he called him thus, ANATOT.

88. אָמַר רַבִּי חִיָּיא בְּמִסְכְּנוּתָא הֲוָה עָלְמָא, מִיּוֹמָא דַּעֲבַר אָדָם, עַל פִּקוּדֵי קֻדְשָׁא בְּרִיךְ הוּא, עַד דְּאָתָא נֹחַ, וְקָרֵיב קָרְבָּן, וְאִתְיַישַׁב עָלְמָא. אָמַר ר׳ יוֹסֵי לָא אִתְיַישַׁב עָלְמָא וְלָא נַפְקָא אַרְעָא מִזוּהֲמָא דְּנָחָשׁ, עַד דְּקַיְימוּ יִשְׂרָאֵל עַל טוּרָא דְּסִינַי, וְאִתְאֲחִידוּ בְּאִילָנָא דְּחַיֵּי, כְּדֵין אִתְיַישַׁב עָלְמָא.

88. Rabbi Chiya said that the world was in a state of poverty from the time that Adam transgressed the command of the Holy One, blessed be He, until the time when Noah came forward and offered his sacrifice, thereby settling the world. Rabbi Yosi said that the world was not settled and the land was not pure from the pollution of the serpent until Yisrael stood at Mount Sinai and held onto the Tree of Life. Only then did the world settle properly.

89. וְאִלְמָלֵא דְּהָדְרוּ יִשְׂרָאֵל וְחָאבוּ קַמֵּיה קֻדְשָׁא בְּרִיךְ הוּא, לָא הֲווֹ מֵתִין לְעָלְמִין, דְּהָא אִתְפַּסַּק מִנַּיְיהוּ זוּהֲמָא דְּנָחָשׁ. כֵּיוָן דְּחָבוּ, כְּדֵין אִתְבָּרוּ אִינוּן לוּחֵי קַדְמָאֵי, דַּהֲווֹ בְּהוֹ חֵירוּ דְכֹלָּא, חֵירוּ דְּהַהוּא נָחָשׁ, דְּאִיהוּ קֵץ כָּל בָּשָׂר.

89. And had Yisrael not sinned before the Holy One, blessed be He, they would have never died, for the pollution of the serpent had been purged from them. But because of their sin, the first tablets, which brought freedom from all sins, freedom from the serpent – who is "the End of all Flesh," THIS IS THE ANGEL OF DEATH – were broken.

90. וְכַד קָמוּ לֵיוָאֵי, לְקַטְלָא קַטְלָא, כְּדֵין אִתְעַר חִוְיָא בִּישָׁא, וַהֲוָה אָזִיל קַמַּיְיהוּ, וְלָא יָכִיל לְשַׁלְטָאָה בְּהוֹ, בְּגִין דַּהֲווֹ יִשְׂרָאֵל מִזְדַּרְזִין כֻּלְּהוֹ בְּחַגִּירוּ מְזַיְינָן, וְלָא יָכִיל הַהוּא נָחָשׁ לְשַׁלְטָאָה בְּהוֹ. וְכֵיוָן דְּאָמַר לְמֹשֶׁה וְעַתָּה הוֹרֵד עֶדְיְךָ מֵעָלֶיךָ. אִתְיְיהִיב רְשׁוּ לְהַאי נָחָשׁ לְשַׁלְטָאָה עֲלַיְיהוּ.

90. And when the Levites rose up to slay the guilty, THAT IS WHEN MOSES TOLD THEM, "PUT EVERY MAN HIS SWORD BY HIS SIDE...AND SLAY EVERY MAN HIS BROTHER (SHEMOT 32:27), then the evil serpent walked in front of them. Nevertheless, he could not dominate them because all Yisrael were girt with a special armor that protected them against his attacks. THIS SPECIAL ARMOR IS THE ORNAMENT THAT THEY RECEIVED AT MOUNT HOREB. Thus, the serpent could not have prevailed against them. However, when He said to Moses, "Therefore now put off your ornaments from yourself" (Shemot 33:5), permission to rule over Yisrael was given to the serpent.

91. תָּא חֲזֵי, מַה כְּתִיב, וַיִּתְנַצְּלוּ בְּנֵי יִשְׂרָאֵל אֶת עֶדְיָם מֵהַר חֹרֵב. וַיִּתְנַצְּלוּ וַיִּנָּצְלוּ מִבָּעֵי לֵיהּ. אֶלָּא, וַיִּתְנַצְּלוּ, עַל יְדָא דְּאַחֲרָא, בְּגִין דְּאִתְיְיהִיב רְשׁוּ לְנָחָשׁ לְשַׁלְּטָאָה. אֶת עֶדְיָם מֵהַר חֹרֵב, דְּקַבְּלוּ מִטּוּרָא דְּחוֹרֵב, כַּד אִתְיְיהֵיב אוֹרַיְיתָא לְיִשְׂרָאֵל.

91. Come and behold: it is written: "And the children of Yisrael were stripped of their ornaments by the mount Horeb" (Ibid. 6). SO HE ASKS: "Were stripped?" It should have been written 'stripped themselves!' AND HE ANSWERS THAT the words "were stripped" SHOW US that they were actually stripped by another POWER, as permission was given to the serpent to rule over them. "Their ornaments by the mount Horeb," REFERS TO the ornament they received from mount Horeb when the Torah was given to Yisrael.

92. אָמַר רַבִּי חִיָּיא נֹחַ דַּהֲוָה צַדִּיק, אַמַּאי לָא הֲוָה בָּטֵיל מוֹתָא מֵעָלְמָא. אֶלָּא, בְּגִין דְּעַד לָא סָלְקַת זוּהֲמָא מֵעָלְמָא. וְעוֹד דְּאִינּוּן לָא הֲווֹ מְהֵימְנִין בֵּיהּ בְּקֻדְשָׁא בְּרִיךְ הוּא, וְכֻלְּהוּ אֲחִידָן בְּטַרְפֵּי אִילָנָא לְתַתָּא, וּמִתְלַבְּשָׁאן בְּרוּחַ מְסָאֲבָא.

92. Rabbi Chiya asks: why, if Noah was a righteous man, did he not cancel death over the world, JUST AS IT WAS CANCELED AT THE TIME OF THE GIVING OF THE TORAH? AND HE ANSWERS: Because the pollution of the serpent had not yet been removed from the world and because the people of the world had no faith in the Holy One, blessed be He. As a result, they clung to the 'leaves of the lower Tree,' THE EXTERNAL FORCES, and covered themselves with the spirit of defilement.

93. וְתוּ, לְבָתַר אוֹסְפוּ לְמֶחֱטֵי וּלְמֵהַךְ בָּתַר יֵצֶר הָרָע, כַּד בְּקַדְמֵיתָא,
וְאוֹרַיְיתָא קַדִּישָׁא דְּאִיהִי אִילָנָא דְחַיֵּי, אַכַּתֵּי לָא נָחִית לָהּ קֻדְשָׁא
בְּרִיךְ הוּא בְּאַרְעָא. וְתוּ דְּאִיהוּ אַמְשִׁיךְ לֵיהּ בְּעָלְמָא לְבָתַר, דִּכְתִיב
וַיֵּשְׁתְּ מִן הַיַּיִן וַיִּשְׁכָּר וַיִּתְגַּל בְּתוֹךְ אָהֳלֹה. וְהָא אִתְּמָר.

93. Not only that, but WHEN THEY LEFT THE ARK, they continued to sin and follow the Evil Inclination, as they had before. Also the holy Torah, which is the Tree of Life, had not yet been brought down to earth by the Holy One, blessed be He. In addition to all this, Noah himself brought death again upon the world. As it is written: "And he drank of the wine and was drunk, and was uncovered within his tent" (Beresheet 9:21). This has already been explained.

14. The Jew

The following section reveals the hidden secrets and mysteries concerning the holidays of Rosh Hashanah (the Jewish New Year), Yom Kippur (Day of Atonement), Sukkot (the Holiday of the Booths), and the First Day of each new month. The Zohar reveals the process by which we utilize these spiritual tools to cleanse our world, and our souls, of the negative residues from our egotistic behavior. We can help facilitate all these processes as we meditate and intently browse through the ancient text.

94. עַד דַּהֲווֹ אָזְלֵי, חָמוּ חַד יוּדָאי דַּהֲוָה אָתֵי, אָמַר רַבִּי יוֹסֵי, הַאי בַּר נָשׁ יוּדָאי אִיהוּ, וְאִתְחֲזֵי. כַּד מָטָא גַּבַּיְיהוּ, שָׁאִילוּ לֵיהּ, אָמַר לוֹן, שְׁלִיחָא דְּמִצְוָה אֲנָא, דְּהָא אֲנַן דַּיְירֵי בִּכְפַר דְּרָאמִין, וּמָטֵי זִמְנָא דְּחַג, וַאֲנַן צְרִיכִין לוּלָב, וְזִינִין דְּעִמֵּיהּ, וַאֲנָא אָזֵיל לְקַטְעָא לוֹן לְמִצְוָה, אַזְלוּ כַּחֲדָא.

94. As they were walking along, they saw a Jew coming toward them. Rabbi Yosi said that this person is a Jew, because he looks like a Jew. When he reached them, they asked him WHO HE WAS. He told them that he was on a religious errand, as he lived in the village of Dramin and the time of Sukkot having arrived, they needed a Lulav and the other three kinds. He was on his way to cut them down for the purpose of the commandment. They walked together.

95. אָמַר לְהוּ הַהוּא יוּדָאי, הָנֵי אַרְבַּע מִינִין דְּלוּלָב, דִּבְכֻלְּהוּ אָתָאן לְרַצּוּיֵי עָלְמָא, שְׁמַעְתּוּן אַמַּאי אֲנַן צְרִיכִין לוֹן בַּחַג. א"ל כְּבָר אִתְעָרוּ בְּהוּ חַבְרַיָּיא, אֲבָל אִי מִלָּה חַדְתָּא אִיהוּ תְּחוֹת יְדָךְ אֵימָא לָהּ.

95. The Jew spoke to them and asked: Have you heard why we need the four kinds of the Lulav to appease the world during this holiday, BUT NOT AT ANY OTHER TIME? They told him: The friends have already explained this subject BY TELLING THE REASON, but if you have a new explanation, then say it.

96. אָמַר לוֹן, וַדַּאי הַהוּא אֲתָר דַּאֲנַן דַּיְירֵי בֵּיהּ, הוּא זְעֵיר, וְכֻלְּהוּ

עָסְקֵי בְּאוֹרַיְיתָא. וְאִית עֲלָן צוּרְבָּא מֵרַבָּנָן, רַבִּי יִצְחָק בַּר יוֹסֵי מֵחוֹזָאָה
שְׁמֵיהּ, וּבְכָל יוֹמָא וְיוֹמָא אֲמַר לָן מִלִּין חַדְתִּין בְּאוֹרַיְיתָא. וַאֲמַר,
דְּהָא בְּחַג זִמְנָא הוּא, לְשַׁלְטָאָה. אֲזֵי עָבַר עַל נַפְשֵׁנוּ הַמַּיִם הַזֵּידוֹנִים,
בָּרוּךְ ה' שֶׁלֹּא נְתָנָנוּ טֶרֶף לְשִׁנֵּיהֶם, וְכִי אִית שִׁנַּיִם לַמַּיִם. אֶלָּא אִינּוּן
שְׁאָר עַמִּין. אִינּוּן רַבְרְבִין מְמַנָּן עַל שְׁאָר עַמִּין עכו״ם וּמִתְבָּרְכָאן
מִסִּטְרַיְיהוּ דְיִשְׂרָאֵל, וְקָרִינָן לוֹן מַיִם הַזֵּידוֹנִים, כְּמָא דְּאַתְּ אָמַר הַמַּיִם
הַזֵּידוֹנִים.

96. He said to them: the place where we live is indeed a small one, but all indulge in the study of the Torah. We have a rabbi, who is well known among the Rabbis, whose name is Rabbi Yitzchak and who is the son of Rabbi Yosi from Mechoza'a. He teaches us new explanations of the Torah each and every day. And he said that during this holiday, it is the time for domination, WHEN YISRAEL OBTAIN DOMINATION OVER THE MINISTERS OF THE SEVENTY NATIONS. SO IT IS WRITTEN: "then the proud waters have gone over our soul. Blessed be Hashem, who has not given us as a prey to their teeth" (Tehilim 124:5-6). AND HE ASKS, "Does water have teeth?" AND HE REPLIES THAT they – THE PROUD WATERS – refer to the other nations, AND THE "TEETH" REFER TO the supernal ministers of these nations, who are worshippers of the planets and constellations. They are blessed through Yisrael, and they are called proud waters, as it says "the malicious waters."

97. וּבְגִין לְשַׁלְטָאָה עֲלַיְיהוּ אָתֵינָא בְּרָזָא דִשְׁמָא קַדִּישָׁא, בְּאִינּוּן
אַרְבַּע מִינִין שֶׁבַּלּוּלָב, לְרַצּוּיֵי לֵיהּ לְקֻדְשָׁא בְּרִיךְ הוּא, וּלְשַׁלְטָאָה
עֲלַיְיהוּ בְּרָזָא דִשְׁמָא קַדִּישָׁא, וּלְאִתְעָרָא עֲלָן מַיִין קַדִּישִׁין, לְנַסְּכָא עַל
גַּבֵּי מַדְבְּחָא.

97. To dominate THE MINISTERS OF THE NATIONS, we come with the Holy Name that is represented by those four kinds with the Lulav: THE MYRTLE IS THE SECRET OF CHESED, GVURAH AND TIFERET, FROM THE LETTER *YUD* OF THE YUD HEI VAV HEI; THE WILLOW BRANCHES ARE THE SECRET OF NETZACH AND HOD, FROM THE FIRST LETTER *HEI* OF THE YUD HEI VAV HEI; THE LULAV IS THE SECRET OF YESOD, FROM THE

LETTER *VAV* OF THE YUD HEI VAV HEI; AND THE ETROG IS THE SECRET
OF MALCHUT OF THE LOWER *HEI*. Together they appease the Holy One,
blessed be He, and rule over the proud waters by means of the Holy Name.
They bring and arouse upon us the holy waters, NAMELY THE ABUNDANCE
OF THE UPPER WATERS, for the water libation ceremony at the altar,
WHICH IS MALCHUT. AND THESE UPPER WATERS OVERCOME THE
PROUD WATERS.

98. תּוּ אֲמַר לוֹן, בְּר"ה אִתְעֲרוּתָא קַדְמָאָה אִיהוּ בְּעָלְמָא. מַאי
אִתְעֲרוּתָא קַדְמָאָה, דָּא בֵּי דִינָא דִלְתַתָּא, דְּאִתְעַר לְמֵידַן עַלְמָא,
וְקֻדְשָׁא בְּרִיךְ הוּא יָתֵיב עַל עָלְמָא בְּדִינָא, וְדָאִין עָלְמָא.

98. And he went on to say that on Rosh Hashanah, the first awakening,
WHICH IS THE FEMALE PRINCIPLE, reoccurs and appears in the world.
THIS MEANS THAT THE FEMALE PRINCIPLE RETURNS TO ITS PREVIOUS
STATUS ON THE FOURTH DAY OF CREATION. AND HE ASKS: What is this
first awakening? AND HE ANSWERS: It is the lower courthouse that is
aroused in order to judge the world. It is when the Holy One, blessed be He,
sits on the throne of Judgment and judges the world.

99. וְשַׁלְטָא הַאי בֵּי דִינָא, לְמֵידַן עָלְמָא, עַד יוֹמָא דְכִפּוּרֵי, דְּנָהֲרִין
אַנְפָּהָא, וְלָא אִשְׁתְּכַח חִוְיָא דִלְטוֹרָא בְּעָלְמָא, דְּאִיהוּ אִתְעַסַּק בַּמֶּה
דְּאַתְיָין לֵיהּ הַהוּא שָׂעִיר, דְּאִיהוּ מִסִּטְרָא דְרוּחַ מְסָאֲבָא, כְּדְקָא חֲזֵי
לֵיהּ. וּבְגִין דְּאִתְעַסַּק בְּהַהוּא שָׂעִיר, לָא קָרֵיב לְמַקְדְּשָׁא.

99. This courthouse rules and judges the world until Yom Kippur (the Day
of Atonement), when her face, of the Female Principle, lights up, THIS
MEANS THAT THE FEMALE PRINCIPLE RECEIVES THE UPPER THREE
SFIROT – KETER, CHOCHMAH AND BINAH – CALLED THE 'FACE.' At this
time, the slanderous serpent leaves the world alone, because he is busy with
the scapegoat which has been offered to him. This offering is from the side
of the spirit of defilement, which is appropriate FOR THE SLANDEROUS
SERPENT, WHO IS THE PROSECUTOR. So while he is occupied with his
scapegoat, he does not approach the Temple, OR THE FEMALE PRINCIPLE.
THAT IS, HE DOES NOT APPROACH THE CHILDREN OF YISRAEL IN ORDER

TO PROSECUTE THEM ANYMORE, AND DOES NOT SEPARATE THE MATING
OF ZEIR ANPIN AND THE FEMALE PRINCIPLE.

100. וְשָׂעִיר דָּא כְּהַהוּא שָׂעִיר דְּר"ח דְּאִתְעַסַּק בֵּיהּ, וְאַנְהִירוּ אַנְפָּהָא
דְּמַקְדְּשָׁא. וְעַל דָּא יִשְׂרָאֵל כֻּלְּהוּ, מַשְׁכְּחִין רַחֲמֵי קַמֵּי קֻדְשָׁא בְּרִיךְ
הוּא, וְאִתְעֲבַר חוֹבַיְיהוּ. וְרָזָא חֲדָא, אָמַר לוֹן, וְלָא אִתְיְיהִיב רְשׁוּ
לְגַלָּאָה, בַּר לַחֲסִידֵי קַדִּישִׁין עִלָּיוֹנִין חַכִּימִין. אָמַר רַבִּי יוֹסֵי מַאן אִיהוּ,
אָמַר לוֹן, עַד לָא בְּדִיקְנָא בְּכוּ.

100. This scapegoat is like the sin offering of the he-goat on the first day of
the month. Because he is occupied with it, the face of the Temple, WHICH IS
THE FEMALE PRINCIPLE, lights up. And this is how all Yisrael find mercy
in the eyes of the Holy One, blessed be He, and He removes their sins. But
there is one secret, he told them, that may not be revealed, except to
exceedingly wise, saintly, and pious men. Rabbi Yosi asked him: And what
is that secret? So he answered: I have not yet checked you out, SO I
CANNOT TELL WHETHER YOU ARE FIT TO HEAR THIS SECRET.

101. אֲזָלוּ, לְבָתַר אֲמַר לוֹן, כַּד סִיהֲרָא אִתְקְרֵיבַת בְּשִׁמְשָׁא, אִתְעַר
קֻדְשָׁא בְּרִיךְ הוּא סִטְרָא דְּצָפוֹן, וְאָחִיד בָּהּ בִּרְחִימוּ, וּמָשִׁיךְ לָהּ לְגַבֵּיהּ,
וְדָרוֹם אִתְעַר מִסִּטְרָא אָחֳרָא, וְסִיהֲרָא סַלְקָא וּמִתְחַבְּרָא בְּמִזְרָח, וּכְדֵין
יָנְקָא מִתְּרֵין סִטְרִין, וְנָטִיל בִּרְכָּאן בַּחֲשַׁאי, וּכְדֵין אִתְבָּרְכָא סִיהֲרָא,
וְאִתְמַלְיָא. וְהָכָא אִתְקְרֵיבַת אִתְּתָא בְּבַעְלָהּ.

101. They proceeded on their way, and after a while he said: When the
moon, WHICH IS THE FEMALE PRINCIPLE, approaches the sun, WHICH IS
ZEIR ANPIN, then the Holy One, blessed be He, stirs up the northern side,
WHICH IS THE LEFT COLUMN, and He grasps her lovingly and draws her
toward Himself. THIS IS THE SECRET OF ASKING PERMISSION AND
APPEASEMENT. And then the southern side, WHICH IS THE RIGHT
COLUMN, is aroused from the other side. And eventually the moon, WHICH
IS THE FEMALE PRINCIPLE, rises and joins the east, WHICH IS ZEIR ANPIN.
Thus, She draws sustenance from both sides, FROM THE SOUTH AND FROM
THE NORTH, and receives the blessing OR THE ABUNDANCE OF THE
MATING, in silence. And now the moon is blessed and filled WITH THE

ABUNDANCE, as a woman approaches her husband. THIS MEANS THAT A COMPLETE MATING HAS OCCURRED, IN WHICH THE ENTIRE MOCHIN ARE REVEALED TO THE WORLD.

102. כְּמָה דְאִית רָזָא דְיוֹקְנָא שַׁיְיפֵי דְאָדָם, וְתִיקוּנוֹי. הָכִי נָמֵי אִית רָזָא דִדְיוֹקְנֵי דְּשַׁיְיפֵי נוּקְבָא, וְתִקוּנֵי דְנוּקְבָא. וְכֹלָא פָּרֵישׁ בִּגְוָון. הָכִי נָמֵי אִית לְעֵילָא, אָחִיד בָּה, וְאִתְּעַר לְקַבֵּל בִּרְחִימוּ, ה"נ אִית לְתַתָּא, רָזָא וְתִקוּנָא דְאָדָם תַּתָּאָה אָחֳרָא, תְּחוֹת סִיהֲרָא.

102. Just as there is a secret pertaining to the shape of the parts of the body of man, ZEIR ANPIN and its composition, so too there is a secret pertaining to the shape of the parts of the body of the Female Principle OF ZEIR ANPIN and its composition. And the only difference between them is their color: THE COLOR GREEN IS THE SECRET OF ZEIR ANPIN, WHILE RED IS THE SECRET OF THE FEMALE PRINCIPLE. NEVERTHELESS, THE SHAPES OF THEIR PARTS ARE SIMILAR. And as there is that above which joins her and rises to receive her with love, so below ATZILUT, beneath the moon, lies the secret of another, lower man OF THE OTHER SIDE. HE ALSO HAS THE SAME PARTS OF THE BODY, NAMELY THE LEFT AND RIGHT AND SO ON. WHAT WE LEARN FROM THIS IS THAT ALL THE LEVELS ARE MODELED AFTER ONE ANOTHER, SUCH THAT THE SHAPES OF THE UPPER LEVEL CARRY DOWN TO THE LOWER ONE. AND THE AROUSAL OF ANY ONE OF THESE ASPECTS, AROUSES AN OPPOSITE ASPECT IN THE OTHER LEVELS, AS SHALL FURTHER BE EXPLAINED.

103. כְּמָה דִדְרוֹעָא שְׂמָאלָא לְעֵילָא אָחִיד בָּה, וְאִתְּעַר לְקַבְלָה בִּרְחִימוּ, הָכִי נָמֵי אִית לְתַתָּא, הַאי נָחָשׁ, אִיהוּ דְרוֹעָא שְׂמָאלָא דְרוּחַ מְסָאֳבָא, וְאָחִיד בֵּיה מַאן דְּרָכִיב בֵּיה, וְקָרְבָא לְגַבֵּי דְסִיהֲרָא, וּמָשִׁיךְ לָה בֵּינַיְיהוּ דְקוּטְפָא וְאִסְתָּאֳבַת.

103. Above, the left arm OF ZEIR ANPIN holds THE FEMALE PRINCIPLE and rises lovingly toward her. Simlary below the FEMALE PRINCIPLE, the serpent, which is the left arm of the spirit of defilement, is THE FEMALE PRINCIPLE OF DEFILEMENT. He who rides upon THE SERPENT, WHO IS THE MALE OF THE DEFILEMENT, GRASPS AND MATES WITH IT. By this he approaches the moon, WHICH IS THE FEMALE PRINCIPLE, and draws her toward him, MEANING THAT HE IS NURISHED FROM HER from between those that are clinging – MEANING THE PLACE OF THE MATING – and thus, she is defiled.

104. וּכְדֵין יִשְׂרָאֵל לְתַתָּא, מְקָרְבִין שָׂעִיר. וְהַהוּא נָחָשׁ, אִתְמְשַׁךְ אֲבַתְרֵיהּ דְּהַהוּא שָׂעִיר, וְסִיהֲרָא אִתְדַּכְּיַאת, וְסַלְקָאת לְעֵילָא, וְאִתְקְשָׁרַת לְעֵילָא, לְאִתְבָּרְכָא, וּנְהִירִין אַנְפָּהָא, מַה דְּאִתְחַשְׁכַת לְתַתָּא.

104. Then, Yisrael below offer the scapegoat ON THE FIRST DAY OF THE MONTH. The serpent is drawn to it FOR ITS ENTIRE CRAVING IS FOR THE ILLUMINATION OF THE LEFT. THROUGH THE SCAPEGOAT, YISRAEL DRAW THE SWEETENING OF MALCHUT IN BINAH AND THE ILLUMINATION OF THE LEFT FROM BELOW UPWARD. Then the moon is purified AND BECOMES FIT TO RECEIVE THE ABUNDANCE FROM HER HUSBAND, ZEIR ANPIN. She then climbs up and clings above TO ZEIR ANPIN in order to be blessed. While before, when she was below AND HAD NOT YET MATED WITH ZEIR ANPIN, she was dark, now her face lights up.

105. כְּדֵין הָכָא בְּיוֹמָא דְכִפּוּרֵי, כֵּיוָן דְּהַהוּא חִוְיָא בִּישָׁא, אִתְעַסַּק בְּהַהוּא שָׂעִיר, סִיהֲרָא אִתְפָּרְשַׁת מִנֵּיהּ, וְאִתְעַסְּקַת לְאוֹלְפָא עֲלַיְיהוּ סָנֵיגוֹרְיָא, וְסוֹכְכַת עֲלַיְיהוּ, כְּאִמָּא עַל בְּנִין, וְקֻדְשָׁא בְּרִיךְ הוּא בָּרֵיךְ לוֹן מִלְעֵילָא, וּמָחֵיל לוֹן.

105. The same is true of Yom Kippur, another day on which the evil serpent is kept busy with the scapegoat, WHICH IS THE ILLUMINATION OF THE LEFT. JUST AS ON THE FIRST DAY OF THE MONTH, WHEN THE SERPENT IS BUSY WITH THE SCAPEGOAT, the moon is separated from it and may busy herself in protecting Yisrael as a mother protects her children. Then the Holy One, blessed be He, blesses Yisrael from above and forgives them for their sins.

106. לְבָתַר, יִשְׂרָאֵל כַּד מָטוּ לַחַג, מִתְעָרֵי סְטְרָא דְּיָמִינָא לְעֵילָא, בְּגִין דְּיִתְקַשַּׁר בֵּיהּ סִיהֲרָא, וְיִתְנְהִירוּ אַנְפָּהָא כְּדְקָא חָזֵי. וּכְדֵין פְּלֵגַת חוּלָקָא דְּבִרְכָאן, לְכָל אִינּוּן מְמַנָּן דִּלְתַתָּא, דְּיִתְעַסְּקוּן בְּחוּלָקֵהוֹן, וְלָא

יֵיתוּן לְיָנְקָא וּלְקָרְבָא בְּסִטְרָא דְחוּלְקֵהוֹן דְיִשְׂרָאֵל.

106. Later, when Yisrael reach the holiday of SUKKOT, the Right COLUMN of above is aroused, AS ALLUDED TO IN THE VERSE, "AND HIS RIGHT HAND EMBRACES ME" (SHIR HASHIRIM 2:6). This allows the moon, WHO IS THE FEMALE PRINCIPLE, to attach herself to him, NAMELY TO THE RIGHT, and then her face is fittingly illuminated. Then she shares her blessings with all the ministers below, NAMELY THE SEVENTY MINISTERS OF THE NATIONS. By keeping them occupied with their blessings, they are distracted from approaching and sucking from Yisrael's portion. AS IS DESCRIBED WITH THE SERPENT AND THE FEMALE PRINCIPLE, ITS OCCUPATION WITH THE SCAPEGOAT DEFLECTS ITS PROSECUTION OF THE FEMALE PRINCIPLE.

107. כְּגַוְונָא דָא לְתַתָּא, כַּד שְׁאָר עַמִּין אִתְבָּרְכוּן, כֻּלְּהוֹן אִינוּן מִתְעַסְּקִין בְּאַחְסָנַת חוּלְקֵהוֹן, וְלָא הֲווֹ אַתְיָין לְאִתְעָרְבָא בַּהֲדַיְיהוּ דְיִשְׂרָאֵל, וּלְחַמְדָא חוּלַק אַחְסַנְתְּהוֹן, וּבְגִין כָּךְ יִשְׂרָאֵל, אִינוּן מָשְׁכִין בִּרְכָאן לְכָל אִינוּן מִמַּנָן, בְּגִין דְיִתְעַסְּקוּן בְּחוּלְקֵהוֹן, וְלָא יִתְעָרְבוּן בַּהֲדַיְיהוּ.

107. The same applies below IN THIS WORLD. When all the other nations are blessed, they all become occupied with their portion and do not meddle with Yisrael or covet their portion. JUST AS WE DESCRIBED PREVIOUSLY – THE SERPENT WITH THE FEMALE PRINCIPLE AND THE SEVENTY SUPERNAL MINISTERS WITH YISRAEL – SO IS THE CASE WITH THE SEVENTY NATIONS AND YISRAEL BELOW. This is why DURING SUKKOT, WHEN THEY OFFER THE SEVENTY BULLS AS A SACRIFICE, Yisrael draw blessings down to all the supernal ministers OF THE SEVENTY NATIONS, so they will be occupied with their portion and not meddle with Yisrael.

108. וְכַד סִיהֲרָא אִתְמְלֵי בִּרְכָאן לְעֵילָא, כִּדְקָא יָאוֹת, יִשְׂרָאֵל אַתְיָין וְיָנְקִין מִנָּה בִּלְחוֹדַיְיהוּ. וְעַל דָּא כְּתִיב בַּיּוֹם הַשְּׁמִינִי עֲצֶרֶת תִּהְיֶה לָכֶם, מַאי עֲצֶרֶת, כְּתַרְגוּמוֹ, כְּנִישׁוּ. כָּל מַה דְבַנְישׁוּ, מֵאִינוּן בִּרְכָאן עֲלָאִין, לָא יָנְקִין מִנֵיהּ עַמִּין אָחֲרָנִין, בַּר יִשְׂרָאֵל בִּלְחוֹדַיְיהוּ, וּבְגִין כָּךְ כְּתִיב, עֲצֶרֶת תִּהְיֶה לָכֶם, לָכֶם וְלָא לִשְׁאָר עַמִּין, לָכֶם וְלָא לִשְׁאָר מִמַּנָן.

108. When the moon is full of blessings from above as she aught, Yisrael come and draw sustenance from her for themselves alone. That is why it is written: "On the eighth day you shall have a solemn assembly (Heb. *Atzeret*)" (Bemidbar 29:35). What is this assembly? It indicates the assembling of the blessings from above, from which only Yisrael may draw sustenance. And that is why it is written: "There shall be a solemn assembly for you," REFERRING SPECIFICALLY to 'you' and not to the other nations; to you and not to the other supernal ministers.

109. וְעַל דָּא אִינּוּן מְרַצִּין עַל הַמַּיִם, לְמֵיהַב לוֹן חוּלָק בִּרְכָאן, דְּיִתְעַסְּקוּן בֵּיהּ, וְלָא יִתְעָרְבוּן לְבָתַר, בְּחֶדְוָותָא דְיִשְׂרָאֵל, כַּד יָנְקִין בִּרְכָאן עִלָּאִין. וְעַל הַהוּא יוֹמָא כְּתִיב, דּוֹדִי לִי וַאֲנִי לוֹ, דְּלָא אִתְעָרַב אוֹחֲרָא בַּהֲדָן.

109. This is the reason why YISRAEL appeases THE HOLY ONE, BLESSED BE HE, with water libations UPON THE ALTAR. THIS gives the supernal ministers OF THE NATIONS part of the blessings, so that they are occupied with it and do not meddle with the joy of Yisrael when they come to draw the blessings from above. And of this day, it is written: "My beloved is mine and I am his" (Shir Hashirim 2:16), MEANING that there is no stranger interfering with us.

110. לְמַלְכָּא דְּזַמַן רְחִימוֹי בִּסְעוּדָתָא עִלָּאָה, דַּעֲבֵיד לֵיהּ לְיוֹמָא רְשִׁימָא. הָא רְחִימוֹי דְּמַלְכָּא יָדַע, דְּמַלְכָּא אִתְרְעֵי בֵּיהּ. אָמַר מַלְכָּא הַשְׁתָּא אֲנָא בָּעֵי לְמֶחֱדֵי עִם רְחִימַאי, וְדָחִילְנָא דְּכַד אֲנָא בִּסְעוּדָתָא, עִם רְחִימַאי, יַעֲלוֹן כָּל אִינּוּן קַסְטוֹרֵי מְמַנָּן, וְיִתִּיבוּן עִמָּנָא לְפָתוֹרָא, לְמִסְעַד סְעוּדָתָא דְּחֶדְוָה, עִם רְחִימַאי. מָה עֲבַד, אַקְדִּים הַהוּא רְחִימוֹי קוֹסְטוֹרִין דִּירוֹקֵי, וּבִשְׂרָא דְּתוֹרֵי, וְאַקְרִיב קַמַּיְיהוּ, דְּאִינּוּן קַסְטוֹרֵי מְמַנָּן לְמֵיכַל. לְבָתַר יָתִיב מַלְכָּא עִם רְחִימוֹי, לְהַהִיא סְעוּדָתָא עִלָּאָה, מִכָּל עִדּוּנִין דְּעָלְמָא. וּבְעוֹד דְּאִיהוּ בִּלְחוֹדוֹי, עִם מַלְכָּא, שָׁאִיל לֵיהּ כָּל צָרְכּוֹי, וְיָהִיב לֵיהּ. וְאַחֲדֵי מַלְכָּא עִם רְחִימוֹי, בִּלְחוֹדוֹהִי, וְלָא אִתְעָרְבִין אַחֲרָנִין בֵּינַיְיהוּ. כָּךְ יִשְׂרָאֵל, עִם קֻדְשָׁא בְּרִיךְ הוּא, בְּגִין כָּךְ כְּתִיב בַּיּוֹם הַשְּׁמִינִי עֲצֶרֶת תִּהְיֶה לָכֶם.

110. This day is like the day on which a king invites a close friend to a special feast, prepared on a special day, so that his friend will know his deep love. The king thinks to himself: Now I wish to feast and be merry with my beloved alone, but I fear that during my feast all the other ministers will come and join us at our table to be together and take part in the festive meal that I have prepared for my beloved and myself. So what does the king do? He first regales his governors and ministers with dishes of vegetables and beef. Only after they are satisfied can he sit in peace with his friend and enjoy the supernal banquet with the world's finest delicacies spread before them. And while alone with the king, his friend puts before him all his petitions and requests, which the king grants. So just as the king enjoys the company of his beloved alone, with no stranger disturbing them, the Holy One, blessed be He, enjoys Yisrael. Hence it is written: "On the eighth day you shall have a solemn assembly."

111. אָמְרוּ רַבִּי יוֹסֵי וְר׳ חִיָּיא, קֻדְשָׁא בְּרִיךְ הוּא אַתְקִין אוֹרְחָא קַמָּן. זַכָּאִין אִינּוּן דְּמִשְׁתַּדְּלֵי בְּאוֹרַיְיתָא. אָתֵי נְשָׁקוּהוּ. קָרָא עֲלֵיהּ ר׳ יוֹסֵי וְכָל בָּנַיִךְ לִמּוּדֵי ה׳ וְרַב שְׁלוֹם בָּנַיִךְ. כַּד מָטוּ בֵּי חֲקַל, יָתִיבוּ. אָמַר הַהוּא בַּר נָשׁ, מַאי שְׁנָא דִּכְתִיב וַה׳ הִמְטִיר עַל סְדוֹם וְעַל עֲמוֹרָה וְגו׳. וּמַאי שְׁנָא בְּטוֹפָנָא, דִּכְתִיב אֱלֹקִים אֱלֹקִים בְּכָל אֲתַר, וְלָא כְּתִיב וַה׳.

111. Rabbi Yosi and Rabbi Chiya said: The Holy One, blessed be He, established the right way for us; happy are those who delve into the Torah. They approached THE JEW and kissed him. Rabbi Yosi applied to him the verse: "And all your children shall be taught of Hashem, and great shall be the peace of your children" (Yeshayah 54:13). When they reached a field, they all sat down. That man asked what changed when the verse says, "And Hashem rained upon Sodom and upon Gomorrah" (Beresheet 19:24), AND DID NOT USE THE TERM 'ELOHIM'? And what changed during the Great Flood, when the term 'Elohim' is used, while the term Hashem, AS MENTIONED IN THE OVERTHROWING OF THE CITIES OF SODOM AND GOMORRAH, IS NOT USED AT ALL?

112. אֶלָּא תָּנֵינָן בְּכָל אֲתַר דִּכְתִיב וַה׳ הוּא וּבֵית דִּינוֹ. אֱלֹקִים סְתָם, דִּינָא בִּלְחוֹדוֹי. אֶלָּא בִּסְדוֹם אִתְעֲבֵיד דִּינָא, וְלָא לְשֵׁיצָאָה עָלְמָא, וּבְגִין כָּךְ אִתְעָרֵב אִיהוּ בַּהֲדֵי דִינָא. אֲבָל בְּטוֹפָנָא, כָּל עָלְמָא שֵׁצֵי,

וְכָל אִינוּן דְּאִשְׁתַּכָּחוּ בְּעָלְמָא.

112. We have learned that everywhere the term "and Hashem" is mentioned, IT INDICATES Him and His courthouse, NAMELY ZEIR ANPIN, WHICH IS MERCY, TOGETHER WITH HIS FEMALE PRINCIPLE, WHICH IS JUDGMENT. But when the term Elohim is mentioned alone, this indicates only the courthouse, NAMELY THE FEMALE PRINCIPLE WITHOUT ZEIR ANPIN. In the case of Sodom, Judgment was passed not to destroy the world, and thus, ZEIR ANPIN was involved in carrying out Judgment. THAT IS WHY IT IS WRITTEN "AND HASHEM," VAV - YUD HEI VAV HEI, INDICATING THE ATTRIBUTE OF MERCY WHICH IS ZEIR ANPIN, TOGETHER WITH HIS COURT OF JUSTICE, WHICH IS HIS FEMALE PRINCIPLE, FOR THE LETTER *VAV,* WHICH CARRIES THE MEANING OF THE ENGLISH WORD 'AND', THAT IS JOINED WITH YUD HEI VAV HEI, INDICATES THE FEMALE PRINCIPLE. But in the case of the Great Flood, the whole world and all of its inhabitants were destroyed. THAT IS WHY THE EVENT IS DESCRIBED WITH THE TERM 'ELOHIM,' INDICATING THE ATTRIBUTE OF JUDGMENT ALONE, UNTEMPERED BY MERCY.

113. וְאִי תֵימָא נֹחַ וּדְעִמֵּיהּ. סְתִים מֵעֵינָא הֲוָה, דְּלָא אִתְחֲזֵי, וְעַל דָּא כָּל מַה דְּאִשְׁתְּכַח בְּעָלְמָא שֵׁצֵי לֵיהּ, וְעַל דָּא וַה' בְּאִתְגַּלְיָא, וְלָא שֵׁצֵי כֹּלָּא. אֱלֹקִים בָּעֵי סְתִימוּ, וּבָעֵי לְאִסְתַּמְּרָא, דְּהָא כֹּלָּא שֵׁצֵי, וְעַל דָּא אֱלֹקִים בִּלְחוֹדוֹי הֲוֵי.

113. And although you may say that Noah and all who were with him WERE SAVED AND NOT ALL WERE DESTROYED, IT IS ONLY BECAUSE THEY were hidden from sight and unseen BY THE ANGEL OF DESTRUCTION. Thus, IT IS CONSIDERED THAT everything, NAMELY, EVERYTHING THAT WAS SEEN BY THE EYES OF THE ANGEL OF DESTRUCTION, that existed in the world was destroyed. That is why the term "And Hashem," indicates that He does not destroy all that is revealed to the eye, AS IN THE CASE OF THE DESTRUCTION OF SODOM. However, the term Elohim indicates that all should be carefully concealed, because He destroys everything, NAMELY ALL THAT IS REVEALED TO THE EYE. That is why the term Elohim REFERS TO THE FEMALE PRINCIPLE alone, WITHOUT ZEIR ANPIN, WHO IS MERCY.

114. וְרָזָא דָּא ה׳ לַמַּבּוּל יָשָׁב, מַהוּ יָשָׁב, אִלְמָלֵא קְרָא כְּתִיב, לָא
יָכְלִינָן לְמֵימַר, יָשָׁב בִּלְחוֹדוֹי, דְּלָא אַתְיָא עִם דִּינָא, כְּתִיב הָכָא יָשָׁב,
וּכְתִיב הָתָם בָּדָד יֵשֵׁב, בִּלְחוֹדוֹי.

114. And this is the secret of the verse, "Hashem sat at the Flood" (Tehilim 29:10). SO HE ASKS, What is THE MEANING OF THE TERM "sat?" AND HE ANSWERS THAT if it had not been written in the scriptures, we could not have said it, BECAUSE THE TERM "SAT" INDICATES that He sat alone, by Himself and was distinct from the Judgment THAT WAS PASSED AT THE GREAT FLOOD. THIS IS BASED ON THE ANALOGY THAT here it is written: "HASHEM sat," while in another place it is written: "He shall sit alone" OUTSIDE THE CAMP (Vayikra 13:46). THE MEANING, IN BOTH CASES, IS THAT HE WAS ALONE, by himself. ALL THIS LEADS TO THE FACT THAT AT THE SENTENCE OF THE FLOOD, YUD HEI VAV HEI SAT ALONE; HE DID NOT JOIN IN THAT JUDGMENT. AND THAT IS WHY THE SENTENCE WAS IMPOSED AS JUDGMENT WITHOUT MERCY.

115. וּבְגִין דְּנֹחַ הֲוָה סָתִים מֵעֵינָא, לְבָתַר כַּד אִתְעֲבֵיד דִּינָא, וְשֵׁצֵי
עָלְמָא, וְנָח רוּגְזֵיהּ, מַה כְּתִיב, וַיִּזְכֹּר אֱלֹקִים אֶת נֹחַ וְגו׳. דְּהָא כַּד שֵׁצֵי
עָלְמָא, לָא אִדְכַּר דְּסָתִים מֵעֵינָא הֲוָה.

115. Now because Noah was out of sight after the sentence was passed, the world was destroyed, and His temper was quiet, it is written: "And Elohim remembered Noah" (Beresheet 8:1). For UNTIL NOW when He was destroying the world, Noah was not remembered, because he was out of sight.

116. וְרָזָא אוֹלִיפְנָא, קַדְשָׁא בְּרִיךְ הוּא סָתִים וְגַלְיָא. גַּלְיָא: הוּא בֵּי
דִינָא דִּלְתַתָּא. סָתִים: הוּא אֲתַר דְּכָל בִּרְכָּאן נָפְקֵי מִתַּמָּן. וּבְגִין כָּךְ כָּל
מִלּוּי דְּבַר נָשׁ, דְּאִינוּן בִּסְתִימוּ, בִּרְכָּאן שַׁרְיָין עֲלוֹי. וְכָל דְּאִינוּן
בְּאִתְגַּלְיָא, הַהוּא אֲתַר דְּבֵי דִינָא שַׁרְיָאן עֲלוֹי, בְּגִין דְּאִיהוּ אֲתַר
בְּאִתְגְּלֵי, וְהַהוּא דְּאִקְרֵי רַע עַיִן, שַׁלִּיט עֲלֵיהּ, וְכֹלָּא הוּא בְּרָזָא עִלָּאָה,
כְּגַוְונָא דִּלְעֵילָּא.

116. I have learned a secret that the Holy One, blessed be He, is revealed

and concealed. He is revealed when presiding over the lower courthouse, WHICH IS THE FEMALE PRINCIPLE CALLED RACHEL WHO STANDS FROM THE CHEST OF ZEIR ANPIN DOWNWARD, and He is concealed when He is AT the place from where come out all the blessings, WHICH IS THE STATE IN WHICH ZEIR ANPIN MATES WITH LEAH. LEAH STANDS FROM THE CHEST OF ZEIR ANPIN UPWARD, AND FROM THIS MATING ALL BLESSINGS COME FORTH. This is why all the affairs of man that are hidden from sight are blessed from above, while all those exposed to view are under the influence of the court of justice, NAMELY THE FEMALE PRINCIPLE WHO IS FROM THE CHEST OF ZEIR ANPIN DOWNWARD, because this is the place that is revealed, NAMELY THE REVEALED WORLD. IN OTHER WORDS, CHASSADIM are REVEALED IN HER BY THE ILLUMINATION BY CHOCHMAH. The one who is called the 'Evil Eye' rules over it, MEANING THAT ALL JUDGMENT AND KLIPOT CLING TO THE PLACE WHERE THE ILLUMINATION OF CHOCHMAH IS REVEALED. BUT IN THE FEMALE PRINCIPLE ABOVE THE CHEST THERE ARE HIDDEN CHASSADIM, WHICH IS WHY IT IS CALLED THE HIDDEN WORLD. NO KLIPAH CAN SEIZE IT. THUS, BLESSING FROM THE HIDDEN WORLD REST ON HIM WHOSE AFFAIRS ARE CONCEALED FROM SIGHT, BUT JUDGMENT FROM THE REVEALED WORLD REST ON HIM WHOSE AFFAIRS ARE FOR ALL TO SEE. Thus, all is according to the supernal secrets of above.

117. בָּכָה רַבִּי יוֹסֵי וַאֲמַר, זַכָּאָה דָּרָא דְּרַבִּי שִׁמְעוֹן שַׁרְיָא בְּגַוֵּיהּ, דְּהָא זְכוּתָא דִּילֵיהּ אַזְמִין לָן בְּטוּרֵי, מִלִּין עִלָּאִין כְּאִלֵּין. אָמַר רַבִּי יוֹסֵי הַאי בַּר נָשׁ לְאוֹדָעָא לָן מִלִּין אִלֵּין קָא אָתֵי, וְשַׁדְרֵיהּ קֻדְשָׁא בְּרִיךְ הוּא לְגַבָּן. כַּד אָתוֹ וְסִדְּרוּ מִלִּין קַמֵּיהּ דְּרִ' שִׁמְעוֹן, אֲמַר, וַדַּאי שַׁפִּיר קָא אֲמַר.

117. Rabbi Yosi wept and said: Happy is the generation who has Rabbi Shimon among it. His merit has brought us to these mountains, so that we could hear such supreme matters. He continued: This man has come for the SOLE purpose of revealing these matters to us. The Holy One, blessed be He, sent him to us. And when they came to Rabbi Shimon and repeated ALL THAT THEY HEARD, he said: Definitely, all that he said is true.

15. The secrets of the sacrifices

Here the Zohar discusses the mysteries that surround the ritual of
sacrifice. We connect to the Light through the sacrifices that were
made during the time of the Temple. The secret of this ritual
concerns the sacrifice that must occur within the self. We must
become the sacrifice, spiritually speaking, by giving up our own
ego and Evil Inclination. This section gives us the strength of
character to approach the people in our lives with honesty, and to
sacrifice our own egos by admitting any jealousies and insecurities
in our relationships with them.

118. רַבִּי אֶלְעָזָר, הֲוָה יָתֵיב יוֹמָא חַד קַמֵּיה דְּר״ש אֲבוֹי. אָמַר לוֹ הַאי
קֵץ כָּל בָּשָׂר, אִתְהַנֵּי מֵאִינּוּן קָרְבָּנִין דַּהֲווֹ יִשְׂרָאֵל מְקָרְבִין עַל גַּבֵּי
מַדְבְּחָא אוֹ לָא. אָמַר לֵיה כֹּלָּא הֲווֹ מִסְתַּפְּקֵי כַּחֲדָא, לְעֵילָּא וְתַתָּא.

118. Rabbi Elazar was sitting one day before his father, Rabbi Shimon, and
asked him, if the 'End of all Flesh,' WHICH IS THE OTHER SIDE, enjoys
those sacrifices that Yisrael offered upon the altar or not. He answered that
all derived their nourishment, both above and below.

119. וְתָא חֲזֵי, כַּהֲנֵי וְלֵיוָאֵי וְיִשְׂרָאֵל, אִינּוּן אִקְרוּן אָדָם, בְּחִבּוּרָא
דְּאִינּוּן רְעוּתִין קַדִּישִׁין דְּסָלְקִין מִגַּוַּויְיהוּ. הַהוּא כְּשָׂבָּא אוֹ אִמְּרָא, אוֹ
הַהִיא בְּהֵמָה דְּקָרְבִין, אִצְטְרִיךְ עַד לָא יִתְקְרֵיב עַל גַּבֵּי מַדְבְּחָא,
לְפָרָשָׁא עֲלָה כָּל חַטָּאִין וְכָל רְעוּתִין בִּישִׁין, לְאִתְוַדָּאָה עֲלָה. וּכְדֵין
הַהִיא אִתְקְרֵי בְּהֵמָה בְּכֹלָּא, בְּגוֹ אִינּוּן חַטָּאִין וּבִישִׁין וְהִרְהוּרִין.

119. Come and behold: the priests, the Levites and Yisrael are THE SECRET
OF THE THREE COLUMNS – RIGHT, LEFT AND CENTRAL – AND ARE
called 'man', through the union of the holy desires that rise from them, AS
MAYIN NUKVIN (FEMALE WATERS). DESIRE RISES FROM THE PRIESTS
BY THEIR WORK; FROM THE LEVITES BY THEIR SINGING; AND FROM
YISRAEL BY THEIR ATTENDANCE AT THE TIME OF THE OFFERINGS OF
THE SACRIFICE. And when a sheep, or a deer or any other animal is brought
to be sacrificed, all sins and evil desires and intentions must be confessed
over them. Then the sacrifice is called 'a beast,' as it is now burdened with
all the sins and evil intentions THAT WERE CONFESSED OVER IT.

120. כְּגַוְונָא דְּקָרְבָּנָא דַּעֲזָאזֵל, דִּכְתִיב וְהִתְוַדָּה עָלָיו אֶת כָּל עֲוֹנוֹת בְּנֵי יִשְׂרָאֵל וגו'. הָכֵי נָמֵי הָכָא, וְכַד סָלְקָא עַל גַּבֵּי מַדְבְּחָא, מָטוּ לָהּ עַל חַד תְּרֵין, וּבְגִין כָּךְ, דָּא סַלְקָא לְאַתְרֵיהּ, וְדָא סַלְקָא לְאַתְרֵיהּ, דָּא בְּרָזָא דְּאָדָם, וְדָא בְּרָזָא דִּבְהֵמָה, כְּמָה דְּאַתְּ אָמַר אָדָם וּבְהֵמָה תּוֹשִׁיעַ ה'.

120. This is similar to the sacrifice of the scapegoat, of which it is written: "and he shall confess over him all the iniquities of the children of Yisrael" (Vayikra 16:21). So here as well, OVER EVERY SACRIFICE, THERE SHOULD BE A CONFESSION OF THE SINS. Because when the sacrifice is raised upon the altar AND IS NOT SENT TO THE DESERT, it bears a twofold burden, each of which is raised to its own place. The first is the secret of man, WHICH IS ALSO THE SECRET OF THE THREE COLUMNS; the latter is in the secret of the beast, WHICH IS THE SECRET OF THE ILLUMINATION OF THE LEFT COLUMN ONLY, as it is written: "Hashem, You preserve man and beast" (Tehilim 36:7).

121. חֲבִיתִין, וְכָל שְׁאָר מִנְחוֹת, לְאִתְעָרָא רוּחָא קַדִּישָׁא, בִּרְעוּתָא דְּכַהֲנֵי וְשִׁירָתָא דְּלֵיוָאֵי, וּבִצְלוֹתָא דְּיִשְׂרָאֵל. וּבְהַהוּא תְּנָנָא וְשַׁמְנָא וְקִמְחָא דְּסָלֵיק מִתְרַוְּון וּמִסְתַּפְּקִין כָּל שְׁאָר מָארֵי דְּדִינִין, דְּלָא יָכְלִין לְשַׁלְטָאָה בְּהַהוּא דִּינָא דְּאִתְמְסַר לוֹן וְכֹלָא בְּזִמְנָא חֲדָא. תָּא חֲזֵי, כֹּלָא אִתְעֲבֵיד בְּרָזָא דִמְהֵימְנוּתָא לְאִסְתַּפְּקָא דָּא בְּדָא, וּלְאִסְתַּלְּקָא לְעֵילָא, מָאן דְּאִצְטְרִיךְ, עַד אֵין סוֹף.

121. Fried meal offerings and all other meal offerings arouse the Holy Spirit, NAMELY THE ASPECT OF MAN, through the desire of the priests, the singing of the Levites and the prayer of Yisrael, WHO COLLECTIVELY ARE THE SECRET OF THE THREE COLUMNS. And from the smoke, the oil and the flour that rise UPON THE ALTAR, all the prosecutors replenish themselves, and are appeased. Once appeased, they become powerless to pursue the indictment that has been delivered into their hands, AND THEY ARE CONSIDERED TO BE THE ASPECT OF THE BEAST. SO THE MEAL OFFERINGS PERTAIN TO MAN AND BEAST ALIKE, and both are drawn at the same time. IN OTHER WORDS, BOTH MAN AND BEAST ARE DRAWN AT THE

TIME OF THE SACRIFICIAL OFFERING. Come and behold: everything is arranged in accordance with the secret of faith – both sides are replenished and sent above up to the Endless Light.

16. Raising the hands during prayer

The essence of this passage from the Zohar concerns the hands, and their inherent nature of constantly attracting negative forces. Since the hands are the tools by which we carry out most of our actions in life, the forces of darkness latch onto them in order to influence our deeds. We can infuse our hands with the positive energy that dwells in the Upper Worlds so that they bring blessing and good fortune to all endeavors.

122. אֲמַר רַבִּי שִׁמְעוֹן אֲרֵימַת יְדַאי בִּצְלוֹתִין לְעֵילָּא, דְּכַד רְעוּתָא עִלָּאָה, לְעֵילָּא לְעֵילָּא, קַיְימָא עַל הַהוּא רְעוּתָא, דְּלָא אִתְיְדַע, וְלֹא אִתְפַּס כְּלָל לְעָלְמִין, רֵישָׁא דְּסָתִים יַתִּיר לְעֵילָּא, וְהַהוּא רֵישָׁא אַפִּיק מַאי דְּאַפֵּיק, וְלָא יְדִיעַ, וְנָהֵיר מַאי דְּנָהֵיר, כֹּלָּא בִּסְתִימוּ.

122. Rabbi Shimon said: "I raise my hands in high to prayer," AS HE BEGAN TO REVEAL THE ORDER OF THE EMANATIONS OF THE UPPER THREE SFIROT OF ARICH ANPIN, WHICH ARE CALLED KETER, THE 'BRAIN (HEB. MOACH) OF AIR,' AND THE 'CONCEALED BRAIN (MOACH).' HE BEGAN, TOO, TO REVEAL HOW TO RISE UP TO THE 'UNKNOWN HEAD,' WHICH IS THE SECRET OF THE ENDLESS WORLD (HEB. EIN-SOF), BLESSED BE HE. BECAUSE THIS ISSUE IS AN EXALTED AND VERY SECRET MATTER, HE PRAYED SO THAT THE REVELATION OF THESE SECRETS WOULD BE ACCEPTED BEFORE HASHEM, BLESSED BE HE. When the supernal desire at the highest point above, WHICH IS THE SECRET OF KETER OF ARICH ANPIN, is established upon the forever unknown and ungraspable desire, WHICH IS THE SECRET OF THE HEAD OF ATIK CALLED THE 'UNKNOWN HEAD,' KETER OF ARICH ANPIN becomes the most concealed Head above. And that Head emanates something that is unknown, WHICH IS THE BRAIN OF AIR OF ARICH ANPIN. And He illuminates all that He illuminates in a concealed manner, WHICH IS THE CONCEALED BRAIN OF ARICH ANPIN, AS SHALL BE FURTHER EXPLAINED.

123. רְעוּ דְּמַחֲשָׁבָה עִלָּאָה לְמִרְדַּף אֲבַתְרֵיהּ, וּלְאִתְנַהֲרָא מִנֵּיהּ. חַד פְּרִיסוּ אִתְפְּרֵיס, וּמִגּוֹ הַהוּא פְּרִיסָא, בִּרְדִיפוּ דְּהַהִיא מַחֲשָׁבָה עִלָּאָה,

מָטֵי וְלָא מָטֵי. עַד הַהוּא פְּרִיסָא, נָהֵיר מַה דְּנָהֵיר. וּכְדֵין אִיהוּ מַחֲשָׁבָה עִלָּאָה, נָהֵיר בִּנְהִירוּ סָתִים דְּלָא יְדִיעַ, וְהַהוּא מַחֲשָׁבָה לָא יָדַע.

123. The desire of the supernal thought, WHICH IS KETER OF ARICH ANPIN, CALLED THE SUPERNAL WILL. AFTER IT HAS BEEN ESTABLISHED AS THE HEAD, IT IS CALLED "SUPERNAL THOUGHT." But as it desires to run after THE UNKNOWN HEAD TO SHINE FROM IT, a veil spreads BETWEEN THE UNKNOWN HEAD AND KETER, and from within the veil the light reachs yet does not reach it. THE VEIL HINDERS IT FROM REACHING THERE. Something shines upward toward the veil, BUT NOT FROM THERE DOWNWARD. Therefore supernal Thought shines with unrevealed illumination TO THE CONCEALED BRAIN, and with light unknown TO THE BRAIN OF AIR." But Thought itself, WHICH IS KETER – is considered not knowing.

124. כְּדֵין בָּטַשׁ הַאי נְהִירוּ דְּמַחֲשָׁבָה דְּלָא אִתְיְידַע, בִּנְהִירוּ דְּפַרְסָא דְּקַיְימָא, דְּנָהֵיר מִמַּה דְּלָא יְדִיעַ וְלָא אִתְיְידַע, וְלָא אִתְגַּלְיָיא. וּכְדֵין דָּא נְהִירוּ דְּמַחֲשָׁבָה דְּלָא אִתְיְידַע בָּטַשׁ בִּנְהִירוּ דְּפַרִיסָא, וְנָהֲרִין כַּחֲדָא, וְאִתְעֲבִידוּ תֵּשַׁע הֵיכָלִין.

124. Then, the illumination of the Unknown Thought hits upon the illumination of the veil that stands and shines from what is unknown BY THE 'BRAIN OF AIR,' from what is not known, BY KETER, and what is unrevealed IN THE 'CONCEALED BRAIN.' Thus, the illumination of the Thought that is not known, WHICH IS THE UNKNOWN HEAD, hits upon the veil's illumination, and they shine together. And from them, nine chambers are made IN THE UNKNOWN HEAD.

125. וְהֵיכָלִין, לָאו אִינּוּן נְהוֹרִין, וְלָאו אִינּוּן רוּחִין, וְלָאו אִינּוּן נִשְׁמָתִין, וְלָא אִית מָאן דְּקַיְימָא בְּהוֹ. רְעוּתָא, דְּכָל תֵּשַׁע נְהוֹרִין, דְּקַיְימֵי כָּלְּהוּ בְּמַחֲשָׁבָה, דְּאִיהוּ חַד מִנַּיְיהוּ בְּחוּשְׁבָּנָא, כָּלְּהוּ לְמִרְדַּף בַּתְרַיְיהוּ, בְּשַׁעֲתָא דְּקַיְימֵי בְּמַחֲשָׁבָה וְלָא מִתְדַּבְּקָן וְלָא אִתְיְידָעוּ, וְאִלֵּין לָא קַיְימֵי לָא בִּרְעוּתָא, וְלָא בְּמַחֲשָׁבָה עִלָּאָה תָּפְסִין בָּהּ, וְלָא תָּפְסִין. בְּאִלֵּין קַיְימֵי כָּל רָזֵי דִמְהֵימְנוּתָא, וְכָל אִינּוּן נְהוֹרִין מֵרָזָא

דְּמַחֲשָׁבָה עִלָּאָה כֻּלְּהוּ אִקְרוּן אֵין סוֹף. עַד הָכָא מָטוּ נְהוֹרִין וְלָא מָטוּן, וְלָא אִתְיְיְדָעוּ, לָאו הָכָא רְעוּתָא, וְלָא מַחֲשָׁבָה.

125. These chambers are not lights, AS ARE THE NINE LIGHTS OF ARICH ANPIN IN THEIR ORIGINAL LOCATION. And they are neither Ruchot nor Neshamot, and nobody can understand what they are. BECAUSE THE LIGHT OF THE EIN SOF, BLESSED BE HE, SHINES UPON THE UNKNOWN HEAD, THE NINE CHAMBERS THEREIN ARE AS THE EIN SOF, WHICH NO MIND CAN GRASP, AS SHALL BE EXPLAINED. The desire of all nine lights OF THE THREE HEADS OF ARICH ANPIN which can be grasped by thought, NAMELY IN THEIR LOCATION IN ARICH ANPIN, WHICH IS CALLED THOUGHT that is also considered one of them. THE DESIRE OF ALL IS to pursue THE NINE CHAMBERS IN WHICH THEY ARE LOCATED WITHIN THE UNKNOWN HEAD, while THE NINE LIGHTS are located in Thought, WHICH IS ARICH ANPIN. Nevertheless, THE CHAMBERS are not attained and not known TO THE NINE LIGHTS because they are not established as either AN ASPECT OF desire or as AN ASPECT OF supernal Thought, WHICH IS ARICH ANPIN. They grasp it yet do not grasp. All the secrets of Faith are present in AND BASED ON THESE NINE CHAMBERS. And all of these lights come from the secret of supernal Thought, WHICH IS ARICH ANPIN, AND ALL OF THE NINE CHAMBERS ORIGINATE FROM IT and all are called Ein Sof. Because the lights reach and do not reach this point, and are unknown, there is no desire nor thought at this point.

126. כַּד נָהִיר מַחֲשָׁבָה, וְלָא אִתְיְידַע מִמַּאן דְּנָהֵיר, כְּדֵין אִתְלַבֵּשׁ וְאַסְתִּים גּוֹ בִּינָה, וְנָהֵיר, לְמַאן דְּנָהֵיר וְאָעֵיל דָּא בְּדָא, עַד דְּאִתְכְּלִילוּ כֻּלְּהוּ כַּחֲדָא.

126. When Thought shines from an unknown source, NAMELY FROM THE BRAIN OF AIR, IT IS ENCLOTHED AND COVERED BY BINAH. It shines upon whom it shines, and they enter each other until they are as one.

127. וּבְרָזָא דְּקׇרְבְּנָא כַּד סָלֵיק, כֹּלָּא אִתְקַשַּׁר דָּא בְּדָא, וְנָהִיר דָּא בְּדָא, כְּדֵין קַיְימֵי כֻּלְּהוּ בִּסְלִיקוּ, וּמַחֲשָׁבָה אִתְעַטַּר בְּאֵין סוֹף. הַהוּא נְהִירוּ דְּאִתְנְהֵיר מִנֵּיהּ מַחֲשָׁבָה עִלָּאָה, אִקְרֵי אֵין סוֹף. וּמִנֵּיהּ אִשְׁתְּכַח

וְקַיְימָא וְנָהֵיר לְמַאן דְּנָהֵיר, וְעַל דָּא כֹּלָא קָאֵים. זַכָּאָה חוּלָקֵיהוֹן
דְּצַדִּיקַיָּיא בְּעָלְמָא דֵין וּבְעָלְמָא דְּאָתֵי.

127. Returning to the secret of the sacrifice: when it rises ON THE ALTAR, all
are enmeshed within one another and shine one upon the other. Now all the
grades are in a state of rising and, WHEN IT ASCENDS TO THE UNKNOWN
HEAD, THOUGHT, WHICH IS ARICH ANPIN, it is crowned by the Ein Sof.
And FROM EIN SOF comes ARICH ANPIN. It is established and shines upon
whom It shines. All is based upon this, ON THE DRAWING OF THE LIGHT OF
EIN SOF BY ARICH ANPIN TO THE WORLDS, AS HAS BEEN EXPLAINED.
Happy are the righteous WHO RAISE UP THE 'FEMALE WATERS' AND
UNIFY THE AFOREMENTIONED EXALTED COMBINATIONS in this world and
the World to Come, (AS THEY INHERIT BOTH WORLDS.)

128. תָּא חֲזֵי הַאי קֵץ כָּל בָּשָׂר, כְּמָה דְּקִשּׁוּרָא אִשְׁתְּכַח לְעֵילָא בְּחֶדוּ,
אוּף הָכֵי נָמֵי לְתַתָּא, בְּחֶדְוְותָא וּרְעוּתָא, לְאִסְתַּפְּקָא כֹּלָא לְעֵילָא
וְתַתָּא, וְאִימָא קַיְימָא עֲלַיְיהוּ דְּיִשְׂרָאֵל כִּדְקָא יָאוֹת.

128. Come and behold: this 'End of all Flesh,' means that the attachment
takes place in joy above IN BINAH AND IN ARICH ANPIN. The same applies
below TO ZEIR ANPIN, THE FEMALE PRINCIPLE, AND THE LOWER
WORLDS. AND THE ATTACHMENT OF EVERY LOWER GRADE TO EVERY
UPPER ONE OCCURS in happiness and in a desire to share fulfillment with
everything above and below, EVEN TO THE 'END OF ALL FLESH;' and Ima,
WHICH IS THE SHECHINAH, dwells properly upon Yisrael.

129. תָּא חֲזֵי בְּכָל רֵישֵׁי יַרְחָא וְיַרְחָא, כַּד סִיהֲרָא מִתְחַדְּשָׁא יָהֲבִין לֵיה
לְהַאי קֵץ כָּל בָּשָׂר, חוּלָקָא חֲדָא יַתִּיר עַל קָרְבָּנִין, לְאִתְעַסְּקָא בֵּיה,
וְיִשְׁתַּמֵּשׁ בְּחוּלָקֵיה, וְיֵהֵא סִטְרָא דְּיִשְׂרָאֵל בִּלְחוֹדַיְיהוּ, בְּגִין דְּיִתְאַחֲדוּן
בְּמַלְכֵּיהוֹן, וְדָא אִיהוּ שָׂעִיר, בְּגִין דְּאִיהוּ בְּחוּלָקָא דְּעֵשָׂו דִּכְתִיב בֵּיה
שָׂעִיר, הֵן עֵשָׂו אָחִי אִישׁ שָׂעִיר. וְעַל דָּא אִיהוּ אִשְׁתַּמַּשׁ בְּחוּלָקֵיה.
וְיִשְׂרָאֵל אִינוּן מִשְׁתַּמְּשִׁין בְּחוּלְקֵיהוֹן, וּבְגִין כָּךְ כְּתִיב כִּי יַעֲקֹב בָּחַר לוֹ
יָה יִשְׂרָאֵל לִסְגֻלָּתוֹ.

129. Come and behold: every first day of the month, when the moon renews herself, OR, IN OTHER WORDS, THE FEMALE PRINCIPLE RENEWS HERSELF BY MATING WITH ZEIR ANPIN. Then, the 'End of all Flesh' is given an extra portion, WHICH IS THE SCAPEGOAT OF THE NEW MOON, which is added to the REGULAR sacrifices. Thus, he is occupied by it and uses his portion. SO, THE NEW MOON'S SCAPEGOAT RENEWS THE ILLUMINATION OF THE LEFT SIDE, FROM WHICH THE 'END OF ALL FLESH' IS REPLENISHED. Hence, the RIGHT side of Yisrael remains for them alone so that they can unify with their King. This is why THEY OFFER THE SCAPEGOAT, ALSO CALLED 'Hairy' (Heb. *se'ir*), because it belongs to the part of Esau, who is described as being hairy, as it is written: "Esau my brother is a hairy (Heb. *sa'ir*) man" (Beresheet 27:11). Thus, THE 'END OF ALL FLESH' uses his part OF ESAU, WHICH IS THE LEFT SIDE, while Yisrael uses their part, WHICH IS THE RIGHT. Thus, it is written: "For Yah has chosen Jacob to Himself, Yisrael for His peculiar possession" (Tehilim 135:4).

130. תָּא חֲזֵי, הַאי קֵץ כָּל בָּשָׂר כָּל רְעוּתֵיה לָאו אִיהוּ, אֶלָּא בְּבִשְׂרָא תָּדִיר, וּבְגִין כָּךְ תִּקוּנָא דְבִשְׂרָא תָּדִיר לְגַבֵּיה, וְעַל דָּא אִקְרֵי קֵץ כָּל בָּשָׂר. וְכַד אִיהוּ שַׁלִּיט, שַׁלִּיט עַל גּוּפָא וְלָא עַל נִשְׁמָתָא, נִשְׁמָתָא סָלְקָא לְאַתְרָא וּבִשְׂרָא אִתְיְהִיב לַאֲתַר דָּא. כְּגַוְונָא דָא, בְּקָרְבָּנָא, דִרְעוּתָא סָלְקָא לַאֲתַר חַד, וּבִשְׂרָא לַאֲתַר חַד.

130. Come and behold: the sole desire of this 'End of all Flesh' is flesh alone. All that is done with the flesh in any instance is only for his sake. That is why he is called the 'End of all Flesh.' And when he rules, he rules over the body, WHICH IS THE FLESH, but not over the soul. The soul returns to its place, WHILE THE BODY, NAMELY the flesh, is given over to this place, NAMELY THE 'END OF ALL FLESH.' It is the same with the offering, as the desire goes to one place and the flesh to another.

131. וב"נ דְּאִיהוּ זַכָּאָה, אִיהוּ קָרְבָּנָא מַמָּשׁ לְכַפָּרָה, וְאָחֳרָא דְלָאו אִיהוּ זַכָּאָה, לָאו אִיהוּ קָרְבָּנָא, בְּגִין דְּבֵיה מוּמָא, דִכְתִיב כִּי לֹא לְרָצוֹן וְגו'. וְעַל דָּא צַדִּיקַיָּא כַּפָּרָה אִינוּן דְּעָלְמָא, וְקָרְבָּנָא אִינוּן בְּעָלְמָא. תָּא חֲזֵי, וַיֹּאמֶר אֱלֹקִים לְנֹחַ, קֵץ כָּל בָּשָׂר בָּא לְפָנַי, לְמֵיטַל רְשׁוּ לְאַחְשָׁכָא

אַפַּיְיהוּ דִּבְנֵי עָלְמָא, וּבְגִינֵי כָךְ הִנְנִי מַשְׁחִיתָם אֶת הָאָרֶץ.

131. A person who is righteous is HIMSELF a sacrifice given for atonement, BECAUSE HE SACRIFICES HIS OWN DESIRE, OVERCOMING HIS WILL. But a person, who is not righteous, is not accepted as a sacrifice because he is blemished. As it is written: "For it shall not be acceptable for you" (Vayikra 22:20). So the righteous alone atone for the world and are accepted as sacrifices in this world. Come and behold: "And Elohim said to Noah, the End of all Flesh is come before Me" (Beresheet 6:13), NAMELY, THE OTHER SIDE. And it came to receive permission to darken the faces of humankind. So that is why "I will destroy them with the earth" (Ibid.).

132. תָּא חֲזֵי, מַה כְּתִיב וְנֹחַ בֶּן שֵׁשׁ מֵאוֹת שָׁנָה וגו', וְכִי אַמַּאי אָתָא חוּשְׁבְּנָא דָא לְמִמְנֵי, אֶלָּא אִילוּ לָא הֲוָה נֹחַ בֶּן שֵׁשׁ מֵאוֹת שָׁנָה, לָא יֵיעוֹל לְתֵיבוּתָא, וְלָא יִתְחַבַּר בַּהֲדָהּ, כֵּיָּן דְּאִשְׁתְּלִים בְּשֵׁשׁ מֵאוֹת שָׁנָה, כְּדֵין אִתְחַבַּר בַּהֲדָהּ.

132. Come and behold: it is written: "And Noah was 600 years old" (Beresheet 7:6). AND HE ASKS: Why does the verse count THE YEARS OF NOAH? AND HE ANSWERED If Noah was not 600 years old, he would not have entered the ark and unit with it. Because he became complete with 600 years, he unit with it.

133. וְעַל דָּא, מִן יוֹמָא דְּאִשְׁתְּלִים דִּבְנֵי עָלְמָא, אוֹרִיךְ לוֹן קֻדְשָׁא בְּרִיךְ הוּא, עַד דְּאִשְׁתְּלִים נֹחַ, בְּשֵׁשׁ מֵאוֹת שָׁנָה, וְאִשְׁתְּלִים דַּרְגֵּיהּ כִּדְקָא יָאוֹת, וַהֲוָה צַדִּיק שְׁלִים וּכְדֵין עָאל לְתֵיבוּתָא, וְכֹלָּא כְּגַוְונָא דִּלְעֵילָא. וְנֹחַ בֶּן שֵׁשׁ מֵאוֹת שָׁנָה. כְּמָה דַּאֲמָרָן. וּבְגִינֵי כָךְ לָא אִתְמַר כְּבֶן שֵׁשׁ מֵאוֹת שָׁנָה.

133. From the day that the sins of the people were completed, FROM THE TIME THEY WERE DESERVING OF RECEIVING THEIR PUNISHMENT, the Holy One, blessed be He, still waited for them. He waited until Noah completed his 600 years and perfected himself as a righteous man. Only then did Noah enter the ark. And everything below is as above. IN OTHER

WORDS, EVERYTHING WAS DONE BY DIVINE INSPIRATION FROM THE UPPER YESOD AND MALCHUT. THAT IS WHY IT IS WRITTEN: "And Noah was 600 years old," and not 'approximately 600.' FOR, AS WE HAVE SAID, HE HAD TO BE EXACTLY 600 YEARS OLD.

17. "And, behold, I will bring flood of waters"

No matter how far one may fall spiritually, the Light of the Creator is always present the moment we decide to rise above our negativity. This awareness, together with the positive influences radiating from the text, is the way we can begin our ascent.

134. תּוּ פָּתַח וְאָמַר, וַאֲנִי הִנְנִי מֵבִיא אֶת הַמַּבּוּל מַיִם. מ"ט הִנְנִי, כֵּיוָן דַאֲמַר וַאֲנִי, אֶלָּא אֲנִי הִנְנִי, כֹּלָּא מִלָּה חָדָא הִיא. תָּא חֲזֵי בְּכָל אֲתַר אֲנִי, אִתְעֲבִיד גּוּפָא לְנִשְׁמָתָא, וַדַּאי, דִּמְקַבְּלָא מִמַּה דִּלְעֵילָא, וּבְגִין כָּךְ, אִתְרְמִיז בְּאָת קַיָּימָא, דִּכְתִיב אֲנִי הִנֵּה בְּרִיתִי אִתָּךְ, אֲנִי דְּקַיְימָא בְּאִתְגַּלְיָא, מְזוּמֶנֶת לְמִנְדַּע. אֲנִי, כָּרְסְיָא לְמַה דִּלְעֵילָא. אֲנִי, דַּעֲבִידְנָא נוּקְמִין לְדָרֵי דָרִין. וַאֲנִי, כָּלִיל דְּכַר וְנוּקְבָּא כַּחֲדָא, לְבָתַר אִתְרְשִׁים בִּלְחוֹדוֹי, דְּאִזְדַּמַּן לְמֶעְבַּד דִּינָא. הִנְנִי מֵבִיא אֶת הַמַּבּוּל מַיִם.

134. And he continued, quoting the verse: "And, behold I will (Myself) bring flood of waters" (Beresheet 6:17). HE ASKS: Why DOES THE VERSE SAY "Myself" after already saying "And I?" AND HE ANSWERS: The words "I" and "Myself" are the same. But, come and behold: wherever it is written "I," a body has been made for the soul. THIS MEANS THAT "I" IS THE FEMALE PRINCIPLE, WHICH IS AS A BODY FOR ZEIR ANPIN. CONVERSELY, ZEIR ANPIN IS CONSIDERED TO BE HER SOUL. And she certainly does receive from above, FROM ZEIR ANPIN. That is why THE WORD "I" is hinted in the sign of the covenant BY THE LETTER VAV (LIT. 'AND'), WHICH IS YESOD OF ZEIR ANPIN. As it is written: "As for Me (lit. 'I'), behold, My covenant is with you" (Beresheet 17:4), FOR THE FEMALE PRINCIPLE RECEIVES FROM THE COVENANT OF ZEIR ANPIN. "I" means that I am ready to be revealed and am achievable; "I" means that it is a throne of what is above; "I" means that I am the one who shall seek revenge for generations upon generations. But the words "and (Heb. ve) I," APPEARING IN THIS PASSAGE, INCLUDE THE LETTER VAV, AND refer to the union of the Male and Female. THE VAV OF "AND I" REFERS TO THE MALE, WHO IS ZEIR ANPIN. Afterwards, THE FEMALE PRINCIPLE is mentioned alone, WITHOUT ZEIR ANPIN, at the time when she is ready to execute Judgment, as it is written: "Myself, will bring the flood of waters upon the land."

135. כֵּיוָן דַּאֲמַר, מֵבִיא אֶת הַמַּבּוּל, לָא יִדְעֲנָא דְּאִיהוּ מַיִם, אֶלָּא אֶת הַמַּבּוּל, לְאַסְגָּאָה מַלְאַךְ הַמָּוֶת, דְּאַף עַל גַּב דְּמַיָּא הֲווֹ, מְחַבְּלָא אָזִיל בְּעָלְמָא, לְשֵׁיצָאָה בְּאִינוּן מַיִין.

135. HE ASKS: if it has been already stated, "will bring the flood," do we not understand that He refers to water? IF SO, WHY IS IT THEN NECESSARY TO MENTION "FLOOD OF WATERS?" AND HE ANSWERS: Flood implies the presence of the Angel of Death, even though it was only water. The Angel of Destruction went in the world to destroy it with these waters.

136. אֲנִי ה'. הָכֵי תָּנִינָן, נֶאֱמָן אֲנָא, לְשַׁלְּמָא אֲגַר טוֹב לְצַדִּיקַיָּא, וּלְאִתְפְּרַע מֵרַשִׁיעַיָּא, וּבְגִין כָּךְ, אַבְטַח לוֹן קְרָא לְצַדִּיקַיָּא, בָּאֲנִי, לְשַׁלְּמָא אֲגַר טַב דִּלְהוֹן, לְעָלְמָא דְּאָתֵי. וְאַגְזִים לְרַשִׁיעַיָּא, לְאִתְפְּרַע מִנַּיְיהוּ לְעָלְמָא דְּאָתֵי, בָּאֲנִי.

136. HE CONTINUED BY SAYING: We have learned that the words, "I am Hashem" show that 'I am faithful to the recompense of the righteous and the punishment of the wicked.' So, here, in this verse, "I" means to promise to reward and repay the righteous well in the World to Come. Likewise, it describes the threat to the wicked, who will be punished in the World to Come, by the term "I".

137. לְשַׁחֵת כָּל בָּשָׂר, כְּמָה דְּאוֹקִימְנָא, דְּדָא הוּא מְחַבְּלָא דְעָלְמָא. וְעַל דָּא כְּתִיב וְלֹא יִתֵּן הַמַּשְׁחִית לָבֹא אֶל בָּתֵּיכֶם לִנְגּוֹף. וְדָא הוּא לְשַׁחֵת כָּל בָּשָׂר, מִסִּטְרָא דְּקֵץ כָּל בָּשָׂר בָּא לְפָנַי. דְּהָא כֵּיוָן דְּמָטָא זִמְנָא, דְּאוֹרִיךְ לוֹן קֻדְשָׁא בְּרִיךְ הוּא, עַד דְּאַשְׁלִים נֹחַ לְשֵׁשׁ מֵאוֹת שָׁנָה, כְּדֵין לְשַׁחֵת כָּל בָּשָׂר. אָמַר הָכֵי אוֹלִיפְנָא מִשְּׁמֵיה דְּרַבִּי יִצְחָק דַּאֲמַר לָן.

137. As we previously explained, the words "To destroy all flesh" (Beresheet 6:17) refer to the Angel of Destruction. This is why it is also written: "And He will not allow the Angel of Destruction to come into your house to smite you" (Shemot 12:23). THIS MEANS THAT HE DOES NOT

GIVE HIM PERMISSION TO DESTROY. To "destroy all flesh" is from THE ANGEL OF DESTRUCTION, WHICH IS HINTED IN THE VERSE, "The End of all Flesh is come before Me," MEANING THAT HE CAME BEFORE HIM TO ASK PERMISSION TO DESTROY. The time the Holy One, blessed be He, had waited for them to repent had passed. That is, Noah had reached 600 years of age, AND IT WAS POSSIBLE TO REWARD HIM, TO UPHOLD THE REWARDING OF THE RIGHTEOUS. THE TIME HAD ALSO ARRIVED FOR THE PUNISHMENT OF THE WICKED. THAT IS WHY HE GAVE PERMISSION TO THE ANGEL OF DESTRUCTION "to destroy all flesh." He said: This is what we learned in the name of Rabbi Yitzchak, who told us all this.

18. "I said, I shall not see Yah"

Many dark forces attempt to sway us from our spiritual path, tempting our eyes with the illusions of physical reality. But we can draw the Light to assist us in seeing through these illusions. In this way, we can follow the path that leads to the Light of the Creator, rather than the path that leads to punishment.

138. פָּתַח וַאֲמַר, אָמַרְתִּי לֹא אֶרְאֶה יָהּ יָהּ בְּאֶרֶץ הַחַיִּים לֹא אַבִּיט אָדָם עוֹד עִם יוֹשְׁבֵי חָדֶל. אָמַרְתִּי לֹא אֶרְאֶה יָהּ, כַּמָּה אֲטִימִין אִינּוּן בְּנֵי נָשָׁא, דְּלָא יָדְעִין וְלָא מַשְׁגִּיחִין בְּמִלֵּי דְּאוֹרַיְיתָא, אֶלָּא מִסְתַּכְּלֵי בְּמִלּוֹי דְּעָלְמָא, וְאִתְנְשֵׁי מִנַּיְיהוּ רוּחָא דְחָכְמְתָא.

138. He began by saying, "I said, I shall not see Yah, Yah, in the land of the living; I shall behold man no more with the inhabitants of cessation" (Yeshayah 38:11). How obtuse, he said, are the people who do not know or pay heed to the words of the Torah, but look only upon worldly matters. The spirit of wisdom is forgotten from them.

139. דְּכַד בַּר נָשׁ אִסְתַּלָּק מֵהַאי עָלְמָא, וְיָהִיב חוּשְׁבְּנָא לְמָארֵיהּ, מִכָּל מַה דַּעֲבַד בְּהַאי עָלְמָא, בְּעוֹד דְּאִיהוּ קָאֵים רוּחָא וְגוּפָא כַּחֲדָא, וְחָמֵי מַה דְּחָמֵי, עַד דְּאָזִיל לְהַהוּא עָלְמָא, וּפָגַע לֵיהּ לְאָדָם הָרִאשׁוֹן, יָתִיב לְתַרְעָא דְּגִנְתָּא דְעֵדֶן, לְמֶחֱמֵי כָּל אִינּוּן, דְּנַטְרוּ פִּקּוּדֵי דְמָארֵיהוֹן, וְחָדֵי בְּהוּ.

139. When a person departs this world, that person gives an account to his Master of all his worldy actions. He does this while his body and spirit are still joined together and he can see all that he sees until he reaches the World of Truth, where he meets Adam, the first man, sitting at the gate of the Garden of Eden, waiting to see and rejoice with all who have observed the commandments of their Master.

140. וְכַמָּה צַדִּיקַיָּא סַחֲרָנֵיהּ דְּאָדָם, אִינּוּן דְּאִתְמַנְעוּ מֵאָרְחָא דְּגֵיהִנֹּם, וְסָטוּ לְגַבֵּי אָרְחָא דְּגַן עֵדֶן· וְאִלֵּין אִקְרוּן יוֹשְׁבֵי חָדֶל. וְלָא כְּתִיב יוֹשְׁבֵי חָלֶד, בְּגִין דְּלָא הֲווֹ כְּמוֹ חוּלְדָּה דְּגָרְרָא, וּמַנְחָא, וְלָא יָדְעָא לְמַאן

שַׁבְקָא, אֶלָּא יוֹשְׁבֵי חָדֶל. כד״א חִדְלוּ לָכֶם מִן הָאָדָם וגו'. דְּאִתְמְנַע
לוֹן מֵאָרְחָא דְּגֵיהִנֹּם וְאִתְקִיפוּ בְּהוּ לְאַעֲלָא לְהוּ בְּגִנְתָּא דְּעֵדֶן.

140. And many are the righteous around Adam, who instead of walking along the path that leads to Gehenom, followed the path to the Garden of Eden. These are the ones who are called "Inhabitants of the Cessation" (Heb. *chedel*). AND HE ASKS: Why is it not written: "Inhabitants of the world (Heb. *cheled*)"? HE ANSWERS: Because they are not like the mole (Heb. *chulda*), a creature who is laboriously storing and hiding provisions, knowing not for whom. They are the inhabitants of cessation, as in "Cease (Heb. *chidlu*) from man, though his breath be in his nostrils" (Yeshayah 2:22). BECAUSE THE HEBREW WORD *CHEDEL* MEANS TO AVOID, THEY ARE CALLED THE INHABITANTS OF CESSATION. They avoided walking the path of Gehenom and disciplined themselves to walk along the path leading to the Garden of Eden.

141. דָּבָר אַחֵר יוֹשְׁבֵי חָדֶל אִינוּן מָרֵיהוֹן דִּתְשׁוּבָה, דִּמְנָעוּ גַרְמַיְיהוּ
מֵאִינוּן חוֹבִין דְּחַיָּיבַיָּא, וּבְגִין דְּאָדָם הָרִאשׁוֹן, תָּב בְּתִיוּבְתָּא קַמֵּי
מָארֵיהּ, יָתִיב עַל אִינוּן דְּאִתְמְנָעוּ מֵחוֹבֵיהוֹן, וְאִינוּן בְּנֵי חָדֶל, כד״א
אֵדְעָה מֶה חָדֵל אָנִי. וּבְגִין כָּךְ אִיהוּ יָתִיב לְתַרְעָא דְּגִנְתָּא דְּעֵדֶן, וְחָדֵי
בְּהוּ בְּצַדִּיקַיָּיא, דְּאַתְיָין בְּהַהוּא אוֹרְחָא דְּגִנְתָּא דְּעֵדֶן.

141. Another explanation is that "inhabitants of cessation" REFERS TO all those who repented and ceased performing the sins of the wicked. Because Adam repented before his Master, he sits among others who also repented, ceased sinning, and are called "inhabitants of cessation." As it is written: "I will know how frail (Heb. *chadel*) I am" (Tehilim 39:5). And therefore, Adam sits at the gate of the Garden of Eden, and he is happy with the righteous who walk along the path and arrive at the Garden of Eden.

142. תָּא חֲזֵי, מַה כְּתִיב, אָמַרְתִּי לֹא אֶרְאֶה יָהּ, וְכִי מַאן יָכִיל לְמֶחֱמֵי
יָהּ. אֶלָּא סוֹפָא דִּקְרָא אוֹכַח, דִּכְתִיב יָהּ בְּאֶרֶץ הַחַיִּים, תָּא חֲזֵי, כַּד
סַלְקִין נִשְׁמָתִין לַאֲתַר צְרוֹרָא דְּחַיֵּי, תַּמָּן מִתְהַנָּן, בְּזָהֲרָא דְּאִסְפַּקְלַרְיָאה
דְּנָהֲרָא, דְּנָהִיר מֵאֲתַר עִלָּאָה דְּכֹלָּא, וְאִילוּ לָא מִתְלַבְּשָׁא נִשְׁמָתָא,
בְּזָהֲרָא דִּלְבוּשָׁא אָחֳרָא, לָא תֵּיכוֹל לְאִתְקָרְבָא לְמֶחֱמֵי הַהוּא נְהוֹרָא.

142. Come and behold: it is written: "I said, I shall not see Yah." So HE ASKS: Who can ever see Yah now? AND HE REPLIES THAT the end of the verse reveals the intention of the words, as it is written: "Yah, in the land of the living." Come and behold: when the souls ascend and reach the place of the Bundle of Life, they enjoy the illumination of the radiant mirror, which shines and brings forth light from the most elevated place of all. A soul not enclothed in the radiance of another garment could neither approach nor get close enough to see that light.

143. וְרָזָא דְמִלָּה, כְּמָה דְּיַהֲבֵי לְנִשְׁמָתָא, לְבוּשָׁא דְּמִתְלַבְּשָׁא בֵּיהּ, לְמֵיקַם בְּהַאי עָלְמָא. הָכִי נָמֵי יַהֲבֵי לָהּ לְבוּשָׁא, דְּזָהֲרָא עִלָּאָה, לְמֵיקַם בֵּיהּ בְּהַהוּא עָלְמָא, וּלְאִסְתַּכְּלָא בְּגוֹ הַהוּא אַסְפַּקְלַרְיָאה דְּנָהֲרָא, מִגּוֹ הַהוּא אֶרֶץ הַחַיִּים.

143. And the secret of the matter is that as the soul is given garments to don so it can exist in this world, WHICH IS THE BODY, so it is also given garments of supernal radiance. These allow it to exist in the World to Come and to see into the radiant mirror, WHICH IS ZEIR ANPIN, from that land of the living, THE FEMALE PRINCIPLE OF ZEIR ANPIN. THUS THE PROBLEM THAT AROSE IN THE VERSE, "I SAID, I SHALL NOT SEE YAH," IS SOLVED. THE INTENTION IS THAT BY THESE TWO IMPLEMENTS – (1) BY THE GARMENT OF THE SUPERNAL RADIANCE AND (2) BY THE FEMALE PRINCIPLE OF ZEIR ANPIN, CALLED THE LAND OF OF LIVING – THE RIGHTEOUS PEOPLE DESERVE TO SEE INTO THE RADIANT MIRROR, WHICH IS THE SECRET OF YAH (YUD-HEI) IN THE LAND OF THE LIVING.

144. תָּא חֲזֵי, מֹשֶׁה לָא יָכִיל לְקָרְבָא. לְאִסְתַּכְּלָא, בַּמֶּה דְּאִסְתַּכַּל, אֶלָּא כַּד אִתְלַבַּשׁ בִּלְבוּשָׁא אָחֳרָא, כְּדֵ"א וַיָּבֹא מֹשֶׁה בְּתוֹךְ הֶעָנָן וַיַּעַל אֶל הָהָר. וְתַרְגּוּם בִּמְצִיעוּת עֲנָנָא. וְאִתְלַבַּשׁ בָּהּ, כְּמַאן דְּאִתְלַבַּשׁ בִּלְבוּשָׁא, וּבְגַ"ד, וּמֹשֶׁה נִגַּשׁ אֶל הָעֲרָפֶל אֲשֶׁר שָׁם הָאֱלֹקִים, וּכְתִיב וַיָּבֹא מֹשֶׁה בְּתוֹךְ הֶעָנָן וְגוֹ'. וַיְהִי מֹשֶׁה בָּהָר אַרְבָּעִים יוֹם וְאַרְבָּעִים לַיְלָה. וְיָכִיל לְאִסְתַּכְּלָא בַּמֶּה דְּאִסְתַּכַּל.

144. Come and behold: Moses would not have been able to approach what he was looking at had he not been dressed in another garment. As it is written: "And Moses went into the midst of the cloud, and went up into the mountain" (Shemot 24:18). And he covered himself with the cloud as a person wears a garment. And then, it is written: "and Moses drew near to the thick darkness where Elohim was" (Shemot 20:18), and "Moses was in the mountain forty days and forty nights" (Shemot 24:18) and was able to see what he saw.

145. כְּגַוְונָא דָא, מִתְלַבְּשִׁין נִשְׁמַתְהוֹן דְּצַדִּיקַיָּא, בְּהַהוּא עָלְמָא, בִּלְבוּשָׁא, כְּגַוְונָא דְּהַהוּא עָלְמָא, דְּלָא יִתְנַהֵג אֶלָּא בִּלְבוּשָׁא, כְּגַוְונָא דָא. וְקַיְימֵי לְאִסְתַּכְּלָא בִּנְהוֹרָא דְּנָהִיר, בְּהַהוּא אֶרֶץ הַחַיִּים. וְזֶהוּ יָהּ, יָהּ בְּאֶרֶץ הַחַיִּים. דַּהֲוָה סָבִיר דְּלָא יִזְכֵּי לְהַהוּא נְהוֹרָא, וּלְהַהוּא אִסְתַּכְּלוּתָא, בְּגִין דְּנַהֲרָא דְּנָגִיד, פָּסִיק לֵיהּ, וְלָא אוֹלִיד. לֹא אַבִּיט אָדָם עוֹד, דָּא אָדָם קַדְמָאָה כְּמָה דְּאִתְּמַר.

145. In the same way, the souls of the righteous in the World of Truth dress themselves in garments and act in accordance with that world. So dressed, they are prepared to gaze into the light that shines in the land of the living, MEANING THAT THEY COVER THEMSELVES WITH THE LIGHT OF THE FEMALE PRINCIPLE, FROM WHICH THEY ARE ABLE TO GAZE INTO THE LIGHT OF THE RADIANT MIRROR. WHEN HEZEKIAH CALLED, "Yah, Yah, in the land of the living," he was afraid that he might no longer be worthy of gazing on that light and meriting that vision. The stream that flows FROM THE GARDEN OF EDEN, he stopped it, and did not beget any children. AND WHOEVER DOES NOT INDULGE IN THE ACT OF PROCREATION, BLEMISHES THE RIVER THAT FLOWS FROM THE GARDEN OF EDEN, WHICH IS YESOD OF ZEIR ANPIN. THIS IS INDICATED IN THE VERSE: "I shall behold man no more." This refers to the first man, as has already been explained. ADAM SITS AT THE GATE OF THE GARDEN OF EDEN AND RECEIVES THE SOULS OF THE RIGHTEOUS WHO ARRIVE THERE. HEZEKIAH FEARED THAT HE WAS NOT WORTHY OF SEEING ADAM AT THE GATE.

146. וְכָל דָּא לָמָה, בְּגִין דַּאֲמַר לֵיהּ נְבִיאָה, כִּי מֵת אַתָּה, בְּהַאי עָלְמָא, וְלָא תִחְיֶה, לְהַהוּא עָלְמָא, בְּגִין דְּמַאן דְּלָא אוֹלִיד בְּנִין בְּהַאי עָלְמָא, כַּד נָפִיק מִנֵּיהּ, מִתַּרְכִין לֵיהּ, מִכָּל מַה דַּאֲמָרָן, וְלָא שַׁרְיָא

לְמֶחֱמֵי בְּהַהוּא נְהוֹרָא דְּנָהֵיר. וּמַה חִזְקִיָּה, דַּהֲוָה לֵיהּ זְכוּת אָבוֹת, וְאִיהוּ זַכָּאָה צַדִּיקָא וַחֲסִידָא כָּךְ, כָּל שֶׁכֵּן מַאן דְּלֵית לֵיהּ זְכוּת אָבוֹת וְחָטֵי קַמֵּי מָארֵיהּ.

146. And what was the reason for all this, NAMELY WHY DID HEZEKIAH FEAR THIS? Because the prophet told him, "for you shall die" in this world "and not live" (Yeshayah 38:11) in the World of Truth. For, upon death, he who has not begotten any children in this world is expelled from all that is mentioned above and cannot stay to gaze upon that shining light. If this was the case with Hezekiah, who was a pure, righteous man, so much more for those who do not have ancestral merit to support them and have even sinned before their Master.

147. הַאי לְבוּשָׁא דְּקָאֲמָרָן, אִיהוּ מַה דַּאֲמָרוּ חַבְרַיָּיא, חֲלוּקָא דְּרַבָּנָן, דְּאִתְלְבִישׁוּ בְּהַהוּא עָלְמָא. זַכָּאָה חוּלָקֵיהוֹן דְּצַדִּיקַיָּיא, דְּגָנֵיז לוֹן קֻדְשָׁא בְּרִיךְ הוּא, כַּמָּה טָבִין וְעִידוּנִין, לְהַהוּא עָלְמָא, עֲלַיְיהוּ כְּתִיב, עַיִן לֹא רָאָתָה אֱלֹקִים זוּלָתְךָ יַעֲשֶׂה לִמְחַכֵּה לוֹ.

147. This garment, previously mentioned, has already been discussed by the friends. There is a "robe of the sages" that they wear in the World of Truth. Happy are the righteous with their inheritance, as the Holy One, blessed be He, has put aside many blessings and delights for them in the World of Truth. It has been written of them: "Neither has the eye seen, that an Elohim, beside You, should do such a thing for him that waits for Him" (Yeshayah 64:3).

19. "And, behold, I will bring the flood of waters," part two

The spiritual insight conveyed here by the Zohar concerns an individual who commits a terrible deed, but still retains a spark of shame, a degree of embarrassment, or a slight awareness of the wrongfulness of his actions. There is still hope for this person and the path of repentance remains open to him. But those who commit wanton acts of evil, without any remorse for their actions, are considered to be past the point of no return. This section helps us maintain awareness of what constitutes positive and negative spiritual actions.

148. וַאֲנִי הִנְנִי מֵבִיא אֶת הַמַּבּוּל מַיִם עַל הָאָרֶץ, ר' יְהוּדָה פְּתַח, הֵמָּה מֵי מְרִיבָה אֲשֶׁר רָבוּ בְנֵי יִשְׂרָאֵל אֶת ה' וַיִּקָּדֵשׁ בָּם, וְכִי בַּאֲתַר אָחֳרָא לֹא רָבוּ בְּנֵי יִשְׂרָאֵל אֶת ה', מ"ש הָכָא דְּקָאָמַר הֵמָּה מֵי מְרִיבָה, וְלָא אָחֳרָנִין. אֶלָּא הַנֵּי מֵי מְרִיבָה הֲווֹ וַדַּאי, דְּיָהֲבוּ חֵילָא וְתוּקְפָּא לְמָארֵיהוֹן דְּדִינָא לְאִתְתַּקְּפָא, בְּגִין דְּאִית מַיִין מְתוּקִין, וְאִית מַיִין מְרִירָן, אִית מַיִין צְלִילָן, וְאִית מַיִין עֲכִירָן, אִית מַיִין שְׁלָם, וְאִית מַיִין קְטָטוּ. וְע"ד הֵמָּה מֵי מְרִיבָה אֲשֶׁר רָבוּ בְּנֵי יִשְׂרָאֵל אֶת ה', דְּאַמְשִׁיכוּ עֲלַיְיהוּ, לְמַאן דְּלָא אִצְטְרִיךְ, וְאִסְתְּאָבוּ בֵּיהּ, הֲדָא הוּא דִכְתִיב וַיִּקָּדֵשׁ בָּם.

148. "And, behold, I will bring the flood of waters upon the earth" (Beresheet 6:17). Rabbi Yehuda opened the discussion with the verse: "These are the waters of strife, wherein the children of Yisrael strove with Hashem and He was sanctified by them" (Bemidbar 20:13). AND HE ASKS: This is not the only place where the children of Yisrael strove with Hashem. Why does the text say "waters of strife" here, but not at any other place? AND HE REPLIES: These waters in particular are the waters of strife, for they gave strength and power to the Prosecutor. There are sweet water and bitter waters, WHICH ARE THE SECRET OF HOLINESS AND ITS OPPOSITE – OF THE RIGHT COLUMN. And there are pure and mucky waters, WHICH ARE THE SECRET OF HOLINESS AND ITS OPPOSITE – OF THE LEFT COLUMN. And there are waters of peace and of strife, WHICH ARE THE SECRET OF HOLINESS AND ITS OPPOSITE – OF THE CENTRAL COLUMN. That is why IT IS WRITTEN: "These are the waters of strife, wherein the children of Yisrael strove with Hashem," THIS SHOWS THAT THE WATERS REFERS TO THE OPPOSITE SIDE OF THE CENTRAL COLUMN. As they drew

upon themselves that which they should not have DRAWN, NAMELY THE OPPOSITE SIDE, CALLED THE WATERS OF STRIFE and they were defiled by them. And this is why it is written: "and He was sanctified by them."

149. אָמַר לוֹ רַבִּי חִזְקָיָה, אִי הָכֵי, מַאי וַיִּקַּדֵשׁ, וַיִּקַּדְשׁוּ מִבָּעֵי לֵיהּ, אֶלָּא מִלָּה אִסְתְּלִיקַת, וַיִּקַּדֵשׁ, אִתְפְּגַם מַאן דְּלָא אִצְטְרִיךְ, כִּבְיָכוֹל, דְּאִתְפְּגֵימַת סִיהֲרָא. וַיִּקַּדֵשׁ לָאו לִשְׁבָחָא אִיהוּ הָכָא. וַאֲנִי הִנְנִי מֵבִיא אֶת הַמַּבּוּל, כְּמָה דְּאוֹקִימְנָא, לְאַיְיתָאָה מְחַבְּלָא עֲלַיְיהוּ, כְּמָה דְּאִינוּן אִסְתָּאֲבוּ בֵּיהּ.

149. Rabbi Chizkiyah asked him: If it is so, then why is it written: "and He was sanctified,"? It should have been written: 'and they were sanctified' IN THE PLURAL, REFERRING TO THE CHILDREN OF YISRAEL. AND HE REPLIES THAT there is a hidden meaning to the words "He was sanctified." THEY INDICATE THAT something that should not be damaged is damaged. It is as if the moon, WHICH IS THE FEMALE PRINCIPLE, has been damaged. So the word "sanctified" is not mentioned here for praise, WHICH ACCOUNTS FOR THE DISCRETION EXPRESSED IN THE SCRIPTURES. AND RABBI YEHUDA CONCLUDED THAT "And, behold, I will bring the flood of waters" means that He shall send the Angel of Destruction upon them, just as they defiled themselves with him, as we have stated previously.

150. אָמַר רַבִּי יוֹסֵי, וַוי לוֹן לְרַשִּׁיעַיָּא, דְּלָא בָּעָאן לְאָתָבָא, קַמֵּי קֻדְשָׁא בְּרִיךְ הוּא עַל חוֹבֵיהוֹן בְּעוֹד דְּאִינוּן בְּהַאי עָלְמָא, דְּכַד בַּ"נ אָתֵיב, וְאִתְנַחָם עַל חוֹבוֹי, קֻדְשָׁא בְּרִיךְ הוּא מָחִיל לֵיהּ. וְכָל אִינוּן דְּמִתְתַּקְּפִין בְּחוֹבַיְיהוּ, וְלָא בָּעֵי לְאָתָבָא קַמֵּי קֻדְשָׁא בְּרִיךְ הוּא עַל חוֹבֵיהוֹן, לְבָתַר יִנְפְּלוּ לַגֵּיהִנֹּם וְלָא יִסְקוּן לֵיהּ מִתַּמָּן לְעָלְמִין.

150. Rabbi Yosi said: Woe to the wicked who do not want to repent of their sins before the Holy One blessed be He, while they are still in this world, because when a person repents and feels sorry for his sins, then the Holy One, blessed be He, forgives him. But those who cling to their sins and refuse to repent will eventually fall into Gehenom and never be brought up again.

151. תָּא חֲזֵי, בְּגִין דְּאִתְקִיפוּ לְבַּיְיהוּ, כָּל אִינּוּן דָּרָא דְּנֹחַ, וּבָעוּ
לְאַחֲזָאָה חוֹבַיְיהוּ בְּאִתְגַּלְיָא, קֻדְשָׁא בְּרִיךְ הוּא אַיְיתֵי דִינָא עֲלַיְיהוּ,
בְּהַהוּא גַּוְונָא. אָמַר רַבִּי יִצְחָק, וַאֲפִילוּ כַּד חָטֵי ב"נ בְּאִתְכַּסְיָא, קֻדְשָׁא
בְּרִיךְ הוּא רַחֲמָן, וְאִי תָּב ב"נ לְגַבֵּיה, חָפֵי עֲלֵיה, וּמָחִיל לֵיה וְשָׁבִיק
לֵיה, וְאִי לָא, גָּלֵי לֵיה לְעֵינֵי כֹלָּא, מְנָלָן, מִסּוֹטָה.

151. Come and behold: Because the generation of Noah was stubborn and bold enough to sin openly, the Holy One, blessed be He, brought Judgment upon them in the same manner. Rabbi Yitzchak said that if a person sins, and he does so secretly, then the Holy One, blessed be He, is merciful. If he repents, he is pardoned and forgiven. But if he does not repent his sins, He reveals them for all to see. How do we know this? We learn this from the way in which the faithless wife WHO SINS SECRETLY IS TREATED AND FROM HOW THE HOLY ONE, BLESSED BE HE, REVEALS HER SIN OUT IN THE OPEN WITH THE CURSING WATERS.

152. וְהָכֵי נָמֵי אִתְמְחוּן אִלֵּין חַיָּיבַיָּא מֵאַרְעָא בְּאִתְגַּלְיָא, וְהֵיךְ
אִתְמְחוּן. אֶלָּא דַּהֲווֹ נָפְקֵי מַיָּיא, וַהֲווֹ רְתִיחָן, מִן תְּהוֹמָא, וְסָלְקֵי
וְאַעֲבַר מִנַּיְיהוּ מָשְׁכָא, וְכֵיוָן דְּאַעֲבַר מִנַּיְיהוּ מָשְׁכָא, הָכֵי נָמֵי בִּשְׂרָא,
וְלָא אִשְׁתְּאָרוּ אֶלָּא בְּגַרְמַיְיהוּ לְחוֹד, לְקַיְימָא דִכְתִיב וַיִּמָּחוּ מִן הָאָרֶץ.
וְכָל אִינּוּן גַּרְמֵי, אִתְפָּרְדָן דָּא מִן דָּא, וְלָא אִשְׁתְּאָרוּ כַּחֲדָא, וּמִכֹּלָּא
אִתְעֲבָרוּ מֵעָלְמָא. רַבִּי יִצְחָק אָמַר, וַיִּמָּחוּ מִן הָאָרֶץ, מַאי וַיִּמָּחוּ, כד"א
יִמָּחוּ מִסֵּפֶר חַיִּים, מִכָּאן אוֹלִיפְנָא דְּלֵית לוֹן תְּחִיָּה לְעָלְמִין, וְלָא
יְקוּמוּן בְּדִינָא.

152. In the same manner, the wicked, NAMELY THE GENERATION OF THE FLOOD, were openly destroyed and wiped from the face of the earth. And how were they wiped out? The scalding waters spurted up from the abyss, skinning them alive. As skin was torn from flesh, they were left only with their bones – and then the bones came asunder. As it is written: "They were destroyd from the earth" (Beresheet 7:23). Rabbi Yitzchak said: "And they destroyed from the earth." What is meant by the expression "destroyed out?" It is similar to, "Let them be blotted out from the book of living"

(Tehilim 69:29). We learn from this that they shall not participate in the resurrection and will not stand for judgment.

20. "But with you will I establish My covenant"

The vital importance of the *Covenant* between man and God can remain in our consciousness through the spiritual forces released by the letters of this section. This *Covenant* is founded primarily upon the greatest power that humanity was given for revealing spiritual Light into this world and into our own lives – that is, sexual relations between husband and wife. The Kabbalists teach us that because this action has the most potential and influence for revealing Light, it is given the most attention by the Evil Inclination and the negative forces that dwell in our midst.

153. וַהֲקִימוֹתִי אֶת בְּרִיתִי אִתָּךְ, אָמַר ר' אֶלְעָזָר, מֵהָכָא קַיּוּמָא דִּבְרִית לְעֵילָא, כְּקִיּוּמָא דִּבְרִית לְתַתָּא, מַשְׁמַע דִּכְתִיב אִתָּךְ. וְאָמַר רַבִּי אֶלְעָזָר, מִכָּאן אוֹלִיפְנָא, דְּכַד זַכָּאִין אִינוּן בְּעָלְמָא, אִתְקַיַּים עָלְמָא לְעֵילָא וְתַתָּא.

153. "But with you will I establish My covenant" (Beresheet 6:18). Rabbi Elazar said that from this we learn that the establishment of the covenant above is equivalent to the establishment of that below. This is concluded from the term, "with you." Rabbi Elazar continued to say that from this we learn that when there are righteous in the world, the worlds above and below are firmly established.

154. אָמַר רַבִּי שִׁמְעוֹן מִלָּה סְתִים אִיהוּ, כַּד אִתְעֲרוּתָא דִּדְכוּרָא לְגַבֵּי נוּקְבָא, כַּד אִיהוּ מְקַנֵּי לָהּ. תָּא חֲזֵי, רָזָא דְּמִלָּה, כַּד צַדִּיקָא אִיהוּ בְּעָלְמָא, מִיָּד שְׁכִינְתָּא לָא אִתְעֲדִיאַת מִנֵּיהּ, וְתֵיאוּבְתָּא דִּילֵהּ בֵּיהּ, כְּדֵין תֵּיאוּבְתָּא דִּלְעֵילָא לְגַבָּהּ בִּרְחִימוּ, כְּתֵיאוּבְתָּא דִּדְכוּרָא לְנוּקְבֵיהּ, כַּד אִיהוּ מְקַנֵּי לָהּ, וְעַל דָּא וַהֲקִימוֹתִי אֶת בְּרִיתִי אִתָּךְ. אִתְעַר תֵּיאוּבְתָּא בְּגִינָךְ. כְּגַוְונָא דָּא וְאֶת בְּרִיתִי אָקִים אֶת יִצְחָק.

154. Rabbi Shimon said that this is a hidden matter, because the arousal of the male to the female happens when he feels jealousy toward her. Come and behold: When there is a righteous person in the world, the Shechinah immediately attaches Herself to him and never leaves him. And She therefore desires him. The upper desire is then aroused toward Her with

love that is similar to the desire of a man for a woman when he feels jealousy toward her. That is why it is written: "But with you will I establish My covenant." THIS MEANS THAT My desire is aroused because of you. The verse, "My covenant will I establish with Isaac" (Beresheet 17:21), has a similar meaning THAT IT IS BECAUSE OF ISAAC, AS BY NOAH.

155. וַהֲקִימוֹתִי אֶת בְּרִיתִי אִתָּךְ, לְמֶהֱוֵי אָת בְּרִיתִי בְּעָלְמָא, וּלְבָתַר וּבָאתָ אֶל הַתֵּיבָה, דְּאִלְמָלֵא לָאו אִיהוּ צַדִּיק, לָא יֵיעוֹל לְתֵיבוּתָא, דְּהָא לָא אִתְחַבַּר לַתֵּיבָה, בַּר צַדִּיק, וּבְגִינֵי כָּךְ, וּבָאתָ אֶל הַתֵּיבָה, וְהָא אִתְּמַר.

155. "But with you will I establish My covenant," MEANS THAT you shall be My covenant in the world. And after that, "and you shall come into the ark." Because had he not been righteous, he would not have entered the ark, as only a righteous man may be connected with the ark. That is why it is written: "you shall come into the ark," AFTER IT HAS BEEN STATED THAT "WITH YOU WILL I ESTABLISH MY COVENANT."

156. אָמַר רַבִּי אֶלְעָזָר, בְּכָל זִמְנָא, דִּבְנֵי נָשָׁא, יִתְאַחֲדוּן בִּבְרִית דָּא, וְלָא יִשְׁבְּקוּן לֵיהּ, לֵית עַם וְלִישָׁן בְּעָלְמָא, דְּיֵיכוֹל לְאַבְאָשָׁא לוֹן, וְנֹחַ אַתְקִיף בִּבְרִית דָּא, וְנָטַר לֵיהּ, בְּגִינֵי כָּךְ, קֻדְשָׁא בְּרִיךְ הוּא נָטַר לֵיהּ. וְכָל בְּנֵי דָרֵיהּ לָא נָטְרוּ לֵיהּ, בְּגִין כָּךְ קֻדְשָׁא בְּרִיךְ הוּא אַעֲבַר לוֹן מֵעָלְמָא, וְהָא אִתְּמַר, בְּהַהוּא חוֹבָא מַמָּשׁ, דְּאִינוּן חָאבוּ, בְּהַהוּא גַּוְונָא אִתְמְחוּן מֵעָלְמָא.

156. Rabbi Elazar said that as long as people hold on to the covenant, no nation nor tongue in the world can harm them. And because Noah kept and protected the Covenant, the Holy One, blessed be He, protected him. But the rest of his generation did not observe the covenant, so the Holy One, blessed be He, removed them from the world. And it has been said that in the same way that they sinned, they were also erased from the world.

21. "And he repaired the altar of Hashem that was broken down"

The *covenant* between mankind and God connects to the Sfirah of *Yesod*, which correlates to the reproductive organs of man. There is also a vital spiritual link to the circumcision of a newborn male child.

The underlying lesson of this section is the Kabbalistic doctrine that all war, natural disasters, famine, slaughter, and massacre can be traced to destructive spiritual forces arising from humanity's negative sexual acts. Negative sexual acts are defined as those that are not for the purpose of procreation or for the bringing of Light to the world.

Sexual relations between man and wife mirror the metaphysical forces at work in the Upper Worlds. The male corresponds to the realm of *Yesod*, and the woman to the world of *Malchut*. Whenever any kind of positive Light and fulfillment reaches our lives, it is a direct result of the enjoining of *Yesod* and *Malchut*.

Sexual relations accomplish this mating of the two Upper Worlds. However, negative forces constantly try to sever this connection. These negative forces are so cunning and clever, they have deceived us into believing they do not even exist.

Through our own meditation and desire to share, the power of these words of the Zohar can awaken a genuine understanding of the role sexual relations play in the revelation of Light into the world.

157. רַבִּי יְהוּדָה הֲוָה שְׁכִיחַ קַמֵּיהּ דְּר"שׁ, וַהֲווֹ עָסְקֵי בְּהַאי קְרָא דִּכְתִיב וַיְרַפֵּא אֶת מִזְבַּח ה' הֶהָרוּס. מַאי וַיְרַפֵּא, תָּא חֲזֵי, בִּימֵי אֵלִיָּהוּ, יִשְׂרָאֵל כֻּלְּהוּ שָׁבְקוּ לֵיהּ לְקֻדְשָׁא בְּרִיךְ הוּא, וְשָׁבְקוּ בְּרִית קַיָּימָא דִּלְהוֹן, כַּד אָתָא אֵלִיָּהוּ וְחָמָא דְּקָא שָׁבְקוּ בְּנֵי יִשְׂרָאֵל הַאי בְּרִית קַיָּימָא, וְאַעֲבָרוּ מִנַּיְיהוּ הַאי בְּרִית.

157. Rabbi Yehuda was sitting before Rabbi Shimon, and both were studying the text, in which it is written: "And he repaired the altar of Hashem that was broken down" (I Melachim 18:30). What is the meaning of the term 'repaired' in this verse? Come and behold: "In the days of Elijah, all Yisrael left the Holy One, blessed be He, and in so doing, left their holy covenant. And when Elijah came and saw that the children of Yisrael had

left the holy covenant and therefore it had been taken away from them, HE FIXED IT AND BROUGHT IT BACK TO ITS PLACE. THAT IS, HE FIXED YESOD, MAKING IT CAPABLE OF MATING WITH MALCHUT. AND THIS IS CONSIDERED TO BE THE REPAIR OF THE ALTAR, WHICH IS MALCHUT, AS SHALL BE FURTHER EXPLAINED.

158. כֵּיוָן דְּחָמָא אֵלִיָּהוּ כָּךְ, אָתָא לְאַתְקָנָא מִלָּה לְדוּכְתֵּיה, כֵּיוָן דְּקָרִיב מִלָּה לְדוּכְתֵּיה, אִתְסֵי כֹּלָּא, הה"ד וַיְרַפֵּא אֶת מִזְבַּח ה' הֶהָרוּס, דָּא בְּרִית קַיָּימָא, דַּהֲוָה שָׁבִיק מֵעָלְמָא. וּכְתִיב וַיִּקַּח אֵלִיָּהוּ שְׁתֵּים עֶשְׂרֵה אֲבָנִים לְמִסְפַּר שִׁבְטֵי בְנֵי יַעֲקֹב, דָּא הוּא תִּקּוּנָא דְּמִזְבַּח ה'.

158. Because he brought it back to its place, NAMELY BECAUSE HE REPAIRED YESOD AND BROUGHT IT BACK TO MALCHUT, all was healed! This is why it is written: "And he repaired the altar of Hashem that was broken down" – a reference to the covenant that had been forsaken. It is therefore written: "And Elijah took twelve stones, according to the number of the tribes of the sons of Jacob" (Ibid. 31), which alludes to the repair of the altar of Hashem, THE FIXING OF THE DAMAGE AND THE 'HEALING' OF THE ALTAR.

159. אֲשֶׁר הָיָה דְבַר ה' אֵלָיו לֵאמֹר יִשְׂרָאֵל יִהְיֶה שְׁמֶךָ. מ"ט אִדְכַּר הָכָא יִשְׂרָאֵל, אֶלָּא וַדַּאי יִשְׂרָאֵל יִהְיֶה שְׁמֶךָ, וַדַּאי לְאִסְתַּלְקָא לְעֵילָּא, וְלַאֲתָבָא בְּרִית קַיָּימָא לְאַתְרֵיה, וְהַיְינוּ דִּכְתִיב כִּי עָזְבוּ בְרִיתְךָ בְּנֵי יִשְׂרָאֵל, וּבְגִין כָּךְ, אֶת מִזְבְּחוֹתֶיךָ הָרָסוּ.

159. "To whom the word of Hashem came, saying, Yisrael shall be your name" (Ibid.). HE ASKS: What is the reason for mentioning the name 'Yisrael' upon the altar? AND HE ANSWERS: Assuredly, "Yisrael shall be your name..." signifies FIXING HER to raise her up, NAMELY TO RAISE MALCHUT TO THE SUPERNAL ABA AND IMA, and to return the holy covenant to its place. IT SIGNIFIES THAT YESOD OF ZEIR ANPIN COULD UNITE AGAIN WITH MALCHUT, FOR THERE CAN BE NO UNION BETWEEN ZEIR ANPIN AND MALCHUT UNLESS THEY RETURN TO THE PLACES OF ABA AND IMA. That is why it is written: "For the children of Yisrael have forsaken Your covenant" and have therefore "ruined Your altars" (I Melachim 19:10), WHICH IS MALCHUT. AND BY THE SECRET OF FIXING

OF THE COVENANT, SHE SHALL BE REBUILT.

160. תָּא חֲזֵי, כָּל זִמְנָא דְּיִשְׂרָאֵל נָטְרוּ קְיָימָא קַדִּישָׁא, כְּדֵין עָבְדֵי
קִיּוּמָא, לְעֵילָּא וְתַתָּא. וְכַד שָׁבְקֵי לְהַאי בְּרִית, כְּדֵין לָא אִשְׁתְּכַח קִיּוּם
לְעֵילָּא וְתַתָּא. דִּכְתִיב אִם לֹא בְרִיתִי יוֹמָם וָלַיְלָה חֻקּוֹת שָׁמַיִם וָאָרֶץ
לֹא שָׂמְתִּי, וּבְגִין כָּךְ, וַיְרַפֵּא אֶת מִזְבַּח ה' הֶהָרוּס. וְכִי רְפוּאָה אִיהוּ.
הָכִי הוּא וַדַּאי, דְּהָא מְקַיֵּים לְהַהוּא אֲתָר, דִּמְהֵימְנוּתָא תַּלְיָא בֵּיה.

160. Come and behold: As long as Yisrael observed the holy covenant, they maintain the higher and lower worlds. But when they forsake the covenant, the worlds above and below cannot exist. As it is written: "If My covenant be not day and night, it were as if I had not appointed the ordinances of heaven and earth" (Yirmeyah 33:25). This is why it is written: "And he repaired the altar of Hashem that was broken down." HE ASKS if this is considered to be "healing?" AND HE ANSWERS: Yes, most certainly! Because he maintains the place upon which faith is dependent. IN OTHER WORDS, HE OBSERVES THE COVENANT, WHICH IS YESOD, AND MAINTAINS THE PLACE ON WHICH MALCHUT THAT IS CALLED FAITH DEPENDS.

161. תָּא חֲזֵי, אוֹף הָכִי פִּנְחָס, בְּשַׁעֲתָא דְּקַנֵּי לְעוֹבָדָא דְזִמְרִי, אַתְקִין
לְהַאי בְּרִית בְּאַתְרֵיה, וּבְגִין כָּךְ כְּתִיב, הִנְנִי נוֹתֵן לוֹ אֶת בְּרִיתִי שָׁלוֹם.
וְכִי ס"ד, דְּבְגִין פִּנְחָס הֲוָה, וּמַה קְטָטָא הֲוָה לֵיה לְפִנְחָס, בְּהַאי בְּרִית,
אֶלָּא הָכָא אִתְקְשַׁר מִלָּה בְּדוּכְתֵּיה, הִנְנִי נוֹתֵן לוֹ אֶת בְּרִיתִי, וּמַה אֶתֵּן
לוֹ שָׁלוֹם, לְאִתְחַבְּרָא בְּרִית בְּאַתְרֵיה. וְעַל דָּא הִנְנִי נוֹתֵן לוֹ אֶת בְּרִיתִי.
וּמַה, שָׁלוֹם, דְּאִיהוּ אַתְרֵיה לְאִתְחַבְּרָא בַּהֲדֵיה, מַה דְּאִתְפָּרַשׁ מִנֵּיה
בְּחוֹבַיְיהוּ, בְּגִינֵיה אִתְחַבַּר בֵּיה, וְעַל דָּא, הוֹאִיל וְהוּא אַתְקִין מִלָּה
בְּדוּכְתֵּיה, מִכָּאן וּלְהָלְאָה, וְהָיְתָה לּוֹ וּלְזַרְעוֹ אַחֲרָיו בְּרִית כְּהֻנַּת עוֹלָם
תַּחַת אֲשֶׁר קִנֵּא לֵאלֹקָיו וְגוֹ'.

161. Come and behold: The same applies to Pinchas, who was zealous because of what Zimri had done. By his action, he reinstated the covenant and returned it to its proper place. That is why it is written: "Behold, I give to him My covenant of peace" (Bemidbar 25:12). Can one really accept the idea that Pinchas was the reason for the peace? And upon what is this controversy between Pinchas and the covenant based? That here, IN THE WORD PEACE, everything was connected to its right place, meaning "Behold, I give to him My covenant of peace." But what shall I give him, THE COVENANT? "Peace," WHICH MEANS SUPERNAL MATING, so that the covenant can be connected to its proper place, WHICH IS MALCHUT. That is why it is written: "I give to him My covenant of peace." And what is "peace?" It is the place with which to connect; IT IS THE MATING WITH MALCHUT REFERRED TO BY THE TERM 'PEACE.' MALCHUT THAT was disconnected from it, FROM YESOD, as a result of the sins OF YISRAEL was attached to it by PINCHAS. He was the person who returned the covenant to its place for all time. "And he shall have it, and the covenant of an everlasting priesthood shall belong to his seed after him, because he was zealous for his Elohim" (Ibid.).

162. אָמַר רְבִּי שִׁמְעוֹן, לֵית לָךְ מִלָּה בְּעָלְמָא, דְּקַדְשָׁא בְּרִיךְ הוּא קַנִּי לֵהּ, כְּמוֹ חוֹבָא דִּבְרִית, כְּד"א חֶרֶב נוֹקֶמֶת נְקַם בְּרִית. וְתָא חֲזֵי לָא אִשְׁתְּלֵים חוֹבָא דְּדָרָא דְּטוֹפָנָא אֶלָּא בְּגִין דְּחָבוּ בְּחַבִּילוּ דְּאָרְחַיְיהוּ עַל אַרְעָא. וְאַף עַל גַּב דַּהֲווֹ מְקַפְּחֵי דָּא לְדָא, כְּדִכְתִיב וַתִּמָּלֵא הָאָרֶץ חָמָס, וּכְתִיב כִּי מָלְאָה הָאָרֶץ חָמָס מִפְּנֵיהֶם, מִכָּל מָקוֹם, וַתִּשָּׁחֵת הָאָרֶץ לִפְנֵי הָאֱלֹקִים, וְהִנְנִי מַשְׁחִיתָם, מִדָּה כְּנֶגֶד מִדָּה, הִנְנִי מַשְׁחִיתָם בְּחוֹבָא דְּחַבָּלוּתָא.

162. Rabbi Shimon said that there is nothing in the world which so provokes the zealousness of the Holy One, blessed be He, as the sin of disregarding the covenant. As it is written: "A sword that shall execute the vengeance of the covenant" (Vayikra 26:25). Come and behold: The sin of the generation of the Flood was not completed until they sinned by corrupting their ways on earth. And even though they were violent with each other – as it is written: "And the earth was filled with violence" (Beresheet 6:11) and "for the earth is filled with violence through them" (Ibid. 13) – "I shall destroy them" (Ibid.) was because of the sin of letting semen spill in vain. THAT IS, THEIR SENTENCE WAS NOT SEALED UNTIL THE COVENANT WAS BLEMISHED. "The earth was also corrupt before the Elohim" (Ibid. 11) and "I shall destroy them" was measure for measure.

163. וְאִית דְּאָמְרֵי, דְּלָא אִשְׁתְּלִים קַסְטַיְיהוּ, אֶלָּא בְּחוֹבָא דְּחָמָס, דַּהֲווֹ
מְקַפְּחִין דָּא לְדָא דַּהֲווֹ בִּישִׁין לַשָׁמַיִם וְלַבְּרִיּוֹת. תָּא חֲזֵי כַּמָּה אִינוּן
מְמַנָּן מִלְעֵילָא, דְּאִתְפָּקְדָן עַל קָלֵי דְּאִינוּן דְּמָסְרֵי דִּינָא עַל חַבְרֵיהוֹן,
עַל מַה דְּעָבְדֵי לוֹן, וְעַל דָּא כְּתִיב כִּי מָלְאָה הָאָרֶץ חָמָס מִפְּנֵיהֶם.
וּבְגִין כָּךְ כְּתִיב, וְהִנְנִי מַשְׁחִיתָם אֶת הָאָרֶץ.

163. And there are those who say that their measure of guilt was not completed when they sinned with violence and were cruel with each other. FOR BY THIS they were wicked toward heaven and to other people. Come and behold: There are many ministers above, who are appointed to the voices of those who declare the sentences of their neighbors TO HEAVEN for what has been done to them. And for this sin, it is written: "The earth is filled with violence through them." This means that each and every one passed judgment on his neighbor before heaven. That is why it is said: "I will destroy them with the earth."

22. "Come you and all your house"

The home is a magnet for both positive and negative spiritual forces. Negative people who visit our homes can instill harmful energy, and this section gives us the protection against any such forces.

164. וַיֹּאמֶר ה' לְנֹחַ בֹּא אַתָּה וְכָל בֵּיתְךָ, אָמַר רַבִּי שִׁמְעוֹן אַמַּאי בְּכֻלְּהוּ אֱלֹקִים וְהָכָא ה', מַאי שְׁנָא הָכָא דְּאִתְּמַר ה', שְׁמָא עִלָּאָה דְּרַחֲמֵי. אֶלָּא רָזָא אִיהוּ, דְּאוֹלִיפְנָא, לָאו אוֹרַח אַרְעָא, לְקַבְּלָא אִתְּתָא אוּשְׁפִּיזָא בַּהֲדָה אֶלָּא בִּרְשׁוּ דְּבַעְלָה.

164. "And Hashem said to Noah, Come you and all your house" (Beresheet 7:1). Rabbi Shimon asked: Why does the term "Elohim" appear in all the verses of the text, while here the name Hashem, YUD HEI VAV HEI, is mentioned? What is different here that Yud Hei Vav Hei, which is the supernal name of Mercy was mentioned? This hints at the secret we have already learned, that it is not proper for a woman to invite a guest into her house without the permission of her husband.

165. אוּף הָכִי נֹחַ, בָּעָא לְאַעֲלָא בְּתֵיבוּתָא, לְאִתְחַבְּרָא בַּהֲדָה, וְלָאו הֲוָה יָאוּת עַד דְּבַעְלָה דְּתֵיבָה, יְהַב לֵיהּ רְשׁוּ לְאַעֲלָאָה, דִּכְתִיב בֹּא אַתָּה וְכָל בֵּיתְךָ אֶל הַתֵּבָה. וּבְגִין כָּךְ אִקְרֵי הָכָא ה', בַּעְלָה דְּתֵיבָה, וּכְדֵין עָאל נֹחַ וְאִתְחַבַּר בַּהֲדָה. וְכֵן אוֹלִיפְנָא, דְּלֵית לֵיהּ רְשׁוּ לְאוּשְׁפִּיזָא לְמֵיעָאל לְבֵיתָא, אֶלָּא בִּרְשׁוּ בַּעֲלָה, מָארֵיהּ דְּבֵיתָא, הֲדָא הוּא דִּכְתִיב לְבָתַר, וַיָּבֹא נֹחַ וְגוֹ'.

165. It was the same when Noah was asked to enter the ark, WHICH IS MALCHUT, and to unite with Her. It was not yet proper for him to enter until the 'husband' of the ark gave him permission to do so. As it is written: "Come you and all your house into the ark." And this is why the name Yud Hei Vav Hei, who is the husband of the ark, is mentioned there, FOR YUD HEI VAV HEI IS ZEIR ANPIN AND THE ARK IS MALCHUT. Only after the husband gave permission did Noah enter and unite with the ark. Thus, we have learned that a guest does not have permission to enter a house without

-362-

the consent of the husband, the owner of the house. This is why after the mention of Yud Hei Vav Hei, it is written: "And Noah went in" (Idib. 7).

166. תָּא חֲזֵי, מַה כְּתִיב כִּי אוֹתְךָ רָאִיתִי צַדִּיק לְפָנַי בַּדּוֹר הַזֶּה. מִכָּאן אוֹלִיפְנָא, דְּלָא יְקַבֵּל ב"נ אוּשְׁפִּיזָא בְּבֵיתֵיה, אִי אִיהוּ חָשִׁיד בֵּיה דְּאִיהוּ חַיָּיבָא, אֶלָּא אִי אִי קָאֵים בְּעֵינוֹי לְזַכָּאָה, דְּלָא חָשִׁיד בְּעֵינוֹי כְּלָל, הה"ד בֹּא אַתָּה וְכָל בֵּיתְךָ אֶל הַתֵּבָה, מַאי טַעְמָא בְּגִין כִּי אוֹתְךָ רָאִיתִי צַדִּיק לְפָנַי בַּדּוֹר הַזֶּה.

166. Come and behold: What is written? "For you I have seen righteous before Me in this generation" (Ibid. 1). From this we learn that a person should never accept a guest into his house if he suspects that he might be wicked. And he should accept him only if he considers him to be righteous and is not at all suspicious of him. That is why it is written: "Come you and all your house into the ark." Why? Because "you I have seen righteous before Me in this generation."

167. וְאוֹלִיפְנָא, דְּאִי יָהֵיב לֵיה רְשׁוּ בִּלְחוֹדוֹי, וְלָא יָהֵיב רְשׁוּ לְכָל אִינּוּן דְּאַתְיָין עִמֵּיה, לָא יֵיעוֹל לוֹן לְבֵיתָא, הה"ד בֹּא אַתָּה וְכָל בֵּיתְךָ אֶל הַתֵּבָה, לְכֹלָּא יָהֵיב רְשׁוּתָא לְמֵיעַל. וּמִקְרָא דָא אוֹלִיפְנָא, רָזָא דְּאוֹרְחוֹי דְּאַרְעָא.

167. And we have also learned that if the husband gives permission to the guest alone, but not to his companions, the guest should not bring them into the house. In the verse, "Come you and all your house into the ark," permission was given to all of Noah's companions to enter the ark, and from this passage we learn a secret concerning proper manners and ways of conduct.

23. "The earth is Hashem's and the fullness thereof"

Sexual relations that are not founded upon spiritual principles cause a drying up of the connection between Malchut and Yesod, like a river whose waters have ceased to flow. This withdrawal of Light manifests as all forms of natural and man-made turmoil.

168. רַבִּי יְהוּדָה פָּתַח, לְדָוִד מִזְמוֹר לַה' הָאָרֶץ וּמְלוֹאָהּ תֵּבֵל וְיוֹשְׁבֵי בָהּ. הָא תָּנִינָן, לְדָוִד מִזְמוֹר, דַּאֲמַר שִׁירָתָא, וּלְבָתַר שָׁארַת עֲלֵיהּ רוּחַ קֻדְשָׁא, מִזְמוֹר לְדָוִד, דְּשָׁארַת עֲלֵיהּ רוּחַ קַדִּישָׁא, וּלְבָתַר אֲמַר שִׁירָתָא.

168. Rabbi Yehuda quoted: "For David, a psalm. The earth is Hashem's, and the fullness thereof; the world, and they that dwell in it" (Tehilim 24:1). We have learned that wherever it is written: "For David, a psalm," it means that he chanted a song and afterward the Holy Spirit rested upon him. But where it is written: "A psalm of David," it means that the Holy Spirit rested upon him and then he chanted the song.

169. לַה' הָאָרֶץ וּמְלוֹאָהּ, הַאי קְרָא עַל אַרְעָא דְיִשְׂרָאֵל אִתְּמַר, דְּאִיהִי אַרְעָא קַדִּישָׁא. וּמְלוֹאָהּ, דָּא שְׁכִינְתָּא, כד"א כִּי מָלֵא כְבוֹד ה' אֶת בֵּית ה', וּכְתִיב וּכְבוֹד ה' מָלֵא אֶת הַמִּשְׁכָּן. מַהוּ מָלֵא וְלָא מִילָא. אֶלָּא מָלֵא וַדַּאי, דְּאִתְמַלְיָא מִכֹּלָּא, דְּאִתְמַלְיָא מִן שִׁמְשָׁא, סִיהֲרָא שְׁלִים בְּכָל סִטְרִין. מָלֵא, מִכָּל טוּבָא דִלְעֵילָּא, כְּאַסְקוֹפָא דָא, דְּאִתְמַלְיָא מִכָּל טוּבָא דְעָלְמָא, וְעַל דָּא כְּתִיב לַה' הָאָרֶץ וּמְלוֹאָהּ. תֵּבֵל וְיוֹשְׁבֵי בָהּ, דָּא שְׁאָר אַרְעָאן.

169. "The earth is Hashem's, and the fullness thereof." This verse refers to the land of Yisrael, which is the Holy Land, while "the fullness thereof" refers to the Shechinah. As it is written: "For the glory of Hashem had filled (lit. 'is full') house of Elohim" (II Divrei Hayamim 5:14) and, also, "and the glory of Hashem filled the Tabernacle" (Shemot 40:35). SO THE WORDS "FILLED" AND "THE FULLNESS THEREOF" REFER TO THE SHECHINAH. But, why IS IT WRITTEN "full" and not "filled?" Because, assuredly, She is full of everything; meaning that She is filled by the sun. The moon, WHICH IS THE SHECHINAH, is filled and completed BY THE RIGHTEOUS; She is

filled with all the goodness from above, like a treasure box filled with the riches of the world. That is to what the verse, "The earth is Hashem's and the fullness thereof," refers. But the words, "the world, and they that dwell in it" were said in reference to countries OTHER THAN THE LAND OF YISRAEL.

170. דָּבָר אַחֵר לַה׳ הָאָרֶץ וּמְלוֹאָהּ. דָּא אַרְעָא קַדִּישָׁא עִלָּאָה, דְּקֻדְשָׁא בְּרִיךְ הוּא אִתְרְעֵי בָהּ. וּמְלוֹאָהּ, אִלֵּין נִשְׁמַתְהוֹן דְּצַדִּיקַיָּיא, אִתְמַלְיָא מִנַּיְיהוּ, מֵחֵילָא דְּעַמּוּדָא חַד, דְּעָלְמָא קַיְימָא עֲלֵיהּ.

170. Another explanation of the verse, "The earth is Hashem's and the fullness thereof" is that these words refer to the upper Holy Land, NAMELY THE FEMALE PRINCIPLE, that the Holy One, blessed be He, desires. And the term 'fullness' refers to the souls of the righteous, which fill THE FEMALE PRINCIPLE with the power of pillar THAT IS YESOD OF ZEIR ANPIN, upon which the whole world stands. IN OTHER WORDS, ALL THAT EXISTS IN THE WORLD, WHICH IS THE FEMALE PRINCIPLE, IS RECEIVED FROM YESOD OF ZEIR ANPIN. AND THIS IS WHY THE WORLD IS CONSIDERED TO STAND UPON IT.

171. וְאִי תֵימָא עַל חַד קַיְימָא, תָּא חֲזֵי מַה כְּתִיב כִּי הוּא עַל יַמִּים יְסָדָהּ. כִּי הוּא, מַאן הוּא, דָּא קֻדְשָׁא בְּרִיךְ הוּא, כד״א כִּי הוּא עָשָׂנוּ. וּכְתִיב כִּי הוּא לִקְצוֹת הָאָרֶץ יַבִּיט.

171. If you wonder, Does THE WORLD stand upon one PILLAR? Come and behold: In the verse: "For He has founded it upon the seas" (Tehilim 24:2), the words "For He" refer to the Holy One, blessed be He. The meaning of this is similar to that of the words: "It is He who made us" (Tehilim 100:3) and that of, "For He looks to the ends of the earth" (Iyov 28:24).

172. עַל יַמִּים יְסָדָהּ וְעַל נְהָרוֹת יְכוֹנְנֶהָ, אִלֵּין שִׁבְעָה עַמּוּדִים דְּקַיְימָא עֲלַיְיהוּ, וּמַלְיָין לָהּ. הִיא אִתְמַלְיָא מִנַּיְיהוּ, הֵיךְ אִתְמַלְיָא מִנַּיְיהוּ, בְּשַׁעֲתָא דְּאַסְגִּיאוּ זַכָּאִין בְּעָלְמָא, כְּדֵין אַרְעָא דָּא עַבְדַת פֵּירִין, וְאִתְמַלְיָא מִכֹּלָּא.

172. The words, "For He has founded it upon the seas and established it upon the floods" refer to the seven pillars upon which THE FEMALE PRINCIPLE is founded and by which she is filled. THESE ARE THE SEVEN SFIROT: CHESED, GVURAH, TIFERET, NETZACH, HOD, YESOD AND MALCHUT OF ZEIR ANPIN. SO RABBI YEHUDA ASKS: How is she filled by them? AND HE ANSWERS: When the righteous multiply in the world, the land, WHICH IS THE FEMALE PRINCIPLE, produces fruit and is filled with everything.

173. וּבְשַׁעֲתָא דְּאַסְגִּיאוּ חַיָּיבִין בְּעָלְמָא, כְּדֵין כְּתִיב אָזְלוּ מַיִם מִנִּי יָם וְנָהָר יֶחֱרַב וְיָבֵשׁ. אָזְלוּ מַיִם מִנִּי יָם, דָּא אַרְעָא קַדִּישָׁא, דַּאֲמָרָן דְּאִשְׁתַּקְיָא מִשַּׁקְיוּ עִלָּאָה, וְנָהָר יֶחֱרַב וְיָבֵשׁ, הַהוּא עַמּוּדָא חַד, דְּקָאֵים עֲלָהּ, לְאִתְנַהֲרָא מִנֵּיהּ, וְנָהָר יֶחֱרַב וְיָבֵשׁ, כְּמָא דְאַתְּ אָמֵר הַצַּדִּיק אָבָד.

173. But the verse says that when the wicked multiply in the world, "the waters fail from the sea, and the river is parched, and dries up" (Iyov 14:11). The place where "The waters fail from the sea" is the Holy Land, as previously mentioned. AND THE FEMALE PRINCIPLE is watered by the supernal stream. "THE WATERS FAIL," while "the river is parched, and dries up" refers to the pillar upon which she is founded, NAMELY YESOD, WHICH IS NOW ARID – PARCHED AND DRY. "The river is parched, and dries up" IS THE EQUIVALENT OF "The righteous perishes" (Yeshayah 57:1), THE RIGHTEOUS BEING YESOD, WHICH IS CALLED 'RIGHTEOUS.'

24. The sinners are destroyed from the world

When negative forces are abundant as a result of the collective sins of mankind, they have the power to harm even innocent people who unwittingly cross their paths. The Zohar provides us with protection as we meditate upon its words. Our intent to share this protection with others brightens the Light for entire world.

174. וְאָמַר רַבִּי יְהוּדָה, בְּהַהוּא זִמְנָא דְּאִתְאֲבִידוּ, אִינוּן חַיָּיבִין מֵעָלְמָא, קֻדְשָׁא בְּרִיךְ הוּא אִסְתַּכַּל עַל עָלְמָא, וְלָא חָמָא מַאן דְּאָגֵין עֲלֵיה. וְאִי תֵימָא הָא נֹחַ, דַּהֲוָה לֵיה לְאַגָּנָא עַל דָּרֵיה, וּלְאַפָּקָא מִנֵּיה תּוֹלְדִין לְעָלְמָא, הה"ד כִּי אוֹתְךָ רָאִיתִי צַדִּיק לְפָנַי בַּדּוֹר הַזֶּה. בַּדּוֹר הַזֶּה דַּיְיקָא.

174. Rabbi Yehuda continued: At the time that the wicked are destroyed from the world, the Holy One, blessed be He, watches the world but cannot find anyone to protect them. And you might ask, If Noah was there to protect his generation DURING THE GREAT FLOOD and was able to bring forth offspring, WHY DID HE NOT PROTECT HIS GENERATION? The verse reads: "For you have I seen righteous before Me in this generation" (Beresheet 7:1). "In this generation" is a precise term, FROM WHICH WE MAY LEARN THAT IN ANOTHER GENERATION HE WOULD NOT HAVE BEEN CONSIDERED RIGHTEOUS. AND FOR THIS REASON, HIS MERIT WAS NOT ENOUGH TO PROTECT THE GENERATION OF THE FLOOD.

175. רַבִּי יוֹסֵי אָמַר, בַּדּוֹר הַזֶּה, דָּא שְׁבָחָא דִּילֵיה, דַּהֲוָה בְּהַהוּא דָּרָא חַיָּיבָא, וְאִשְׁתְּכַח כּוּלֵי הַאי אִישׁ צַדִּיק תָּמִים, וַאֲפִילוּ בְּדָרָא דְמֹשֶׁה, אֲבָל לָא הֲוָה יָכִיל לְאַגָּנָא עַל עָלְמָא, בְּגִין דְּלָא אִשְׁתַּכְּחוּ עֲשָׂרָה בְּעָלְמָא, כד"א אוּלַי יִמָּצְאוּן שָׁם עֲשָׂרָה, וְלָא אִשְׁתַּכְּחוּ תַּמָּן. אוּף הָכָא, לָא אִשְׁתַּכְּחוּ עֲשָׂרָה, אֶלָּא הוּא, וּתְלַת בְּנוֹי, וְנוּקְבַיְיהוּ, וְלָא הֲווֹ עֲשָׂרָה.

175. Rabbi Yosi said that the words "In this generation" are a tribute to Noah, who lived in such a wicked generation and nevertheless remained a righteous man and perfect. NOT ONLY IN HIS GENERATION IS HE

CONSIDERED RIGHTEOUS, BUT even in the generation of Moses WOULD
HE HAVE BEEN SO CONSIDERED. But he was not able to protect the world,
because there were not even ten RIGHTEOUS PEOPLE in it. This was the
case as described IN THE DESTRUCTION OF SODOM: "perhaps ten shall be
found there" (Beresheet 18:32). As not even ten were found, SODOM WAS
DESTROYED. The same happened here. Ten RIGHTEOUS people were not to
be found; only Noah, his three sons and their wives. Because they did not
add up to ten, THEY COULD NOT PROTECT THEIR GENERATION.

176. רַבִּי אֶלְעָזָר שָׁאִיל לֵיהּ לְרַבִּי שִׁמְעוֹן אֲבוֹי, הָא תָּנֵינָן, בְּשַׁעֲתָא
דְעָלְמָא אִתְמַלְיָא חוֹבֵי בְּנֵי נָשָׁא, וְדִינָא נָפַק, וַוי לְהַהוּא זַכָּאָה
דְאִשְׁתְּכַח בְּעָלְמָא, דְאִיהוּ אִתְפַס בְּחוֹבוֹי דְחַיָּיבַיָּא בְּקַדְמֵיתָא. נֹחַ אֵיךְ
אִשְׁתְּזֵיב, דְּלָא אִתְפַס בְּחוֹבַיְיהוּ. אָמַר לוֹ הָא אִתְמַר, דְּקֻדְשָׁא בְּרִיךְ
הוּא בָּעָא לְאַפָּקָא מִנֵּיה תּוֹלְדִין לְעָלְמָא מִגּוֹ תֵּיבוּתָא. וְתוּ דְּהָא דִינָא
לָא יָכְלָא לְשַׁלְטָאָה עֲלוֹי, בְּגִין דַּהֲוָה טָמִיר וְגָנִיז בַּתֵּיבָה, וְאִתְכַּסְיָיא
מֵעֵינָא.

176. Rabbi Elazar asked his father, Rabbi Shimon: We have learned that
when the world is full of the sins of mankind and Judgment is pronounced,
woe to the righteous man who is found in the world. For he is the first to be
punished for the sins of the wicked. How did Noah escape the Flood without
being punished for the sins OF HIS GENERATION? And RABBI SHIMON
answered him: It is said that because the Holy One, blessed be He, wanted
to bring from Noah offspring into the world, HE SPARED HIM. Not only
that, but Judgment could not be applied to him, because he was covered in
the ark and hidden from view.

177. וְתָּא חֲזֵי כְּתִיב בַּקְּשׁוּ צֶדֶק בַּקְּשׁוּ עֲנָוָה אוּלַי תִּסָּתְרוּ בְּיוֹם אַף ה'.
וְנֹחַ בִּקֵּשׁ צֶדֶק, וְעָאל בִּגְוֵוּה דְּתֵיבוּתָא, וְאִסְתַּתַּר בְּיוֹם אַף ה'. וְעַל דָּא,
דִינָא לָא יָכִיל לְשַׁלְטָאָה, וּלְקַטְרְגָא לֵיהּ.

177. Come and behold: It is written: "Seek righteousness, seek humility; it
may be you shall be hidden on the day of Hashem's anger" (Tzefanyah 2:3).
Noah did seek righteousness. He entered the ark and was hidden there on

the day of Hashem's anger." And that is why Judgment could neither be applied to nor hurt him.

178. הָכָא אִתְרְמִיז לְאִינוּן קַדִּישֵׁי עֶלְיוֹנִין, לְמִנְדַע בְּרָזָא דְּאַתְוָון קַדִּישִׁין עִלָּאִין, הִפּוּכָא דְּאַתְוָון כ״ב לְאִתְמְחֵי לְאִינוּן חַיָּיבַיָּא. וְעַל דָּא, וַיִּמָּחוּ מִן הָאָרֶץ. וּכְתִיב, בֹּא אַתָּה וְכָל בֵּיתְךָ.

178. Here, we find a hint of the secret of the holy supernal letters, reserved for the holy supernal men to learn and know: The reverse order of the 22 Hebrew letters can bring the destruction of the wicked, and this is why it is written: "they were destroyed from the earth" (Beresheet 7:23), and "Come you and all your house into the ark."

25. The difference between Moses and other people in the world

Placing others ahead of ourselves is counter to the foundations of human nature. Even a righteous soul such as Noah did not possess a complete and selfless love for all mankind. The only person willing to sacrifice himself for all humanity was Moses. Though Noah did all that God asked of him pertaining to the building of the Ark, Noah did not argue with God on behalf of the people of his generation who were destined to perish in the flood. The people of Moses' generation were a stiff-necked and unappreciative lot, who knew no boundaries when it came to brazen, intolerant and negative behavior. But Moses still fought with God to spare his fellow man. Moses offered his own life in place of theirs, despite their constant betrayal and insurgency. We must begin the near impossible task of truly considering others before ourselves. The spiritual attributes that Moses possessed are available through the influences of the Hebrew letters that spell out this story.

179. רַבִּי יִצְחָק פָּתַח, מוֹלִיךְ לִימִין מֹשֶׁה זְרוֹעַ תִּפְאַרְתּוֹ, בּוֹקֵעַ מַיִם מִפְּנֵיהֶם לַעֲשׂוֹת לוֹ שֵׁם עוֹלָם. דָּא זְכוּתָא דְּאַבְרָהָם, דְּאִיהוּ יָמִינָא, מִמֹּשֶׁה, תִּפְאֶרֶת דְּמֹשֶׁה. וּבְגִין כָּךְ בּוֹקֵעַ מַיִם מִפְּנֵיהֶם. דְּהָא זְכוּתָא דְּאַבְרָהָם בּוֹקֵעַ מַיִם אִיהוּ. וְכָל דָּא לָמָּה, לַעֲשׂוֹת לוֹ שֵׁם עוֹלָם.

179. Rabbi Yitzchak analyzed the words: "He who caused His glorious arm to go at the right hand of Moses, that divided the water before them to make Himself an everlasting name" (Yeshayah 63:12). He said that "His glorious arm" is the merit of Abraham, WHO IS THE EMBODIMENT OF CHESED and who is to the right side of Moses, Tiferet of Moses. IN OTHER WORDS, MOSES IS THE SECRET OF TIFERET AND CHESED IS TO HIS RIGHT. SO THE TERM "ARM" INDICATES THE RIGHT ARM OF THE TIFERET OF MOSES. And, therefore, "that divided the water before them" indicates that the merit of Abraham, WHO IS CHESED, divides the water. And for what reason? "To make Himself an everlasting name."

180. תָּא חֲזֵי, מַה בֵּין מֹשֶׁה לִשְׁאָר בְּנֵי עָלְמָא, בְּשַׁעֲתָא דא"ל קֻדְשָׁא בְּרִיךְ הוּא לְמֹשֶׁה וְעַתָּה הַנִּיחָה לִי וְגוֹ' וְאֶעֱשֶׂה אוֹתְךָ לְגוֹי גָּדוֹל וְגוֹ'. מִיָּד אָמַר מֹשֶׁה, וְכִי אֶשְׁבּוֹק דִּינְהוֹן דְּיִשְׂרָאֵל בְּגִינִי. הַשְׁתָּא יֵימְרוּן כָּל

אִינּוּן בְּנֵי עָלְמָא, דַּאֲנָא קַטְלִית לוֹן לְיִשְׂרָאֵל, כְּמָה דַּעֲבַד נֹחַ.

180. Come and behold: What is the difference between Moses and other people? When the holy One, blessed be He, said to Moses, "Now therefore let Me alone...and I will make you a great nation" (Shemot 32:10), Moses immediately asked, 'Shall I abandon Yisrael, forget their punishment, AND NOT PLEA FOR MERCY FOR THEM, FOR MY OWN WELFARE? The world now shall say that I have killed Yisrael, and that I did the same as Noah had done before me.'

181. דְּכֵיוָן דַּאֲמַר לֵיהּ קֻדְשָׁא בְּרִיךְ הוּא, דִּישֵׁזִיב לֵיהּ בְּתֵיבוּתָא, דִּכְתִיב וַאֲנִי הִנְנִי מֵבִיא אֶת הַמַּבּוּל מַיִם וְגוֹ'. וּכְתִיב וּמָחִיתִי אֶת כָּל הַיְקוּם אֲשֶׁר עָשִׂיתִי מֵעַל פְּנֵי הָאֲדָמָה. וַאֲנִי הִנְנִי מֵקִים אֶת בְּרִיתִי וְגוֹ'. וּבָאתָ אֶל הַתֵּבָה. כֵּיוָן דַּאֲמַר לֵיהּ דְּיִשְׁתְּזִיב הוּא וּבְנוֹי, לָא בָּעָא רַחֲמִין עַל עָלְמָא, וְאִתְאֲבִידוּ. וּבְגִין כָּךְ אִקְרוּן מֵי הַמַּבּוּל עַל שְׁמֵיהּ. כְּד"א כִּי מֵי נֹחַ זֹאת לִי אֲשֶׁר נִשְׁבַּעְתִּי מֵעֲבוֹר מֵי נֹחַ.

181. Noah did not plea for mercy on behalf of the world, and they all perished, because the Holy One, blessed be He, had told him that he and his children would be saved by the ark – as the verses state: "and, behold, I will bring the flood waters..." and "and every living substance that I have made will I destroy from off the face of the earth (Beresheet 7:4) and "As for Me, behold, I establish my covenant..." and "Come you...into the ark." Because Noah did not plea for them, the Flood waters are named after him, as it is written: "for this is as the waters of Noah to Me; as I have sworn that the waters of Noah should no more go over the earth" (Yeshayah 54:9).

182. אָמַר מֹשֶׁה, הַשְׁתָּא יֵימְרוּן בְּנֵי עָלְמָא, דַּאֲנָא קְטִילַת לוֹן, בְּגִין דַּאֲמַר לִי, וְאֶעֱשֶׂה אוֹתְךָ לְגוֹי גָדוֹל. הַשְׁתָּא טַב לִי דְּאֵימוּת, וְלָא יִשְׁתֵּצוּן יִשְׂרָאֵל, מִיָּד וַיְחַל מֹשֶׁה אֶת פְּנֵי ה' אֱלֹקָיו. בָּעָא רַחֲמִין עֲלַיְיהוּ, וְאִתְעַר רַחֲמֵי עַל עָלְמָא.

182. Moses said: Now all the people shall say that I have killed them, because Hashem has told me that He shall make me a great nation. Now it is best for me to die rather than have Yisrael destroyed. Then immediately, "Moses besought Hashem his Elohim" (Shemot 32:11). He prayed for mercy, and indeed mercy for the world was aroused.

183. וְאָמַר רַבִּי יִצְחָק, שֵׁירוּתָא דְּבָעָא רַחֲמֵי עֲלַיְיהוּ, מַאי קָאָמַר, לָמָּה ה' יֶחֱרֶה אַפְּךָ בְּעַמֶּךָ. וְכִי מִלָּה דָא אֵיךְ אָמַר לָהּ מֹשֶׁה לָמָּה, וְהָא עָבְדוּ כו"מ, כד"א עָשׂוּ לָהֶם עֵגֶל מַסֵּכָה, וַיִּשְׁתַּחֲווּ לוֹ וַיֹּאמְרוּ אֵלֶּה וְגוֹ'. וּמֹשֶׁה אָמַר לָמָּה. אֶלָּא הָכֵי אוֹלִיפְנָא, מַאן דִּמְרַצֶּה לְאַחֲרָא, לָא בָּעֵי לְמֶעְבַּד הַהוּא חוֹבָא רַב, אֶלָּא יַזְעֵיר לֵיהּ קַמֵּיהּ. וּלְבָתַר יַסְגֵּי לֵיהּ קַמֵּיהּ אַחֲרָא, דִּכְתִיב אַתֶּם חֲטָאתֶם חֲטָאָה גְדֹלָה.

183. Rabbi Yitzchak continued: At first, when he pleaded for mercy for them, what did he say? He said, "Hashem, why does Your wrath burn against Your people?" (Ibid.). AND HE ASKS: Why did Moses ask why? They sinned by idol worshipping – for it is written: "…they have made them a molten calf and have worshiped it" (Ibid. 8) – nevertheless Moses asked why! AND HE ANSWERS THAT we have already learned that when a person is trying to appease a friend who has been offended by another, he should not magnify, but should rather minimize, the offense in the eyes of the offended. Later, he should maximize it in the eyes of THE OFFENDER. SO THIS IS WHY MOSES ASKED BEFORE THE HOLY ONE, BLESSED BE HE: "WHY DOES YOUR WRATH BURN AGAINST YOUR PEOPLE?" HE MINIMIZED THE SIN, BUT AFTERWARD MAGNIFIED IT TO THE PEOPLE OF YISRAEL, saying: "You have sinned a great sin!" (Ibid. 30).

184. וְלָא שָׁבִיק לֵיהּ לְקֻדְשָׁא בְּרִיךְ הוּא, עַד דְּמָסַר גַּרְמֵיהּ לְמוֹתָא. דִּכְתִיב וְעַתָּה אִם תִּשָּׂא חַטָּאתָם וְאִם אַיִן מְחֵנִי נָא מִסִּפְרְךָ אֲשֶׁר כָּתַבְתָּ. וְקֻדְשָׁא בְּרִיךְ הוּא מָחִיל לוֹן דִּכְתִיב וַיִּנָּחֶם ה' עַל הָרָעָה וְגוֹ'. וְנֹחַ לָא עֲבַד כֵּן, אֶלָּא בָּעָא לְאִשְׁתְּזָבָא וְשָׁבִיק כָּל עָלְמָא.

184. He did not relent, but kept pleading with the Holy One, blessed be He, for mercy, to the point of offering his own life FOR THE SAKE OF YISRAEL. As it is written: "and if not, blot me, I pray You, out of Your book which You have written" (Ibid. 32). And then the Holy One, blessed be He, forgave them, as it is written: "and Hashem relented of the evil…" (Ibid. 14).

But Noah did not act AS DID MOSES, he only pleaded to be saved and left the world to its fate.

185. וּבְכָל זִמְנָא דְדִינָא שַׁרְיָא עַל עָלְמָא, רוּחַ קוּדְשָׁא אֲמַר וַוי, דְּלָא אִשְׁתְּכַח כְּמֹשֶׁה. דִּכְתִיב וַיִּזְכֹּר וְגוֹ', אַיֵּה הַמַּעֲלֵם מִיָּם וְגוֹ'. דִּכְתִיב וַיֹּאמֶר ה' אֶל מֹשֶׁה מַה תִּצְעַק אֵלָי. דְּהָא אִיהוּ בִּצְלוֹתָא, סָלִיק לוֹן מִן יַמָּא. וּבְגִין דְּשַׁוֵּי גַרְמֵיהּ, בִּצְלוֹתָא עֲלַיְיהוּ דְיִשְׂרָאֵל בְּיַמָּא, אִקְרֵי הַמַּעֲלֵם מִיָּם, דְּאִיהוּ אַסִּיק לוֹן מִן יַמָּא.

185. So whenever Judgment is upon the world, the Holy Spirit says, "Alas! There is no one like Moses." As it is written: "Then He remembered the days of Moses... Where is he who brought them up out of the sea...?" (Yeshayah 63:11). The verse tells us, "Hashem said to Moses, 'why do you cry to Me?'" (Shemot 14:15), showing that he himself brought them up out of the sea through prayer and because he prayed for Yisrael upon the sea, he was called "he who brought them up out of the sea," as he did bring them out from the sea.

186. אַיֵּה הַשָּׂם בְּקִרְבּוֹ אֶת רוּחַ קָדְשׁוֹ. דָּא אִיהוּ מֹשֶׁה, דְּאַשְׁרֵי שְׁכִינְתָּא בֵּינַיְיהוּ דְיִשְׂרָאֵל. מוֹלִיכָם בַּתְּהֹמוֹת. כַּד אִתְבְּקָעוּ מַיָּא, וַאֲזָלוּ בְּגוֹ תְּהוֹמֵי בְּיַבֶּשְׁתָּא, דִּגְלִידוּ מַיָּא, בְּגִין דְּאָמְסַר גַּרְמֵיהּ עַל יִשְׂרָאֵל.

186. "Where is he that put His holy spirit within them?" (Yeshayah 63:11) refers to Moses; to he who caused the Shechinah to reside among Yisrael and led them through the depths on dry land when the waters were cleft, as if frozen. And all this happened because he was willing to offer his life to save Yisrael.

187. אָמַר רַבִּי יְהוּדָה, אַף עַל גַּב דְּזַכָּאָה הֲוָה נֹחַ, לָאו אִיהוּ כְּדַאי דְּקֻדְשָׁא בְּרִיךְ הוּא יָגִין עַל עָלְמָא, בְּגִינֵיהּ. תָּא חֲזֵי, מֹשֶׁה לָא תָּלָה מִלָּה בִּזְכוּתֵיהּ, אֶלָּא בִּזְכוּת אֲבָהָן קַדְמָאֵי, אֲבָל נֹחַ לָא הֲוָה לֵיהּ, בְּמַאן דְּיִתְלֵי בִּזְכוּתָא, כְּמֹשֶׁה.

187. Rabbi Yehuda said that even though Noah was righteous, it was still

not worthwhile for the holy One, blessed be He, to protect the world because of him. Come and behold: Moses did not ask anything on the basis of his own merit. He depended on the merit of the Patriarchs. But Noah, unlike Moses, had no other person on whose merit he could depend.

188. אָמַר רַבִּי יִצְחָק, וְעִם כָּל דָּא, כֵּיוָן דַּאֲמַר לֵיהּ, קֻדְשָׁא בְּרִיךְ הוּא, וַהֲקִמֹתִי אֶת בְּרִיתִי אִתָּךְ. הֲוָה לֵיהּ לְמִבְעֵי רַחֲמֵי עֲלַיְיהוּ, וְקָרְבְּנָא דְּאַקְרִיב לְבָתַר, דְּיַקְרִיב לֵיהּ מִן קַדְמַת דְּנָא, דִּלְמָא יִשְׁכֵּךְ רוּגְזָא מֵעָלְמָא.

188. Rabbi Yitzchak said that even though this was the case, when the Holy One, blessed be He, said to him "But with will I establish My covenant," he should have asked for mercy for them as well. And he should have sacrificed the offering he sacrificed AFTER THE FLOOD, before it happened. Maybe that would have calmed the Judgment of wrath that hung over the world.

189. אָמַר רַבִּי יְהוּדָה, מַאי הֲוָה לֵיהּ לְמֶעְבַּד, דְּהָא חַיָּיבֵי עָלְמָא, הֲווֹ מַרְגִּיזִין קַמֵּי קֻדְשָׁא בְּרִיךְ הוּא, וְאִיהוּ יַקְרִיב קָרְבְּנָא. אֶלָּא וַדַּאי נֹחַ, דָּחִיל עַל גַּרְמֵיהּ הֲוָה, בְּגִין דְּלָא יְעָרַע בֵּיהּ מוֹתָא, בְּגוֹ חַיָּיבֵי עָלְמָא, דַּהֲוָה חָמֵי עוֹבָדֵיהוֹן בִּישָׁא כָּל יוֹמָא, וְהֵיךְ מַרְגְּזָן קַמֵּי קֻדְשָׁא בְּרִיךְ הוּא כָּל יוֹמָא.

189. Rabbi Yehuda asked: What should NOAH have done? For the wicked of the world provoked the Holy One, blessed be He! Should he have offered a sacrifice on their behalf? He was certainly afraid for himself, that death might reach him among the wicked. He had seen their wicked deeds and how they had provoked the Holy One, blessed be He, day in and day out.

190. רַבִּי יִצְחָק אָמַר, כָּל זִמְנָא דְּחַיָּיבֵי עָלְמָא אַסְגִּיאוּ, זַכָּאָה דְּאִשְׁתְּכַח בֵּינַיְיהוּ, הוּא אִתָּפַס בְּקַדְמֵיתָא. דִּכְתִיב וּמִמִּקְדָּשִׁי תָּחֵלוּ. וְתָנִינָן אַל תִּקְרֵי מִמִּקְדָּשִׁי, אֶלָּא מִמְּקוּדָּשִׁי. וְנֹחַ הֵיךְ שֵׁזִיב לֵיהּ קֻדְשָׁא בְּרִיךְ הוּא, בֵּין כָּל אִינוּן חַיָּיבַיָא. אֶלָּא בְּגִין, דְּיִפְקוּן מִנֵּיהּ, תּוֹלְדִין בְּעָלְמָא דַּהֲוָה צַדִּיק כִּדְקָא יָאוֹת.

-374-

190. Rabbi Yitzchak said: As long as the wicked multiply in the world, when a righteous person is found among them, he is punished first. As it is written: "and begin at My sanctuary" (Yechezkel 9:6), and we have learned to read this not as *mimikdashi* ('at My sanctuary'), but rather as *mimkudashai* ('from My holy ones'). AND THIS BEING THE CASE, how did the Holy One, blessed be He, save Noah who was righteous among the wicked? AND HE ANSWERS: He was saved so that he could bring further generations into the world. For he was truly righteous AND FIT TO BEGET PROPER CHILDREN.

191. וְתוּ, דְּאִיהוּ אַתְרֵי בְּהוּ כָּל יוֹמָא וְיוֹמָא, וְלָא קַבִּילוּ מִנֵּיה, וְקַיָּים בְּנַפְשֵׁיה, קְרָא דִּכְתִיב, וְאַתָּה כִּי הִזְהַרְתָּ רָשָׁע וְגוֹ'. וּכְתִיב וְאַתָּה אֶת נַפְשְׁךָ הִצַּלְתָּ. מִכָּאן כָּל מַאן דְּאַזְהַר לְחַיָּיבָא, אַף עַל גַּב דְּלָא קַבִּיל מִנֵּיה, הוּא שֵׁזִיב לֵיה לְגַרְמֵיה, וְהַהוּא חַיָּיבָא אִתְפַּס בְּחוֹבֵיה. וְעַד כַּמָּה יַזְהַר לֵיה, עַד דְּיִמְחֵי לֵיה. הָא אוּקְמוּהָ חַבְרַיָּיא.

191. Not only that, but he warned them every day, but they did not pay heed. And the verse: "yet if you warn the wicked...but you have saved your soul" (Yechezkel 3:19), is applied to him. From this we learn that whoever warns the wicked – even if the wicked do not heed him – that person saves himself, while the wicked are punished according to their sins. HE ASKS: How far should he go in warning them? AND HE ANSWERS: To the point of hitting them. This issue has already been explained by the friends.

192. רַבִּי יוֹסֵי הֲוָה שְׁכִיחַ קַמֵּיה דְּר"ש יוֹמָא חַד, א"ל, מַאי חָמָא קֻדְשָׁא בְּרִיךְ הוּא לְשֵׁיצָאָה כָּל חַיּוֹת בָּרָא, וְעוֹף שְׁמַיָּא, עִמְּהוֹן דְּחַיָּיבַיָּא, אִי בְּנֵי נָשָׁא חָטָאן, בְּעִירֵי וְעוֹפֵי שְׁמַיָּא וּשְׁאָר בִּרְיָין, מַה חָטוּ. אָמַר לוֹ, בְּגִין דִּכְתִיב כִּי הִשְׁחִית כָּל בָּשָׂר אֶת דַּרְכּוֹ עַל הָאָרֶץ. כֻּלְּהוֹ, הֲווֹ מְחַבְּלֵי אָרְחַיְיהוּ, שַׁבְקֵי זִינַיְיהוּ וְדָבְקוּ בְּזִינָא אָחֳרָא.

192. Rabbi Yosi was staying with Rabbi Shimon. One day he asked him: What was the motive of the Holy One, blessed be He, in extirpating all the animals of the field and the birds of the air along with the wicked? Men sinned, but what wrong had the animals, birds, and other creatures committed? Rabbi Shimon answered him: The reason is given in the words,

"For all flesh had corrupted its way upon the earth" (Beresheet 6:12). This means that all creatures corrupted their way, THAT IS, they mated with other species.

193. תָּא חֲזֵי, אִינוּן חַיָּיבֵי עָלְמָא, גָּרְמוּ הָכֵי לְכָל בִּרְיָין, וּבְעוֹן לְאַבְּחָשָׁא עוֹבָדָא דִּבְרֵאשִׁית, וְאִינוּן גָּרְמוּ לְכָל בִּרְיָין, לְחַבְּלָא אוֹרְחַיְיהוּ, כְּמָה דְּאִינוּן מְחַבְּלָן. אֲמַר קֻדְשָׁא בְּרִיךְ הוּא, אַתּוּן בְּעֵיתוּ לְאַבְּחָשָׁא עוֹבָדֵי יְדַי אֲנָא אַשְׁלִים רְעוּתָא דִּלְכוֹן, וּמָחִיתִי אֶת כָּל הַיְקוּם אֲשֶׁר עָשִׂיתִי מֵעַל פְּנֵי הָאֲדָמָה. אַהֲדַר עָלְמָא לְמַיִין, כְּמָה דַּהֲוָה בְּקַדְמֵיתָא, מַיִין בְּמַיִין, וְהָא אִתְּמַר. מִכָּאן וּלְהָלְאָה, אַעֲבֵיד בִּרְיָין אָחֳרָנִין בְּעָלְמָא, כִּדְקָא יָאוֹת.

193. Come and behold: The wicked of the world caused all the creatures TO MATE WITH SPECIES NOT THEIR OWN. They thereby sought to destroy the work of Creation BY MIXING AND ALTERING SPECIES. They caused all the creatures to pervert their ways on earth, as they themselves had done. The Holy One, blessed be He, said to them, 'As you seek to destroy My work of Creation, I shall fully grant your wish. "And every living substance that I have made, will I destroy from off the face of the earth" (Beresheet 7:4). I shall bring the world back to water, as in the beginning, cover it with water, and then make other creatures who are fit to exist in the world.'

26. "And Noah went...into the ark"

Here the Zohar reveals the concept of *Evil Eye*. Evil eye pertains to the negative glances and resentful looks that we receive from those who may harbor envious feelings. The Kabbalist attributes the majority of common ailments and misfortunes to *evil eye*. When we cast the *evil eye* towards others, we create an opening within ourselves that attracts even more negative glances. We ourselves become more vulnerable to its effects, and a vicious circle is created. This action brings equal harm to both the bearer of Evil Eye and to the recipient.

194. וַיָּבֹא נֹחַ וּבָנָיו וְאִשְׁתּוֹ וּנְשֵׁי בָנָיו אִתּוֹ. רַבִּי חִיָּיא פָּתַח וַאֲמַר, אִם יִסָּתֵר אִישׁ בַּמִּסְתָּרִים וַאֲנִי לֹא אֶרְאֶנּוּ נְאֻם ה'. כַּמָּה אִינוּן בְּנֵי נָשָׁא אֲטִימִין לִבָּא, סְתִימִין עַיְינִין, דְּלָא מַשְׁגִּיחִין וְלָא יָדְעִין, בִּיקָרָא דְמָארֵיהוֹן, דִּכְתִיב בֵּיה, הֲלֹא אֶת הַשָּׁמַיִם וְאֶת הָאָרֶץ אֲנִי מָלֵא. הֵיךְ בָּעוֹן בְּנֵי נָשָׁא, לְאִסְתַּתְּרָא מֵחוֹבַיְיהוּ, וְאָמְרֵי מִי רוֹאֵנוּ, וּמִי יוֹדְעֵנוּ. וּכְתִיב וְהָיָה בְמַחְשָׁךְ מַעֲשֵׂיהֶם. לְאָן יִתְטַמְּרוּן מִקַּמֵּיה.

194. "And Noah went in, and his sons and his wife and his son's wives with him" (Beresheet 7:7). Rabbi Chiya opened the discussion with the verse, "Can anyone hide himself in secret places that I shall not see him? says Hashem" (Yirmeyah 23:24). How blind and obtuse are the people who neither seek nor know the honor of their Master, of whom it is written: "Do not I fill heaven and earth?" (Ibid.). How do people expect to hide from their sins? They ask, "Who sees us? And who knows us?" (Yeshayah 24:15). And also, "They toil in the dark" (Ibid.). Where can they hide from Him?

195. לְמַלְכָּא, דְּבָנָה פַּלְטְרִין, וַעֲבַד תְּחוֹת אַרְעָא טְמִירִין פְּצִירִין, לְיוֹמִין מָרְדוּ בְּנֵי פַּלְטְרִין בְּמַלְכָּא, אַסְחַר עֲלַיְיהוּ מַלְכָּא בְּגַיְיסוֹי, מָה עֲבַד, עָאלוּ וּטְמִירוּ גַּרְמַיְיהוּ, תְּחוֹת נוּקְבֵי פְּסִירִין. אָמַר מַלְכָּא, אֲנָא עֲבַדִית לוֹן, וּמִקַּמַּאי אַתּוּן בָּעָאן לְאִתְטַמְּרָא. הה"ד אִם יִסָּתֵר אִישׁ בַּמִּסְתָּרִים וַאֲנִי לֹא אֶרְאֶנּוּ נְאֻם ה'. אֲנָא הוּא דַּעֲבַדִית, נוּקְבֵי פְּסִירִין וַעֲבַדִית חֲשׁוֹכָא וּנְהוֹרָא, וְאַתּוּן אֵיךְ יָכְלִין לְאִתְטַמְּרָא קַמָּאי.

.195. This is similar to the story in which a king builds a palace with hidden fortified, subterranean caves. And it came to pass that the inhabitants of the palace revolted against the king. So he surrounded them with his troops. And what did they do? They hid themselves inside the fortified hiding places. The king asked: As I made these caves, how can you expect to hide from me in them? This is why it says, "Can anyone hide himself in secret places that I shall not see him? says Hashem." It was I who made these fortified caves. It was I who made light and darkness. How can you hide from Me?

196. תָּא חֲזֵי, כַּד ב״נ חָטֵי קַמֵּי מָארֵיה, וְאַמְשִׁיךְ גַּרְמֵיה לְאִתְכַּסְיָא, קֻדְשָׁא בְּרִיךְ הוּא עָבֵיד בֵּיה דִּינָא בְּאִתְגַּלְיָא. וְכַד ב״נ אַדְכֵּי גַּרְמֵיה, קֻדְשָׁא בְּרִיךְ הוּא בָּעֵי לְאַסְתָּרָא לֵיה, דְּלָא יִתְחֲזֵי בְּיוֹם אַף ה׳. דְּוַדַּאי אִבְעֵי לֵיה לְאִינִישׁ דְּלָא יִתְחֲזֵי קַמֵּי מְחַבְּלָא, כַּד שַׁרְיָא עַל עַלְמָא, דְּלָא יִסְתַּכַּל בֵּיה, דְּהָא כָּל אִינוּן, דְּיִתְחַזּוּן קַמֵּיה, אִית לֵיה רְשׁוּ לְחַבְּלָא.

196. Come and behold: When a person sins before his Master and sins further by hiding himself AND MAKING HIMSELF BELIEVE THAT NOBODY IS WATCHING HIM, then the Holy One, blessed be He, punishes him openly. But when that person purifies himself AND REPENTS, then the Holy One, blessed be He, seeks to hide him so that he should not be seen on the day of the wrath of Hashem. For, certainly, every person should hide himself so as not to be seen by the Angel of Destruction, when the latter dwells in the world. He should not see him, as he is authorized to destroy all those whom he sees.

197. וְהַיְינוּ דְּקָאֲמַר ר׳ שִׁמְעוֹן, כָּל ב״נ דְּעֵינֵיה בִּישָׁא, עֵינָא דִּמְחַבְּלָא וְשַׁרְיָא עֲלוֹי, וְאִיהוּ מְחַבְּלָא דְּעָלְמָא אִקְרֵי. וְלִבְעֵי לֵיה לְאִינִישׁ לְאִסְתַּמְּרָא מִנֵּיה, וְלָא לְאִתְקָרְבָא בַּהֲדֵיה, דְּלָא יִתְּזַק, וְאָסִיר לְמִקְרַב בַּהֲדֵיה בְּאִתְגַּלְיָא. וּמִשּׁוּם הָכִי, מֵאִישׁ רַע עַיִן בָּעֵי לְאִסְתַּמְּרָא מִנֵּיה. מִקַּמֵּי מַלְאַךְ הַמָּוֶת עַל אַחַת כַּמָּה וְכַמָּה.

197. Rabbi Shimon said that every person who has the evil eye, has upon him the eye of the Angel of Destruction, who is called the 'Destroyer of the world.' Therefore, all should beware of such a person and not come close to him. By avoiding him, one shall be protected. It is forbidden to openly approach such a person, EXPOSING OURSELVES TO HIS EVIL EYE. If we must beware a person with the evil eye, so much more must we beware the Angel of Death AND HIDE OURSELVES ON THE DAY OF THE WRATH OF HASHEM.

198. מַה כְּתִיב בְּבִלְעָם וּנְאֻם הַגֶּבֶר שְׁתֻם הָעָיִן. דְּעֵינָא בִּישָׁא הֲוָה לֵיהּ, וּבְכָל אֲתַר דַּהֲוָה מִסְתַּכֵּל בֵּיהּ, הֲוָה אַמְשִׁיךְ עֲלֵיהּ רוּחַ מְחַבְּלָא. וּבְגִין כָּךְ הֲוָה בָּעֵי לְאִסְתַּכְּלָא בְּהוּ בְּיִשְׂרָאֵל, בְּגִין דִּישֵׁצֵי, בְּכָל אֲתַר דְּעֵינֵיהּ הֲוָה מִסְתַּכֵּל. מַה כְּתִיב, וַיִּשָּׂא בִלְעָם אֶת עֵינָיו. דְּזָקִיף עֵינָא חַד. וּמָאִיךְ עֵינָא חַד, בְּגִין לְאִסְתַּכְּלָא בְּהוּ בְּיִשְׂרָאֵל, בְּעֵינָא בִּישָׁא.

198. Of Bilaam, it is written: "The speach of the man whose eyes are open" (Bemidbar 24:3), meaning that he had an evil eye, and wherever he looked, he drew the spirit of destruction on it. That is why he wanted to gaze on Yisrael, so that he could destroy all that his eye could see. Thus, it is written: "And Bilaam lifted up his eyes" (Ibid. 2), meaning he raised one eye and lowered the other, attempting to gaze on Yisrael with the evil eye.

199. תָּא חֲזֵי, מַה כְּתִיב, וַיַּרְא אֶת יִשְׂרָאֵל שׁוֹכֵן לִשְׁבָטָיו. וְחָמָא דִּשְׁכִינְתָּא חַפְיָא עֲלַיְיהוּ, וּרְבִיעָא עֲלַיְיהוּ, מִתְתַּקְנָא בִּתְרֵיסַר שִׁבְטִין תְּחוֹתָהּ, וְלָא יָכִיל לְשַׁלְטָאָה עֲלַיְיהוּ עֵינֵיהּ. אָמַר, אֵיךְ אֵיכוֹל לְהוֹן, דְּהָא רוּחַ קַדִּישָׁא עִלָּאָה, רְבִיעָא עֲלַיְיהוּ, וְחָפַת לוֹן בְּגַדְפָהָא. הה"ד כָּרַע שָׁכַב כַּאֲרִי וּכְלָבִיא מִי יְקִימֶנּוּ. מִי יְקִימֶנּוּ מֵעֲלַיְיהוּ, בְּגִין דְּיִתְגַּלְיָין, וְשָׁלְטָא עֵינָא עֲלַיְיהוּ.

199. Come and behold: It is written: "and he saw Yisrael dwelling according to their tribes" (Ibid.), and he also saw that the Shechinah hovered and brooded over them. Because She was made whole by the twelve tribes beneath Her, the eye of Bilaam could not have power over them. He said: How can I overcome them, as the supernal Holy Spirit, NAMELY BINAH is hovering over them and protecting them with its wings? As it is written: "He couches, he lay down like a lion, and like a great lion; who shall stir him up?" (Ibid. 9) THAT IS, who shall raise it, THE SUPERNAL HOLY

SPIRIT, THAT IT SHOULD STOP PROTECTING THEM, so that they might be revealed to the eye, which would then rule them?

200. וְעַל דָּא קֻדְשָׁא בְּרִיךְ הוּא בָּעָא לְחַפְיָא לְנֹחַ, לְאִסְתַּתְּרָא מֵעֵינָא, דְּלָא יָכִיל רוּחַ מְסָאֲבָא לְשַׁלְטָא עֲלֵיהּ, בְּגִין דְּלָא יִתְחַבֵּל. וְהָא אִתְּמַר. וַיָּבֹא נֹחַ, כְּמָה דְּאִתְּמַר, לְאִסְתַּתְּרָא מֵעֵינָא. מִפְּנֵי מֵי הַמַּבּוּל, דְּמַיְיִן דַּחֲקוּ לֵיהּ. אָמַר רַבִּי יוֹסֵי, חָמָא מַלְאַךְ הַמָּוֶת דַּהֲוָה אָתֵי, וּבְגִין כָּךְ עָאל לְתֵיבוּתָא.

200. Therefore, the Holy One, blessed be He, wanted to protect Noah by hiding him out of sight, so that the impure spirit could not rule him and destroy him, as has already been explained. The words, "And Noah went in" apply to what has previously been said – that he entered the ark to be hidden from sight. The words, "because of the waters of the flood" indicate that the waters actually pushed him INTO THE ARK, meaning that he saw the waters of the Flood and was afraid. As a result, he "went...into the ark." Rabbi Yosi added that Noah saw the Angel of Death arrive WITH THE WATERS OF THE FLOOD and that is why he entered the ark.

201. וְאִסְתַּמַּר בָּהּ, תְּרֵיסַר יַרְחֵי. וְאַמַּאי תְּרֵיסַר יַרְחִין, פְּלִיגֵי בָּהּ, ר' יִצְחָק וְר' יְהוּדָה, חַד אָמַר י"ב יַרְחִין, דְּכָךְ אִיהוּ דִּינָא דְּחַיָּיבַיָּא. וְחַד אָמַר, לְאַשְׁלָמָא צַדִּיק דַּרְגִּין תְּרֵיסַר, וּשְׁאָר דַּרְגִּין דְּאִתְחֲזֵי לְאַפְקָא מִן תֵּיבָה.

201. And he protected himself BY STAYING IN THE ARK for twelve months. Why twelve months? On this point, Rabbi Yitzchak and Rabbi Yehuda have different opinions. One says that the twelve months are the period of the sentence of the wicked IN GEHENOM; the other says that the purpose of the twelve months was to enable NOAH the righteous to complete himself through twelve stages, so that he and all the others could emerge from the ark. BECAUSE EACH STAGE REQUIRES ONE MONTH FOR COMPLETION, THEY WERE DELAYED FOR TWELVE MONTHS.

202. ר' יְהוּדָה אָמַר, שִׁיתָּא יַרְחֵי אִינוּן בְּמַיָּא, וְשִׁיתָּא יַרְחֵי בְּאֶשָּׁא. וְהָא הָכָא מַיָּיא הֲווֹ, אַמַּאי תְּרֵיסַר יַרְחֵי. אָמַר רַבִּי יוֹסֵי, בִּתְרֵי דִּינִין

דְּגֵיהִנֹּם אִתְדָנוּ, בְּמַיָא וְאֶשָּׁא. בְּמַיָא: דְּמַיִין דְּנָחֲתוּ עֲלַיְיהוּ מִלְּעֵילָא, הֲווֹ צְנִינִין כְּתַלְגָּא. בְּאֶשָּׁא: דְּמַיִין דְּנַפְקֵי מִתַּתָּא, הֲווֹ רְתִיחָן כְּאֶשָּׁא. וְעַל דָּא בְּדִינָא דְּגֵיהִנֹּם אִתְדָנוּ, בְּאֶשָּׁא וּמַיָּא, עַד דְּאִשְׁתְּצִיאוּ מֵעָלְמָא. וְנֹחַ, הֲוָה מִסְתַּתֵּר בְּתֵיבוּתָא, וְאִתְכַּסֵּי מֵעֵינָא, וּמְחַבְּלָא לָא קָרִיב לְגַבֵּיהּ, וְתֵיבוּתָא אִיהוּ הֲוָה שַׁטְיָא עַל אַנְפֵּי מַיָא. כְּמָה דְאַתְּ אָמֵר וַיִּשְׂאוּ אֶת הַתֵּבָה וַתָּרָם מֵעַל הָאָרֶץ.

202. Rabbi Yehuda said: IN GEHENOM, THE WICKED ARE PUNISHED with water for six months and with fire for six months. So why DURING THE FLOOD WERE THEY PUNISHED only by water for twelve months? SIX MONTHS SHOULD HAVE BEEN ENOUGH. Rabbi Yosi told him that they were sentenced to both punishments of Gehenom: water and fire. THEY WERE PUNISHED by water, and the water that fell upon them from above was cold as snow. And THEY WERE ALSO PUNISHED by fire, because the water that sprouted from the deep was scalding. Thus, they were punished for twelve months, receiving the full sentence of Gehenom – six by water and six by fire. This continued until they were completely removed from the face of the world. During this time, Noah was hidden in the ark. As a result, the Angel of Destruction did not approach him, and the ark roamed upon the waters, as it is written: "And they bore up the ark, and it was lifted above the earth" (Beresheet 7:17).

203. אַרְבָּעִים יוֹם לָקוּ. דִּכְתִיב וַיְהִי הַמַּבּוּל אַרְבָּעִים יוֹם עַל הָאָרֶץ וְגוֹ'. וְכָל שְׁאָר זִמְנָא אִתְמְחוּן מֵעָלְמָא. הה"ד וַיִּמָּחוּ מִן הָאָרֶץ. וַוי לוֹן לְאִינּוּן חַיָּיבַיָא, דְּהָא לָא יְקוּמוּן לְאַחֲיָיא בְּעָלְמָא לְמֵיקַם בְּדִינָא. הה"ד וַיִּמָּחוּ. כד"א שְׁמָם מָחִיתָ לְעוֹלָם וָעֶד. דַּאֲפִלּוּ לְמֵיקַם בְּדִינָא לָא יְקוּמוּן.

203. They were smitten for forty days. As it is written: "And the Flood was forty days upon the earth" (Ibid.). For the duration of the 12 months, they were being erased, as it is written: "They were destroyed from the earth" (Ibid. 23) Woe to those wicked people, because they shall not rise from the dead and appear in the world to be judged, for "they were destroyed from the earth" as is described in the verse: "You have blotted out their name for ever and ever" (Tehilim 9:6). So they shall not even be allowed to stand to be judged, WHICH MEANS THAT THEY SHALL NOT EVEN BE AMONG THOSE WHO SHALL RISE AND STAND EVERLATIVNG CONTAMPT AS IS WRITTEN IN DANIEL (12:2).

27. "And they bore up the ark"

Every negative action we commit literally pushes away God's presence – the Shechinah – from our midst. The further away we push this Light, the dimmer our reality becomes. With each new level of darkness, more chaos and turmoil manifest in our lives. This section of Zohar helps us arouse the Light to remove the darkness created by our iniquities.

204. וַיִּשְׂאוּ אֶת הַתֵּבָה וַתָּרָם מֵעַל הָאָרֶץ. רַבִּי אַבָּא פָּתַח, רוּמָה עַל הַשָּׁמַיִם אֱלֹקִים עַל כָּל הָאָרֶץ כְּבוֹדֶךָ. וַוי לוֹן לְחַיָּיבַיָּא. דְּאִינּוּן חָטָאן, וּמַרְגִּיזִין לְמָארֵיהוֹן בְּכָל יוֹמָא, וּבְחוֹבַיְיהוּ דַּחְיָין לָהּ לַשְּׁכִינְתָּא מֵאַרְעָא, וְגָרְמִין דְּתִסְתַּלֵּק מֵעָלְמָא, וּשְׁכִינְתָּא אִקְרֵי אֱלֹקִים, וַעֲלָהּ כְּתִיב, רוּמָה עַל הַשָּׁמַיִם אֱלֹקִים.

204. "And they bore up the ark, and it was lifted up above the earth." Rabbi Aba began by saying, "Be You exalted above the heavens, Elohim, let Your glory be above all the earth" (Tehilim 57:6). Woe to the wicked who sin and provoke their Master, every day. For by their sins they push the Shechinah out of the earth and cause Her to leave this world. Because the Shechinah is called 'Elohim,' it is said about Her, "Be you exalted above the heavens, Elohim."

205. תָּא חֲזֵי, מַה כְּתִיב, וַיִּשְׂאוּ אֶת הַתֵּבָה, דְּדַחְיָין לָהּ לְבַר. וַתָּרָם מֵעַל הָאָרֶץ דְּלָא שַׁרְיָיא בְּעָלְמָא, וְאִסְתַּלְּקַת מִנָּהּ. וְכַד אִסְתַּלְּקַת מֵעָלְמָא, הָא לֵית מַאן דְּיַשְׁגַּח בְּעָלְמָא. וְדִינָא שַׁלְטָא כְּדֵין עֲלוֹי. וְכַד יִתְמְחוּן חַיָּיבֵי עָלְמָא, וְיִסְתַּלְּקוּן מִנֵּיהּ, שְׁכִינְתָּא אַהֲדְרַת מְדוֹרָהּ בְּעָלְמָא.

205. Come and behold: It is written: "And they bore up the ark," MEANING that they pushed THE SHECHINAH OUT, FOR THE ARK IS THE SHECHINAH. The words, "and it was lifted up above the earth," MEAN THAT THE SHECHINAH no longer resided in the world, having removed Herself from it. When She left the world, no one was left to protect it any longer and Judgment prevailed. But after the wicked were destroyed and removed from the world, the Shechinah made Her dwelling in the world again.

206. אָמַר לוֹ רַבִּי יֵיסָא, אִי הָכֵי, הָא אַרְעָא דְיִשְׂרָאֵל דְּאִתְמְחוֹן חַיָּיבַיָּא, דַּהֲווֹ בְּהַהוּא זִמְנָא, אַמַּאי לָא אַהְדְרַת שְׁכִינְתָּא לְאַתְרָה, כִּדְבְקַדְמֵיתָא. אָמַר לוֹ בְּגִין דְּלָא אִשְׁתְּאָרוּ בָה, שְׁאָר זַכָּאֵי עָלְמָא. אֶלָּא בְּכָל אֲתַר דַּאֲזָלוּ, נַחְתַּת, וְשַׁוִּיאַת מְדוֹרָה עִמְּהוֹן. וּמַה בְּאַרְעָא נוּכְרָאָה אָחֳרָא, לָא אִתְפָּרְשַׁת מִנַּיְיהוּ, כָּל שֶׁכֵּן אִי אִשְׁתְּאָרוּ בְּאַרְעָא קַדִּישָׁא.

206. Rabbi Yesa asked him: If it is so, then why after the wicked who had lived in the land of Yisrael during THE DESTRUCTION OF THE TEMPLE were blotted out, did the Shechinah not return to Her place? Rabbi Aba answered him: Because AFTER THE DESTRUCTION, the righteous of the world did not remain in THE HOLY LAND, BUT LEFT FOR EGYPT, AS DESCRIBED IN THE BOOK OF JEREMIAH. Wherever they went in exile, THE SHECHINAH followed and resided among them. If She did not leave them even in a strange land, then certainly, had the people stayed in Yisrael, SHE WOULD HAVE RETURNED TO THEM AFTER THE DESTRUCTION.

207. וְהָא אִתְּמָר, בְּכָל חוֹבִין, דְּחַיָּיבֵי עָלְמָא, דַּחֲיָין לָה לַשְּׁכִינְתָּא, חַד מִנַּיְיהוּ מַאן דִּמְחַבֵּל אוֹרְחֵיה עַל אַרְעָא, כִּדְאַמְרָן. וּבְגִין כָּךְ, לָא חָמֵי אַנְפֵּי שְׁכִינְתָּא, וְלָא עָאל בְּפַלְטֵרִין. וְעַל דָּא כְּתִיב בְּאִלֵּין, וַיִּמָּחוּ מִן הָאָרֶץ. אִתְמְחוֹן מִן כֹּלָּא.

207. So it is clear by now that the sins of the wicked caused the Shechinah to depart. One of those sins is the sin of man corrupting his way upon the earth, as we have previously explained. Such a person shall not see the face of the Shechinah, nor shall he enter the palace OF THE KING. This is why it is written that "they were destroyed from the earth," destroyed completely.

208. תָּא חֲזֵי, בְּהַהוּא זִמְנָא דִּזְמִין קֻדְשָׁא בְּרִיךְ הוּא, לְאַחֲיָאָה מֵתַיָּיא, כָּל אִינוּן מֵתִין דְּיִשְׁתַּכְּחוּן לְבַר, בִּשְׁאָר אַרְעִין נוּכְרָאִין, קֻדְשָׁא בְּרִיךְ הוּא יִבְרָא לוֹן גּוּפַיְיהוּ, כִּדְקָא חֲזֵי. דְּהָא גַּרְמָא חַד, דְּאִשְׁתְּאַר בֵּיה בְּבַר נָשׁ, תְּחוֹת אַרְעָא. הַהוּא גַּרְמָא יִתְעֲבִיד כַּחֲמִירָא בְּעִיסָה, וַעֲלֵיה יִבְנֵי קוּדְשָׁא בְּרִיךְ הוּא כָּל גּוּפָא.

208. Come and behold: When the time comes and the Holy One, blessed be He, resurrects the dead, He shall make all the dead in countries other than THE LAND OF YISRAEL rise and stand in their bodies, for one bone is left from the human body as it lies underground, and it is like a lump of dough from which the Holy One, blessed be He, shall rebuild the whole body.

209. וְלָא יָהֵיב לוֹן קֻדְשָׁא בְּרִיךְ הוּא נִשְׁמָתִין, אֶלָּא בְּאַרְעָא דְיִשְׂרָאֵל. דִּכְתִיב הִנֵּה אֲנִי פוֹתֵחַ אֶת קִבְרוֹתֵיכֶם וְהַעֲלֵיתִי אֶתְכֶם מִקִּבְרוֹתֵיכֶם עַמִּי וְהֵבֵאתִי אֶתְכֶם אֶל אַדְמַת יִשְׂרָאֵל, דְּיִתְגַּלְגְּלוּן תְּחוֹת אַרְעָא, וּלְבָתַר מַה כְּתִיב, וְנָתַתִּי רוּחִי בָכֶם וַחְיִיתֶם וגו'. דְּהָא בְּאַרְעָא דְיִשְׂרָאֵל יְקַבְּלוּן נִשְׁמָתִין, כָּל אִינוּן בְּנֵי עָלְמָא. בַּר אַלֵּין דְּאִסְתָּאֲבוּ וְסָאִיבוּ אַרְעָא, בְּאַלֵּין כְּתִיב, וַיִּמָּחוּ מִן הָאָרֶץ. מִן הָאָרֶץ דַּיְיקָא וְאַף עַל גַּב דְּאַקְשׁוּ וְאַפְּלִיגוּ קַדְמָאֵי עַל דָּא. וַיִּמָּחוּ, כד"א יִמָּחוּ מִסֵּפֶר חַיִּים.

209. But He shall not restore their souls to them until they are in the land of Yisrael, as it is stated: "Behold I will open your graves and cause you to come up out of your graves, My people, and I will bring you into the land of Yisrael." They will roll through underground passages AND COME TO THE LAND OF YISRAEL. Next, it is written: "I will put My spirit in you and you shall live" (Yechezkel 37:12-14). Only in the land of Yisrael will they receive their souls, except those who have defiled themselves and the land, NAMELY THE GENERATION OF THE FLOOD. As for them, it has been declared, "They were destroyed from the earth." From the earth MEANS PRECISELY THAT THEY SHALL NOT RISE DURING THE RESURRECTION OF THE DEAD AND SHALL NOT COME TO THE LAND OF YISRAEL TO RECEIVE THEIR SOULS. Although some of the ancient sages differ in their opinion, CLAIMING THAT THEY SHALL BE RESURRECTED, WHAT HAS BEEN SAID STANDS. FOR the term "destroyed" is similar to the expression: "Let them be blotted out of the book of the living" (Tehilim 69:28), MEANING THAT THEY SHALL NEVER BE RESURRECTED.

210. אָמַר לוֹ רַבִּי שִׁמְעוֹן, וַדַּאי לֵית לוֹן חוּלָקָא בְּעָלְמָא דְאָתֵי, דִּכְתִיב וַיִּמָּחוּ מִן הָאָרֶץ. וּכְתִיב, לְעוֹלָם יִרְשׁוּ אָרֶץ. אֲבָל יְקוּמוּן בְּדִין, וַעֲלַיְיהוּ כְּתִיב וְרַבִּים מִישֵּׁנֵי אַדְמַת עָפָר יָקִיצוּ אֵלֶּה לְחַיֵּי עוֹלָם וְאֵלֶּה

לַחֲרָפוֹת וּלְדֵרָאוֹן עוֹלָם. וּפְלוּגְתָּא בְּהָא, אֲבָל כֹּלָא כְּמָה דְאוֹקְמוּהָ חַבְרַיָּיא.

210. Rabbi Shimon said to him: Undoubtedly, THE GENERATION OF THE FLOOD will have no share in the World to Come, as it is written: "They were destroyed from the earth." Analogously, it is written: "they shall inherit the land (earth) forever" (Yeshayah 60:21). AND WE LEARN THAT THE WORD "EARTH" HAS THE SAME MEANING IN BOTH SENTENCES. Nevertheless, they shall rise and stand for Judgment. As they are described: "and many of them that sleep in the dust of the earth shall awake, some to everlasting life and some to shame and everlasting contempt" (Daniel 12:2). Even though opinions differ on this matter, everything is as the friends have explained.

28. "And He destroyed every living substance"

Destruction caused by our own negative actions not only affects our world, but also harms the angels who watch over us in the Upper Worlds. By directing the spiritual influences of the Zohar in their direction, we can fortify these angelic forces.

211. וַיִּמַח אֶת כָּל הַיְקוּם אֲשֶׁר עַל פְּנֵי הָאֲדָמָה. ר' אַבָּא אָמַר, לְאַכְלָלָא כָּל אִינּוּן שַׁלִּיטִין דְּשָׁלְטִין, מְמַנָּן עַל אַרְעָא, וְדָא הוּא, הַיְקוּם אֲשֶׁר עַל פְּנֵי הָאֲדָמָה. דְּכַד עָבִיד קֻדְשָׁא בְּרִיךְ הוּא דִּינָא בִּבְנֵי עָלְמָא, אַעֲבַר לְאִינּוּן שַׁלִּיטִין, דִּמְמַנָּן עֲלַיְיהוּ בְּקַדְמֵיתָא, וּלְבָתַר לְאִינּוּן דְּיַתְבֵי תְּחוֹת גַּדְפַיְיהוּ, דִּכְתִיב, יִפְקוֹד ה' עַל צְבָא הַמָּרוֹם בַּמָּרוֹם. וּלְבָתַר עַל מַלְכֵי הָאֲדָמָה עַל הָאֲדָמָה.

211. "And He destroyed every living substance which was upon the face of the ground" (Beresheet 7:23). Rabbi Aba said that THE VERSE INDICATES THAT the ministers who rule and govern upon the earth, NAMELY THE ANGELS WHO GOVERN THE PEOPLES OF THE WORLD, WERE also DESTROYED. This is the meaning of, "every living substance which was upon the face of the ground." For when the Holy One, blessed be He, executes His Judgment and punishes the people of the earth, He starts with the supernal ministers who rule them and, after they are destroyed, continues with the people who abided beneath the shelter of their wings. As it is written: "Hashem will punish the host of the heavens on high," and then, "the kings of the earth upon the earth" (Yeshayah 24:21).

212. וְהֵיךְ מִתְעַבְּרָן קַמֵּיהּ, אֶלָּא אַעֲבַר לוֹן בְּנוּרָא דְּדָלִיק, הה"ד כִּי ה' אֱלֹקֶיךָ אֵשׁ אוֹכְלָה הוּא אֵל קַנָּא. אֶשָּׁא דְּאָכִיל אֶשָּׁא, הַהוּא יְקוּם דְּעֲלַיְיהוּ בְּאֶשָּׁא. וְאִינּוּן דְּיַתְבֵי תְּחוֹתַיְיהוּ בְּמַיָּא. וּבְגִינֵי כָּךְ, וַיִּמַח אֶת כָּל הַיְקוּם אֲשֶׁר עַל פְּנֵי הָאֲדָמָה. וּלְבָתַר מֵאָדָם וְעַד בְּהֵמָה עַד רֶמֶשׂ וְעַד עוֹף הַשָּׁמַיִם וַיִּמָּחוּ מִן הָאָרֶץ. כָּל אִלֵּין דִּלְתַתָּא. וַיִּשָּׁאֶר אַךְ נֹחַ. אַךְ לְמִעוּטֵי, דְּלָא אִשְׁתָּאֲרוּ בְּעָלְמָא, בַּר נֹחַ וּדְעִמֵּיהּ בְּתֵיבוּתָא. רַבִּי יוֹסֵי אוֹמֵר, חַגִּיר הֲוָה, דְּאָכִישׁ לֵיהּ אַרְיָא. וְהָא אוּקְמוּהָ.

212. But how were these ministers removed? A DIFFICULTY WAS RAISED CONCERNINGTHIS POINT. BECAUSE DEATH HAS NO CONTROL OVER THEM, HOW SHALL HE REMOVE THEM? AND HE REPLIES: "He drove them through burning fire," as it is written: "for Hashem your Elohim is a devouring fire, a zealous El" (Devarim 4:24). Thus, the 'living substance' of above, WHICH INCLUDES THE SUPERNAL MINISTERS, was driven through fire, while those who were governed by them AND RESIDED BELOW THEM, NAMELY PEOPLE, were erased by water. This is why THE VERSE BEGINS, "And He destroyed every living substance," and then continues, "man, cattle and creeping things, and the birds of the heaven; they were destroyed from the earth." In, "Only Noah was left," the word "only" signifies that nothing and nobody remained in the world – except Noah and whoever was with him in the ark. Rabbi Yosi said that THE WORD "ONLY" INDICATES THAT NOT EVEN NOAH'S BODY WAS SPARED, for he was smitten by a lion and became lame, as was previously explained.

29. "And Elohim remembered Noah"

The Zohar discloses a secret concerning the word *remembered,* and its connection to having our prayers answered. Prayer alone will not yield a response if, metaphorically speaking, the Creator cannot see the alarm lights flashing. The coverings that block our alarm signals are negative entities called *Klippot,* which are brought into existence through our own negative deeds. These coverings become more dense with each new negative action. The words that tell of these spiritual secrets help our prayers pierce through all the dense layers of Klippot, so that our cries are heard above. This is the mystery behind the word *remembered.*

213. וַיִּזְכֹּר אֱלֹקִים אֶת נֹחַ וְאֶת כָּל הַחַיָּה וְאֶת כָּל הַבְּהֵמָה אֲשֶׁר אִתּוֹ בַּתֵּבָה. רַבִּי חִיָּיא פָּתַח עָרוּם רָאָה רָעָה וְנִסְתָּר. הַאי קְרָא, אִתְּמַר עַל נֹחַ, דְּעָאל לְתֵיבוּתָא, וְאִסְתַּתַּר בָּהּ. וְעָאל לְגוֹ תֵּיבוּתָא, בְּזִמְנָא דְּמַיָּיא דְּחֲקוּ לֵיהּ. וְהָא אִתְּמַר, דְּעַד לָא עָאל לְתֵיבוּתָא, חָמָא לֵיהּ לְמַלְאַךְ הַמָּוֶת, דְּאָזִיל בֵּינַיְיהוּ, וְאַסְחַר לוֹן. כֵּיוָן דְּחָמָא לֵיהּ, עָאל לַתֵּיבָה, וְאִסְתַּתַּר בְּגַוֵּהּ, הה"ד עָרוּם רָאָה רָעָה וְנִסְתָּר. רָאָה רָעָה, דָּא מַלְאַךְ הַמָּוֶת, וְנִסְתָּר מִקַּמֵּיהּ, הה"ד מִפְּנֵי מֵי הַמַּבּוּל.

213. "And Elohim remembered Noah, and every living thing, and all the cattle that were with him in the ark" (Beresheet 8:1). Rabbi Chiya quoted the verse, "A prudent man foresees evil, and hides himself" (Mishlei 22:3), saying that this verse refers to Noah who entered the ark and hid himself in it. And he entered the ark only when the waters forced him to do so. As was previously explained, before he went into the ark, he saw the Angel of Death walking among the people and encircling them. Because Noah saw the Angel of Death, he entered the ark and hid. Thus, it is written: "A prudent man foresees evil, and hides himself." "Foresees evil" refers to the Angel of Death from whom he hid, as it is written: "from the waters of the flood." OR IN OTHER WORDS, FROM THE ANGEL OF DEATH WHOM HE SAW ON THE WATERS OF THE FLOOD.

214. רַבִּי יוֹסֵי אָמַר, עָרוּם רָאָה רָעָה וְנִסְתָּר. אַהֲדַר עַל מַה דְּאִתְּמַר בְּזִמְנָא דְּמוֹתָא שַׁרְיָא בְּעָלְמָא, בַּר נָשׁ חַכִּים יִסָּתֵר, וְלָא יָקוּם לְבַר, וְלָא

יִתְחֲזֵי קַמֵּי מְחַבְּלָא. בְּגִין דְּכֵיוָן דְּאִתְיְיהִיב לֵיהּ רְשׁוּ, יְחַבֵּל כָּל אִינוּן דְּיִשְׁתַּכְּחוּן קַמֵּיהּ וְיַעַבְרוּן קַמֵּיהּ בְּאִתְגַּלְיָיא, וְסוֹפָא דִּקְרָא, וּפְתָאִים עָבְרוּ וְנֶעֱנָשׁוּ. עָבְרִין קַמֵּיהּ, וְאִתְחַזְיָין קַמֵּיהּ, וְנֶעֱנָשׁוּ. דָּבָר אַחֵר עָבְרוּ, עָבְרוּ פִּקּוּדָא דְּמָארֵיהוֹן, וְנֶעֱנָשׁוּ. דָּבָר אַחֵר, עָרוּם רָאָה רָעָה וְנִסְתָּר, דָּא נֹחַ. וּפְתָאִים עָבְרוּ וְנֶעֱנָשׁוּ אִלֵּין בְּנֵי דָרֵיהּ.

214. Rabbi Yosi said that the verse "A prudent man foresees evil, and hides himself" means, as has been stated, that when death rages throughout the world, a wise man will hide and not appear in the open. This prevents the Angel of Destruction from seeing him, because when THE ANGEL OF DESTRUCTION gets permission to destroy, he destroys everything in front of him and everyone who openly passes before him. An allusion to this appears at the end of the verse that reads, "but the simple pass on, and are punished" (Ibid.), referring to those who pass in front of him, are seen by him, and therefore punished. Another explanation is that "pass on (Heb. avru)" means that those who transgress (Heb. avru) the commandments of their Master are therefore punished. According to yet another explanation, a "prudent man foresees evil, and hides himself" refers to Noah, while "the simple pass on, and are punished" refers to the people of his generation.

215. כֵּיוָן דְּאִסְתַּתַּר וְאִשְׁתָּהֵי תַּמָּן כָּל הַהוּא זִמְנָא. לְבָתַר, וַיִּזְכֹּר אֱלֹקִים אֶת נֹחַ. אָמַר רַבִּי שִׁמְעוֹן תָּא חֲזֵי, בְּשַׁעְתָּא דְּדִינָא אִתְעֲבֵיד, לָא כְּתִיב בֵּיהּ זְכִירָה כֵּיוָן דְּאִתְעֲבֵיד דִּינָא, וְאִתְאֲבִידוּ חַיָּיבֵי עָלְמָא, כְּדֵין כְּתִיב בֵּיהּ זְכִירָה. דְּהָא כַּד דִּינָא שַׁרְיָא בְּעָלְמָא, אִתְחַבְּרוּתָא לָא אִשְׁתְּכַח, וּמְחַבְּלָא שַׁרְיָא עַל עָלְמָא.

215. He hid himself IN THE ARK, and remained inside IT all this time. What does it say afterward? It says, "And Elohim remembered Noah." So Rabbi Shimon said: Come and behold: While Judgment is executed, there is no remembrance. But after Judgment has been executed and the wicked have been removed from the world, then the word "remember" is mentioned. THIS IS because when Judgment prevails in the world, there is no SUPERNAL mating above and the Angel of Destruction rages throughout the world. THUS THERE IS NO POSITIVE REMEMBRANCE, AS REMEMBRANCE MEANS MATING.

216. כֵּיוָן דְּאִתְעֲבַר דִּינָא, וְאִשְׁתַּכֵּיךְ רוּגְזָא, תָּב כֹּלָּא לְאַתְרֵיהּ. וּבְגִין כָּךְ כְּתִיב הָכָא, וַיִּזְכֹּר אֱלֹקִים אֶת נֹחַ. דְּבֵיהּ שַׁרְיָא זָכוֹר, דְּנֹחַ, אִישׁ צַדִּיק כְּתִיב בֵּיהּ.

216. But after Judgment is passed and is completed, and the wrath is appeased, everything returns to its proper order, NAMELY THE SUPERNAL MATING COMMENCES AND MERCY IS REVEALED IN THE WORLD. This is why the text reads, "And Elohim remembered Noah." Because the term "remember," WHICH MEANS MATING, applies to Noah, as indicated by the words, "Noah was a righteous man." AND HE IS A THRONE FOR THE SUPERNAL MATING, SO THAT WHEN THE MATING COMMENCED, ELOHIM REMEMBERED NOAH.

217. כְּתִיב אַתָּה מוֹשֵׁל בְּגֵאוּת הַיָּם בְּשׂוֹא גַלָּיו אַתָּה תְשַׁבְּחֵם. בְּשַׁעֲתָא דְּיַמָּא קָפִיץ בְּגַלְגְּלוֹי, וּתְהוֹמֵי סַלְקֵי וְנָחֲתֵי, קֻדְשָׁא בְּרִיךְ הוּא שָׁדַר חַד חוּטָא, מִסִּטְרָא דִּימִינָא, וּמָשִׁיךְ גַּלְגְּלוֹי, וְשָׁכִיךְ זַעְפֵּיהּ, וְלֵית מָאן דְּיָדַע לֵיהּ.

217. It is written: "You rule the raging of the sea; when the waves thereof rise up, You still them" (Tehilim 89:10). When the sea is stormy, the waves mount on high and the waters of the deep go up and down, the Holy One, blessed be He, sends forth a thread OF CHESED from the right side, pulls back its waves, and appeases its rage; but there is nobody who can grasp Him.

218. יוֹנָה נָחַת לְיַמָּא, וְאִזְדַּמַּן לֵיהּ הַהוּא נוּנָא, וּבָלַע לֵיהּ, הֵיךְ לָא נָפְקַת נִשְׁמָתֵיהּ מִנֵּיהּ, וְלָא פָּרְחָא מִיָּד. אֶלָּא, בְּגִין דְּקֻדְשָׁא בְּרִיךְ הוּא שַׁלִּיטָא בְּהַהוּא גֵּאוּתָא דְּיַמָּא.

218. Jonah fell into the sea and a fish swallowed him. SO HE ASKS: Why did his soul not leave him at once? AND HE ANSWERS: Because the Holy One, blessed be He, controls the raging of the sea.

219. וְהַהוּא גֵּאוּתָא דְּיַמָּא, הוּא חַד חוּטָא דִּשְׂמָאלָא, דְּסָלִיק לֵיהּ לְיַמָּא לְעֵילָא, וּבֵיהּ אִסְתַּלַּק. וְאִי לָאו הַהוּא חוּטָא, דְּמָטֵי לֵיהּ מִסִּטְרָא

29. "And Elohim remembered Noah"

דְּיַמִּינָא, לָא סָלְקָא לְעָלְמִין, דְּכֵיוָן דְּהַהוּא חוּטָא נָחִית לְיַמָּא, וְיַמָּא אִתְאֲחִיד בֵּהּ, כְּדֵין אִתְעָרִין גַּלְגְּלוֹי, וְשָׁאֲגָן לְמִטְרַף טַרְפָּא. עַד דְּקֻדְשָׁא בְּרִיךְ הוּא אָתִיב לֵיהּ לַאֲחוֹרָא. וְתָבִין לְאַתְרַיְיהוּ.

219. The 'raging of the sea,' is the thread from the left, which causes THE WAVES OF the sea to rise, and rises with it. But had the other thread OF CHESED, not arrived from the right, it would have never risen. For when that thread FROM THE LEFT goes down to the sea and is held by the sea, the waves 'awaken' and begin to 'roar' for prey, until the Holy One, blessed be He, restrains the waves, holds them back, and they return to their place.

220. הה"ד בְּשׂוֹא גַלָּיו אַתָּה תְשַׁבְּחֵם. תְּשַׁבְּחֵם, לְאִינוּן גַּלֵּי יַמָּא, תְּשַׁבְּחֵם: תִּתְבַּר לוֹן, לַאֲתָבָא לְאַתְרַיְיהוּ. דָּבָר אַחֵר, תְּשַׁבְּחֵם מַמָּשׁ, שְׁבָחָא הוּא לוֹן, בְּגִין דְּסַלְּקִין בְּתֵיאוּבְתָּא לְמֶחֱמֵי. מִכָּאן כָּל מָאן דְּכָסִיף לְאִסְתַּכְּלָא וּלְמִנְדַּע, אַף עַל גַּב דְּלָא יָכִיל, שְׁבָחָא אִיהוּ דִּילֵיהּ, וְכֹלָּא מְשַׁבְּחָן לֵיהּ.

220. As it is written: "You rule the raging of the sea: when the waves thereof rise up, You still (lit. 'praise') them." ONE INTERPRETATION IS THAT PRAISE (HEB. *TESHABECHEM*) IS THE SAME AS breaking (Heb. *teshabrem*) and pulling them back to their place WITH THE THREAD OF CHESED. A different interpretation is that the meaning is literally 'You praise them.' That is, the fact that the waves rise with the desire to see is praiseworthy. From this we can learn that whoever seeks and longs for knowledge, even if he is incapable of attaining it, is praised for his effort.

221. אָמַר רַבִּי יְהוּדָה, נֹחַ כַּד הֲוָה בַּתֵּיבָה, דָּחִיל הֲוָה, דְּלָא יִדְכַּר לֵיהּ קֻדְשָׁא בְּרִיךְ הוּא לְעָלְמִין. וְכֵיוָן דְּאִתְעֲבֵיד דִּינָא, וְאִתְעֲבָרוּ חַיָּיבָא עָלְמָא, כְּדֵין מַה כְּתִיב וַיִּזְכֹּר אֱלֹקִים אֶת נֹחַ.

221. Rabbi Yehuda said that when Noah was in the ark, he was afraid that the Holy One, blessed be He, might never remember him. But after Judgment was executed and the evil people were removed, what does the scripture say? It says, "And Elohim remembered Noah." AND THE REASON FOR THIS SHALL BE EXPLAINED PRESENTLY BY RABBI ELAZAR.

222. רַבִּי אֶלְעָזָר אָמַר, תָּא חֲזֵי בְּשַׁעֲתָא דְדִינָא שַׁרְיָא בְּעָלְמָא, לָא לִיבָּעֵי, לֵיהּ לְאֵינַשׁ דְּיִדְכַּר שְׁמֵיהּ לְעֵילָא, דְּהָא אִי אַדְכַּר שְׁמֵיהּ, יִדְכְּרוּן חוֹבוֹי, וְיֵיתוּן לְאַשְׁגָּחָא בֵּיהּ.

222. Rabbi Elazar says: Come and behold: When Judgment prevails in the world, it is inappropriate for a person's name to be mentioned above, because if his name is mentioned, his sins will be remembered and they will come to judge him.

223. מְנָלָן, מִשּׁוּנַמִּית, דְּהַהוּא יוֹמָא, יוֹם טוֹב דְּרֹאשׁ הַשָּׁנָה הֲוָה, וְקֻדְשָׁא בְּרִיךְ הוּא דָּאִין עָלְמָא. וּכְדֵין אָמַר לָהּ אֱלִישָׁע, הֲיֵשׁ לְדַבֶּר לָךְ אֶל הַמֶּלֶךְ. דָּא קֻדְשָׁא בְּרִיךְ הוּא. דִּכְדֵין אִקְרֵי מֶלֶךְ, מֶלֶךְ הַקָּדוֹשׁ, מֶלֶךְ הַמִּשְׁפָּט. וַתֹּאמֶר בְּתוֹךְ עַמִּי אָנֹכִי יוֹשֶׁבֶת. לָא בָּעֵינָא דְּיִדְכְּרוּן לִי וְיַשְׁגְּחוּן בִּי, אֶלָּא בְּתוֹךְ עַמִּי. מַאן דְּעַיֵּיל רֵישֵׁיהּ בֵּין עַמָּא, לָא יַשְׁגְּחוּן עֲלֵיהּ, לְמֵידַן לֵיהּ לְבִישׁ, בְּגִינֵי כָךְ אָמְרָה בְּתוֹךְ עַמִּי.

223. From where do we know this? From the story of the woman of Shunam. On the Holy Day of Rosh Hashanah, the Holy One, blessed be He, was judging the world. Elisha the prophet asked the woman, "Would you be spoken for to the king?" (II Melachim 4:13). The "King" here refers to the Holy One, blessed be He, who is called on that day "the King," "the Holy King," and "the King of Justice." "And she answered, 'I dwell among my own people'" (Ibid.), MEANING, 'I do not want to be scrutinized on my own. Therefore I dwell among my own people!' He who puts himself in the middle of his own people does not draw attention to himself and is not judged for his wrongdoings. She thus said, "among my own people."

224. תָּא חֲזֵי, נֹחַ, בְּשַׁעֲתָא דְרוּגְזָא שַׁרְיָא בְּעָלְמָא, לָא אִדְכַּר, כֵּיוָן דְּדִינָא אִתְעֲבַר, מַה כְּתִיב, וַיִּזְכֹּר אֱלֹקִים אֶת נֹחַ. הַשְׁתָּא אַדְכַּר שְׁמֵיהּ. דָּבָר אַחֵר וַיִּזְכֹּר אֱלֹקִים אֶת נֹחַ. כְּמָה דְאַתְּ אָמַר וְאָזְכֹּר אֶת בְּרִיתִי.

224. Come and behold: During the time when the wrath OF JUDGMENT was raging throughout the world, Noah was not mentioned. But after the Judgment was completed, what does the scripture say? It says, "And Elohim

remembered Noah." Now was his name mentioned. A different explanation of "And Elohim remembered Noah" is that it is similar to "And I remembered My covenant" (Shemot 6:5), WHICH MEANS THAT HE CAUSED THE SUPERNAL MATING!

30. "And Noah built an altar"

After the great flood, the metaphysical lines of communication between the Upper and Lower worlds were destroyed, and the flow of Light into our world was cut off. In order to reestablish a link, Noah rebuilt the *metaphysical cables* that run throughout the worlds. This concept is the mystery behind the Alter that Noah built.

225. רַבִּי חִזְקִיָּה, הֲוָה אָזֵיל מִקַפּוֹטְקִיָּא לְלוּד, פָּגַע בֵּיה רַבִּי יֵיסָא, אָמַר לוֹ תְּוַוהְנָא עֲלָךְ, דְּאַתְּ בִּלְחוֹדְךָ. דְּהָא תָּנִינָן, דְּלָא יִפּוֹק בַּר נָשׁ יְחִידָאִי בְּאוֹרְחָא. אָמַר לוֹ רַבְיָא חַד אָזֵיל בַּהֲדַאי, וְאִיהוּ אָתֵי אֲבַתְרָאי. אָמַר לוֹ וְעַל דָּא תְּוַוהְנָא, אֵיךְ אָזֵיל בַּהֲדָךְ, מַאן דְּלָא תִשְׁתָּעֵי בֵּיה מִלֵּי דְאוֹרַיְיתָא, דְּהָא תָּנִינָן, כָּל מַאן דְּאָזֵיל בְּאָרְחָא, וְלָאו עִמֵּיה מִלֵּי דְאוֹרַיְיתָא, אִסְתַּכַּן בְּנַפְשֵׁיה. אָמַר לוֹ הָכֵי הוּא וַדַּאי.

225. Rabbi Chizkiyah was on his way from Cappadocia to Lod, when Rabbi Yesa ran into him. He addressed him saying: You surprise me! Why are you walking alone, since we have learned that a person should not go on a journey alone! Rabbi Chizkiyah replied: There is a young boy following and accompanying me. Rabbi Yesa said to him: This is what surprises me! Why are you accompanied by someone with whom you are not able to discuss the Torah? We have learned that whoever goes on a journey and does not delve into the matters of the Torah, endangers his life! Rabbi Chizkiyah replied: It is certainly so!

226. אַדְהֲכֵי מָטָא הַהוּא רַבְיָא, אָמַר לוֹ רַבִּי יֵיסָא, בְּרִי, מֵאָן אֲתַר אַנְתְּ, אָמַר לוֹ מִקַּרְתָּא דְלוּד, וְשָׁמַעְנָא דְּהַאי ב"נ חַכִּים, אָזֵיל תַּמָּן, וְזַמִּינָא גַרְמַאי, לְפוּלְחָנֵיה, וּלְמֵיהַךְ בַּהֲדֵיה.

226. In the meantime, the young boy caught up with them. Rabbi Yesa asked him: My son, from where do you come? The boy answered: From the city of Lod. I heard that this learned man was heading toward there, so I offered to work for him – TO SERVE HIM AND to walk with him.

227. אָמַר לוֹ בְּרִי יָדַעְתְּ מִלֵּי דְאוֹרַיְיתָא, אָמַר לוֹ יְדַעְנָא, דְּהָא אַבָּא

הֲוָה אוֹלִיף לִי בְּפָרָשַׁת קָרְבָּנוֹת, וְאַרְכִינָא אוּדְנָאי לְמַאי דַּהֲוָה אָמַר, עִם אָחִי, דְּאִיהוּ קַשִּׁישָׁא מִנָּאי, אָמַר לֵיהּ רַבִּי יֵיסָא, בְּרִי, אֵימָא לִי.

227. Rabbi Yesa then asked him: My son, are you familiar with matters of the Torah? And he answered: Yes, I am. My father used to teach me the section of the sacrifices, and I also used to listen to what he taught my elder brother. Rabbi Yesa then said to him: My son, speak to me!

228. פָּתַח וְאָמַר, וַיִּבֶן נֹחַ מִזְבֵּחַ לַה' וַיִּקַּח מִכָּל הַבְּהֵמָה הַטְּהוֹרָה וּמִכָּל הָעוֹף הַטָּהוֹר וַיַּעַל עוֹלֹת בַּמִּזְבֵּחַ. וַיִּבֶן נֹחַ מִזְבֵּחַ, דָּא אִיהוּ מִזְבֵּחַ דְּאַקְרִיב בֵּיהּ אָדָם קַדְמָאָה. נֹחַ אַמַּאי קָרֵיב עוֹלָה, דְּהָא עוֹלָה לָא סַלְקָא, אֶלָּא בְּגִין הִרְהוּרָא דְלִבָּא, וְנֹחַ, בַּמֶּה חָב. אֶלָּא נֹחַ הִרְהֵר וְאָמַר, הָא קֻדְשָׁא בְּרִיךְ הוּא גָּזַר דִּינָא עַל עָלְמָא דְּיִתְחָרַב, דִּילְמָא בְּגִין דְּשֵׁזִיב לִי, כָּל זְכוּתָא פָּקַע לִי, וְלָא יִשְׁתָּאַר לִי זָכוּ בְּעָלְמָא. מִיָּד וַיִּבֶן נֹחַ מִזְבֵּחַ לַה'.

228. The young boy started with the verse: "And Noah built an altar to Hashem and took of every clean beast and of every clean fowl, and offered burnt offerings on the altar" (Beresheet 8:20). He said, "And Noah built an altar" indicates the altar on which Adam offered his sacrifice. THEN HE ASKS: Why did Noah offer a burnt offering, as a burnt offering is only offered TO ATONE for wrongful thoughts of the heart? What was Noah's sin? AND HE REPLIES: Noah thought to himself, The Holy One, blessed be He, judged the world and sentenced it to destruction. Perhaps in being spared, I used up all the merit that I have and am now left with none. So immediately, "Noah built an altar to Hashem."

229. הַהוּא מִזְבֵּחַ דְּאַקְרִיב בֵּיהּ אָדָם הָרִאשׁוֹן הֲוָה. אִי הָכִי, אַמַּאי וַיִּבֶן. אֶלָּא, בְּגִין דְּחַיָּיבֵי עָלְמָא, גָּרְמוּ דְּלָא קָיְימָא בְּדוּכְתֵּיהּ, כֵּיוָן דְּאָתָא נֹחַ כְּתִיב בֵּיהּ וַיִּבֶן.

229. This was the altar on which Adam offered his sacrifices. SO THE BOY ASKS: If it is so, then why does it say that he "built it?" IT WAS ADAM WHO BUILT IT. AND HE REPLIES: It says this, because the wicked of the world had caused the altar not to stand in its place, THE PLACE WHERE IT CAN TRANSFER ABUNDANCE TO HOLINESS. When Noah came TO OFFER HIS SACRIFICE ON IT, the verse states, "And Noah built it" BECAUSE HE BROUGHT IT BACK TO THE PLACE WHERE ABUNDANCE IS DIRECTED TOWARD HOLINESS.

230. וַיַּעַל עוֹלוֹת. עֹלת כְּתִיב, חֲדָא. כְּתִיב עֹלָה הוּא אִשֶּׁה רֵיחַ נִיחֹחַ לַה'. עוֹלָה סַלְקָא דְּכַר, וְלָא סַלְקָא נוּקְבָּא, דִּכְתִיב זָכָר תָּמִים יַקְרִיבֶנּוּ. אַמַּאי כְּתִיב אִשֶּׁה, דְּהָא אֵשׁ בָּעֵי לְאִשְׁתַּכְּחָא תַּמָּן.

230. "And offered burnt offerings (Heb. olot)." Olot has a defective spelling, WITHOUT THE LETTER VAV, WHICH WOULD HAVE INDICATED THE PLURAL FORM, BECAUSE HE OFFERED ONLY one BURNT OFFERING. It is written: "It is a burnt offering, an offering made by fire (Heb. isheh), of a sweet savor to Hashem (Vayikra 1:13). THE BOY SAID: The burnt offering is a male and not a female, as it is written: "He shall offer it a male, without blemish" (Vayikra 1:3). THEREFORE, why is the term isheh spelled WITH A FINAL HEI, INDICATING THE FEMININE FORM OF THE WORD? Esh (fire), WITHOUT HEI, should have been used instead, WHICH IS THE MASCULINE FORM.

231. אֶלָּא, אַף עַל גַּב דְּעוֹלָה אִתְקְרִיב דְּכַר, וּלְאַתְרֵיה אִתְקְרִיב, נוּקְבָּא לָא בָּעְיָא לְאִתְפָּרְשָׁא מִנֵּיה, אֶלָּא בָּה אִתְקְרֵיב, בְּגִין לְחַבְּרָא דָּא בְּדָא. דְּסַלְקָא נוּקְבָּא לְגַבֵּי דְּכוּרָא, לְאִתְחַבְּרָא כַּחֲדָא. וְאַף עַל גַּב דְּאִשֶּׁה לְשׁוּם אִישִׁים.

231. AND HE EXPLAINS THAT even though the burnt offering is male and is sacrificed to its place, NAMELY TO ZEIR ANPIN WHO IS THE MALE ASPECT, the Female Principle should not be separated from ZEIR ANPIN AS A RESULT OF THE OFFERING. Thus, it is offered to THE FEMALE PRINCIPLE, uniting ZEIR ANPIN AND HIS FEMALE PRINCIPLE. THROUGH THE OFFERING, the Female Principle rises up to ZEIR ANPIN and unites with him. Even though we find the explanation that the fire offering is for the Ishim, THE MASCULINE PLURAL FORM AND NOT FOR THE RAKINGS, WE LEARN FROM THE ALLUSION TO THE FEMALE PRINCIPLE.

232. נֹחַ אִצְטְרִיךְ לֵיהּ, לְמִקְרַב עוֹלָה, דְּאִיהוּ, בַּאֲתַר דִּדְכוּרָא עֲבַד לֵיהּ קֻדְשָׁא בְּרִיךְ הוּא, לְאִתְחַבְּרָא וּלְאַעֲלָאָה בַּתֵּיבָה. וְעַל דָּא, אַקְרִיב עוֹלָה. עוֹלָה הוּא אִשֶּׁה. אֵשׁ ה׳, דְּאִתְחַבַּר שְׂמָאלָא בְּנוּקְבָא, דְּהָא נוּקְבָא מִסִּטְרָא דִשְׂמָאלָא, קָא אַתְיָא, דְּאִתְדַּבַּק דָּא בְּדָא, וּבְגִין כָּךְ אִקְרֵי נוּקְבָא אִשָּׁה. אִשָּׁה קְטִירוּ דִרְחִימוּ, דְּאָחִיד בָּהּ שְׂמָאלָא, לְסַלְּקָא לָהּ לְעֵילָא, וּלְאִתְקַשְּׁרָא כַּחֲדָא. וּבְגִין כָּךְ, עוֹלָה הוּא אִשֶּׁה, קְשִׁירוּ דִּדְכַר וְנוּקְבָא, דָּא בְּדָא.

232. Noah should have sacrificed a burnt offering. For the Holy One, blessed be He, had established him in the place of the male, so that he could enter the ark, THE SECRET OF THE FEMALE PRINCIPLE, and be united with it. He offered a burnt offering, AND NOT ANY OTHER KIND OF SACRIFICE, BECAUSE HE DID NOT REALLY SIN. HE ONLY THOUGHT THAT HE HAD NO MERIT LEFT. "It is a burnt offering, an offering made by fire (isheh)," meaning the fire of Hei (esh Hei). This indicates that the left OF ZEIR ANPIN, WHICH IS CALLED 'FIRE,' joined with the Female Principle, CALLED HEI. The Female Principle comes from the left side, WHICH IS CALLED FIRE, AND when THE FEMALE PRINCIPLE and THE FIRE are joined, she is called a woman (Heb. isha). THE WORD ishah INDICATES the bond of love, as the left, WHICH IS FIRE, HOLDS HER, THE SECRET OF THE HEI. The fire raises her TO ZEIR ANPIN, binding them together as one. This is why the verse reads, "It is a burnt offering, an offering made by fire," INDICATING the bond of a male and female with each other.

31. "And Hashem smelled the sweet savor"

This complex section concerns the power of aroma to awaken and arouse great Lights. The various processes and conduits that spiritual currents must travel are revealed here by the Zohar. A contemporary example can shed some light on the ideas that are being presented. A computer contains a processor, which must make billions of computations per second in order to accomplish a task. In essence, the Zohar is describing the metaphysical computations taking place within the Ten Sfirot whenever the aroma of incense arouses the spiritual forces of Light. Perusing the Aramaic words connects us to these forces.

233. וַיָּרַח ה׳ אֶת רֵיחַ הַנִּיחֹחַ. וּכְתִיב, אִשֶּׁה רֵיחַ נִיחֹחַ. אִשֶּׁה, הָכֵי שְׁמַעְנָא תְּנָנָא וְאַשָּׁא מְחַבְּרִין כַּחֲדָא, דְּהָא לֵית תְּנָנָא, בְּלָא אֶשָּׁא, כְּמָה דִּכְתִיב וְהַר סִינַי עָשַׁן כֻּלּוֹ מִפְּנֵי אֲשֶׁר יָרַד עָלָיו ה׳ בָּאֵשׁ.

233. "And Hashem smelled the weet savor" (Beresheet 8:21). It is also written: "An offering made by fire, of a sweet savor" (Vayikra 1:13). I have heard that THE TERM "an offering made by fire" REFERS TO AN OFFERING IN WHICH smoke and fire are conjoined, since there is no smoke without fire. This is similar to the verse: "Now Mount Sinai was altogether smoke, because Hashem descended upon it in fire" (Shemot 19:18).

234. תָּא חֲזֵי, אֵשׁ נָפִיק מִלְּגָיו, וְאִיהוּ דַק, וְאָחִיד בְּמִלָּה אַחֲרָא לְבַר, דְּלָאו אִיהוּ דַק הָכֵי. וְאִתְאַחֲדָן דָּא בְּדָא, וּכְדֵין תְּנָנָא סַלְקָא, מַאי טַעְמָא, בְּגִין דְּאִתְאַחִיד אֶשָּׁא, בְּמִלָּה דְּרַגִּישׁ. וְסִימָנָךְ, חוּטְמָא דְּנָפִיק בֵּיהּ תְּנָנָא, מִגּוֹ אֶשָּׁא.

234. Come and behold: Fire comes from inside and is tenuous. It must attach itself to something on the outside that is not so tenuous. When fire and matter hold on to each other, smoke rises. Why? Because fire affects whatever reacts to it. An example is the nose, which reacts to the smoke that issues from the fire.

235. וְע״ד כְּתִיב, יָשִׂימוּ קְטוֹרָה בְּאַפֶּךָ. בְּגִין דְּאִתְהֲדָר אֶשָּׁא לְאַתְרֵיהּ,

וְחוֹטְמָא אִתְכְּנִישׁ, בְּהַהוּא רֵיחָא לְגוֹ לְגוֹ, עַד דְּאִתְאַחִיד כֹּלָּא, וְתָב לְאַתְרֵיהּ, וְאִתְקְרִיב כֹּלָּא לְגוֹ מַחֲשָׁבָה, וְאִתְעֲבֵיד רְעוּתָא חָדָא. וּכְדֵין רֵיחַ נִיחֹחַ דְּנָח רוּגְזָא וְאִתְעֲבֵיד נַיְיחָא.

235. Hence it is written: "They shall put incense before You (lit. 'in Your nose')" (Devarim 33:10), MEANING THAT THE JUDGMENTS WHICH ARE THE FIRE AND SMOKE ISSUING FROM THE NOSE ARE APPEASED BY INCENSE. It sends the fire FROM THE NOSE back to its place. Because of the smell of the incense, the nose contracts and reaches its innermost levels, until all are united. THEN EVERYTHING returns to its point of origin and they all come closer to Thought, WHICH IS ARICH ANPIN. Then they are combined into one desire, which is a sweet (Heb. *nichoach*) savor, which appeases anger and restores satisfaction (Heb. *nachat*).

236. דְּהָא תְּנָנָא אִתְכְּנִישׁ, וְעָיֵיל וְקָמִיט בְּאֶשָׁא, וְאֶשָׁא אָחִיד בִּתְנָנָא, וְעָיְילֵי תַּרְוַוייְהוּ לְגוֹ לְגוֹ, עַד דְּנָח רוּגְזָא. וְכַד אִתְאַחִיד כֹּלָּא דָּא בְדָא, וְנָח רוּגְזָא, כְּדֵין הוּא נַיְיחָא, וְקַשִׁירוּ חַד, וְאִתְקְרֵי נַיְיחָא דְרוּחָא. חֶדְוָותָא דְכֹלָּא כַּחֲדָא. נְהִירוּ דְבוֹצִינִין. נְהִירוּ דְאַנְפִּין. וּבְגִין כָּךְ כְּתִיב, וַיָּרַח ה' אֶת רֵיחַ הַנִּיחֹחַ. כְּמַאן דְּאָרַח וְכָנִישׁ כֹּלָּא, לְגוֹ אַתְרֵיהּ.

236. When the smoke is gathered, it enters and folds itself onto the fire, and the fire catches on to the smoke. Together, they enter the innermost levels, until anger is appeased. After they are all united and anger is appeased there is satisfaction and all are bonded together, and it is called 'appeasement', satisfaction, and universal rejoicing, all together. They are the radiance of the candles FROM THE LEFT SIDE and the brightness of the faces FROM THE RIGHT. Thus, it is written: "And Hashem smelled the sweet savor," as one who smells and gathers everything to himself.

237. אָתָא ר' יֵיסָא וּנְשָׁקֵיהּ. אֲמַר, וּמַה כָּל הֲדֵין טָבָא, אִית תְּחוֹת יְדָךְ וְלָא יְדַעְנָא בֵּיהּ. אֲמַר, אַהֲדַרְנָא מִן אוֹרְחָא, וְנִתְחַבֵּר בַּהֲדָךְ. אֲזְלוּ, אֲמַר רַבִּי חִזְקִיָּה, אָרְחָא דָא, בַּהֲדֵי שְׁכִינְתָּא נְהַךְ, דְּהָא מִתַּקְנָא קַמָּן.

אָחִיד בִּידָא דְּהַהוּא יְנוּקָא, וְאַזְלוּ. אָמְרוּ לֵיה, אֵימָא לָן קְרָא חַד,
מֵאִינּוּן דַּאֲמַר לָךְ אֲבוּךְ.

237. Rabbi Yesa then approached THE YOUNG BOY and kissed him, saying
that he did not realize that the boy possessed all these precious goods, and
added that he would change his route in order to accompany the boy. So
they all proceeded together. Rabbi Chizkiyah said: We are walking along
this route accompanied by the Shechinah, so it is cleared for us! He then
took hold of the young boy's hand and walked on. Then both rabbis
requested that he tell them one of the scriptural expositions that his father
has told him.

238. פָּתַח הַהוּא יְנוּקָא וְאָמַר, יִשָּׁקֵנִי מִנְּשִׁיקוֹת פִּיהוּ, דָּא הוּא
תְּאוּבְתָּא עִלָּאָה, דְּיִפּוֹק רְעוּתָא מִפּוּמָא. וְלָא נָפִיק מֵחוֹטְמָא, כַּד אֶשָׁא
נָפְקָא, דְּהָא כַּד אִתְחַבַּר פּוּמָא לְנַשְּׁקָא נָפִיק אֶשָׁא, בִּרְעוּתָא, בִּנְהִירוּ
דְּאַנְפִּין, בְּחֶדְוָה דְּכֹלָּא, בְּאִתְדַּבְּקוּתָא דְּנַיְיחָא.

238. The young boy started with the verse, "Let him kiss me with the kisses
of his mouth" (Shir Hashirim 1:2). This, he continued, is the supernal
passion. Because when the fire was issued, the desire came from the mouth
and not from the nose. Because when one mouth is connected TO SOMEONE
ELSE'S for the purpose of a kiss, fire emerges in the form of desire,
brightness of face, the rejoicing of all, and satisfied union.

239. וּבְגִין כָּךְ כִּי טוֹבִים דּוֹדֶיךָ מִיָּיִן. מֵהַהוּא יַיִן, דִּמְחֶדֵי וְנָהִיר אַנְפִּין,
וְחַיְיכִין עַיְינִין, וְעָבִיד רְעוּתָא. וְלָאו מִיַּיִן דִּמְשַׁכֵּר, וְעָבִיד רוּגְזָא,
וְאַחְשִׁיךְ אַנְפִּין וְלָהֲטָאן עַיְינִין, יַיִן דְּרוּגְזָא.

239. This is also why IT IS WRITTEN: "For your love is better than (also
'from') wine" (Ibid.). That is wine, it is come from the wine that brightens
the face and causes the eyes to laugh, bringing affection and friendship. It is
not from the wine that leads to drunkenness and that brings anger and rage,
causing darkening of the face and burning of the eyes.

240. וְעַל דָּא, בְּגִין דַּחֲמַר דָּא טַב, נָהֵיר אַנְפִּין, וְחַדֵי עַיְינִין, וְעָבִיד

תֵּיאוּבְתָּא דִּרְחִימוּ, מַקְרִיבִין לֵיהּ כָּל יוֹמָא, עַל גַּבֵּי מַדְבְּחָא. שִׁעוּרָא
דְּמַאן דְּשָׁתֵי לֵיהּ, חָדֵי לֵיהּ, וְעָבִיד לֵיהּ נַיְיחָא, דִּכְתִיב וְנִסְכּוֹ רְבִיעִית
הַהִין. וּבְגִין כָּךְ, כִּי טוֹבִים דּוֹדֶיךָ מִיָּיִן. מֵהַהוּא יַיִן, דְּאִתְּעַר רְחִימוּתָא
וְתֵיאוּבְתָּא.

240. Therefore, because this wine is good, it brightens the face, makes the
eyes merry, and arouses the passion for love. Thus, it is offered daily as a
sacrifice on the altar in a specific amount that makes whoever drinks it
merry and satisfied. As it is written: "And the wine offering thereof shall be
a fourth part of a *hin*" (this is a unit of measurement) (Bemidbar 28:7). This
is the reason IS, "your love is better from wine," for wine induces love and
passion.

241. וְכֹלָּא, כְּמָה דִּלְתַתָּא, אִתְּעַר רְחִימוּתָא דִּלְעֵילָא. תְּרֵין שְׁרַגִּין כַּד
אִתְדְּעַךְ נְהוֹרָא דִּלְעֵילָא, בִּתְנָנָא דְּסָלִיק, מֵהַהוּא דִּלְתַתָּא, אִתְדְּלִיק
הַהוּא דִּלְעֵילָא. אָמַר רָבִּי חִזְקִיָּה, הָכִי הוּא וַדַּאי, דְּעָלְמָא עִלָּאָה,
תַּלְיָא בְּתַתָּאָה, וְתַתָּאָה בְּעִלָּאָה וּמֵזִמְנָא דְּאִתְחָרִיב בֵּי מַקְדְּשָׁא,
בִּרְכָאן לָא אִשְׁתְּכָחוּ לְעֵילָא וְתַתָּא. לְאַחֲזָאָה דְּדָא בְּדָא תַּלְיָא.

241. And all, as it occurs below arouses love above. For there are two
candles, and when the light of the one on high is extinguished by rising
smoke from the one below, the upper one is lit. Rabbi Chizkiyah then said
that it is clearly true that the upper world, WHICH IS BINAH, depends on the
lower world, WHICH IS THE FEMALE PRINCIPLE. FOR, THE FEMALE
PRINCIPLE REKINDLES THE EXTINGUISHED BINAH. The lower world, THE
FEMALE PRINCIPLE, depends on the upper world, BINAH, BECAUSE THE
LIGHT THAT THE FEMALE PRINCIPLE MADE SHINE IN BINAH IS MERITED
BY THE FEMALE PRINCIPLE AS WELL. The fact that since the destruction of
the Temple, there are no more blessings above IN BINAH or below IN THE
FEMALE PRINCIPLE, shows that the two depend on each other.

242. וְאָמַר רָבִּי יוֹסֵי, בִּרְכָאן לָא אִשְׁתְּכָחוּ, וּלְוָוטִין אִשְׁתְּכָחוּ, דְּהָא
יְנִיקוּ דְּכֹלָּא, בְּהַהוּא סִטְרָא נָפְקֵי. מַאי טַעְמָא, בְּגִין דְּיִשְׂרָאֵל לָא שַׁרְיָין
בְּאַרְעָא, וְלָא פָּלְחֵי פּוּלְחָנָא דְּאִצְטְרִיךְ, לְאַדְלָקָא בּוֹצִינִין, וּלְאִשְׁתְּכָחָא

בִּרְכָאן, וּבְגִין כָּךְ לָא מִשְׁתַּכְּחֵי לְעֵילָא וְתַתָּא, וְעָלְמָא לָא יָתֵיב בְּקִיּוּמֵיהּ כִּדְקָא יָאוֹת.

242. And Rabbi Yosi said that there are no blessings, but curses do exist, because sustenance is drawn from that side, NAMELY, FROM LIGHTING THE UPPER CANDLE WITH THE SMOKE THAT RISES FROM THE LOWER ONE. Why? Because Yisrael do not reside in the land of Yisrael and do not worship properly. To worship properly is to light the candles, TO LIGHT THE UPPER CANDLE WITH THE LOWER ONE, and to draw down the blessings TO BE PASSED ONTO THE WORLDS. This is why there are no blessings above or below. Therefore the world is not maintained as it should.

243. וְאָמַר רַבִּי חִזְקִיָּה, לֹא אוֹסִיף לְקַלֵּל עוֹד אֶת הָאֲדָמָה בַּעֲבוּר הָאָדָם. מַאי הוּא, אָמַר רַבִּי יֵיסָא הָכֵי שְׁמַעֲנָא מֵרַבִּי שִׁמְעוֹן, דַּאֲמַר כָּל זִמְנָא דְּאֶשָּׁא דִּלְעֵילָא אוֹסִיף לְתָקְפָּא, תְּנָנָא דְּאִיהוּ דִּינָא דִּלְתַתָּא, אַתְקֵיף רוּגְזָא, וְשֵׁיצֵי כֹּלָּא. בְּגִין דְּכַד נָפִיק אֶשָּׁא, לֵית לֵיהּ פֶּסֶק, עַד דְּיִשְׁתְּלִים דִּינָא. וְכַד דִּינָא דִּלְתַתָּא לָא אוֹסִיף לְאִתְתַּקְפָא בְּדִינָא דִּלְעֵילָא, עָבִיד דִּינָא וּפָסִיק, וְלָא יִשְׁתַּלַם דִּינָא לְשֵׁיצָאָה. וּבְגִין כָּךְ כְּתִיב לֹא אוֹסִיף. לְמֵיהַב תּוֹסֶפֶת, לְאִתְתַּקְפָא דִּינָא דִּלְתַתָּא.

243. Then Rabbi Chizkiyah asked: What is the meaning of the verse that reads: "I will not again curse the ground any more for man's sake" (Beresheet 8:21)? COULD IT BE THAT THE HOLY ONE, BLESSED BE HE, FEELS REGRET? Rabbi Yesa answered that he had heard it was so from Rabbi Shimon, who said that as long as the upper fire OF BINAH spreads, THEN the smoke, which is the lower Judgment OF THE FEMALE PRINCIPLE intensifies the anger and destroys everything. For when the fire FROM BINAH comes forth, it does not stop until the punishment OF THE FEMALE PRINCIPLE, WHICH IS SMOKE, is carried out completely. So when the Judgment from below, THE SMOKE, ceases to gain strength by the Judgment from above, FROM THE FORCE OF THE FIRE, then the Judgment is done and stopps, and is not executed until destruction. That is why it is written: "I will not again," MEANING I WILL NOT CONTINUE TO ADD TO THE FIRE in order to intensify the Judgment down below, WHICH IS THE SMOKE.

244. אָמַר הַהוּא יְנוּקָא, שְׁמַעְנָא, בְּגִין דִּכְתִיב, אֲרוּרָה הָאֲדָמָה בַּעֲבוּרֶךְ. דְּהָא בְּהַהִיא שַׁעֲתָא דְּאִתְלַטְיָא אַרְעָא, בְּחוֹבָא דְּאָדָם. אִתְיְיהֵיב רְשׁוּ לְשַׁלְטָאָה עֲלָה, הַהוּא חִוְיָא בִישָׁא, דְּאִיהוּ מְחַבְּלָא דְּעָלְמָא, וְשֵׁצֵי בְּנֵי עָלְמָא. מֵהַהוּא יוֹמָא דְּקָרֵיב נֹחַ קָרְבָּנָא, וְאָרַח לֵיהּ קֻדְשָׁא בְּרִיךְ הוּא, אִתְיְיהֵיב רְשׁוּ לְאַרְעָא, לְנַפְקָא מִתְּחוֹת הַהוּא נָחָשׁ, וְנַפְקָא מִמְּסָאֲבָא. וְעַל דָּא מַקְרִיבִין יִשְׂרָאֵל קָרְבָּנָא לְקֻדְשָׁא בְּרִיךְ הוּא, בְּגִין לְאַנְהָרָא אַפֵּי אַרְעָא. אָמַר רָבִּי חִזְקִיָּה, יָאוּת הוּא, וְהַאי הֲוָה תָּלֵי עַד דְּקַיְימוּ יִשְׂרָאֵל עַל טוּרָא דְסִינַי.

244. The young boy said: I heard that the words, "Cursed is the ground for your sake" (Beresheet 3:17), indicate that the land has been cursed because of the sin of Adam, when the evil serpent received permission to rule over it. And as it is the destructive force in the world, THROUGH WHOM EVIL WAS SLOWLY REVEALED UNTIL IT BROUGHT THE FLOOD UPON THE EARTH and destroyed all the people of the world. IN OTHER WORDS, THE FLOOD REVEALED EVIL AND MADE IT POSSIBLE TO SEPARATE THE BAD FROM THE GOOD. But from the day when the Holy One, blessed be He, smelled Noah's sacrifice, HE SEPARATED THE BAD FROM THE GOOD, AND granted permission to the land to leave the dominion of the serpent and depart from the defiled side. FOR EVIL WAS SEPARATED FROM THE LAND. Therefore, Yisrael offer sacrifices to the Holy One, blessed be He, to brighten the face of the earth, WHICH IS MALCHUT. THAT IS, BECAUSE NOAH HAD NOT YET COMPLETED THE CORRECTION, YISRAEL STILL NEED TO OFFER SACRIFICES. Rabbi Chizkiyah said that this is indeed so, because THAT CORRECTION did not occur until Yisrael stood at Mount Sinai. THEN THE EVIL COMPLETELY SEPARATED FROM THE LAND, THE POLLUTION CEASED, AND THERE WAS FREEDOM FROM THE ANGEL OF DEATH, AS IS KNOWN.

245. אָמַר ר' יֵיסָא, קֻדְשָׁא בְּרִיךְ הוּא אַזְעֵיר לֵהּ לְסִיהֲרָא, וְשַׁלְטָא הַהוּא נָחָשׁ, אֲבָל בְּגִין חוֹבָא דְּאָדָם, אִתְלַטְיָיא, בְּגִין לְמֵילַט עָלְמָא. בְּהַהוּא יוֹמָא, נַפְקַת אַרְעָא מֵהַהִיא קְלָלָה, וְקַיְימָא סִיהֲרָא בְּהַהִיא גְּרִיעוּתָא, בַּר בְּשַׁעֲתָא דְּקוּרְבָּנָא אִשְׁתְּכַחוּ בְּעָלְמָא, וְיִשְׂרָאֵל יַתְבִין עַל

-404-

אַרְעֲהוֹן. אֲמַר רַבִּי יֵיסָא לְהַהוּא יְנוּקָא, מַה שְׁמָךְ, אֲמַר לוֹ אַבָּא. אֲמַר
לוֹ אַבָּא תְּהֵא בְּכֹלָּא, בְּחָכְמָה וּבִשְׁנִין. קָרָא עֲלֵיהּ יִשְׂמַח אָבִיךָ וְאִמֶּךָ
וְתָגֵל יוֹלַדְתֶּךָ.

245. Rabbi Yesa said that the Holy One, blessed be He, diminished the moon, WHICH WAS THE FEMALE PRINCIPLE, EVEN BEFORE ADAM SINNED and the serpent took over. But because of Adam's sin, it was cursed as well, in order to curse the world THAT RECEIVES LIGHT FROM IT. On the day THAT NOAH OFFERED HIS SACRIFICE, only the land, WHICH IS THE FEMALE PRINCIPLE was freed from the curse, but the moon's light was still diminished. Only when there is an offering in the world and the nation of Yisrael live in their land WILL MOON'S DEFICIENCY BE SET RIGHT. THIS REFERS TO THE TIME OF KING SOLOMON, AND CONTRADICTS THE WORDS OF THE YOUNG BOY, WHO SAID THAT NOAH'S OFFERING RESULTED IN PERMISSION FOR THE EARTH TO LEAVE THE DOMINION OF THE SERPENT. HE CLAIMED THAT THE CURSE HAD BEEN CANCELED, BUT THE DOMINION OF THE SERPENT STILL PREVAILED. THAT IS WHY THE OFFERINGS OF YISRAEL ARE REQUIRED IN THE TEMPLE. Rabbi Yesa then asked the young boy for his name. He replied: Aba (which means father). Rabbi Yesa continued, "You shall be a father in all things; you shall be A FATHER in wisdom and in years." And he applied to him the verse: "Your father and your mother will be glad and she that bore you shall rejoice" (Mishlei 23:25).

246. אֲמַר רַבִּי חִזְקִיָּה, זַמִּין קֻדְשָׁא בְּרִיךְ הוּא לְאַעֲבָרָא רוּחַ מִסְאֲבָא
מִן עָלְמָא, כְּמָה דִּכְתִיב וְאֶת רוּחַ הַטֻּמְאָה אַעֲבִיר מִן הָאָרֶץ. וּכְתִיב
בִּלַּע הַמָּוֶת לָנֶצַח וּמָחָה ה' אֱלֹקִים דִּמְעָה מֵעַל כָּל פָּנִים וְחֶרְפַּת עַמּוֹ
יָסִיר מֵעַל כָּל הָאָרֶץ כִּי ה' דִּבֵּר.

246. Rabbi Chizkiyah said that the Holy One, blessed be He, shall remove the spirit of uncleanliness from the world, as it is written: "And I will cause...the unclean spirit to pass out of the land" (Zecharyah 13:2) and also, "He will swallow up death forever, and Hashem Elohim will wipe away tears from off all faces, and the insult of His people shall He take away from off all the earth, for Hashem spoke" (Yeshayah 25:8).

247. וְזַמִּין קָדְשָׁא בְּרִיךְ הוּא לְאַנְהָרָא לְסִיהֲרָא, וְלָאֲפָקָא לָהּ מֵחֲשׁוֹכָא, בְּגִין הַהוּא חִוְיָא בִּישָׁא. כְּמָה דִּכְתִיב וְהָיָה אוֹר הַלְּבָנָה כְּאוֹר הַחַמָּה וְאוֹר הַחַמָּה יִהְיֶה שִׁבְעָתַיִם כְּאוֹר שִׁבְעַת הַיָּמִים. מַאי אוֹר, הַהוּא אוֹר, דְּגָנִיז לֵיהּ קָדְשָׁא בְּרִיךְ הוּא, בְּעוֹבָדָא דִּבְרֵאשִׁית.

247. And the Holy One, blessed be He, shall restore the moon to its full brightness and remove it from the darkness into which the evil serpent caused it to fall. As it is written: "And the light of the moon shall be as the light of the sun, and the light of the sun shall be sevenfold, as the light of the seven days" (Yeshayah 30:26). So HE ASKS: What is the light OF THE SEVEN DAYS? AND HE ANSWERS: IT is the light that the Holy One, blessed be He, hid away in the seven days of Creation!

32. "And Elohim blessed Noah"

The Zohar offers us the opportunity to draw in and manifest all the blessings that are generated though this passage.

248. וַיְבָרֶךְ אֱלֹקִים אֶת נֹחַ וְאֶת בָּנָיו וַיֹּאמֶר לָהֶם פְּרוּ וּרְבוּ וגו'. רַבִּי אַבָּא פָּתַח וַאֲמַר בִּרְכַּת ה' הִיא תַעֲשִׁיר וְלֹא יוֹסִיף עֶצֶב עִמָּהּ. בִּרְכַּת ה' דָּא שְׁכִינְתָּא, דְּאִיהִי אִתְפַּקְּדָא עַל בִּרְכָאן דְּעָלְמָא, וּמִנָּהּ נָפְקֵי בִּרְכָאן לְכֹלָא.

248. "And Elohim blessed Noah and his sons, and said to them, 'Be fruitful, and multiply, and replenish the earth'" (Beresheet 9:1). Rabbi Aba started the discussion by saying: "The blessing of Hashem, it makes rich, and He adds no sorrow with it" (Mishlei 10:22). So "the blessing of Hashem" is the Shechinah, who is in charge of the blessings of the world and from whom come all blessings.

249. תָּא חֲזֵי מַה כְּתִיב בְּקַדְמֵיתָא, וַיֹּאמֶר ה' לְנֹחַ בֹּא אַתָּה וְכָל בֵּיתְךָ אֶל הַתֵּבָה וגו'. כְּמָה דְאִתְּמַר, דְּמָארֵיהּ דְּבֵיתָא יְהַב לֵיהּ רְשׁוּ לְמֵיעָאל. לְבָתַר אִתְּתָא אֲמָרָה לֵיהּ לְנַפְקָא. בְּקַדְמֵיתָא עָאל בִּרְשׁוּתָא דְּבַעֲלָהּ, לְסוֹף נָפַק בִּרְשׁוּ דְּאִתְּתָא. מִכָּאן אוֹלִיפְנָא, מָארֵיהּ דְּבֵיתָא יָעִיל, וְאִתְּתָא תָּפֵיק, הה"ד וַיְדַבֵּר אֱלֹקִים אֶל נֹחַ לֵאמֹר צֵא מִן הַתֵּבָה. דְּרְשׁוּ הֲוָה בִידָהָא, לְאַפָּקָא לֵיהּ לְאוּשְׁפִּיזָא, וְלָא לְאַעֲלָא לֵיהּ.

249. Come and behold: What is written before THE VERSE THAT READS "AND ELOHIM BLESSED NOAH?" IT IS WRITTEN: "And Hashem said to Noah: Come you and all your house in the ark" (Beresheet 7:1). WHEN THEY ENTERED THE ARK THEY WERE ADDRESSED BY YUD HEI VAV HEI WHO IS ZEIR ANPIN, BUT WHEN THEY LEFT THE ARK THEY WERE ADDRESSED BY ELOHIM, WHO IS THE FEMALE PRINCIPLE OF ZEIR ANPIN. As has already been stated, the master of the House, WHO IS ZEIR ANPIN, gave NOAH permission to enter. Afterward, the Lady of the House, WHO IS THE FEMALE PRINCIPLE OF ZEIR ANPIN, allowed him to leave. SO HE ENTERED WITH THE PERMISSION OF THE HUSBAND, ZEIR ANPIN, AND LEFT BY PERMISSION FROM THE WIFE, WHO IS THE FEMALE

PRINCIPLE OF ZEIR ANPIN. From this we learn that the landlord should welcome THE VISITOR INTO THE HOUSE and the wife should escort him out. As it is written: "And Elohim spoke to Noah saying; go forth out of the ark" (Beresheet 8:15-16). Permission to leave is granted by the wife; permission to enter is not.

250. כֵּיוָן דְּנָפַק, יָהַב מַתְּנָן לָהּ, בְּגִין דְּאִיהִי בְּבֵיתָא, וּבֵיתָא בִּידָהָא. וְאִינּוּן מַתְּנָן דִּיהַב לָהּ, בְּגִין לְאַסְגָּאָה לָהּ רְחִימוּתָא בְּבַעֲלָהּ. מִכָּאן אוֹלִיפְנָא אוֹרַח אַרְעָא לְאוּשְׁפִּיזָא. וְעַל דָּא לְבָתַר דְּיִהַב לָהּ מַתְּנָן, לְאַסְגָּאָה לָהּ רְחִימוּתָא בְּבַעֲלָהּ, בֵּרְכָא לֵיהּ, דִּכְתִיב וַיְבָרֶךְ אֱלֹקִים אֶת נֹחַ וְאֶת בָּנָיו וַיֹּאמֶר לָהֶם פְּרוּ וּרְבוּ וְגוֹ'. וּבְגִין כָּךְ כְּתִיב בִּרְכַּת ה' הִיא תַעֲשִׁיר. וַדַּאי כְּמָה דְאִתְּמָר.

250. Because he left THE ARK, he presented her with gifts, NAMELY THE OFFERING OF A SACRIFICE. For she is in the "House," and it was in her hands. He offered her gifts to make her more lovable to her husband. From this we can learn how a guest should behave. HE SHOULD PRESENT THE LADY OF THE HOUSE WITH DEPARTING GIFTS. After he gives her the presents, so her husband will become fonder of her, she will bless him. As it is written: "And Elohim blessed Noah and his sons, and said to them, 'Be fruitful, and multiply,'" and also, "The blessing of Hashem, it makes rich," which definitely indicates THAT THE SHECHINAH, WHO IS RESPONSIBLE FOR THE BLESSINGS OF THE WORLD, IS HASHEM'S BLESSING.

251. וְלֹא יוֹסִיף עֶצֶב עִמָּהּ. רָזָא, דִּכְתִיב בְּעִצָּבוֹן תֹּאכְלֶנָּה, עִצָּבוֹן: עֲצִיבוּ וְרוּגְזָא בְּלָא נְהִירוּ דְאַנְפִּין. כַּד אִתְחֲשַׁךְ סִיהֲרָא וּבִרְכָאן לָא מִשְׁתַּכְחֵי. בְּעִצָּבוֹן: סִטְרָא דְּרוּחָא אָחֳרָא, דְּאַמְנַע בִּרְכָאן מֵעָלְמָא, וּבְגִין כָּךְ וְלֹא יוֹסִיף עֶצֶב עִמָּהּ. וְדָא הוּא רָזָא דִּכְתִיב לֹא אוֹסִיף לְקַלֵּל עוֹד אֶת הָאֲדָמָה.

251. "And He adds no sorrow with it" (Ibid.). This is the secret of the verse, "In sorrow shall you eat of it" (Beresheet 3:17). The word "sorrow" indicates sadness and anger, it means without a bright face. When the moon grows darker the blessings disappear. "In sorrow" refers to the spirit of the

Other Side, OR THE KLIPOT, which prevents blessings from reaching our world BY CAUSING PEOPLE TO SIN. The words, "And He adds no sorrow with it" hint at the secret of the verse: "I will not again curse the ground anymore" (Beresheet 8:21). FOR "SORROW" MEANS THAT THE OTHER SIDE TAKES HOLD, BRINGING CURSES UPON THE WORLD. THEREFORE, WHEN HE DOES NOT ADD ANY SORROW WITH IT, HE ALSO DOES NOT "AGAIN CURSE." BECAUSE BOTH ARE ONE AND THE SAME.

33. "And the fear of you and the dread of you"

Man has two bodies, one composed of Light – *Tzelem Elohim*, or Image of God – and the other composed of physical matter. The Light body is our protective shield that shines and projects outward from our physical selves. The Zohar explains that even deadly animals fear us when this force radiates at maximum power. Negative actions gradually weaken and dim this protective Light. This arouses fears within us, which in turn create vulnerabilities to destructive external forces.

This secret is concealed in the Torah story of God blessing Noah and his children so that all the animals shall fear them. Knowing this secret rekindles the Light aspect of our body.

252. וּמוֹרַאֲכֶם וְחִתְּכֶם יִהְיֶה. מִכָּאן וּלְהָלְאָה, יְהֵא לְכוֹן דְּיוֹקְנִין דִּבְנֵי נָשָׁא, דְּהָא בְּקַדְמֵיתָא לָא הֲווֹ דְּיוֹקְנִין דִּבְנֵי נָשָׁא. תָּא חֲזֵי, בְּקַדְמֵיתָא כְּתִיב בְּצֶלֶם אֱלֹקִים עָשָׂה אֶת הָאָדָם. וּכְתִיב בִּדְמוּת אֱלֹקִים עָשָׂה אוֹתוֹ. כֵּיוָן דְּחָטוּ אִשְׁתַּנּוּ דְּיוֹקְנַיְיהוּ, מֵהַהוּא דְּיוֹקְנָא עִלָּאָה, וְאִתְהַפְּכוּ אִינּוּן לְמִדְחַל מִקַּמֵּי חֵיוָון בָּרָא.

252. "And the fear of you and the dread of you shall be" (Beresheet 9:2) MEANS THAT from now on, you shall take the form of human beings, FROM WHICH THE WILD BEASTS FEAR. FROM THE TIME OF ADAM'S SIN UNTIL THIS POINT, they did not take the form of human beings. Now come and behold: In the beginning it is written: THE WILD BEASTS WERE AFRAID OF MAN "for in the image of Elohim made He man" (Ibid. 6), and also, "in the likeness of Elohim made He him" (Beresheet 5:1). But as people sinned, they no longer maintained the supernal image, and they became afraid of the beasts of the field.

253. בְּקַדְמֵיתָא, כָּל בִּרְיָין דְּעָלְמָא, זָקְפָן עַיְינִין, וְחָמָאן דְּיוֹקְנָא, קַדִּישָׁא עִלָּאָה, וְזָעָאן וְדָחֲלִין מִקַּמֵּיה. כֵּיוָן דְּחָטוּ אִתְהַפַּךְ דְּיוֹקְנַיְיהוּ, מֵעַיְינַיְיהוּ, לְדִיוֹקְנָא אַחֲרָא. וְאִתְהַפַּךְ דִּבְנֵי נָשָׁא זָעִין וְדָחֲלִין קַמֵּי שְׁאָר בִּרְיָין.

253. Formerly, the creatures of the world looked upon man and saw the holy supernal image and trembled with fear. But as people sinned, their image was transformed in the eyes of the beasts. This is why human beings now tremble with fear of other creatures.

254. תָּא חֲזֵי, כָּל אִינּוּן בְּנֵי נָשָׁא, דְּלָא חָטְאן קַמֵּי מָארֵיהוֹן, וְלָא עָבְרִין עַל פִּקּוּדֵי אוֹרַיְיתָא. זִיו דְּיוֹקְנָא דִּלְהוֹן, לָא אִשְׁתַּנֵּי מֵחֵיזוּ דִּדְיוֹקְנָא עִלָּאָה. וְכָל בְּרִיָּין דְּעָלְמָא, זָעִין וְדַחֲלִין קַמֵּיהּ. וּבְשַׁעֲתָא דִּבְנֵי נָשָׁא עָבְרִין עַל פִּתְגָּמֵי אוֹרַיְיתָא, אִתְחַלַּף דְּיוֹקְנָא דִּלְהוֹן, וְכֻלְּהוֹ זָעִין וְדַחֲלִין מִקַּמֵּי בְּרִיָּין אַחֲרָנִין, בְּגִין דְּאִתְחַלַּף דְּיוֹקְנָא עִלָּאָה, וְאִתְעֲבַר מִנַּיְיהוּ, וּכְדֵין שָׁלְטֵי בְּהוּ חֵיוַת בְּרָא, דְּהָא לָא חָמוּ בְּהוּ, הַהוּא דְּיוֹקְנָא עִלָּאָה כִּדְקָחֲזֵי.

254. Come and behold: All the people who do not sin before their Master and do not transgress against the precepts of the Torah, retain the divine splendor of the image OF ELOHIM. Therefore all the creatures of the world tremble with fear of them. But when the people transgress against the precepts of the Torah, their shape changes and they tremble and fear other creatures, because the supernal shape has left them. Because the beasts cannot see the supernal form in them anymore, they are ruled by the beasts of the field.

255. וְעַל כָּךְ, הַשְׁתָּא כֵּיוָן דְּעָלְמָא אִתְחַדַּשׁ כְּמִלְּקַדְמִין, בָּרִיךְ לוֹן, בִּרְכָה דָא, וְשַׁלִּיט לוֹן עַל כֹּלָּא, כד"א וְכָל דְּגֵי הַיָּם בְּיֶדְכֶם נִתָּנוּ. וַאֲפִילּוּ נוּנֵי יַמָּא. ר' חִיָּיא אֲמַר, בְּיֶדְכֶם נִתָּנוּ. מִקַּדְמַת דְּנָא. דְּכַד בְּרָא קֻדְשָׁא בְּרִיךְ הוּא עָלְמָא מְסַר כֹּלָּא בִּידֵיהוֹן, דִּכְתִיב, וּרְדוּ בִדְגַת הַיָּם וּבְעוֹף הַשָּׁמַיִם וְגו'.

255. When THEY LEFT THE ARK AND the world was renewed, He blessed them by granting them dominion over all THE CREATURES, even over the fish in the sea. As it is written: "And upon all the fishes of the sea; into your hand they are delivered" (Beresheet 9:2). Rabbi Chiya said that "into your hand they are delivered," indicates that when the Holy One, blessed be He, created the world, He delivered everything into the hands of man. As it is written: "and have dominion over the fish of the sea, and over the birds of the air..." (Beresheet 1:28). THAT IS TO SAY, THEY WERE SUBJUGATED TO PEOPLE ON THE DAY THAT ADAM WAS CREATED.

256. וַיְבָרֶךְ אֱלֹקִים אֶת נֹחַ, רַבִּי חִזְקִיָּה פָּתַח, לְדָוִד מַשְׂכִּיל אַשְׁרֵי נְשׂוּי פֶּשַׁע כְּסוּי חֲטָאָה. הַאי קְרָא אוּקְמוּהָ, אֲבָל קְרָא דָא, בְּרָזָא דְּחָכְמְתָא אִתְּמַר. דְּהָא תָּנִינָן, בַּעֲשָׂרָה זִינֵי שְׁבָחָא, שַׁבַּח דָּוִד לְקֻדְשָׁא בְּרִיךְ הוּא, וְחַד מִנַּיְיהוּ מַשְׂכִּיל. וְהוּא דַּרְגָּא חַד מֵאִינוּן עֲשָׂרָה. וְדָוִד אַתְקִין גַּרְמֵיהּ עַד לָא יִשְׁרֵי עֲלוֹי הַאי דַּרְגָּא.

256. "And Elohim blessed Noah." Rabbi Chizkiyah opened his discourse on the verse, "Of David, Maskil. Blessed is he whose transgression is forgiven, whose sin is covered" (Tehilim 32:1). He said that although this passage has been explained, it contains deep secrets of wisdom. We have learned that King David praised the Holy One, blessed be He, with ten levels of praises, WHICH ARE: CONDUCTING; PLAYING MELODY; MASKIL; EPIGRAMS (MICHTAM); PSALMS; SONG; BLESSING; PRAYER; THANKSGIVING, AND HALLELUYAH. THROUGH THESE PRAISES, KING DAVID ESTABLISHED THE BOOK OF TEHILIM. Maskil is the level THAT REFERS TO THE SECRET OF CHOCHMAH, and David perfected himself before attaining this level.

257. אַשְׁרֵי נְשׂוּי פֶּשַׁע: דְּהָא בְּשַׁעֲתָא דְּקֻדְשָׁא בְּרִיךְ הוּא, אַתְקִיל חוֹבֵי וְזַכְוָון דִּבְנֵי נָשָׁא, דְּהַהוּא תִּיקְלָא, דְּבִסְטַר חוֹבִין מִסְתַּלְּקִין, וְאִינוּן אוֹחֲרָנִין, זַכְיָין דְּאִינוּן בְּתִיקְלָא אָחֳרָא, מַכְרִיעִין לְתַתָּא, דָּא הוּא נְשׂוּי פֶּשַׁע.

257. "Blessed is he whose transgression is forgiven." THIS MEANS THAT when the Holy One, blessed be He, weighs the sins and the merits of men, transgression is forgiven when the merits overcome the sins and are pulled downward on the scale. THIS MEANS THAT HE HAS MORE MERITS THAN SINS. When this happens, his "transgression is forgiven."

258. כְּסוּי חֲטָאָה: בְּשַׁעֲתָא דְּדִינָא שַׁרְיָא בְּעָלְמָא, דִּיהֵא מְחַפְיָא, דְּלָא יִשְׁלוֹט עֲלוֹי מְחַבְּלָא, כְּמָה דַּהֲוָה לְנֹחַ, דְּכַסֵּי לֵיהּ קֻדְשָׁא בְּרִיךְ הוּא, מֵהַהוּא חֲטָאָה, דְּאַמְשִׁיךְ עֲלֵיהּ אָדָם עַל עָלְמָא. דְּכֵיוָן דַּחֲטָאָה דָא, אַנְגִּיד אָדָם עַל עָלְמָא, שְׁאָר בְּרִיָּין שָׁלְטָאן, וּבַר נָשׁ דָּחִיל מִנַּיְיהוּ, וְעָלְמָא לָא אַתְקִין בְּתִקּוּנֵיהּ. וּבְגִין כָּךְ, כַּד נָפַק נֹחַ מִתֵּיבוּתָא, קֻדְשָׁא

בְּרִיךְ הוּא בִּרְכֵיהּ. דִּכְתִיב, וַיְבָרֶךְ אֱלֹקִים אֶת נֹחַ וְאֶת בָּנָיו וְגוֹ'.

258. The verse, "Whose sin is covered," means that when Judgment prevails in the world, sin should be covered so that the Angel of Destruction does not take control of it. This is what happened with Noah DURING THE FLOOD, when the Holy One, blessed be He, shielded him from Adam's sin OF THE TREE OF KNOWLEDGE OF GOOD AND EVIL, that Adam brought down upon the world. BECAUSE THE ANGEL OF DESTRUCTION DID NOT SEE NOAH, HE WAS UNABLE TO TAKE HOLD ON HIM AND PUNISH HIM. But because Adam brought sin upon the world, WE FIND THAT the other creatures were given control, the human being is afraid of them, and the world has not reached perfection. So when Noah left the ark, the Holy One, blessed be He, blessed him. As it is written: "And Elohim blessed Noah and his sons…" . AND, ALSO, "THE FEAR OF YOU AND THE DREAD OF YOU SHALL BE UPON EVERY BEAST OF THE FIELD…" WHICH MEANS THAT HIS FORM BECAME LIKE THAT OF ADAM BEFORE THE SIN OF THE TREE OF KNOWLEDGE, WHEN ALL THE CREATURES FEARED HIM.

259. וְאַתֶּם פְּרוּ וּרְבוּ. בְּהַנֵּי בִּרְכָאן, לָא אִשְׁתַּכְּחוּ נוּקְבֵי, אֶלָּא אֶת נֹחַ וְאֶת בָּנָיו, אֲבָל נוּקְבֵי לָא אָמַר קְרָא. אָמַר רִבִּי שִׁמְעוֹן, וְאַתֶּם כְּלָלָא דִּדְכוּרֵי וְנוּקְבֵי כַּחֲדָא. וְתוּ, אֶת נֹחַ, לְאַסְגָּאָה נוּקְבֵיהּ. וְאֶת בָּנָיו, לְאַסְגָּאָה נוּקְבֵי דִּלְהוֹן.

259. "And as for you, be fruitful, and multiply" (Beresheet 9:7). HE RAISED THE ISSUE THAT women do not seem to be included in these blessings, as the verse mentions only Noah and his sons, but not women. Rabbi Shimon said that the term "and you" WITH AN ADDED *VAV*, WHICH MEANS 'AND,' indicates that the males and the females were both included. THE LETTER *VAV* THAT APPEARS HERE INDICATES THE FEMALE PRINCIPLE. Not only that, but in the verse, "And Elohim blessed Noah," THE PARTICLE *ET* BEFORE 'ELOHIM' IS THE NAME OF THE FEMALE PRINCIPLE. AND IT IS ALSO MENTIONED HERE to include NOAH'S wife. And in the line, "And (et) his sons," THE PARTICLE *ET* IS USED to indicate that their wives are included.

260. וּבְגִין כָּךְ כְּתִיב, וְאַתֶּם פְּרוּ וּרְבוּ. לְמֶעְבַּד תּוֹלָדוֹת. מִכָּאן וּלְהָלְאָה

שָׁרְצוּ בָאָרֶץ. וְהָכָא יָהֵיב לוֹן קֻדְשָׁא בְּרִיךְ הוּא שֶׁבַע פְּקוּדֵי אוֹרַיְיתָא.
לוֹן וּלְכָל דְּאָתוּ אֲבַתְרַיְיהוּ, עַד דְּקַיְימוּ יִשְׂרָאֵל בְּטוּרָא דְסִינַי, וְאִתְיְיהַב
לוֹן כָּל פְּקוּדֵי אוֹרַיְיתָא כַּחֲדָא.

260. Because it is written: "And as for you, be fruitful, and multiply," propagate your kind, WE KNOW THAT WOMEN WERE ALSO BLESSED. And from here onward, "bring forth abundantly in the earth" (Beresheet 9:7), in which the Holy One, blessed be He, gave them – to all of them who followed after – seven precepts of the Torah. When Yisrael stood on Mount Sinai, they were given all the precepts of the Torah together.

34. "I have set My rainbow in the cloud"

The Zohar explains that the rainbow is a sign indicating that a great destruction was forthcoming, but it has been prevented by the hand of God. Reading this section infuses us with the same Light of protection expressed by the sign of the rainbow.

261. וַיֹּאמֶר אֱלֹקִים לְנֹחַ וגו׳. זֹאת אוֹת הַבְּרִית אֲשֶׁר אֲנִי נוֹתֵן בֵּינִי וּבֵינֵיכֶם וגו׳. אֶת קַשְׁתִּי נָתַתִּי בֶּעָנָן. נָתַתִּי מִקַּדְמַת דְּנָא. רָבִּי שִׁמְעוֹן פָּתַח וּמִמַּעַל לָרָקִיעַ אֲשֶׁר עַל רֹאשָׁם כְּמַרְאֵה אֶבֶן סַפִּיר דְּמוּת כִּסֵּא. מַה כְּתִיב לְעֵילָא, וָאֶשְׁמַע אֶת קוֹל כַּנְפֵיהֶם כְּקוֹל מַיִם רַבִּים כְּקוֹל שַׁדַּי בְּלֶכְתָּן. אִלֵּין אַרְבַּע חֵיוָון רַבְרְבָן עִלָּאִין קַדִּישִׁין, דְּהַהוּא רְקִיעַ מִתְתַּקְנָא עֲלַיְיהוּ. וְכֻלְּהוּ גַּדְפַיְיהוּ מִתְחַבְּרָאן דָּא בְּדָא, לְחַפְיָיא גּוּפַיְיהוּ.

261. "And Elohim said to Noah... this is the sign of the covenant which I make between Me and you... I have set My rainbow in the cloud" (Beresheet 9:8, 12-13). The words, "I have set," SHOW THAT He had already set the rainbow. Rabbi Shimon commented on the verse: "And above the firmament that was over their heads was the likeness of a throne, with the appearance of a sapphire stone" (Yechezkel 1:26). Before this, it is written: "And when they went out I heard the noise (voice) of their wings, like the noise of great waters, as the voice of Shadai" (Ibid. 24). These words refer to the four sacred and mighty supreme living creatures upon whom the firmament rests. Their wings are joined together to cover their bodies.

262. וּבְשַׁעֲתָא דְּאִינוּן פָּרְשֵׂי גַּדְפַיְיהוּ, אִשְׁתְּמַע קוֹל גַּדְפִין דְּכֻלְּהוּ, דְּאָמְרֵי שִׁירָתָא, הה״ד כְּקוֹל שַׁדַּי. דְּלָא אִשְׁתְּכִיךְ לְעָלְמִין. כְּמָה דִּכְתִיב לְמַעַן יְזַמֶּרְךָ כָבוֹד וְלֹא יִדֹּם. וּמַאי אָמְרֵי, הוֹדִיעַ ה׳ יְשׁוּעָתוֹ לְעֵינֵי הַגּוֹיִם גִּלָּה צִדְקָתוֹ.

262. When they spread their wings, the singing voice of all their wings is heard, and the words, "as the voice of Shadai," indicate that this voice is never silent. As it is also written: "may sing praise to You, and not be silent" (Tehilim 30:13). HE THEN ASKS: What do they say? AND HE

ANSWERS: They say: "Hashem has made known His salvation, His righteousness He has revealed in the sight of the nations" (Tehilim 98:2).

263. קוֹל הַמְּלָה כְּקוֹל מַחֲנֶה, כְּקוֹל מַשִׁרְיָיתָא קַדִּישָׁא, כַּד מִתְחַבְּרָן כָּל חֵילִין עִלָּאִין לְעֵילָא. וּמַאי אָמְרֵי, קָדוֹשׁ קָדוֹשׁ קָדוֹשׁ ה' צְבָאוֹת מְלֹא כָל הָאָרֶץ כְּבוֹדוֹ. אַהְדְּרוּ לְדָרוֹם, אָמְרוּ קָדוֹשׁ, אַהְדְּרוּ לְצָפוֹן אָמְרוּ קָדוֹשׁ. אַהְדְּרוּ לְמִזְרָח, אָמְרוּ קָדוֹשׁ. אַהְדְּרוּ לְמַעֲרָב, אָמְרוּ בָּרוּךְ.

263. The words: "The noise of commotion, as the noise of a host" (Yechezkel 1:24), signify the noise of the holy camp, with its supernal armies assembled on high. HE ASKS: "And what do they say?" AND HE ANSWERS: THEY SAY "Holy, holy, holy is Hashem Tz'vaot, the whole earth is full of His glory" (Yeshayah 6:3). They face south and say "Holy," then they face north and say "Holy," then they face east and say "Holy," and then they face west and say "blessed."

264. וְהַאי רָקִיעַ קָאִים עַל רֵישֵׁיהוֹן. וּבְכָל אֲתַר דְּאִיהִי אַזְלָא, אַסְחֲרוּ אַפִּין לְהַהִיא סִטְרָא, דְּאִתְכְּלִילוּ אַנְפִּין בֵּיהּ. אַסְחֲרוּ אַנְפִּין לְאַרְבַּע זְוְיָין, וְכֻלְהוּ מִסְתַּחֲרִין לְתַתָּא.

264. And that firmament rests on top of their heads, so wherever THE LIVING CREATURE moves, it turns its head and faces all four faces gathered within. They turn and face all four corners of the world, ALL FOUR DIRECTIONS OF THE WINDS, and they are all brought back and spread downward.

265. בְּרִבּוּעָא דִילֵיהּ, אִתְגְּלִיפַת בְּאַרְבַּע אַנְפִּין, אַנְפֵּי אַרְיֵה. אַנְפֵּי נִשְׁרָא. אַנְפֵּי שׁוֹר. אַנְפֵּי אָדָם. גָּלִיף בְּכֻלְהוּ, אָדָם. אַנְפֵּי אַרְיֵה, אָדָם. אַנְפֵּי נֶשֶׁר, אָדָם. אַנְפֵּי שׁוֹר, אָדָם. כֻּלְהוּ כְּלִילָן בֵּיהּ. וּבְגִין כָּךְ כְּתִיב, וּדְמוּת פְּנֵיהֶם פְּנֵי אָדָם.

265. The four faces OF THESE LIVING CREATURES are imprinted on all four sides OF THE FIRMAMENT, WHICH ARE THE "FOUR WINDS" – SOUTH,

NORTH, EAST AND WEST. The face of a lion IS IMPRINTED TO THE SOUTH; the face of an ox TO THE NORTH; the face of an eagle TO THE EAST; and the face of a man TO THE WEST. All of the faces are also imprinted with the face of man: the face of a lion IS IMPRINTED WITH the face of a man, the face of an eagle with the face of a man, and the face of an ox with the face of a man. All faces are included in the face of a man, and this is why it is written: "As for the likeness of their faces, they each had the likeness of a man (Yechezkel 1:10). THIS MEANS THAT ALL FOUR HAVE THE FACE OF A MAN.

266. וְהַאי רָקִיעַ דְּאִתְרַבַּע, כָּלְהוּ גְּוָונִין כְּלִילָן בֵּיהּ, אַרְבַּע גְּוָונִין אִתְחַזְיָין בֵּיהּ, גְּלִיפִין בְּאַרְבַּע אַרְבַּע. בְּאַרְבַּע גְּלִיפִין, רְשִׁימִין טְהִירִין, עִלָּאִין וְתַתָּאִין. כַּד מִתְפָּרְשָׁאן גְּוָונִין דְּאִינּוּן אַרְבַּע, סָלְקִין תְּרֵיסַר. גְּוָון יָרָק. גְּוָון סוּמָק גְּוָון חִוָּור, גְּוָון סַפִּיר, דְּאִתְכְּלִילוּ מִכָּל גְּוָונִין. הה״ד כְּמַרְאֵה הַקֶּשֶׁת אֲשֶׁר יִהְיֶה בֶעָנָן בְּיוֹם הַגֶּשֶׁם כֵּן מַרְאֵה הַנּוֹגַהּ סָבִיב הוּא מַרְאֵה דְּמוּת כְּבוֹד ה׳. חֵיזוּ דִגְוָונִין דְּכֹלָּא. וּבְגִין כָּךְ, אֶת קַשְׁתִּי נָתַתִּי בֶּעָנָן.

266. Now the firmament is a square THAT POINTS IN FOUR DIRECTIONS AND contains all of the colors, four of which – WHITE, RED, GREEN AND BLACK – are seen in it. EACH OF THESE COLORS IS imprinted with all four colors, SO WE HAVE SIXTEEN COLORS ALTOGETHER. The upper ones are imprinted with four engravings. The same applies to the lower ons. When these four colors spread out, they become twelve, AND NOT SIXTEEN. THE COLORS ARE green, red, white and sapphire, which is a combination of the first three colors. IN OTHER WORDS, THE COLOR SAPPHIRE, WHICH IS MALCHUT, IS NOT REALLY A COLOR BY ITSELF, BUT A COMBINATION OF THE THREE OTHER COLORS. SO WE HAVE THREE COLORS MULTIPLIED BY FOUR, WHICH ADDS UP TO TWELVE. This is why it is written: "As the appearance of the rainbow that is in the cloud in the day of rain...so was the appearance of the brightness round about. This was the appearance of the likeness of the glory of Hashem" (Ibid. 28). THIS APPEARANCE AND LIKENESS, MALCHUT, contains all three colors, MEANING THAT MALCHUT HAS NO COLOR OF HER OWN, BUT CONTAINS THE OTHER THREE COLORS. That is why it is written: "I have set My rainbow in the cloud."

267. מַאי קַשְׁתִּי, כְּמָה דְּאִתְּמַר בְּיוֹסֵף, דִּכְתִיב וַתֵּשֶׁב בְּאֵיתָן קַשְׁתּוֹ.

בְּגִין דְּיוֹסֵף צַדִּיק אִקְרֵי, וּבְגִין כָּךְ, קַשְׁתּוֹ: דָּא בְּרִית דְּקֶשֶׁת, דְּאִתְכְּלִיל בְּצַדִּיק, דִּבְרִית, דָּא בְּדָא אִתְאַחֵיד. וּבְגִין דְּנֹחַ הֲוָה צַדִּיק, קָיְימָא דִילֵיהּ קֶשֶׁת.

267. HE ASKS: What is meant by "My rainbow"? AND HE REPLIES: 'It is similar to what has been said about Joseph, "But his bow (rainbow) abode is strength" (Beresheet 49:24). THE RAINBOW SUGGESTS MALCHUT, AND since Joseph is called righteous, WHICH IS THE ATTRIBUTE OF YESOD, "his rainbow" refers to the "covenant of the rainbow," YESOD OF MALCHUT. THE COVENANT IS YESOD AND THE RAINBOW MALCHUT. The rainbow is incorporated in the Righteous because the covenant, YESOD united with it. And because Noah was righteous, HIS COVENANT was established AND INCLUDED in THE SECRET OF the rainbow.

268. וַיָּפֹזּוּ. מַאי וַיָּפֹזּוּ, אַנְהִירוּ בַּחֲמִידוּ דְכֹלָּא. כד"א הַנֶּחֱמָדִים מִזָּהָב וּמִפַּז רָב וּמְתוּקִים. אִתְנְהִירוּ בִּנְהִירוּ עִלָּאָה, כַּד נָטַר בְּרִית. וּבְגִין כָּךְ, אִקְרֵי יוֹסֵף הַצַּדִּיק. עַל דָּא, אִקְרֵי הַקֶּשֶׁת בְּרִית, כָּלִיל דָּא בְּדָא.

268. "Were made supple (Heb. *vayaphozu*)" (Ibid.). HE ASKS, what is the meaning of *vayaphozu* (lit. 'to make strong')? AND HE REPLIES THAT HIS HANDS were shining from the light that is AS PURE GOLD (HEB. *PAZ*) AND desired by all. This relates to the verse, "More to be desired are they than gold, even much fine gold (Heb. *paz*); sweeter... " (Tehilim 19:11). This means that HIS HANDS shone with the supernal light because he observed the covenant. This is why WHEN HE MERITED THE COVENANT, he was called "Joseph the Righteous." The rainbow was also called the covenant, because he and the rainbow are combined and included within each other, AS PREVIOUSLY EXPLAINED.

269. וְדָא זָהֲרָא יְקָרָא עִלָּאָה, חֵיזוּ דְּכָל חֵיזוּ. חָזוּ כְּחֵיזוּ טְמִירִין, גְּוָונִין טְמִירִין. גְּוָונִין דְּלָא אִתְגַּלְיָין. וְלֵית רְשׁוּ לְאִסְתַּכְּלָא בְּעֵינָא בַּקֶּשֶׁת, כַּד אִתְחֲזֵי בְּעָלְמָא, דְּלָא יִתְחֲזֵי קְלָנָא בִּשְׁכִינְתָּא. וְכֵן גְּוָונִין דְּקֶשֶׁת הוּא חֵיזוּ סוֹסְטִיפָא קְטִירָא, כְּחֵיזוּ יְקָרָא עִלָּאָה, דְּלָא לְאִסְתַּכְּלָא.

269. And THE RAINBOW is the splendor of the supernal glory, the sight beyond all sights. MALCHUT, CALLED THE SUPERNAL GLORY, CONTAINS ALL THE SIGHTS. It is also the sight of the hidden LIGHTS, WHICH ARE the hidden and unrevealed colors. The eye is not permitted to look at the rainbow when it appears in the world. For the rainbow exposes fault in the Shechinah. Furthermore, the colors of the rainbow are connected with the "appearance of the mist and the cloud," WHICH MEAN THAT THEY ARE COVERED UP. Like the appearance of the supernal glory, it should not be gazed upon.

270. וְכֵיוָן דְּאַרְעָא חָמָאת לְהַאי קֶשֶׁת, קַיְימָא קַדִּישָׁא, אִתְקָיְימַת בְּקִיּוּמָא. וְעַל דָּא, וְהָיְתָה לְאוֹת בְּרִית בֵּין אֱלֹקִים וְגוֹ'. הַאי דַּאֲמָרָן, דְּאִלֵּין תְּלַת גְּוָונִין, וְחַד דְּאִתְכְּלֵיל בֵּינַיְיהוּ, כֻּלְּהוּ רָזָא חֲדָא. וּבְגוֹ עֲנָנָא סָלְקָא לְאִתְחֲזָאָה.

270. But because the earth looks at the rainbow, MALCHUT, CALLED THE EARTH, IS COMPLETED BY THE RAINBOW AND then the sacred COVENANT is properly established. Therefore, "it shall be for a sign of a covenant between Elohim... " (Beresheet 9:13). What we previously stated, that these are three colors – WHITE, RED AND GREEN – and one OTHER COLOR that is comprised of the other three, all form one secret. THIS MEANS THAT THE RAINBOW IS FORMED BY THESE THREE COLORS AND A FOURTH THAT IS A COMBINATION OF THEM. And THE RAINBOW climbs to the clouds to show itself, BECAUSE IT CAN ONLY BE SEEN FROM WITHIN A CLOUD.

271. וּמִמַּעַל לָרָקִיעַ אֲשֶׁר עַל רֹאשָׁם כְּמַרְאֵה אֶבֶן סַפִּיר. הַאי הִיא אֶבֶן שְׁתִיָּה, דְּאִיהִי נְקוּדָה חֲדָא, דְּכָל עָלְמָא. וְקָיְימָא עֲלָהּ קֹדֶשׁ הַקֳּדָשִׁים. וּמַאי הִיא כָּרְסְיָיא קַדִּישָׁא עִלָּאָה, דְּאִיהִי מְמַנָּא עַל אִלֵּין אַרְבַּע. דְּמוּת כִּסֵּא, בְּאַרְבַּע סָמְכִין, וְדָא הוּא תּוֹרָה שֶׁבְּעַל פֶּה.

271. "And above the firmament that was over their heads was the likeness of a throne, as the appearance of a sapphire stone" (Yechezkel 1:26). This SAPPHIRE STONE is the Foundation Stone, which is one point upon which the whole world stands. Upon it, the Holy of Holies is established. What is this POINT? It is the supernal holy throne, which is appointed over the four COLORS. It bears a resemblance to a throne and its four supports, WHICH

ARE THE FOUR COLORS, WHITE, RED, GREEN AND SAPPHIRE. This THRONE is the Oral Law, MALCHUT.

272. וְעַל דְּמוּת הַכִּסֵּא דְּמוּת כְּמַרְאֵה אָדָם עָלָיו מִלְמַעְלָה. דָּא הוּא תּוֹרָה שֶׁבִּכְתָב. מִכָּאן דְּתוֹרָה שֶׁבִּכְתָב יְשַׁוּוּן יָתָהּ, עַל תּוֹרָה שֶׁבְּעַל פֶּה. בְּגִין דְּהַאי כָּרְסְיָיא לְדָא, כְּמַרְאֵה אָדָם. דְּאִיהוּ דְּיוֹקְנָא דְּיַעֲקֹב, דְּאִיהוּ יָתִיב עֲלָהּ.

272. "And upon the likeness of a throne was the likeness as the appearance of a man upon it above" (Ibid.). This refers to the Written Law, NAMELY ZEIR ANPIN. From this we learn that the Written Law should be placed above the Oral Law, because the one is a throne for the other. "As the appearance of a man" refers to the image of Jacob, WHO IS ZEIR ANPIN, because he sits upon this throne.

35. "And this stone which I have set for a pillar"

Within this discussion, the Zohar stresses the importance of properly preparing oneself – mind, body and soul – before entering the gates of Torah study. The reason given by the Zohar concerns the supernal forces and the souls of the righteous, who traverse many worlds to join us whenever we learn. True spiritual study does not pertain to the acquisition of external knowledge. Learning and studying the secrets of the Torah is the sum and substance of Light Itself. Specifically, *study* and *Light* are one and the same. Therefore, when we study, we are, in reality, bringing the spiritual forces of Light into full manifestation. This understanding helps us prepare our entire being, so that we may become worthy vessels for the Light of the Creator to fill.

273. רַבִּי יְהוּדָה, קָם לֵילְיָא חַד לְמִלְעֵי בְּאוֹרַיְיתָא, בְּפַלְגוּ לֵילְיָא, בְּבֵי אוּשְׁפִּיזָא, בְּמָתָא מַחְסְיָא. וַהֲוָה תַּמָּן בְּבֵיתָא, חַד יוּדָאי, דְּאָתָא בִּתְרֵי קִסִירָא דִקְטְפִירָא. פָּתַח רַבִּי יְהוּדָה וַאֲמַר, וְהָאֶבֶן הַזֹּאת אֲשֶׁר שַׂמְתִּי מַצֵּבָה יִהְיֶה בֵּית אֱלֹקִים. דָּא הִיא אֶבֶן שְׁתִיָּה, דְּמִתַּמָּן אִשְׁתִּיל עָלְמָא, וַעֲלָהּ אִתְבְּנֵי בֵּי מַקְדְּשָׁא.

273. Rabbi Yehuda woke up one night to study Torah. It was midnight in a guest house in the town of Mata-Machesya. There was a Jew staying there, who had arrived with two sacks of clothes TO SELL. Rabbi Yehuda opened the discussion, saying, "And this stone which I have set for a pillar shall be the house of Elohim" (Beresheet 28:22). That STONE, he continued, is the Foundation Stone, on which the world was planted. And on that stone the Temple was built!

274. זָקַף רֵישֵׁיהּ, הַהוּא יוּדָאי וְאָמַר לוֹ הַאי מִלָּה אֵיךְ אֶפְשָׁר, וְהָא אֶבֶן שְׁתִיָּה עַד לָא אִתְבְּרֵי עָלְמָא הֲוַת, וּמִינָהּ אִשְׁתִּיל עָלְמָא, וְאַתְּ אֲמַרְתְּ וְהָאֶבֶן הַזֹּאת אֲשֶׁר שַׂמְתִּי מַצֵּבָה. דְּמַשְׁמַע דְּיַעֲקֹב שַׁוֵּי לָהּ הַשְׁתָּא, דִּכְתִיב וַיִּקַּח אֶת הָאֶבֶן אֲשֶׁר שָׂם מְרַאֲשׁוֹתָיו. וְתוּ, דְּיַעֲקֹב בְּבֵית אֵל הֲוָה, וְהַאי אַבְנָא הֲוָה בִּירוּשְׁלֵם.

274. The Jew raised his head up and said: How can this be possible? As the

Foundation Stone existed before the world was created and from it the world was planted. You claim that "this stone which I have set for a pillar" means that until Jacob set it AS A PILLAR, IT WAS NOT PROPERLY SET AND DID NOT STAND IN ITS PLACE. As it is written: "And he took the stone he had put under his head" (Beresheet 22:11). BUT THE FOUNDATION STONE WAS ESTABLISHED AND STOOD IN ITS PLACE BEFORE THE CREATION OF THE WORLD. And furthermore, Jacob was in Bethel, while the FOUNDATION Stone was in Jeruslaem, WHERE IT STANDS IN THE PLACE OF THE TEMPLE.

275. רַבִּי יְהוּדָה, לָא אַסְחַר רֵישֵׁיה לְגַבֵּיה, פְּתַח וַאֲמַר הִכּוֹן לִקְרַאת אֱלֹקֶיךָ יִשְׂרָאֵל. וּכְתִיב הַסְכֵּת וּשְׁמַע יִשְׂרָאֵל. מִלֵּי דְאוֹרַיְיתָא בָּעְיָין כַּוְונָה. וּמִלִּין דְאוֹרַיְיתָא, בָּעָאן לְאִתְתַּקְנָא בְּגוּפָא וּרְעוּתָא כַּחֲדָא. קָם הַהוּא יוּדָאי, וְאִתְלַבַּשׁ, וְיָתֵיב לְגַבֵּיה דְרַבִּי יְהוּדָה, וַאֲמַר זַכָּאִין אַתּוּן צַדִּיקַיָּא, דְמִשְׁתַּדְּלֵי בְּאוֹרַיְיתָא יוֹמָא וְלֵילֵי.

275. Rabbi Yehuda, without turning his face toward him, quoted the verse, "Prepare to meet your Elohim, O Yisrael" (Amos 4:12). He continued, as it is written: "Take heed and hear, O Yisrael" (Devarim 27:3). This means that the words of Torah require full attention and that it should be approached with the body and soul properly focused. The Jew rose, dressed, sat by Rabbi Yehuda's side, and said: 'Happy are you righteous who study the Torah day and night!'

276. אֲמַר לוֹ רַבִּי יְהוּדָה, הַשְׁתָּא דְכַוְונַת גַּרְמָךְ, אֵימָא מִילָךְ, דְנִתְחַבַּר כַּחֲדָא. דְהָא מִלֵּי דְאוֹרַיְיתָא בָּעְיָין תִּקּוּנָא דְגוּפָא, וְתִקּוּנָא דְלִבָּא. וְאִי לָאו, בְּעַרְסָאי שְׁכִיבְנָא וּבְלִבָּאי אֲמַרְנָא מִלִּין. אֶלָּא הָא תָּנִינָן, דַּאֲפִילוּ חַד דְּיָתֵיב וְלָעֵי בְּאוֹרַיְיתָא שְׁכִינְתָּא אִתְחַבְּרַת בַּהֲדֵיה, וּמַה שְׁכִינְתָּא הָכָא, וַאֲנָא שָׁכִיב בְּעַרְסָאי. וְלָא עוֹד, אֶלָּא דְבַעְיָין צָחוּתָא.

276. Rabbi Yehuda said to him: Now that you have properly prepared yourself, we shall join one another and you can say what you want to say. For before discussing Torah, a person has to properly prepare his body and heart. If this were not so, I would lay in bed and think of these things in my heart. But we have learned that even one person, sitting and studying Torah,

is accompanied by the Shechinah. And if the Shechinah is already here, how can I lay in bed? Also, IN ORDER TO DELVE INTO TORAH, a person requires a clear mind. AND HE WHO LIES IN HIS BED DOES NOT HAVE A CLEAR MIND.

277. וְתוּ, דְּכָל בַּר נָשׁ, דְּקָם לְמִלְעֵי בְּאוֹרַיְיתָא, מִפַּלְגוּ לֵילְיָא, כַּד אִתְעַר רוּחַ צָפוֹן, קֻדְשָׁא בְּרִיךְ הוּא אָתֵי לְאִשְׁתַּעְשְׁעָא עִם צַדִּיקַיָּא בְּגִנְתָּא דְעֵדֶן. וְהוּא וְכָל צַדִּיקַיָּא דִּבְגִנְתָּא, כֻּלְּהוּ צַיְיתִין לְאִלֵּין מִלִּין דְּנָפְקֵי מִפּוּמֵיהּ. וּמַה קֻדְשָׁא בְּרִיךְ הוּא, וְכָל צַדִּיקַיָּא, מִתְעַדְּנִין לְמִשְׁמַע מִלֵּי דְאוֹרַיְיתָא בְּשַׁעֲתָא דָא. וַאֲנָא אֱהֵא שָׁכִיב בְּעַרְסָאי. אָמַר לֵיהּ, הַשְׁתָּא אֵימָא מִילָךְ.

277. Furthermore, when a person gets up to study Torah in the middle of the night, when the northern wind awakes, the Holy One, blessed be He, enters the Garden of Eden and enjoys Himself with the righteous. And He, together with the righteous in the Garden, listen to the words that come from such a person's mouth. So if the Holy One, blessed be He, and the righteous delight in hearing the words of Torah at this hour, how can I lay in my bed? Now, RABBI YEHUDA said to THE JEW: Say what you have to say.

278. אָמַר לוֹ, שָׁאֵילְנָא עַל מַה דַּאֲמַרְתְּ בִּפְסוּקָא דָא, וְהָאֶבֶן הַזֹּאת אֲשֶׁר שַׂמְתִּי מַצֵּבָה יִהְיֶה בֵּית אֱלֹקִים, דְּדָא אֶבֶן שְׁתִיָּה. הֵיךְ אֶפְשָׁר, דְּהָא אֶבֶן שְׁתִיָּה, עַד לָא אִתְבְּרֵי עָלְמָא הֲוַת, וּמִנָּהּ אִשְׁתִּיל עָלְמָא, וְאַתְּ אֲמַרְתְּ, אֲשֶׁר שַׂמְתִּי, דְּמַשְׁמַע דְּיַעֲקֹב שַׁוֵּי לָהּ הַשְׁתָּא. וּכְתִיב וַיִּקַּח אֶת הָאֶבֶן אֲשֶׁר שָׂם מְרַאֲשׁוֹתָיו.

278. He told RABBI YEHUDA that he had a question about the statement regarding the verse, "And this stone which I have set for a pillar shall be the house of Elohim." You said it refers to the Foundation Stone: How can that be? The Foundation Stone existed even before the creation of the world. From this Stone the world was planted. And you say that "which I have set" means that Jacob has just set it, and it is written: "And he took the stone that he had put under his head."

279. וְתוּ, דְּיַעֲקֹב בְּבֵית אֵל הֲוָה, וְאַבְנָא דָא הֲוַת בִּירוּשְׁלֵם. אָמַר לוֹ כָּל

אַרְעָא דְיִשְׂרָאֵל אִכְפַּל תְּחוֹתוֹי, וְהַהוּא אֶבֶן תְּחוֹתֵיהּ הֲוַת. אָמַר לוֹ, אֲשֶׁר שָׁם כְּתִיב. וּכְתִיב, וְהָאֶבֶן הַזֹּאת אֲשֶׁר שַׂמְתִּי מַצֵּבָה. אָמַר לוֹ אִי יָדַעְתְּ מִלָּה אֵימָא לָהּ.

279. Also, Jacob was in Bethel, while the stone was in Jeruslaem. Rabbi Yehuda answered that Jacob folded up the Land of Yisrael and placed it under his head, EVEN THOUGH HE WAS IN BETHEL. The Jew continued: It is written: "he took the stone that he had put" and, also, "And this stone which I have set for a pillar," MEANING THAT JACOB ESTABLISHED IT NOW. SO HOW CAN IT BE THE SAME STONE WHICH HAD EXISTED BEFORE THE WORLD WAS CREATED? Rabbi Yehuda said: If you know anything, say it!

280. פְּתַח וַאֲמַר, אֲנִי בְּצֶדֶק אֶחֱזֶה פָנֶיךָ אֶשְׂבְּעָה בְהָקִיץ תְּמוּנָתֶךָ. דָּוִד מַלְכָּא, חֲבִיבוּתָא וּדְבֵקוּתָא דִילֵיהּ, בְּהַאי אֶבֶן הֲוָה. וַעֲלָהּ אָמַר אֶבֶן מָאֲסוּ הַבּוֹנִים הָיְתָה לְרֹאשׁ פִּנָּה. וְכַד בָּעָא לְאִסְתַּכְּלָא, בְּחֵיזוּ יְקָרָא דְמָרֵיהּ, נָטַל לְהַאי אֶבֶן בִּידֵיהּ, בְּקַדְמֵיתָא, וּלְבָתַר עָיֵיל.

280. The Jew then began: It is written: "As for me, I shall behold Your face in righteousness, I shall be satisfied, when I wake up, with beholding Your likeness" (Tehilim 17:15). King David felt great affection for and devotion to this stone. THE STONE IS MALCHUT, AND IT IS CALLED THE "FOUNDATION STONE" AND ALSO "RIGHTEOUSNESS." Therefore, David said of it: "The stone which the builders rejected has become the cornerstone" (Tehilim 118:22), and when he wanted to look at the reflection of his Master's glory, he would simply take the stone into his hands and enter.

281. בְּגִין דְּכָל מַאן דְּבָעֵי, לְאִתְחֲזָאָה קַמֵּי מָרֵיהּ, לָא אָעֵיל אֶלָּא בְּהַאי אֶבֶן. דִּכְתִיב בְּזֹאת יָבֹא אַהֲרֹן אֶל הַקֹּדֶשׁ. וְדָוִד מְשַׁבַּח גַּרְמֵיהּ, וַאֲמַר אֲנִי בְּצֶדֶק אֶחֱזֶה פָנֶיךָ. וְכָל אִשְׁתַּדְּלוּתֵיהּ דְּדָוִד, לְאִתְחֲזָאָה בְּהַאי אֶבֶן, כִּדְקָא יָאוֹת, לְגַבֵּי דִלְעֵילָא.

281. Whoever wants to appear before his Master can enter only by that stone, as it is written: "Thus (Heb. *bezot*), WITH MALCHUT THAT IS CALLED

THIS (HEB. *ZOT*) shall Aaron come into the holy place" (Vayikra 16:3). King David was glorifying himself, saying, "As for me, I shall behold Your face in righteousness," WHICH IS MALCHUT. His main intention was to show himself and appear with the stone turned heavenward.

282. תָּא חֲזֵי, אַבְרָהָם אַתְקִין צְלוֹתָא דְּצַפְרָא וְאוֹדַע טִיבוּ דְּמָארֵיהּ בְּעָלְמָא. וְאַתְקִין הַהִיא שַׁעֲתָא, בְּתִקּוּנָהָא כְּדְקָא יָאוֹת. דִּכְתִיב וַיַּשְׁכֵּם אַבְרָהָם בַּבֹּקֶר. יִצְחָק, אַתְקִין צְלוֹתָא דְמִנְחָה. וְאוֹדַע בְּעָלְמָא, דְּאִית דִּין וְאִית דַּיָּין, דְּיָכוֹל לְשֵׁזָבָא וּלְמֵידַן עָלְמָא.

282. Come and behold: Abraham instituted the morning prayer, WHICH CORRESPONDS TO THE SFIRAH OF CHESED OF ZEIR ANPIN, and in so doing, he made known the essence of his Master in the world, and he fixed the time OF MORNING, as it should properly be, as it is written "And Abraham rose up early in the morning" (Beresheet 22:3). THIS MEANS THAT HE ESTABLISHED THE ATTRIBUTE OF CHESED, THAT PREVAILS IN THE MORNING. Isaac instituted Minchah (the afternoon prayer), WHICH CORRESPONDS TO THE SFIRAH OF GVURAH OF ZEIR ANPIN, and made the world know that there is Judgment and a Judge who can save the world and judge it. THIS MEANS THAT HE ESTABLISHED THE ATTRIBUTE OF GVURAH.

283. יַעֲקֹב, אַתְקִין צְלוֹתָא דְּעַרְבִית, וּבְגִין צְלוֹתָא דָא, דְּאַתְקִין מַה דְּלָא אַתְקִין ב"נ מִקַּדְמַת דְּנָא, כְּדְקָא יָאוֹת. בְּגִין כָּךְ, שַׁבַּח גַּרְמֵיהּ, וְאָמַר וְהָאֶבֶן הַזֹּאת אֲשֶׁר שַׂמְתִּי מַצֵּבָה. דְּעַד הַהִיא שַׁעֲתָא, לָא שַׁוִּי לָהּ אָחֳרָא כַּוָּותֵיהּ.

283. Jacob instituted Arvit (the evening prayer), WHICH CORRESPONDS TO MALCHUT, OF THE FEMALE PRINCIPLE OF ZEIR ANPIN. Through this prayer, he established what no man had before, and he therefore praised himself, saying, "And this stone WHICH IS MALCHUT, "which I have set for a pillar." HE FIXED IT PROPERLY, because until that time, nobody had established it as he had!

284. וּבְגִין כָּךְ, וַיִּקַּח אֶת הָאֶבֶן אֲשֶׁר שָׂם שָׁם מְרַאֲשֹׁתָיו וַיָּשֶׂם אֹתָהּ

מַצֵּבָה. מַאי מַצֵּבָה, דַּהֲוָה נְפִילָה, וְאוֹקִים לָהּ. וַיִּצוֹק שֶׁמֶן עַל רֹאשָׁהּ. דְּהָא בְּיַעֲקֹב תַּלְיָא מִילְתָא, לְמֶעְבַּד יַתִּיר מִכָּל בְּנֵי עָלְמָא.

284. This is why he "took the stone that he had put under his head, and set it up for a pillar" (Beresheet 28:18), but what is the meaning of "a pillar?" It means that MALCHUT had fallen and he "set her up." "And he poured oil on the top of it" (Ibid.) means that her positioning depended on Jacob more than on any other person in the world. FOR JACOB IS HER HUSBAND, THE CHARIOT OF TIFERET. THEREFORE ALL SETTINNGS MADE TO MALCHUT, WHO IS HIS FEMALE PRINCIPLE, ARE DEPENDENT ON HIM.

285. אָתָא רַבִּי יְהוּדָה וּנְשָׁקֵיהּ, אָמַר לוֹ, וְכָל הַאי יָדַעְתְּ וְאַתְּ מִשְׁתַּדֵּל בִּסְחוֹרְתָא, וּמַנַּח חַיֵּי עָלְמָא. אָמַר לוֹ דַּהֲוָה דְּחִיקָא לִי שַׁעְתָּא, וְאִית לִי תְּרֵין בְּנִין, וְקַיְימִין כָּל יוֹמָא בְּבֵי רַב, וַאֲנָא אִשְׁתַּדְּלָנָא עַל מְזוֹנַיְיהוּ, וּלְמֵיהַב לוֹן אֲגַר לְמוֹרַיְיהוּ, בְּגִין דְּיִשְׁתַּדְּלוּן בְּאוֹרַיְיתָא.

285. Rabbi Yehuda then came, kissed THE JEW, and said to him, You know all this and still you deal in commerce and neglect eternal life? The Jew answered: Times are pressing, and I have two sons studying daily in a house of Torah. I have to care for their expenses and pay their teacher's fees so that they can continue to study.

286. פְּתַח וְאָמַר, וּשְׁלֹמֹה יָשַׁב עַל כִּסֵּא דָוִד אָבִיו וַתִּכּוֹן מַלְכוּתוֹ מְאֹד. מַאי שְׁבָחָא דָא. אֶלָּא, דְּאַתְקִין אֶבֶן שְׁתִיָּה, וְשַׁוֵּי עֲלָהּ קֹדֶשׁ הַקֳּדָשִׁים, וּכְדֵין, וַתִּכּוֹן מַלְכוּתוֹ מְאֹד.

286. He continued, quoting the verse: "And Solomon sat upon the throne of David, his father. And his kingdom was established firmly" (I Melachim 2:12). AND HE ASKS, what is the reason for SOLOMON'S praise? HE REPLIES THAT he established the Foundation Stone and set over it the Holy of Holies, and thereby "his kingdom was established firmly."

287. וּכְתִיב, וּרְאִיתִיהָ לִזְכֹּר בְּרִית עוֹלָם. דְּהָא קֻדְשָׁא בְּרִיךְ הוּא, תֵּיאוּבְתָּא דִילֵיהּ בָּהּ תָּדִיר, וּמַאן דְּלָא אִתְחֲזֵי בָּהּ, לָא עָאִיל קַמֵּי מָארֵיהּ. וְעַ"ד כְּתִיב, וּרְאִיתִיהָ לִזְכֹּר בְּרִית עוֹלָם.

287. It is written: "And I will look upon it, that I may remember the everlasting covenant" (Beresheet 9:16), meaning that the Holy One, blessed be He, always desires her, MALCHUT. Whoever is not seen by her does not enter before his Master. That is why it is written: "And I will look upon it, that I may remember the everlasting covenant," BECAUSE THE SEEING IS ONLY FOR HER.

288. וּרְאִיתִיהָ. מַאי וּרְאִיתִיהָ, רָזָא הוּא, כד״א וְהִתְוֵיתָ תָּיו עַל מִצְחוֹת וגו'. לְאִתְחַזָּאָה עֲלַיְיהוּ. וְאִיכָּא דְּאָמְרֵי, דָּא רְשִׁימוּ דְאָת קַדִּישָׁא, דִּי בְּבִשְׂרָא.

288. HE ASKS: What is meant by "And I will look upon it"? AND HE ANSWERS THAT it is a secret relating to the words, "and set a mark upon the foreheads…" (Yechezkel 9:4). THIS MARK IS THE LETTER *TAV* THAT SHALL BE 'SEEN' ON THEIR FOREHEADS. But there are those who say that the 'seeing' is related to the impression of the holy sign in the flesh (the circumcision).

289. אָמַר רָבִּי יְהוּדָה, וַדַּאי כֹּלָּא הוּא. אֲבָל, הַאי קֶשֶׁת דְּאִתְחֲזֵי בְּעָלְמָא, בְּרָזָא עִלָּאָה קַיְימָא. וְכַד יִפְקוּן יִשְׂרָאֵל מִן גָּלוּתָא, זְמִינָא הַאי קֶשֶׁת לְאִתְקַשְּׁטָא בְּגַוְונוֹי, כְּכַלָּה דָא, דְּמִתְקַשְּׁטָא לְבַעֲלָהּ.

289. Rabbi Yehuda said: Certainly everything, BOTH THE ASPECT OF THE LETTER TAV AND THE DIADEM, IS IMPLIED IN THE EXPRESSION "LOOK UPON IT." Nevertheless, the rainbow that is seen in the world is based on a supernal secret, and when Yisrael will come out of the exile, this rainbow will be adorned with its colors likes a bride who adorns herself for her husband.

290. אָמַר לוֹ הַהוּא יוּדָאי, כָּךְ אָמַר לִי אַבָּא, כַּד הֲוָה מִסְתַּלֵּק מֵעָלְמָא, לָא תְצַפֵּי לְרַגְלֵי דִמְשִׁיחָא, עַד דְּיִתְחֲזֵי הַאי קֶשֶׁת בְּעָלְמָא, מִתְקַשְּׁטָא בְּגַוְונֵי נְהִירִין, וְיִתְנְהִיר לְעָלְמָא. וּכְדֵין צָפֵי לֵיהּ לְמָשִׁיחַ.

290. The Jew then told him: This is what my father said to me while he was departing from this world: Do not expect the coming of Messiah until this rainbow is seen in the world, adorning itself in shining colors and shining to the world. Only then expect Messiah.

291. מְנָלָן, דִּכְתִיב וּרְאִיתִיהָ לִזְכֹּר בְּרִית עוֹלָם. וְהַשְׁתָּא דְּאִתְחַזְיָא בִּגְוָונִין חֲשׁוֹכִין, מִתְחַזְיָא לְדוּכְרָנָא, דְּלָא יֵיתֵי מַבּוּל. אֲבָל בְּהַהִיא זִמְנָא אִתְחַזְיָיא בִּגְוָונִין נְהִירִין, וּמִתְקַשְּׁטָא בְּתִקּוּנָא כְּכַלָּה דְּמִתְקַשְּׁטָא לְבַעֲלָהּ. וּכְדֵין לִזְכֹּר בְּרִית עוֹלָם. וְיִדְכַּר קֻדְשָׁא בְּרִיךְ הוּא לְהַאי בְּרִית, דְּאִיהוּ בְּגָלוּתָא, וְיָקִים לָהּ מֵעַפְרָא, הה"ד וּבִקְשׁוּ אֶת ה' אֱלֹהֵיהֶם וְאֶת דָּוִד מַלְכָּם. וּכְתִיב וְעָבְדוּ אֶת ה' אֱלֹהֵיהֶם וְאֶת דָּוִד מַלְכָּם אֲשֶׁר אָקִים לָהֶם, אֲשֶׁר אָקִים מֵעָפָר, כד"א אָקִים אֶת סֻכַּת דָּוִד הַנּוֹפָלֶת. וְע"ד וּרְאִיתִיהָ לִזְכֹּר בְּרִית עוֹלָם, וּלְאַקְמָא לָהּ מֵעַפְרָא.

291. From where do we know this? From the verse that says, "And I will look upon it, that I may remember the everlasting covenant." Because now, DURING THE EXILE, when the rainbow is seen with darkened colors, it is a reminder to prevent the Flood from returning to the world. But, WHEN MESSIAH APPEARS, it shall shine brightly and be ornamented, like a bride who adorns herself for her husband. And what is predicted in the verse: "to remember the everlasting covenant," SHALL COME TO PASS. Then the Holy One, blessed be He, will remember that covenant and raise it (her) from the dust, as it is written: "And they will seek Hashem their Elohim and David their king" (Hoshea 3:5). "DAVID THEIR KING" REFERS TO MALCHUT THAT IS THE SECRET OF THE RAINBOW. It is also written: "But they shall serve Hashem their Elohim and David their king, whom I will raise for them" (Yirmeyah 30:9), MEANING, "whom I will raise" from the dust. As you say, "I will raise up the tabernacle of David that is fallen" (Amos 9:11). It is therefore said at that time "I will look upon it, that I may remember the everlasting covenant" and raise it (her) from the dust.

292. וַאֲמַר הָכֵי אַבָּא, דִּבְגִין כָּךְ, אִדְכַּר בְּאוֹרַיְיתָא, פּוּרְקָנָא דְּיִשְׂרָאֵל, וּדְכוּרָנָא דִּילָהּ. וְדָא הוּא דִּכְתִיב אֲשֶׁר נִשְׁבַּעְתִּי מֵעֲבוֹר מֵי נֹחַ עוֹד עַל הָאָרֶץ כֵּן נִשְׁבַּעְתִּי מִקְּצֹף עָלַיִךְ וּמִגְּעָר בָּךְ.

292. My father said that the reason the redemption of Yisrael and the

-428-

remembrance OF MALCHUT are mentioned in the Torah IS THAT "REMEMBER THE EVERLASTING COVENANT" REFERS TO THE REDEMPTION OF YISRAEL AND THE COMPLETION OF MALCHUT. That is why, IN REFERENCE TO THE TIME OF REDEMPTION, it is written: "For as I have sworn that the waters of Noah should no more go over the earth, so have I sworn that I would not be angry with you, nor rebuke you" (Yeshayah 54:9).

36. "And the sons of Noah that went forth from the ark"

Rabbi Shimon discloses a secret to explain this verse. It concerns a process of revelation of great Light. When we scan this portion, may we all merit the Light that shines from these secrets.

293. וַיִּהְיוּ בְּנֵי נֹחַ הַיּוֹצְאִים מִן הַתֵּבָה. רַבִּי אֶלְעָזָר אָמַר, כֵּיוָן דִּכְתִיב וַיִּהְיוּ בְּנֵי נֹחַ. אַמַּאי אָמַר הַיּוֹצְאִים מִן הַתֵּבָה. וְכִי בְּנִין אָחֳרָנִין הֲווֹ לֵיה, דְּלָא נָפְקֵי מִן תֵּיבוּתָא.

293. "And the sons of Noah that went forth from the ark..." (Beresheet 9:18). Rabbi Elazar said: it is written, "the sons of Noah that went forth from the ark." Could it be that there were others who did not emerge from the ark?"

294. אָמַר לֵיה רַבִּי אַבָּא, אִין. דְּהָא לְבָתַר, אוֹלִידוּ בְּנוֹי בְּנִין. דִּכְתִיב, וְאֵלֶּה תּוֹלְדוֹת שֵׁם וגו'. וְאִינוּן לָא נָפְקֵי מִגּוֹ תֵּיבוּתָא. וּבְגִין כָּךְ כְּתִיב, הַיּוֹצְאִים מִן הַתֵּבָה שֵׁם חָם וָיָפֶת.

294. Rabbi Aba answered: Yes. His sons bore other children afterward, as it is written: "These are the generations of Shem..." (Beresheet 11:10). They did not go forth from the ark, and it is therefore written: "that went forth from the ark were Shem, Ham and Japheth."

295. רַבִּי שִׁמְעוֹן אָמַר, אִילּוּ הֲוֵינָא שְׁכִיחַ בְּעָלְמָא, כַּד יָהֵיב קֻדְשָׁא בְּרִיךְ הוּא סִפְרָא דַּחֲנוֹךְ בְּעָלְמָא, וְסִפְרָא דְּאָדָם, אַתְקִיפְנָא, דְּלָא יִשְׁתַּכְּחוּן בֵּינֵי אֱנָשָׁא, בְּגִין דְּלָא חַיְישׁוּ כָּל חַכִּמָאן לְאִסְתַּכְּלָא בְּהוֹ, וְטָעָן בְּמִלִּין אָחֳרָנִין, לְאַפָּקָא מֵרְשׁוּ עִלָּאָה, לִרְשׁוּ אָחֳרָא. וְהַשְׁתָּא הָא חַכִּימֵי עָלְמָא יָדְעִין מִלִּין, וְסָתְמִין לוֹן, וּמִתַּתַּקְפֵי בְּפֻלְחָנָא דְּמָארֵיהוֹן.

295. Rabbi Shimon said: Had I been alive, when the Holy One, blessed be He, gave people the Books of Enoch and Adam, I would have tried my best to prevent them from circulating among people. For at that time, wise men

were not afraid to look into them. THEY twisted the books' ideas and took them from the supernal dominion of holiness to another dominion, WHICH IS NOT HOLY. Now, however, the wise of the world know things but conceal them, THAT IS, THEY DO NOT REVEAL THE SECRETS and they strengthen themselves in serving their Master. THAT IS WHY NOW IT IS ALLOWED TO DELVE INTO THE SECRETS OF THE TORAH.

296. וְהַאי קְרָא, אַשְׁכַּחְנָא בְּרָזָא דְרָזִין. דְּכַד אִתְּעַר חֶדְוָה דְּכָל חֶדְוָון, טְמִירָא סְתִּימָא, סָבְתָּא דְּסַבְתִּין, אַנְהֵיר מִנֵּיה נְהִירוּ דַּקִּיק. חֶדְוָה דְּכָל חֶדְוָון, נָהֵיר לִימִינָא, בְּמִשַׁח רְבוּת עִלָּאָה. וְנָהֵיר לִשְׂמָאלָא בְּחֶדְוָוה דְּחַמְרָא טַב, נָהֵיר לְאֶמְצָעִיתָא בְּחֶדְוָוה דִּתְרֵין סִטְרִין. רוּחַ אִתְּעַר, וְרוּחַ סָלְקָא, וְאִתְּיְיהֵיב בְּרוּחָא.

296. I found this passage ABOUT THE SONS OF NOAH WHO WENT FORTH FROM THE ARK hidden among the secrets of the secrets. When the hidden and unknown bliss that is above all bliss, WHICH IS BINAH WHEN IT ASCENDED TO THE HEAD OF ARICH ANPIN, is aroused, the cause of all causes, WHICH IS ARICH ANPIN, produces from within Himself a thin light. THIS MEANS THAT, using the supernal anointing oil, THE ILLUMINATION OF CHASSADIM, WHICH IS THE SECRET OF CHOLAM, the bliss above all bliss shines its light on the Right COLUMN. And it shines its light on the Left COLUMN with the gaiety of good wine, THAT IS, ILLUMINATIONS OF CHOCHMAH, WHICH IS THE SECRET OF SHURUK. And it shines its light on the Central COLUMN with the gaiety of both THE RIGHT AND THE LEFT Columns, WHICH IS THE SECRET OF CHIRIK. For the spirit, WHICH IS ZEIR ANPIN, has been aroused AND HAS JOINED THE CENTRAL COLUMN OF BINAH, WHILE THE SPIRIT OF THE LEFT COLUMN HAS ASCENDED and been placed in the spirit OF THE RIGHT COLUMN. THEN ALL THREE COLUMNS OF BINAH ARE JOINED TOGETHER AND INCLUDED IN EACH OTHER.

297. דָּבְקָן דָּא בְּדָא. תְּלַת עָאלִין בִּתְלַת. מִגּוֹ תְּלַת, נָפְקָא חַד בְּרִית, וְדָבְקָא בִּבְרִית. אִתְעַבְּרַת רוּחַ דְּסָלְקָא, מִתְעַבְּרַת מִנֵּיה. כַּד אִתְּיְיהֵיבַת בִּתְרֵין סִטְרִין, אִתְדַּבְּקוּ רוּחָא בְּרוּחָא, וּמִתְעַבְּרָאן מִתְּלַת בְּנִין. וְנָח וְתֵיבָה, נָפְקוּ מִנַּיְיהוּ תְּלָתָא, כְּגַוְונָא דִּתְלָתָא עִלָּאִין, וְאִלֵּין אִינוּן

דְּנָפְקוּ מִגּוֹ תֵּיבוּתָא: שֵׁם וְחָם וְיֶפֶת. שֵׁם: דְּבִסְטַר יָמִינָא, חָם: דְּבִסְטַר שְׂמָאלָא. יֶפֶת: אַרְגְּוָונָא דְּכָלִיל לוֹן.

297. They cling to each other. ZEIR ANPIN CLINGS TO BINAH, and then all three enter into the other three – THE THREE COLUMNS OF BINAH ENTER AND BECOME THE THREE COLUMNS OF ZEIR ANPIN. From the three COLUMNS OF ZEIR ANPIN, one goes forth. THIS ONE IS the covenant, YESOD, and THE FEMALE PRINCIPLE is attached to the covenant. AFTERWARD, the rising spirit, WHICH IS THE SPIRIT OF THE LEFT COLUMN, leaves Him and THE FEMALE PRINCIPLE is impregnated by him. THIS MEANS THAT THE LEFT COLUMN LEAVES ZEIR ANPIN AND IS PASSED ONTO THE FEMALE PRINCIPLE. Afterward, when THE FEMALE PRINCIPLE receives the two Columns OF ZEIR ANPIN, WHEN SHE RECEIVES THE CHASSADIM OF THE RIGHT and SHE AND ZEIR ANPIN are attached spirit to spirit, THE FEMALE PRINCIPLE becomes pregnant with three sons. Then from Noah and the ark, three SONS emerged. These sons who emerged from the ark, Shem, Ham, and Japheth, were similar to the supernal three COLUMNS. Shem was the Right one, Ham the Left one, and Japheth THE CENTRAL ONE – whose color is purple and which includes the other two.

298. וְחָם הוּא אֲבִי כְנַעַן. זוּהֲמָא דְּדַהֲבָא, תְּחוֹת קַסְטִיפִין. אִתְעֲרוּתָא דְּרוּחָא מְסָאֲבָא, דְּנָחָשׁ קַדְמָאָה. וּבְגִין כָּךְ, רְשִׁים וַאֲמַר, וְחָם הוּא אֲבִי כְנַעַן. דְּאַיְיתֵי לְוָוטִין עַל עָלְמָא. הַהוּא כְנַעַן, דְּאִתְלַטְיָא. הַהוּא כְנַעַן, דְּאַחְשִׁיךְ אַנְפֵּי בְּרִיָּין.

298. "And Ham is the father of Canaan" (Beresheet 3:18). CANAAN is the filth under the refuse of gold, NAMELY THAT WHICH SETTLES AT THE BOTTOM OF THE POT DURING THE MELTING OF GOLD. And he is also the arousal of the ancient serpent's spirit of impurity. HAM IS THE LEFT COLUMN, WHICH IS THE SECRET OF GOLD, AND CANAAN, WHO REPRESENTS THE ANCIENT SERPENT, IS HIS REFUSE. This is why the verse specifically reads, "And Ham is the father of Canaan," THE SAME CANAAN who brought curses on the world, the same Canaan who was himself cursed and who darkened the faces of the creatures. IN OTHER WORDS, HE IS THE SERPENT WHO SEDUCED EVE AND BROUGHT

CURSES ON THE WORLD, AND WHO WAS CURSED HIMSELF AND DARKENED THE FACES OF CREATURES BY BRINGING DEATH UPON THEM.

299. וּבְגִין כָּךְ, לָא נָפֵיק מִגּוֹ כְּלָלָא דְּכָלְּהוּ, אֶלָּא דָא. דִּכְתִיב, וְחָם הוּא אֲבִי כְנָעַן. הַהוּא דְּאַחְשִׁיךְ עָלְמָא, וְלָא כְתִיב בִּכְלָלָא דָא, וְשֵׁם הוּא אֲבִי כָּךְ, אוֹ יֶפֶת הוּא אֲבִי כָּךְ, אֶלָּא מִיָּד קָפַץ וַאֲמַר, וְחָם הוּא אֲבִי כְנָעַן. וַדַּאי.

299. Only Ham was separated from the rest, because, as is written: "And Ham is the father of Canaan." THIS REFERS TO the one who brought darkness upon the world: THE POWER OF THE SERPENT. Nobody else is described in this fashion. It does not say, 'Shem is the father of so and so', or 'Japheth is the father of so and so'. The Scriptures say immediately, "And Ham is the father of Canaan."

300. וְעַל דָּא, כַּד אָתָא אַבְרָהָם, מַה כְּתִיב, וַיַּעֲבֹר אַבְרָם בָּאָרֶץ. דְּעַד לָא הֲוָה קִיּוּמָא דַּאֲבָהָן, וְלָא אָתוּ זַרְעָא דְיִשְׂרָאֵל בְּעָלְמָא, דְּיִפּוֹק שְׁמָא דָא, וְיֵיעוֹל שְׁמָא עִלָּאָה קַדִּישָׁא. כַּד הֲווֹ זַכָּאִין יִשְׂרָאֵל, אִקְרֵי אַרְעָא, עַל שְׁמָא דָא, אֶרֶץ יִשְׂרָאֵל. כַּד לָא זָכוּ, אִקְרֵי אַרְעָא עַל שְׁמָא אָחֳרָא, אֶרֶץ כְּנָעַן.

300. Hence, what does it say about Abraham? It says, "and Abram passed through the land... And the Canaanite was then in the land" (Beresheet 12:6). The Patriarchies, THE MOCHIN THAT WERE DRAWN DOWN FOR THE FEMALE PRINCIPLE, CALLED 'THE LAND,' were not yet established, and the seed of Yisrael had not yet appeared in the world. The name OF CANAAN therefore could not yet be removed FROM THE LAND and replaced with the sacred supernal name OF YISRAEL. But when Yisrael were righteous AND DREW DOWN THE THREE COLUMNS OF ZEIR ANPIN, CALLED 'YISRAEL,' TO MATE WITH THE FEMALE PRINCIPLE, the land came to be called by the name, 'land of Yisrael.' IT WAS NAMED AFTER YISRAEL BELOW, WHO PERFECTED THE FEMALE PRINCIPLE, AND AFTER HER HUSBAND, ZEIR ANPIN. But when they were not worthy AND THE FEMALE PRINCIPLE WAS LEFT WITH THE LEFT COLUMN, WITH THE GOLD'S REFUSE, CALLED 'CANAAN,' it was called by a different name, 'the land of Canaan.'

301. וְעַל דָּא, כְּתִיב וַיֹּאמֶר אָרוּר כְּנַעַן עֶבֶד עֲבָדִים יִהְיֶה לְאֶחָיו. דְּאִיהוּ אַיְיתֵי לְוָוטִין עַל עָלְמָא. וּבְנָחָשׁ מַה כְּתִיב אָרוּר אַתָּה מִכָּל הַבְּהֵמָה. הַיְינוּ דִכְתִיב עֶבֶד עֲבָדִים. וְעַל דָּא כְּתִיב, שֵׁם חָם וָיֶפֶת. תְּלַת אִלֵּין בְּנֵי נֹחַ הַיּוֹצְאִים מִן הַתֵּיבָה כִּדְקָאֲמְרֵינָן.

301. Therefore, it is written: "And he said: Cursed be Canaan, a slave of slaves he shall be to his brothers" (Beresheet 9:25), for he brought curses upon the world, and HE REPRESENTS THE ANCIENT SERPENT. And what is said of the serpent? "You are cursed above all cattle" (Beresheet 3:14). HE WAS CURSED AS WELL IN THE PASSAGE, "CURSED BE CANAAN...a slave of slaves SHALL HE BE TO HIS BROTHERS." BECAUSE CATTLE ARE SLAVES TO PEOPLE AND BECAUSE HE IS WORSE THAN THE CATTLE AND MORE CURSED, HE IS THE SLAVE OF SLAVES. This is why it is written that Shem, Ham, and Japheth are the three sons of Noah who emerged from the ark, as has previously been explained. THEY ARE THE SECRET OF THE THREE COLUMNS: THE FEMALE PRINCIPLE, THAT IS CALLED 'THE ARK,' RECEIVED THEM FROM ZEIR ANPIN, BECAME PREGNANT WITH THEM, AND BROUGHT THEM FORTH INTO THE WORLD.

37. "These are the three sons of Noah"

Three unique energy forces permeate all existence. The Zohar explains that this supernal secret is denoted by the *Three sons of Noah*.

These three spiritual forces are known as *Right Column, Left Column* and *Central Column*. That is, the positive *desire to share*, the negative *desire to receive* and the *free will* to balance these desires into *receiving for the sake of sharing*. In our physical world they also manifest as the proton, electron, and neutron. The Zohar further reveals that Noah's three sons are the source of all the souls who have come to this world.

302. שְׁלֹשָׁה אֵלֶּה בְּנֵי נֹחַ. קִיּוּמָא דְּכָל עָלְמָא, קִיּוּמָא דְּרָזָא עִלָּאָה. וּמֵאֵלֶּה נָפְצָה כָל הָאָרֶץ. הַיְינוּ רָזָא דִּתְלַת גְּוָונִין עִלָּאִין. דְּכַד הַהוּא נָהָר דְּנָגִיד וְנָפִיק, אַשְׁקֵי לְגִנְתָּא, בְּחֵילָא דִּתְלַת אִלֵּין עִלָּאִין. וּמִתַּמָּן אִתְפָּרְשָׁן גְּוָונִין דִּלְתַתָּא, כָּל חַד וְחַד כָּלִיל בְּחַבְרֵיה, לְאַחֲזָאָה דִּיקָרָא דְּקֻדְשָׁא בְּרִיךְ הוּא, אִתְפַּשַּׁט לְעֵילָא וְתַתָּא, וְאִיהוּ חַד, בְּעֶלָּאֵי וְתַתָּאֵי.

302. "These are the three sons of Noah" (Beresheet 9:19). They are the existence of the entire world. THE WORD 'EXISTENCE' INDICATES THE MOCHIN OF THE FEMALE PRINCIPLE, WHICH IS CALLED 'THE WORLD.' THEY ARE the existence of the supernal secret, THE MOCHIN OF BINAH. THE WORDS, "and of them was the whole earth overspread" (Ibid.), MEANS THAT ALL HUMAN SOULS ARE DESCENDED FROM THEM. THEY ARE the secret of the three supernal colors OF BINAH, WHICH ARE THE THREE COLUMNS. When the river that comes out FROM EDEN AND WHICH IS ZEIR ANPIN watered the Garden, WHICH IS THE FEMALE PRINCIPLE, it watered it by the power of the three supernal COLUMNS, BY THE POWER OF THE SUPERNAL BINAH. Then, the lower colors, WHITE, RED, AND BLACK, WHICH ARE THE SECRET OF THE LOWER THREE COLUMNS OF THE FEMALE PRINCIPLE, expanded. Each of these colors is included in the other, to show that the glory of the Holy One, blessed be He, extends up TO BINAH and down TO MALCHUT, and is one, above and below.

303. אֲמַר רַבִּי אֶלְעָזָר, תְּלַת גְּוָונִין אִלֵּין, בְּכָל אִינוּן דְּאַתְיָין, מִסְטַר דִּקְדוּשָׁה, וּמֶחֱזוּ דִּתְלַת גְּוָונִין אִלֵּין, מִתְפָּרְשָׁאן לְכָל אִינוּן דְּאַתְיָין

מִסְּטְרָא דְּרוּחָא אַחֲרָא. וְכַד תִּסְתַּכֵּל בְּרָזָא דְּדַרְגִּין, תִּשְׁכַּח הֵיךְ מִתְפָּרְשָׁן גְּוָונִין, לְכָל אִינּוּן סִטְרִין, עַד דְּעָיְילִין לְתַתָּא, בְּרָזָא דְּאִינּוּן שִׁבְעָה וְעֶשְׂרִין צִנּוֹרִין, דְּדַשֵׁי. דְּחָפְיָין לִתְהוֹמֵי.

303. Rabbi Elazar said that these three colors exist in all OF THE MOCHIN that originate from the holy side. Their appearance, WHICH IS MALCHUT, INCLUDES all three colors, which expand into the colors coming from the side of the other spirit. And when you look into the secret of the levels, you will find that the colors spread out in all directions: RIGHT, LEFT AND CENTER, until they enter below INTO MALCHUT. This is the secret of the 27 channels of doors that cover the deep.

304. וְכֹלָּא יְדִיעָא לַחֲכִימִין עֶלְיוֹנִין. זַכָּאָה חוּלָקֵהוֹן דְּצַדִּיקַיָּיא, דְּקֻדְשָׁא בְּרִיךְ הוּא אִתְרְעֵי בִּיקָרֵיהוֹן, וְגַלֵּי לוֹן סִתְרִין עִלָּאִין דְּחָכְמְתָא, עֲלַיְיהוּ כְּתִיב סוֹד ה' לִירֵאָיו וּבְרִיתוֹ לְהוֹדִיעָם.

304. All this is known to the exalted sages. Worthy are the righteous with their lot that the Holy One, blessed be He, wants to glorify them and reveal to them the supernal secrets of Wisdom. Of them, it is written: "The secret of Hashem is to those who fear Him, and He will reveal to them His covenant" (Tehilim 25:14).

305. פָּתַח רַבִּי אֶלְעָזָר וַאֲמַר: ה' אֱלֹקַי אַתָּה אֲרוֹמִמְךָ אוֹדֶה שִׁמְךָ כִּי עָשִׂיתָ פֶּלֶא עֵצוֹת מֵרָחוֹק אֱמוּנָה אֹמֶן. כַּמָּה אִית לוֹן לִבְנֵי נָשָׁא, לְאִסְתַּכְּלָא בִּיקָרָא דְּקֻדְשָׁא בְּרִיךְ הוּא, וּלְשַׁבְּחָא לִיקָרֵיה. בְּגִין דְּכָל מַאן דְּיָדַע לְשַׁבְּחָא לְמָארֵיה, כִּדְקָא יָאוֹת, קֻדְשָׁא בְּרִיךְ הוּא עָבִיד לֵיה רְעוּתֵיה. וְלָא עוֹד, אֶלָּא דְּאַסְגֵּי בִּרְכָאן לְעֵילָא וְתַתָּא.

305. Rabbi Elazar said: "Hashem, You are my Elohim; I will exalt You, I will praise Your name; for You have done wonderful things, even counsels of old, in faithfulness and truth" (Yeshayah 25:1). How important it is for people to pay attention to the glory of the Holy One, blessed be He, and praise His glory. For the desires of he who knows how to praise his Master as He deserves will be fulfilled. Not only that, but he also causes an increase of blessings above and below!

306. וְעַל דָּא מַאן דְּיָדַע לְשַׁבְּחָא לֵיהּ לְמָארֵיהּ, וּלְיַחֲדָא שְׁמֵיהּ, חָבִיב הוּא לְעֵילָא, וְחָמִיד לְתַתָּא. וְקֻדְשָׁא בְּרִיךְ הוּא מִשְׁתַּבַּח בֵּיהּ. וַעֲלֵיהּ כְּתִיב, וַיֹּאמֶר לִי עַבְדִּי אַתָּה יִשְׂרָאֵל אֲשֶׁר בְּךָ אֶתְפָּאָר.

306. So whoever is able to praise his Master and proclaim His unity is held in affection on high and is beloved below. And the Holy One, blessed be He, is proud of him. Such a person is described by the verse: "And said to me, you are My servant, Yisrael, in whom I will be glorified" (Yeshayah 49:3).

38. "And Noah began to be husbandman, and he planted a vineyard"

The Zohar explains that both Noah and Adam sinned under the influence of wine. Kabbalah teaches that wine is a powerful tool for drawing in Light, as the grape is a potent conduit of spiritual energy. Wine is therefore used as a tool in blessings to reveal God's Light into our physical world. When, through the absence of a blessing, we do not prepare a large enough Vessel, or if we consume wine for reasons not related to spirituality, the torrent of Light aroused becomes uncontrollable. This is the mystery that explains wine's ability to induce intoxicated behavior.

307. וַיָּחֶל נֹחַ אִישׁ הָאֲדָמָה וַיִּטַּע כָּרֶם. ר' יְהוּדָה וְר' יוֹסֵי. חַד אָמַר, מִגַּן עֵדֶן אִתְתְּרַכַת, וּנְצִיב לָהּ הָכָא. וְחַד אָמַר בְּאַרְעָא הֲוַת, וְעָקַר לָהּ, וְשָׁתַל לָהּ, וּבְהַהוּא יוֹמָא, עֲבָדַת אִיבִּין וְנִיצַת לְבִלְבִּין, וַעֲנָבִים וַהֲוָה סָחִיט לָהּ, וְשָׁתֵי מִן חַמְרָא וְרָוֵי.

307. "And Noah began to be a husbandman, and he planted a vineyard" (Beresheet 9:20). Rabbi Yehuda disagreed with Rabbi Yosi's interpretation of this verse. One said the vine was thrown out of the Garden of Eden, and that Noah planted it IN THE GROUND. The other said, IT IS WRITTEN: "AND HE PLANTED," BECAUSE the vine had already been in the ground and Noah plucked it out FROM ITS PLACE and replanted it ELSEWHERE. It blossomed and gave fruit on the same day, and he squeezed the grapes, drank their wine, and got drunk.

308. רַבִּי שִׁמְעוֹן אָמַר, רָזָא דְחָכְמְתָא, אִיהוּ הָכָא, בְּהַאי קְרָא. כַּד בָּעָא נֹחַ לְמִבְדַּק בְּהַהוּא חוֹבָא, דְּבָדַק אָדָם הָרִאשׁוֹן. לָאו לְאִתְדַּבְּקָא בֵּיהּ, אֶלָּא לְמִנְדַע, וּלְאַתְקָנָא עָלְמָא, וְלָא יָכִיל. סָחַט עֲנָבִים לְמִבְדַּק בְּהַהוּא כָּרֶם. כֵּיוָן דְּמָטָא לְהַאי, וַיִּשְׁכָּר וַיִּתְגַּל. וְלָא הֲוָה לֵיהּ, חֵילָא לְמֵיקָם. וּבְגִין כָּךְ, וַיִּתְגַּל: גַּלֵּי פִּרְצָה דְעָלְמָא, דַּהֲוָה סָתִים. בְּתוֹךְ אָהֳלֹה, כְּתִיב בְּה"א. וְע"ד כְּתִיב, וְאַל תִּקְרַב אֶל פֶּתַח בֵּיתָהּ. בְּתוֹךְ אָהֳלֹה, דְּהַהוּא כָּרֶם.

308. Rabbi Shimon said that there is a sublime secret hidden in this passage.

Noah had come to reexamine Adam's sin OF THE TREE OF KNOWLEDGE, so that he could refrain from repeating it and could make reparations in the world. But he was unable TO ACCOMPLISH THIS, HOWEVER, because after squeezing the grapes, so that he could examine them, he got drunk, was uncovered, and had no strength to get up. This is why THE VERSE SAYS, "and was uncovered," MEANING THAT he 'uncovered' a gap in the World, which had been covered until that time. "Within his tent (Heb. *ohaloh*)" is spelled with a final *Hei*. It is not spelled OHALO WITH A VAV. Therefore, it is written: "and do not come near the door of her house" (Mishlei 5:8), "his tent" – indicating the vineyards tent AND NOT HIS OWN TENT. FOR THIS REASON, IT IS SPELLED WITH A *HEI* AND NOT WITH A *VAV*.

309. כְּגַוְונָא דָא, בְּנֵי אַהֲרֹן, דְּתָנִינָן שְׁתוּיֵי יַיִן הֲווֹ. וְכִי מַאן יָהִיב לוֹן חַמְרָא, בְּהַהוּא אֲתַר לְמִשְׁתֵּי. אִי ס"ד, דְּאִינּוּן חֲצִיפִין הֲווֹ, דְּרָווּ חַמְרָא. לָאו הָכִי, אֶלָּא וַדַּאי, מֵהַהוּא חַמְרָא רָווֹ. דִּכְתִיב, וַיַּקְרִיבוּ לִפְנֵי ה' אֵשׁ זָרָה. כְּתִיב הָכָא, אֵשׁ זָרָה, וּכְתִיב הָתָם לִשְׁמָרְךָ מֵאִשָּׁה זָרָה. וְכֹלָּא חַד מִלָּה.

309. The same thing happened with the sons of Aaron, who, as we have learned, were drunk. AND HE ASKS: Who gave them wine to drink in such a place? Could you ever think that they were so impertinent as to get drunk! No, this cannot be so, but indeed they did drink from that certain type of wine and became drunk, as is it is written: "and they offered strange fire before Hashem" (Vayikra 10:1). It says here "a strange fire (Heb. *esh*)" and elsewhere "That they may keep you from the strange woman (Heb. *isha*)" (Mishlei 7:5), and both verses apply to the same thing. Everything amounts to the same explanation.

310. וְכֵן כְּגַוְונָא דָא, וַיֵּשְׁתְּ מִן הַיַּיִן וַיִּשְׁכָּר וַיִּתְגַּל. וְעַל דָּא, אִתְּעַר חָם אֲבִי כְנָעַן, כְּמָה דְּאִתְּמַר. וְאִתְיְיהִיב אֲתַר לִכְנַעַן לְשַׁלְטָאָה, וּמַאי דַּהֲוָה הָדֵין צַדִּיק, בְּרָזָא דִּבְרִית, סָרְסוֹ. וְתַנְיָא דְּאַעֲבַר מִינֵּיהּ הַהוּא קִיּוּמָא.

310. We find the same meaning in the words: "And he drank of the wine and was drunk, and he was uncovered" (Beresheet 9:21). This aroused Ham, the father of Canaan. And we have learned that Canaan was given a place to

rule. And he castrated NOAH, thereby removing the secret of the covenant, which had made him a righteous man. As we have learned that he removed the covenant (the male organ) from him, MEANING THAT HE REMOVED THE MOCHIN OF BEGETTING, WHICH ARE GIVEN ONLY BY THE POWER OF THE HOLY COVENANT. THIS REMOVAL IS CONSIDERED CASTRATION.

311. וּבְגִין כָּךְ אֲמַר, אָרוּר. דְּהָא לְוָוטִין, אִתְּעָרוּ בְּקַדְמֵיתָא, עַל יְדֵיהּ בְּעָלְמָא. עֶבֶד עֲבָדִים יִהְיֶה. כד"א אָרוּר אַתָּה מִכָּל הַבְּהֵמָה וגו'. כֹּלָּא יִתְתַּקַּן לְזִמְנָא דְּאָתֵי, וְהוּא לָא יִתְתַּקַּן. וְכֹלָּא יִפְקוּן לְחֵירוּ, וְהוּא לָא יִפּוֹק. וְרָזָא אִיהוּ לְאִינוּן דְּיָדְעֵי אָרְחוֹי, וּשְׁבִילֵי דְּאוֹרַיְיתָא.

311. This is why NOAH said, "Cursed be Canaan," because curses were initially brought upon the world by him. FOR HE IS THE SECRET OF THE SERPENT, AS IT IS WRITTEN: "A slave of slaves he shall be," and, also, "You are cursed above all cattle" (Beresheet 3:14). Everything shall be corrected in the future except for CANAAN. All THE SLAVES EXCEPT CANAAN shall be freed from their slavery. And this is the secret known to those who are familiar with the ways and the paths of the Torah.

39. Bathsheba and Uriah

Through a story pertaining to King David and Bathsheba, the Zohar reveals that a person's negative action brings about the creation of an actual negative entity. These negative influences are not presented as metaphors. They are actual forces that directly affect the activities of mankind, individually and collectively. They are as real as an unseen atom, and as influential in our lives as the invisible force of gravity. The Kabbalists reject entirely the concept of a Creator who administers punishments and rewards. By way of illustration, electrical energy benefits our society in countless ways. If a person inadvertently placed his finger in a light socket and was electrocuted, it would be senseless to suggest that the electricity *punished* the individual. The Zohar is offering us a lesson on accountability. This, along with repentance, is the only way we can eradicate all negative forces.

312. פְּתַח וְאָמַר, כִּי פְשָׁעַי אֲנִי אֵדָע וְחַטָּאתִי נֶגְדִּי תָמִיד. כַּמָּה אִית לוֹן לִבְנֵי נָשָׁא, לְאִסְתַּמְרָא מֵחוֹבַיְיהוּ, מִקַּמֵּי קֻדְשָׁא בְּרִיךְ הוּא. דְּהָא לְבָתַר דְּחָטָא בַּר נָשׁ, רָשִׁים הוּא, חוֹבֵיהּ לְעֵילָא, וְלָא אִתְמְחַק, בַּר בְּתוֹקְפָּא דִּתְיוּבְתָּא סַגִּיא. כְּד"א כִּי אִם תְּכַבְּסִי בַּנֶּתֶר וְתַרְבִּי לָךְ בּוֹרִית נִכְתָּם עֲוֹנֵךְ לְפָנָי.

312. He opened the discussion by quoting: "For I acnowledge my transgressions; and my sin is ever before me" (Tehilim 51:5). People should be staunchly on guard against sinning before the Holy One, blessed be He, because after a person has sinned, his sin is recorded in the upper world and may only be blotted out through the power of great repentance. This is as it is written: "For though you wash yourself with nitre, and take yourself much soap, yet the stain of your iniquity is before Me" (Yirmeyah 2:22).

313. תָּא חֲזֵי, כֵּיוָן דְּחָב ב"נ קַמֵּי קֻדְשָׁא בְּרִיךְ הוּא זִמְנָא חָדָא, עָבִיד רְשִׁימוּ. וְכַד חָב בֵּיהּ זִמְנָא תִּנְיָינָא, אִתְתַּקַּף הַהוּא רְשִׁימוּ יַתִּיר. חָב בֵּיהּ זִמְנָא תְּלִיתָאָה, אִתְפַּשַּׁט הַהוּא כִּתְמָא, מִסִּטְרָא דָּא לְסִטְרָא דָּא, כְּדֵין כְּתִיב, נִכְתָּם עֲוֹנֵךְ לְפָנָי.

313. Come and behold: The first time a person sins before the Holy One,

blessed be He, he leaves a mark. If he sins a second time, the mark is darkened. If he sins a third time, the stain spreads to all sides. This is suggested by the words: "the stain of your iniquity is before Me" (Yirmeyah 2:22).

314. תָּא חֲזֵי, דָּוִד מַלְכָּא, כֵּיוָן דְּחָב קַמֵּי קֻדְשָׁא בְּרִיךְ הוּא, עַל עִסְקָא דְּבַת שֶׁבַע, חָשִׁיב, דְּהַהוּא חוֹבָא, אִתְרְשִׁים עֲלֵיהּ לְעָלְמִין. מַה כְּתִיב, גַּם ה׳ הֶעֱבִיר חַטָּאתְךָ לֹא תָמוּת. אַעֲבַר הַהוּא רְשִׁימוּ מִקַּמֵּיהּ.

314. Come and behold: When King David sinned with Bathsheba before the Holy One, blessed be He, King David thought that the stain of this sin would last forever. But what is written? "Hashem also has put away your sin, you shall not die" (II Shmuel 12:13), MEANING THAT the stain was blotted out.

315. אָמַר לוֹ רַבִּי אַבָּא, וְהָא תָּנִינָן דְּבַת שֶׁבַע, דִּילֵיהּ דְּדָוִד מַלְכָּא הֲוַת מִן יוֹמָא דְּאִתְבְּרֵי עָלְמָא, אַמַּאי, יָהֲבָה קֻדְשָׁא בְּרִיךְ הוּא לְאוּרִיָּה הַחִתִּי, מִן קַדְמַת דְּנָא.

315. Rabbi Aba then asked him: If Bathsheba belonged to King David from the day the world was created, why did the Holy One, blessed be He, give her first to Uriah the Hittite?

316. אָמַר לוֹ, הָכֵי אוֹרְחוֹי דְּקֻדְשָׁא בְּרִיךְ הוּא, אַף עַל פִּי דְּאִתְּתָא אַזְמִינָא לֵיהּ לְבַר נָשׁ, לְמֶהֱוֵי דִּילֵיהּ, אַקְדִּים אַחֲרָא וְנָסִיב לָהּ, עַד דְּמָטָא זִמְנֵיהּ דְּהַאי. כֵּיוָן דְּמָטָא זִמְנֵיהּ, אִתְדַּחְיָיא הַאי דְּנָסִיב לָהּ, מִקַּמֵּי הַאי אָחֳרָא, דְּאָתֵי לְבָתַר, וְאִסְתַּלָּק מֵעָלְמָא. וְקַשֵּׁי קַמֵּיהּ קֻדְשָׁא בְּרִיךְ הוּא לְאַעֲבָרָא לֵיהּ מֵעָלְמָא, עַד לָא מָטֵי זִמְנֵיהּ, מִקַּמֵּי הַאי אָחֳרָא.

316. Rabbi Shimon told him that these are the ways of the Holy One, blessed be He. Although a woman may be destined to become a certain man's wife, another man may marry her first. But as soon as the time has come for the destined man to marry her, the latter is removed from this

-442-

world, because of the other that comes after him. And it is very hard and for the Holy One, blessed be He, to remove that person from the world before his time has come, for someone else's sake.

317. וְרָזָא דְּבַת שֶׁבַע, דְּאִתְיְיהִיבַת לְאוּרִיָּה הַחִתִּי בְּקַדְמֵיתָא, פּוֹק וְדוֹק, אַמַּאי אִתְיְהִיבַת אַרְעָא קַדִּישָׁא לִכְנַעַן, עַד לָא יֵיתוּן יִשְׂרָאֵל. וְתִשְׁכַּח מִלָּה דָּא. וְכֹלָּא רָזָא חֲדָא אִיהוּ, וּמִלָּה חֲדָא.

317. The secret of why Bathsheba was given first to Uriah the Hittite lies in the answer to the question of why the Holy Land was given first to Canaan, before Yisrael existed. From this, you shall understand WHY BATHSHEBA WAS GIVEN FIRST TO URIAH. Both questions are connected to one secret and one matter.

318. תָּא חֲזֵי, דָּוִד, אַף עַל גַּב דְּאוֹדֵי עַל חוֹבֵיהּ, וְתָב בְּתִיּוּבְתָּא, לָא אֲדֵי לְבֵיהּ וּרְעוּתֵיהּ מֵאִינּוּן חוֹבִין דְּחַב, וּמֵהַהוּא חוֹבָא דְּבַת שֶׁבַע, בְּגִין דְּדָחִיל עֲלַיְיהוּ תָּדִיר, דִּילְמָא גָּרִים חַד מִנַּיְיהוּ, וִיקַטְרֵג עֲלֵיהּ בְּשַׁעֲתָא דְּסַכָּנָה. וּבְגִין כָּךְ, לָא אַנְשֵׁי לוֹן, מִינֵּיהּ וּמֵרְעוּתֵיהּ.

318. Come and behold: Even though David confessed his sins and repented, he was not able to completely forget and extirpate them from his heart, especially the sin related to Bathsheba. Because he always feared that one of his sins might reappear and persecute him in time of danger, he never forgot them or blotted them out of his memory. HE SAID, "FOR I AKNOWLEDGE MY TRANSGRESSION, AND MY SIN IS EVER BEFORE ME ALWAYS."

319. דָּבָר אַחֵר, כִּי פְשָׁעַי אֲנִי אֵדָע. כָּלְּהוּ דַּרְגִּין, דְּתַלְיָין בְּהוֹ חוֹבֵי בְּנֵי נָשָׁא, אֲנִי אֵדָע. וְחַטָּאתִי נֶגְדִּי תָמִיד. דָּא פְּגִימוּ דְּסִיהֲרָא, דְּלָא נָפְקָא מִסְאוֹבְתָּא, עַד דְּאָתָא שְׁלֹמֹה, וְאִתְנְהִירַת בְּאַשְׁלָמוּתָא. וּכְדֵין אִתְבַּסַּם עָלְמָא, וְיָתִיבוּ יִשְׂרָאֵל לִרְחַצָן. דִּכְתִיב וַיֵּשֶׁב יְהוּדָה וְיִשְׂרָאֵל לָבֶטַח אִישׁ תַּחַת גַּפְנוֹ וְתַחַת תְּאֵנָתוֹ. וְעִם כָּל דָּא, וְחַטָּאתִי נֶגְדִּי תָמִיד. וְלָא אִתְפְּסָק מֵעָלְמָא. עַד דְּיֵיתֵי מַלְכָּא מְשִׁיחָא, לְזִמְנָא דְּאָתֵי. כְּמָה דְּאִתְּמָר וְאֶת רוּחַ הַטֻּמְאָה אַעֲבִיר מִן הָאָרֶץ.

39. Bathsheba and Uriah

319. Another interpretation of the verse, "For I acknowledge my transgression" is, 'I am familiar with all the levels whence the sins of humankind originate.' IN OTHER WORDS, HE HAD ALREADY CORRECTED THEM. On the other hand, "my sin is ever before me" refers to the defect of the moon, WHICH HE DID NOT CORRECT. The moon's defect was not corrected until Solomon appeared. AT THAT POINT, IT SHONE FLAWLESS AND FULL. Then, the world was joyful (lit. 'perfumed') and Yisrael dwelled in security. As it is written: "And Judah and Yisrael dwelled safely, every man under his vine and under his fig tree" (I Melachim 5:5). "My sin is ever before me" SIGNIFIES THAT EVEN IN THE DAYS OF KING SOLOMON, THE MOON'S DEFECT WAS NOT COMPLETELY CORRECTED. FOR THE TEMPLE WAS DESTROYED A SECOND TIME, AND THE MOON, WHICH IS THE FEMALE PRINCIPLE, RETURNED TO ITS UNCORRECTED STATE. THIS DEFECT shall not be removed from the world until the King Messiah appears, as is described in the verse: "and also I will cause...the unclean spirit to pass out of the land" (Zecharyah 13:2).

40. "He was a mighty hunter"

According to the Zohar, Nimrod used the clothes of Adam to gain strength. *Clothes* is a code word that alludes to the physicality that conceals the Light, as garments conceal the body. Nimrod, we are told, connected only to the material world, without any regard or consideration for the spiritual essence of reality. This is considered to be a form of *idol worshipping*. It is falling under the delusion and control of the physical world.

A deeper awareness for the spiritual essence of life is awakened within us by these passages, so that we are not controlled by illusion.

320. הוּא הָיָה גִבּוֹר צַיִד לִפְנֵי ה' עַל כֵּן יֵאָמַר כְּנִמְרוֹד גִבּוֹר צַיִד לִפְנֵי ה'. תָּא חֲזֵי, הוּא הֲוָה גְּבַר תַּקִּיף. לְבוּשׁוֹי דְּאָדָם הָרִאשׁוֹן הֲוָה לָבֵישׁ. וַהֲוָה יָדַע לְמֵיצַד צֵידָה דִּבְרִיָּיתָא בְּהוֹ.

320. "He was a mighty hunter before Hashem; therefore, it is said, 'even as Nimrod the mighty hunter before Hashem'" (Beresheet 10:9). Come and behold: Nimrod was a brave man, who wore the garments of Adam and knew how to hunt. ALL LIVING BEINGS SURRENDERED TO HIM BECAUSE OF THOSE GARMENTS, THOSE "COATS OF SKIN," AS THE VERSE READS: "TO ADAM ALSO AND TO HIS WIFE DID HASHEM ELOHIM MAKE COATS OF SKIN, AND CLOTHED THEM" (BERESHEET 3:21).

321 אָמַר רַבִּי אֶלְעָזָר, נִמְרוֹד הֲוָה מְפַתֵּי לִבְרִיָּיתָא, לְמֵיהַךְ בָּתַר פּוּלְחָן דַּע"ז. וַהֲוָה שַׁלִּיט בְּאִינּוּן לְבוּשִׁין, וְנָצַח בְּנֵי עָלְמָא. וַהֲוָה אֲמַר דְּאִיהוּ שַׁלִּיטָא בְּעָלְמָא, וּפָלְחִין לֵיהּ בְּנֵי נָשָׁא. וְאַמַּאי אִקְרֵי שְׁמֵיהּ נִמְרוֹד. דְּמָרַד בְּמַלְכָּא עִלָּאָה. דִּלְעֵילָא. דְּמָרַד בְּעִלָּאֵי, וּמָרַד בְּתַתָּאֵי.

321. Rabbi Elazar said that Nimrod used to entice people into idol worshipping. He used the power of those garments to rule all other people. He proclaimed himself ELOHIM, the ruler of the world, so all other people served him. But why was he called Nimrod? Because he rebelled (Heb. *marad*) against the High King of above, against the power of SUPERNAL HOLINESS, and also against the lower beings, THE PEOPLE OF THIS WORLD.

322. בְּאִינּוּן לְבוּשִׁין, שַׁלִּיט עַל כָּל בְּנֵי עָלְמָא, וּמָלַךְ בְּהוּ. וּמָרַד
בְּמָארֵיהּ. וַאֲמַר, דְּאִיהוּ שַׁלִּיטָא דְעָלְמָא, וַהֲוָה מְפַתֵּי לִבְרִיָּיתָא
אֲבַתְרֵיהּ, עַד דְּמָשַׁךְ בְּנֵי נָשָׁא, לְמֵיפַק מִבָּתַר פּוּלְחָנָא דְּמָארֵי עָלְמָא.
אֲמַר רָבִּי שִׁמְעוֹן בְּאִלֵּין לְבוּשִׁין, יָדְעֵי בְּהוּ חַבְרַיָּיא רָזָא עִלָּאָה.

322. By the power of these garments, he was able to rule over all mankind. He rebelled against THEM AND his Master by saying that he was the ruler of the world, THAT IS, HE DECLARED HIMSELF ELOHIM. He seduced people into following him, leaving the service of the Master of the universe, and serving him. Rabbi Shimon said that the friends knew a great secret about these garments.

41. "And the house, when it was in building"

If we make a complete connection to the Light of God, we need only begin a new endeavor and the Light finishes the work on our behalf. This unusual concept is further understood through the example of planting a seed. Once the seed is planted, the forces of nature take over, eventually giving birth to a full grown tree. When our connections to the Light are secure and complete, we can plant seeds of positive energy in all areas of our lives. We gain this ability through the metaphysical powers that are emitted through the medium of the letters.

323. מַתְנִיתִין. וַיְהִי כָל הָאָרֶץ שָׂפָה אַחַת וּדְבָרִים אֲחָדִים. ר' שִׁמְעוֹן פָּתַח, וְהַבַּיִת בְּהִבָּנוֹתוֹ אֶבֶן שְׁלֵמָה מַסַּע נִבְנָה וּמַקָּבוֹת וְהַגַּרְזֶן כָּל כְּלֵי בַרְזֶל לֹא נִשְׁמַע בַּבַּיִת בְּהִבָּנוֹתוֹ. וְהַבַּיִת בְּהִבָּנוֹתוֹ. וְכִי לָא הֲוָה בָּנֵי לֵיהּ שְׁלֹמֹה, וְכָלְּהוּ אוּמָנִין, דַּהֲווֹ תַּמָּן, מַהוּ בְּהִבָּנוֹתוֹ.

323. Mishnah "And the whole earth was of one language and of one speech" (Beresheet 11:1). Rabbi Shimon began by quoting: "And the house, when it was building, was built of stone made ready before it was brought there: so that there was neither hammer nor ax nor any tool of iron heard in the house, while it was being built" (I Melachim 6:7). HE ASKS IF THE WORDS, "And the house, when it was in building," MEAN THAT THE HOUSE BUILT ITSELF. Could it be that Solomon and all his artisans did not build it? Why does it read, "when it was in building?"

324. אֶלָּא, כָּךְ הוּא, כְּמָה דִכְתִיב, מִקְשָׁה תֵּעָשֶׂה הַמְּנוֹרָה. אִם הִיא מִקְשָׁה, מַהוּ תֵּעָשֶׂה. אֶלָּא, וַדַּאי כֹּלָּא בָּאת וְנִיסָּא אִתְעֲבֵיד אִיהוּ מִגַּרְמֵיהּ. כֵּיוָן דְּשָׁרָאן לְמֶעְבַּד עֲבִידְתָּא אוֹלִיף לְאוּמָנִין לְמֶעְבַּד בָּהּ, מַה דְּלָא הֲווֹ יָדְעִין מִקַּדְמַת דְּנָא.

324. We read: "And you shall make a candelabra. In one piece of pure gold shall the candelabra be made" (Shemot 25:31). Now a candelabra is to be made of beaten work, MEANING IF THE ARTISANS ARE TO BEAT THE BAR OF METAL WITH A SLEDGEHAMMER, why does the verse continue, "shall the candelabra be made?" THAT IS TO SAY, SHALL IT BE MADE BY ITSELF! But, of course, IN THE TEMPLE everything happened, and all objects made

themselves, by miracles and signs. As soon as the artisans began to work, the art crafted itself, showing them how to work in ways they had not known before THEY STARTED.

325. מ״ט, בְּגִין דְּבִרְכָתָא דְּקַדְשָׁא בְּרִיךְ הוּא, שָׁרָא עַל יְדַיְיהוּ, וְע״ד כְּתִיב, בְּהִבָּנוֹתוֹ, אִיהִי אִתְבְּנֵי מִגַּרְמֵיהּ, דְּהוּא אוּלְפָא אוּלְפַן לְאוּמָנִין, הֵיאךְ שָׁרָאן לְמֶעְבַּד, וְלָא אִסְתַּלַק מֵעֵינַיְיהוּ רְשִׁימוּ דְּהַהוּא עֲבִידְתָּא מַמָּשׁ, וּמִסְתַּכְלָאן בֵּיהּ וְעָבְדֵי, עַד דְּאִתְבְּנֵי כָּל בֵּיתָא.

325. Why was that so? Because the blessings of the Holy One, blessed be He, was upon their hands. Therefore, it says, "when it was in building," to indicate that it was built by itself. The building taught the artisans how to start their work by guiding their hands with signs. The artisans did not turn their eyes away from the vision of the form until the house was completely built.

326. אֶבֶן שְׁלֵמָה מַסַּע נִבְנֶה. שְׁלֵמָה כְּתִיב, חָסֵר יוד, אֶבֶן שְׁלֹמָה וַדַּאי. מַסַּע: דְּאִתְנְטִיל וְאַתְיָיא וְשַׁרְיָיא עֲלַיְיהוּ, וְאִתְעֲבִיד עֲבִידְתָּא. מַסַּע: דְּאַנְטֵיל יָדָן לְמֶעְבַּד, דְּלָא מִדַעְתַּיְיהוּ. כְּתִיב הָכָא מַסַּע. וּכְתִיב הָתָם וּלְמַסַּע אֶת הַמַּחֲנוֹת.

326. The words "stone made ready (Heb. *shlema*; lit. 'whole') before it was brought there (Heb. *masa*; lit. 'journey');" *shlema* is spelled without a *Yud*. AS A RESULT, IT CAN BE ALSO PRONOUNCED SHLOMOH (ENG. 'SOLOMON'), AND NOT JUST *SHLEMA*. THAT REFERS TO THE FEMALE PRINCIPLE, CALLED THE STONE OF THE KING OF PEACE (HEB. *SHALOM*). Now the word *masa* indicates that A WHOLE STONE, THE FEMALE PRINCIPLE, TRAVELED FROM ABOVE AND came to dwell upon them and accomplish the work. ANOTHER INTERPRETATION IS THAT THE STONE made the hands "travel" or work involuntarily. For here, it is written *masa*, just as it appears in the verse, "and for the journeying (*masa*) of the camps" (Bemidbar 10:2). BECAUSE THE WORD IN THE LATTER VERSE REFERS TO AN ACTION, WE MAY CONCLUDE THAT IN THE FIRST ONE IT ALSO DESCRIBES AN ACTION.

327. וּמַקָּבוֹת וְהַגַּרְזֶן כָּל כְּלֵי בַרְזֶל לֹא נִשְׁמַע. בְּגִין, דְּשַׁמִּיר בָּזַע כֹּלָּא,

וְלָא אִשְׁתְּמַע מִלָּה, דְּלָא אִצְטְרִיכוּ לִשְׁאָר מָאנִין לְמֶעְבַּד. וְכֹלָּא בְּאָת וְנִיסָא הֲוָה.

327. "There was neither hammer nor ax nor any tool of iron heard in the house," because a CERTAIN WORM CALLED shamir (Eng. 'emery') split everything noiselessly, and thus, they did not require other tools. Everything occurred by a miracle.

328. אֲמַר רַבִּי שִׁמְעוֹן, כַּמָּה חֲבִיבִין אִינּוּן מִלֵּי דְאוֹרַיְיתָא. זַכָּאָה חוּלָקֵיה, מָאן דְּאִתְעַסַּק בְּהוּ, וְיָדַע לְמֵיהַךְ בְּאֹרַח קְשׁוֹט. וְהַבַּיִת בְּהִבָּנוֹתוֹ. כַּד סָלְקָא בִּרְעוּתָא דְקֻדְשָׁא בְּרִיךְ הוּא, לְמֶעְבַּד יְקָרָא לִיקָרֵיה, סָלְקָא מִגּוֹ מַחֲשָׁבָה רְעוּתָא, לְאִתְפַּשְּׁטָא, וְאִתְפַּשְּׁטַת מֵאֲתַר דְּאִיהִי מַחֲשָׁבָה סְתִימָא, דְּלָא אִתְיְידַע.

328. How pleasant it is to hear the words of the Torah; how good is the lot of he who delves in them and knows how to walk the path of truth, said Rabbi Shimon. So, "the house, when it was in building" MEANS THAT the desire of the Holy One, blessed be He, to be glorified arose from within the Thought and spread forth. IN OTHER WORDS, BINAH, WHICH IS CALLED 'DESIRE,' CAME FROM THE HEAD OF ARICH ANPIN, WHICH IS CALLED 'THOUGHT,' and spread forth from the place that is called 'Concealed Thought.' THAT IS, IT SPREAD FORTH FROM THE 'CONCEALED CHOCHMAH' OF ARICH ANPIN, which is a mystery.

329. עַד דְּאִתְפַּשְּׁטַת וְשַׁרְיָיא לְבֵי גָרוֹן, אֲתַר דְּאִיהוּ נְבִיעַ תָּדִיר, בְּרָזָא דְּאִיהוּ רוּחַ חַיִּים. וּכְדֵין כַּד אִתְפַּשְּׁטַת הַהִיא מַחֲשָׁבָה, וְשַׁרְיָא בַּאֲתַר דָּא, אִקְרֵי הַהִיא מַחֲשָׁבָה, אֱלֹקִים חַיִּים. דִּכְתִיב הוּא אֱלֹקִים חַיִּים.

329. BINAH spread forth until it lodged inside the 'throat' OF ARICH ANPIN, from where it constantly flows by the secret of the 'spirit of life.' Afterward, Thought, CHOCHMAH OF ARICH ANPIN, had expanded and settled in that place. Thus, Thought is called 'Living Elohim', as is written: "He is the living Elohim" (Yirmeyah 10:10).

330. עוֹד בָּעָא, לְאִתְפַּשְּׁטָא וּלְאִתְגַּלְיָא, מִתַּמָּן נָפְקוּ, אֶשָּׁא וְרוּחָא

וּמַיָּא, כְּלִילָן כַּחֲדָא, וּנְפַק יַעֲקֹב, גְּבַר שְׁלִים, וְאִיהוּ קוֹל חַד דְּנָפִיק
וְאִשְׁתְּמַע. מֵהָכָא, מַחֲשָׁבָה דַּהֲוָה סְתִימָא בַּחֲשַׁאי, אִשְׁתְּמַע לְאִתְגַּלְיָא.

330. THE EMANATOR wanted to continue expanding and revealing Himself, so He caused THE SECRET OF THE THREE COLUMNS, fire, wind, and water, to come forth. Thus, Jacob, the perfect man, WHO IS ZEIR ANPIN, came forth. And his was the one voice that came through and was heard. From this, we learn that Thought that was secretly hidden – BINAH – was revealed and made audible BY JACOB, WHO IS ZEIR ANPIN.

331. עוֹד, אִתְפַּשְׁטַת הַאי מַחֲשָׁבָה, לְאִתְגַּלְיָא. וּבָטַשׁ הַאי קוֹל וְאַקִּישׁ
בְּשִׂפְוָון, וּכְדֵין נָפְקָא דִּבּוּר, דְּאַשְׁלִים כֹּלָּא, וְגָלֵי כֹּלָּא. אִשְׁתְּמַע דְּכֹלָּא
אִיהוּ הַהִיא מַחֲשָׁבָה סְתִימָא דַּהֲוַת לְגוֹ, וְכֹלָּא חַד.

331. This Thought kept expanding so that it could be revealed, and this voice struck upon the lips and speech came out, completing and revealing everything. We learn from this that everything is Thought that was concealed internally, and therefore all are one.

332. כֵּיוָן דְּמָטָא אִתְפַּשְׁטוּתָא דָא, וְאִתְעֲבֵיד דִּבּוּר בְּתִקִּיפָא דְּהַהוּא
קָלָא, כְּדֵין, וְהַבַּיִת בְּהִבָּנֹתוֹ. כַּאֲשֶׁר נִבְנֶה לֹא כְּתִיב, אֶלָּא בְּהִבָּנֹתוֹ,
בְּכָל זִמְנָא וְזִמְנָא. אֶבֶן שְׁלֵמָה, כְּמָה דְּאִתְּמַר. וּכְתִיב בָּעֲטָרָה שֶׁעִטְּרָה
לוֹ אִמּוֹ.

332. Speech was an extension OF BINAH, MEANING THAT BINAH WAS DRAWN TO THE FEMALE PRINCIPLE and was formed by the power of the voice. THE VOICE IS ZEIR ANPIN, WHO RECEIVES FROM BINAH AND PASSES ON TO THE FEMALE PRINCIPLE. The words, "And the house, when it was in building," REFER TO THE FACT THAT IT BUILT ITSELF BY SIGNS AND MIRACLES. The verse reads, "when it was in building" and not "when it was built." IF THE PHRASE WAS MEANT TO INDICATE THAT THE HOUSE BUILT ITSELF, IT WOULD HAVE READ, 'AND THE HOUSE WHEN IT WAS BUILT,' WHY DOES IT READ, "WHEN IT WAS IN BUILDING?" AND HE EXPLAINS THAT THIS IS TO TEACH US THAT it is so at all times. "Stone made ready" is THE STONE OF SOLOMON as we said before. It is also written:

"with the crown with which his mother crowned him" (Shir Hashirim 3:11), REFERRING TO BINAH, WHICH IS CALLED IMA. THUS, WHEN THE FEMALE PRINCIPLE RECEIVES THESE CROWN, SHE IS CALLED THE STONE OF SOLOMON.

333. מַסַּע: דְּנַפְקָא מִלְגוֹ, וְשַׁרְיָא וְנָטִיל לְבַר, נַפְקָא מִלְעֵילָא, וְשַׁרְיָא וְנָטִיל לְתַתָּא. וּמַקְבוֹת וְהַגַּרְזֶן כָּל כְּלִי בַּרְזֶל: אִלֵּין שְׁאָר דַּרְגִּין תַּתָּאִין, דְּכֻלְּהוּ תַּלְיָין בֵּיהּ, וְלָא אִשְׁתְּמָעוּ, וְלָא אִתְקַבְּלָן לְגוֹ, כַּד אִיהִי סַלְקָא לְאִתְאַחֲדָא לְעֵילָא, וּלְיָנְקָא מִתַּמָּן. וְדָא הוּא בְּהִבָּנוֹתוֹ.

333. "It was brought there," INDICATES THAT THE ILLUMINATION OF THE MOCHIN emerged from the internal aspect OF BINAH. THAT IS, ALL THE WORK WAS COMPLETED and came FROM BINAH. It then remained outside IN ZEIR ANPIN, emerging from the upper level – BINAH – and traveling down TO THE FEMALE PRINCIPLE. The "hammers and ax and all other tools of iron" are the lower levels that depend on THE FEMALE PRINCIPLE. They were neither heard nor received by the internal aspect when THE FEMALE PRINCIPLE ascended to unite with the it, ENCLOTHE ABA AND IMA, and be nourished from there. BECAUSE THEY USED THE SHAMIR INSTEAD OF OTHER TOOLS, THEY WERE NOT HEARD. This is why the verse uses the phrase "when it was n building" TO INDICATE THAT IT WAS BUILT WITHOUT ANY OF THE HANDIWORK OF THE LOWER BEINGS.

334. וּכְדֵין כַּד אִיהִי יָנְקָא, כֻּלְּהוּ קַיְימֵי בְּחֶדְוָותָא, וְיָנְקִין וְאִתְמַלְיָין בִּרְכָאן. וּכְדֵין, קַיְימִין עָלְמִין כֻּלְּהוּ, בְּרָזָא חֲדָא, בְּיִחוּדָא חַד, וְלָא הֲוֵי בְּהוּ בְּכֻלְּהוּ עָלְמִין פְּרוּדָא. לְבָתַר דְּנַטְלֵי חוּלָקְהוֹן כָּל חַד וְחַד, כֻּלְּהוּ מִתְפַּשְּׁטָן וּמִתְפָּרְשָׁן לְסִטְרַיְיהוּ, לְמָה דְּאִתְמַנָּן.

334. When THE FEMALE PRINCIPLE is nourished FROM ABA AND IMA, all the worlds are happy. They nourish themselves FROM THE FEMALE PRINCIPLE, and are filled with blessings. They are united by one secret, one unity, and there is no separation in the worlds. After all THE WORLDS, each and every one, have taken their share FROM THE FEMALE PRINCIPLE, they expand and return to the purposes for which they were created.

42. "A city and a tower"

Kabbalah differs from other spiritual teachings in that we are not called upon to separate ourselves from the physical world of chaos. Instead, we embrace chaos to eradicate our negative traits and to nurture transformation. Throughout history, this has been a difficult endeavor. The peoples of the past, such as the Tower of Babel generation, chose the easy path to spiritual Light, with dire consequences. We must be careful not to fall into that same trap.

In the biblical story, a group of evil people seek to build a tower that will reach Heaven. They intend to challenge God and seek world domination.

The Zohar quotes the verse from the Torah: *And they said, come, let us build us a city and a tower, whose top may reach to heaven: and let us make ourselves a name.*

The Zohar reveals that the terms *City* and *Tower* allude to the highest levels of the dark spiritual forces. The word *name* refers to the Names of God, or the power of the Hebrew letters. It is the letters that will allow the evil ones to access negative spiritual forces. God then confuses their language, creating seventy other tongues so that the power of the Hebrew letters can never be used for destructive purposes.

This section helps us to remain true to our spiritual path, and stops us from falling to the temptations of paths that always appear easier.

335. תָּא חֲזֵי, וַיְהִי כָל הָאָרֶץ שָׂפָה אַחַת וְגוֹ'. לְבָתַר מַה כְּתִיב, וַיְהִי בְּנָסְעָם מִקֶּדֶם. מֵהַהוּא קַדְמָאָה דְּעָלְמָא. וַיִּמְצְאוּ בִקְעָה בְּאֶרֶץ שִׁנְעָר. דְּהָא מִתַּמָּן, מִתְפָּרְשָׁן לְכָל אִינוּן סִטְרִין, וְאִיהוּ רֵישׁ מַלְכוּ לְאִתְבַּדְּרָא.

335. Come and behold: Observe WHAT HAS BEEN WRITTEN: "And the whole earth was of one language, and of one speech" (Beresheet 11:1). What is written next? "And it came to pass, as they journeyed from the east (also, 'yore')" (Ibid. 2). FOR THEY REMOVED THERMSELVES from the Originator of the world. IN OTHER WORDS, THEY DREW DOWN THE ILLUMINATION OF THE LEFT, WHICH THE ORIGINATOR OF THE WORLD HAD FORBIDDEN THEM TO DO. THEREFORE, THE PASSAGE CONTINUES, "they found a plain in the land of Shinar" from where JUDGMENTS spread out in all directions. This is the beginning of Malchut's separation FROM

HOLINESS. IT IS DESCRIBED BY THE PHRASE, "YOU ARE THIS HEAD OF
GOLD" (DANIEL 2:38), BECAUSE "ELOHIM HAS MADE THE ONE AS WELL
AS THE OTHER" (KOHELET 7:14). IN THE KLIPOT, THERE ARE ALSO
FOUR ASPECTS: CHOCHMAH, BINAH, TIFERET AND MALCHUT. AND THE
KLIPAH OF BABYLON IS CHOCHMAH OF THE KLIPAH. HENCE, IT IS THE
HEAD OF ALL OF THE KLIPOT.

336. וְאִי תֵימָא, הָא כְּתִיב וְנָהָר יוֹצֵא מֵעֵדֶן לְהַשְׁקוֹת אֶת הַגָּן וּמִשָּׁם
יִפָּרֵד. וַדַּאי הָכֵי הוּא, דְּכֵיוָן דְּנָטְלֵי מִתַּמָּן, הֲוֵי פְּרוּדָא, וְכַד אִינּוּן
כְּנִישִׁין תַּמָּן לְיַנְקָא לָא הֲוֵי פְּרוּדָא. וְכַד נָטְלִין הֲוֵי פְּרוּדָא, דִּכְתִיב
וַיְהִי בְּנָסְעָם מִקֶּדֶם, וַיִּמְצְאוּ בִקְעָה. כְּמָה דְאִתְּמָר.

336. You might ask: Since it has already been written: "And a river went
out of Eden to water the garden, and from thence it was parted" (Beresheet
2:10), HOW CAN WE SAY THAT THE PLAIN (LIT. 'PARTITION') IN THE LAND
OF SHINAR WAS THE BEGINNING OF THE SEPARATION? AND HE
REPLIED: It is certain THAT THE SEPARATION STARTS AFTER OR BEYOND
MALCHUT OF ATZILUT, WHICH IS THE SECRET OF THE GARDEN. When
they journeyed from THE GARDEN, THEY FOUND THE PLAIN IN THE LAND
OF SHINAR, and the separation was complete. If they gathered IN THE
GARDEN for nourishment, BUT DO NOT DRAW THE ILLUMINATION OF THE
LEFT, then there was no separation. THAT IS WHY THE VERSE STATES
THAT FROM THE GARDEN "IT WAS PARTED." Only when they journeyed
away FROM THE GARDEN did the separation occur, as it is written: "as they
journeyed from the east," OR FROM THE GARDEN, they "found a plain," as
previously explained. HAD THEY NOT LEFT THE GARDEN, THEY WOULD
NOT HAVE FOUND A PLAIN IN THE LAND OF SHINAR AND THEY WOULD
NOT HAVE BEEN SEPARATED FROM HOLINESS. THIS IS WHY THE PLAIN
IN THE LAND OF SHINAR IS CONSIDERED TO BE THE BEGINNING OF THE
SEPARATION.

337. וַיְהִי כָל הָאָרֶץ שָׂפָה אֶחָת וּדְבָרִים אֲחָדִים. דְּהָא כְּדֵין עָלְמָא,
בִּיסוֹדָא וְעִקָּרָא וְשָׁרְשָׁא חֲדָא, וּמְהֵימְנוּתָא חֲדָא, בֵּיהּ בְּקֻדְשָׁא בְּרִיךְ
הוּא. מַה כְּתִיב, וַיְהִי בְּנָסְעָם מִקֶּדֶם. מִקַּדְמָאָה עִקָּרָא דְעָלְמָא,
מְהֵימְנוּתָא דְכֹלָּא. וַיִּמְצְאוּ בִקְעָה. מְצִיאָה אַשְׁכָּחוּ, וְנָפְקוּ בָהּ מִתְּחוֹת
מְהֵימְנוּתָא עִלָּאָה.

337. "And the whole earth was of one language, and of one speech," because it had one basic and essential foundation, MERCY. All peoples had faith in the Holy One, blessed be He, AND WOULD NOT SIN BEFORE HIM. But what does it say? It says, "And it came to pass, as they journeyed from the east" – MEANING THAT THEY "DRIFTED AWAY" from the First and Foremost of the world and from the universal faith, and "they found a plain." They did indeed find something, something that would cause them to leave the supernal faith, AS SHALL BE EXPLAINED.

338. תָּא חֲזֵי, נִמְרוֹד מַה כְּתִיב בֵּיה, וַתְּהִי רֵאשִׁית מַמְלַכְתּוֹ בָּבֶל. דְּהָא מִתַּמָּן נָטַל לְאִתְאַחֲדָא בִּרְשׁוּ אָחֳרָא. וְהָכָא, וַיִּמְצְאוּ בִקְעָה בְּאֶרֶץ שִׁנְעָר. מִתַּמָּן נָטְלוּ בְּלִבַּיְיהוּ, לְאַפָּקָא מֵרְשׁוּתָא עִלָּאָה, לִרְשׁוּ אָחֳרָא.

338. Come and behold: What is said of Nimrod? It is said: "And the beginning of his kingdom was Babylon" (Beresheet 10:10). For he drew POWER from Babylon that helped him to cling on to the dominion of the Other SIDE. IT ALSO READS, "they found a plain in the land of Shinar," MEANING they filled their hearts WITH DESIRE derived from Shinar, to leave the upper dominion and join a different power. FOR THE LAND OF SHINAR, WHICH IS BABYLON, IS THE HEAD AND ROOT OF SEVERENCE FROM THE HOLY ONE, BLESSED BE HE.

339. וַיֹּאמְרוּ הָבָה נִבְנֶה לָנוּ עִיר וּמִגְדָּל וְרֹאשׁוֹ בַשָּׁמַיִם וְנַעֲשֶׂה לָנוּ שֵׁם. ר' חִיָּיא פְּתַח, וְהָרְשָׁעִים כַּיָּם נִגְרָשׁ וְגוֹ'. וְכִי אִית יָם נִגְרָשׁ. אִין. דְּכַד יַמָּא נָפְקָא מִתִּקּוּנֵיהּ, וְאָזִיל בְּלָא חַבָּלָא, כְּדֵי נִגְרָשׁ וְאִתְתְּרַךְ מֵאַתְרֵיהּ, כְּמַאן דְּרָוֵי חַמְרָא, וְלָא יָתִיב עַל בּוּרְיֵיהּ, וְסָלְקָא וְנָחֲתָא. מ"ט בְּגִין, כִּי הַשְׁקֵט לֹא יוּכַל וְיִגְרְשׁוּ מֵימָיו רֶפֶשׁ וָטִיט. דְּמַפְּקוּ מֵימוֹי, כָּל הַהוּא טִינָא דְיַמָּא, וְכָל טִנוּפָא לִשְׂפַוָּותֵיהּ.

339. "And they said, Come, let us build us a city and a tower, whose top may reach to heaven; and let us make us a name" (Beresheet 11:4). Rabbi Chiya quoted the verse: "And the wicked are like the troubled sea" (Yeshayah 57:20). HE ASKS: Is there a "troubled sea?" AND HE REPLIES: Yes, indeed, because when the sea leaves the bed, in which it belongs and starts to sway uncontrollably, ATTEMPTING TO OVERCOME THE

BOUNDARIES OF THE SAND THAT HOLDS IT IN PLACE AND POUR OVER THE LAND, it is troubled and driven from its place. It is like a drunkard who cannot sit steadily in his place and sways up and down. Why is that? Because "it cannot be still, and whose waters cast up mire and dirt" (Ibid.), FROM ITS FLOOR up to its shore.

340. כְּגַוְונָא דָא, אִינּוּן רְשָׁעִים, דְּנָפְקָא מֵאָרְחָא דְּתָקְנָא, וְאָזְלֵי כְּרָוֵי חַמְרָא, בְּלָא תִּקּוּנָא, דְּנָפְקֵי מֵאוֹרַח מֵישָׁר, לְאוֹרַח עָקִים. מ״ט בְּגִין, כִּי הַשְׁקֵט לֹא יוּכָל. דְּהָא עֲקִימוּ דְּאָרְחַיְיהוּ גָּרִים לוֹן, לְמֵהַךְ בְּלָא תִּקּוּנָא, וּבְלָא שְׁכִיכוּ.

340. Similarly, the wicked GENERATION OF THE TOWER OF BABYLON CALLED 'THE GENERATION OF SEPARATION', left the right and proper way FIXED BY THE ORIGINATOR OF THE WORLD, and were as directionless and purposeless as drunk men. THEY ATTACHED THEMSELVES TO BINAH OF THE KLIPAH, straying from the straight path and taking a crooked one. THE CROOKED PATH WAS THE PLAIN OF THE LAND OF SHINAR AND THE FLAW THAT THEY FOUND THERE. Why did this happen? Because it "cannot rest." The crookedness of their way, WHICH IS THE FLAW THAT THEY FOUND IN IT, caused them to be purposeless and restless, UNTIL THEY SAID, "LET US BUILD US A CITY AND A TOWER..." – THAT IS THEY BUILT CHOCHMAH AND BINAH OF THE KLIPOT.

341. וְלָא עוֹד, אֶלָּא, דְּכָל רוּגְזָא דִּידְהוּ, בְּשַׁעֲתָא דְּאָמְרֵי מִלָּה מִפּוּמַיְיהוּ, הַהוּא מִלָּה, רֶפֶשׁ וָטִיט. כֻּלְּהוּ מַפְקֵי טְנוּפָא וְגִיעוּלָא, מִפּוּמַיְיהוּ לְבַר, עַד דְּמִסְתָּאֲבֵי, וּמְסָאֲבֵי לוֹן.

341. Not only that, but they were full of anger when they uttered these words. THAT IS, WHEN THEY SAID, "LET US BUILD US A CITY AND A TOWER," THEY INTENDED TO FULFILL THEIR LUST, SINCE A GLUTTON IS ALWAYS IRATE. Their words were "mire and dirt," AND THE VERSE DESCRIBES THEIR ACTION AS, "WHOSE WATERS CAST UP MIRE AND DIRT," WHICH IS A REFERENCE TO THE ASPECTS OF THE KLIPAH CALLED "MIRE AND DIRT." They brought up filth and abomination from their mouths. THEY BROUGHT ON THE DEFILEMENT OF THE SERPENT, WITH THE WORDS, "LET US BUILD US...", until they were themselves defiled BY THE SERPENT.

342. תָּא חֲזֵי, וַיֹּאמְרוּ הָבָה נִבְנֶה לָנוּ עִיר וּמִגְדָּל וְרֹאשׁוֹ בַּשָּׁמַיִם. לֵית הָבָה: אֶלָּא הַזְמָנָה בְּעָלְמָא. נִבְנֶה לָנוּ עִיר וּמִגְדָּל וְרֹאשׁוֹ בַּשָּׁמַיִם. כֻּלְּהוּ בְּעֵיטָא בִּישָׁא, אָתוּ לְסַרְבָא בֵּיהּ, בְּקֻדְשָׁא בְּרִיךְ הוּא. בִּשְׁטוּתָא אָתוּ בְּטִפְּשׁוּ דְּלִבָּא.

342. Come and behold: "And they said, come, let us build us a city and a tower whose top may reach to heaven." The word "come" is an invitation. The words, "let us build us a city and a tower whose top may reach to heaven," WERE UNACCOMPANIED BY ACTIONS. THE UTTERANCE OF THE WORDS ALONE CAUSED THE BUILDING OF THE CITY AND TOWER IN THE UPPER WORLDS. The people took bad advice, following the stupidity and vanity of their hearts, and going against the Holy One, blessed be He.

343. אָמַר ר' אַבָּא, שְׁטוּתָא נְסִיבוּ בְּלִבַּיְיהוּ. אֲבָל בְּחָכְמָה דְרָשִׁיעוּ אָתוּ, בְּגִין לְנָפְקָא מֵרְשׁוּ עִלָּאָה, לְרְשׁוּ אָחֲרָא, וּלְאַחְלָפָא יְקָרֵיהּ, לִיקָרָא נוּכְרָאָה. וּבְכֹלָּא אִית רָזָא דְּחָכְמְתָא עִלָּאָה.

343. Rabbi Aba then said that they followed the stupidity of their hearts, but they used the Chochmah of the Klipah to leave the upper dominion OF HOLINESS and enter the dominion OF THE KLIPOT, exchanging the glory of the blessed One, with that of a strange El. This whole matter contains a secret of supreme wisdom.

344. הָבָה נִבְנֶה לָנוּ עִיר וּמִגְדָּל. תָּא חֲזֵי, כַּד מָטוּ לְהַאי בִּקְעָה, דְּאִיהוּ רְשׁוּ נוּכְרָאָה, וְאִתְגְּלֵי לְהוּ, אֲתַר דְּשַׁלְטָנוּתָא דָּא   תְּקִיעַ בְּגוֹ נוּנֵי יַמָּא. אָמְרוּ, הָא אֲתַר, לְמֵיתַב וּלְאִתְתַּקְּפָא לִבָּא, לְאִתְהַנָּאָה בֵּיהּ תַּתָּאֵי. מִיָּד הָבָה נִבְנֶה לָנוּ עִיר. נַתְקִין בַּאֲתַר דָּא, עִיר וּמִגְדָּל.

344. "Let us build us a city and a tower whose top may reach to heaven." Come and behold: When they reached the plain that was the foreign dominion, THE PLACE WHERE THE FLAW OF BINAH OF THE KLIPAH WAS, AND SETTLED, it was revealed to them that the place was stuck among the fishes of the sea. They said, "This is the place to settle and strengthen our hearts, and let the lower beings enjoy themselves, AND DRAW THE LIGHT

DOWNWARD, BECAUSE THIS IS THE PLACE OF THE KLIPOT." Having found the place, they immediately said, "let us build us a city" and establish a city and a tower for ourselves.

345. וְנַעֲשֶׂה לָנוּ שֵׁם. אֲתַר דָּא יְהֵא לָן לִדְחַלָּא, וְלָא אָחֳרָא, וְנִבְנֶה לַאֲתַר דָּא, עִיר וּמִגְדָּל. לָמָּה לָן לְסַלְקָא לְעֵילָּא, דְּלָא נֵיכוֹל לְאִתְהַנָּאָה מִנֵּהּ. הָא הָכָא אֲתַר מִתְקָנָא. וְנַעֲשֶׂה לָנוּ שֵׁם. דַּחֲלָא לְמִפְלַח תַּמָּן. פֶּן נָפוּץ: לְדַרְגִּין אָחֳרָנִין, וְנִתְבַּדַּר לְסִטְרֵי עָלְמָא.

345. "And let us make us a name" – this place shall be Elohim for us. REFERRING TO THE PLACE OF THE KLIPOT, and not any other. The words, "build us a city and tower," indicate THAT THEY PLANNED TO DRAW DOWN CHOCHMAH AND BINAH OF THE KLIPOT, WHICH ARE CALLED A CITY AND A TOWER. Why should we climb up AND DRAW THE LIGHT FROM HERE UPWARD, when we are unable to enjoy anything that is above. Here, we have found a vantage point from which TO DRAW DOWNWARD. And we shall "make us a name," AN Elohim to worship here, "lest we be scattered abroad" to the other levels and to all FOUR corners of the world.

סתרי תורה

346. קוּמְטוּרָא דְּהַרְמָנָא, מְמַלְּלָן בְּלִשּׁוֹן הַקֹּדֶשׁ, דְּמַה"שׁ אִשְׁתְּמוֹדְעָן בֵּיהּ, וְלָא הֲווֹ מְמַלְּלִין בְּלִישָׁן אָחֳרָא. בְּגִין כָּךְ כְּתִיב וְעַתָּה לֹא יִבָּצֵר מֵהֶם וְגוֹ'. דְּאִלְמָלֵי מִשְׁתָּעָאן בְּלִישָׁן אָחֳרָא דְּמַלְאֲכֵי עִלָּאֵי לָא הֲווֹ אִשְׁתְּמוֹדְעָן בֵּיהּ, גָּרַע חֲשִׁיבוּ דְּאִינּוּן חָשְׁבִין לְמֶעְבַּד. בְּגִין, דְּעוֹבָדָא דְּשֵׁדִין, לָאו אִיהוּ אֶלָּא בְּרִגְעָא חֲדָא, לְחֵזוּ בְּנֵי אֲנָשָׁא, וְלָא יַתִּיר.

Sitrei Torah (Concealed Torah)

346. The builders of the city and the tower spoke only the holy language (Hebrew) known to the ministering angels. That is why it is written: "and now nothing will be withheld from them..." (Beresheet 11:6). Had they spoken a different language, one unknown to the supernal angels, they would not have succeeded in carrying our their plan. For the actions of demons do not last for long, only long enough for human beings to see and not longer.

347. וּדְבָרִים אֲחָדִים. דַּהֲווֹ יַדְעִין דַּרְגִּין עִלָּאִין, כָּל חַד וְחַד, עַל
בּוּרְיֵיהּ, וְלָא אִתְחַלַּף לְהוּ דַּרְגָּא. וּבְגִין כָּךְ כְּתִיב, וּדְבָרִים אֲחָדִים.
וּבְגִין כָּךְ, אִתְיָעֲטוּ בְּעֵיטָא בִּישָׁא, עֵיטָא דְּחָכְמְתָא, דִּכְתִיב הָבָה נִבְנֶה
לָנוּ עִיר וּמִגְדָּל.

347. "And of one speech," indicates that, they were familiar with the levels
on high. They confused no level with another. It says, "and of one speech,"
BECAUSE THE LEVELS WERE AS CLEAR TO THEM AS "ONE SPEECH."
THEY HAD NO PROBLEM IN KNOWING THEM. But they took bad advice, the
advice of Chochmah. Therefore, it is written: "come, let us build us a city
and a tower," REFERRING TO THE CHOCHMAH OF THE KLIPAH.

348. כֹּלָּא בְּרָזָא דְּחָכְמְתָא הוּא, וּבָעוֹ לְאִתַּקְּפָא בְּאַרְעָא, סִטְרָא אָחֳרָא,
וּלְמִפְלַח פּוּלְחָנָא דִילֵיהּ. בְּגִין דַּהֲווֹ יַדְעִין, דְּהָא כָּל דִּינִין בִּישִׁין,
מִתַּמָּן נַחֲתִין לְעָלְמִין. וּבָעְיָין לִדְחוּיֵי דַּרְגָּא דְּקַדְשָׁא.

348. All was according to the secret of wisdom. They planned to strengthen
the power of the Other Side in the world and worship it because they knew
that all evil Judgments descend from there to the worlds. In so doing, they
hoped to drive away the level of Holiness.

349. עִיר וּמִגְדָּל: דָּא חָכְמְתָא עִלָּאָה. הֲווֹ יַדְעֵי דִּשְׁמָא קַדִּישָׁא, לָא
אִתְתַּקַּף בְּאַרְעָא, אֶלָּא בְּעִיר וּמִגְדָּל. עִיר: דִּכְתִיב עִיר דָּוִד הִיא צִיּוֹן
וְגו'. מִגְדָּל: דִּכְתִיב כְּמִגְדַּל דָּוִד צַוָּארֵךְ. וּבְחָכְמְתָא עֲבְדוּ, לְמֶהֱוֵי
שָׁלְטָנָא דְּסִטְרָא אָחֳרָא בְּאַרְעָא, דְּדַחְיָיא אָדוֹן כָּל הָאָרֶץ מֵאַתְרֵיהּ.
וּלְמֶהֱוֵי דִיּוּרָא לְסִטְרָא אָחֳרָא בְּאַרְעָא.

349. "A city and a tower" relates to supernal Chochmah. They knew that the
Holy Name, MALCHUT, is only strengthened on earth by a city and a tower.
A city is required, as it says: "the city of David which is Zion" (I Melachim
8:1), and a tower, as it says: "Your neck is like the tower of David" (Shir
Hashirim 4:4). THAT IS, THE HOLY NAME, WHICH IS THE KINGDOM OF
DAVID, IS ALSO CALLED A CITY AND A TOWER. THESE NAMES SUGGEST
MALCHUT DRAWING DOWN CHOCHMAH. They also acted upon the wisdom

of the Other Side, in order to establish its dominion on earth, WHICH IS THE OPPOSING POWER OF MALCHUT. They wanted it to drive MALCHUT – CALLED the 'Master of all the earth – from its place.

350. וְנַעֲשֶׂה לָנוּ שֵׁם. כְּמָה דַּאֲחִידָא אִיהוּ שֵׁם לְעֵילָא, נַתְקִיף לָהּ בֵּינָנָא, לְמֶהֱוֵי שֵׁם בְּאַרְעָא. פֶּן נָפוּץ. יְדִיעָא הֲוֹו יָדְעִין, דְּיִתְבַּדְּרוּן מֵעַל אַפֵּי אַרְעָא. וּבְגִין כָּךְ, הֲווֹ מִתְיַחֲדִין לְמֶעְבַּד עֲבִידְתָּא דָא בְּחָכְמָא.

350. "And let us make us a name" like that of the other, HOLY SIDE in the upper worlds. We will strengthen it, so that it will stay with us and we will have a name in the land. AS THE HOLY SIDE SHINES FROM BELOW UPWARD, WE WILL DRAW THE LIGHT FROM ABOVE DOWN TO EARTH. "Lest we be scattered abroad" : they knew that they were about to be scattered all over the face of the earth, and therefore joined together to accomplish their goal and build THE CITY AND THE TOWER with Chochmah.

351. סִטְרָא אָחֳרָא, אִיהוּ דְּכַר וְנוּקְבָּא, תּוּקְפָּא דְּזוּהֲמָא דְּדִינָא קַשְׁיָא. וּכְמָה דְּאָדָם חָב בְּהוּ, וְאִתְקְפוּ בְּגִינֵיהּ עַל עָלְמָא. אוֹף הָכֵי אִינּוּן עָבְדִין דְּאִתְתַּקַף יַתִּיר, דִּכְתִיב אֲשֶׁר בָּנוּ בְּנֵי הָאָדָם. בְּנוֹי דְּאָדָם קַדְמָאָה, דְּאַיְיתֵי וְאַשְׁלִיט סִטְרָא אָחֳרָא עַל עָלְמָא, סִטְרָא בִּישָׁא. כְּמָה דְּסִטְרָא דִּקְדוּשָׁה, לַאו שָׁלְטָנֵיהּ בְּהַאי עָלְמָא, אֶלָּא בְּעִיר וּמִגְדָל. אוֹף הָכֵי חֲשִׁיבֵי אִינּוּן, לְמִבְנֵי עִיר וּמִגְדָל, לְמִשְׁלַט הַאי סְטַר בִּישָׁא בְּעָלְמָא.

351. The Other Side includes male and female, and they are the strength of the filth of harsh Judgment. When Adam sinned BY EATING OF THE TREE OF KNOWLEDGE, THE MALE AND FEMALE OF THE OTHER SIDE were strengthened in the world. They too caused THE OTHER SIDE to be strengthened. As it is written: "which the children of man built," referring to Adam's children, who brought the dominion of the Other Side, which is the side of evil, upon the world. Like the Holy Side, the Other Side has no power to rule in the world without a city and a tower. Therefore, they built a city and a tower to give it dominion in this world.

352. וַיֵּרֶד ה' לִרְאוֹת, נָחַת הַאי שְׁמָא דְקַדִּישָׁא, לְמֶחֱזֵי עוֹבָדֵיהוֹן דִּבְנְיָינָא דִּבְנוֹ. וְאִינוּן הֲווֹ מְמַלְּלָן בִּלְשׁוֹן קֹדֶשׁ, לְגַבֵּי כָּל אִינוּן דַּרְגִּין קַדִּישִׁין, וַהֲווֹ מַצְלִיחִין. כֵּיוָן דְּנַחֲתַת קְדוּשָׁה, אִתְבַּלְבְּלוֹ כָּל אִינוּן דַּרְגִּין, עִלָּאִין נָחֲתוּ, וְתַתָּאִין סְלִיקוּ, וְלָא הֲווֹ קַיְימִין בְּאֹרַח מֵישָׁר, כְּמָה דַּהֲווֹ. וּלְבָתַר בִּלְבֵּל לִישַׁנְהוֹן בְּע' לִישָׁן, וְאִתְבַּדָּרוּ לְכָל סִטְרֵי עָלְמָא.

352. "And Hashem came down to see" (Beresheet 11:5). The Holy Name came down to observe their deeds, the building they built, and how they spoke the holy language and successfully communicated and adjured with all the holy levels. When Holiness came down, the levels became confused, the upper ones descending and the lower beings rising. Because the levels were no longer properly placed AND BECAUSE THEIR NAMES HAD BEEN CHANGED, THEY COULD NO LONGER INVOKE THEM. He confused their language, dividing it into seventy languages, and scattered them to all FOUR corners of the world.

353. חַד מְמַנָּא הוּא בִּרְקִיעָא, וּבֵיהּ קַיְימִין כָּל מַפְתְּחָן, דְּעוֹבָדֵי עָלְמָא. וְאִיהוּ קַיְימָא זַמִּין, בְּשַׁעֲתֵי וְרִגְעֵי דְיוֹמָא. וְאִינוּן הֲווֹ יָדְעִין בְּרָזָא דְּחָכְמְתָא, גִּנְזָא דְּהַאי מְמַנָּא. וַהֲווֹ פָּתְחֵי וְסַגְרֵי, וּמַצְלְחֵי בְּעוֹבָדֵיהוֹן, בְּמֵימְרָא דְּפוּמְהוֹן. כֵּיוָן דְּאִתְבַּלְבֵּל מֵימְרָא דִּלְהוֹן, כֹּלָּא אִתְמְנַע מִנַּיְיהוּ.

353. There is one governor in heaven who holds all the keys to the happenings of the world. He stands waiting FOR THOSE WHO SEEK HIM, but he is only available at certain hours and times of the day. They were familiar with the secret of the wisdom and they knew all the secrets of this governor. They used utterances to open and close THE GATES OF THE HIDDEN MYSTERIES. USING WORDS, they succeeded BY INVOKING THE SUPERNAL GOVERNOR, THE GREATEST GOVERNOR AND THE LEADER OF THE WORLD, IN BUILDING THE CITY AND THE TOWER. When their language became confused, everything became impossible. THEY WERE NO LONGER ABLE TO BIND THIS GOVERNOR WITH OATHS.

354. וַאֲתַר מְתֻקָּן אַשְׁכָּחוּ, בְּהַהוּא בִּקְעָה. סִטְרָא דְּסִתְרִין. וַיִּמְצְאוּ בִקְעָה. אֲתַר מְתֻקָּן לְהַאי סִטְרָא בִּישָׁא דְּבָעוּ אִנּוּן לְאִתְתַּקָּא וְאִתְמְנָעוּ.

תּוּקְפָּא דְּהַהוּא סִטְרָא הֲוָה תַּלְיָא לְאִתְפְּרָעָא בְּהַהִיא בִּקְעָה, עַד דְּנָטְלָא תַּמָּן חֵילִין וּמַשִּׁירְיָין, כְּגַוְונָא דְּאִינּוּן דְּבָנוּ קַרְתָּא וּמִגְדְּלָא. וְאִתְיְהִיבוּ כֻּלְּהוּ בִּידָהָא, וְאִתְקְטָלוּ תַּמָּן.

354. In that plain, which is most hidden, they found ready a place for strengthening the evil side, but were still unable to fortify it. So, the power of the Other Side remained latent in that plain until the armies and camps like those who built the city and the tower, NAMELY THE SONS OF EPHRAIM, traveled and reached it. AS HE CONCLUDES, there they came under the influence of that side and were killed.

355. אִנּוּן, דְּלָא בָּעוּ לְמֵיפַק בְּקֵץ הַיָּמִין, אִתְבְּהִילוּ וּנְפָלוּ בְּקֵץ הַיָּמִים. בְּהַהוּא אֲתַר, דְּאִתְחַלַּשׁ תַּקְפָּא בְּקַדְמֵיתָא, בְּהַאי בִּקְעָה. וְעַ״ד כְּתִיב, וְהִיא מְלֵאָה עֲצָמוֹת.

355. Those who did not wish to leave under the influence of the End of the Right, THE CHILDREN OF EPHRAIM WHO LEFT EGYPT BEFORE THE END OF THE TIME OF EXILE, panicked. They fell under the influence of the End of Days, on this plain, the strength of which had been weakened AT THE TIME OF THE GENERATION OF THE TOWER OF BABYLON. NOW, BECAUSE OF THEIR MISDOINGS, THE OTHER SIDE RETURNED TO POWER AND KILLED THEM ALL. This is why the verse says: "the valley which was full of bones" (Yechezkel 37:1).

356. וְאִתְתַּקְפַת בְּהַהוּא צוּלְמָא, דְּאָקֵים נְבוּכַדְנֶצַּר. וְאִתְבַּר תּוּקְפָּא לְבָתַר, בְּאִנּוּן גַּרְמִין, וּבְהַהוּא צוּלְמָא דְּאִינּוּן קַדְמָאֵי קָיְימוּ, וְקָמוּ עַל רַגְלֵיהוֹן. וְהַהוּא צוּלְמָא אִתְבַּר.

356. THE OTHER SIDE was strengthened by the idol that Nebuchadnezzar built, and then it was weakened by the bones OF THE SONS OF EPHRAIM, WHICH EZEKIEL BROUGHT BACK TO LIFE. Therefore, the idol THAT NEBUCHADNEZZAR ESTABLISHED was shattered by the image, DRAWN FROM THE HOLY SIDE, of the forefathers who were brought back to life and rose and stood on their feet.

357. וּכְדֵין יָדְעוּ כָּל עַמִּין דְּעָלְמָא, דְּלֵית אֱלוֹהַ בַּר קֻדְשָׁא בְּרִיךְ הוּא בִּלְחוֹדוֹי. וְתוּ דְּאִתְקַדַּשׁ שְׁמֵיהּ, עַל יָדָא דַחֲנַנְיָה מִישָׁאֵל וַעֲזַרְיָה. וְכֹלָּא בְּחַד יוֹמָא, וְעַ"ד כְּתִיב וְהִקְדִּישׁוּ אֶת קְדוֹשׁ יַעֲקֹב וְגו'.

עַד כָּאן סִתְרֵי תוֹרָה.

357. Then all the peoples of the world realized that there is no Eloha besides the Holy One, blessed be He. Not only that, but His Name was sanctified by Hananiah, Mishael, and Azariah, BECAUSE OF WHOM THE POWER OF THE OTHER SIDE WAS BROKEN. And all THESE EVENTS occurred in one day. Therefore it says: "they shall sanctify My name, and sanctify the Holy One of Jacob" (Yeshayah 29:24). BECAUSE THESE THREE EVENTS – THE RESURRECTION OF THE DEAD THAT EZEKIEL PERFORMED, THE SANCTIFICATION OF THE HOLY NAME BY HANANIAH, MISHAEL AND AZARIAH, AND THE SHATTERING OF THE IDOL OF NEBUCHADNEZZAR – ALL OCCURRED IN A SINGLE DAY. SIX MIRACLES OCCURRED IN THAT ONE DAY.

(End of Sitrei Torah)

358. וַיֵּרֶד ה' לִרְאוֹת אֶת הָעִיר וְאֶת הַמִּגְדָּל. דָּא הוּא חַד מֵאִינוּן עֲשַׂר זִמְנִין, דְּנָחֲתָא שְׁכִינְתָּא לְאַרְעָא. וְכִי מַה הוּא לִרְאוֹת, וְלָא הֲוָה יָדַע מִקַּדְמַת דְּנָא. אֶלָּא, לִרְאוֹת: לְאַשְׁגָּחָא בְּדִינָא. כד"א, יֵרֶא ה' עֲלֵיכֶם וְיִשְׁפֹּט.

358. "And Hashem came down to see the city and the tower." This was one of the ten times that the Shechinah came down to earth. HE ASKS: What did He see that He did not know beforehand? AND HE ANSWERS: To see means to observe with Judgment. As it is written: " May Hashem see and judge" (Shemot 5:21).

359. אֶת הָעִיר וְאֶת הַמִּגְדָּל. הָכָא אִית לְאִסְתַּכְּלָא, דְּהָא לָא כְּתִיב, לִרְאוֹת אֶת בְּנֵי הָאָדָם, אֶלָּא, לִרְאוֹת אֶת הָעִיר וְאֶת הַמִּגְדָּל. אַמַּאי. אֶלָּא, בְּשַׁעֲתָא דְּאַשְׁגַּח קֻדְשָׁא בְּרִיךְ הוּא בְּדִינָא, בְּקַדְמֵיתָא יַשְׁגַּח

-462-

בְּדַרְגָּא דִלְעֵילָא, וּלְבָתַר בְּדַרְגָּא דִלְתַתָּא. בְּקַדְמֵיתָא בְּעִלָּאֵי, וּלְבָתַר בְּתַתָּאֵי. וּבְגִין דְּהַאי מִלָּה מָטָא לְעֵילָא, אַשְׁגָּחוּתָא דִלְעֵילָא הֲוָה בֵיהּ בְּקַדְמֵיתָא. דִּכְתִיב, לִרְאוֹת אֶת הָעִיר וְאֶת הַמִּגְדָּל.

359. "The city and the tower:" We should note what is written here, because it does not say 'to see the people,' but rather, "to see the city and the tower." Why? Because when the Holy One, blessed be He, observes TO EXECUTE His Judgment, He first observes the upper levels, WHICH ARE THE ROOTS, and then the lower beings, WHICH ARE THE BRANCHES. The matter OF THE CITY AND TOWER reached high above TO THE WORLDS ABOVE and therefore the observance was first on high. As it is written: "to see the city and the tower," INDICATES THE CITY AND TOWER OF THE WORLDS ABOVE.

360. אֲשֶׁר בָּנוּ בְּנֵי הָאָדָם. מַאי בְּנֵי הָאָדָם, בְּנוֹי דְּאָדָם קַדְמָאָה, דְּמָרַד בְּמָרֵיהּ, וְגָרַם מוֹתָא לְעָלְמָא. אֲשֶׁר בָּנוּ בְּנֵי הָאָדָם, בִּנְיָינָא וַדַּאי, אָמְרוּ וּבָעוּ לְמִבְנֵי לְעֵילָא.

360. "Which the children of man (Heb. *Adam*) built." HE ASKS: Why does it say the "children of Adam?" AND HE ANSWERS THAT THE VERSE IMPLIES THAT THEY ARE the children of Adam, who rebelled against His Master and brought death upon the world. THAT IS, THEY FOLLOWED IN HIS FOOTSTEPS. The words, "which the children of Adam (Man) built," indicate that they actually built it. EVEN THOUGH THEIR WORDS, "COME, LET US BUILD US..." WERE MERE WORDS, as soon as they uttered them, they caused it to be built in the upper worlds. THEY UTTERED OATHS WITH THEIR MOUTH AND WITH THEM THE CITY AND TOWER WERE BUILT.

43. "The gate of the inner court"

As the spiritual energy center of the earth, Israel cannot be overtaken by any negative forces. Though evil nations throughout history have conquered Israel, they eventually lost all their power after occupying the land. When we attach ourselves to Israel's power through these words, we receive the supernal Light of protection.

361. רַבִּי שִׁמְעוֹן פָּתַח כֹּה אָמַר ה' אֱלֹקִים שַׁעַר הֶחָצֵר הַפְּנִימִית הַפּוֹנֶה קָדִים יִהְיֶה סָגוּר שֵׁשֶׁת יְמֵי הַמַּעֲשֶׂה וּבְיוֹם הַשַּׁבָּת יִפָּתֵחַ וּבְיוֹם הַחֹדֶשׁ יִפָּתֵחַ. הַאי קְרָא אִית לְאִסְתַּכְּלָא בֵּיה, וְאִיהוּ רָזָא, כְּמָה דְאִתְּמָר, יִהְיֶה סָגוּר שֵׁשֶׁת יְמֵי הַמַּעֲשֶׂה. אֲמַאי.

361. Rabbi Shimon started by quoting: "Thus says the Hashem Elohim. The gate of the inner courtyard that faces the east shall be shut the six days of work; but on the Shabbat day it shall be opened, and on the day of the new moon it shall be opened" (Yechezkel 46:1). He said that we should closely examine this verse, because there is a secret here. It says, "shall be shut the six days of work;" but why SHOULD IT BE SHUT?

362. אֶלָּא, אִלֵּין יְמֵי חוֹל, דְּתַרְעָא דָא יִהְיֶה סָגוּר. דְּלָא לְאִשְׁתַּמְּשָׁא חוֹל בְּקוּדְשָׁא. וּבְיוֹם הַשַּׁבָּת יִפָּתַח וּבְיוֹם הַחֹדֶשׁ יִפָּתַח. דְּהָא כְּדֵין, שִׁמּוּשָׁא דְקוּדְשָׁא בְּקוּדְשָׁא. וּכְדֵין, אִתְנְהֵיר סִיהֲרָא לְאִתְחַבְּרָא בְּשִׁמְשָׁא.

362. Because the six days are the ordinary (non holy) days, and the gate should be shut so that the ordinary does not make use of the sacred. "But on the Shabbat day it shall be opened, and on the day of the new moon it shall be opened," because at those times, the sacred makes use of the sacred, and the moon, WHICH IS THE FEMALE PRINCIPLE, shines in order to unite with the sun, WHICH IS ZEIR ANPIN.

363. תָּא חֲזֵי, תַּרְעָא דָא, לָא אִתְפַּתַּח בְּאִינּוּן שִׁתָּא יוֹמֵי דְחוֹל. בְּגִין דְּהָא בְּאִינּוּן יוֹמֵי דְחוֹל, עָלְמָא תַּתָּאָה אִתְזָן, וְשָׁלְטִין כָּל אִנּוּן שִׁית

יוֹמִין דְּחוֹל עַל עָלְמָא. בַּר בְּאַרְעָא דְיִשְׂרָאֵל.

363. Come and behold: This gate is not opened during the six ordinary days because during these days, the lower world, WHERE THE KLIPOT AND THE EXTERNAL FORCES RESIDE, is nourished. These common days, WHICH ARE THE OTHER SIDE, rule over all the world except the land of Yisrael.

364. וְאִינּוּן דְּשָׁלְטֵי, לָא שָׁלְטֵי בְּאַרְעָא קַדִּישָׁא. בְּגִין, דְּהַשַּׁעַר הַזֶּה, אִיהוּ סָגוּר. אֲבָל בְּיוֹם הַשַּׁבָּת וּבְיוֹם הַחֹדֶשׁ, כֻּלְּהוּ מִתְעַבְּרָן, וְלָא שָׁלְטִין. בְּגִין, דְּהַשַּׁעַר הַזֶּה, אִיהוּ פָּתוּחַ, וְעָלְמָא אִיהוּ בְּחֶדְוָה, וְאִתְּזָן מִתַּמָּן, וְלָא אִתְיְיהֵיב עָלְמָא לִרְשׁוּ אָחֲרָא.

364. And these COMMON DAYS that rule OUTSIDE THE LAND OF YISRAEL have no rule over the Holy Land, because of the closed gate. But on Shabbat and the new moon, THE KLIPOT are all removed FROM THIS WORLD and do not rule it. When the gate is opened, the world is happy and receives nourishment from it, and the world is not under the influence of the another power.

365. וְאִי תֵימָא, דְּכָל אִינּוּן שִׁית יוֹמִין, אִינּוּן שָׁלְטִין בִּלְחוֹדַיְיהוּ. תָּא חֲזֵי. הַפּוֹנֶה קָדִים: עַד לָא יְקוּמוּן לְשַׁלְטָאָה, אִיהוּ אִסְתַּכַּל תָּדִיר בְּעָלְמָא. אֲבָל לָא אִתְפַּתַּח לְאַתְזְנָא עָלְמָא מְקוּדְשָׁא, בַּר בְּיוֹמָא דְּשַׁבַּתָּא, וּבְיוֹמָא דְּחַדְשָׁא. וְכֻלְּהוּ יוֹמִין, כֻּלְּהוּ אִתְדַּבְּקָן בְּיוֹמָא דְּשַׁבַּתָּא, וְאִתְזְנוּ מִתַּמָּן. דְּהָא בְּיוֹמָא דְּשַׁבַּתָּא כֻּלְּהוּ תַּרְעִין פְּתִיחָן, וְנַיְיחָא אִשְׁתְּכַח לְכֹלָּא, לְעֶלָּאֵי וְתַתָּאֵי. תָּא חֲזֵי. וַיֵּרֶד ה' לִרְאוֹת. נָחַת מְקוּדְשָׁא לְחוֹל, לְאַשְׁגָּחָא בַּמֶּה דְּבָנוֹ, וְקַיְימוּ קַיּוּמָא לְאַתְעָרָא עַל עָלְמָא, לְדַחֲלָא לוֹן.

365. If you claim that these six days can rule alone, come and behold: the words, "that which faces the east (lit. 'before')" REFER TO THE GATE THAT FACES the time BEFORE when THE KLIPOT took over. It used to perpetually look at the world, EVEN DURING THE SIX DAYS OF THE WEEK. But now

THE GATE is only open to allow for the world's nourishment from Holiness on Shabbat and the new moon. THEREFORE, all the days, NAMELY ALL THE SIX DAYS OF WORK, cling onto the day of Shabbat and are replenished by it. On that day, all the gates are opened and all, the upper and the lower beings, are pleased. THE SIX DAYS WOULD NOT BE ABLE TO SHINE IF THEY WERE NOT ATTACHED TO THE DAY OF SHABBAT, BECAUSE THEY WOULD BE MALNOURISHED. Come and behold: "And Hashem came down to see." He came down from the holy to the ordinary to see what they had built, TO SEE THE CITY AND THE TOWER, WHICH ARE CHOCHMAH AND BINAH OF THE KLIPAH, THAT THEY HAD ERECTED for the world to worship.

366. רַבִּי יִצְחָק, הֲוָה יָתִיב קַמֵּיהּ דְּרַבִּי שִׁמְעוֹן, אָמַר לוֹ, מָה חָמוּ אִלֵּין, דְּעַבְדוּ שְׁטוּתָא דָא, לְמָרְדָא בֵּיהּ בְּקֻדְשָׁא בְּרִיךְ הוּא, וְכֻלְּהוּ, בְּעֵיטָא חָדָא אִתְקָיְימוּ בְּדָא. אָמַר לוֹ, הָא אִתְּמַר, דִּכְתִיב, וַיְהִי בְּנָסְעָם מִקֶּדֶם. אִתְנְטִילוּ מֵעֵילָּא לְתַתָּא. אִתְנְטִילוּ מֵאַרְעָא דְיִשְׂרָאֵל, וְנָחֲתוּ לְבָבֶל. אָמְרוּ, הָא הָכָא אֲתָר לְמִדְבַּק.

366. Rabbi Yitzchak was sitting in front of Rabbi Shimon, and asked him: What did these people see that caused them to do such a foolish thing as to unite to rebel against the Holy One, blessed be He? Rabbi Shimon answered that we have already learned from the words, "and it came to pass, as they journeyed from the east," that they traveled from above downward, from the land of Yisrael, and went down into Babylon. There they said, 'This is the place in which to settle.'

367. וְנַעֲשֶׂה לָנוּ שֵׁם וְגו'. וְיִתְדַּבַּק סִיּוּעָא דִלְתַתָּא, בַּאֲתָר דָּא. בְּגִין דְּכַד דִּינָא אָתֵי לְאַשְׁרָאָה בְּעָלְמָא, הָא אֲתָר דָּא לְקַבְּלֵיהּ. וּמֵהָכָא אִתְהֲנֵי עָלְמָא, וְיִתְּזָן. דְּהָא לְעֵילָּא, דְּחִיקוּ אִיהוּ לְאִתְחֲזָנָא עָלְמָא מִנֵּיהּ. וְלָא עוֹד, אֶלָּא, אֲנַן נִסַּק לִרְקִיעָא, וְנַגַּח בֵּיהּ קְרָבָא, דְּלָא יֵחוֹת טוֹפָנָא בְּעָלְמָא. כִּדְבְקַדְמֵיתָא.

367. "And let us make us a name..." And the help from below shall be connected to this place, OUTSIDE OF THE LAND OF YISRAEL. For when

Judgment comes to abide in the world, this place will be in opposition to it. From this place, the world will gain its sustenance and joy, because from above, FROM THE LIGHTS THAT ARE DRAWN FROM BELOW UPWARD, the world has scarce nourishment. And not only that, but we shall ascend and rise up to the heavens and declare war on Him, so that He shall not bring a Great Flood on earth as He did before.

44. "And Hashem said, 'Behold, the people is one"

The biblical story of the Tower of Babylon holds within it secrets concerning the power of unity. After the great Flood, the people of the world spoke a single language, which was Hebrew. A group of people living in the city of Babylon were using mystical black arts in an attempt to control and dominate the world. These black arts were empowered by spiritual forces transmitted via the Hebrew letters. The Zohar states that even the Creator could not stop these evil magicians as long as they were unified by speaking the same language. The Creator therefore caused a fragmenting of their language, severing their lines of communication, and this shattered their unity. Unified evil will always have the capability to defeat and conquer good if disunity exists among the righteous. The only way to defeat unified evil is through total unity among the good. This portion of the Zohar helps inspire us to seek unity in all our relationships. We begin to recognize that the cause of any disunity is our own ego

368. וַיֹּאמֶר ה' הֵן עַם אֶחָד וְשָׂפָה אַחַת לְכֻלָּם. בְּגִין דְּכֻלְּהוּ כַּחֲדָא, בְּיִיחוּדָא דְּכֻלְּהוּ יַעַבְדּוּן וְיִצְלְחוּן בְּעוֹבָדַיְיהוּ. יִתְבַּדְּרוּן דַּרְגִּין, כָּל חַד לִסְטְרֵיהּ. וּבְגִין כָּךְ, יִתְבַּדְּרוּן כָּל הַנֵּי דִלְתַתָּא. מַה כְּתִיב וַיָּפֶץ ה' אוֹתָם מִשָּׁם.

368. "And Hashem said, 'Behold, the people is one, and they have all one language'" (Beresheet 11:6). Because their unity had enabled them to succeed in what they were doing, all the levels and all the nations below, THE BRANCHES OF THOSE LEVELS, they shall be scattered. And what is written? "So Hashem scattered them abroad from there" (Ibid. 8). THIS MEANS THAT THE HOLY ONE, BLESSED BE HE, PASSED JUDGMENT AND BROUGHT JUDGMENT UPON THE UPPER ROOTS, BECAUSE THE BRANCHES ARE AFFECTED BY THEIR ROOTS.

369. וְאִי תֵימָא, לִישָׁנְהוֹן אַמַּאי אִתְבַּלְבַּל. אֶלָּא, בְּגִין דְּכֻלְּהוֹן מְמַלְּלִין בִּלְשׁוֹן הַקּוֹדֶשׁ. הַהוּא לִישָׁנָא, קָא עָבִיד לוֹן סִיּוּעָא, בְּגִין, דִּבְעוֹבָדָא, וּבְמִלּוּלָא דְּפוּמָא, תַּלְיָין מִלִּין אִלֵּין, לְאַדְבְּקָא כַּוָונָה דְלִבָּא, וּבְדָא עָבְדֵי סִיּוּעָא לְהַהוּא אֲתַר, דְּבָעֵי לְאוֹקְמָא.

369. And if you ask: Then why was their language confounded? The answer is, because they all spoke the holy language, they were able TO COMMAND THE SUPERNAL GRADES WITH OATHS. Achieving the right intention of the heart depends on actions and words. By THE POWER OF THEIR INTENTIONS, they strengthened and aided the establishment of the place.

370. וְעַל דָּא אִתְבַּלְבֵּל לִישָׁנְהוֹן, דְּלָא יָכִילוּ לְאִתַּתְקְפָא רְעוּתְהוֹן, בִּלְשׁוֹן הַקוֹדֶשׁ. כֵּיוָן דְּאִתְחַלַּף לִישָׁנְהוֹן, לָא אַצְלְחוּ בְּעוֹבָדָא. בְּגִין דְּחֵילָא דִלְעֵילָא, לָא יָדְעֵי, וְלָא אִשְׁתְּמוֹדְעֵי בַּר בִּלְשׁוֹן הַקֶּדֶשׁ. וְכַד אִתְבַּלְבֵּל לִישָׁנָא דִלְהוֹן, אִתְחַלַּשׁ חֵילַיְיהוֹן, וְאִתְבַּר תּוּקְפָּא דִלְהוֹן.

370. For that reason, their language was confounded, and they were no longer able to strengthen their intentions using the holy language. The supernal powers know only the holy language, AND when their language was confounded, their strength flagged and their power was broken. THE CONFUSION OF THEIR LANGUAGE weakened their strength BELOW AND BROKE THEIR CONCENTRATION. THUS, their power was broken ABOVE.

371. תָּא חֲזֵי, דְּהָא מִלָּה דְּאָמְרֵי תַּתָּאֵי בִּלְשׁוֹן הַקֶּדֶשׁ, כָּלְהוּ חֵילֵי שְׁמַיָא יָדְעֵי בֵּיה, וְאִתְתַּקְפֵי בֵּיה. וְלִישַׁן אָחֳרָא לָא יָדְעִין, וְלָא אִשְׁתְּמוֹדְעֵי בֵּיה. וְעַל דָּא, אִלֵּין, כֵּיוָן דְּאִתְבַּלְבֵּל לִישָׁנָא דִלְהוֹן, מִיָּד וַיַּחְדְּלוּ לִבְנוֹת הָעִיר. דְּהָא אִתְבַּר חֵילַיְיהוּ, וְלָא יָכִילוּ לְמֶעְבַּד מִדֵּי, בִּרְעוּתָא דִלְהוֹן.

371. Come and behold: Any words, OATHS, the lower beings spoke in AND the holy language was known by all the hosts of heaven. They are strengthened by AND RECEIVE EXTRA POWER from it. They neither understand nor accept any language other than the holy language. Once the language of the people was confounded, "they ceased to build the city" (Beresheet 11:8). Their power was broken and they could do nothing more with their intentions.

372. לֶהֱוֵי שְׁמֵיה דִּי אֱלָהָא מְבָרַךְ מִן עָלְמָא וְעַד עָלְמָא דִּי חָכְמְתָא וּגְבוּרְתָא דִּי לֵה הִיא. דְּהָא בְּגִין דְּאַנְחֵית קַדְשָׁא בְּרִיךְ הוּא רָזֵי

דְּחָכְמְתָא לְעָלְמָא, אִתְקַלְקֵלוּ בֵּיה בְּנֵי נָשָׁא. וּבָעוּ לְאִתְגָּרָא בֵּיה.

372. "Blessed be the name of Elohim, from everlasting to everlasting; for wisdom and might are His" (Daniel 2:20). Because the Holy One, blessed be He, brought the secrets of supernal wisdom down to earth, the people became corrupt and wanted to provoke Him.

373. יְהַב חָכְמְתָא עִלָּאָה לְאָדָם הָרִאשׁוֹן, וּבְהַהִיא חָכְמָה דְּאִתְגְּלֵי לֵיהּ, יָדַע דַּרְגִּין, וְאִתְדְּבַק בְּיֵצֶר הָרָע, עַד דְּאִסְתַּלְּקוּ מִנֵּיהּ מַבּוּעֵי דְחָכְמְתָא. וּלְבָתַר תָּב קַמֵּי מָארֵיהּ. וְאִתְגַּלְיָין לֵיהּ מִנַּיְיהוּ, וְלָא כְּקַדְמֵיתָא. לְבָתַר, בְּהַהוּא סִפְרָא דִּילֵיהּ, יָדַע חָכְמְאן, וּלְבָתַר, אָתוּ בְּנֵי נָשָׁא, וְאַרְגִּיזוּ קַמֵּיהּ.

373. He passed the supernal wisdom onto Adam, and through this wisdom, Adam recognized the grades. Adam stuck to the Evil Inclination until the sources of Knowledge left him. Then he returned to his Master and part of this wisdom came back to him, but not as it had been before. And after that, through the book THE ANGEL RAZIEL GAVE HIM, he was able to achieve wisdom again. Later, people sinned, BY MISUSING THIS WISDOM before THE HOLY ONE, BLESSED BE HE.

374. יְהַב חָכְמְתָא לְנֹחַ, וּפָלַח בָּהּ לְקֻדְשָׁא בְּרִיךְ הוּא, לְבָתַר מַה כְּתִיב, וַיֵּשְׁתְּ מִן הַיַּיִן וַיִּשְׁכָּר וַיִּתְגָּל. כְּמָה דְאִתְּמַר. יְהַב חָכְמְתָא לְאַבְרָהָם, וּפָלַח בָּהּ לְקֻדְשָׁא בְּרִיךְ הוּא. לְבָתַר, נָפַק מִנֵּיהּ יִשְׁמָעֵאל, דְּאַרְגִּיז קַמֵּי קֻדְשָׁא בְּרִיךְ הוּא. וְכֵן יִצְחָק, נָפַק מִנֵּיהּ עֵשָׂו. יַעֲקֹב נָסַב תְּרֵין אֲחָתָן.

374. Adam passed this wisdom to Noah, who used it to serve the Holy One, blessed be He. But what is written next? "And he drank of the wine and was drunk; and he was uncovered" (Beresheet 9:21). He then passed it onto Abraham, who also used it to serve the Holy One, blessed be He. But then Ishmael, who was descended from him, angered the Holy One, blessed be He. From Isaac, came Esau. Jacob married two sisters.

375. יְהַב חָכְמְתָא לְמֹשֶׁה, מַה כְּתִיב בֵּיה, בְּכָל בֵּיתִי נֶאֱמָן הוּא. וְלָא

הֲוָה כְּמֹשֶׁה שַׁמָּשׁ מְהֵימָן, בְּכָלְהוּ דַּרְגִּין, וְלָא סָטָא לִבֵּיהּ, בְּתֵיאוֹבְתָּא דְּחַד מִנַּיְיהוּ, אֶלָּא קָאֵים בִּמְהֵימְנוּתָא עִלָּאָה, כִּדְקָא יָאוֹת.

375. He passed the wisdom to Moses, of whom it was said: "He is the trusted one in all My house" (Bemidbar 12:17). There was no one like Moses, who was faithful man in all of the levels and whose heart was seduced by none, and who stood firmly in his supernal faith.

376. יְהַב חָכְמְתָא עִלָּאָה לִשְׁלֹמֹה מַלְכָּא. לְבָתַר, מַה כְּתִיב בֵּיהּ בְּמִשְׁלֵי שְׁלֹמֹה, הַמַּשָּׂא נְאֻם הַגֶּבֶר לְאִיתִיאֵל לְאִיתִיאֵל וְאֻכָל. אָמַר שְׁלֹמֹה אִתִּי אֵל, וְחָכְמְתָא דִּילֵיהּ הוּא. וְאוֹכַל: וְאֵיכוֹל לְמֶעְבַּד רְעוּתִי. לְבָתַר וַיָּקֶם ה' שָׂטָן לִשְׁלֹמֹה וגו'.

376. He passed the supernal wisdom on to King Solomon. And what is written in the Proverbs of Solomon? "the burden. Thus says the man to Itiel, even to Itiel and I am consumed (Heb. *ukal*)" (Mishlei 30:1). Solomon said: "Itiel," meaning El is with me (Heb. *iti*), and since wisdom is His, I shall be able (Heb. *uchal*) to do what I want WITHOUT FAIL. THAT IS, EVEN THOUGH THE TORAH SAYS THAT A KING SHOULD NOT TAKE MANY WIVES SO THAT HIS HEART WILL NOT TURN AWAY, KING SOLOMON SAID: 'I SHALL MARRY MANY WOMEN AND MY HEART WILL NOT TURN AWAY. FOR *ITI-EL*, EL IS WITH ME, AND HAS GIVEN ME HIS WISDOM.' BUT after that, IT IS WRITTEN: "Hashem raised up an adversary (Heb. *Satan*) for Solomon" (I Melachim 11:14), ALLUDING TO THE FACT THAT IN HIS OLD AGE, HIS WIVES DID TURN AWAY HIS HEART AND HE WAS PUNISHED.

377. תָּא חֲזֵי, בְּגִין זְעֵירוּ דְּחָכְמְתָא, דְּאַשְׁכָּחוּ אִלֵּין מֵהַהוּא חָכְמָה דְּקַדְמָאֵי, אִתְגְּרוּ בֵּיהּ בְּקֻדְשָׁא בְּרִיךְ הוּא, וּבְנוּ מִגְדָּל, וַעֲבָדוּ כָּל מַה דַּעֲבָדוּ, עַד דְּאִתְבַּדָּרוּ מֵאַנְפֵּי אַרְעָא, וְלָא אִשְׁתְּאַר בְּהוּ חָכְמָה, לְמֶעְבַּד מִדֵּי.

377. Come and behold: Because of part of the wisdom that the generation of the Tower of Babylon received from their forefathers, they provoked the

Holy One, blessed be He, and built the tower. They persisted until they were scattered all over the face of the earth, lost all their wisdom, and could accomplish nothing.

378. אֲבָל לְזִמְנָא דְּאָתֵי, קֻדְשָׁא בְּרִיךְ הוּא יִתְעַר חָכְמְתָא בְּעָלְמָא, וְיִפְלְחוּן לֵיה בָּהּ. הה״ד וְאֶת רוּחִי אֶתֵּן בְּקִרְבְּכֶם וְעָשִׂיתִי. לָאו כְּקַדְמָאֵי, דַּחֲבִילוּ בֵּיה עָלְמָא. אֶלָּא וְעָשִׂיתִי אֶת אֲשֶׁר בְּחֻקַּי תֵּלֵכוּ וְאֶת מִשְׁפָּטַי תִּשְׁמְרוּ וַעֲשִׂיתֶם.

378. But in the future, the Holy One, blessed be He, shall arouse this wisdom in the world and all shall serve Him with it. As it is written: "And I will put My spirit within you, and cause you..." (Yechezkel 36:27). I will not cause you as I caused the first ones to corrupt the world by using it, BUT I WILL "cause you to follow My statutes, and you shall keep My ordinances, and do them."

379. ר׳ יוֹסֵי וְר׳ חִיָּיא, הֲווֹ אָזְלֵי בְּאָרְחָא. אָמַר לוֹ ר׳ יוֹסֵי לְר׳ חִיָּיא, נִפְתַּח בְּאוֹרַיְיתָא וְנֵימָא מִלָּה. פָּתַח רַבִּי יוֹסֵי וְאָמַר כִּי ה׳ אֱלֹקֶיךָ מִתְהַלֵּךְ בְּקֶרֶב מַחֲנֶךָ לְהַצִּילְךָ וְלָתֵת אוֹיְבֶיךָ לְפָנֶיךָ וְהָיָה מַחֲנֶיךָ קָדוֹשׁ וְלֹא יִרְאֶה בְּךָ עֶרְוַת דָּבָר וְשָׁב מֵאַחֲרֶיךָ. כִּי ה׳ אֱלֹקֶיךָ מִתְהַלֵּךְ, מְהַלֵּךְ מִבָּעֵי לֵיה. אֶלָּא, כד״א מִתְהַלֵּךְ בַּגָּן לְרוּחַ הַיּוֹם. וְדָא הוּא אִילָנָא, דְּאָכַל מִנֵּיה אָדָם הָרִאשׁוֹן. מִתְהַלֵּךְ: נוּקְבָא. מְהַלֵּךְ: דְּכַר.

379. Rabbi Yosi and Rabbi Chiya were walking together. Rabbi Yosi addressed Rabbi Chiya, saying: Let us discuss Torah. So Rabbi Yosi began by quoting: "For Hashem your Elohim walks in the midst of your camp, to deliver you, and to give you your enemies before you; therefore your camp shall be holy, that He does not see an unseemly thing in you and turn away from you" (Devarim 23:15). SO HE ASKS: Why does it say, "For Hashem your Elohim walks," using the word *mit'halech* and not the more common term *mehalech*? AND HE REPLIES THAT this is similar to "walking (Heb. *mit'halech*) in the garden in the breeze of the day" (Beresheet 3:8). This HAS BEEN SAID OF the Tree OF KNOWLEDGE from which Adam ate, WHICH IS THE FEMALE PRINCIPLE, THE SECRET OF THE TREE OF KNOWLEDGE. So the word *mit'halech* refers to the Female Principle, while

mehalech refers to the male aspect.

380. וְדָא הוּא, דְּאָזִיל קַמַּיְיהוּ דְיִשְׂרָאֵל, כַּד הֲוֹוֹ אָזְלֵי בְּמַדְבְּרָא. דִּכְתִיב, וַה' הוֹלֵךְ לִפְנֵיהֶם יוֹמָם וְגוֹ'. הוּא דְּאָזִיל קַמֵּיה דְּב"נ כַּד אָזִיל בְּאוֹרְחָא, דִּכְתִיב צֶדֶק לְפָנָיו יְהַלֵּךְ וְיָשֵׂם לְדֶרֶךְ פְּעָמָיו. וְדָא הוּא, דְּאָזִיל קַמֵּיה דְּב"נ בְּשַׁעֲתָא דְּאִיהוּ זָכֵי. וְלָמָּה, לְהַצִּילְךָ וְלָתֵת אוֹיְבֶיךָ לְפָנֶיךָ. לְאִשְׁתְּזָבָא בַּר נָשׁ בְּאָרְחָא, וְלָא יִשְׁלוֹט בֵּיה אָחֳרָא.

380. And it was He, THE FEMALE PRINCIPLE, who went in front of the children of Yisrael as they walked in the desert, as it is written: "And Hashem went before them by day" (Shemot 13:21). THE PHRASE "AND HASHEM" REFERS TO HIM AND HIS COURTHOUSE, WHICH IS THE FEMALE PRINCIPLE. AND THE SAME THING APPLIES TO he who walks in front of another person, while going on his way. Because the verse reads, "Righteousness shall go before him, and walk in the way of his steps" (Tehilim 85:14), RIGHTEOUSNESS REFERS TO THE FEMALE PRINCIPLE. And it is that which walks in front of a person, when he is worthy of it. But why DOES HE WALK IN FRONT? As it is written: "to deliver you and to give you your enemies before you" (Devarim 23:15), or to guard a person while he is walking on his way and save him from being overcome by the Other SIDE.

381. וּבְגִין כָּךְ לְבָעֵי לֵיה לְב"נ לְאִסְתַּמְּרָא מֵחוֹבוֹי. וּלְדַכָּאָה לְגַרְמֵיה. מַאי דַכְיוּ. דָּא דִּכְתִיב וְהָיָה מַחֲנֶךָ קָדוֹשׁ. מַאי קָדוֹשׁ, קְדוֹשִׁים מִבָּעֵי לֵיה, אֶלָּא, מַחֲנֶךָ קָדוֹשׁ: אִלֵּין שַׁיְיפֵי גוּפָא. דְּגוּפָא אִתְחַבַּר וְאִתְתַּקַּן בְּהוּ. וּבְגִין כָּךְ, וְהָיָה מַחֲנֶךָ קָדוֹשׁ. וְלֹא יִרְאֶה בְךָ עֶרְוַת דָּבָר.

381. That is why a person should be careful, guard himself from his own sins, and purify himself. SO HE ASKS: What is it to purify? AND HE REPLIES THAT as it is written: "therefore your camp shall be holy." Why does it say holy in the singular when it should have said holy in the plural? Because "your camp shall be holy" implies the members from which the body is assembled and completed. So it says OF THE BODY, "your camp shall be holy, that He does not see an unseemly thing in you."

382. מַאי עֶרְוַת דָּבָר. דָּא מִלְּתָא דְּעֶרְיָין, דְּדָא הוּא מִלָּה דְּקֻדְשָׁא בְּרִיךְ

הוּא מָאִיס בָּהּ יַתִּיר מִכֹּלָּא. כֵּיוָן דְּאָמַר וְלֹא יִרְאֶה בְךָ עֶרְוַת, אַמַּאי דָּבָר. אֶלָּא, הָנֵי חַיָּיבֵי עָלְמָא, דִּגְעָלֵי וּמְסָאֲבֵי גַרְמַיְיהוּ, בְּמִלָּה דִּלְהוֹן דְּנָפְקֵי מִפּוּמַיְיהוּ, וְהָא אִיהוּ עֶרְוַת דָּבָר.

382. AND HE ASKS: What is the meaning of "unseemly thing"? AND HE REPLIES: it means sexual immoral behavior, which is the thing that the Holy One, blessed be He, despises most of all. AND HE ASKS why the verse reads, "that He does not see an unseemly thing," using the unnecessary word 'thing'? AND HE ANSWERS THAT this refers to wicked people in the world, who defile and befoul themselves with the things they say BY CURSING AND USING FOUL LANGUAGE. This is the meaning of "unseemly thing." NOW THE ZOHAR HAS COMPLETED THE EXPLANATION OF THE WORD 'PURIFY,' ABOUT WHICH IT HAD PREVIOUSLY ASKED. 'PURIFY' INDICATES THAT A PERSON SHOULD GUARD AGAINST BEING EXPOSED TO INDECENCY AND SHOULD GUARD HIS MOUTH FROM SAYING FOUL THINGS.

383. וְכָל כָּךְ לָמָּה. בְּגִין דְּאִיהוּ אָזִיל קַמָּךְ, וְאִי אַתְּ עָבֵיד כְּדֵין, מִיָּד וְשָׁב מֵאַחֲרֶיךָ. דְּלָא יֵזִיל בַּהֲדָךְ, וְיֵיתוּב מֵאַחֲרֶיךָ, וַאֲנַן הָא אַזְלִינָן קַמֵּיהּ, בְּאָרְחָא, נִתְעַסֵּק בְּמִלֵּי דְּאוֹרַיְיתָא. דְּהָא אוֹרַיְיתָא אִתְעַטְּרָא עַל רֵישֵׁיהּ דְּבַר נָשׁ, וּשְׁכִינְתָּא לָא אַעֲדִיאַת מִנֵּיהּ.

383. SO HE ASKS: Why is the Torah so strict about this matter? AND HE ANSWERS, because He, THE SHECHINAH, walks in front of you. And if you say foul things, then, it will "turn away from (lit. 'behind') you." That is, He will no longer walk alongside you, but go behind your back. AND RABBI YOSI CONCLUDED THAT As for us, we go on our way walking before Him, BEFORE THE SHECHINAH. We should delve into the Torah, because the person WHO OCCUPIES HIMSELF WITH IT is crowned and perpetually accompanied by the Shechinah.

384. פָּתַח ר' חִיָּיא וְאָמַר, וַיֹּאמֶר ה' הֵן עַם אֶחָד וְשָׂפָה אַחַת לְכֻלָּם וְגוֹ' תָּא חֲזֵי, מַה כְּתִיב, וַיְהִי בְנָסְעָם מִקֶּדֶם. מַאי מִקֶּדֶם. מִקַּדְמוֹנוֹ שֶׁל עוֹלָם. וַיִּמְצָאוּ. וַיִּרְאוּ מִבְעֵי לֵיהּ, מַאי וַיִּמְצָאוּ. אֶלָּא מְצִיאָה אַשְׁכָּחוּ תַּמָּן, מֵרָזֵי דְּחָכְמְתָא מִקַּדְמָאֵי, דְּאִתְנְעַר תַּמָּן, מִן בְּנֵי טוֹפָנָא, וּבָהּ

-474-

אִשְׁתַּדְּלוּ לְמֶעְבַּד, בְּהַהִיא עֲבִידְתָּא דַּעֲבָדוּ, לְסָרְבָא בֵּיה בְּקֻדְשָׁא בְּרִיךְ
הוּא, וַהֲווֹ אָמְרֵי בְּפוּמָא, וְעַבְדֵי עֲבִידְתָּא.

384. Rabbi Chiya then quoted: "And Hashem said, Behold; the people is
one, and they have all one language..." Come and behold: What is written?
It says, "And it came to pass, as they journeyed from the east (also, 'yore')"
But what is the meaning of 'yore'? It refers to the Originator of the world.
SO HE ASKS: WHY DOES IT SAY, "And they found," WHEN IT SHOULD
HAVE SAID, 'And they saw?' What did they find? AND HE ANSWERS: They
found part of the secrets of wisdom of their forefathers, THE GENERATION
OF THE FLOOD, which was shaken off at SHINAR (LIT. 'THE PLACE OF
SHAKING OFF'). And with the wisdom that they found, they strove to do the
deed they performed to rebel against the Holy One, blessed be He. They
uttered OATHS TO BIND THE UPPER MINISTERS and worked TO BUILD THE
CITY AND THE TOWER.

385. חֲמֵי, מַה כְּתִיב, הֵן עַם אֶחָד וְשָׂפָה אַחַת לְכֻלָּם. בְּגִין, דְּאִינּוּן
בְּלִבָּא חַד, וּרְעוּתָא חַד, וּמְמַלְּלֵי בִּלְשׁוֹן הַקֹּדֶשׁ. וְעַתָּה לֹא יִבָּצֵר מֵהֶם
כָּל אֲשֶׁר יָזְמוּ לַעֲשׂוֹת. וְלֵית מַאן דְּיִמְנַע עוֹבָדָא דִּלְהוֹן. אֲבָל מַאי
אַעֲבֵיד, אֲבַלְבֵּל לוֹן דַּרְגִּין דִּלְעֵילָא, וְלִישַׁן דִּלְהוֹן לְתַתָּא. וּכְדֵין
אִתְמְנַע עוֹבָדָא דִּלְהוֹן.

385. Come and Behold: It is written that "the people is one, and they have
all one language." Because they are of one heart and one desire to speak the
holy language, THEREFORE, "now nothing which they have planned to do
will be withheld from them." Nobody could prevent their acts, but THE
HOLY ONE, BLESSED BE HE, SAID, 'What shall I do? I shall confound the
celestial grades above and their language below, and then their work will be
withheld.'

386. וּמַה, בְּגִין דַּהֲווֹ בִּרְעוּתָא וְלִבָּא חַד, וּמְמַלְּלֵי בִּלְשׁוֹן הַקֹּדֶשׁ כְּתִיב,
לֹא יִבָּצֵר מֵהֶם כֹּל אֲשֶׁר יָזְמוּ לַעֲשׂוֹת, וְדִינָא דִּלְעֵילָא, לָא יָכִיל
לְשַׁלְּטָאה בְּהוּ. אֲנַן, אוֹ חַבְרַיָּיא דְּמִתְעַסְּקִין בְּאוֹרַיְיתָא, וַאֲנַן בְּלִבָּא
חַד, וּרְעוּתָא חַד, עַל אַחַת כַּמָה וְכַמָה.

386. And if they, because they were of one heart and one desire, all spoke the holy language, it is written: "nothing that they have planned to do, will be withheld from them," and they will not be subject to the supernal Judgment. For us, and the friends who occupy themselves with the Torah and are of one heart and one desire, this will be all the more true, FOR NOTHING THAT WE WANT TO DO WILL BE WITHHELD FROM US.

387. אָמַר רָבִּי יוֹסֵי, מִכָּאן לְאִינּוּן מָארֵי דְמַחְלוֹקֶת, לֵית לוֹן קִיּוּמָא. דְּהָא כָּל זִמְנָא, דִּבְנֵי עָלְמָא, אַלֵּין עִם אַלֵּין, בִּרְעוּתָא חָדָא, וְלִבָּא חַד, אע״ג, דְּמָרְדֵי בֵּיה בְּקֻדְשָׁא בְּרִיךְ הוּא, לָא שָׁלְטָא בְּהוּ דִינָא דִּלְעֵילָא. כֵּיוָן דְּאִתְפַּלְגוּ, מִיָּד, וַיָּפֶץ ה׳ אוֹתָם מִשָּׁם וגו׳.

387. Rabbi Yosi said that from this we learn that people who are quarrelsome do not survive. As long as people are of one heart and one desire, even though they might rebel against the Holy One, blessed be He, the supernal Judgment is powerless against them. As soon as THE GENERATION OF THE TOWER differed with each other, Hashem "scattered them abroad from there..." SO WE LEARN THAT QUARRELSOME PEOPLE DO NOT SURVIVE LONG.

388. אָמַר רָבִּי חִיָּיא, אִשְׁתְּמַע, דְּכֹלָּא בְּמִלָּה דְפוּמָא תַּלְיָיא. דְּהָא, כֵּיוָן דְּאִתְבַּלְבַּל, מִיָּד וַיָּפֶץ ה׳ אֹתָם מִשָּׁם. אֲבָל בְּזִמְנָא דְאָתֵי, מַה כְּתִיב, כִּי אָז אֶהֱפֹךְ אֶל עַמִּים שָׂפָה בְרוּרָה לִקְרֹא כֻלָּם בְּשֵׁם ה׳ וּלְעָבְדוֹ שְׁכֶם אֶחָד. וּכְתִיב וְהָיָה ה׳ לְמֶלֶךְ עַל כָּל הָאָרֶץ בַּיּוֹם הַהוּא יִהְיֶה ה׳ אֶחָד וּשְׁמוֹ אֶחָד. בָּרוּךְ ה׳ לְעוֹלָם אָמֵן וְאָמֵן.

388. Rabbi Chiya then concluded that everything therefore depends upon the utterings of the mouth. As soon as THEIR LANGUAGE was confounded, "Hashem scattered them abroad..." But what does it say of the future? It says: "For then I will convert the peoples to a purer language, that they may all call upon the name of Hashem, to serve Him with one consent," (Tzefanyah 3:9) and, also, "and Hashem shall be King over all the earth; in that day shall Hashem be one, and His name one" (Zecharyah 14:9). Blessed be Hashem forever. Amen and Amen!

NOTES

NOTES

NOTES

NOTES

NOTES

NOTES

NOTES

NOTES

NOTES

NOTES

NOTES

NOTES

NOTES

NOTES

NOTES

NOTES

FROM TIME IMMEMORIAL

FROM TIME IMMEMORIAL

THE ORIGINS OF THE ARAB-JEWISH CONFLICT OVER PALESTINE

JOAN PETERS

1817

HARPER & ROW, PUBLISHERS, New York
Cambridge, Philadelphia, San Francisco, London
Mexico City, São Paulo, Sydney

Copyright acknowledgments appear on page 603.

Designer: Sidney Feinberg
Maps by Frank Ronan.

Library of Congress Cataloging in Publication Data
Peters, Joan, date
  From time immemorial.
  Bibliography: p.
  Includes index.
  1. Palestine—Emigration and immigration.
2. Palestinian Arabs. 3. Jews—Arab countries.
4. Jewish-Arab relations—1917-1949. I. Title.
JV8749.P3P47 1984   325.5694   83-48374
ISBN 0-06-015265-6

84 85 86 87 88 10 9 8 7

This book is dedicated to many: to the countless thousands whose lives have been lost in Arab-Jewish conflict; to the courageous on both sides whose longing for lasting peace between Arabs and Jews transcends politics; to my endlessly tolerant friends; to Bill, to Cora, to Lori, and especially to Stanley, the most indulgent and supportive of all.

Contents

Acknowledgments

Special thanks must go to Professor Philip M. Hauser, for many hours of explaining, correcting, checking, and rechecking the demographic study produced for this book. Professor Bernard Lewis extended encouragement, introductions to invaluable contacts and sources, and generous sharing of his personal archival resources, for which I am especially appreciative. I am grateful to Professor P. J. Vatikiotis for sharing his recollections, and for leading me to the research skills of Arlene Jones, whose diligence shortened my hours in London libraries, enabling me to extend my time at Kew Gardens and Oxford. Thanks also to Professor Elie Kedourie, who provided encouragement and directed me to the locations of important papers; to Martin Gilbert, for valuable reference clues that provided a more expeditious route to some of the secrets buried in the Public Record Office; to Professor Fred Gottheil, who provided a singular technical understanding of what I was onto; to Professor Walter Laqueur, for facilitating my access to both the Public Record Office and the Wiener Library in London; to James Cook at *Forbes* magazine; to Professor Bruce Reinhardt of the University of Michigan, for his aid at the United States Department of Labor; to John McCarthy of the United States Catholic Conference; to Dr. George Gruen, editor of the *American Jewish Yearbook,* for current data and statistics about the Jews in Arab countries; to Dr. Paul Riebenfeld, for making available his data concerning the Palestine Mandate, and to Beshara Ghorayeb, for offering his time and his insights.

I want to express my appreciation to the Library of International Relations in Chicago, whose staff graciously afforded me access to its records even during its moving headaches, in the critical first period of research; I am grateful to the staffs of the Public Record Office in Kew Gardens; the Old Bodleian Library and Rhodes House at Oxford; the Zionist Archives; the Israel State Archives in Jerusalem, for complying with the seemingly endless summoning of file after file filled with British immigration forms; to Don Fisher and Mary Bain, assistants to my Congressman, Sidney Yates of Illinois, for unlimited and indefatigable cooperation in expediting Library of Congress and other data; to the Regenstein Library at the University of Chicago, the Asher Library at Chicago's Spertus

College, the New York Public Library, and the Wiener Library, then in London, all of whom provided painstaking assistance and infinite patience; and to various other archives that rendered briefer but meaningful assistance.

Whatever investigative fortitude I possess is owed primarily to Herman Kogan, my esteemed former editor; the book was greatly benefited by the long, generous, and important counsel and assistance of Alistair Cooke, and the late Professor Hans Morgenthau. I am also indebted to Ambassador Angier Biddle Duke, the late Ambassador Kenneth Keating, Professor George Schwab, Professor Frank Notestein, Professor Raymond Tanter, and Sidney Hyman. Through Professor Kemal Karpat's contemporary study of the demographic composition in the Ottoman Empire I found a new route to the discovery of the truth behind the heretofore mysterious population phenomenon in Palestine.

To the many unnamed friends and colleagues who read parts or all of the manuscript in its different stages, responded cordially to queries, or otherwise lent important sustenance and critical judgment, I am appreciative beyond measure. Frances Goldin has represented this book with loyalty and provided important encouragement. Above all, I am pleased to thank my editor, Aaron Asher, for judicious, penetrating, and sensitive advice and guidance, as well as for the constancy of his regard and enthusiasm.

For yeoman services in typing, proofreading, translation, and myriad other chores, my warmest thanks go to Diane Levin; also to Judith Matsuta, Nathan Snyder, Leora Zaidenberg, Victor Seckler, Jacob Weisberg, Joseph Weisberg, Don Anderson, Reuven Resnick, Marthe Muller, Celia Goldman, and Nancy Galanos. I am especially indebted to Judith Hayner, a talented woman who originally signed on as temporary typist for the completed manuscript and then stayed, dedicatedly protecting the fidelity of the book to its reference sources throughout the period of its reproduction.

Finally, for infinite patience, inspiration, and support, all offered freely and with good humor, I take great pleasure in expressing my profound gratitude to my husband, Stanley.

In the seven-year period of producing this work, I was often accorded gracious hospitality within the concerned Middle Eastern states, and numerous persons lent unsolicited support or assistance in many unexpected ways; however briefly, I was bolstered by every gesture and I am grateful for every one.

We may with advantage
at times forget what we know.

Publilius Syrus, *Maxims*

Every tradition grows ever more venerable—
the more remote is its origin, the more confused
that origin is. The reverence due to it increases from
generation to generation. The tradition finally
becomes holy and inspires awe.

Nietzsche, *Human, All Too Human*

THE MIDDLE EAST REFUGEES—
RECOGNIZED AND UNRECOGNIZED

The Puzzle's Extra Pieces

Alice: There's no use trying . . . one
can't believe impossible things.
The Queen: I dare say you haven't had much
practice. Why sometimes I've
believed as many as six impossible
things before breakfast.
—*Alice in Wonderland*

. . . conscience does make cowards of us all.
—*Hamlet*

It was not until this book was well under way that I reluctantly confronted the historical factors underlying the "Palestinian problem." The book was originally meant to be solely an investigation of the current plight of the "Arab refugees," as that subject was then still generally known.

The deprivation of Arab refugees' human rights and the political manipulation of their unfortunate situation were unconscionable to me, particularly because it seemed their plight had been prolonged by a mechanism funded predominantly by contributions from the United States. As an ardent advocate of civil rights I had been in Mississippi during the early days of the Civil Rights movement, to join hands in concern for equality. I'd investigated and written about Ku Klux Klan activities, against the judgment of my editor, who at first felt that such an assignment was too "dangerous" for a woman.

By the time I went to the Middle East during the 1973 Yom Kippur War as a free-lance writer with a CBS assignment, women were no longer excluded from consideration for such tasks. When I went to Lebanon after the war had ended, I managed to make contact with a leader of the Palestine Liberation Organization (PLO). After I was led by one of his workers from my hotel through a series of purposeful mazes, to disguise the apartment building currently housing his headquarters—headquarters were constantly moved to avoid detection by either Israelis or enemy Arab factions—the PLO leader gave me an interview in his office. On a desk were intricately detailed maps, charts and plans for the invasion of Safed, in Israel, and a book lying open, about the strategies of Israeli generals. As we were talking, a familiar hum of approaching planes grew louder. That sound can be ominous directly after a war, and we rushed out to the tiny iron-railed balcony to learn the cause of the sudden commotion. They were Israeli jets, strafing the area, as the PLO members said they did every day. When the planes flew directly overhead, the staff in the makeshift office dramatically threw themselves flat on the floor, face down, out of sight to evade a camera's identification, I was told, and thus prevent the Israelis from learning the whereabouts of the latest headquarters.

Afterward I was taken by a roundabout route to tour one of the poorer refugee camps on the outskirts of Beirut. It was there, in a refugee camp, where children were counting out arsenals of Kalashnikovs on the shelves of a small "hospital supply" warehouse, that I fully realized the unfairness and the futility of these perpetual "refugee camps." It was 1974, two and a half decades after the war against Israel's statehood, with two other Arab-Israeli wars since, and these appealing, victimized people were still refugees, with weapons as the remedy prescribed for their collective wound. Where were *their* civil rights? Why were the Arab refugees, unlike refugees on other continents, not yet rehabilitated but still in camps?

From that starting point, I came to learn that the Arabs weren't the only unfortunates who fled from their homes at the time of the Arab-Israeli War of Independence. Because I'd assumed that Arab refugees from Israel were *the* "Middle East refugees," I was startled to find that, also around 1948, whole Jewish populations from numerous Arab countries had been forced to flee as refugees to Israel and elsewhere in the world.

Though I read through stacks of documents concerning the refugees, looking for official consideration of these "other," Jewish "Middle East refugees," I found little or none. But in the process, some other key beliefs in the popular (and my personal) understanding of the Arab-Israeli conflict were shaken. For example, while I was examining United Nations data from 1948 onward, a seemingly casual alteration of the definition of what constitutes an Arab "refugee" from Israel caught my attention. I passed it by at first, and only returned to it after investigation of refugee transfers in other parts of the world had led me to note what the general definition of refugee eligibility was. In *other* cases the more or less universally used description of eligibility included those people who were forced to leave "permanent" or "habitual" homes. In the case of the *Arab* refugees, however, the definition had been broadened to include as "refugees" any persons who had been in "Palestine" for only *two years* before Israel's statehood in 1948.

Even after I'd noted the disparity, that alteration made little impression. However, during the subsequent rhetorical and political evolution of a new image for these Arabs—from "refugees" to "Palestinian people excluded from plots of land inhabited by them from time immemorial"—I found myself returning uneasily to that "two-year" clause.

The question that began to nag and unravel the outline of my book was: "Why was it necessary to amend that Arab refugee definition?" First, that the alteration was important enough to be incorporated into the official "refugee" definition indicated the existence of a significant condition: such a blanket change would not have been required if only a few refugees had just recently arrived, in what became Israeli terrain. Since that was the logical deduction, the claim that the "Palestinian refugees" had been settled for "millennia" for the first time activated my curiosity. The two situations were not compatible: what the altered "two-years-presence" definition of an "Arab refugee" implied was a direct contradiction of assumed historical factors that are the very foundation of the current Arab claim of "legitimate rights of the Palestinian people to their homeland for a thousand" or "two thousand years."

Yet, the assumed historical setting had become so cemented into political dialogue and authoritative works about the Arab-Israel issue that it was the "two-year" clause I questioned, not the Arab historical claim. Why was that amendment there? Even then my research, already directed into the history of those overlooked Jewish refugees, assumed that those Jews were the only unknown quantity in this political equation. It was undoubtedly a common oversight, probably caused by an undue deference to the sheer pervasiveness of the popular "facts" about the Palestinian homeland; when Western governments and influential voices were reiterating only those axiomatic themes, then they must be true—or so, perhaps unconsciously, went the reasoning.

To many of us considering the Arab-Israel conflict, the "Palestinian Problem" had become a sticking point. The notion of the Arabs' "throwing Israel into the sea" was anathema to all the civilized world. Those who had learned of or personally witnessed the Holocaust of World War II were especially alarmed by any questioning of the right of the Jewish state to exist secure. Yet, there were disturbing elements in the plight of the embittered Palestinian people.

Recollections of the Arab world's saber rattling at the time of its war against Israel's independence in 1948 have become abstract and dulled; for those of us too young to have had political awareness or personal memories of that time, the "facts" as they were reported then are obscure and less important now than the persistent call for a "Palestinian homeland" for the "four million" Arab people who were said to have lived on their farms in the Holy Land "from time immemorial." In almost any given week of the last few years, Middle East specialists —the United States State Department, the British Foreign Office, esoteric strategy centers, university seminars, international forums, media columnists, and fledgling reporters in the field—all have been pursuing the gospel of the current Mideast problem, the "legitimate rights of the Palestinians." The Pope, and United States Presidents Carter and Reagan have in turn echoed, with only slight variation, the theme of the Palestine Liberation Organization—in PLO leader Yasser Arafat's words: "The main issue" of the Arab-Israel conflict "is the Palestinian state!"

Inherent in that claim are a number of fundamental, disquieting assumptions, so long and so often reiterated that they are considered unchallengeable: "The Arabs, Palestinians and otherwise, have nothing against Jews—Arabs and Jews lived harmoniously in Arab lands before 1948; it was only the alien European

'Zionists' who came back after two thousand years to usurp the property of the Palestinian Arab native throngs," it is said. "Jewish 'terrorists' intruded into the Arabs' traditionally poor but tranquil existence in 'Palestine,' " and "when Palestine became Israel" in 1948, "Jews forced the exodus of millions of Arabs from their plots of land inhabited by them from time immemorial."

As the Arab leaders shifted from outraged proclamations avowing Israel's destruction to sympathetic concern for Palestinian "rights," the adjusted approach dimmed general understanding of the Arab world's role in the conflict: in fact, the "Arab-Israeli" conflict has recently been regarded as only ancillary to the real "heart of the matter," the problem of the "Palestinians." "Once the Palestinians' plight is solved, the Arab-Israeli dispute can be settled," recent analyses have concluded. Lately the Arab world has been joined by humanitarian voices everywhere, raised in defense against the "wrongs" done to Palestinian Arabs when the Jewish state got its rights.

As a consequence, perturbation with Israel grows. Many who continue to believe in and defend Israel's rights must now reconcile the claims of other "rights"; they bear an oft-unnamed fear that their own championing of the Jewish state may have imposed an unfair burden upon the Palestinians. The very moral standards and principles by which Israel is judged a necessity now require that the "Palestinians' inalienable rights" must also be considered.

What once seemed clear-cut and indisputable becomes uncomfortably vague and confusing. The Palestinian problem has grown into a perplexing situation, with a competing set of claims that seem complicated and relevant to those of us who believe in justice and humanitarian treatment for all. "Surely the Jews had to have their homeland after the Holocaust, but to attain it only at the expense of displacing another people. . . ." If it is as the Arabs are telling it, it is at the very least, tiny nation against tiny nation, right against right, "diaspora against diaspora," a "twice promised land." Some of us put the Palestinian subject away, in a sort of side pocket, so that the uncertainties raised by persistent accusations need not be faced. That is one way to postpone indefinitely learning something one doesn't want to know. The discovery might be too painful—because the matter to be looked into is what the Jews may have brought upon the "Palestinians."

But the increasingly insistent depiction of the Arab Palestinians as victims of Israel's existence is difficult to avoid. The high visibility causes nagging doubts. The provoking of doubts is well financed and carefully orchestrated: a mere phone call to request refugee estimates from the United Nations Relief and Work Agency (UNRWA) brings to me, by return mail, not only the requested data, but politically focused brochures and eight giant elegantly printed photographic posters, eloquently and sympathetically depicting Palestinian women and children—"Survivors who go on surviving." News cameras that once captured "terrorist" Yasser Arafat with his revolvers in the United Nations later find him cuddling infants in the smoking ruins of Lebanon, and still later, as the "moderate" under siege by "extremists."

The popular angle of vision has been sufficiently adjusted so that even the conservative United States President Reagan, who long had insisted that the Palestinian problem was not a conflict of nationalities but only a "refugee problem," had altered his thinking and his formula by 1982, to a program that included solving the problem of the "Palestinian homeland." The somewhat vague "historical facts" central to the validity of the Palestinians' claims are becoming ever more decisive in the perception of what the Arab-Israel conflict is about. An additional, impressive element of credibility comes from the well-publicized fact that many dissenting Israeli voices have joined the chorus protesting the Palestinians' plight and charging Israel with "responsibility." The answers given by Israeli officialdom have never effectively quelled those doubts.

Given the wide acceptance of the conventional wisdom about the "Palestinians," the standard avoidance mechanism has also been at work. While allaying doubt, perhaps, it has also discouraged investigation. For instance, TV documentaries about the Middle East conflict that begin by describing the horrors of the Nazis' extermination of six million Jews are always assumed to be supportive of the Israeli position. Because they start with such descriptions, when the documentaries next invariably set forth the assumed "historical facts" of the "Palestinians," these presentations, with their built-in implications of Jewish, or Israeli, fault, are regarded as "even-handed" and accurate. As a consequence, they tend to cause bewildering, squeamish reactions, either expressed or unexpressed, of doubt or guilt—among even some of the strongest of Israel's defenders, even within Israel itself. Any intimation of guilt on the part of Jews causes particular distress and amplified effect: the Jews are perceived as a people with "special" responsibility. They who suffered the Holocaust must be more humane, more sanctified than anyone else.

For all the above reasons, and perhaps a few I cannot fathom, this book was nearly two years along and its outline still contained the assumptions of conventional wisdom about the pivotal past, unwittingly supporting and reinforcing central misconceptions of the Arab-Israel conflict even while I was attempting to uncover the truth. Despite some Arab writings I'd read that strayed from those assumptions, it was only after I had happened upon some rather definite statements describing *massive Arab immigration to Palestine,* by such persons as Winston Churchill and Franklin Roosevelt, that I began to speculate about what these various pieces really meant to the puzzle. What, for instance, might the impact be of evidence of significant *Arab* immigration *into* Palestine before 1948?

Once that challenge to popular assumptions had become too compelling to disregard, I found myself troubled by other previously isolated and disparate items that had gone unrecognized during earlier research. The whole fabric of historical presuppositions unraveled upon close inspection. No sooner had one error been examined than another was revealed. What began as a closer look at the refugees led to reflecting on the lengths the Arabs were willing to go to, including their cruel indifference to the well-being of their own brethren, in their hostility toward a Jewish state. Concern and curiosity prompted a closer look at the "harmony" between Muslims and Jews that had allegedly existed traditionally in Arab countries before the existence of Israel, from time immemorial.

The result of that historical penetration of the actual traditional relationship and its effect on contemporaries was so contrary to expectations that it literally directed me to an investigation into the Palestinian background of the Arab refugees. Were the actual historical traditions in Palestine perhaps as greatly at variance from conventional assumptions as what I'd learned about the relationship of Jews and Muslims in Arab lands? What really had caused the Arab leaders to treat their own countrymen so shabbily? Was it purely political behavior stemming from hostility toward Israel or were there other, more deeply rooted traditions responsible? My initial investigative efforts revealed hints of a set of conditions that, while logical on hindsight, were so unexpected and so contradictory to prevalent theories that, at first, they were staggering, and I found myself backing away. If the logical conclusions of the clues were established, they must alter the very basis of our understanding of the Arab-Israel conflict and destroy the foundation upon which the "Palestinian" claims have rested.

Thus I tentatively labeled one of my files "Arab immigration?" and set it aside; another was called "Zionism in Arab countries," and others, "Arab feudalism: traditional exploitation?", "Jews in early Palestine," "usury and corruption in the 19th Century"—and on it went. The thicker those files swelled with references and notes, the more disruptive they became, until ultimately they changed the focus of my book. The tension literally tore apart the fabric of the assumed "facts" of the Arab-Israeli question and blew away all the remnant "complications." Those files ultimately dictated the subjects for the book's chapters.

But this book is not strictly "about" the Arab peasants' plight in and around Palestine. Nor is it alone a history of the Jews' plight in the Arab world or their Zionism there, although several of the beginning chapters concentrate on a little-known background that is seminally influential to the later "conflict." It is not, either, a comprehensive recounting of the Jewish presence in Palestine following the defeat by the Romans, or a complete chronology of the conquests and population changes in Palestine since then. It is neither an exhaustive survey of the geographical details of all "Palestine," tracing the distribution of all its peoples, nor is it a sociological exposition of all Palestine's traditions throughout the ages. It does, however, try to ascertain how and why certain vital information has remained largely unknown.

As a result, I've had to search into all sorts of varied subjects, combining first-hand interviews with research on population movements and the presumptuous undertaking of an original demographic study. From investigating the history of violence in Palestine, and Turkish government attitudes toward Palestinian Jews, I was led into a laborious inquiry of the British-Arab-Jewish-Palestine relationships before England pulled out. It is now five years since I began to follow the unforeseen lead of those files. From start to finish, this book took roughly seven years. Indeed, by the date of its completion, it undoubtedly appeared, to anyone who'd cared to follow its progress, as it does to me, to have been forthcoming "for millennia."

In the process, there were many trips to the region—Syria, Egypt, Israel–West Bank–Gaza, Jordan, and Lebanon. I spent weeks virtually camping in the Kew Gardens' Public Record Office outside London, where recently opened or over-looked "secret" correspondence files, pertaining to the British Mandatory government from the 1920s until the late 1940s, are inconspicuously mixed in among infinitely categorized clerical minutiae and diplomatic reports. The first sight of all that material was paralyzing: not the correspondence itself but just the subject-file *categories* occupied roomfuls of files and books, and needed an expert guide. Many more hours were spent at Oxford wading through personal papers and memoirs of British officials key to the administration of the Palestine Mandate, which had been willed to assorted archives there. Later, there was seemingly interminable but worthwhile sifting to do among the boxes of paperwork left behind in Palestine by the British, now largely in disuse in Israel's State Archives in Jerusalem. Whether in those formidable archives or obscured in the United Nations, the United States Library of Congress, and other document files, the buried records relevant to the conflict were indeed available to be found. Only after those records could be examined and then connected to other important sources was it possible to understand fully how extensively the conclusions contradict popular perceptions.

I had hunted in vain for a book that combined once-recognized factors with those that are newly traced here. The task that seemed to remain was to fill that void. It was to reveal the integral *connection* between what is and what is not known or considered about the Arab-Jewish conflict over Palestine, and to remind about the amalgam of pivotal, once-familiar facts that today are obscured or known only to experts.

For that reason, this book has combined original research and narrative of personal experience with a synthesis of relevant evidence from recognized authorities and primary documents—often in their own words.

With that synthesis as a background for the new materials, the events in today's headlines can be understood and evaluated in context. Combining previously known factors with the more original information provides new insights into the conflict, and produces a further net result: the muddy "complications" that have wrecked many proposed simplistic solutions became identifiable *not* as "complications" but, rather, as logical, natural, and tragic progressions from the real roots of the conflict.

The background information is presented here only to the extent that is essential. It is just a sampling of the important existing sources that have been largely forgotten in the current Mideast dialogue. Principally British, Arab, Turkish, and other earlier authorities were sources for the Arab and the Palestine past and present. Jewish sources, and Arab sources when available, provided the historical data on Jews in Arab countries, although Jews and Jewish culture were noted sparingly in Arab and Arabic literature, only when they were regarded as relevant to Islam. For detailed information concerning Jewish settlement in nineteenth- and twentieth-century Palestine, Zionist, German, and some British sources were obtainable.

The thesis is developed in much the same way as the jigsaw puzzle is assembled. One must take care, because it is clarifying a picture jumbled for so long that it has become perhaps the most pervasively misconceived image of any political situation in the world. The completing of the puzzle has restored many pieces whose critical absence had not even been missed. Those "extra" pieces have filled in a vast space between perception and reality.

This book analyzes fundamental concepts in the West's perception of the Arab-Israel-Palestine conflict, against the background of the movements of the region's peoples.

The remaining chapters of Part I examine all the "refugees" displaced by the creation of Israel in 1948—where they are and what traditions created the unacknowledged "other" refugees: the Arab-born Jews who are the mass of Israel's "Sephardic" majority, and whose history and flight as refugees are somehow never adequately connected to the observation that they have since "orientalized" the Jewish state.

Part II traces the earlier composition of Palestine's peoples and their traditions, a combination of conditions that created unrecognized factors which alter the perception of the Arab-Israeli conflict today.

Part III illustrates how the twentieth-century continuation of earlier tradition was an unknown instrument in creating the circumstances of Arab refugees. At the same time, the third part of the book reveals how that tradition exercised an undetected influence so powerful that the cruel effect of its implementation has already thwarted justice—and the magnitude of the general ignorance of its consequences has thus far allowed history to be turned upside down.

In a strict sense, then, the book focuses on the quintessential and unrecognized role played by unknown or unconsidered traditions, particularly the importance of traditional population movements, in the reality of the Arab-Israeli-Palestinian conflict. In the human sense, it is about the onrushing of peoples—about flight from conquest, from persecution, from corruption, from habit, and from poverty.

In essence, it is about the flight from fact.

2

The Invitation

> The people are in great need of a "myth" to fill
> their consciousness and imagination. . . .
>
> —Musa Alami, 1948

> Since 1948 Arab leaders have approached the
> Palestine problem in an irresponsible manner. . . .
> They have used the Palestine people for selfish
> political purposes. This is ridiculous and, I
> could say, even criminal.
>
> —King Hussein of Jordan, 1960

> The nations of western Europe condemned
> Israel's position despite their guarantee of her
> security. . . . They understood that . . . their
> dependence upon sources of energy precluded
> their allowing themselves to incur Arab wrath.
>
> —Al-Haytham Al-Ayubi, Arab Palestinian
> military strategist, 1974

A strange and unlikely invitation was extended through the Palestine Liberation Organization (PLO) in 1975. Farouk Kaddoumi, then the PLO political department head, declared that all the Jews who had fled from Arab states since 1948 were welcome "to return and exercise their full rights."[1]

One day later an Iraqi broadcast from Radio Baghdad echoed the PLO offer to "return," particularly to the 140,000 Iraq-born Jews who are now in Israel.[2] The Iraqi government underscored its invitation two weeks afterward, with paid advertisements in selected newspapers around the world. Readers of the *New York Times,* the *Toronto Star,* or *Le Monde* would have found the ad difficult to overlook; in half-inch boldface letters, "Iraqi Jews" were "invited to return to Iraq."[3] The invitation excluded Jews who were Zionists, because "the latter is . . . racist . . . directed against Palestinian Arabs. . . ."[4]

The day after the ad appeared, the *New York Times* reported that the Arab offer "was scoffed at" by the Jews "as a propaganda move." The *Toronto Star* expressed disdain for the ad's "ostensibly generous invitation." In its editorial, entitled "Iraq's Phony Invitation," the *Star* observed that "the militantly anti-

11

Israel" dictatorship "knows that the vast majority of Jews . . . support Israel and are therefore Zionist in sympathy." According to the Toronto paper, the "real purpose" of the ad was to emphasize the "Zionism-is-racism" United Nations resolution and "to deny the validity of Israel's existence." The editorial concluded that "Iraq's 'come-home' . . . hypocritical gesture . . . won't fool any Jews in Canada, and it shouldn't mislead any other Canadians. . . ."[5]

The Arab invitations* were not simply a sales device to convince Israeli sympathizers that Zionism is guilty of the evils alleged by the Arabs and by the Arab-inspired United Nations resolutions. Most knew little or nothing about even the existence of such a Jewish community. Neither were the invitations designed to fool the Jews. The PLO's Kaddoumi has never pretended to hospitality toward them. In fact, almost simultaneously with his invitation, Kaddoumi had told *Newsweek*, "This Zionist ghetto of Israel must be destroyed."[7]

More likely, the Arabs' invitations were orchestrated for quite a different purpose. They were in all probability an attempt to offset little-known facts that were gradually emerging—facts with the potential to discredit one of the central themes relating to the "right" of the Palestinian refugees to "return."

Before the crushing 1967 "Six-Day" defeat of the Arab countries by Israel, the "Palestine-for-the-Palestinians" cause was met by "complacency, and . . . crass ignorance." The prominent Arab Palestinian activist, writer, and innovator Musa Alami tried virtually singlehandedly to interest the Arab world in this propaganda program in 1948.

> In Iraq he was told by the Prime Minister that all that was needed was "a few brooms" to drive the Jews into the sea; by confidants of Ibn Saud in Cairo, that "once we get the green light from the British we can easily throw out the Jews."[8]

But the reality was much more complicated than the Iraqi Prime Minister had suggested. The Arabs had initiated hostilities in Palestine[9] upon the November 1947 United Nations' partition of Palestine into a Jewish and an Arab state,[10] employing outside forces and arms from Arab states as distant as Iraq[11] to prevent the creation of the Jewish state, "a series of killings and counterkillings that would continue for decades.†"[12] Thousands of Arabs, including the more affluent, left for nearby Arab states before Jewish statehood.[13] When Israel's independence was declared in 1948, the Arab forces combined to crush it.[14]

Beckoning to the Arabs

At the time of the 1948 war, Arabs in Israel too were invited by their fellow Arabs —invited to "leave" while the "invading" Arab armies would purge the land of

---

*Among others, Libya in 1970 and 1973, Sudan in 1975 (although the number of former Sudanese Jews now in Israel is "minute"), and Egypt in 1975.[6]
†See Chapters 9ff.

Jews.[15] The invading Arab governments were certain of a quick victory; leaders warned the Arabs in Israel to run for their lives.[16]

In response, the Jewish Haifa Workers' Council issued an appeal to the Arab residents of Haifa:*

> For years we have lived together in our city, Haifa. . . . Do not fear: Do not destroy your homes with your own hands . . . do not bring upon yourself tragedy by unnecessary evacuation and self-imposed burdens. . . . But in this city, yours and ours, Haifa, the gates are open for work, for life, and for peace for you and your families.[17]

While the Haifa pattern appears to have been prevalent, there were exceptions. Arabs in another crucial strategic area, who were "opening fire on the Israelis shortly after surrendering,"[18] were "forced" to leave by the defending Jewish army to prevent what former Israeli Premier Itzhak Rabin described as a "hostile and armed populace" from remaining "in our rear, where it could endanger the supply route . . ."[19] In his memoirs, Rabin stated that Arab control of the road between the seacoast and Jerusalem had "all but isolated" the "more than ninety thousand Jews in Jerusalem," nearly one-sixth of the new nation's total population.

> If Jerusalem fell, the psychological blow to the nascent Jewish state would be more damaging than any inflicted by a score of armed brigades.[20]

According to a research report by the Arab-sponsored Institute for Palestine Studies in Beirut, however, "the majority" of the Arab refugees in 1948 were not expelled, and "68%" left without seeing an Israeli soldier.[21]

After the Arabs' defeat in the 1948 war, their positions became confused: some Arab leaders demanded the "return" of the "expelled" refugees to their former homes despite the evidence that Arab leaders had called upon Arabs to flee.† At the same time, Emile Ghoury, Secretary of the Arab Higher Command, called for the *prevention* of the refugees from "return." He stated in the *Beirut Telegraph* on August 6, 1948: "it is inconceivable that the refugees should be sent back to their homes while they are occupied by the Jews. . . . It would serve as a first step toward Arab recognition of the state of Israel and Partition."

Arab activist Musa Alami despaired: as he saw the problem, "how can people struggle for their nation, when most of them do not know the meaning of the word? . . . The people are in great need of a 'myth' to fill their consciousness and imagination. . . ." According to Alami, an indoctrination of the "myth" of nationality would create "identity" and "self-respect."[22]

However, Alami's proposal was confounded by the realities: between 1948

---

*See British report in Appendix II.

†Such as President Truman's International Development Advisory Board Report, March 7, 1951: "Arab leaders summoned Arabs of Palestine to mass evacuation . . . as the documented facts reveal. . . ."

and 1967, the Arab state of Jordan claimed annexation of the territory west of the Jordan River, the "West Bank" area of Palestine—the same area that would later be forwarded by Arab "moderates" as a "mini-state" for the "Palestinians." Thus, that area was, between 1948 and 1967, called "Arab land," the peoples were Arabs, and yet the "myth" that Musa Alami prescribed—the cause of "Palestine" for the "Palestinians"—remained unheralded, unadopted by the Arabs during two decades. According to Lord Caradon, "Every Arab assumed the Palestinians [refugees] would go back to Jordan."[23]

When "Palestine" was referred to by the Arabs, it was viewed in the context of the intrusion of a *"Jewish* state amidst what the Arabs considered their own exclusive environment or milieu, the *'Arab* region.' "*[24] As the late Egyptian President Gamal Abdel Nasser "screamed" in 1956, "the imperialists' 'destruction of Palestine' " was "an attack on *Arab* nationalism," which " 'unites us from the Atlantic to the Gulf.' "*[25]

Ever since the 1967 Israeli victory, however, when the Arabs determined that they couldn't obliterate Israel militarily, they have skillfully waged economic, diplomatic, and propaganda war against Israel. This, Arabs reasoned, would take longer than military victory, but ultimately the result would be the same. Critical to the new tactic, however, was a device designed to whittle away at the sympathies of Israel's allies: what the Arabs envisioned was something that could achieve Israel's shrinking to indefensible size at the same time that she became insolvent.

This program was reviewed in 1971 by Mohamed Heikal,[26] then still an important spokesman of Egypt's leadership in his post as editor of the influential, semi-official newspaper *Al Ahram.* Heikal called for a change of Arab rhetoric —no more threats of "throwing Israel into the sea"—and a new political strategy aimed at reducing Israel to indefensible borders and pushing her into diplomatic and economic isolation. He predicted that "total withdrawal" would "pass sentence on the entire state of Israel."

As a more effective means of swaying world opinion, the Arabs adopted humanitarian terminology in support of the "demands" of the "Palestinian refugees," to replace former Arab proclamations of carnage and obliteration. In Egypt, for example, in 1968 "the popularity of the Palestinians was rising," as a result of Israel's 1967 defeat of the Arabs and subsequent 1968 "Israeli air attacks inside Egypt."[27] It was as recently as 1970 that Egyptian President Nasser defined "Israel" as the cause of "the expulsion of the Palestinian people from their land." Although Nasser thus gave perfunctory recognition to the "Palestinian Arab" allegation, he was in reality preoccupied with the overall basic, pivotal Arab concern. As he continued candidly in the same sentence, Israel was "a permanent threat to the *Arab** nation."[28] Later that year (May

*Emphasis added.

1970), Nasser "formulated his rejection of a Jewish state in Palestine," but once again he stressed the "occupation of *our* [Pan-Arab] lands,"* while only secondarily noting: "And we reject its [Israel's] insistence on denying the legitimate rights of the Palestinian people in their country."[29] Subsequently the Arabs have increased their recounting of the difficulties and travail of Arab refugees in the "host" countries adjacent to Israel. Photographs and accounts of life in refugee camps, as well as demands for the "legitimate" but unlimited and undefined "rights" of the "Palestinians," have flooded the communications media of the world in a subtle and adroit utilization of the art of professional public relations.[30]

A prominent Arab Palestinian strategist, Al-Haytham Al-Ayubi, analyzed the efficacy of Arab propaganda tactics in 1974, when he wrote:

> The image of Israel as a weak nation surrounded by enemies seeking its annihilation evaporated [after 1967], to be replaced by the image of an aggressive nation challenging world opinion.†[31]

The high visibility of the sad plight of the homeless refugees—always tragic —has uniquely attracted the world's compassion.[33] In addition, the campaign has provided non-Arabs with moral rationalization for abiding by the Arabs' anti-Israel rules, which are regarded as prerequisites to getting Arab oil and the financial benefits from Arab oil wealth. Millions of dollars have been spent to exploit the Arab refugees and their repatriation as "the heart of the matter," as the primary human problem that must be resolved before any talk of overall peace with Israel.

Reflecting on the oil weapon's influence in the aftermath of the 1973 Yom Kippur War, Al-Ayubi shrewdly observed:

> The nations of western Europe condemned Israel's position despite their guarantee of her security and territorial integrity. They understood that European interests and their dependence upon sources of energy precluded their allowing themselves to incur Arab wrath.[34]

Thus Al-Ayubi recommended sham "peace-talks," with the continuation, however, of the "state of 'no peace,' " and he advocated the maintaining of "moral pressure together with carefully-balanced military tension . . ." for the "success of the *new* Arab strategy."‡ Because "loss of human life remains a sore point for the enemy," continual "guerrilla" activities can erode Israel's self-confidence and "the faith" of the world in the "Israeli policeman."

Al-Ayubi cited, as an example, "the success of Arab foreign policy maneuvers" in 1973, which was

---

*Emphasis added.

†As Rosemary Sayigh wrote in the *Journal of Palestine Studies,* "a strongly defined Palestinian identity did not emerge until 1968, two decades after expulsion." It had taken twenty years to establish the "myth" prescribed by Musa Alami.[32]

‡Emphasis added.

so total that. . . . With the exception of the United States and the racist African governments, the entire world took either a neutral or pro-Arab position on the question of legality of restoring the occupied territories through any means—including the use of military force.

As Al-Ayubi noted, "The basic Arab premise concerning 'the elimination of the results of aggression' remains accepted by the world." Thus the "noose" will be placed around the neck of the "Zionist entity."

But the Arabs' creation of the "myth" of nationality did not create the advantageous situation for the Palestinian Arabs that Musa Alami had hoped for. Instead, the conditions he complained of bitterly were perpetuated: the Arabs "shut the door" of citizenship "in their faces and imprison them in camps."[35]

Khaled Al-Azm, who was Syria's Prime Minister after the 1948 war, deplored the Arab tactics and the subsequent exploitation of the refugees, in his 1972 memoirs:

> Since 1948 it is we who demanded the return of the refugees . . . while it is we who made them leave. . . . We brought disaster upon . . . Arab refugees, by inviting them and bringing pressure to bear upon them to leave. . . . We have rendered them dispossessed. . . . We have accustomed them to begging. . . . We have participated in lowering their moral and social level. . . . Then we exploited them in executing crimes of murder, arson, and throwing bombs upon . . . men, women and children—all this in the service of political purposes. . . .[36]

Propaganda has successfully veered attention away from the Arab world's manipulation of its peoples among the refugee group on the one hand, and the number of those who now in fact possess Arab citizenship in many lands, on the other hand. The one notable exception is Jordan, where the majority of Arab refugees moved,* and where they are entitled to citizenship according to law, "unless they are Jews."[37]

The Needy and the Numbers

According to various estimates, the accurate number of Arab refugees who left Israel in 1948 was somewhere between 430,000 and 650,000.† An oft-cited study that used official records of the League of Nations' mandate and Arab census figures[38] determined that there were 539,000‡ Arab refugees in May 1948.[39]

There was heated controversy over the exact number of Arab refugees who left Israel. In October 1948, there were already three "official" sets of figures: The

---

*The critical implications of the "exception" and the historical factors of "Palestine" which demanded Jordan's actions are discussed in Chapter 12.

†The Statistical Abstract of Palestine in 1944–45 set the figure for the total Arab population living in the Jewish-settled territories of Palestine at 570,800.

‡Walter Pinner began with a total of 696,000 Arabs living within the Armistice lines in 1948, from which he subtracted the 140,000–157,000 who remained in their homes when Israel became independent. Pinner further asserts that no more than 430,000 were "genuine refugees" in need of relief. See the population study in Chapter 12 for new information and a detailed breakdown.

United Nations had two, the higher of which estimated the number would "shortly increase to 500,000";[40] the Arab League's official figures reported a total already greater by almost 150,000 than the higher of the UN figures. The swollen Arab League figures could never be verified because the Arabs refused to allow official censuses to be completed among the refugees.[41] Observers have deduced that the Arab purpose was to seek greater world attention through an exaggerated population figure and thereby induce the UN to put heavier pressures upon Israel, to force "repatriation."

But the propaganda use of erroneous, inflated, or otherwise manipulated population statistics was not a recent phenomenon restricted to the Arab refugee camps. As subsequent chapters reveal, this practice has long played a critical, underestimated role in shaping the perceptions and the resolution—or the lack of resolution—of the Arab-Israeli conflict.*

The former Director of Field Operations for the United Nations Disaster Relief Project reported in July 1949 that

> It is believed that some local [Arab] welfare cases are included in the refugee figures.[42]

When the United Nations Relief and Work Agency (UNRWA) was established as a singular, special unit to deal with Arab refugees, practically its first undertaking, in May 1950, was an attempted refugee census to separate the genuinely desperate from the "fradulent claimants." After a year's time and a $300,000 expenditure, UNRWA reported that "it is still not possible to give an absolute figure of the true number of refugees as understood by the working definition of the word."[43] For the purpose of that census, the definition of "refugee" was "a person *normally resident* in Palestine who had lost his home and his livelihood as a result of the hostilities and who is in need." A reason given by UNRWA for falsified numbers was that the refugees "eagerly report births and . . . reluctantly report deaths."[44]

One of the first official reports to question the accuracy of the refugee figures stated that there could be "no true refugee population" figures because the agency director "did not consider it practicable to ask the operating agencies to impose any kind of eligibility test and . . . had no observers of his own for this purpose."[45] The report stated it was having difficulty excluding "ordinarily nomadic Bedouins and . . . unemployed or indigent local residents" from genuine refugees, and

> it cannot be doubted that in many cases individuals who *could not qualify as being bona fide refugees are in fact* on the relief rolls.†

---

*A more current example of the traditional swelling of numbers was described by *New York Times* correspondent David Shipler during the 1982 Israeli routing of the PLO foundation in Lebanon. On July 14, Shipler wrote, "It is clear to anyone who has traveled in southern Lebanon . . . that the original figures . . . reported by correspondents quoting Beirut representatives of the Red Cross during the first week of the war, were extreme exaggerations."

†Emphasis added.

One of the camp workers in Lebanon who was questioned about the accuracy of the refugee count answered,

> We try to count them, but they are coming and going all the time; or we count them in Western clothes, then they return in *aba* and *kaffiyah* and we count the same ones again.[46]

UNRWA's relief rolls from the beginning were inflated by more than a hundred thousand,* including those who could not qualify as refugees from Israel even under the newer, unprecedentedly broad eligibility criterion for the refugee relief rolls. UNRWA now altered its definition of "refugees" to include those people who had lived in "Palestine" a minimum of only *two years* preceding the 1948 conflict.[48] In addition, the evidence of fraud in the count, which accumulated over the years, was given no cognizance toward reducing the UN estimates. They continued to surge.

According to the Lebanese journal *Al-Hayat,* in 1959 "Of the 120,000 refugees who entered Lebanon, not more than 15,000 are still in camps."[49] A substantial de facto resettlement of Arab Palestinian refugees had actually taken place in Lebanon by 1959. Later that year *Al-Hayat* wrote that "the refugees' inclination—in spite of the noisy chorus all about them—is toward immediate integration."[50] The 1951–1952 UNRWA report itself had determined that "two-thirds of the refugees live elsewhere than in camps," and that "more fortunate refugees are not even on rations, but live rather comfortably . . . and work at good jobs."[51] The recognition in the United Nations and in Arab journals that the refugee camps had largely been emptied, through absorption and resettlement, raised appropriate subjects for inquiry with regard to correcting the number of persons receiving rations and seeking "repatriation."

After their 1960 investigation, Senators Gale McGee and Albert Gore[52] reported the surfeit of

> Ration cards [which] have become chattel for sale, for rent or bargain by any Jordanian, whether refugee or not, needy or wealthy. These cards are used . . . almost as negotiable instruments. . . . many have acquired large numbers of ration cards . . . rented or bartered to others who unjustifiably receive . . . rations, much of which are now in the black market.

At the same time, the UNRWA Director admitted that the *Jordan ration lists alone* "are believed to include 150,000 ineligibles and many persons who have died."[53] Officials told the two senators of twenty percent to thirty percent inflation of the relief rolls,[54] and an American representative on the UNRWA Advisory

---

*UNRWA Director Howard Kennedy on November 1, 1950, reported to the United Nations Ad Hoc Political Committee that "a large group of indigent people totalling over 100,000 . . . could not be called refugees, but . . . have lost their means of livelihood because of the war and post-war conditions . . . The Agency felt their need was even more acute than that of the refugees who were fed and housed." In November 1950, Kennedy referred to "the 600,000 [Arab] refugees," although he had reported in May 1950 that UNRWA had distributed 860,000 rations, citing the hundreds of thousands of "hungry Arabs" who were not bona fide refugees but who claimed need.[47]

Board added, "I have actually seen merchants openly weighing and buying supplies from recipients of distribution centers."*[55]

In 1961, UNRWA Agency Director John Davis acknowledged that the United Nations refugee counts included "other victims of the conflict of 1948," and that it would be wrong to deny them aid merely because they weren't legally qualified.[56] However, they were persons neglected by their own Arab governments, and they should not have been counted among the Arab refugees from Israel; by continuing to be unfaithful to its own mandate, UNRWA contributed to further distortion of an already misrepresented and misunderstood refugee situation. In fact, what were originally intended as humanitarian endeavors to aid needy Arab resident populations by the Red Cross and others would unwittingly contribute to the use of hapless humans for an entire political and military campaign.[57]

Resettlement Opportunities: Dignity Denied

Over the last thirty-odd years, numerous projects have been proposed, international funds provided, studies undertaken, all indicating the benefits that could be derived by the Arab refugees from their absorption into the brethren cultures of the Arab host countries. Various international bodies and independent Arab voices over the years have clearly challenged as immoral the position of the Arabs in promoting the continued languishing of the Arab émigrés who came within their borders; also deplored on occasion is the Arab states' departure from the free world's unvarying precedent: of granting to refugees around the world the dignity of resettlement within a compatible environment where they can become productive citizens. From the beginning, the Arab host governments were offered unprecedentedly broad opportunities based on the refugees' rehabilitation, which could help develop their countries' vast potential under the proposed aid programs.

International experts reported and published undisputed evidence that integration and resettlement of those who were refugees, when implemented by the community of Arab nations, would benefit not only the Arab refugees but also the underpopulated areas within the Arab world, which needed additional labor forces to implement progress. Iraq and Syria were judged by many specialists in the area to be ideal for resettlement of the Arab refugees.[58] Among many such findings was the report by President Truman's International Development Advisory Board. Headed by Nelson Rockefeller, the board asserted that under proper development Iraq alone could absorb an Arab refugee population of 750,000. According to the report,

*According to the *Mideast Mirror,* a weekly news review published by Arab News Agency of Cairo: "There are refugees who hold as many as 500 ration cards, 499 of them belonging to refugees long dead. . . . There are dealers in UNRWA food and clothing and ration cards to the highest bidder. . . . 'Refugee capitalists' is what UNRWA calls them." July 23, 1955.

... Israel [which] in the three years of its existence *has absorbed a Jewish refugee population, about equivalent in number to the Arab refugees,* ... in flight from Moslem countries in the Middle East and North Africa, cannot reabsorb the Arabs who fled its borders, but it can and indeed has, offered to contribute to a fund for Arab resettlement. The exchange of the Arab population of Palestine with the Jewish population of the Arab countries was favored by the ... League of Nations as an effective way of resolving the Palestine problem. In practical effect, such an exchange has been taking place. The resettlement of the Arab refugees is ... much simpler ... in Arab lands.*[59]

Another of the authoritative studies reported:

Iraq could contribute most to the solution of the refugee problem. It could absorb agriculturists as well. This would benefit the refugees and the country equally.[60]

Pointing to Iraq's special availability for resettlement and countering the Arab argument that the Arab refugees were "unemployable"—the same study emphasized that

In the years 1950–51 100,000 Iraqi Jews left the country. . . . They left a big gap in the life of the city. Many of them were shopkeepers, artisans or white collar workers, while 15,000 belonged to the well-to-do. The gap could be . . . filled. . . . Again Iraq would also benefit. . . .

The study concluded that "host countries should take over responsibility for the refugees at the earliest possible date," and that "redistribution of the refugees among these countries is a primary requisite."

According to yet another study, by S.G. Thicknesse,[61] Iraq's were the "best long-range prospects" for resettlement of the Arabs from Palestine. Herbert Hoover suggested that "this would clear Palestine . . . for a large Jewish emigration. . . ."[62]

El-Balad, an Arab daily paper in the Jordan-held "old city" of Jerusalem, stressed the value to the Arabs of the Jews' flight from Iraq, since "roughly 120,000" Jewish refugees had fled Baghdad for Israel, leaving all of their goods and homes behind them.[63] Salah Jabr, former Prime Minister of Iraq and leader of Iraq's National Socialist Party had stated that

the emigration of 120,000 Jews from Iraq to Israel is beneficial to Iraq and to the Palestinian Arabs because it makes possible the entry into Iraq of a similar number of Arab refugees and their occupation of the Jewish houses there.[64]

A survey by the League of Red Cross Societies determined that thirty-five percent of the Palestine refugees were "townspeople" and could "easily fill the vacuum" left by the Jews.

*Emphasis added.

... Their departure created a large gap in Iraq's economy. In some fields, such as transport, banking and wholesale trades, it reached serious proportions. There was also a dearth of white collar workers and professional men.[65]

Syria was also proposed by many experts as an area with great potential for absorbing refugees: according to one report, Syria required more than twice as many inhabitants as its then-current population of a little more than two million (after World War II.)[66] According to Arab Palestinian writer Fawaz Turki, Syria "could have absorbed its own refugees, and probably those in Lebanon and Jordan."[67] The British Chatham House Survey[68] estimated that, with Syria's agreement, "Syria might well absorb over 200,000 Palestine refugees within five years in agriculture alone." Chatham House also recommended that about 350,-000 refugees could be resettled in Iraq, further noting that the refugees themselves would "not offer serious resistance" if they were encouraged to realize that their lives would become more productive.

In 1949 a newspaper editorial from Damascus stated that

Syria needs not only 100,000 refugees, but 5 million to work the lands and make them fruitful. *[69]

The Damascus paper, earlier recognizing that Arab refugees were not to be "repatriated," suggested that the government place these "100,000 refugees in district[s] . . . where they will build small villages with the money appropriated for this purpose."†[70]

In 1951, Syria was anxious for additional workers who would settle on the land. An Egyptian paper[71] reported,

The Syrian government has officially requested that half a million Egyptian agricultural workers . . . be permitted to emigrate to Syria in order to help develop Syrian land which would be transferred to them as their property. The responsible Egyptian authorities have rejected this request on the grounds that Egyptian agriculture is in need of labor.‡

Near East Arabic Radio[72] reported that Syria was offering land rent free to anyone willing to settle there. It even announced a committee to study would-be settlers' applications.

*Emphasis added.
†On June 27, 1949, Near East Arab Broadcasting, a British-run station, broadcast (in Arabic): "The Arabs must forget their demand for the return of all refugees since Israel, owing to her policy of crowding new immigrants into the country at such a rate that the territory she holds is already too small for her population, is physically unable to accept more than a small number of Arab refugees. The Arabs must face the facts before it's too late, and must see to the resettlement of the refugees in the Arab states where they can help in the development of their new lands and so become quickly assimilated genuine inhabitants, instead of suffering exiles." "Daily Abstracts of Arabic Broadcasts," Israel Foreign Office. Similar broadcasts were recorded on 10/31/50, 11/11/50, 11/29/50, 12/31/50.
‡200,000 Arab "refugees" were languishing in Gaza, along with "80,000 original residents who barely made a living before the refugees arrived," according to the UNRWA report in 1951–52, yet a project with "hope" to accommodate "10,000 families" in the "Sinai area" was "suspended."

In fact, Syrian authorities began the experiment by moving 25,000 of the refugees in Syria into areas of potential development in the northern parts of the country, but the overthrow of the ruling regime in August 1949 changed the situation, and the rigid Arab League position against permanent resettlement, despite persistence on the part of isolated leaders, prevailed.[73]

Notwithstanding the facts,[74] the Arab world has assiduously worked to build the myth that no jobs were available in Arab lands for Arab refugees in 1948 or since, and that the refugees had become surplus farm workers "in an era when the world at large and Arab countries in particular already has too many people in the rural sector."[75]

At around the same time, the Egyptian Minister for Foreign Affairs, Muhammad Saleh ed-Din, in a leading Egyptian daily, demanded the *return* of the refugees:

> Let it therefore be known and appreciated that, in demanding the restoration of the refugees to Palestine, the Arabs intend that they shall return as the masters of the homeland, and not as slaves. More explicitly: they intend to annihilate the state of Israel.[76]

Thus, while the "refugee" count kept growing, Arab leaders' confusion over "return" or "not return" had been more or less clarified: they proclaimed that the "refugees" must indeed "return," but not before Israel was destroyed.

The Lebanese paper *Al-Ziyyad*[77] anticipated a current expressed goal of the PLO charter, though it was less candid. In a sophisticated assessment, it suggested the *recognition of Israel* as a strategy that would accomplish the following results:

> The return of all the refugees to their homes would be secured, thereby we should, on the one hand, eliminate the refugee problem, and on the other, create a large Arab majority that would serve as the most effective means of reviving the Arab character of Palestine, while forming a powerful fifth column for the day of revenge and reckoning.

Despite findings of the 1950 United Nations Palestine Conciliation Commission,[78] which recommended "concentration on Arab refugees' resettlement in the Arab countries[79] with both the technical and financial assistance of the United Nations and coupled with compensation for their property," the Arab League[80] insisted that

> relief projects should not prejudice the right of the refugees to return to their homes or to receive compensation if unwilling to return . . .[81]

The *Revue du Liban* was among many dissenters who challenged the Arab League's position and discouraged Arab refugees from "return":

> . . . it is a fact that many Arabs leave Israel today of their own free will.

The paper pointed out that "in the event of a return of the refugees they will constitute a minority . . . in a foreign environment . . . unfamiliar . . . , together with people who speak a language they do not understand." Also, the paper stated, the refugees would "encounter the economic difficulties of Israel," and

> their settlement in Israel will cost much more than their absorption in the countries where they live today. After three years it is not human and not logical to compel them to wait without giving them concrete help. Syria and Iraq can easily absorb additional refugees. . . . They should form a productive force which might help to improve the economic conditions in the countries where they will be absorbed.[82]

Despite tacit recognition of the actual "resident"—as opposed to "refugee"—identity of so many of those involved, projects unparalleled for refugees elsewhere continued to offer to facilitate the Arab world's resettlement of all its "refugees."[83] Yet the Arabs rebuffed every effort to secure realistic well-being for their kinsmen. At a refugee conference in Homs, Syria, the Arabs declared that

> any discussion aimed at a solution of the Palestine problem which will not be based on ensuring the refugees' right to annihilate Israel will be regarded as a desecration of the Arab people and an act of treason.[84]

In 1958, former director of UNRWA Ralph Galloway declared angrily while in Jordan that

> The Arab states do not want to solve the refugee problem. They want to keep it as an open sore, as an affront to the United Nations, and as a weapon against Israel. Arab leaders do not give a damn whether Arab refugees live or die.[85]

And King Hussein, the sole Arab leader who, for reasons that later become clearer, directed integration of the Arabs, in 1960 stated,

> Since 1948 Arab leaders have approached the Palestine problem in an irresponsible manner. . . . They have used the Palestine people for selfish political purposes. This is ridiculous and, I could say, even criminal.[86]

Eleven years after the Arab leavetaking, the late United Nations Secretary-General Dag Hammarskjöld reiterated that there were ample means for absorbing the Arab refugees into the economy of the Arab region; he asserted further that the refugees would be beneficial to their host countries, by adding needed manpower to assist in the development of those countries. Hammarskjöld detailed the estimated cost of the refugee absorption, which he proposed be financed by oil revenues and outside aid. But again, plans for permanent rehabilitation of the refugees were rejected by the Arab leaders, because such measures would have terminated the refugees' status as "refugees"; the Arab leaders reasoned that once the refugees accepted their new homes, they would eventually abandon their desire to "return" to former homes, as have other refugees. Such action would have resulted in the Arab world's loss of a weapon against Israel,[87] and would have falsely implied acceptance of the Jewish state.

While the vast majority of refugees has now left the camps for greater opportunities among their brethren—many in the oil-rich Gulf states—most have been denied citizenship in the Arab countries to which they had moved. Regardless of their contributions as "law-abiding" citizens de facto, and regardless of their length of time there, they have largely been discriminated against. As one Palestinian Arab in Kuwait told *Forbes* editor James Cook in 1975,

> They owe me citizenship. I've been here for nearly 20 years and I helped create this country's great wealth. I did. I haven't simply earned my citizenship, they owe it to me.[88]

This Arab refugee, whose plight is representative of so many, according to Cook, was "unlikely to get it," although it is said that some of the Arabs who left Western Palestine for Kuwait have finally obtained Kuwaiti citizenship. In Iraq, Palestinians have been "allowed to live in the country but not to assume Iraqi nationality," despite the fact that the country needs manpower and "is encouraging Arab nationals to work and live there by granting them citizenship, with the *exception* of Palestinians.*[89]

In this endeavor, the Arab world has received inordinate support from the United Nations, as a candid former United Nations Palestinian Conciliation Commission official admitted in 1966. Dr. Pablo de Azcarate wrote:

> . . . solemn proclamation [of the "right of the refugees to return . . ."] by the [General] Assembly and its incorporation into the text of the resolution of December 14, 1948, have had three results.
>
> In the first place, a platform has been provided, of inestimable value to all those Arab political elements who are more interested in keeping alive the political struggle against the State of Israel than in putting an end, by means of a practical and reasonable compromise formula, to the tragic situation of the refugees. The truth is that since the resolution, . . . the Arab states, whenever the question arose, have done nothing but attack Israel. . . .
>
> The second result of the proclamation . . . has been complementary to the first —to paralyze any possible initiative on the part of those who would have preferred to give priority, not to the struggle against Israel, but to the solution of the refugee problem by means of a reasonable and constructive compromise formula.
>
> [And third,] the proclamation and the propaganda surrounding it have created a state of mind among the refugees based on the vain hope of returning to their homes, which has immobilized their cooperation, . . . an indispensable condition if a way is to be opened to a solution at once practical and constructive of their distressing problem. . . .
>
> . . . after years of effort, the sole achievement has been to feed and shelter the refugees in some sort of fashion, without taking a single step along the road to their economic and social rehabilitation.[90]

*Emphasis added.

Arab propaganda has also managed thus far to direct all attention to one aspect of the Middle East refugee problem as if it were the only aspect of that problem, and thus to mask the overall reality. One crucial truth, among many that have been obscured and deprecated, is that there have been as many Jewish refugees who fled or were expelled from the Arab countries as there are Arab refugees from Israel, and that the Jews left of necessity and in flight from danger.

The Exchange of Populations

For every refugee—adult or child—in Syria, Lebanon, or elsewhere in the Arab world who compels our sympathy, there is a Jewish refugee who fled from the Arab country of his birth. For every Arab who moved to neighboring lands, a Jew was forced to flee from a community where he and his ancestors may have lived for two thousand years. The Jews escaped to their original homeland, where their roots are even older; the Arabs also arrived where they were in the majority, where they shared the same language and culture with fellow Arabs, and often only a few dozen miles from their places of origin.

An exchange of populations has in actuality taken place and been consummated; by coincidence, even the *total* number of Arabs who reportedly left Israel is almost exactly equaled by the number of Jews exchanged. There has been a completed exchange of minorities between the Arabs and the Jews, and a more-than-even tradeoff of property for the Arabs. The Jews who fled Arab countries left assets behind in the Arab world greater than those the Arabs left in Israel.[91] Jewish property that the Arabs confiscated in Iraq, Syria, Libya, and Egypt apparently has more than offset Arab claims of compensation from Israel.

In fact, the concept of an "exchange of Arab and Jewish populations" was introduced by an *Arab leader* as a solution to the "disturbances" in the Middle East *long before* Israel or the actual exchange came about. In 1939, Mojli Amin, a member of the Arab Defense Committee for Palestine, drew up a proposal, published in Damascus and distributed among Arab leaders, entitled "Exchange of Populations." Amin proposed that

> all the Arabs of Palestine shall leave and be divided up among the neighboring Arab countries. In exchange for this, all the Jews living in Arab countries will go to Palestine. . . .
>
> The exchange of populations should be carried out in the same way that Turkey and Greece exchanged their populations. Special committees must be set up to deal with the liquidation of Jewish and Arab property. . . .
>
> I fear, in truth, that the Arabs will not agree. . . . But in spite of this, I take upon myself the task of convincing them. . . .[92]

At least a decade before the 1947 resolution to partition Palestine into a Jewish and an Arab state, the British had proposed the exchange of "Arab population in Palestine" for Jews elsewhere.[93] In 1945 Herbert Hoover stated that "The Arab population of Palestine would be the gainer from better lands in exchange for their present holdings. Iraq would be the gainer, for it badly needs agricultural population. Today millions of people are being moved from one land to another." Therefore, Hoover suggested "financing" Iraq to "complete" the population transfer with greater facility.[94]

From the time Israel attained modern statehood, independent humanitarian pleas attempted to reveal the actualities of all the "Middle East refugees" and to spotlight the potential permanent relief. One example was clergyman Carl Hermann Voss, who hoped through his books to change the world's faulty perception. He wrote,

> Some appeals for aid have implied that there is only an Arab refugee problem, enabling Arab propagandists to blame the Arab refugee plight on Israel. If proper attention is called to both Jewish and Arab refugee problems, much ill-will may be avoided and genuine human need, regardless of race or creed, will be served.[95]

Sui Generis?

Why was this de facto exchange of Arab and Jewish populations treated differently from all other population exchanges? Virtually all mass movements of refugees—even those which went one way and were not reciprocal, as are population exchanges—have been solved by resettlement or absorption of the refugees in either the original host country or another designated area.[96]

In the roster of the world's unfortunate shifts of population the number of refugees is staggering: from 1933 to 1945, a total of 79,200,000 souls were displaced;[97] since the Second World War at least 100,000,000 additional persons have become refugees. In times of conflict throughout history those who became insecure migrated to regions where they felt safer. Most are no longer refugees, because the resettlement and integration of these refugee transfers by the host country has been considered by the world community to be the normal and humanitarian course of action. The international legal precedent of granting refugees the privilege to live in dignity as citizens in their countries of asylum has been consistently urged for all refugees.[98] There has been no successful mass repatriation by any refugee group except after a military victory; further, in instances of refugee *exchanges* there is no historical, moral, or other basis for one-way repatriation.

The exchange between India and Pakistan in the 1950s was overwhelming in magnitude: 8,500,000 Sikhs and Hindus from Pakistan fled to India, and roughly 6,500,000 Muslims moved from India to Pakistan.[99] Even in "crowded, waterlogged West Bengal," according to the *New York Times,*[100] where refugees streamed from East Pakistan, the refugees "felt their only hope for solace was among people who spoke their language, had the same dietary habits and shared their customs and traditions." This exchange had not come about peacefully. As reported by the *Times* of London,[101]

Moslems have been murdering Hindus and Sikhs, Hindus and Sikhs have been murdering Moslems. Each side blames the other with passionate vehemence and refuses to admit that its own people are ever at fault.

Yet, contrary to Arab attitudes, Pakistani President Mohammed Ayub Khan, at a Cairo press conference in 1960, announced that he had directed his people to deal with their own refugees, without "substantial support from Muslim brethren over the world"; he suggested that Pakistan's settlement of its nearly seven million refugees from India might act as an example for the "three-quarters of a million refugees from Palestine" in the Arab countries.[102]

The modern precedent was set in 1913 when Turkey and Bulgaria began their equal population exchange; and in 1923, Turkey and Greece exchanged 1,250,000 Greeks and 355,000 Turks. An agreement was signed in 1930 abandoning individual appraisal in favor of wholesale liquidation of accounts by lump-sum compensation between Greece and Turkey.[103] Since almost all the property of the Indians and Pakistanis who changed homelands had been taken over and put to use by the respective governments, India and Pakistan eventually had to reach a similar solution.[104]

Millions of refugees who left their homes because of religious, ethnic, or political pressures have been successfully resettled. Many millions more are now being absorbed slowly into the life of their respective countries of asylum. The United States Committee for Refugees' (USCR) latest official figure (1982)[105] estimated a current "Worldwide Total" of more than 10,000,000 refugees. As that committee reported, ". . . few resettled refugees ever require assistance again from the UN," although the Office of the United Nations High Commissioner for Refugees (UNHCR) "lists resettled people as refugees until they acquire a new nationality."[106]

Among the dozens of countries to which tens of millions of refugees have fled for asylum, the only instance in which the "host countries refused," as a bloc, to assist properly, or even to accept *aid* in the *permanent* rehabilitation of their refugees, occurred in the "Arab states."[107] In March 1976, the director of the United States Committee for Refugees said that while "everyone must accept their refugees—that's the world situation," still, the "Arab refugees are a special case."[108]

Why is the "Palestinian refugee" problem treated as a special case? The United States Catholic Conference's eminent expert, John McCarthy, attempted to put the circumstances of the Arab refugees into the broader context, through his decades of first-hand worldwide experience with refugees. McCarthy's own private affiliations—he has worn "several hats" in Catholic-sponsored refugee resettlement organs—have accomplished the resettlement of roughly one hundredth of the world's hundred million refugees rendered homeless since World War II. During an interview in December 1978, he was asked:

> Q: Is the world really receptive to observing the precedent of finding new homes for refugees?

McCarthy: We've settled about a million people in the past 30 years. At the present time we have from Southeast Asia—we can provide homes and jobs for 7,000 people a month, without regard to race, religion, what-have-you. There's no problem with this—it works. We're carrying out resettlement programs in Canada, Switzerland, Austria, Germany, Nordic countries, also New Zealand, Australia—all Southeast Asians. We're working with Egyptians, and out of Europe we're taking care of Ethiopians, Kurds, Iraqis, and the whole Iron Curtain. So we have quite a movement of people. There isn't any problem. It always works—if they're told the story as it should be told. You must remember that in any structure—black, white, green, yellow—there's always a certain resistance to the newcomer. If we can show that these people can contribute—that these people have a problem, that these people are good—if we can show that they're your brother, it works.

Q: In the case of the Palestinian Arab refugees—why hasn't it worked there?

McC: It *has* worked there.

Q: You mean *un*officially?

McC: You must remember—it's such an involved political structure. I've worked in the Palestinian structure, trying to say, "Let's resettle these people." The governments of Egypt and so on, they all said, "Wait a while," or "No, we won't do it. The only place they're going to resettle is back in Israel, right or wrong." You must remember—well—these people are simply pawns.

Q: What can be done?

McC: We can do things with people if we have the help, just the permission of the governments. But you must remember one thing: the Arab countries don't want to take Arabs. It's discriminating against their own. . . . Our only job is to see if we can create new life opportunities.

The most important thing is to get the refugees, the people, resettled.[109]

"Permanent resettlement" remains the general goal of the United States government as well.[110] Yet the current dialogue omits any mention of the rehabilitation or resettlement of Palestinian Arab refugees. It is the "right of the Palestinians to their homeland" that is consistently reiterated.

The abuse of the refugees, their deprivation of real "human rights" from 1948 onward, and the true motive behind their rejection by the Arab world have all been buried by propaganda slogans and omissions. Humanitarian voices of concern for "human need" and dignity are now muted by the louder and increasingly prevalent trumpeting of the "rights" of the "Palestinians" to "return."

Amid that campaign, the belated recognition of the *"other"* Middle East refugees, the Jews, was termed an ill-timed "complication" by United States officials during the Carter administration.[111] To the benefit of the Arab propaganda mechanism, and perhaps to the ill fortune of many perpetual Arab refugees, Israel has not made an effective case for its own Jewish refugee claim; Israelis say that they have reserved the matter of the population exchange for overall peace negotiations, although they have referred to the exchange during discussions of refugee compensation, and in forums such as the United Nations.

However, if the Israelis chose virtually to ignore the propaganda benefits to be gained from exploitation of their refugees, the Arabs predicted otherwise.

Perhaps because of the Arab world's own political use of its refugees, some Arabs have anticipated with apprehension the Israelis' eventual use of what the Arabs see as a strong claim for Israel and its resettled Jewish refugees from Arab countries.

There have been sophisticated warnings that the existence of those hundreds of thousands of Jewish refugees who fled to Israel from Arab states would trump the Arab refugee "propaganda card." Even before the propaganda line substituted the term "Palestinians" to replace the term "Arab refugees," the Arab world manifested popular recognition that its demand for the "return" of the Arab refugees to Israel was implausible: in 1966, a prominent Egyptian newspaper published an editorial stating that "we all know that Zionist influence . . . brought about the transfer to Israel, of thousands of Jews from Yemen . . . thousands of Moroccan Jews, the same thing was done in Tunisia, and Syria also tried to follow the same policy . . ."

As a result, the editorial reasoned, Israel can claim that, if "tens of thousands of Jews who previously lived in the Arab countries" are settled in Israel, "why should the Arab refugees not be settled in their stead? . . . This proposal . . . can serve as a propaganda card to arouse the interest of world public opinion."[112]

In 1974 the question was obliquely raised again by the Arabs—this time by an Arab-born Israeli journalist, interviewing the head of the PLO delegation to the United Nations at that time, Dr. Nabil Shaat. The Israeli journalist asked, "Why did you send your people to kill innocent people in Ma'alot and Kiryat Shemona . . . knowing they were mostly populated by Oriental Jews, whom you call brothers?" At the reference to the Arab-born Jewish refugees, Dr. Shaat responded, "I have no answer to that. I will personally raise the question in our organization when I return to Beirut. . . ."[113]

The PLO's Dr. Shaat granted another interview months later, which he used as a platform for his answer: Shaat called for a "charter of rights of Arab citizens of Jewish persuasion."[114] Shortly afterward the series of "invitations" from the Arab world to "its Jews" resumed.

Continuing Arab concern was indicated in May of 1975 by an unusually candid article written for the Beirut journal *Al Nahar*. Sabri Jiryis, an Arab researcher, author, and member of the Palestinian National Council, wrote that "the Arabs were very active" in the creation of Israel, although

> this is hardly the place to describe how the Jews of the Arab states were driven out of their ancient homes, . . . shamefully deported after their property had been commandeered or taken over at the lowest possible valuation. . . . This is true for the majority of the Jews in question.

Jiryis warned that "Israel will air this issue in . . . any negotiations undertaken regarding the rights of the Palestinians. . . . Israel has been assembling the minutest details about the Jews who left the Arab states after 1948 . . . so that these can be used when the time comes."

Jiryis concluded that

Israelis will put these claims forward: . . . "It may be . . . that we Israelis entailed the expulsion of some 700,000 Palestinians. . . .

"However, you Arabs have entailed the expulsion of just as many Jews from the Arab states. . . . Actually, therefore, what happened was a . . . 'population and property exchange,' and each party must bear the consequences.

"Israel is absorbing the Jews, . . . *the Arab states for their part must settle the Palestinians in their own midst and solve* their problems."[115]*

Lebanese Arabs demanded in 1977 that the "Palestinian refugees be relocated to all Arab nations . . . each according to its own capacity."[116] That the motives for the Lebanese proclamation were political and not strictly humanitarian was evident: the PLO had contributed greatly to the transformation of Lebanon from international playground to countrywide battlefield. Significantly, however, the demand went to the *Arab* countries and not to Israel. Thus the responsibility for the refugees was placed, albeit briefly, by Arabs upon the Arab world.

Nonetheless, rumblings of renewed external recognition of this Middle East population exchange continued to appear in the late 1970s, nearly thirty years after the fact.

University of Chicago population expert Philip Hauser, former United States Census Director, who represented the United States on the United Nations' Population Commission from 1947 to 1951, stated in 1978 that

> the exchange of populations between out-migrant Arabs and out-migrant Jews is real—precedents have been established. As far as the unprecedented refusal by the Arabs to accept Arab refugees—some quarters call this a deliberate means of destroying Israel. What the out-migration of Arabs from newly-created Israel did was to provide in Arab countries a milieu in which the Arab refugees had access to a common culture and language . . . a unique historical situation, in the sense that most refugee populations are faced with the necessity of living in a new cultural and linguistic world. . . . In light of the total situation—and now I will speak not in the demographic vein but in the less familiar political vein—it would be absurd for the Arabs to insist on what would be double compensation from Israel. . . .[117]

Moreover, perhaps in view of the Israeli government's relegation of its refugee equation to a state of suspended animation, the Jewish refugees themselves finally began to coalesce into independent bodies; in several countries such organizations grew up. One international body calls itself WOJAC—World Organization of Jews from Arab Countries—with delegations of Arab-born Jews representing sixteen countries of asylum. The Jewish refugees, who never had been clearly identified or adequately discussed in world forums, decided to become recognized, to explain why they can never go back to their lands of origin, and to demand "even-handedness."[118]

It was precisely when WOJAC announced the convening of its organizing conference in Paris that the Arabs issued several of their invitations to the

*Emphasis added.

Arab-born Jews to "come back." The Jews disdained the gesture of "hospitality," and composed a response. They enumerated the "miseries" they had endured in the Muslim Arab society at a press conference called to communicate their negative answer to the invitation.*

In 1981, the United States Committee for Refugees noted, as it had not done in many previous reports, the "600,000 Jewish refugees resettled from Arab countries . . . three decades ago."[119] By the next survey, however, that important recognition was singularly negated.[120] Had the Jews initially drawn worldwide attention to their Arab-born Jewish refugees in Israel, had they broadcast the persecution of the Jews and other minorities in the Arab countries—and the social and economic burden of absorbing the Jewish refugees from Arab countries—the Arab demand for one-sided repatriation might be perceived today in a different, more evenhanded and objective perspective, and other, critical unknown elements in the conflict might have by now intruded into the consideration of "justice."

As we have seen, all those hapless peoples counted as "refugees" were not in fact refugees: many were needy souls of other nationalities who found sustenance in the camps, and in the process became—and their children became—unwitting human weapons in a holy war that never ends.

The immediate objective of the Arab world's propaganda strategy has been one-sided Arab "repatriation," a "return" in the name of "self-determination" of those Arab refugees who have been perceived as *the* Palestinian people from time immemorial, with "rights" to "their land." In the foundation for those claims, one cornerstone is the popular perception that the Arabs are the *only* hapless refugees who were uprooted in 1948.

The Arabs well know how Jews were—and in least one case, still are—treated in Arab countries,† however they may have publicly congratulated themselves for "traditionally benign" treatment of "their" Jews. Consequently, they have grounds for concern for the success of one aspect of their program. If the world recognizes that there has been an irreversible exchange of Jewish and Arab refugee populations, this Arab political maneuver, perhaps, might be expected to reach an impasse.

And yet, as illustrated earlier here, some in the world community *have* recognized the Arab world's cynical and heartless manipulation of those Arab brethren—men, women, and children who found themselves in refugee camps in

---

*In January 1976, the American Sephardi Federation "representing more than 1½ million Jewish refugees from Arab lands" took a full-page advertisement in the *New York Times* to "decline" the Iraqi government's "invitation." A photograph of two bodies suspended from a scaffold, surrounded by angry-looking onlookers was identified as a "News Service Photo: Iraqis watch the bodies of Sabah Haim (left), and David Hazaquiel, both Jews, dangle from the scaffold after they were hanged in Baghdad." Beneath the photograph the organization responded: "INVITATION DECLINED."

"We, the Jewish refugees from Arab lands whose history in those countries goes back more than 2,000 years, long before Islam—suggest that the Arab governments finance the welfare of their own brothers instead of using them as political pawns, while they spend huge amounts for hypocritical propaganda, half truths and outright lies." (January 11, 1976, *New York Times.*)

†See Chapter 7.

search of a better life. Why has that recognition failed to bring about a reasonable solution? Why is this refugee problem different from other refugee problems?

Why has UNRWA spent well over a billion humanitarian-contributed dollars —mostly from the United States—to perpetuate the refugee dilemma? More important, why does the Arab world of nearly 200 million people and millions of miles of territory remain so steadfast in its rejection of one minuscule Jewish state that the Arabs have been willing to sacrifice the human rights and often the very lives of their own people? And, given the honorable and predominantly well-intentioned motives of the free world community—oil-benefit seekers aside —how have the Arabs managed to perpetuate this status quo ante?

The answers lie in what is known—and what is not known—about the region.

Having worked to obliterate from the practical dialogue the history of the Jews as "Palestinian people," and having in fact denied Jewish historical ties to their Holy Land (as in, for example, Article 20 of the PLO Covenant), the Arabs have consistently claimed that in the proposed "secular democratic state of Palestine," most of the Jews who are now in their homeland of Israel would have to depart,[121] presumably back to their countries of origin—including the little-known major component of Arab-born Jews.

But a mutual repatriation obviously could not be demanded if one side of an exchange of populations had fled from intolerable conditions and could not return. Hence the need for a revised scenario, the Arab "invitation" to Jews to return, and the alteration from "Arab refugees" to "Palestinians." Armed by myths, prevalent among outsiders, that the "alien" Jews lived harmoniously among the "native" Arabs before Israel became a state, the Arabs have tried, through consistent diplomatic and media repetition of statements by Arab leaders, to convince world opinion that the Jews would be "welcome again" in the Arab states if they were forced out of their homeland in Israel, the "Palestinian homeland" of the "Palestinian people from time immemorial."

Because there are extensive contradictions to important popular perceptions and reports—discernible by reading the sentiments and strategies expressed by Arab writers and by visiting the Arab "confrontation" states—the purported "facts" and the "legitimate rights" that are part of the current rhetoric of the Arab-Israel conflict become recognizable as persistent and troubling questions.

Despite the Arab nations' splintered, disparate reactions to what they consider greater threats than Israel—for some the primary danger is seen as the Soviet Union, for others Muslim Fundamentalism, and for the Gulf states its retention of the power of oil—the Arab world remains adamant and uncharacteristically united in its goal, as Al-Ayubi stated it—to tighten a "noose" around the "Zionist entity."

It is the motive for the unchanging, overarching Arab strategy vis-à-vis Israel, the historical factors behind that motive, and the maneuvers that created a climate where that strategy is advocated as "morally" acceptable, which must now be traced.

3

The Arab Jew

> Before the Jewish state was established,
> there existed nothing to harm good relations
> between Arabs and Jews.
>
> —The late King Faisal of Saudi Arabia,
> November 1973, to Henry Kissinger
>
> We are not against the Jews.
> On the contrary, we are all Semites
> and we have been living with each
> other in peace and fraternity, Muslims,
> Jews and Christians, for many centuries.
>
> —Yasser Arafat, head of the PLO

Since the rebirth of Israel, hundreds of thousands of Jews from Arab lands have swarmed into the new state. In 1948 more than 850,000 Jews lived in the Arab world. Today there are fewer than 29,000, a shadow of the former ancient community. Most of those Jewish refugees fled to Israel. Where did they come from with such urgency—and why?

Contrary to the myth that Jews lived in harmony with the Arabs before the Zionist state, innumerable authoritative works document decisively the subjugation, oppression, and spasmodic anti-Jewish eruptions of violence that darkened the existence of the Jews in Muslim Arab countries.

In truth, before the seventh-century advent of the Prophet Muhammad and Islam, Jews and Arabs did have harmonious relations, and words of praise regarding the noble virtues of the Jews may be found in ancient Arab literature.[1]

Before the Arab conquest, in fact, some rulers of Arabia "had indeed embraced Judaism," as Muslim historians attest.

The Koran itself has been witness to the Jewish nature of the "Israelite communities of Arabia": Koranic references appear about the rabbis and the Torah which they read, and the prestige and reverence with which the earlier community viewed them.[2]

The Koran "contains so many legends and theological ideas found in Talmudic literature that we are able to draw a picture of the spiritual life of the Jews with whom Mohammad must have come into contact."[3]

It was the Prophet Muhammad himself who attempted to negate the positive image of the Jew that had been prevalent earlier. According to historian Bernard

33

Lewis, the Prophet Muhammad's original plan had been to induce the Jews to adopt Islam;[4] when Muhammad began his rule at Medina in A.D. 622 he counted few supporters, so he adopted several Jewish practices—including daily prayer facing toward Jerusalem and the fast of Yom Kippur—in the hope of wooing the Jews. But the Jewish community rejected the Prophet Muhammad's religion, preferring to adhere to its own beliefs, whereupon Muhammad subsequently substituted Mecca for Jerusalem, and dropped many of the Jewish practices.

Three years later, Arab hostility against the Jews commenced, when the Meccan army exterminated the Jewish tribe of Quraiza.[5] As a result of the Prophet Muhammad's resentment, the Holy Koran itself contains many of his hostile denunciations of Jews[6] and bitter attacks upon the Jewish tradition, which undoubtedly have colored the beliefs of religious Muslims down to the present.

Omar, the caliph who succeeded Muhammad, delineated in his Charter of Omar the twelve laws under which a *dhimmi,* or non-Muslim, was allowed to exist as a "nonbeliever" among "believers." The Charter codified the conditions of life for Jews under Islam—a life which was forfeited if the *dhimmi* broke this law. Among the restrictions of the Charter: Jews were forbidden to touch the Koran; forced to wear a distinctive (sometimes dark blue or black) habit with sash; compelled to wear a yellow piece of cloth as a badge (blue for Christians); not allowed to perform their religious practices in public; not allowed to own a horse, because horses were deemed noble; not permitted to drink wine in public; and required to bury their dead without letting their grief be heard by the Muslims.[7]

As a grateful payment for being allowed so to live and be "protected," a *dhimmi* paid a special head tax and a special property tax, the edict for which came directly from the Koran: "Fight against those [Jews and Christians] who believe not in Allah . . . until they pay the tribute readily, being brought low."[8]

In addition, Jews faced the danger of incurring the wrath of a Muslim, in which case the Muslim could charge, however falsely, that the Jew had cursed Islam, an accusation against which the Jew could not defend himself.

Islamic religious law decreed that, although murder of one Muslim by another Muslim was punishable by death, a Muslim who murdered a non-Muslim was given not the death penalty, but only the obligation to pay "blood money" to the family of the slain infidel. Even this punishment was unlikely, however, because the law held the testimony of a Jew or a Christian invalid against a Muslim, and the penalty could only be exacted under improbable conditions—when two Muslims were willing to testify against a brother Muslim for the sake of an infidel.[9]

The demeanment of Jews as represented by the Charter has carried down through the centuries, its implementation inflicted with varying degrees of cruelty or inflexibility, depending upon the character of the particular Muslim ruler. When that rule was tyrannical, life was abject slavery, as in Yemen, where one of the Jews' tasks was to clean the city latrines and another was to clear the streets of animal carcasses—without pay, often on their Sabbath.

The restrictions under Muslim law always included the extra head tax regardless of the ruler's relative tolerance. This tax was enforced in some form until 1909 in Egypt, Iraq, Syria, Lebanon, and Turkey; until 1925 in Iran; and was still enforceable in Yemen until the present generation. The clothing as well as the tax and the physical humiliation also varied according to whim. Thus, in Morocco, Jews had to wear black slippers,[10] while in Yemen, Jewish women were forced to wear one white and one black shoe.[11]*

Jews were relegated to Arab-style Jewish ghettos—*hara, mellah,* or simply Jewish Quarter were the names given the areas where Jews resided—recorded by travelers over the centuries, as well as by Jewish chroniclers. A visitor to fourteenth-century Egypt, for example, commented in passing[12] on the separate Jewish quarter, and five hundred years later another visitor in the nineteenth century verified the continuation of the separated Jewish existence: "There are in this country about five thousand Jews (in Arabic, called 'Yahood'; singular, 'Yahoodee'), most of whom reside in the metropolis, in a miserable, close and dirty quarter, intersected by lanes, many of which are so narrow as hardly to admit of two persons passing each other in them."[13]

In 1920, those Jewish families in Cairo whose financial success had allowed them out of the ghetto, under relatively tolerant rule, had been replaced by "poor Jewish immigrants." Thus, although the character of the population may have changed, the squalor and crowding remained. As one writer, a Jew, observed:

> Our people are crowded and clustered into houses about to collapse, in dark cellars, narrow alleys and crooked lanes choked with mud and stinking refuse, earning their meagre living in dark shops and suffocating workshops, toiling back to back, sunscorched and sleepless. Their hard struggle for existence both inside and outside the home is rewarded by a few beans and black bread.[14]

Under no circumstances were Jews considered truly equal. Among the Jews in Arab lands were many individual personal successes and regionalized intermittent prosperity, but the tradition of persecution was characteristic throughout most of Jewish history under Arab rule.[15] If the *dhimmi* burdens were light in one particular region, the Jew had the residue of fear left from the previous history of pogroms and humiliations in his area. These harsh and ancient *dhimma* restrictions persisted even up to the present time to some degree, in some Arab communities, and their spirit—if not their letter—continued generally throughout the Arab world.[16]

Throughout the centuries, the Jews were the first to suffer persecution in times of economic turmoil or political upheaval,[17] and the cumulative effect of the sporadic mass murders left their mark on the Jews even in periods of relative

---

*The edict set by the Sultan of Morocco in 1884 varies somewhat, as did most interpretations of the *dhimma* law. His restrictions also included insistence that Jews work on their sacred day of rest; carry heavy burdens on their backs; work without pay; clean foul places and latrines; part with merchandise at half price; lend beasts of burden without payment; accept false coinage instead of negotiable currency; take fresh skins in return for tanned hides; hold their beds and furniture at the disposal of government guests, etc.

quiescence. In Syria, the infamous blood libel of 1840 brought about the death, torture, and pillage of countless Jews falsely accused of murdering a priest and his servant to collect the blood for Passover matzoth![18] Before the Jews were finally vindicated of this slander, word of the charges had spread far from Damascus, causing terror in numerous Jewish communities.

The scurrilous blood libel has not been purged from Arab literature, however. In fact, the Arabs seem in the past two decades to have seized upon this primitive old calumny with renewed vigor. In 1962 the UAR (Egyptian) Ministry of Education published "Human Sacrifices in the Talmud" as one of a series of official "national" books. Bearing on its cover the symbol of the Egyptian Institute for Publications, this modern book is a reprint of an 1890 work by a writer in Cairo.[19] In the introduction, the editor shares his discovery: "conclusive evidence . . . that this people permits bloodshed and makes it a religious obligation laid down by the Talmud." The editor's description becomes more vile as it purports to become more explicit regarding the "Indictment."[20]

Two years later, in 1964, a professor at the University of Damascus published his own affirmation of the nineteenth-century blood libel, stating that the wide attention given the story served a valid purpose: to warn mothers against letting their children out late at night, "lest the Jew . . . come and take their blood for the purpose of making matzot for Passover."[21] Still another version, also published in the 1960s, "The Danger of World Jewry to Islam and Christianity," alleges that thousands of children and others disappear each year, and all of them are victims of guess who?[22]

They've even dramatized the infamous canard for the theater. In November 1973, a former minister in the Egyptian Foreign Service published a play based on the 1840 blood libel in Damascus—replete with gory descriptions—in a widely circulated Egyptian weekly.[23] During the same month the late Saudi Arabian King Faisal stressed the importance of the blood libel of 1840 in Damascus as a requisite to understanding "Zionist crime."[24] And in 1982, shortly after Israel transferred its much coveted Sinai territory to Egypt for a more coveted peace, the Egyptian press (government-run) dredged up inflammatory variations on the horrible theme. Two examples: ". . . The Israelis are Israelis and their favorite drink is Arab blood. . . ."[25] and "A Jew . . . drinks their blood for a few coins."[26]

The departure of European colonists in the twentieth century brought into being a highly nationalistic group of Arab states, which increasingly perceived their Jews as a new political threat.* The previous Arab Muslim ambivalence—an ironic possessive attitude toward "their" Jews, coupled with the omnipresent implementing of the harsh *dhimma* law—was gradually replaced by a completely demoniacal and negative stereotype of the Jew. Traditional Koranic slurs against the Jews were implemented to incite hostility toward the Jewish national move-

---

*The Arab reaction seems not dissimilar to that of a Ku Klux Klansman in the United States, responding vehemently to the question I once asked about his attitude toward integration: "They're our 'Niggers,' and we've taken good care of 'em, but I'll be damned if I'll let 'em take over. . . . Our 'Niggers' don't really wanna vote, y'know." (The epithet is his.) *Chicago Daily News,* April 10, 1965.

ment. The Nazi anti-Semitism in the 1930s and 1940s flourished in this already receptive climate.

Although Arabs themselves frequently speak of "anti-Semitism" as synonymous with anti-Jewishness—before the 1947 partition, for example, Egyptian UN Representative Haykal Pasha warned the General Assembly that partition would bring "anti-Semitism" worse than Hitler's[27]—frequently they justify or obscure an anti-Jewish action by saying, "How can I be anti-Semitic? I'm a Semite myself." According to Professor S. D. Goitein, "the word 'semitic' was coined by an 18th-century German scholar, concerned with linguistics. . . . The idea of a Semitic race was invented and cultivated in particular in order to emphasize the inalterable otherness and alien character of the Jews living in Europe."[28]

Another eminent Arabist, Bernard Lewis, dates the invention of the term "anti-Semitism" to 1862, although "the racial ideology that gave rise to it was already well established in the early 19th century. Instead of—or as well as—an unbeliever . . . the Jew was now labeled as a member of an alien and inferior race. . . ."[29]

As early as 1940 the Mufti of Jerusalem requested the Axis powers to acknowledge the Arab right "to settle the question of Jewish elements in Palestine and other Arab countries in accordance with the national and racial interests of the Arabs and along lines similar to those used to solve the Jewish question in Germany and Italy."[30]*

Hitler's crimes against the Jews have frequently been justified in Arab writings and pronouncements. In the 1950s, Minister Anwar Sadat published an open letter to Hitler, hoping he was still alive and sympathizing with his cause. Important Arab writers and political figures have said Hitler was "wronged and slandered, for he did no more to the Jews than Pharaoh, Nebuchadnezzar, the Romans, the Byzantines, Titus, Mohammed and the European peoples who slaughtered the Jews before him." Or that Hitler wanted to "save . . . the world from this malignant evil. . . ."[31]

Arab defense of the Nazis' extermination of the Jews has persisted: prominent Egyptian writer Anis Mansour wrote in 1973 that "People all over the world have come to realize that Hitler was right, since Jews . . . are bloodsuckers . . . interested in destroying the whole world which has . . . expelled them and despised them for centuries . . . and burnt them in Hitler's crematoria . . . one million . . . six millions. Would that he had finished it!"[32]

Mansour alleged at another time that the vicious medieval blood libel was historical truth: "the Jews confessed" that they had killed the children and used their blood; thus he justifies persecution and pogroms of "the wild beasts."[33] That article was followed by a "report," after Mansour returned from representing Egypt at the Fortieth International PEN (writers') Conference in 1975 in Vienna. In it, Mansour continued the theme: "The Jews are guilty" for Nazism; ". . . the world can only curse the Jews . . . The Jews have only themselves to blame."

*For a discussion of Jewish-Arab relations in Palestine, see Chapter 9; additional information on the Arab leadership's sympathies is found in Chapter 17.

Mansour was angry that "the whole world" protested "all because" a "teacher" told the Jewish waiter serving him in Vienna that " '. . . Hitler committed a grave error in not doing away with more of you. . . .' "[34]

It was from such a climate that the Jews had escaped, seeking refuge in Israel.

Yemen

The entire Yemenite community of Jews, who swarmed almost 50,000 strong into Israel via "Operation Magic Carpet," believed that "King David" Ben-Gurion was actually the Messiah calling them home. Jewish settlements in Yemen existed more than 2,000 years ago,[35] and some claim the Jews' presence there has been longer—from the Jews' Babylonian captivity and the fall of the First Temple in 586 B.C. Yemenite Jewry fled to Israel from what historian S. D. Goitein described as "the worst aspect" of the Arab mistreatment of Jews. A Yemenite law decreed that fatherless Jewish children under thirteen be taken from their mothers and raised in Muslim homes as Muslims.

"Children were torn away from their mothers," according to Goitein. Despite attempts of family and friends to adopt the children secretly, "very often the efforts . . . were not successful. . . . To my mind, this law, which was enforced with new vigor about fifty years ago, more than anything else impelled the Yemenite Jews to quit that country to which they were very much attached. . . . The result was that many families arrived in Israel with one or more of their children lost to them . . . some widows . . . [were] bereaved in this way of all their offspring."[36]

Persecution was constant and extreme—stoning Jews, an "age-old" custom, according to "an old doctor of Muslim law,"[37] was still common tradition at the time of the 1948 exodus—although the bearability of life throughout the centuries of Muslim domination often depended upon whether the rule was Turkish or Arab.

The Yemenite Jews' situation changed drastically for the worse in the seventh century, with the Arab conquest. After the Jews who lived in what is now part of Saudi Arabia[38] were either expelled by the Prophet Muhammad or obliterated, Jewish communities in the rest of the conquered Muslim territory fell under the new infidel status.[39] The Jews of Yemen were subjected to the severest possible interpretation of the Charter of Omar, plus carefully devised brutal improvisations on the *dhimmi* theme. For about four centuries, the Jews suffered under the fierce fanatical edict of the most intolerant of all Islamic sects.[40]

In the twelfth century the conditions were so punishing, and formerly repugnant forced conversion to Islam was so eagerly sought by terrified Jews, that the "Great Rambam"—the venerated Rabbi Moses Maimonides—was prompted to write the famous "Yemen Epistle,"[41] in which he commiserated with Yemen's Jewry and besought them to keep the faith.

The eighteenth century was one of almost unbearable burden, bringing the

1724 famine, in addition to insidiously varied humiliations and violence. Fanatical rulers ordered synagogues destroyed, and public prayers were forbidden. Many thousands attempted to follow "false messiah" Shabbetai Zevi on his pilgrimage to the Holy Land, but they were attacked on the way, and the Chief Rabbi of San'a was "tortured to death."[42]

One overlord decided to rid the Arabian peninsula of Jews by offering them a choice of religious conversion or banishment; the overwhelming number chose to leave the capitals and head for the Red Sea coast. Those who had not died of starvation, thirst, or illness during the torturous journey—for many, on foot—were allowed to settle in a town called Mauza', where more casualties were caused by the cruelties of the climate. The Jews' exile at Mauza' was terminated by decree in 1781,[43] according to one report, because the exiled Jews had been the only craftsmen in the country and their work was keenly missed.

The latter eighteenth century, with its more tolerant ruler, allowed Yemen's Jews brief respite from both hunger and humiliation. One Jew was even accorded an official position as Minister of Currency—he was imprisoned for two years by his ruler, however, after many years of prominence.

A visit was paid to Yemen in 1762 by a Danish-German explorer who described life in the Jewish ghetto under the "improved" circumstances of the eighteenth century:

> Completely shut off from the city of San'a is the Jewish village . . . where 2,000 Jews live in great contempt. Nevertheless they are the best artisans, potters, goldsmiths, engravers, minters and others. By day they work in their shops in San'a, but by night they must withdraw to their isolated dwellings. . . . Shortly before my arrival, twelve of the fourteen synagogues of the Jews were torn down, and all their beautiful houses wrecked. . . .[44]

Throughout the nineteenth century Jews were victims of hunger and of Arab attacks on the ghetto, which resulted in murder and pillage.

In the middle of the nineteenth century a writer from Jerusalem described the Yemenite Jews' plight during the two years he lived with them:

> The Jews who have been living in Yemen for many hundreds, perhaps even thousands of years, are now in a position of inferiority, and are oppressed by a people which declares itself holy and pious but which is very brutal, barbarous and hard-hearted. The natives consider the Jew unclean, but his blood for them is not unclean. They lay claims to all his belongings, and if he is unwilling, they employ force. . . . The Jews . . . live outside the town in dark dwellings like prison cells or caves out of fear for murderers and robbers. Whoever has any money or valuables conceals them in the earth or in such secret holes as they have in their little houses so that nobody may see them. . . .
>
> It is particularly bad for the Jew if he is himself accused of a crime. There is then no mercy. For the least offense, he is sentenced to outrageous fines, which he is quite unable to pay. In case of non-payment, he is put into chains and cruelly beaten every day. Before the punishment is inflicted, the Cadi addresses him in gentle tones and urges him to change his faith and obtain a share

of all the glory of this world and of the world beyond. His refusal is again regarded as penal obstinacy. On the other hand, it is not open to the Jew to prosecute a Muslim, as the Muslim by right of law can dispose of the life and the property of the Jew, and it is only to be regarded as an act of magnanimity if the Jews are allowed to live. The Jew is not admissible as a witness, nor has his oath any validity.[45]

Beginning at the turn of the century, the Yemenite Jews were even prohibited from fleeing the country to escape persecution. "Those who live in a country which discriminates against them most blatantly want to have, at least, one right: to leave that country," historian Goitein believes. But the Shi'ite Muslims in Yemen adhered to the "strictly inner Islamic legal basis"—that "a Jew, a 'protected' subject, was not allowed" into "enemy territory"—which to the Shi'ites meant any region ruled by non-Shi'ites. The few who managed to emigrate "had to leave everything behind," and "for the great masses . . . the old prohibition was a source of great suffering."[46]

In one town, however, the Jews became the center of a power struggle between two Arab tribes: as a result, the town's ruler loosened Jewish restrictions to the extent that some Jews became wealthy and a few were allowed to have houses even higher than the Muslims'.[47]

There have always been conflicting reports on the number of the Jews in Yemen, but because famine often struck the Yemenite Jews, death through starvation was "a common event." (Thus, even though the birth rate was high and polygamy occurred among the Yemenite Jewish community, the rate of natural increase was kept down in Yemen, into the twentieth century.) One visitor wrote, "Nothing moves the Jewish traveler so much as the sight of many places where all of the Jewish inhabitants have been carried off by the last famine. The average rate of mortality is terrible."[48]

A teacher was sent from Beirut in 1910 to assess the constant reports of travail for the Yemenite Jews. He noted that, after

more than a week, I have made myself acquainted with the life of the Jews in all its phases. . . . They are exceedingly unfortunate. . . . If they are abused, they listen in silence as though they had not understood; if they are attacked by an Arab boy with stones, they flee.[49]

There were some Yemenite Jews who fled on foot over the desert in pilgrimage to the Holy Land, particularly during the nineteenth century, and into the twentieth. One group of Jews decided to sell their possessions for half their worth, and a movement to the Holy Land commenced. "In 1912 alone, over 2,000 Yemenite Jews disembarked at Jaffa." They kept embarking on the hazardous pilgrimage, even during World War II, and many had to disguise themselves as Arabs to avoid being intercepted and imprisoned. Often it was the Jewish children who unwittingly exposed the disguise—when the Arabs tested them by offering *un-kosher* food (not edible by Jewish Orthodox law).[50]

As late as 1946, an American missionary reported that a Yemenite Jewish mother and son had been put into chains for accepting a ride in the American's jeep.[51]

Nearly 50,000 traditionally religious Yemenites, who had never seen a plane, were airlifted to Israel in 1949 and 1950.[52] Since the Book of Isaiah promised, "They shall mount up with wings, as eagles," the Jewish community boarded the "eagles" contentedly; to the pilot's consternation some of them lit a bonfire aboard, to cook their food!

Aden

"When I stood in the ancient graveyard of the Jewish community of Aden—from which tombstones 700 and 800 years old had been taken away to museums, and looked toward the natural harbor where ships of local design were still being built, it occurred to me that King Solomon's ships, not very different from those I saw there, might have anchored nearby. . . ."[53]

"Archeological evidence puts us on firmer ground," Goitein tells us. A room in Beth She'arim, Palestine, "dating from approximately 200 A.D. . . . was reserved for Jews from . . . South Arabia."[54]

Thus Jews are certain to have appeared in Aden in A.D. 200, and although the Jewish community seems to have eluded thorough historical documenting,[55] a letter yet remains, "sent by a Jewish merchant from Aden in South Arabia to Cairo about 850 years ago. In this letter he asks his business correspondent in Cairo to buy for him all kinds of goods for the needs of his household."[56]

That there were prominent Jewish merchants in Aden in the early twelfth century hints at a difference in opportunities between the Jews of Yemen and Aden at that period.[57] Documentary evidence exists that some of the Aden Jewish community was substantial enough so that they could contribute "ample donations to a well-known Spanish poet" in the thirteenth century.[58]

Still, the general quality of life for Aden's Jews during the Arab reign was hardly "golden." The proximity to Yemen and the same dominating power indicate that Jews of Aden suffered conditions of humiliation under Muslim rule similar to those of the Yemenite Jews "until Aden was conquered by the British in 1839."[59]

Through the middle of the nineteenth century, most of Aden's Jewry continued to languish under the intermittent persecution and degradation that was the lot of the Jews in that area of Arabia. The exceptions were the "few Jews in Hadramaut and its environs (an area which was known as the Protectorate of Aden)." The Jews in the Protectorate paid their traditional head taxes to the Arabs but in return they were given "more comfortable conditions" than the hapless Jews of Yemen and of the rest of Aden.[60]

In twentieth-century Aden,

> The Jews . . . always knew that they were living on sufferance; the local Arab population never harbored anything but hatred towards them. They (the Jews)

remembered that "light" pogrom in 1933, when a few people were beaten up and wounded outside the Jewish Quarter, when there was some stoning and when a number of rioters entered a Jewish house and did some looting.

That reminiscence of the 1933 anti-Jewish uprising in Aden was contained in an eye-witness "memorandum" which described the "Disaster of the Jews of Aden," the Arab-led mass murder, pillage, and destruction that came down on Aden's Jews in December 1947.[61]

An Englishman who was in Aden from 1931, and was appointed Aden's governor in 1951, later described a traditional enmity between Arabs and Jews that preceded the Palestine partition by decades. His report contradicted others, which blamed the bloody pogrom in 1947 on outside factors and incitement in behalf of the Palestinian Arabs.[62] Sir Tom Hickinbotham wrote that

> The Jews are disliked by the Arabs whom they fear. . . . Therefore, we are always liable to have trouble between the Arabs and the Jews which might well spread to the Hindu community. . . .
>
> [The Jews], generally speaking, kept very much to themselves, were self-effacing and their contacts with the Arabs were reasonably good. . . . The Arabs consider that the Jews are their social inferiors and, provided they keep their own place, or what the Arabs consider to be their place, there is no trouble at all and the two communities may live side by side in peace for years; but as soon as the Jews tended to forget that they were Jews and began to assert themselves as men, then there was always a likelihood of serious trouble.[63]

The British Commissioner of Police in Aden testified in 1947 that "Since I arrived in Aden there has been a steady growing antagonism between Jews and Arabs . . . shown by many petty assaults and by children throwing stones at each other."[64]

The antagonism that was evident in 1933 and more so in 1942 was inflamed by anti-Jewish broadcasts from Egypt just before the partition of Palestine. The messages of hate were relayed in public meeting places and helped to incite Arabs against Jews in Aden.[65]

In addition to the Egyptian broadcasts, "Orders [were] issued by the Arab League to arrange strikes and protests against the decision to partition Palestine," and rumors were spread that the Jews had been killing Arabs.[66]

The pogrom that erupted on December 2, 1947, was devastating—82 Jews were murdered and 76 wounded; 106 out of the 170 existing Jewish shops in Aden were robbed bare and eight were partially emptied. Four synagogues were "burnt to the ground" and 220 Jewish houses were burned and looted or damaged.[67]

There were a few wealthier Jewish families who lived in an area called "Steamer Point," where passengers disembarked from the large liners.[68] But after the 1947 massacre most of Aden's Jews were isolated for their own security and "for months did not dare to venture out of" the Jewish Quarter. A visiting Jewish official reported in January 1949 that "one felt that the pogrom had taken place not a year ago but a week ago . . . the Jews still live in a state of tension and anxiety. . . . the Jews still erect barricades at night."[69]

Many thousands of the Aden Jews boarded the "wings of eagles" for Israel along with the Yemenite refugees.[70] In 1958 some were victimized by murder and looting, and those diehard Jews who had remained in Aden after the 1947 massacre were alarmed.[71]

A visitor at the time of the 1958 riots observed,

> It would seem that the problem of this Jewish community is not where to turn, but when to turn. They might be wise to remember that "he who hesitates is lost." They would not be the first Jewish community that waited too long.[72]

The remnant of the Jewish community in Aden was victimized again after the 1967 Six-Day War. Murder, looting, new destruction to the synagogues—Jews were finally evacuated with the help of the British, when they discovered the Arabs were planning to massacre what remained of the Jewish community. The Jewry of Aden became virtually "the community that was."[73]

Iraq

The Jews of Iraq, too, flew to Israel—between 1949 and 1952 alone, more than 123,000[74] Iraqi Jews escaped or were forced to flee to Israel and to leave their assets and communal holdings behind.

The Iraqi Jews took pride in their distinguished Jewish community, with its history of scholarship and dignity. Jews had prospered in what was then Babylonia for twelve hundred years before the Muslim conquest in A.D. 634;[75] it was not until the ninth century that *dhimma* laws such as the yellow patch, heavy head tax, and residence restrictions were enforced. Capricious and extreme oppression under some Arab caliphs and Mamluks brought taxation amounting to expropriation in A.D. 1000, and in 1333 the persecution culminated in pillage and destruction of the Baghdad synagogues. In 1776, there was a slaughter of Jews at Basra, and the bitterness of anti-Jewish measures taken by Turkish-Muslim rulers in the eighteenth century caused many Jews to flee.[76]

Just after the turn of the present century, the British vice-consul in Mosul wrote a report that illustrated the nature of the "traditional relationship" between Muslim and Jew in a less volatile moment:

> The attitude of the Moslems toward the Christians and Jews, to whom as stated above, they are in a majority of ten to one, is that of a master towards slaves whom he treats with a certain lordly tolerance so long as they keep their place. Any sign of pretension to equality is promptly repressed. It is often noticed in the streets that almost any Christian submissively makes way even for a Moslem child. Only a few days ago the writer saw two respectable looking, middle-aged Jews walking in a garden. A small Moslem boy, who could not have been more than 8 years old, passed by and, as he did so, picked up a large stone and threw it at them—

and then another—with the utmost nonchalance, just as a small boy elsewhere might aim at a dog or bird. The Jews stopped and avoided the aim, which was a good one, but made no further protest.[77]

There was a particularly fearsome period just before the British Mandate; with the outbreak of the First World War, Jews were forced to finance the military expenses of the army stationed nearby. If they refused, they were tortured, and if they hid, they were caught and hanged.[78] The Jews of Iraq actually welcomed the Arab revolt against the Turkish governors, and they rejoiced after the war when the state of Iraq was established under British Mandate.[79]

Some Jews were allowed to hold official posts; under the British Mandate Iraqi Jews were supposed to be treated as "equals." Many were writers, traders, and physicians, and some became quite wealthy through commerce and banking.

Near the end of the British reign, Hitler's accession to power began, and by the time Iraq declared independence in 1932, the German minister in Baghdad had organized an efficient and influential power base for Nazi propaganda.[80] Within the first year of Iraq's sovereignty, the new government benignly pronounced that minorities would continue to have some measure of freedom.

Almost immediately afterward, in August 1933, the Iraqi army massacred the Assyrians and the Jews began to feel increased foreboding. The *London Daily News* reported[81] that ". . . when the Iraq army returned after the weekend [following the Assyrian atrocity], not one Christian or Jew was seen on the streets." By now the increasingly violent demonstrations over the "Palestine problem" added to deteriorating conditions for the Jewish community; many Jews were murdered by agitated mobs,[82] nitric acid was thrown by terrorists upon Jews in the street, and bombs were flung into synagogues.[83]

In 1941 the violence exploded into a bloody *farhud*—massacre—of the Jews, with the police openly participating in the attack. The investigating committee appointed by the Iraqi government determined that "all these attacks were carried out by the army with the assistance of some civilians"; the massacre was executed "without the police arresting anyone or protecting the Jews," and "large British forces stood at the gates of the city, none of them lifting a finger."[84] "Judaism" was "a threat to mankind," the Iraqi Minister of Justice declared.[85]

According to the eminent Iraqi-born historian Professor Elie Kedourie, ". . . once the disorders started, . . . the soldiers and the police, debauched by Nazi propaganda, and bereft of leadership, ran amuck and themselves began the attacks on the Jews." None of the officials "were willing to assume the responsibility. . . ."

Cowardice was universal. . . . As for the police, the report of the investigating committee pertinently pointed out that they had no need to seek orders from their superiors for firing on looters and murderers caught in *flagrante delicto*. The director-general of police and his assistants and the *mutasarrif* forgot or feigned to forget, the report declared, that every member of the police had the right to fire in such circumstances.[86]

The number killed is uncertain—estimates range between 150 and "hundreds,"[87] but one member of the investigating committee "later told the chronicler Hasani (who had the story confirmed by the then-Baghdad chief of police) that the true figure was nearer six hundred but that the government was anxious for the lower figure only to appear in the official report."[88] Hundreds more were wounded, and more than a thousand Jewish-owned houses and businesses looted and destroyed.

From that time, Arab documents chronicle a systematic attempt by the government, using official means, to destroy the Iraqi Jewish community.[89] Jews suffered indiscriminate torture, imprisonment without charge, and relentless persecutions. When Iraq joined the Arab war against Israel's independence, in May 1948, government terror increased; Jews, who had been restricted to some degree from travel, now were forbidden to leave the country, and many fortunes were extorted or confiscated. Despite the law, thousands escaped illegally by paying heavy bribes.

After Israel's 1948 victory and official recognition of Jewish statehood, Nuri Said, fourteen times Prime Minister of Iraq, who "ruled the country in the 1950s irrespective of whether or not Nuri headed the cabinet himself,"[90] recommended a final Jewish solution for Iraq. Nuri Said proposed to the British Ambassador in Jordan at that time, Sir Alec Kirkbride, that "the majority of the Jewish community in Iraq" should be forcibly evicted "in army lorries escorted by armoured cars . . . to the Jordanian-Israel Frontier." There the "Iraqi Jews" would be ordered to "cross the line."[91]

Kirkbride later assessed the fate of Iraqi Jews, had Nuri Said's plan been enacted: "Either the Iraqi Jews would have been massacred or their Iraqi guards would have had to shoot other Arabs to protect the lives of their charge."[92] The likelihood of the Jews' protection by the Iraqi guards was remote, considering the precedent established by the police and army participation in the 1941 massacre. Nuri Said's solution, then, was unambiguous, as was the temper of Iraq toward its Jews.

Zionism became a capital crime, and Jews were publicly hanged in the center of Baghdad, with an enthusiastic mob as audience. Although no laws authorized the confiscation of Jewish property in Iraq before 1950,[93] the Jews were stripped of millions of dollars through economic discrimination, "voluntary donations" appropriated by the government, and other subterfuges.[94]

An Egyptian journal[95] reported in 1948 that all Iraqi Jews who went to Palestine and did not return would be tried in absentia as criminals. Those who were tried in absentia were sentenced to hang or serve extended prison sentences. There had been more than 130,000 Jews in Iraq in 1947, 100,000 of them living in or near Baghdad. Although some part of the Jews' property had already been expropriated, the bulk still remained in Jewish hands, while vast amounts were taken by officials who participated in illegal escapes.

Perhaps because of the desperate financial condition of the Iraqi government, Jewish "emigration" was legalized—upon confiscation of property and permanent loss of citizenship. In 1950, Iraq enacted a law that allowed Jews to "leave Iraq for good."[96] The Jews left their vast accumulated holdings behind, and within the first three years of the law, most of them were flown to Israel, with the Iraqi government taking "a handsome share of the profits" produced by the flights.[97]

Thus, the Jews—who, according to Nuri Said, "have always been and will forever be a source of evil and mischief"—had largely been forced from Iraq.[98]

Between 1969 and 1973 at least seventeen Jews were hanged in a public square, and twenty-six others were "slaughtered" in their homes or in Iraqi prisons.[99] As of 1982, most of Iraq's Jewry had found refuge in Israel, and several thousand had found sanctuary elsewhere.

Egypt

In 1948, 75,000 Jews lived in Egypt, in a community dating back to before the Babylonian captivity.[100] After the Arab conquest, Jews in Egypt, as in other Arab countries, lived at the whim of erratic Arab sovereignty. One Arab caliph invoked *sunna* ("the Muslim term for customs ascribed to Mohammed") to tyrannize the Jews and Christians in Cairo in the ninth and tenth centuries.[101] Under the caliphs of Baghdad[102] life was restrictive at times, and generally unpredictable.

One caliph, al-Hakim of the Fatimids, devised particularly insidious humiliations for the Jews in his attempt to perform what he deemed his role as "Redeemer of Mankind." First the Jews were forced to wear miniature golden calf images around their necks, as though they still worshiped the Golden Calf. But the Jews refused to convert. Next they wore bells, and after that, six-pound wooden blocks were hung around their necks. In fury at his failure, the caliph had the Cairo Jewish Quarter destroyed, along with its Jewish residents, in 1012.[103]

The rule of the Ayyubids (1171–1250) continued the demeaning *dhimma* laws,[104] and during the thirteenth-century reign of the Burji Mamluks, Jews were particularly sought out for attack, with the result that the Jewish population "greatly declined."[105] At the end of the thirteenth century, the poll tax, or head tax, was "reintroduced in Egypt, where it had fallen into oblivion,"[106] and in the fourteenth century Jews were subject to "anti-dhimmi" mob "riots." With the reign of "mainly" Circassian-born Mamluks, "the prevailing attitude . . . was more severe than ever."[107] In the sixteenth century, a religious fanatic wreaked terror among the Jews in Cairo. "He regarded himself as a religious and moral reformer and whipped and mulcted the Jews . . . in Cairo, where the Mamluk sultan Kanush al-Ghauri was then in power."[108]

From even those scholars who have documented the Arab persecution of Jews, there are accounts of a "flourishing" Jewish community in Egypt under the Ottoman rule.[109] Yet Edward Lane's definitive report of the first half of the nineteenth century, which asserts that "the Jews . . . are under a less oppressive government in Egypt than in any other country of the Turkish empire,"[110] puts the Jews' role in general, and the relatively "flourishing" Egyptian Jewry, into a somewhat more realistic perspective by that report's description of Egypt's "less oppressed" Jews:

> They [the Jews] are held in the utmost contempt and abhorrence by the Muslims in general . . . the Jews are detested by the Muslims far more than are the Christians. Not long ago, they used often to be jostled in the streets of Cairo, and sometimes beaten merely for passing on the right hand of a Muslim. At present, they are less oppressed; but still they scarcely ever dare to utter a word of abuse when reviled or beaten unjustly by the meanest Arab or Turk; for many a Jew has been put to death upon a false and malicious accusation of uttering disrespectful words against the Kur-an or the Prophet. It is common to hear an Arab abuse his jaded ass, and, after applying to him various opprobrious epithets, end by calling the beast a Jew.
>
> A Jew has often been sacrificed to save a Muslim, as happened in the following case.—A Turkish soldier, having occasion to change some money, received from the seyrefee (or money-changer), who was a Muslim, some Turkish coins called 'adleeyehs, reckoned at sixteen piasters each. These he offered to a shopkeeper, in payment for some goods; but the latter refused to allow him more than fifteen piasters to the 'adleeyeh; telling him that the Básha had given orders, many days before, that this coin should no longer pass for sixteen. The soldier took back the 'adleeyehs to the seyrefee, and demanded an additional piaster to each; which was refused: he therefore complained to the Básha himself, who, enraged that his orders had been disregarded, sent for the seyrefee. This man confessed that he had been guilty of an offence; but endeavored to palliate it by asserting that almost every money-changer in the city had done the same, and that he had received 'adleeyehs at the same rate. The Básha, however, disbelieving him or thinking it necessary to make a public example, gave a signal with his hand, intimating that the delinquent should be beheaded. The interpreter of the court, moved with compassion for the unfortunate man, begged to the Básha to spare his life. "This man," said he, "had done no more than all the money-changers of the city; I, myself, no longer than yesterday, received 'adleeyehs at the same rate." "From whom?" exclaimed the Básha. "From a Jew," answered the interpreter, "with whom I have transacted business for many years." The Jew was brought, and sentenced to be hanged; while the Muslim was pardoned. The interpreter, in the greatest of distress of mind, pleaded earnestly for the life of the poor Jew: but the Básha was inexorable: it was necessary that an example should be made; and it was deemed better to take the life of a Jew than that of a more guilty Muslim. I saw the wretched man hanging at a window of a public fountain which forms part of a mosque in the main street of the city.* One end of the rope being passed over one of the upper bars of the grated window, he was hauled up; and as he hung close against the window, he was enabled, in some slight degree, to support himself by his feet against the lower bars; by which his suffering was dreadfully protracted. His relations offered large sums of money for his pardon; but the only

---

*"It is surprising that Muslims should hang a Jew against a window of a mosque, when they consider him so unclean a creature that his blood would defile the sword. For this reason a Jew, in Egypt, is never beheaded."

favour they could purchase was that of having his face turned towards the window, so as not to be seen by the passengers. He was a man much respected by all who knew him (Muslims, of course, excepted); and he left a family in a very destitute state; but the interpreter who was the unintending cause of his death contributed to their support.[111]

One historian has documented persistent blood libel persecutions throughout nineteenth-century Egypt—six separate instances between 1870 and 1892 alone, preceded by others—in 1844 in Cairo, where "Muslims . . . despised and sometimes abused the Jews," and even in such cosmopolitan communities as Alexandria, in 1869.[112] That such acts "undermined the confidence of the Egyptian Jews" was the cautious conclusion drawn by the definitive historian of the subject.

Among the populous Muslim peasant (*fellahin*) community, the Jews were not better off. A Britisher long connected with the *fellahin* through his Egyptian government job, reported in 1888 that "Armenians, Syrians, Circassians, Jews, are all hated as well as the Turk himself. I think it would be difficult to discover which particular race is most hated (by the Egyptian *fallahin*) [*sic*] but I fancy that the Jew or Armenian would take the palm. I mention Jews because one of the most powerful and disliked Pashas . . . is spoken [of] by many as a Jew, and always in terms of disgust."[113]

In 1890 an Egyptian version of the false charge "documenting" the "Human Sacrifices in the Talmud" was published in Cairo.[114] Anti-Jewish "agitation" and persecution of the Jews in Port Said was frequent between the 1880s and 1908, when a Jewish leader in Cairo wrote of concern for the "insecurity of Port Said's Jews."[115]

In 1926 the first Egyptian Nationality Code established that Egyptian citizenship would be offered only to those who belonged "racially to the majority of the population of a country whose language is Arabic or whose religion is Islam."[116] From the late 1930s, Egyptian nationalism, Arab unity against Zionists, and Nazi propaganda fused with traditional prejudice to ignite violently against the Jews.[117] Often the destruction victimized other infidels. One such major incident was the burning of synagogues and churches, and other communal buildings belonging to non-Muslims.[118]

Beginning in the forties, many Jews were killed or injured in organized anti-Jewish riots, putting into fearsome perspective the 1946 report that "the general position of the Jews in Egypt is beyond comparison better than any [Arab and Muslim] country so far. . . ."[119] Jews suffered extensive economic losses when the Egyptians passed a law that largely precluded Jews from employment; the government confiscated much Jewish property and "wrecked" the economic condition of the Jews within a few months.[120] In the days following the November 1947 vote to partition Palestine, Jews in Cairo and Alexandria were threatened with death, their houses were looted, and synagogues were attacked.[121]

Anti-Jewish riots were rampant in 1948. According to an eyewitness account, in one seven-day period, 150 Jews were murdered or seriously wounded.[122] Perhaps the letter to the editor of an Egyptian newspaper from a Muslim provides an insight to the hazards of Jewish life then:

> It seems that most people in Egypt are unaware of the fact that, among the Moslem Egyptians, there are some of white skin. Every time I take the tramway I hear people around me saying, while pointing at me with their fingers, "A Jew . . . a Jew. . . ." I have been beaten more than once because of this. This is why I beg you kindly to publish my photo, specifying that I am not a Jew and that my name is Adham Moustafa Ghaleb.[123]

With the outbreak of the 1948 war, Egyptian Jews were barred from leaving Egypt, whether for Israel or elsewhere. Then, early in August 1949, the ban was abruptly lifted, and much sequestered Jewish property was returned.

From August until November of 1949, more than 20,000 of Egypt's 75,000 Jews fled, many to Israel.[124] There was a brief and surprising period under the more tolerant leadership of General Muhammad Naguib, but he was overthrown by General Gamal Abdel Nasser, who authorized mass arrests and property confiscation. At the beginning of 1955 the Nasser regime hanged two Egyptian Jews as "Zionist spies," an action the Egyptian Embassy in Washington justified by distributing a pamphlet called "The Story of the Zionist Espionage in Egypt," claiming that "Zionism and Communism" both sought "world domination."[125] After the Sinai Campaign of 1956, thousands of Jews were interned without trial,[126] while still other thousands were served with deportation papers and ordered to leave within a few days; their property was confiscated, their assets frozen.[127]

Worldwide concern for Egypt's Jews was evidenced in 1957 by the statement issued at an international conference of Jewish organizations:

> Large numbers of Jews of all nationalities have either been served with orders of expulsion or were subjected to ruthless intimidation to compel them to apply for permission to depart. Hundreds who have reached lands of refuge have testified that they were taken in shackles from prison and concentration camps to board ships. In order to ensure that this deliberate creation of a new refugee problem should not evoke protests from international public opinion, documents proving expulsion were taken away from expellees before departure. Furthermore, they were compelled to sign statements that they left voluntarily. The victims of this barbaric process were deprived of their possessions.[128]

The 1926 Nationality Code, with its racist tone, was "reinforced" by a 1956 version excluding "Zionists."[129] That law was "regulated" still further in 1958 by the Egyptian Minister of the Interior, stating in "unambiguous terms that all Jews between the ages of 10 and 65, leaving Egypt, are to be added to the list of persons who are prohibited from returning to Egypt."[130]

In 1964 President Gamal Abdel Nasser declared, in an interview, that Egypt still pledged allegiance to the old Nazi cause: "Our sympathy was with the Germans." Nasser gave an example of that loyalty: "The president of our Parliament, for instance, Anwar Sa'adat, was imprisoned for his sympathy with the Germans."[131] Anti-Jewish publications deluged Egypt—including the infamous "Protocols"—many of them circulated by the Egyptian government.[132] When the Six-Day War began, Jews were arrested and held in concentration camps, where they were beaten and whipped, deprived of water for days on end and forced to chant anti-Israel slogans.[133] By 1970, these Jews too had escaped the country. "Egypt," according to the officer in charge of an internment camp, ". . . had no place for the Jews. . . ."[134]

Morocco

From the Maghreb, known as North Africa, more than 300,000 Jews have crowded into Israel[135] since 1948. Almost 250,000 of them arrived from what is now Morocco, where Jews have lived since 586 B.C. The history of the Jews under Arab rule in North Africa is turbulent and erratic. The conditions of their lives as infidels under the Charter of Omar might have been bearable under a more tolerant Arab caliph of one region, while at the same time, in another, Jews would have been under siege, or massacred.[136]

Practically from the beginning of the seventh-century Arab conquest, Jews were forced to live separately—in Morocco the ghetto was called *mellah,* while in Tunisia the Jewish area was a *hara.* Some "Jewish tribes" had lived separately for "reasons of convenience," in some pre-Islamic periods, but now Jewish Quarters were *imposed* by the Arab conquerors of North Africa, with their "special Maghrebi" type of Islam—the "Malakite *madhhab,* school most intolerant of non-Muslims," and "the establishment of the *tariqas,* mystical fraternities headed by religious fanatics."[137]

Because most of the Christian minority fled—those who had not been massacred or converted to Islam by the twelfth century[138]—restrictions became increasingly harsh toward the Jew. Native Jews were the sole *dhimmi* group who had neither the inclination toward conversion nor the Christian's claim to his European community's protection.[139] Although the *dhimma* law was amended in the eleventh century to allow a Jew to hold office—with authority limited to taking orders, not giving them—the one Jew who rose to real power in the thirteenth century was murdered with his family when he became the object of envy among his Muslim rivals.[140]

Despite their general misery and deprivation, some Jews managed to accumulate wealth.[141] However, most Jews were outcasts who suffered not only the traditional contempt of the *dhimma* code, but were subject to imaginative interpretations thereof. Slaps in the face upon payment of the head tax, bullying, and insults were everyday occurrences. Rapes and looting, burning of synagogues, ripping of sacred Torah scrolls, even murder—all were "so frequent that it is impossible to list them."[142]

In 1032, 6,000 Jews of Fez were murdered, and still others were "robbed of their women and their property."[143] In 1146, Fez was attacked by the Almohads, leaving "one hundred thousand persons killed." Marrakesh suffered similarly, when an unbelievable "one hundred twenty thousand" were slaughtered. According to an account of "eye-witness" reports, "On entering, . . . the Almohads tried to convert the Jews to Islam by debate and persuasion . . ." until "a new commander . . . solved the problem by a more efficient method. One hundred and fifty were killed . . . the remainder converted. . . ."[144]

One of the frequent violent power struggles among Muslims that especially affected the Jews, the Almohad atrocities left a deep imprint on Jews throughout North Africa. Those few Christians still in the region were "completely wiped out" by the Almohads, leaving the Jews as lone infidel survivors to suffer "the spite of the second Almohad generation."[145] Forced conversion to Islam, death, or exile were the choices for the survivors of the Almohad massacres.

It was the brutality of the persecution against Morocco's Jews that inspired Moses Maimonides to write the "Epistle Concerning Apostasy," in 1160, exhorting the Jews to remain true to Judaism.[146]

Maimonides reminded the persecuted Moroccans:

> Now we are asked not to render active homage to heathenism but only to recite an empty formula which the Moslems themselves knew we utter insincerely in order to circumvent the bigot. . . . Indeed, any Jew who, after uttering the Moslem formula, wishes to observe the whole 613 precepts in the privacy of his home, may do so without hindrance. Nevertheless, if, even under these circumstances, a Jew surrenders his life for the sanctification of the name of God before men, he has done nobly and well, and his reward is great before the Lord. But if a man asks me, "Shall I be slain or utter the formula of Islam?" I answer, "utter the formula and live. . . ."[147]

Because of the practical advice Maimonides gave to the Jews—keep the faith while appearing to go through the motions of conversion in order to stay alive—Maimonides became a marked man among the Arabs. He had written his letter in Arabic, so that all the Jews in the area would be able to read it, but Maimonides made enemies among the Muslims, who also read it. He was warned by a Muslim poet that suspicion had "already fallen on the writer of the *Letter*."[148]

At the same time, his friend, Ibn Shoshan, was "attacked and hacked to death in the course of an aroused religious frenzy." Perhaps that was the moment Maimonides decided to leave his home in Fez.

Some Jews chose conversion. But those who chose to be Islamicized, rather than the inexorable alternative, found they were considered "Muslims of Jewish origin," ordered to continued demeanment and separateness. A thirteenth-century Arab historian quoted one ruler of the twelfth century who insisted that "the new Muslims" wear humiliating garments despite their conversion. Abu Yusif Ya'qub confided,

> If I were sure that these Jews have wholeheartedly embraced Islam, I should permit them to mix with the Muslims by marriage and in every other way. And

if I were certain that they are infidels, I should put the men to death, sell their children into slavery and confiscate their property in favour of the believers. But I am perplexed about the matter.[149]

In the latter part of the thirteenth century, "immediately before the founding of the New City [of Fez], the Muslims in the Old City rioted against the Jews."[150]

One of the cruelest of the "forced Muslim" deprivations was denial of the right to raise children, "who were considered Muslims from birth," while the converted parents were deemed not to be true Muslims. "According to Islamic law, a non-Muslim cannot be the natural . . . guardian of Muslim children."[151]

Many Jews among those who had chosen conversion over death or slavery continued to practice Judaism in secret. Whole Jewish movements were developed from their furtive but persistent fidelity to their faith.[152] And into modern times, the words "hypocrite" and "hypocritical" and other expressions of suspicion run throughout the modern writings of Arab theologians paraphrasing the Koran—"saying with their lips what was not in their hearts." "When they meet those who believe, they say: 'we believe.' " The converts were rarely if ever trusted despite their apparent renunciation of Judaism.[153]

A relatively small number, particularly Jewish scholars of the Maghreb, sought asylum and escape from the death-or-conversion dilemma in Syria, Palestine, Egypt or Italy.[154] But exile was generally unlikely—the North African Jews had hardly anywhere to go. In fact, it was *to* Morocco that many of the exiled Spanish and Portuguese Jews escaped, seeking sanctuary in 1391. Their reception was described thus: ". . . those who went to Arab countries endured untold suffering. . . . Especially the villagers rose against them—saying that they were protecting their religion—and put them in chains . . . part were impelled by their tribulations to say: Let us make a captain, and let us return. . . ."[155]

While Jewish martyrs had impotently defended themselves against insuperable odds, most Jews learned that the only comparative safety was to take cover in their *mellahs* until the storm had passed. Fez was the scene of repeated anti-Jewish scourges in the early fifteenth century. Jews were "plundered" by the Moors "from time to time," as "upon the death of a king." They were eventually "transferred to the new city of Fez."[156] But anti-Jewish propaganda was used to incite Muslim masses in a power struggle and many Jewish lives were taken. In 1465 Muslims of Fez attacked the collective Jewish community, accusing the Jews when they found a slain Muslim. "Men, women and children were killed . . . and only a few families escaped."[157]

The fact that "a few Jews" were appointed to the service of the Merenid rulers in the thirteenth through fifteenth centuries "ought not to be interpreted" as evidence of harmony between the Muslims and Jews; according to Norman Stillman's comprehensive study *The Jews in Arab Lands,* it was the "marginal" status of Jews in Morocco—without any "power base"—that made the Jews at times most desirable as courtiers: because they found "no sympathy among the Muslim masses," they were "totally dependent upon their masters."[158]

The bulk of Moroccan Jewry suffered still greater humiliation and brutality when Morocco was cut off from the rest of the Maghreb.[159] Although a Jewish elite existed—one that achieved intellectual recognition as well as commercial and diplomatic success in the sixteenth century[160]—"indeed, there were few [Jewish] communities in Morocco and Algeria which escaped pillage and even massacre."[161]

The "fierce persecution of 1640, called the al-Khada," was described by a victim of another assault, in a rare ancient manuscript; this report illustrates that in rare instances of Jew insulting Muslim, the Muslims reaped vengeance upon the entire Jewish community with utter disregard for individual innocence or guilt.

> . . . in Fez, . . . the persecution . . . occurred because the Jews had become so arrogant and lawless that they went to the Great Mosque, stopped up the source of the water pouring forth there and filled the marble basin from which the water poured with wine and drank there all night, and at daybreak they went away, leaving one Jew there drunk and asleep. And the Gentiles came and found him there, and they killed all the male Jews who were there, and only those escaped who changed their religion. And they killed children and women and brought Jews from another place and settled them in their stead. And during the second persecution, it was decreed that the Jews might only wear a garment made of hair. All this I found written on some faded paper, and I copied it in order that it might be remembered. I, the poorest of my clan, the smallest on earth, the lowliest of all, Moses the son of the honorable teacher and rabbi, Rabbi Jacob Gavison, may the Lord protect him and keep him alive. Tuesday, the 17th day of Tammuz (may God turn it to the good), 5449/1689.[162]

Down through the nineteenth century, the Jews' existence in Morocco remained insecure and tenuous, their misery often recorded by foreigners. The Jews were subjected at various times under Islam to *"such repression, restriction and humiliation as to exceed anything in Europe."*[163]*

Charles de Foucauld, a French officer who posed for two years as a rabbi in an intelligence-gathering mission, was one of many who recorded Jewish life under Arab rule in nineteenth-century Morocco:

> Bled white without restraint, . . . they are the most unfortunate of men. . . . Every Jew . . . belongs body and soul to his seigneur, the sid. . . . He came into the sid's possession through inheritance, as part of his personal belongings under the rules of Moslem law. . . . If he had settled only recently in the place where he lived, then immediately on his arrival, he had to become some Moslem's Jew. Once having rendered homage, he was bound forever, he and his descendants. . . . Nothing in the world protected the Jew against his seigneur: he was entirely at his mercy.[164]

*Emphasis added.

De Foucauld was not sympathetic to the Jews generally, as many of his descriptions in "Reconnaissance au Maroc" illustrate, yet his accounts are poignant—of Jewish children being snatched, slaves sold at auction, robbery followed by expulsion of whole *mellahs* and Arab enjoyment of Jewish wives; when "the *sid* was headstrong and a spendthrift, his treatment of his Jews [was] like the squandering of an inheritance."

In even the "most fortunate of *mellahs,*" the miserable physical existence of Jews prevailed. Yet those regions which the Turks had captured for their empire found the Jews less desperate, occasionally affluent, and even wealthy by contrast. The wealth was accumulated through those limited occupations that Jews' political subjection would allow; although there were exceptions, the Jews became mainly occupied in trades that allowed for quick departure, and in which they could take their accumulations with them—namely, hard currency.

The brutal carnage, however, did not cease for long. Five hundred Jews were killed in Marrakesh and Fez by "Muslim mobs" in 1864.[165] Two decades afterward, a "savage anti-Jewish" attack on the Jews of Demnate created a furor in the world's Jewish press.[166]

French rule came to Morocco in 1912, and brought welcome relief for the Jews, despite yet another pogrom in Fez that killed sixty Jews and left 10,000 homeless.[167] Because Moroccans were not granted French protection in the same fashion as Algerian or Tunisian Jewry, local Arab rule continued and the Jews remained *dhimmi;* nonetheless, their confusing situation—between French rule and Muslim tradition—was measurably improved.[168]

By 1948, Jews had become nominally involved in local politics. When Israel was established, French authorities kept vigilant watch, struggling to maintain an equilibrium between the Muslim and Jewish communities, and the Muslim sultan appealed to his subjects to restrain violence against the Jews—reminding them of the protection Morocco had always given to its Jews.[169]

Early in June 1948, mob violence erupted simultaneously against the Jewish communities of several towns in northern Morocco, resulting in dozens of Jewish deaths. Shortly afterward, the first major group of Moroccan Jews—30,000—fled to Israel. The fate of Morocco's Jewish community fluctuated with each strong political wind: Moroccan independence as an Arab state was declared in 1956, and although emigration to Israel was declared illegal, 70,000 more Jews managed to arrive in the Jewish state. The sultan's return was followed by appointment of Jews to major government posts—then, in 1959, Zionism became a crime. Two years later a new king ascended the throne and attempted to ease the panic among the Jews by legalizing emigration, but when he lifted the ban, another hundred thousand made their way to Israel.

Israeli victory in the 1967 war brought heightened hostilities from Muslim mobs, and by 1982 Moroccan Jewry had shrunk to less than ten percent of its former number.

Algeria

The fate of Algeria's Jewish community was harsh; despite some historians' judgments that life for the Jews there was relatively calmer than nearby Morocco's, the two were often interchangeable. At the end of the fourteenth century, the Jews of the town of Tlemcen were persecuted to such extremes that one eminent historian states that there is no indication of "how the indigenous Jews managed to survive the period of tribulations."[170]

Even on the edge of the Sahara Desert, the Jews were plundered and murdered. In late-fifteenth-century Tu'-at, an "oasis" town, a sheikh incited the Muslims by accusing the Jews of "sorcery" and of the arrogance of their failing to conform to the "discriminatory" codes; many Jews were killed and others forced to wear conspicuous and peculiar garb. This took place, ironically, in 1492, when the Jews were expelled from Spain and were wearily arriving in North Africa in search of respite from persecution.[171]

In the sixteenth century, Tlemcen was still a site of tribulation for its Jewish community. The town was an important power base and, regardless of who the changing parties to the power struggle happened to be, the Jews were invariably attacked. Some were forcibly converted, others were sold into slavery, still others "thrown into prison" to await their redemption, which sometimes came, but in the form of "a heavy ransom."[172]

The Algerian Jewish community continued to bear the outrages of local "protectors," even after Algeria came under Turkish domination. In 1801 a would-be ruler promised, in return for assisting the overthrow of a rival, to give the soldiers "8 times their pay, white bread and the right to sack the Jews for three days."[173] In the next fifteen years, hundreds of Jews were massacred; during one episode three hundred Jews were slaughtered within a few hours, while as the result of another carnage, the Algerian Chief Rabbi was decapitated. The murder of a Jew by a soldier sparked yet another bloodletting: while desecrating a synagogue, it claimed among its victims more than a dozen Jews who were at prayer.

An American consul in Algiers from 1816 until 1828 described conditions thus:

> The Jews suffer frightful oppressions. They are forbidden to offer resistance when they are maltreated by a Moslem, no matter what the nature of the violence. They do not have the right to bear arms of any sort, not even a cane. . . . A number of times when the janissaries [army] revolted, the Jews were pillaged indiscriminately; they are still tormented by the fear of similar occurrences. . . . Their lives [are] nothing but . . . debasement, oppression and outrage. I believe that today the Jews of Algiers are perhaps the most unhappy remnant of Israel.[174]

Recognizing the history of frequent ravages, one historian writes, nevertheless, that "Algeria was relatively peaceful"[175] compared with Morocco, while another asserts the Algerian government was "most oppressive."[176] Perhaps the reason for what appears to be a historians' dispute can be clarified somewhat by an eminent scholar's description of the limitations imposed even upon Jews of "wealth": because "Jews were the only non-Muslims, . . . Jews were the only persons who traveled to European countries on political missions, and were agents and vice-consuls of European states. . . . At the same time, that wealthy stratum that had access to the authorities . . . did not enjoy a favored status with the Muslim rulers; they were subject to the same humiliations as their fellow Jews."[177] For the relatively few Jews who possessed it, wealth, that universal symbol of success, tended to be misleading, and the trappings of affluence encouraged misinterpretation, when applied as a measure of freedom for the Jews in Arab lands.

In 1830 Algeria was occupied by the French, marking the end of North Africa as a single political entity. The French colonization also signaled Algerian Jews' release from their unpredictable fate under Muslim rule. Although the French culture never was to penetrate local customs or alter religious rites,[178] the French were greeted by a deliriously happy Jewish community, which burst into freedom with exuberance. Jews became prime organizers in establishing schools, and in 1870 they were granted the dignity of French citizenship.

There was resentment at the new Jewish freedoms, however, and Jews once again became the target for hostile action—in Tlemcen, 1881; Oran, 1883; and Algiers, 1882, 1897, and 1898.[179] This time, however, the Muslims were not solely responsible; it was the European political element that incited a smear campaign in the press. Synagogues were once again desecrated, Jews were robbed and murdered, and anti-Jewish riots and massacres commenced. In 1898 anti-Jewish riots erupted in all the principal communities of Algeria.[180]

The ascent of Nazi Germany gave rise to new waves of anti-Semitism, which reinforced compatible Muslim attitudes of the past. "The swastika appeared everywhere."[181] The massacre at Constantine in 1934 left twenty-five Jews slain, dozens wounded, and Jewish property once again pillaged.[182] Muslims involved in the massacre were apprehended and the year afterward they came to trial, where "it became clear that the almost criminal ineffectiveness of the local authorities" had facilitated the attack.[183]

The appointment of a Jew as Premier of France[184] further inflamed the Nazi-incited Algerians. Then, in 1940, the Nazi-allied Vichy government took over. Jews were stripped of French citizenship, banned from schools and public activities, and rendered "pariahs"[185] through the passage of a new law.[186] Only the Allies' landing prevented the transfer of Algerian Jews to European death camps. It should be noted particularly, however, that Messali Hadj, the "father of the Algerian Nationalist movement," refused to support Nazi Germany's policies.[187]

The Jews struggled against the Vichy regime along with the Algerian Resistance.[188] After World War II, when they attempted neutrality between the French and the Nationalists, during the struggle for Algerian independence, their neutrality backfired—the Jewish Algerians were hit by both factions. In addition,

Algeria now had forged stronger links with the Arab League, which redounded to the detriment of the Jews. In 1960, Jewish Agency officials were kidnapped and assassinated; the historic and venerated Great Synagogue in Algiers and the Jewish cemetery in Oran were desecrated.[189] Jews were threatened ominously by the Arab Liberation Party.

The Jews, a people who had "arrived with the victory of the first conquerors" (the Phoenicians), left 2,500 years afterward.[190] The Jewish community of Algeria, which had numbered 140,000 in 1948, diminished within months; many thousands of Jews fled to Israel, and 125,000 went to France. In 1962 Algeria gained independence as an Arab state—one that the Algerian Liberation Front had touted as a "secular democratic state"; that the Jews of Algeria had largely disappeared was fortunate, because the Nationality Code of 1963 permitted "secular democratic" Algerian citizenship only to those residents whose father and paternal grandfather were Muslim.[191]

Tunisia

Tunisian Jewry, along with the other Maghrebi Jewish communities, has been relegated to "a backwater of Jewish history"—mainly because of the comparatively meager supply of source material readily accessible until recently to Jewish historians, and also because, generally, the Arab historians understandably dwelt upon the Islamic chronicles, touching only peripherally the infidel communities.[192] Painstaking research by present-day scholars has closed the historical gap. The Jews of Tunisia "existed continuously for about 2300 years," numbering among them important intellectual and religious leaders, and, sporadically, prominent international traders.

An apparently paradoxical role as detested *dhimmi* was allotted to the Jews at the same time: it is important to understand the special "otherness" of the Jew even in what some historians have judged to be the periods of "splendour" for the Jews in Arab lands.

For example, perhaps the definitive historian on the North African Jews, H. Z. Hirschberg, notes that in fifteenth-century Tunis, several Jews held "positions of honor." To a Western-oriented reader, the "position of honor" would indicate freedom from persecution. Yet an authenticated and respected document of that period, written by a visiting Flemish nobleman, describes Tunisian Jews as "despised and hated." After noting the privileged positions of local Christians, the nobleman wrote:

> The Jews, on the other hand, have no freedom. They must all pay a heavy . . . tax. They wear special clothes, different from those of the Moors. If they did not do so, they would be stoned, and they therefore put a yellow cloth on their heads or necks; their women dare not even wear shoes. They are much despised and hated, more than even the Latin Christians. . . .[193]

When confronting the fact that the Flemish nobleman's observations contradicted his findings, the historian explained that the "special yellow headgear of the Jews" was a mark of "native-born [Jewish] residents and not foreign traders. . . . The contempt shown to the wearers of the yellow headgear, and their fear of transgressing the discriminatory regulations, likewise indicate that the reference is to people not enjoying the protection of a European state."[194] Those foreign Jewish traders wore a "round cape" to distinguish them.[195]

Yet the historian notes that even "wearers of round capes" were subject to similar "humiliations." The point is that, through the careful, even hair-splitting research that establishes fact, academic disputes can result in the spreading of erroneous assumptions, which have had important political consequences in the Middle East refugee matter. While one scholar might argue that the Arab Muslims' massacres of Jews were "not necessarily specifically anti-Semitic," and another might conclude, from a superficial look at the incomplete source material readily available, that Jews in Arab countries were "better off than Jews in Europe," their statements, out of context, are misleading, and when quoted often enough, can serve as a conduit to the misconception that "harmony" and "equality" existed for Jews in Arab lands. Such obviously was not the case.

From the seventh-century Arab conquest down through the Almohad atrocities, Tunisia fared little better than its neighbors.[196] The "complete expulsion" of Jews from Kairouan, near Tunis, occurred after years of hardship, in the thirteenth century, when Kairouan was anointed as a holy city of Islam.[197] In the sixteenth century, the "hated and despised" Jews of Tunis were periodically attacked by violence, and they were subjected to "vehement anti-Jewish policy" during the various political struggles of the period.[198]

An Arab historian offered insight into the enormous uncertainty of Jewish life in Tunisia at that time: in 1515, the "fanatically religious" founder of the Saad Dynasty in Morocco incited the Muslims to anti-Jewish hostilities as he was "passing through Tunis on a pilgrimage to Mecca" by delivering inflammatory speeches against the Jews. He even extorted "contributions" from the objects of his capricious chastisement.[199]

Tunisian Jews were somewhat better off than either their Algerian or Moroccan brothers at times throughout the last few centuries,[200] but the separate Jewish Quarter, or *hara,* of Tunisia was not much less squalid and miserable than were other North African ghettos before French rule began. Jews were permitted to live as *dhimmis,* and as such, they led an uncertain existence at the alternating inclinations of their overlords. The smaller community of Jewish elite in Tunisia was allowed by more moderate sovereigns to engage in commerce and, from earliest times, eminent scholars and rabbis emerged from the Tunisian ghettos.

Yet, a historian reminds us,

The success that Tunisia's Jews achieved in the various trades and professions should not . . . obscure the fact that there also existed . . . a large group of Jews of the lowest social status—the Jew of the *hara*. This urban proletariat was only slightly less unfortunate than that of the Moroccan *mellah* and there were many thousands of people who . . . were permanently unemployed, the . . . misfits. . . .[201]

An Italian observer described the *hara* of the mid-nineteenth century: "the . . . hara appears as a labyrinth of muddy narrow alleys lined with ancient tumble-down buildings, at times frighteningly so, with middens of filth at the entry to the house. It lodges thousands of persons who live a life of hardship. . . ."[202]

When Muhammad Bey ascended the throne in 1855, he abolished the special *dhimma* tax for Jews, the first real attempt at legal reform of the contemptible infidel status.[203] The reaction in the Muslim community was hostile and immediate: the old *dhimma* law—whereby the word of a Jew was unacceptable in defense of a Muslim's charge of blasphemy against Islam—was invoked against a Jew. The Bey refused to intervene, and the Jew was decapitated.[204]

The Muslim society had been unprepared for the Bey's attempt at uprooting its traditional persecution, and the revolution of 1864 sufficiently intimidated the Bey so that he was compelled to revoke the new liberal laws. Some ravages in the aftermath of that 1864 revolt are described among eyewitness reports.[205] One witness wrote:

> Another disaster to report! Muslim fanaticism . . . unleashed against our brethren on the island of Djerba. . . . Arab tribes . . . turned upon . . . the Jewish Quarters, which they sacked, destroying everything. . . . [On] Yom Kippur . . . synagogues profaned and defiled. The Scrolls . . . torn in pieces and burnt . . . men injured and trampled . . . all the women and girls raped. . . . My pen refuses to set down the terrifying . . . atrocities . . . in all [their] horror. . . . The governor of the island refused to intervene to re-establish order; . . . the pillage did not cease for 5 days and nights. . . .[206]

Another complained of the Tunisian ruler's deviations:

> The Sovereign of Tunis found nothing better to do to pass the . . . Ramadan than to take by force—on the pretext that he had become a Muslim—a Jewish youth . . . not yet 15! He had the victim shut up in the men's seraglio and obstinately refuses to give him up to his parents. . . .[207]

An outraged writer bitterly assailed the government's "protection":

> Eighteen Jews have already fallen in a few months to the knives of fanatical [Muslim] murderers; and His Highness's Government, far from punishing the guilty, protects and apparently encourages them.
>
> The Government's conduct toward us is macchiavellian beyond words. *We are not directly persecuted but such is the scornful treatment we receive, when we ask for justice from the Bey or his ministers, that open persecution would be a hundred times better. Acknowledged persecution however, would expose the executioner and his victim to the world, and the Tunisian Government wishes to appear*

impartial, whilst masking killers surreptitiously. * . . . We do not seek an eye for an eye, blood for blood, but that the guilty should be . . . legally condemned.†[208]

A Jew from Tunis protested assassinations in a neighboring community:

Nabel is a town of fanatics, and we must unfortunately record six other murders of our co-religionists, the perpetrators of which have not been punished. . . .[209]

The violence spread in 1869 to the city of Tunis, where Muslims butchered many Jews in the defenseless ghetto. The French Protectorate was established in Tunisia in 1881, and life improved considerably for many Tunisian Jews. In 1910 they were allowed to become French citizens, though they were not fully accepted in Muslim and French societies.[210]

The subsequent Nazi occupation and Vichy regime did not improve conditions; the Great Synagogue in Tunis was put into use as a Nazi stable. When Tunisia became independent in 1956, a Jew was included in the Bourguiba cabinet, while at the same time, paradoxically, an authoritative report published in 1956 stressed that "the Jew in Tunisia has lost his position of middle man in the distributive industry—with commerce becoming more and more the privilege of a Moslem caste. . . ."[211]

The Jews of Tunisia soon began to flee from the extremism that the "Arabization" policy of the government had fostered. Of 105,000 Jews in 1948, 50,000 emigrated to Israel and roughly the same number have gone to France and elsewhere.

Syria

Jewish history in Syria began in biblical times. By A.D. 70, 10,000 Jews dwelt in Damascus, and a consistent Syrian Jewish presence was maintained for more than two millennia. From the time of the Arab conquest, the Jews' position in Syria was found by a Christian Arab scholar to be ". . . outside the community; they were not allowed to carry weapons, to bear witness against Moslems in courts of law, or to marry Moslem women; . . . they were subject to special . . . taxation. But they were permitted to retain their beliefs and their property, . . . and to manage the internal affairs of the communities according to their own laws and customs. . . ."[212]

The Jewish community of Syria became a refuge for Jews fleeing the Spanish Inquisition.[213] For centuries under Ottoman rule, it has been maintained, the Jews were allowed to live "relatively secure," often "prosperous" lives—chiefly as

---

*The nineteenth-century complaint about the "government's wish to appear impartial" to the world while "masking" its persecution illustrates the sophisticated aptitude for image making that was practiced more than a hundred years ago. The "invitation" from the Arab world to its Jews (see Chapter 2 above) is one modern example of the continued tradition.

†Emphasis added.

merchants—in their *mellahs.* Spanish exiles were responsible for establishing many Jewish religious schools in Damascus and Aleppo, and more than one Jew held the post of Finance Minister.

But in Syria, as elsewhere in the Arab world, the "position of Jews was in many ways precarious."[214]

A thirteenth-century Syrian Arab writer provided a classic example of the durability and consistency of the Muslims' traditional Koran-inspired demoniacal image of "the Jew"—the image through which the Prophet Muhammad and his followers sought to avenge the Jews for favoring Judaism over the "new," seventh-century religion. The Syrian wrote that

. . . this [Jewish] group is the most cursed of all God's creation, the most evil-natured, and the most deeply rooted in infidelity and accursedness. They are the most evil-intentioned of mankind in their deeds, even they are the most ostentatious in humility and self-abasement. . . . When they manage to be alone with a man, they bring him to destruction, they introduce, by trickery, a stupefying drug into his food, and then they kill him.[215]

As *dhimmis* they paid the special tax, and their testimony against Muslims was invalid in the Syrian courts. Jews bore many traditional *dhimma* discriminatory burdens: forbidden to ride a horse in town; forbidden to wear Muslim apparel; forbidden to carry arms; and "usually" prohibited from building or repairing places of worship. To those consistent humiliations were added the intermittent "oppression, extortion and violence by both the local authorities and the Muslim population."[216]

One Jew who rose to the post of "treasury manager," at the end of the eighteenth century, ran the gamut of the schizoid Jewish existence under Muslim rule. In the first stage of his ascendancy, he was arrested, an eye was gouged out, and his nose and ears cut.[217] In the second stage, he gained prominence "unique" for Jews, under the tolerant reign of a new pasha—a Christian writer in Damascus wrote that "Hayim the Jew . . . doing whatever he wishes . . . a Jewish person dominates the Muslims and Christians . . . without any restriction."[218]

A Swiss writer observed at the actual time (1811) of "Hayyim the Jew's" influence, "There is scarcely an instance in the modern history of Syria of a Christian or Jew having long enjoyed the power or riches . . . he may have acquired. These persons are always taken off in the last moment of their greatest apparent glory."[219] True to this prophecy, "Hayyim the Jew" was executed in 1820 and his property was confiscated by yet another successor to the Syrian reign.[220]

According to nineteenth-century historians, some Jewish families in Aleppo —which, like Alexandria, was an atypically tolerant cosmopolitan center of international commerce—were affluent and relatively safe. Others, even in Aleppo, who were less well-connected were "subject to violence and oppression from various quarters."[221] Money was extorted by officials on every pretext, petty bullying was commonplace, and one Jew reported that "When a Jew walked among them [the Muslims] in the market, one would throw a stone at him in order to kill him, another would pull his beard and a third his ear lock, yet another spit on his face and he became a symbol of abuse."[222]

In 1831, Egyptian rule improved markedly the lot of non-Muslims; Christians finally gained full equality. Not quite so for the Jews, although some at times were now allowed to repair their synagogues, and extortion through illegal taxes was officially forbidden. Muslims and particularly Egyptian soldiers were "severely punished" for abusing Jews.[223]

According to reports from the Jewish community in 1839, however, it was the European consuls who insisted on the protection of the Jews—not entirely the beneficence of the occupying Arab government: "Had it not been [for] the consuls' supervision, we would have all been destroyed and lost, since the gentiles wish but to eat the Jews and to accuse them falsely."[224]

A gradual decline of the Jews' position continued during the Egyptian occupation. European settlers began to usurp the Jews' role as traders.[225] Then, in 1840 a general economic slump, and incitement by means of the vicious "ritual murder" canard, exploded into riots and a pogrom against the Jews—the infamous Damascus blood libel of 1840.[226] The Arabs adopted the inflammatory mechanism as their own and have used it until the present day, despite the fact that the false charge was eventually proved fraudulent in a Turkish court.[227] As the Egyptians were forced out of Syria, a Turkish imperial *firman* was issued, exonerating the Damascus Jews from the foul accusation,* and stating "that the charges made against them . . . are nothing but pure calumny. . . . The Jewish nation shall be protected and defended."[228]

During the 1850s the Muslims began to concentrate violence upon the Christian community in Syria, and the nonplussed Jewish community remained unharmed. The Jews enjoyed a greater measure of religious freedom—to the extent that a synagogue was designed by the sultan's architect. Ottoman officials revered the chief rabbis, and life for the Jewish *dhimmi*—still forced to observe the discriminatory practices—was noticeably relieved.[229]

The French were assigned mandatory rights over Syria in 1920, and in 1925, the time of the Druse revolt against the French, the Jewish Quarter of Damascus was attacked; many Jews were murdered, dozens were wounded, and homes and shops were looted and set afire. The French persistently attempted to protect Jews from the increasing attacks brought about by Arab resentment of foreigners in general and of the French in particular.

But the rise of the Palestine antagonism crystallized hostility, and anti-Jewish riots were hurled upon the Jews of Damascus in 1936. The fact that the Jewish community made known its support of the Arab nationalists[230] was to no avail; Syrian Jews were accused of being Zionists, and the late '30s were fraught with

---

*Earlier, similar absurd charges were levied against Syrian Jews in Aleppo—1810, in Homs—1824, and in Anatakia—1826.

anti-Jewish violence.[231] Jews were stabbed by activist Muslims, and demands were made to boycott the Jewish Quarters.

Damascus was now a headquarters of anti-Jewish activities, and in 1937 a Nazi delegation, conferring with its Nazi representative in the Middle East, paid a visit to Damascus. As a result, anti-Jewish propaganda intensified and closer affiliations grew up between German and Arab youth organizations. An armed extremist group, the Arab National Youth Organization, declared a boycott against Arab merchants who bought "Zionist goods from Palestine."[232]

From Damascus the Arab Defense Committee warned the Jewish Agency president that "Your attitude will lead you and Jews of the East to the worst of calamities that has been written in history up to the present."[233] Despite the then-dominant Nazi-allied Vichy regime, local French authorities continued to defend the Jews from Arab extremist attack, although Jews were dismissed from official posts and penalized by economic restrictions. The Allied occupation in 1941 restored equilibrium somewhat, but Nazi propaganda continued.

In 1942 the Axis radio in Damascus caused additional alarm through broadcast of the false report that Roosevelt and Churchill had promised Syria to the Jews as part of a post-war Jewish state. The Jewish Quarter was raided in 1944 and 1945,[234] and the end of World War II intensified the persecution and restrictions against the Jews. Tens of thousands of Syrian Jews had fled between the world wars and after. The Jews numbered roughly 35,000 in 1917; in 1943 about 30,000 still remained.[235] In June 1945 the director of the Alliance Jewish-affiliated school was murdered.

That same year Syria won its independence, and the Damascus Mufti warned at a religious conference that if Jewish immigration into Palestine was not halted, all countries of Islam would declare a "holy war" against the Jews.[236] Shortly afterward a Syrian student mob celebrated a Muslim holiday by desecrating the Great Synagogue of Aleppo, beating upon Jews at prayer and burning prayer books in the street.[237]

Intimidation by the government was initiated, and Jews were prohibited from leaving. Jewish leaders were informed that unless they publicly denounced Zionism and surrendered Jewish refugees en route to Palestine, all refugees captured would be put to death along with their helpers. When the Jews protested, the Syrian Prime Minister amended the law to provide life imprisonment instead of death. But he exacted three conditions from the Jews: "Surrender all persons aiding the movement of refugees; cooperate with security forces in capturing refugees, and issue a public statement denouncing Zionism and calling on all Jews in the Arab states to support the struggle against Zionism."[238]

It was through such scare tactics that Syrian Jews were induced to testify that "Jews of Syria were happy and not discriminated against; that their situation was excellent under the present Syrian government; and that they had absolutely nothing whatever to do with Zionism." A member of the Anglo-American Committee, investigating the precarious position of Jewish minorities in Arab states, reported that after the Syrian Jews raced through the "45-seconds of testimony," they fled to their seats amid "murmurs of sly amusement from the Moslem audience which said, as clearly as words, 'They knew what was best for them.' "[239]

By early 1947, only 13,000 Jews remained; thousands more Jewish refugees had fled, many of them covertly, and the Syrian government, according to the *New York Herald Tribune,* [240] launched "an investigation into the disappearance of some 17,000 Syrian Jews since the last government census [1943]."

Letters were smuggled out of Syria; one told of

> the war against Zionism [which] has turned into a war against the entire Jewish people, . . . Anti-Jewish propaganda is rampant in the press, over the radio and in special pamphlets. . . . Poisonous articles, full of degradation and employing the lowest form of expression, are read over the radio and in the mosques. The masses follow faithfully, since the sheikhs promise them . . . paradise. . . . I am writing anonymously as I cannot give you my name for fear of vengeance. . . ."[241]

Around the same time as the hate campaign, various restrictions brought Jewish economic life to a halt. Jewish leaders accused the Syrian government of "making their livelihood impossible by denying them jobs in the government, withholding import and export licenses, and making virtually impossible the admission of Jewish youths into secondary schools."[242] Jews were still forbidden to leave the country, and terrified of venturing even near to the edge of the ghettos.[243]

In December 1947 anti-Jewish riots climaxed in a vicious pogrom; Syrian mobs poured into the *mellah* of Aleppo, burnt down most of the synagogues, and destroyed 150 Jewish homes, five Jewish schools, fifty shops and offices, an orphanage, and a youth club. Holy scrolls, including a priceless ancient manuscript of the Old Testament, were burned, while the firemen stood by and police "actively helped the attackers."[244] In the aftermath, the Syrian president asserted to a visiting Jewish delegation that "Incidents of this sort occur even in advanced countries. . . ."[245] and the Minister of Finance rejected the request for a loan to repair one of the synagogues so that the Jews could continue to worship.[246]

A bomb tossed into the heart of the Damascus Jewish Quarter, in front of the Alliance Israelite Universelle, caused inestimable damage; most important, it reinforced terror among the Damascus Jews. On the eve of the establishment of the State of Israel, in April 1948, several Aleppo rabbis wrote to a Brooklyn congregation:

> This is the third day we are in hiding. The Arab mobs are raging and threatening our lives. Pray for us. Act in our behalf before your government. Our lives are in total danger . . . help us![247]

Addressing its Jewish former citizens, the government ludicrously warned all "Syrian" citizens that unless they returned immediately,[248] they would lose Syrian citizenship. Compounding the orders prohibiting Jews from leaving the country, they were forbidden to change their places of residence,[249] sell private property, or acquire land.[250] In 1949 all bank accounts held by Jews were frozen.

In summer 1949, following the ascendance of a regime that promised "equality," the synagogue at Damascus was bombed during Sabbath preparations, with more than a score dead and twenty-six wounded. The new Syrian president called for an investigation and arrests, and when a Palestinian Arab confessed, the president promised justice based on the evidence.[251] But the new leader was killed in another military coup, with his successor's subsequent government becoming more unremitting in its severity than ever before.

Palestinian Arabs, many militantly anti-Jewish, were given the Jewish public buildings and the vacant former living quarters of Jewish escapees in the *mellah;* there they confronted their Jewish neighbors with omnipresent threats, often fulfilled. Such was the quality of terrorizing that some members of the normally close-knit protective Jewish community became informers when an Israeli escaped from prison in 1953 and sought sanctuary at the Damascus synagogue:

> The congregation was in consternation. The hostile regime and the suffering it had caused them had destroyed their self-respect. Anyone suspected of aiding Israel only brought disaster on himself, and now an Israeli prisoner, escaped from jail. . . . [His] fate was sealed the moment he crossed the threshold of the synagogue. . . . A squad broke in and removed the "dangerous Zionist" . . .[252]

The Jews were kept strictly within the confines of the ghetto, with penalties for escape as harsh as those of a prison. Yet many remained unintimidated—those Jews took great risks through carefully guarded secret routes, leaving everything behind, to escape from the oppressive existence; hundreds of Jews, including women and children, were arrested and tortured in the attempt to be smuggled out.[253]

Since then, except for brief periods,[254] Syria's Jewish community has huddled together, its collective and individual human rights and dignity distinctly cut off.[255]

Lebanon

Jews have been in the Mediterranean coastal region now called Lebanon since A.D. 70, if not earlier.

Although all thirty-five Jewish families living in Beirut were slaughtered by the Crusaders,[256] Jews survived elsewhere in Lebanon and their population was infused with Spanish Jews who fled from Spain in 1492. During the Turkish reign, Jews in Lebanon, as elsewhere in the Ottoman Empire, paid the poll tax to ensure their protection,[257] along with other infidels in the Muslim state, and at times were subject to severe dress codes or harsh legal restrictions.[258]

But life for the small Jewish community in Lebanon—fifty-five families in 1826—was comparatively easy,[259] until the infamous blood libel charges spread —to Beirut in 1824 and to (Lebanese) Tripoli in 1834.[260]

With the calumnies came the predictable attacks and suffering, which were compounded by the anti-Jewish attacks during the Druse Rebellion[261]—the uprising wiped out the Jewish community in the town of Dir el-Qamar in 1847.

Under the early twentieth-century French occupation, Jews were less discriminated against in Lebanon than elsewhere in the Middle East; only "a few" recorded incidents of anti-Jewish attacks marred Jewish life there in the thirties. In 1945, the time of Lebanese independence, twelve Jews were murdered in the Muslim-populated town of Tripoli; following the 1947 partition of Palestine, houses and synagogues were attacked by Muslims.[262] In 1948 a Beirut Jew was murdered; in 1950 a Jewish school was bombed and its director killed—acts predominantly executed by Muslim groups.[263] Money extorted from the Lebanese Jews as "contributions" often went directly to finance Arab Palestinian sabotage.

Yet, on the whole, historians note that Jews were protected by authorities as Lebanese independence emerged in 1946. During the anti-Zionist demonstrations at the time of Israel's declaration of statehood, "police forces were posted" in Beirut's Jewish Quarter "day and night when required"—sharp contrast to the official behavior in other Arab states at the time.[264]

During the 1948 war, Maronite Christians as well as Christian authorities protected the Jews from "Muslim fanatics"[265] and offered assistance to Jewish refugees fleeing from Iraq and Syria. Jews retained their jobs, even as civil servants, until 1957, and authorities continued to guard the Jewish community from the Muslim opposition's attacks.[266]

Until 1958, Lebanon was the sole Arab state where Jews had increased in number—to about 9,000—after the war of Israel's independence. When Lebanon officially began to finance terrorist activities by the newly inspired Arab Palestinian "Revolution" in 1968, many of the remaining Jews left.

Although no Lebanese Jews were employed by the government, and the Lebanese could not communicate with the "enemy territory" of Israel, Jews were allowed to travel freely, even within the Middle East, before Lebanon's Arab-versus-Arab bloodletting was renewed in the early 1970s. But few of them visited the Arab countries of their own volition.[267]

The Jews of Lebanon enjoyed greater freedom than any other Jewish group living in the Arab world, primarily because of the Christian-dominated government. It was not until the advent of Muslim revolt—the demise of "secular democracy" in the Arab world—that the Lebanese Jews became sufficiently insecure to flee in great numbers.

Libya

Libya's Jewish community has virtually disappeared, its roots dug up after millennia of deep attachment to the North African terrain that is Libya today.

Jews were attracted to the country before the destruction of Jerusalem—many from the "Egyptian diaspora."[268] According to Josephus Flavius, "100,000 Jews [were] transferred from Palestine" by Egyptian ruler Ptolemy around 300 B.C., and thousands of those Jews were "settled" in Libyan cities employed as a human shield to protect Egypt from its enemies.[269] The Jewish community was reportedly destroyed in the anti-Roman rebellion of A.D. 73, reappearing in Tripoli before the fourth century.[270]

The seventh-century Arab conquest, taking fifty years to subjugate all of North Africa, brought Libyan Jews under the same fluctuating oppressive *dhimma* restrictions as elsewhere in the Maghreb. Once again the Jews became a buffer against attack—this time protecting the Arabs of Tripoli against the Byzantines.[271]

From that period forward, the Jewish population was, in one city or another, sacked, cheated, and pillaged alternately by nomads and Bedouins, with sterner penalties and banishment meted out arbitrarily, according to the whim of whichever Muslim tribal leader had at that moment defeated his rival.[272] In addition to the reverberations of feuds, disease, and poverty, the Jews of Libya—then Tripolitania—were subject to the "nomad invasions, highway robbery and piracy" of the general populace.[273]

The twelfth century brought the barbarity of the Almohads to the eastern plains, and the Jews were severely persecuted "for the purpose of conversion" about 1140.[274]

> . . . the blood of sons and daughters was spilt on a sabbath day. . . . There is not a Jew, not a single one, in Dajayya or al-Mahdiya, and for Sabrat and Tura my eye always weeps.[275]

The remaining historical fragments on twelfth-century "sufferings of African Jewry" are few: the above was excerpted from one, and the following mid-twelfth-century description from another:

> . . . years of distress, oppression and persecution to Israel, and they were exiled from their localities: such as were for death, to death and such as were for the sword, to the sword, and . . . to the famine, and . . . to the captivity. . . . and such as were destined to leave the community left because of the sword of Ibn Tūmart, who went forth into the world in the year 4902 (1141/2) and who had decided to eliminate Israel. . . . And so he left no name of them in the whole of his kingdom nor remnant . . . , from the end of the world to the city of al-Mahdiya."[276]

European travelers through the region have recorded the persistence of various compulsory *dhimma* demeanments inflicted by the Berber and Arab Muslims, who "despised and vilified" the Jews. Though there are writers who speak of the relative "haven" Spanish exiles found as refuge from the Inquisition, Tripolitania proffered something short of the sanctuary that the fleeing Spanish Jews had hoped for.[277]

Because of the Maghrebi Jews' imposed "otherness"—the miserable living conditions in many ghettos and the stubbornness that resistance to conversion must spawn—the more cosmopolitan Jewish refugees from Europe reportedly "scorned" the peculiar, unfamiliar North African Jewish "locals," with whom the Spaniards were reluctant to identify. One historian admitted the difficulty of "merging the two strata"—which "took centuries and is still not complete"[278] in the 1970s. Another claimed the "confrontation . . . passed on the whole harmoniously . . . with a minimum of communal damage. . . . [the] diversity . . . minimized."[279] Yet he, too, later reported the "friction" that developed between native and newcomer.

In the late sixteenth century many of the Libyan Jews whose ancestors had fled the forced conversion of Spain ironically were faced with the choice of death —or conversion to Islam.[280] "Hundreds" of Jews were murdered during the persecutions of Ali Gurzi Pasha's reign.[281]

The Ottoman conquest of Tripolitania in 1835 brought a measure of relief to Jews in Tripoli and some other cities. At the same time, Jews in other regions of Tripolitania did not benefit from the Turkish rule; they were subjected to forced conversion and anti-Jewish pogroms, and they shared the ghetto miseries suffered in other parts of North Africa. Numerous complaints were registered by Jewish leaders in Tripolitania.[282] A few excerpts might color one's perspective regarding the "relative security" of Jews among the Arab Muslims. Regarding the burning of a synagogue in Zliten—

. . . everyone knows what the Arabs, the *Cadi* [judge], the Ulema were doing to the Israelites. . . . If the Governor here had rendered justice to the Jews of Zliten, both with regard to their cemetery and their synagogue, the people of Zliten would not have dared to carry out this disgraceful act . . . if, God forbid, they do not obtain ample satisfaction, . . . the Jews will be obliged to emigrate to save their lives and their few possessions.[283]

Also at Zliten—

. . . some Muslims attacked the house of a Jew, and stole all he had after seriously injuring him. . . . [others] entered the house of another Jew, stripped him of all his possessions, struck and injured both him and his wife, and killed his son aged about 20. . . . robbed [another] Jew . . . injured him and killed a young child at its mother's knees. Finally . . . at Zawiya Gharibya, only 7 hours away from here, the Sacred Synagogue was plundered and profaned in every . . . way. . . .[284]

Another plea came from the entire Jewish community of Tripoli—

. . . The situation of the Jews in all parts of Tripolitania is very dangerous. From all the rights . . . we are unfortunately excluded by reason of extreme ill-treatment and persecution at the hands of the Muslims in our country, under the . . . present [Governor] . . . who does not wish to . . . protect us against the cruel and inhumane Muslim population. . . . Last Thursday, a Jew on the way to his village was killed by Arabs and his companion was injured. . . . the authorities have not attempted to find the criminals. . . . to the Muslims, Jews are of no account, and our personal safety is in jeopardy and our belongings are not our own.[285]

A final example is from the Sahara region—

. . . In these out-of-the-way places . . . the Jew may not ride a horse or ass in an Arab's presence. The Jewish rider, on seeing an Arab coming, must dismount quickly and go on foot, leading his mount until the Arab disappears. . . . If the Jew forgets this or takes too long to dismount, the Arab brutally reminds him . . . by throwing him to the ground. . . . The Jews of Gebel (one of these regions) told me that within the last 20 years three Israelites had been killed in this way. The testimony of a Jew is not accepted and he would never dare to accuse anyone of robbing him. . . . Along all this part of the Tripolitanian coast, small communities of Jews are living amongst the Arabs, more or less subjected to them.[286]

The Libyan Jews, enjoying the "easier" conditions under the Ottomans, confronted arbitrary anti-Jewish cruelties, and taxation amounting to extortion, in most of the country through the end of the nineteenth century. Jewish religious institutions survived, but the *hara,* or ghetto, was at best barely above poverty level. With the Italian occupation in 1911, the Jews escaped from *dhimmi* status and the Jewish community thrived until the mid-thirties, when Libya, as the only Arabic-speaking Italian possession, became Mussolini's Muslim center for fascist propaganda.[287]

The Second World War brought a great wave of persecution—in 1941 and 1942 Benghazi's Jews were attacked;[288] Jewish property in Benghazi was pillaged and nearly 2,600 Jews were sent to a forced labor camp in the desert, where more than 500 died. Later in 1942, thousands more Jews from Tripoli and other towns were condemned to forced labor.

On the eve of the Allied victory in Tripoli, Axis troops stormed the Jewish Quarter and slaughtered the leaders of the Jewish community. As the Allies freed the Jews from concentration camps and the British took control of Libya, anti-Jewish crowds stormed Tripoli and other communities.[289] Nonetheless, Jewish activities were revived. "Palestinian Jewish soldiers serving with the British army opened Hebrew schools for liberated Jewish children,"[290] and peace brought some restoration of security to Libya's Jews.

The struggling community was totally unprepared for the violent anti-Jewish bloodbath that began November 4, 1945. The Tripoli pogrom was inspired by anti-Jewish riots in Egypt a couple of days earlier, but the ravages in Tripolitania were even more devastating. Whereas the Egyptian violence was directed to pillage and looting, Arab nationalism and religious fanaticism in Tripoli was aimed at the physical destruction of Jews.

According to the *New York Times'* Clifton Daniel,

Many of the attacks were premeditated and coldly murderous in intent.[291]
Babies were beaten to death with iron bars. Old men were hacked to pieces

where they fell. Expectant mothers were disemboweled. Whole families were burned alive in their houses. Two brothers lost 27 relatives in one attack. . . . When the riots were raging, the thirst for blood seemed to have supplanted the desire for loot and revenge.[292]

Forced conversion, girls raped with their families looking on—the Muslim gangs' bestiality was directed specifically against Jews, and only Jewish dwellings and businesses were devastated. Just one week after the atrocity had ended, an Arab leader was interviewed:[293] he warned that because of "Zionist activity"— Libyan Jewish Boy Scouts sang "Zionist" hymns and Zionist clubs were formed —the Arabs "have become annoyed" and the Jews must disavow "militant Zionism." In the short period following the November 1947 vote to partition "Palestine" into a Jewish state and an Arab state, the Libyan mobs murdered more than 130 Jews.[294] Another Tripoli horror was perpetrated the following year, with impassioned zeal, and the erstwhile unswervable Jewish community began to flee. Libya's Jewish population in 1948 was 38,000; by 1951 only 8,000 Jews remained.[295]

The precarious position of Libyan Jewry deteriorated further when the British began to move Arab families into the former homes of departed Jews, in the walled *hara*. Where before the Jews had felt some measure of security in isolation, now there was hostility on the doorstep.[296] By the time Libya achieved independence in 1952, there were relatively few Jews left to take advantage of the purported equality offered under the new constitution. From the time of Libya's entry into the Arab League, Jewish clubs were closed, and life, while less violent, was no more secure.

By the 1960s, only some hundreds of Jews remained, and with the renewal of Arab mob violence after the Six-Day War,[297] practically all of Libya's remaining Jewish population was forced literally to run for their lives.[298] Leaving behind everything they owned, most became a part of the 37,000-member Libyan refugee community in Israel.

In 1970, President Qaddafy confiscated Jewish-owned property that the fleeing Libyan-born Jews had left behind.[299] The expatriate Libyan Jewish community in Rome protested the property takeover, claiming that such action contradicted the Libyan constitutional decree of citizen equality. Thereupon a Libyan official invited the Libyan Jews to return to the country, and assured them that their property would then be released. Libya's "invitation" came on the heels of a new government regulation that prohibited those few Libyan Jews who remained from leaving Libya, no matter how short the duration of the requested visit.[300]

When Qaddafy visited France during the 1973 Arab-Israeli Yom Kippur War to press the Arab oil embargo and negotiate arms, the Tunisian-born writer Albert Memmi responded to Libya's invitation to Jews in a personal address to Qaddafy:

Is it true that you have said that the Jews have always lived at peace in the Arab countries? And that you have nothing against Jews, only Zionists? . . .

The error which may have been made at Deir Yassine[*] is constantly being thrown in our faces. Ah, but we have undergone a hundred Deir Yassines, a thousand Deir Yassines![†] And not only in Russia, Germany or Poland, but also at the hand of Arab people; yet the world has never been upset over it! . . .

. . . if you really wanted to avoid having us come together on this particular bit of land, . . . Israel . . . , then why did you hound us and expel us from the regions over which your power extends? . . .

Do you believe that the Jews born in Arab countries can go back and live in the countries from which they were expelled, before being plundered and massacred? . . .

. . . your constant affirmation [is] of the unity of the Arab nation. . . . When you come right down to it, the Palestinian Arabs' misfortune is having been moved about thirty miles within one vast nation. Is that so serious? Our own misfortune, as Jews from the Arab countries, is much much greater, for we have been moved thousands of miles away, after having also lost everything. And today [we] are . . . half the population of Israel. . . . And no one has the right to challenge our possibility of taking in our past and also, alas!, our future survivors.[302]

The Arab world had been virtually emptied of its Jews, and the fledgling Jewish state would bear the burden of its hundreds of thousands of Jewish Arab-born refugees almost in secret.

So unknown and undisclosed are these Arab-born Jews and the plight they have faced—the camps, squalor, uprooting, loss of property and security, discontent, unemployment, and what they sensed to be neglect of their problems in Israel—that in countless conversations outside the Middle East with academics or professionals, from university graduates to blue-collar workers, including Jews as well as non-Jews, when the question of the "Middle East refugees" is raised, almost without exception the response is, "You mean the Palestinians—the Arabs, of course." It is as though the sad and painful story of the Arab-born Jewish refugees had been erased, their struggle covered over by a revision of the pages of history.

---

*An Arab village harboring Iraqi and other Arab troops, blocking the supply route to Jerusalem, during battles immediately before Israel gained statehood. Although the Palestinian Jewish Irgun and Stern troops who bombarded Deir Yaseen in April 1948 first warned the community and called for surrender, their subsequent attack killed an estimated 250 villagers along with the regular Arab army troops in the village. Jewish authorities punished the renegade force, and British investigations found it to be one of the "few" Jewish reprisals, among a "law-abiding" Jewish population, after years of "almost unbelievable self-restraint" from retaliation for continuous Arab terrorist attacks upon Palestinian Jews. Arab propaganda has used "Deir Yaseen" as a "justification" for unlimited international acts of Arab terrorism.[301]

†See Chapter 9.

4

Ideology of the East, Rhetoric
of the West

> Because of the wrongdoing of the Jews. . . .
>
> distorting with their tongues and slandering religion. . . .
>
> The most vehement of mankind in hostility [be] the Jews
> and the idolators. . . .
>
> the greediest of mankind. . . .
>
> desire nothing but your ruin. . . .
>
> commit evil and become engrossed in sin.
>
> Allah hath cursed them for their disbelief.
>
> Taste ye the punishment of burning.
>
> —The Koran, from quotations excerpted in this chapter
>
> The Jews . . . lived exiled and despised since by their nature
> they are vile, greedy and enemies of mankind.
>
> —Syrian second-year junior high school textbook, 1963–1964

The pages of history unfolded in the foregoing chapter, to which this chapter is in essence an epilogue, reveal the traditional treatment by the Arab world of "its Jews." By no means is it an exhaustive study; it is merely a drawing of characteristic features sufficiently detailed to preclude distortion or doubt. The causes for Jewish tribulation in Arab lands may be subject to interpretation or even in some minds to justification; the historical record itself, however, cannot be subject to opinion or obfuscation—that record exists.

Despite that record, modern Arab claims to the contrary have been allowed to supplant the facts. The Arabs currently have been painting a specious propaganda portrait of the "tranquility" and peace attained by "their Jews" before the independence of Israel. The late King Faisal of Saudi Arabia told Henry Kissinger that ". . . Before the Jewish state was established, there existed nothing to harm good relations between Arabs and Jews. . . ."[1] Ironically, no Jews were allowed to enter or live in Saudi Arabia.

Jordan's King Hussein stated, "The relationship that enabled Arabs and Jews to live together for centuries as neighbors and friends has been destroyed by

72

Zionist ideas and actions."² Yet the Jordanian Nationality Law states that "a Jew" cannot become a citizen of Jordan.³

It was "Zionism"—Israel—that drove a wedge between Arabs and Jews, Arab rulers have insisted. Yet King Faisal subsequently distributed illuminated copies of one of the most infamous and durable of all anti-Jewish libels—the czarist forgery known as "The Protocols of the Elders of Zion"—along with an anthology of other anti-Jewish calumnies, to journalists who accompanied French Foreign Minister Jobert to Jedda in January 1974. Saudi officials were reported to have asserted that these defamatory books were the King's "favorites."⁴

Sheikh Goshah, Grand Cadi (Chief Judge) of Jordan, spoke of the happy past together shared by the Jews and Arab Muslims, "stressing the Mosaic roots of Islam."⁵ But when Goshah spoke at Al-Azhar University to Muslim theologians at the Fourth Conference of the Academy of Islamic Research, he said, "Treachery was the business of Jews throughout their ages and times. . . . Allah backed Muslims until they gained victory throughout all incursions and battles against the treacherous hypocritic Jews."⁶

Implicit within many such statements is the intention of enforcing the religious command that Jews shall be "returned" to their former status as humiliated infidels in the Arab lands, according to the will of the Koran. The message seems to be that "these Jews who have always been 'our Jews,' are insolent in daring to insist upon treatment as equals in the Arab world." Whoever heard of a *Dhimmi* State?

Determining to a great extent the Arab world's historical subjugation and mistreatment of Jews, the Koran, and to some extent the *Hadith*—statements attributed to the Prophet Muhammad—have been pivotal in creating the modern Jewish stereotype for Muslims.⁷ One *Hadith* of the Prophet Muhammad appeared in Egyptian publications in the 1930s and 1940s:

> The resurrection of the dead will not come until the Muslims will war with the Jews and the Muslims will kill them; . . . the trees and rocks will say, "O Muslim, O Abdullah, here is a Jew behind me, come and kill him."⁸

The holy writings of Islam also contain benign references to Jews, which often are cited to support the fantasy of "harmonious relations between Muslims and Jews in Arab lands." Wherever Jews have lived under Arab Islam, however, their conditions appear to have been determined by the *negative* images of Jews within the *Hadith* Reports and the Koran, the juridical source of Islamic law, images found in such statements as the following:

> Ignominy shall be their portion [the Jews'] wheresoever they are found. . . . They have incurred anger from their Lord, and wretchedness is laid upon them. . . . because they . . . disbelieve the revelations of Allah and slew the Prophets wrongfully. . . . because they were rebellious and used to transgress.⁹

> And thou wilt find them [the Jews] the greediest of mankind. . . .¹⁰

Evil is that for which they sell their souls. . . . For disbelievers is a terrible doom.[11]

Taste ye [Jews] the punishment of burning.[12]

Those who disbelieve Our revelations, We shall expose them to the fire. As often as their skins are consumed We shall exchange them for fresh skins that they may taste the torment.[13]

Because of the wrongdoing of the Jews. . . . And of their taking usury . . . and of their devouring people's wealth by false pretenses. We have prepared for those of them who disbelieve a painful doom.[14]

Allah hath cursed them [the Jews] for their disbelief.[15]

They [the Jews] will spare no pains to corrupt you. They desire nothing but your ruin. Their hatred is clear from what they say, but more violent is the hatred which their breasts conceal.[16]

In truth the disbelievers are an open enemy to you.[17]

And thou seest [Jews and Christians] vying one with another in sin and transgression and their devouring of illicit gain. Verily evil is what they do. Why do not the rabbis and the priests forbid their evilspeaking and their devouring of illicit gain? . . . . evil is their handiwork.[18]

O ye who believe! Take not the Jews and Christians for friends.[19]

The most vehement of mankind in hostility [are] the Jews and the idolators.[20]

Fight against such of those [Jews and Christians] . . . until they pay for the tribute readily, being brought low.[21]

Allah fighteth against them [the Jews]. How perverse they are![22]

Believers, many are the rabbis and the monks who defraud men of their possessions. . . . Proclaim a woeful punishment to those that hoard up gold and silver and do not spend it in Allah's cause. . . . their treasures shall be heated in the fire of Hell. . . .[23]

They [the Jews] spread evil in the land. . . .[24]

[The Jews] knowingly perverted [the word of Allah], know of nothing except lies . . . commit evil and become engrossed in sin.[25]

Many of these words of holy hatred and others were repeated amid religious fervor at a Cairo "religious" conference in 1968.[26] The tone of that conference, *Arab Theologians on Jews and Israel,* was unambiguous. First the introductory remarks:

I welcome you in the name of Islam which gathered you under the banner of righteousness and good . . . as active prominent scholars, and to reinforce through you brotherhood in religion. [Dr. Mahmud Hubballah, Secretary General of the Islamic Research Academy][27]

Then the proceedings, including the following unbrotherly interpretations:

The Jews . . . had resorted to their former policy and thus they deserved to be called, the worst of beasts in the Quran . . .

They are characterized by avarice and many other vices. . . . [Sheikh Abd Allah Al Meshad][28]

. . . it behoves us to refer to the distortion of the Jewish creed that filled the life of Jews with perfidy and evil. . . .

Islamic tolerance is in complete contrast with Jewish intolerance and cruelty . . . I should like to say before I conclude that I have thoroughly scrutinized the nature of the Jews. They are avaricious, ruthless, cruel, hypocrite and revengeful. These traits govern their lives. [Mohammed Taha Yahia][29]

The Jews' wicked nature never changes. . . . Evil, wickedness, breach of vows and money worship are inherent qualities in them. Many a time were they punished for their evil, but they never repented or gave up their sinfulness. [Kamal Ahman Own, Vice-Principal, Tanta Institute][30]

Against the turbulent, uncertain, and unmistakably iniquitous background of the Arab world's Jewry, it is commonly claimed that the Jews were, during certain periods in the Arab lands, "better off" than they were in Christian lands of Europe. They were not burnt in ovens, and perhaps in part because more twentieth-century Arab-born Jews escaped with their lives, however subjugated, many contemporary Jews have romanticized their historical relations with the Arabs.

Some have not. In the mid-nineteenth century, "Benjamin II," a Rumanian Jewish traveler, wrote about his five years in the Orient and told the "Jews of Europe,"

How happy I would be if (by my book of travels) I could interest the Jews of Europe in the plight of their coreligionists who are the victims of oriental barbarism and fanaticism. Our free brethren who have the good fortune to live under liberal regimes, where they are governed by wise laws and are treated humanely will understand how deplorable and urgent is the abnormal situation of their brothers in the Orient. . . . May the Almighty One lessen the burden of so many tribulations, may he reward their heroism after centuries of slavery as well as their indomitable faith under such cruel persecutions.[31]

Non-Jewish European observers, too, determined that the more brotherly "spirit" enjoyed by the Jews of Europe had not penetrated the Middle East. The British consul in Jerusalem in 1839 reported:

The spirit of toleration towards the Jews is not yet known here to the same extent it is in Europe . . . still, the Jew in Jerusalem is not estimated in value much above a dog. . . .[32]

A Christian clergyman and traveler to the Middle East in 1858 commented sorrowfully:

It is said that in Rome the Jews never pass under Titus' Arch, but if they also keep such long memories and grudges in Muslim lands, I do not see where they can walk.[33]

Somehow the brutal facts have been replaced by crueler fiction. Even some Jewish historians—who have themselves placed time and cause of Arab persecution, who have themselves chronicled a detailed calendar of horrors over many centuries in their own works—even these historians have demonstrated an inability to fathom or, perhaps, to accept the implications of the history they themselves have uncovered. Thus, among the presentations of documented Arab atrocities perpetrated against the Jews, there is in some volumes a recurrent theme of the particular author's discomfort with the subject and his findings, and even a peculiar sort of apologia for having bared them. "Although the slaughter was violently anti-Jewish, we cannot say that this was true anti-Semitism. Anti-Semitism did not exist historically in Arab countries." The problem lies in the susceptibility to misinterpretation, in the risk of being taken literally—but out of context. In the example just quoted above, the "fact" that might remain in the reader's mind is "Anti-Semitism did not exist historically in Arab countries." Although one or two or a dozen experts might understand that the writer was making an obtuse differentiation, the vast majority of readers, using the work for superficial reference or information, might be expected to perpetuate the myth further.

In one case, a historian wanted to make the point that, "though violent, these crises were of a passing nature." "These crises" were the senseless bloodlust, brutality, and premeditated torture of Jews by the Almohads in the twelfth and thirteenth centuries, which the author had just described on the preceding pages in the following fashion: "The chronicles of the Jewish communities of North Africa repeat the same phrases *again and again:* 'They plundered all the Jews. . . . They carried off so many Jews. . . . They slaughtered so many women, so many children, so many Jews. . . . Who can know our unhappiness. . . . Those that survived the mob were mowed down by death . . .' " and more. The historian cited the "plaint" of a famous Jewish poet in his illustration of the "sufferings of the Jews of North Africa," where "Jews became the victim of every crisis."[34] Yet, perhaps unwittingly supporting the contention that the "crises were . . . *passing,* "* that otherwise extensively helpful compilation omitted the pivotal fact that the Sephardic (Oriental, non-European) Jewish world's leading scholar of the period, Maimonides, was forced to leave his home in Fez as the result of Muslim rage at his letter to the Moroccan and Tunisian Jews, an "epistle" commiserating with their persecution. The historian in question wrote that Maimonides' family stayed in Fez, Morocco, "so safe a town" that they lived in a house in the Moslem medina, "he taught in the Mosque," and only noted cryptically that "he left Fez in 1165 for Palestine and later for Egypt." Then, a few paragraphs later, the same

---

*Emphasis added.

historian wrote that, "In Morocco, the condition of the Jews deteriorated further."[35] Allowing for poor translation—a possibility—this book and some others, when examined closely, seem to exhibit a prevalent tendency to reject the unpleasant conclusions that follow from their own findings, even though the works contribute valuable documentation in little-known areas. One such ambivalent historian was interviewed for this book, and his revealing comments to a Syrian escapee appear in Chapter 6.

Some noted historians have confronted the myth of "equality" for Jews among Arabs. A few concluded significantly that it might be *Muslims* who inspired the *Christians* to certain anti-Jewish discriminations. One historian pointed out that it was "the [12th century] *Almohad* example which *decided Christendom to adopt the . . . measure"* of forcing Jews to wear the humiliating yellow badge or other "distinctive mark,"* which Christians did not institute until a century later.[36]

Another distinguished Orientalist, Bernard Lewis, reached the conclusion that

> The golden age of equal rights was a myth, and belief in it was a result, more than a cause, of Jewish sympathy for Islam. The myth was invented by Jews in 19th century Europe as a reproach to Christians—and taken up by Muslims in our own time as a reproach to Jews.
> . . . European travelers to the East in the age of liberalism and emancipation are almost unanimous in deploring the degraded and precarious position of Jews in Muslim countries, and the dangers and humiliations to which they were subject. Jewish scholars, acquainted with the history of Islam and with the current situation in Islamic lands, can have no illusions on this score.[37] [Arminius] Vambery is unambiguous: "I do not know any more miserable, helpless, and pitiful individual on God's earth than the *Jahudi* in those countries. . . . The poor Jew is despised, belabored and tortured alike by Moslem, Christian and Brahmin. . . ."[38]

In some places and under special circumstances, life was allowed to be more civil, when the individual ruler was just or kindly or where the colonial protector tempered or restrained the inclinations of the local populace. During those intermittent periods when the Arab countries were under Turkish, French, or British colonial rule, at some times a relatively less insecure, occasionally even financially flourishing—albeit unequal and separated—Jewish community was permitted. But the operative word is *"relatively"*—the conditions for Jews under the "best" of circumstances in the Arab world must be viewed in the proper perspective.

During isolated periods, Christians in the lands of Islam were more severely persecuted and oppressed by pogroms than were Jews. In the Middle Ages, for instance, and to some extent ever since, the Christians became an enemy threat to the Muslims, suspected as a potential fifth column, and regarded as a security risk.

*Emphasis added.

Most of the Christian community fled to more comfortable, Christian-dominated regions, however. The Jews remained—at best the sole *dhimmi* minority to be "tolerated" in many of the Arab countries, particularly North Africa —with no place to go and no outside affiliation or political power sufficient to protest against their oppressive "protected" treatment.

It was with the advent of Israel, when the Jews finally gained the political protection of their own liberation movement, that the contemptible *dhimmi* role was replaced. To the Arabs, the Jews became perceived as Zionists—the infidel European-inspired "fifth column."

An eloquent illustration of the Arabs' altered attitude toward the Jews was expressed in 1951 during a private conversation between the Iraqi Prime Minister and an eminent Arab historian. The historian asked whether it would not be wiser for the Iraqi government to defer lifting the ban on Jewish exits from Iraq until "the Palestinian and refugee problems are settled."* The Iraqi Premier replied,

> The Jews have always been and will be forever a source of evil and mischief for Iraq. They are spies. . . . They do not possess land which they can sow. So how will they live? What would they do if they remained in Iraq? No, my friend, we had better get rid of them, so long as the opportunity for getting rid of them is open.[40]

The transformation of the Arab attitude toward Jews—from capricious "toleration" and prejudice of a harmless, safely scorned, and intimidated minority, to fierce and active hatred of the Jewish presence as an enemy force—was evidenced frequently in Arab statements such as the following:

> The Jews in the Arab countries have not respected the defense that Islam has given them for generations. They have encouraged World Zionism and Israel in every way in its aggression against the Arabs. . . . The Congress hereby declares that the Jews in the Muslim countries whose ties with Zionism and Israel are proved shall be regarded as fighters against the Muslims, unfit for the patronage and protection which the Muslim faith prescribes for adherents of peaceful protected faiths.[41]

Numerous official Arab Ministry of Education materials have been produced to prepare the present adult Arab generation for its continuation of "harmony" among Arabs and Jews.

The following are a few examples from publications officially distributed by the Ministries of Education in various Arab countries:[42]

---

*Another Iraqi, ex-Premier Muzahim el Pachachi, also urged Iraq to delay the Jews' leavetaking. Pachachi recognized the implications of the massive Jewish exodus to Israel and Iraq's confiscation of their property. Thus, he suggested, the government should consult the member states of the Arab League so that a united policy on Jewish immigration from Arab countries could be formulated. "We should study the question of whether it would not be possible to *exchange* our Jews for the Arabs of Israel or the Palestine Arab refugees."[39] (Emphasis added.)

Jordan, 1966, for third-year junior high school: *Modern World History.* For example, "The Jews in Europe were persecuted and despised because of their corruption, meanness and treachery."

Jordan, 1964, department for school curricula and textbooks, for first-year high school: *Glances at Arab Society,* p. 117. An exercise: "Israel was born to die. Prove it."

Syria, Damascus, 1963–64, for second-year junior high school: *The Religious Ordinances Reader,* p. 138. For example: "The Jews . . . lived exiled and despised since by their nature they are vile, greedy and enemies of mankind."

Syria, 1963, fifth-year elementary school: *Basic Syntax and Spelling.* An exercise: "We Shall Expel All the Jews." For example, "Analyze the following sentences: 1. The merchant himself travelled to the African continent. 2. We shall expel all the Jews from the Arab countries."

Egypt, 1965, Egyptian State Seal, for first-year junior high school: *Grammar,* p. 244. An exercise: "The Arabs do not cease to act for the extermination of Israel."

U.A.R. (Egypt), for ninth-grade secondary schools: *Zionist Imperialism,* by Abbad Muhmud Al-Akkad, p. 249. ". . . Israel hopes to be the homeland of the Jew, and they have the stubbornness of 4,000 years of history behind them. But Israel shall not live if the Arabs stand fast in their hatred. She shall wither and decline. Even if all the human race, and the devil in Hell, conspire to aid her, she shall not exist."[43]

Among the many examples, a Jordanian textbook for use in second-year high school asserts that the God of Judaism "is a God who . . . is bloodthirsty, fickleminded, harsh and greedy . . . pleased with imposture and deceit."

The anti-Semitic literature published by the Arabs since World War II has been voluminous, and is continually increasing, despite the almost total evacuation of the Arab world's Jews.[44]

The virulence of this literature is disturbing, but even more significant is the official or governmental origin of the publications—not from an extremist fringe, which might be lightly dismissed, but from Arab governments, including those called "moderate."

Arab propagandists and sympathizers have persisted in the charge that Israel is a foreign outpost of Western civilization, the intruding offspring of Europe inhabited by European survivors of Nazi brutality. In actuality, more than half of the people in Israel today are Jews or offspring of Jews who lived in Arab countries and have fled from Arab brutality; Israel's present population consists mainly of refugees and their descendants from two oppressions, European-Nazi and Arab. As the Arab writer Sabri Jiryis has acknowledged, either by official edict or by the Arab's own harsh mistreatment of the Jews among them, the Arab world has expelled or has caused Jews to flee to Israel. Were the facts popularly recognized, the Arab propaganda claim of a "European" Israel would long ago have been refuted. The Arabs have long helped to make the Jewish state predominantly an "Oriental" Israel of Jews from Arab lands.

5

Last Year and Next Year in Jerusalem: Zionism in the Arab World and the Holy Land

> My heart is in the East and I am at the
> uttermost West.
> —Judah Halevi, 1086–1141

> The mode of conducting Jewish affairs
> among themselves . . . is entirely
> in Hebrew, which ancient custom
> they are very tenacious of and
> desirous to maintain.
> —W. T. Young, British Consul in Jerusalem, 1839

Clearly the massive exodus of Jewish refugees from the Arab countries was triggered largely by the Arabs' own Nazi-like bursts of brutality, which had become the lot of the Jewish communities. Walter Laqueur writes: "History has always shown that . . . men and women have chosen to leave their native country only when facing intolerable pressure."[1] But the history is long of persecution against Jews by the Arabs, a chronicle of "intolerable pressure" that had its beginnings in and took its inspiration from the seventh-century book of the creator of Islam.

History has also illustrated that persecution and its pressures become "intolerable" only when an alternative other than death is provided. The Arab-born Jews suffered in silence until they learned that they could act out their hope of getting to a Jewish state.

They bore their burdens as did many peoples of the world before and until the United States became the universal haven of the oppressed. Yet the hapless black peoples who had been brought to America as slaves could not even begin to alleviate *their* oppression and exploitation here until they began to gain the freedoms and thus the strength to resist and insist upon their rights—rights that are in some areas yet to be achieved.

There is no doubt that the long-sought Jewish national homeland was finally brought into being by a horrified, conscience-stricken international community, which viewed Israel as a necessary refuge for Jews throughout the world who had become victims of the Nazis or their followers. However, after World War I, in 1918, nearly half of the total Jewish population in Jerusalem consisted of "Sephardic" Jews—that is, the Jews of the Middle East, non-European Jewry.[2] And it cannot be denied that the overwhelming majority of hundreds of thousands of Jewish refugees fleeing from Arab persecution *also* poured directly into Israel— in fulfillment of an unflagging, little-known "Zionism," a national liberation movement among Arab-born Jews whose gestation period had lasted roughly two thousand years.

From the Arab conquest, hundreds of thousands of Jews in the Arab world managed to survive between traditional ravages. Most had religious affiliations. The Arabs' general prohibition against political activities by their Jewish *dhimmis* might have been a factor that inhibited and submerged the growth of Zionism as a political phenomenon among the Sephardic Jews. But what may be called a "spiritual Zionism" took root in biblical times in the Sephardic Jewish community; those Jews, who are uniquely indigenous to the terrain that now is the Arab world, have retained in their liturgy the steady longing for "return" to the Land of Israel, a longing that has been mistakenly assumed to be exclusively "European."

Jews from Arab countries often become incensed when confronted with the argument that Zionism originated in Europe. Every Sephardic Jew interviewed had the same immediate reaction: the Sephardim are just as truly believers in Zion, and their ancient uninterrupted Jewish history led directly from the destruction of the Temple at Jerusalem.

They too were descendants of the original exiles, and, unlike their Western Jewish brothers, their empathy with the Bible was not dependent upon "unyielding interpretations," because Sephardic Jews lived in close proximity to the world of the Bible and could more easily relate to it. During an interview with an eminent Jewish scholar from Tunisia, I mistakenly likened the Sephardic Jewish communities, which have burgeoned in Israel and elsewhere since the Jews' exodus from Arab countries, to the European "shtetl." The scholar promptly corrected that assumption, somewhat bitterly and with alacrity. He explained that

They are more like our own *"mellah"* or *"hara,"* which many people probably never heard of. Zionism was in the Arab countries with every prayer we uttered —for millennia before Herzl.

The Jewish Presence

The Jewish presence in "the Holy Land"—at times tenuous—persisted throughout its bloody history. In fact, the Jewish claim—whether Arab-born or European-born Jew—to the land now called Palestine does not depend on a two-thousand-year-old promise. Buried beneath the propaganda—which has it that Jews "returned" to the Holy Land after two thousand years of separation, where they found crowds of "indigenous Palestinian Arabs"—is the bald fact that the Jews are indigenous people on that land who never left, but who have continuously stayed on their "Holy Land." Not only were there the little-known Oriental Jewish communities in adjacent Arab lands, but there had been an unceasing strain of "Oriental" or "Palestinian" Jews in "Palestine" for millennia.[3]

The Reverend James Parkes, an authority on Jewish/non-Jewish relations in the Middle East, assessed the Zionists' "real title deeds" in 1949.[4]

> It was, perhaps, inevitable that Zionists should look back to the heroic period of the Maccabees and Bar-Cochba, but their real title deeds were written by the less dramatic but equally heroic endurance of those who had maintained the Jewish presence in The Land all through the centuries, and in spite of every discouragement. This page of Jewish history found no place in the constant flood of Zionist propaganda. . . . The omission allowed the anti-Zionists, whether Jewish, Arab, or European, to paint an entirely false picture of the wickedness of Jewry trying to re-establish a two thousand-year-old claim to the country, indifferent to everything that had happened in the intervening period. It allowed a picture of The Land as a territory which had once been "Jewish," but which for many centuries had been "Arab." In point of fact any picture of a total change of population is false. . . .

It was only *"politically"* that the Jews lost their land, as Parkes reminded us. They never abandoned it physically, nor did they renounce their claim to their nation—the only continuous claim that exists. The Jews never submitted to assimilation into the various victorious populations even after successive conquerors had devastated the Jewish organizational structure. But, more important, despite becoming "much enfeebled in numbers and deprived both of political and social leaders and of skilled craftsmen,"[5] the Jews, in addition to their spiritual roots, managed to remain in varying numbers *physically at all times* on the land.

Thus, despite "physical violence against Jews and pagans" by the post-Roman Christians, more than forty Jewish communities survived and could be traced in the sixth century—"twelve towns on the coast, in the Negev, and east of the Jordan [land that was part of the Palestine Mandate, called Transjordan in 1922, and declared the "Hashemite Kingdom of Jordan" only thirty-odd years ago] and thirty-one villages in Galilee and in the Jordan Valley."[6]

In A.D. 438 the Jews from Galilee optimistically declared, "the end of the exile of our people" when the Empress Eudocia allowed the Jews to pray again at their holy temple site.[7] Recent archaeological discoveries determine that in A.D. 614 the Jews fought along with the Persian invaders of Palestine, "overwhelmed the Byzantine garrison in Jerusalem," and controlled that city for five years.[8] By the time the Arabs conquered the land two decades later, the Jews "had suffered three centuries of Christian intolerance, and monkish violence had been spasmodic during at least half of that period."[9] And the Jews hopefully welcomed the Arab conquerors.

The Muslim Arabs who entered seventh-century Jerusalem found a strong Jewish identity. At that time, *"we have evidence that Jews lived in all parts of the* *country and on both sides of the Jordan, and that they dwelt in both the towns and the villages, practicing both agriculture and various handicrafts.* "* A number of Jews lived in Lydda and Ramle—which have been identified by modern propaganda and even by more serious documents as historically "purely Arab" towns. "Large and important communities" of Jews lived "in such places as Ascalon, Caesarea and above all Gaza, which the Jews . . . had made a kind of capital [when] . . . they were excluded from Jerusalem."[10]

Jericho was home to many Jews[11]—the seventh-century Jewish refugees from Khaibar in Arabia among them. Khaibar had been a thriving Jewish community to the north of Mecca and Medina. After the Jews had "defended their forts and mansions with signal heroism," the Prophet Muhammad had "visited upon his beaten enemy inhuman atrocities," and "by the mass massacre of . . . men, women and children," the Prophet of Islam exterminated "completely" two Arabian Jewish tribes.[12]

> The consequences of the war were catastrophic. For centuries the Jews of Khaibar had led a life of freedom, peace, labor and trade; now they had to bow under the yoke of slavery and degradation. They had prided themselves on the purity of their family life; now their women and daughters were distributed among and carried away by the conquerors.[13]

An Arab "notable" from Medina, who visited the site of hostilities afterward, was quoted by a ninth-century Arab historian:

> Before the Moslem occupation, whenever there was a famine in the land, people would go to Khaibar. . . . The Jews always had fruit, and their springs yielded a plentiful supply of water. After the conquest of Khaibar, the Jews were said to design evil schemes against the Moslems. But hunger pressed us to go to their fields. . . . We found the landscape completely changed. We met none of the rich Khaibar landowners, but only destitute farmers everywhere . . . When we moved on to Kuteiba we felt much relieved. . . .[14]

The Jewish survivors from the area surrounding Khaibar were expelled from "the Arabian Peninsula" when the extent of the Muslim conquest was sufficient to add enough Arab farmers and replace the detested Jews.† Based on the Prophet Muhammad's theory, Caliph Omar implemented the decree "Let not two religions co-exist within the Arabian Peninsula."[15]

The Arab theologians' 1968 conference, 1,300 years later, continued to justify the Khaibar extermination of its Jews. One participant explained:

> . . . Omar . . . got experience that the Jews were the callers and instigators of the sedition at any time and everywhere. He purified Arabia from them. Most of them dwelt at Khaibar and its neighborhood. That was because he was informed that the Prophet said while he was dying: "Never do two religions exist in Arabia." [Sheikh Abd Allah Al Meshad][16]

*Emphasis added.
†See Chapter 8.

Another Arab participant at that conference emphasized,

> All people want to get rid of the Jews by hook or by crook. . . . People are not prejudiced against them but the Jewish evil and the various wicked aspects . . . are quite clear. . . .
>
> When Bani Qoraiza were punished, an end was put to the Jews of Madina. Those Jews had been the strongest, the richest and the most pernicious and harmful ones. They had been deeply rooted in the society and they had had a high rank and an important status. . . .
>
> Some orientalists ignore the various reasons why the Jews of Khaibar and others were punished. . . . These orientalists alleged that the invasion of Khaibar was launched because the Prophet wished to reward the Muslims of Hodaibeya and comfort them. . . . but we have mentioned the most evident reasons of the punishment befalling the Jews. The question of the booty is casual and always subsidiary for waging the wars of the Prophet. It is mentioned in the Verses of the Quran about *Jihad* [holy war] as a secondary reason for striving against the Unbelievers. [Muhammad Azzah Darwaza][17]

The seventh-century Jewish refugees from Khaibar's environs joined the indigenous Jewish population in "Transjordan, especially in Dera'a." In fact, Arabian Jewish exiles settled "as far as the hills of Hebron," but had they not "intermarried" with the established Jewish communities and connected somehow to the "Diaspora centers, they [the Jewish settlements] could hardly have survived as Jewish communities for hundreds of years." A settled Jewish community was present then in the northern Transjordanian city of Hamadan, "or Amatus" —"a city famed for its palms"—in the area that one day would be part of the League of Nations'* Mandated "Jewish National Home" in Palestine.[18]

The Christian Crusaders of the eleventh century were merciless but unsuccessful in their efforts to remove any vestige of Jewish tradition. In 1165, Benjamin of Tudela, the renowned Spanish traveler, found that the "Academy of Jerusalem" had been established at Damascus. Although the Crusaders had almost "wiped out" the Jewish communities of Jerusalem, Acre, Caesarea and Haifa, some Jews remained, and whole "village communities of Galilee survived."

Acre became the seat of a Jewish academy in the thirteenth century. And while "many may have merged themselves into the local population, Christian or Muslim," the Jews "stayed, to share and suffer from the disorder" of the aftermath of the Crusaders' "feudalism,"[19] resisting conversion. During the twelfth and thirteenth centuries, "there was a constant trickle of Jewish immigrants into the country . . . some from other Islamic territories and especially North Africa."[20]

Jews from Gaza, Ramle, and Safed were considered the "ideal guides" in the Holy Land in the fourteenth century, as Jacques of Verona, a visiting Christian monk, attested. After the Christian had "noted the long established Jewish community at the foot of Mount Zion, in Jerusalem," he wrote,

*See Chapter 12.

A pilgrim who wished to visit ancient forts and towns in the Holy Land would have been unable to locate these, without a good guide who knew the Land well, or without one of the Jews who lived there. The Jews were able to recount the history of these places since this knowledge had been handed down from their forefathers and wise men.

So when I journeyed overseas I often requested and managed to obtain an excellent guide among the Jews who lived there.[21]

In 1438 a rabbi from Italy became the spiritual leader of the Jewish community in Jerusalem,[22] and fifty years afterward, another Italian scholar, Obadiah de Bertinoro, founded the Jerusalem rabbinical school that dealt authoritatively "in rabbinic matters among the Jewish communities of the Islamic world."[23]

The Jews, meanwhile, were plentiful enough so that in 1486 "a distinguished pilgrim" to the Holy Land, the Dean of Mainz Cathedral, Bernhard von Breidenbach, advised that both Hebron's and Jerusalem's Jews "will treat you in full fidelity—more so than anyone else in those countries of the unbelievers."[24]

The "Ishmaelite," or Islamic-born, Jewish immigration to the Holy Land was prominent, and became intensified after the Spanish Inquisition. The Holy Land's throbbing, spirited Jewish life continued, even in Hebron, where "the prosperous Jewish community . . . had been plundered, many Jews killed and the survivors forced to flee" in 1518, three years after Ottoman rule began. By 1540, Hebron's Jewry had recovered and reconstructed its Jewish Quarter, while the first Jewish printing press outside Europe was instituted in Safed in 1563.[25]

Under Turkish rule the Jews in Jerusalem and in Gaza maintained "cultural and spiritual unity," and Sultan Suleiman I allowed many Jews "to return to the Holy Land." In 1561, "Suleiman gave Tiberias, one of the four Jewish holy cities, to a former 'secret' Jew from Portugal, Don Joseph Nasi, who rebuilt the city and the villages around it." Nasi's efforts attracted Jewish settlement from many areas of the Mediterranean.[26] And those "Ishmaelite" Jewish communities that did not or could not make the pilgrimage were nonetheless spiritually attached to their brothers in the Holy Land.

Sephardic Zionism

Nearly every one of the recurrent "false Messiahs" who attempted to play the Messianic role in leading the Jewish people back to Israel were apparently Sephardic Jews.[27] One Messianic movement was started by two Sephardic Jews who attempted to negotiate with the Pope in 1524. When they failed to convince him of a plan that would liberate Palestine for the Jews, another proposal was made to the German emperor, Charles V, after which both would-be Messiahs were arrested and jailed.[28] One, Solomon Molcho, was burned to death, "a martyr's death," and the other, David Reubeni, "a mysterious character," disappeared, leaving his diary behind.[29]

Shabbetai Zevi, who along with his prophet, Nathan of Gaza, is considered "the most outstanding" Messianic pretender, was born in 1626 in Asia Minor, son of "Mordechai of Smyrna." Zevi's followers came from "Amsterdam to Yemen, from the eastern frontier of Poland to the outlying villages in the Atlas Mountains of North Africa." His unparalleled ability to lead the receptive Jewish people "back" was attributed by Gershom Scholem, the foremost authority on Zevi and his Sabbatean movement, to "the general atmosphere within Jewry," which was "more decisive in shaping the movement than the peculiar spiritual state of the youthful . . . Sabbatai Sevi."[30] Because the seventeenth century was fraught with persecution for both Sephardic and Western (Ashkenazic) Jews, "penitents and seekers of liberty—rich and poor, scholars and the ignorant—thus united round" the Messianic movement.

It was Zevi himself who was the "weakest of its leaders"—"in 1666 . . . the Jews who saw him entering the sultan's palace" never dreamed that "the messiah had adopted . . . Islam." But Zevi had done exactly that, upon "being threatened with great physical punishment and even death." Because of Zevi's conversion, one writer says that "The greater part of Jewry was shaken to the core. The blow was even greater than the crucifixion of Jesus had been to his followers."[31] The disillusionment was shattering; "Jesus had paid the highest price that could be demanded from a man, but Shabbetai had not."[32] Zevi "fell into a state of deep depression" after his conversion, then recovered and "went wandering from community to community, preaching . . ." and committing "strange actions" afterward. The letter of renunciation of his former visions, which Zevi had been "compelled" by a "strict rabbinical court" to sign in Venice two years after his conversion, remained intact:[33]

> Although I have declared that I saw the *Merkava* as Ezekiel the prophet saw it and the prophecy declared that Shabbetai Zevi is the Messiah, the Rabbis and Geonim of Venice have ruled that I am in error and there was nothing real in that vision. I have therefore admitted their words and say that what I prophesied regarding Shabbetai Zevi has no substance.[34]

Shabbetai Zevi died at fifty in 1676.

Another prominent Sephardic Zionist was Spanish-born Rabbi Manasseh ben Israel, a major seventeenth-century Jewish scholar. Rabbi ben Israel became convinced that England—which had no Jewish population for three hundred years—was holding back the redemption and return to the Holy Land. The horror of the Spanish Inquisition, he maintained, had fulfilled part of the biblical requisite—the suffering—but the Bible had promised to restore the Jews to Israel only after they had also been dispersed to every part of the world.

Since ben Israel had ascertained that some settlers in America were Jewish, he concluded that only England—bereft of Jews—stood in the way of "return." In a formal "declaration" to the British, he explained that " . . . before the Messiah come . . . first we must have our seat here likewise." For good measure, he strengthened his argument by stressing the economic benefits England could derive through imports and exports from Jewish merchants throughout the world. The British may have considered other factors more determinative, but some historians credit Rabbi ben Israel as the direct force that brought about the re-entry of the Jews to England.[35]

There have been Sephardic Jewish "Zionists" from the time of the biblical exile of the Jews from Jerusalem in 586 B.C. "It is common knowledge that religious life in the Diaspora was bound up with the Holy Land and with the Temple so long as it existed. The connection of Cyrene, Carthage and the rest of North Africa with Palestine was in fact quite strong."[36]

"Jason of Cyrene" wrote a five-volume work about Palestine, where he arrived during the Hasmonean Revolt.[37] The pilgrimages to Jerusalem by Libyan Jews were recorded in the Bible,[38] as was the Jerusalem synagogue that was named after them.[39] "Simon the Cyrenian" was one of many of the Libyan pilgrims who remained in Jerusalem. It was Simon who was reported by the New Testament to have been " a chance passerby just arrived from the country," who "was forced to take part in the crucifixion."[40]

The holiday of Passover, commemorating the Jews' return from exile in Egypt to the Holy Land of Israel, was not celebrated differently by eleventh-century "Palestinian Jews" than by modern Jews around the world. It was when the Jews left Egypt, no longer slaves, that they became organized—a people with the prospect of returning to their land.[41] Passover service for Jews everywhere concludes with the words, "Next year in Jerusalem." Sephardic clergy explain rather impatiently that the basic Sephardic liturgy is "much the same" as the European, although the Sephardim are particularly proud of the indigenous poetry that enhances their religious literature.

In fact, much of the universal Jewish liturgical devotion to the Holy Land has been adopted from Sephardic Jewish scholars. An important example is the venerated twelfth-century rabbinical scholar and poet, Jehudah Halevi, whose words became a prominent part of the universal Jewish liturgy—"My heart is in the East and I at the uttermost West . . ." and "Ode to Zion,"[42] among others.

Halevi was also a pragmatist who wrote serious treatises on the theme that became the foundation of modern Zionism—rather than languish in exile, he stressed, the Jews themselves must take the first step and the Messiah would come later. Faithful to his enjoinder, Halevi left his thriving family and career as a physician, and set out from Spain in the twelfth century on what was then the hazardous journey to Palestine.

Halevi was warned by friends and compatriots when he broke journey in Egypt, according to his German biographies. But after resting, he resisted their attempts to dissuade him from continuing: "In Egypt, Providence showed itself in a hurry as it were; it settled down permanently in the Holy Land only," Halevi wrote. His German biographer likened Goethe's Faust to Halevi's "highest moment"—"when he first set eyes on the Holy City, as it came into his view between the mountains." Halevi "wanted to walk barefooted over the heap of ruins that had once been the Temple." According to traditional history, he had barely arrived at the gates of Jerusalem and was kissing the stones of hallowed land, when he was slain by an Arab tribesman.[43]

The concept of the "return" of the Jews from exile to the biblical homeland in Zion—the promised land—was an integral part of Jewish life everywhere, but nowhere was it more fervently held or more inextricably interwoven with daily life and long-range hope than among the Sephardim. They were intense in their religious observances. Some of the most perceptive and distinguished Jewish scholars came from "Arab" countries, and the revered Babylonian Talmud was compiled in what is now Iraq. The Sephardic Jews were diligent in their religious pursuits, and would have disdained any open attempt to deviate from the flexible norm of religious observance. The synagogues in many *haras* or *mellahs* were the hub of social life as well as a moral duty.

Jewish communities were tightly knit, and their interpersonal relationships attained the close warmth of an extended family. They spoke their prayers with understanding and expectation of eventual fulfillment. Their implorations for deliverance from the austerity of exile in foreign lands, and the promised ingathering of the Jews back in the Holy Land was, for many of them, not mere cant recited by rote, but a sincere profession of anticipation and desire.

Scattered throughout the vast extent of what became the Arab world, and isolated within it during all the centuries of harsh Arab rule that came after their exile, the Sephardic Jews looked forward to this realization of a prophecy. Although from time to time manifested in the temporary acceptance of one Messianic pretender or another who would lead them back to Zion, the eventual debunking of these self-anointed zealots did not diminish hope.

Their synagogues, as every synagogue in the world theoretically, were constructed so that the worshiper would be directed toward Jerusalem—when he entered, upon facing the Torah (holy scrolls), and when he or she stood to pray.[44] Even in the most isolated Jewish troglodyte communities of southern Tunisia or the remote island of Djerba, the prayers which were offered were much the same as those in the services of a modern American synagogue.[45] Whether said three times a day, as prescribed by pre-eminent religious Jewish scholars in Arab and European countries alike, or recited at dawn and sunset—when the Tunisian Jews from troglodyte villages around Matmata[46] came out of their limestone caves to pray—the prayers always[47] included the plea to

> . . . Sound the great Shofar for our freedom; . . . bring our exiles together and assemble us from the four corners of the earth. Blessed art thou, O Lord, who gatherest the dispersed of thy people Israel to return in mercy to the city Jerusalem; . . . rebuild it soon, in our days. . . . Blessed art thou, O Lord, Builder of Jerusalem.[48]

Perhaps the most unfortunate among the Jews in Arab countries took their prayers more literally than the relatively secure. Many orthodox Jewish victims of European persecution also turned inward toward hope of redemption, while many others observed fewer symbolic traditions—European Jewish citizens who obstinately believed themselves "assimilated" up until the decree of a death sentence by Hitler's Nuremberg Laws or their precursors. But for the Jews in the Arab Muslim world, "assimilation" was a contradiction in terms, as impossible in the twentieth century as it had been a thousand years before.

For virtually all Sephardic Jews, religious life was active, and was integrally connected to the "Palestinian center."[49] Because Jerusalem had been sacred to Jews fifteen centuries before the Prophet Muhammad was born—just as Mecca and Medina are sacred to Muslims because the Prophet Muhammad lived and worked there[50]—over the centuries the dispersed Oriental Jews continuously sent offerings to Jerusalem. There a Jewish center had been established near the "Western" or "Wailing Wall," the sacred ruin at the site of the original Temple built by King Solomon, and the site too of the Jews' Second Temple that the Romans had destroyed in A.D. 70.

Though the Jewish refugees from Arab lands in the twentieth century had no international multigovernment assistance agency, as the Arab refugees have had UNRWA, the latter-day outpouring of Jewish funds to modern Israel for its refugees stemmed from an ancient tradition. Historian S. D. Goitein tells of the disgrace that befell an eleventh-century Tunisian Jewish community because it had failed to make its "annual appeal for the Academy of Jerusalem" promptly. However, the community "assures us that the Jerusalem appeal was carried through, . . . albeit belatedly," and thus, redeemed itself.

As an amusing example of the geographical diversity of "Palestine's" jurisdiction over the Jews in Diaspora,

> A Jewish court in *India* . . . issues, in the year 1132, a [proprietary] document for a local girl and a merchant from *Tunisia* in the name of exilarch of *Baghdad* and of the *Palestinian* Gaon [Chief Rabbi], who at that time had his seat at Cairo.*[51]

Jewish schools in the Mediterranean Diaspora prayed for the "welfare of dedicated community leaders at the holy places in Jerusalem."[52] The "synagogue of the Palestinians,"† which described itself in legal documents as "acting on behalf of the High Court of the yeshiva [academy] of Jerusalem and its head . . ."[53] was the main synagogue of Old Cairo, Alexandria, Ramle, Damascus, and Aleppo in the eleventh century. Documents have been found attesting to Jewish

---

*Emphasis added.

†The centuries-old traditional use of the term "Palestinian" to describe Jews provides forceful repudiation of the present popular usage of "Palestinian"—to denote exclusively the Arab refugees. The psychological propaganda benefit derived by the Arabs from annexing the word "Palestinian," to designate only Arabs, is considerable: if the Arab refugees are seen as *the* "Palestinians," the world reaction becomes conditioned to identifying the Arab "Palestinian" refugees with Palestine. Although the greatest bulk of Palestine is known today as Jordan, this fact has become obscured. There appears today no popularly known "Palestine" except the smaller area which became Israel, so the perceived connection between Arab Palestinian refugees and Israel will follow. Thus, the misstatement now in common use: "Palestine became Israel." See Chapters 8 and 12.

cultural and spiritual life in a "sizeable" fourteenth-century Jewish community at Bilbays, a town "on the caravan route from Cairo to Palestine," even after it had been subjected to forced conversion to Islam *en masse,* and its synagogue turned into a mosque.[54]

Pilgrimages such as Rabbi Halevi's or Maimonides' were frequently made with great difficulty from all corners of the Arab world. And the inspiration for the Spanish-born Halevi was provided by the writings of a native of Fez, Morocco, the eleventh-century Rabbi Isaac Alfassi, who was called "the symbol of Hebrew scholarship in North Africa."[55] Complaints were in fact registered about the heavy burden of maintaining the way stations in Egypt's Jewish community, where Jewish pilgrims en route to the Holy Land "expected to be equipped" for the rest of the arduous trip.[56]

Documents recording the modern history of the Jewish national liberation movement give sparse credit to the significant role of Sephardic Jews' devotion over the centuries to the philosophical and spiritual nationalism that undoubtedly prepared a base for modern Zionism. Indeed, a Sephardic Jew, Rabbi Yehudah Alkalay (1798–1878), has been called the precursor of modern Zionism. Walter Laqueur,[57] in a study dealing primarily with the European Zionist movement, states: "It should be noted at least in passing that another rabbi, Yehuda Alkalay, writing in Serbia . . . had already drawn up a practical program toward . . . the return to Zion"; Sephardic "Zionist" Alkalay's development came *twenty years before* the European Zionist whose work Laqueur was discussing.[58]

That some Jews from Arab lands were already "home" in Alkalay's time is attested to by many recorded visits and foreign consulate communications. One dispatch from the British Consulate in Jerusalem in 1839 reported that "the Jews of Algiers and its dependencies, are numerous in Palestine. . . ."[59] In 1843, a Christian missionary from England wrote of "the arrival" in Jerusalem of an additional "150 Jews from Algiers," and he noted: "There is now a large number of Jews here from the coast of Africa, who are about to form themselves into a separate congregation."[60]

Not only were the Sephardic Jews "numerous" in the Holy Land, but their language, Hebrew, was popularly used "in the ordinary affairs of life" long before the "new Jewish immigration of the early eighteen-eighties."[61] In 1839 British Consul Young, in Jerusalem, reported that "the mode of conducting Jewish affairs among themselves . . . is entirely in Hebrew, which ancient custom they are very tenacious of and desirous to maintain. . . ."[62] Young had found it "necessary" to hire a Hebrew interpreter "immediately upon his appointment in 1838."[63] Another British consul, James Finn, in 1850 transmitted the "translation" of a Hebrew petition from "the Moghrabi or African Jews settled in Jerusalem . . . [who] form a considerable body, increasing in numbers. . . ."[64]

In 1862 Finn suggested sending a Hebrew-speaking member of his staff to "the Jews of Galilee,"[65] and he noted in his memoirs that, "With regard to pure Hebrew, the learned world in Europe is greatly mistaken in designating this a dead language. In Jerusalem it is a living tongue of everyday utility." In fact,

Hebrew was "spoken" and widely used in the "English Consulate."[66] His wife, in her own book, *Reminiscences of Elizabeth Anne Finn*, related that in everyday life as well as official business, "all the men spoke Hebrew, and I have seen men from Kabul, India and Jerusalem, meeting as total strangers, at once fall to conversing in Hebrew, which was still a thoroughly living language, for speaking as for literary and religious purposes."[67] Thus, Sephardic "Zionists" found a "living" Hebrew when they arrived at "The Land."

Simultaneously, non-Jewish "Zionists" were urging the "regeneration of Palestine" as a Jewish homeland, in part due to their horror at learning of the tortures and persecution of the Jews of Damascus following the blood libel of 1840. In June of 1842 Colonel Charles Churchill, the Duke of Marlborough's grandson, wrote that, "in his view, the Jews ought to promote the regeneration of Palestine and the eastern Mediterranean region. Were they to do so, they would, Churchill believed, 'end by obtaining the sovereignty of at least Palestine.' Charles Churchill felt strongly that the Jews should resume what he described . . . as their 'existence as a people.' "[68]

Another non-Jew reportedly espousing the Jewish nation was Napoleon Bonaparte, who launched his campaign to conquer Palestine in 1799 with a pledge to "restore the country to the Jews."[69] While Napoleon was unsuccessful in his attempt, some believe he was a catalyst for

> a distinguished gallery of writers, clerics, journalists, artists and statesmen [who] accompanied the awakening of the idea of Jewish restoration in Palestine. Lord Lindsay, Lord Shaftesbury (the social reformer who learned Hebrew), Lord Palmerston, Disraeli, Lord Manchester, George Eliot, Holman Hunt, Sir Charles Warren, Hall Caine—all appear among the many who spoke, wrote, organized support, or put forward practical projects by which Britain might help the return of the Jewish people to Palestine. There were some who even urged the British government to buy Palestine from the Turks to give it to the Jews to rebuild.[70]

Sir George Gawler, who had fought in the battle of Waterloo, wrote in 1845 that "the most sober and sensible remedy for the miseries of Asiatic Turkey" was to "Replenish the deserted towns and fields of Palestine with the energetic people whose warmest affections are rooted in the soil." Gawler published a series of pamphlets on the theme, one on "the emancipation of the Jews," and in 1849 he made a pilgrimage to Palestine with his friend, Jewish leader Sir Moses Montefiore.[71]

In 1847, Lord Lindsay declared his hopes that

> The Jewish race, so wonderfully preserved, may yet have another stage of national existence opened to them, may once more obtain possession of their native land. . . . The soil of Palestine still enjoys her sabbaths, and only waits for the return of her banished children, and the application of industry, commensurate with her agricultural capabilities, to burst once more into universal luxuriance, and be all that she ever was in the days of Solomon.[72]

In Britain, the idea of increasing the Jewish population in Palestine to form a Jewish state took on such popular appeal[73] that the press repeated false rumors that Lord Beaconsfield—Benjamin Disraeli—had attempted and failed to achieve the restoration of Jewish Palestine, and asserted that "If he had freed the Holy Land and restored the Jews, as he might have done instead of pottering about Roumelia and Afghanistan, he would have died dictator."[74]

Meanwhile, thousands of miles distant, more than 2,000 Yemenite Jews were setting out on the perilous journey to their homeland, where they would arrive in 1881. There the "first enduring Jewish agricultural settlement in modern Palestine"—Petach Tikvah—was founded on the "deserted and ruined" Sharon Plain by "old-time" Palestinian Jewish families who left "the overcrowded Jewish Quarter of the Old City of Jerusalem" in 1878. It was four years later that what is called the first *aliyah* (Hebrew), a great wave of Jewish European refugees, would settle on the land.[75] Theodor Herzl came with his own concept of modern Zionism, but not until many years afterward. In fact, Theodor Herzl's grandfather reportedly attended the Sephardic Zionist Yehudah Alkalay's synagogue in Semlin, Serbia, and the two frequently visited. The grandfather "had his hands on" one of the first copies of Alkalay's 1857 work[76] prescribing the "return of the Jews to the Holy Land and renewed glory of Jerusalem." Contemporary scholars conclude that Herzl's own implementation of modern Zionism was undoubtedly influenced by that relationship.[77]

Alkalay was subjected to "scornful criticism" for his unorthodox dream: "that all of Israel should return to the land of our fathers." Alkalay was perhaps the first to write of the "Damascus Affair"—the blood libel of 1840—and that episode apparently crystallized his "daring" ideas. "Complacent dwellers in foreign lands" must be chastened by the suffering of the Jews in Damascus.[78] Intent upon unifying a worldwide Jewish coalition for nationhood, in 1874 Alkalay immigrated to Jerusalem at the age of seventy-six.[79] Although he is cited in some authoritative chronicles and anthologies,[80] his achievement remains little-known. Alkalay and Sephardic Jews in general are given greater cognizance in a contemporary French study: "From the period of the 'golden age' of Spain to the death of Alkalay . . . the contribution of the Sephardim—beyond its extraordinary cultural influence on Judaism—to the rebirth of the Jewish national entity . . . resides incontrovertibly in their" overwhelming adoption of the Jewish state, "the intensity of their love for Zion and their unshakeable belief in the coming of the Messiah."[81]

A dramatic illustration of this point is the 2,500-year-old Jewish community in Yemen, which in 1948 picked up its collective self and boarded "the wings of eagles" to Israel. As discussed at some length in the last chapter, the Yemenite Jews had remained singularly adherent to the ancient Jewish tradition despite, or perhaps because of, the constant persecution and degradation to which they were subjected by the Arabian Muslims. They seemed still faithful to the reminder that the venerated philosopher, Maimonides, had written them, in his "Epistle to Yemen" in 1172:

It is, my coreligionists, one of the fundamental articles of the faith of Israel, that the future redeemer of our people will . . . gather our nation, assemble our exiles, redeem us from our degradation, propagate the true religion, and exterminate his opponents as is clearly stated in Scripture. . . .

Remember, my coreligionists, that on account of the vast number of our sins, God has hurled us in the midst of this people, the Arabs, who have persecuted us severely, and passed baneful and discriminatory legislation against us, as Scripture has forewarned us, "Our enemies themselves shall judge us" (Deut. 32:31). Never did a nation molest, degrade, debase, and hate us as much as they. . . . Although we were dishonored by them beyond human endurance, and had to put up with their fabrications, yet we behaved like him who is depicted by the inspired writer, "But I am as a deaf man, I hear not, and I am as a dumb man that opens not his mouth" (Ps. 38:14). Similarly our sages instructed us to bear the prevarications and preposterousness of Ishmael in silence. . . .[82]

The general Sephardic stoicism and steadfast rejection of conversion to Islam in the face of constant abuse was an impressive monument to cultural and spiritual Zionism, yet in Yemen this quality was perhaps most pronounced. There the Jews were poor. The Koran has ordained "twice" (2:1; 3:112) that Jews be poor. The Muslims in Yemen and other Muslim countries took the words "literally": "Yemenite Jews . . . always were clothed like beggars . . . some of the older generation cling to this habit even in Israel" and at times "Jewish property, even houses, were taken away from them" by Muslims because "they presented a picture of wealth incompatible with the state assigned to the Jews by God."[83] Western culture had barely penetrated anywhere in Yemen, but Yemenite Jews were extremely clean, and their pious community sent its children to synagogue at the age of two. By the time they were three or four, they were learning the Torah (Jewish law and tradition).

The Yemenite Jews seemed, to those who visited there, to be waiting, in what they also deemed was their necessarily miserable exile, for the return to the "Perfect World"[84]—and, in costume, they rehearsed the celebration of their redemption on every Sabbath on which they were not forced to work. Israelis who received the Jews from Yemen upon their arrival in Israel reported that the deliriously happy Yemenites could not be dissuaded from referring to the Israeli greeters as "prophets." Some of them were disappointed that "King David" was not on hand.

For many more sophisticated Jews from the Arab centers, the drive toward Israel was based not as strictly on the mystical or religious aspect of the "return," but on their cultural identification with a "people." One young Tunisian Jew was described very succinctly in a study:

His fate . . . lies not in his birthplace, Tunisia, but in his ethnic homeland of Israel. There is no future for him in Tunisia, whereas in Israel, there is a possibility . . . of a great existential experience. "If I have only one life, I want to dedicate my life to something greater than me."[85]

When, in the familiar Jewish wedding tradition, the bridegroom stomps on a glass, the crushed goblet is a reminder of the destruction of the temple in Jerusalem: nowhere is this observed more passionately than among Sephardic Jews.

The identification with a Jewish homeland, a Jewish nationality, remained a strong influence even upon the young Sephardic Jews, whose education and social life broadened with the liberalizing influence of non-Arab colonials. In twentieth-century Iraq, for example, during a period when Turkish rule allowed for many young Jews to expand further into the intellectual mainstream, there was a break with many elements inherent in traditional Jewish life. Yet the Iraqi Jews continued to observe the symbolic traditions; they were still fasting on the Day of Atonement and "maintaining" various traditions "even in recent years."[86]

Significantly, very few of the Jews whose day-to-day religious observance has dwindled have converted.[87] The pattern that has evolved in the latter twentieth century, it seems—although the regular religious observance has assumed less importance as a daily ritual than it had for their forebears—is that their ethnic or cultural identification as "the Jewish people" has stood constant and perhaps even strengthened. Had the Jews from Arab countries enjoyed the same manifold freedoms and opportunities that are the right of every citizen from many Western nations, it is uncertain whether the unprecedented virtual emptying of Jews from Arab countries would have been precipitated by the re-creation of the Jewish state. Perhaps they would have continued to adhere to the pattern set by American Jews, of whom a minuscule percentage have moved to Israel.

The hardships faced by hundreds of thousands of refugees once they arrived in the embryonic Jewish state were multiple—for Jews born in Arab countries, a new language, modern Hebrew, had to be learned, and the swarms of homeless had to be housed. The refugee camps and "temporary" housing—*maabarot*—were bulging.

Raphael Patai described some of the conditions encountered by the hopeful hordes of refugees when they arrived in the "land of milk and honey":

> The great majority of them were housed in tents which were drenched from above and flooded from below during the heavy rains of the winter of 1949 and 50. The original plan called for a sojourn of a few weeks only in the immigrants' camps after which each immigrant was to be sent to a permanent place of settlement. Actually, however, in view of the large number of immigrants the rate of evacuation from the camps lagged constantly behind the rate at which the new immigrants were brought into Israel, and the period of sojourn in the camps was prolonged from three months, to four months, to six months, to eight months . . .
>
> One of the main immigrant's reception camps was that of Rosh Ha'ayin, in which at the height of its occupancy in 1950 there were some 15,000 Yemenite Jewish immigrants, all lodged in tents, fifteen of them in each tent. The few buildings in the camp were used to house the hospital and the clinics. . . . When

the immigrants arrived many of them were very weak. Mortality was high, and as many as twenty deaths occurred daily. . . . very soon, mortality decreased and generally the strength of the people increased. Practically all the immigrants (98 percent to be exact) suffered from trachoma when they arrived at Rosh Ha'ayin. After a four months' sojourn in the camp, and constant medical treatment—often administered against the wishes of the patients—this percentage sank to 20 percent. The health of the children was also in very bad shape.[88]

In 1951, 256,000 Jewish refugees—or one-fifth of Israel's population then, which was 1,400,000—were still living in "temporary" settlements.[89] Mordechai Ben Porath, an Iraqi-born Israeli, and long a member of Israel's Parliament, told of the camps in the '50s:

> I arrived in Israel penniless and, in the early 1950's, directed a transit camp for tens of thousands of Jews from Arab countries. There my family and I lived with them. I saw those people housed in makeshift huts without water, without electricity, exposed to rain, wind, and even flood. Professional people were helpless: they didn't have their licenses or any other certificates with them. These had been torn to shreds by Arab officials in certain Arab countries when they left.[90]

The refugees had little in common with their brothers who had immigrated to the Holy Land generations before. This was particularly true of the Yemenite Jews. More than two thousand "Zionists" from Yemen had managed to get to Palestine in 1881. By the time of the refugee deluge of 1948 and onward, more than 45,000 Jews from Arab lands already were living in the country. In fact, relative to the total populations of Jews in Asia and Africa from 1919 to 1948, more Oriental Jews immigrated from the East than from Europe and America, with approximately one-third of Yemenite and Syrian Jews becoming immigrants; "as far as is known, there was no other Jewish community from which such a high percentage immigrated" to the land of Israel between 1919 and 1948.[91]

Carl Hermann Voss, a theologian and, in 1953, Chairman of the American Christian Palestine Committee, discussed the "125% increase of population" during Israel's first five years: "A difficult adjustment was necessary. . . . The Israel of 1948 had only meager natural resources, limited capital, and no friendly states on its borders. . . . The fabric of this swiftly growing society was strained by the heterogeneity of . . . the several hundred thousand Oriental Jews who came from Iraq, North Africa, and Yemen."[92]

Voss wrote of his "memorable experience" to see Jews

> coming home from lands of death and dispersal to a land of life and light . . . a fulfillment of the prophecy of Isaiah . . . for Jews who had left the caverns and cellars of North Africa or the bleak wastes of feudal Yemen.
>
> In a Ma'abara work village on the slopes of Mt. Carmel not far from Elijah's cave, I talked to a bizarre type of Jew—a Jew from Baghdad, purportedly descended from those who did not return with Ezra and Nehemiah from the Babylonian exile to rebuild the Temple 2,500 years ago. In garb that made him almost

indistinguishable from his Arab cousin, and speaking the Arabic tongue, he seemed incongruous in this modern setting of the new Israel; yet this Iraqi Jew gave new meaning to a sentence I had learned in my youth: "Behold I shall bring them from the north country and I shall gather them from the coasts of the earth. A great company shall return thither."[93]

For Jews born in Arab countries, the many freedoms in Israel often had to be learned. One poignant scene was described by historian Goitein, who visited a refugee way-station camp in Aden, where Jews fleeing from Yemen were waiting to get to Israel.

[It was] in the receiving camp of Hashid near Aden in November 1949. The scene occurred between two Yemenites, one an Israeli, a man who had lived in Palestine long enough to become socially naturalized, and the other an immigrant who had arrived at the camp only a few days previously.

The Israeli Yemenite, an attendant working in the camp, of course mixed on terms of complete equality with everyone else there, with the director of the camp, the chief doctor and with a university professor. One day I was standing near him when an immigrant Yemenite ran up to him and in a fraction of a second threw himself on the ground before the attendant, kissing his feet and embracing his legs, while making some trivial request. The mere physical aspect was quite remarkable. Throwing oneself down on the ground with such force without getting hurt showed that the man must have had long practice in such matters. Yemen is, of course, one of the more backward Arab countries; still, that unforgettable little scene illustrates a tremendous contrast."[94]

There are Jews who sought refuge from Arab countries, who are dedicated to their Jewish homeland, but who retain many happy memories of their lives in the very communities from which they fled. Yet during long conversations, as they recalled the past, these people from different Arab lands related individual experiences so similar in their discriminatory character that, despite their distances from one another, they seemed to speak in unison. Although they never had met and probably never would meet, they narrated a collective chronicle of a buoyant, resilient, close-knit community life punctuated by fear and demeanment, and by intermittent terrorizing and anti-Jewish violence.

Their ambivalent remembrances indicated a kind of nostalgia for the land and customs of their origin and childhood. For some, the nostalgic tendency is enhanced by the passage of time and tempered by dissatisfaction at the frequent conditions of austerity and hardship in Israel. However, even the mass, admittedly happier within their own Jewish nation, might wish to erase the blemish of painful memories.

But this wistful turning to the lovely scenes of their native lands, their joy in the colorful traditions they knew in their youth, and the universal, perhaps healthier tendency to prefer recollection of the sweet moments of life rather than the bitter, should not obscure the actualities. Many Iraqi or Syrian or North

African Jews have wistful and moving recollections of the streets and the rivers and the flowers they loved; they long to see Damascus or Cairo or Baghdad again. But in evaluating the nostalgia, one must remember that there were many German Jews who had similar memories of Berlin.

6

Invitation Declined

... there was always some riot in Baghdad
against the Jews, I guess just for the fun of it or something.
—Rafi, about Iraq in 1929

... if he was lucky, he was just slapped on the
face for nothing and told, "You are a dirty Jew."
—Shlomo, about Egypt in 1946

Only when the Syrians are free can they tell the
truth about their life in Syria.
—Shoshana, about Syria in 1982

You can never feel equal because you don't
know what will happen next.
—Helena, about Morocco in 1982

The preceding harsh chronicle of historical data places in perspective the Arab claims of traditional tolerance and just treatment for "their Jews."

A number of Jewish refugees from Arab countries have been interviewed for this book—in Israel, in France, in England and in the United States—so that the tradition can be traced down to the present generation.

Some, who fled at the time of the Jewish refugees' mass exodus around 1948, described the quality of their lives *before* Israel's statehood. Other Jews, who remained in their Arab birthplaces *after* the Arab world brought war against Israel's modern re-creation in 1948, told of experiences in which their traditional demeanment as the Jewish lower-caste *dhimmi* was compounded by another ingredient: the Arab-Muslim community intensified its persecution of the Jews as "Zionists," branded as members of an enemy fifth column, until they escaped or were expelled.

Their stories vividly indicated the probable quality of life that awaited the average Arab-born Jew who might accept the Arab governments' "invitations" to return "home." The recollections also verified and gave individual life to the historical evidence: that the Arab world was united not against "Zionism" as such, but against any Jew, and perhaps any non-Muslim, who deemed himself or herself truly equal. Further, the accounts may offer insight into the so-called "hard-line" attitudes of the Sephardic Jewish majority that now prevails in Israel.

Among the many powerful and moving interviews, each one of the little-recognized "other" Middle East refugees chronicled a little-known life history, and the lives of his or her family. It was wrenching to be forced to choose, from so many often-painful memories that were breathed earnestly and patiently into a tape recorder, those that would then be pressed into the pages of this book. But the scope of the subject of the "Palestine Problem" still to be discussed in following chapters dictated brevity.

The following personal experiences, as told by Jews who themselves fled from those Arab countries where they were born, are varied by each individual's style, and by the quality of the intimidation their countries of origin practiced.

However, those selected here to describe their respective Arab birthplaces draw a sketch that is representative of experiences that were recounted time after time, in more than one hundred individual personal interviews conducted over the past several years.[1]

Rafi

Rafi, an Iraq-born Jew, was anxious to "tear away" the "myth" that "Arabs' hostility toward Jews began in 1948." He recalled bitterly his childhood in Baghdad before "the family ran to Israel" in the early thirties.

When I was born, in 1923, I was the last of a big family of eleven children, and my biggest brothers had been already abroad. If a Jew was, say nineteen or twenty, and if he could afford it, he went abroad. But still they continued their ties with their family in Iraq. Things changed very drastically for the Jews when the mandate in Iraq was over and the power was turned over to the Iraqis. There was now a nationalistic attitude among the Arabs, and it coincided with the activities in Palestine at that time against the Jews.

I recall as a kid, before I left Iraq, in 1929, I was at that time about six years old. But I do recall 1929. Some riots had taken place against the Jews in Palestine. Whenever there has been any problem in Palestine—even though the British were here still—if the Jews had been attacked somewhere, there was always some riot in Baghdad against the Jews, I guess just for the fun of it or something.

Before this time, I cannot tell you out of my personal experience. I was too young. All history of the Jewish community in Iraq was all the time between, in the middle—on the one side, they were a fairly well-to-do community, a very old community, about two thousand five hundred years old, and it started with the construction of the first Temple that the Jewish community started there. Highly educated, or, in any case, much higher than the average population.

Many of the Arab leaders at that time were sent to Jewish schools, because the only schooling system that was existing at that time was Jewish. So, on the one hand, Jews were fairly well-to-do, fairly well educated, some of them with property—

Still, and always, whenever anything happened—the first to be victims were the Jews. The reason is that they were a minority from all aspects. Religious minority, national minority, and so when there is a disease all of a sudden, and thousands of people die, it is because "the Jews did this and that," and you have the religious prejudice.

I cannot say if it's anti-Semitism, but for a Jew, if he would have touched food that was supposed to go to an Arab, it was supposed to be "poisoned." I mean all kinds of ideas and beliefs from a *religious* point of view.

Now, another thing that influenced the situation in the Arab world for the Jews was the rise of Hitler and the Nazis in Europe, which found a very encouraging area of influence in the Arab countries. This was one of the ways the power of British and the French at that time could be undermined. Apparently, the Nazis found in the Arab countries a great response to the ideas of power and the ideas of patriotism. I mean, this combination appealed very much to the Arabs at this time.

By 1933, many Jews decided that they had to leave Iraq, even though the economical situation was still good and all that. That is why my family and I came to Israel in the early thirties. I know that after that things went from bad to worse.

By the way, the first thing that Iraqis did when they got their independence [1932] was the mass pogrom of a Christian community—not Jews, but *Christians.* This was the first "act of independence" and this was a sign of what was going to happen later on. Even though the first king in Iraq was supposed to be one of the most moderate and reasonable leaders in the Arab world at that time, the superiority the Arab felt toward all minorities was immediately shown. . . .

When the War started in '48, it was absolutely out of question to run away to Israel because all the desert between Iraq and Israel was full of Arab armies and all that, so Jews started running away to Persia, which is Muslim, but not an Arab country, and lately Persia had more fairly tolerated Jews. . . .

Apparently the international conscience was a little bit better than what it looks like today, and when stories started to come out about youngsters who had just been tortured because they wanted to run away for their lives from Iraq, there was a big outcry in the United Nations, which in 1948 and '49 was different from what it looks like today. The Iraqis found themselves under a certain pressure and so they thought, "The hell with it. Whoever wants to leave the country, give them permission to give up their nationality"; they also had in mind that they can also confiscate the property, which they did, openly, It is one of the cases where you have laws issued openly like the Nazi laws, which managed to confiscate the Jews' property.

A question for Rafi: Some Arabs claim that Iraqi Jews like Rafi who are now in Israel would love to go back. They have a saying that "one day in Baghdad, and then they would be willing to die." Rafi interrupted, saying, "Yes, one day —they would not be able to survive more than that!"

I do not say that there has been no good Arabs. But there have been as many Jew refugees from the Arab countries as there has been Arab refugees from Palestine. The only difference is that the Jews' property has been openly confiscated. So help me God, I have never understood—in the ministry of foreign affairs, our delegation to the United Nations—why we Israelis never stressed this point enough. In my mind it was a stupid thing to allow the myth that "the Jews have been loved in the Arab countries, and then all of a sudden there came some evil, the evil of Hitler."

There is also the myth that only Jews are coming to this country, and sending Arabs out. But Arabs were immigrating to Israel, as much as the Jews. You have Arabs from Sudan and Arabs from Iraq, and—someone must do research on the West Bank and see who has been here more than three generations.

Why does an Arab, that did not exist here a few generations before, have more right than a Jew who has been here many generations, and sometimes his ancestors for twenty generations, in Israel? Why was this issue never raised by the Jews? It seems too great an issue to have been just shoved under the rug.

Shaul

Shaul is one of many Iraqi Jews who had to escape illegally to Israel in 1950, even though the law had already been passed allowing the Jews to depart. He recalled his childhood, beginning long before the 1948 war against Israel:

I remember when I was four or five, my mother used to threaten me—"The Muslims will beat you," she said. I am conscious when I was three, four, five years old, that Muslims hate Jews. In 1931, when I was four years old, I remember from then. My parents knew from their own experience. I experienced it in some cases, when I was alone and I went to buy something in the area where Muslims are with Jews.

Shaul had to attend Muslim schools from the age of twelve because of financial reverses in his family.

We are five brothers, and if we paid the Jewish school, it was very difficult for us, so I left to go to the Muslim school in 1940 and they used to really beat me and I suffered from the students. Every Jew was a Zionist in their eyes.

One of the teachers I recall was really anti-Zionist. Even a Jewish communist group there was anti-Zionist—but that particular teacher was *particularly* anti-Zionist, and usually he was responsible for the school on Thursday, and he used to ask us to sing a song which reminds Arabs of Palestine. It was called "Palestino, Palestino" in Arabic—"Palestine, Palestine, . . . no Zionist can come to you" and so on.

He used to watch every Jew in the school to see that he was singing that. And we used to sing it. I know the Arabic verses even now, because this strikes me and I still remember. You know, for us, Zionism was even stronger than in European shtetls, in a way. We were yearning to go and see our land; yes, yearning. In our prayer it is mentioned, we cannot get rid of it. For example, even in the Jewish schools we have Solomon the King, Joseph and all this, and it reminds us of our country, so this is automatic, we want our land to come back to us. It's a way of life.

You know, before Western Zionism came to Israel, Zionism was existing in Iraq. We prayed every day, and every Passover that we are saying "Next year in Jerusalem," we are emotionally really aroused, and we *mean* it. We dream to come to Israel—but there is no government. The minute the government was established, suddenly a hundred thousand Jews of Iraq left . . .

Shaul told of two poignant experiences when an Arab saved members of his family from the violence of an inflamed Arab mob:

When I was seventeen or eighteen years I almost was killed. We were in a group and it was the last day of Passover. We were returning from the other part of town, and we were singing and so on. We were a majority of Jews in the bus, and we are singing Jewish songs and they hit one of our Jewish people. Then the Arabs threw us from the bus and we went walking the rest of the way to our area. They waited for us in the square, close to the bus stop. Not one, not two, hundreds of Arabs on the street. I'm not exaggerating. They knew we were walking down, and they gathered hundreds, hundreds, honestly.

I was able to slip away. But they caught one of my friends and beat him and beat him on the head. And I couldn't move. I saw him. I just froze. An Arab Muslim religious man said to me, "Come here my boy, poor boy," and then he took his stick and he hit me on the head, and they threw me into the street. There was no transportation any more; cars couldn't move, and they started to hit me, kick me—soldiers in their big shoes.

The soldiers cursed at us and said that the Jews cursed Muhammad. They just said that. The truth is that I sang Hebrew. Yes, and some of them listened to me. They didn't know, but they thought it was Hebrew, it must be. And I was seventeen, I was enthusiastic and so I did it. We were impudents. I sang Hebrew. Can you ask me how I was saved? A prostitute! Honestly. She came with her car. She wanted to know, she was curious to know what was going on. And suddenly she found a young boy, and all people are hitting me. "Come, my son, come," she said. And I found the door open and threw myself inside the car. She pushed them and shouted at them in Arabic and she took me home. Really, it was just a miracle.

You know, all the Arab countries are clearly hostile, not only Iraq. My sister-in-law was from Egypt. She was very beautiful. And when she used to walk, when people see someone who is fair or white in color—even though she is not Jew—they run after her saying, "She is Jew, let's do something to her."

So it happened that my sister-in-law was walking in a Cairo street and all the people ran in the street and said, "Here is a Jew, let's run after her"—all, one after the other. They shouted at each other and asked, "Who are you running after?" They answered, "After a Jew," and it happened that she was so scared that she ran into a house and ran upstairs, and the people saved her in their apartment. The crowd was waiting downstairs, and the crowd said, "If you are not going to let her come out, we will burn the building." And the people in the apartment said, "She is not a Jew, she's our cousin, she's one of us." And they saved her just by saying, "She's not a Jew."

Menachem

You could live there as long as no alternative existed—where could you go? When Israel came into existence, there was someplace to go.

These were the words of Menachem, a former Iraqi Jew who escaped to Israel in 1950 when he was fifteen. His first cousin was one of those hanged in Baghdad in 1969. Why was his cousin hanged?

They needed nine and he was one of them. I heard it from his widow that he had been hanged. It was one of the Ba'ath Party factions that wanted to show strength, and the bodies of the victims were exposed for four days. I came from a very, very wealthy family. We left everything, everything was confiscated. The regime in Iraq have always been unstable, they have always practiced the most severe persecutions of Jews. My grandfather was the chief rabbi of Baghdad, one known in our Jewish community for his judgments and his reading of the Torah. We were always involved in a spiritual Zionism.

But one of the reasons I became active was that in 1947, before Israel's partition, I was more than once beaten by Muslim children at the Hebrew school. They used to beat us up regularly, and more than once we had to be locked up for days in our house, because whenever things got hot, they took it out on the Jews.

And that was *before* Iraqi nationalism. Even if Israel was never to exist, they *never* saw us as part of the Iraqi people. We were Jews first, not as Iraqis, but as "Jews living in Iraq." When Israel came into being, we found a natural outlet for our way of life, for things we could not do in Iraq. Now there are only a few Jews left in Iraq. Old people, a few hundred Jews. You know, there is something inbuilt —you pray for Jerusalem all the time. The younger you are, the more enthusiasm you have to find the things you're denied.

I left without my family. My parents paid some Muslims a handsome amount of money to have me smuggled across the border to Iran, along with four other escapees. They took us in a bus, but not to the border. We were beaten, all five of us, by the four Muslims, who took us for ten days on horseback in the desert with little food. But we had a code word which we invented with our parents which we would only give to the Muslims after we had crossed the border—then they would go back with the code word and be paid. We were not to give them the word until after we were across the border, so we weren't murdered. It was our only way—we could not contact our family or they'd have been hanged.

Shimon

Shimon, an Israeli who escaped from Baghdad in 1950, is now about forty-five.

My memory and my family's memory is of fear—the feeling that we were different. We left with two conditions from Iraq. We lose citizenship and possessions; we could take only clothes. Our fear is we can be beaten in the streets. My father, my mother taught me to speak Arab and have two names; my Arab name is Fouad—but we Jews *look* different.

In 1941, because the prime minister was close to the Nazis, we were in the pogroms. I was four years old; I remember. They closed the Jewish ghetto. Arabs came and killed one hundred and eighty Jews and took everything. We escaped from one roof to another for a couple of days. Yes, I remember well. Later on, when the Zionist movement became stronger, conditions were much more difficult. In 1949, searches began in homes. They took away heads of families after five-hour searches.

They found a history book of World War I and said it was a Zionist book, and they took my father, but we were lucky—he came back. Sometimes, they just picked them up and never found them again.

I loved Baghdad, and was homesick as a new immigrant here in Israel. We were so miserable in Israel, in camps, with not enough food. But nothing will happen to you in Israel, we are Jews. We don't have to hide. I started to work at thirteen in Israel and studied at night. Some research people doing research for Hebrew University asked my father one day, "Wouldn't you like to go back? It's so bad here." I thought my father would say yes, but he said, "No—my children can go out late here." Part of Iraqi Jews left Israel for the United States, but most of us stay because it is our homeland, because we are safe.

Someday, I want to go back to Baghdad, I want to see my river, the ghetto, the synagogue. Most Jews from Muslim countries are not so orthodox, but we went to synagogue on *Shabat* [Sabbath] once a week, and then we had a Jewish community club and social life. Israel is very difficult; a Western civilization which Iraqis, with their extended family, had difficulty in understanding. In Israel we had to change. I took over because my father never recovered from the crisis of coming to Israel. Recently, my sister left our apartment in Israel, in the same city—to live alone. We didn't believe this—unheard of. This happened ten years ago and my mother never forgave her yet. I am a mixture of personality—I love the East, I learned a lot from the West.

When my father wanted to leave Iraq, my mother was pregnant. He was afraid of the Arabs. As long as he remembers, from time to time Arabs persecuted Jews. In '70 there were 4,000 Jews. Why did they remain? Part of the families had father or relative in prison and didn't want to leave them there. Others, rich with lands, were "waiting for Godot." The government took their lands, but they thought they'd get them back.

My father knew this; I admire and respect him. Since I remember, he said, "My son, we don't have any future in this country and we have to leave for Israel. They will take everything from us here." I want you to understand, my father was not a genius—he was not well educated, a common man. You're talking with an average Jew from Iraq. Things you would hear in most families there.

Yaacov and Shlomo

In a conversation with a couple of ex-Egyptian Jewish men now living in Israel, the late President Sadat's avowal of Egypt's historically fair treatment of its Jews was rebutted somewhat ironically. Yaacov, a teacher, spoke first:

Sure, there was nothing to complain about. We came back alive from school . . . when we took the train to school, I have to be very careful to lock the door in my compartment or to be with other Jewish students.

And many times I had incidents, as I was ten, eleven years old—this was in 1946 to 1948 or '49. It was a fact of life. Nothing to complain about. I mean just to say, well it was raining today. So what? Nothing extraordinary. It was part of everyday life to be beaten for being a Jew; you could expect it.

Shlomo, his companion, broke in:

That is, if I can compare it with what I had as a kid, it is like being lower-class Indian. You can't do anything about it. You have been born there and you belong to disgust. You are a *dhimmi,* that's all. That is, your shadow is not holy. In India, it is clearcut; but in Egypt, it's a little bit different.

Jews as a group mix a little bit more, but still they belong to . . . you're not the same. It is not the Zionist movement or something that was creating it. It existed for a long time.

Killings, it happened once in every two years, about. You should expect that too. Every now and then, for one reason or another, though you have done nothing—I mean nothing concerning you directly—you must expect, in every two years, something like that. You try to avoid it. The same as cholera and typhoid and malaria. I must compare it to these. The Jew is the bright fellow, but yet his life is never sure. That is, tomorrow someone can get and kill him and he will not be punished as if this fellow killed the same person of his own community.

Shlomo (the Israeli name he has taken) would not give his former family name, because he has an aged relative living in Egypt. A teacher formerly, now a businessman, Shlomo insisted that the foreign colonial powers in Egypt didn't protect the Jews from demeaning treatment.

With the Turks and later on with the British, the Jews still lived in unsafety. The Jew had to be afraid that something would happen to him. If he was lucky, he was just slapped on the face for nothing and told "You are a dirty Jew." If he was unlucky, he suffered a little bit more than that. And I think during the modern history—the war history—even though there has always been someone else who was responsible, Jews suffered, and were ill-treated and were persecuted and molested in the streets.

I can tell only of my own experiences. It was very normal for me to return back from school as a kid and to be beaten for no reason. That was in '46 and '47.

Yaacov interjected an oft-expressed observation:

There is also another aspect which we did not speak of. The Arabic wording, the Arabic life has much more value. The term "Jew" in itself, without saying "dirty Jew" is already a dirty word. There is kind of a myth that the Jews were not treated as badly in Arab countries as they were in the countries of Europe.

Arabs never killed six million Jews because they never had the chance. They could have participated—with great pleasure—in the killing of six million. You are unfair to them, because they were never given the chance. I mean, you expect them to do things they couldn't do, and there's a difference. Probably one of the things that annoyed them is that they didn't kill six million Jews.

Shlomo nodded somber agreement with his friend and added:

Let me make a point here. You see, I think that many of the Jews are very taken by the idea that in our lifetime we can see the peace and the Arabs accepting our existence and all that. But the world must put pressure on the Arabs—the Israelis are not the ones who need the pressure—we want too much that the Arabs will stop warring with us. We are a tiny and poor country—they are so rich and great. It is them—the Arabs—that the world must help to understand, that we can live together, to let us live.

Sarah

Sarah left Egypt after the 1967 war. She told of her family's flight to Israel after her husband's arrest and imprisonment in a "concentration camp where the Jewish men from sixteen to seventy years were taken when the '67 war started."

... Finally, after six months my husband is in concentration camp; I tried to get him out, but I needed help. ... So finally, I wrote this letter to my sister in France and I say, "Please, if you can, help me to do something to help my husband." ... And finally, the French Embassy sent a letter to the Egyptian Embassy.

So after six months of working so hard we get this small paper that we can go out of Egypt. My husband and my brother, they were released like criminals. When I saw them going out, they had handcuffs on their hands. It's like they were criminals just because they were Jewish. They were not Zionists, nothing. Jews.

When my husband leaves the prison . . . they give us five dollars for each person. They tell us we never can return to Egypt.

Would Sarah go back to Egypt under peaceful conditions?

When my husband is in the concentration camp we had to sign a paper that we are not being pushed out of Egypt. I had to sign papers that I'm not going to come back to Egypt. You can never tell what would happen. With what heart would I have to go back to Egypt? You can never trust the Arab people. Never. I would never trust them after what happened to my husband . . .

... No, never would I go back. You see, in school, the children six, seven years old, in the playground, they are pretending to shoot the Jewish people. Starting the day having a war! And the Arab teacher teaches the kids that they should really be against the Jews—that "the Jews are killing" their people, that "the Jews are taking" their land. Giving them a very, very black view of the Jewish people. Not the *Israeli* only, but the *Jew.*

Singing songs against Jews—so figure it out, a Jewish child should be in the school, singing against his own blood? Suppose that I meet people, in Egypt, like now I am meeting you, and I don't know you. Do you think I will tell you that I am Jewish? If you ask me what religion I am, I say, "Well, I am Christian." My kids—when they were in Egypt, I say "I am Christian." Well, they can *hear* me. And they want to be proud of being Jewish!

Mordecai

I spoke to a number of people from Libya, among them Mordecai, who gave an account often repeated:

I remember that in the 1950s, although Libya had a relatively low crime rate, I felt threatened by the man on the street.

When my family told me we hadn't any reason to worry because the Libyan leaders were sympathetic to the Jews, I became confused, because why then should I feel threatened? Possibly because just five or six years earlier—in 1945 —the Jews had been the victims of a terrible pogrom. Around one hundred and fifty Jews were killed in Tripoli. The murders were bestial and whole families were brutally massacred.

But all the Arabs who were accused by the British of these crimes were let free, and the only people who were put in prison were ten Jews—they were in prison for self-defense. They tried it again in 1948, but this time the Jews were ready for them so there was less damage, and this time, the British interrupted the violence.

Qadaffi can't really be serious when he says we should go back to Libya. After Libya became an independent country in 1951, I remember that we were no longer able to send letters or packages to Israel. The next year, they closed the Jewish schools; we had to go to either Arab schools or Christian schools, and we had to learn Arabic for two hours daily.

Since the Jews felt helpless to do anything, they did nothing, and because they were seen to be weak by the Arabs, the Arabs kept creating new laws which restricted us further. We were unable to conduct our holiday services without vandalism and disruption by the Arabs, and we couldn't get any reply when we asked the police to assist us. From 1956, we were no longer free, and at the same time, we were no longer free to leave the country. No one could leave the country with his whole family, and after a while, there were no visas available at all.

It went from bad to worse. Our Jewish girls were the victims of Arab lust and the Arabs even installed an Arab treasurer to check on the funds of the Jewish community. In 1967, after the Six-Day War, Jews were killed wantonly, thrown from balconies into the street—it was horrible—riots, burning the synagogue . . . After that debacle, I was taken together with the rest of the Jews of the country (about three thousand five hundred of us) to military camps, supposedly to protect us from the anger of the Arabs. Finally I was "allowed" out of Libya forever—with only 50 pounds sterling and my clothes.

Now I want to know why they think all of us Jews ran from Arab countries as refugees in a world that didn't understand, taking with us none of the fruits of our labors for many centuries! Fortunately, I found a homeland, the State of Israel—just as the Arab refugees could have established themselves in any number of countries among the Arab nations, twenty or twenty-one, I don't know. If the Palestinians are demanding compensation for their property, we Jews from Arab lands left more property behind—by four or five times.

Helena

Helena, a woman in her late thirties from Morocco, needed no time at all to recall the anxieties of her life in Marrakesh, and her attitude toward Israel.

Zionism is a way of life. In Morocco we were born with the security of it, we grew up with it and we looked forward to one day go back to our land—because the Arabs reminded us every day, in our day-to-day living, that we were "foreigners"—no matter how many centuries we had been there [in Morocco].

If you had a fight, they would—the Arabs would still say to you, "Get out, go back to your country, go back to where the Jews are . . . This is not your country." And we would say, "But look, we have been here for centuries." And that's the truth, because we existed there long before Muhammad started to preach Islam, and so we have more right to be Moroccan than they have.

But we never, NEVER had the full right of being Moroccans. As an example: we were under the French protection, and then we turn into Moroccan citizens. But the people, the day-to-day people that we encountered had the resentment to see us being there and every day they would say, "Well, most of you left, you Jews —what are you waiting for?" As a child, that impressed on me that I was a foreigner. If I wanted to give something to Morocco, to be of service—there was no way, because I was not part of that society.

Let's put it this way; there is no stability. [King] Hassan is really flexible, supposed to be very nice and Western and the whole thing. He has a European education and in fact he tolerated a Jewish cabinet member. Then the right-wing man came in and got rid of the Jews. Hassan is a tolerant man, but he cannot control the mass. When there is a war in Israel, the mass are crying to get vengeance on us. Oh, there have been "functionaries" in government—Jews were very much in business and commerce. But when Hassan's father was in power— Muhammad—we had our share of concentration camps. You can never feel equal, because you don't know what will happen next.

Helena married an American and lives in the United States, but she and her family are moving to Israel, because

In Morocco I was number one and first a Jew, and the only land that accepts a Jew, as far as I am concerned and so far as I have been *impressed*—is Israel. And the soonest for us—the future for me and for all my children is to assemble and go to Israel and make a life for ourselves. And that's where the migrations are going.

And really they pushed us into becoming stronger Zionists; see, if the Arabs really wanted us we could have stayed and learned to live perhaps in harmony . . . if they did not have so much prejudice. But Zionism is a way of life—Zionism is Judaism, to them.

Now that we went back to our country, "where the Jews are," like the Arabs said we should—now they say we should not be *THERE!*

I heard many conflicting opinions from Moroccans about the conditions of life for the Jews there. Some insisted that the Moroccan community should be separated from the others because "Morocco was better to the Jews than most." One man said he and his family had been free to leave whenever they wanted to go, and an older woman warned me not to write about the Jewish community in Morocco because she is "afraid of what will happen to them if King Hassan dies."

Many believed, as the Tunisian-born writer Albert Memmi suggested, that life in Morocco appeared "better" because it compared favorably to that of Jews who had lived elsewhere among the Arabs.

A Note on the ex-Syrian Interviewees

All the Jewish refugees from Syria with whom I spoke were truly terrified lest their families behind in Damascus or Aleppo or Qamishli be identified. Because they fear that Syrian authorities would penalize their relatives for their "indiscretion," they requested that the genders of the persons interviewed be changed in some cases, that the number and kind of their families left behind be altered, and that facts identifying shop or home locations should be as vague as possible. The statements have all been recorded on tape, with one exception: one person refused to have a rather distinctive voice recorded, despite assurances that the tapes were for convenience and for record only. The person concerned was afraid "they" would "get hold of the tapes" and abuse the relatives still held in Syria.

Shoshana

An Israeli named Shoshana escaped from Syria in 1974, when she was in her mid-twenties.* She "feels guilty" about having left her family because she remembers "the fright in the eyes" of the younger children in her family, expecting some support from her:

> They wanted to know why they were being shouted at, "Jews, Jews!" and why they are different from the others. They wanted to have someone explain that to them.
> The fear is that at any time of day or night the security people might knock at the door and take either the father or one of the elder brothers—and they really don't know what is happening. I know that this is happening, I see it, but I don't know why. Ever since I was a child, I felt there was something wrong with my life and I wasn't getting the rights I was entitled to, and I have been living in constant fear. The teachers treat you differently, and I was being treated differently because I live in the ghetto, and I came home many times weeping too, and asked my mother, "Why are we different?"

I asked Shoshana why she felt so "different," since she was living in a ghetto with other Jews. She said,

> It is not true. In the same place where I lived there were Palestinians and other Arabs, and they knew I was Jewish. They called me "Jew." They used to beat me. I would like to have beaten them back, but I wouldn't dare. Because if I did that, they would bring their whole family to fight—but I couldn't bring mine. I would go home and lock myself in and start living in my dream, crying.

It was because "the Arabs lived differently" that Shoshana "knew" that people can live differently than the way the Jews lived in Syria.

The TV reports on "60 Minutes" contradicted her own. Were there two

*Because Shoshana preferred Hebrew, I engaged a Hebrew interpreter, who stopped Shoshana after every few sentences, for the purpose of greater accuracy. The interview lasted several hours.

separate Jewish communities? "No," Shoshana replied; she knew all the families who were on television.

> They have to say what they say, because they have absolutely no choice. It would have been a terrible thing had they said other than what they did because the security people were there. They had to say that they lived well because the security people were listening, and when the television people would have gone —as they would go—then these people would have been in trouble had they spoken differently.
>
> I know that some of that "happy family" had *escaped* from Syria. Why? Why do those escaped ones tell of misery now, if it is not true? In Syria no person must dare. If anyone—a foreigner—were to take a Syrian Jew out alone and speak to him, he would say something completely different from what he told Mike Wallace— But . . . maybe they wouldn't dare speak to someone anyhow. The police would learn of it. . . . It's pathetic. It is not possible. Only when the Syrians are free can they tell the truth about their lives in Syria.

Shoshana was imprisoned because she participated in a demonstration, which she described:

> When they brought the bodies of the girls they murdered, those who tried to cross the border—three sisters who were killed were members of my family.
>
> When the girls tried to escape—according to how *I* heard it, these sisters and their friend couldn't bear life there any longer and that's why they tried it on their own without having a boy escorting them— What happened is that a shepherd saw three men go into a cave with the four girls and he said afterward that he thought they were just out for fun. He said the reason he didn't go in after them was because the men who pushed the girls into the cave were armed.
>
> And then, the shepherd saw the men go out alone and he didn't know what happened to the girls. But then he started to smell something burning. So he went into the cave and found the bodies burning. The Syrians told everybody that the shepherd smelled something burning and went into the cave—but they didn't say that he saw the men going in. The shepherd is an eyewitness, and he notified the police, but it was ten days afterwards that there was an announcement on the radio. Before that the parents had received a fake letter saying that the girls did make it across the border. The special office which takes care of Jews, the "Palestinian Bureau," they have a free hand where Jews are concerned.
>
> The bodies were burned to such a state that they couldn't be identified; that's why it took ten days . . . I will never forget that day. The whole ghetto went insane when they saw how they brought back the bodies—in sacks—and threw them on the floor of the doorsteps of the families' homes. So everybody in the ghetto saw how it looked. It wasn't that they just came and looked; they were all together for the funeral and they saw the sacks with the bodies spilled out of them . . . and they just went berserk.

Before the murders, Shoshana said that many of her friends had planned to escape, but after this incident, they were

. . . scared to death that it would happen to them, so we started sitting home, in the dark—even the animals were living better than we were. We wanted to breathe the air and see the light—but to be confronted with such deaths was more than we could take. The whole community went to the synagogue to demonstrate— in the ghetto—and someone from the police came and said they would try to find the killers and bring them to trial.

We demanded to the police that we wanted freedom, we wanted to work freely, live freely. They started arresting people and there were so many that it got to the point where we didn't know whether our neighbors were at home or in prison. But we didn't dare go out to find out.

I was arrested ten days later.

Shoshana was visibly proud to have demonstrated; she said that this is something that is not done by "anyone in Syria."

We were so desperate that it really didn't matter. We knew the consequences, but I was at the point where nothing mattered—so I decided to do it. I know it's forbidden, and it's not only forbidden for the Jews; it's forbidden for everyone.

What worries me is the look on my mother's face when I went to prison, and I couldn't even ask where they were taking me. One of my parents was ill—not well. I prayed to God that I would die in prison because I couldn't take it any longer. I won't forget those three days—not one moment of those three days. I kept looking around the room for a way to kill myself; I was looking for a window to throw myself out of in jail.

She described, with great difficulty, her imprisonment:

In the van taking me from home to prison, I was put in the middle and there were two policemen on either side. All the way there they kept telling me they were going to beat me. "I'm a girl—they can do anything with me." I was scared —I was very scared.

I kept being pushed from one room to another, and in every room there was a person with a torture device. Nobody talked to me, but they kept showing me the electric chair and other things. They told me, "If you're not going to tell us that you're spying for Israel, that you're in contact with Israel, then this is what is going to happen to you."

I told them they don't even let me breathe—how could I know what Zionism was? After this, the torture started—the beatings. If these people were to see me on the street, they would stab me to death—let alone being in prison with them.

They would use the water torture: cold water dripping on her head. "Don't forget, this was winter," she said.

Even if it was an old man, they would do it to him—the water torture. And at night they came into my room. . . .

At this point, the translator attempted to comfort Shoshana, who had begun to weep quietly. After a few minutes the translator explained emotionally, "She said she's ashamed to tell us what they did to her."

After three days, they said they had made a mistake: she wasn't the girl they were looking for.

> They destroyed me for life, because what I have gone through has become part of my life, and I can't get rid of it. I can't believe that my family is there and they live this kind of life.

She became angry:

> I just do not understand how things like that can happen and people don't do anything about it. It's a discovery—being out of Syria—that the world is so really big and strong. Is it maybe just because we are Jews that we can't do anything?

Joseph

Among the many Jewish escapees from Syria was Joseph, who "got away" in 1975 at the age of twenty-two:

> After '67 they put the PLO, thousands of them, to live with the Jews in ghetto. It's more violent with the PLO living among us. Eight persons were killed two months after the '67 war, by the Palestinians.
>
> My father was arrested three times for "making Jewish religious objects." He didn't make Jewish religious objects, but for four days he disappear. Nobody knows where he is for four days. Two men take my father in the car and some articles that, maybe they say, "look Jewish." I run after the car and then can't run any more. Nobody allowed to be out after ten in the evening. They take sometimes the family to prison, if someone is not home on time, and they are beaten. If the secret police or—not only secret police—anybody who comes to the Jews and says, "Come with me," we go, because we are afraid not to go. I get no letter now for five months from my family. Before, I got a letter each month. Since I gave a press conference and some Arabs from the Syrian embassy in Washington see me and recognize me, now I don't get mail any more. . . .
>
> My father manufactured tourist items, but from 1970 and '71 there are no tourists allowed to see the Jews in Damascus, because Jews in Damascus may give secrets of how we live in Syria. My father was factory owner forty years, a little bit wealthy. They [the Syrian government] took all his money from the bank as of 1967. Also, no more collection of credit was allowed by Jews. We could not collect if a soldier came and took something.
>
> Now is more worse; since 1973, when Arabs—the Palestinians mostly—hear "Jewish" they want to kill them. Part of my family is here—my parents and others are still there. The Syrian government tries to find out who is telling about them —I'm afraid. Mix up the facts, please . . . I finished high school. I couldn't get permit from secret police to go to university, because they want Jews to be low. Jews are used to learning.
>
> It's all Jewish United States money which supports the Jewish schools in Syria, but now it goes to Muslim teachers, who teach the Koran in every class, and the secret police have their children planted in every class. A lot of times those children inform on their classmates from class talk, regarding radio programs the Jews might listen to or other communications.

Now they are afraid because they want the United States' money, so they send token Jews to this country. Just now there is one Syrian Jew sent to the United States for medical treatment. His wife and children—five children—are back in Syria. He will come and go back so they look "moderate." They sent about five persons out this way in one and half years.

Moshe and the Professor

While talking in Israel with a young ex-Syrian, Moshe, the young man was joined by a distinguished Algerian-born professor and scholar, whose special area was the history of the Jewish communities of North Africa. For a while, Moshe spoke uninterruptedly. He managed to arrive in Israel before the October 1973 war; he escaped from Syria through measures he would not describe.

I paid the man who makes for me an identity card, saying I was an Albanian. I showed my identity card and so I passed the borders. When I got out from Syria, I got out without money, and without any documents whatsoever of what I studied in Syria. And I didn't tell my parents or friends I was leaving because, you know, let's say a Jew he is arrested, there is no law that says how many . . . how long he will be in prison. The Syrians are very intelligent, I suppose, because all the restrictions of Jews—the Jews have no contact with the police. But they have contact with the Army. So all are the laws of the Army. Nobody can know what is going on with the Jews because it is secret. If I were arrested, it would be in Maza prison. It depends, maybe for one year, or two, maybe for three years.

I didn't take money with me, because I know if a Jew escapes with money it is a problem. If I take money, they'll know the Jew had escaped from Syria to go to Israel, maybe he'll be with the enemy Israeli army. And if I go with my certificate to prove that I had studied something, maybe they think these documents can be very important for Israel.

What had prompted Moshe to leave Syria?

I remember that the Moslem boys threw stones at me and I remember too the education I received in school. The Jewish school, but the majority is Muslim. I remember it is written that the Jews are evil, I don't know why. And their God is a God who wants to drink the blood of all the other peoples. This was in the Arabic book at the education system. I was taught this in the Jewish school, because I am a student and want to pass through these schools to graduate.

I remember that in 1967 Israel had a victory, so the Syrians must—maybe as a psychological reaction—they must take it out on the Jews. After that, for eight months, the Jews can't go out from their houses. I remember that in Damascus a man from the Citizen's Bureau came to our house and he was looking for a reason to take somebody to prison.

The Jewish professor, who had been quietly listening, broke in now:

It is a mistake to make something very, very tragic of the relations with the Jews and the Arabs—"No hope," and so on . . . because if we had no hope to be on good terms with the Arabs, what is our future?

I think that the Jews were discriminated against, but the Arab countries were not founded on a democratic basis. *Everyone* was discriminated against. The Jews were not involved in politics. They were a strong organization, a community.

Moshe asked the professor whether Jews were allowed to be in politics. "No, . . . not in politics," the professor said. "But," Moshe asked, "didn't Jews—don't Jews today love politics when they are allowed?" The professor paused, then answered,

But they had no ambition. I think that we must distinguish between the people and the regime. I think that the regime are more responsible than the real Arab people.

At this point Moshe interjected,

In my Jewish school is one course in Arabic studies. A book said that the Jews were "craven" and so on, and "murderers and barbarians," and that they had a God who "preached that they must drink the blood of non-Jews." This book, this official teaching, talked only of Jews—no other minorities, only Jews. Only Jews had to have this!

Moshe asked the professor if he knew the literature of the nineteenth century that described the alleged "blood libels" of the Jews. The professor, who unbeknownst to Moshe, has published books about Jews in Arab lands, said cryptically that he was aware of them, then continued:

If we cannot live with Islam, then we have no future in this part of the world. And if I believed that . . . I should not stay in this country. I lived in Morocco and Algeria. For six centuries my family was there. My family administered in it.

"Were you average Jews there?" Moshe interrupted. The professor didn't acknowledge the question but went on:

Now the Arabs are in the driver's seat, they have no democratic cities, they have none of the modern technology that Europe has. They are not in the twentieth century.

Moshe wanted to know whether the professor agreed to the "secular democratic state" that the PLO proposed. The professor replied,

. . . with the Palestinian thinking, Israel will be finished. I am for the Arab state federated within Jordan, but in the power fight between Arabs and Arafats, they will kill us.

But then, you had a hate really deep between France and Germany. From one day to the next, they kissed and you had no problem, because the level of life was the same. The psychological level was more or less the same. And the *hate,* you can change—especially in our century. But you cannot change the fact that the Arab countries are living with two hundred dollars a year, and the Jew or the Christian cannot make a living with that. It is impossible, that is the point!

The professor left, and Moshe resumed his description of life in Syria.

I remember we received a book of prayers from New York, and we prayed a benediction written for Johnson, President Johnson, of the United States. And it was a problem for us, because the Army came to the synagogue and they asked if we pray for Johnson because he sends arms to Israel.

The journalists come from Europe and United States, especially from France, to visit our quarter, and I remember that the agent of the police came to tell us what to say. From time to time they would come back and tell us that "tomorrow at twelve o'clock, if we come to see you and they ask you about the Jews in Syria, you have to say so-and-so. If you tell them other than what we have told you, you will be in bad condition."

I asked Moshe who these police were.

The agents of the Citizens Bureau—the Department of Anti-Spies of the Syrian Army—I think that's how to say it.

From time to time they come to the houses of the Jews and take someone to prison, generally Maza prison. I remember they took our neighbor to Maza prison, and after ten months—no, after eight months—they told him, "You can go home."

That's all. You know, we have no rights—I can't tell you everything, because the Syrians have records for all Jews from fifteen years old to sixty-five. All the information about Jews, how much education, when I was at the university, I can't tell you; you know my family is there and they will persecute my family, I am sure . . .

I think that with time, maybe they will accept Israel, and accept that it is not easy to "throw Israel into the sea." Why are they so against us? Maybe they will say, "We can't throw this state away." It is better for the Arab lands one day to see that. It is more better for them to accept Israel.

7

Remnant of a Tradition:
The Arab-Jewish Diaspora

> . . . Jewish people living in Syria today are
> subjected to the most pervasive and inhuman
> persecution. . . . Even a four-year-old has been jailed. . . .
>
> —Ramsey Clark, 1974

> One thing is certain: . . . the Syrian Jewish
> community . . . are not likely to complain openly. . . .
>
> —Donald Kirk, *Chicago Tribune,* 1976

> Many of our Jewish members sharply criticized
> us for not delineating in greater detail the harsh
> conditions under which that small [Syrian
> Jewish] community has been forced to exist. . . .
> After months of carefully reviewing the evidence,
> we have concluded that our critics were right, we erred.
>
> —*National Geographic,* 1974

Of more than 850,000 Jews in Arab lands before Israel's statehood, fewer than 29,000 remain.[1]

Many of the Arab states, as illustrated in the table above, have been rendered virtually *judenrein* (free of Jews—Hitler's term).

Saudi Arabia has been excluded from the chart because Jews have long been forbidden to enter, much less live in what has been deemed "moderate" Saudi Arabia—with the notable exceptions of Henry Kissinger, when he was the United States Secretary of State; Secretary of Defense Harold Brown in 1979; and per-

TABLE A. Estimated Jewish Population in Arab Countries

	pre-1948	1979–1982		pre-1948	1979–1982
Iraq	125,000–135,000	200–300	Morocco	265,000	18,000
Egypt	75,000	250	Algeria	130,000–140,000	300–400
Syria	30,000	4,300–4,800	Tunisia	105,000	2,500–4,000
Yemen	55,000 }		Lebanon	5,000	200
Aden	8,000 }	1,200	Libya	38,000	15–20

116

haps a few selected Jewish academicians, businessmen, or journalists. Saudi Arabia, where thriving and influential communities of Arabian Jews existed at the time of Islam's creation in the seventh century,[2] has maintained a "moderate" policy that totally excludes Jews. As the Saudi Arabian Ambassador to The Hague said, upon Dutch Foreign Minister Max Van Der Stoel's proposed visit to Saudi Arabia in 1975,

> No Jewish journalist will be allowed into Saudi Arabia to cover Mr. Van Der Stoel's visit. . . . Official policy has always been to refuse entry to Jews because they support Israel as a state.[3]

Noting the bigotry inherent in the Saudis' avowed institutionalized discriminatory practices, Foreign Minister Van Der Stoel cancelled that visit. He advised the Dutch Parliament that

> The government of Saudi Arabia has informed me that it will not issue an entry visa for the Netherlands journalist representing *Urij Nederland.* Naturally, every government has the right to decide which foreigners it wishes to allow into its country. On the other hand, I want to emphasize that the government of the Netherlands utterly rejects any form of discrimination on the grounds of race or religion,[4] which might form the basis for granting such an entry permit.[5]

That same month, a London journalist reported that, during his visit to Saudi Arabia,

> My guide insists on giving me a copy of that horrifying old forgery about the Jews' plot to conquer the Arabs: *The Protocol of the Elders of Zion.* It turns out that all visiting journalists are given it.[6]

The Kingdom of Jordan also has been excluded from the table, because no Jews lived there in 1948, although the Jewish presence in the major portion of Palestine—which is presently "Jordan"—had existed long before the seventh-century creation of Islam. In fact, many of the Jews who had survived Muslim-led massacres in Arabia, only to be expelled in the seventh century from their lands in the Arabian Peninsula, had fled and found refuge in the large Jewish settlements of Eastern Palestine*—more than a thousand years before that eastern territory of mandated Palestine became perceived as a separate "kingdom" of "Transjordan" in 1922.

Jews who had dwelt on historical Palestinian terrain both east of the Jordan River and in the area called "the West Bank" were driven out of that land's Arab-dominated towns over the past half century by sporadic pogroms and pillage, so that by the 1940s the Palestinian towns in Transjordan and the West Bank were considered "purely Arab"—already purged of their former Jewish population. The Jews once living in the area of Palestine known as Jordan and the West Bank had become "Palestinian Jewish refugees" as the result of Arab violence. And the fact that there are Jewish "Palestinian refugees" of twentieth-

---

*See further discussions in Chapters 8 and 12.

century vintage is overlooked even in Israel. These refugees found safety only in the predominantly Jewish-settled areas of Palestine's coastal plain, which today is Israel. By 1948, the more than seventy-five percent of Palestine that the British had allocated to the Arabs as "Transjordan" already had been efficiently purged of all Jews, through periodic Arab onslaughts upon the various long-established Jewish communities. Despite that fact, the Jordanian government's nationality law of 1954 sought to safeguard its would-be racial purity: According to that law, a "Palestinian" living in Jordan was entitled to Jordanian citizenship unless he was a Jew.[7]

Conditions vary within those few Arab countries where more than a token remnant of their ancient-rooted Jewish communities still persist. Life for Morocco's remaining Jewish community—by far the largest remnant with an estimated 18,000 Moroccan Jews (compared with 265,000 before 1948)—is marginal and relatively tolerable, apparently by the grace of King Hassan II.[8] Foreign Jews are permitted to study and travel outside the country, and American Jewish leaders have been encouraged to visit the country.[9] As Dr. George Gruen, Director of Middle East Affairs for the American Jewish Committee, reported in June 1981, the Moroccan Minister of Tourism pointed out that, "In contrast to such Arab countries as Syria and Jordan," which, the Minister of Tourism said, " 'use the Palestine problem as a pretext and as an instrument,' " Morocco wished to play a " 'constructive, moderate role to achieve a pacific solution.' "[10] Morocco played an active part in secret peace negotiations between Israeli and Arab leaders, yet Morocco contributed fighting forces to both the Syrian and Egyptian fronts in their 1973 Yom Kippur War against Israel.

Jonathan Tumin, who worked with the American Jewish Joint Distribution Committee in Morocco, reported in 1976 that the Jews there were not living well.

> . . . Most of that community is impoverished. What is surprising is that at least a portion of those still there *do* live well, as they are small businessmen. However, the reason that they are still there is that they do not have enough money to persuade the right officials to allow them to leave with their possessions. . . . Discrimination makes it virtually impossible for Jews to get jobs in Arab firms. . . . Much of the Jewish community subsists on food and payments from the Joint Distribution Committee.[11]

In 1979, veteran *New York Times* correspondent Marvine Howe concluded an optimistic report on a note of caution: "The big problem for the Jews who have stayed is the young people. Parents are increasingly sending their children abroad . . . because their future here is restricted."[12]

Dr. Gruen's report two years later concluded on a somewhat similar note: "After we heard the ubiquitous Moroccan phrase 'pas de problème' (no problem), one Jew whispered to me, 'pas de problème sauf tous les problèmes' (no problem, except for all the problems!)."[13]

Syria

While the quality of life may be "tolerable" in Morocco or Tunisia, the situation in Syria is intolerable. A description of the contemporary conditions for Syrian Jews, with firsthand, eyewitness reports by this writer and others, may give further insight into this special situation.

There are still some 4,500 Jews in Syria,[14] all forbidden to emigrate. Whatever measure of safety and well-being was provided by the Jews' isolation in the Syrian ghettos, that isolated security is no longer because thousands of Palestinian Arab refugees are now housed in the homes left by those Jews who escaped. In the past several years, visitors to the Damascus ghetto have reported that, immediately upon arrival there, they were greeted by a kind of "surveillance" from young Arab Palestinians, who often as not led them directly to the police.[15]

The persons interviewed for this book spoke of their Arab neighbors with a terror that could not have been feigned.[16] Journalistic reports have been myriad of the tortures and imprisonments inflicted by a totalitarian S.S.-styled special Bureau of Intelligence "for Palestinians," concerned mainly with "Jewish Affairs." According to a 1981 report, "The government has unleashed the special Defense Brigades," headed by the brother of Syrian President Hafez al-Assad,

> and allowed the *Mukhabarat,* the secret police, to conduct a reign of terror and intimidation, including searches without warrant, detention without trial, torture, and summary execution.[17]

After a visit to Syria in 1980, one American scholar observed that

> the *Mukhabarat* has made itself a greater menace to the citizenry than the Muslim Brotherhood ever was.[18]

The only candid reports available on the living conditions of the Jews in Syria have been those from the escapees—there were still escape attempts across the Lebanese border between bloodlettings in Lebanon until the Syrian takeover closed that route.

Journalists periodically have tried to learn the extent to which Jews are suffering persecution: the *London Observer*[19] reported in 1974 that

> Syria's Security Service arrested 11 Syrian Jewesses in Aleppo . . . and tortured them in prison until they revealed who had smuggled their children out of the country.

The *Observer,* like others, had interviewed recent refugees who escaped to give shocking testimony of torture. Less common but no less bestial have been the reports of Jews caught attempting to escape and later murdered by the Syrians, who then framed other innocent Jews for the deaths.[20]

Because the Syrian Jews' condition has been reported internationally, "Syrian

Jewry's plight" became a human rights issue, and world attention has occasionally focused on the Syrian government's repressive tactics, but only sporadically and with little effect.

U Thant, as UN Director General, in 1970 deplored the situation through diplomatic means although he refused, owing to Arab pressure, to authorize a UN investigation,[21] despite appeals from international public figures. Alain Poher, President of the French Senate, and the writer Jean-Paul Sartre expressed reactions similar to that of Ramsey Clark, who stated in 1974:[22]

> . . . Jewish people living in Syria today are subjected to the most pervasive and inhuman persecution. . . . Young women and children are harassed in the streets. Old people are knocked down. Homes are stoned. Jews are barred from most employment. . . . Much of the Syrian population is forbidden to trade with Jews. . . . Even a four-year-old has been jailed. . . . Syrian Jews are rarely seen by visitors from the outside world. . . . They are forbidden to leave in peace and cannot remain in dignity. They are alone and hated.
>
> Many have been arrested, detained, tortured and killed. Recently, four young Jewish women seeking to escape from Syria were caught, raped, murdered and mutilated. Two young Jewish men with two others were immediately arrested and charged with the atrocity. Only when they were brought to trial did world protest compel the Syrian government to change the charges. . . . The right to leave a country is a fundamental human right recognized by the Universal Declaration of Human Rights. . . . The Syrian Jews are denied their . . . rights. No nation can deny its people such rights and defend its acts as a domestic policy. . . . Are human rights unimportant?

In the past, reporters' requests for interviews with Syria's Jews were summarily rejected by authorities—particularly in the Jewish Quarter. Several years ago the present leader, President Hafez al-Assad, apparently chose to practice public relations, aimed at the West. At least a half dozen articles appeared, all featuring interviews with the same Syrian-Jewish persons, all of whom repeated —with little variation—"life-is-happy-under-this-regime." A selected Jewish cast was designated for the interviews by the Syrian government to represent faithfully the proper line. To make certain, however, at least one Intelligence police escort was usually present.[23]

In every interview held by this writer with a refugee from Syria, it was made clear that a visitor hadn't much chance of getting a candid report inside Syria: the police in every case had visited the interviewees in advance and had made perfectly clear what was expected of them; if not a run-through of their lines, the police visit itself was tantamount to a threat. Even without the official "visit," the interviewees could be expected to do the right thing, or else. "They knew what was best for them."[24]

The staged interviews fooled some—in 1974 the *National Geographic* published a free-lance article on Syria that spoke of Damascus as "the city still tolerantly [embracing] significant numbers of Jews. . . ."[25] Some months later, after further inquiry, the *National Geographic* stated:

Many of our Jewish members sharply criticized us for not delineating in greater detail the harsh conditions under which that small community has been forced to exist since 1948. We began to wonder if we had unwittingly failed to reflect the true situation. Now, after months of carefully reviewing the evidence, we have concluded that our critics were right, we erred.[26]

A "60 Minutes" report of Syria from Mike Wallace in 1975[27] understated the severity of the repression and restraints borne by the Jews of Syria. Wallace noted that Syrian Jews could not travel in Syria or emigrate, and that they must carry identity cards stamped "Jew." Yet the program naively implied widespread financial prosperity and religious freedom in the Syrian-Jewish community, and gave a misleading—albeit well-meaning—impression of Syrian "moderation." Through interviews with "selected" Syrian Jews, the report tended to support indirectly the Syrian government's claim that charges of brutality toward Syrian Jews were exaggerated.

As such, it becomes a case in point for current media coverage of Syria: the Syrians who were interviewed on "60 Minutes" could not be unaware of the consequences that candor would have brought to themselves and their families from Syria's brutal secret police. Perhaps the seriously uncritical reporting was attributable to the government-imposed limitations; if the facts were censored in Syria, this could have been explained at the program's beginning when it was aired in the United States—as the preordained, built-in censorship prevailing in other Arab countries, such as Egypt, could and ought to be consistently reported. If no appropriate explanation of any kind was feasible without endangering the persons interviewed, then the interviews must be dismissed as misleading. In either case, the accuracy and objectivity of the resulting report was fundamentally impaired, in a series long before and since admired for its fearless in-depth coverage.

Because of a general furor created by the program among Jews in the United States, "60 Minutes" planned a repeat visit to Syria.[28] In his "second look," Wallace concluded that

Syria is a police state . . . difficult, totalitarian—and for the Jews it is more difficult than for the others.[29]

The second "60 Minutes" program was believed by concerned American-Jewish groups to be important and beneficial:[30] they pointed out that in anticipation of the imminent TV visit, one discriminatory practice—the red-inked scrawl "Musawi" (denoting Jews, followers of Moses)—began to disappear (temporarily) from Syrian identity cards "only two weeks before" the CBS staffers returned for the follow-up.[31]

Since then, the pettier persecutions have been amended in and out of Syrian law as the occasion arises, but the right to leave is the only right that should matter. The Syrian government has violated the international code of civil rights.[32] Because only the young can even attempt the rigors of an escape route, most of the escapees have been young people—mostly men. The Syrian Jewish community has complained that there were, in fact, too many nubile young girls left behind who as a consequence would never marry. Yet the Syrian President insisted that the reason he was keeping the Jews locked in was to keep them from bolstering the Israeli enemy's army—hardly a credible claim, considering the shortage of young Jewish men, the potential army recruits, in Syria.

While Syria has been overtly and undeniably identified as a "rejectionist" or "steadfast" Arab state, and a staunch Soviet ally antagonistic to the West, at the same time Western observers and officials have frequently offered unquestioning acceptance of Syrian claims to President Assad's "moderation." During a briefing in Damascus in 1977, one candid United States Embassy staffer there commented to this writer that the reason "President Assad and President Carter got along so well [at their 1977 Geneva meeting] was that nothing was asked from Assad," other than the promised token release of about a score of young Syrian-Jewish women, as "proxy brides" to young men in the United States.

The charade hasn't fooled everyone: Donald Kirk of the *Chicago Tribune* reported an interview in Syria[33] in March of 1976:

> "So many journalists write about the Jews of Damascus," the Syrian says proudly. . . . "They see there is no discrimination. . . . We treat the Jews as we do any other Arabs. It is only Zionist propaganda that tries to make the world think we persecute them."

Kirk then wrote his reaction:

> Whatever one may think of such claims, one thing is certain: Members of the Syrian Jewish community can talk to foreigners only when escorted by Syrian information officials, and they are not likely to complain openly. . . ."

Kirk regarded the show of "15 Jewish doctors, 3 lawyers, 7 or 8 pharmacists and 7 or 8 rabbis" as "tokenism," and he was not impressed by the Syrian government's declared intention to strike out the red scrawl—"Musawi" (Moses)—which continued to appear on Jews' identity cards. Although sometimes in black ink and computerized, by latest reports, it still does appear.

Between long moratoriums on information, the media will become rife with stories contradicting each other within a matter of months, depending on the sophistication of the journalists and the extent of Syrian repression. In any six-month period, headlines can be found that state both that "Syria Tightens Persecution of Damascus Jews" and "Syria Eases Pressure on Jews." Both are in all probability accurate and indicate the arbitrary nature of the harshness of Jewish life in Syria. The fact is that, in the ancient tradition, pettier restrictions can be hurled at them or relieved according to official whim.

Moderation in Damascus' Jewish Quarter

Perhaps a personal experience best serves as an illustration of that arbitrary and unpredictable bullying. In the summer of 1977, President Carter met Syria's President Assad in Europe, where they had agreed in theory that some Jewish brides might leave Syria and be married by proxy to American Jews.

Just after that meeting, I traveled with a small group of former or between-posts State Department officials, media persons and private citizens, to Syria. Our "fact-finding committee" was told by the U.S. State Department authorities at the American Embassy in Damascus that Syria had become "moderate."

One member of our mission, former Ambassador Angier Biddle Duke, requested a visit to the Jewish Quarter and was told that he was welcome to go, that the visit would present no problems, that "things had cleared up," and that we were free to visit the homes of the Syrian Jews "if they invited us."

The next day we went to the Jewish Quarter in Damascus. We had no "escort." We were told none was necessary and we were driven in our bus down to the edge of the Jewish Quarter. Beshir, our tour guide, was to wait at the bus.

We bounded off the bus with Beshir shouting after us, "Turn left and walk. It is ahead." We turned into a narrow unpaved road and passed countless dilapidated buildings with Arabic scrawls on doors, past smiling toddlers and sullen teenagers who gazed curiously as the peculiar-looking group of half a dozen enthusiastic tourists strode by. We were looking for something—we didn't know what—some sign that might tell us we were among Jews. Ambassador Duke was pleased at the chance to verify the relative well-being of the Syrian Jews, and the group was intrigued at the opportunity to tour an exotic corner and see firsthand what we'd been assured were improved living conditions for the Jews.

We scanned faded whitewashed walls and the faces of local passersby, searching for some sign. Scrutinizing the Syrians we passed, we realized somewhat sheepishly that we could never tell who among these locals were the Jews. There were Palestinian Arabs living in homes left behind by Jews who had escaped from Syria since 1948, there were Cretans and Syrians of many complexions. Finally, we stopped to question a cluster of kindergarteners who'd been observing us with great delight and amused asides to each other. One asked me to remove my sunglasses so that he could see the color of my eyes. I asked in French, "Where is the Jewish Quarter?"

They laughed, and a man walked up to offer assistance. He pointed out that the children crowding around us were Jewish, and then identified himself as a "Cretan." He asked where we were from, and we told him. Just then someone walked up to our assemblage and whispered into the Cretan's ear. The Cretan watched us, nodding as the other man was talking, and when they'd finished, he turned to us and said, *"There* is a Jewish house and they would like you to come in and talk to them." He pointed across the narrow road at a high whitewashed wall, where a gate was being opened from within. We thanked him, walked toward the entrance, and looked in hesitantly; we were beckoned inside.

As we entered, we saw several people, mostly women, sitting around a yard directly inside the gate. It was a tiny unpaved dirt patio from which many doors led to the separate dwellings of many different families, with stairways in several directions. As we clustered in the center of the courtyard, we saw that because of the early-afternoon heat and traditional "siesta," we had caught people napping. As word of our arrival must have spread, however, the little courtyard began to fill with people who seemingly appeared from nowhere.

A couple of elderly women were quite terrified of speaking with us. As several younger people began to speak to our group, the older women harshly reprimanded them, repeating over and over, "J'ai peur" (I am afraid). The others first tried to calm them and then disregarded the warnings. They asked if we were from Israel. When we told them that we were American they asked "what kind of life" there was for Jews in America. Was it true that there were as many Jews in America as they had heard?

One attractive woman, a bookkeeper in her early thirties, told us that she had lost her job in a hotel "outside," because "they found out" she was Jewish. She explained that, although the laws had recently been amended so that Jews purportedly could work outside the Jewish Quarter, "When they found out that you were Jewish you were automatically fired." She was "desperate" to keep a job that paid enough to care for her family. Several other women expressed fear for their families' safety because of the Palestinians who lived on their doorsteps—who taunted and terrorized the Jewish children.

Some of the younger Jews were obviously fearful—and they spoke tentatively —while others were defiant and angry. All of them were determined that we learn "the truth" about the Jews who had been interviewed on "American television programs" and particularly on what they called the "Wallace program." Those Jews were "special" Jews, who appeared in most interviews conducted by the foreign press and were given "special privileges." But "they did not speak the truth," we were told. "Yes," Syrian authorities *promised* that the word *Musawi,* stamped in red ink across all Jews' identity cards, would be deleted. But some of these Jews literally ran into their homes and rushed out with their cards to show us that the red stamp had not been removed. When we told them that President Assad and President Carter had met to try to alleviate the situation for young Jewish girls, they exchanged wry grins.

One woman smirked bitterly, charging, "They'd rather see our children dead than married!" She seemed to give courage to the others and their mood snapped from reticence to anxiety—two or three spoke at once, softly but in such urgent tones that the travelers were visibly moved.

As though a dam of silence had burst, their fears poured forth and they complained of the harshness of their lives with rushing words, weeping tears of frustration that they impatiently wiped away.

As we talked, people were now crowding the courtyard. Shabbily but meticulously dressed, many seemed well educated. A woman in her forties started to tell of what was obviously an unhappy incident that had involved her son, but one of the elderly who had earlier expressed concern at our visit sharply cut her off, her voice raised harshly. The younger woman mutely nodded and then remained silent. We'd been speaking for about an hour when one of the residents suggested that the authorities might wonder what we were doing there, and so we began to say our good-byes. They requested a "promise": would we try to help them? They wanted their daughters to be able to marry and there were no young men to marry them. They wanted freedom. They begged us to "tell the world" that they were "not free," and that the Jews who said they were free did so because they were afraid for their safety—for their very lives and the lives of their families —if they told the truth.

Several of them began to cry openly then, and men and women in our group were weeping with them. After some difficult moments we all shook hands warmly, waved good-byes, and the troubled visitors began to file out of the courtyard. Some headed off down the road, and two of us lagged behind for a few moments. As Ambassador Duke and I headed out of the courtyard into the street we expected to see the others but they were nowhere in sight. Just then a young man ran up to us in great agitation, speaking with difficulty in broken French. Someone had been "arrested." Ambassador Duke ran after him to find out what had happened and after ten minutes another Syrian rushed up to say that Duke was also "arrested."

At that point I made a mad dash in the other direction, toward the exit to the main street where the bus was waiting outside the Jewish Quarter. When I arrived there, Beshir, our guide, wanted no part in assisting us. "It was your own fault," he said—he didn't want to be blamed, because he had "told" us "not to go." When he was reminded that, earlier, he had cheerfully waved us off on our tour with his "blessings," Beshir shrugged uneasily and looked away.

I wanted the nearest phone. The only place to look was down a row of tiny vendors' or artisans' shops lining the street on the edge of the Jewish Quarter. Beshir said they were "not Jewish-owned" but Muslim shops. At my first stop I was coldly refused the use of the phone. I ran into a second shop where I first, hurriedly, bought two cassettes to become a "customer," and then told the Syrian proprietors—largely in sign language—that I must use a telephone. After a few minutes of conversing between themselves the two men behind the counter finally agreed. Luckily I had the list of phone numbers that the American Embassy had given us earlier in the week and, after a maddeningly long series of trial-and-errors, I finally heard an American voice on the other end—ironically, it was the official who had briefed us on the "calm" within the Jewish Quarter. When he heard that Ambassador Duke and another visitor had been arrested, his reaction was, "That's impossible. How could that happen?" My response was not to consider how or why, but to get them out of there. The American staffer said he was "mortified"; he'd do what he could, he assured me, and then he hung up.

About an hour later, Ambassador Duke and friend appeared back at the bus, looking harassed and angry. Duke, white-faced and worn, explained that a plain-clothes Syrian agent had followed us throughout, from our entrance into the Jewish Quarter. The agent had stood outside the courtyard listening, while we were speaking with the Syrian Jews. He informed Duke of this later, in his role as one of the interrogators at the "headquarters" in the Jewish Quarter. Perhaps because Duke's irate indignation and his formidable list of titles intimidated the agents, the two Americans were released after what Duke cryptically described as "a rough time" with "some petty bullying." Although they hadn't physically molested him, Duke said he felt as though he'd been "beaten up."

That capricious police action made more poignant the travails and pleas for help of the people we had just met in the tiny courtyard, who have no titles to protect them. We were particularly uncomfortable that we had been given such positive assurances by our Embassy that "all was well in the Jewish Quarter." We left Syria the next day. At the Damascus airport Duke received a phone call from President Assad himself; Assad wanted us to stay and have lunch with him, and he promised that afterward he would charter a plane to take us to Cairo in time to keep an appointment with President Sadat in Egypt. Duke tersely de-clined, saying that he was "not feeling well." As a veteran State Department loyalist who believed in the soundness of State Department policies, he was more jolted than the rest of us by the fact that it had been U.S. State Department foreign service officers at the Embassy who had assured us of a condition that was totally contradicted by the facts.

In October of 1978, a year after Duke's arrest, Kevin Murphy, of the *Evening News* in London, reported that

> Life for Jews living in Syria is harsh—as I soon found out. I was arrested by armed police and marched off for interrogation when I tried to talk to a rabbi in Damas-cus. I had been in the rabbi's home only about ten minutes when a leather-jacketed scruffy policeman—pistol clipped to his trousers—walked in and demanded to know who I was and what I was doing.
>
> A policeman with a submachine gun stands guard at the entrance to the area. . . . There are approximately 3,000 Jews marooned in Damascus, living in a squalid rabbit warren of back alleys in the old part of the city. Ironically, they share the distressing area with the archenemy of the Israelis, the Palestinians.

According to Murphy, who had been in Syria to "examine the plight of the Jewish community in Damascus," the "police station . . . consisted of a stark gray painted room with two beds, a desk and a few wooden chairs," and there, he said, "The police demanded to know whether I had taken any photographs in the Jewish Quarter. . . ." While they were interrogating him in English, they were asking the same questions of the rabbi in Arabic, with one of the younger men in plain clothes making a "great show" of fiddling with a pistol. Murphy reported,

> I was later allowed to interview the rabbi through the interpreter with the chief of police and his deputy sitting between us. The supervised answers painted a pleasant picture of Jewish life in Syria.[34]

In 1978, some 400 Syrian Jews, including entire families, escaped via secret routes; as a consequence, in early 1979 the Syrians increased surveillance and restrictions. In 1981, even the "handful of Jews" who could afford to hold passports found their travel documents "cancelled," while in early 1983 some Jews were permitted to travel. Jewish property has been "seized," and many Jews "have had to pay rent to the government to live in their own homes."[35]

Since the PLO and other radical groups were reinforced by returnees from the 1982 war in Lebanon,[36] the Jewish community has reportedly become increasingly alarmed: according to reporter Elenore Lester, "in addition to their fear of becoming scapegoats in the crossfire between the Suni [*sic*] Muslim majority . . . and [President] Assad's Alawite minority, the Jews fear the PLO . . . many of whom have settled in Jewish areas of Damascus and Aleppo. . . ."[37]

An American representative of the Syrian Jews after his visit to Syria several years ago summed up the situation as it yet remains:

> The Jews are living in a jail. Most escapees are the young and agile—when they flee, the youngsters disappear overnight without telling their families, because it's safer for their relatives not to know. What must it be like to know that you may lose your child overnight and never see him or her again?
>
> They want to get out—they want to be free. Those few Jews who have traveled briefly abroad—who left families as hostage and could afford the huge security bond necessary—came back in shock. They had tasted a free Jewish life, and now that they *know* it exists, they want more than ever to get out of jail.[38]

Egypt

In Egypt, perhaps 250 Jews are left of the ancient long-persevering Jewish community that once comprised many tens of thousands. Among the Egyptian Jews, most are aged, and some are unmarried women. They were allowed to worship in the synagogue in Cairo at the time of my visits to that city in 1974 and 1977. The quality of life for those few remaining Egyptian Jews had long been more complex in nature than that of Syria.

Since the 1979 Egyptian-Israeli peace treaty was signed, however, the climate of receptivity among Egyptians for a "return" of its Jews is surely a study in ambivalence, as was the somber reception Egypt gave to Israeli Prime Minister Begin when he arrived in Cairo for the first official visit.[39]

Egypt had been significantly recognized as the "most moderate" of Arab states due to the uniquely publicized, precedent-breaking program of peace efforts by Egyptian President Anwar Sadat, beginning with his historic visit to Israel's capital city of Jerusalem in November 1977. Before that important gesture to the Jewish state, the Egyptian attitudes had already long been perceived by American officials and press as "moderate" with regard to acceptance of Jewish "equality" and a Jewish entity in the Middle East. Yet when President Sadat issued his invitation to former Egyptian Jews to "return" to Egypt in September 1977, the Egyptian-born Jews charged that Sadat's "welcome" was cynical, that Jews could never "go back," and that Sadat "knew it"—because his "invitation" had excepted any Jews who were "Zionists."

The invitation had been issued less than two months before Sadat's peace journey to Jerusalem, and even after that image-changing visit the Egyptian-born Jews' response remained adamantly negative. To understand fully the Egyptian-born Jews' disdain for Egypt's "invitation," one must examine the contemporary Egyptians' attitude toward "their Jews."

On my first trip to Cairo, armed with high hopes and twin assignments—"moderation" and an analysis of Egypt's population explosion, which was reportedly crippling progress and Egypt's economy—I arrived into a community uniquely hospitable to the American journalist. Never had I been so quickly connected, never more graciously received. I had expected to find the widely publicized "new" Egyptian "moderation."

Even before the fighting ended in the 1973 war, memory of the Egyptian-Syrian aggression against Israel was fading; President Sadat was lauded for "fighting for the sake of peace." Reports had begun to circulate in the West about the new reasonableness in Egypt. These hopeful beginnings were accompanied by a new kind of rhetoric emanating from Egyptian officialdom in which the old bellicosity and threats of throwing Israel into the sea were replaced by announcements of a readiness and a desire for peace.

For this change of rhetoric President Sadat was hailed as "that most moderate of Arab leaders"; from that time, "Egypt" was synonymous with "moderation." Editorials that now seem prophetic—in the New York Times and other important newspapers around the country—saw "clear signs that Egypt . . . has already come around to accepting the desirability of coexistence with Israel."[40] The Times's Henry Tanner, just four months after the 1973 October war, reported with elation that he had seen a book on self-taught Hebrew in a Cairo display window, an "illustration of the psychological and political transformation that Cairo has undergone since the war under Anwar el-Sadat's presidency."[41] Tanner, in his reports from Cairo, consistently stressed what he saw as the "psychological trend in the Arab world toward accepting the existence of Israel." Jesse Zel Lurie wrote in the New Leader that he, as editor of Hadassah magazine, could talk politics openly with an Egyptian in the Cairo Hilton coffee shop: "Under Nasser [his Egyptian companion] would have feared [the waitress] reporting us to the secret police."[42]

Ignorant at that time of the Jews' past in Egypt, I accepted without question the prevailing notion that "before Israel," traditional "equality" and historical "tolerance" of Jews had existed in Egypt. Consequently, before setting out for Cairo, I immersed myself in the literature attesting to the positive change in Egyptians' attitudes toward the Jewish state—without understanding their underlying attitude toward Jews or how inextricably that traditional sentiment was woven into their hostility toward Zionists and Israel.

Once in Egypt I interviewed as representative a cross section of Egyptians as I could find—government officials, writers, academics, scientists, demographers, doctors, architects, engineers, housewives, shopkeepers, students, soldiers, salesmen, cab drivers, waiters, women's-rights activists, secretaries, carpenters, travel agents; Communists, leftists, nationalists, and right-wing conservatives. The consensus that emerged, so far from conforming to the prevailing Western perception of Egypt, seemed rather to suggest its opposite. The views expressed, far from being provoked by the interviewer, were often fiercely intruded, whether an interview on demography, a conversation about Egyptian archaeology, or a discussion of Egyptian "moderation." Vehement anti-Israeli—and, what is more, deeply rooted anti-Jewish—sentiments were the norm among Egyptians and were characteristic of government officials at the highest levels no less than of the man in the street.

As an example, a law professor whom I had been assured was "well-informed, a man of the regime," a former politician of "common sense," and a "moderate," wanted to be of assistance in helping me to fulfill my assignments. I asked if he could arrange an informal gathering of students—young people—and he promised to try.

The meeting with Professor Ali's group* was held after hours, in one of the offices of an old and somewhat deteriorated enclosed court building that Ali told me had once been the grand meeting place of Egypt's aristocrats. Unfortunately Ali could not remain at the meeting, but he introduced me to his friends and settled me in. Dr. Amin, a lawyer and former member of the foreign ministry, rose from behind his desk to greet me; he was a tall, powerfully built, well-dressed man with silver hair and a mustache, and a deep reverberating voice. There were only two young people, he apologized—a young man who studied at Cairo University, and Dr. Amin's secretary, a girl about nineteen. The other guests included a well-turned-out woman lawyer in her thirties, a balding former judge, and a fortyish "engineer-businessman." Comfortably ensconced in couches and chairs around Dr. Amin's desk, they exchanged a few reserved, awkward remarks, taking the official line of the "conflict" and the prospects for "peace." But after thirty minutes Dr. Amin and his guests were passionately reacting to one another—never in dispute, but in corroboration of their common position. Except for the retired judge's occasional angry lapses into French, everyone spoke English, often all at once.

The only reason for Israel's existence, the group agreed, was to "make trouble all over the world." But Israel was fated to "fade out, disappear," because "there is no real reason for it to exist." As soon as Israel became "secure"—which meant shrinking to the size of a "very small state" with "no political activities" and few resources—the world would forget about it. They expressed exasperation at America's rejection of Arafat's "secular state." Was it so impossible to accept the dissolution of the Jewish state? Dr. Amin quoted long passages from a 1970 *Foreign Affairs* article by the late, controversial Jewish personality, Nahum Goldmann—he said he knew it by heart. According to Dr. Amin, Goldmann proved that Zionism was based on fallacious premises. The Palestinians *would* have

*The professor requested the use of fictitious names.

"their" land, and the Egyptians would get back the Sinai, which they'd held for "six thousand years"—even if it took "a hundred wars to get it." They seemed genuinely unaware that the Sinai had come into Egypt's possession only after World War I.

The world has "no time for religious fanatics," they continued. Israel is "finished" because it "does no good to anybody."

> The Jews dominate England, France, the United States. Once upon a time a madman started persecuting the Jews . . . maybe he had a grudge against them. Maybe it was justified?

In fact, the Bible itself—they purported to know it well—told of "incest" and "social diseases" that Jews "like Abraham" had brought to Egypt. Jews had always "asked for trouble" and made a "show."

> When Shakespeare wrote his Shylock, he drew him well.
> Shylock is the universal Jew of all time, all places . . . not just Israel.
> You see, the Jews want their pound of flesh.

They passionately defended PLO terrorism:

> What should matter is to kill as many Jews—as many Israelis as they can.
> The terrorist attempts are never successful because the boys are not really destructive, they don't want to be barbarians, they don't have it in their blood, not like the Irish.
> They are peaceful people, not like the cold-blooded Jews.
> That is the difference between Shylock and Muhammad—the Jews are Shylock all over . . . not a peace-loving people.
> Even when the Arabs were in domination of the world, they were never bloodthirsty, always peaceful, loving and idealistic [sic].

"Most of the time," they affirmed, the acts of Arab Palestinian terrorism "are really maneuvered by the Jews themselves, by Israel." It is "more than just coincidence," they believed, that

> every time the Jews . . . antagonize world opinion, the Arab commandos do something that arouses sympathy for the Jews.

The Munich massacre of Israeli Olympic players had been "maneuvered by Israel." "They [the Jews] are very clever."

"Maybe the United States will force Israel into accepting a settlement," they suggested. "That's why Egyptians spend so much hard hope on the United States —not on idealistic grounds." The Arabs were all "very anxious" for a settlement, but

> Israel would never sign to any borders whatsoever, because once the borders are settled, Israel won't exist anymore. They know that and we know it better!

Everyone was laughing now, but the tension seemed unrelieved. I forced a smile, mumbled something about the lateness of the hour—we'd been "discussing" for almost three hours—and thanked them for their kind cooperation. All assured me they'd had "a very good time," and hoped I'd "take [their] good ideas" back home with me, and "do good work." It was very important to "do good work," because

> Jews dominate mass communications. There is no place for Arab voices to express their opinion in Europe or the United States.

During another interview, Foreign Minister Ismaïl Fahmy warned that, if I wrote "the truth," *they* would be after me, *they* would never leave me alone. I would lose my job. Who?

> The Jewish lobby in your country. I guarantee you . . . you will lose your job. *I am warning you!* I'm afraid for your future.

Yet, several Egyptians in Cairo confided quite candidly that Jewish writers from abroad were then being given "special treatment." One former General predicted:

> Once we can convince the Jews—especially the six million in the U.S.—that it is *Egypt* who is the "moderate" and *Israel* is "intransigent" and "standing in the way of peace," we will have won the two hundred million Americans. Who among the two hundred million will be for Israel if the six million American Jews are not?

In an article about the above,[43] I wrote of what I found to be a significant and alarmingly "immoderate," anti-Jewish Egypt in 1975. Later, while reading translations of Arabic religious doctrine and official Arab government educational texts of the 1960s, like those mentioned in Chapter 4, the sentiments expressed in the 1970s by the Egyptians became recognizable: their expressions in many instances were verbatim or paraphrased renditions that parroted the Muslim clergy and the schoolbooks.

In mid-1977 I returned to Egypt. There, two State Department staffers from the U.S. Embassy privately advised me, over coffee in the snack bar of a Cairo hotel, that they had "heard about" my earlier reports, and "no, nothing has changed—because Egypt hasn't even begun" what they called "the process of socialization of an attitude of accepting a Jewish state in their midst." During the same trip, I met with President Sadat, a few months before his precedent-breaking pilgrimage to Jerusalem. In that interview the Egyptian president acknowledged that "Seventy percent of this Arab-Israeli conflict is a psychological problem— it has only thirty percent substance."[44] In all probability Sadat was planning then to change the circumstances under which, as he put it, "Both of us have no confidence in the other."

Afterward the political relations of the two nations had alternated between the triumphs of both leaders' visits to each other's countries and the tribulations brought about by the hard negotiations for peace. Perhaps nobody was more surprised than the countries concerned when the on-again, off-again efforts culminated in the historic peace treaty of 1979.

Prime Minister Menachem Begin, the first Israeli leader to pay an official call on Cairo since the founding of his country, seemed impervious to the fact that he was received by a less-than-jubilant Egypt. The joyous welcome President Sadat had received from Israel upon his 1977 Jerusalem mission was conspicuously absent from Cairo during Prime Minister Begin's visit—which caused some observers to become skeptical of the Egyptians' sincerity.

Despite the peace implemented, most Egyptian-born Jewish refugees now in Israel were doubtful of the sincerity of Egypt's welcome. While they joyously and incredulously received the visit of Sadat to Jerusalem in 1977, by 1979 they expressed distrust and fear at the fact that, although Israeli Prime Minister Begin included all the Jewish-settled Sinai territory in the Israeli government's concessions to gain peace, not one Jewish resident among the thousands who had settled in the Sinai after the 1967 Israeli victory was allowed by Egypt to remain. Many such Israelis, and their refugee counterparts from other Arab states, maintained that the peace treaty was in fact no more than a "temporary" ploy used by Sadat and Egypt. These detractors argued that Egypt was merely using the Israelis' long-sought desire for the end of hostility to "take what the Israelis gave"; they claimed that the negotiations were an "apartheid truce" and not a peace treaty.

But when Begin arrived in Cairo, for many,

the most remarkable aspect of the Begin visit was . . . that it was taking place at all

amid the raising of an Israeli flag with its emblazoned blue-and-white Star of David, and accompanied by the premiere Egyptian performance of the Jewish national anthem.[45]

When President Sadat was murdered in 1981, his political foes and Israel's enemies hoped the assassin's bullet that cut him down would sever the flow of peace and the formal ties between Egypt and Israel. Those eager to keep the peace process alive placed their aspirations in the policies of Sadat's successor, President Hosni Mubarak; there the momentous groundwork of Sadat and Begin would lie uneasy and more fragile, stalled in the political wake of the 1980s war waged by Israel against PLO terror in Lebanon.

For the handful of Jews still in Egypt, mostly the elderly, perhaps the question is purely academic. As for the rest of Egypt's erstwhile Jewish community, as Mr. Begin said in Cairo, although

only a small remnant remains, . . . we can take solace in that most of those who are left are in the land of Israel.[46]

It is certain that the courage of Anwar el-Sadat changed Arab-Israeli history and established a precedent of peace; however tenuous, it was once done. Those of us who watched breathlessly in the Tel Aviv airport as Egypt's presidential plane first touched down on Jewish soil, felt tangibly the tremors of that first step in a peace path and were immeasurably moved.

No reasonable observer ought to expect that, within the Egyptians' deep-rooted attitudes toward Jews, an abrupt change of heart can take place. Even with totalitarian-styled control, a political peace cannot artificially induce the will of a people to "love thy neighbor." Some of the sentiments greeting Begin in the Egyptian press on his arrival in Cairo after the peace accords—including words like "Shylock" and "bloodsucker"—were uncomfortably reminiscent of a hostility I'd heard years before. And that some in our media identified those press reactions as "anti-Semitic"[47] reminded me of words written at another time about re-education in another context by the eminent physicist Leo Szilard: "How many years would it take . . . to be slightly malicious without being outright offensive?"[48] The devout desire was that such Egyptian "psychological" residue in time would diminish and disappear into the black hole of Egypt's historical hostility toward Jews. Whether the dynamics of peace be the stronger, only time would tell.

A Backward Glance

In truth, there is only a small fraction left throughout the entire Arab world of its once near-million Jewish population, and some of those Jews do not remain by choice. Far fewer Jews have chosen to continue living under hostile Arab rule than, for instance, Jews who remained in Germany, where—despite the officially declared anti-Jewish policy and the opportunity, albeit hazardous, to flee between 1933 and 1939—nearly two-thirds did not leave. As the German-born scholar Rabbi Joachim Prinz observed:

> The Jews seem to have a perverse talent for developing an unhappy and totally uncritical patriotism for the countries in which they live. They were Frenchmen who adored the tricolor when, during the days of Dreyfus, the streets were full of mobs yelling "A bas les juifs!" They were loyal Germans and faithful Englishmen, and loving children of Russia, in spite of the storm troopers, degradation and pogroms. And by 1492 they had been Spaniards for centuries.[49]

There were many reasons for the difference between the mass exodus of the Arab-born Jewish refugees and the reluctant leave-taking by the German Jews who escaped from Hitler: Arab-born Jews realized that the Arab threats would be carried out, because they had lived as second-class citizens—*dhimmis*—with reminders of pogroms in their own or their families' past experiences, whereas the German Jews felt themselves "assimilated," part of the German mainstream. They expressed initial "disbelief" that any such bigotry as the Nazis' could be more than a cruel political joke. It was justified disbelief—never had there occurred so massive or systematic a genocide—even of Jews—in the Western world. The German Jews' incredulity was shared by the rest of the world—rumors of the Nazi intentions were eschewed as "Zionist" or "Jewish" propaganda, and even when unmistakable evidence filtered through of the awful truth, Western officials judged that evidence to be exaggerated.

By the time of their exodus in 1948, the Arab-born Jews had the advantage of hindsight—not only had they learned of the Nazi holocaust, but they had lived in the Arab lands that zealously had embraced the Nazi dogma and had adopted it within their own Arab anti-Jewish *Muftism*. And the *most important difference* of all was that by 1948 Arab-born Jews had a place to go—Israel.

Why then would *any* Arab-born Jew persist in living in a hostile Arab community that avowedly views him or her an "enemy," when there is an alternative? Unquestionably there are many surface explanations—loss of livelihood, fear of change, reluctance to abandon aged relatives who refused to uproot from familiar surroundings. The process of rejection of one's perilous predicament, however, is nearly analogous, by its very existence, to the avoidance mechanism that Jews have employed in so many unfortunate periods of Jewish history. They avoided perhaps because the knowledge or acceptance of such history required an awareness too painful to bear—that flight for the Jews was inexorable, at some point, from everywhere, and that any haven other than Israel was only transient.

II

THE CREATION OF YESTERDAY:
EARLY POPULATION
AND DEPOPULATION
OF THE HOLY LAND

8

"Palestina": A Precedent of Prey

> . . . How often in talks with Rogers,
> Kissinger, Sisco and others has Egypt heard
> the Americans say, in effect, "We're not
> interested in raking over the past: let's
> look at the situation as it is today." *But
> today's situation is the creation of yesterday.* *
>
> —Mohamed Heikal, *The Road to Ramadan*

> . . . some [Jews] you slew and others you took
> captive. *He [Allah] made you masters* of their *land,*
> their *houses* and their *goods,* and of yet *another
> land on which you had never set foot before.*
> Truly, Allah has power over all things.*
>
> —The Koran, The Clans, surah XXXIII

> Yes, the existence of a separate Palestinian
> identity serves only tactical purposes. The
> founding of a Palestinian state is a *new* tool
> in the continuing battle against Israel . . .
>
> —Zuheir Muhsin, late Military Department head
> of the PLO and member of its Executive
> Council, Dutch daily *Trouw,* March 1977

> The Prophet Muhammad said, "War is deception."
>
> —al-Bukhari, al-Jami al Sahih

Although a politically based mythology has grown up around and smothered the documented past of the land known as "Palestine," there is recognition among preeminent scholars of what one of them has called "the more chauvinist Arab version of the region's history as having begun with the Arabs and Islam."[1]

The claim that Arab-Muslim "Palestinians" were "emotionally tied" to "their own plot of land in Palestine"—based upon a "consistent presence" on "Arab" land for "thousands of years"[2]—is an important part of that recent mythology. It was contrived of late in a thus far successful Orwellian propaganda effort—an

*Emphasis added.

137

appeal to the emotions that would "counter Zionism" and that "serves" tactical purposes as "a *new* tool in the continuing battle against Israel," as the late PLO official Muhsin stated candidly in an interview, quoted at the beginning of this chapter.

In order to understand how that tool, aided by a general near-ignorance of the "unrelenting past," has distorted the perception of the present, a look at the "yesterday" of "Palestine" is necessary.

The inspection will be focused upon completing a circle—tracing the actual conditions and events that have been glossed over or omitted from the dialogue about the Arab-Israeli conflict; they are conditions and events that shaped the real political, economic, and demographic circumstances in the area. Those circumstances in turn critically affected what "justice" really consists of—for the Jewish and Arab refugees, or the "Palestinian Problem"—for the Arab-Israeli conflict. Illuminating that situation reveals and fills in the chasm between the documented facts and the Arab claims, and gives perspective to those contentions and assumptions that have become key in interpreting what is "just" for the population in question today.

"The only Arab domination since the Conquest in 635 A.D. hardly lasted, as such, 22 years . . .," the Muslim chairman of the Syrian Delegation attested in his remarks to the Paris Peace Conference in February 1919.[3]

The British Palestine Royal Commission reported in 1937 that "it is time, surely, that Palestinian 'citizenship' . . . should be recognized as what it is, as nothing but a legal formula devoid of moral meaning."[4]

That the claim of "age-old Arab Palestinian rights to Arab Palestine" is contradicted by history has been pointed out by eminent historians and Arabists.

According to the Reverend James Parkes, "The Land was named *Palestina* by the Romans to eradicate all trace of its Jewish history. . . . "

> It may seem inappropriate to have devoted so much time to "a situation which passed away two thousand years ago." But it is only *politically* that the defeat by Rome, and the scattering of the Jewish population, made a decisive change in the history of The Land. That which had been created by more than a thousand years of Jewish history [a thousand years before A.D. 135] remained, as did that which was beginning to be created in the thoughts of the young Christian Church.*[5]

Many authorities have addressed the misconceptions surrounding the word *Palestine.* The name derived from "other migrants from the northwest, the Philistines. Though the *latest arrivals,* and though they only exercised control over the whole country for a few uncertain decades, they had been the cause of its name of Palestine. These *Philistines* were an *Aegean* people, driven out of Greece and the Aegean islands around about 1300 B.C.E. They moved southward along the Asiatic coast and in about 1200 attempted to invade Egypt. Turned back, they

*Emphasis added.

settled in the maritime plain of southern 'Palestine', where they founded a series of city-states."[6]

According to Bernard Lewis, an eminent authority, "The word Palestine does not occur in the Old Testament. . . . Palestine does not occur in the New Testament at all."

> The official adoption of the name Palestine in Roman usage to designate the territories of the former Jewish principality of Judea seems to date from after the suppression of the great Jewish revolt of Bar-Kokhba in the year 135 C.E. . . . it would seem that the name Judea was abolished . . . and the country renamed Palestine or Syria Palestina, with the . . . intention of obliterating its historic Jewish identity. The earlier name did not entirely disappear, and as late as the 4th century C.E. we still find a Christian author, Epiphanius, referring to "Palestine, that is, Judea."

As many, including Professor Lewis, have pointed out, "From the end of the Jewish state in antiquity to the beginning of British rule, the area now designated by the name Palestine was not a country and had no frontiers, only administrative boundaries; it was a group of provincial subdivisions, by no means always the same, within a larger entity."[*7]

In other words, it appears that Palestine never was an independent nation and the Arabs never named the land to which they now claim rights. Most Arabs do not admit so candidly that "Palestinian identity" is a maneuver "only for political reasons" as did Zuheir Muhsin. But the Arab world, until recently, itself frequently negated the validity of any claim of an "age-old Palestinian Arab" identity.

The Arabs in Judah-cum-Palestine were regarded either as members of a "pan-Arab nation," as a Muslim community, or, in a tactical ploy, as "Southern Syrians."[8] The beginning article of a 1919 Arab Covenant proposed by the Arab Congress in Jerusalem stated that "The Arab lands are a complete and indivisible whole, and the divisions of whatever nature to which they have been subjected are not approved nor recognized by the Arab nation."[9] In the same year, the General Syrian Congress had the opposite view; it expressed eagerness to stress an exclusively Syrian identity: "We ask that there should be no separation of the southern part of Syria, known as Palestine . . ."[10] The Arab historian George Antonius delineated Palestine in 1939 as part of "the whole of the country of that name [Syria] which is now split up into mandated territories. . . ."[11] As late as the 1950s, there was still a schizoid pattern to the Arab views. In 1951, the Constitution of the Arab Ba'ath Party stated:

> The Arabs form one nation. This nation has the natural right to live in a single state and to be free to direct its own destiny . . . to gather all the Arabs in a single, independent Arab state.[12]

*See the map "Ancient Palestine" in Appendix I.

A scant five years later, a Saudi Arabian United Nations delegate in 1956 asserted that "It is common knowledge that Palestine is nothing but Southern Syria."[13] In 1974, Syria's President Assad, although a PLO supporter, incorporated both claims in a remarkable definition:

> . . . Palestine is not only a part of our Arab homeland, but a basic part of southern Syria.[14]

The one identity *never seriously* considered until the 1967 Six-Day War—and then only as a "tool"—was an "Arab Palestinian" one, and the absence was not merely disregard. Clearly there was no such age-old or even century-old "national identity." According to the British *Palestine Royal Commission Report*,

> In the twelve centuries or more that have passed since the Arab conquest Palestine has virtually dropped out of history. . . . In economics as in politics Palestine lay outside the main stream of the world's life. In the realm of thought, in science or in letters, it made no contribution to modern civilization. Its last state was worse than its first.[15]

Before the Arab Conquest

But long before the Arab conquest, as a British Member of Parliament pointed out in 1939,

> a thousand years before the Prophet Mohammed was born, the Jew, already exiled, sitting by the waters of Babylon, was singing: "If I forget thee O Jerusalem, may my right hand forget its cunning."[16]

The Reverend Parkes says that the theme that "gives to Jewish history characteristics which begin by being unusual and end by being unique" is that "the religion which was developing into a universalistic ethical monotheism never lost its root in The Land."[17]

> . . . Jewry has nowhere established another independent national centre; and, as is natural, the Land of Israel is intertwined far more intimately into the religious and historic memories of the people; for their connection with the country has been of much longer duration—in fact it has been continuous from the 2nd millenium B.C.E. up to modern times. . . . The Land therefore has provided an emotional centre which has endured through the whole of their period of "exile", and has led to constant returns or attempted returns, culminating in our own day in the Zionist Movement.[18]

Israel had already become a nation about 1220 B.C.—nearly two thousand years before the first Arab invasion began.[19] The Jews' persistent presence on the land survived periodic attempts to extinguish them throughout their history. Around the first century,

> Many Diaspora Jews observed the commandments of pilgrimage, and on the High Holidays in Jerusalem one might have met Jews from such different lands as

Parthia, Media, Elam, Mesopotamia, Cappadocia, Pontus, Asia Minor, Phrygia, Pamphylia, Cyrene, Crete, Rome and Arabia.[20]

By the time of the Roman conquest of Judea the Jews were considered "turbulent and troublesome people to deal with," according to the *Encyclopaedia Britannica,*[21] when they stubbornly refused to surrender their country to Roman rule.

The Emperor Hadrian, "determined to stamp out this aggressive Jewish nationalism," ruled that henceforth Jewish traditions such as circumcision, the Sabbath, reading of the law—in fact, the beliefs of Judaism itself—were illegal and "forbidden."[22] Hadrian was "determined to convert the still half-ruined Jerusalem into a Roman colony." After the Jews' Temple was destroyed in A.D. 70, the revolt of Jewish leader Bar Kochba—who had "200,000 men at his command" —recaptured Jerusalem and many "strongholds and villages throughout the country." The "full-scale country-wide war . . . raged with fierce bitterness for four years, the Romans having to bring in legion after legion of reinforcements to suppress the insurgents."[23]

Although the Romans ultimately regained political reign, "sacked the city [of Jerusalem] . . . and expelled the bulk of the Jewish survivors from the country,"[24] the cost of victory was shattering—"It is said that as many as 580,000 men were slain!"—Romans as well as Jews. It was after the debacle that Hadrian changed the name of the city of Jerusalem to Aelia Capitolina, ordered the building of a temple of Jupiter on the Jewish Temple site and "forbade any Jew, on pain of death, to appear within sight of the city."[25]

But in the same way that the name Judea did not disappear, neither did the Jews abandon their land. A number had obstinately remained, and many others quickly returned to rebuild their world. Some Jews, however, fled the Roman conquest for other points—including Arabia, where they formed some new settlements and in many instances joined Jewish Arabian communities established at the time of release from the captivity in Babylon or existing even before then. Thus evolved the flight of the *first* "Palestinian" refugees—the Judeans, or Jews.

The Haven in Arabia

A look at the haven where these "Palestinian" or "Judean" Jewish refugees from the Romans found sanctuary is important to understanding the "heart of the matter" in the Middle East today—the conflict between Arab and Jew. The circumstances of the Arabian Jewish communities in the Arabian Peninsula— both *before* and *after* the Arab Conquest—bear importantly upon Arab-Jewish relationships until this day, because the pattern that developed in Arabia established a tradition that has been followed ever since.

According to Arabist scholar Alfred Guillaume, Jews probably first settled in Arabia in connection with the fall of Samaria in 721 B.C.:

. . . it is almost certain that the self-contained Jewish military colony in Aswan and upper Egypt, about which the world knew nothing until a few years ago, was founded just after the fall of Samaria, and consequently it is not impossible that some Jewish settlements in Arabia were due to fugitives fleeing from the old northern capital of the Hebrews.

Guillaume is certain that "in the first and second centuries A.D., . . . Arabia offered a near asylum" to the Jews who had been victimized by the "utterly ruthless" Romans.[26]

In the Arabian land considered by many to be "purely Arab," the land which would spawn Islam many centuries later,

Numbers of Jewish and Christian settlements were established in different parts of Arabia, both spreading Aramaic and Hellenistic culture. The chief southern Arabian Christian centre was in Najrān, where a relatively advanced political life was developed. Jews and Judaised Arabs were everywhere, especially in Yathrib, later renamed Medina. They were mainly agriculturists and artisans. Their origin is uncertain and many different theories have been advanced.[27]

Although the fact is little recognized, more than one historian has affirmed that the Arab world's second holiest city, Medina, was one of the allegedly "purely Arab" cities that actually was first settled by Jewish tribes.[28] Bernard Lewis writes:

The city of Medina, some 280 miles north of Mecca, had originally been settled by Jewish tribes from the north, especially the Banū Nadīr and Banū Quraiza. The comparative richness of the town attracted an infiltration of pagan Arabs who came at first as clients of the Jews and ultimately succeeded in dominating them. Medina, or, as it was known before Islam, Yathrib, had no form of stable government at all. The town was torn by the feuds of the rival Arab tribes of Aus and Khazraj, with the Jews maintaining an uneasy balance of power. The latter, engaged mainly in agriculture and handicrafts, were economically and culturally superior to the Arabs, and were consequently disliked. . . . as soon as the Arabs had attained unity through the agency of Muhammad they attacked and ultimately eliminated the Jews.[29]

In the last half of the fifth century, many Persian Jews fled from persecution to Arabia, swelling the Jewish population there.[30] But around the sixth century, Christian writers reported of the continuing importance of the Jewish community that remained in the Holy Land. For the dispersed Arabian Jewish settlers, Tiberias in Judea was central. In the Kingdom of Himyar on the Red Sea's east coast in Arabia, "conversion to Judaism of influential circles" was popular, and the Kingdom's rule stretched across "considerable portions of South Arabia."

The commoners as well as the royal family adopted Judaism, and one writer reports that "Jewish priests (presumably rabbis) from Tiberias . . . formed part of the suite of King Du Noas and served as his envoys in negotiations with Christian cities."[31]

According to Guillaume,

At the dawn of Islam the Jews dominated the economic life of the Hijaz [Arabia]. They held all the best land . . . ; at Medina they must have formed at least half of the population. There was also a Jewish settlement to the north of the Gulf of Aqaba. . . . What is important is to note that the Jews of the Hijaz made many proselytes [or converts] among the Arab tribesmen.[32]

The first "Palestinian" or Judean refugees—the *Jews*—had resettled to become prosperous, influential *Arabian* settlers.

The prosperity of the Jews was due to their superior knowledge of agriculture and irrigation and their energy and industry. Homeless [Jewish] refugees in the course of a few generations became large landowners in the country, [the refugees who had come to the Hijaz when the Romans conquered Palestine] controllers of its finance and trade. . . . Thus it can readily be seen that Jewish prosperity was a challenge to the Arabs, particularly the Quraysh at Mecca and . . . [other Arab tribes] at Medina.

The Prophet Muhammad himself was a member of the Quraysh tribe, which coveted the Jews' bounty, and

when the Muslims took up arms they treated the Jews with much greater severity than the Christians, who, until the end of the purely Arab Caliphate, were not badly treated.[33]

One of the reasons for "this discrimination" against the Jews is what Guillaume called "the *Qurān's* scornful words" regarding the Jews.[34] The Jews' development of land and culture was a prime source of booty in the Arabian desert peninsula. Beginning at the time of the Prophet Muhammad and Islam[35] —from the expulsions, depredations, extortion, forced conversions or murder of Jewish Arabians settled in Medina to the mass slaughter of Jews at Khaibar— the precedent was established among Arab-Muslims to expropriate that which belonged to the Jews. Relations between the Prophet Muhammad and the Jews were "never . . . easy":

They had irritated him by their refusal to recognize him as a prophet, by ridicule and by argument; and of course their economic supremacy . . . was a standing irritant.[36]

It appears that the first "instigation" by the Prophet Muhammad himself against the Jews was an incident in which he had "one or two Jews . . . murdered and no blood money was paid to their next of kin."

. . . Their leaders opposed his claim to be an apostle sent by God, and though they doubtless drew some satisfaction from his acceptance of the divine mission of Abraham, Moses, and the prophets, they could hardly be expected to welcome the inclusion of Jesus and Ishmael among his chosen messengers.[37]

. . . the existence of pockets of disaffected Jews in and around his base was a cause of uneasiness and they had to be eliminated if he [Muhammad] was to wage war without anxiety.[38]

Because the Jews preferred to retain their own beliefs,

> a tribe of Jews in the neighborhood of Medina, fell under suspicion of treachery and were forced to lay down their arms and evacuate their settlements. Valuable land and much booty fell into the hands of the Muslims. . . . The neighboring tribe of Qurayza, who were soon to suffer annihilation, made no move to help their co-religionists, and their allies, the Aus, were afraid to give them active support.[39]

The Prophet Muhammad's pronouncement: "Two religions may not dwell together on the Arabian Peninsula."[40] This edict was carried out by Abu Bakr and Omar I, the Prophet Muhammad's successors; the entire community of Jewish settlements throughout northern Arabia was systematically slaughtered. According to Bernard Lewis, "the extermination of the Jewish tribe of Quraiza" was followed by "an attack on the Jewish oasis of Khaibar."[41]

Messengers of Muhammad were sent to the Jews who had escaped to the safety and comfort of Khaibar, "inviting" Usayr, the Jewish "war chief," to visit Medina for mediations.

> Usayr set off with thirty companions and a Muslim escort. Suspecting no foul play, the Jews went unarmed. On the way, the Muslims turned upon the defenseless delegation, killing all but one who managed to escape. "War is deception,"[42] according to an oft-quoted saying of the Prophet.[43]

The late Israeli historian and former President, Itzhak Ben-Zvi, judged the "inhuman atrocities" of the Arabian communities as unparalleled since then:

> . . . the complete extermination of the two Arabian-Jewish tribes, the Nadhir and Kainuka' by the mass massacre of their men, women and children, was a tragedy for which no parallel can be found in Jewish history until our own day. . . .[44]

The slaughter of Arabian Jews and the expropriation of their property became Allah's will. According to the Koran,

> . . . some you slew and others you took captive. He [Allah] made you masters of their [the Jews'] *land,* their *houses* and their *goods,* and of yet *another land* [*Khaibar*] *on which you had never set foot before.* Truly, Allah has power over all things.*[45]

Guillaume reports that the anti-Jewish attack at Khaibar was fiercely fought off, but "though the inhabitants fought more bravely here than elsewhere, outnumbered and caught off their guard, they were defeated."[46] Those who somehow survived constituted the formula for Islam's future successes. Some of the Jews, as "non-Muslims" or infidels, "retained their land," at least until Muslims could be recruited in sufficient numbers to replace the Jews. Meanwhile, the Arabian Jews paid a fifty-percent "tribute," or tax, for the "protection" of the new plun-

*Emphasis added.

derers. As Professor Lewis writes, "The Muslim victory in Khaibar marked the first contact between the Muslim state and a conquered non-Muslim people and formed the basis for later dealings of the same type."[47]

Thus the Jewish *dhimmi* evolved—the robbery of freedom and political independence compounding the extortion and eventual expropriation of property. "Tolerated" between onslaughts, expulsions, and pillages from the Arab Muslim conquest onward, the non-Muslim *dhimmi*—predominantly Jewish but Christian too—provided the important source of religious revenue through the "infidel's" head tax. He became very quickly a convenient political scapegoat and whipping boy as well.

Other Jewish colonies succumbed in much the same way: "Jews were allowed to keep their land on condition that they surrendered half the produce to Medina." But, "the arrangement did not last long. . . ." Virtually all of Khaibar's and Medina's surviving Jews—along with "all the other Jews and Christians in the peninsula"—were dispossessed and expelled through the Prophet Muhammad's edict, zealously implemented by his caliph Omar.[48]

> Much of the wealth of the country which had been concentrated in the hands of the Jews had now been seized by the Muslims, *who were no longer indigent immigrants but wealthy landowners,* men of substance, owning camels and horses and their own weapons. . . . Muhammad's fame spread far and wide, and the bedouin flocked to him in thousands.*[49]

The Precedent of Prey

Thus evolved the formation of the successful pattern that was to be perpetuated in the propagation of the Arabian Muslim creed. Those Jews who escaped with their lives became perhaps the first Arabian refugees. They were the beginning link in the long chain of Jews to be plundered by "immigrant" Muslims of the "Arab" world, who would exact their reward as their new faith permitted, even prescribed them to do.

It is likely that among the Jewish refugees fleeing from Arabia were numbers of Jews whose "Palestinian"—or Judean—ancestors had fled from the Romans. Now they returned to seventh-century Palestine, joining their Jewish brethren who had never left. Ironically, the Jewish refugees' return coincided with the introduction of the Arab conquerors from the desert; the very invaders who had forced themselves in and the Jews out of their homes in Arabia would now plunder Judah-Palestina in the identical pattern.

And the Jews who inhabited many towns of "Palestine" uninterruptedly would one day in the twentieth century be forced out as the Arabian Jews had been—by slaughter or expropriation and terrorizing. The towns would then, in the later twentieth century, be touted as "purely Arab Palestinian areas since time

*Emphasis added.

immemorial," just as the Arabian Peninsula had come to be perceived as "purely Arab," when in fact the holy Arab Muslim city of Medina had been originally settled by Jews.

After the seventh-century invasion of Medina—the beginning of the Arab conquest in Arabia—where we have seen the settled Jews conquered by the "Arabians," Caliph Omar was ruling over the vanquished tribes when he received word from his general that Arabian invaders had conquered Alexandria:

> "I have captured a city from the description of which I shall refrain. Suffice it to say that I have seized therein 4,000 villas with 4,000 baths, *40,000 poll-tax paying Jews* and four hundred places of entertainment for the royalty."*[50]

The Arabs who invaded Judah-cum-Palestine followed that precedent. Upon the invasion of Palestine, the "Arabians of the desert" found a Palestinian Jewish community of major proportion. Shortly after the Arab conquest, the Jews would again assert their nationalistic goals, rising in part from the infliction of the new *dhimma* restrictions and humiliations that were to become the fate of all non-Muslims.

> Omar II was the religious zealot who instituted many of the restrictions. . . . These restrictions were, no doubt, responsible for the rising of the pseudo-Messiah Syrene, . . . a Syrian Jew, [who had] promised to . . . regain possession of the Holy Land for Jewish people."[51]

Those Jews who had remained in Roman "Palestine," together with the Jewish communities who quickly returned after the Roman conquest, had succeeded in "mould[ing] Judaism in a new stamp."[52] Although the revered Temple had been destroyed, the synagogue remained to "soften the blow" and Jewish leaders who had escaped from the siege of Jerusalem were permitted by Roman leaders to return, and to teach the form of Judaism that was to preserve and perpetuate the "aggressive Jewish nationalism" that finally achieved political reclaiming of the land nearly twenty centuries later.

Ironically, it was thus those very Roman leaders who had *conquered* the Jewish State and destroyed the Jewish Temple who helped unwittingly to initiate the means by which the Jewish National Liberation movement would remain intact. Had the Romans permitted the Jews to retain their sovereignty, the Jews might have been relegated to archaic history as had the Hittites, the Philistines, and other long-extinct peoples of the region. Although the tenacious Jewish history before the Romans would indicate otherwise, one might ponder the Jews' fate if the Jewish people and their way of worship had been a matter of indifference rather than the traditional object of resentment and suspicion born of imitation.

In the centuries between the Roman dismantling of the Jewish sovereign state

*Emphasis added.

and the Arab invasion, the Jews' population had "remained as . . . before the loss of independence, primarily peasants and landowners." The Jewish population—between five and seven million in A.D. 70, according to Josephus[53]—still numbered around three million, despite large numbers of Jews who were deported or had fled just before the Jewish revolt and defeat of Bar Kochba. According to Roman figures, nearly 600,000 Jews alone fell during that revolt, but the Jews managed to remain on the land and to accomplish significant achievements afterward.[54]

The centers of Jewish life occasionally shifted in importance—after the revolt of Bar Kochba the nucleus of the Jewish community moved to Galilee for a time.[55] But the Romans, because they recognized the Jewish hereditary Patriarchate as "the supreme . . . authority" for the total Jewish community in the empire, inadvertently provided the Jews with a political-religious center that had the practical effect of replacing—though never pre-empting—the grievously lost Temple.[56] The result was that the Jewish identity with the Jewish nation remained steadfast.

As the British Royal Commission would report in 1937, almost 2,000 years afterward,

> Always . . . since the fall of the Jewish state some Jews have been living in Palestine. . . . Fresh immigrants arrived from time to time . . . [and] settled mainly in Galilee, in numerous villages spreading northwards to the Lebanon and in the towns of Safad and Tiberias.[57]

According to reports of the various periods of history, some of the Jewish enclaves managed to remain in their original places for thousands of years.

The Jews were numerous in Judah-cum-Palestine and the Christians proportionately few in the third and fourth centuries.[58] And for a rare and brief moment there was peace. The historian de Haas wrote that

> The East breathed more freely, and enjoyed even a spell of real peace during the reign of Alexander Severus (222–235), . . . His predilections brought him the nickname of Archisynagogus, or rabbi. He flirted with the Jews, and his mother, Julia Mammae, protected the great church father, Origen. This catholicity was even exhibited in the imperial palace, where pictures of Orpheus, Jesus, and Abraham, hung side by side.[59]

But Professor Lewis reminds that

> *In Palestine, the Jews, still an important element, if no longer the majority of the population, had suffered even more grievously than the heretical Christians* from Byzantine repression, and had little love for their masters."*[60]

The "bullying orthodoxy" of the growing Byzantium diminished the Jews' political, civil, and even religious rights in the fifth century. The Reverend Parkes

*Emphasis added.

reports that, by the time the Persians invaded in A.D. 611, the Jews had been persecuted long enough so that the "Persians received substantial help from the Jews of Galilee"—an estimated 20,000 to 26,000 Jewish soldiers. The Persians' occupation ended after fifteen years.[61]

On the eve of the introduction of the Arabian to Palestine, the Christians briefly reoccupied Palestine in A.D. 629. Because the Jews had cooperated with the Persians, "the clergy of Jerusalem thought only of revenge," and inspired a "bloody massacre . . . of Jews."[62]

Neither Christian nor Jew realized that within a few years the Arabian invasion would bring Byzantine rule to an end, and many of those inhabitants who had once converted to Byzantine now would adopt the tongue, religion, and, briefly, the rule of the Arabs.

> When we look back over the history of the early Caliphates—and we must do so, since the present hopes and pretensions of the Arabs, and the popular belief in their coming Renaissance rest equally on ancient history—we find the period of genuine Arab Empire extraordinarily short. Arabs governed Arabs, through Arabs on an imperial scale for much less than a century. It is just the Omayyad Caliphate—the Damascus period and no more.

Thus was the comparatively recent Arab propaganda claim of Palestine as an "Arab" country for "millennia" disproved by the historian David George Hogarth in 1877.[63] Hogarth was described by eminent Arab writers as "one of the greatest authorities of his time on Arabian history."[64]

The Reverend James Parkes has agreed that

> The period during which the empire was ruled from Damascus and can be called an "Arab" empire, lasted less than a century and even in that short time it had begun to decline.[65]

Noting that decline, the prominent Arab historian Philip Hitti also explained how the "Arab" invaders were "diluted" by converts:

> Through their intermarriages with the conquering stock they served to dilute the Arabian blood and ultimately to make that element inconspicuous amidst the mixture of varied racial strains.[66]

> . . . the invaders from the desert brought with them no tradition of learning, no heritage of culture, to the lands they conquered.[67]

The "Arab" rule as such had been precluded before A.D. 750. According to Hitti,

> Shortly before the middle of the eighth century a caliph ascended to the Umayyad throne who had been born of a slave mother. . . . His two successors, the last in the dynasty, were also sons of slave women. . . . That the reigning family could no longer boast pure Arab blood was symptomatic of a loosening of moral standards throughout society.[68]

Hitti pointed out the destructive element of tribal warfare that contributed heavily to the ravages of Palestine.

The position of the Omayyad dynasty, weakened by this decadence, was further undermined by the increasingly sharp division of North Arabian as against South Arabian tribes. *This racial tendency to separatism, apparent even in pre-Islamic days,* now became complete and was the cause of boundless dispute.*[69]

The findings of even those historians most vaunted by the Arab world have been specific in their contradiction of Arab claims to historical right of sovereignty in the land of "Palestine." The Arabs never created their own name for the land they now claim as their own. Neither was there ever an independent country of Palestine, nor a "Palestinian" rule. The word "Palestine" was given to the land of Judea by the Romans when Roman conquerors unsuccessfully attempted to purge the land of the "nationalistic," obstinate Jews.

"The brevity of purely Arab Empire was determined less by the force of non-Arab elements than by the inability of Arabs themselves to develop any system of imperial administration more adequate than the Patriarchal," Hogarth determined.[70]

"The short . . . Meccan period was all conquest and raiding accompanied by no more organization of territories overrun than would secure their payment of tribute."[71]

"The long Baghdad period" was, according to Hogarth, *"not . . . government of Arabs by Arabs."*

If the Abbassids were Meccan, their ministers, great and often small, were Iranians or Turanians, and their trust was in mercenaries, at first Persian, then Turk, Circassian, Kurd—*any race but the Arabian."*[72]

Hogarth found that the same "formula" applied to Egypt and North Africa, where the ruled people as well as their governors were "non-Arab."

"What we now call 'Arab civilization' was Arabian neither in its origins and fundamental structure nor in its principal ethnic aspects," according to Philip Hitti.

Throughout the whole period of the caliphate, the Syrians, the Persians, the Egyptians and others, as Moslem converts or as Christians and Jews, were the foremost bearers of the torch of enlightenment and learning, just as the subjugated Greeks were in their relation to victorious Romans. The Arab Islamic civilization was at bottom the Hellenized Aramaic and the Iranian civilizations as developed under the aegis of the caliphate and expressed through the medium of *the Arabic tongue."*[73]

*Emphasis added.

The "Arab identity" is in fact largely a linguistic commonality. Hitti defines "Arabs" as *a term which in our usage would comprise all Arabic-speaking peoples, including the Arabians, that is, the inhabitants of the Arabian peninsula.*[*74]

According to Hogarth, even the "extraordinarily short" Arab rule was mechanical and not innovative.

The Omayyads alike in Syria and Spain seemed to have carried on with the machinery they found, insisting only after a time on expression in Arabic.[75]

To speak historically of original inhabitants of Judah-cum-Palestine as "Arab" peoples, then, is categorically inaccurate. Not only was there no country of "Palestine," never a "Palestinian" Arab rule, there was only an "extraordinarily short" period of time—a matter of decades—when *any* Arabs ruled Arabs on that land.

The first Arabian use of the word Arab occurs in the ancient southern Arabian inscriptions, . . . dating from the late pre-Christian and early Christian centuries. In these, Arab means Bedouin, often *raider,* and is applied to the nomadic as distinct from the sedentary population. . . . *For Muhammad and his contemporaries the Arabs were the Bedouin of the desert, and in the Qur'ān the term is used exclusively in this sense and never of the townsfolk of Mecca, Medina and other cities.*[*76]

Islam was the "national religion and war-cry" and the new empire was "their booty" as the conquering Arabians—or Arabs—briefly invaded and ruled over "a vast variety of peoples differing in race, language and religion, among whom they [the Arabs] formed a . . . minority," according to Professor Bernard Lewis.[77]

The use of the adjective Arab to describe the various facets of this civilization has often been challenged on the grounds that the contribution to "Arab medicine," "Arab philosophy," etc. of those who were of Arab descent was relatively small. Even the use of the word Muslim is criticized, since so many of the architects of this culture were Christians and Jews. . . .[78]

The Prophet Muhammad, Arabian creator of Islam, had quickly determined that, to gain followers, plunder must be bountiful.

So little was the first wave of the Arab conquest an exclusive product of religious fanaticism, offering the conquered Islam or the sword, that many of the bedouin bands who formed the armies of Islam were in all probability still pagans when they took part in the first great surge out of the [Arabian] peninsula.[79]

Because the "Arabian Moslems" subscribed widely to the Koranic invocation to "Make war . . . upon such of those to whom the Book has been given until they pay tribute offered on the back of their hands, in a state of humiliation" (9:29), Hitti concluded that

*Emphasis added.

Not fanaticism but economic necessity drove the Bedouin hordes . . . beyond the confines of their arid abode to the fair lands of the north. . . . Far from being entirely the result of deliberate and cool calculation, the campaigns seem to have *started as raids* to provide new outlets for the warring spirit of the tribes now forbidden to engage in fratricidal combats, *the objective in most cases being booty and not the gaining of a permanent foothold.* "*[80]

The Arabs ruled Arabs for only some decades, not millennia, and only under the Omayyads, who were the lone dynasty of "Arab" stock. The victory of Abassids was Islamic, not Arab, and "it was Islam and not Arab blood which formed the basis of unity."[81] Within a hundred or so years, the "successive usurpers" of power were almost entirely "of Turkish origin."[82]

Depopulation of a Melting Pot

In Palestine the "small" number of Arab invaders who had been imported by the Arabian conquerors were wiped out by disease. Thus the "myth" of the "Palestinian Arab" descending "from the Arab conquerors" appears to be factually incorrect for all but perhaps a few. Supporting Hogarth, Hitti, and Lewis, the Reverend Parkes found that

> During the first century after the Arab conquest the caliph and governors of Syria and The Land [Palestine] ruled almost entirely over Christian and Jewish subjects. Apart from the bedouin [nomads], in the earliest days the only Arabs west of the Jordan (not all of whom were themselves Muslims) were the garrisons. . . ."

They "were small," and were "decimated" by epidemics within two years after the capture of Jerusalem. After a law, prohibiting the Arabs from owning land there, had been rescinded, "rich Arabs" came into ownership of "a good deal of the country."[83]

"But this change of owners"*—often through the dispossession of Christian owners—"did not involve any extensive change in the nature of the population." *Jews and Christians still worked the land,* because the Arabs had neither the desire nor the experience for agricultural toil; they "heartily despised" both the toil and "the tiller."[84]

In fact, during the brief time of actual Arab rule—the Omayyad from Damascus—that rule was military only.

> The clerical or theological view favoring a providential interpretation of Islamic expansion, corresponding to the Old Testament interpretation of the Hebrew history and to the medieval philosophy of Christian history, *has a faulty philological basis. . . .*
> *Not until the second and third centuries of the Moslem era did the bulk of the*

---

*Emphasis added.

people in Syria, Mesopotamia and Persia profess the religion of Muhammad.
Between the military conquest of these regions and their religious conversion a
long period intervened. *And when they were converted the people turned primarily
because of self-interest—to escape tribute and seek identification with the ruling
class.* *[85]

Islam and the Arabic language were disseminated by a multi-ethnic Muslim
community that at first included "numbers of Arabians in the provinces," but by
"the tenth century onwards," yet another "new ruling race, the Turks" joined the
seemingly endless parade of conquest—a kind of periodic rape of the Holy Land.

"From the tenth century" a multi-ethnic native population, which perhaps
still included some few descendants of the Arabian invaders—all together under
the rule of the Turks—commingled, and the possibility of singling out the Arabs
as a people became unworkable; *Arabic-speaking* people would be a more accurate term. Already in the tenth century "the word Arab reverts to its earlier
meaning of Bedouin or nomad, becoming in effect a social rather than an ethnic
term."[86]

With the Crusaders' slaughters—including mass murder in 1099 of all the
70,000 Muslims in Jerusalem—the deterioration of the land in Palestine accelerated.

> . . . Massacres and the fear of massacre had greatly reduced the number of Jews
> in Palestine and Christians in Syria.[87]

The "vast majority" remaining in Palestine was "native Christians," of "mixed
origin . . . carelessly known as Christian Arabs."[88]

Because the population was "decimated" by the endemic massacres, disease,
famine, and wars, one Muslim ruler "brought in Turks and Negroes." Another
"had Berbers, Slavs, Greeks and Dailamites." The Kurdish conqueror,[89] "Saladin, introduced more Turks, and some Kurds."[90]

"The flower of the Saracenes who fought the Crusaders were Turks," chronicled Philip Graves.[91] "The Mamluks brought armies of Georgians, and Circassians. For his personal security each monarch relied on his own purchase."[92] "In
the Palestinian towns Greek was the common tongue. . . ."[93] In 1296, 18,000
"tents"—families—of Tartars entered and settled in the land of Palestine.[94]

Thus, not only was Arab rule "extraordinarily short," but the "pure Arab
peoples in Palestine for millennia"—a romanticized notion discredited by serious
scholars—actually consisted of a non-Arabian, multi-ethnic procession of immigrants.

In the fourteenth century, the identity was specifically a religious one. According to Bernard Lewis,

> The majority belonged to . . . the community or nation of Islam. Its members
> thought of themselves primarily as Muslims. When further classification was

*Emphasis added.

Palestina: A Precedent of Prey   153

TABLE B. A Partial Chronology of Judah-Cum-Palestine[95]

A.D.	
70	The Romans conquer Jerusalem.
132–136	Jewish revolt under Bar Kochba; final defeat of Judah and loss of political sovereignty.
351	Jewish revolt to end foreign rule; Roman Empire adopts Christianity.
395	Palestine part of the Eastern Roman (Byzantine) Empire, still called Judea or Judah.
438	Empress Eudocia allows Jews back to Temple site, misinterpreted by Jews as return to nationhood.
614	Persian conquest under Chosroes (with the support of a Jewish army).
628	Palestine reconquered by the Byzantines.
633–637	Arab conquest; shortly afterward, attempt by Jews to restore their nation.
639	Muawiyah Arab governor.
660	Muawiyah is made the first Omayyad Caliph of Damascus.
661	Murder of Ali; Omayyad Dynasty begins.
750	Last Omayyad Caliph defeated; reign of the Abbassid Caliphs of Baghdad (Persian, Turk, Circassian, Kurd).
878	Ahmad, b. Tūlūn, a Turkish general and governor of Egypt, conquers Palestine; reign of the Tulunides (Turks).
904	The Abbassids of Baghdad reconquer Palestine.
906	Inroads of the Carmathians.
934	The Egyptian Ikhshidi princes conquer Palestine; their reign begins.
969	The Fatimid Caliphs of Cairo conquer Palestine.
969–971	War with the Carmathians.
970–976	Byzantine invasion.
1070–1080	Seljuq Turks conquer Palestine.
1099	The Crusaders conquer Jerusalem, massacre the Jewish and Muslim populations; reign in parts of Palestine until 1291.
1187	Saladin of Damascus, a Kurd, captures Jerusalem and the greater part of Palestine.
1244	The Kharezmians, instigated by Genghis Khan, invade Palestine; Jerusalem's population is slaughtered, the city sacked.
1260	Mameluk Sultans of Egypt defeat Mongols at Ain Jalut, in Palestine; their reign begins.
1260	Mongol invasion; Jerusalem sacked.
1291	End of the Latin (Crusaders) Kingdom.
1299–1303	Mongol invasion.
1516–1517	The Ottomans conquer Palestine.
1799	Napoleon conquers Palestine, but is defeated at Acre.
1831	Ibrahim Pasha, adopted son of Egypt's Viceroy, occupies Palestine.
1840	Ibrahim Pasha compelled by the Powers to leave Palestine; Turkish rule restored.
1840 on	English writers and statesmen begin to discuss the possibility of a Jewish restoration.
1871–1882	First Jewish agricultural settlements.
1909	Foundation of the all-Jewish city of Tel Aviv.
1917–1918	Allies occupy the whole of Palestine, east and west of the Jordan River; British military administration, end of Ottoman reign.
1917–1918	Balfour Declaration granting "Jewish Homeland" internationally approved.
1920	British (pre-Mandate) civil administration; Turkish sovereignty renounced, treaty includes Balfour Declaration.

TABLE B. A Partial Chronology of Judah-Cum-Palestine (cont'd)

A.D.	
1922	Palestine Mandate; Jewish National Home confirmed.
1923	Palestine Mandate comes into operation.
1923	Seventy-five percent of Palestine is set aside as an independent Arab "Palestinian" state, Transjordan.
1925	Hebrew University of Jerusalem opened.
1927	High Commissioners receive Commission for Transjordan.
1929	Arab revolt.
1936–1939	Arab revolt and civil war.
1946	Establishment of Arab state of Transjordan.
1948	End of Mandate for Palestine; establishment of State of Israel; Arab-Jewish war.
1948	Eastern Palestine—Transjordan—occupies the West Bank area of Western Palestine, becomes "Jordan," constituting over eighty percent of Palestine.

necessary, it might be territorial—Egyptians, Syrian, Iraqi—or social—townsman, peasant, nomad. It is to this last that the term Arab belongs. *So little had it retained of its ethnic meaning that we even find it applied at times to non-Arab nomads of Kurdish or Turkoman extraction.* *[96]

The new Arab "identity" derives, according to Lewis, from "the impact of the West . . . in the last fifty years. . . . It is that which regards the Arabic-speaking peoples as a nation or group of sister nations in the European sense, united by a common territory, language and culture and a common aspiration to a political independence."[97]

Hogarth deduced:

History tells us that, in fact, Ahmad Ibn Tulun was a Turk and Saladin was a Kurd. . . . the Turk has assimilated not a few Semites, while fewer Turks have ever come to regard themselves as Arabs—probably none at all during these last four centuries of the subjection of the one race [Arabs] to the other [Turks].[98] . . . Arab civilization owes a heavy obligation to the Greek, to the Persian, to the Jewish. . . . So much for ancient history.[99]

When Mark Twain toured the country in the late 1860s, he bemoaned his disillusionment at confronting the realities of the Holy Land, and expressed his displeasure at having been so misled:

I am sure, from the tenor of books I have read, that many who have visited this land in years gone by . . . came seeking evidences in support of their particular creed; . . . and they had already made up their minds to find no other, though possibly they did not know it, being blinded by their zeal. . . .

Honest as these men's intentions may have been, they were full of partialities and prejudices, they entered the country with their verdicts already prepared and

*Emphasis added.

they could no more write dispassionately and impartially about it than they could about their own wives and children. . . . These authors write pictures and frame rhapsodies. . . .

I claim the right to correct misstatements . . .[100]

Whatever propaganda claims to the contrary, the territory that appears qualifiable to be claimed by the Arabs as historically "Arab land" consists solely of the "Island of the Arabians," the Arabian desert peninsula; Hitti concluded that there existed "an almost unique example of uninterrupted relationship between populace and soil." Yet even in Arabia, as we have noted, historians are unambiguous when and if they deal at all with the Jews there;[101] the fact is clearly recorded that dominant Arabian-Jewish communities were established within a somewhat Judaized Arabian Peninsula dating from well before the time of Jewish political exile from their homeland—possibly a thousand years before the advent of the Prophet Muhammad and Islam.

The Jews were invaded, slaughtered, expelled, or converted and displaced by the conquering "Arabians." The seventh-century surviving Jewish refugees fleeing to Judah-cum-Palestine from Arabia were victims of the *dhimma* "protection" that would carry down over 1,300 years—sometimes less violent, but unaltered in concept. The Jewish refugees who fled Arab countries in 1948 were also escaping from the "protection" of Arab-Muslims—with one important difference: the seventh-century refugees found themselves bereft of their political sovereignty, while in 1948 the Jewish refugees went "home" to their restored nation.

The "chauvinist Arab version of history," then—so important to the current claim of "Palestinian" rights to "Arab Palestine," which Arab Palestinians purportedly inhabited for "thousands of years"—*omits* several relevant, *situation-altering facts.*

History did not begin with the Arab conquest in the seventh century. The people whose nation was destroyed by the Romans were the Jews. There were no Arab Palestinians then—not until seven hundred years later would an Arab rule prevail, and then briefly. And not by people known as "Palestinians." The short Arab rule would be reigning over Christians and Jews, who had been there to languish under various other foreign conquerors—Roman, Byzantine, Persian, to name just three in the centuries between the Roman and Arab conquests. The peoples who conquered under the banner of the invading Arabians from the desert were often hired mercenaries who remained on the land as soldiers—not Arabians, but others who were enticed by the promise of the booty of conquest.

From the time the Arabians, along with their non-Arabian recruits, entered Palestine and Syria, they found and themselves added to what was "ethnologically a chaos of all the possible human combinations to which, when Palestine became a land of pilgrimage, a new admixture was added."[102] Among the peoples who have been counted as "indigenous Palestinian Arabs" are Balkans, Greeks, Syrians, Latins, Egyptians, Turks, Armenians, Italians, Persians, Kurds, Germans, Afghans, Circassians, Bosnians, Sudanese, Samaritans, Algerians, Motawila, and Tartars.

John of Wurzburg lists for the middle era of the kingdom, Latins, Germans, Hungarians, Scots, Navarese, Bretons, English, Franks, Ruthenians, Bohemians, Greeks, Bulgarians, Georgians, Armenians, Syrians, Persian Nestorians, Indians, Egyptians, Copts, Maronites and natives from the Nile Delta. The list might be much extended, for it was the period of the great self-willed city-states in Europe, and Amalfi, Pisans, Genoese, Venetians, and Marseillais, who had quarters in all the bigger cities, owned villages, and had trading rights, would, in all probability, have submitted to any of the above designations, only under pressure. Besides all these, Norsemen, Danes, Frisians, Tartars, Jews, Arabs, Russians, Nubians, and Samaritans, can be safely added to the greatest human agglomeration drawn together in one small area of the globe.[103]

Greeks fled the Muslim rule in Greece, and landed in Palestine. By the mid-seventeenth century, the Greeks lived everywhere in the Holy Land—constituting about twenty percent of the population—and their authority dominated the villages.[104]

Between 1750 and 1766 Jaffa had been rebuilt, and had some five hundred houses. Turks, Arabs, Greeks and Armenians and a solitary Latin monk lived there, to attend to the wants of the thousands of pilgrims who had to be temporarily housed in the port before proceeding to Jerusalem.[105]

"In some cases villages [in Palestine] are populated wholly by settlers from other portions of the Turkish Empire within the nineteenth century. There are villages of Bosnians, Druzes, Circassians and Egyptians," one historian has reported.[106]

Another source, the Encyclopaedia Britannica, 1911 edition (before the "more chauvinist Arab history" began to prevail with the encouragement of the British), finds the "population" of Palestine composed of so "widely differing" a group of "inhabitants"—whose "ethnological affinities" create "early in the 20th century a list of no less than fifty languages"*—that "it is therefore no easy task to write concisely . . . on the ethnology of Palestine." In addition to the "Assyrian, Persian and Roman" elements of ancient times, "the short-lived Egyptian government introduced into the population an element from that country which still persists in the villages."

. . . There are very large contingents from the Mediterranean countries, especially Armenia, Greece and Italy . . . Turkoman settlements . . . a number of Persians and a fairly large Afghan colony . . . Motawila . . . long settled immigrants from Persia . . . tribes of Kurds . . . German "Templar" colonies . . . a Bosnian colony . . . and the Circassian settlements placed in certain centres . . . by the Turkish government in order to keep a restraint on the Bedouin

*See a list of languages and birthplaces, circa 1931, in Chapter 11.

. . . a large Algerian element in the population . . . still maintain(s) [while] the Sudanese have been reduced in numbers since the beginning of the 20th century.

In the late eighteenth century, 3,000 Albanians recruited by Russians were settled in Acre. The *Encyclopaedia Britannica* finds "most interesting all the *non-Arab** communities in the country . . . the Samaritan sect in Nablus (Shechem); a gradually disappearing body" once "settled by the Assyrians to occupy the land left waste by the captivity of the Kingdom of Israel."[107]

The disparate peoples recently assumed and purported to be "settled Arab indigenes for a thousand years" were in fact a "heterogeneous" community[108] with no "Palestinian" identity, and according to an official British historical analysis in 1920, no *Arab* identity either: "The people west of the Jordan are not Arabs, but only Arabic-speaking. The bulk of the population are fellahin. . . . In the Gaza district they are mostly of Egyptian origin; elsewhere they are of the most mixed race."[109]

The Land in Waste

A review of Palestine, before the era of prosperity began with the late nineteenth-century renewal of Jewish land settlement, shows that periodically Palestine was virtually laid waste, and its population suffered acute decline.

An enormous swell of Arab population could only have resulted from immigration and in-migration to the area, a movement considered at some length in the following chapters of this book. First, however, it is helpful to see the land that was virtually emptied—and why.

Dio Cassius, writing at the time, described the ruin of the land beginning with the destruction of Judah:

Of their forts the fifty strongest were razed to the ground. Nine hundred and eighty-five of their best-known villages were destroyed. . . .

Thus the whole of Judea became desert, as indeed had been foretold to the Jews before the war. For the tomb of Solomon, whom these folk celebrate in their sacred rites, fell of its own accord into fragments, and wolves and hyenas, many in number, roamed howling through their cities.[110]

One historian after another has reported the same findings.

In the twelve and a half centuries between the Arab conquest in the seventh century and the beginnings of the Jewish return in the 1880's, Palestine was laid waste. Its ancient canal and irrigation systems were destroyed and the wondrous fertility of which the Bible spoke vanished into desert and desolation. . . . Under the Ottoman empire of the Turks, the policy of disfoliation continued; the hillsides were denuded of trees and the valleys robbed of their topsoil.[111]

*Emphasis added.

In 1590 a "simple English visitor" to Jerusalem wrote, "Nothing there to be scene but a little of the old walls, which is yet Remayning and all the rest is grasse, mosse and Weedes much like to a piece of Rank or moist Grounde."[112]

"While Tiberias was being resettled by Jews from Papal states, whose migration was approved by a papal Bull, Nazareth was continuing its decline." A Franciscan pilgrim translated a Latin Manuscript that reported that " 'A house of robbers, murderers, the inhabitants are Saracens. . . . It is a lamentable thing to see thus such a town. We saw nothing more stony, full of thorns and desert.' "[113] A hundred years afterward, Nazareth was, in 1697, "an inconsiderable village. . . . Acre a few poor cottages . . . nothing here but a vast and spacious ruin." Nablus consisted of two streets with many people, and Jericho was a "poor nasty village."[114]

In the mid-1700s, British archaeologist Thomas Shaw wrote that the land in Palestine was "lacking in people to till its fertile soil."[115] An eighteenth-century French author and historian, Count Constantine François Volney, wrote of Palestine as the "ruined" and "desolate" land.

In "Greater Syria," which included Palestine,

> Many parts . . . lost almost all their peasantry. In others, . . . the recession was great but not so total.[116]

Count Volney reported that, "In consequence of such wretched government, the greater part of the Pachilics [Provinces] in the empire are impoverished and laid waste." Using one province as an example, Volney reported that

> . . . *upwards of three thousand two hundred villages were reckoned; but, at present, the collector can scarcely find four hundred.* Such of our merchants as have resided there twenty years have themselves seen the greater part of the environs . . . become depopulated. The traveller meets with nothing but houses in ruins, cisterns rendered useless, and fields abandoned. Those who cultivated them have fled . . .[117]
>
> . . . And can we hope long to carry on an advantageous commerce with a country which is precipitately hastening to ruin?*[118]

Another writer, describing "Syria" (and Palestine) some *sixty years later in 1843,* stated that, in Volney's day, "the land had not fully reached its last prophetic degree of desolation and depopulation."[119]

From place to place the reporters varied, but not the reports: J. S. Buckingham described his visit of 1816 to Jaffa, which "has all the appearances of a poor village, and every part of it that we saw was of corresponding meanness."[120] Buckingham described Ramle, "where, as throughout the greater part of Palestine, the ruined portion seemed more extensive than that which was inhabited."[121]

After a visit in 1817–1818, travelers reported that there was not "a single boat of any description on the lake [Tiberias]."[122] In a German encyclopedia published

*Emphasis added.

in 1827, Palestine was depicted as "desolate and roamed through by Arab bands of robbers."[123]

Throughout the nineteenth century the abandonment and dismal state of the terrain was lamented. In 1840 an observer, who was traveling through, wrote of his admiration for the Syrian "fine spirited race of men" whose "population is on the decline."[124] While scorning the idea of Jewish colonization, the writer observed that the once populous area between Hebron and Bethlehem was "now abandoned and desolate" with "dilapidated towns."[125] Jerusalem consisted of "a large number of houses . . . in a dilapidated and ruinous state," and "the masses really seem to be without any regular employment." The "masses" of Jerusalem were estimated at less than 15,000 inhabitants, of whom more than half the population were Jews.[126]

The British Consul in Palestine reported in 1857 that

> The country is in a considerable degree empty of inhabitants and therefore *its greatest need is that of a body of population.* . . . [127]*

In the 1860s, it was reported that "depopulation is even now advancing."[128] At the same time, H. B. Tristram noted in his journal that

> The north and south [of the Sharon plain] land is going out of cultivation and whole villages are rapidly disappearing from the face of the earth. Since the year 1838, no less than 20 villages there have been thus erased from the map [by the Bedouin] and the stationary population extirpated.[129]

Mark Twain, in his inimitable fashion, expressed scorn for what he called the "romantic" and "prejudiced" accounts of Palestine after he visited the Holy Land in 1867.[130] In one location after another, Twain registered gloom at his findings.

> Stirring scenes . . . occur in the valley [Jezreel] no more. There is not a solitary village throughout its whole extent—not for thirty miles in either direction. There are two or three small clusters of Bedouin tents, but not a single permanent habitation. One may ride ten miles hereabouts and not see ten human beings.[131]

In fact, according to Twain, even the Bedouin raiders who attacked "so fiercely" had been imported: "provided for the occasion . . . shipped from Jerusalem," by the Arabs who guarded each group of pilgrims.

> They met together in full view of the pilgrims, after the battle, and took lunch, divided the *baksheesh* extorted in the season of danger and then accompanied the cavalcade home to the city! The nuisance of an Arab guard is one which is created by the sheikhs and the Bedouins together, for mutual profit . . .[132]

To find ". . . the sort of solitude to make one dreary," one must, Twain wrote dramatically,

*Emphasis added.

Come to Galilee for that . . . these unpeopled deserts, these rusty mounds of barrenness, that never, never, never do shake the glare from their harsh outlines, and fade and faint into vague perspective; that melancholy ruin of Capernaum: this stupid village of Tiberias, slumbering under its six funereal palms. . . . We reached Tabor safely. . . . We never saw a human being on the whole route.[133]

Nazareth is forlorn. . . . Jericho the accursed lies a moldering ruin today, even as Joshua's miracle left it more than three thousand years ago; Bethlehem and Bethany, in their poverty and their humiliation, have nothing about them now to remind one that they once knew the high honor of the Savior's presence; the hallowed spot where the shepherds watched their flocks by night, and where the angels sang, "Peace on earth, good will to men," *is untenanted by any living creature.* . . . Bethsaida and Chorzin have vanished from the earth, and the "desert places" round about them, where thousands of men once listened to the Savior's voice and ate the miraculous bread, sleep in the hush of a *solitude that is inhabited only by birds of prey and skulking foxes.* *[134]

"Palestine sits in sackcloth and ashes. . . . desolate and unlovely . . . ," Twain wrote with remorse. ". . . it is dreamland."[135]

Jaffa, a French traveler wrote late in the nineteenth century, was still a ruin.[136] Haifa, to the north, had 6,000 souls and "nothing remarkable about it," another Frenchman, the author of France's foremost late-nineteenth-century Holy Land guidebook, commented. Haifa "can be crossed in five minutes" on the way to the city of Acre, he judged; that magnificent port was commercially idle.[137]

Many writers, such as the Reverend Samuel Manning, mourned the atrophy of the coastal plain, the Sharon Plain, "the exquisite fertility and beauty of which made it to the Hebrew mind a symbol of prosperity."

But where were the inhabitants? This fertile plain, which might support an immense population, is almost a solitude. . . . Day by day we were to learn afresh the lesson now forced upon us, that the denunciations of ancient prophecy have been fulfilled to the very letter—"the land is left void and desolate and without inhabitants."*[138]

Report followed depressing report, as the economist-historian Professor Fred Gottheil pointed out: "a desolate country";[139] "wretched desolation and neglect";[140] "almost abandoned now";[141] "unoccupied";[142] "uninhabited";[143] "thinly populated."[144]

In a book called *Heth and Moab,* Colonel C. R. Conder pronounced the Palestine of the 1880s "a ruined land." According to Conder,

so far as the Arab race is concerned, it appears to be decreasing rather than otherwise.[145]

Conder had also visited Palestine earlier, in 1872, and he commented on the continuing population decline within the nine or ten-year interim between his visits:

*Emphasis added.

The Peasantry who are the backbone of the population, have diminished most sadly in numbers and wealth.[146]

Pierre Loti, the noted French writer, wrote in 1895 of his visit to the land: "I traveled through sad Galilee in the spring, and I found it silent. . . ." In the vicinity of the Biblical Mount Gilboa, "As elsewhere, as everywhere in Palestine, city and palaces have returned to the dust; . . . This melancholy of abandonment, . . . weighs on all the Holy Land."[147]

David Landes summarized the causes of the shriveling number of inhabitants:

As a result of centuries of Turkish neglect and misrule, following on the earlier ravages of successive conquerors, the land had been given over to sand, marsh, the anopheles mosquito, clan feuds, and Bedouin marauders. A population of several millions had shrunk to less than one tenth that number—perhaps a quarter of a million around 1800, and 300,000 at mid-century.[148]

Palestine had indeed become "sackcloth and ashes."

The Migrants

Just as today the myths are being perpetuated about the "Palestinian Arab identity for thousands of years" and about the "golden age of Jews in Arab Lands," so public opinion of the world was swayed by Arab propaganda to blame the plight of the wretched *fellah* (peasant) driven off his land "since time immemorial"—on the "moneyed Jews of the world." The story goes: "But poor and neglected though it was, to the Arabs, who lived in it, Palestine . . . was still their country, their home, the land in which their people for centuries past had lived and left their graves."[149]

In fact some Arab—or Arabic-speaking—peasants *were* displaced, but they were displaced by *Arabs* beginning long before the Jews' mass restoration of the land had begun, and continuing long after Jewish settlements thrived, as we will see in other chapters. It was those peoples—peasants crippled by the corruption in Palestine and land nearby—along with migrants by tradition, and immigrants "planted" by the Turks—who would flood into the area of opportunity, the Jewish-settled areas of Western Palestine. And it was those *same* "Arabic" migrant-peasants and immigrants to the Jewish-settled areas who would later be counted as "settled" Muslims on their land "from time immemorial" who were being "displaced by the Jews."

The barrenness of the land, the bleak desolation of its disintegration from the once fertile biblical "milk and honey" to sour decay, resulted in and from the same conditions—ravages of conquest, epidemics, earthquakes, abandonment, and corruption.

As historians' findings indicate earlier in this book, the spoils system predominated from the time of the Prophet Muhammad and was regulated by his successor, Caliph Omar. According to the commandments of Allah,

Know that whenever you seize anything as a spoil, to God belongs a fifth thereof and to his Apostle. . . .[150]

The rest belonged to the conquering Muslims as a collective group, not to any individual.[151]

In the Prophet Muhammad's time, that fifth of the booty of conquest was portioned out to members of his family and purportedly to "the needy" as well. But as the booty passed to the leaders who succeeded Muhammad, it appears that patterns for an unequal distribution of wealth were set "as early as the days of Omar I."[152]

In the centuries that followed, as spoils became spoilage, Palestine's wide open, virtually lawless state encouraged a perpetuation of the corrupt system. The dwindling number of peasants were so heavily taxed and extorted by whatever fiefdom or feudal state existed at the particular moment that those who might have remained sedentary were compelled to join the traditional ranks of the wandering migrant population.

The fiefdom of the Mamluks (1260–1516) was replaced when the Ottomans conquered the country in 1516. The Ottoman feudal system only exacerbated the conditions of corruption. Bernard Lewis reports that

> Harsh, exorbitant, and improvident taxation led to a decline in cultivation, which was sometimes permanent. The peasants, neglected and impoverished, were forced into the hands of money-lenders and speculators, and often driven off the land entirely. With the steady decline in bureaucratic efficiency during the seventeenth and eighteenth centuries . . . the central government ceased to exercise any check or control over agriculture and village affairs, which were left to the unchecked rapacity of the tax-farmers, the leaseholders, and the bailiffs of court nominees.[153]

Another study of the land system found that

> . . . Every day the law was circumvented, because the rich used to take over all the tenancies with the purpose of again letting them privately, and at a great profit to themselves, to sub-tenants, in clear contradiction to the express object of the State that the lands should remain in the hands of the actual tenants all their lifetime. These sub-tenants also endeavoured to squeeze out profit for themselves by laying an intolerable burden on the peasants.[154]

In 1730 reforms were attempted to abolish life tenancies, but "Various attempts made to introduce reforms in the fief system ended in failure."[155]

Recognized authorities of the day traveled to the country and their recorded findings were unanimous. At the end of the eighteenth century, Count Volney found a wasteland,[156] where ". . . nothing is more destructive to Syria, than the shameful and excessive usury customary in that country."[157]

Historians, sociologists, official visitors, tourists—all have described the devastating conditions of existence in the country. Tax farmers, who "were supposed to raise from the peasants only a stipulated amount . . . enjoyed great power," and ". . . owing to the increasing weakness and corruption of the government, the peasants had practically no legal redress. . . ."[158]

By the nineteenth century there was "cash farming," which prompted "a tendency for village or tribal lands to be appropriated by some powerful individual, e.g., tribal shaikhs, local landlords, or urban money lenders."[159]

> In order that the tax-gatherers—the *multazim*—might be able to extract from their venture the money which they had paid to the Government and a profit besides, they exploited and ransacked the peasants to the last penny, robbing them of half their produce and even more. *The fellah was delivered hand and foot to the tax-collectors,* since he had not the slightest protection against their tyranny.*[160]

As a result, most peasants were "impoverished" and "could not . . . seek a living in town for, by the 1840's, industrial production was sharply declining." The relative few among the peasantry who worked their own farms were "forced" to attempt to remain, "thus falling prey to the usurer."[161] And those in the towns were reported, by witnesses of the time, to be equally poor, as the inhabitants of Jerusalem, who "really seem to be without any regular employment."[162]

The Arabs' migratory pattern of living had long been common in the region of Palestine. Well into the twentieth century the nomadic life was still the custom. As Sir John Hope Simpson wrote in 1930, "the fellah . . . is always migrating, even at the present time."[163] And in 1937, Lord Ormsby-Gore, Secretary of State for the Colonies, testified that "There has always been a certain amount of migration inside the Arab world."[164]

The coming and going of the populace was a constant throughout the literature of the eighteenth- and nineteenth-century scholars who visited the area. In the last decades of the eighteenth century there is evidence that many of the peasants migrated throughout the region in search of work.[165]

John Lewis Burckhardt graphically described the migratory patterns he found in the early 1800s:

> The oppressions of the government on one side, and those of the Bedouins on the other, have reduced the Fellah of the Haouran to a state little better than that of the wandering Arab. Few individuals . . . die in the same village in which they were born. Families are continually moving from one place to another; in the first year of their new settlement the Sheikh acts with moderation towards them; but his vexations becoming in a few years insupportable, they fly to some other place, where they have heard that their brethren are better treated, but they soon find that the same system prevails over the whole country. . . . they are always permitted to depart.[166]

Burckhardt found that not only robbery but also incessant migration were largely responsible for the land's corrosion:

*Emphasis added.

This continued wandering is one of the principal reasons why no village in the Haouran has either orchards, or fruit trees, or gardens for the growth of vegetables. "Shall we sow for strangers?" was the answer of a Fellah, to whom I once spoke on the subject. . . .[167]

In his journal Burckhardt noted, for example, that when he passed through the village of Merjan in 1819, only one family lived there. Two years later, he returned to the village to find nearly a dozen families. Many were Druses who had come from another village, which in 1810 had many inhabitants but two years later was deserted.[168]

One historian noted, in passing, "the emigration of many Druzes from Lebanon to Jebel Druze [Syria],"[169] and another found "analogous" situations in Palestine in the 1840s, "where peasants from remote villages came to . . . grain cultivation areas." The writer "struck up an acquaintance in the region of Hebron with a peasant from the village of Bait Jala. . . ."[170]

The traditional roving was endemic: ". . . Trans Jordanian peasants . . . left their villages in 1847 owing to famine [and] found work in various villages near Hebron."[171] Peasants from Western Palestine, west of the Jordan River, moved to cultivate land in Eastern Palestine. Other "Palestinian peasants" were "brought in" by prosperous merchants to cultivate a "considerable stretch of territory" and the émigrés' efforts made the merchant "a wealthy notable."[172]

Such was the custom.

In 1858 a reform was attempted, with destructive results.[173] According to Professor Elie Kedourie, it was "a new, European-model land law."

The Land Code did not create a European-style small landed peasantry with a stake in the land. On the contrary, *the small agriculturist, whether member of a settled village community, or of a tribe which had never known individual ownership of land, found his customary rights and interests squeezed and destroyed by a law, the operation of which was made even more vicious by the corruption and malpractices that a large, unwieldy, centralized bureaucracy naturally entailed.* *[174]

In the 1860s and 1870s, here is one graphic example among the myriad reports of the unrelenting ruination of the peasant:

[The tax-collectors] extort from [the peasants] nearly all the produce of their lands in return for the doubtful advantage of having them stand between them and the officers of the government. . . . The farmer [tax-farmer] of a village . . . is, in fact, a petty tyrant who takes *all* if he cannot otherwise get back what he has spent, and the iniquitous interest also.

This system of tax-gathering greatly multiplies the petty lords and tyrants who eat up the people as they eat bread.[175]

The oppression of the peasant swept across the traditional barriers of Islam. With regard to exploitation,

*Emphasis added.

The line of basic demarcation ran . . . not between Muslim and Christian, Turk and non-Turk, but between ruler and ruled, oppressor and oppressed. . . .

The maligned Turkish peasant . . . was generally no better off than the ordinary non-Muslim and as much oppressed by maladministration.[176]

But those barriers—separating Muslim from non-Muslim infidel—were powerful forces against reform. The leaders who sought reform were faced with an "imposing obstacle"—"the conviction of superiority, which Muslim Turks possessed." It was a formidable "conviction," a bias bound to undermine a "reform based on equality of all Ottoman subjects. . . . Christians and Jews were inevitably considered second-class citizens" not only "in the light of religious revelation" but also because of "the plain fact that they had been conquered and were ruled by the Ottomans. The common term for the infidel, *gavur,* carried this implication of Muslim superiority."[177]

Compounding the difficulties of reform, the Muslims "opposed innovation. Cevdet Efendi (later Pasha) who began to learn French in 1846, had to do so secretly for fear of criticism."[178] In 1868 a Muslim writer estimated that only about two percent of the Muslim population were literate.[179] Another bemoaned the fact that most were "without pen and without tongue."[180] "Suleyman Pasa [*sic*] in the same period guessed that in the capital itself only twenty thousand Muslims could read a newspaper."[181]

The widespread illiteracy sustained and fed the coffers of the feudal extortionists. The peasant had to borrow to pay the taxes, and the debts he incurred from outrageous usurious rates of interest forced him to sell his land, often to the wealthy *effendis*—landlords—in the town.[182]

But even *after surrendering* his *property,* the peasant still had to deal with moneylenders and their viselike usury, because the unstable conditions—Bedouin raids, earthquakes, epidemics, high prices—prevented the *fellah* from supporting himself through farming.[183]

A writer described the moneylending, a practice that carried on into the twentieth century:

Money lending . . . was one of the curses of Palestine. Nearly everyone borrowed money, and the rate of interest was fantastic, not because the surety for the loan was not satisfactory, but because the borrower was completely in the hands of the lender. The *fellah,* even if he was in a good position, had practically never a penny to bless himself with. One day the Government official turns up and demands a large sum in cash. What is the *fellah* to do? But here comes a merchant from the town, or a Moslem *frangi* (i.e., a man in European dress) happens to be walking about in the village with his pockets bulging with money, and one of them is willing to accommodate the *fellah.* But the lender requires not only substantial security, but a good rate of interest also—20, 25, and even 30 or 40 per cent. "What can I do," thinks to himself the needy *fellah.* He knows very well that just at this moment he will not be getting in any money, and if he will not be able to bribe the tax-collector and postpone the payment he will in the end be imprisoned as a defaulter. He also knows that to get out of prison will cost him a lot of money, much more than paying the interest to the lender, not to reckon his loss of time. On the other side it is clear to him that if the grain or olive crop is a failure he will not be able to liquidate his debt, and the interest payments which he will have to make every year will go on increasing.*[184]

Another blight was the centuries-old traditional incursion by Arab raiders, which befell the few "sedentary peasant-farmers" who remained on the land.

> . . . unless checked by firm government action, the nomads have always sought to thrust into the settled areas, terrorizing and exploiting the villagers and eventually causing them to give up cultivation and flee.[185]

One historian contrasted the "excellent roads and fortifications, . . . and judicious alliances" of Judeo-Roman times with the spoiled, debauched Ottoman-ruled land at the end of the eighteenth century, following the emigration of the 'Anza tribes from Central Arabia.[186] In 1785, Volney recorded the scene:

> The peasants are incessantly making inroads on each others' lands, destroying their corn (durha), sesame and olive trees and carrying off their sheep, goats, and camels. . . . The Bedouin whose camps occupy the level country are continually at open hostilities with them (the Turks), of which the peasants avail themselves to resist their authority or do mischief to each other. . . . The mutual devastation of the contending parties renders the appearance of this part of Syria more wretched than that of any other.[187]

As a direct result of the tribal raiding, "large portions of the country went out of cultivation, and hundreds of villages were depopulated."[188]

In the nineteenth century a great number of Bedouin tribes continued to filter into the region. "Arabia has always periodically overpeopled herself and, at this time, the emptiness of the Syrian plains and their almost absolute lack of defenses tempted the . . . Arabia tribes. Once the movement was under way, this attraction communicated itself to other tribes." In addition, the "disturbances" in the warring Arabian plains caused still other tribes to emigrate. Tribes who lived in Syria and environs were forced, by raiding and tribal warfare among the new émigrés, to flee into the "fringes of the desert," and plundering prevailed.[189]

Burckhardt recorded graphically a predatory practice long common to that terrain—one that is known in the latter-twentieth-century western world as the "protection racket."

> The . . . most heavy contribution paid by the peasants, is the tribute to the Arabs. . . . Constant residents in the Haouran, as well as most of the numerous tribes of Aeneze, who visit the country only in the summer, are, from remote times, entitled to certain tributes called Khone (brotherhood), from every village in the Haouran. In return for this Khone, the Arabs abstain from touching the harvest of the village, and from driving off its cattle and camels, when they meet them in their way. Each village pays Khone to one Sheikh in every tribe; the village is

*Emphasis added.

then known as his Ukhta or Sister, as the Arabs term it, and he protects the inhabitants against all the members of his own tribe. It may easily be imagined, however, that depredations are often committed, without the possibility of redress, the depredator being unknown, or flying immediately towards the desert. The amount of the Khone is continually increasing, for the Arab Sheikh is not always contented with the quantity of corn he received in the preceding year, but asks something additional, as a present, which soon becomes a part of his accustomed dues.[190]

The journal of the Christian traveler H. B. Tristram was another among the plethora of documents that totally contradicted the widely believed propaganda claim by the Arabs that it was "Jewish immigration and settlement" that disrupted the Palestinians' "tranquility and stability." Tristram wrote in 1865 that,

A few years ago, the whole ghor (Jordan Valley) was in the hands of the Fellahin and much of it cultivated for corn. *Now the whole of it is in the hands of the bedouin,* who eschew agriculture except in a few spots, cultivated here and there by their slaves. And with the bedouin, come lawlessness, and the uprooting of all Turkish authority. No government is now acknowledged on the east side; and unless the porte acts with greater firmness and caution than is his wont . . . *Palestine will be desolated and given up to the nomads.* *[191]

A French writer reported that, during travels in Palestine and Syria in the late 1870s, he found that in order to buy seeds, the peasant paid an interest rate as high as 200 to 300 percent.[192] According to one scholar,

This state of affairs was made possible by the *fellahin's* misery and lack of rights, which were the result of the high degree of feudal exploitation in villages.[193]

Not only regional rich *effendis* snatched up the land, but also enterprising foreigners saw the chance to reap the local profits.

Buyers operating in Syrian villages were usually agents of foreign merchants. Foreign capital found a fertile soil for its commercial and usurious activities in villages pressed beneath the feudal yoke.[194]

And these were Arab profiteers, not Jewish settlers, though a small number of native Jews and Yemenite Jewish immigrants were already assuming the task of developing and reclaiming future farmland.† Most of the "Palestinian" Jews were still "paupers,"[195] eking out an existence in the towns and villages of the "Holy Land."[196] The great wave of Jewish settlement would not begin until 1882.[197] Meanwhile, the *effendis* were gaining from their monopolistic grip on the land.

The British Consul in Jerusalem from 1845 to 1863 reported that a group of prominent landholding families in Jerusalem, exerting the influence of their wealth, had gained control of "all the municipal offices. In consequence they hold certain villages or groups of villages in a species of serfdom."[198] By the end of the

*Emphasis added.
†See Chapter 10.

nineteenth century the political power was in the hands of those Muslim families "with names like al-Husayni, al-Khalidi and al-Nashashibi."[199] The "parasitic landlord class" had acquired, through the *fellahins'* ruinous indebtedness, huge landholdings, which the landlords seldom if ever visited, and almost never farmed.[200]

In the late 1880s, several years after the new major Jewish immigration had begun, the migratory patterns remained unchanged.

> When the debts reach a certain figure the *fellah* takes his bundle of bedclothes, along with his cooking pan and water can, and if he is very fortunate, his small water jug and his shoes, and having loaded the whole on his one ass, if he has managed to retain an ass, and on to his wife, he flees on a dark night and crosses the Jordan Valley, until he reaches the Hauran or Ajlun, where he finds a tolerably secure refuge from his pursuers and oppressors.[201]

As late as 1908, a German historian found that the *fellah* had turned Bedouin to escape the grip of his indebtedness. If the *fellah* sensed peril, he packed his family and they fled across the Jordan, where they became members of a nomad tribe.[202] "The land was left without owners and without workers, and became *mahlul*"—a kind of state domain.[203]

So thorough was the plundering of the Bedouins, so corrupt the government and its feudal system, that despite the imported replenishment of peoples from near and far, Doughty, in his account of travels in the region, was moved to write in 1876 that

> "The desert" (says the Hebrew prophet) "shall become a ploughland," so might all this good soil, . . . return to be full of busy human lives; there lacks but the defense of a strong government.[204]

Doughty found a "desert" that was devoid of but a few "human lives" at the precise moment when the Jews had begun to develop their settlements—on the semi-abandoned territory where one day the Arab propaganda would claim that *Jews* had crowded out, "displaced," and rendered the "Palestinian" Arabs "landless."

Thus, we are faced with the facts of the land once called Judah, Judea, and later, the Romans' "Palestina" and "Southern Syria," a once fertile "ploughland" laid waste, whose inhabitants sadly diminished in number through natural disaster—and the greed of goat and man.

The peoples who roamed the country in the nineteenth century were not the peoples who conquered, with the Prophet Muhammad's troops, the land of Judah-Palestine. Those peoples were not indigenous to the land. They did not stay on the land. Of the sparse population who were later counted as "original" settled "Arabs" in the nineteenth century when the arriving Jewish immigrants united with the native Palestinian Jewish population, many were in fact imported Muslim peoples from Turkey and other lands, whom the Turks, in many cases, had recently brought, to protect against the wandering Bedouin tribes—a kind of landed pirates who periodically attacked that settled multi-ethnic populace. "The Land's" vicious cycle of conquest and destruction had relentlessly claimed its inhabitants. Thus each new conqueror brought his own measure of the population with him as protective force, while other thousands went in and out from lands as distant as the Caucasus.

The government was often "directly responsible" for importing immigrants to spur development.

For example, Circassian and other colonists were deliberately planted on the frontier of settlement, especially from 1870 onwards.[205]

About 1860 several hundred tents of the Wulda tribe crossed the Euphrates and eventually settled down about thirty miles south of Aleppo, in Jebel Samaane. Sections of other tribes, such as the Bu Shaikh, Lheib, and Aquedat also drifted west, usually after being defeated in raids or wars, half fleeing from the powerful desert tribes and half attracted by the possibilities of settlement.[206]

Kurds, Turcomans, Naim, and other colonists arrived in Palestine around the same time as the Jewish immigration waves began. Eighteen thousand "tents" of Tartars,[207] the "armies of Turks and Kurds," whole villages settled in the nineteenth century[208] of Bosnians and Moors and "Circassians" and "Algerians" and Egyptians, etc.—all were continually brought in to people the land called Palestine.

This melting pot will be seen in following chapters to have been counted as "original settled Muslims" in "Palestine." However, it is clear by now that the claim that a numerous "descended Arab Palestinian people" exists, with "family ties to the land for thousands of years," is historically inaccurate.

"In 1878 the first Circassians arrived. . . . Two years later a second group settled. . . . In 1885 Circassian immigrants arrived to found three villages. . . ." The Circassians "effectively fulfilled the role allotted to them: to occupy and cultivate land, to weaken and to act as a buffer against the bedouin"[209]—in short, to fulfill the same function as the protective forces of Ibrahim Pasha: Ibrahim, Palestine's Egyptian conqueror, had left behind him "permanent colonies of Egyptian immigrants at Beisan, Nablus, Irbid, Acre, and Jaffa, where some five hundred Egyptian soldiers' families established a new quarter"—500 alien families, at least 2,000 persons, imported at a single moment—and that was only one among countless similar situations. "With this aid and the resettlement of the Jews, which dates from 1830, Jaffa began to grow."[210] In another area, "The Muslims of Safed are mostly descended from . . . Moorish settlers and from Kurds. . . ."[211]

The land called Palestine was never considered a nation at all, and surely could not have been regarded by the later immigrants as their "ancestral" homeland, any more than a Norwegian immigrant to the United States would consider that his "ancestral" home was the United States when his ancestors were born in Norway.

As late as the time coinciding with Jewish reclamation and development, the land was so sparsely populated that "landlords [were] bringing in peasants and former semi-nomadic tribesmen" from other areas "to work on their land." The Turkish land laws enacted in 1858 had worked to the disadvantage of the peasant, but "made it easy for landlords and speculators to gain control of disproportionately great areas of land." When the peasants and semi-nomads "fell prey to the usurer" and lost their tenancies, they fled and were replaced by new immigrants.[212]

The majority of genuine "Arabs" among the sparse population in the "ruined" country when the Jewish settlers began to buy land for restoration were Arabian tribal nomads. The multi-ethnic "Arab" peasants who remained were so few—despite the consistent replenishment of peoples—and generally so impoverished that an Arab writer was prompted to sum up the harsh conditions thus:

> . . . At the turn of this century, Palestine was no longer the land of milk and honey described by the Bible, but a poor Ottoman province, a semi-desert covered by more thorns than flowers. The Mediterranean coast and all the southern half of the country were sand, and the rare marshy plains were fens of Malaria which decimated the sparse, semi-nomadic population, clinging to slopes and bare hills.[213]

Much of the Muslim population that remained in the country was transient. As the Arab leader Sherif Hussein observed in 1918,

> The resources of the country are still virgin soil and will be developed by the Jewish immigrants. One of the most amazing things until recent times *was that the Palestinian used to leave his country, wandering over the high seas in every direction. His native soil could not retain its hold on him* . . . *[214]

How then does the profusion of evidence of an uninhabited Palestine jibe with the Arab propaganda claim of an overwhelming Arab settled population in a Palestine so crowded that the "Jews displaced the Arabs who had been there for thousands of years?" The rotation of multi-ethnic Muslims and Christians had been imported either by various conquerors or through traditional migratory patterns to Judah-cum-Palestine, where they had met with the omnipresent Jewish and Christian inhabitants—all have been abundantly documented. That they were "Arabs" who had been for "thousands of years," or even hundreds, as a consistent presence in Palestine is known to be inaccurate. Moreover, according to the Arab writer Ameen Rihani, confusion abounded with respect to an "Arab" identity "achieved mainly by exciting the fanatical spirit of the tribes." The Arabic-speaking peoples in Palestine were not motivated toward Palestinian nationalism or Pan-Arabism, and there were no prominent Arab negotiators in Palestine even to protest the "giveaway [of] Syria and Palestine."[215]

It was the *Arabs* themselves—by tradition as well as corruption—who

*Emphasis added.

prompted Arabic-speaking Muslims to disregard or abandon the land, and it was the *Jews* who would create a climate of opportunity that drew the peasant-migrants by the thousands to the Jewish-settled area of Palestine. But, as we will see, it was long *after, not before,* the Jews settled their new farms that the first claims of "Palestinian Arab" identity and an "age-old" tie to the land would be invented.

Even the Arabs' impressive propaganda effort could not obscure the unassailably recorded persistence of Jewish nationalism, or the lesser-known obstinate Jewish presence in Judah-cum-Palestine—a combination of historical factors that resulted in the international recognition of the Jews' renewed national liberation. So the Arab world has attempted to match the Jewish history by inventing an "identity" for the "Palestinian Arabs" that *would,* they reason, "counter Zionism." Thus has been largely accomplished the cynical rewriting of history, which in turn can only result in a perversion of "justice."

9

Dhimmi in the Holy Land

His right derived from time immemorial in his
family, to enter Jewish houses, and take toll or
contributions at any time without giving account.

—A "Muslim in Hebron," as reported
by James Finn, British Consul in
Jerusalem, 1858

I have learned with horror of the
atrocious acts committed by bodies of ruthless
and blood-thirsty evil-doers, of savage murders
perpetrated upon defenseless members of the
Jewish population, regardless of age or sex . . .
acts of unspeakable savagery. . . .

—J. R. Chancellor, High Commissioner and
Commander-in-Chief in Palestine, September 1, 1929

[The Jews] always did live previously in Arab
countries with complete freedom and liberty, as
natives of the country. In fact, Moslem rule has
always been known for its tolerance . . .
according to history Jews had a most quiet and
peaceful residence under Arab rule.

—Mufti Haj Amin al-Husseini, 1937

Before proceeding to the evidence and indications of the "systems" of immigration and their crucial consequence in Palestine, it is important to look at the
conditions under which the Palestinian Jews lived during the generations *prior
to* the "new," late-nineteenth-century Jewish settlements.

In order to assess accurately the responsibility for the plight of the Arab
refugees, the true role must be seen of the Jews in Palestine among the many
ethnic groups constituting the Muslim inhabitants who are all called—and for the
sake of convenience will be called here—Arabs.

Although the same as in Arab countries in some fundamental respects, the
relationships in the Holy Land developed special qualitative differences. Those
attitudes were the residual of a long tradition of intrinsic prejudice inflamed by
cynical political manipulation. That tradition has been perpetuated for genera-

tions—and for more than three decades at the cost of the well-being of some of the Arab refugee-émigrés themselves.

The violence that the PLO's Yasser Arafat and others now claim was "only begun against Jews with the 1948 rebirth of Israel"—"Palestinian" terrorism—was actually a critical factor in the early developments that instigated the pivotal population conditions in Palestine. In their Holy Land, the Jews, as well as Christians, suffered long from harsh discrimination, persecution, and pogroms. According to the British Consulate report in 1839, the Jew's life was not "much above" that of a dog.[1]

The inverting of facts—*turnspeak**—has had the propaganda effect of perpetuating the false claim of "displaced" and "terrorized" Arabs in the Jewish-settled area of Palestine until the current time—long after the charge had been disproved by investigations. In fact, as following chapters will show, it was the Jews who were displaced by Arabs—the Arab immigrant flocks would migrate into the Jewish areas of development, filling the places that the Jews were clearing for other Jews—on land designated at that very time as the mandated "Jewish Homeland."

Those few "Arab effendi" families—like the Husseinis and the Nashashibis and the Khalidis—who had been dispossessing and then continuing to exploit the hapless peasant-migrant in underpopulated Palestine would become threatened *by the spectacle of* dhimmi *Jews living on the land as equals,* tilling their own soil and granting previously unknown benefits to the Arabic-speaking non-Jewish worker. The Jews would undoubtedly upset the "sweets of office," which had been accruing to the *effendis.* Thousands of peasant-migrants would be emigrating to reap the better wages, health benefits, and improvements of the Jewish communities. Although the *effendis* would charge scalper's prices for land they sold to the Jews, at the same time they would lose thousands of their former debtors who saw an escape from the stranglehold of usury and corruption prevalent in Palestine for generations.

Yet perhaps most galling of all to *effendi* leadership was the Jew who would settle the land. This was not the *dhimmi* Jew—cowering to survive, as in Arab lands—but a person who commanded equal treatment. The outrage which that insistence created, among those weaned on the tradition of Muslim supremacy, would infect the multi-ethnic Arabic-speaking Muslim workers of Palestine as well: for centuries Jews had been objects to oppress and despise.

As a Muslim in Hebron retorted when he was confronted with his theft and vandalism of Jews in 1858, *"his right derived from time immemorial in his family, to enter Jewish houses, and take toll or contributions at any time without giving account."*[2]† This attitude and its prevalence in Palestine cannot be overlooked. It is perhaps the most powerful factor in the Middle East conflict today and cer-

---

*Turnspeak—the cynical inverting or distorting of facts, which, for example, makes the victim appear as culprit.

†Emphasis added.

tainly at the core of the "Palestinian" question—the true "heart of the matter."

When the Jews' revival of their nation was still a persistent dream in the prayers of worldwide Jewry, and most "Palestinian Jews" were still clinging to their holy cities, the Koranic-inspired discriminatory practices, along with periodic pillage and slaughter of the Jew, had extended to Palestine. The myth of "harmony among Jews and Arabs," of "equality," and "fraternity" for Jews within a Muslim, Arabic-speaking Palestine has been invented, as the means to an unequal end.

Through the centuries of conquest and oppression, as the Palestine Royal Commission reported in 1937, despite seemingly insurmountable odds, "a number of . . . [Jews] clung throughout the centuries . . . to what had once been their national soil."[3] The history of those Jews who stubbornly survived other massacres in their homeland to confront Muslim "fraternity" is stained by the same Muslim Jew-hatred that permeated Muslim communities throughout the Arab world. The same myth of harmony that has been perpetuated about the Arab world—in Yasser Arafat's assertion that ". . . we have been living with each other in peace and fraternity, Muslims, Jews and Christians, for many centuries"[4]—has been engaged specifically as a weapon to attack the Jewish state. The "peaceloving Palestinians," goes the myth, were running from "Jewish terrorism."

In fact, so thorough has the rewriting of history been that some Jews themselves have accepted the allegation that the "Palestinian Arabs" are simply using "Jewish tactics" to gain statehood when the Arab terrorists attack in and outside Israel.[5] The Arab propaganda slogan today is that the Jews are "Nazis" in "Palestine."[6]

Perhaps an apt illustration of the turnspeak tactic was the protestation discussed earlier by the group in Egypt who sought to prove that the Arab terrorists' Munich massacre of Israeli Olympics athletes was "really masterminded by the Jews."[7]

The Arabs have faithfully followed the agitator's manifesto—the best defense is attack. Loudly and repeatedly they have attributed their own historical foul deeds to their victims while the victims were still paralyzed by those deeds, and before the victims had stopped reeling long enough to retaliate. Thus a writer who was allowed to examine the textbooks of the recruits at a Fatah terrorist training camp reported:

> There are political books available: Castro, Guevara, Mao Tse-tung, Giap, Rodinson; General de Gaulle's memoirs; and also *Mein Kampf*. When I expressed surprise at the presence of this last volume, the political commissar replied that it was necessary to have read everything, and that *since the Israelis behaved like Nazis it was useful to know precisely what Nazism was.*[8]

—a graphic example of turnspeak, quickwitted and cunningly designed to mask the underlying attitude of the Arabic-speaking community in Palestine, whose sentiments, for somewhat different reasons, matched *Mein Kampf* and its doctrines.

Israel's attempt to destroy the PLO terror network in Lebanon brought a barrage of such rhetoric. For instance, from an important Egyptian daily, only weeks after the Israel-Egypt peace had culminated in the Israelis' return of the Sinai:

> It is now clear to us from the behavior of the Nazi Zionist regime in Israel that Zionism wishes to come in the place of the fascist Nazi tyrants.[9]

And from the influential Egyptian magazine, *October,* on the same day:

> . . . what Hitler did in 12 years cannot be compared to what Israel has done in twelve days.[10]

In truth, "Arab" terrorism in the Holy Land originated centuries before the recent "tool" of the "Palestinian" cause was invented. In towns where Jews lived for hundreds of years, those Jews were periodically robbed, raped, in some places massacred, and, in many instances, the survivors were obliged to abandon their possessions and run.

At the beginning of this century Jews were recorded in nearly every town[11] that is today considered to have been "purely Arab"—in other words, without Jewish inhabitants "from time immemorial." Those same towns decades later had been purged of their Jews through the arbitrary oppression of the Jews within the Muslim communities.[12] Thus, we find Jewish refugees who have not been heretofore recognized—those Palestinian Jewish refugees who were forced to flee from their homes within Palestine to other areas in Palestine. The Jews were refugees in Palestine once again: "Palestinian Jewish" refugees.

The same inversion of fact, by which today's totalitarian regimes are called "democratic," has created the corruption of the term "legitimate rights of the Palestinians." The original theme of "legitimate rights," certainly a legitimate and righteous quest, has been twisted instead into a carefully designed slogan pointing the finger of guilt at the Jews for acts that the Arab-Muslim world has committed against the Jews and against its own brothers.[13]

As we have seen, beginning with the Prophet Muhammad's edict demanding racial purity—that "Two religions may not dwell together . . ."—the Arab-Muslim world codified its supremacist credo, and later that belief was interpreted liberally enough to allow many non-Muslim *dhimmis,* or infidels, to remain alive between onslaughts in the Muslim world as a means of revenue. The infidel's head tax, in addition to other extortions—and the availability of the "nonbelievers" to act as helpless scapegoats for the oft-dissatisfied masses—became a highly useful mainstay to the Arab-Muslim rulers. Thus the pronouncement of the Prophet Muhammad was altered in practice to: two religions may not dwell together *equally.* That was the pragmatic interpretation.

Thereafter, whatever reigning power after the Arab conquest, whoever the conqueror, the attitude of its Muslims toward unbelievers, and the infidel's subjugation, reinforced by terrorizing, were never abandoned in the Holy Land. The following is a general summary that may provide some insight into the foundation that could foment a PLO.

By the time the "short" Arab rule of Palestine from Damascus had ended in the eighth century—more than eleven hundred years ago—"Muslim intolerance and even fanaticism were beginning to show . . . at the level of the street and the marketplace . . ." in Palestine.[14] A new Muslim assumption of superiority toward the unbeliever—Islam was then less than a hundred years old—was compounded by resentment and coveting of the prosperity and power that a small number among the predominant Christian and Jewish *dhimmis* had managed to retain through special official protection or connections.[15]

Because the "Palestinian" Jewish population was prey not only to epidemics and earthquakes, but also to periodic slaughter and persecution, the constant trickle of immigration and the following of messianic exhortations to "return to the Holy Land" never boosted the total number of Jews. But a hard core persisted there and in time outnumbered the once-greater Christian population. In 1491 a Bohemian pilgrim wrote of Jerusalem:

> There are not many Christians but there are many Jews, and these the Moslems persecute in various ways. Christians and Jews go about in Jerusalem in clothes considered fit only for wandering beggars.
> The Moslems know that the Jews think and even say that this is the Holy Land which has been promised to them and that those Jews who dwell there are regarded as holy by Jews elsewhere, because, in spite of all the troubles and sorrows inflicted on them by the Moslems, they refuse to leave the Land.[16]

About the same time, another pilgrim noted that the Jews in Jerusalem spoke mainly Hebrew,[17] while yet another visitor recorded in his journal that the Jewish community of Jerusalem was hopeful of restoring its nation.[18]

From the beginning of Turkish rule in the sixteenth century, the infidel *dhimma* code of oppressions against nonbelievers was maintained in Palestine.* The humiliation was a given; the degree of harshness of injunctions against Jews depended on the whim of the ruler, local as well as the lord of the empire. Among the constants of *dhimma* restrictions in the Holy Land:

> Jews had to pass Muslims on their left side, because that was the side of Satan. They had to yield the right of way, step off the pavement to let the Arab go by, above all make sure not to touch him in passing, because this could provoke a violent response. In the same way, anything that reminded the Muslim of the presence of alternative religions, any demonstration of alternative forms of worship, had to be avoided so synagogues were placed in humble, hidden places, and the sounds of Jewish prayer carefully muted.[19]

When the Turks conquered the land in 1516, "Not only were governors at all times vexatious in their demands, but the Muslims were often hostile to their Jewish neighbors."

*See Chapter 3.

The gentleness of 'Omar was the mantle that hid the Arab-Jewish relations for three centuries, the early Othman [Turkish] hospitality obscured the actualities of Jewish life in the Near East. . . .[20]

The Muslims' subjection of Jewish infidel communities was heightened by the rise of the "first anti-Jewish" sultan, Murad III.[21] Murad decreed that all Jews throughout his empire be executed, because they were too well dressed, but a well-placed Jewish subject interceded and Murad reduced the death sentence for Jews to a law prohibiting them from wearing silk and forcing them to wear special headdresses.[22]

In sixteenth-century Judah-cum-Palestine—particularly in Jerusalem and Safed, two of their "holy" cities—the Jews were persecuted with zeal. "The community gradually withered; of seven hundred Jewish widows in Jerusalem, six hundred died of hunger."[23] The Jewish community was, however, consistently replenished by the constant influx of faithful immigrants "returning" to their country. No matter how hazardous the journey was for the Jews, they appear to have managed, even when their presence was forbidden, to keep their goal alive and their population extant.[24] For those European Jews who braved the journey in the Middle Ages and before, there was certain danger of

> . . . the whole range of persecution from mass degradation to death after torture. For a Jew who could not and would not hide his identity to make his way from his own familiar city or village to another, from the country whose language he knew through countries foreign to him, meant to expose himself almost certainly to suspicion, insult, and humiliation, *probably to robbery and violence,* possibly to murder. *All travel was hazardous.* For a Jew in the thirteenth, fourteenth, or fifteenth century (and even later) to set out on the odyssey from Western Europe to Palestine was a heroic undertaking, which often ended in disaster.*[25]

Two Christians who made a pilgrimage to Jerusalem in 1479 reported the circuitous route of travel for Jewish immigrants from Germany, starting at Nuremberg:[26]

Nuremberg to Posen	300 miles
Posen (Poznań) to Lublin	250 miles
Lublin to Lemberg (Lvov)	120 miles
Lemberg to Khotin	150 miles
Khotin to Akerman	150 miles
Akerman to Samsun	6 days
Samsun to Tokat	6–7 days
Tokat to Aleppo	15 days
Aleppo to Damascus	7 days
Damascus to Jerusalem	6 days

*Emphasis added.

In 1576 Sultan Murad III enacted legislation to uproot and deport a thousand of Safed's prosperous Jews to Cyprus, where the economy needed boosting. The same order was given again a year later, although no document establishes that his dictates were followed.[27] Safed at that time, according to the British investigation by Lord Peel's committee, "contained as many as 15,000 Jews in the 16th century," and was "a centre of Rabbinical learning." The Jews spoke Arabic as well as Hebrew, "they were equally exposed to the raids of marauding tribesmen," and "public security deteriorated." The population generally declined.[28]

In the early seventeenth century a pair of Christian visitors to Safed told of life for the Jews: "Life here is the poorest and most miserable that one can imagine." Because of the harshness of Turkish rule and its crippling *dhimmi* oppressions, the Jews "pay for the very air they breathe."[29] Yet at the turn of the century, the Jewish population had grown from 8,000–10,000 (in 1555) to between 20,000 and 30,000 souls.[30]

With Murad's anti-Jewish innovations and the economic upset of the Turkish Empire came lawlessness. "Public security was undermined," and Turkey had very quickly lost—a matter of decades after its conquest—its widely heralded tolerance of Jewish infidels. "Turkey ceased to be a lodestar for exile Jewry."[31]

In sixteenth-century Jerusalem, the Jews' taxation was tantamount to extortion, and the last remaining synagogue—a monument from the time of Nachmanides—was expropriated in 1586. As a result, most of Jerusalem's Jewry hastened off to Hebron, Gaza, and Tiberias.[32]

But the marauders were everywhere—Bedouin raiders, general anarchy, tax corruption—with the additional tax burden that aimed only at Jews.[33] Yet the Jewish communities of Judah-cum-Palestine "still held on all over the country. . . . in Hebron . . . Gaza, Ramle, Sh'chem [Nablus], Safed, . . . Acre, Sidon, Tyre, Haifa, Irsuf, Caesarea, and El Arish; and Jews continued to live and till the soil in Galilean villages."[34]

Those Jews remaining in Jerusalem were "bitterly persecuted" during the seventeenth-century reign of an Arab ruler who purchased his governorship and arrested the Jewish leaders.[35] Under the next ruler, while the hapless Jews were "speculating on the advent of the Messiah," a great number of them were massacred.[36]

> In 1625, the local ruler of Jerusalem persecuted the Jews mercilessly in defiance of orders from the authorities in Damascus and Constantinople. It was not unusual, when the countryside suffered from drought, for the Moslem mob to attack "Jewish sinners who drank wine and thus caused the rains to stop!" To buy off the attackers, Jews had to borrow money from rich Moslems at compound interest, under threats of further attacks if they failed to repay.[37]

When the Jewish community of its holy city of Safed was "massacred in 1660," and the town "destroyed by Arabs," only one Jew managed to evade death.[38] In 1674 Jerusalem's Jews were similarly impoverished by the oppression of the Turkish-Muslim rule, according to the Jesuit Father Michael Naud, "paying heavily to the Turk for their right to stay here."

> . . . They prefer being prisoners in Jerusalem to enjoying the freedom they could acquire elsewhere. . . . The love of the Jews for the Holy Land, which they lost through their betrayal . . . is unbelievable. Many of them come from Europe to find a little comfort, though the yoke is heavy.[39]

The eighteenth century saw the increasing decline of order and the further waste of the terrain, and with it all came violence and persecution of the Jewish *dhimmi*. Yet, one ruling sheikh brought tolerance and improvements to the Jews of Galilee. Although only a brief respite, the Jews of Safed and Tiberias were given hope when the kindly sheikh welcomed a rabbi from Smyrna to "come and inherit the land of his ancestors." The rabbi's grandfather had been "Rabbi of Tiberias" a century earlier and his arrival in 1742 brought back the Jewish community of Tiberias, which had been virtually purged of Jews for seventy years.[40]

Near the end of the eighteenth century, this Galileean tolerance ended abruptly, with the fairminded sheikh's overthrow. His successors reinforced the code of humiliation and harassment of "their" Jews as it had been maintained elsewhere in the country.[41]

In 1775, the anti-Jewish blood libel was spread throughout the holy Jewish city of Hebron, inciting mob violence, as that vicious canard has wrought havoc for Jews in Arab and European communities alike.[42] Safed's Jewish Quarter, which had again been revived during the reign of the kindly sheikh a few decades before, "was completely sacked by the Turks" in 1799.[43]

The Muslims in Nablus prohibited Christians from settling in the town.[44] The year 1783 brought the rise of an Albanian-born Mamluk "Arab," nicknamed "The Butcher"—*el Djezzar*—whose sadistic, wanton exploits became legend.[45] The Latin Patriarch's correspondence in 1805 reports:

> Mohammad Djezzar, pasha of Jerusalem and Damascus, began to take by force twenty-five thousand piastres more than it was customary to pay. This continued for seven years, during which he was at different times governor, to say nothing of other exactions with which he was incessantly harassing us. All our representations to the Porte were unavailing as this pasha obeyed none of its firmans.[46]

As his power grew, industry and agricultural production declined further, "so that his chief source of revenue became what he could extract out of the district of Damascus and the Palestinian churches."[47] The inhabitants of his dominion—stretching at one point from Beirut to the Egyptian border[48]—were so intimidated that few fought off his harsh decrees. "The limit of his extensive pashalic [district] . . . might be easily known by the air of gloom and desolation with which it was overspread."[49]

Hayim Farhi, the one Jew who had risen to some power in the area (about whom more was mentioned in Chapter 3), was imprisoned by The Butcher, and some "milder forms of punishment"[50] were administered—"ear cropping, nose slitting and the gouging out of an eye." The Butcher branded most of his aides by one or another of the mutilations. "His cavalry scoured the country, levying tribute or committing any atrocity he was pleased to enjoin."[51]

He was known to travel accompanied by an executioner. When The Butcher encountered a subject who was adjudged to be misbehaving, "the criminal bowed his neck, the executioner struck, and the head fell."[52] The Butcher's brutality was contagious, and persecutions of many Palestinian minorities were rife under his encouragement.[53] At one point his popularity among the masses prompted him to pronounce an order to massacre all Christians under his authority. Thereupon Sir Sidney Smith sent The Butcher an outraged message: if one Christian head were to fall, so would The Butcher's seat of power. According to a prominent historian of the period, Sir Sidney's threat worked. "I have often heard both Turks and Christians exclaim [that Sir Sidney's word] was like God's word, it never failed."[54]

The Jews in Palestine had no such power—worldly or otherwise. The nineteenth century ushered in an even lower ebb to the perilous existence of "Palestinian" Jewry. Some historians believe that The Butcher's mistreatment of the French merchants in Acre and other cities under his authority—in 1791 he decreed confiscations of their property and expulsion with only a few days' notice—caused Napoleon's invasion of Palestine.[55]

When Napoleon Bonaparte planned his invasion of Jerusalem at the end of the eighteenth century, he tried to enlist the African and Asiatic Jews to march with him by promising to return their Holy Land and restore Jerusalem. But the Turks spread the word that the French "treated Jews particularly in a cruel manner." Thus the Jews of Jerusalem "encouraged and even assisted" the Turks to their defense buildup of the Holy City. Some believe "it was only a trick" by Bonaparte to gain the support of Hayim Farhi, the Jew who briefly rose to power in Syria.[56]

Farhi was assassinated in 1820. Napoleon's vision of himself as Emperor of the East had already evaporated into the dust of other conquests in the Holy Land, and his debatable "promise" of the country to the Jews was never tested.[57]

In the 1800s the Jews continued to suffer the same discriminatory practices as other non-Muslim "infidels,"[58] which "in many places throughout Syria and Palestine" meant "oppression, extortion, and violence by both the local authorities and the Muslim population."[59]

The Christians in their holy town of Nazareth were also forced through maltreatment into fleeing.

> Even as late as 1801 Djezzar sent troops to destroy the standing crops in the environs of Nazareth. Ramleh, however, bore the brunt of the Muslim wrath. During the three days of pillage, the local Latin Christians were either murdered, or lost all their property and fled.[60]

But there were additional oppressions reserved for the Palestinian Jewish community. The Jews were "at the bottom"[61] of the heap of peoples in status.

Among the special extortions that their Holy Land extracted from the Jews, paid to "local officials, Arab notables, and Arab neighbors":[62] in Jerusalem the *effendi* whose property was adjacent to the Sacred Wall on the site of the Jews' temple dunned the Jews 300 pounds annually for the right to pray there. They paid another 100 pounds to Siloam's inhabitants—a village on the outskirts of Jerusalem[63]—as protection against destruction or vandalism of the Jewish burial grounds at the Mount of Olives. Fifty pounds a year went to an Arab community to ensure against assault upon Rachel's Tomb, and Sheikh Abu Gosh collected 10 pounds "not to molest Jewish travelers on the road to Jerusalem, though he was already paid by the Turkish government to maintain order on that road."[64]

The first latter-day Jewish defense volunteers may have been the group protecting against marauders, which was described in a British Consulate correspondence in 1840:

> Last year when Sir Moses Montefiore travelled through Palestine, and when the publick roads were infested with bands of Robbers and depredators, *some of the Jews of the above-mentioned villages together with others of their Brethren gallantly volunteered to conduct him safely through the Country and they accompanied him armed with swords and pistols all the way to Beyrout,* and such was the formidable and imposing appearance of this armed party that Sir Moses was in consequence distinguished by the title of King of the Jews. This armed party halted at the same quarter where I was staying, and I had the pleasure and the novelty of living in the midst of a little camp of Jewish warriors who would have proved a match for any strolling party of Arabs.*

According to the correspondent, "the faithfulness and most probably the courage too of the Jewish soldiers" had so impressed the "Russian Despot" that he had assigned them "to form a party of his bodyguard."[65]

As earlier pages have shown, extortion and *baksheesh,* or bribery, were rampant, and the Jews, who had no protection of their own as did the Christians, were most easily victimized. The historian-traveler Burckhardt recorded the unpredictability of their existence—even when their community was the "largest." During his visit of 1810–1816 in Safed, where the Jews had been "sacked" just a decade before, Burckhardt wrote,

> The town is built upon several low hills, which divide it into different quarters; of these the largest is inhabited exclusively by Jews, who esteem Szaffad as a sacred place. The whole may contain six hundred houses, of which one hundred and fifty belong to the Jews, and from eighty to one hundred to the Christians. . . . The town is governed by a Mutsellim, whose district comprises about a dozen villages. The garrison consists of Moggrebyns [North Africans]. . . .
>
> During the life of Djazzar Pasha [the Jews] were often obliged to pay heavy fines; at present they merely pay the Kharadj. Their conduct, however, is not so

*Emphasis added.

prudent as it ought to be, in a country where the Turks are always watching for a pretext to extort money; they sell wine and brandy to the soldiers of the town, almost publicly, and at their weddings they make a very dangerous display of their wealth.[66]

Despite the canards to the contrary, most Jews who clung to Judah-cum-Palestine were impoverished, and the burden of discriminatory taxes through all their insidious forms kept them poor, for the most part. Burckhardt reported that although there were some Jews of enough means in Safed to warrant their being pillaged, most young Jews who made their perilous way to Palestine were disillusioned when they came face to face with the conditions of the Holy Land for Jews. According to Burckhardt,

> . . . several of them have absconded from their parents, to beg their way to Palestine, but no sooner do they arrive in one or other of the four holy cities, than they find by the aspect of all around them, that they have been deceived.[67]

Hardships notwithstanding, the native Jews and new immigrants alike appear to have considered themselves transcended by living in their Holy Land. One letter, written by a group of new immigrants in 1810, was perhaps particularly illustrative of the point:

> Truly, how marvelous it is to live in the good country. Truly how wonderful it is to love our country. . . . Even in her ruin there is none to compare with her, even in her desolation she is unequaled, in her silence there is none like her. Good are her ashes and her stones.[68]

Perhaps it was that inexplicable joy at being there at all which sustained them in Palestine in the nineteenth century, and which led them to survive by forebearance where revolt would have led to extinction. In the mid-1800s James Finn, British Consul in Jerusalem, found:

> It was distressing to behold the timidity which long ages of repression had engendered. Many times a poor Jew would come for redress against a native, and when he had substantiated his case, and it had been brought by the consulate before the Turkish authorities, he would, in mere terror of future possible vengeance, withdraw from the prosecution, and even deny that any harm had been done to him; or if that was too manifest, declare that he could not identify the criminal, or that the witnesses could not be produced. Still, even then, the bare fact that some notice had been taken had a deterrent effect upon the criminals who had hitherto regarded the defenseless Jews as their special prey.[69]

In the 1830s havoc was created during an Egyptian reign of Palestine, and the Jews were persecuted brutally throughout the small country.[70] The Egyptian Pasha Mehmet Ali, after his conquest of Syria and Palestine, "oppressed the inhabitants of these countries more severely even than those of his own pashalic [district] in order to fill his coffers."[71]

The rebellion of the Druses caused violence and pillage of the Jews in Galilee and Safed, and when the Egyptian ruler Ibrahim Pasha levied conscription on the entire population in 1834, the inhabitants of Eastern Palestine crossed the Jordan River to join natives of Nablus, Hebron, and Bethlehem in the insurrection.

> Forty thousand fellahin rushed on Jerusalem. . . . The mob entered, and looted the city for five or six days. The Jews were the worst sufferers, their homes were sacked and their women violated.[72]

Now the Jews became victims of the Egyptian soldiers as well as the multi-ethnic "Arab" natives. That same year the Jews of Hebron were massacred by "Egyptian soldiers who came to put down a local Muslim rebellion."[73] And the Safed Jewish community was once again "brutally attacked by Muslim and Druzes"[74] who destroyed the printing presses which the Jews had built and used for centuries. "The types were converted into bullets" by the invaders from Nablus.[75]

The Jews under siege were as defenseless as their counterparts in the Arabic-speaking Muslim "Arab" world and as powerless as perhaps the black slaves called "Niggers" by the Southern whites—they too "knew what was good for them," and any attempt at redress for their grievances would only result in more extreme persecution. Both had to "keep their place."

Some assistance was attempted by those among the locally headquartered foreign diplomats who were sympathetic to the plight of the luckless *dhimmis* in Palestine.[76] The Christian infidels had long derived benefits from foreign protection due to the Christian dominance of the countries represented. But the Jews had to rely on the few representatives who were courageous enough to complain about the conditions and therefore confront the local authorities and interfere with the status quo. According to an eminent authority on the period, Professor M. Ma'oz, "A noticeable number of Christians and Jews, particularly children, were forced to adopt Islam,"[77] but even the converts were persecuted as Jews.

The earthquake that hit Safed in 1837 brought another onslaught from the surviving Muslims into the Jewish quarter, and the blood libel of Damascus in 1840 brought heightened waves of persecution and murder of Jews throughout Palestine, against which the foreign consulates could offer little protection.[78] But lest it be supposed that the foul canard was newly imported by the Europeans, the 1775 persecution of Jews in Hebron—which was based on the same old calumny—must be recalled.[79]

The receptive anti-Jewish masses who would later adopt and influence Nazism by their own *Muftism* in Palestine—calling it a "nationalistic" reaction to "Zionism"—were actually responding to centuries-long traditional religious hatred and discrimination.

For example, *before* the 1840 Damascus blood libel against the Jews, in one period of a brief few months the British Consul filed claim after lamenting claim of the unrelenting Muslim attacks on Jews. In one report, the Consul included the following complaint from a Jew, Joseph Amzalek:

As a British Subject I beg leave to address you the following statement of the manner in which I have this day been outraged by an Officer of the Pacha's Army—

About 4 o'clock this afternoon I was standing with my Son-in-law outside the door of my house which is nearly opposite the Castle—some of the miserable objects who have lately been taken here for the Army happened to be led out of the Castle—A number of Towns people collecting to look on, the Officer (of the grade of Captain) fell upon them with a large stick and drove them away—As I was standing at my own door with some other respectable persons at a considerable distance from the scene, there could have been no pretence for attacking me and yet the said officer returning from the crowd ran up and gave me such a blow with his stick as brought me to the ground, and had not Dr. Giorgio Grasso (also a British subject) who was standing by me interposed, he would have continued his blows. . . .[80]

Like a rape victim who is blamed for being there to be raped, in this case the victimized Jew was deemed by the British officer in charge to be the guilty party.* The official reply to the Jerusalem consul three months later was: "I think that Mr. Amzalek was in the wrong, and in great measure brought his difficulties upon himself, and I shall not therefore interfere farther in this case."[81]

Thus the status quo proceeded uninterruptedly.

In May 1839, for instance, the complaints registered with the British Foreign Office by Consul Young in Jerusalem were appalling. In one day, in one report:

I think it my duty to inform you that there has been a Proclamation issued this week by the Governor in the Jewish quarter—that no Jew is to be permitted to pray in his own house under pain of being severely punished—such as want to pray are to go into the Synagogue. . . .

There has also been a punishment inflicted on a Jew and Jewess—most revolting to human nature which I think it my duty to relate—

In the early part of this week, a House was entered in the Jewish Quarter, and a robbery was committed—the House was in quarantine—and the guardian was a Jew—he was taken before the Governor—he denied having any knowledge of the thief or the circumstances. In order to compel him to confess, he was laid down and beaten, and afterwards imprisoned. The following day he was again brought before the Governor, when he still declared his innocence. He was then burned with a hot iron over his face, and in various parts of the body—and beaten on the lower parts of his body to that extent that the flesh hung in pieces from him. The following day the poor creature died. He was a young Jew of Salonica about 28 years of age—who had been here but a very short time, he had only the week before been applying to enter my service.

A young man—a Jew—having a French passport—was also suspected—he fled—his character was known to be an indifferent one—his mother an aged woman was taken under the suspicion of concealing her son—She was tied up and beaten in the most brutal way . . .

*Consider the bombing of a Paris synagogue in 1980, where many Frenchmen perceived the Jewish victims as culprits and presented the bills for damages to the bombed-out synagogue's rabbi.

I must say I am sorry and am surprised that the Governor could have acted so savage a part—for certainly what I have seen of him, I should have thought him superior to such wanton inhumanity—but it was a Jew—without friends or protection—it serves well to show, that it is not without reason that the poor Jew, even in the nineteenth century, lives from day to day in terror of his life.[82]

One can only speculate unhappily about those acts of violence that went *unreported* by a predominantly intimidated Jewish society that had been long terrorized into silence.

Perhaps an account by Winston Churchill's favorite writer, A. W. Kinglake, best illustrates the climate of "protection" and "brotherhood" under which the Jews lived in Palestine "before the Zionists and Israel." It might be considered a particularly noteworthy perspective because of Kinglake's own admittedly ambivalent reactions toward Jews, vacillating between disdain and sympathy, and his delight and admiration for the "Mussulman" (Muslim) onslaught or "experiment." In the following excerpt from *Eothen,* published in 1844, Kinglake told of his own involvement with the Jews in the town of Safed sometime after the "insurrection of 1834":

> . . . At length I drew near to the city of Safet. . . . It is one of the holy cities of the Talmud; and according to this authority, the Messiah will reign there for forty years before He takes possession of Sion. The sanctity and historical importance thus attributed to the city by anticipation render it a favorite place of retirement for Israelites; of these it contains, they say, about four thousand, a number nearly balancing that of the Mohammedan inhabitants. I knew by my experience of Tabarieh [Tiberias] that a "holy city" was sure to have a population of vermin somewhat proportionate to the number of its Israelites, and I therefore caused my tent to be pitched upon a green spot of ground at a respectful distance from the walls of the town.
>
> When it had become quite dark (for there was no moon that night), I was informed that several Jews had secretly come from the city, in the hope of obtaining some help from me in circumstances of imminent danger. . . . It was arranged that the two principal men of the party should speak for the rest, and these were accordingly admitted into my tent. One of the two called himself the British Vice-Consul, and he had with him his consular cap; but he frankly said that he could not have dared to assume this emblem of his dignity in the daytime, and that nothing but the extreme darkness of the night rendered it safe for him to put it on upon this occasion. The other of the spokesmen was a Jew of Gibralter, a tolerably well-bred person, who spoke English very fluently.
>
> These men informed me that . . . about the beginning of that year [1834] a highly religious Mussulman called Muhammed Damoor went forth into the marketplace, crying with a loud voice and prophesying that on the fifteenth day of the following June the true Believers would rise up in just wrath against the Jews, and despoil them of their gold, and their silver, and their jewels. . . . When that day dawned, the whole Mussulman population of the place assembled in the streets, that they might see the result of the prophecy. Suddenly Mohammed Damoor rushed furious into the crowd, and the fierce shout of the prophet soon

ensured the fulfillment of his prophecy. Some of the Jews fled, and some remained, but they who fled and they who remained alike and unresistantly left their property to the hands of the spoilers. The most odious of all outrages, that of searching the women for the base purpose of discovering such things as gold and silver concealed about their persons, was perpetrated without shame. The poor Jews were so stricken with terror that they submitted to their fate, even where resistance would have been easy. In several instances a young Mussulman boy, not more than ten or twelve years of age, walked straight into the house of a Jew, and stripped him of his property before his face, and in the presence of his whole family.* When the insurrection was put down, some of the Mussulmans (most probably those who had got no spoil wherewith they might buy immunity) were punished, but the greater part of them escaped; none of the booty was restored, and the pecuniary redress which the Pasha had undertaken to enforce for them had been hitherto so carefully delayed that the hope of ever obtaining it had grown very faint. . . . the Jews complained; and either by the protection of the British Consul at Damascus, or by some other means, had influence enough to induce the appointment of a Special Commissioner—they called him "the Modeer"—whose duty it was to watch for and prevent anything like connivance on the part of the Governor, and to push on the investigation with vigour and impartiality. . . .

. . . the result was that the investigation had made no practical advance, and that the Modeer, as well as the Governor, was living upon terms of affectionate friendship with Mohammed Damoor, and the rest of the principal spoilers.

Thus stood the chance of redress for the past, but the cause of the agonizing excitement under which the Jews of the place now laboured was recent, and justly alarming: Mohammed Damoor had again gone forth into the market-place, and lifted up his voice, and prophesied a second spoliation of the Israelites. This was grave matter; the words of such a practical and clearsighted prophet as Mohammed Damoor were not to be despised. I fear I must have smiled visibly, for I was greatly amused, and even, I think, gratified at the account of this second prophecy. Nevertheless, my heart warmed towards the poor oppressed Israelites, and I was flattered, too, in the point of my national vanity at the notion of the far-reaching link by which a Jew in Syria, because he had been born on the rock of Gibralter, was able to claim me as his fellow-countryman. . . . It seemed to me that the immediate arrest of Mohammed Damoor was the one thing needful to the safety of the Jews, and I felt sure (for reasons which I have already mentioned in speaking of the Nablous affair) that I should be able to obtain this result by making a formal application to the Governor. I told my applicants that I would take this very step on the following morning; they were very grateful, and were *for a moment much pleased* at the prospect of safety thus seemingly opened to them, but the *deliberation of a minute entirely altered their views, and filled them with a new terror.* They declared that any attempt or pretended attempt on the part of the Governor to arrest Mohammed Damoor would certainly produce an immediate movement of the whole Mussulman population, and a consequent massacre and robbery of the Israelites. My visitors went out, and remained I know not how long consulting of their brethren, but all at last agreed that *their present*

*"It was after the interview which I am talking of, and not from the Jews themselves, that I learnt the fact."

perilous and painful position was better than a certain and immediate attack, and that if Mohammed Damoor was seized, their second estate would be worse than their first. I myself did not think that this would be the case, but I could not, of course, force my aid upon the people against their will, and moreover the day fixed for the fulfillment of this second prophecy was not very close at hand; a little delay, therefore, in providing against the impending danger would not necessarily be fatal. The men now confessed that although they had come with so much mystery and (as they thought) at so great risk to ask my assistance, they were unable to suggest any mode in which I could aid them, except, indeed, by mentioning their grievances to the Consul-General at Damascus. This I promised to do, and this I did.

My visitors were very thankful to me for my readiness to intermeddle in their affairs, and the grateful wives of the principal Jews sent to me many compliments, with choice wines and elaborate sweetmeats.

The course of my travels soon drew me so far from Safet that I never heard how the dreadful day passed off which had been fixed for the accomplishment of the second prophecy. If the predicted spoliation was prevented, poor Mohammed Damoor must have been forced, I suppose, to say that he had prophesied in a metaphorical sense. This would be a sad falling off from the brilliant and substantial success of the first experiment.*[83]

The above extract reveals not only the treatment of Jews that was tradition, but also the poignant, tenuous position of those Jewish communities who nonetheless remained in Palestine.

It was in such a predatory climate that the preposterous blood libel[84] against the Jews could thrive—a climate of "fraternity" and "peace" according to the Grand Mufti, his successor and relative Yasser Arafat, and even his more moderate Arab compatriots. It was that same climate that provided the life for Jews described in 1839 by British Consul Young:

> . . . scarcely a day passes that I do not hear of some act of Tyranny and oppression against a Jew—chiefly by the soldiers, who enter their Houses and *borrow* whatever they require without asking any permission—sometimes they return the article, but more frequently not. In two instances, I have succeeded in obtaining justice for Jews against Turks—But it is quite a new thing in the eyes of these people to claim justice for a Jew—and I have good reason to think that my endeavors to protect the Jews, have been—and may be for some little time to come, *detrimental* to influence with other classes—Christians as well as Turks. . . .
>
> Like the miserable dog without an owner he is kicked by one because he crosses his path, and cuffed by another because he cries out—to seek redress he is afraid, lest it bring worse upon him; he thinks it better to endure than to live in the expectation of his complaint being revenged upon him. Brought up from infancy to look upon his civil disabilities everywhere as a mark of degradation, his heart becomes the cradle of fear and suspicion—he finds he is trusted by none —and therefore he lives himself without confidence in any.[85]

*Emphasis added.

The Muslims' anti-Jewish indoctrination began at an early age, with added incentives from other cultures: one book reported the game "Burn the Jew," a Christian-Arab children's pastime at Lent in Jaffa in the 1830s.[86]

The hostilities surrounding the 1840 blood libel in Damascus inflamed Muslim and Christian[87] equally against Jews in Palestine, and were more widely known than other similar instances. The dreaded false charge, however, was dredged up in the Holy Land "on at least nine occasions" in the same region "in the nineteenth century alone."[88] As a result of the violent barrage upon the Jews in the Muslim world, which went "public" with the Damascus ritual murder accusation, British Jewish leader Sir Moses Montefiore helped organize the Alliance Israelite Universelle "to do philanthropic and educational work among the Jews in Arab countries." It undoubtedly hoped to offer some protection as well.

Under Western pressure and pleas from "Jewish notables to the Sultan," the Turkish authority issued an edict, commanding "full equality of Jews before the law and strict justice for them and their property before all courts of justice."[89]

In Palestine, the "Evil," which made the proclamation of "equality" for Jews no more than an ironic exercise in futility for the Holy Land, was reported:

> It is a fact that the Jewish Subjects . . . especially in Palestine, do not enjoy the privileges granted to them. . . . This Evil may in general be traced to the . . . following causes:
>
> I. To the absence of an adequate protection whereby they are more exposed to cruel and tyrannical treatment.
> II. *To the blind hatred and ignorant prejudices of a fanatical populace.*
> III. To the several peculiarities which alienate them from the other inhabitants.
> IV. To the starving state of numerous Jewish population, resident in Palestine, hitherto subsisting in a great measure upon the charity of their occidental Brethren.
>
> The weakness of the Porte on the one hand and on the other the dispersion of the Jews throughout so manifold a population prejudiced against them, together with the want of pecuniary resources and state of despondency occasioned by the existing distress, render the removal of the aforesaid evils impracticable if the above obstacles are allowed to continue. It is therefore *necessary* to fix upon *a place* which from its situation would be beyond the reach of fanatical attacks, in contact with European civilization—easily protected by the Porte,—and a spot to which the Jews might feel themselves attracted.*[90]

At the same time British Foreign Secretary Palmerston was encouraging the Sultan to allow Jews to settle on the land in Palestine. In 1840, he presented evidence to Constantinople from Jewish sources in England that,

*Emphasis added.

. . . no sooner should there be an opening to cultivate the soil in Palestine, than the Jews from the Russian Dominions would flow into it. . . . In mentioning to them the probability of a way being opened to their Nation to return to the land of their Fathers and to become cultivators of the soil, they became almost frantic with joy and thousands of Jews would have followed . . . their leader to Jerusalem.[91]

Palmerston suggested that it would be "highly advantageous to the Sultan" if "scattered" Jews were "induced to go and settle in Palestine."[92]

But the "Mussulman" population adamantly and "constantly manifested" its "state of feeling" in the Jerusalem environs, and the British Consul "begs aid to check this evil," against "Christians and Jews."

Reports from Sidon, Tyre, Acre and Caiffa [Haifa] complain of bigotry and outrages toward Christians: Confirmed by what is observed here in Jerusalem towards Christians and Jews. Executive too feeble and indifferent to act effectively.[93]

In 1841, just after the proclamation issuing "equal treatment" was issued to the Jews, Foreign Secretary Palmerston defended British encouragement of the new edict:

. . . the Turkish Government must know how difficult it is in any country to carry into strict effect at once or for a long time any new Laws which tend to prevent one part of the subjects of a State from oppressing another part *upon whom they have been accustomed to commit violence and injustice with impunity;* and the Turkish Ministers must also be aware *how difficult it would be for the Jews in Palestine to make their complaints known at Constantinople,* and unless the existence of abuses be brought to the knowledge of the Sovereign Power, it is impossible that any remedy can be applied to such abuses. For these reasons it is, and strictly *therefore in the interest of the Sultan himself,* that Her Majesty's Government have made this request to the Porte, and Her Majesty's Government cannot conceive that such an arrangement could be looked upon as in the slightest degree infringing upon the independence of the Sultan.*[94]

According to Muslim law, Jews could not give evidence against Muslims, nor could Christians. Lord Palmerston exhorted the Turkish Ambassador to England to engage the Sultan's immediate attention "for preventing the Muftis in Syria from acting on the obsolete and antiquated doctrine" of refusing to accept such evidence against Muslims.[95]

Emphasizing the waste of potential in Palestine, Foreign Secretary Palmerston further instructed his ambassador in Constantinople

. . . to impress upon the minds of the Turkish Ministers that it would be highly advantageous to the Sultan that the Jews who are scattered through other countries in Europe and Africa should be induced to go and settle in Palestine. . . .

*Emphasis added.

The Jews, Palmerston wrote, would bring "wealth" and "industry," which would "tend greatly to increase" Turkish resources and "promote the progress of civilization therein."

But, Palmerston noted, the Jews would never leave the European countries' "security" [sic] for the "violence, injustice and oppression to which the Jews have hitherto been exposed in the Turkish Dominions." If the Sultan could not "give the Jews some real and tangible security, he cannot expect the benefit which their immigration into Palestine would afford him."[96]

Another British official, Colonel George Gawler, published a booklet entitled *Tranquilization of Syria and the East. Observations and Practical Suggestions in furtherance of the Establishment of Jewish Colonies in Palestine; the most sober and sensible remedy for the miseries of Asiatic Turkey.*

On the same theory as Lord Palmerston's, Gawler promoted Jewish agricultural settlements with local autonomy, and national control by the British Consul coordinating with the Turks. He proposed the funding be given by a number of countries, who had ungratefully persecuted the Jews despite having learned their religion from Judaism.[97]

As though in defiance of the edict of "equality," another false ritual murder charge was hurled against the Jewish community in Jerusalem in March of 1847. The British Consul reported:

> . . . On Monday, 8th Instant—A Greek boy assaulted a Jewish boy in the street, the latter ran into a house to hide himself, but on leaving the house afterwards, found his adversary still lying in wait for him—he then threw a stone at him which cut his foot—The Greeks raised a tumult and declared that a Jewish boy had stabbed an innocent Christian with a knife. The case was brought before the Pasha, who refused to examine so childish a quarrel, and dismissed the complaint.
>
> On Thursday however the Greeks directly, and other Christians indirectly persisted in having the enormity further investigated . . . of the horrible crime so often imputed to the Jews—The Christians pleaded that their most venerated theologians in all ages had uniformly asserted this accusation, *The Moslem Mufti, Cadi, &c. asserted that their Sacred books declared the same indirectly and by implication,—* while the Jews appealed to their divine Law and its Expositors to prove that not only is such practice not enjoined, but that the principles universally pervading those writings are diametrically opposed to it—Finally they referred to the Firman received in 1841 from His Majesty the Sultan after the dreadful cruelties exercised on this same account in Rhodes and Damascus, which Firman declares that strict search had been made into all the Jewish writings and that no trace of such practice is there to be found.[98]

A Jewish visitor who made a pilgrimage to Palestine in 1847 reported the sorry situation and his fellow Jews' conditioning to their plight:

> They do not have any protection and are at the mercy of policemen and the pashas who treat them as they wish . . . they pay various taxes every now and then . . . their property is not at their disposal and they dare not complain about

an injury for fear of the Arabs' revenge. Their lives are precarious and subject to daily danger of death.[99]

The anti-Jewish sentiments sometimes took another, more devious form:

There is another species of persecution to which the Jews are subject here. . . .
So soon as the Plague is reported to be in the City, the Jews at once become the object of cupidity, to every employee in the quarantine service, who, with the Native practitioners in medicine, rob and oppress them to the last degree. From one individual alone, of the better class, they succeeded lately in obtaining 4,000 piastres, equal to L40 sterling, in bribes—his son was sick with fever—they declared it to be the Plague—set a guard on his house, deprived him of all means of obtaining medical assistance—the patient died, and then, on his refusing to satisfy their demands—they threatened to burn everything in his house. *This My Lord is not a solitary instance.*
What the Jew has to endure, at all hands, is not to be told.*[100]

In 1848 about four thousand armed peasants and "numerous Bedouin allies acted as gangs for "two great chiefs," and lawlessness spread. Hebron's local governor was overthrown by an oppressive chief whose brutal tactics earned him the admiration of Jerusalem's Pasha and the award of the "robe of honour." In Hebron, one of the holy Jewish cities, Jews were still "helpless" and "plundered" and the new ruler managed to confiscate booty of those trying to flee by sending "agents to rob travellers on the road."[101]

In the following few decades (1848–1878) scores of incidents involving anti-Jewish violence, persecution, and extortions filled page after page of documented reports from the British Consulate in Jerusalem. A chronology would be overwhelming, but perhaps a few extracts from those complaints will show the pattern of terror that continued right into the period of the major Jewish immigration beginning about 1878.

May, 1848: I have the honor to report that after the disturbance in the Church of the Holy Sepulchre Easter Eve, in beating the Jew who had imprudently entered there—The Prussian Acting Consul here, informed me that he had been told by the Pasha, and also by the Greek Patriarch, that a Firman exists, which allows Christians to beat Jews if found within that Church, or even if passing along the street in front of it—and which declares that in case of a Jew being killed under such an infliction, the price of blood should be rated at only ten paras—value about three farthings.[102]

March, 1849: Reporting the complaint of a Jew . . . of being assaulted and stabbed by a soldier, while his house was searched and his females beaten. . . .[103]

September, 1850: Last month I visited Hebron to do what I could for the protection of the Jews. . . . Abderahhman [a "brigand chief"] vexes them with irregular extortions, but in return he keeps them in security from other oppressors,

*Emphasis added.

however He has had himself enrolled on the books of the Jewish Treasury, as a pensioner for 100 piastres a month, and always sends for his pension two days before the day of due.

During my last visit there I had a Moslem summarily bastinadoed in the open street, for pulling a Jew's beard—the Mutesellim in his eagerness to satisfy me, inflicted the punishment with his own hands, to my great astonishment. Abderrahhman was absent at Dura but one of his sons was present at the scene. This forms a strange contrast to the fact of the Austrian Jewish Agent being frequently beaten in the streets there. . . .[104]

July, 1851: It is my duty to report to Your Excellency that the Jews in Hebron have been greatly alarmed by threats of the Moslems there at the commencement of Ramadan—For several days my Cancelliere staid there with two Kawasses and obtained from the Governor Abderrahhman the punishment of some offenders: but others were released from prison on the self-same night of their condemnation.

The Cancelliere reports that the old feuds between the partisans of Abderrahhman and his brothers still exist—that the partisans of the latter steal cattle by force of arms during the night from Hebron itself, and that they did so close to his tent—also that in one day the vines were cut down from twenty feddans of vineyard—but that such proceedings are sure to cease instantly on every approach of Abderrahhman himself, which however is not frequent.

The Jews having complained that a freed slave named Saad Allah was more obnoxious to them than any other person in Hebron,—and that Abderrahhman had released him almost immediately after sentencing him to imprisonment. . . .
. . . the enormous avarice of Abderrahhman is peculiarly oppressive to them.[105]

December, 1851: . . . the murder of a Jew named Gershon ben Abraham, under English Protection, in Jerusalem, . . .
. . . the victim was extricated from the well . . . he was found to be stabbed in the throat, heart and ribs, besides injured in a horrible manner for the mere purpose of torture. . . .

A Moslem (he whose house I had examined in the morning) named Mohammed Damiatti, was immediately arrested on suspicion of having perpetrated the murder. . . .

The distress of the bereaved family is very great—it is not too much to expect that Moslems will prefer claims and swear falsely in matters of debt and credit, as the poor man carried his ledger about with him, and this has not been found —and it is remarkable that his father was some years ago murdered in a Moslem house in Saloniki, and his only brother killed in Jerusalem two years ago by a fall from a scaffold.[106]

December, 1851: . . . the Samaritans of Nablus . . . consist of about thirty-five taxable men, with a synagogue and sacred books. . . .

They have probably for many generations, and especially within the last century, been exposed to cruel persecutions from the dominant Moslems—and Nablus is always noted as an especially fanatic town. . . .

They generally contrive to have the cleverest man belonging to them employed as government Secretary for the district, by which means they have warded off much of fiscal oppression, just as Jews do in other countries, and Copts in Egypt—but even this has not been able to protect them from violence, murder and spoliation in their houses or streets in past times. . . .

I am informed by a Christian in Nablus that there is too much reason to fear evil consequences from the loss of their Secretary, as the Moslems are reviling them in the streets with menaces for the future.[107]

May, 1852: . . . I proceeded to Hebron and lodged there in a Jewish house. The Jews were all so alarmed . . . that they would tell me nothing of news: they protested that Abderrahhman had done no harm to any one, no houses had been rifled &c. and one of the leading Rabbis implored me not to inform Abderrahhman if he should visit me, that I had come to protect the Jews, as he would inevitably punish them the more for it after my departure. . . .

As for the accusations preferred by Abderrahhman against the Effendis here —I cannot tell how true they are—but I know that these personages are constantly taking bribes in other cases, the sums however which are laid against each seem incredibly large. I should rather imagine that much of the bribery money was spent in Damascus and Beyroot.[108]

November, 1852: Having learned that the peasantry levy of 4000 men from the Nablus district had committed excesses in the houses of British protected Jews in Tiberias I repaired thither, to induce the commander to keep better order. . . . Remonstrance was made against petty thefts "and of their having brought their horses and asses during the rain into the Jewish Synagogues."[109]

July, 1853: . . . The Christians and Jews of Jerusalem were in a state of absolute terror, and especially on the preceeding day had been announcing to each other house to house that the Moslems were to massacre them after the prayers at noon. Persons shut themselves up in their houses, and shops were closed, and some persons are still ill in bed from the effect of that day's fear.[110]

October, 1853: The Jews in their Quarter of the city have had to suffer many insults of late from town's people of which I only hear some time after their occurence, as the subjects of the violence are afraid to acquaint me with the circumstances, lest they should draw upon themselves greater injuries by way of revenge after the Consul has obtained redress.[111]

December, 1853: [Regarding] the Algerine Jews of Caiffa [Haifa] . . . I beg to represent to Your Lordship that the blessing of British Protection is a boon of inestimable value to these people. It would be a blessing to be exempted from Turkish oppression at any time, and peculiarly so at the present period, when fanaticism is liable at any minute to break out into violence and when the local governors are endeavouring to extort money by every possible means. And these people fear that if left to Turkish rule they will be required to pay arrears of taxes for all the past years of their residence in this country. . . .

A similar renunciation of Algerine Jews has been made in Safed, Tiberias and Shefa Amer as shown in Enclosure No. 2. . . .

A peculiarity of the French Consulates as far as they have come within my observation, is that they always show a strong desire to get rid of Jewish Subjects. I have had frequent evidences of this in Jerusalem, where that desire has been often expressed to me—and in Caiffa I regret to add that the Jews have complained of direct persecution from the French and Turkish authorities combined.[112]

July, 1858: I have the honour to report that in consequence of a series of disgusting insults offered to Jews and Jewesses in Hebron, I obtained such Orders as I could from the Pasha's Agent in this city, during His Excellency's absence —which I sent by my Dragoman Rosenthal and a Kawass. . . .

The streets of the town were paraded by fanatic Durweeshes—and during my stay there a Jewish house was forcibly entered by night, iron bars of the window broken, and heavy stones thrown from invisible hands at every person approaching the place to afford help.

One of the Members of the Council affirmed that they were not obliged to obey Orders from the Pasha's Deputy—and *another declared his right derived from time immemorial in his family, to enter Jewish houses, and take toll or contributions at any time without giving account.*

When others present in the Council exclaimed against this he said—"Well then I will forbear from taking it myself, but things will happen which will compel the Jews to come and kiss my feet to induce me to take their money."*[113]

November, 1858: . . . although the thief had previously confessed to the robbery in presence of Jews, the Kadi would not proceed without the testimony of two Moslems—when the Jewish witnesses were offered, he refused to accept their testimony—and the offensive term adopted towards Jews in former times (more offensive than Giaour for Christians) was used by the Kadi's servants.

I have no doubt of being able to set all this to rights (except perhaps the matter of Jewish testimony in that Court) but such circumstances exhibit the working of the present Turkish government in Jerusalem.[114]

May, 1863: . . . Galilee, comprising the modern towns of Nazareth, Safed and Tiberias, in which two latter places there are living upwards of 600 Jews in the enjoyment of British protection. The existence of so many protected subjects in these retired spots, residing as they do in the midst of a Moslem population, naturally gives rise to numerous questions with the local Governors who are prone to *oppress them unless their interests are constantly cared for.* My predecessor was required to make an Annual tour to those towns, in order that his appearance from time to time amongst our protected subjects there might keep within proper bounds *the ill-concealed aversion which their presence never fails to excite amongst their Moslem neighbors . . .* *[115]

March, 1864: . . . the circumstances attending the death of the British subject Peter Meshullam, and to try Abdalla Abu Kakoora, the individual charged with his murder. . . . they declare, as the result of their enquiry, that P. Meshullam

*Emphasis added.

died in consequence of the fall from his mare, and, consequently that Abdalla is innocent of charges preferred against him.

I confess I was hardly prepared for such a finding and verdict. . . . I addressed to His Excellency a reply conveying my entire dissent from the decision of the Commission . . .[116]

June, 1864: . . . Her Majesty's Government have little doubt that Mr. Mashullan's death was caused by violence and not by a fall from his horse. . . .[117]

The tradition of contemptuous "fraternity" continued—a tradition that illuminates what measure of credibility may be given to modern promises concerning a "Palestinian Arab state," which would "value people, independent of race and religion."[118]

Over the decades, as the nineteenth-century *dhimmi* Jews were reinforced by successive waves of Jewish pioneers, anti-Jewish violence erupted spasmodically in the Holy Land. Observers labeled these outbreaks as "European anti-Semitism," "Ottomanism," and later, "anti-Zionism."*

British officials attributed the violence—so-called "disturbances"—to the manifestation of "Arab nationalism." The British, however, were never able to discover any manifestation of such nationalism on the part of the Arabs in Palestine other than the oppression and intolerance shown toward their *dhimmi.* This narrowly based "nationalism" of violence continued to grow as the Jews continued to struggle out of *dhimmi* status toward freedom and equality. British investigators were eventually forced to concede, and officially to note, that "Arab nationalism in Palestine has been artificially puffed up. . . . Only a little firmness is needed to deflate it."[119] Unlike the "insurgent nationalism elsewhere,"

in Palestine Arab nationalism is inextricably interwoven with antagonism to the Jews.[120]

Yet by so perverse a rationale was a movement of enmity dignified and the legend of Palestinian nationalism initiated.

*See Chapter 10.

10

The Population Under the Turks: Mid-Nineteenth Century to 1918

> The same Arab politicians who protested that
> they cared nothing for the money the Jews
> brought into the country. . . . showed no such
> contempt for money when it came to the
> treatment of their own peasantry.
> —The Reverend James Parkes, *Whose Land?*

> The Palestinians who are today's refugees in
> the neighboring countries . . . know all this . . .
> that their present nationalist exploiters are the
> worthy sons of their feudal exploiters of
> yesterday, and that the thorns of their life are of
> Arab, not Jewish origin.
> —Abdel Razak Kader, 1969

We have seen strong evidence that the Holy Land was inhabited only sparsely in the nineteenth century. For centuries the non-Jewish, particularly the Muslim, peoples who did inhabit the land had been largely composed of a revolving immigrant population of diverse ethnic origins who could not possibly have constituted a substantial indigenous "Palestinian" population, much less a nation of inhabitants for "a thousand" or "two thousand years." Rather, the majority of those inhabitants were migrants and peasants originating from other lands, many of whom had been unscrupuluously exploited by feudal or absentee landlords, moneylenders, and corrupt officials of the Turkish government. They in turn traditionally exploited and preyed upon the oppressed *dhimmi* Jewish population.

How does the history of those relationships mesh with the Arab claim that "displacement" and "landlessness" of Arab "natives" was caused by the Jews? If that claim is false, it is long-perpetuated. As such, it must be traced to its beginnings, in the Palestine of Turkish rule, when the Arab notables' charge of "Jews displacing Arabs" was devised.

It was 1878. Harsh conditions prevailed.[1] Into Palestine[2] came groups of Circassians, Algerians, Egyptians, Druses, Turks, Kurds, Bosnians, and others. One historian deduced that of 141,000 settled Muslims living in all of Palestine (all areas) in 1882, "at least 25% of those 141,000 . . . were newcomers or descendants of those who arrived after 1831 (Egyptian conquest)."[3]

A prominent British official had observed as early as 1840 that the barren Palestinian land needed the collective political return of the Jews:

> If we consider their return in the light of a new establishment or colonization of Palestine, we shall find it to be the cheapest and the safest mode of supplying the wastes of these depopulated Regions. . . .[4]

Throughout the nineteenth century Palestine's occupying government had officially settled many foreigners. The "Egyptian" conqueror Ibrahim Pasha, son of the Turkish-speaking Ottoman Muhammad Ali, had "left behind him permanent colonies of Egyptians at Beisan, Nablus, Irbid, Acre and Jaffa . . ." In Jaffa, "some five hundred Egyptian soldiers' families established a new quarter."[5] Into Jaffa alone, then, "at least two thousand people" had been imported.[6] In 1844, "the American expedition under Lynch" recorded fewer than 8,000 "Turks" in Jaffa in a population of 13,000.[7] In 1857, Elizabeth Finn, the wife of James Finn, British Consul in Jerusalem, reported that "Greek and Latin foreigners hostile to Turkish power are endeavoring to grasp piecemeal and occupy the Holy Land so valuable to them both. The corrupt Pashas and Effendis [notables] allow them for [*sic*] money to do so as they list."[8] In 1858 Consul Finn reported the "Mohammedans of Jerusalem" were "scarcely exceeding one-quarter of the whole population."[9]

In 1860 Algerian tribes moved from Damascus *en masse* to Safed, and the Muslims there were "mostly descended from these Moorish settlers and from Kurds who came earlier to the city."[10]

In that same year, the British Consul wrote:

> From Caiffa [Haifa] I learn the arrival of about 6,000 of the Beni Sukhr Arabs at Tiberias (who are very seldom seen on this side of the Jordan). . . .[11]

> . . . I have omitted to mention the increase of Mahometan agriculturalists and pastoral Arabs from countries of Barbary, forming a small colony in the district north of Lake Tiberias.[12]

A report on "Disturbances" noted that "The Plain of Esdraelon is full of Turkoman Bedouins. . . ."[13] The restored Turkish government was continuously adding its own numbers in order to replenish and guard its administration, as had the Egyptians before them, as had dozens of conquerors over the centuries.[14]

> I have the honour to report to your Lordship that the excess of the Druses in the Lebanon remaining unchecked by The Turkish Government, the same practices are being extended southwards, among the Metawalis.
>
> These are a sect of Mahometans differing from the orthodoxy of the Turks, inhabiting a hilly district south of the Lebanon; their creed is the same as that of the Persians, and called the Sheah.
>
> . . . but now they are acting on their own account. They have plundered the

large village of Bassa on the verge of the plain of Acre, and plundered the village of Kefir Beraan near Safed. . . .[15]

Landlords imported workers to keep up their great areas, but the peasants and former nomads who came were subjected to the robbery of the usurers, until they ran off, to be replaced by new immigrants.[16]

Despite the constant immigration into Palestine, the land remained largely depopulated. However observers, travelers, and field workers may have differed[17] in their observations—one found "fertility" and "the flush of green on the desert,"[18] while another found Sharon and the Upper Galilee barren[19]—records descriptive of Palestine concur on the state of depopulation and of the official wholesale importing of newly arrived émigrés who continued to constitute a great part of the populace that did exist there.

As historians have noted, "The real source of the interest in the problem was the condition of Palestine":[20] "empty"[21]—"silent"[22]—"waste"—"ruin."[23] Between 1840 and 1880 "writing travellers learnt on the spot . . . to mistrust and hate the Turk and despise the Muslim population."

The village lands belonged in reality to the crown . . . if uncultivated.[24] The population was hopelessly incompetent and lethargic, owing to the taxation.[25]

In Jerusalem, 1859, the British consul identified part of the "thinly scattered population":[26]

The Mohammedans of Jerusalem are less fanatical than in many other places, owing to the circumstances of *their numbers scarcely exceeding one quarter of the whole population*—and of their being surpassed in wealth *(except among the Effendi class)* in trade and manufactures by both Jews and Christians.*[27]

At the same time, an official report on "Disturbances" affirmed that *"the Mahometan population is dying out, I can scarcely say slowly,*" and that the government had to supply a populace to "places formerly unknown." (Note below the reference to *"not sufficient"* numbers of "Mohametans"—*Muslims*— *immigrating* at the *same* time as the *"large numbers"* of *Jews*):

Hence, for the present *we are supplied* with low-bred ignorant Turks, reigning in small towns or rural districts, and farming taxes. . . . While the Jews from Russia come also in large numbers and settle in Jerusalem and Safed . . . I cannot tell whether the recent immigration of Algerine Mohametans in the North is invited or fostered by Turkish Governors. These bring fanaticism with them, but their numbers are not sufficient as yet.*[28]

However distasteful he found the impoverished Arab immigrants who were "supplied," the British Consul complained that there were too few inhabitants of any sort in Palestine. "Palestine," he reported, was almost "empty of inhabi-

*Emphasis added.

tants," and urgently needed a "body of population irrespective of religious considerations."[29] In fact, another official British report—contradicting the alleged
grounds for its own future policy*—attested to the abandonment of the land
when renewed Jewish development began. In one area, for example:

> In 1878 Commission of Enquiry visited Beisan, as did another Commission
> 50 years later, to report on land situated there. The commission appeared to have
> reported that they found the lands in disorder, exposed to raids by marauding
> Bedouin from across the Jordan, abandoned by the cultivators and only scantily
> cultivated.
>
> There is, then, evidence for assuming that it is doubtful that any of the
> present-day cultivators can prove their occupation before 1870.[30]

Meanwhile, the Jewish population had been growing. They were the majority
in Safed and Tiberias by 1851,[31] and by the late 1850s Jews formed at least half
of the population of Jerusalem. Most of them were the "class called sephardem,"[32]
and the Jews "greatly exceed the Moslems in number."[33]

The Turkish Sultan had enacted laws that promised "every encouragement
to the cultivation of the land."[34] In 1856, Sir Moses Montefiore was granted an
edict by the Sultan permitting Jews to buy land in Palestine.[35] At mid-nineteenth
century, a "considerable number" of Jewish immigrants had come and settled—
in the four holy cities of Jerusalem, Safed, Hebron, and Tiberias, largely—but also
on the land.[36] (They were not the first European, or Ashkenazi, Jews to join the
native Sephardim; following the 1769 earthquake at Safed, "a new influx" of
Russian Jews had refounded the town, about 1776.)[37]

In 1860 Sir George Gawler, a non-Jewish "Zionist," one of a group in England who had been staunchly advocating Jewish nationalism for decades, wrote:

> I should be truly rejoiced to see in Palestine a strong guard of Jews established
> in flourishing agricultural settlements and ready to hold their own upon the
> mountains of Israel against all aggressors.
>
> I can wish for nothing more glorious in this life than to have my share in
> helping them to do so.[38]

By the 1870s, despite the traditional attacks—"sometimes to death"—on
Palestinian Jews by "their Muslim neighbors," the situation was reportedly more
secure.[39] Jews had "more redress."[40] And foreign-born Jewish pioneers were
coming to join the Jewish *fellahin* who had clung to Palestine's soil.

> The Jewish fellaheen—those who have worked the land for centuries . . . are not
> differentiated in their external appearance, their dress, their language or their
> daily life, from their non-Jewish neighbors.[41]

Contrary to other parts of the Ottoman Empire of the nineteenth century, in
Judah-cum-Palestine Jews had remained on the Holy Land.

*See Chapter 14 and 15.

A significant characteristic of theirs [Jews] is that, *except in Palestine,* they are almost all city dwellers.*[42]

Together they were beginning the Jewish development of depopulated land, decades before Theodor Herzl's "Zionism" was implemented in 1901. The newcomers' settlement of newly purchased areas would enable many native Palestinian Jews to shed the historically persecuted, poverty-stricken *dhimmi* existence.[43]

But Jews had lived principally in *urban* areas of the Holy Land—their "sacred" Jewish cities.[44] However "preferable" it might have been to hire Jews for land development, Jewish agricultural labor was scarce. Furthermore, most who were available were totally inexperienced and nearly useless. For generations in many countries Jews had not been permitted to own land, and most Jews in the Holy Land had been relegated to accepting religious charity as a means to survive. By 1859, however, the British Consul could observe that

> The Jews are increasing in numbers, and the Rabbis tightening the ecclesiastical control; yet the mechanical class among them are learning, though slowly, to work for their own living, instead of depending solely for subsistence upon alms from Europe, distributed by the Rabbis.[45]

The "principle of using exclusively Jewish labor" would take longer to introduce to some areas.[46] One pioneer supposedly commented,

> The transformation of a "tribe of *schnorrers*" [beggars, Yiddish] . . . into a new breed of Spartan, self-reliant, technically accomplished tillers and reapers could not be accomplished overnight.[47]

In 1878, Petach Tikvah, the first modern Jewish colony, was founded, principally by native Palestinian Jews from Jerusalem.[48] Jews such as Edmond Rothschild believed projects should be "carried out with Jewish rather than Arab labour," even though "relatively few Jewish manual labourers could be found in Jaffa or Petach Tikva," and those were "at least twice as expensive as their Arab counterparts."[49] As a consequence, on the new settlement non-Jews were hired to assist for a time with the reclamation work by which the Jews would transform the country.

Many of the Arab laborers hired were new immigrants themselves. "After 1870," for instance, the Turks' "forward policy . . . included the planting of Circassian colonies" in the country.[50] Circassians "surrounded" the Jewish settlement of Sedjera, which had been purchased from an "absentee Arab landlord" in the late 1890s.[51]

At Hadera, founded in 1891, Egyptian workers were contracted because there was not enough local Arab labor, and those few locals available were not willing to run the "risk of malaria and yellow fever." At Zikhron Yaacov, founded in 1882, there were twenty-one Jewish workers to six Arab workers in 1893; five

---

*Emphasis added.

years later, in 1898, there were twenty-seven Jews to twenty-one Arabs.[52]

And in 1889, the forty Jewish families in the Jewish settlement Rishon l'Tsion (founded in 1882) had been followed by more than ten times as many Arab families from Egypt and elsewhere. The following letter from a pioneer provides a vivid illustration:

> In Rishon L'tzion, there are now forty Jewish families, and most of them are financially supported by the noble. . . . Besides this forty, more than four hundred families are settled in the areas surrounding the moshava. The Arab village of Sarafand that stood ruined to the south of the moshava (Rishon L'tzion) is now called Srefand Harib, and is a large, spreadout village; many Bedouin and Egyptian families have settled within it. Those who left their villages to come here all find work. They, along with their wives, daughters and sons have split up into a wide variety of trades and vocations. Dozens of families have gathered in Bet Dagon (Badazshak), in Yadzor, in Safria, in Srafand Amar, in Agar and elsewhere (a few thousand dunam that was, and until today is, desolate and empty and used for putting sheep and bulls out to graze). Those who have come to the area are wretchedly poverty-stricken and destitute, and came with nothing to plant. Grains (income) were taken by the government, and they were left lacking of all. About one thousand Arabs work on occasion and (during the winter in Rishon), and how many in the villages? We ourselves are giving them plough blades that are sharpened—into the hand of those who someday may stand as enemies against us.[53]

By 1897, at Petach Tikvah, one of the largest Jewish settlements, Jews were in a "rotating work force of some thirty-two hands" in an attempt to "avoid the need for Arab labour," and strengthen the spirit of the settlers.[54] Still, in 1914, Petach Tikvah's population would number 2,600 Jewish settlers, 600 resident Arab workers, and 1,100 "floating" Arabs.[55]

Jewish Development and the Arabs

Quickly the opportunities for the Arab migrants and immigrants had become evident to three critical Arab groups: 1) the masses of traditionally "landless" impoverished wanderers who are endemic to the Middle East—in Sir John Hope Simpson's words, "He goes to any spot where he thinks he can find work";[56] 2) the former landed Arab peasants, who had been rendered landless, sucked dry by Arab moneylenders, absentee landlords, *effendis* (notables) or feudal-lord families, and Turkish taxes; 3) the *effendis,* who were selling land to the Jews at astronomical profits, and at the same time "losing the sweets of office"[57]—their viselike hold over the wages of the Arab migrant-peasants who made them rich. It is this last group, a disproportionately powerful few families, which would, on the one hand, encourage the Jews' purchase of land, and, on the other hand, incite racist violence against the Jewish presence. While the *effendi* Arabs coveted the profits, they sought to prevent Jews from offering the advantages that would set free Arab laborers throughout the neighboring areas, who flooded into Jewish-settled areas as they learned of the better wages and unparalleled opportunities there.

202 THE CREATION OF YESTERDAY

In the early nineteenth century, particularly the 1830s, the village sheikhs and religious notables had been nearly locally autonomous under Turkish rule in Palestine. The corruption rampant in earlier centuries continued to flourish. Despite the conquest of the Egyptian Ibrahim Pasha at Acre, one historian notes, "the chiefs and religious notables . . . were the true masters of the country."[58] Their power was directly drawn from their role as tax collectors for the Turkish Empire, a position that was generally inherited. With the advent of Ottoman reform measures in mid-century came a new method of collecting taxes and an attempt to reduce the power of the village chiefs. The chiefs' loss was the great gain of influence by the urban Muslim first families, who not only wielded political power in their districts, but concentrated in their coffers the wealth of landed property.[59]

When the first wave of Jewish pioneer immigrants arrived, this small cluster of Arab notables had already ascended to power, and as their influence increased, so did the number of land parcels they controlled.[60] At the end of the century the *effendis'* group controlled most of the private land and "bought [additional] stretches of land" for speculation, "selling them as soon as their value went up."[61]

> Thus an Arab capitalist from Egypt bought valuable holdings in the regions of Beisan and Samakh.[62]

Most of the land purchased by the Jews came from two sources. One was foreign absentee landlords:

> Virtually all of the Jezreel Valley, for example, belonged in 1897 to only two persons: the eastern portion to the Turkish Sultan, and the western part to the richest banker in Syria, Sursuk "the Greek."[63]

The other sellers were the notables—*effendis.* The *effendis* "rarely" lived on their own lands—"The fields of Moab, for instance, belonged for the most part to rich effendis" from Hebron.[64] The *effendis* now collected taxes for the Turkish administration, and they controlled the populace from their seats on the governing councils. They were known, in Arabic, as "a'yan"—"eyes."[65] They were increasingly the "fist" as well.

Turkish Restrictions: Nature and Consequences

The greatest areas of land in the country were in the state domain,[66] in depopulated and "abandoned" condition according to official British investigation and traveler alike. Yet by the 1870s the local Turkish ruler of the Jerusalem district enforced laws restricting the entry of Jewish immigrants into that one area which Jews were then most actively developing. In addition, he attempted to create obstacles for those Jews already in the country, blocking the sale of land and its use by Jews.[67]

With encouragement from the Arab notables, the Turkish government began more actively to limit Jewish immigration. At the time when Jews most needed their own laborers so that Jews could once again become self-sufficient on what they considered their natural soil, Jewish immigration was severely restricted.[68] Arab laborers from impoverished areas both within Palestine east and west of the Jordan River, and from other lands—Egypt, Syria, Sudan, Libya, and others— found their way in to gain the higher wages paid by the Jews.* While Arabs were moving in, Jews were being kept out.

Because Christians and Jews had to depend on foreign relief for their subsistence, most of Jerusalem's populace was reported in 1880 to be "mendicants and beggars."[69] The years 1880 to 1884 brought the Egyptian War, cholera, and other plagues, all of which contributed to a severe economic backslide.[70] According to the United States Consul in 1890, "depression" had become a "chronic ailment."[71]

It was into such sanctuary that the Jews from Russia and Rumania fled from persecution in the 1880s. The American Consul reported that not even a thousand among the estimated 40,000 Jews in Palestine in 1881 were agriculturalists,[72] and that there had been a "partial failure of the various Jewish colonies near [Jaffa]."[73] Jewish immigration was at times limited and other times totally forbidden by Turkish restrictions, already in effect in 1880–1881,[74] and continuing in varying degrees of harshness until the Turks' defeat in 1918 at the end of World War I by the British. The reasons given by historians for the Turks' forbidding Jews to enter in large numbers, or to buy adequate land for settlement, vary.[75]

The British traveler Laurence Oliphant, who had proposed a Jewish development in Palestine on the Jordan River's East Bank (now Jordan) in 1879, surmised that the anti-Jewish forces in Constantinople and the clash between Turkey and England over Egypt inspired the bans.[76] Palestinian Jews blamed each other for the immigration restrictions—local Sephardic Jews felt threatened by newly arrived Ashkenazi Jews, who might further upset the Muslims; pauperized Jews feared their alms would be diminished by the newcomers. They also suspected that the Mutasarrif, Rauf Pasa, had instigated the restrictions himself, since he reportedly found Jews distasteful.[77] According to an exhaustive study of the Ottoman policy restricting Jewish immigration, the "real reasons" were the Ottoman fear of "another national problem in the Empire," and their reluctance to allow more foreign nationals "in its domain."[78]

Whatever the causes, the fact remains that

every sale from local owner to Jew was subject to endless graft in Palestine and in Constantinople, and titles were withheld on one pretext or the other.[79]

The result was that "the purchase price of a tract of land at Atlit, near Haifa, *rose eight times* over between 1886 and 1892.†"[80]

One report in 1887 noted that

*See Chapter 12.
†Emphasis added.

The restraints the Turkish Government makes against the Jews coming to Palestine are becoming gradually severe. When coming, they are allowed only to stay one month, and then have to return; when not returning themselves they are sent back by the police and such desiring to become Turkish subjects could formerly do so without much difficulty, now a very high tax has been imposed.[81]

Because of the stringent enforcement of existing laws beginning in July of 1891, barely a single Jew settled in Palestine for a whole year.[82] Some historians claim that Turkish restrictions anticipated and preceded Arab leaders' awareness of how the Jews' settlements might liberate the peasantry.[83]

Other scholars believe that it was the Arab-Muslim protests against the Jews which had provoked or incurred the following restrictions:

> [Jewish] immigrants will be able to settle as scattered groups throughout the Ottoman Empire, *excluding Palestine*. They must submit to all the laws of the Empire and become Ottoman subjects.*[84]

Whether the announcement of the restrictions was fostered or merely encouraged by Arab leaders' sentiment, the history of the traditional Arab-Muslim racial hostility, suspicion, and violence toward Jews in Palestine indicates that the *effendis* were not displeased by the prohibition of Jews. However, the *effendis* must have suffered mixed emotions. On one hand, by offering living wages, the infidel Jews were indeed interfering with the traditional extortionate payments that *effendis* could exact from the Arab migrants they exploited and displaced. On the other hand, the enormous profits from land sales, often transacted in some measure despite restrictions, were tantalizing to the powerful absentee landlords.

On one occasion, king of moneylenders and landowner Elias Sursuq of Beirut, was "upbraided" by a Jew "in his own office in Beirut" in 1906, for exploiting the *fellah's* oppression. The Jew, as a result of his civic concerns, paid more for less land.[85]

As for the Turks, in 1907 a "prominent Turkish official," when told by the British Consul in Jerusalem that there were twelve million Jews in the world, exploded, " 'Good Lord! They are not all coming to Palestine, are they?' "[86] The Turks seem to have operated on that premise from the first. They had become "absolutely opposed to the settlement of the Jews, and the more Jews settled, the greater would be their opposition."[87]

One example of Turkish diligence and intentions was Constantinople's reactions to a tiny group of Russian Jewish "Lovers of Zion" (Hovevei Zion), whose boat arrived at the Turkish capital on its way to Jaffa in June 1882. The Turkish decree issued two months earlier had rendered their entry into Palestine illegal, but fourteen of them[88] (there had been only eighteen in all), who called themselves BILU,†[89] defied the law and sailed for Jaffa.[90] The Turkish government, on that

---

*Emphasis added.

†Hebrew acronym of the Hebrew initials representing the biblical command "House of Jacob, Come you and let us go."

same day, sent word to Jerusalem, "forbidding Russian, Rumanian, and Bulgarian Jews to land at Jaffa or Haiffa,"[91] and prohibited the "Biluim" from entering the "holy" cities in which Palestinian Jewry was then still largely based.[92]

The "Biluim" hopefuls managed to remain, however, and settled first in the Jewish colony of Rishon l'Tsion.[93] Finally, in 1884, the BILU gave up "the ideal of a colony based on the principles of democracy . . . which would serve as a focal point in the settlement of Palestine . . ."[94] and nine of them settled into the Gedera colony. The Biluim, like many of the earlier idealists, had found the Turks' land obstructions, the harassment of "Arab neighbors," the extreme physical travail, and the pressure to join the established Jewish colonies all to be insurmountable.[95] "About sixty" members of BILU had eventually made their way to Palestine. Of those, only twenty-seven actually settled there, fourteen of whom were "farmers in the colonies."[96] In other words, less than half of the BILU had been able to remain in Palestine. Similarly, it is likely that the number of Jews in general who managed to remain and survive in Palestine represents at least twice as many who would have stayed on, had the obstacles they faced been less formidable.[97]

In 1884,

> . . . only Jewish *pilgrims* could enter Palestine. Their passports were to be properly visaed by Ottoman consuls abroad; on arrival they were to hand over a deposit guaranteeing their departure, and they were to leave after thirty days.[98]

The Palestinian Jews could not promote new settlements,[99] and each group of prospective settlers that managed to "infiltrate" Palestine faced greater hardships than the last.[100] Because Jewish immigration was materially cut, progress on the existing settlements was painfully slow, "scarcely greater" in the 1890s "than that made in the previous decade."[101]

The Arab population, however, with no limits imposed, kept growing, supplemented largely by immigrants who were paid better there by far than anywhere else in the bordering or nearby lands.[102] The sparse local Arab population was beginning to show signs of breaking free from the bonds of the *effendis* and Arab moneylenders.

When "news" was "spread" that a new wave of Jewish immigrants was headed for Jerusalem, the city's "leading Moslems"—*effendis*— wired to "His Highness the Grand Vizier," issuing in effect a warning not to allow the Jews into Palestine.[103] Little more than a week later, the Grand Vizier complied with the Arab *effendis*' demands: he issued a "telegraphic Order stating, that, the Settlement of the Jews in the Sandjak of Jerusalem being forbidden, they are not to be permitted to remain in the Sandjak after they visit the country,"[104] nor to acquire land.[105]

One scholar specializing in the period places surprising emphasis on that early example of Muslim leaders pressuring Turkish authorities. He calls it "the first Arab protest against modern Jewish settlement in Palestine." His implications are susceptible of misinterpretation. To represent what was another extension of the long-manifest Muslim resentment of Jews as a singular "first Arab protest against modern Jewish settlement in Palestine" implies a *political* protest where none is evidenced.

Further, description of the Arab leaders' telegram as a "first Arab protest" might mislead the reader about what went before between Muslims and Jews in Palestine. Without an awareness of the tradition of terror that prevailed prior to the telegram, one might misinterpret from this description that the notables—or "leading Moslems"—were manifesting their "first Arab protest" against Jews in Palestine and that it was singularly caused by the recent Jewish immigration and settlement. It is from such unintentional ambiguities that destructive myths have grown up.

Not all the Jews were Eastern European immigrants. Along with that Jewish community identified as indigenous Palestinians, the Jews in Palestine in 1914 represented the Oriental Jewish world. Besides the hundreds of Yemenite Jews who had survived their journey in 1881–1882,[106] there were

> Persians, Kurds, Bokharians [*sic*], Babylonians, Orafalians, Moroccans, Maghrabians, Syrians . . . , and Jews from Daghestan.[107]

Considering the depressed conditions of Jews living in Middle Eastern countries in general, and their particular isolation as *dhimmis*,[108] a surprising number of these Sephardic Jews managed to get to Palestine, particularly from Yemen and Aden, and from Persia.

They, too, were set upon by the Muslims, although most were in appearance indistinguishable from Muslims, and certainly not mistakable for "alien Europeans." A Presbyterian minister's report to the British Consul in 1892 of one such incident is particularly revealing of life in this period:

> Last Tuesday at 3 P.M. there was a large crowd of Jews and others before the new stores, or shops, on the Jaffa road, in front of Fiel's Hotel, and in coming near I heard piteous female cries issuing from one of those stores. Those inside were trying hard to force the doors open, while police and a set of Moslem roughs were piling big stones against the doors, the police striking any who succeeded in putting head or hands out. I at once realized what the violent scene meant.
>
> As you know several groups of Persian Jews, driven away, it is avowed, by persecution, have, within the last two months arrived in Jerusalem, via Jaffa. They are computed at 50, 80 and 100 families but I have found no evidence to warrant an estimate exceeding 50 to 60 at most, or of over 150 individuals, children included. . . .
>
> . . . The Pasha . . . thereupon telegraphed to the Porte, and received orders to expel them from the country.
>
> Accordingly the police had been all day and were still hunting for the Persian Jews on every side and driving them by blows into that extemporised store-prison, to be kept penned up like wild beasts, till all could be collected and marched away back to Jaffa to be shipped off.
>
> I was told of a woman caught in the street and marched off by brute force, and she was shrieking piteously for the baby she left in her miserable hovel.

Another, I was assured, being "enceinte" was taken with pains under the blows which hurried her to the prison store. The scene was heart-rending and outrageous to all humane feelings.

I remonstrated with the police against this inhuman, cruel treatment of these poor exiles, particularly the women and girls, but they were too excited and frustrated, and replied roughly that they were acting by superior orders. To the question had they committed any crime, there was no reply except that it was no business of mine.[109]

Despite the benefits brought by Jewish settlement to Arab indigents from all over the area, "not a single colony was established without some loss of life resulting from Bedouin attacks." And the *fellahin*—peasant-migrants—appear to have continued to consider the individual Jews as legitimate prey, however important to the peasants' new well-being the Jews as a group might be.[110]

In 1893, before the theme of "displacement" had been adopted as a propaganda technique, grievance after grievance was filed by the bolder among the Jewish populace. Jews were "oppressed," "morally injured by being robbed of all rights, even that of defending ourselves against insult," and they protested that "false representations" by the Arab leaders were "influencing" the Turkish officials.[111] "Jew" was a "term of reproach" in the Holy Land, and immigrants and Jewish Palestinians alike were "generally despised . . ." A letter from the Jewish leaders to the British Consul pled for "mediation" to "bring about . . . our rights which have been . . . unjustly withheld for no other reason than 'that we are Jews.' "[112]

Pierre Loti described his reactions to the Jerusalem he found in the 1890s in *La Galilee,* published in 1895. Regarding the Jews' "holiest place," the Temple mount known as the "Wailing Wall," Loti found:

> . . . I arrive at the foot of the Wall. Old velvet robes, gray old forelocks, old hands raised to curse, they are there, as expected, the elders of Israel, who soon will be nourishing the grass in the valley of Jehosaphat; . . . There before us, . . . there is already a band of Arab children, there to torment them: little ones disguised as animals, as dogs, under burlap sacks, coming up on all fours with wild laughs to bark at their feet. On that occasion these Jews did rouse me to profound pity, in spite of everything . . . ![113]

The British Consul reports of Jaffa in 1895 were indicative of the same conditions. "Offences of military officials" reported during a one-month period of 1895 in Jaffa included the following:

> Abd-el-Wahad Yaseen Shaweesh beat and wounded a Jew . . . up to the present, he has not been condemned. . . .
> Mahmound Effendi. . . . Forcibly entered the house of an honest Ashkinazi Jew for an indecent purpose.

Under the heading of "Offences by the Civil Officials and Officers of Justice," were such reports as the following:

Moslems are allowed to go unpunished when found in the streets at night without lanterns, while Christians and Jews are imprisoned if they go with or without lanterns.

Disorders committed by the Mussulman Inhabitants &c.

False witness always ready to appear in any accusation or claim brought by Mussulmans against Christians or Jews.[114]

. . . a Jew was murdered in the Jewish colony of Mulabas [Petach Tikvah] near Jaffa, by some Mussulmans, . . . the crime having apparently been committed without any provocation on the part of the victim.[115]

One exhaustive Yale University study concluded that the peasant-migrants understandably did not show "overt opposition to Jewish settlement during the first period of Zionist work in Palestine";[116] another source maintains that it was the large land purchases by Jews that "alarmed Arab peasants in the Tiberias region."[117] The presence of a more deeply rooted, traditional religious intolerance as motivation for Jews there being "molested" is erroneously overlooked.

It was not until 1896—a date by which the Jews, however hindered and oppressed, already had been in the process of resettling the Holy Land for at least a generation—that Herzl would publish *The Jewish State (Der Judenstaat)*.[118] Herzl's document became widely renowned as the inspiration for the Jewish national liberation movement and for the theme of establishing a homeland and haven for persecuted Jews throughout the world. If earlier "Zionists," in fact, had already begun to implement the Jews' aspirations,[119] the founding of the Zionist movement per se in 1897 was directly attributable to Herzl's writings. He became the head of the Zionists, and the first Zionist Congress was held the same year.[120]

Despite the eminent French study published in 1895 which concluded that *no more* than *one-tenth* of the land in Palestine had been tilled by anyone,[121] the portents of a first "Zionist Congress" in 1897 brought increased difficulties for the Jewish settlers.[122] From that time, Turkish authorities enforced the old restrictions with greater zeal than ever, and added newly devised obstacles. "Entry of foreign Israelites into Palestine was prohibited"[123] and instructions were given to keep them from landing.[124] Already native Ottoman Jews from other Turkish areas had been prohibited from entering the country.

Those Ottoman Jews who were already in Palestine were prevented from buying land in the Ottoman state domain—*miri* lands. Since the bulk of the country's land was *miri* (state-owned),[125] the restriction of *miri* land transfer to Jews was a formidable limitation.[126]

The impositions were enforced more rigorously at one time than another, depending on the extent of local corruption, susceptibility to traditional *baksheesh* (bribery), and the amount of influence the Arab notables could exercise over particular Turkish officials. The observance of official restrictions was often honored in the breach, since by "unofficially relaxing . . . the existing restrictions . . . [an official might gain] personal advantage."[127]

For instance, "red tickets"—a kind of permit for Jews "good from 30 to 90 days"—were introduced in 1899,[128] presumably as a method of keeping close track of Jews who entered as pilgrims or in other categories. However, this measure proved to be, in fact, a relaxation of the restrictions, since with the red tickets some Jews got in. Once having gained entry, they might remain permanently if they got protection from their local consuls, because it appears the Turkish authority was ordered "not to permit . . . problems" to develop "with foreign embassies."[129] Nonetheless, inconsistent or inefficient though the Turks may have been, a degree of effectiveness was achieved in the effort to keep out the Jews.

That the powerful *effendi* families could impel *local* Turkish authorities to anti-Jewish policies was predictable. However, in Constantinople too the Sultan's policies were decided with an eye to appeasing the incitable Muslim mobs: "He feared that the masses would be aroused."[130] The Sultan Abdulhamed thus turned down an offer by Theodor Herzl, who was willing to "pay any requested sum to the Imperial Treasury" if persecuted Jews could be permitted to settle in Palestine. The Sultan, according to a French historian, replied in "un oui negatif":

> The great confidence which I have in the Jewish nation, does not prevent me from rejecting your proposal. It is probable that it will be acceptable when I shall consult my Council of Ministers on this subject, which, if it finds it is just, will prepare the means by which to give it a practical form. Are you satisfied with my answer?[131]

The Sultan, according to some sources, "made up his mind categorically against any agreement with the Jews."[132] But the Sultan himself expressed more enthusiasm to a friend, Dr. Atif Huseyin:

> They [the Zionists] have a goal in our country. They want to purchase land in the area of Jaffa and Jerusalem. I think that now they can purchase. There was an editor of a paper published in Vienna. He was a Jew. He was a man of knowledge. Now he died [referring to Herzl]. Some time ago, the rich Jews sent him to me as a delegate. They wanted to purchase land in the neighborhoods of Jaffa and Jerusalem, and to settle Jews from all parts [of the world] there. They really wanted to create a government there. Their offer was to take full responsibility for the state's Public Debt. It is a good thing, since there exists a danger that if a day will come when we will not be able to pay our debts, the finance of the state will be taken under the control [of the Powers]. I then put forward some conditions to them. Afterwards this man died, the revolution broke out, and the matter remained incomplete.
>
> The power of money can do anything. They are not going to create a government today; it is a preliminary stage. It is an aim and a hope. They will commence their work now, and after many years, even if it will be a thousand years they might be successful in their aim; and I think they will be.[133]

Although many who are familiar with the history of persecution calculate that the Palestinian Jews' lot improved after 1860,[134] when "Jews were no longer legal objects of annoyance,"[135] the traditional Muslim hostility, coupled with a Christian-Arab resentment toward his fellow *dhimmi,* was always there, inflammable and destructive. It was racist in nature, and could be detonated—not by political fanaticism, or fear of displacement, which they knew well was the opposite of the case—but by incitement of "deep-rooted" and "virulent racial feeling."[136]

As one historian wrote of Palestine,

> The trouble about the Arab is that his ruling classes, moved by interest . . . can easily inflame the Moslem masses, who add to a religious fanaticism an inborn if latent hatred of the Jew. This conflict between Jacob and Esau is as old as history: it is splitting Palestine to-day.[137]

Fanning the flame was the more recent Christian anti-Semitic influence, at work artificially inseminating "justification" to the Muslims for their traditional anti-Jewish violence. A native Arabic-speaking Palestinian Jew reported in 1899 that

> . . . foreign missionaries and priests were heightening Arab feeling against the Jews. Protestant missionaries, aiming at conversion, indirectly spread anti-Semitism. Sapir cites as evidence, *Ben Hur,* an evangelical novel containing a passage about the death of Jesus at the hands of the Jews, which was translated into Arabic in 1897 by Dr. Cornelius van Dyke, an influential missionary and educator at the Syrian Protestant College. Much more damage . . . was being done by Catholics, especially Jesuits, through their literature and in their schools.[138]

But although many Christian Arabs joined Muslims in anti-Semitic campaigns and initiated attacks on their own in an effort to overcome their own "infidel" status as "non-believers," many other Christians supported the Jewish struggle in "Syria" because they believed that strengthening the Jewish minority would help balance the Christians' minority role amongst Muslims.

Some Christians even welcomed a Jewish majority:

> We even wish that the Jews would form the majority in Palestine and succeed in establishing there a Jewish autonomy properly speaking which would split in two that compact Muslim mass which peoples such vast contiguous regions as Iraq, Syria, Egypt, the Hijaz and Yemen.[139]

One influential Christian Arab wrote a pamphlet praising the Palestinian Jews, particularly the Jewish settlers, for the "immense good" they did "in reviving their own barren land."[140]

The Arab notables themselves were split on finer points. All might object to the long-term economic losses, and the diminution of power over the migrants and peasants that they would suffer because of Jewish settlements, but how they could still benefit from the Jewish purchases while demanding that Jewish purchases be banned—this became a problem.[141] One of the al-Husseini notables, Sa'id Bey, determined that while Palestine could not "support large-scale Jewish immigration," some "small number of Jews" might still bring "advantages to Palestine."[142]

A member of the al-Khalidi family was more defensive: while he allowed that "individual Jews" might be permitted to "enter," their "financial capacity" to purchase land threatened the Arabs.[143] Neville Mandel noted the "Muslim in Haifa" who spent "eighteen hours a day" thinking of the "benefits" brought by the Jews, and the other "six hours . . . he suspected them of wanting to establish a Jewish state in Palestine."[144]

By 1908, Arab deputies held 60 of the 288 seats in the Parliament. The Turkish powers "could not afford to alienate" the influential Arabs, which was certain if the Turks acceded to Zionist request.[145] Within the next few years, the Arab notables were reported to have organized to "oppose land sales to Jews";[146] they were headed by the Nashashibi family of Jerusalem.[147] That same year, one of the younger Nashashibis wrote an anti-Jewish story called "The Wizard and the Jew" for a Jaffa publication,[148] attributing his enlightenment to the "great Frenchmen . . . masters and teachers"—Edouard Drumont, writer of anti-Semitic literature, and his disciples.[149]

However resentful some migrant-peasants may have been, many others were infiltrating the Jewish-settled areas. The flow was persistent of Arab immigration from surrounding lands in Egypt, Transjordan, and elsewhere, as well as migration from the sections in Palestine that lay outside the area that would one day be Israel—from sections of the country that did not offer even the employment, much less the wage scale, of the Jewish-settled areas.

The Arab newcomers managed to fill those openings for workers that the Jewish settlements had to fill—places meant for Jewish refugees to come to, places which the erratic Turkish immigration restrictions had deprived Jews from taking. It was largely those Arab migrants or immigrants to the Jewish-settled areas —who never ceased but increasingly flooded those areas of opportunity under the British Mandate (1919–1948)—who would later be called, by ironic inversion, the "displaced" Arabs. In actuality, only the Jews lost their rightful places—to the unlimited, ignored flow of Arabs. The only displacement of Arabs in Palestine was and would be attributable to their fellow Arab leaders.

Throughout the definitive historical works that document this period appears the schizoid pattern of anti-Jewish action sponsored by those Arabs who are themselves selling land to Jews. However they may have objected to losing the "sweets" of stranglehold over the migrant-peasants in the long run, they coveted the shorter-range advantages to be seized from land-sale profits. Apparently, they were succeeding in keeping both.[150] The restrictions did take a toll, however: land sales may have continued to some extent before 1914, but "the figures of 1913 showed no advance in acreage acquired" by the Jews since 1897.[151]

Meanwhile, though the eastern-European pogroms had abated between 1885 and the end of the century, the Russian authorities enforced existing anti-Semitic measures such as the "May Laws" with "even greater savagery and ingenuity,"[152] and the twentieth century would bring a new wave of violence beginning with the "great pogrom of Kishinev" in 1903.

Thus, "in spite of the imposed restrictions, Jews were immigrating to Palestine."[153] If the foreign Jews had originally imagined that life for their native

Palestinian Jewish brothers was relatively undisturbed by racial violence or religious persecution in Palestine, they might be forgiven. Most of the world outside the Middle East knew little or nothing of the subjugation of the *dhimmi* Jew or that the mandatory badge writ for Jews had not been first devised in Europe, but a hundred or hundreds of years earlier by Muslims. Yet even when the newly arrived Jewish hopefuls had learned the hazardous reality, the evidence of real Jewish progress in Palestine apparently sustained them.

Regardless of the murders and violent assault in Palestine, Jews found methods of circumventing bans or restrictions and accepted with alacrity the terms of bribery offered by the corrupt Turkish official involved. "No doubt *baksheesh* was a great power in Turkey, and the greatest men in the country were unable to resist it."[154] In Judah-cum-Palestine Jews might, however painful, however hazardous, join their people in settling their holy land. In Rumania or Russia, by contrast, anti-Semitism was not offset by hope. Martin Gilbert has written of a poignant example:

> On 25 November 1913 Ruppin [a Jewish pioneer] received a telegram from the Galilee: "Moshe Barsky, Deganiah, murdered Saturday. Yesterday worker Joseph Salzmann, Kinneret, murdered." Barsky, a boy of eighteen, had come to Deganiah from Russia. On learning of his death, Barsky's father, who was still in Russia, urged his younger son to go out to Palestine in Moshe's place, and he did so. News of this soon spread, encouraging others to go.[155]

From the first, ways had been found to circumvent the laws; some Jews were able to enter Palestine by land via Egypt and then might purchase land either in the names of Ottoman Jews, or local Arabs, consuls, or consular-agents, for a "consideration."[156] The compulsory "temporary structures" remained standing, and "dug-outs" were utilized as an alternative to the prohibited above-the-ground structures.[157] Russian Jews sometimes were able to obtain permits in Constantinople, allowing them to travel within the Ottoman Empire and thus enter Palestine "legally."[158] Since attention was focused on curtailing Jewish *settlers,* other Jews were allowed entry either as pilgrims or on business, and many simply remained; those practices continued in spite of harsher enforcement of Turkish restrictions as early as 1883.[159]

In 1901, the Council of Ministers ruled that, as a foreigner, the Jewish Colonization Association (JCA) President could buy land in the Vilayet of Beirut, provided that no foreign Jews were installed on it.[160] In fear that these new regulations would allow Jews to enter freely, the Arab *fellahin* from several villages were alerted, became "alarmed," and on "a number of occasions" molested JCA workers who had come to survey the land for sales.[161]

Unhampered by the *effendis'* mixed emotions, the Muslim masses would react predictably to the planted rumors and public statements by al-Khalidi, al-Husseini, al-Nashashibi, and others.[162] What would evolve in Arab-Muslim countries later, when Israel became a state in 1948, began now to occur in Palestine: the

Palestinian Jew began to be seen not as the traditional *dhimmi* whipping boy for Muslims, but as a Jew who would be equal.

One condition was unique to Palestine, however: it was solely in Judah-cum-Palestine that the traditional Jewish *dhimmi* not only would be equal, but he or she would 1) help wrench the *effendis'* historical hold over the peasant-migrants and 2) create independence for the Jews.

As a counter, the *effendis* would set about inflaming the entrenched Jew-hatred of the Muslim masses by instilling fear in the only way the masses understood: by ominous warnings that Jews might begin to oppress Muslims as the Muslims had for so long oppressed the Palestinian Jews. According to one account,

> In all eyes the Jew is becoming . . . the traitor prepared to plunder his neighbor to take possession of his goods.[163]

It was in 1909, at the time when leading *effendis* felt their grip over the lives and fortunes of their erstwhile prey was getting too loose, that *effendi* Ruhi Bey al-Khalidi warned that the Jews would *"displace* the Arab farmers from their land and their fathers' heritage. . . . The Jews were not here when we conquered the country."[164] It mattered little that the *effendi*'s argument was false. It served his group's long-range economic interests, and at least some of his misstatements would be swallowed whole by a surprisingly large part of the world for the better part of a century.

In 1911, an Arab land official from a notable family based in Damascus charged that the Jewish settlers in Palestine wanted "solely to expel the poor Arab peasants from their land,"[165] while "treacherous Arab landowners" sold lands to the Jews.[166] In case some among the impoverished masses might question the sincerity of sudden concern shown by the Arab absentee landlord in question— whose wealth and holdings came from precisely the activities he was attributing to the Jews—a more emotional and basic appeal was added to ensure the desired mass reaction: the Damascus landlord warned that the Jews were "disloyal" Ottoman soldiers and would "later shoot the Arabs."[167]

As *Jew* had been plundered by Arab, so now would *Arab* be plundered, the leaders alleged. As Arab had been stripped of land and money by Arab, so now the Jews would be blamed. Most important, as Jew was displaced by Arab in Palestine—with each restriction on Jewish immigration, Arabs were coming into the Jewish-settled areas to take places and employment that the Jews were creating for other Jews—so Arab would charge Jew with the Arab's action. The implanted fear that the new, bolder Jews would turn the tables on the Muslims fomented the desired violent reaction. It was the same tactic that would later throw fuel on the "Palestinian refugees" flight in 1948.

The *effendis'* somewhat disingenuous tactic in 1909 may have been the first specious charge of Jews specifically "displacing" Arabs. But the same *effendi* tactic had succeeded in pressuring the Turks to halt Jewish immigration to the

Holy Land nearly thirty years before that. And the same tool would be cynically employed later by the Arabs with British support: later, "Arabs" in "Palestine" would be seen by the world as having been "displaced" and "excluded" from "their homeland" in 1948.

Despite the anti-Jewish solicitation inherent in his positions, as early as 1911 Ruhi Bey al-Khalidi proclaimed he was not an "anti-Semite, but an anti-Zionist."[168] It was perhaps the premiere performance of that protest of qualification that is prevalent today. One benefit accruing from prominent *effendi* al-Khalidi's pronouncement could have been that Jews might be more likely to continue to buy land surreptitiously from one who disclaimed any support of "anti-Semitism."

But the distinction was aimed only at influencing the Jews. As other non-Jews pointed out, the "masses were incapable of making the distinction" between one Jew and another.[169] One influential Arab writer candidly observed that there should be no distinction between "Zionists" and "non-Zionists," since all shared common goals.[170]

Anti-Jewish attitudes were the "daily bread in Palestine."[171] Sheikh Sulayman al-Taji, an "Ottomanist" patriot and landlord who, paradoxically, himself sold land to Jews, wrote a poem called "The Zionist Danger" about "Jews, the weakest of all peoples and the least of them . . . sons of clinking gold, stop your deceit . . ."[172] The "poem" was published in November 1913, and that same month, murders were committed in Jewish kibbutzes (kibbutzim) of the Jewish-settled area of the country.[173]

By the time of World War I, the active Arab anti-Semitism, whether called "Ottomanism," "anti-Zionism," or "Arab nationalism,"[174] had evolved into a kind of *Muftism* after Haj Amin al-Husseini, Grand Mufti and scion of the al-Husseini notables.

As Britain's Commander in Chief and Palestine's High Commissioner would conclude a generation later, in 1938, Arab "terrorism was not a national movement but bands of banditti of no genuine political significance [or] Arab peasants who are restless and anti-Jew, and who are not averse to joining violent action" for a fee. But, said the Commissioner, the "moderate" Arabs in Palestine who opposed terror feared they would become the victims if they took "a lead against the terrorists." "Other political leaders might arise," if Grand Mufti Haj Amin al-Husseini weren't "sitting just across the border."[175] But the terrorist leader and his *effendi* colleagues in Palestine had been "sitting" in control of the country's security for decades. As an anti-Jewish movement, *Muftism* would not only cooperate with the Nazis, but would actually succeed in efforts to cause the deaths of additional hundreds of thousands of European Jews whom the Nazis had earmarked for Palestine, as is documented later.*

In January 1914, the Turkish authorities did away with the "red ticket" restrictions on Jewish immigration and supposedly relaxed the prohibition of land

*See Chapter 17.

sales to Jews as well.[176] But the restrictions against purchase of land actually remained intact. Although the Turkish Power wanted to show "its good intentions" to the Jewish settlers, fear of "Arab reactions" had intimidated the government.[177]

Nevertheless, the British Consul in Jerusalem reported on the eve of World War I that the Jews' "nationalist spirit" was manifested with "increased vigour" —particularly regarding Zionist education.[178] The Zionist and scholar Arthur Ruppin noted in his memoirs that

> Today I succeeded in buying from Sir John Gray Hill his large and magnificently situated property on Mount Scopus, thus acquiring the first piece of ground for the Jewish university in Jerusalem.[179]

Ruppin was enthusiastic: "On Passover [1914] many rich Zionist" tourists "were prepared to invest money," and "our work was increasing from day to day."

Then World War I broke out "at the end of July," Ruppin wrote, and "settled like a blight on our work and our hopes." In November 1914, Baha-ud Din, the principal officer of the 4th Army Commander, returned from the Turks' heinous mass slaughter of the Armenian people, and "openly boasted of doing much the same to the Jews if ever he got the chance."[180]

On December 17, 1914, Baha-ud Din ordered all Jews in Jaffa who were not then Ottoman subjects to be immediately deported, and he had entire families thrown in jail—"nursing mothers and infants included"—by four that afternoon to set an example.[181] Daily life was altered: Hebrew, which had been in use for generations,[182] was banned—"newspapers, posters, signs and the like all had to be done away with."[183] Postage stamps picturing Herzl and Nordau became illegal, as was the local money used in the largest settlements (Zikhron, Petach Tikvah and Rishon).[184]

The Jewish settlers were cut off from funds abroad and from import outlets for their products. New crippling "patriotic contributions" were demanded, to add to their existing stiff taxes. Thousands of Jews somehow mustered funds to buy naturalized citizenship, and those Jewish males between eighteen and fifty who couldn't meet payments that exempted them from the hostile Turkish army (2,500 francs in gold or 10,000 in Turkish notes a year, at its peak)[185] were put in labor battalions as punishment.

"Epidemics of typhus and cholera, conscription to remote parts of the Caucasus or Mesopotamia, and the near-famine conditions of 1917 all took their toll,"[186] and all were partly responsible for the drop in population from 85,000 in 1914 to about 58,000 at the war's end in 1918. But most of the reduction was due, predictably, to emigration; by mid-1915, already "over 11,000 had left the country, voluntarily or otherwise."[187] Hospital beds and offices were confiscated for use as military quarters.[188]

Equipment vital to the struggling Jewish settlements—"farm carts and wagons, and the mules and oxen which pulled them"—were confiscated just before the harvest was to begin. Following the ousters and persecution at Jaffa, Petach

Tikvah and Tel Aviv were "evacuated" brutally. In a few settlements where the Jews in authority were personally friendly to the local Turkish official, "life proceeded almost as though there were no war," according to one historian,[189] but for most, the combination of disease, arbitrary discrimination, and panic had taken its toll on those Jews remaining in Palestine.

While the powerless Jewish community was wincing and warding off the blows once again, a few individual Jews attempted to overcome the impossible odds: led by Avshalom Feinberg, a Palestinian native, and Aaron Aaronson, a renowned scientist, in the belief that Britain was their only hope, the small group formed "Nili" in 1915,[190] an intelligence unit working for the British behind enemy Turkish lines. During the period of Nili's perilous activities, prominent Palestinian Jews wired a chilling message to the British Foreign Office:

> During Passover the entire Jewish population of Jaffa expelled towards North. Homes, property sacked, population in flight, robbed in connivance with Turkish authorities. Jews, resisting, pillaged, hanged. Thousands wandering helplessly on roads, starving. Overcrowding of Colony increasing misery, disease. Masses of young Jerusalem Jews deported, northward, destination unknown.[191]

The British were advancing toward Jerusalem by 1917. They were bringing with them long-awaited encouragement to the Jews' hope for the restoration of their political independence, because many in England were resuming proposals for what was stated by the British Press as the "liberation"[192] of the Jews in Palestine. There, they declared, a "Zionist State under British Protection had much to commend it."[193] "A British Palestine must be a Jewish Palestine."[194]

When the British suffered defeat at Gaza, which temporarily dimmed their enthusiasm for Jewish goals, the Zionists remained undaunted. British Prime Minister Lloyd George had already "instructed" in April about "the importance of not prejudicing the Zionist movement and the possibility of its development under British auspices." Jews, he noted, could be of "more assistance than the Arabs."[195] Sir Mark Sykes responded that "the Arabs probably realized that there was no prospect of their being allowed any control over Palestine."[196]

Germany too had been wooing the Jews, because of "the war-value of Jewish sympathy." A Turkish-German "proposition" was founded to compete with the British pro-Zionist forces: "a kind of chartered company . . . for German Zionists," with "limited form of local self-government and right of immigration."[197] The Turks had agreed to the plan, but before Constantinople could officially accept the proposal of its German ally, Palestine was "in General Allenby's hands."[198]

Meanwhile, the war's ravages wracked the Holy Land, and locusts devastated the harvest in many settlements where the Turkish ruler had not. When Jews were sent loans from abroad, the money was trimmed so materially by Turkish authorities that precious little finally got to the settlers.[199] Some were forced to resort to the Arab moneylenders' extortion. By 1917 the previous two years' ruined harvests and prohibition from obtaining sustenance abroad brought disaster. "In

Jerusalem . . . 300 of the poor and mostly aged Jewish . . . population were dying each month," and the Turks confiscated any goods they fancied. Exemptions from the draft were beyond reach, torture was the norm upon arrest, and all the country including its new settlements had been plundered.[200]

The non-Jewish population in Palestine also diminished temporarily; the number of "Arabs" and other groups dropped between thirteen percent and twenty-one percent from the effects of the war, epidemics, and *traditional low natural increase.* [201] The Nili network was uncovered by the Turks just two months before the momentous Balfour Declaration could have afforded them the protection they had fought for.[202] Two Nili members were hanged in Damascus, and their bodies exhibited to the public;[203] one woman shot herself between torture sessions;[204] and many others were tortured and incarcerated. Some of the punishments were averted, however, by Britain's victory.[205]

The British "delayed" formal recognition of the renewed Jewish national liberation movement in Palestine "till . . . the success of General Allenby's invasion of Palestine seemed certain."[206] Then, on November 2, 1917, with approval from its cabinet and the United States,[207] the British Government published a "statement of policy" that became known as the Balfour Declaration:*[208]

> His Majesty's Government view with favour the establishment in Palestine of a National Home for the Jewish People, and will use their best endeavors to facilitate the achievement of this object, it being clearly understood that nothing shall be done which may prejudice the civil and religious rights of existing non-Jewish communities in Palestine, or the rights and political status enjoyed by Jews in any country.

If it were not for Turkish restrictions on Jews entering and buying land, perhaps hundreds of thousands more Jews would have settled in Palestine even before the turn of the century. As it was, compared to non-Jews—called Arabs —who lived in the Jewish-settled area of Palestine, the proportion of Jews was far greater than has ever been recognized.

*See Chapter 12.

III

THE POLITICAL INFLUENCE
OF TRADITION:

IMMIGRANTS AND IN-MIGRANTS—

RECOGNIZED AND UNRECOGNIZED

III

11

Popular Misconceptions About the Population of "Palestine"

> . . . a sad condition was created for the Palestinian people who were excluded from their homeland.
> —Pope John Paul II, 1980

> . . . it is very difficult to make a case out for the misery of the Arabs if at the same time their compatriots from adjoining states could not be kept from going in to share that misery.
> —British Governor of the Sinai from 1922 to 1936

> . . . the Arabs watch the immigration figures with close and anxious concern.
> —*Palestine Royal Commission Report,* 1937

In October 1980 Pope John Paul II said that while "the Jewish people . . . gave birth to the state of Israel" in 1948 after "the extermination of so many sons and daughters" in the Holocaust, "at the same time, a sad condition was created for the Palestinian people who were excluded from their homeland. These are facts everyone can see."[1] Emanating from the Vatican, the pontiff's sympathetic statement of humanitarian concern is perhaps the definitive example of a perception that pervades most of the world today.

That a popular understanding and expression of the "facts" as represented above were registered officially by a body as undisputable as the Vatican and the Pope is testimony to the effectiveness of the distortions with which Arab propaganda machinery has obscured all existing evidence of the actual conditions pertaining to the Arab-Jewish conflict, now under the umbrella of the "problem of the Palestinian People."

The image of the Arab-Israeli conflict as popularly conjured is based upon the myth that "the Jews only arrived in 1948, where they displaced a teeming Arab population from its rooted homeland since time immemorial." What went before Israel was declared an independent state is, in the minds of most, somewhat vague. Some of us had little or no awareness that an extensive Jewish development program had in fact already been taking place for decades in Palestine by 1917, the time the land was declared and internationally mandated as the "Jewish National Home." All the "depopulated" and "wasted" land, delineated as "Palestine" or "South Syria"—east of the Jordan River to the Hejaz (Arabia) and west of the Jordan River to the Mediterranean Sea—in 1917 would be pledged by League of Nations mandate to "close settlement" by the Jews for their "Jewish National Home."

Even fewer of us recognized that the development of depopulated land in Judah-cum-Palestine, in fact, had been started by Jewish pioneers decades *before* Theodor Herzl's "Zionism" was implemented in 1901, or that among the scattering of *fellahin* in the Holy Land—native peasants working the soil—were impoverished Jewish farmers.[2]

Before 1948, the common picture among observers was that the Jews "displaced" the "Arab heirs," in Palestine, who were "son[s] of the soil to be replaced from a land of his country," according to one British report in 1931.[3] A pivotal British report that supported Arab propaganda and became a justification for the heightened British restrictions against Jewish immigration to the Jewish National Home in Palestine, the Hope Simpson *Report* of 1930,[4] claimed that

> Everywhere there is the complaint that many of the cultivators have lost their land.[5]

Since the inception of modern Israel in 1948, that perception has been embellished. The Jewish "aliens" came as "refugees from Europe" and "stole" land from the Arab settled population, it is claimed. No doubt the Jews did suffer from the monstrosities of the Holocaust, but Jewish suffering should not be salved by inducing the suffering of the "Palestinian people," and "excluding" or "expelling" them from their land since "time immemorial," it is thought.

Inherent in the evolution of the present Arab claim of "displacement" and "exclusion" or "expulsion"—depending on the interpretation—is that theme— that the "Arab" is the native "son of the soil" who has always been on his plot of land in Palestine and who was "increasing rapidly and has lost land." As one population expert put it, the Jew was "immigrant" and "culturally very distinct from the Arab" native.[6]

Immigration: Government Reports and Their Contradictions

While the "Jewish population" of Palestine was "predominantly immigrant in character," according to the 1931 census of Palestine[7] the Muslims were assumed to be "the natural population"—"Not quite two percent of the Moslem population are immigrants." By 1945, the Anglo-American Committee of Inquiry would report that, although the Jewish population had risen from 84,000 in 1922 to 554,000, and "three-fourths of this . . . [Jewish] expansion was accounted for by immigration," the Arabs had increased "by a greater number" than the Jews. "The expansion of the Arab community *by natural increase** has been in fact one of the most striking features of Palestine's social history," the report stated.[8] The same sponsor, in an earlier report, has assessed that "the speed with which the Moslems have followed Western patterns in reduction of mortality has been very remarkable, probably more than could be expected by any observer twenty years ago."[9]

The Arabs allegedly were following the trends of improvements in the Jewish-settled areas and were "the gainers" from the Jews' higher health standards;[10] the death rate, which is central to determine the rate of natural population increase between 1922 and 1944, decreased proportionately, as would be expected, since standards improved as time passed. The Jews' death rate therefore was at its highest in 1922. Contradicting that logic, in the 1922–1944 period the death rate for the Arabs was reported at its *lowest* in 1922.[11] According to demographic experts, that phenomenon would have been incredible, considering the conditions in Palestine and the factors influencing the inhabitants at that time.[12]

Occasionally the British administration, noting "disproportions" and disparities in its data on Arab population growth, attempted to justify the conflicting assumptions in nonscientific terms, but the so-called "unprecedented"[13] rate of "natural increase" among the non-Jews was never satisfactorily broken down or explained.

A very great disproportion is evident between the Moslem and Jewish death-rates and has been accentuated by a steady decline in the Jewish death-rate over the period under review.[14]

Nevertheless, a pivotal report during the same period concluded that

It must be observed that a smaller population may overtake a larger population in numbers as time goes on. This depends on the relative age-constitutions and potential fertilities of the two communities considered. Jewish immigration adds a yearly increment to the Jewish population which is potentially highly reproductive. The time might come some scores of years ahead when the Jewish natural increase exceeded the Arab natural increase, but it would take a very long time for the Jews to obtain a majority in Palestine by that means alone.[15]

The various reports usually acknowledge in one place or another that the Arab population of Palestine would have remained stable at the figure—actually 300,000 to 400,000[16]—where it had remained for the last two centuries,[17] if it were not for the better conditions introduced by the Jewish settlements and/or the British administration. "Fluctuations [were] cancelled out" by war, disease, natural disasters, and so on. An official 1937 report found that "The growth in their numbers [Arab *fellahin*-peasants] has been largely due to the health services,

*Emphasis added.

combating malaria, reducing the infant deathrate, improving water supply and sanitation," commencing with the advent of both the Jewish and the British mandatory influence.[18]

The actual thinly settled "existing" Arab population of the early 1900s—to which the Balfour Declaration and Mandate give testimony—would not have been "prejudiced" by immigration of Jews. But the Arabs, it is claimed, had grown "naturally" by an unprecedented number—a number greater even than the enormous swell of Jewish immigration between 1922 and 1944 could raise the Jewish population. Even Zionist historians[19] accepted the phenomenon of the Arabs' soaring "natural increase" without question, despite the fact that the evidence which contradicted that assumption often was noted on other pages of the same official British Government report that had made the "natural increase" assumption.

As late as the mid-1940s, the 1945–1946 *Survey of Palestine* stated that "It is probable that the high rate of natural increase of the population of Palestine is a phenomenon of the mandatory period. . . ."[20]

One source cited earlier—a population expert who assumed that a populous indigenous Arab community had been in Palestine for a millennium—noted elsewhere in the same chapter that, by the date of his book, 1936, well into that Mandatory period, "fall in the death-rate" was the "likely" cause of the Arabs' population increase. And yet, he contradicted his own explanation by stating that in fact by 1936, fourteen years into the Mandatory period, "Medical and sanitary progress has made little headway among the Palestinian Arabs as yet, and cannot account for any considerable fall in the death-rate." After disqualifying all other excuses, that writer was left with one rather lame possibility: that perhaps the phenomenal rate of increase among Arabs in Palestine could be attributed solely to British "administrative measures" like "quarantine"![21]

In other words, the new "phenomenal" rise in the Arab population of Palestine, which had remained sparse and static for two hundred years despite constant replenishing, was attributed to a sudden, hyped natural increase of the "existing" long-settled indigenes. That phenomenon, or so went the rationalization, resulted from *new* conditions. Yet, it was *also* acknowledged that because of its recent timing, the introduction of those new conditions *could not in fact have been responsible* for the population increase in the period of time for which it was credited!

That same self-contradictory expert source was heavily relied upon by the Palestine Partition Commission in 1938, which tried to reconcile contradictory "facts": for example,

> We thus have the Arab population reflecting simultaneously two widely different tendencies—a birthrate characteristic of a peasant community in which the unrestricted family is normal, and a death-rate which could only be brought about under an enlightened modern administration, with both the will and the necessary funds at its disposal to enable it to serve a population unable to help itself. It is indeed an ironic commentary on the working of the Mandate and perhaps on the science of government, that this result which so far from encouraging *has almost*

certainly hindered close settlement by Jews on the land, could scarcely have been brought about except through the appropriation of tax-revenue contributed by the Jews."*[22]

The same report referred to "a combination of circumstances unique in modern history." For the Jews, "an unusually high (though not unprecedented) rate of immigration"[23] and for the "Arabs," that is, Muslims, "an abnormally high (and *possibly unprecedented*) rate of natural increase in the *existing indigenous* population."*[24]

Note the words *"existing"* and *"indigenous."* They were not simply modifiers; their use, as we will see in following chapters, became central to our seriously uncritical acceptance of Arab propaganda's misrepresentation of migrants and immigrants as "displaced" and "landless Arabs" deprived of their homeland by the Jews.

While the Arabs were reportedly growing in number "naturally" by phenomenal leaps, the Jews were immigrating—in all but depression times—as heavily as the British immigration restrictions on Jews would allow. The 1937 *Palestine Royal Commission Report*— often called the Peel Report—noted that

> The pace and extent of the development of the Jewish National Home must obviously depend on the rate and volume of Jewish immigration over a series of years. Having regard to their fear of being overwhelmed and therefore dominated by Jewish immigrants, the Arabs watch the immigration figures with close and anxious concern.[25]

Another practically unknown and unrecognized condition was indicated: the same report observed also that *Arab immigration* into Palestine might exist.

> No accurate estimate can be made of the numbers of Arabs who have come into Palestine from neighboring Arab lands and settled there, but it may be reckoned that roughly nine-tenths of growth has been due to natural increase, and it has been a growth of over 50 percent in 17 years. Those are remarkable figures especially in view of the general belief that the population of Palestine under the Ottoman regime was more or less stationary.[26]

Other references reported similar observations. Some examples:

> Immigration has accounted in large part for the increase of the Jewish section of the population, though the Arabs have also received some reinforcement from this source.[27]

> The collection and compilation of the data of migration are beginning to reach a tolerable degree of precision; but in one main repect they remain incomplete since it has not yet been possible to arrange for a reasonably complete record of the movement of people to and from Trans-Jordan.[28]

*Emphasis added.

4,866 travellers who entered Palestine during the year were registered as immigrants. Of these 4,114 were Jews and 752 non-Jews.[29]

Yet the possibility of *substantial* Arab entry into Palestine was dismissed, despite the "remarkable" growth of the Arab population compared to the admittedly "stationary" number of the "Arab" population for centuries, before and until the "Jewish National Home" was mandated.[30]

Reported Arab Immigration

If there had not yet been sufficient time for the improved health standards to affect the Arabs' rate of natural increase, then another, artificial factor had to cause the otherwise scientifically unexplainable Arab population increase.

The only demographic possibility remaining was that Arabs, like the Jews, had immigrated to swell their numbers. Yet, no record of substantial Arab immigration was recorded in Palestine by the British government. According to all the reports of the period, Arab "recorded" immigration to Palestine was minimal, casual, and unquantifiable.[31]

Any observer at the time, however, might have found strong indications that questioned the accuracy of the government's assumptions from the beginning.

The British Department of Migration itself quite candidly acknowledged that the "records" in respect to *non-Jewish* immigration from neighboring countries such as "Syria" and "the Lebanon" were "defective"; that defect was deemed "of no great consequence," however, because, as the reports stated, the Department's records were intended to check only *"Jewish* immigration into Palestine according to the capacity of the country to absorb immigrants." The report assured, "in *that aspect* of the matter that the statistics may be held to have a high degree of accuracy."*[32]

Thus we find that in the British immigration system there was not even a serious gauge for considering the incidence of Arab immigration into "Palestine." The verbose description of the "mandatory policy" assumed that only *"Jewish* immigration" must be measured.

Yet, in the 1931 census, at least twenty-three different languages were reported in use by "Moslems," and most of those plus an additional twenty-eight were in use by "Christians"—many of whom were known as, or represented as "Arabs"—a total of at least fifty-one languages.[33]

And the *non-*Jews in Palestine in 1931 listed as their "birthplaces" at least twenty-four different countries, in addition to the Americas and Europe. In Jerusalem alone, twenty different places of birth (outside the Americas and Europe) were reported by the "Moslems"; those plus another four countries were listed by "Christians."[34]

The *"illegal"* Jewish immigration was fastidiously reported—"One case is

*Emphasis added.

TABLE C. Birthplaces of Inhabitants of Jerusalem District circa 1931

JEWS	NON-JEWS		
	Moslems	*Christians*	*Others*
Palestine	Palestine	Palestine	Palestine
Syria	Syria	Syria	Syria
Greek Islands	Transjordan	Transjordan	Egypt
Cyprus	Cyprus	Cyprus	Persia
Other Mediterranean Islands	Egypt	Malta	Czechoslovakia
	Hejaz-Nejd	Other Mediterranean Islands	Poland
Abyssinia	Iraq		Rumania
Egypt	Yemen	Abyssinia	Switzerland
Iraq	Other Arabian Territories	Egypt	United Kingdom
Yemen		Hejaz-Nejd	U.S.S.R.
Other Arabian Territories	Persia	Iraq	
	Turkey	Other Arabian Territories	
Persia	Central Asiatic Territories		
Turkey		Persia	
Central Asiatic Territories		Turkey	
	Indian Continent	Central Asiatic Territories	
Indian Continent			
Far Eastern Asia	Far Eastern Asia		
Other Asiatic Territories		Indian Continent	
	Algeria		
Algeria	Morocco	Far Eastern Asia	
Morocco	Tripoli		
Tripoli	Tunis	Algeria	
Tunis	Other African Territories	Morocco	
Other African Territories		Tripoli	
	Albania	Tunis	
Austria	France	Other African Territories	
Belgium	Greece		
Bulgaria	Spain	Albania	
Czechoslovakia	United Kingdom	Austria	
Denmark		Belgium	
Estonia	U.S.S.R.	Bulgaria	
Finland	U.S.A.	Czechoslovakia	
France	Central & South America	Denmark	
Germany		France	
Gibraltar	Australia	Germany	

TABLE C. Birthplaces of Inhabitants of Jerusalem District circa 1931 (cont'd)

JEWS	NON-JEWS		
	Moslems	*Christians*	*Others*
Greece		Gibraltar	
Holland		Greece	
Hungary		Holland	
Italy		Italy	
Latvia		Latvia	
Lithuania		Lithuania	
Poland		Norway	
Portugal		Poland	
Rumania		Portugal	
Spain		Rumania	
Switzerland		Spain	
United Kingdom		Sweden	
U.S.S.R.		Switzerland	
Yugoslavia		United Kingdom	
Canada			
U.S.A.		U.S.S.R.	
Central & South America		Yugoslavia	
		Canada	
Australia		U.S.A.	
		Central & South America	
		Australia	

TABLE D. Languages in Habitual Use in Palestine circa 1931

JEWS	NON-JEWS		
	Moslem	*Christian*	*Other*
Arabic	Afghan	Abyssinian	Arabic
Aramaic (Targum)	Albanian	Arabic	Czech
Armenian	Arabic	Armenian	English
Bokharian	Bosnian	Basque	French
Bulgarian	Chinese	Brazilian [*sic*]	German
Caucasian dialect	Circassian	Bulgarian	Hebrew
Circassian	English	Catalan	Persian
Danish	French	Chaldean	Polish
Dutch	German	Chinese	Russian
English	Greek	Circassian	Spanish
Español (Jewish dialect)	Gypsy	Czech	Yiddish
Finnish	Hebrew	Danish	
French	Hindustani	Dutch	
Georgian	Indian dialects	English	
German	Javanese	Estonian	
Greek	Kurdish	Finnish	
Hebrew	Persian	Flemish	
Hindustani	Portuguese	French	
Italian	Russian	German	
Kurdish	Spanish	Greek	

TABLE D. Languages in Habitual Use in Palestine circa 1931 (cont'd)

JEWS	NON-JEWS		
	Moslem	*Christian*	*Other*
Lithuanian	Sudanese	Hebrew	
Magyar	Takrurian	Hindustani	
Persian	Turkish	Indian dialects	
Polish		Irish	
Rumanian		Italian	
Russian		Kurdish	
Serbian		Latin	
Slavic		Magyar	
Swedish		Malayalam	
Swiss		Maltese	
Tatar Group		Norwegian	
Turkish		Persian	
Tuscan (Italian)		Polish	
Yiddish		Portuguese	
		Rumanian	
		Russian	
		Serbian	
		Slavic	
		Spanish	
		Sudanese	
		Swedish	
		Swiss	
		Syrian	
		Turkish	
		Welsh	

Source: *Census of Palestine—1931*, volume I, *Palestine*; Part I, *Report* by E. Mills, B.A., O.B.E., Assistant Chief Secretary Superintendent of Census (Alexandria, 1933), p. 147.

known in which a small party of Jews endeavored to enter Palestine via Trans-Jordan"[35]—while the Arabs who immigrated illegally were addressed only when their "detection" had become "flagrant."[36] The British Colonial officials were "thinking of Jews" in matters of immigration as we will see later in some detail.

But the British Government, which recorded comings and goings within Palestine, occasionally was forced by its prevalence to give mention to the "illegal *Arab* immigration."[37] The movement, however, was underestimated and minimized, deemed "casual," and was never introduced as a factor in determining the population increase in the portion of Palestine area being settled by the Jews:

> In addition to this increase by recorded immigration, a number of persons are known to enter Palestine *illegally* from both adjacent and European countries and to remain there permanently.*[38]

In fact, in some instances the conclusion that Jews were increasing through immigration while Arabs were increasing only through natural increase was

*Emphasis added.

alleged in the same reports which observed elsewhere in their pages that "considerable" illegal Arab immigration was indeed proceeding without restriction or record from such areas as Syria, Egypt, Transjordan, and Lebanon, among others.[39]

Most Government acknowledgments of *Arab* "illegal immigration" were concealed from recognition by the cryptic nonspecific heading of "Unrecorded Illegal Immigration" or were obscured by discussion of "Jews and Arabs" together.[40] When "illegal entry" of *Arabs* was recognized separately in that regard, invariably the report in question would note that the volume "must be insignificant."[41]

Although the Jewish "illegal" immigration—comparatively small until Hitler rose to power in the 1930s—was meticulously recorded, minutely detailed, and later even estimated in advance and deducted from the government's strict Jewish quota, the references to Arab "illegal immigration" were always presented ambiguously.[42] Almost without exception, the matter was obscured, negated, and overwhelmed by preponderant concentration on Jewish immigration as the primary issue.

Hints of Substantial Unrecorded Immigration

It was while studying documents pertinent to Palestine among the Winston Churchill papers[43] that the author first noticed a statement that challenged the very foundation of the current claim that Jewish settlement in Palestine had caused the uprooting of hundreds of thousands of Arabs.[44] Churchill said in 1939,

> . . . So far from being persecuted, the Arabs have crowded into the country and multiplied till their population has increased more than even all world Jewry could lift up the Jewish population.[45]

For the British statesman—a veteran of the first days in Britain's administration of the Mandate—to make that statement, surely he had to have become aware of significant evidence to back his assertion. And indeed, buried by the more recent propaganda campaign, politically targeted "fact sheets" distributed by organs of the United Nations and the Palestine Liberation Organization, and the gospel according to the British Foreign Office, substantial evidence does exist to support Churchill's challenge of the Arab propaganda.

For example, according to the *Minutes* of the Permanent Mandates Commission of the League of Nations,[46] *La Syrie* had published, on August 12, 1934, an interview with Tewfik Bey El-Hurani, Governor of the Hauran. Governor El-Hurani stated that *"in the last few months* from 30,000 to 36,000 Hauranese [Syrian] had *entered Palestine* and *settled* there."*

The Mandates Commission—which was overseer to all League of Nations Mandatory Administrations—took special "note" in its *Minutes* of the fact that the Hauranese, not merely passing through, had indeed "settled." Yet no official

---

*Emphasis added.

account of that important wave of Arabs who entered illegally appears in British immigration records.

In "private" and "secret" British correspondence files, however, there were innumerable references to Syrians from the Hauran district "admitted" freely to "Palestine" "without passport or visa"[47] from the beginning of the British Mandate after World War I and consistently into the 1940s.[48] British reports were at times obliged by the prevalence of "Syrian countrymen in Palestine" to acknowledge the "illegal . . . large proportion of Arab immigrants from the Hauran."[49]

But the data quoted from directly above were not included in any official report until after extensive evidence had been given in 1937* and consequent pressure exerted by the Permanent Mandates Commission.[50] Even then, in that belated acknowledgment, the recorded "number of Hauranis illegally in the country" was grossly underestimated.[51] Some of them had "fled" back to Syria and elsewhere to avoid prosecution for violence in the riots of 1936—but that factor will be examined later, along with more detailed evidence of the British policy of benign blinking.

The Permanent Mandates Commission had also addressed the incidence of illegal Arab immigrants from "Trans-Jordan." Its members had spoken of "free admission of Transjordanians into Palestine," which might "lead to abuse" since a number of them "remained in the country"; the Commission had indicated Arab illegal immigration from other countries as well, all of which is addressed in following pages.

For the moment, however, we turn back to the Syrian-Haurani influx, of "thirty to thirty-six thousand" Arab illegal immigrants from one area in just "a few months" of 1934, verified by an official international document and attested to by a Syrian leader.

That is, from spring to summer of 1934, from just one area in only one of the many depressed neighboring Arab countries from which impoverished citizens were known to be emigrating into Palestine—particularly into the Jewish-settled portion of the country—an Arab official's unequivocal report indicated that *more Arabs illegally entered and remained in Palestine than the total number of Jews for twice that length of time in 1934 who were "approved" to immigrate into their designated "Jewish National Home."*[52] Yet the official British record of immigration to Palestine for the entire year of 1934[53] reports "recorded immigration" of just 1,784 "non-Jews," with only about 3,000 as "travelers remaining illegally," and those figures supposedly included *Arab immigrants* from all points into all of Palestine.

Although carefully categorized records were kept for age groups, occupations, amount of capital, etc. of those *Jews* who immigrated, there was no specific accounting of the "non-Jews" in the official reports. None except for one phenomenon—despite the mandatory government's rigorous application of immigration laws for Jews and the official winking at the incidence of Arab illicit entry, the

*See Chapter 14.

number of *"non-Jews"* recorded as having been "deported for immigration offences" was more than twice as great as the number of Jews.[54] The question arises: if there were so many illegal Arab immigrants that even an official policy which concentrated almost solely on limiting *Jews* was forced to identify and deport more than twice as many *Arabs* as Jews, then is it not possible or even likely that the number of illegal Arab immigrants had to be so much larger than recorded that it constituted a massive wave of entry?

Yet, in autumn of 1934 the Palestine High Commissioner stated that during that year "We do not consider that the numbers of those illegal immigrants exceed 100 per month."[55] In 1935, the number of deportations of *non-*Jews was even more significant: in a system admittedly overlooking all but the most blatant cases of illicit Arab immigration, the 1935 Annual Report stated that of 2,455 deported, 2,152 were *"non-Jews."*[56]

Churchill's recognition of massive Arab immigration into Palestine was confirmed by many, including the British Governor of the Sinai from 1922 to 1936, who wryly observed that

> This illegal immigration was not only going on from the Sinai, but also from Transjordan and Syria and it is very difficult to make a case out for the misery of the Arabs if at the same time their compatriots from adjoining states could not be kept from going in to share that misery.[57]

Nonetheless, Arab leaders and their British supporters attempted to make exactly that case. In order to appease the small but powerful Arab *effendi* community, the Mandatory power began imposing stricter limitations upon Jewish immigration.

While counting the newly arrived Arab illicit immigrants as indigenous deeply rooted Palestinians, the British explained that it was the Jews who were flooding the country beyond its "absorptive capacity" and crowding out Arabs. The Hope Simpson *Report* of 1930 announced its seminal conclusion that Arabs were being "displaced" by Jews, even though in its own pages the report revealed that there was an *uncontrolled influx of illegal Arab immigrants from Egypt, Trans-Jordan and Syria.*[58]

Speaking unmistakably of *"other* than *Jewish* labour,"* the report states

> The Chief Immigration Officer has brought to notice that illicit immigration through Syria and across the northern frontier of Palestine is material.[59]

Further, the *Report* speaks of "the case of the *'pseudo-traveller'* who comes in with permission for a limited time and *continues* in Palestine after the term of his permission has expired" as being "present practice," a method that was *"injustice"* to the Jews.[60]*

The broad implications of that seemingly casual observation within the Hope

*Emphasis added.

Simpson *Report* will become evident in the following pages. If large-scale Arab immigration was a recognized "practice," how could official reports justify a conclusion that only Jewish population was increasing through immigration and forcing out Arabs? If Arabs were incoming also, then might their increase in number be attributable not to the natural increase of natives present since time immemorial on the land, but instead, an increase swelled as importantly—perhaps even more importantly—by immigration than that of the Jews?

One British official conducted an investigation on the "displaced" and "landless" Arab situation. Despite an enormous unrecorded Arab influx—and even adding the illicit Arab immigrant community into the category of "native population" that had supposedly been displaced—the official concluded, after investigating the areas, that the allegation was largely inaccurate, as we will see later from excerpts of his testimony during an official investigation.[61]

The official would be slain shortly thereafter.[62] The land being cleared by Palestinian Jews, for Jewish victims of persecution in Europe, had been and still was being appropriated by Arabs. Yet the White Paper of 1939 was in the works. That legislation by the British at the instigation of the Arabs would so harshly restrict *Jewish* immigration to Palestine that hundreds of thousands of Jews would be prevented from entering what was to have been their sanctuary and thus be condemned to the fateful inferno of the Nazis. And that White Paper would be justified by the premise that the Jews were usurping the Arabs' places in "Palestine."

According to the British Government's 1937 Report to the League of Nations,[63] the number of Arabs in Palestine had indeed soared higher, in Churchill's words, than "even all world Jewry could lift up the Jewish population." Yet this crucial and incompatible evidence went disregarded or unrecognized and was never figured into the political equation of Palestine.[64]

12

A Hidden Factor in Western Palestine: Arab In-Migration

> The Palestinian Arabs have at present no will of their own. Neither have they ever developed any specifically Palestinian nationalism. . . . It would seem as though in existing circumstances most of the Palestinian Arabs would be quite content to be incorporated in Trans-Jordan.
>
> —Folke Bernadotte, *To Jerusalem,* 1950–1951

> The Arabs cannot say that the Jews are driving them out of their country. If not a single Jew had come to Palestine after 1918, I believe that the Arab population of [Western] Palestine today [over a million in 1938] would still have been around about the . . . figure at which it had been stable under the Turkish rule.
>
> —Malcolm MacDonald, British Secretary of State, 1938

The prevalent perception is that Jewish immigrants arrived in "Palestine" amidst a crowded Arab populace around 1917, at the time the Balfour Declaration established a "Jewish National Home." Few Middle East observers have been aware of the extent to which the Jewish Settlement had begun to develop in the nineteenth century. The Jews, many believe, infringed upon the "natives" on "millennia"-settled "Palestinian Arab land."

Contrary to that assumption, of the sparse Muslim population found in "Palestine" at that time, many were transient and most were landless, as we have seen. As Arab leader Sherif Hussein had commented in a 1918 article discussed in earlier pages, the "native soil" of Palestine could not keep the Arabs from "wandering . . . in every direction."

Defining the Native Soil: A Critical Error Identified

One of the most confusing matters of the "Palestinian problem" is the location of "Palestine." What area in fact constituted the "native soil"? In most discussions of the Middle East today, Israel is considered equivalent to all Palestine.

But the *land* on which Israel was located contained only a fraction of the Palestine Mandate originally dedicated to the Jews as their homeland, incorporating the Balfour Declaration.[1] The League of Nations and the British had designated the land called "Palestine" for the "Jewish National Home"—east and west of the Jordan River from the Mediterranean to Arabia and Iraq, and north and south from Egypt to Lebanon and Syria.[2] Historian Arnold Toynbee observed in 1918 that the "desolate" land "which lies east of the Jordan stream,"[3] was

> capable of supporting a large population if irrigated and cultivated scientifically. . . . The Zionists have as much right to this no-man's land as the Arabs, or more.

Thus, the territory known variously as "Palestine," as "South Syria," as "Eastern and Western Palestine," or as part of "Turkey" had been designated by international mandate as a "Jewish National Home," concerning which the United States declared,

> That there be established a separate state of Palestine. . . . placed under Great Britain as a mandatory of the League of Nations . . . that the Jews be invited to return to Palestine and settle there. . . . and being further assured that it will be the policy of the League of Nations *to recognize Palestine as a Jewish state as soon as it is a Jewish state in fact.* . . . England, as mandatory, can be relied on to give the Jews the privileged position they should have without sacrificing the [religious and property] rights of non-Jews.*[4]

The Arabs of that day achieved independent Arab statehood in various lands around Palestine but not within Palestine itself. Sovereignty was granted after World War I to the Arabs in Syria and Iraq; in addition, Saudi Arabia consisted of approximately 865,000 square miles of territory that was designated as "purely Arab."[5]

Considering all the "territories" that had been given to the Arabs, Lord Balfour "hoped" that the "small notch" of Palestine east and west of the Jordan River, which was "being given" to the Jewish people, would not be "grudged" to them by Arab leaders.[6]

But, in a strategic move, the British Government apparently felt "the need to assuage the Emir's [Abdullah's] feelings."[7] As one of the royal sons of the Hejaz (Saudi Arabia), Abdullah was a recipient of British gratitude; the Arabians of the Hejaz had been, among all the Arab world, of singular assistance to England against the Turks.[8]

The insertion of Abdullah and his emirate into mandated Palestine, in the area east of the Jordan River that was part of the land allocated to the "Jewish National Home," might be partially traced to a suggestion received by Colonial Secretary Winston Churchill from T. E. Lawrence. In a letter of January 1921, Lawrence informed Churchill that Emir Feisal (Abdullah's brother, and Lawrence "of Arabia's" choice to lead the Arab revolt)[9] had "agreed to abandon all

*Emphasis added.

Britain and the Palestine Mandate: the Jewish National Home

SYRIA

IRAQ

Mediterranean Sea

PALESTINE MANDATE

EGYPT

HEJAZ
(SAUDI ARABIA)

Palestine Mandate, granted to Britain in 1920 at San Remo Conference, approved 1922 by League of Nations as Jewish National Home

Separated from Palestine by Britain in 1921–1922, bestowed upon Emir Abdullah by Britain, called Transjordan

Ceded by British to French Mandate of Syria in 1923

Sources: Martin Gilbert, *The Arab-Israeli Conflict. Its History in Maps;* Esco Foundation,
Palestine. A Study of Jewish, Arab, and British Policies.

The Mandate of Palestine: "Small Notch" in the Arab World

claim of his father to [Western] Palestine," if Feisal got in return Iraq and Eastern Palestine as Arab territories.*

Further explanation was found in a "secret dispatch from Chief British Representative at Amman" later in 1921. He cautioned that the local "Transjordanian Cabinet" had been replaced by a "Board of Secretaries,"

> responsible for all internal affairs, referring to his highness Abdullah for a decision in the event of any disagreement. . . .

All the "Board" members, according to the Eastern Palestine envoy, were

> Syrian exiles, who with perhaps one exception, are more interested in designs on the French in Syria than in developing Trans-Jordania. . . . In his Highness' opinion, the allies had not dealt fairly with the Arab nation and Great Britain had not treated him as he deserved. He was one of the most chiefly instrumental in bringing about the Arab revolution and when Feisal, during the war, was inclined to accept the overtures of the Turks he had opposed that policy. . . . When he came to Trans-Jordania "with the consent of the British", he had agreed to act in accordance with Mr. Churchill's wishes and with British policy, as he did not wish to be the cause of any friction between the British and their allies, the French. . . . The allies had not dealt fairly with the Arabs because, whereas they had agreed to form one Arab nation, forming different Arab states, and even in Syria, as small as it is, they had divided that country into six or seven states. He had come to Trans-Jordania hoping for great things and now he realized that he had no hope either north or east. *If he went back from here to the Hejaz, he would look ridiculous.* †[10]

Winston Churchill proposed his plan for Transjordan to Prime Minister Lloyd George in March 1921:

> We do not expect or particularly desire, indeed, Abdullah himself to undertake the Governorship. He will, as the Cabinet rightly apprehend, almost certainly think it too small. . . . The actual solution which we have always had in mind and for which I shall work is that which you described as follows: while preserving Arab character of area and administration to *treat it as an Arab province or adjunct of Palestine.* [11]

It was a British Jew, Palestine High Commissioner Sir Herbert Samuel, who supported and even extended Winston Churchill's formulations. Samuel sent a telegram to Churchill in July 1921; while discouraging Churchill from submitting to Abdullah's predicted eventual "demand" for "attachment of Trans-Jordania to the Hejaz," as being "contrary to Article V of the Mandate and open to much objection in relation to future development," High Commissioner Samuel suggested the following:

---

*See Feisal-Weizmann agreement in Appendix IV.
†Emphasis added.

I concur in proposal that Abdullah should visit London and had written to you suggesting it. . . . At the end of six months, the following settlement might be arranged: (1) the Arab governor mutually agreed upon by his majesty's government and Abdullah or King Hussein. (2) British officer(s) to have real control. (3) Reserve force commanded by British officer(s), Air Force and armored cars as at present. (4) A small British garrison to be stationed in District temporarily. (5) A declaration in accordance with new article to be inserted in mandate that *Jewish National Home provisions do not apply east of Jordan.* This would *not prevent* such *Jewish immigration* as political and economic conditions allowed but without special encouragement by Government.*[12]

Feisal got his wishes and became King of Iraq;[13] his brother Abdullah was installed in the British mandatory area as ruler of the "temporary" emirate on the land of eastern Palestine, which became known as the "Kingdom of Transjordan."

Palestine High Commissioner Harold MacMichael later offered some evidence of the original "temporary" nature of British intentions in a "private, personal and most secret" cipher; MacMichael reported in 1941 that Abdullah now harbored greater ambitions, because of

the part he [Abdullah] played in the last war, his position in the Arab world as a senior member of a royal house, [and] the purely *temporary* arrangements whereby in 1921 having narrowly missed being made King (a) of Iraq and (b) of Syria in turn, he was left to look after Trans-Jordan. . . .*[14]

Britain nevertheless quietly gouged out roughly three-fourths of the Palestine territory mandated for the Jewish homeland[15] into an Arab emirate, Transjordan,[16] while the Mandate ostensibly remained in force but in violation of its terms.[17] Historians and official government documents concerned with the area continued to call it "Eastern Palestine," despite the new appellation. That seventy-five percent of the Palestine mandate was described by England's envoy to Eastern Palestine:[18] "a reserve of land for use in the resettlement of Arabs [from Western Palestine], once the National Home for the Jews in Palestine"† resulted in the "Jewish independent state."

The League of Nations Mandate for Palestine remained unchanged even though Britain had unilaterally altered its map and its purpose.[19] The Mandate included Transjordan until 1946, when that land was declared an independent state.[20] Transjordan had finally become the *de jure* Arab state in Palestine *just two years before* Israel gained its Jewish statehood in the remaining one-quarter of Palestine; Transjordan comprised nearly 38,000 square miles; Israel, less than 8,000 square miles.

---

*Emphasis added.

†As the next chapters will illustrate, instead, Arabs poured *from* Eastern Palestine as well as from Arab areas within Western Palestine—*into* the *Jewish-settled areas* in Western Palestine. The course of action which followed from that unrecognized population movement brought ramifications which are as *critical* to the question of political "justice" as they are *unknown* or disregarded today.

Thus, about seventy-five percent of Palestine's "native soil," east of the Jordan River, called Jordan, is literally an independent Palestinian-Arab state located on the majority of the land of Palestine; it contains a majority of Palestinian Arabs in its army as well as its population. In April 1948,[21] just before the formal hostilities were launched against Israel's statehood, Abdullah of Transjordan declared:[22] "Palestine and Transjordan are one, for Palestine is the coastline and Transjordan the hinterland of the same country." Abdullah's policy was defended against "Arab challengers" by Prime Minister Hazza al-Majali:

> We are the army of Palestine. . . . the overwhelming majority of the Palestine Arabs . . . are living in Jordan.[23]

Although Abdullah's acknowledgment of Palestinian identity was not in keeping with the policy of his grandson, the present King Hussein, Jordan is nonetheless undeniably Palestine, protecting a predominantly Arab Palestinian population with an army containing a majority of Arab Palestinians, and often governed by them as well. Jordan remains an independent Arab Palestinian state where a Palestinian Arab "law of return" applies: its nationality code states categorically that all Palestinians are entitled to citizenship by right unless they are Jews.[24] In most demographic studies, and wherever peoples are designated, including contemporary Arab studies, the term applied to citizens of Jordan is "Palestinian/Jordanian." In 1966 the Arab League's Ahmed Shukeiry declared that[25]

> The Kingdom of Palestine must become the Palestinian Republic. . . .

Yasser Arafat has stated that Jordan is Palestine. Other Arab leaders, even King Hussein and Prince Hassan of Jordan, from time to time have affirmed that "Palestine is Jordan and Jordan is Palestine." Moreover, in 1970–1971, later called the "Black September" period, when King Hussein waged war against Yasser Arafat's Arab PLO forces, who had been operating freely in Jordan until then, it was considered not an invasion of foreign terrorists but a *civil* war. It was "a final crackdown" against those of "his people"[26] whom he accused of trying to establish a separate Palestinian state, under Arab Palestinian rule instead of his own, "criminals and conspirators who use the commando movement to disguise their treasonable plots," to "destroy the unity of the Jordanian and Palestinian people."[27]

Indeed, the "native soil" of Arab and Jewish "Palestines" each gained independence within the same two-year period, Transjordan in 1946 and Israel in 1948. Yet today, in references to the "Palestine" conflict, even the most serious expositions of the problem refer to Palestine as though it consisted only of Israel —as in the statement, "In 1948 Palestine became Israel."[28] The term "Israel" is commonly used as if it were the sum total of "Palestine."

However, *within* what Lord Balfour had referred to as that "small notch" sometimes called Palestine, the "Jewish National Home" had been split into *two* separate unequal Palestines: Eastern Palestine—or the Arab emirate of Transjordan—and Western Palestine, which comprised less than one-fourth of the League of Nations Mandate. The portion of the "notch" of land on which the Jews settled and in which most Jews actually lived—from the 1870s and 1880s through the 1940s—was in fact only a segment of the area of *Western* Palestine.

The only part of Palestine which is pertinent to the persistent Arab allegation that Jews "displaced" Arabs is that fraction of Western Palestine where the Jews were placed, and where they settled and lived.[29] From the beginning of the "new" Jewish reclamation and land development during the 1870s until Israel became a state in 1948, that area of Jewish settlement remained roughly the same.

As we have seen, the corner of Palestine that eventually became Israel was sparsely inhabited by any permanent indigenous settled peoples when the Jews' organized redevelopment is said to have commenced, in 1870–1880.[30] It was an underpopulated land, its revolving populace perennially depleted in number because of exploitation, reckless plundering, nomadism, endless tribal uprisings, and natural disaster.

Interestingly, Eastern Palestine's Arab population was usually excluded from consideration as part of "Palestine's" total population, for several reasons: 1) despite several attempts by Jewish developers and supporters of the Mandate, no Jews were permitted to settle in that eastern portion of the mandated area of "the Jewish National Home," from the beginning of British administration of the Mandate in 1922; 2) it was politically expedient for the Arabs concerned, and their British supporters, to *eradicate* the qualifying adjective "Western." By so doing, they would eliminate the otherwise automatic interconnection to an "Eastern" Palestine, which was already being treated as an Arab state; 3) if Western Palestine were not perceived as "all of Palestine," then it would have been clearly recognized that Arab Palestine was a *fait accompli* in Transjordan-Jordan just as a Jewish Palestine was a *fait accompli* in Israel; and 4) the Zionists were too preoccupied with the hazards of protecting and developing the small area they had already purchased in *Western* Palestine to concentrate on the eastern territory filched from their National Home, where few if any Jews still survived.

In many areas of *Western* Palestine, Jews were prohibited from settling; in some places, they were murdered or forced to flee for their lives,* and some areas of Western Palestine, where few if any Jews then lived, were excluded from Israel's territory in 1949. Obviously, one cannot charge the Jews with "displacement of Arabs" in those areas of Western Palestine where there were no Jews. Yet that is precisely what is alleged and promulgated by the vagaries of today's propaganda, assisted by the general unfamiliarity with facts about the country at the time.

When the Arab and Jewish total populations in Western Palestine at about the beginning of the twentieth century are compared to show the preponderance of non-Jews over Jews, the comparison is in every case erroneous. It is wrong because invariably the *Arab* total population figure cited takes in the *overall Arab*

*See Chapter 9.

population of *all* Western Palestine, while the Jewish total population figure relates only to the Jewish-settled area.

Such a specious comparison is tantamount to describing the population of Harlem by comparing as equal situations the total population of the whites in all of New York State with the number of blacks living in Harlem—assuming for this hypothesis that blacks lived *only* in Harlem—and using the much greater number of the whites *throughout the whole state* as a basis for claiming that "the whites are the overwhelming majority in Harlem." Keeping that in mind, note the following examples of official descriptions of Palestine's population:

> At present, however, the Jews form barely a sixth of the total population of 700,000 in Palestine. . . .[31]

> In 1919 the total estimated population of Palestine was 590,000. The Jewish population of Palestine was 55,000 or nine per cent.[32]

> In 1918 there had been less than 100,000 Jews in Palestine and over a half a million Arabs.[33]

In other words, the "less than 100,000 Jews" who all lived in the *Jewish-settled area* of Western Palestine are being compared with "over half a million Arabs" who inhabited all the territory *throughout* Western Palestine, including mostly those Arabs who lived *away* from Jews or their settlements.

As an American Presbyterian clergyman later pointed out,

> Malcolm MacDonald, one of the principal authors of the Chamberlain-Mac-Donald White Paper of 1939 and thus no friend of the Zionists, had this significant comment to make about Jewish benefits to Arabs in Palestine (in 1939):
> "The Arabs cannot say that the Jews are driving them out of their country. If not a single Jew had come to Palestine after 1918, I believe that the Arab population of [Western] Palestine today [over a million in 1938] would still have been round about the 600,000 figure at which it had been stable under the Turkish rule."[34]

Even in the above statement—which was intended to illustrate that Jews were responsible not for "displacing" Arabs, but for bringing Arabs *into* Western Palestine—the cited "600,000 figure" for Arabs referred to the whole of Western Palestine, not just the relevant Jewish-settled area. Unwittingly, the statement, and others like it, have fostered false interpretations. As in the "Harlem" hypothesis, if all Arabs throughout (Western) "Palestine" are compared with the small total Jewish population, then the Arab and Jewish populations are all necessarily assumed, incorrectly, to live on the same part of the terrain. In discussions of a vast "Arab majority," then, the Jewish-settled area is presumed to cover all of "Palestine."

The figures cited universally for Palestine have never been broken down into an accurate assessment of how many Muslim Arabs had been living permanently and for a long period in the areas of heavy Jewish settlement, when the Jews came to settle—that is, when, allegedly, the "natives were displaced by Jews."

Because of the skewed statistics universally cited, the popular misconception is that Jewish settlers had arrived among a half-million "Arabs" and usurped the land from a teeming population of "native Palestinian Arabs from time immemorial" on "Palestinian Arab land for millennia." One has gathered from that framework that 1) all those non-Jewish Arabic-speaking inhabitants have "always" been there and 2) that all of them originated in the areas of Jewish settlement in Western Palestine, where they would *have* to have lived in order to justly forward the claim that they were "displaced" by Jews. The first assumption—of a "millenary Arab-Palestinian character, nationality and population" in Palestine[35]—was discussed in earlier pages.[36]

The second assumption—that the population (as well as the land) in the Jewish-settled area of Western Palestine was synonymous with all the population in all of Western Palestine—is pivotal to the current Arab claim to Israel as the "inalienable right of the Palestinian people." To make that assumption discards the weight of evidence available from the beginning of the period of broader Jewish agricultural settlement, dated generally as 1872–1882.

To compare the total number of Jews who all settled in a *portion* of Western Palestine with the number of Arabs *throughout* Western Palestine is incompatible and inaccurate. Moreover, to use such a comparison is to paint a falsely diabolical picture of Jews converging and taking over a crowded area where all of the larger number of Arabs were concentrated. Any survey beginning with that distorted assumption must proceed from its premise to an unfair, one-sided, and faulty conclusion—no less faulty than to assume, as in the earlier specious formula, that "whites are the majority of Harlem."

The Jewish-settled areas have been assumed incorrectly to be *all* of Palestine, when in fact the Jewish-settled areas were only a fraction of an already-truncated Palestine,* a Palestine of which about seventy-five percent had been already delivered to Arab control—in violation of international mandate. It is primarily because that erroneous geographical assumption has been ingrained in the dialogue and perceptions of the Middle East Arab–Israeli conflict that the claim of "Palestinian Arabs excluded from Palestine" has gained a measure of credibility.

The recorded Arab population figures in that fraction of Western Palestine which was the Jewish-settled area (later in Israel) must be examined in order to determine the nature and density of the population in that area. The only Arab population which can fairly be compared with the Jewish population is that number of the Arabs who in fact lived within the Jewish-settled area at the time of comparison: that is, when the Jews settled. Further, the only Arab population which can accurately be considered the *"existing* non-Jewish population" when the Jewish National Home was developed is that part which was settled on the land *before* the Jews' resettlement began. Those Arabs who arrived in Jewish-settled areas *with* the Jews, or *after* the Jews arrived and had begun to develop

*See map, p. 246.

their land in Western Palestine, obviously cannot be "indigenous millennia-settled Arab Palestinians" living on their plot of land in the Jewish-settled area "since time immemorial."

As we have seen, the later nineteenth-century Muslim population of Palestine "was continuously replenished from the tribes of the Arabian desert," with "colonies of Turkomans, Circassians, Kurds and others planted about," mainly because the "Arab race" had "diminished most sadly."[37] This might explain the statements by British observers and official reports that "fluctuations cancelled out" any possible increase in Western Palestine, leaving a static small number of inhabitants which had not changed "for two centuries." It was a condition that, but for the Jewish development, might have continued to "remain the same."

In the area then part of "Southern Syria," later called "Western Palestine" —and today mistaken for all of "Palestine"—the total population when Jewish colonization began (1872–1882) was between 300,000 and 400,000 souls, according to the most reliable estimates.[38] Thirty-four thousand were Jews, living largely in their four "holy cities."[39] Less than half the population was "settled" Muslim, 65,000 were Bedouin-nomadic,[40] and roughly 55,000 were Christians. Thus, a total of roughly 200,000 Muslims* were living in all of Western Palestine in 1882.

However imprecise the estimates of population in "Palestine" or "Southern Syria" may have been, there are a few among the geographers, field workers, and researchers of that time who have been cited consistently in historical studies of the period, and whose population estimates have been generally accepted as reliable.

According to perhaps the most detailed and scientific of these, the study by the French geographer Vital Cuinet,[41] the population of Western Palestine by 1895 had grown to more than 450,000, of which Muslims numbered roughly 252,000 throughout Western Palestine.

1882: 141,000 "settled" Muslims†
1895: 252,000 "settled" Muslims

The above figures for the Muslim population would indicate that their number almost doubled in the thirteen years between 1882 and 1895. This hardly seems possible. Even if we assume a high rate of natural increase‡ of 1.5 percent per annum for that thirteen-year period, the population would not have increased to more than 170,000 or so.

The rate of natural increase we have assumed in order to reach even the 170,000 figure is unduly high by all demographic indications and observations of the time: depending on the angle of vision, reportedly the "Arab race" was "decreasing," had "diminished in number" between 1872 and 1882, or at best,

*Settled and nomadic.
†Nomads excluded.
‡Natural increase = births − deaths: in other words, "natural" population growth exclusive of in-migration, out-migration, immigration, or emigration.

"fluctuations" in the population had "cancelled out," with the result that the population figure remained static.

Even assuming that unlikely rate were accurate,[42] if we also assume that the 1895 figure of 252,000 is accurate, then what must be accounted for is the difference of 82,000 between the Muslims' maximum population growth due to natural increase (170,000) and the total figure of 252,000. The only plausible answer is that at least the remainder of roughly 82,000 of the Muslim Arabic-speaking "settled" population in Palestine in 1895 had to be *immigrants* and *in-migrants,* * whose arrival coincided exactly with the time Jewish development commenced.

As we will see, in greater detail, not only the time, but the *place*—the Jewish-settled area of Western Palestine—where the Jewish immigrants and the Arab immigrants and in-migrants were headed was the same. The Arabs were moving into the very areas where Jewish settlement had preceded them and was luring them.

The statistics from 1893 onward, which will be described in the following pages, are more definitive and solid. However, the earliest estimates for 1882–1895, although approximate, are important as a gauge to view the impact that the Jewish settlements had upon the population growth in Western Palestine *as a whole,* from the very beginning. Further, they illustrate clearly the pattern that Arab propaganda has obscured. It was a pattern so clear that it prompted unambiguous and apolitical observations such as the following in 1953 by Dr. Carl Hermann Voss, then Chairman of the American Christian Palestine Committee:

> *The Arab population of Palestine was small and limited until Jewish resettlement restored the barren lands and drew to it Arabs from neighboring countries.* †[43]

When organized Jewish colonization began in 1882, there were fewer than 150,000 Arabs in the land. The great majority of the Arab population in recent decades were comparative newcomers—either late immigrants or descendants of persons who had immigrated into Palestine in the previous seventy years.[44]

The Jewish-Settled Area: Identifying the Population

Once the layout, general population figures, and trends for the period have been established for *all* of Western "Palestine," the *specific* area of relevance—the Jewish-settled area of Western Palestine—must be examined more close-

---

*See Chapter 8. When used in this book, the term "in-migrant" means a person who moves into the Jewish-settled area of Western Palestine from another part of Western Palestine. (The term "in-migrant" might properly be applied also to those who moved from Eastern Palestine—part of the same country, in fact. However, this study used the population data to trace Western Palestine population movements exclusively in its calculations.) "Immigrant" means a person who comes into Western Palestine from a place outside Western Palestine; the term "emigrant" means a person who moves out of Western Palestine.

†Emphasis added.

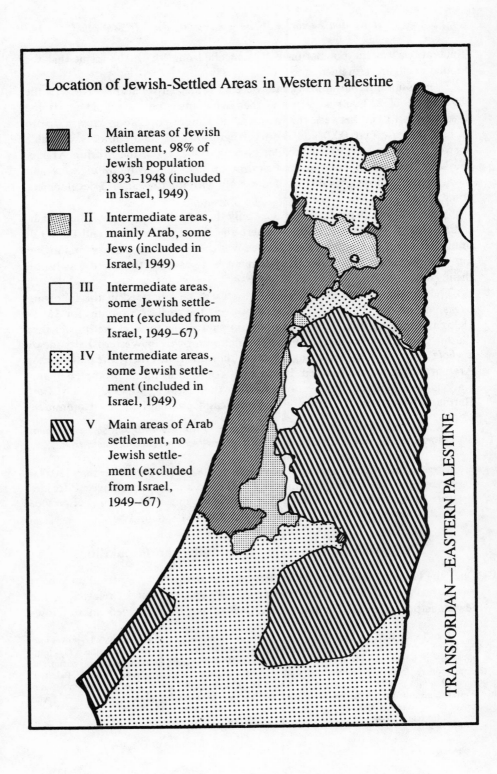

Location of Jewish-Settled Areas in Western Palestine

I   Main areas of Jewish settlement, 98% of Jewish population 1893–1948 (included in Israel, 1949)

II   Intermediate areas, mainly Arab, some Jews (included in Israel, 1949)

III   Intermediate areas, some Jewish settlement (excluded from Israel, 1949–67)

IV   Intermediate areas, some Jewish settlement (included in Israel, 1949)

V   Main areas of Arab settlement, no Jewish settlement (excluded from Israel, 1949–67)

TRANSJORDAN—EASTERN PALESTINE

ly. Therein lies the Arab claim of "displacement" and "exclusion" by Jews.*

In order to establish the true demographic picture of Jews and Arabs in Jewish-settled territory of Western Palestine, the actual number of *non-Jews* who were settled inhabitants when modern Jewish immigration began—and not *non-Jewish in-migrants* from other areas in Western Palestine who followed the Jews for work, or *immigrants* of recent vintage—must be determined.

As Kemal Karpat, who has recently published his important analysis and findings concerning the 1893 Turkish census, observed in 1972:

> Ottoman documents as well as British consular reports indicate clearly that the area to be known as Palestine was divided among several administrative subcenters. Consequently, any demographic study of Palestine shall have to deal separately with each major town and its environments included in this area in order to establish the number of people inhabiting it.[45]

To excavate the facts, a population breakdown of the period has been calculated. The results of that study have revealed, with greater accuracy than statistics or estimates in the past, how many non-Jews were actually inhabiting the land within the Jewish-settled area of Western Palestine when Jewish colonization began—it was that land which constituted virtually all the territory in which the Jews lived until 1948 when Israel became a state. (The barren southern half of Western Palestine, the Negev Desert, included in Israel in 1948, is not relevant, since no Jews lived on that land until a handful pioneered the area in 1944, and no Arabs had settled it before then. Also excluded are Western Galilee and the "Jerusalem corridor" where Jewish settlement was scattered.)

Before discussing the results, perhaps a review of the factors which prompted that examination would be of interest to the reader. Surely the matter of an unrecorded bloc of thirty-some thousand Arab immigrants entering Palestine illegally in only "a few months" seemed to contradict the British reports that Arab in-migration and immigration were "insignificant," and it piqued curiosity.

The "unprecedented" sudden "natural" increase among the Arabs of Western Palestine after centuries of static population figures was intriguing. That extraordinary increase was represented as a countrywide "phenomenon."

And the concept of an earlier "depopulated" and "barren" land did not jibe with the popular propaganda picture of Jews barging into the midst of a teeming Arab populace. The alleged displacement by Jews of a vast majority of "millennia-settled" Arab inhabitants in Jewish-settled areas of Western Palestine conflicts with readily available evidence; migration and landlessness among the peasantry were traditional and commonplace in that region.

There were more tangible indications that the history of the Arab population in the Jewish-settled area of Western Palestine was incomplete and therefore susceptible to misinterpretations and distortion. British reports admittedly con-

*See map, p. 246.

centrated on quantifying *Jewish* immigration; the British obviously had not even attempted to quantify *Arab* in-migration or illegal Arab immigration, and yet their reports consistently referred to the apparently unavoidable, "unquantifiable illicit Arab immigration" from neighboring lands as a problem that needed control.

In 1939 Winston Churchill had unambiguously pointed out that "Arabs have crowded into the country" in greater numbers than Jews.[46] Investigations conducted by the British government—even those which were judged by others among the plethora of British reports as biased toward the Arabs[47]—cautioned against continuing the habit of freely allowing illegal Arab immigrants into Palestine.*

Based upon the challenges arising from contradictory reports, and ambiguous, vague generalities used by official and expert sources to describe both the whereabouts of the Western Palestine population and the identification of what in fact *was* "Palestine," a series of originally uninformed questions eventually evolved through research into some revealing answers. (A map can be found on page 246; a detailed corresponding chart is in Appendix V.)

The findings have provided a logical explanation for some of the unknowns inherent in prevalent assumptions—crucial questions that somehow never have been considered—about the history of the population of "Palestine." They are questions that must be answered if the Arab-Israeli conflict is to be understood.

Tracing the Peoples: Tools and Categories

We have extrapolated a rough breakdown of the non-Jewish population into the number of "Arabs" or non-Jews who lived inside and outside the area of Jewish settlement in Western Palestine: it was that area which constituted Jewish settlement focus during the half century before the state of Israel was established.

The basic data and statistics were primarily drawn from the 1893 Turkish census statistics[48] for non-Jewish population figures according to Turkish subdistricts within Western Palestine; those figures, in turn, were broken down into Jewish-settled areas. British and Arab data and British[49] census statistics were used for the later non-Jewish population figures according to British subdistricts (which closely corresponded to the Turkish subdistricts).

With those tools, employing traditional demographic methods,† it has been possible to calculate[50] the non-Jewish population that existed in the Jewish-settled areas of Western Palestine in 1893, according to the official Turkish census.‡ Also

*See Chapter 14.
†Natural increase= births minus deaths; total population minus natural increase = immigration.
‡See description of methodology for study of population in Western Palestine in Appendix VI.

extracted from the census data was the number of the non-Jewish population *outside* the Jewish-settled areas, in the rest of Western "Palestine," where Jews were not permitted to purchase land for settlement after 1939, where the majority of Arabs lived in 1893 and afterward, and much of which was excluded from Israel in 1948.

The resulting calculations have drawn a more accurate picture of the population distribution and movement in Western "Palestine"—both in the Jewish-settled area included in Israel and in the areas within Western Palestine that, although allocated to the "Jewish National Home," were never or were only negligibly settled by Jews between 1882 and 1948.

The results have provided an answer to the following question: *at a minimum, how many of the Arab population, of whom all were counted as "indigenous existing natives" by Arab leaders and by the British government, were actually in-migrants —that is, newcomers to the Jewish-settled areas from other, "Arab areas" of Western Palestine?* The point was *not* to prove that no remnant of long-time Arab settled population existed. The purpose of the study was to determine whether in fact there was a large-scale displacement of Arab natives by Jews in Western Palestine before and at the time of the November 1947–1948 war of Arabs against Jewish independence.

What the calculations indicate is that, rather than a situation in which a teeming Arab people, present "from time immemorial," was forced off or excluded from its land, the situation is almost the exact opposite, of a people—the Jews—whose presence attracted Arab migrants, and the Jews' land, earmarked as their Home, was usurped by the arrival of these Arab in-migrants from outside Jewish-settled areas.

From this point we shall call the entire non-Jewish population "Arabs" when discussing the calculations of the study. For purposes of these discussions, which project Turkish population figures through the British period, a common criterion had to be employed, one that could most accurately trace the "Arab" population and its increase throughout the 1893–1947 span.

In spite of the fact that to identify persons accurately as "Arabs," in ethnic terms,* requires notice and recognition of ethnic origin,[51] and that a great number in Western Palestine were *not* "Arab," *all* the Arabic-speaking peoples in Palestine who were *non-Jewish* were identified at times, inconsistently, as "Arabs," particularly in British records; non-Arab Muslims, Christians, and "others" were all at various times, for purposes of categorizing, listed as "Arabs."[52] In the British Records the categories applied were inconsistent and ambiguous. For instance, within the category of "Non-Jews" may arbitrarily fall Christians, Moslems, Armenians, Russians, Druses, and others. The inexactness of the records allows for wide interpretation of the data. More specifically, it can conceal particular data, perhaps unintentionally; for example, the use of the "Non-Jew,

*See Chapter 8.

Jew" delineation when reporting immigration/emigration data allows for one to interpret that the proportion of Arabs and Muslims entering the country was low, relative to other non-Jewish groups. In this way, an influx of Arab immigrants might be neatly camouflaged.[53]

In a typical presentation following Arab propaganda claims, the Arab population is defined as Muslims plus Christians:

> The combined Muslim and Christian population, that is the Arab population, of Palestine. . . .[54]

In the 1930s, as discussed earlier, the (Western) Palestine Department of Migration Reports explained that, if there were "defects" in the system of identifying Arab population changes, the "defects were of no great consequence . . . ," because

> . . . the consideration of the records of . . . *Jewish* immigration into Palestine according to the capacity of the country to absorb immigrants . . . may be held to have a high degree of accuracy.*[55]

As another report would underscore, for the Arab population movements, "*different* considerations from those relevant to Jewish immigration" had been applied.[56]

In addition, Turkish and British demographic statistics employed different criteria in their data[57]—the Turks by religion, the British sometimes by religion, other times only by ethnic breakdown. Thus, for consistency in tracing the population movement in Western Palestine through the 1893–1948 period, the "Arab" category used in calculations was compelled to include all non-Jewish inhabitants in Western Palestine—even though not Arab—and is in fact equivalent to "non-Jewish."

The term "Arab," then, has been employed by this study only to simplify the logical conclusions to be drawn therefrom. But as a result, the figures that this study calculated in order to determine "Arab" population actually include a percentage of Christians who were not Arab, as well as other groups, such as Circassians, Armenians, and Druses, living in Western Palestine between 1893 and 1947–1948.

1893 in the Jewish-Settled Area of Western Palestine: Findings and Indications

The first finding is typical and central. In 1893 at most 92,300 non-Jews apparently lived in Jewish-settled areas of Western Palestine.† In other words, within the area where organized Jewish settlements began in 1872–1882—the area where more than ninety-eight percent of the Jews would live during the fifty or sixty

*Emphasis added.
†See the table in Appendix V.

years between the beginning of modern settlement and Israel's independence—the entire *non-Jewish* population, Muslims, Christians and "others," of that Jewish-settled area was little more than 92,000 in 1893.

The data indicate that the proportion of Arabs to Jews in Western Palestine was far smaller than the conventional wisdom has assumed. At that time the Jews there numbered nearly 60,000, despite Turkish restrictions against Jewish immigration, which by 1893 the Turkish government had already been enforcing for years.

There is also reliable evidence from another source that within that non-Jewish population of about 92,000, nearly 38,000 were Christians. The total of 92,300 "non-Jews," as recorded by the Turkish census, corroborates Vital Cuinet's estimate in 1895 of roughly 93,600 "non-Jews"—37,853 Christians and 55,823 Muslims—compared to 59,431 Jews, in the Jewish-settled areas.[58]

In Jewish-settled areas of Palestine, then, the Jews were at least as numerous as the Muslims. However, because of the use of the categories that would correspond to both Turkish and British records in order to project population figures accurately, the projected calculations counted as "Arabs" undoubted thousands of non-Jews who were *not* in fact either "settled Muslims" or "Arab" Christians in 1893. This illustrates that what the study concludes to be the "Arab" settled indigenous population in 1893 already includes a built-in inflation of "Arab" population; it must do so, for the sake of accuracy.

In actuality, the Jewish settled area, which *today* holds the majority of the nearly four million souls in Israel, contained less than 155,000 people before the turn of the century—a decade or two after modern Jewish settlement commenced.

In fact, the true picture of the peoples in Jewish-settled Western Palestine in 1893–1895 would be likely to show that *Jews* were perhaps actually a marginal *majority* of the population in that area which nearly all of the Jews would inhabit throughout the period between that date and 1948, when Israel gained modern statehood.[59]

Yet, even for those who go behind the propaganda to check its charges, the fuzzy picture commonly drawn is that, around the turn of the century, the Jews intruded into a land crowded with hundreds of thousands of Arabs, and began "displacing" Arab cultivators "on their land from time immemorial."

The unadulterated situation in 1893 was that about 92,300 non-Jews (including non-Arabs) were on the land that Jews had begun to settle *a decade earlier.* On that Jewish-settled land within Western Palestine, only 59,000 of the non-Jews were Muslim Arabs. Throughout the whole of Western Palestine, the total non-Jewish population numbered about 450,000–465,000:[60] only about twenty percent (92,300) of that limited non-Jewish (called "Arab") population of Western Palestine was located in the Jewish-settled area in 1893; moreover, only 55,000 to 60,000 of that 92,300 was Arab-Muslim.[61]

This precisely supports the evidence of "abandonment" and "depopulated" land cited earlier. The majority of non-Jewish Arabic-speaking inhabitants who, it was later claimed, had lived consistently in *Jewish*-settled areas "since time immemorial" were instead undoubtedly new arrivals from other Arab regions in Western Palestine who followed on the heels of the Jews.

Another Qualifying Factor

In addition to this study's necessary inclusion, as "Arabs," of those non-Jews *other* than "Arabs," the figures for 1893 that represent "settled Arabs" also undoubtedly included earlier in-migrants and immigrants who, by the time of the Turkish census, had only recently arrived in the area of Jewish settlement. The new economic attractions of the Jewish areas had an immense pull for the poor peasant-migrants in the Middle East lands adjacent to the hitherto "deserted" Palestine; their "crushing burdens" of confiscatory taxation and extortionate loan practices, added to the bedouin raiding and tribal warfare, were all factors that had both contributed to and resulted from the migratory patterns of the inhabitants. As discussed earlier, Burkhardt had reported of the 1810–1816 period that

> Few individuals . . . die in the same village in which they were born. Families are continually moving from one place to another . . . in a few years . . . they fly to some other place, where they have heard that their brethren are better treated . . .[62]

The 1893 Turkish census was reporting statistics that were applicable *after* the formal beginning of the first Jewish development when the Jews began to leave their four sacred cities and spread into agricultural settlements. That census was completed fifteen years after the first Palestinian Jews had left their homes in Palestine to develop the Petach Tikvah settlement in 1878.[63] Consequently, it can safely be assumed that even the comparatively sparse Arab population that the census reported to be in *all* of Western Palestine was not entirely an "indigenous settled Arab population" in 1893; of that the evidence leaves little doubt.

That population included, in addition, many immigrants "planted" by the Turkish government who had arrived between the 1870s and the 1893 census date.* For example, in the Jewish settlement Rishon l'Tsion (founded in 1882), by the year 1889 the "forty Jewish families" settled there had attracted "more than four hundred Arab families," most of them "Bedouin and Egyptian." They had come to "surround the moshava" (settlement) in a "now-thriving village" that, before the founding of Rishon l'Tsion, had been Sarafand—"a forsaken ruin."[64]

The report from Rishon pointed out that many other Arab villages had sprouted in the same fashion.

An analogy to the 400 Arab families who followed after the Rishon l'Tsion settlement of 40 Jewish families could possibly be assumed to hold similarly true for fifteen other Jewish settlements[65] that were founded before 1893 (see the table on p.253): for instance, a Libyan tribe from Tripolitania "settled in the neighbor-

*See Chapter 8.

TABLE E. Jewish Agricultural Settlements of Palestine Before 1893

Name [sic]	Founded	Population (1914)
1. Mikveh Israel	1870	100
2. Rishon I'Zion*	1882	1,500
3. Wadi Hanin (Ness Tsionah)	1882	200
4. Rehobot	1890	1,100
5. Ekron (Mazkeret Batiah)	1884	360
6. Katrah (G'derah)	1885	180
7. Petach Tikvah	1878	3,300
8. Kfar Saba	1892	100
9. Hadeirah	1891	300
10. Zichron Jacob	1882	1,000
11. Shveyah	1891	50
12. Um el Djemal	1891	80
13. Rosh Pinah	1882	700
14. Mishmar ha-Yarden	1890	100
15. Yessod ha-Maalah	1883	160
16. Ain-Seitun	1891	30

*Including the laborers' settlement Nachlat Yehudah.

Source: *Syria: an Economic Survey,* by Dr. Arthur Ruppin (translated and abridged by Nellie Straus), published by The Provisional Zionist Committee (New York, 1918), pp. 29–31.

hood" of the Jewish settlement Gedera just after its founding in 1885.[66] If anything like the same ratio were applied to those fifteen settlements—40 Jewish families followed by 400 Arab families—the very founding of a Jewish settlement could possibly have promoted as high as a ten-to-one ratio of Arab migrants and immigrants to the Jews in the Jewish-settled areas in question well *before* the Turkish census in 1893.

Were we to apply the ratio of one Jew followed by ten "Arabs" to the rest of the new Jewish-settled area—the pattern set by the actual condition in Rishon l'Tsion[67]—the additional 900 Jews on the other fifteen settlements might have been followed by 9,000 Arabs into the Jewish area by about 1890–1893.

It is intriguing to speculate whether indeed 9,000 Arabs may have followed 900 Jews,* and could afterward have increased in number by at least a rate of immigration similar to the Jews'. In 1914 that 900-odd Jewish population had actually grown to some 7,700. Might 9,000 Arabs have increased to 77,000 by 1914? From that hypothesis—using the most conservative and favorable rate of natural increase for the Arabs in the Jewish-settled area between 1893 and 1947 —that hypothetical number, or another number of Arab "informal" entrants to the Jewish-settled areas who came *after* the Jews' settlements were established, conceivably may have been counted as part of the 92,300 "original Arab settled population" in 1893, who were projected forward to 1947–1948 by this study.

If so, the possibility arises that even the study calculated for this book—whose

*This figure even excludes the aforementioned population of Rishon l'Tsion.

purpose is to distinguish between Arab in-migrants and actual long-settled Arab inhabitants in the Jewish-settled area of Western Palestine—has counted many thousands—anywhere from 45,000 to 350,000—of Arabs as long-time "settled" population of 1893-and-their-descendants present in 1947, when in reality that group may have *followed the Jewish settlers* into Jewish-settled areas of Palestine.

The weight of evidence leaves no question that the movement of Arab migration from other parts of Western Palestine was already under way when the Ottoman census was conducted in 1893. The numbers of the above hypothesis can only be speculative; however, the speculation serves to demonstrate that the estimate of some 92,000 non-Jews drawn from that census as being in the Jewish-settled area in 1893, and thus represented here as "original settled Arab population," is the *maximum* number possible.

Western Palestine, 1893–1947: Explaining the "Unprecedented" Numbers

From 1893 the Arab population of Western Palestine could be more easily divided between *Jewish* and *non-Jewish* areas. The figures emerging from the study, even though conservatively drawn, were indicative of the unmistakable trend: massively supplementing the diminished "existing" Arab population there, an Arab *in-migrant* population from within Western Palestine moved to the Jewish-settled areas *with* and mostly *after* the Jews. The Jews could not be said to have "displaced" those people who only came after them.

By dividing Western Palestine into 1) those subdistricts that were heavily or mainly settled by Jews,[68] 2) those regions that had little Jewish development,[69] and 3) those areas from which Jews were being expelled, it has been possible to determine the surge of Arab in-migrants into the Jewish-settled area of Western Palestine, in the continuation of a traditional pattern—moving into "any spot where he thinks he can find work."[70]

In the main areas of heaviest Jewish settlement there were a maximum 92,300 Arabs, including nomads, in 1893. In 1947 the number of non-Jews, called here "Arabs," living in the main Jewish-settled area of Western Palestine had grown from 92,300 in 1893 to nearly 463,000—*five* times the 1893 number, or an increase of 400 percent.

In those areas in which few Jews lived, but where some did live and the areas were near Jewish settlements, the Arab population in 1947 numbered *almost two and one half* times as many as in 1893.

The main non-Jewish, or "Arab" area of Western Palestine that was not included in Israel—that is, the West Bank, Gaza, and so on—in 1893 contained 233,500 Arabs; in 1947, their population numbered 517,000, little more than two times as many as in 1893.

Thus the Arab population appears to have increased in direct proportion to the Jewish presence.* Surely, however, within the radius of a few miles, the Arabs' physical proximity to the Jews could not be seriously considered as a factor altering the Arabs' *natural* rate of increase. That factor could not account for the immense disparity between the rate of natural increase among Arabs *with* or *near* Jews and the rate of Arabs *away* from Jews—all within that part of Palestine falling west of the Jordan River. In fact, the Arab population *outside* the mainly Jewish-settled areas had only increased by 1947 to *about two times its 1893 total.* The Arabs there had moved into the Jewish-settled areas.

The Arabs within the Jewish-settled area should have multiplied at roughly the same rate as in all of Western Palestine (somewhat over two and one half times), because the rates of increase—*natural* increase—of a group within the same small country at the same moment do not vary by more than a marginal amount.

The 92,300 Arabs in the primarily Jewish-settled area in 1893 thus could have increased naturally by 1947 to as much as 249,000 and little more. Instead,

TABLE F. Arab Population Within Main Jewish-Settled Areas†

1893 total	92,300
1947 total	462,900
Arab settled population (1893 population and descendants)	249,200
Arab nomads	8,800
Arab recorded "legal immigrants"	27,300
Arab recorded "illegal immigrants"	9,500
Arab unrecorded in-migrants (minimum)	168,100
1947 difference between "settled" and total Arab population	213,700
1947–1948 total Arab unrecorded immigrants and in-migrants	213,700

†See map of Jewish-settled areas in this chapter.

TABLE G. Arab Population According to Areas of Settlement†

Geographical area	1893	1947
Main area of Jewish settlement	92,300	462,900
Some Jews, mainly Arab	38,900	110,900
Intermediate	14,300	39,900
Intermediate	87,400	173,100
Main areas of Arab settlement—no Jewish settlement	233,500	517,000
Overall total for Arab population of Western Palestine	466,400	1,303,800

†See map of Jewish-settled areas in this chapter.

*See map on p. 246 and population chart in Appendix V.

however, the Arab population there had grown to 462,900, *five* times as many Arab inhabitants by 1947 in the Jewish-settled areas as in 1893.

Subtract the highest possible total population by *natural* increase—249,200 by 1947 (based on the rate of natural increase of the overall *non-Jewish* Western Palestine population between 1893 and 1947)—from the *actual* population increase of non-Jews ("Arabs") in Jewish-settled Area I—which totaled 462,900 in 1947. The remainder—213,700—*had to be* "Arabs" migrating to the Jewish-settled area. Then, if we subtract the minimal number of Arab immigrants—"legal" and "illegal" from outside Western Palestine—that the British *did* report, as well as nomads, the remainder of 170,000 is the *minimum* total of Arab in-migrants from local Arab areas to Jewish-settled areas before 1948.

In other words, *by the most conservative calculation,* 170,000 Arab in-migrants were never recorded by the government, were never figured into the political equations. And yet they had moved in.

Allowing the highest rate of natural increase possible, the calculations assumed that the total populations in the Arab areas of Western Palestine were long-settled indigenes. To maintain the highest possible degree of accuracy, it had to be assumed that in the areas not settled by Jews—the "Arab" areas where Jews either did not settle or where Jews had been forced out—all the population increase was natural. That assumption was based on the fact that the Arab population increase was so much lower in those Arab areas than in the Jewish-settled areas.

But evidence provided by the British censuses indicates that, even into the non-Jewish sectors of Palestine west of the Jordan River, some *immigration* of Arabs from neighboring lands was taking place during the period of the Mandate.[71] Thus, for example, the figure of 249,200 that has been calculated to be the actual total of "settled Arab" population in the main Jewish-settled area in 1947 (based upon that assumed rate of natural increase from 1893) is the *highest possible* number.

In fact, if the number of Arabs counted in *non-Jewish* or "Arab" areas also included unrecorded Arab *immigrants,* as is likely, then to consider all of them as "settled" population, growing in number only by *natural* increase, is to attribute a *higher* rate of natural increase to the Arabs in Jewish-settled areas than actually existed. However low the rate of natural increase might appear to be in the Arab areas by the calculations, by applying that rate of natural increase to the Jewish-settled areas, this study has perhaps assumed a higher rate of natural increase for the Arab population in the Jewish-settled areas than held true.[72] It follows, then, that what the study has established as Arab in-migration gives only the *minimum* number of Arab migrants who flocked into the Jewish-settled areas from the hills of Western Palestine until 1947–1948. It is probable that the actual increase through migration is substantially greater.

In other words, the number of the "existing" Arab indigenous people from that area of Western Palestine in which the Jews lived was grossly exaggerated until now—even by conservative, less inflated estimates. Using the conventional

TABLE H. Actual Numbers of Arab Refugees—1948*

	Arab settled population (1893 population and descendants)	Arab nomads	Arab "legal" and "illegal" immigrants, as reported by British administration†	Arab in-migrants (from main areas of Arab settlement and intermediate areas) and descendants since modern Jewish settlement began	Total
Areas included within Israel, 1949–1967					
Present in 1947	483,000	56,800	36,800	170,300	746,900
Remained in 1948	140,200	19,800	–	–	160,000
"Refugees"	342,800	37,000	36,800	170,300	586,900‡

*See Appendix V.

†See Chapters 14–15.

‡ This total figure exceeds most reliable estimates (see Chapter 2) and may be assumed to represent the highest possible total figure. Moreover, that total for "refugees" includes Arab immigrants who were never calculated by the government, as the following pages illustrate.

built-in distortion, the vague inference that all "native" Arabs lived in Jewish-settled areas, those "natives" were reported to be reproducing "naturally" at an "unprecedented" and "phenomenal" rate, with only negligible in-migration or immigration, from the beginning of the British Mandate and before.

The stock description—"600,000 Arabs and 50,000 Jews in 1918"—was the widely mistaken image of the original population composition in "Palestine" (Western Palestine) when a high British official fatefully concluded afterward that "we could not have known how Arab *existing* population would grow."

By the same token, the number of genuine Arab refugees "excluded from their homeland" in 1948, where they had lived "since time immemorial," diminishes considerably.[73] According to the calculations—and *not counting unrecorded immigrants*—there were in fact at the very least 170,000 "returnees" to Arab areas in Western Palestine who were included as refugees.

Perhaps we should recount the significance of the findings thus far: if the original 1893 Arab population in the Jewish-settled area had increased proportionately to the average for the whole Arab population of all Western Palestine, the total by natural increase could have amounted to as much as 249,200 by 1947. In fact, it amounted to 462,900. The difference of 213,700 (minus reported Arab immigration and nomads) had to be in-migrants from the hill country. Some had originally shuttled back and forth, and then later made their homes in the Jewish-settled area.

Including the minimal government-reported number of "legal" and "illegal" Arab immigrants and nomads (see the population table in this chapter), a total of 213,700 Arabs who were counted as the "settled Arab population for millennia" in Jewish-settled Western Palestine were actually newcomers. Many if not all are probably counted among the refugees; it seems likely that those 140,000 Arabs who remained in the main *Jewish-settled areas* when Israel gained statehood in 1948 were the ones with the deeper and more lasting roots.

From the evidence, then, among the estimated 430,000–650,000 Arab "refugees" reported in 1948, well over 170,000 are apparently Arabs who were *returning* to "Arab areas" in Western Palestine (the West Bank or Gaza) from the Jewish-settled areas where those Arabs had recently arrived in search of better opportunities.[74]

That minimum figure does not include the other classification of Arab population movement: unrecorded Arab immigration. The probabilities, which are considered in the following pages, are that the combined, identifiable 170,000 Arab in-migrants and the "unquantifiable" Arab immigrants together indeed accomplished what Winston Churchill characterized as a greater "lifting up of the population than all World Jewry could raise."

What becomes startlingly clear is that in the area where more than ninety-eight percent of Jews in Palestine lived consistently throughout the 1893–1948 period, the number of "Arabs" (including all non-Jews) was little more than 92,000 in 1893, compared to 58,000–60,000 Jews.

The relevant Jewish-settled area, which today contains the majority of the nearly four million Israeli population, contained *not* "500,000 or 600,000 *existing* Arabs" at the beginning of the century, but less than a hundred thousand "Arabs," including thousands who were actually non-Arabs but were necessarily included, as "non-Jews," to assure the accuracy of the trends revealed in these calculations.

The impact of those central facts on the present-day "Arab Palestinian" claim to the Jewish-settled area of Western Palestine must be properly recognized and fairly evaluated.

The Jewish-settled areas within Western Palestine that spawned modern Jewish development in 1878–1882 were so sparsely settled that by 1893—when the Ottoman census was taken—the Arab numbers had already been repeatedly replenished by the Turks in order to populate the area. Yet the prospective Jewish population had cynically been restricted from immigrating and adding to the population as heavily as it otherwise would have. We see graphically that the grandiose Arab claims today—that "Jews displaced Arabs" who were later "excluded from their homeland" when Israel became an independent state—cannot be the case.

What has become evident is that, instead, the Arabs migrated from the depressed areas to those places where they could gain greater economic advantage, taking the places in the Jewish-settled areas of Palestine that Jews were clearing for other Jews to pioneer or to use as a haven from outside oppression.[75]

It must be repeated that, in the interest of accuracy and fairness, and in order to remain consistently faithful to all the official data and sources between 1893 and 1947 that were compiled to complete the calculations, limitations were imposed:

1) All non-Jews living in the Jewish-settled area of Western Palestine—from 1893 through 1947—were counted as "Arabs" in the study's calculations, despite the established fact that many thousands included were actually not Arabs—for example, Circassians, Druses, Turks, Armenians, Algerians, non-Arab Christians.

2) Because this study began with the Ottoman census of 1881–1893, years after Jewish settlement is said to have been "officially" launched, many who were counted as "original settled Arab population" in 1893 had arrived only shortly before 1893, attracted by the opportunities of the new Jewish development. Thus, even in this study, which attempts to differentiate, some newcomers were necessarily included as "settled Arabs" in 1893.

3) Since the Ottoman census supplied no data on births and deaths, the study applied as a rate of natural increase the *highest* possible rate—in other words, the exact rate of increase of Arabs in non-Jewish Western Palestine between 1922 and 1947—to the Jewish-settled area's Arab population of 1893 and forward; this rate was applied despite the fact that until the end of World War I, "there is no evidence that the population increased or diminished during the last two centuries."[76]

4) The rate of natural increase applied to the Arabs in the Jewish-settled area of Western Palestine was the *total* reported increase of all the Arabs throughout the rest of Western Palestine. Thus the study assumed *all* population increase

among Arabs *outside* the Jewish-settled area was *natural.* Since some immigration into those areas from other lands also took place, a number of newcomers were counted as "native" population who only increased by reproduction; consequently, that rate of "natural" increase which was applied probably is higher than the one that actually obtained.

It would be difficult to overestimate the advantages that have accrued to Arab propaganda from the representation of a miraculously explosive rate of natural increase as the explanation for the high population growth among the Arabs in the Jewish-settled areas—an alleged rate that was assumed long before improved health and other benefits from the Jews' development could actually begin to affect population growth positively or explain it to any great extent.

The population was never accurately identified by location, or analyzed according to Jewish and non-Jewish areas. All "Palestine" was assumed to be Jewish-settled and Jewish-settled Palestine was assumed to be all of "Arab Palestine."

The five-times-its-1893-population increase of Arabs within the Jewish-settled areas *always was averaged* with the lowest, less-than-two-times-its-1893-population increase in the non-Jewish or "Arab" areas where few Jews settled before 1948. By *averaging* that increase in the Arab population over the whole of Western Palestine, including the non-Jewish Arab-populated areas where there was much less than half the numerical increase of that in the Jewish-settled areas, the resultant average increase—that which was consistently officially reported— "had the effect of favoring or supporting a *higher natural* increase than that which actually took place."[77]

In other words, the incorrect oft-reported Arab "phenomenal natural rate of increase," generally assumed to have taken place because of improved conditions in the Jewish-settled areas, and so high that it was considered by experts to be "unprecedented," *had already been artificially lowered.*[78] Had the actual scope of the Arab rate of population increase in the Jewish-settled areas been differentiated and accurately reported, without reducing the appearance of increase through averaging it with the far lower rate elsewhere in Western Palestine, the "natural" rate of increase would have been recognized as not merely "unprecedented" but incredible.

Between 1893 and 1922, the "Arab" rate of increase in Jewish-settled areas of Western Palestine was so similar to the Jews' rate of increase, which was admittedly due to immigration, that the inferences from those figures alone should have posed certain questions. Moreover, the *reported* rate of "natural" increase of Arabs in Palestine—even *after* averages had lowered the appearance of increase—when compared with Arab groups in similar conditions in neighboring Arab countries, should have been suspect.

How could the far greater rate in Palestine be accepted by more scientific studies without serious question as to the incidence of other than "casual" Arab in-migration? Even considering improved standards caused by efforts and revenues of the Jews, the length of time necessary for improved conditions to substantially affect Arab health and quality of life was not sufficient to explain the supposed "natural" rate of increase. Moreover, even in neighboring Egypt, seat of one of the world's highest population "explosions," applying the "unprecedented" rate of "natural increase" attributed to Palestinian Arabs between 1922 and 1947 would have been incompatible with demographic realities.[79]

Emphasizing the disparity between the Arab rate of increase inside Jewish-settled areas and that of non-Jewish areas in Western Palestine, the Arab population also escalated dramatically in the "three major Jewish cities"—far beyond the rate of natural increase between World War I and World War II. At the same time, in "predominantly Arab towns" the Arab population "rose only slightly (if at all)" and in one case—Gaza—actually decreased.[80]

Thus, first-rate scholars on the subject have figured the assumption of "9-per cent-Jews vs. vast-Arab-majority-in-Palestine" and the "unprecedented rate of natural increase of Arabs" into the demographic and political equations as "facts." Perhaps because of the British Mandatory Government's adoption of the myths, those numbers, as statistics often do, became sacred, immutable, somehow superseding logic.

The turnspeak has spread from authoritative and widely respected studies to political analyses. It has also extended to the major media, and even shows up frequently in letters-to-editor columns: thus the terrorism of the Palestine Liberation Organization (PLO) and "self-determination" for "the Palestinians" are still being defended and justified by the single assertion that

since 1917 . . . the population of Palestine was 90 percent Arab.[81]

Had the real conditions of "Palestine" surfaced and been given official currency by the British and other influential powers—1) that the Jewish-settled area was only a fraction of "Palestine"; 2) that most of the sparse "*existing* Arab" population "since time immemorial" was living outside and away from the Jewish settled area when Jews' organized settlement began and afterward; 3) that, within a few years after Jewish development commenced, Jews were actually the largest religious group in the areas that they settled near the end of the nineteenth century, rather than "9%"; 4) that an Arab "Palestinian" homeland containing seventy-five percent of "Palestine" existed; 5) that a large percentage of Arabs in Jewish-settled Palestine were landless in-migrants who, like millions of their brothers in the Arab world, were understandably in search of better opportunities and were not "millennia-long natives" with a special right to Jewish-settled areas of Western Palestine, and 6) that in 1948, when Arabs fled at the time of the war, a considerable percentage was actually "returnees" and not refugees— had those conditions been revealed and properly considered, countless injustices to all peoples might have been averted.

The fact is that the Arab population of Western Palestine's Jewish-settled area was greatly increased by Arab in-migrants from the rest of Western Palestine, the Arab areas outside the primarily Jewish-settled areas. Thus the claim that the Jews were taking away employment opportunities from the "native, indigenous" Arab population in the Jewish-settled area is insupportable. On the contrary, it was Jewish development and the Jews' presence that attracted workers in the first place from outside the areas of Jewish settlement.

In 1947–1948, there were about 747,000 "Arabs" in Israel-to-be (including for the purposes of the calculations Areas II and IV*, which were included in the territory of Israel but contained few Jews); of that number, about 57,000 were nomads, 37,000 were immigrants reported by the government, and 170,000 were in-migrants from Arab areas of Western Palestine. The remainder totaled about 483,000 Arabs. This figure represents the number of Arabs in Israel, then, in 1947–1948 who were neither nomads nor those immigrants who *were* reported by the British Mandatory Government. That group constituted the maximum Arab "settled" population in Israel in 1948.

During the 1948 exodus of Arab refugees, 140,000 Arabs remained in the Jewish-settled areas, becoming "Israeli Arabs." According to the calculations, then (747,000 "Arabs" were counted in the areas included in Israel minus 263,-000: nomads, in-migrants, and reported immigrants), 483,000 settled Arabs were in the Jewish-settled areas in 1947. A total of 140,000 Arabs in the Jewish-settled areas remained in Israel after the 1948 war; the balance of roughly 343,000 Arabs (out of 483,000), who fled in 1948, according to the calculations, is the maximum number possible of genuine refugees—not nomads, not in-migrants originating from areas of Western Palestine outside Israel (outside "Jewish-settled areas"), and not recorded as immigrants in the British reports.

Now that the relevant areas of Western Palestine have been delineated, their populations identified, and their numbers calculated to the extent feasible, we see an Arab "settled" population of possibly 483,000 in Israel-to-be in 1947–1948[82] —a population present from roughly 1893. Of that 483,000, 343,000 fled in 1948. Thus only 343,000 of the Arab refugees in 1948 were fleeing from Jewish-settled territory in which they had presumably lived permanently—or since 1893, after Jewish settlement had commenced and the large Jewish immigration wave of 1872–1882 had begun. That 343,000 figure is a *maximum* number, as explained earlier: 1) because of the probable inclusion of Arab immigrants who came later, attracted by opportunities for employment in Jewish settlements, and 2) because the rate of natural increase assumed in the calculations was possibly higher than the actual rate in non-Jewish Western Palestine.

It should especially be noted that the maximum figure of 343,000 is *less than half* the number of refugees claimed by the Arabs immediately after their leaving, before the numbers were reportedly further "inflated" in the refugee camps.

What the population study could not calculate is how many among 343,000 Arab "settled population" were in fact illegal immigrants to Western Palestine, following the time-honored tradition, to get to where their brethren were better off. Arab *immigration,* unlike the in-migration, is not calculable. No comprehensive records of Arab immigration exist.[83] But on the basis of evidence of infectious immigration seen earlier and in following pages, illegal Arab immigrants could

---

*See map on p. 246 and table in Appendix V.

account for a very substantial number among the Arabs included in the 343,000 refugee figure.

The actual historical conditions have been acknowledged by some: as Kemal Karpat observed, there was a "convergence toward Palestine of several ethnic groups. . . . A considerable number of newcomers. . . . were *non-Arabic* speaking." These "were probably assimilated into the Arabic population," in addition to Algerians, Iraqis, Turks, Circassians, Egyptians and, others.[84]

Fred M. Gottheil, through his studies of economic conditions in Western Palestine, found that between 1922 and 1931 "Arab immigration comprised 36.8% of the total immigration into pre-State Israel," while "in non-Israel" areas of Western Palestine, "Arab migration was positive, but inconsequential."[85]

It is interesting to note that, according to the population expert Riad Tabbarah, in the late 1940s, when the population growth of Kuwait rose to five percent a year as a result of the oil boom, fully half of that growth was recognized as immigrant Arab labor, and of that immigrant group most were Arabs identified as "Palestinians."[86] However, although in Palestine the immigrant Arab laborers somehow had been statistically absorbed into the "settled population" and the Arab sector of the population growth of Palestine was mistakenly assumed to be "almost totally due to natural increase," that *same* "Palestinian Arab" population, which supposedly was reproducing phenomenally in Jewish-settled Palestine, once it arrived in Kuwait, increased only more or less according to the norms within the region. The behavior of Palestinian Arabs in Kuwait corresponded to that of other Arabs with respect to the rate of natural increase, without being distorted by the abnormally fertile air of Palestine.

The "oil-generated economic boom" that began to prompt "heavy" immigration of Arab labor to Kuwait, "in the late 1940's,"[87] can be compared to the Jewish-development-generated economic boom that prompted the Arab in-migration and immigration into the Jewish-settled areas of Western Palestine beginning in the 1870s, proceeding after the First World War, and continuing through the British administration of Palestine until 1946 or 1947. In Kuwait, however, the element of immigration within the late 1940s population growth—"population growth rates reached around 5 percent a year (possibly half of which was due to immigration)"—was factored into the total Kuwaiti population picture.

In the case of Western Palestine and its own, earlier economic boom, the Arab in-migration and immigration factors were drastically overlooked.

It is ironic to recall that the only group immigration meticulously accounted for by the British was Jewish immigration, the development from which caused the boom that attracted the Arabs. To quantify the one—the Jew—without considering the other—the Arab—is tantamount to attempting to describe a game of cricket by counting the score of only one team.

Other Indications of Population Movement

Recent regional studies indicate there is further reason to believe, in addition to the minimum figure of 170,000 Arab in-migrants who became, overnight, "natives since time immemorial excluded from their homeland," that in Jewish-settled Western Palestine the Arab immigrant movement from other Arab lands was perhaps at least as significant.

Those regional studies were not focused on the composition of the population of Palestine or its political ramifications; the population findings were incidental to other research. Consequently the evidence revealed lends a greater degree of credibility to the indications.

The first, a geographic "survey of the Arab villages, engaged in the investigation of changes occuring therein . . . examining matters of land ownership . . . analyzing the geographic implications of the social structure . . . ," was conducted in more than 200 Arab villages within Israel since 1968. This study has found that

> . . . the major increase in the population of the Arab villages in the coastal plain, during the British period, had come largely from immigrants from neighboring countries.[88]

According to the geographer who headed the study, Professor Moshe Braver, of Tel Aviv University,

> We found that in many cases these people arrived [in what is now Israel, i.e., Jewish-settled areas] in the 1930's.[89] For example, although I have lived in this country almost since my birth and I know the country quite well—the villages and all—when I investigated an Arab village in 1941, I was amazed to find that the village of Beit Girga was more Egyptian in character than Palestinian. A very substantial part of the population—especially the elders—wore Egyptian styled dress, you know, the *gallabya.* I spoke to the people of Beit Girga and found that the great majority of the village population had been born in Egypt, some of them came here toward the end of World War I, with the British army, and some of them infiltrated into Palestine later on to join members of their families or friends in Beit Girga and neighboring villages.
>
> That is only one example. The same condition was quite evident in other villages. It was a conspicuous fact in the human landscape—that there was a substantial population which was foreign. There were Arabs from Egypt, from Jordan, from Syria and even further away—from Yemen. Now, many of those villages in which the immigrants concentrated were on the fringes of the Jewish areas, which Israel conquered during the Arab war against Israel's independence, in 1948, and these immigrants fled. The village of Beit Girga—it does not exist any more—it was ruined during the 1948 war and the villagers fled.

In addition, the Braver study "went one step further": it investigated some of the areas the immigrants had originated from, primarily "villages in Jordan." Braver explained:

> I asked geographers working for German, British and other universities outside Israel, who were doing research in Jordan, to inquire in the villages whether there are any families who have relatives in refugee camps. If they have refugee relatives —who had left coastal plain of Israel where the Jews were—we wanted to estab-

lish approximately when those refugee parts of the family migrated or immigrated from Jordan.

These geographers managed to establish in at least two-to-three-hundred cases—in villages which they investigated for their own purposes—the fact that these Jordanian people had relatives who had gone to [Western] Palestine, and that those who had become refugees had migrated within their lifetime—which means within the last fifty or sixty years to "Palestine." Some of them of course are still refugees. You see, the benefits of being refugees are so considerable that they didn't go back to their villages, or even if they did go back to their original Jordanian villages after 1948, they went and registered as refugees when the refugee camps were established, in order to get the refugee benefits.

It became quite obvious that there was very substantial emigration from Jordan, especially from the northern part of Jordan to [Western] Palestine, during the time of the British Mandate. In fact—I cannot give you his name because he will not be allowed back into Jordan if his name is published—but only a few months ago we got information from a foreign doctoral candidate who did work on this subject. He stayed in Jordan for many months, and he established without the slightest doubt that in the Adjloun area there was very substantial immigration into Palestine during the 1920s and '30s.[90]

According to Braver, Egyptians continued to come and settle, mainly in Jaffa and its neighborhood, and "in villages and towns along the coastal strip between Jaffa and Gaza," until after the Second World War. The "final wave" of immigrants from Egypt came to fill places opened for laborers by the British war effort.

Transjordanians, Syrians, and Lebanese "poured into the country from the early 1920's until 1947,"[91] Braver said.

The extent of the settlement of Arab immigrants and the format of their diffusion along the coastal plain and the hills to the east of it parallel the scope and volume of growth in the citrus industry, urban construction and other development processes. When economic growth slowed down there was a drop also in immigration from neighboring countries, while in periods of prosperity it rose again.

On the other hand, [as opposed to economic prosperity along the coastal plain], several times it was economic distress and other events in the adjacent countries which sent streams of immigrants to Palestine. A large wave of immigrants from Southern Syria (the Hauran) came in the wake of a drought and changed the complex of the population and the labor market.[92]

Another example among more recent works on the region is *Arab Village,* a careful sociological study of a Transjordanian peasant community by Richard T. Antoun, in which the author assumes that Kufr al-Ma—the Transjordanian village studied—was generally representative, or "traditional." Antoun reports that a majority of the inhabitants of Kufr al-Ma had immigrated to Western Palestine for economic reasons during the British Mandatory period.[93] Even village *mukhtar* (chief) Muflih al-Hakim and his family had "spent much of their lives in [Western] Palestine,"[94] and he returned with his family to the village of his origins in 1951 after fighting against Israel in the Arab Legion.[95]

TABLE I. Villages Settled Primarily by Egyptian Immigrants:
Growth of Population in Arab Villages Along Southern Coastal Plain

Village	Population, 1922	Population, 1944	Increase in percentage (approx.)
Beit Girga	397	940	137
Julis	481	1,030	115 [sic]
Zarnuka	967	2,380	147 [sic]
Harbiyya	1,037	2,240	116
Yibneh	1,791	5,420	203
Qubeba (near Rehovot)	519	1,720	211 [sic]
Qestina	406	890	119

Source: Moshe Braver, "Immigration as a Factor in the Growth of the Arab Village in Eretz-Israel," *Economic Review—Problems of Aliyah and Absorption,* vol. 28, no. 7–9, Jerusalem, 1975 (July–Sept.), p. 17.

TABLE J. Villages Settled Primarily by Egyptians, Transjordanians,
Syrians, and Others: Growth of Population in Arab Villages in the Central Coastal
Plain

Village	Population, 1922	Population, 1944	Increase in percentage (approx.)
Bet Dajan	1,689	3,840	127
Jaljuliyya	123	740	500
Yehudiyya	2,437	5,650	132
Yazur	1,284	4,030	214
Sawalma	70	800	1,040
Salameh	1,187	6,730	476
Safariyya	1,306	3,070	143
Saqiyya	427	1,100	157
Faja	164	1,200	630

Source: Moshe Braver, "Immigration as a Factor in the Growth of the Arab Village in Eretz-Israel," *Economic Review—Problems of Aliyah and Absorption,* vol. 28, no. 7–9, Jerusalem, 1975 (July–Sept.), p. 18.

A final example is an anthropological study led by Professor Gideon Kressel that is focused upon marriage traditions among Arabs "in the center of Israel" (the Jawarish).[96] It was learned, as a by-product of the investigation, that 144 of the 166 families of the community had their origins in Egypt, Libya, and Sudan. Arab immigrants—as of December 1971, the completion of the study—still "continue to arrive and camp in tents . . . while awaiting the completion of the 'rent houses.' "

For instance, one group of families arrived from Libya to the Jewish-settled area in 1885, and first "encamped" around the new Russian-Jewish pioneer settlement Gedera, where friends and family later immigrated to join them. They moved to their present village after 1949, where they number forty-nine families, and "they and their descendants are considered the social elite of the community" (as of December 1971).[97]

From first-person accounts within the study, as well as the map tracing the "annals of the five Jawarish subgroups," it becomes clear that the immigrant families have branches in cities and villages throughout southern and coastal areas, from Haifa to Gaza and Beersheba, where

> The British occupation of . . . Palestine (1918) increased [the flow of western immigration] particularly after the completion of the railway across the Sinai.[98]

From the "representative" first-person case histories, an example:

> First we were peasants in Egypt. . . . we lived in Gaza and later in Dimrah where all of us were Egyptians (Masarwah). . . . Jadalla's father . . . used to sell his produce to the kitchen of the Kibbutz Yad Mordekhay [*sic*] . . . as far as Kibbutz Doroth. . . . Dimrah was destroyed in 1948. . . . The lands of Dimrah were split by the new border, and on the Israeli side Kibbutz Erez was established. They provided us substitute houses in Ramla or in Lod.[99]

While the "cultural identity of the Egyptian-fellahin apparently faded away during the recent past," because "they lived under the patronage of Negev Bedouin," the Libyan immigrant community—*Magharbah*—"maintained their identity of a Libyan diaspora *(ej-jaliah el-libiah)* and have continued to foster linguistic forms and traditional rituals of the original homeland,"[100] according to Kressel.

In an interview with this writer in the summer of 1979, Dr. Kressel described and exhibited the data of his comprehensive research project, which he began just after the 1967 Six-Day War; in the course of his exhaustive study of marriage patterns, he has conducted hundreds of interviews in Arabic with Arabs[101] living in Israel, and under friendly, nonpolitical conditions.

It was perhaps only under such circumstances that the true origins of the Arabs concerned could be revealed.[102] However proud they might be of their rightful and actual origins and family heritage, fear of extremist violence from the PLO and associated gangs would undoubtedly silence any such revelations in the context of a politically inspired interview. The tragedy of having to conceal their origins, or in the case of the twelve-year-old "Palestinian Arab," of having his or her real identity buried by indoctrination, however, cannot be rectified by sweeping the truth under a rug of revised history.

Arab immigrants who found their way to benefits within Jewish settlements and were counted as "existing indigenous" Arab population can be accurately said to have displaced Jews whose immigration was supposed to be "facilitated" into their Jewish National Home.

If those who live in Jordan—Eastern Palestine—deny the documented history which testifies to the fact that they are Palestinian Arabs living in Arab Palestine, then they are disregarding the very "history" by which they might claim *any* "right" to Palestine. Even were we to set aside the historical evidence that contradicts the claim of a "Palestinian Arab" identity, if Arabs call upon the "Palestinian's historical" claims to Palestine, then the Arabs must conform those claims to the actual history they invoke, not to arbitrary fictions.

They cannot both claim that history has afforded them "rights" and at the same time deny the nature of other "historical rights" and facts—that segment of history which may contradict their claims and does not conform to their political goals. Such demands are unjust—to the Palestinian Jews in Israel, and to the Palestinian Arabs, who in fact, by virtue of their history and their numbers in Palestine-cum-Jordan, are more legitimately entitled to self-determination in what is the Jordanian three-fourths of Palestine. As with Israel, Jordan is no less Palestine because it is currently called by another name.

The historical reality is analogous to the following parable.*

In the state of Georgia, there is a population of nearly 600,000 farmers— 500,000 white farmers and 85,000 black farmers. The white farmers are sprinkled on land throughout the state. The black farmers have been permitted to dwell and buy land in a small, generally undeveloped, and abandoned coastal county of that state; they have toiled to drain and reclaim its swampland and have begun to build up its sandy wastes.

Although the majority of the state's land is state domain, the whites exert pressure and utilize violence in order to keep the Georgia administration from selling to the blacks that state territory which is their right. The Georgia government passes spuriously based legislation that has the effect of impeding the sales of state domain land to the black would-be settlers, and enacts restrictions on entry into Georgia in order to keep out the blacks. The only land left available to them is the outrageously overpriced land that the whites sell to the blacks, most of which has become dunes and swampland.

Meanwhile white migrant workers from throughout Georgia, and from neighboring states as well, begin flooding into the area that has been promised to and allocated by federal legislation for black settlement. Having been hired by the blacks to assist in development, those white migrants are then designated by the government of Georgia to be the "original settled inhabitants" of the area. Then the white so-called "original settlers" charge that the blacks are "dispossessing" the whites, and must be kept out, although all the states surrounding Georgia— as well as the majority of territory *inside* Georgia—are dominated by whites, all in areas where Klu Klux Klan persecution and lynching of blacks have been occurring with regularity. The white farmers resent the prosperity and the equality accruing to those whom they regard as their "niggers" and therefore claim that the previously deserted land was "expropriated from whites," insisting that the blacks' farms belong to the whites from time immemorial.

Would any reasonable jury today respect such a claim?

And yet, so buried by layer upon layer of propaganda is the actual historical situation of Arabs and Jews in the Jewish-settled area of Western Palestine that just such Arab demands have been given acceptance by many who, while in search of justice, lack the facts.

*The blacks in the Georgia parable are analogous to the Jews in "Palestine"; the whites analogous to the Arabs; the federal government to the League of Nations Mandate; and the Georgia government is analogous to the British administration in Palestine.

13

A Hidden Movement: Illegal Arab Immigration

> Arab immigration into Palestine? Why, it did not exist. There was no such thing. No one ever kept track of *that*.
>
> —Veteran archivist, British Public Record Office, 1979

> It is agreed that refugees who would appear to be Syrian, Lebanese or Palestinian by nationality may be admitted into Palestine without passport or visa.
>
> —Controller of Permits, Jerusalem, 1926

> Identity card system should be imposed forthwith. French did it in 15 days in 1926. Without this system control of movements of the population is impossible.
>
> —Colonel Gilbert MacKereth, British Consul in Damascus, October, 1937

> I am not sure that Col. MacKereth has always appreciated the wider issues . . . vis a vis the Arab world. . . . I think we should . . . replace him. . . .
>
> —George W. Rendel, Head of Eastern Department of British Foreign Office, 1937

Why was illegal Arab immigration dismissed as "insignificant" or as "about 1% of the population"? One must pause here to question—how could a condition as chronic and serious in its implications as the artificial inflation of "existing" Arab population by Arab immigration into Jewish-settled areas of Western Palestine remain unchallenged and unrecorded by the British Mandatory Government? As evidenced earlier, the reports of the government might note the general condition with some alarm on one page and then dismiss it on another, within the same report.

In fact, during an extended study at the formidable archives of the Public Record Office in London's Kew Gardens the author spent dozens of hours in the reference rooms in search of material on *Arab immigration* into Palestine. There were hundreds of references in both the Foreign Office and Colonial Office records on *Jewish* immigration—legal and illegal. But, except for the few compulsory references filed in annual Reports to the Administration—reports that vastly underestimated Arab immigration—no category covering the incidence of incoming Arabs could be found.

When a thirty-year veteran archivist—a specialist in the Foreign Office and Colonial Office records on the Middle East for the Public Record Office—was asked to assist in finding the records on immigration to Palestine, he led briskly to the varied references on Jewish immigration and to the general "emigration-immigration" category, under which all the headings that indicated Jews' arrival were to be found. But what of Arab immigration, illegal and otherwise, he was asked. "Arab immigration into Palestine? Why, it did not exist. There was no such thing," he scoffed. "No one ever kept track of *that.*" When he was told of citations from Syrian, Egyptian, and British officials, which challenged his assurance, the archivist seemed genuinely astonished. "Indeed," he pondered. "Hmnn, well, you have come up with something completely new!"

In fact, an examination of the "private" and "secret" correspondence files of the Mandatory government reveals evidence that the British were not unaware of the magnitude of illegal Arab immigration or, indeed, of the possible political ramifications of that condition should it become known.

Although explicit evidence of the prevalence of illicit Arab immigration into Palestine—particularly to the Jewish-settled area—was not catalogued or referenced so as to be easily located among the reams of documentation labeled *Jewish* immigration, the British occasionally did record that which they were forced to acknowledge.[1]

For example, an "Urgent" order in 1925 went from the Controller of Permits to the Northern District Commissioner (with a "copy to Chief Secretary"):

Subject: Refugees from Syria
    ... to the officer in charge at Ras-El-Nakurah. ... Will you be so good as to ... furnish him as speedily as possible with a mimeographed supply of the blank passes.[2]

January 3, 1926:
To: "Palestine Gendarmerie, Samakh"
From: Controller
Subject: Entry of Refugees into Palestine
    So long as the Hauran and neighborhood remain disturbed it is agreed that refugees who would appear to be Syrian, Lebanese or Palestinian by nationality may be admitted into Palestine without passport or visa.[3]

October 25, 1926:
To: Controller of Permits, Jerusalem
From: District Offices, Nablus
Subject: Damascene Refugees
    ... many a Damascene have found their way into Palestine without a proper permit. These refugees are scattered all over Palestine. ... .[4]

In one 1931 memo to Chief Immigration Officer, *"Syrian Affairs,"* a "Deputy Commandant" noted that although the Syrians had been provided amnesty by the French and could return "to their country of origin," many "residing in the Northern District [Safed, Haifa, and elsewhere] and others, less in number, living in other parts of Palestine are now reported to have remained in the country."[5]

In an Immigration memo, *"Druzes who are in Palestine without permission,"* a *mukhtar* (village chief) could vouch for the illegals: "In the cases of those persons who claim that they were born in Palestine they should be called upon to produce satisfactory documentary evidence to that effect from the Mukhtar of their respective villages. . . ." From Immigration Officer, December 22, 1931.[6]

In the urban areas the practice was similar: in another memo, the Southern District Commissioner reported that

> in the case of persons who have been unable to produce documents in authentication of their right to British Protection, I have endeavored to obtain the testimony of a prominent citizen of Jaffa that the person concerned is, in fact, a native of British Protected Territory.[7]

Thus Arab immigrants were apparently provided the loophole *and* the "official" fraudulent means to prevent their deportation as illegals.

An occasional conscientious official brought the condition to the attention of his seniors, unaware of British officialdom's policy of deliberately ignoring the Arab illegal immigration. A rare memorandum on "Deportation of Persons in Palestine Without Permission,"[8] written in June 1933, unmistakably referred to Arab or non-Jewish illegal immigrants—as well as Jews—"Syrians, Egyptians, etc.," or "native of a neighboring country. . . ." According to that memo, "deportation for illegal presence" should be processed "without delay" and the party arrested "so that (the man or woman) could not conceal himself and be untraceable. . . ."

The official complained:

> This procedure has never really been applied. Consideration . . . has been spread over months during which a new crop of difficulties has arisen and at the end of which the object . . . cannot be found.

He also protested the "new practice" which "had arisen" in addition—"prosecuting instead of taking steps to deport"; the official said that as a result of that practice, "in a still greater number of cases deportation has been made impossible." Among examples given was a woman "bound over in the sum of one pound for a year. The result is . . . that the woman who was deportable when proceedings were taken against her is free to remain in the country . . . in effect as much longer as she wishes." In another example,

> charge was dismissed on the ground that the offender had friends in Palestine who would look after him.[9]

No mention was made, no record was found either in official reports or in the correspondence files specifically concerning the "30,000–36,000 Hauranese" who had immigrated to Palestine in 1934. However, as a result of the anti-Jewish riots and strikes in 1936, "countrymen from Hauran" were among a smaller number of Arab immigrants who "applied urgently and pleadingly to be sent back to their homes for the reason that there was no work . . . and they did not wish to be involved in more trouble."[10]

Although the Hauranis' entry had been ignored, their hasty leavetaking to avoid trouble was noted in private correspondence in some detail. The "arrangements" were agreed to by the Chief Secretary:

> providing that he obtained a written statement (that he should if he could obtain) from these men or their representatives that they were being repatriated at their own request, so that no questions would arise afterwards that we had deported them.[11]

A "confidential" note handwritten by the High Commissioner confirmed that

> every encouragement should be given to countrymen to return to their own country without compulsion. When the port is reopened fully probably none will want to go without compulsion.[12]

Another memo, headed simply "Hauranis," reported that "128 have left today. Many more are expected to ask to leave tomorrow . . ." Handwritten minutes responded to the report:

> Dear Hall, Hauranis proper are here illegally. They are a turbulent lot. The sooner they go the better at their own request. Next week they may not want to go.

Arthur Wauchope, the High Commissioner of Palestine and Transjordan, added,

> As long as they go voluntarily I fear no Arab comments.[13]

In general there is sparse mention of any government policy toward Arab immigration in the correspondence files, and practically no record of the *numbers* of Arab immigrants[14] (except for the explanation of those thousands of Arab "illegal" immigrants officially imported during World War II. That practice is discussed in Chapter 16).

However, during the period following the 1936 Arab riots and strikes, the British officials in "Palestine" appear to have become suddenly preoccupied with requests for "repatriation" by numbers of Sudanese, Egyptian, Syrian, South Arabian, and Somali illegal immigrants who "entered Palestine without permission." Dozens of memos and "confidential" communications, for instance, were exchanged in the one month of May 1936, the time of the so-called "Arab Revolt." Here are representative extracts from just a few:

From: Chief Immigration Officer, Jerusalem
   . . . Egyptian Authorities are willing to take at Kantara [*sic*] batches of 20

Egyptians containing not more than 10 from any one quarter. . . . *Provided, however, that documents are held by all of them for their return to Palestine* if they are not admitted at Kantara.*[15]

From: Minute No. 19
. . . the Egyptian Consul is prepared to grant visas to Egypt to any Soudanese sent . . . for repatriation to Soudan, on the understanding that Palestine will accept back again any persons whose Soudanese nationality is not established. There are 14–15 Soudanese, of whom 5 have Soudan passports; the remainder have apparently no documents of identity. C.M.S. will issue temporary travel documents where necessary.[16]

From: Minute No. 15
. . . The Soudanese and South Arabians will be dealt with as soon as C.M.S. has further particulars of their identity and travel documents.[17]

Telegram: . . . reporting numerous Egyptians anxious return urgently without passports stop, apply ordinary procedure reference person for interrogation stop . . . *Request provide each with travel document valid return Palestine* stop. . . .*[18]

It is interesting to note that the immigrants were often required by their home governments to get permission to "return" to Palestine.[19]

The enclosure to a memorandum in that same month, May 1936, is perhaps indicative: the names and origins of fifty Arabs who had approached the Southern District Commander in Palestine for assistance because of unemployment are listed. Not one is "Palestinian" and "in many cases they entered Palestine without permission." Nearly half immigrated after 1930, none before World War I, from Nigeria, Sudan, Somaliland via Egypt, Syria, and the Hejaz. Many came "with the British Army," or "with Transjordan Frontier Force," a few as "pilgrims," and others simply by "camel" or "on foot."[20] (See examples of original British documents in Appendix VII.)

It is difficult to grasp the extent of the murderous assaults, rioting, and strikes that triggered the Arab immigrants' temporary flight, from High Commissioner Wauchope's cryptic description (throughout his 1936 correspondence regarding the "voluntary repatriation")—the *present circumstances* under which their presence may be undesirable." Once again the long tradition of violence and terrorism must be seen in context—here, as the singularly important factor that influenced British Colonial policy in Palestine. As an essential to understand the reversal of British pledges to uphold the Mandated "Jewish homeland," it must be underscored that the small Arab power clique's racial incitement to terrorize, which had achieved with some effect the Turk's restrictions against Jewish immigration and land settlement, would succeed in far greater measure during the British administration.

*Emphasis added.

British placation of the anti-Jewish campaign of the deceptively "mild-mannered little man of great courtesy and benign expression,"[21] *effendi* Haj Amin al-Husseini, was an exercise in futility equaled only perhaps by the 1938 appeasement of the Nazis in Czechoslovakia. A British historian wrote that ". . . the Mufti mixed religion with politics so cleverly that it is impossible to say where the one begins and the other leaves off."[22]

According to documentary records submitted to the United Nations in 1947, al-Husseini was "responsible for the Arab riots in 1920."[23]

Savage attacks were made by Arab rioters in Jerusalem [on Easter Sunday] on Jewish lives and property. Five Jews were killed and 211 injured.[24]

"Cries directed against the Jews were shouted by leaders in the procession" of thousands of Muslim pilgrims at the Muslim festival of Nebi Musa in Jerusalem, "and agitators incited an attack," whereupon "marchers in the procession fell upon the Jews with sticks and knives; the Arab police remained passive or in some instances joined the rioting."[25]

Haj Amin, only twenty-seven in 1920, was already a longtime foe of the Jews following the tradition of his powerful forebears.[26] British Officer R. Meinertzhagen reported later that Haj Amin had been informed by British Colonel Waters-Taylor four days before the Easter pogrom in Jerusalem that

he had a great opportunity at Easter to show the world that the Arabs of Palestine would not tolerate Jewish domination in Palestine; that Palestine was unpopular not only with the Palestine Administration but in Whitehall; and if disturbances of sufficient violence occurred in Jerusalem at Easter, both General Bols and General Allenby would advocate the abandonment of the Jewish Home.[27]

Colonel Meinertzhagen, a senior British officer stationed in Palestine in 1920, a non-Jew, was charged with being "pro-Zionist" and sent back to a "desk job" in London, where he later protested British policy against the Jews:

Much has been written about injustice to the Arabs. There is nothing in a Jewish State which conflicts with Arab rights. And, moreover, be it remembered that the Arabs are the only nation in the world with at least three kings and several sovereign states. The Jews are a nation without a home.[28]

In fact, that outbreak was notable as the only and last act of Arab terrorism that did not directly instigate anti-Zionist policy by Great Britain: "On the contrary, it helped to expedite the decision of the Peace Conference [Paris] to grant the Mandate to Great Britain, with the responsibility of the Balfour Declaration attached."[29] Indirectly, however, even the 1920 Nebi Musa violence and related acts instigated by al-Husseini and his followers had their desired consequences.

Haj Amin al-Husseini's anti-Semitic *Muftism,* as we shall see in later pages, would one day ultimately insist upon and cause the "extermination program of the Nazis" to be "carried out even in those satellite countries which were willing to permit the rescue of Jews."[30]

However, even as the Mandate was embraced by Britain and Lloyd George in April 1920, with its instruction to "facilitate Jewish immigration" and "close settlement by Jews on the land, including State Lands and waste lands not required for public purposes"[31] to "secure the establishment of the Jewish national home,"[32] by August of that same year a first "Jewish immigration quota" was "fixed."[33] From that time the preoccupation of Palestine's administration would be concentrated solely upon *limiting* the immigration of the *Jews*. As a British report attested, for "Arab immigration," a "different" set of rules applied.[34]

The pattern continued. From the Jewish-development-despite-*Turkish*-restrictions, followed by Arab-migrants-seeking-better-opportunities, the only change was the government setting the restrictions. But the *British* letter and enforcement would prove to be more harsh and discriminatory than those of the Turks. Britain's enforcement was to turn justice on its head, because the British purportedly would be administering Palestine after the land had been internationally mandated as a "national home" for the Jews. And the incidence of Arab illegal immigration during the British mandatory period would grow more prevalent, following the exact same pattern as under the Turks but with its hidden numbers concealing what was evidently an immigration movement great enough to compare with admittedly immigration-based increase of the Jews.

The League of Nations' Permanent Mandates Commission, which alone had noted officially the massive Hauranese illegal immigration of 1934, expressed concern in its role as the League's international regulating body for Mandates: an unreasonably high number of Jews were being deducted from the Jewish immigration quota, the Commission noted, despite the fact that

> . . . of 1,079 persons deported in the year 1935, 245 were Jews and 834 *other persons*. Who were those other persons?*[35]

Commission members asked the question of Mr. Trusted, the British representative. According to the Mandates Commission minutes,[36]

> Mr. Trusted said that, generally speaking, they were mainly Arabs from Syria or Transjordan. . . . Some persons had also been deported to Egypt.

Reading further from the same report:[37]

> Count de Penha Garcia asked whether the figures . . . showing that of 1,354 persons summarily deported to Syria and Egypt only 38 were Jews, meant that illegal immigration was greater among Arabs than among Jews.†[38]

---

*Emphasis added.

†In the 1935 Report to the Administration under discussion by the Mandates Commission, only "Jewish Immigration into Palestine" was catalogued; that was the only heading, although "other persons" deported, under at least three separate categories, totaled *more than ten times* the number of Jews. Yet the predominant focus throughout that section of the report is the Jewish "illicit

If so, he felt inclined to support the suggestion of the Jewish Agency that stricter steps should be taken to prevent illegal immigration. . . .*

Mr. Trusted said that the figures to which Count de Penha Garcia referred were simply those relating to cases of deportation. If the whole figures of illegal immigration were considered it would be seen that the proportion was very different.

. . . He agreed that the phraseology was somewhat misleading.

M. Orts, *referring to Count de Penha Garcia's question concerning illegal immigration, noted that,* at its 27th session (pages 46, 47, 48 of the Minutes of that session), *the Commission had been told by the accredited representative that rigorous control had been instituted in the matter of Trans-Jordanians and Haurani entering the country.* If such control had been maintained, why did the 1935 report[39] . . . state that no reliable statistics are available as to the "number of Trans-Jordanians who enter Palestine and leave after the seasonal work is done"?

His question was not unconnected with the present troubles. Certain Jewish documents complained that elements from Trans-Jordan and the Hauran had played a very active part in the Jaffa riots. Consequently, several hundreds of these individuals had been expelled. *Had they entered and remained in Palestine without the knowledge of the authorities?*

Mr. Trusted said he appreciated the difficulty of interpretation experienced by the Commission. The question centered round the fact that Trans-Jordanians were granted by law special facilities to enter the country for a specified period for seasonal work, and that other persons had in the past availed themselves of those facilities to enter Palestine surreptitiously. There was now a system of identity documents for all Trans-Jordanians entering Palestine: these documents were prepared and controlled by the local authorities in Trans-Jordan. Furthermore, as the new Statistical Department progressed it would be easier to keep an ever closer watch on persons from outside Palestine sojourning in that territory.[*] He could assure the Commission that Trans-Jordanians were not allowed to stay beyond the specified time. The Commission could assume that this class of temporary immigrant did not present a serious problem.†[40]

Despite Trusted's assurances, members of the Permanent Mandates Commission (PMC) registered doubts in their reports following the meeting. Among their observations:

---

settlement," which "Government has employed every means at its disposal, both through the agency of his Majesty's Consular Officers abroad and by the employment of a special preventive force on land and sea, as well as through the usual control arrangements at ports and frontiers, to prevent. . . . Deductions, corresponding to the number of illicit settlers who it is estimated will enter and remain in the country during the following period of six months, are made from the number of certificates authorized for distribution by the Jewish Agency under each Labour Schedule." It is significant that despite the rigorous application of methods described above to prevent Jewish immigration, and the institutionalized blinkered vision regarding the Arab immigration, still the number of "other" or non-Jews detected for deportation was far greater. The report, nonetheless, discussed *only* the factors relating to *Jewish immigration,* while the major "other" persons enumerated were ignored.

*According to the annual report on the Administration for 1936, "The control of travel to and from Trans-Jordan is the duty of a special section of Arab Legion, etc.," p. 324.

†Emphasis added.

Illegal immigration exists, but it is not confined to Jews;[41] . . . convictions for illegal immigration apply much more to non-Jews than to Jews. This is a situation which deserves to be studied for, as against 283 Jews convicted for illegal entry into Palestine, there were 2,150 non-Jews.[42]

The "secret" handwritten comments of a British official in response to the Mandates Commission reports indicate that Government was both well aware of the "illicit" Arab immigration[43] and resented the challenge to its one-sided selective "system" of immigration into Western Palestine:

I think we can ignore the peevish reaction about illicit immigration in May PMC's report.[44]

In the year following those PMC reports, the correspondence between British officials clearly underscores an official awareness and recognition of the Arabs' illegal entry over the borders from Syria and Transjordanian Palestine into the Jewish-settled areas of Palestine.

A "secret" report in January 1937 from High Commissioner Wauchope told Britain's Colonial Secretary that

. . . the British resident in Transjordan has examined the possibility of preventing the passage of men and arms from Iraq to Palestine via Transjordan . . . at times of disturbance. . . . I shall be glad . . . if his Majesty's minister at Jeddah may be required to take up the matter with the Saudi authorities with a view to securing their agreement in principle that in the event of a situation necessitating such a measure they will prevent the passage from the KAF area into Transjordan of all persons coming from Iraq *except bonafide merchants and migrating tribes.* *[45]

In other words, only in the "event" of "disturbance" would even the *possibility* of control be considered. And *even then* "migrating tribes" would still be exempt from the scrutiny of border authorities.

A month later, Lacy Baggallay, a British Foreign Service officer, discouraged even that diluted token effort to control Arab immigration, because it might offend the Saudis:

. . . while we appreciate the . . . desirability of controlling entrants into Transjordan . . . we much doubt whether this object will be best attained by representation to Ibn Saud at this stage. . . . to ask him now to make promises which might prove difficult or even dangerous for him about a hypothetical situation, would be putting a strain on his friendship which would be most imprudent, seeing how valuable it may be to us. . . .

If any attempt to extract these promises were made, Ibn Saud might conclude either (a) that we doubted whether he would continue to act as a good neighbor and wished to give him a hint to do so—which would be insulting, or else (b) that we took it for granted that whatever policy His Majesty's government adopted it was for him to put into force a control system on Saudi territory . . . which would be presumptuous.

*Emphasis added.

For those reasons, we would prefer *even at the risk of losing valuable time when the emergency arises* to make no representations in advance, *although we recognize* that it may be desirable and *even necessary* . . . *[46]

The British representative in Jeddah "shared Foreign Office views" and "strongly deprecated proposal."[47]

The British officials' comments, further, reveal that even when the illicit immigrants were "thugs" and "terrorists" entering Palestine for the purpose of wreaking terror in the officials' own midst—imported agitators who incited mob violence—the government deemed the outbreaks "nationalism" and resisted those security measures that might have controlled the situation, for fear of offending Arab leaders.

The Case of the Stifled Solution

There were those who insisted that the violence was criminal outbreak only loosely masquerading as "nationalism" to gain sympathy for Arabs in their attack against the Jews. Two or three British officers persisted in identifying the imported agitators as mercenaries† hired to incite mobs against the Jews and the British and proposed that force must be used to prevent further bloodshed in Palestine; they were ridiculed among their colleagues privately and their proposals to halt the Arabs' illegal entry were generally thwarted.

The following series of "secret" communications concerns a diehard among the few dissenting British officials, Colonel Gilbert MacKereth, British Consul in Damascus. His frustrated effort is vividly illustrated. But the next pages, excerpted from "secret" and confidential correspondence, are included to the extent that they are because they offer a dramatic disclosure of the circumstances and the British attitudes that prevailed in the 1930s.

While Colonel MacKereth's warnings were corroborated by the reports of some of his colleagues, those who at first supported him and even initiated "intensified patrolling" themselves (Shuckburgh and Battershill, for example) appear to have been persuaded later to a position of greater personal political advantage. A policy that understood or overlooked the terrorism and justified it by raising the myth of "nationalist Arab patriotism" would be more favorably looked upon by Arabs and British alike than the unromantic reality. Like "the Good Soldier Schweik," Gilbert MacKereth became the lone dissenter, against a British administration attitude that from the beginning discouraged any "assistance" in patrolling Palestine's borders.

The exchange begins with the Palestine High Commissioner's request to halt the "temporary" Syrian assistance in patrolling the borders:

*Emphasis added.
†The argument over whether "terrorism" or "guerrilla national liberation" maintains today.

To: High Commissioner, Syria
From: High Commissioner, Palestine and Transjordan
July 30, 1937

The moral and practical aid given by the presence and active patrolling of your troops has been a great service to us during the past three weeks. Now the situation has become so much more quiet that I consider there is no further need for me to ask for their further services at the present time. Our difficulties being over for the present I shall be happy if you care now to recall all those troops who have rendered us such valuable services. . . .[48]

To: Sir John Shuckburgh of the Colonial Office
From: W. D. Battershill
October 12, 1937

I recently discussed with the police the lack of success which they have had in tracing any terrorist from months past, and the suggestions which follow are the result of my deliberations. I put the matter to you privately in the first instance.

It is, I think, established that the terrorist gang is an offshoot of the Sheikh Kassab gang which appeared in 1930. . . . They are, I am informed, a very fanatical lot. What their numbers amount to is not known. It is believed that the actual gunmen live in Palestine scattered amongst the villages near and around Haifa and in the North generally. They are directed by some Palestinians who live in Damascus. *We have reasonably good evidence to connect the murder of [Lewis] Andrews with those who killed Khalim Basta in Haifa.* It is clear that the gunmen are well directed and take considerable pains to insure success. So much for the bare facts about the terrorist organization. I must add that few of the facts could be proved in a court of law, but nonetheless I believe them to be substantially true. . . . I feel convinced that this administration cannot stand another murder of a British official at the moment. And information which I have is that the gang will make further attempts on British officers in the near future. The morale of the administration generally is satisfactory now. But another murder of a British official will shake the administration very badly indeed. I suggest that the following suggestions might be considered.

(A)The small band of desperadoes who are living in Damascus should be ordered to leave Syria and should be handed over to our police on the border and they should be then interned in Iraq. I realize to the full the difficulties in the way of doing this but I have telegraphed about this today. If we could get these people inside Accre (prison), I think the directing hand of the gang would be removed. We are not asking for all the Palestinians in Damascus to be sent to us though I should have liked to have asked for that. There is no doubt that there are some hundreds of Palestinians there preaching open in the streets of Damascus sedition of the worst kind against H. M. G. The Syrian government which is supposed to be friendly to us and also the French seem powerless to stop this.*[49]

From: W. D. Battershill
October 16, 1937

. . . *the French were patrolling the frontier which they would have been*

*Emphasis added.

prepared to continue doing had they not been asked by this administration to stop.
. . . no thanks had been given to the French in the report for all the work they
had done on the frontiers in 1936. The French thought there should have been
no reference to the possibility of the formation of an Arab agency. They felt that
such a recommendation would make it difficult for them in Syria. . . . the French
and Syria still definitely had the whiphand over the Arabs there. *He thought that
they would hand over to this government anyone against whom there was a warrant
out provided pressure was brought to bear.* *[50]

To: Sir John Shuckburgh
From: W. D. Battershill
October 16, 1937
    . . . When I was administering the government on the occasion of the High
Commissioner's visit to England just prior to the publication of the Royal Commission's Report, amongst other steps which I took at the suggestion of the police
to insure that there would be no disturbances on the publication of the report was
to ask the French to cooperate on the northern frontier.
    The actual wording of the telegram I had drafted to the Consul General in
Beirut was:—"recent reports suggest the possibility of the incursion of Syrians
into Palestine after the publication of the Royal Commission's Report and the
conclusions of His Majesty's government. I should therefore be grateful if the
French authorities might be asked to intensify patrolling on the frontier." Actually the forces used by the French amounted to three squadrons of Circassian
levies with armored cars commanded by French officers. . . .
    The High Commissioner [Wauchope] on his return from England and on the
question of liaison being raised wrote to [Lieut.-General] Dill [commander of the
British Forces in Palestine] who replied on the 24th July stating inter alia "it was
very good of the French to put out these posts but I really don't know why they
did. I certainly never asked them to do it but I did write and thank General
Huntziger for having so very kindly given his voluntary help."
    The High Commissioner spoke to me about this matter on the 30th of July
and I gather that *he thought I had made a mistake* in seeking for French cooperation of this kind and also in omitting to consult Dill. It was suggested that I should
write an apologetic note to Dill which I did. The High Commissioner sent the
telegram of which a copy is enclosed. I feel sure that the High Commissioner had
no knowledge that the French wished to keep these arrangements in force. And
the circumstances as they were then, there was no necessity to trouble the French
with these additional patrols. . . .
    . . . I have already telegraphed to you regarding some of our terrorists in Syria
and now that the Mufti is there the question has become of the greatest importance.*[51]

To: Anthony Eden, the Principal Secretary of State for Foreign Affairs
From: Gilbert MacKereth, British Consul in Damascus
October 18, 1937
    . . . I availed myself of the opportunity to which Jamil Mardem Bey gave me

*Emphasis added.

of putting before him frankly my views regarding the apparent indifference of the Syrian authorities toward the active and almost open conspiracy in Syria to . . . continuance of the public disorders in Palestine.

2. I was careful to explain to Jamil Mardem and the two other members of his cabinet, Shukri Quwatli and Dr. Abdurrahman Kayali, who joined us, that I had no instructions whatever to broach this question with him officially; any formal representations which might need to be made at the present time would, of course, be made to the French authorities, with whom alone I was in direct and official contact. . . .

3. I first of all pointed out that we were fully aware, as was the whole city of Damascus, of the activities of Mahomet al Ashmar and several well known Palestinian political agitators now living here. . . . he repeated what he had frequently told me in the past, that Syria had enough troubles of her own. I said that from what I had heard, I was very skeptical about mere verbal cautions in the case of a person of al Ashmar's calibre. I told Jamil Mardem and his ministers that it was internationally intolerable that the Syrian government should not do everything in its power to stop this plotting. Pan Arabian sentiment, laudable in itself, was no excuse. I had noticed, I said, with growing concern for Syria, many outspoken articles which had been recently appearing in the *British press stating openly* and with some truth, they must admit, *that troubles in Palestine were being actively fomented in Damascus.* . . . I said I could readily conceive of a . . . reaction, were public disturbances to continue in Palestine when so much of its inspiration could be laid at the door. I allowed myself to suggest that one result of rising public opinion in England might conceivably be an uncompromising refusal to countenance the admission of Syria to the League of Nations. . . . I suggested he was possibly inclined to overestimate *Pan Syrian and Pan Arab feeling in Syria.* It was perhaps not so ardent as some people thought, nor was it so wholeheartedly interested in the Palestine problem. I did not think the security of his government really rested on it at all.

4. I believe I was successful in shaking the complacency of Shukri Quwatli, who has hitherto been in the forefront of those who have facilitated the machinations of the Palestinian agitators in Damascus. The Prime Minister was urgent in his assurances that the Government, notwithstanding its difficulties, which he knew I understood, would make a very real effort to put an end to these objectionable activities. Admittedly, these were only words, but I had left my host with a hopeful feeling that I had sewn seed the real alarm in their minds which would grow and embolden them to face public opinion and to take some practical steps to stop the abuses of which I had complained. I am further fortified in my hope by learning this evening from Commandant Bonnot, head of the French Intelligence Service, that four emissaries have today been sent from Damascus to urge upon the Arabs in Palestine cessation of their terrorist activities.

I have also been informed that four Assyrians who have been engaged in Damascus to join the Palestinian bandits and who were attempting to enter TransJordan from Syria, have just been arrested by the Syrian police; a hitherto unheard of proceeding.*[52]

*Emphasis added.

To: Secretary of State, Eden
From: W. D. Battershill
October 18, 1937

In view of possible incursion of armed bands from Syria of which there are *unconfirmed rumors locally* I should be glad if French authorities could be asked to intensify their patrolling along this bare side of northern frontier of Palestine. I have not made this request direct as I should normally have done because I understand negotiations are now proceeding between His Majesty's government and French government regarding the Mufti and because such a request will have greater force coming from His Majesty's government. If however, such cooperation has only to be obtained on the understanding that we declare some form of martial law in Palestine and assume firmer control of TransJordan (see telegram number 17, foreign office from Consul at Damascus) then I would rather forego cooperation of French at present for time has not yet come for delegation of powers and *I am unable to agree that control in Trans-Jordan needs greater firmness than is in force at present.* If French find themselves unable to intensify patrols I intend to close northern frontier posts to all traffic during all hours of darkness. I found out French opinion as to this proposal last week through Consul General at Beirut and is clear that the French while not feeling able in the circumstance to oppose proposal would like to avoid its being put into force largely on account of the trade between Syria and Palestine. If on the other hand the French will cooperate fully then I shall not take step of closing frontier posts without further consultation with them. General Wavell concurs in the terms of this telegram.*[53]

To: Right Honorable A. Eden, His Majesty's Principal Secretary of State for Foreign Affairs
From: Gilbert MacKereth
October 19, 1937

The purpose to my telegrams numbers 14, 15, 16 and 17 concerning the activities of certain Palestinian and Syrian political agitators to commence terrorist acts in Palestine, it may now be convenient to record in greater detail recent happenings in this connection.

2. After the Bludan Congress, Palestinian and Syrian extremists held many secret meetings. The conclave which was described in annex 6 of my memorandum on the Bludan Congress was typical of them.

3. I have been in the closest touch with Mr. Kingsley Heath and from a copious exchange of information with him it soon became abundantly clear that not only was there substantial traffic in arms going on from Syria into Palestine, *but that active preparations were being made to engage unemployed Syrians for service in bands to commit acts of banditry in Palestine with the object of creating a general state of public disorder out of which the Palestine Arab irredentists hoped to achieve their political aims. . . .* These thugs, led by Shaikh Aptiweh, were able to plot unmolested in Damascus and there was strong grounds for believing that

*Emphasis added.

they had organized at least seven recent assassinations in Palestine. They appear to have no direct connection with Mahomet al Ashmar and the Palestine agitators. Nevertheless, it was significant that when the Mufti of Jerusalem visited Damascus, Shaikh Aptiweh was frequently in touch with him. . . .

5. On the 13 September, *having obtained positive information on the recruiting of bandits at the instigation of the Arab higher committee in Jerusalem and its agents in Damascus,* notably Fakhri Abdel Hadi and Mu'in al Madi, I informed you of the fact and *suggested that the French government,* who are ultimately responsible for the state of affairs in Syria, *should be asked to oblige Syrian authorities* to take suitable steps to *prevent the Syrian,* Mohamet [sic] al Ashmar, who was taking a permanent part in *exhorting his compatriots to go to Palestine* to fight there in the "Arab cause" *from repeating his exploits of last year; leaving Syria to lead guerilla bands in Palestine.* . . .

9. By the 11th October I was able to establish beyond reasonable doubt that small bands of Syrians had been formed [with] new group leaders, had received earnest money in amounts varying between 2 and 4 Palestinian pounds, a rifle, a few rounds of ammunition, a warm Jalabieh, and a water bottle. They were only awaiting a signal from Palestine to make their way across the frontier in parties of *three or four, till they rendezvous somewhere in the Nablus Hills. I also had testimony, of which I was less sure, that some similar parties had already gone.* There were unmistakeable signs of careful and concerted organization. Experience last year showed that even with active French military patrols and complete French control over the Syrian police and gendarmerie, *factors which do not obtain today, it proved impossible to prevent Syrian bandits from slipping between the frontier posts.* The only hope, therefore, of preventing Syrian participation in public disturbances in Palestine which appear again to have broken out, was to force the reluctant hand of the Syrian authorities, with whom we are not in direct relations, and to oblige them to assume responsibility for preventing these subversive activities.

10. I informed the acting high commissioner in Palestine of the state of affairs. . . . On the 12th October I called on the delegate and laid before him all the evidence in my possession, giving him four lists of persons who, according to my information, should be placed under especial restraint or observation. The lists contained respectively (1) the names of nine political agitators, (2) five terrorists, (3) 27 known bandits, who had agreed to sell their services to the Arab cause in Palestine, and (4) 47 traffickers in arms who, according to their accomplices or to intercepted messages, have been concerned recently in the sale of arms to persons in Palestine. Comte Ostrorog and M. Perisse, Chef de la Surete, who was at my request, present at the interview, expressed themselves impressed by the completeness of the evidence I was able to present to them. Comte Ostrorog promised to get in touch with High Commissioner and, with the added weight of M. deMartel's authority, again confront the Syrian Prime Minister with these grave developments.

. . . M. deMartel had received instructions from Paris to call upon the Syrian government to bring the present state of affairs to an end. This appeared most satisfactory. It came later to my notice however that the same evening Mahomet al Ashmar had held a large political recruiting meeting in his house and had declared in public that he had retorted to the Syrian Prime Minister's admonition that he had no intention of being dictated to by the Syrian or any other government. . . .

12. The situation was, as I think you will agree, far from satisfactory, and the only other immediate course seemed to be that of direct military intervention by the French, but it did not seem to me that we were in a position to demand this in view of the fact that events in Palestine have not led us to a declaration of partial or complete martial law. Moreover, it is impossible to close our eyes to a fact which is remembered with some bitterness against us; we failed in 1925 and 1926 to show adequate sympathy with the difficulties the French had themselves in Syria at that time.

It is a noteworthy fact that the British authorities in Palestine and particularly in TransJordan showed a hospitality to Syrian bandits and rebels which now we must truthfully regret. A sharp thorn at our side today is Mahomet al Ashmar. A bandit chief from the Jabrun mountains of Syria, who was directly responsible for the death of two French officers and three French non-commissioned officers in 1925, he had a previous criminal record and was condemned to death by French court martial. He escaped into Palestine where we insisted on treating him as a political refugee. His case like that of Fawzi Kawokji, a deserter from the French forces, was only one of many. Most of those *then benefited from British asylum are now planning to go, or had already gone, to Palestine, to continue their acts of terrorism, this time directed against the British administration.*

13. You will see sir that the position is a delicate one. . . . Nevertheless, if we find it necessary to declare martial law in Palestine and what is equally important, assume a more evident control of the situation in *TransJordan which,* notwithstanding recent measures taken to improve matters in that country, *is still an open door to Palestine for arms and rebel bands,* then we should be in a position to ask the French to reassume a more direct control themselves in Syria.

14. Faced with this dilemma, I took the unusual course and opportunity provided. I'm endeavoring to frighten the Syrian government into taking steps which may prove sufficiently effective, provided the situation in Palestine itself does not markedly deteriorate. I hesitate at this stage to feel unduly sanguine, nevertheless the information I received today that a number of people, whose names were in a list I gave Comte Ostrorog, have been summoned to the Syrian police headquarters; that four Syrians bound for the Nablus Hills have been arrested by the Syrian police when about to cross the TransJordan frontier; and that a party of men who had left Homs yesterday stopped in Damascus, encourages that the position locally is improving. Signed Gilbert MacKereth.*[54]

To: Sir George Rendel, Head of the Eastern Department of the Foreign Office
From: J. R. Shuckburgh, Head of the Middle East Department
October 21, 1937

In our official letter number 75156/37 of the 14th October we enclosed a copy of a telegram from Battershill in which he asks that the French government may be approached with a view to the expulsion from Syria of a number of Palestinian

*Emphasis added.

"bad hats." In connection with that letter I think you ought to see the enclosed extracts from a personal letter which I had from Battershill which reinforces his official telegram.[55]

From: Gilbert MacKereth, British Consul in Damascus
October 21, 1937

1. At present time all Syrians hired to proceed to Palestine *are going* unarmed. Efforts made to arrest them are thus rendered largely negative especially if they invariably travel by night. Syrians have caught about 20 so far but my information is that many get through.

2. *Identity card system should be imposed forthwith. French did it in 15 days in 1926. Without this system control of movements of the population is impossible. . . .*[*56]

To: Eden, Secretary of State for the Colonies
From: Battershill, Officer Administrating the Government of Palestine
October 22, 1937

. . . 2. *Question of identity card system was considered and rejected some months ago for political and other reasons. Scheme is in being* should it ever be decided to enforce it and village registers covering the whole of the northern frontier have been prepared. Question of curfew on roads and adjoining frontier already considered and *rejected for good reasons* but will come under review from time to time.[*57]

From: Gilbert MacKereth in Damascus
October 23, 1937

(1) I am aware of additional measures taken. I consider them insufficient in themselves.

(2) Having no information numbers of persons arrested after illegally crossing the frontier I cannot judge just how efficacious the new measures have been. I am on the other hand aware that many parties of Syrians have succeeded evading both the Syrian and Palestinian patrols during the past ten days. During this period of fairly willing cooperation by Syria some 25 have been caught attempting surreptitiously to cross the frontier to join Palestinian rebels; five have been passed to French military courts. It is impossible to stop every one but if Palestinian authorities have not been able to achieve at least equal results by their intensive activity it appears to me that method should be changed at once.

(3) I am aware of the many political and other reasons that militate against adoption of identity card system which some years ago I urged unsuccessfully in respect of illegal immigration into Palestine. Nevertheless, I am unshaken in my opinion that without it Palestine public security will always be in great danger, a danger which will increase as French control system diminishes. *The French faced with the same difficulty rapidly brought 1925–1926 revolt in Morocco to an end by instituting this system within 15 days in 1926; they then found the dreaded political consequences had been greatly exaggerated.*

*Emphasis added.

(4) Curfew on roads is not enough as bandits easily avoid the roads. What is required is authority to hold and send for detailed examination any person found outside his house at night in the frontier zone.

(5) On the other hand if something in the nature of these measures is not done quickly all the Syrian bandits will have gained the vastnesses of Palestine hills despite all my and the French efforts. Sufficient arms are, I believe, already in Palestine to provide ample for all Assyrian and other bandits who can move about unarmed apparently innocent.*[58]

Minute Written by Sir George Rendel, Head of the Eastern Department of Foreign Office
October 26, 1937
Colonel MacKereth is certainly showing great zeal and energy in trying to prevent Syria becoming a base for the operations of the Arab nationalists in Palestine. It is obviously necessary that all British should make every possible effort to bring the campaign of murder and terrorism to an end, and Colonel MacKereth has, therefore, in principle, acted quite rightly.

But I confess that I am somewhat disturbed by the threat he used with Jamil Mardem that we might veto the admission of Syria to the League when the time came, if the present situation goes on. This statement will certainly be regarded as having been made under instructions, and will probably be reported to the French as such. The French may or may not complain to us about it, but they are likely to be much annoyed, especially as we've already promised them to make things as easy as possible when the emancipation of Syria comes before the League. It might be well, therefore, to give Colonel MacKereth the word of warning.

Apart from this my only criticism of Colonel MacKereth's attitude is that he seems to regard the whole question as purely a local criminal one. The Arab rebels are something more than mere 'thugs.' The code upon which they are acting, however misguidedly, has a passionate desire to prevent territory which they regard as their own from being given—as they think, unjustly—by a third party (i.e. His Majesty's government) to an *alien invader.* * We must clearly resist rebellion and try to stop murder. But it is merely foolish not to recognize that the rebels may be acting on at any rate explicable motives and are not necessarily all "bad hats."[†]

Queries: Copy to colonial office and quite privately to Colonel MacKereth giving him, in cautious language—so as not to discourage him unduly—the substance of the above minute.[59]

___

*Emphasis added.
†The generally negative reaction to MacKereth's plea for stricter enforcement at borders to prevent terrorist murders in Palestine by senior foreign officer Rendel and others—"that the Arab 'rebels' have a 'passionate' desire to prevent territory which they regard as their own from being given . . . to an 'alien invader' . . . it is merely foolish not to recognize that the rebels may be acting on at any rate explicable motives"—is an attitude that approximates apologia for the terrorism. Further, the reaction of Rendel, that Jews are "alien invaders," is not unlike French minister Barre's statement in France in 1980 after the bombing raid in a Paris synagogue, that "innocent Frenchmen" were also killed or in danger because of the bombing. The implication was that the Jews were neither innocent nor French.

George Rendel's Foreign Office Memorandum Entitled:
"Palestine. Immediate Problem"

   . . . bands of Arabs from neighboring countries are waiting to take the first opportunity to cross into Palestine to assist in the guerrilla warfare which is being proposed against the Mandatory powers.

   . . . we have as many enemies in Europe, and there are clear signs that the Arabs are already turning to them for help against us. Our Palestine policy will thus not only earn us the hostility of all the Arabs, both inside and outside Palestine, but is calculated to bring about increasingly close association between those Arabs and our European rivals, the consequence of which may be far-reaching and extremely serious to ourselves.

   . . . no local Zionist success in Palestine could be worth the sacrifice involved.

   The trouble in Palestine is political and not criminal, though naturally our political opponents are using criminal measures, since no others are at present open to them.[60]

To: Gilbert MacKereth, British Consul in Damascus
From: Sir George Rendel, Head of the Eastern Dept. of Foreign Office
October 28, 1937

   . . . there is one aspect of your dispatch on which I feel I ought to send a few purely personal and private comments. . . .

   3. *The Palestine problem is one of extreme complexity and is in our view, very far from being merely one of a rebellion by criminal elements against constituted authorities as such. You are of course thoroughly familiar with the aspect of the question from your reading of the Royal Commission's Report. But some of your recent references to the Arabs as "bandits," "bad hats," and "thugs" (cf. your telegram 21 of October 23rd) make me wonder whether there may not be a certain danger in regarding the Arab nationalist movement rather too much as a purely criminal outbreak, and rather too little as a manifestation of Arab feeling against the proposals to create a new state in Palestine mainly for the sake of the central European Jews, whom the Arabs, in spite of our pledges not unnaturally regard as alien invaders. . . .*

   5. Finally let me repeat that I put forward these caveats *not with any intention of criticizing what you have done, but merely as a probably quite unnecessary hint of warning for your future guidance.*

   It may, of course, be wise to continue to take the line in dealing with Assyrians that any Arabs who cross into Palestine to take part in the campaign are merely ordinary criminals. But I am not sure that it will help us to get over our difficulties if we are too ready ourselves to assume that this is the case. *[61]

To: Right Honorable A. Eden, His Majesty's Principal Secretary of State for Foreign Office
From: Gilbert MacKereth, British Consul at Damascus
October 30, 1937

   . . . I have the honor to enclose a translation of a letter which I received yesterday from the Black Hand, the secret terrorist society. The same day I

*Emphasis added.

translated the original to the French delegate for such action as he considered proper to take.

2. . . . This is the third time I've been threatened by Palestinian terrorists during the past 2½ months. . . .

3. These incidents smack of melodrama, but as my latest correspondent observes, they should not be mocked at. During the past two years the astonishing inability of the Palestinian authorities to bring to book the perpetrators of a large number of political assassinations has emboldened beyond all previous measure the thugs of today, and since the French hold on Syria public security has weakened they are not as constrained as they once were in this country. Mr. Ogden and myself, the targets in Syria for Palestinian malcontents enjoying Syrian asylum, have naturally been taking all reasonable precautions. I have now made arrangements to have the consular canvasses suitably armed. Signed Gilbert MacKereth.

[*Enclosure:*] preserved as a memorandum of a threat to the Consul and his oppressive government threat in defense of the Arab countries.

To his Honor the respected Consul of Britain. An Arab salutation of note from Northern and Southern Syria. I have written these lines as a warning that you shall know what will happen. Beware of the murderous resolve of the Arabs and "Fidaiyyin" (desperados) should we decide to use violence. You must remember that you who are English are among us. You eat our vegetables, our fruit, you drink our water and enjoy your sojourn in our land under our sky.

How haughty you are you English. *We know how wickedly you deal with the Arabs of southern Syria. We know too how corrupt you are in sustaining certain people whom all the world hates and whom Allah, the all powerful, also hates.* Understand that we are a secret society that has sworn an oath that you and every Englishman in this city are liable to be slain should our Grand Mufti the Sheikh Amin al Hussani be even slightly injured. You will then be aggressors and will have caused it. This is perfectly reasonable and logical. Therefore, notify your government of this threat and of this letter.

This is, however, not enough: As soon as you receive this message ask two policemen to watch over you, for we are not afraid of the police, or of the soldiers or of any force whatever. We are "believers" who fear no one no matter how great he may be. We fear only Allah. Be assured that by the will of Allah we can carry out the threats made in this letter should the slightest harm be done to the Grand Mufti who is a refugee in this country. Bear all this in mind, reflect upon what we say and mock not at it.

Signed "Kufuf Saudeh" (black hands) tinged with blood.*[62]

To: Secretary of State for the Colonies
From: W. D. Battershill, Acting High Commissioner
November 1, 1937

. . . 2. Between 1st October and 29th October, 288 persons of whom 188 were Arabs have been arrested after illegal crossing of frontier. A similar number of Arabs was turned back through the frontier.

3. *Identity card system would be welcomed by* the general officer commanding

*Emphasis added.

but in order to be made effective this would have to cover an area from our northern frontiers far south of that of Akur-Safad/Tiberius Road and would entail issue of cards to all men and women over age of 16 to an estimated approximate number of 60,000 persons. . . . Apart from time involved estimated at about three months and practical difficulties involved of imposing on district administration additional duties of introducing the system when they are already so fully occupied with other security measures, *the political consequences might be considerable.* It is inferred [by MacKereth] that like the French we may find the political difficulties have been greatly exaggerated. *I disagree.* It will be maintained in spite of government assurances to the contrary that institution of this system is connected with partition and removal of population and it is possible that we should be faced with mass non-cooperation in which case enforcement must fail. At present there is very strict enforcement of bon voisinage agreement. Anyone seen crossing the frontier is asked for his bon voisinage.

If he has none he's detained until he satisfies the police as to his identity. I am assured that strangers in villages can easily be identified as such at present. Anyone moving by night in this area is at once arrested and detained for investigation. In the circumstances I do not think that identity card system should be introduced and the general officer commanding agrees though with some reluctance.*[63]

Recommendation by George W. Rendel, Head of the Eastern Dept. of the Foreign Office, regarding Gilbert MacKereth:
November 1, 1937
Col. MacKereth is an admirable and extremely energetic officer who has shown enormous activity in helping the Palestine authorities in trying to keep Arab discontent under control. . . .

At the same time, I feel bound to record that I am not altogether happy about the proposal. [This refers to the transfer of MacKereth to Jerusalem] I am not sure that Col. MacKereth has always appreciated the wider issues involved in this question, which he has inevitably looked at from a somewhat *local* point of view. His very energy and enthusiasm make this loss of perspective more conspicuous than it would be in a less active man, and I think it is important that, if he goes to Jerusalem, any measures which he and the Palestine authorities may agree upon vis a vis the French should be referred to us for our approval before being embarked on. *There are questions connected with extradition of political refugees, and affecting the position of the French authorities vis a vis the Arab world which are inevitably rather beyond Col. MacKereth's immediate sphere, and which will need watching.* *[64]

From: Gilbert MacKereth
November 2, 1937
From my own observations and direct experience I remain unconvinced that administrative difficulties of instituting an indentity card system would be in practice as onerous as feared by Mr. Battershill. To take the case of Syria: with

*Emphasis added.

a population three times as great as Palestine, operation was carried out with sufficient effectiveness within three weeks. It was found, on 15 days warning being given, all persons anxious to avoid being inconvenienced hastened to take out identity cards. I consider as do experienced French officials that system should be directly offered without delay to the whole of Palestine not merely limited to northern frontier zone which in my view would be of little value. Immediate additional labor would be ultimately regained by increased administrative advantages. It should not be forgotten I venture to suggest that there has been but little peace from thuggery in Palestine since 1929 quite apart from recent open revolts. The efficacy of identity card system is surely shown an advantage taken in frontier zones of bon voisinage passes, it is not in the frontier zones where the worst acts of terrorism have occurred but in the interior of the country.

2. If the principle is accepted the system should be instituted as an urgent measure of public security under emergency orders in council without explanation or assurances. Should massed non-cooperation, which after 16 years residence amongst Arabs and Pseudo-Arabs I do not anticipate, render measure negatory, position would merely revert.[65]

Foreign Office Memorandum
From: Rendel
November 3, 1937

I have heard indirectly that the colonial office are not being strongly urged to take a line that His Majesty's government should meet Arab opposition to our partition policy by pressing forward that policy as rapidly and drastically as possible. I understand that, in the view of those who are giving this advice, once Palestine Arabs understand that His Majesty's government are prepared to carry their policy through, irrespective of any agitation against it, that agitation will subside and we shall have no more trouble. . . .

The line of policy indicated above, if sufficiently ruthlessly applied, will almost certainly succeed—for a time at any rate—in Palestine itself. The Palestine Arabs are mostly poor and ignorant, and much divided among themselves. We should have the whole-hearted support of the 400,000 Jews in the country, and should command sufficient military resources to be able to hold down the other elements of the population by force without undue difficulty. We should appear to have solved the problem by "firm action," and could go to the League and to Parliament with every prospect of getting our policy endorsed.

4. But I submit that this attitude completely ignores the fact that the Middle East is an organic whole. The frontiers shown on the maps, at any rate, as between the Arabic-speaking countries, are largely artificial post-war creations, resting on no true national, geographical or ethnographical basis. Strong measures in one country are likely to produce strong reactions at its neighbors', and there are many European powers only too ready to seize on any such reactions that exploits them to our disadvantage. . . . I submit that it is not only useless, but quite extraordinarily dangerous to deal with the Palestine question in isolation. As I represent it in another paper, the Palestine problem could be effectively settled—provided we do not delay much longer—if it could be dealt with independently of that of central Europe. But to continue to look at the Palestine problem in the light of

our alleged commitments to the central European Jews, while refusing to look at it in the light of the situation, and of our vital Imperial interests, in the neighboring Arab countries and the Middle East as a whole, can only lead to a catastrophe.[66]

To: Foreign Office
From: George Rendel
November 3, 1937
... he [Ibn Saud] has *now* realized that the formation of a compact homogeneous and independent Jewish state on the Mediterranean coast of the Arab countries, with some six million Jews from Central Europe desperately trying to get into it, will mean so serious a threat to any hopes of the creation of an independent and prosperous Arabia that it is his duty, as the leading independent Arab sovereign, to make almost any sacrifice to try to prevent it.[67]

Minute by George Rendel, Head of Eastern Dept. of Foreign Office
November 4, 1937
... The bands [of terrorists] may ... operate from TransJordan, where it is very possible there might be a widespread rebellion, which it would be very difficult for us to control with our very exiguous troops. As soon as the bands begin to operate, organized assistance to the rebels and to the guerilla bands will be furnished from Syria and Iraq, however much the governments of those countries may try to prevent it. This will probably be followed soon afterward by a relaxation of the frontier control by Ibn Saud, and the *penetration of Saudi tribesmen into TransJordan and possibly across into Palestine.*

Each development will produce another on a somewhat larger scale. We shall be obligated to send out strong reinforcements which will be met in turn by more highly organized and more widespread resistance. . . .*[68]

"Secret" Minutes of meeting attended by MacKereth, British Consul to Damascus, Col. Peake, the officer commanding the Arab legion, the officer administering the government, W. D. Battershill, and recorded by Mr. R. Scott, assistant Secretary.
November 5, 1937
Col. MacKereth stated that in some respects the situation might be said to have deteriorated, due to the fact that the French authorities who for some time have been cooperating closely with the Palestine government have now found themselves unable to move the Syrian government to adopt stronger measures against those agitators in Damascus, who aim at the promotion of a Syrian insurrection in Palestine. The Syrian Prime Minister had even threatened to resign if the High Commissioner for Syria and the Lebanon insisted on the adoption of these measures. More vigorous action could not, therefore, be expected.

The group of agitators in Damascus which have been financed with the funds of the former Arab Higher Committee was still awaiting an opportunity to proceed to Palestine for the purpose of stirring up insurrection. Col. MacKereth considered that there were numbers of persons in Syria, where there were many out of work and much poverty, who might be persuaded to come to Palestine for

*Emphasis added.

money or loot. In particular, there were the dangerous ruffians who emanate from the Black Mountain region between Damascus and Homs. The measures to be taken by the government of Palestine have, however, made the adventure definitely more dangerous and this was recognized by the gunmen, whose price had gone up. At this point when MacKereth was asked what the government could do "short of surrounding Palestine with an electric fence" MacKereth said "When the French had been faced with the great difficulties in Syria in 1926 they had adopted a system of identity cards which were of a simpler nature than the ordinary cartes d'identite. They had found that the system enabled them to eventually catch the gang leaders and consider that this happy result was almost entirely due to the existence of a card system."[69]

Rendel note: Foreign Office Papers
November 5, 1937
[Rendel noted that the "terrorists" and "thugs" of MacKereth report were actually "sincere Arab patriots."][70]

George Rendel, Head of the Eastern Dept. of the Foreign Office
Foreign Office Minute
November 12, 1937
. . . As will be seen from the attached green papers we have for some time realized that Col. MacKereth's activities against the organizers of the campaign of violence in Palestine might expose him to serious risks. I understand that a few weeks ago he arranged to have a bulletproof waistcoat sent out to him, and I then discussed with Mr. Scott how far we were justified in continuing to allow him to take such risks.

That these risks are very serious indeed there is no doubt. Col. MacKereth has, in my opinion, misunderstood the nature of the trouble in Palestine, which he regards as nothing more than a criminal outbreak against constituted authority as such. We have reason to note, however, that the present campaign of violence is only part of a very widespread and deepseated national movement spreading to all the Arabic-speaking countries against our policy in Palestine. . . . The best service we could render Col. MacKereth and his fellow British officials in the Middle East would be to reconsider our Palestine policy. This question is to come up before the Cabinet shortly and until a decision has been reached there is no more I think that we can do.[71]

From: Foreign Officer in London [presumably Eden]
November 13, 1937
I am disturbed that Mr. Rendel thinks that Col. MacKereth "is only too likely to lose his life in any case." I am not clear whether this unhappy eventuality is likely to occur because of Col. M's anti-terrorist activities or whether it is simply because he is our Consul at Damascus. If the former, and if a successor too is less likely to be assassinated, then I think that we should move Col. MacKereth and replace him by an officer who could be instructed to confine himself to pure consular work. I really do not feel that it is fair that our Consul should be exposed to this kind of risk through doing work which should be done by the Palestine

and Syrian authorities in collaboration. [Signed by foreign officer in London—possibly Eden.][72]

To: George Rendel
From: Gilbert MacKereth
November 15, 1937

Thank you for your kind letter, etc. . . . I confess a glow of self-satisfaction on Wednesday when the Palestinian authorities finally adopted my persistently urged use of military courts for arms cases. It is sad however, to think that it seemed to need vile assassinations of a district commissioner and unarmed private soldiers finally to sweep away all the unsubstantial objections raised against this use of military courts. I carry on, you will see, the fight for an identity card system. When this is brought in, provided it is done quickly, tranquility in Palestine should come speedily. When terrorism is supressed and both we and the Arabs generally will view one another with more friendly eyes. . . . It seems to me a pity that it is only when the country is in a mess and our relations with Arabs have generally been severely strained as a consequence that I, who live in the nerve center of Pan Arabism and mix intimately with many of its more active protagonists, am asked for an opinion. It is in no spirit of boastfulness that I can claim to see the Arab aspect of the Palestine problem in a more accurate perspective than the Palestine administration, with its enforced parochiality and more clearly and in greater detail than those in London. In this connection Battershill wrote to me about my visit to Jerusalem last Friday "the talk we had was of great value to me. . . ."

I much appreciated your views about the use of the word "bandit" and the like. I confess I preferred it to the Americanism "gunmen" used by the Palestine administration. The complexity of the Palestine problem holds, I think little mystery for me. *But I allow myself to wonder whether many of the difficulties are not of our own creation.*

There is one point about the present situation in Palestine where I think there's been some confusion of thought at home as well as in neighboring Arabic speaking countries. There are two aspects to it and they should, for the clearer understanding, be rigidly separated. The first, with which we can allow ourselves to sympathize, is the purely Pan Arab one. And, Palestine has centered itself on an unrelenting hostility to the Zionist movement. The second aspect, which is the one with which I have dealt with in my recent dispatches, is the thuggery which many Palestinian political leaders have deliberately encouraged and developed as a means of gaining their fairly laudable political aims. It should not be thought that the Arab nationalists, either in Palestine or Syria, offer themselves as heroes in a noble cause. Far from it. During the past two months they have been scouring the slums of Syrian towns for known criminals (many of whom already served long terms as punishment for savage assaults.) I have myself compiled in the course of my efforts to prevent them from going to Palestine a list of about 150 Syrians in Palestinians residence in Syria who have in this way been canvassed; *many have been hired and have gone to Palestine with a sordid and purely mercenary mission to create what havoc they can. So far, though I write subject to correction, not a singly honorably known Syrian or Palestinian from Syria has* *crossed the frontier to join any of the groups of bandits who in Palestine pass their time blowing up passenger trains, menacing and murdering officials, defenseless soldiers, policemen and civilians, extorting money at the point of the revolver from Arab, Christian and Jew alike . . . and performing a hundred antisocial acts. I do not refer to Arabs generally as bandits, bad hats, and thugs, but I believe I can fully justify the use of these epithets in the cases where I have used them. . . . I would go even farther, though I have been careful not to do so in my official dispatches, and say that where the genuine nationalists (agitators and others) become accessories before and after the odious crimes I've enumerated, they earn my contempt and loathing and do the Arab cause, which I personally favor but despair over, an inestimable amount of harm. Their contribution toward it may be likened to that of Burke and Hare to medical science. The situation in Palestine is not at present a political revolt, although it may yet grow into one if it does not soon mend, but a state of terrorism started by the Mufti and his party and now continuing of its own momentum, one with a background, not of Arab nationalism, but of Islamic fanaticism.* What I was striving for is not to prevent the nationalist Arabs of Palestine from drawing political assistance from Syria. It is to prevent common highwaymen and criminals being hired by Palestinian and Syrian nationalists in Damascus and sent into Palestine to raise hell there. This, I fear, may sound to you farfetched and melodramatic; it is, alas, the fact. The trouble is that the laudable and despicable aspects tend to become combined with the result that mere banditry eventually takes on a patriotic or heroic glamour as was the case of the massacre of the Syrians in 1933. There is no Syrian politician of my acquaintance who does not openly or secretly look upon that deed as noble, patriotic and requiring no justification. I would however like to stress the point that the Syrian government are fully aware of the danger, the spread of terrorism, an infectious disease, presents to them and are genuinely anxious to see it suppressed, although they fear to take too open a stand against it in Palestine. Yours forever, Gilbert MacKereth.*[73]

To: Anthony Eden
From: Gilbert MacKereth
November 16, 1937
    As a result of my observations concerning the use made of TransJordan as a jumping off ground and arms depot for Syrian ruffians hired to go to Palestine, I was able to impress on Sir Henry Coggs and Col. Peake the necessity for a more strict control of the TransJordanian police to the northern district of that country. Since I first drew attention to the gravity of this matter a British officer has been stationed permanently at Irbid. I have information that the mere fact of his presence there has given pause to the activities of the arms traffic as in gang organizers. . . .
    7. . . . The French High Commissioner asked me to assure Mr. Battershill of his desire to cooperate in every possible way with the Palestine government, and in particular, he offered to re-establish a military cordant along the Syrian and Lebanese frontier. I should again like to draw your attention to the sympathetic assistance I am receiving from the local French authorities. It is certainly not their

---

*Emphasis added.

fault that altered political conditions in Syria make the assistance less efficacious than it might otherwise be, but it is nonetheless valuable and has undoubtedly served to stem the flood of men and arms to Palestine. In the absence of such reinforcements and supplies the efforts of the Palestinian and Syrian nationalists to raise a general insurrection, which has been and still is their aim, seems likely to prove abortive.[74]

RE: "Memorandum drafted by Rendel, amended and initialed by Eden and circulated to the Cabinet on 11/19/37, as though Eden himself had written it." *November 19, 1937*

It has been suggested to me that there is only one way in which we can now make our peace with the Arabs, and avoid the dangers I have indicated above, that is, by giving the Arabs some assurance that the Jews will neither become a majority in Palestine, nor be given any Palestinian territory in full sovereignty....[75]

Perhaps because the unfortunate MacKereth admittedly "favored Arab causes" he did not perceive the full significance of the failure to institute the effective identity-card system he so earnestly sought. Afterward, Colonel Mac-Kereth's zeal was transferred to areas outside the conflict in question. However, because he had demonstrated his penchant for fearless and vocal opposition, the Foreign Office did not make the predictable blunder of demoting him: he died as *Sir* Gilbert MacKereth, having served a distinguished and lengthy service as Ambassador to Colombia.[76]

The Arab immigrants' virtual free access to the Jewish-settled areas of Western Palestine—throughout the British administration of the Mandate—would have the effect of distorting critical future political and demographic assessments prevailing until today and—literally—would prevent the rescue of those tens, even hundreds, of thousands of Jews whose lives had depended upon filling the places in Palestine that the Palestinian Jews had opened for them. Those places were taken instead by Arab immigrants—whose own origins and tradition of immigration would be obliterated—since, officially, "there was no such thing as Arab immigration." The Arab newcomers, like the in-migrants from Western Palestine,* immediately acquired the status of "indigenous native population since time immemorial," who—the British decided—would be further "displaced" by what senior official Rendel called the "alien Jewish invaders," if Jewish immigration were not severely curtailed.

*See Chapter 12.

14

Official Disregard of Arab Immigration

> Such Arab entrants will quickly satisfy all
> demands for additional labour . . . and will thereby
> virtually leave no room in the labour category for
> Jewish immigrants from outside for Palestine.
> —Palestine Partition Report, 1938

> If you debar various people from Trans-Jordan, and Hauranis
> from coming in . . . it would give more opportunities
> for Jewish labour? Is that your contention?
> —Palestine Royal Commission member
> to witness at hearings, 1936

> . . . it is probably sufficient to maintain the present
> practice, under which he is counted against the Labour
> Schedule, though this method does a certain injustice
> to the Jewish immigrant outside the country whose
> place is taken by the traveller concerned.
> —The Hope Simpson Report, 1930

Perhaps one of the greatest paradoxes of the history of the "Palestinian Problem" is that the Hope Simpson Report, which by itself contributed substantially to the myth of "displaced" and "landless" Arabs brought about by Jews—a myth that prevails today, although its contentions were proved false[1] within a short time after the report was published—also contains in its pages its own authors' *recognition* of the evidence and factors that *contradict* and refute the very foundation of the myth.

The pivotal Hope Simpson Report literally admitted not only that it was the "present practice" of British officials to blink at all but the most "flagrant" of the thousands of Arabs immigrating into Western Palestine, but also acknowledged that the illegal Arab immigration was an "injustice" that was *displacing* the prospective *Jewish* immigrants. As the Hope Simpson Report had put it in 1930,

Where the case is flagrant, recourse should certainly be had to expulsion. In cases of no special flagrancy, and where there is no objection to the individual, it is probably sufficient to *maintain the present practice, under which he is counted against the Labour Schedule, though this method does a certain injustice to the*

Jewish immigrant outside the country whose place is taken by the traveller concerned. *²

Thus we learn, as we suspected from such hard evidence as 35,000 Arabs coming unreported from the Hauran, that the elusive "secret" British correspondence that *did* deal with Arab deportation in large numbers dealt in fact only with "flagrant" cases, and that the "deportations" of Arabs annually *reported*—however large their number might be—must represent a far *larger unreported* incidence of illegal Arab immigration gone unrecorded.

Not only did the illicit Arab immigration go unrecorded, it was clearly *recognized in 1930* that by allowing the immigration of Arabs into Palestine de facto, the British were cooperating in and even fostering what Hope Simpson himself branded as "injustice" to the Jewish immigrant, whose place—cleared frantically and against powerful odds—was being taken by an illicit Arab immigrant (or by one of the 170,000-plus Arab in-migrants), in the mandated "Jewish National Home."

The Hope Simpson Report was riddled with facts that refuted its convoluted conclusions; according to that Report, evidence of Arab immigration abounded:

Egyptian labour is being employed;³ unemployment lists being swollen by immigrants from Trans-Jordania;⁴ illicit immigration through Syria and across the northern frontier of Palestine is material. . . .⁵

The Report described the ease with which a

number of persons evade the frontier control and enter Palestine without formality of any kind. . . . such control as exists is carried out at police posts on the roads. The immigrant who wishes to evade the control naturally leaves the road before reaching the frontier and takes the footpaths over the Hills.⁶

The Report suggested that "when" the illicit immigrants "are discovered"—in other pages called "flagrant"—"it should be the rule that they are at once returned to the country whence they came." Although it might be harsh, so the Report went, "unless it is understood that detection is invariably followed by expulsion the practice will not cease. It is probable that it will cease entirely as soon as it is discovered that the rule is actually in force."

This is exactly the discipline MacKereth and others urged upon the British administration seven years later, in 1937. But by 1942, the injustice persisted still. As British officials would attest in their confidential correspondence,

The police have no instructions to concentrate on picking up *Arabs* who are in Palestine illegally.*⁷

*Emphasis added.

Further, Arab unemployment was claimed when in fact such was not the case; according to the Report, Arab unemployment figures were inflated. The importance of inflating such reports was described:

Arab unemployment is liable to be used as a political pawn.

Arab politicians are sufficiently astute to realize at once what may appear an easy method of blocking that [Jewish] immigration to which they are radically averse, and attempts may and probably will be made to swell the list of Arab unemployed with names which should not be there, or perhaps to ensure the registration of an unemployed man in the books of more than one exchange. It should not prove difficult to defeat this manoeuvre.[8]

Yet, despite that evidence to the contrary in its own pages, the Report concluded—with no further mention of the Arabs' abuse of unemployment claims for political purposes—that it was *Jews' immigration* which was responsible for "prejudicing" the Arabs. The Report protected the so-called "existing" indigenous Arab population, the same community that the Report itself had proved was largely composed either of immigrants or Arab in-migrants, who were not in fact indigenous or "existing" in Western Palestine's Jewish-settled areas—but it was *Jewish* immigration that, according to the Hope Simpson Report, should be reduced or "if necessary, suspend(ed)." As the Report stated,

It is evident that any interference with freedom of immigration is a limitation to the admission of Jews who desire to take part in . . . [the Jewish National] Home. Article 6 of the Mandate, however, directs that the rights and position of other sections of the population shall not be prejudiced by Jewish immigration. Clearly, in cases in which immigration of Jews results in preventing the Arab population obtaining the work necessary for its maintenance, it is the duty of the Mandatory Power under the Mandate, to reduce and if necessary, to suspend, such immigration, until immigration will not affect adversely the opportunities of the Arab for employment.[9]

The authors of the Hope Simpson Report had disingenuously invoked the Mandate's qualifications regarding Article 6—not prejudicing the "existing" non-Jewish population's rights—to profess fidelity to the Mandate. At the same time, in its own pages the Report had strongly indicated 1) that the Arab population for whom they invoked the Mandate's protective caveat was actually largely immigrant and not indigenous—thus not entitled to the Mandate's protection—without ever mentioning the faulty statistical assumptions* that disguised the tens of thousands of Arab in-migrants, who became regarded as part of the "existing" population in the Jewish-settled area upon their arrival; and 2) that the condition of Arab "unemployment" was being blown up out of all semblance to reality by the Arab leaders who had indeed found the "method of blocking that [Jewish] immigration to which they are radically averse."

*See Chapter 12.

The 1930 Hope Simpson Report, according to a later British report, was "inclined towards the Arab side."[10] It had been induced by the government on the heels of the 1929 Arab massacres of Jews and other widespread "disturbances," to show cause for limiting Jewish land purchases and immigration and to justify the accompanying 1930 White Paper[11] that—according to the official "report"—"inclined even more towards the Arab side than had either the Shaw or Hope Simpson Reports."[12]

It is the height of irony that the Hope Simpson Report, while testifying to the situation of Jews' places in their "National Home" being taken by illicit Arab immigrants, nonetheless became instead the official conduit for the false Arab claim that Jews were displacing "landless" Arabs. The only Hope Simpson Report findings that were acted upon were those which supported Arab demands. Thus the operative Hope Simpson "opposed . . . further Jewish immigrants as settlers on the land"[13] and recommended "close settlement . . . by both Arabs and Jews,"[14] which was the obligation of the Mandate.* There would be "no room for a single additional [Jewish] settler,"[15] according to the Report.

The actions that followed from the erroneous conclusions of the Hope Simpson Report, and the like, bear importantly on subsequent and, indeed, *present* claims, charges, and conditions of the "Palestinian problem." It is for this reason that we pause here to examine briefly the results of those actions, not only as they weighed upon official disregard of the illegal Arab immigration, but as they shaped general British attitudes and policy in the years to come.

The Passfield White Paper of 1930 sought to give the right to acquire State lands—not to the Jews for their close settlement as Article 6 of the Mandate prescribed and directed—but to "landless Arab cultivators." Furthermore, the "landless Arabs" need not have owned land before, nor was it necessary that they had been inconvenienced by the Jews' land purchases.

Despite Hope Simpson's own obscured admission—that Arab unemployment was inflated for political purposes—he had correlated Arab unemployment with Jewish immigration. Therefore, ignoring the all-important factor of the *Arab*

---

*John Hope Simpson wrote in 1937, "I have just reread the mandate, and cannot think that the intention was to flood Palestine with a Jewish urban population . . . it would seem (Article VI) that the Jewish immigration was to be facilitated especially with the object of close settlement on the land. . . .

"I cannot but think that agricultural settlement was the original object of the policy announced in the Balfour Declaration and there may be some record prior to the Declaration which would elucidate this point.

"The political importance of Jewish immigration of large scale is enhanced by Mussolini's obvious attempt to constitute himself protector of the Muslims. He is following, in this, in the footsteps of the late Kaiser. But the Arabs are probably quite clever enough to use Mussolini to our detriment, if we are going to side definitely with those Zionists.

"The alternative appears to me to be (1) Give up the Mandate as unworkable. (2) Close Jewish immigration at once, on the ground that the National Home is overcrowded. Or (3) let the thing rip —encourage as many Jews to immigrate as can do so, but make them defend themselves."[16]

Hope Simpson's "confidential" and apparently candid view of the Jews' right to immigration and land settlement as prescribed in the Mandate is startling in light of the fact that his report cynically contended the reverse.

immigration taking place illegally, the 1930 White Paper directed that *Jewish* immigration should depend on *Arab* unemployment as well as Jewish, with no regard for the fact that "Jewish Capital was imported solely for the employment of Jewish labour. . . ."[17]

Jewish immigration and settlement should be suspended, according to the White Paper, until the "landless Arab" situation and primitive Arab farming methods had been improved. The Jews, who had been explicitly granted the position "as of right and not on sufferance" by international Mandate, were now being relegated to a permanent minority status. Jewish spokesmen were in a state of shock. Chaim Weizmann protested to Lord Passfield that the White Paper was "inconsistent with the terms of the mandate, and in vital particulars marks the reversal of the policy hitherto followed by His Majesty's Government in regard to the Jewish National Home."[18]

In 1931 Prime Minister Ramsay MacDonald temporarily alleviated some of the restrictions of the Passfield White Paper by the publication of a letter to Weizmann.[19] Only "such Arabs" who could show that they had "been displaced from the lands which they occupied in consequence of the lands passing into Jewish hands, and who have not obtained other holdings on which they can establish themselves, or other equally satisfactory occupation" could qualify as "landless Arabs" who would be given the right to State lands by the 1930 White Paper.

Despite the government's unprecedented generosity and concern, however, the records illustrate that only a minuscule part of the Arab population of Western Palestine even registered as landless Arabs who had been displaced. In all, *less than one percent* of the rural non-Jewish population of Arabs proved to be bona fide "displaced Arabs."[20]

It is a curious fact that none among the "very considerable landless class" of Arabs in Transjordanian–Eastern Palestine—where no Jews were allowed to settle[21]—were given such an opportunity. While Hope Simpson had asserted that 29.4 percent of the Arab population of (Western) Palestine were "landless," and that "Everywhere there is the complaint that many of the cultivators have lost their land,"[22] two salient facts were missing from consideration.

First, a "landless" condition among part of the population was common to most countries of the Middle East[23] and was not an indication that there was a shortage of land—as witness the British Government's very different attitude toward "Trans-Jordan" in its 1935 Annual Report:

> *Except for the very limited professional and artisan classes, Trans-Jordanians are dependent for their livelihood on agriculture, but although the land is not intensively cultivated there is a very considerable landless class;* these landless people in the slack times of the agricultural year obtain employment on the roads and railway and sometimes go as far as Haifa.*[24]

*Emphasis added.

Second, the widespread illegal Arab immigration—which is, coincidentally, actually indicated in the above Government description concerning "Haifa" and is clearly described in other pages of Hope Simpson's report as we have seen— could easily have accounted for at least the "29.4 percent" Hope Simpson claimed were "landless"—and more. Even had as large a "displaced" Arab population existed as Hope Simpson alleged, the above factors should not have been ignored. As it turned out,

> seldom, indeed, has a report by a responsible British Commission been so completely and so soon falsified by events as the report of the Simpson Commission.[25]

According to the investigation by the Department of Development,

> on the Arab side the number of landless Arabs has, no doubt, been exaggerated and no account has been taken of the sources of employment opened to displaced tenant-cultivators by the development of the larger towns or the increase of the area under citrus, but in my view, the real basis of the outcry was not so much the existing state of affairs, as apprehension for the future.[26]

For example, an "Arab expert" witness before the 1929 Shaw Commission had claimed "about" 1,746 families were affected in the Jezreel area, where most of the Arab claims were based.

> By the time the matter was discussed in Parliament the number of families involved had been inflated to 10,000. The results of the Government investigation made in 1931, when every claim was closely scrutinized by a legal assessor, completely demolished all these figures.[27]

As a measure of the few "displaced" Arabs who took up the offers of the government, in 1934 *eleven* "new claims" were brought; the Annual Report for 1934 explained that the minuscule number of claims was due to the employment opportunities in the towns and citrus groves.[28] In 1935, there were altogether *thirty-five.* Those few were *not recently* "displaced" but had "delayed" filing their claims "for various reasons." All had long been off the land. The Annual Report for 1935 stated:

> As none of the remaining registered Arabs have signified their willingness to take up holdings upon Government estates, no new schemes have been put in hand this year. *[29]

"Landless Arab Cultivators" continued to be rewarded if their transient farming employment was interrupted by the sale of land. After a year's notice, they received either cash or land elsewhere under the various "Cultivator's Protection Ordinances," which began in 1929[30] and by 1933 had been amended and replaced to the extent that, if his animal had grazed on the area in question, an Arab must be given subsistence area or remuneration based on his landlord's earnings.[31]

*Emphasis added.

In all, "only 664" applications were "admitted" up to January of 1936 from "landless Arabs," according to the Palestine Royal Commission Report.[32] Those "proved displaced cultivators" either were given lands purchased by the government "at a cost of 72,240 [pounds sterling]" or they "declined the land offered them on the grounds that they were accustomed neither to the climate of the new area nor to irrigated cultivation."

In 1936, on the eve of the British Palestine Royal Commission's investigation of "disturbances," John Hope Simpson, the author of the 1930 Report on "landless" and "displaced" Arabs that had rationalized stricter British policy against Jewish immigration, had expressed the ever-widening sentiment among the British Foreign Officers: Hope Simpson wrote, "What of the Palestine Royal Commission? Are they men of independent mind? Is there any chance that the Arab case will be properly presented? One realizes clearly that the Jewish advocacy will be admirable. One of the Arab misfortunes is Ormsby-Gore's Zionist bias. Another is his Jewish vote and the Jewish wealth in England."[33]

That Lord Ormsby-Gore, Colonial Secretary, was *not* encumbered by a "Zionist bias" may be evidenced by a letter he wrote at the time of the Royal Commission *Report.* He rejected the "proposal" to give "a general service medal" to those "personnel of the services" who had acted to "suppress" the "disturbances" of 1936:

> . . . I am sorry to say that I feel I must submit reasons against the proposal on political and general grounds, particularly at this stage of events.
> The first point I should like to make is that if such a medal is given, *it can only be regarded as a medal for services against the Arabs.* We do not want it to go out to the world, especially the Islamic world that we have been at war with the Arabs; and politically, I should find the effect of such an award most embarrassing, more particularly at this time when we are anxious to avoid doing anything unnecessarily to provoke resentment in neighboring Arab countries. . . .*[34]

When the Palestine Royal Commission heard public testimony that confirmed widespread illegal Arab immigration to Jewish-settled areas and other parts of Western Palestine—and the crucial political ramifications that might follow from official recognition of "the thousands" of Arabs who had, and were still, "flooding" the country—the Commission members were incredulous, as following excerpts from the December 1936 hearings illustrate:†[35]

> *Answer* [Witness]: Immigration from neighboring countries is causing a number of social and economic evils. . . . illegal immigration . . . illicit infiltration from neighboring countries. . . . The movement is continuous of people coming over. . . . There is always a large residue remaining . . . once they have come over many of them find it is better for them to stay on and work for wages

*Emphasis added.
†In the following testimony, emphasis added.

than to go back to their fields in the Hauran and Trans-Jordan. . . . In the port of Haifa . . . about fifty percent of the Arabs working there are Trans-Jordanians. . . .

Question [Commission]: *Are these matters of public knowledge? Do they appear in the papers?*

Answer: Yes, they are matters of public knowledge.

There are cases . . . where an Arab peasant takes on a Haurani as a farm hand, leaving him in charge of the farm while he himself goes to a Jewish colony to be employed by a Jewish orange grower, in view of the difference between the wage he gets from the Jewish orange grower and the wages paid to the Haurani. In this and other ways the infiltration of Haurani labour releases an unwarrantable supply of Arab labour for Jewish employers.

Besides the Hauranis and the Trans-Jordanians there are also Egyptians scattered all over Palestine, many of whom have settled permanently. There are also Bedouin from Sinai coming into Palestine with their flocks every year, some of whom are not only present here as nomads but enter the labour market. It is not exceptional to find in Palestine Arabs who have come from as far as the Sudan, Northern Syria, the Hedjaz and the Yemen.

Question: As regards these people from the Sudan and so forth, have you yourself seen a Sudanese Arab in Palestine?

Answer: Yes. . . . I will give you an example. I was once travelling in Trans-Jordan, and in the desert between Ama'an and Ma'an: I suddenly saw from my car two people walking, and I was astonished because it was a very hot day. We stopped and asked them if they needed something. The first thing we asked them was where did they come from and they told me they had come from the Hedjaz, from Tibuk if I am not mistaken. We asked them where they were going and they said, *"We are going to Palestine; we heard from some pilgrims, Moslems going to Mecca and Medina, about the good and prosperous conditions in Palestine, so we are going there."*

When evidence was given that Government not only knew of, but knowingly "employed and encouraged" the illegal Arab immigrants, the chairman of the Royal Commission was astonished. He asked, "Do you suggest that the Government, either directly or indirectly through contractors, employs these Hauranis at these low rates of wages that you spoke of?" The witness responded, "That is our definite suggestion. The first point is that they employ them, *well knowing they are in the country illegally.* . . . these people who come in illegally are *employed* by the Government, which is also an encouraging factor."

Question: As regards Government employment, of course, the Government do not employ them; Government contractors may?

Answer: Not only Government contractors, but Government *does* employ them in the port of Haifa for porterage.

Question: Hauranis?

Answer: Yes, for porterage. There may be Trans-Jordanians among them also, but those people are employed by the Government and the Government cannot but know that they are in the country illegally or that they have taken work in the country illegally.

Question: If you debar various people from Trans-Jordan and Hauranis from coming in to work in the port, your contention is that the Government would then be able to employ Jews, it would give more opportunities for Jewish labor? Is that your contention?

Answer: Yes, that would be one of the effects of it. It would also mean a better position of security for Palestine.

. . . when we began discussing this with Government in 1932 and 1933, at the beginning the Government denied the existence of a serious problem; not that they denied the fact that some people were coming, but they maintained that the numbers were very few and that they were purely seasonal, that there was no residue, and that it was causing no problem at all, and we found ourselves in a controversy with the Government, first of all, on a point of fact. Our estimate of the Hauranis in Palestine was much larger than the figure the Government was prepared to accept. Then a time came when Government itself began to use figures approximating to our own and our impression was, after this had gone on for some time, that Government largely came round to our point of view and accepted our information as basically correct. Then Government said that, although this was so, it was unavoidable that there should be a certain seasonal influx . . . of people from the neighboring countries into Palestine for work in the ports and in the season of orange picking. We maintain that there is a succession of seasonal works in Palestine constituting a practically continuous chain, a *permanent capacity* of *absorption,* and that this capacity of absorption should really serve the purpose of allowing more Jews to come into Palestine and that the position should not be that, through an inadequate labour immigration, a vacuum should be suffered to develop in the labour market, which would suck in people from outside. So that after we had had our argument with the Government on the question of size we had a serious argument with the Government on the question of whether this was seasonal or permanent.

Question: That may have been a very long argument, I take it?

Answer: Yes, it went on for years and in the meantime *those people were coming in in their thousands.*

The Jews' introduction of the evidence of illegal Arab immigration was intended to show displacement of Jews by Arabs and the injustice inherent in the British enforcement of quotas upon only the Jewish immigrants.

Question: Would it be right to say this? Your contention is briefly that, unless this illicit immigration is stopped and properly stopped, it is impossible for Government to arrive at any satisfactory conclusion as to the absorptive capacity of the country for immigrants?

Answer: My submission is that, unless it is stopped the *absorptive capacity* of Palestine, which is continually being expanded, and which it is not always possible to estimate in advance for any length of time is *going to serve the purpose of absorbing people from the neighboring countries.*

Question: It comes to much of the same thing. In the matter of immigration, you want to get, as we have been told, at the economic absorptive capacity of the country?

Answer: Yes, for any given period.

Question: Yes, for any given period. If previous to that period or during that period there has been a considerable illicit immigration, to that extent the figures must be falsified, is that not so?

Answer: Yes, that is so. . . . I would mention this also as one of the *proofs that Government's estimates of absorptive capacity were erroneous,* they were an under-estimate, because the country actually proved itself capable of absorbing many more people than those allowed for in the schedules given *us* by the Government, which were supposed to exhaust the whole supply of labour immigration.

. . . our main contention is that, so far as there is an absorptive capacity in Palestine for immigrants from outside, that it should be primarily used to allow Jews to come in and get that employment.

The . . . main point is that the allotments of certificates for labour immigrants have been inadequate in the course of the last few years and continue to be so. They are not sufficient to cover the demands for labour that exist in this country.

. . . it is a very serious problem, from the point of view of the Jewish future and the future of Palestine. This happens to be the only country, in comparison with the whole of the countries surrounding it, in which development is going on at a fairly rapid pace. Development is going on and absorptive capacity is being created and, to a certain extent, it is being filled by Jewish immigration, not to the full extent by any means, and at the same time *the country is becoming a magnet for the neighboring countries.* It attracts people . . . particularly when there is a vacuum in the labour market and those people are virtually being sucked in from neighboring territories, where conditions remain much as they have always been.

Question: That means, of course, the labour schedule?

Answer: Yes.

Question: [Chairman] You have been talking about illicit immigration. I understand you have not the same objection to licit immigration? Supposing the absorptive capacity in any year was settled by the Government at, say, 30,000 immigrants, labour immigrants. You would not object, I suppose, or criticise the Government for allotting to those licit immigrants from Arabian countries a certain proportion of Arabs? You would not say, "We the Jews, claim the whole of the 30,000," would you?

Answer: We would certainly say that the Jews claim the whole of 30,000 save in exceptional cases. . . . the Government is here under obligation to facilitate Jewish immigration into Palestine and the emphasis is both on the word "facilitate" and on the word "Jewish," and it is not here to facilitate the immigration of other races into Palestine.

Question: That is an important interpretation. You think the words "facilitate Jewish immigration into Palestine" mean that, subject to the exceptional cases you have mentioned, the Government must not admit immigrants, we will say, from Arab countries, but that the whole of the absorptive capacity—because we are talking of the labour schedule—must be Jews? Is that so?

Answer: Yes. The question of immigration was mentioned in the Mandate *only* in connection with the *Jewish* people. I submit that, in point of fact, were it not for the Jewish efforts in Palestine there would have been no Arab immigration into Palestine in any case. The problem of Arab immigration has arisen only because of the Jewish development and Jewish immigration into Palestine, which has created room for more people than the number of Jews allowed by the Government to come in.

The evidence of illicit *Arab* infiltration from other countries also served to show the real roots of the "disturbances" in Palestine—agitation perceived as "nationalism" or "patriotism"—and economic problems as a result.

Question: Do they employ them at that low rate or do they pay them a rate of wages more approximating to what we should call a Trade Union rate?

Answer: I suppose when the Hauranis are employed directly by the Government they get the current rate, but when they are employed by Government contractors Government has no control over the wages which the contractors pay.

Question: Are they not supposed to pay any recognised rate of wages in practice?

Answer: No. An interesting fact in connection with that is that there is now a strong *Arab opposition* to this great infiltration of cheap labour from neighboring countries. The labourers are appreciating the way in which it affects them and the dangers it may have for them. I can bring forward examples if necessary.

I submit that there are also undesirable elements among these immigrants from neighboring countries from the point of view of public security. Many illicit immigrants from the Hauran were prominent during the riots of 1933, especially in Haifa, and the same happened to an even larger extent at the beginning of the riots on the 19th April this year. In addition, many of the immigrants coming from the Hauran are involved in small crimes and there are frequent disorders among themselves. . . . For instance, just recently a gang of Haurani thieves was detected in Haifa and there are also cases of shop-breaking in which Hauranis are involved in Haifa, Jaffa, Tel Aviv and Tiberias.

While there was no reaction to that evidence by the Commission, regarding the "quality" of *Arabs* entering the country illegally, there was pointed questioning about "undesirables" among the "legal" *Jewish* immigrants.

Question: One more point and that is as regards the quality of the [Jewish] immigrants who are coming into the country. You are doing your utmost to try to see that the quality of the immigrants is a good one, that a good class of immigrant comes into the country, are you not?

Answer: Yes, we do that.

Question: I just want to ask you this question. On the occasion of the Jaffa Riots in 1921 the report says this:

"It was only when Arab discontent with Zionist manifestations and resentment against the new immigrants reached its climax that a demonstration of Bolshevik Jews became the occasion for a popular explosion. The appeal of a pamphlet circulated in Jaffa by the Bolsheviks inciting the working class to civil war, was by a cruel coincidence of causes accepted, and the co-religionists of its authors supplied the majority of the victims."

All I want to know is whether you find that there are among the immigrants who come in under the labour schedule undesirables. You do eventually find Bolsheviks and so on?

Answer: We exercise very considerable control over this and we go to great lengths to prevent the entrance of Communists into this country. That is a very fixed and rigid rule with us. Even if a man is only suspected of being a Communist or having Communistic affiliations his application is put aside and the case very carefully investigated. Sometimes we find that it is a mistake, to our satisfaction, but we always try to be on the safe side even at the cost of hardship to an innocent man. We say, "We have reason to doubt you. You must wait until we can clear it up."

Question: You do not think that there are any number of Bolshevik Jews in the country?

Answer: There may be people who turn Communist as they do in any other country. All I can say is that in the selection of our immigrants we take the greatest possible care to prevent people already holding Communist views coming here but I do not say there are no cases of Jews in Palestine who have turned Communist. Their proportion however must be very low.

Question: They might slip in as illegal immigrants?

Answer: They might slip in as illegal immigrants.

The "obvious" answer, that the "Jews' presence" constituted provocation, was once again employed by the British. The agitation by Sudanese, Nigerian, Syrian, Egyptian, Algerian, and other entrants was ignored.

When the Commission asked for "a remedy," the matter of identity cards was pivotal, and the arguments identical to those that would be set forward in the MacKereth-Government exchange.[36]

Question: Then the chief traffic is gunrunning and illicit immigration, is it?

Answer: Illicit immigration, which partly devotes itself to gun-running. Of course, there are people who go on business; there are people who go to sell their produce; there are people who go from Jerusalem or Nablus or Es Salt or Ama'an or other towns of Trans-Jordan to sell things, or to visit their relatives, and vice versa, but that is over much greater distances than just across the Jordan.

Question: Would you make them take out passports?

Answer: I do not see why they should not be made to take out a pass in order to cross. That would not mean that they would have to wait to make their visits, but they would have to call at the police post and get a pass. They could be given a pass on the bridges as they crossed them without any condition, but with the warning that they must not accept employment and that if they do so without permission they render themselves liable to punishment or deportation.

If some accounting and limit was implemented at the borders, more Jews could immigrate to the Jewish National Home in the stead of those "seasonal"-turned-permanent Arab immigrant laborers, the witness insisted:

. . . we would rather see a certain number of Jews unemployed in the off-season and devise some means for them to tide over the off-season than to acquiesce in

a position where the demand for seasonal labour must necessarily be covered by
. . . an uncontrolled infiltration from the neighboring countries.

Question: You realise what you are asking for . . . ? It means practically a
labour census of the whole of Palestine for Government to get at the facts, which
would probably take two years, really to get all the facts and, . . . it would involve
the suspension of immigration during that period so that they could absolutely
get at the facts?

Answer: The suspension of *legal* immigration?

. . . Even if such a census were necessary then I do not see why this should
not be begun in the meantime and some measures taken to strengthen the control
at the frontiers, without stopping legal immigration at all. I really do not see why
legal immigration should be stopped.

Ten days after the public evidence was heard, in one of several "secret" and
"private" hearings,[37] Commission member Sir Laurie Hammond advised witness
Chaim Weizmann, the preeminent Zionist leader,[38] that, to issue identity cards
—"carte de visite"—"it means not only stopping gun-running, but stopping illicit
immigration of the Arabs on the frontiers."

In order to do so, Hammond would *stop all immigration of Jews.* Why would
this punitive action be justified?

Hammond answered peevishly, "Because there is a limit to what the Administration can undertake, and if they are concentrating all their energies on what I
like to regard myself as making the foundations of your national home secure,
if they are directing all their energies to that, you must relieve them of the great
pressure of work that is thrown on them by these continual waves of immigration."

Thus the witnesses were squelched. The British had perceived the evidence
and its proposed remedy as a threat to their neat "system" of immigration. The
response was to defend that system with a threat of their own—an insidious threat
that seems to have effectively muzzled any further serious argument over the
crucial issue of illegal Arab immigration.

Arab political historian and activist George Antonius, whose 1939 book, *The
Arab Awakening,*[39] staunchly advocated "Arab Nationalism," also testified before
the Palestine Royal Commission, in January 1937.[40]

At that time Antonius attempted to preempt the question of Arab illegal
immigration, by raising the subject himself:

There have been complaints, growing in volume in the last two or three years,
about illegal immigration. The government came down with all its resources on
illegal immigration and what was the result? The result was that in casting its net,
it caught three times as many Arabs as it did Jews, and it deported them, at a
time when the Arab population of the country was excited and up in arms because
not a few hundred, but thousands of Jews, on everybody's admission, were coming
into the country, and as against that, a few hundred Hauranis were coming to eke
out a living and then go back; they were not coming in as illegal immigrants, they

were coming in as illegal travellers, and yet the government, having solemnly promised to do what it could to put an end to illegal immigration and to deport the illegal immigrants who were already in the country, as I say, cast its net and caught a large number of Arabs and a few Jews.

Now there may be other reasons than willful discrimination for that; I am not sure of that, but what I say is there is the net result, and that is how it appears to the Arab population here, that the Government, when they promised to put an end to illegal immigration, are behind the backs of the people and in secret working to favor it and come down on the Arab illegal travelers and deport them.

After disposing of the question by his gratuitous remarks,* which drew no serious challenges from the Commission, Antonius also sought to deny Arab "racial hatred" of Jews:

There is no anti-Semitism in the Arab mind. The Arab mind throughout its history has been singularly free from any such thing as anti-Semitism, which, as we all know, is a European and not an Arab invention, and I am sorry to say, a European Christian invention; but the Arabs throughout their history, and more particularly the Moslems, have been entirely free from the taint of anti-Semitism, and it is a fact that *the greatest days* of *Jewish efflorescence* have taken place when the Jews were under *Moslem rule,* whether in Baghdad, Cordoba, or Cairo, or anywhere else where large Jewish communities were living under the rule of Moslems. Those were the days in which the Jews attained their greatest intellectual, moral and material efflorescence under the direct patronage, encouragement, and tolerance of the Moslem rulers.†

At the same sessions, Mufti Haj Amin al-Husseini, of Jerusalem, whose efforts as zealous collaborator of Adolf Hitler in the "final solution of the Jewish problem" will be outlined later, stated in testimony before the Royal Commission‡ that the Jews

always did live previously in Arab countries, with complete freedom and liberty, as natives of the country. In fact Moslem rule has always been known for its tolerance. . . . According to history, Jews had a most quiet and peaceful residence under Arab rule.[41]

In fact, it had been the Mufti who was considered largely responsible from the beginning of the twentieth century for organized anti-Jewish pogroms throughout Palestine. The Mufti understood—as the British only privately would acknowledge—that the attempts to form a "nationalism" among the multiethnics of Palestine had proved to be ineffectual—even the might and main of T. E. Lawrence had ended in his disillusionment. It was only by invoking the deeply

*Another Arab witness contradicted Antonius's assertion that only "a few hundred Houranis" had entered (Western) Palestine: Auni Abdul Hadi acknowledged that Houranis and others were going to "Palestine" because of the higher wages offered there.[42]
†Emphasis added.
‡See the Mufti's testimony in Appendix VIII.

rooted religious prejudice of the masses against the Palestinian Jews that al-Husseini and other *effendi* families could hope to regain the extent of power that had once been allowed to the feudal barons of the country by the Turks.*

The Palestine Royal Commission published its much-awaited report[43] in July 1937; it was one of the more important among the constant stream of British "investigations" that punctuated the inexorable veering of British policy away from implementing "the Jewish National Home" toward a policy that would not "be hateful to the Arabs."[44]

Embodied in the Report were the "axioms" evolved from Arab propaganda and perpetuated by earlier British reports issued to justify Arab claims: namely, the Jews had provoked unrest by their presence; the "vast Arab majority, indigenous" since "time immemorial," had grown through "natural increase"; the Jewish-settled area of Western Palestine was to be treated as though it were all of Palestine.

Still, the evidence of illegal Arab immigration had taken some effect. The "Arab immigrants," particularly "Hauranis" from Syria, the Report stated, "probably remain permanently in Palestine."[45]

But, although the number of Hauranis who illegally immigrated was "authoritatively estimated" at 10,000–11,000 during a "bad" year in the Hauran, only the unrealistically, perhaps disingenuously low Government estimate of 2,500 were concluded to be "in the country at the present time."[46]

The *Palestine Royal Commission Report* did enumerate several "proposed steps for dealing with illegal immigration"; it presented "suggestions" to the Government:

the following steps might be taken to prevent illegal immigration:
(i)   Legalizing of the position of illegal immigrants already in the country.
(ii) Institution of an identity card.
(iii) Enactment of an Immigration Ordinance placing the onus of proof on the
      immigrant to show that he is in the country legally.
(iv) Creation of a special frontier control force.
(v)   A secret fund for intelligence.
(vi) Separate naturalization of wives.

We are not sure on the evidence before us whether it is possible to enforce a system of identity cards. If the system is administratively possible, it is clear that the control of the police will be far more effective. We are, however, prepared to endorse proposals (i), (iii), (iv), (v), and (vi).[47]

Moreover, the Report had stated significantly, in its opening pages,

Unquestionably . . . the primary purpose of the Mandate, *as expressed in its preamble and its articles,* is to promote the establishment of the Jewish National Home.†[48]

*See Chapters 8 and 10.
†Emphasis in original.

The Report further noted that the evidence "seemed to show that the Jews have been able to enlarge the economic *absorptive capacity* of the country for Jews,"* and that the capacity to absorb Jews "need only be limited by . . . funds" provided by the Jews.

One of the unsung herculean tasks of the Palestinian Jews during the Mandatory period was their efficiency in enlarging that so-called "absorptive capacity" and the "cultivable" land area. Not only did the Zionist efforts to reclaim and develop force the British to continue the limited flow of Jews—even after it was estimated that the "absorptive capacity" had been reached and no more Jews could be allowed. In addition, that "absorptive capacity" had stretched wide enough to include the thousands upon thousands of illegal Arab immigrants who were counted as "indigenous Arab population from time immemorial."

Despite the fact that large numbers of unacknowledged Arab *newcomers* must have been included among the claimed-to-be "Palestinian landless" Arabs, all but those "few" who brought "landless" claims at the urgings of the British Government had found work, and even among those few, many had chosen to "drift back to" the easier work in the towns.[49] All of that had been definitely illustrated in the evidence taken by the Palestine Royal Commission.

Yet, disregarding its own finding that the Mandate's purpose was primarily the Jewish National Home, the *Palestine Royal Commission Report* came to the conclusion that such "expansion" was "not organic but is unnatural, since it ignores . . . the hostile attitude of the Arab inhabitants of Palestine."[50]

Here was the bottom-line actuality—not that the Arabs were increasing naturally at the claimed "phenomenal" rate, but that even the supposedly limited "absorptive capacity" invented to restrict Jewish immigration had been "enlarged"—not only for Jews, but especially for the Arabs whose in-migration and immigration went largely unrecorded. It was the "hostile attitude" of the Arab inhabitants—whose number grew faster than the Jews and the Arab hostility growing commensurately—which was responsible for, and increasingly appeased by, the British administration of "Palestine."

Thus the Royal Commission Report, in a contradiction of many of its own basic findings and a misrepresentation of the truth, recommended "partition" of "Palestine," under which "the Arabs must acquiesce in the exclusion *from their sovereignty* of a piece of territory, long occupied and once ruled by them."*[51]

Among Jews, there were many who rejected anything less than the area of Palestine that had been internationally pledged to a Jewish National Home. Martin Gilbert, the biographer of Winston Churchill, has disclosed the "private" correspondence between Zionist activist Jabotinsky and Churchill, in which Jabotinsky wrote that, although the Jews may not "fully realize" all the treacherous implications of the *Palestine Royal Commission Report* recommen-

*Emphasis added.

dation, the proposed partition "kills all their hopes."[52]

Others more pragmatic opposed only the fact that, within that "small notch" called Palestine, the fraction of land that the proposed partition allotted to Jews was too small to provide defensible borders or economic stability. The Jewish "non-Zionists" opposed *any* Jewish State, "still believing" that the Jewish political entity might "in some way prejudice their rights as citizens in other countries."[53]

Despite the "deep cleavages of opinion" among the Jews,[54] the Zionist Congress of August 1937 accepted the principle of partition, but they voted the proposed distribution of land "unacceptable."[55]

Meanwhile, however indifferent or encouraging the British policy remained toward illegal Arab immigration—which their reports and correspondence confirm in other pages—the broad scope of evidence attesting to that Arab movement which was disclosed during the Palestine Royal Commission's investigations prompted Government to take certain token measures: In January 1937, the weekly *Palestine* reported that[56] "Palestine Government have given instructions not to employ Arabs who enter the country illegally. These instructions are the result of Jewish testimony before Royal Commission at Haifa."

Of course, Government was not unduly altering the reality, since according to its immigration records, few Arabs entered the country illegally. Thus the system prevailed and "present practices" were continued.

And still another "Commission," the "Woodhead" Palestine Partition Commission, was sent into the area to investigate possible alternative plans for "Partition."

The Woodhead Commission was thrust upon its arrival into the midst of what its Report would call the "widespread campaign of murder and intimidation" that followed from the "Arab side's" reaction to the Palestine Royal Commission's Report.[57]

> . . . the Arabs remain inflexibly hostile to partition. During our stay, no Arab came forward to submit evidence or to co-operate in any way with us: the boycott was complete.

It was little wonder that "no Arab came forward to submit evidence." Because of what the *Palestine Royal Commission Report* had called "toleration by the Government of subversive activities, more especially those of the Mufti of Jerusalem,"[58] not only Jews but moderate Arabs and those *effendis* engaged in a power struggle with the Mufti were murdered. As the *Palestine Royal Commission Report* had observed, with uncharacteristic indignation,

> . . . intimidation at the point of a revolver has become a not infrequent feature of Arab politics. Attacks by Arabs on Jews, unhappily, are no new thing. The novelty in the present situation is attacks by Arabs on Arabs. For an Arab to be suspected of a lukewarm adherence to the nationalist cause is to invite a visit from a body of "gunmen." Such a visit was paid to the editor of one of the Arabic newspapers last August shortly after he had published articles in favour of calling

off the "strike." Similar visits were paid during our stay in Palestine to wealthy Arab landowners or businessmen who were believed to have made inadequate contributions to the fund which the Arab Higher Committee were raising to compensate Arabs for damage suffered during the "disturbances." Nor do the "gunmen" stop at intimidation. It is not known who murdered the Arab Acting Mayor of Hebron last August, but no one doubts that he lost his life because he had dared to differ from the "extremist" policy of the Higher Committee. The attempt to murder the Arab Mayor of Haifa, which took place a few days after we left Palestine, is also, we are told, regarded as political. It is not surprising that a number of Arabs have asked for Government protection.[59]

Many Christian Arabs, as well as the Muslims, opposed the Jews—now predominantly Zionists—and this common hostility toward Jews served to cool down the Muslim-versus-Christian resentments. As an example of the contributions to terror and violence directed by some among the Christian Arabs, Professor S. F. Albright cited an instance during one anti-Jewish onslaught, in which a prominent Christian Arab editor

called his little boy of five into the room and told him what he must do to a Jewish boy if he should get a chance. He even put cruel words into the little chap's mouth: "I will take a knife and stab him; I will take a pistol and shoot him."[60]

But the Christian Arabs were not exempt from Arab terrorism. The Christians were compelled at gunpoint to abandon their traditional head covering, the tarbush, and adopt the Muslim *keffiyah* instead. The compulsory Muslim veil was forced upon Christian women. Christian Arab shopkeepers were forced to close on the Muslims' Friday sabbath as well as on Sundays, thus losing a day's revenue.[61]

As in the past, the Arab masses responded only to "the appeal of religious fanaticism and . . . their tradition of violence which a single generation of British rule had not eradicated."[62] The ruling families had never pretended to any sort of reform: the *fellahin* were, in the 1930s, still plagued by "indebtedness and ruinous charges exacted from them by the Arab landowners and moneylenders."[63]

The *effendi*-led attacks upon Jews and their supporters still were designed 1) to keep the "sweets" of feudalism and 2) to prevent the traditional *dhimmi* Jew from an "inconceivable" elevation to equality with Muslims.[64] As one British eyewitness press report described the situation,[65]

. . . For the most part the villagers are decent law abiding folk who have no great sympathy with the Arab rebels who are fighting to stem the tide of Jewish immigration and demanding an Arab Government for Palestine.

They merely want to be left alone to sow and harvest; to marry and find the wherewithal in these troubled times to bring up their families.

Then one night a rebel band descends on the village. The rebel chief goes straight to the house of the village headman and orders him to produce 50 young men to come out on the hills to snipe at the British, and for another 100 men to tear up Government roads.

Hospitals were not exempted from the wanton violence. On June 24, 1938,

". . . Two Arabs working in a Jewish-owned stone quarry near Haifa were wounded by Arab raiders. The wounded men were taken to hospital, but two of the raiders entered the hospital in search of them, killing by mistake another Arab, a patient from Nablus."[66]

The "collection" of contributions to fund the terrorists was equally effective, following the same traditional methods that the Arabs had applied to extract funds for "protection" against raiding. According to the Chief of Staff under Lieutenant General Dill's command in 1936,

The collection of funds for "distressed Palestine" was carried out by methods similar to those employed by the racketeer. Large sums were collected under pressure from firms as well as from individuals. There was always the threat of the gun. At the same time pressure was exerted on individuals, and sometimes there was the use of the gun.[67]

Even though the Mufti had fled to Syria upon the "resurgence of violence"[68] that he had instigated, Jews, British, and rival or moderate Arabs alike became the objects of his continued wrath. As the *Times* of London observed a year after the Mufti's flight,

. . . Many of the leaders of the National Defence Party [opposition to Mufti] have been murdered; others have been compelled by threats to leave the country. . . . It is certainly true that during the last four months far more Arabs than Jews or British soldiers have been killed by Arab terrorists.[69]

From April 1936, the Mufti's "systematic extermination" caused the murder or flight from the country of any Arab suspected of less than total loyalty to the rebels: mayor, affiliated official, sheikh, village *mukhtar* (headman), rival Arab notable, and even prominent Muslim religious figures—all were victims.

The mayor of Hebron, Nasr el Din Nasr, murdered August 4, 1936, was a close ally of the Mufti's chief opponent, Ragheb Bey Nashashibi; the wife and daughter of the mayor of Bethlehem were wounded July 1937; the mayor of Nablus, Suleiman Bey Toukan, who publicly warned the government of chaos if terrorism was not squelched, fled after attempted assassination in December of 1937. No fewer than eleven *mukhtars* were slain, along with family members, between February of 1937 and November of 1938.*[70]

Muslim religious leaders murdered or wounded included the following:

March 1938   Sheikh Yunis el Husseini, head of El Aqsa Mosque administration, was wounded.
July 1938   Sheikh Ali Nur el Khatib, of El Aqsa Mosque, was murdered.

*A similar list of "moderate" Arabs who have been exterminated recently by the PLO—the modern "Muftism"—could be compiled today.

Dec. 1938   Sheikh Dauoud Ansari, Imam of El Aqsa Mosque, was killed (after fourth attempt).

Other Sheikhs who were murdered then by Arab terrorists included:

July 1938   Sheikh Nusbi Abdul Rahim, Counsel to the Moslem Religious Court, murdered at Acre.

Sept. 1938   Sheikh Abdul el Badawi, murdered at Acre.

Nov. 1938   Sheikh El Namouri, murdered at Hebron.[71]

As the MacKereth-versus-British Foreign Office correspondence (cited earlier) indicated, the terrorists, or "rebels," were viewed by an increasing number of British officials and observers as "sincere Arab patriots" whose violence was "justified."

There were, however, those who resisted appeasement of the terrorist tactics for a time. One communication with a British "correspondent in Palestine," transmitted to the former Palestine High Commissioner Chancellor, expressed outrage at the reports in the London *Times* early in 1937:

. . . Who is "the Times" correspondent out here? This is obvious Arab propaganda. The Mufti has gone to Mecca with the avowed intention of getting help to continue the contest and as to objecting to violence, it is absolutely false; "Courage to disavow his own tactics"! It is their usual method always to disavow anything when convenient, and unless he wished it, it would not appear in any Arab newspaper. They are openly saying that the lawlessness will soon begin again, but if the "disavowal" is in the Arab newspapers . . . the Arabs would merely laugh knowing quite well it was said just to deceive the foolish English. It is pure bluff. The correspondent is obviously pro-Arab and against his own country and ought to be shown up. It is disgraceful. The murders continue, as you will see in the paper I am sending you.

. . . The Arabs hate civilisation and would like to keep the country in its present backward state but it is horrible to see it being spoilt. The goats are allowed to eat off all the young plants and the women take what is left for fuel. Fortunately, the Jews are enclosing their land and they are the one hope for the prosperity of the land. The Arabs don't care for taking any trouble. They talk big about *their* country but what have they ever done for it? *They tread down the poor and take bakshish and that is all they care for.*

You know all this as well as I do, but I can't help repeating it.*[72]

Just before the Mufti fled to Syria, the British Commander of the Arab Legion was convinced that

the Arabs . . . are still out of hand, and in my opinion we shall have in the end to teach them a lesson. Besides the Mufti's party which is bad enough we have all the young Effendi class, products of our education, and beyond them and probably most dangerous and well-organized are the Communists. That, a few

*Emphasis added.

weeks ago a police officer could be murdered in the middle of Haifa, and the assailants get clear away is an eye-opener; and now the same thing happens in Jerusalem. *I am quite sure that lots of people knew all about those crimes, and probably many Arab members of the police do also, but they would be murdered if they came forward with their evidence.* *[73]

Upon the Mufti's arrival in Syria, a local British officer wired the Foreign Office that "Surveillance exercised over Mufti appears to be little short of a farce . . . Mufti . . . thanking French and Lebanese for their warm welcome here."[74]

Perhaps it was Ormsby-Gore's apparent outrage at the newest "reign of terror" that reversed his previous attitude toward offending the Arab world. Whatever the reason, in his capacity as Colonial Secretary, Ormsby-Gore wrote in a "secret Cabinet memorandum"[75] that although the Jewish "mini" state "may temporarily accentuate Arab hostility in the countries surrounding Palestine," the Jewish state must be supported.

> Compromise with the demands of the Arab world within and without Palestine . . . involve at the best the toleration of the Jews in Palestine as a permanent minority.

The "increase" of "Arab intransigence" would be caused more by the continuation of the "present uncertainty" of the British, he asserted, than by a firm position supporting the Jewish state.

It was Ormsby-Gore who had clung to the proposed "partition" by sending forth the Woodhead Commission, which, it was rumored, in the end "would decide against partition."

In August 1938, British Secretary of State Malcolm MacDonald communicated a "secret note" to friends in the Cabinet, confiding that

> Great harm had already been done in Palestine by rumours that the wisdom of Partition had been questioned in the Cabinet, which have encouraged the Arab terrorists and those behind them to believe that if only they persist in their campaign they will force us to abandon this policy.

MacDonald noted that the terrorist leaders "virtually dictate Arab Policy."[76]

MacDonald had resisted pleas by influential Arabs, ranging from the Egyptian Prime Minister to the head of London's Arab Centre, to "recall" the Mufti and his supporters "from their exile . . . to negotiate with them"; MacDonald insisted then that "the Mufti and his colleagues" were "in general" behind the "campaign of violence in Palestine." There was "plenty of information on that point." The terrorism was "being encouraged from a source outside Palestine. Terrorism could not continue without that encouragement. . . . I would not," MacDonald vowed, "trust the word of the leaders who had been exiled," nor would he allow them to come back.[77]

The Woodhead Commission, as the Arabs had anticipated, recommended

*Emphasis added.

against partition, after which the British government abandoned the proposal.[78] The fact that "Arab opposition was a decisive factor in" the retraction of Government's partition plan was "generally understood," although the Woodhead Commission claimed its "rejection" to be "based . . . on practical grounds."[79] Malcolm MacDonald expressed the fear that if partition were implemented, "We should forfeit the friendship of the Arab world."[80]

The Permanent Mandates Commission complained of the British "policy of appeasement."

> Mr. Van Asbeck . . . reverting . . . to the seeming leniency shown by the Palestine Government to the Arab population in suppressing the revolt, asked whether that leniency did not place other elements of the population in a very serious situation—the Jews in their agricultural settlements were particularly exposed to raids and attacks by the Arab gangsters. Further, had it not the serious effect of weakening the authority of, and lessening the respect of, the Arab population for the Government? Had it not engendered the feeling that they could be as lawless as they like without feeling the strong hand of the Government on their neck?[81]

PMC member Rappard in particular deplored the "Policy of appeasement" (in 1937) and "felt obliged to confess that he was himself troubled on that point; he could not help feeling that the reputation of undue leniency . . . was well established."[82]

Underscoring that observation, a British colonel explained to the president of the Jewish ex-officers association in Tel Aviv, "I am afraid that merely asking for justice . . . is useless. In my experience, especially in times of difficulty, governments give way only to action. . . ."[83]

Within the Woodhead *Palestine Partition Commission Report,* however, was the clearly marked Jewish-settled area of Western Palestine, differentiated from the rest of the country and divided according to population of Arabs and Jews. As the Report stated unequivocally,

> . . . no impartial person would think the Arabs justified in claiming sovereign rights over persons and property of Jews who have settled in other parts of Palestine on the faith of the Balfour Declaration and the Mandate.[84]

It was the *only* one of the plethora of policy papers and reports which gave more than just a hint that the Jewish-settled areas were *not* all of Western Palestine, and that the Arabs who claimed rights to those areas were neither justified nor displaced.

More importantly, the Woodhead *Partition Commission Report* posed at least the possibility—albeit presented as though it was not already a fact—that *if* no identity cards were introduced, *"unlimited numbers"* of Arab immigrants from "the Arab State" *would* "enter the Mandated Territories."

> . . . such Arab entrants will quickly satisfy all demands for additional labour . . . and will thereby virtually leave no room in the labour category for Jewish immigrants from outside Palestine.[85]

TABLE K. Mandated "Jewish National Home": Chronology of Some Jewish Immigration/Land Restrictions and Related Factors

Year	"Disturbances" and Influences	Immigration/Land Restrictions
1920	Riots and "Nebi Musa." Mandate and Balfour Declaration for Jewish National Home internationally enforced at San Remo. Hitler's anti-Semitic "25 points" spread by speeches.	Jews' immigration quota set.
1921	Haj Amin al-Husseini appointed Mufti of Jerusalem by British High Commissioner. Arab onslaught against Jews in Jaffa, Petach Tikvah, "abetted" by "British officials" (de Haas, *History*, p. 501). Haycraft Commission Report on riots, October 1921.	Suspension of Jewish immigration.
1922	Eastern Palestine, Transjordan—roughly 75 percent of the Mandated Jewish National Home—separated: forms de facto Arab Palestinian state (Anglo-American Committee, *Survey of Palestine*, pp. 13–14).	Churchill White Paper limits Jewish immigration to "capacity to absorb new arrivals"—absorptive capacity (*Survey*, p. 20).
1928	"Organic Law" provides "separate Commissions for Palestine and Transjordan respectively" (*Survey of Palestine*, p. 14), against Mandate. Wailing Wall incident—Arabs incited by Mufti Haj Amin al-Husseini and followers to anti-Jewish attacks (Gabbay, *Political Study*, p. 31; *Survey*, p. 23).	Jews prohibited from settlement in Transjordan.
1929	"Ratification" of "Agreement" regarding Transjordan; Arab massacre of Jews, Safad and Hebron, rioting and assaults on Jewish settlements and in Jerusalem by "deliberate religious inflammation for which Mufti and his party bear the sole responsibility" (Parkes, *History*, p. 315). High Commissioner Chancellor's Proclamation, Sept. 1, 1929. "Protection of Cultivators Ordinance" enacted for "displaced" Arabs.	Shaw Commission finds Jewish immigration of 1925–26 was "excessive" and recommends restriction of Jewish immigration and land sales.
1930	Hope Simpson Report alleges Arabs rendered "landless" and unemployed by Jewish immigration. State lands allocated for "landless Arabs" instead of Jewish settlement as Art. VI of Mandate had prescribed—regardless whether Jewish purchases had caused "landlessness" and whether or not	1930 Passfield White Paper restricts Jewish immigration and land acquisition, based on "absorptive capacity."

Arabs in question had previously possessed any land. Hitler's plan for Jews of Europe gaining popularity.

1931 Hope Simpson findings disproved by investigation and other British studies; see Chapter 14.

"Protection of Cultivators' Ordinance" amended to further benefit "landless" and "displaced" Arabs (*Survey*, p. 290; also see Laws of 1929, Vol. I, p. 299; Laws of 1931, vol. I, p. 3).

1933 Muslims incited at Festival of Nebi Rubin by Musa Kasem Pasha al-Husseini's "violent speech against Jewish immigration" (*Survey*, p. 31). Strikes and anti-Jewish riots. Government accused of favoring Jews. Hitler comes to power.

Cultivators' Ordinance of 1933 replaces earlier laws, institutes allowance of subsistence area or remuneration for any Arab "statutory tenant" not "grossly neglecting" areas of grazing or occasional presence (Cultivators' Ordinance of 1933, Drayton, vol. 1, p. 506, cited in *Survey*, pp. 290–291).

1934 Influx of 30,000–35,000 Arab immigrants from the Hauran—Syria—to the Jewish-settled areas in Western Palestine, during a period of approximately three months. The population movement recognized by Syrian leadership and League of Nations Permanent Mandates Commission, but denied by and omitted from British Mandatory Government data, records, and statistics.

Government institutes practice of deducting estimated numbers of illegal Jewish immigrants from Jewish immigration quotas (*Report for the Year 1934*, p. 28; *Report for the Year 1935*, p. 13; Report, Department of Migration, 1935, p. 19).

1936 Anti-Jewish pogroms, riots, Arab strikes with imported assistance of hired Syrian and Iraqi mercenaries—known as "Arab Revolt."

1937 Royal Commission appointed to investigate "deteriorating" Palestine conditions. Lewis Andrews, District Commissioner for Galilee, assigned to administer Commission's tour, murdered outside his church by Arab terrorists. "Moderate" Arabs murdered (Gilbert, *Exile*, p. 186; see also the periodical *Palestine*, Oct. 6, 1937, vol. XII, note 40 for list of names of Arab victims). Nearly 100 Jews, Arabs (according to Esco-Yale, *Palestine*, hereafter Esco-Yale, p. 880, 246 deaths resulted) and Government personnel murdered, around 150 wounded (*Survey*, p. 43).

Palestine Royal Commission Report recommends partition into one Jewish, one Arab, state.

1938 Mufti-led guerrilla warfare aided by imported Arab rebels, including anti-Jewish pogroms, assassinations of other Arabs, ambushes of the military, and general sabotage

Unemployment rises, Jewish immigration restrictions continued, "illegal" Jewish immigration rises

Mandated "Jewish National Home": Chronology of Some Jewish Immigration/Land Restrictions and Related Factors (cont'd)

Year	"Disturbances" and Influences	Immigration/Land Restrictions
	leading to occupation of the Old City of Jerusalem (Esco-Yale, pp. 876–889). Mufti "engaged in plan of systematic extermination of his opponents" (Esco-Yale, p. 888). "Casualties" during 1938 totaled 3,717 (Royal Institute of International Affairs, *Great Britain and Palestine 1915–1939*, p. 103). "These figures are based on a report in *The Times* of January 2, 1939. *The Survey of International Affairs 1938*, gives slightly different figures: 77 British, 98 Palestinian members of the security forces, 206 Jewish civilians and 458 Arab civilians. It does not state the number of armed rebels killed. The figures are based on a report of the Administration of Palestine (*Survey of International Affairs 1938*, vol. I, p. 414," cited in Esco-Yale, p. 880). Woodhead Commission Report advises against partition; Government abandons partition proposal. The Munich Pact between Hitler and Chamberlain is signed. Evian conference decides not to modify immigration of allied nations to accommodate German and other European Jews.	Government White Paper enforces new, rigidly pro-Arab, anti-Mandate policy: restricting Jewish immigration to a token number for five years, and afterwards at the discretion of "Arabs of Palestine." Prohibits transfers of most land in (Western) Palestine "except to a Palestinian Arab" (Great Britain, *Palestine Land Transfer Regulations*, Command Paper 6180, 1940; see Esco-Yale, p. 933 ff).
1939	Violence of Husseini-Nashashibi rivalry and rebellion continues, 348 "deaths in the first quarter" of the year (Esco-Yale, p. 879). England declares war. Nazi atrocities against Jews of Europe; Arab leaders collaborate with Axis.	
1940	Land Transfer Regulations enforced by White Paper of 1940.	

The Woodhead Report attempted to dispose of the problem of "Arab entrants" by representing it as only a probability for the future, ignoring the evidence of a condition that had been recognized as prevailing nearly a decade before by the Hope Simpson Report.

While High Commissioner Wauchope asserted that the situation had worsened in 1936, and that additional measures should be taken to "protect" the small farmer as well as the tenant-cultivator, the Annual Report for 1937 noted that the total of Arabs who claimed to be dispossessed—six families—were compensated by Government lands.[86]

An example of how the actual conditions at the time were distorted by purportedly fair-minded "reports" is illustrated in the case of the Wadi Hawarith Arabs. As reported in the 1945–1946 Anglo-American *Survey of Palestine,* the Wadi Hawarith Arabs were "the first landless Arabs to be dealt with." Their "eviction" made it "imperative" to "find other land" for them, so Government

> undertook the reclamation and deep ploughing of some 10,000 dunums of the land which it had purchased in the *Beisan* subdistrict, with a view to settling these Arabs upon it, and by the 31st of August, 1933, the major portion of the area was ready for occupation. On being evicted from the Wadi Hawarith, the Arabs, however, refused to settle on the lands prepared for them *on the grounds* that they were used neither to the climate nor to irrigated cultivation; their settlement in the Beisan subdistrict had accordingly to *be abandoned.* *[87]

Yet the lands in the Beisan subdistrict that Government offered to the "landless Arabs"—whose "landless" counterparts in Transjordan, Palestine, or Egypt were offered no such benefits—had been found to be deserted and without cultivation for "a period of between 20 and 30 years" during a 1921 investigation.[88] As such, the lands might have become state domain, and thus would be subject to the Mandatory requirement of "close settlement" by Jewish immigrants. Yet the land was treated as "Arab land" and *still* only 43 families accepted the land, the "new houses, water and irrigation works," because, as Government explained, employment opportunities abounded elsewhere.[89] Those facts were omitted from the *Survey,* however.

The Royal Commission Report "regretted" that Government did not buy lands for "hired labourers" or those who had sold land to Arab moneylenders, who in turn sold to Jews—that it "only" allowed "Arabs who had lost their land as tenants and cultivators."[90] But a Woodhead Commission member challenged that premise the following year. Sir Alison Russell commented,

> It does not appear to me that to permit an Arab to sell his land for three or four times its value, and to go with the money to a different part of the Arab world where land is cheap, can be said to "prejudice" his rights and position within the meaning of Article 6 of the Mandate for Palestine. Indeed, the attempts that have been made to prevent the sale of land by Arabs have been resisted.[91]

*Emphasis added.

The Arab Palestinian notable Musa Alami pointed out that most of the Jewish purchases had been from "absentee landlords." Arab small landholders "in general would only part with their land when hopelessly in debt to moneylenders." Alami lamented that

> So far all the Higher Arab Committee had done to discourage such sales was to disapprove them and bring such pressure as was possible on would-be sellers. . . .[92]

In fact, no blame was attached to the Jewish land purchasers by the various reports.[93] And as one British writer pointed out,

> In point of fact, an exhaustive inquiry by the Government showed, as we have seen, that the displacement of Arabs was infinitesimal and although defenders of the Arab case deny this, they have so far produced no fact or figures to shake the statement in the Annual Report of 1935[94] *that the dispossessed Arabs represented about three-fifths of 1 percent of the rural non-Jewish population as shown by the 1931 census.* *[95]

Indeed, the "ban on the sale of land to Jews," which since the anti-Jewish uprisings by the Arabs had "headed all the Arab programs," was subverted by the actions of many Arab landowners themselves. The "ban" meant partly to channel traditional intolerance and frustration into political foment among the Arab masses, "particularly the rural population." But it was assessed in 1931 as only a "slogan" to incite, while at the same time

> men who, as politicians, everywhere brand the sale of land to Jews as a crime, are offering their own land for sale as landowners, like all other landowners in financial difficulties.

Because of the violence visited upon those who publicly would do business with the Jews, many of the landowners "prefer the method of indirect negotiation through dummies—out of fear of public opinion." However, there was no question that

> they [Arab landowners] are ready to transfer their lands—for hard cash—to the Jews.[96]

Where problems existed for the peasantry,

> every one of the inquiries into rural development which took place during the early '30's revealed that the real problems of the fellahin were, apart from the land system itself, indebtedness and the ruinous charges exacted from them by the Arab landowners and moneylenders—usually the same class, and often the same individuals.[97]

The paralyzing "burden of debt" had been perpetuated by Arab moneylenders well into the '30s.[98]

*Emphasis added.

It was "not in the interest of the Arab governing classes that the Arab-fellahin and laborers should improve their economic position or learn new methods,"[99] which was exactly what the Jewish development offered.

A British Colonial officer, noting the Arab Executive Committee's *rejection* of Government aid for the "landless" Arabs,* remarked,

> This shows how much sympathy for displaced Arabs exists among Arab landowners, and how little displaced Arabs want to get "back to the land."[100]

As the Royal Commission Report noted, "the Arab peasant proprietor" was being "gradually but inevitably" absorbed—not by Jews but "by the Arab *effendi* or capitalist landlord."[101]

The propaganda allegations that Jewish immigration caused a shortage of Arab employment omitted carefully the fact that the Arab labor in question would have been, in great part, illegally immigrating into the Jewish-settled areas of Western Palestine. Further, in cases where no Arab laborers were hired,

> The propagandists usually forget to add that in the co-operative and communal settlements . . . *no hired labor of any kind was employed.* But in any case . . . a large proportion of the Arab rural population found employment . . . such as they had never known before.†[102]

Wages were rising.[103] In 1937 land prices soared and it was solely Arab landsellers who were the beneficiaries, even while "in public" they might be helping incite the Arab peasants to anti-Jewish violence and "denouncing" the land sales.[104]

But while the charge that a large landless class had been created by Jewish settlers had been quickly disproved and discredited by the plethora of British studies following the Hope Simpson Report, the devices for preventing the volume of Jewish immigration that the country actually was capable of accommodating remained in force. The "absorptive capacity" was limited by "unemployment" and supposed "natural increase" of "native Arabs," while "cultivable" lands were misrepresented as "uncultivable" when estimating the number of *Jews* who could find space in Western Palestine.

When Lewis Andrews, District Commissioner and Director of Development for the Galilee, was grilled by the Palestine Royal Commission in November 1936, he debunked the alleged "displacement-by-Jews."[105] Several Commission members expressed disbelief at the "comparatively few complaints and applications" by "landless and displaced" Arabs that Andrews had received. Even though new Arab immigrants were doubtless being counted as long time inhabi-

---

*The same attitudes that motivated the Arab Executive Committee to refuse government aid for the alleged "landless Arabs"—mostly new Arab entrants—also would be seen more than a decade later in 1948, when the Arab world adamantly rejected universally-offered funds and guidance to rehabilitate and resettle the Arab "refugees": in both cases, the real traditions and circumstances of the peoples involved, and the actual culpability for those circumstances, was disguised and then exploited—at cost to the "landless" or "refugee" Arabs themselves.

†Emphasis added.

tants (since Andrews did not make mention of Arab illegal immigration as a condition), still there were very few Arabs who took advantage of Andrews' and his assistants' invitations to come forward.

The line of questioning attempted to discern whether there were not "another number of persons who were displaced when the Jews acquired land. . . ." (Andrews had earlier testified that a number of Arabs had been "displaced in consequence of the purchase of land by *non-Jews*" but because, "under the definition [of a 'landless Arab'] he must be displaced as a result of the sale of land to *Jews,*" that subject was categorically dropped from the hearings.[106]) Andrews said he had "no record of" another group of "complaints." When the question was repeated Andrews added, somewhat peeved, that

> In fact we had a very good "scout round" to get people to put in applications and we were accused at the time of forcing people to put in applications *unnecessarily.* *

Many Arabs who had worked on the lands had drifted to the towns, Andrews said. When his staff "put" them "back," he explained, "they had to work harder than they anticipated," so "they gradually drifted back," into what Andrews called "town life."[107] At the conclusion of Andrews' testimony, he was asked again "why there were so comparatively few complaints. . . . " Andrews said,

> The only answer I can give is that there were not so many people displaced as we imagined.[108]

Lewis Andrews was murdered by Arab terrorists ten months later,[109] shot down as he left his church services, "where he had read the lessons."

Colonial Secretary Ormsby-Gore announced the circumstances surrounding Andrews' murder at a Cabinet meeting on September 29, 1937:

> Mr. Andrews was perhaps the most promising member of the Palestine Civil Service and had been attached to the Royal Commission during their visit. It was at his house that the Royal Commission had met the Arab leaders and it was known that his name had been placed on the Mufti's black list. The circumstances of the murder were most despicable. . . .

"This murder had been accompanied by *many other murders of moderate Arabs,* and a reign of terror seems to have been inaugurated.*[110]

Despite, or perhaps because of the terrorism, Government policy continued to "facilitate close settlement by"—Arabs: in the Jewish-settled plains, within the Jewish National Home. And the Jews were *prevented* from settling elsewhere in Palestine as compensation for the land pulled out from under them, land that had been granted "as of right." The Royal Commission Report stated that,

*Emphasis added.

at present, and indeed for many years to come, the Mandatory Power should not attempt to facilitate the close settlement of Jews in the hilly districts generally . . .[111]

No land in the "hilly" or "Arab" area could be settled by Jews as compensation.
Thus, as Hope Simpson's critical, obscured observation testified, "injustice" was
done "to the Jewish immigrant outside the country whose place is taken" by the
Arab immigrants.

The Arabs and their supporters continued to focus on the ploys begun in
Turkish times, the "landless" and "displaced Arab" myths, promoting terror to
instigate policies that would prevent Jews from immigrating. Meanwhile the truth
—that Arabs were in fact displacing Jews in the "Jewish National Home"—was
buried in the pages of the Hope Simpson Report, put there perhaps by John Hope
Simpson or his assistants as a concession to a nagging conscience. It remained
generally unrecognized and ignored.

15

Britain's Double Standard

> I can only hope and expect that the other world,
> which has such deep sympathy for these criminals,
> will at least be generous enough to convert this
> sympathy into practical aid. We, on our part, are
> ready to put all these criminals at the disposal of these
> countries, for all I care, even on luxury ships.
> —Adolf Hitler, 1938

> If we must have preferences, let me murmur in
> your ear that I prefer Arabs to Jews.
> —Anthony Eden, 1943

The Arab population that migrated and emigrated from surrounding Arab areas to become beneficiaries of the Jews' efforts unquestionably were following a traditional pattern and a natural inclination to better themselves. But the "injustice"—as Hope Simpson observed—follows from the fact that these émigrés from other areas were allowed to flood into the new projects in such numbers that they filled the places—which the Palestinian Jews developed and reclaimed at great personal sacrifice—places meant to provide space for the hundreds of thousands, if not millions, of Jewish refugees fleeing to their homeland from oppression throughout the world.

It was because these Arab immigrants were counted, from the time of their arrival, as "original settlers" in the Jewish-settled area who would be "displaced" after "two thousand years"[1] if more Jewish refugees entered the land—it was this claim, along with the wanton terrorist violence by Arab provocateurs, that resulted in, first, the Turkish and, eventually, the British Mandatory power's restrictions upon Jewish immigration based on the specious charge that "Arabs" were "displaced" by Jewish land purchases.

Despite all the lands with great potential for development in the Arab world, it was the deteriorated, comparatively minuscule "Jewish Homeland" in "Palestine" that the Arabs predominantly sought. Although we may understand and sympathize with the natural inclination of man and woman to better themselves, that trend cannot be justification for distorting and misrepresenting the conditions of the League of Nations Palestine Mandate, which England was legally

obligated to observe. The evidence indicates, however, that England honored its
obligation in the breach.

The fact is that Jews were allowed to settle only on a very limited and
restricted portion of the land. As an illustration, even if one utilized the prevalent
distorted population comparison—Jews-within-Jewish-settled-areas compared
with the Arabs-throughout-Western Palestine—the Jews still would have constituted 33 percent (about 400,000) of the 1935 population of Western Palestine.[2]
Yet in 1935 Jews had acquired only 9.3 percent of the land of Western Palestine
—a far smaller proportion than their population would justify even had the land
of Palestine not been allotted as the "Jewish Homeland" many years before. But
the land of Palestine had been recognized as the haven for Jews, where Jews
would be unrestricted in their "close settlement with the land"; even preceding
the Nazi holocaust the Jews had needed that haven from persecution and desolation in Arab lands and in Europe. Still, the only immigration restrictions imposed
by the British, and they were vigilantly adhered to, were the restrictions on the
Jews.

The "humaneness" of advocating a Jewish nation reborn had been for some
a politically motivated tactic. When it failed as effective foreign policy, some
among the British hoped to nullify or at least neutralize the Jewish homeland
in a fruitless attempt to appease the Arab Muslim world. (It must be pointed
out that this discussion bears upon the British only insofar as they were convinced by the Arabs' intransigence and violence that there was only one course
—against the Jews.[3]) It is not to "beat a dead horse" that the British role in
assisting the Arab cause is reiterated. The British, in attempting to gain the
support of the predominantly Arab-Muslim Middle East against the Nazis, mistakenly calculated that capitulation to the Arab demands would gain such support. As will be illustrated, subsequent events proved that British appeasement
was to no avail.

From the beginning of the British Mandate, support from high British quarters had been given to the implementation of the Jewish homeland with which
England had been charged.

International expectations for Britain's administration of the Palestine Mandate and the purpose of the Mandate's incorporation of the Balfour Declaration
for "The Jewish National Home" were unambiguous. Against Arab demands for
repudiation of the Balfour Declaration and a halt of Jewish immigration, the
British Colonial Secretary, Duke of Devonshire, stated in a 1923 speech before
the House of Lords,

The Mandate is not merely a national obligation, it is an international obligation,
and the Balfour Declaration was the basis on which we accepted from the principal Allied Powers the position of Mandatory Power in Palestine. . . . It is not
possible for us to say that we wish to reserve certain portions of the Mandate and
dispense with others.[4]

But, also from the beginning, double and conflicting signals were evidenced in stated policy and unofficial communications, actions, and attitudes of British officials concerned.

As John Gunther observed,

> From the beginning Zionism faced not only political watering down of the Mandate but deep-seated antipathy from anti-Semitic British officials. The Jews were violently discriminated against—in what was presumably to be their own country.[5]

What was an inbred Arab abhorrence of the *dhimmi* Jews' intimations of equality, coupled with the drive of *effendi* leadership to keep its general stranglehold over the country and those "sweets of office," found sympathy, compatibility, or both among some in England.

Compounding the effect of the Arabs' intimidation by terror on British policy was a predisposition of certain key British officers toward the Arab anti-Jewish attitudes. Certainly England's acquiescence to Arab demands of restrictions against Jews, for the oft-stated reason that the British then would gain the Arabs as long-hoped-for allies against the Axis, bore scant credibility on the basis of logical British foreign policy. The *Palestine Royal Commission Report* recalled that in World War I, among "the Arabs of Palestine . . . while some Palestinian conscripts deserted, others continued fighting in the Turkish army." None fought for the British against the Turkish and German forces. "Ten thousand Arabs and five hundred of their officers had deserted" in 1917, one German historian observed in 1926.[6]

The Arabs' potential "reliability" as allies must have been known to British officials: the fact was well chronicled that those who were active among the "inert"[7] Arab population of East and West Palestine, "far from contributing anything towards ultimate victory," had "actively opposed" the British.[8] David Lloyd George wrote:

> No race has done better out of the fidelity with which the Allies redeemed their promises to the oppressed races than the Arabs . . . the Arabs have already won independence in Iran, Arabia, Syria and Trans-Jordania, *although most of the Arab races fought throughout the War for their Turkish oppressors.* Arabia was the only exception in that respect. *The Palestinian Arabs fought for Turkish rule.* *[9]

As a grand vizier of the Turkish Empire said in 1917, "The Fatherland of a Muslim is the place where the Holy Law of Islam prevails."[10] Bernard Lewis observed,

> . . . A Muslim Iraqi would feel far closer bonds with a non-Iraqi Muslim than with a non-Muslim Iraqi. . . . the imported western idea of ethnic and territorial nationhood remains, like secularism, alien and incompletely assimilated.[11]

*Emphasis added.

T. E. Lawrence "of Arabia," whose exploits in the quest to raise an Arab national movement greatly romanticized the image of the Arab world in the West, was more realistic in his private appraisals than his public expectations. In 1916 Lawrence wrote:

> . . . Unless we, or our allies, make an efficient Arab empire, there will never be more than a discordant mosaic.[12]

> There is no national feeling.[13]

Lawrence had come to realize that, for the Arab—whom Lawrence called "Semite"—the "ideal of national union was episodic combined resistance to an intruder. Constructive policies, an organized state, an extended empire, was not so much beyond their sight as hateful in it. They were fighting to get rid of the [Turkish] Empire, not to win it."[14] "Arab unity is a madman's notion."[15]

Lawrence "meant to make a new nation,"[16] but even he had his reservations. In a startling, prophetic insight, Lawrence noted,

> They [the Arabs] were weak in material resources, and even after success would be, since their world was agricultural and pastoral, *without minerals,* and could never be strong in modern armaments. Were it otherwise, we should have had to pause before evoking in the strategic centre of the Middle East new national movements of such abounding vigor.*[17]

Whatever the past record of the Muslim Arabs in Palestine, the Haycraft Commission of 1921 investigating anti-Jewish attacks by the Muslims in Jaffa and the violent attack on the Jews at the Khedera settlement, established a precedent that was to be inimical to the "Jewish National Home." The Haycraft Report cited the fact that in the Muslim-populated villages around the Jewish settlements,† "Jews were not tolerated," and that Muslims had spread false rumors to incite against the Jews. Nevertheless, the same report found the anti-Jewish onslaught "grossly exaggerated." The Haycraft Report attributed the action—not to scapegoating of the *dhimmi* Jew, which had long been the tradition in Southern Syria-Palestine, but to "Zionist manifestations" by " 'new' Jews" and "Bolsheviks," which quite understandably, it was implied, brought "Arab discontent."[18]

A month after the Haycraft Report was issued, in an attempt to mollify the Arabs who charged that the British were favoring Jews, Winston Churchill told a meeting of the Deputation of Arabs that

> Many of the British Officials in Palestine are very, very friendly to the Arabs, more so than to the Jews. The Jews make continued outcry on that subject, that the British officials and the British military authorities are unduly partial towards the Arabs. No one has harmed you, and no one is harming you. . . . Give the Jews their chance.[19]

---

*Emphasis added.

†Many of the "Arabs" surrounding Khedera had immigrated to the neighborhood following founding of the Jewish settlement. See Chapter 12.

The Hope Simpson and the Palestine Royal Commission Reports, discussed earlier, are classic examples of the double signals issued throughout the British Mandatory administration; they contained both the false Arab allegations and the facts that contradicted those allegations—but the "injustice" to the Jews was disregarded. Twisted and buried among the reams of rhetoric in the various "Reports," the crux of the population issue was there—but the Arabs refuted and fiercely denied it, alternately terrorizing and charming the British authorities into incorporating Arab propaganda charges as "facts" in the determination of British policy.

The inflammatory Arab press continued its "campaign against Jewish immigration," stepping it up in 1933, the year Adolf Hitler came to power.[20] The proved facts notwithstanding, Arab newspapers accused the British Government of "flooding the country with Jews with the object of displacing Arabs from the land and depriving them of employment."[21]

Despite the fact that the mythical, prohibitive "absorptive capacity"—employed solely against Jewish immigration—had been proved inaccurate many times since its invention in 1922, Arab propaganda was working its way ever more comprehensively into British perceptions. The "secret Report on the Political Situation" for October 1933, from the British Foreign Officer at Amman, Transjordan, told the Foreign Office that, according to "His Highness," the Emir, Palestine can "hold no more" Jews

> and is, indeed, over full already as is proved by the reports of those experts who have visited Palestine to examine the situation. Any further influx of Jews is therefore, he [Emir] considers, an indication that this excess is destined for neighboring Arab States, and of this these neighboring States are highly apprehensive.[22]

Transjordanian Palestine's "Emir" needn't have worried about Western Palestine's "neighbors." Illustrating a noticeable double standard that stood the stated purpose of the Mandated "Jewish National Home" on its head, the Transjordanian Arabs were admitted freely to *Western* Palestine with its shrunken Jewish-settled area, but the Jews, without exception, were not allowed to settle in Transjordan. The League of Nations Permanent Mandates Commission had repeatedly underlined the duty of the Mandatory power (Britain): to "provide *special* facilities for the immigration of Jews," throughout Palestine, their "National Home."[23] That included Transjordanian, or Eastern, Palestine, the "beautiful Trans-Jordanian plateaux . . . neglected and uninhabited. . . ." In 1921 it had a "total population" of "considerably less than 200,000. . . ."

Chaim Weizmann had written to Winston Churchill in 1921 that[24]

> Eastern Palestine . . . may bulk much larger in the economic future of the Jewish National Home. . . .
>
> The economic progress of Cis-Jordania itself is dependent upon the development of these Trans-Jordanian plains, for they form the natural granary of all Palestine and without them Palestine can never become a self-sustaining, eco-

nomic unit and a real National Home. The evidence of competent and impartial authorities . . . gives abundant proof of this. . . .

It is confidently hoped, therefore, that there will be no thought of any further diminution of the legitimate claims of Palestine when the eastern and southern frontiers come under discussion. The unsatisfactory character of the settlement on the north makes it all the more vital that the Jewish National Home be generously dealt with on the east and south.[25]

Over the years, the actuality restricted Jewish immigration even in the small, Jewish-settled portion of Western Palestine. "Government" forbade Jewish settlement in the eastern area of Palestine called Transjordan, while at the same time it was blinking at the broad-scale Arab in-migration and illicit Arab immigration into the Jewish-settled area of Western Palestine. The situation created was in fact diametrically opposed to the express purpose of the Jewish National Home—it facilitated instead Arab influx and imposed its restrictions only on the Jews. One member of the Permanent Mandates Commission observed,

> While Trans-Jordanians might go freely into [Western] Palestine Jews were not allowed to settle in Trans-Jordan.[26]

Although according to the Mandates Commission, "There could be no doubt that quite a large number of Trans-Jordanians did settle in [Western] Palestine,"[27] the attitude prevalent among the British was that a reciprocal agreement allowing Jews into *Eastern* Palestine—or Transjordan—must be avoided. As Major J. B. Glubb, "Glubb Pasha," head of the Arab Legion, wrote in 1938,

> The entry of foreigners into Trans-jordan would lead to a deterioration of law and order. . . . It would probably increase the total revenues of Trans-Jordan. It might be for the general benefit of the human race. But let us be quite clear and honest —it would not be for the benefit of the tribesmen.[28]

Here we can observe the typical predisposition of the British to regard the Jews, whether native or newcomer, as "foreigners," or troublemakers, and the Arabs, from however distant a place, as "tribesmen," or natives. Glubb concluded that the improvement achieved in Jewish-settled coastal Palestine was unnecessary in Transjordanian Palestine, and that "Human beings in the last resort, cannot be won by money." The anti-Semitic inference to the Jew and his money is unmistakable there, and his final statement is significant:

> The introduction of foreign capital would not benefit the tribesmen of Trans-Jordan even if it gave them increased financial prosperity, because it would introduce a smiling, simple people to the hell of race-hatred. It may be necessary to do such things to gain higher or greater objects, but it is an error to suppose that it would be helpful to the Arabs of Trans-Jordan.[29]

Glubb's article reflects, perhaps as well as any expression might, the prevailing sentiment that governed the actions of the British Mandatory power between the two world wars and until their departure in 1948.

The "Jewish National Home," which "His Majesty's Government is responsible for," may be "quite proper," wrote a Colonial official to George Rendel, the influential future assistant and often the voice of Anthony Eden, in 1933:

> But the last thing we want is to slip into the position of posing as the protector of Jews all over the world. Quite apart from any other consideration, that would lead to trouble with many countries."[30]

A book published in 1937 by the Secretary of the Arab Executive, Matiel E. T. Mogannam, repeated the warning of "danger" from a "largely Arab Palestine," invaded by the "new arrivals." It was *"natural,"* Mogannam wrote, that the "aggressiveness of the new arrivals" and the "strong bolshevist element" should offend "Arab Palestine," where "matters of social etiquette, decorum and tradition" were of "great importance."[31]

The Arab propaganda was recited again and again to the staccato accompaniment of Mufti-led terrorist violence, strikes, and "disorder,"[32] until the evidence that existed to challenge the theme was effectively muted by the deafening propaganda blows. Thus, the *Palestine Royal Commission Report also* found the "Arab reactions" of violence to "all these Jewish men and women . . . quite *natural.* "[33] The same year, Lord Hailey, a "distinguished Colonial civil servant," argued to the Permanent Mandates Commission at Geneva that

> the British public would never with any conviction support . . . the subordination of an *indigenous Arab population* to a *new* population largely consisting of Polish and German colonists.*[34]

The pivotal fact confirmed by John Hope Simpson's report seven years before —that the Arab immigrants were an even "newer population," following the Jewish trail—was conspicuously absent, as was the plentiful evidence of widespread Arab illegal immigration contained in the Palestine Royal Commission Notes of Evidence of 1936.

A Crucial Moment: The Gesture

Meanwhile the prospective Jewish "colonists" in Poland, Germany, and other European lands, whom the British Government deprecated as "aliens" and rejected as immigrants to their "Home," were by 1937–1938 victimized by riots, murder, pillage and government-approved persecution in their homes throughout Europe.[35]

> Political anti-Semitism acquired an irresistible momentum as a force in European politics.[36]

Germany's "enthusiasm for Jewish emigration" led its government to "facilitate some 40,000" German Jews' emigration to Palestine between 1933 and 1938.

*Emphasis added.

The German government "remained anxious to encourage Jewish emigration," and "expressed dissatisfaction with . . . the slow progress" in getting rid of the unwanted "non-Aryans."[37] In October of 1938, "more than fifteen thousand" Polish-born Jews who had "long" been living in Germany, were "rounded up," expelled from the Reich, and dumped at the Polish border, one of many "similar" actions.

When Hitler marched on Vienna in March of 1938, however, "there was a total of sixteen immigration certificates" for the whole Austrian Jewish community.[38] The late prominent Zionist activist Ehud Avriel, a Viennese-born Jew, in his book *Open the Gates* described the scene:

> . . . my parents were still in Vienna when the Nazis took over. . . . when they did leave for Palestine, soon after, they did so together with the "optimists"—those who had never believed the catastrophe could occur but who now, too, were refugees.[39]

The Austrian Jews "overnight" were stripped of security and "in many cases also all their property." By the end of April "more than 500 Austrian Jews had committed suicide."[40] The Jews in Vienna, as elsewhere, "turned down by one foreign consulate after the other," were faced with the fact that "no country would take them in."[41]

President Franklin D. Roosevelt called an international conference at Evian, France, to be held in July 1938.[42] It was hailed as a humanitarian gesture of concern for the Jewish victims of Nazi persecution and promised a solution to reducing the emigration barriers of the political refugees.[43]

Adolf Hitler responded with alacrity to Roosevelt's announcement:

> I can only hope and expect that the other world, which has such deep sympathy for these criminals, will at least be generous enough to convert this sympathy into practical aid. *We, on our part, are ready to put all these criminals at the disposal of these countries, for all I care, even on luxury ships.* *[44]

Two days before the Evian Conference began, *New York Times* columnist Anne O'Hare McCormick filed this imploration:

> It is heartbreaking to think of the queues of desperate human beings around our consulates in Vienna and other cities waiting in suspense for what happens at Evian. . . . It is not a question of how many unemployed this country can safely add to its own unemployed millions. It is a test of civilization . . . Can America live with itself if it lets Germany get away with this policy of extermination, allows the fanaticism of one man to triumph over reason, refuses to take up this page of battle against barbarism?[45]

By the opening of the Conference, according to the *Times* of London,[46]

*Emphasis added.

... no Jewish family in the country [Austria] . . . has not one or more of its members under arrest. . . . hopelessness and panic . . . can be imagined. . . . The authorities *demand rapid and impossible emigration.* . . . Thousands stand outside the consulates of America, England, and other countries, waiting through the night for admission so that they may register their names. . . . the segregation of Jewish children from "Aryans" is complete. The youngest are not spared; infants . . . can no longer play in public parks and on the door of their school the legend is painted: "Cursed be the Jew."*

At Evian, thirty-two countries[47] met to solve the problem of the refugees. Even "observers from Nazi Germany" were allowed to audit those proceedings,[48] which might well have influenced Hitler's ultimate decision to rid the world of the Jewish "criminals" by extermination. Jews as such, however, were not represented, because they had no state, and leading spokesman Chaim Weizmann was prohibited from speaking even in private session, because Great Britain had protested against it.

The United States set the tone. Precluding any real effect, the Conference had preordained that none of the nations "would be expected or asked to receive a greater number of immigrants than is permitted by *existing* legislation."*[49] Upon that predetermination, America announced that it would continue to honor its legal quota, previously set up as an annual immigration maximum figure of 27,370 for Germany and Austria[50] combined. Thereupon Peru announced its own strict quotas, including a ban on admission of doctors and lawyers for fear of an invasion by intellectuals. The Peruvian representative praised the United States' "shining example that guided the immigration policies" of Peru.[51] Other countries, one by one, followed suit, although some were more candid or generous than others.[52]

The lone exceptions, when the conference concluded, were Santo Domingo, which offered to take in 100,000 refugees,[53] and Holland and Denmark, which for a time "agreed to let in refugees without restrictions."[54]

Government in the Jewish National Home: The Response

The British had no room in the Colonies for the Jews. When "Palestine" was brought up at the Evian's "closing session," the British delegate announced that "only very limited immigration could be considered."[55] The question of the internationally mandated "Jewish National Home east and west of the Jordan River," of which only the small fraction of land that is Israel today holds nearly four million souls, never came up. Its "absorptive capacity" had been pronounced to be "full."[56]

The message of the Evian Conference coupled with the violence and disorder of Muftism in Palestine were the backdrop for the British Government officials'

*Emphasis added.

scenario to turn the League of Nations Mandate upside down.*

The twist in policy had been inexorably established in late 1937, after the violent rejection by Arab leaders of the *Palestine Royal Commission Report*'s recommendation of Western Palestine's partition into a small Jewish state and a larger Arab state. British Secretary of Foreign Affairs, Anthony Eden, then aimed for another plan, "which would not give Jews any territory exclusively for their own use."[57]

There was little attention to inherent "justice" in Government's policy: as Eden later wrote to his private secretary,

If we must have preferences, let me murmur in your ear that I prefer Arabs to Jews.[58]

His secretary noted in his own diary in 1943 that

Unfortunately A.E. is immovable on the subject of Palestine. He loves Arabs and hates Jews.[59]

(Significantly, Eden was Foreign Secretary, 1935–38; Dominions Secretary, 1939–1940; War Secretary, 1940; Foreign Secretary, 1940–1945, and again, 1951–1955. He was England's Prime Minister from 1955–1957.)

That Eden's sentiments were prevalent among British officials† is evidenced by the statement of Neville Chamberlain, Britain's Prime Minister in that most pivotal period of the shaping of British policy, 1937–1940. Chamberlain told his cabinet that,

If we must offend one side, let us offend the Jews rather than the Arabs.[60]

The 1939 White Paper

All that remained was for the British Government to justify that inclination officially. Beginning in January 1939, the oft-repeated mythical Arab claims were embodied uncritically and totally in a new British policy. Malcolm MacDonald,

---

*The documents excerpted in the following pages and in the footnotes and appendix of this book are by no means a comprehensive compendium of the available data relating to the British and the Arab roles in the "Final Solution" to the "Jewish Problem." The illustrations were culled from an immense accumulation of documents, which was itself only a fraction of existing materials, only a small sampling, which hopefully would be adequate to trace the prevailing attitudes and conditions that influenced the immigration of Jewish and Arab populations in Western Palestine. The choice was a difficult one, because *never before* had this writer been aware of the extent to which Arab influence and British bias on British immigration policies in Palestine had determined the fate of countless Jewish victims of the Holocaust.

†The perfidy of British failure to carry out the Mandate, in the violation of its terms and in the history of the British administration of Palestine—this story must be dealt with in detail elsewhere. Much has already been told. What is done here is the detailing of British policy restricting Jewish immigration as compared with British laxity toward Arab immigration and the showing of some quantum of Arab immigration, which was much larger than anticipated, demonstrating the unfairness of Britain's double standard.

All of the immigration data bear on the relationship between the number of Jews and the number of Arabs in Palestine and the status of those Arabs: whether they were settled "existing" population from time immemorial or were recent immigrants to Jewish-settled areas of Western Palestine.

British Colonial Secretary, could not "continue to carry out the Balfour Declaration," he stated in a "secret cabinet memorandum" that spelled out the reversal of policy.

> Arab detestation of the Jewish invasion into Palestine being what it is, it would be wholly wrong to suggest that this large Arab population should one day in their own native land and against their will come under the rule of the newly arrived Jews.[61]

On the one hand, the British Government stated it couldn't continue to honor the Balfour Declaration, although it was part and parcel of the Mandate; on the other hand, paradoxically, the government *justified* its White Paper of 1939 on the theory that the British *were carrying out* the "obligations" of the *Mandate* to "Arabs and Jews" by curtailing Jewish immigration, a logical extension of the myth.[62] The Anglo-American Committee's Chronology of Events later reported the inversion thus:

> It was therefore necessary to devise an alternative policy consistent with the obligations to *Arabs* and *Jews* under the Mandate. The Statement declared unequivocally that it was not part of this policy that Palestine should become a Jewish State as this *would be contrary to the obligations to the Arabs under the Mandate*. . . .*[63]

(Nowhere in that chronology of important "events" would it be noted that seventy-five to eighty percent of the territory under that Mandate—Eastern Palestine/Transjordan—already had been illegally bestowed upon the Arabs.)

The Arabs in Western Palestine rejected any and all additional Jewish immigration, with the "public" support of spokesmen from surrounding Arab nations. But those Arab spokesmen privately "indicated" to Malcolm MacDonald that they might consider an additional 50,000 Jews over a period of five years ". . . provided that the Arabs were in a position to veto the continuance of Jewish immigration after that date."[64]

Two months later, in May 1939, the White Paper codified the Arab agreement with MacDonald.

> Jewish immigration during the five years beginning 1st April, 1939, would be at a rate which, if economic absorptive capacity allowed, would bring the Jewish population up to approximately one-third of the total population of the country. . . . For each of the five years a quota of 10,000 would be allowed . . . and, as a contribution towards the solution of the Jewish refugee problem, 25,000 refugees would be admitted as soon as the High Commissioner was satisfied that adequate provision for maintenance was ensured.
>
> After the period of five years, no further Jewish immigration would be permitted unless the Arabs of Palestine were prepared to acquiesce in it.

*Emphasis added.

Furthermore, an estimated number of the "illegal" Jewish immigrants would be "deducted from the annual quotas."[65]

MacDonald candidly admitted to members of the Cabinet that, had Government considered its new harsh policy on "its strict merits," with less deference to Arab "pressure," "certain points" would have been "omitted."[66]

Thus the myth, which had first been asserted by Arab "notables" to protect their feudal stranglehold over the sparse impoverished populace nearly fifty years before, had been fixed into British decision-making as "fact." Just as, in July of 1891, the Turkish government had halted all Jewish immigration following the ominous wire from "leading Muslims of Jerusalem" to Constantinople,[67]

> praying that the entry of such Jews should be prohibited, as not only was the labour market over-stocked, but also the Muslims themselves would be greatly the sufferers. . . .

so did the British Government, by its 1939 White Paper, bring the Jewish immigration into the "Jewish National Home" to a relative standstill: "Government" thereby shifted the Mandated Jewish Homeland—*and the reality of the demographic situation in the Jewish settled area of Western Palestine*—into reverse.

Malcolm MacDonald was a principal author of the 1939 White Paper, and British Colonial Secretary at that time. He enunciated the Arabs' theme in his disapproval of the Balfour Declaration and its "establishment in Palestine of a national home for the Jewish people." Among Macdonald's criticisms, he judged that

> the authors of the various declarations made to Jews and Arabs . . . were rather confused about the whole business. I doubt whether they realized fully how many Arabs were already living in Palestine at the time when they made their promise to the Jews; they certainly cannot have foreseen how formidably that Arab population would increase after the arrival of Jewish capital and development and British administration.[68]

It was MacDonald who was misled. The 1917 Balfour Declaration stated that the "civil and religious rights" of *"non-Jewish communities"* already *"existing"** in "Palestine" then would not be adversely affected by a resurgence of Jewish development. That inclusion clearly established that the "authors" had indeed considered the sparseness of population and the decay of the land "at the time when they made their promise." Then, the whole of Western Palestine as well as Eastern Palestine was considered the "Jewish National Home," not just the Jewish-settled, restricted segment of Western Palestine that later became Israel.

Had only actual "natural" increase taken place among the *existing* Arabs, without the carefully disguised Arab population increase by in-migration and illegal immigration—that matched or possibly even exceeded the Jews' immigration into their "Jewish National Home"—and had the British firmly supported

*Emphasis added.

their own stated government policy and upheld the international League of Nations Mandate for the Jewish home, the European and Arab-born Jews might have had their sanctuary in time to save countless Jewish lives. Had the British enforced its laws against Arab *effendis'* usury, extortion, and exploitation of the peasantry, instead of defending and encouraging the *effendi*-inspired anti-Jewish racial incitements the Arabs and their British supporters called "nationalism," the "Jewish National Home" would have achieved independence perhaps sooner and certainly in a less hostile atmosphere.

The blinkered vision by which the Shaw Commission reported "excessive immigration [Jewish] of 1925 and 1926,"[69] and by which John Hope Simpson reported in 1930 that

> It is wrong that a Jew from Poland, Lithuania or the Yemen should be admitted to fill an existing vacancy, while in Palestine there are already workmen capable of filling that vacancy. . . .[70]

—these blinders were still operative in 1939, as justification for the White Paper assertion that the country was crowded with citizens seeking employment and it could absorb no more.

That turnspeak has been propagated until the present time, through efforts of today's Arab extremists following the lead of Nazi-supported measures by Haj Amin al-Husseini, who in 1921 had been, ironically, appointed by Palestine High Commissioner Sir Herbert Samuel, a British Jew: Samuel empowered al-Husseini to be the most influential Arab in Palestine, Grand Mufti of Jerusalem and President of the Supreme Moslem Council.[71]

Britain's rationalization of its policy incorporating the Arab claim must be carefully reviewed. Because, as we have seen, the British pledged to uphold the Mandate for the Jewish Homeland, and took administration of Palestine under those conditions, then the land should be "closely settled by Jews." "Jewish immigration" was to be a primary goal, which would not be a physical imposition upon the sparsely populated migrant community inhabiting the Jewish-settled area of development in Western Palestine (as determined in earlier pages). Arab immigration was decidedly not part of the plan for the Jewish home, since *Jewish* immigration was expressly stipulated in conjunction with the "non-Jewish communities" which were then "existing." Thus, had the British officially acknowledged, much less openly encouraged, illegal Arab immigration into the Mandated Jewish homeland, that course would have been condemned as unjust by the international community. Undoubtedly such a course would have been halted by the League of Nations Permanent Mandates Commission, which appears, from the evidence of its minutes, to have had the clear intention to uphold the Mandate for the "Jewish National Home" in Palestine.*

To recognize and give public blessing to the conversion of a Jewish National

---

*In fact, four out of seven of the members protested the 1939 White Paper's violation of the Mandate on several counts.[72]

Home into what the British, perhaps inadvertently, had the effect of creating—a repository for itinerant Arab workers from all over the Arab independent world—would have provoked understandable outrage. Not only Jews and Zionists, but many in the world however apolitical, however unfamiliar with Jews or Judaism, sympathized with the Jewish renewal of political liberation after two millennia. (As Neville Chamberlain said, ". . . Jews aren't a loveable people; I don't care about them myself;—but that is not sufficient to explain the Pogrom."[73])

The British, then, if they were to attempt to reverse the formal Mandated declaration to suit their Arab preference, had to juggle whatever clauses the declaration itself contained, to conform to and justify the British reversal, and at the same time to maintain the appearance of fulfilling the terms of the declaration.

The word *"existing"* became operative and pivotal. Why? Because within the Balfour Declaration was the assessment that the establishment of a home for the Jews would not "prejudice the civil and religious rights of *existing* non-Jewish communities."[74]

If the thousands upon thousands of illicit immigrant and in-migrant Arabs streaming in, who were counted from then on as settled population—as natives who had been on the land in their plot for "two thousand years"—had instead been truthfully identified, as were the Jewish immigrants, then their entry would have been seen to be at cross purposes with the Mandate. The Arab movement would have been condemned as unfair, as diverting places being cleared frantically by Jews for other Jews who sought to escape from persecution, while Arab itinerants, however impoverished, were free from life-threatening racial attack, free to live and migrate within the number of independent Arab states from which they had come. As Malcolm MacDonald himself once observed,*

> If the Jews had not come to Palestine, . . . the Arab population of Palestine would undoubtedly have remained fixed . . . where it had been for ages before.

However, because the Arabs who flooded into the areas of Jewish development were, on the other hand, counted as indigenous, or *existing,*[75] population as fast as they arrived, then all those places being made for Jewish immigrants were viewed as being taken by *existing* Arab population.

One can only speculate how zealously the Jews must have been clearing in order to make places for incoming Jews and Arabs both and enough room for all. And how many more Jews might have been able to live there—live at all—if the British and Arabs had adhered to the Mandate and encouraged Jewish immigration? What would have been the Jews' fate, had the British restricted Arab immigration and respected the rights of those "non-Jews" and Jews and their descendants who actually lived in the relevant areas of Palestine when the Mandate began—the *actual existing* population?

The restrictions against Jewish immigration had been given added weight by the Arab claim that the already limited Jewish land purchase would create a

---

*See Chapter 12.

"landless Arab" class among the purported "existing" Arab population. Many authorities had proved that the "landless" claim was baseless. The tradition of "landless" peasantry throughout the Middle East had no Jewish development as its alleged cause.[76] Other "landless" peasants had lost their lands, if they had once possessed them, through the nefarious schemes and practices of Arab absentee landlords and moneylenders, independent of Jewish enterprises.

While the various British reports had contradicted and disproved the allegation of Jews' "displacing" the "landless Arabs," the British still concentrated on the concerns enunciated by Lewis French and Sir John Hope Simpson—that perhaps the Arabs would be affected "in the future."[77] "Government" heeded reports[78] that alleged:

> . . . owing to the *natural growth of the Arab population* and the steady sale in recent years of Arab land to Jews, there was now in certain areas . . . no room for further transfer of Arab land and expansion in close settlement of the Jews.*[79]

Thus the British official record's inclusion of the percentage of Arab population that was actually newly arrived immigrants and in-migrants into the category of *"settled indigenous Arab population,"* or *existing* population growing only by natural increase, had the direct effect of practically eliminating the Jewish immigration via the White Paper of 1939.

That action was based upon the unfounded "displacement" myth, the same myth that also spawned the now-prevalent distortion—the Arab claim that Jews "dispossessed" Arabs in Israel, beginning in 1948.

*Emphasis added.

16

Jews in Palestine as "Illegals" and as War Allies

From the beginning Zionism faced not only political
watering down of the Mandate but deep-seated
antipathy from anti-Semitic British officials.
The Jews were violently discriminated against—in
what was presumably to be their own country.

—John Gunther, 1939

Hauranis proper are here illegally. They are a
turbulent lot. The sooner they go the better at their own
request. Next week they may not want to go.

—Colonial Official, 1936

"Arab Revolt," Palestine, 1936

As long as they go voluntarily, I fear no Arab comments.

—Palestine High Commissioner Wauchope,

1936 "Arab Revolt"

It is the profound conviction of Christian America
that [British Government] rescind its illegal, unjust,
and indefensible partition of Palestine, to restore
Trans-Jordania to its proper place as part of Palestine
territory, and throw it open to Jewish Settlement.

—Conference of Protestant and

Catholic Leaders, 1936

While the British continued to encourage and wink at Arab immigration into the country, officials were increasingly impatient at stepped-up "illegal" Jewish immigration. Such instances as the immigration of some thirty thousand "Arabs" from the Hauran in a three-month period of 1934 had gone unreported and unrecognized by the Government at the same time Adolf Hitler had ascended to power in Germany, and Jewish immigration had sharply risen.[1] The government had seen to it that those "illegal" Jewish immigrants would be accounted for, however; it was in 1934 that the "Palestine Administration" had first instituted the "practice of . . . deducting [a number for] illegal settlers who might enter the labour-market" on a "half-yearly" basis from the Jewish quota; it was a practice that would be rigidly applied afterward to the Arab-approved 1939 White Paper quota of Jewish immigrants to the Jewish-settled area of Western Palestine during and after World War II.[2]

The British officials' meticulous concern for the welfare of *Arab* "illegals,"* —i.e., High Commissioner Wauchope's enjoinder that "Haurani illegals" leave only "at their own request" because "they may not want to go next week," or his revealing observation that "as long as they go voluntarily I fear no Arab comments"—that obsequiousness was in marked contrast to the official attitude toward *Jews'* entry in the early thirties. Regarding the Jews, High Commissioner Wauchope had been "most anxious that as many as possible of the tourists who remain should be deported . . ."

> . . . advisable to inform Jewish Agency . . . all illegal settlers will be turned out whenever Government has the power to do so. *The hardship of the individual must be ignored* in order to check this illegal custom that has grown to such proportions as to damage the country, and threatens to upset our whole system of immigration.†[3]

The "whole system of immigration"—in the Jewish National Home, where "facilitated" Jewish immigration was mandated—long revolved around circumventing the Mandate's guarantee.

The very concept of Jewish immigration into the Jewish National Home as "illegal" did not appear in British reports until the 1930s. To be sure, from the beginning of the Mandate, the Jews' immigration had been restricted by the British administration (a condition described generally in previous pages, and evidenced by voluminous correspondence on the subject).

In 1921, for example, "a large number of immigrants were refused admission to Palestine during the temporary suspension of immigration . . . ," according to Sir Wyndham Deedes, Chief Secretary to the Palestine Administration.[4] An extensive internal Government summary, "Memorandum on the Control of Immigration to Palestine 1920–1930,"[5] reported that "drastic action was bound to come sooner or later," but after the "outbreaks of riots in Jaffa the High Commissioner issued an order closing the Palestine ports against all Jewish immigrants." Even in 1921, thousands of "men, women and children," many with "valid visas" were already being "turned back from Palestinian ports."

In that official memorandum no reference, no recognition of any kind, was made of Arab influx into the Jewish-settled area of Western Palestine. By contrast, what was termed the "abuse" by Jews "who made it their business to force immigration into the country" was found to be "really amazing." According to the memorandum, "machinery created for control of immigration" was "inade-

*See Chapters 13 and 14.
†Emphasis added.

quate," because of the "horrors and terrors" of "conditions in Eastern Europe," which created "a huge mass of disorganized fugitives." The writers of the memorandum expressed surprise that "the flow . . . was kept within some bounds," since "loopholes" would have allowed in "practically any Jew who desired to go to Palestine" at the beginning of the Mandatory period.[6]

Because of the "utter confusion" caused by "large numbers of Russian and Polish refugees—Jews who fled . . . during the reigns of terror, both White and Red—of 1919–1921 . . . when the Roumanian Government began putting its own house in order, it commenced to sort out these refugees with a view to getting rid of them in some way or other."[7]

The British too had to find their own solution for the "confusion" of the Jews escaping to the "Jewish National Home." A British representative, Sir Wyndham Deedes, reported in 1921:

> The Jews demand a 50% proportion of Jews. I . . . [say] that I hope to give them a 50% "Reliables" in this way:—30% Jews, 10% Circassians, 10% Cypriots. We cannot accept 50% Jews today. . . .[8]

Dr. Chaim Weizmann protested to Deedes at that time that

> The real cause of all the evil is the attitude of the majority of the British in Palestine. In the opinion of Churchill himself nine-tenths of them are against us. The Arabs know that, and know further that by exercising pressure and by threatening the administration in Palestine, they can extract concessions of a political nature. . . . In June the stoppage of immigration was proclaimed without as much as giving us a warning. Then the only privilege which we have ever received viz. the issue of certificates, was withdrawn from us.

Weizmann reminded Deedes that, as Deedes' own letter attested, "The Zionist organization . . . in extraordinarily difficult circumstances . . . have not swamped the country with undesirable immigrants."

> Why was the certificate system destroyed . . . and so a blow to our liberty . . . ? We have been put into a vicious circle. . . ."[9]

This was 1921, months before three-fourths of the "Jewish National Home" was wrenched from the country known as "Palestine" (consisting of Western and Eastern—or Transjordanian—Palestine) in violation of the Mandate, and "given" by the British to an Arab emirate.[10] Thus, Weizmann had continued to believe in the pledge of the Mandate as originally designated,[11] and accordingly, he told Deedes further "of a Jewish company which desired to do some business in TransJordania." According to Weizmann, "every obstacle" had been placed in the Jewish businessman's way:

> For a year a certain political officer in Trans-Jordania has been preaching the doctrine that no Jew could ever be allowed there as the Arabs are definitely hostile. The same . . . officer . . . a violent anti-Semite and one of the patrons of the Arab delegation here, when challenged to explain how he could carry on anti-Zionist

propaganda and still be in the service of HMG which has adopted the Zionist policy, replied . . . that he hoped . . . if he stayed long enough . . . he might contribute to a reversal of this policy.[12]

A few days later, Deedes sent a "secret" communication to young Shuchkburgh (later a high British official influential in the "handling of Colonel Mac-Kereth's identity-card campaign to quash illegal Arab immigration). While Deedes agreed with Weizmann on some issues, he would "save" the Zionists from themselves:

> The national home in Palestine has to be built up with Jews . . . the best that can be found. . . . I am perfectly well aware that the Zionist organization in Europe is placed in very great difficulties [viz. the pogroms] and has great pressure put upon it to allow immigrants to enter, but . . . it [is] the business of the administration . . . to save the Zionists from this very pressure,[*] and . . . the day will come when they will be grateful for what I consider our greater wisdom and foresight.[13]

The year 1922 brought not only the illegal separation of Transjordan from "Palestine"—in addition, the policy of the "Churchill White Paper" was initiated. While continuing to declare "A Jewish National Home in Palestine," where "The Jewish people will be . . . as of right and not on sufferance," now the new policy introduced the mechanism of the "economic capacity of the country at the time to absorb new arrivals."[14] From that time, the official British explanation of policy regarding Jewish immigration was that it "was conducted solely according to the capacity of the country to absorb new arrivals."[15] Thus, in 1922, "the first steps were taken towards concentrating the effective control of immigration . . . ," instituting strict measures which were "a real deterrent" against Jewish immigration. Subsequently, according to the Immigration Memorandum, the Jews resorted to "subterfuges," but when many of the "so-called middle-class" Jews "discovered that life was also difficult in Palestine . . . these people returned to Poland and the flow became a dribble."[16]

Because of the general depression in 1926, Government withheld immigration certificates from qualified Jewish immigrants, including "applicants who claimed to have 500 pounds and . . . all relatives of the working and lower middle-class of 18 to 35 years of age. . . ."[17] (This was the same period in which the British rushed apparently unlimited "blank passes" to the northern borders, to accommodate "Syrian countrymen" wishing to leave the "troubles" in Syria.) By 1927, "the situation grew worse" for the British; despite the fact that, according to the British Immigration Memorandum, "the Palestine Zionist Executive had recognized the necessity for reducing immigration and had not in fact utilized the greater part of the Labour Schedule allotted to them . . . ," the "number of certificates"—Jewish entrants—was reduced "to an absolute minimum."[18]

---

*The recent mode of thought among a group of diplomats and Western commentators—"How to save Israel in Spite of Herself"—is remarkably similar.

In 1928, the British found that the restrictions "were accepted in practice by neither the Jewish population nor the Zionist Executive."

> Almost every case of refusal led to an appeal . . . and the decision of the Chief Immigration Officer rejecting an application overruled.

So the Government "abandoned . . . all the new conditions but a new minimum of 1000 pounds for A (1) immigrants was adopted in place of the earlier one of 500 pounds and the more recent one of 2000 pounds."[19]

Throughout the ten-year period between 1921 and 1931 the Immigration memoranda referred exclusively to "Jewish Agency" and "Zionist organization" matters, which clearly established that the focus was indeed limited to Jews.[20] In 1928, the Palestine Zionist Executive made the following request:

> Powers of the Palestine Government to deport a Jewish immigrant from Palestine (under Article VIII of the Immigration Ordinance) should be cancelled, and . . . Jews entering Palestine should be treated not as foreigners, but as citizens who have returned to their country of origins. . . . The government would escape . . . injustice . . . [of] decisions based on a false conception of the facts. . . .[21]

The Chief Secretary, Sir Harry Luke, who in 1921 had been "Commissioner, Jaffa Riots,"[22] reacted to the Zionists in a "confidential" letter to Leopold Amery, Principal Secretary of State for the Colonies. Luke "cannot subscribe to this contention." Although "No doubt in the majority of cases, such an attitude would be justified," Luke warned of "some Jews who have ulterior political objects, and this Government must reserve their right of deportation, in emergency."

As for the Zionists' plea, that those Jews allotted under the "labor immigration schedule" who were "without means" might be relieved of the substantial "payment of emigration fees" for Jewish immigrants, Chief Secretary Luke "could not . . . defend" the "sacrifice of revenue which would be involved."[23]

However, despite the British Government's obvious annoyance at the "abuses" and "subterfuges" resorted to by the Jewish refugees and other immigrant undesirables into the Jewish National Home—such as "Jewish professional men and women"[24]—no Jewish immigrant or condition of Jewish immigration was found to be described as "illegal" before 1931, in any of the reports or official correspondence in Western Palestine.

The government had in fact treated the Jewish immigrants as foreigners throughout, instituting new restrictions against Jewish immigration on the heels of every broad-scaled Arab attack against Jews, a convoluted breach of the Mandate. However, the actual use of the term "illegal" apparently was not introduced until after the Hope Simpson Report of 1930. In 1931, it was first applied tentatively, as a general term to *all* "persons in Palestine *illegally.*"*[25] But by 1933 the British record, by inverted logic, was focused upon "illegal," or "illicit," entry of "Jewish-settlers," of "Jews."

*Emphasis added.

One 1933 report, in self-contradiction, noted that of "illicit and unrecorded immigration into Palestine, *mostly* of Jews" (totaling 2,000 by official account) *only half* were "Jewish."*[26]

The formalization of the British conception of "illegal Jewish immigration" had evolved through the series of statutory regulation and restrictions drawn up by the Palestine Mandatory administration in submission to Arab acts of terror, Arab leadership's demands, and the bias of British officials. All were directed against immigration of Jews into the "Jewish National Home"—against the Mandate.

While questions had been raised by the League of Nations Permanent Mandates Commission because of the evidence of broad-scale Arab illegal immigration, there never was anything resembling an *Arab* quota, nor would any category exist within the "system" to put such a quota. When illegal immigration was acted upon by Government, that action took the form of deductions from the *Jewish* quota for *Jewish* "illegal" immigration only.

The concept of Jews as "illegals" in their "Home" was never universally accepted, however. In 1936, the Conference of Protestant and Catholic Leaders in New York, "representative of nearly all religious denominations" and "Labor leaders," declared that the British government must uphold "its covenanted pledges to the Jewish people and to the world. . . ." It was "the profound conviction of Christian America" that the British

> rescind its illegal, unjust, and indefensible partition of Palestine, to restore Transjordania to its proper place as part of the Palestine territory, and throw it open to Jewish settlement.[27]

In a concurrent report by United States senators, "The Report on Palestine," Senator Hastings stated that

> There is room for several hundred thousand more Jews in Palestine this side of the Jordan, and several million additional Jewish fugitives could be provided for if they could cross the Jordan and be allowed to settle in the breezy and fertile uplands between it and the desert.[28]

The White Paper

It was the enactment of decrees strictly curtailing the Jews' immigration into Western Palestine that was "illegal" and in violation of Article 6 of the Mandate, according to the League of Nations Permanent Mandates Commission. That Commission protested the 1939 British White Paper in June 1939 as a violation of the Palestine Mandate and its interpretations during the entire period of British administration. The Commission's Report in August confirmed the four-member majority opinion—that the newest and harshest restrictions laid down by the

*Emphasis added.

White Paper, along with its stated recognition of imminent Arab rule, ran counter to the British Mandatory obligation of fulfillment of the Jewish National Home.[29]

President Franklin Roosevelt too questioned the legality of the White Paper's policy, although the State Department supported it. Roosevelt wrote,

Frankly, I do not see how the British Government reads into the original Mandate or into the White Paper of 1922 any policy that would limit Jewish immigration.

At that time he believed the new British policy to be "something that we cannot give approval to by the United States."[30]

The United States' policy, however, never reflected strongly Roosevelt's sentiments of that date.[31] The outbreak of the war in September 1939 and its subsequent pressures would result in a perpetuation of the American policy of concerned disregard that had been evidenced at Evian in 1938.

By 1939, Jewish "illegal" immigrants to the Jewish-settled area of Western Palestine had not only been conceptualized and actions increased against them, but they had become an open wound to the British.

Illegal immigration [is] a dirty, sordid, crooked business,

according to a "confidential" Colonial Office communication directed to British consular corps stationed in the United States. To the Palestine Government, "illegal" immigration had become synonymous with "Jewish" immigration. It was particularly unbecoming, the official memo observed, since it was the Palestinian Jews who had until then adhered to the law even in the face of anti-Jewish attacks and uprisings by the Arabs. Despite the "idea . . . that they are justified . . . by virtue of some super-legal higher morality," because of "the persecutions in Greater Germany and the desperate plight" of "many European Jews," the document asserted further, ". . . they, like so many other lawbreakers . . . fail to realize that what they are doing is fundamentally anti-social—as anti-social as the German persecution of which they complain."[32]

So committed to that strange and perverse analogy had the prevailing British sentiment become that even before the White Paper had been formally implemented, Government officials were invoking it. In its determination to prevent Jewish refugees from succeeding in their escape to the Jewish National Home and "offending the Arabs," the British Foreign Office cabled an order to its ambassador in Berlin in March of 1939; the British envoy was to inform the German government about the means of escape being utilized by Jews, and to ask the German "Authorities" to "discourage such travel. . . ."[33]

Not all of British officialdom was in accord with the Arab appeasement spelled out in the White Paper. In the Parliamentary debate of the new policy on May 22, Winston Churchill, soon to be the most influential of Britain's Prime Ministers, defended the Balfour Declaration once again; he had done so before the Palestine Royal Commission in 1937, and he had so done in 1920, just before he himself was, paradoxically, instrumental in the decision to amputate three-fourths of Palestine from the Jewish National Home and transform it into an Arab emirate.

"I should feel personally embarrassed," Churchill said, "in the most acute manner if I lent myself, by silence or inaction, to what I must regard as an act of repudiation." Churchill branded one particular White Paper declaration, that Arabs must agree to any Jewish immigration after the initial five years, as "the breach";

> there is the violation of the pledge; there is the abandonment of the Balfour Declaration; there is the end of the vision, of the hope, of the dream. . . .
>
> What will our potential enemies think? What will those who have been stirring up these Arab agitators think? Will they not be encouraged by our confession of recoil? Will they not be tempted to say: "They're on the run again. This is another Munich," and be the more stimulated in their aggression by these very unpleasant reflections which they make? . . .
>
> May not this be a contributory factor . . . now—by which our potential enemies may be emboldened to take some irrevocable action . . . ?
>
> We urge that the reputation for fidelity of execution, strict execution, of public contracts, is a shield and buckler which the British Empire, however it may arm, cannot dispense with and cannot desire to dispense with.
>
> Never was the need for fidelity and firmness more urgent than now. You are not going to found and forge the fabric of a grand alliance to resist aggression, except by showing continued examples of your firmness in carrying out, even under difficulties, and in the teeth of difficulties, the obligations into which you have entered.
>
> . . . the policy which you think is a relief and an easement you will find afterwards you will have to retrieve, in suffering and greater exertions than those we are making.[34]

Others in Parliament shared Churchill's outrage. In the debate a day later, Member of Parliament Herbert Morrison reminded Government of the aid being given by Hitler and Mussolini to the upper-class Arab leaders in Palestine[35] ever since British Prime Minister Neville Chamberlain had shown his partiality to "those gentlemen." By giving the Arabs the veto over Jewish immigration, as the White Paper proposed, the British were also giving the Axis that veto. Morrison pleaded with his colleagues to

> stop this evil thing being done. . . . I ask them to remember the sufferings of these Jewish people all over the world. I ask them to remember that Palestine, of all places in the world, was certainly the place where they had some right to expect not to suffer or to have restrictions imposed upon them. Look at the extent of the country—this little patch of territory. Transjordan has been taken away.[36]

Even Neville Chamberlain apparently had not remained unaffected by the foreboding of Nazism. "I believe the persecution arose out of two motives," he wrote in a letter to a sister:

A desire to rob the Jews of their money and a jealousy of their superior cleverness. No doubt Jews aren't a loveable people; I don't care about them myself—but that is not sufficient to explain the Pogrom.[37]

But the White Paper was a *reinforcement* of Chamberlain's policy of appeasement; it had one year earlier culminated in the agreement in Munich, sacrificing Czechoslovakia to the Nazis to gain what Chamberlain proclaimed triumphantly on his return to Britain as "Peace in our time!"[38]

By similar tactics in Western Palestine the British hoped to avert further Arab terrorist violence and disruption of the sort fomented periodically from the beginning of the Mandate, and incessantly reactivated after 1936. With the implementation of the White Paper, the "Arab Revolt" would die down. Even some of the more militant Arabs were privately encouraged by what Arab writer and representative George Antonius called "a substantial advance towards the recognition of Arab rights" and the Jews called "a surrender to Arab terrorism."[39]

Nevertheless, the White Paper was not acceptable to the Arab Higher Committee, "directed from Beirut." The Committee issued a hostile statement, including additional demands such as an immediate halt of Jewish immigration and the right to question the authenticity as "Palestinian" of every Jew entering the country after 1918 if Jewish immigration were to be allowed to continue at all.[40]

The White Paper was approved, by a vote of 268 to 179. (The majority usually expected was 248; it had declined to 89 votes.) The supposedly pivotal Permanent Mandates Commission of the League of Nations, which had protested the White Paper in August, was the last chance to reverse the policy statement. But the war intervened in the few days before that commission was to review the matter.[41] The meeting was to have taken place on September 8; Germany marched on Poland September 1, and Britain declared war on Germany September 3.

England's pledge to observe the tenets of the internationally mandated Jewish homeland in Palestine was unalterably betrayed by the British enforcement of the 1939 White Paper, whereby soon, "only if the Arabs are prepared to acquiesce in it," would "immigration" to "the Jewish National Home" be permitted. In fact that acquiescence to the Arabs was inherent in the White Paper itself. So restrictive was this newest in a series of political deviations that while millions of Jewish refugees would have "swum" to Palestine[42] to escape the Nazis, the White Paper's rigid qualifications prohibited most Jews from entering Palestine.

Thus even the relatively tiny quota for Jewish settlers—10,000 a year for five years, with a bonus of 25,000 more refugees "as soon as the High Commissioner is satisfied that adequate provision for their maintenance is ensured"—was, tragically, not exhausted at the war's end.[43] The places left unfilled resulted in several convenient British distortions: for example, in the Department of Migration Report for 1938, *the unfilled quota was officially interpreted as an indicator that the government's allotment of Jewish places had been ample for their needs.*[44]

By 1945, approximately six million Jews had been systematically slaughtered. Of the Jewish refugees who had reached Palestine, 51,000 were allowed to stay, less than one percent. In all the years of the British Mandatory control, roughly 400,000 Jews had been allowed into the "small notch" of the Middle East that was allocated to the "Jewish National Home," and all 400,000 of those were in only the Jewish-settled area of the "patch" called Western Palestine. Today, little more than that Jewish-settled area—which is Israel—within the "patch" holds almost *four million* souls, with room remaining for countless others.

MacDonald's calculation for the White Paper, which originally called for 450,000 Jewish immigrants over a ten-year period (as of his expectations in July of 1938), had been initially cut to 153,000 over ten years. Eventually it was whittled down to the number approved by the Arabs. Foreign Office Eastern Department head Charles Baxter defended

> the moral right of the Arabs to have some say in . . . admission of aliens into their country.[45]

The injustice to the Jews in the Jewish-settled area of Western Palestine had been buried. Here again was the myth of the "Arab-native" majority crowded out by the "alien" Jew. Now, however, more than a mere bias born of misconception: the myth had been incorporated as policy. That British policy, by its blinkered adherence to the popularized Arab propaganda "justice," would propagate the explosions that reverberate today in the name of the "Palestinian Problem."

Palestinian Peoples and World War II: Immigration Controlled and Uncontrolled

If ever an argument for the necessity of a Jewish state becomes pointedly prescient, it is during a review of the actions taken to prevent that state and what happened to the Jews who tried to get to the homeland reserved for them.

In weighing the Arab efforts and ability to prevent the Jews' rescue because there was not yet a state, several fundamental and startling propositions become self-evident. Had Arab illegal immigration and in-migration into the truncated "Jewish National Home" been checked, the actual smaller number of "existing" Arabs in the Jewish-settled area and that virtual unlimited "absorptive capacity" for Jews would have been given official recognition. Jews would have been immigrating in greater numbers and the Arab "natural" population would have been kept to only its true small number.

A larger "facilitated" Jewish population and a smaller, actual "existing" Arab population growth undoubtedly would have resulted in a Jewish majority before the Second World War. That in turn, according to the Mandate's implications and the United States' declaration in 1919,[46] would have resulted in "a Jewish State as soon as it is in fact a Jewish State"—in other words, *when there was a Jewish majority.* Thus by the time of Hitler's offer to the world of Europe's Jews, there might have existed *some place* on earth for them to go.

As the war progressed, Jewish "restraint" was strained thin. While the doomed Jews were frantically fighting to get into substandard ships surreptitiously headed for the Jewish National Home, Palestine officials were devising additional measures to keep Jewish refugees out. Jews were "only racial refugees," one British officer decided.[47] The White Paper was stringently enforced with no modification despite the news of wholesale persecution and slaughter of the Jews. The policy adamantly remained that

> His Majesty's Government are determined to check illegal immigration, and further preventive measures are being adopted. The numbers of any Jewish illegal immigrants who, despite these measures, may succeed in coming into the country and cannot be deported will be deducted from the yearly quotas.[48]

But it was only *Jewish* immigrants who would be "checked." The *Arab* illegal immigrants streamed in by the thousands meanwhile. Many thousands more would swarm into the country to reap the benefits of the "war effort," as the later official *Anglo-American Survey of Palestine* reported—with the knowledge, consent, and *even at the official order* of the British Government.[49]

In July 1940, however, when the Palestine High Commissioner learned that Polish military personnel were being shipped to Palestine, he directed the Colonial Office to "suggest that only non-Jews be regarded as acceptable," adding that "Polish authorities would be willing to arrange that only non-Jews should come to Palestine."[50]

Despite the Palestinian Jews' bitterness, expressed in a "few" individual violent reprisals against Arab and British hostility, according to the *Anglo-American Survey,*[51]

> With the outbreak of war, the Jews unanimously agreed to put aside their differences with British policy and demonstrated their loyalty to the cause of the democracies.

The isolated few "Jewish terrorist acts ceased completely and the illegal broadcasting station which had previously been operating for some months closed down."[52] The Jewish Agency had "issued an appeal calling on all Jews in Palestine to close their ranks and offer their full assistance to Great Britain."[53]

As past experience had taught the British, the Jews' cooperation with the Allies could be taken for granted. They were not likely to further the Nazi cause, their cooperation with the British until then had been forthcoming, and further, the Jewish "world constituency," particularly in America, was being exposed as impotent against the victimization of its brothers in Europe.

If the Arab world was dissatisfied with near-total submission by the British, the Jews were traumatized. The British had been assured by Joseph Kennedy in April 1939 that they "ought not to over-estimate" the one community which might present problems, "Jewish influence in the United States."[54] That fact was central to many British officials concerned with "placating the Arabs." As one British official, the minister in Egypt, remarked, "The Jews? Let us be practical. They are anybody's game these days." Jewish immigration should cease forth-

352 THE POLITICAL INFLUENCE OF TRADITION

with, suggested the Egyptian-based envoy, and "the pro-Jew element" of British
Parliament could be brought "into line by pleading what is practicable as opposed
to what is desirable."[55] According to the British historian Nicholas Bethell, in his
study of the events leading to the White Paper, the Foreign Office replied that,
in general, "we sympathize with all he says."[56]

British Foreign Secretary Lord Halifax communicated similar views of the
Jewish war effort in his December 1939 letter to Chaim Weizmann:

> While appreciating the Jewish offers of assistance . . . it must not be overlooked
> that these offers were made unconditionally and were welcomed on that footing.

Lord Halifax disregarded Weizmann's alarm at the deadly effect of the White
Paper's virtual cessation of immigration, and its subjugation of Jews in the
"Jewish National Home" into a permanently oppressed *dhimmi* minority at the
whim of the Arab world.[57] Halifax assured Weizmann that by "putting our whole
energy into a life-and-death struggle with Nazi Germany . . . and by ridding
Europe of the present German regime," Halifax hoped "to render a supreme
service to the Jewish people."[58]

The Jews would soon be driven into frantic realization that what was called
a "supreme service to the Jewish people"—allied victory—would be celebrated
too late to matter, as one 1941 Warsaw ghetto report grimly foretold:

> There are pessimists who are afraid the English will finally arrive, declaring, "We
> have conquered. . . . "—to our graves.[59]

Nonetheless, nearly 26,000 "Palestinian Jews served in the British forces,"
according to the British War Secretary in 1945[60]—about half the total number
of Jews, in fact, who actually managed to get to the Jewish-settled area of
Western Palestine during the war. The number of Jews who served the British
Allied cause would have been larger—134,000 Jews had volunteered[61]—but in
an inexplicable gesture of "evenhandedness," the Palestinian Jews' enlistment
was "held down to the Arab rate" of enlistment, which the American Christian
Palestine Committee called "a rather peculiar service to the war effort on the
part of the Palestine Administration." That limit was finally modified, however,
as the "steadily worsening" military situation in the Middle East, the "continued pressure by Jewish volunteers," and the minimal number of Arab enlistees (according to the War Secretary, "9041 Arabs" in all) made the recruiting
of Jews a necessity.[62]

The most "even-handed" of British Reports—even those that ultimately
judged Jewish existence in the midst of Arabs as provocation "responsible" for
Arab terrorism—took for granted the restraint of the Palestinian Jews. One
report noted that

> . . . during the troubles the Jews have behaved themselves extraordinarily well;
> that they have received a great deal of provocation from the Arabs and that, as
> a whole they have not countered that provocation; . . .[63]

Another report observed:

> . . . indeed, throughout the whole series of outbreaks, and under very great provocation, they [the Jews] have shown a notable capacity for discipline and self-restraint.[64]

Even the British official who had—through some perverse logic—determined that the Jews' "illegal" attempts to get to the sanctuary were "as anti-social" as the Nazis' persecution of Jews, was himself forced to mention their "law-abiding" ways. It was not for lack of manpower or ability, as the *Palestine Royal Commission Report* had observed:[65]

> Though it is only on rare occasions that any Jew has resorted to the use of unauthorized firearms, we were informed that, in round numbers the Jews could place in the field 10,000 combatants, trained and armed, with a second line of 40,000.

General Dill, Commander of the British Forces in Palestine, had assured his superior in 1937 that the Royal Commission Report with its then-proposed partition plan, might stir up "armed rebellion" and "political assassinations immediately" among the Arabs, but would bring no serious trouble from the Jews. While "Jewish resistance" would be "strenuous," because the Report so unevenly truncated the Jewish National Home and undercut "Zionist aspirations,"[66] the possibility of Jewish "armed resistance" was "unlikely." If the characteristic "Jewish restraint" shown in "reprisals" for Arab attacks did "weaken" still, Jews would "turn every political stone to undermine Report but unlikely to use force."[67]

British Foreign Officer Charles Baxter similarly assured anxious British officials that there was no danger of a Palestinian Jewish protest similar to the Arabs' violence. Despite the known imminent disaster for the barred prospective Jewish immigrants in Europe, despite the assumption that American Jewry was a formidable opponent, Baxter did "not think that the Jews would be so unwise" as to defy the government White Paper policy.[68]

The Jewish Dilemma

But the British had not reckoned with the reaction of the Jews whose dreams they had given new hope. To the worldwide Jewish panic at the unremitting persecution and terror both in European and in the lesser-known Arab-Muslim communities was added a desperation; that desperation was remnant of the decades of enthusiasm and tenacity of a people finally within reach of regaining political freedom in the state they had nurtured relentlessly. There nobody could any more call the Jews "infidel" or "dhimmi" or "kike" or "zhid"—there an epidemic of dread diseases or a drought need not bring fear of Jews' bearing the blame. There a change in power would not prompt anxiety over the question whether the new regime was "against Jews."

British Member of Parliament Leopold Amery described the Palestinian Jews' dilemma passionately in the House of Commons debate of the White Paper:

> As for the Jews . . . all the hope that they had been encouraged to hold . . . are to be dashed to the ground, all their amazing efforts wasted. . . . That is to be their reward for loyalty, for patience. . . .

Amery noted ironically that the Jews' reward for *"almost unbelievable self-restraint"** against the consistent onslaught of Arab atrocity and pillage was to render Palestinian Jews a "permanent minority" in the land that, "such as it is today, they have created it."[69]

From the enforcement of the White Paper to the end of the British Mandatory administration, the Palestinian Jews, while fighting at the side of the Allies against the Axis during the war, would simultaneously defy the British actions intended to paralyze the Palestinian Jewish community.

Different historians date the change in the Jewish attitude at different moments; one incident or another seemed to suggest the catalyst. Nicholas Bethell, in *The Palestine Triangle,* traces the White Paper's enactment in 1939 as the "blow from which" the Palestinian Jews' "friendly attitude to Britain" had "never recovered," and Bethell notes that the "first serious act of anti-British violence" by the underground Jewish resistance, Irgun Zvai Leumi, took place in August 1939, four months after the White Paper was implemented. The Irgun, a small guerrilla band, was condemned for its acts of violent reprisal thereafter by all the Jewish representative agencies. Irgun would later be denounced as "extremist" and "terrorist."†

At the same time it was pointed out that past instances of Arab terrorism had been rewarded by new concessions at the expense of the Jews. As I. F. Stone wrote, it was not strange

> that some misguided Jewish youths have said to themselves, "Maybe we'd have better luck if we tried those tactics, too?"[70]

There were "one or two occasions" when it was said that "The *Jewish* terrorist groups . . . *copied* Arab Terrorism, . . . especially at [the Arab village] Deir Yassin"‡ in 1948, after the Israel War of Independence had begun in November 1947, and the Arab world had declared a "war of extermination" against the Jews and the United Nations resolution favoring a Jewish state. Reports of Jewish retaliation were broadcast in "exaggerated" accounts that

---

*Emphasis added.

†It was that group—reacting against Arab terror and the brutality of British indifference to the Holocaust—which Arab propaganda would later pounce upon. It would be alleged that the PLO (Palestinian Liberation Organization) had emulated the Irgun, an attempt to justify the PLO terrorist acts throughout the world that had been the tradition among the amalgam of peoples in Palestine for generations, and a diversion from the fact that the PLO was the modern offshoot of Muftism, which the Irgun had been founded to quash.

‡Emphasis added.

"helped to create the atmosphere" to "encourage flight" of the Arabs, wrote the Reverend James Parkes in his historical analysis, *Whose Land?*[71] Since then the West has often adopted the theme of Arab propaganda, citing "Deir Yassin" as the factor by which the world may equate Arab terrorism with "Jewish terrorism." "The Jews were terrorists too" is the not uncommon deduction. In another part of a statement noted earlier here, Albert Memmi, the Tunisian-born writer, answered that propaganda in his open letter to the Libyan strongman and terrorist supporter Muammar Qaddafy:

> The error which may have been made at Deir Yassine [*sic*] is constantly being thrown in our faces. Ah, but we have undergone a hundred Deir Yassines, a thousand Deir Yassines! . . . at the hand of Arab people; yet the world had never been upset over it! (Just as I was correcting the proofs of this book, we learned of the massacre at Qiryat Shemona . . . those unfortunate people machine-gunned in their beds, those children thrown out the window were all North African refugees! "Arab Jews!" . . .)
>
> But what do I need with these historical references and reminders? My own grandfather and father still lived in terror of the blows on the head which any Arab passerby could give them at any time. . . . Now please don't tell me that all that is the result of Zionism. That's another myth.[72]

The Jews of the Jewish-settled area of Western Palestine sought, with desperate zeal, to save lives and to countermand the Nazi death verdict as it was being inflicted upon the Jewish people and their tiny country through the operations of the British immigration policy, which bowed cravenly to Arab pressure. The very premises of justice and mercy must be affronted by the historical distortion, the psychological warp, and the Machiavellian propaganda that could give birth to the following twisted perceptions: that these Palestinian Jews should be equated with the terrorists of the PLO; that the Jewish settlers in Palestine should be perceived as "dispossessors" in the Jewish-settled area of Western Palestine; that the terror of the Arab PLO is "justice" while Jewish resistance to such terror is "injustice"; or that the expulsion of the Jews from the "West Bank" in 1929 and the Arab policy against their return is any different from pogroms in Europe or apartheid in South Africa.

The acceptance of such perverted perceptions may be traceable to any one or a combination of several factors: badly weighted double standards, willful refusal to examine the facts, racial or religious prejudice, reliance upon misunderstanding and misinformation, or, more prevalently, inadequate information and basic lack of awareness of the facts.

The West's "dependence on Arab oil" is said by some to be wholly responsible for such cynical selective perception. The mighty have unquestionably coveted oil power in the last four decades. Their zeal was apparently even more ardent than commonly known. At least in two instances in the 1940s, the Arabs, either under the sting of military inability to defeat the Israelis and the economic compulsion to reduce the burden of military preparedness, or suffering from overwhelming indebtedness, gave an indication of subordinating their inbred hostility to the pressures of necessity and reality. Perhaps only remote possibilities, they were not unprecedented: it had after all been once done, when Emir Feisal and Chaim Weizmann signed their agreement in 1917.* But in later cases, it seems one or another of the "great powers" intervened to bolster existing enmities and disregarded the actual best interests of the region.

As an example, although United States oil companies[73] had begun exporting oil from Saudi Arabia in the 1930s,[74] that underpopulated, underdeveloped terrain remained impoverished during World War II. Thus, to pay his debts in the early 1940s, owed primarily to Britain, Saudi King Ibn Saud reluctantly considered the personally repugnant possibility of borrowing money from Zionist sources, with British support. Ibn Saud might become "boss of bosses" in the Arab world, and would work out, with Chaim Weizmann, a "compromise" settlement of the Palestine dispute, the British assured him.[75] United States State Department officials were extremely upset at the proposal: the head of the Department's Near Eastern affairs stressed the negative result of a "Jewish ascendancy" —a Jewish majority—in Palestine. He argued that "Zionists could extend their influence and activities outside Palestine," suggesting the imposition of "economic imperialism . . . ."[76] As Elie Kedourie observed, the words "economic imperialism, catchwords of Marxism, strike an incongruous note in the memoranda" of a "high State Department official."[77]

Although Undersecretary of State Sumner Welles and President Roosevelt were generally "more enthusiastic" about "Arab-Jewish detente," the Jewish loan was discredited.[78] Waving aside a possible Arab-Jewish rapprochement, State Department officials nonetheless drafted a letter from Roosevelt that gave Saudi Arabia full assurance that no settlement in Palestine would be adopted without first consulting "great and good friend" Ibn Saud and seeking his "agreement."[79] State Department officials were by that time[80] seemingly preoccupied with wooing and winning for themselves the predominant role in Saudi affairs. As Professor Kedourie interpreted it, ". . . if only British influence could be eliminated, a warm and exclusive American-Saudi special relationship" might prevail.[81]

Another example of blocking the pursuit of Arab-Israeli peace concerns the little-known but apparently strenuous British action to prevent militarily devastated Arab leaders from the possibility of dealing with Israel after the Arab world's defeat in 1948. Secret documents of 1949 reveal that British diplomats in some key Arab states had been told of the defeated leader's inclinations to discuss peace with Israel. They were discouraged by high Government officials, on the theory that Britain could lose its dominant ground if a "neutral" Arab-Israel "bloc" were to diverge from perceived British interests.[82]

In a "top-secret" note from Ernest Bevin, then Secretary of State for Foreign

*See copy in Appendix IV.

Affairs, there were no such rhetorical red herrings as "economic imperialism"; the secret nature of the document was apparently sufficient to cloak British priorities from detection and criticism in pro-Israel circles. According to Bevin, Israel must not come "to the point of dominating them [the Arabs] economically and so politically, and thus perhaps imposing her own views of neutrality on the Arab world." Were the Arabs to differ with Britain under the circumstances of independence foreseen as a consequence of such a "neutral bloc," there would no longer be an Arab-Israeli dispute to divert Arabs from Britain's assertion of its ambitions in the Middle East. As Bevin stated it,

> It would be too high a price to pay for the friendship of Israel to jeopardize, by estranging the Arabs, either the base in Egypt or the Middle Eastern oil.[83]

Having initiated, developed, and profited from the subsequent oil boom, the great powers had themselves created their own "oil-dependency." But the "dependency" that really occupied them was the actual dependency of those Arab leaders who were anti-Communist and who well understood that *they* would remain dependent upon continued Western development and patronage. It was the *prospect* of *Arab*—Saudi in particular—*dependency exclusively* on the United States, or Britain, or France, that motivated the apparently frenzied behavior. Had any other influence intruded—even the imaginary Zionist "expansion outside Palestine" warned against by some in the United States, or the "neutral bloc" feared by Britain, reasons given for quashing perhaps improbable but not impossible peace moves—Britain and the United States each feared that they might lose footing in the race.

In both British and American instances, the exaggeration of Arab influence and the definition of Arab desires were apparently dictated not by the real *Arab* desire but by what the Western powers shortsightedly believed to be their own individual best interest. The Arabs were told what, or what not, to want.[84]

The fact that oil was later a factor to exacerbate the Arab-Jewish enmity, and that much which is assumed on the subject of oil-power is not really true, are topics for greater speculation and exploration outside the focus of this volume. Many of the questions raised here have been addressed elsewhere.[85]

However, as this book has revealed, Arab demands were acted upon by the British *before* the United States began exporting oil in 1938. From the review of immigration, first Turkish and then British systems, the direct causal relationship between Arab violence in Palestine and official reactions against Jewish immigration has become clear. Turkish and then British mandatory government solicitation of the Arabs' favor had begun long before Arab oil became a tool, even before "Arab nationalism" was, as T. E. Lawrence described it, "raised up." By the time the leaders of the Arab world were insupportably given what amounted to veto power over what happened in "Palestine"—an area separated from the "Arab states," and internationally assigned to Britain as the Jewish National Home—British patronage was already axiomatic.

What else becomes evident is that, in the Anglo-American scuffling for prime position, the malignant result of the Mandate's inversion in Palestine went overlooked or ignored.

Reinhold Niebuhr touched on the "untouchable" in writing of Jewish immigration laws during World War II:

> . . . When I say the most "generous" immigration laws, I mean, of course, "generous" only within terms of political exigencies. It must be observed that the liberals of the Western World maintain a conspiracy of silence on this point. They do not dare to work for immigration laws generous enough to cope with the magnitude of the problem which the Jewish race faces. *They are afraid of political repercussions, tacitly acknowledging that their theories do not square with the actual facts.* Race prejudice, the intolerance of a dominant group toward a minority group, is a more powerful and more easily aroused force than they dare admit.*[86]

Some in the British Service rejected Chamberlain's delusion of appeasement as solution. In 1938, when Jewish "guerrilla bands" were organized "from among the 'extremists' in the Revisionist party" to defend against the intensifying Arab terror, "manifestos condemning" the Jewish defense were "issued" by the Palestinian Jewish establishment. But as an exhaustive study of "Palestine" pointed out,

> the Jewish terrorists [*sic*] received moral support from some Britishers.[87]

Among those supporters was Colonel Josiah Wedgewood, who wrote to "the President of the Jewish ex-officers association at Tel-Aviv" that

> I am afraid that merely asking for justice . . . is useless. In my experience, especially in times of difficulty, governments give way only to action. . . .[88]

The Palestinian Jews, even those who denounced the guerrilla movements and exhorted the Jews to fight with Britain and its allies in the war, had been mortally wounded by the White Paper, and the moderate Jewish majority felt the pain. In the wake of the first bitter demonstrations by Jews against the White Paper policy in 1939, a British policeman was killed. David Ben Gurion, then Chairman of the Jewish Agency, and personally opposed to the actions of the Irgun, nonetheless revealed his own exasperation; in his significant response to the threat by a British general that, "if rioting occurred again and . . . if blood were shed, it would be on the heads of the Jews," Ben-Gurion answered,

> We deeply deplore and condemn unreservedly the fatal shooting of a British constable. With all due deference I must, however, take exception to your statement this morning that the blood which may be shed will be on the heads of the Jews. . . . *The Jewish demonstration of yesterday marked the beginning of Jewish resistance to the disastrous policy now proposed by His Majesty's Government.* The

*Emphasis added.

Jews will not be intimidated into surrender even if their blood be shed. In our submission the responsibility for what may occur in this country in the course of enforcing the new policy will rest entirely on the Government.*[89]

From that time, when in Austria, Germany, and Czechoslovakia a million Jews had already been "crushed under the heels of Nazism,"[90] and the British government was informing to the Nazis about the boatloads of Jewish refugees headed toward the Jewish National Home, the Palestinian Jews were totally dichotomized: until the war's bitter end, on one hand they were earnestly fighting for the Allies, and on the other hand, they found every conceivable means they could to rescue the "illegal Jewish immigrants" who were anyway being deducted from the shrunken, Arab-approved quota. They bought land in devious ways when the White Paper's land restrictions were published in 1940, prohibiting most sales of land from Arabs to Jews. By 1944, if Arabs sold lands at all,

> Jews paid between $1,000 and $1,100 per acre in [Western] Palestine, mostly for arid or semi-arid land; in the same year, rich black soil in the state of Iowa was selling for about $110 per acre.[91]

Since Jewish-related economic development was considerably diminished as Jewish immigration and land purchase and settlement were curtailed, the potential Arab labor market that had attracted Arab illegal immigration was depressed. It was, however, to be only temporary. The government and private industry would find the need for Arab employment important to the booming war industry. The policy was: jobs for immigrant Arabs, and bullets fired on the disembarking refugee Jews. As High Commissioner Wauchope had evaluated it during the Arab riots of 1936 and 1937, "in the present circumstances" the Arab immigrants' presence may be "undesirable" but "next week they may not want to leave the country."

The Arab rebellion was reported to have been "called off" by the Arab leaders upon the deference paid to their demands and the White Paper's passage. Major-General Bernard Montgomery reported that

> This rebellion is now definitely and finally smashed . . . it is not possible for the rebellion to raise its head again on the scale we previously experienced.[92]

Once the violence was quelled, and only occasional assassinations and pillage occurred, the British hoped to gain the sympathies of the Arab world against the Axis. One British officer protested against the organizing of a Jewish Brigade for fear of offending the Arabs, because

> We always have to face up to the difficulty of their [Arabs'] susceptibility to German propaganda, which has been extremely successful.[93]

The Arabs in general, however, and the Mufti in particular, had already been committed to Hitler.

*Emphasis added.

17

"Muftism" and Britain's Contribution to the "Final Solution"

The greatest contemporary hero [in the Arab world] is Hitler.
—John Gunther, *Inside Asia,* 1939

The Arab riots of 1936 in Palestine were carried
out by the Mufti with funds supplied by the Nazis.
—American Christian Palestine
Committee, 1947

The British were apparently prepared to accept
the probable death of thousands of Jews in
enemy territory because of "the difficulties of
disposing of any considerable number of Jews
should they be rescued."
—Henry Morgenthau, United States Secretary of
the Treasury to President Roosevelt, 1944

I can assure you that the British forces in Palestine
would not try to oppose or fight the Arabs,
because Britain is a real friend of the Arabs.
—Fadel al-Jamali, Iraqi Foreign
Minister, in Cairo, 1948

The one collaboration during the Second World War that has been clearly overlooked was the symbiotic relationship between Muftism and Nazism. In 1920, when Adolf Hitler was still reciting his diatribes in beerhalls,[1] Haj Amin al-Husseini had already fled from Jerusalem to escape from his ten-year sentence for instigating anti-Jewish violence.[2] Five months later he returned by "special pardon," where he would be appointed Grand Mufti of Jerusalem and elected President of the Supreme Muslim Council within the next two years, free to incite the "racial" manifestations of the future with his supporters throughout Palestine.[3]

The Mufti understood that crucial element which the British would tacitly recognize and occasionally acknowledge officially, regardless of Government's frequent apologias and attributions to "displacement" or "nationalism": that only by invoking the deeply rooted religious prejudice of the masses in Palestine—and that with outside agitation—could al-Husseini's and other notable families hope to keep the reins that they enjoyed under the Turks.

As one historian after another has observed, in "Palestine"

> . . . Arab . . . ruling classes . . . can easily inflame the Moslem masses, who add to a religious fanaticism an inborn if latent hatred of the Jew.[4]

In a documented account, "The Arab War Effort," published in 1947[5] by the American Christian Palestine Committee, both the "pre-war links with the Axis" and a country-by-country description of the Arab efforts and collaboration with the Axis forces were traced. The purpose of the Christians' publication was to "reach the general public" with "material which [it] otherwise would almost certainly never" see, the "documented evidence" that

> . . . The [Arab] leaders often cooperated directly with the Axis, . . . *Fascist and Nazi ideologies were not so much imitated as paralleled in the Arab world,* *

where "they fitted into modes of thought already in being and were taken up" by already organized "political organs." These "facts," while not a "revelation" to the Christians' Committee, and while undisputed "in any responsible quarter," were by 1947 being "ignored—as no longer politically relevant." That was "an unfortunate tendency," the Christians' Committee observed. Now

> those peoples have become full-fledged members of the United Nations. Their voices are heard in all international deliberations.

By an "amazing perversion of history," the report observed, "recent" Middle East "discussions omit or slur over" the "Arab collaboration with the Axis," and

> Arab spokesmen [who] believe that the true facts of Arab pro-Nazi activity have been forgotten, . . . are now actually claiming reward for the help which they say the Arabs gave democracies.

Many original documents were reproduced in the American Christian publications, but as the group noted,

> Of the long list of hundreds of Arab agents on the German payroll, only a few are mentioned. Of the numerous cases of sabotage, only a few are recorded. . . . Of the thousands of available documents, fewer than a dozen are published here.[6]

Glubb Pasha, Commander of the Transjordan Arab Legion, reflecting later about the Iraqi revolt of 1941, underscored that evidence:

> The British of course always knew we were going to win the war, but at the time of these operations every Arab was perfectly convinced that Britain was

*Emphasis added.

finished forever, and that it could only be a question of weeks before Germany took over Arabia. The Iraqis were perfectly sure of this or they would not have declared war on us. . . .

In brief, during the six weeks before the fall of Baghdad, every Arab was convinced that we were done for. Every Arab force previously organized by us mutinied and refused to fight for us or faded away in desertions.[7]

In fact, Mufti Haj Amin al-Husseini issued a *fatwa*—"summons to a holy war against *Britain*"* in May 1941.[8] The Mufti's widely heralded proclamation against Britain was declared in Iraq, where he was instrumental in "the pro-Nazi" coup.[9]† Yet the British Government inexplicably was reported by the *Manchester Guardian* several months later to be "readmitting to Palestine former supporters of the Mufti of Jerusalem. It is prepared, apparently, to go to bail for them," the article surmised.[10]

It was the *Jewish immigrants,* attempting to get to Palestine by shiploads at the same time, who were driven off by the Government of Palestine, while, as the *Guardian* put it,

> . . . readmitting former supporters of the Mufti . . . it passes understanding why the victims of Axis brutalities, the shattered fugitives from butcher-states like Roumania, should be thrust back from safety in the home of their race.[11]

The government's justification for considering "wholesale expulsions" of "illegal" Jewish refugees and even "firing on illegal immigrant ships in order to drive them away from Palestinian ports" was set forth in many government communications, discussed later in this chapter.[12] There was, the British claimed, "the possibility of there being agents of the German Government amongst them and the consequent danger to the internal security of Palestine."[13]

Never was a single "German agent" found to justify that fear. Nevertheless, British officialdom put forward such "threats" to defend extreme British actions in forcing shiploads of Jewish refugee families back into the Black Sea,[14] despite the extensive access that British Intelligence gained to information concerning the actual nature of the spy networks in the Middle East.[15]

It was the same double standard by which illegal Arab immigrants' entry into "The Jewish National Home" had been winked at earlier by the British Government, while "Illegal Jewish Immigration" had been considered a "dirty, sordid affair" that had to be prevented by every possible measure, "ignoring the hardship of the individual."

In accordance with that defiance of fairness or reason, while the "threat of enemy agents" among Jewish refugees fleeing from the Nazis was proved to be a "red herring," the reports that "the Arab riots of 1936 in Palestine were carried

---

*Emphasis added.

†See the *fatwa* and examples of original communications between the Mufti and the Nazis in Appendix IX.

out by the Mufti with funds supplied by the Nazis"[16] were smothered. The files of the German High Command in Flensburg, Germany, indicated that

> Only through funds made available by Germany to the Grand Mufti of Jerusalem was it possible to carry out the revolt in Palestine.[17]

The Grand Mufti himself operated at first from headquarters set up in Transjordan, Syria, and Iraq, after he fled Western Palestine at the onset of the revolt he inspired. Then he moved between Teheran and Rome, until November 1941, when he was "established" in Berlin by the Nazis, "with branches organized later in other parts of Germany and Italy"; his "activities"—in espionage, propaganda, establishment of pro-Axis Muslim military units, training of Arabs as Nazi agents, and personal collaboration with Adolf Hitler—have been documented, along with data describing the Nazi collaboration of other *effendi* scions, such as Rasem al-Khalidi, Jamal al-Husseini, Wasef Kamal, and others.[18]

The Grand Mufti of Jerusalem—an inspiration for Arab anti-Jewish "nationalistic" pogroms in Palestine, staunch friend of Hitler and coordinator with Germany in the "final solution" to the "Jewish Problem"—was personally responsible for the concentration camp slaughter of hundreds of thousands of Jews, if not more.[19] (See pages 372–373.)

Among other instances, *when the Mufti learned that the Hungarian government was planning to allow "900 Jewish children" to escape from the Nazis to Palestine, he heatedly demanded they reverse the plan. Because, as the Mufti warned, the Arabs were important to the Nazi effort, his demand was met: the Jewish children were sent instead to the extermination camps in Poland.*[20]

Just before World War II ended, Egypt, Saudi Arabia, Syria, and Lebanon would finally declare war on Germany in February 1945, when Allied victory was assured. Although none participated in "direct military operations," the *formality* of declaring war on the Axis before March 1, 1945, *was required* of any country wanting to join the newly organized United Nations.[21]

Britain had been "deserted" and "betrayed" by the Arabs' "most strategic part of the world by people whose friendship she had strained herself to win," a fact that Britain and the United States had already forgotten, the Christian Committee reminded in 1947. The Committee's New York chairman observed, "Now . . . we seem to be returning to the policy of appeasement," which Britain has not altered since 1939 despite "the failure of appeasement" when "dealing with precisely those Arab leaders who did their utmost to aid the Axis powers."[22]

A young friend of the author's, in reading the preceding account, responded surprisingly—she was "amazed that the Jews were still loyal fighting forces under the British—and that there was not *much more* Jewish defense—or terrorism or . . . whatever." She asked "Why?"

As has been pointed out earlier in this book, the Jews had been uncritically patriotic citizens of unfriendly Spanish, French, and German regimes in other days—they had believed themselves to be considered by others as countrymen of

At the eve of the "final solution" to the "Jewish Problem," the Mufti and Adolf Hitler confer in Berlin, November 21, 1941.

their various places of birth, as they indeed considered themselves. Throughout the Mandatory period administered by the British, the prevailing Jewish establishment had viewed cooperation with the British as their best interests, even when the dissenting Jewish voices pointed out such factors as Arab "illegal" immigration, British double standards, leniency toward Arab terror, and the British enactment of laws treating Jews as the "illegals" and Arabs as the "natural" population—in the Jewish National Home. There was surely no chance of the Jews joining Axis powers and aiding the avowed "final solution to the Jewish problem" of the Nazis, as the British well understood.

Moreover, the Jews had nowhere else in the world to go. The irony was that the very loss of their nation had become the source of much of the anti-Jewish antagonism. The Jews could be pushed around or held suspect, because they weren't "from" any place and no place totally accepted them. The more they clung to their beliefs, the more they seemed to stand out. Conversely, they stood out because the only place the Jews could rightfully "put" their nationality was now withheld by a hostile, artificially increased "majority." In Palestine, their "Home," a slim hope remained that the British might yet relent and recognize that the one place where Jews were to be "as of right and not on sufferance" was available as an alternative "final solution"—which, indeed, it could have been.

The Frantic Forties: British Sympathies

Perhaps the reaction of a group of Rumanian Jews in Bucharest to "a BBC broadcast in Roumanian" is instructive: by 1940 Jews hoping to escape from Europe *knew* that the British were acting to prevent foreign governments from releasing shiploads of Jewish refugees fleeing to the Jewish-settled area of Western Palestine. Yet the "British Embassy in Bucharest . . . warned" that a British broadcast had " 'been interpreted by local Jews to mean that they will all be immediately received [in] some British colony for duration of war.' "[23] Bernard Wasserstein noted, however, that the "primary British object [of the warning] was to prevent, not to stimulate, such an exodus. . . . "[24]

Toward that end, the boatloads of Jews "who had already passed through Dachau and Buchenwald" concentration camps to reach the shores of the "Jewish National Home" were deported.[25] This was 1940, before Nazi policy instituted the Hitlerian "Final Solution" that permitted Jewish exit exclusively through extermination—and the would-be Jewish immigrants had just arrived at what they believed was freedom. The following is an excerpt from the "eye-witness account" of one "deportation" by the British authorities, among the many documents cited in Bernard Wasserstein's study. According to the account, the refugees

> had decided to resist by refusing to pack their few belongings and by refusing to dress: both males and females lay down naked on their beds and did not get up. [British] policemen, armed with sticks, entered the barracks in strength, bela-

boured some of the men with blows, and carried them naked on blankets to
waiting lorries. . . .[26]

"They brought out over a hundred of the first batch of people, all of them
wounded, completely naked . . . The remaining young people walked, quite naked,
pushed from behind by the British police, until they reached the lorry, and they
were then flung into it . . . One immigrant was pushed while he was naked and
clasping a fiddle in his hand . . . Many of the old men fell on the ground and kissed
it. They pleaded with tears before the police officers . . . to have pity on them, that
they had already passed through Dachau and Buchenwald. And the officers paid
no heed to them . . . A British military officer turned very pale, and left the place
in anger.[27]

1,580 Jewish refugees—men, women, and 116 children who were "taken to
the port of Haifa," and who had actually *already become* Jewish immigrants in
the Jewish National Home—were deported to concentration-camp-like facilities
on the island of Mauritius; their "suspicious" possessions—like utensils, razor
blades, and so on—had been taken and their personal possessions, including
cameras, had been "confiscated" and "sold, the proceeds being retained by the
Government of Palestine."* Many refugees died of the typhoid that the British
had known was incubating among them, and which might have been treated had
the refugees been allowed to remain in Palestine a few days longer. "But the
Government did not wait until . . . the disease had subsided." There were
forty-one immediate casualties, nineteen from "privations suffered in the early
stages of the voyage"[29] and twenty-two deaths from typhoid. Most of the 1,310
survivors of the detention were finally allowed to return to Haifa after the war
ended in August 1945.[30]

Those immigrants were among the fortunate 9,000 Jewish passengers who
had eventually made it "home" in the "little ships" by the end of the war. The
list is long of the dilapidated ships whose desperate passengers perished.

But the events of one, the *Struma,* indicated the unmitigated lengths to which
the British would extend their influence to enforce their policy against the "illegal" Jewish immigrants fleeing from Hitler's war against them. The government
had been ever more rigid in its watch against the little refugee ships, lest

it will be spread all over Arab world that Jews have again successfully challenged
decision of British Government and that policy of White Paper is being reversed.

This undoubtedly would be followed, according to the "most immediate"
cable from the British Commander in Chief in the Middle East, by "widespread
disorders in Palestine," which could "greatly enhance influence of Mufti" and
create general distrust among other Arab countries such as Egypt, which was
already heavily engaged in "anti-British propaganda and fifth column activities."[31]

*In 1944 the "threat of unfavorable publicity" in the United States over the sale prompted the
British to, as they put it in one communication, "come clean about it." They eventually paid 3,000
pounds, "about eighteen percent of the amount claimed."[28]

The *Struma* incident occurred against the background of 1) ever-tightening Nazi maneuvers to prevent the Jews' escape in Europe; 2) the readmission into Western Palestine of the Mufti's collaborators; 3) the continuous Arab in-migration to the Jewish-settled areas; and 4) the wholesale immigration to Western Palestine of Arabs from surrounding Arab states, which will be detailed in following pages.

According to the official Anglo-American chronology in its evasive, compressed logging of events,[32] the *Struma* was a "motor vessel" that "arrived at Istanbul [Turkey] with some 750 Jewish refugees from Roumania on board," on December 20, 1941. The Turkish government, according to the terse paragraph in the Report describing the incident, "was unwilling to permit these people to land in Turkey and enquired whether they would be admitted into Palestine." "For security reasons," the Report stressed, ". . . a ban on the admission of persons from Axis and Axis-controlled territory" was in force, hence "the Turkish Government was informed that the 'Struma' passengers would not be admitted to Palestine." However,

> the Palestine Administration ascertained that, given reasonable weather, the vessel should be fit to undertake a Mediterranean voyage.

The Anglo-American chronology continued: when "the Jewish Agency . . . asked that [the security ban] be raised generally and in respect of the 'Struma' passengers," they were "notified that the security ban could not be removed, but that children between the ages of 11 and 16 from the Struma would be admitted to Palestine."

The Report informed its readers of the *Struma*'s tragic end, two months after its arrival at Istanbul, by the following:

> It was later learnt that, before the relevant arrangements had been completed, the Turkish authorities returned the vessel to the Black Sea. It sank on the 24th February as the result of an explosion, with a loss of 760 Jewish passengers.

The Report's bloodless, banal recitation of its version of events up to that point became noticeably less detached thereafter, as this heated description of the aftermath of the *Struma*'s sinking illustrates:

> As soon as the news reached Palestine a violent campaign was launched by the Jews against Government; violently abusive pamphlets and manifestos condemning the "murder" of the passengers by the Palestine Government, demanded the removal of the restrictions on immigration.

Throughout, the abbreviated official account seems to reflect a helpless but blameless British role. Other documents provide another version.

Regarding the Turkish government's reactions, for example: more fully documented accounts of the *Struma* catastrophe show that the Turks were *willing to allow* "and even assist" the ship to Palestine, but the British Ambassador in

Ankara said that his government "did not want these people in Palestine." On December 20, he suggested an alternative:

> If the Turkish Government must interfere with the ship . . . let her rather go toward the Dardanelles. . . . if they reached Palestine, they might despite their illegality receive humane treatment.[33]

London was "dismayed" by the Ambassador's advice—not because it was brutal to send the worn old ship away, but because he had indicated that the refugees on board the *Struma* would perhaps "receive humane treatment." As one Colonial officer complained,

> . . . the first occasion on which . . . the Turkish Government . . . help in frustrating these illegal immigrant ships, and the Ambassador then goes and spoils the whole effect on absurdly misjudged humanitarian grounds.[34]

Others, including High Commissioner MacMichael and Colonial Secretary Lord Moyne, were in ardent agreement. Moyne asserted his prime rationale for turning back every Jewish refugee, although not one instance was ever found— "preventing the influx of Nazi agents under the cloak of refugees." Moyne felt it "difficult to write with moderation about this occurrence, which," he reminded, was

> . . . in flat contradiction of established Government policy and . . . urge that Turkish authorities should be asked to send the ship back to the Black Sea, as they originally proposed."[35]

Regarding the two months when the Jewish Agency begged the British to reconsider the "security" ban while the *Struma* was docked near Istanbul: in that period the Rumanian Jews were attempting to escape from what the United States minister in Bucharest reported were wholesale slayings of Jews whose bodies were hung and displayed on "butcher's hooks."[36] At the same time, British intelligence had unearthed "not a single case" of "any Jewish refugee acting as an enemy agent in Palestine" that might justify Lord Moyne's anxiety.[37] Both Palestine and Home Office officials confirmed that none was ever known to exist, and that "the Jews themselves" would have turned on a Nazi agent.[38]

High Commissioner MacMichael added a further argument against this boat-load: that most of the passengers were "professional people" and would be an "unproductive element in the population."[39] MacMichael had failed to fathom what the Nazis knew and utilized in the concentration camps on an insidiously temporary basis—that able-bodied persons, Jews or otherwise, whatever their former vocation, made productive laborers when their lives depended upon it.

Regarding the rescue of the children on board the *Struma:* the Report's cryptic comment implied that the Turks interfered with British "arrangements" for transferring the youngest refugees to safety. The facts were less unequivocal. Documented accounts tracing the plight of the ill-fated, unequipped boat—originally built in 1867 and designed to hold one hundred rather than the nearly eight hundred souls aboard—indeed found that even the children, without their parents, would not be permitted by the Turkish government to be transported over Turkish land to Palestine.

The British, however, *would* be allowed to send a boat that was in the area to pick up the children from the *Struma*. But no boat was found by the British to rescue them. The possibility of the British rerouting a nearby ship to rescue the Jewish refugee children apparently was never a serious consideration, since a British foreign officer, writing the day after the Turkish ultimatum, enumerated the choices of his government without ever mentioning that measure. Further, he "imagined" that "selecting the children and taking them from their parents off the Struma"—even if the British "got the Turks to agree" to overland transfer —"would be . . . extremely distressing." The Foreign Office official continued, asking,

> Who . . . should undertake it, and has the possibility of the adults refusing to let the children go been considered?[40]

One survivor, David Stoliar,* made an official deposition three months later. Stoliar described the Turkish police boarding the ship "in force" and the Jews' impotent resistance to the orders to go back to Rumania:

> . . . some of the passengers . . . came to blows with the police, but the police overpowered them and there were some 100 to 200 policemen. They took the ship some ten kilometres from the coast and left us. . . . early in the morning . . . an explosion occurred.

Stoliar and "the second Captain . . . jumped into the sea" when "the ship started to sink." The explosion had been "caused by a torpedo which he [the second Captain] saw." Although the ship—only ten kilometers offshore—was visible from the Turkish coast, as the coast was visible to Stoliar,

> Nobody came to our help from ashore. The second Captain who was with me in the sea disappeared about a quarter of an hour before the saving boat arrived.[42]

Turkish Naval Intelligence corroborated the report that the ship was sunk by torpedo.

David Stoliar, after hospitalization and imprisonment,[43] eventually was allowed, along with the other survivor, Medea Salamovici, into Western Palestine through "an act of clemency." But not until High Commissioner MacMichael had been overruled in his objection to the two survivors' entry: MacMichael held the view, shared by so many of his British colleagues, that if these two immigrants were permitted into Palestine, the "floodgate" would "open" and "completely undermine our whole policy regarding illegal immigrants."[44] Who fired the tor-

---

*There was one other survivor—a pregnant woman who managed to escape from the ship to Istanbul, where her baby died. Her husband drowned with the *Struma.*[41]

pedo has never been determined, but the Palestinian Jewish community indeed blamed the tragic drowning of more than 750 men, women, and children on the British letter of the law that killeth. On that point, the Anglo-American Report was deadly accurate.

The drowning of the people on board the *Struma* killed the last remnant of hope among Palestinian Jews that the British might yet honor the Balfour Declaration and observe their legal obligations under the Mandate, the Mandate that had gained for England the right to Palestinian rule.

By 1942 London had publicly received (over a BBC broadcast) the word that the Jews of Eastern Europe were being "physically exterminated on Polish soil, using the Ukrainian and the Lithuanian Fascists for this job."[45] Walter Laqueur writes that the report

> mentioned a great many facts and figures about the number of Jews killed in various places. . . . It gives a figure of 700,000 victims and says that . . . the German Government has begun to carry out Hitler's prophecy that in the last five minutes of the war, whatever its outcome, all the Jews of Europe would be killed.[46]

That news had been published in America in August 1942. Ironically, the Americans' unaltered, minimal prewar-prescribed annual quota—27,370 "German and Austrian" immigrants allotted for 1942—was only 17.8 percent filled.[47]

In Palestine, Government hoped to avoid the embarrassment of another *Struma,* by sending whatever straggler shiploads of Jewish refugees might still slip somehow through the tightened Nazi bonds on to the island of Mauritius. But, to appease Arab protests, Britain declared that after the war the Jews must return to Europe and not enter Palestine.

The awkward alteration of policy—to allay what some British feared would be a Jewish "insurrection" if no concession was offered—was given full if inadvertent cooperation by the Nazis. In 1942, Jews found it "virtually impossible" to escape. "The total number of immigrants to Palestine (both legal and illegal) in 1942 was 3,038, the lowest figure for any year of the war."[48] The Jewish immigrants who made it to the Jewish-settled area of Western Palestine under the status of "illegal" were in fact "placed in a detention camp on arrival." Only if they passed the "careful security check" and were adjudged not to threaten the "overriding principle of *economic absorptive capacity*"* would they be "released." And then they would be "set off"—deducted—from the "quota."[49] This meant that they were in fact not "illegal" at all, since they had merely taken some of the inconceivably few Jewish places that the Arabs had agreed to, those allotted in the White Paper.

Also, it must be remembered that in 1942 the Mufti's cohorts were being allowed to reenter Western Palestine. Miraculously evading detection as Nazi sympathizers and allies, the Arabs in general were still very much an influence in the British government's plans. The plight of the Jewish refugees had thrown

*Emphasis added.

salt on the festering sore of immigration, a condition that Arabs watched with omnipresent hostility. As the Foreign Office official Randall wrote, the British might have to choose "between raising world Jewish opinion against us and trouble with the Arabs."[50]

Disillusioned "world Jewish opinion" decided after the *Struma* debacle to battle the immigration restrictions against Jews into what was after May 1942 formally designated as a "Jewish Commonwealth" in Western Palestine. The Extraordinary Zionist Conference in New York in May 1942, recognizing that the British betrayal of the Balfour Declaration was adamant, voted to further the Balfour-Mandate adoption of a Jewish State, independent and regardless of the Arab-inspired British policy.[51]

The British, however, had made their choice in 1939, although the White Paper restrictions, in the context of Hitler's "war against the Jews,"[52] had become a death warrant. Until the simultaneous events of the May 1948 British leavetaking from Palestine and the 1948 "War of Independence," when Israel was proclaimed internationally as the independent Jewish State, the White Paper would remain the policy of Great Britain. Nonetheless, Palestinian Jews would continue their frantic efforts to smuggle what remained of the prospective community of Jewish refugee immigrants into the Jewish-settled area of Western Palestine throughout the war and afterward.

Meanwhile, England's War Cabinet had declared, in March 1942, that the British would continue to take "all practicable steps . . . to discourage illegal immigration into Palestine,"[53] that "very undesirable trade." The *Struma* was sinking and the Mufti—having declared "holy war against Britain"—was demanding that Hitler, Ribbentrop, and the Bulgarian, Hungarian, and Rumanian governments keep their promise of "the destruction of the so-called Jewish National Home."

That destruction was an "immutable part of the policy of the greater German Reich," the Mufti reminded, and Nazi allies must "do all that is necessary to prohibit the emigration of Jews to Palestine," by sending them to the extermination camps in Poland.

I asked you, Reichsführer, to take all the measures to prevent the Jews from going,

the Mufti had scolded. Those "measures" must be taken, he insisted, to "give a new practical example" to "the Arab Nation" of the "naturally allied and friendly" Arab-Axis relations.[54]

As further proof of his own fidelity, the Mufti offered the Arab Legion for use against the Allies to "Reichsführer and Reichsminister" Heinrich Himmler. The offer was a reaction against the British "establishment of a Jewish military unit to fight against Germany"—the Jewish Brigade.[55]

Mufti Asks Hungary to Send Jews to Poland

As a Sequel to This Request
400,000 Jews Were Subsequently Killed

Rome
June 28, 1943

His Excellency
The Minister of Foreign Affairs for Hungary

Your Excellency:

You no doubt know of the struggle between the Arabs and Jews of Palestine, what it has been and what it is, a long and bloody fight, brought about by the desire of the Jews to create a national home, a Jewish State in the Near East, with the help and protection of England and the United States. In fact, behind it lies the hope which the Jews have never relinquished, namely, the domination of the whole world through this important, strategic center, Palestine. In effect, their program has, among other purposes, always aimed at the encouragement of Jewish emigration to Palestine and the other countries of the Near East. However, the war, as well as the understanding which the members of the Three-Power Pact have of the responsibility of the Jews for its outbreak and finally their evil intentions towards these countries which protected them until now — all these are reasons for placing them under such vigilant control as will definitely stop their emigration to Palestine or elsewhere.

Lately I have been informed of the uninterrupted efforts made by the English and the Jews to obtain permission for the Jews living in your country to leave for Palestine via Bulgaria and Turkey.

I have also learned that these negotiations were successful, since some of the Jews of Hungary have had the satisfaction of emigrating to Palestine via Bulgaria and Turkey and that a group of these Jews arrived in Palestine towards the end of last March. The Jewish Agency, which supervises the execution of the Jewish program, has published a bulletin which contains important information on the current negotiations between the English Government and the governments of other interested states to send the Jews of Balkan countries to Palestine. The Jewish Agency quotes, among other things, its receipt of a sufficient number of immigration certificates for 900 Jewish children to be transported from Hungary, accompanied by 100 adults.

To authorize these Jews to leave your country under the above circumstances and in this way, would by no means solve the Jewish problem and would certainly not protect your country against their evil influence — far from it! — for this escape would make it possible for them to communicate and combine freely with their racial brethren in enemy countries in order to strengthen their position and to exert a more dangerous influence on the outcome of the war, especially since, as a consequence of their long stay in your country, they are necessarily in a position to know many of your secrets and also about your war effort. All this comes on top of the terrible damage done to the friendly Arab nation which has taken its place at your side in this war and which cherishes for your country the most sincere feelings and the very best wishes.

This is the reason why I ask your Excellency to permit me to draw your attention to the necessity of preventing the Jews from leaving your country for Palestine; and if there are reasons which make their removal necessary, it would be indispensable and infinitely preferable to send them to other countries where they would find themselves under active control, for example, in Poland, in order thereby to protect oneself from their menace and avoid the consequent damage.

Yours, etc.

Source: *The Arab Higher Committee. Its Origins, Personnel and Purposes.* Documentary Record Submitted to the United Nations, May 1947, by the Nation Associates.

Rome Le 28 Juin 1943

A Son Excéllence Monsieur le Ministre des
affaires étrangères de H O N G R I E

Excéllence !

Vous savez sans doute ce que fût et ce qu'est encore la lutte entre
Arabes et Juifs en Palestine , lutte sanglante et longue ,dont la raison est
le désir de ces derniers de se créer un foyer national , un Etat juif
dans le proche orient avec l'aide et l'appui de l'Angleterre et des Etats-
Unis d'Amérique . Ceci dévoile en vérité l'espoir que les Juifs n'ont cessé
d'avoir à savoir : la domination du Monde entier par ce centre stratégique
important qu'est la Palestine . En effet leur programme entre autres buts
principaux ,a toujours visé l'encouragement de l'émigration des Juifs en Palestine et vers les autres pays du Proche-Orient . ais la guerre ,la certitu-
ude qu'ont eu les Puissances du Pacte tripartite du rôle joué par les
Juifs dans son déclenchement et enfin leurs mauvaises arrière-pensées
envers les pays qui les abritèrent jusqu'ici sont autant de raisons qui
justifient leur placement sous surveillance vigilante avec laquelle leur
émigration en Palestine ou autre se trouve fermement arrêtée .

Je fus dernièrement mis au courant des efforts ininterrompus prodigués
par les Anglais et les Juifs en vue d'obtenir pour les Juifs résidant dans
votre Pays la permission de le quitter pour la Palestine à travers la Bulgar-
ie et la Turquie .

Je suis également que ces démarches aboutirent avec succès ,puisque

Hungary Promises to End Jewish Problem

A M. KIR. KÖVET
DER KGL. UNG. GESANDTE
360/B.-1944.

Berlin, den 25. Juli 1944.

Eure Eminens !

Ich habe den Auftrag erhalten Euerer Eminens
mitzuteilen, dass der kgl. ungarische Minister des Aeussern
mit Dank Ihr sehr geschätztes Schreiben vom 22. Juni 1944
betreffend die Verhinderung der Auswandrung der Juden nach
Palestina dankend empfangen hat; er wird die darin enthal-
tenen Vorschläge einer Erwägung unterziehen.

Mit dem Ausdruck meiner vorzüglichsten Hochachtung

[signature]
kgl.ungarischer Gesandter

Seiner Eminens

Amin El Hussein
Grossmufti von Palestina

Rubin bei Tittau

Source: *The Arab Higher Committee. Its Origins, Personnel and Purposes.* Documentary Record
Submitted to the United Nations, May 1947, by the Nation Associates.

Illegal Arab Immigration During World War II

The same Arab Legion organization, it might be noted, was in exclusive control of immigration at the borders into Western Palestine through Transjordan.[56]

The principle of "evenhandedness," whereby Jewish volunteers for the war effort had been accepted only in numbers that matched the disproportionately meager number of Arabs who volunteered, had soon been superseded by the British war needs, as we have seen: hence a "Jewish Brigade." However, that so-called evenhandedness had never been applied at the borders to Western Palestine, where Colonel MacKereth had fought for identity cards several years before to prevent "illicit" Arab immigration and gunrunning. The *Palestine Royal Commission Report* in 1937 had determined that the Arab Legion

> Frontier Force could not be used to control and police the Palestine Frontier except at the risk of neglecting the country—Trans-Jordan—from which they are mainly recruited.

The same *Report* had also recognized that Western Palestine's

> open frontier some 250 miles long, bordering on countries in which all the inhabitants are allowed to carry arms is almost impossible [to disarm].

While it was "right that the Arabs if still the aggressors, should first be disarmed," the *Report* cautioned that disarming the Arabs "would be an extremely difficult task."

Yet, while the Palestinian Jews were anxious to have the right to supplement the frontier forces, the *Royal Commission Report* had concluded that

> it is clear that the Jews cannot claim as of right recruitment in a Force towards which the Palestine Government contributes only one-fourth of the cost, and whose duties are primarily outside Palestine.[57]

Not only was the recruitment of Palestinian Jews—whose enforcement could have effectively prevented Arab "gun-running" and what the Report acknowledged as "illicit Arab immigration" discouraged—but the identity cards were never earnestly implemented.

The identity-card system, that one measure which might have deterred[58] "Arab entrants" who would "satisfy all demands for additional labour" and "leave no room in the labour category for Jewish immigrants from outside Palestine," was given, at best, occasional token and ineffectual brief trial.[59] There were still a "serious number of persons who evade the frontier control and enter Palestine without formality of any kind. . . ." The illicit Arab immigration from "Syria and Transjordan," which had "swollen unemployment lists" and was "used as a political pawn" toward "blocking immigration to which they are radically averse" was just as free-moving during World War II as it had been in the 1930s.

The British "practice" was *still* "sufficient"—adding the Arab immigrants into the "economic absorptive capacity" as though they were "indigenous Arab population for millennia." If, as Hope Simpson admitted,[60] it was "injustice" for "illicit" Arab immigrants to "take the places" that Palestinian Jews created for Jewish immigrant hopefuls "outside the country" in all the earlier years of the Mandatory period, the World War II continuation of that casual British "practice," throughout the dark years of the Jews' extermination in Europe, must be viewed as unfathomably disingenuous and callous.

During all "the years of war," as the joint American-British postwar report, *The Survey of Palestine,* cryptically confirmed, "identity cards" were "several times reviewed" for use as a "system" to prevent Arab mercenaries and rebels from entering "Palestine." However, the "system of illegal immigration" in Western Palestine had been otherwise organized:

> *For reasons mainly political* but also related to the practical difficulties involved, it was decided on each occasion that a compulsory system of universal registration should not be introduced. . . .*[61]

As a grudging token response to the earlier British Reports' evidence of illegal Arab immigration, and the League of Nations' challenges of the British administration on the subject, a helter-skelter "method" was applied by the government in 1938; freely admitted to be no more than symbolic, it

> purported solely to establish the holder's identity; and neither the card nor the application form contained any reference to character, antecedents, national status or status under the Immigration Ordinance.[62]

When attempts were made to tighten up the existing farce, effectiveness was soon nullified if indeed any effect had been achieved at all.

For example, in 1941, while the British were justifying the practice of firing on the miserable little rescue ships jammed with hopeful *Jewish* immigrants-to-be, to get them *away* from the "Jewish National Home" in Western Palestine at any cost, Government's District Commissioners actually received instructions *cancelling* its new order to begin to withhold identity cards at the borders to neighboring Arab lands or in Palestine "from persons . . . not . . . legally in Palestine." Because it was seen to "constitute a hardship in numerous instances" and cause "serious inconvenience" to the *Arab* immigrants concerned, even that token "directive" which might cut down Arab immigration was "modified." The *non-Jewish* immigrants "illegally in Palestine" were thus *given cards regardless of their origins,* and allowed to enter or remain in Western Palestine, their

> cards being thereafter stamped . . . *"possession of this card in no way constitutes evidence of legal residence in Palestine."*[63]

*Emphasis added

While no invention was left untested in the British zeal to enforce the prevention of "illegal" Jewish immigrants who were "a very serious embarrassment,"[64] and while the Nazi policy toward Jews was beginning to evolve from the expulsion of the Jews into the more barbarous program of incinerating and gassing those millions of souls who found no place that would accept them—at that very time the hidden immigration of Arabs into Western Palestine was rampant. In the archives the British left behind in Western Palestine there are dozens of cartons stuffed with folders, containing literally reams of forms dated "1940" and "1941," each form stating the name of one (or more) Muslim or other non-Jewish "traveler who is believed to be in Palestine without permission"—all of them dismissed with the stamped or typewritten words: "Could not be traced."[65]

In only a single instance did the files of British correspondence concerning "illegal immigration" refer to "deportation with special reference to Arabs." Saunders, the Inspector General, wrote to the Chief Secretary in April of 1942 that "His Excellency the Officer Administrating the Government raised this question with me recently. . . ." However, Saunders was chided for his mistake. In the handwritten response to his memo about illegal Arab immigration, Saunders was told,

> . . . But I was *not* thinking specially of Arabs. Actually the case which gave rise to my inquiry was Jewish. . . .[66]

In fact, the "practice" that Hope Simpson had identified so many years earlier was the Palestine Government's *clearly delineated policy* in its official *Memorandum on Deportation—Arabs,* of April 9, 1942. The circular directed verbatim that

> The police have *no* instructions to concentrate on *picking up Arabs* who are in Palestine illegally.

Only if a "person who is in the country illegally" should "come to the notice of the Police" will the illegal Arab immigrant be "put up for deportation. . . ."[67]

Thus, in 1942, when London already had received a "detailed account" that Auschwitz concentration camp alone accounted for "4,000 deaths by shooting, 2,900 by gassing, . . . 2,000 by phenol injection . . . 1,200 beaten to death and 800 . . . committed suicide by walking into the camp's electric fence,"[68] the cynical policy toward Arab immigration into Western Palestine was still operative: the illegal Arab immigrants entered unheeded along with Arab in-migrants, and all were counted as "natives" unless they were "flagrant." The lone immigration memo on "Arabs" states that "140 Arabs" were "summarily deported" and "additionally 406 Arabs" were "deported" between January and March 1942— they included "Lebanese, Syrian, Transjordanian, Egyptian, Adenite and [from] Hedjaz." Those "flagrant" illegal immigrants who had "come to the notice of the Police" were then "conducted to the frontier"—which was, it must be remembered, hundreds of miles long and guarded *only* by members of the *Arab Legion.* At the frontier they were "instructed to make their way home."[69]

Since the police were encouraged not to deport illegal Arab immigrants, and the only Arab deportees were those whose presence had become "flagrant" because of "arrest" or "loitering" or "information received" by a third party,[70] the fact that 546 Arabs were "deported" in just two months of 1942 indicates that the number who remained, having found employment and/or other support from other immigrants, members of their families who had arrived earlier—or who simply managed to evade the admittedly permissive, blinkered vision of the authorities—can be estimated to be a number many times the 546 who were deported.

As the later, formal second reply to Saunder's naïve inquiry concerning what actions to take against Arab immigrants once again emphasized,

> the Officer Administering the Government . . . has read with interest . . . and thanks . . . letter (No. 38/G) of the 15th April, 1942. . . . In fact, however, His Excellency was not thinking of Arabs. . . .[71]

Britain's rationalization of its political appeasement to the Arabs, virtually halting Jewish immigration to the Jewish National Home at the time of greatest peril in Europe, was perhaps the most cynical and craven chapter in the tragic record of the Holocaust. It was wrongful enough that the British had continued including newly arrived Arab immigrants against the "labour schedule" in Palestine—in other words, misrepresenting them as "millennia-settled Palestinian Arabs" who would be "displaced" from jobs in Western Palestine if Jewish immigrants were allowed to fill those rightful places that had been created by Palestinian Jews.

Compounding that wrongful "practice," which barred the gates of sanctuary against Jews into the Jewish-settled area of Western Palestine and thus sealed the fate of hundreds of thousands if not millions of would-be Jewish immigrants in the extermination camps of Europe, there was an *additional* and *never-related* factor.

At the very time that the White Paper was defended and rationalized by the British claim that Palestine had reached the outside population limit of its "absorptive capacity" for Jewish workers, the same British Government enacted special legislation that enabled the Palestine administration to import thousands of "illegal" *Arab* workers to meet the increased job needs of the government. *There weren't enough laborers, said the British, to fill those needs.*[72] While there were purportedly no places on the Palestine "labour schedule" for Jews who were instead forced to dig trenches for their own and other Jewish bodies in the death camps of Eastern Europe, the war had in fact created additional countless thousands of jobs in Western Palestine.

The official report pertinent to "Arab illegal immigration . . . by Arabs from neighboring territories in search of employment *during the war years*"* was the Anglo-American Committee's 1945–1946 *Survey of Palestine.* That report began its observations on the subject with "the conclusion . . . that Arab illegal immigra-

---

*Emphasis added.

tion for the purpose of permanent settlement is insignificant."[73] Immediately thereafter, the *Survey* reported that the great majority of Arab "labourers from Syria and the Lebanon" and "Egypt" who were "brought" by "trucks" and "train" to fill the "demand for labour exceeding the local supply" in Western Palestine were presumed to have *"remained in Palestine illegally."**

In the tradition of earlier British reports seeking to dismiss its pivotal importance as a factor, the *Survey* had disposed of the Arab illegal immigration as "insignificant" and then proceeded from that point to contradict its conclusion. Despite the fact that a maze of confusing figures and clinical terminology obscures the data, and despite the undoubtedly understated figures reported, the information that nonetheless emerges is jolting. The *Survey*'s pages reveal a documented account that indicates duplicity and cynicism, bias and double standards, to a degree not thought to have been practiced by any but the fascist governments in World War II.

Because of the "demand for labour exceeding the local supply," according to the Anglo-American *Survey,* "official arrangements were made, in October, 1942," and "under this arrangement" the Report noted that "3,800 labourers" were "admitted" from Syria and Lebanon.[74] Keep in mind that the numbers reported for Arab illegal immigration by the British administration of the Mandate always were understated or minimized, as illustrated earlier in this volume;[75] we find that in another "arrangement," a "police estimate" of Arab illegal immigrants "working for contractors engaged on military R.A.F. construction or in other civil employment" amounted to "9,687."[76]

Since policy only "found" those illegal Arab immigrants who were "flagrant," and because of the design by which Arab immigration was minimized and understated throughout the British Mandatory administration, the true number of thousands of Arabs imported under that legislation can only be speculated about.

Although the author had read and reread the *Survey*'s data describing the Palestine Government's wholesale importation of Arab illegal immigrants, it was not until the paragraphs were taken apart in order to cite them that it became apparent that many of the paragraphs dealing with "Arab illegal immigration" during "the War years" were describing *different* sets of Arab immigrants and different numbers. One was the "Army" workers, another was the "Navy," still another the "R.A.F.," and in addition there were the unquantifiables. In one group of nearly ten thousand reported "foreign workers"—most of whom eventually "deserted" or "remained in Palestine illegally"—the *Survey* states that the Arab

> illegal immigrants [were] Egyptians, Syrians, Lebanese . . . also small numbers from Trans-Jordan, Persia, India, Somaliland, Abyssinia and the Hejaz.[77]

Another group of immigrants noted by the Report:

*Emphasis added.

In addition to these Syrian and Lebanese Labourers who were brought to Palestine under official arrangement, *inhabitants of neighbouring countries, attracted by the high rates of wages offered for employment on military works, entered Palestine illegally during the war in considerable numbers. . . .* For example, in 1942, Egyptian labour was brought into southern Palestine by civilian contractors to the military forces without any agreement with the civil administration; these contractors were employed on the construction camps and aerodromes.*

By stark contrast to the meticulous quota system for Jewish refugees from Hitler, the number in *that* group of "illegal Arab immigrants"—which even in the Report was described as "considerable"—was *omitted* totally from the Report's calculations. As the Report stated unconcernedly,

> *No estimates are available of the numbers of foreign labourers who were so brought into the country or who entered individually in search of employment on military works.* *

In regard to still another group, numbering thousands of "illegal immigrants," the *Survey* reported that by the 1945–1946 date of publication of the report

> The Services authorities are *not able* at present [1945–46 date of publication of the Report] *to find Palestinians* who could suitably replace all these foreigners.*

The authorities, therefore, would "desire to retain" 2,000 of a group of more than 4,000 mostly Egyptian immigrants.[78]

What the official Anglo-American *Survey* of 1945–1946 definitively disclosed —however obfuscated the presentation, however buried in the three-volume postwar report it may be—is that those tens of thousands of "Arab illegal immigrants" *recorded* as having been "brought" into Western Palestine were reported by an administration that was reluctant to record Arab immigration at all. In addition, other *un*estimated "considerable" numbers immigrated "unofficially" or as "individuals" during the war, according to the report. Of the combined masses of Arab illegal immigrants only a small number were "repatriated," and only near the end of the war ("October 1944") was there a token effort to "put the law into force and to deport to their countries of origin the Syrian, Lebanese, Egyptian and other foreign labourers *found* to be illegally in Palestine.* Since the Palestine authorities, as was documented earlier, were under orders *not* to deport Arab illegal immigrants unless they were embarrassingly noticeable, the number deported was predictably minimal. And even then, as later pages of the *Survey* noted, those

> labourers illegally in the country who are employed directly by the Army, Navy or Air Force are not deported, unless local workers can be found to replace them or until they are discharged from their employment.[79]

*Emphasis added.

The evidence clearly stated in the report, however, was ignored as a factor in determining what constituted "justice" for Jews in the area, just as the indications of John Hope Simpson's Report and the corroborating evidence of the Royal Commission, Partition, and other Reports had been similarly ignored.

In the decades before Hitler's Arab-abetted war against the Jews began, however brutal and unfair the policy might have been of barring those Jews who were clamoring to get into the Jewish National Home, in those days at least systematic persecution of Jews in Russia, Poland, Rumania, and elsewhere did not forecast physical annihilation. However biased and double-dealing a policy might have been that appeased Arab demands against and at the expense of the legal requirements of the international Mandate for a "Jewish National Home," until now the actuality of condemning would-be Jewish immigrants—refugees from the crematorium—by prohibiting their entry to Western Palestine *has never been seen in context.*

There has been no connection made between the Arab illegal immigrants being imported to fill the labor demands of Western Palestine—the "Jewish National Home"—and the countless Jewish lives taken because those Jews who would have fled to Palestine were forbidden entry.

Those Jews, the Arabs had protested with the support and legislation of the government, would take the jobs available for the "existing" Arab population from "time immemorial." As we now see, that "existing" unemployed Arab population in fact did not exist. It was fabricated.

> In the final year of the war, when escape from Europe again became a practicable proposition for a few of the Jewish survivors, the British Government resumed its practice of earlier years in seeking to prevent the departure of Jews from Europe.[80]

The combined efforts of the Nazi-allied Arabs and the British government effectively barred from rescue many hundreds of thousands of Jews whose lives might have been spared.

There was an additional element of duplicity involved in the mass import of Arab laborers, for the "labour demands" in Western Palestine that were so great that the need for workers was considered an "emergency." At that very moment it was the Palestinian Jews who were fighting for the Allies, and the British had knowledge of the extermination of Jews in Eastern Europe. Given those facts, to continue to prohibit Jewish immigration into the Jewish-settled area in Western Palestine on *any* basis must be considered callous and inexplicable. To prohibit the rescue of Jews in the one place where they had a right to go, based on the belief that the so-called "absorptive capacity" for workers had been filled— despite the fact that the elastic "absorptive capacity" had been stretched time and time again, enough to accommodate even the thousands upon thousands of unreported Arab illegal immigrants who flooded in throughout the Mandatory period—would have been by itself a cynical appeasement of extreme Arab demands by the British administration. And it was.

That "absorptive capacity," which was so fraudulently used to prevent Jewish immigration, was in fact the actual means by which the illegal *Arab* immigration and in-migration was *facilitated.*

While the Jews were working furiously at clearing land that had been ignored or dismissed by Government "authorities" as "uncultivable," and creating places that Government insisted "did not exist," those opened-up places—which in fact disproved Government's theory that the country was "overfull"—were taken by the illegal Arab immigrants. Having cleared those places only to have them expropriated by the Arab in-migrants and immigrant community—Syrians, Egyptians, Hauranis, Algerians, Hejazis, and others camouflaged as "natural indigenous Palestinian population since time immemorial"—the Jews yet continued their efforts, lest the British halt Jewish immigration entirely, which Government on more than one occasion had threatened to do.

Those thousands upon thousands of places continually created by Palestinian Jews discredited Government's unrealistically low "estimated" capacity of the country to absorb new immigrants. Had those places in the country been left open for the Jews instead of being usurped by illegal Arab immigrants falsely represented as part of the "original" and "existing" Palestinian population for "thousands of years"—many factors would have changed. The Jews would have grown in number at least in direct proportion to the number of places they had cleared for Jewish immigrants to come to from persecution. Concurrently, the number of Arabs would have been reduced to a figure that more plausibly represented the "existing" non-Jewish population and its descendants from the beginning of the century. Thus the Jewish population would have grown substantially—by, at the very least, 200,000 more—while the "non-Jewish" population of Western Palestine would have decreased by the very minimum of 200,000—there would have been at least 200,000 *fewer* "Palestinian Arabs." The resulting proportional changes in the population, plus the evidence which would then have been obvious —that the "absorptive capacity" was inaccurate and begun on a fallacious premise—might have caused the British to "open the gates" to the Jews fleeing to their National Home in Western Palestine, instead of sealing their fates in the extermination camps.

If that act appears as the ultimate cynicism, it at least *might have* presupposed an earnestness on behalf of those who somehow, through blinkered vision, accepted the Arab claim that the land could not hold any more immigrants without "taking jobs away from" the so-called "existing," ostensibly phenomenally growing "native" Arab population. That at least was the purported justification for the White Paper's harsh restrictive measures against the Jews.

But, that the British virtually signed the death warrants for countless Jews in mortal danger by engaging the might of the British Empire to enforce strict laws against Jewish immigration; that simultaneously Government declared an excess of jobs amounting to a need of "emergency" proportions, whereby Government not only encouraged or winked at, but *officially enacted* the illegal immigration of thousands of Arab indigents from neighboring and more distant lands, to take jobs in the Jewish National Home that might have saved the lives of Jewish concentration camp victims—the whole action, seen in context, matches the barbarism that the Allies were battling to defeat.

That deed by Britain's officialdom in Western Palestine is not excusable merely as unwitting complicity in the Mufti-Hitler conspiracy; it may indeed have constituted active participation in the racial genocide of the Jews in Eastern Europe.

In London, meanwhile, the Foreign Office had responded to the news of the genocide with inaction amounting to tacit endorsement. At a moment when Arab "illegals" were being officially and unofficially smuggled over the borders to alleviate the need for workers in the "Jewish National Home," documented evidence shows that whenever the possible rescue of Jews became known, those rescues that were not prevented by the Mufti or other Arab Axis supporters were effectively protested against and eventually foiled by the British Government.

There was at least one notable instance, however, when all the British Empire's might could not prevent one such rescue—a rescue in theory if not in practice. That exception was due to public pressure placed on the British by the United States government, which had chosen to go over the heads of some objecting State Department officials.

In April of 1943, another purportedly sympathetic Anglo-American Conference on refugees had opened and closed in Bermuda; its achievements were as ignominious as the 1938 proceedings at Evian.[81] In the wake of the Bermuda exercise, at the end of 1943 the United States authorized funds necessary to save 70,000 Rumanian Jews—"only a few dollars per head."[82]

The British Foreign Office, however, was

> concerned with the difficulties of disposing of any considerable number of Jews should they be rescued from enemy-occupied territory.[83]

The British hoped that the plan would be "abandoned," although they recognized that American elections were drawing near; as the British Ambassador in Washington reported, the United States

> Administration would certainly not wish to be identified with a British decision which all Jews here, Zionist or non-Zionist, would agree in regarding as inhumane.[84]

The British balancing act was perilous, as one Foreign Office official noted. The Foreign Office was faced with the need for

> helping the State Department and Treasury to meet Jewish electoral pressure, . . . avoiding a crescendo of U.S. criticism about our Palestine policy, and on the other hand, of meeting . . . Arab wishes.[85]

The concern for "Arab wishes" evidently remained the stronger motivation, since Foreign Office opinion "remained hostile to the scheme" although by late 1943 it had long since been known that Rumanian Jews faced certain death.

Another foreign officer's sentiments exemplified, with bloodcurdling candor, the way "Government" reasoned the matter:

> Once we open the door to adult male Jews to be taken out of enemy territory, a quite unmanageable flood may result. (Hitler may facilitate it!)[86]

The United States State Department, however, apparently overrode British objections in this case, based on Treasury Secretary Morgenthau's outrage at the fact that

> in simple terms, the British were apparently prepared to accept the probable death of thousands of Jews in enemy territory because of "the difficulties of disposing of any considerable number of Jews should they be rescued."[87]

One wonders whether the employment boom for Arab immigrants in Western Palestine during the war was kept secret or was, tragically, simply overlooked by the myriad concerned officials purportedly looking for places for the thousands of Jewish refugees. Is it possible that nobody but the Arab immigrants, the British Government, and the various "private contractors" involved were aware of the war boom and its obvious additional opportunities in the "Jewish National Home"? Or that, although known factors, the two counterpoint claims—of emergency need for Arab "illegal immigrant" workers and of the "difficulties of disposing of Jewish refugees"—were never connected? Was the deadly silence on this crucial point caused by the Palestinian Jews' preoccupation with their frantic effort in Europe to save the Jews in the midst of the war's chaos?

Because of the pat anti-Semitic image of the Jew as "cosmopolitan" and "professional," had the British blocked out from their perception of Jews the fact that it was the Palestinian Jewish physical effort as well as economic support that had reclaimed swamps and transformed massive arid, barren plots of land into the Jewish-settled area of Western Palestine? If the British who witnessed it had forgotten that many Jewish immigrant professional people had taken to the land and to physical labor even before the threat to Jewish existence in Europe was imminent, then perhaps it might be argued that the rest of the free world never properly considered that those jobs being given to the thousands of Arab immigrants during the war could have been filled by the Jews.

That tenuous argument, though, was repudiated by one horrible factor, which by 1942 already had been communicated to governments and people of the free world—that in the Nazi "work" camps the Jews were not only laboring furiously at the basest manual tasks the Nazis could devise, just to keep alive for a few precious days longer, but Jewish prisoners were literally digging their own graves.

By November 1947, when the United Nations recommended partition of Western Palestine into a Jewish and an Arab state, the Arab world summarily rejected the very territory that they currently claim as the "mini-state"—the West Bank area later admittedly sought by many Arab strategists as the "first stage" in the dismantling of a Zionist entity. The Arabs' conduct had long been encouraged and given form by the immutable pattern of British precedents. Not only had the British tacitly supported Arab rejection of the *Palestine Royal Commission Report*'s partition plan a decade before, but obsequious *post-World War II* actions by the weary, decaying Palestine Government made the signals clear. As the Anglo-American Committee of Inquiry stated in 1946,

> In the face of actual violence and threats of much more serious violence, possibly approaching the status of civil war, the Palestine Government resorted to drastic emergency legislation which permitted it to modify or suspend normal civil liberties. There can be no gainsaying that Palestine today is governed without the consent of Jews or Arabs by an Administration depending almost solely upon force for the maintenance of a precarious authority.[88]

The Report noted that there were "signs . . . of a revival of Arab secret activities, similar to those which preceded the disturbances of 1936–39."[89] Most active Arab Nazi-sympathizers and supporters had left Western Palestine to lead the 1936–1939 Arab "Revolt" from a safe distance. After the war, these Arabs were permitted back into the country, but the Jewish survivors were kept under a strict quota of "1,500 persons a month."[90]

The typical brief 1946 Anglo-American account of postwar violence concentrated on the "Jews, protesting against restrictions upon [Jewish] immigration," and placed the blame for "threats to public order in Palestine" throughout the entire period of the Mandate upon "Jewish immigration."[91]

Near the end of the war, there were many who evidenced concern that gave hope of a policy change. The British Labour Party had resolved in May 1944 that

> the Arabs should be induced to move out of [Western] Palestine,

presumably to what was then Transjordanian, or Eastern, Palestine.[92] American support was voiced by

> both Democrats and Republicans in the course of the Presidential elections . . . in the autumn of 1944 . . . in particular, a letter by the President . . . in favour of the opening of Palestine to unrestricted Jewish immigration and colonization and such policy as to result in the establishment there of a free and democratic Jewish commonwealth.

These were followed by the June 1945 British Labour Party declarations "in favour of a Jewish State."[93]

But the actual postwar policy of the Palestine government remained unaltered and increasingly hostile to immigration of the Jewish survivors from the death camps. Against the post-mortem of the war, with revelations such as the December 1945 news story headlined, "One Half-Million Jews Offered For Sale," about the Gestapo's offer to "sell" Hungarian Jews "at two dollars each" through the offices of Adolf Eichmann in 1944,[94] the British administration of Palestine remained adamantly opposed to Jewish immigration. On December 27, 1945, the Earl of Halifax, British envoy to Washington, reported anxiously to the Foreign

Office in a "secret telegram" that the United States press was "circulating an allegation":

> in spite of statements that Arab authorities would condescend to an interim in continuation of Jewish immigration into Palestine at the rate of 1,500 a month, all immigration has stopped and no additional immigration certificates are being issued.

Although the qualifications applied to the White Paper's quota of 75,000 into Palestine from 1939 to the war's end in May 1945 were so stringent that not even the minuscule quota had been filled despite the millions who would have swum or crawled to get in,[95] Halifax reported that

> it is further alleged that the authorities in Palestine when approached on the subject replied that they have no instructions to issue further immigration certificates.
>
> These statements are attracting considerable attention here and will undoubtedly result in much criticism. May I be informed by immediate telegram of the position?[96]

The position, in fact, was apparently left up to the Arabs, as a spate of "secret" dispatches in 1946 illustrates, beginning with a January 1946 Foreign Office minute to the British Prime Minister:

> There was a general feeling that immigration into Palestine could not, at this moment, cease altogether and that, while it was right that the concurrence of the Arab States in continued immigration should be sought, His Majesty's Government would in the last resort have to take their own decision in the matter.
> . . . to his Majesty's representatives in the Middle East regarding their approach to the Arab States. These representatives were there authorized to inform the state
> . . . if the question of adherence to the White Paper was raised, that His Majesty's Government, while not adhering to that portion of the 1939 undertaking which left the final word on immigration to the Arabs of Palestine only, proposed to implement the spirit of the assurance that more than 75,000 additional Jewish immigrants would not be admitted into Palestine *save with Arab consent*. Certain of the representatives, in reporting the results of their interviews, stated that they had made use of this assurance. . . .
> In these circumstances it is thought preferable to make no communication to the [Jewish] Agency pending the receipt of the reply from the Arab States. . . .[97]

There was the "general feeling" that Jewish immigration "could not, at this moment, cease altogether"—by 1946 even the general public in England and abroad knew of the "figure of six million" Jews who had been murdered by the Nazis.[98] The Foreign Office responded the next day: His Majesty's Representatives in the Middle East would be instructed to "press the Arab Governments to signify their agreement, at the earliest possible date," to a brief "interim period" for "continued Jewish immigration." The Foreign Office had considered asking the United States Government whether they would be prepared to approach Arab Governments urging them to acquiesce without further delay in continued immigration at [the rate of] 1,500 a month pending receipt of Anglo-American Committee's recommendations but I do not think this would be advisable.[99]

Two days later the British Prime Minister answered a "personal and secret" wire addressing the subject from President Truman with one of his own,[100] informing the President that the Arabs had been "approached":

The quota of 75,000 authorized under the White Paper of 1939 [for Jewish immigration] is now virtually exhausted, balance of only a few hundred remaining, and Arabs have been approached urgently in accordance with the statement made by Bevin in Parliament on 13th November [1945] so as to secure maintenance of immigration at present rate of 1,500, repeat 1,500 persons per month pending consideration of report of the Anglo-American Committee.[101]

The same day Jewish Agency representatives also raised the question of Foreign Secretary Ernest Bevin's promise in Parliament the preceding November. They had been assured

that immigration would continue at the rate of 1,500 monthly without interruption, but now it seemed as if His Majesty's Government were awaiting the acquiescence of the Arab States. What was the position?[102]

The Colonial Office reported on January 7, 1946, that the "present position is . . . that White Paper quota is to all intents exhausted. . . ." As A. Cunningham reported to the Secretary of State for the Colonies, a careful and exacting count had concluded that although 54,166 "legal" Jewish immigrants and 20,304 "illegal" immigrants totaled only 74,470—"under 75,000 quota" by "first January," 1946—

400 authorities . . . have been virtually exhausted to cover cases of 275 illegal immigrants since brought to account.[103]

According to a "Top-Secret-Special-Care-should-be-taken-to-maintain-the-secrecy-of-the-documents-of-this-file" memo, sent later that month, any "further quota" would necessitate a "reply from the Arab States," pending "a meeting of the Arab League."[104] As the memo stated,

The Foreign Office are doubtful whether the Arabs will easily commit themselves to a definite "yes" and I gather that the Foreign Office might not be averse to our taking a line that we had consulted the Arab states and in the absence of a reply we are continuing the quota and the agreed rate until they should make up their minds.

"From the Palestine point of view it is really most embarrassing to have to wait much longer," the memo concluded, because the "uncertainty" was "raising difficulties . . . apart from the problem of what to do with the illegal immigrants. . . ." Enclosed with the memo was a note that clarified the "difficulties apart from" the persistence of Jewish immigration—"It was clear" that "a unilateral pronouncement" by Britain without the concurrence of the Arabs "might damage our relations with the Arab States."[105]

The Arabs' response to the Mandatory government's continuing patronage was forthcoming. Arab troops entered Palestine freely.[106] The Egyptian paper *Al Misri* carried an interview with the Foreign Minister of Iraq, who assessed that

> . . . the Arabs ought not to be afraid of the British. I can assure you that the British forces in Palestine would not try to oppose or fight the Arabs, because Britain is a real friend of the Arabs.[107]

In Western Palestine, conditions were steadily worsening. The Arab strategy was to halt communications between Jewish settlements. In Jerusalem, the Arabs had been unhampered by Government discipline. In December 1947, Golda Meir told the Palestine High Commissioner, Sir Alan Cunningham, that

> Policemen and soldiers were standing around while shops were set on fire and Jews were being attacked, behaving as if it had nothing to do with them.[108]

Striking at the heart of Jerusalem's Old City with its Jewish sanctuaries, the Arabs included among their targets cutting off the water supply.[109] The only highway between Tel Aviv and Jerusalem—the supply route vital to the Jews' survival in Jerusalem—was under siege: villages of non-Jews located at strategic points on the highway were enlisted by the Arabs in Palestine and Iraqi "irregulars." Deir Yaseen, 2,000 feet above sea level, west of Jerusalem toward Bethlehem and Tel Aviv, was one of those villages. At the time of the Jews' widely publicized Deir Yaseen attack on April 9, 1948,[110] every isolated Jewish village was under "massive attack."[111]

> Between November 1947 and May 1948, more than 4,000 Jewish soldiers and 2,000 Jewish civilians had been killed, nearly 1 per cent of the total Jewish population.[112]

Meanwhile, Government's concern for Arab approval—extraordinary, given the Arabs' unequivocal assurances of support for the Axis during the war just ended—continued to color the altogether contrasting hue of the British attitude toward *Arab* illegal immigrants. For example, the Undersecretary of State for the Colonial Office himself wrote to intercede in the case of "Benamar Hedi and Labidi Yousef," two Tunisian stowaways "arrested by the master of the ship and turned over to the immigration authorities. . . ." If they were "sent back to Tunisia, there might be considerable political repercussions," and they would "be shot by the French."[113]

That same day, February 1, 1946, the High Commissioner sent a "secret" telegram to Lord Killearn, His Majesty's Ambassador in Cairo, to placate the Egyptian Prime Minister's concern over the number of Jewish "illegal immigrants who have entered Palestine since exhaustion of White Paper quota." Although there was "some difficulty in giving an answer which will not be open to suspicion of evasion," because "it is impossible to fix the exact date on which the White Paper was exhausted," the British Ambassador in Cairo could assure the Egyptians that

> So far as this Government is aware, 1,350 Jewish illegal immigrants have entered Palestine since the White Paper was exhausted. These of course will be deducted from new interim quota of 1,500 a month.[114]

The much-awaited Anglo-American Committee of Inquiry Report recommended "the admission of 100,000 immigrants, victims of Nazi persecution, as soon as possible," and that

> Palestine should be administered in accordance with the terms of the Mandate . . . which declares with regard to immigration that "The Administration of Palestine, while ensuring that the rights and position of other sections of the population are not prejudiced, shall *facilitate Jewish immigration* under suitable conditions."*[115]

By quoting the Mandate, the Anglo-American Report belatedly had revalidated and underscored the intent of the Mandate. The "100,000 immigrants" recommendation had taken two-thirds of all the European Holocaust survivors into account: only about 150,000 remained, "lingering in the camps . . . who cannot find any place to go. . . ."[116] The Report also boldly underlined the distortion under which "Palestine's system of immigration" had operated throughout British administration: facilitating Arab or "other" immigration instead, without regard for the "prejudice" to existing Jewish population.†

His Majesty's Government, however, had no intention of following the Anglo-American Committee's recommendation.

Earlier in April, just before the publication of the Anglo-American *Report,* the High Commissioner of Palestine had reported to the Secretary of State for the Colonies that

> . . . as from date of White Paper not more than 75,000 Jews plus the 6,000 provided for in the interim quotas for the four months 15th December, 1945–14th April, 1946 should be admitted to Palestine for permanent residence. Consequences of accepting [Jewish] Agency's contention would be to cause excess of this total of 81,000.[117]

The Secretary of State for the Colonies defended the cutoff. It was not that "he had not great sympathy for the refugees," a Foreign Office extract reported.

---

*Emphasis added.

†In the entire "Historical Background" of the Anglo-American Committee of Inquiry Report, and in the specific section called "Illegal Immigration," not one clue or reference was given to the magnitude of Arab illegal immigration, with and without official Government approval and encouragement, into Western Palestine. It was as though what the veteran archivist at the Public Record Office in Kew Gardens had assumed was true—that "there never was any Arab immigration."

It must be admitted, however, that the admission of 100,000 refugees was not a complete solution to the [public] problem. Moreover to give the Jews the 100,000 certificates would be to give them all they had asked for at the moment, and HMG had the obligation of safeguarding the interests of both Jews and Arabs and it was necessary therefore to have regard to the effect of the introduction of 100,000 additional Jews upon the Arabs in Palestine.[118]

The German Jews were especially singled out by the British Government that year. Survivors from the country of origin of the "final solution" were to be selected for particular scrutiny, as advised in a Foreign Office "confidential note" in July:

We must have . . . a clear definition of the term German JEW and must prevent German JEWS from emigrating to PALESTINE [sic].[119]

Britain's attitude toward apprehending war criminals* for the murders of Jews was by no means equally zealous. More "antisemitism under the skin" existed in Britain in 1946, according to Mr. Bevin, than ever before.[121] Despite the number of leading Nazis untouched by the Nuremberg trials,[122] many British agreed with Con O'Neill, a Foreign Office official who argued against continuing the search. As O'Neill put it, "We don't want war crimes trials to become a universal bore."[123]

But by August 1946, the "measures to stop illegal immigration into Palestine" were a matter of increasing agitation to the British Embassy in Washington. The Foreign Office received report of an angry and bitter United States, with the "first press reports" revealing Britain's halting of Jewish immigration into Palestine:

The British are accused of Nazi practices and of attempting to drive the Jews to desperation in order to complete the transformation of Palestine into an armed fortress to safeguard British Imperialist interests in the Near East.

The British "phrase 'illegal immigrant' " was "attacked" by Zionist organizations in the United States as "invalid," since it was based on the 1939 White Paper and

. . . these measures violate the 1924 Anglo-American Convention which provided that no change should be made in the Mandate without United States consent.[124]
Representative Celler (Democrat-New York) also attacks the measures.

United States Representative Emanuel Celler had "Stigmatized the Labor Government as callous and soulless," and he recommended that "further money and credits under the loans be withheld from Britain unless she keeps her pledges."[125] Celler had also reminded Britain that

the labor platform . . . called for unlimited Jewish immigration into Palestine and the removal of the Arabs if there were not enough room for the Jews. The

---

*When the Jewish leadership of Britain requested admission to the Nuremberg hearings, British officials responded that "no Jewish organizations are permanently represented by observers at the trials."[120]

United States Government must insist on the immediate entry of the first 100,000.[126]

And on it went. The violence escalated in Western Palestine—violence from the Muslim Arabs within and without Palestine against the outrage of an equal *"dhimmi"* infidel state, violence after generations of restraint from Palestinian Jews desperate to create homes for the languishing survivors of Nazi genocide and a sanctuary against future onslaughts, by the regaining of their political and cultural independence. There are many documented studies of the bloodletting in Palestine between the war's end and the United Nations' declaration of Israel as an independent state. While the number of fatalities may vary slightly in one account or another, all have been in agreement about the causes of the violence and the British aid and support of the Arabs' attempt to suppress the Jewish state.[127]

The separate forces that had militated against Jews and other *dhimmis* in Arab lands, and in Palestine too with the advent of Muslim, though non-Arab, rule now combined with a ferocity perhaps not even matched by the modern-day mullahs' uprising in Iran. Using every instrument at its disposal—including the short-sighted support of the frazzled British in Western Palestine—the neighboring Arab world virtually went to war months before the declaration of Israel's independence. Arab states sent reinforcements, primarily from Syria, Jordan, and Iraq, fully expecting that, as in past Palestine anti-Jewish onslaughts, the government would buckle under the weight of the violence, ending up in support of Arab claims and penalizing Jewish immigration, because the presence of Jews was a "provocation."

But this time there was not the habitual Jewish restraint, to which both Arab and British had once been accustomed. It had taken the Holocaust to bring effective self-defense to Palestine, where once only the cowering had survived. Now, however, the Jewish "extremist" fringe also attacked. And the British buckling in May 1948 consisted *not* of Government's customary "report" and subsequent imposition of further immigration restrictions against Jews, but of Britain's total retreat and abandonment of "Palestine," one day after Israel—only seventeen percent of the intended "Jewish National Home"—had become the lone, small, mutilated but no less independent Jewish State.

18

The Flight from Fact

> They [the Arabs] were weak in material
> resources, and even after success would be, since
> their world was agricultural and pastoral,
> without minerals, and could never be strong in
> modern armaments. Were it otherwise, we
> should have had to pause before evoking in the
> strategic centre of the Middle East new national
> movements of such abounding vigour.
>
> —T. E. Lawrence, 1918

The "Palestinian problem" is often asserted to be the "heart of the matter," which must be dealt with before any real Middle East peace or any solution can occur. Britain, for example, has never altered its policy. In 1980 the British Foreign Office proposed a "new" Middle East "line": the "Palestinian Question" must be settled before any peace can begin in the region. The British journalist Terence Prittie[1] wrote:

> the media . . . contain many hard-hearted and fair-minded people . . . but [the new policy's] effects are undeniable. Just as water may eventually wear away stone, so Foreign Office arguments which are tirelessly expounded are wearing away doubts and scruples.

The British are still, wistfully, courting Arab "gratitude."

The "heart of the matter," however, is not the Arab refugees or the "Palestinian Arab refugees" or the "rights" of the "Palestinians"—or even Palestine. Were the Jewish-settled independent state on any area within reach of the Arab world—like the Christians in Lebanon, or the Kurds in Iraq—no matter how remote or how barren the location, there might well be another "problem." And very likely there would also be another group of *effendis* to sell land to the Jews. There would be "landless" peasants anxious to better their lot who would migrate into the area of Jewish development.[2] Perhaps they too would be goaded into claiming that the Jews displaced them from their "land since time immemorial." But the chances of the *dhimmi* Jews gaining independence among Arabs in an Arab country, where Islam is the state religion,[3] are not even arguable. Even in the Jews' own Holy Land it took two thousand years and millions of Jewish lives to accomplish the political rebirth of Israel.

The Arabs believe that by creating an Arab Palestinian identity, at the sacrifice of the well-being and the very lives of the "Arab refugees," they will accomplish politically and through "guerrilla warfare" what they failed to achieve in military combat: the destruction of Israel—the unacceptable independent *dhimmi* state. That is the "heart of the matter."

All the myths surrounding the Arab "Palestinians" are based on the same premises: 1) the "Palestinian people" have had an identity with the land; 2) that identity has been present for "thousands of years"; 3) the alien Jews "returned after 2000 years" in 1948 to "displace" the "Palestinian Arabs" in the "new" Jewish state; 4) the Arabs were there first—it was Arab land; 5) the Jews "stole" the Arabs' land; 6) the Jewish terrorists forced the peaceable Arabs to flee from "Palestine"; 7) Palestine is Israel, and Israel constitutes all of Palestine—"In 1948 Palestine became Israel"; 8) only Jews immigrated into "Palestine," while Arabs were natives there for millennia; 9) there are no places for the "homeless" Palestinian "refugees" to go; 10) the Jews were living in equality and tranquility with the "Palestinian Arabs" before Israel became a state, just as Jews had lived traditionally in peace and harmony throughout the benevolent Arab world; 11) the Arab "Palestinians," like other Arabs, have "nothing against Jews—only Zionists."

Contrary to those Arab propaganda claims, 1) in the late nineteenth and early twentieth centuries, Arabs or Arabic-speaking migrants were wandering in search of subsistence all over the Middle East. The land of "Palestine" proper had been laid waste, causing peasants to flee. 2) Jews and "Zionism" never left the Holy Land, even after the Roman conquest in A.D. 70. 3) The traditional land of "Palestine" included areas both east and west of the Jordan River. 4) The Arabic-speaking "masses" in "Palestine"—what few there were—thought of themselves as "Ottomans or Turks," as Southern Syrians or as "Arab people"—but never as "Palestinians," even after *effendis* and the Mufti tried to incite "nationalism," and even after T. E. Lawrence had made herculean attempts to inject the Arabic-speaking residents of "Palestine" with nationalism. 5) Imbued with religious prejudice, the Muslims of Palestine erupted into anti-Jewish violence often, and at the call of the Muslim leaders, long before Israel. 6) Those anti-Jewish, apolitical acts were later, by the British, ascribed to "Nationalism." 7) The bulk of all "Arab" peasantry in the area—East-Palestinian, Syrian, Iraqi, Egyptian, and others—were rendered "landless" by feudal-like societal structures, natural disasters, extortionate taxation, and corrupt loan sharks. Yet the Jews were cynically charged with creating "landless" Arabs in "Palestine." The British gave state domain lands, allocated for the "Jewish National Home," to those "landless" Arabs who claimed they were being "displaced by Jews" in Western Palestine. 8) All the land outside the limited Jewish-settled area of Western Palestine was treated as "Arab" land: more than eighty percent—including even part of *Western* Palestine—was diverted to the Arabs. 9) The overwhelming bulk of Palestine called "Eastern Palestine," or "Transjordan," became the Arab independent state within Palestine, despite the fact that all "Palestine" had been designated as a "Jewish National Home." 10) The "homelands" to which Arab refugees moved in 1948 included lands that many Arab refugees had only recently left in order to gain the economic advantages of the small Jewish region within Palestine. Those "homelands" where many Arab refugees of 1948 originated included the greater part of "Palestine"—Jordan today—to which the Jews claimed historic rights: "Jordan" was no less a "Palestinian state" than was the Jewish-settled fraction named "Israel." 11) Those who deprived the Arab "refugees" of homes among families and within their own Arab nation are the Arab-Muslim leaders. 12) The Arab "refugees-émigrés," who by tradition had been migrating into the Jewish-settled areas, *were* accepted as citizens of Palestine-cum-Jordan, because Jordanians acknowledge that their country is "Palestinian soil." 13) All other adjacent Arab states *refused* to grant the dignity of citizenship to those whom they called their Arab brothers. The migrants had left their nearby Arab homelands to share the new prosperity in the Jewish-settled area of Western Palestine, that fraction of the original Jewish homeland retained by the Jews.

As we have seen, it is only in the Jewish-settled area of Western Palestine that the population distribution is relevant. The charge that "Arab Palestinians were excluded from their homeland" has been levied against the Jewish people, based upon the false assumption that Jews were allowed to settle, unrestricted, throughout their "Jewish National Home" of "Palestine," and thus that Israel was equivalent to all of "Palestine." Since the land of Israel—mainly the Jewish-inhabited land in 1948—accounted for less than a fourth of the land originally designated "Palestine," and if the rest of "Palestine" is inhabited by Jordanian/Palestinians in an *Arab* state carved out of the Palestinian "Jewish National Home"—where Jews are forbidden by law from settling—how, then, can Arabs be said to have been *"excluded"* from a "Palestinian homeland?"

The situation-changing effect of a detailed analysis of the composition and distribution of the population of Western Palestine, and of the nature of immigration and in-migration into that area, is of immense significance; yet these data have heretofore been almost entirely ignored. There was neither map nor measure readily available even to identify accurately the population or territory actually involved in the Jewish-settled areas that constituted the land where ninety-eight percent of all Jews in "Palestine" would live until *after* 1948—a fraction of Western Palestine. There has been no relevant recognition of the British land restrictions against Jews, which limited Jewish settlement to only a portion of *Western* Palestine.

The land in the "Jewish National Home" was treated largely as "Arab Land." The Jews' immigration was brutally restricted, while "illegal" Arab immigration was freely permitted—that was in fact the British "system" of immigration. To appease Arab "discontent," the British violated the international League of Nations Mandate, by "facilitating" *Arab* settlement onto Jewish-settled land, and by treating the Jews only "on sufferance" in their "Jewish National Home." No real measure of Arab in-migrants and immigrants was ever taken, because the prevalent erroneous assumption was and still is that those Arab migrants had "always been there." The omission of such information facilitated the myth of today.

The situation that subsequently evolved brings to mind once more the parable about Georgia set forth earlier.* In the parable, the hypothetical white settlers usurped the lands developed by the blacks and then accused the blacks of "displacing whites" in black-settled land; just so, the Arabs swarmed into the Jewish-settled areas of Western Palestine, took the places that Palestinian Jews were clearing for Jewish refugees, and then charged the Jews with "displacing Arab natives" in the Jewish-settled areas of Western Palestine. Just as the whites could not hope to justify such a claim today, similarly the Arabs, who found "benefits they had never known before," cannot claim to have been victims. The Arab demand for "justice" is seen instead to be "injustice," as John Hope Simpson acknowledged in 1930.†

This Arab movement of peoples stemmed from a tradition of migration and migrants. It is not equivalent to the situation of the German, Russian, Czech, Hungarian, Vietnamese, Cambodian, Afghan, and Lebanese refugees fleeing to become immigrants elsewhere, escaping from persecution, dictatorship, or certain death. Those in-migrants and immigrants among the Arab "refugee" population had been wrongly regarded immediately upon their arrival in Western Palestine as "existing" settled inhabitants "for millennia" within the Jewish-settled area of Western Palestine; they were actually continuing in 1948 their traditional pattern of shifting to where they thought "their brethren were better treated." For the instant "natives," as for those who similarly became instant "refugees," life was better in the UNWRA camp setting than for landless impoverished laborers anywhere in the Arab world.

Many counted as refugees were, more realistically, itinerant workers from neighboring countries; many who became "refugees" fleeing *from* Israel, ostensibly "Palestinians on their plots of land from time immemorial," were in actuality those who had recently gone *into* Israel, where they were treated as the instant "natives," when Israel was still the "Jewish-settled area of Western Palestine."† The fact that they had earned better wages and found improved living conditions among the Jewish settlements was not a strong enough motivating factor to restrain the Arab leavetaking in 1948.

This pattern of movement had been seen earlier, in 1936, when another "Arab Revolt" had begun. Then, some of the Arab immigrants who had never been reported as "entering" the country suddenly appeared in the British record as "requesting to return to their countries." The British, knowing full well the broad-scale illegal Arab immigration into the Jewish-settled areas of Western Palestine, had ordered colonial officials not to discourage those who volunteered to go "at their own request," because "next week they might not want to go"; when the anti-Jewish attacks and the terrorizing riots and strikes died down, the Arabs would want to stay where they might continue to prosper.

Although many of the affluent Arabs and their followers had been leaving

*See Chapter 12.
†See Chapter 14.

since the United Nations resolution for "Palestine's" partition in November 1947, not until the British abdicated and the Jews gained real equality and independence did the greater part of the "refugee flight" from Jewish-settled areas (Israel) take place. That flight, aided and instigated by Arab leaders, was motivated by several powerful factors. The leaders of the Arab world were involved in an intricate series of intra-Arab power thrusts; "Palestine" could perhaps further their respective personal and dynastic ambitions. The motivations and attitudes by which the Arab leaders could goad, direct, and expedite the Arab masses were built-in: the time-honored subjugation of *dhimmi* Jews and the advantages gained therefrom, as well as the deeply imbued belief in Arab-Muslim superiority, gave potency to the Arab leaders' warnings and exhortations.

For centuries, Muslims had been able to incite the Arabic-speaking masses to anti-Jewish attacks by invoking the racially prejudiced "holy words" and by spreading inflammatory fabrications about the Jews. In 1948, two prime related factors were at play: first, the Arab masses believed that, with independence, the Jews would turn the tables on the Arabs and would take retribution from them for the persecution that the Jewish *dhimmi* had suffered at Arab hands in the past. The few "acts of reprisal" by outraged Jews, in response to the Arab violence designed to prevent the Jews' statehood, were novel and unexpected. For so long the *dhimmi* had exhibited "incredible restraint." Word of the Jews' counterattacks was broadcast far and wide, embellished, and vastly exaggerated. For numerous Arabs, among most of whom migration was an easy and deep-rooted tradition, the inclination was to move. Second, the implication of a *dhimmi*-run country in the Middle East, however small in size, was anathema to an Arab-Muslim group; it was one thing for Arabs to exercise their "right" to take advantage of *dhimmi* property and development, but it was an utterly different matter to be under the rule of such *dhimmis*.

Paradoxically, despite the distaste for the existence of a *dhimmi* development, the Arabs had subordinated their emotions for the advantages of living in an area of greater prosperity under British sovereignty. They had followed the Jews into the Jewish-settled areas of Western Palestine from other areas of the country, and from other lands, to be near the Jews. If the Arab numbers hadn't been swelled by in-migration and illegal immigration, the Jews' majority in their own "National Home" would have been far greater, the number of Arab refugees in 1948 would have been far lower, those who were in fact refugees fleeing to lands outside Jordanian Palestine might have been granted their right to citizenship according to international precedent, and the illusion of a "native Palestinian Arab displacement by Jews" could not have achieved a semblance of credibility.

As President Roosevelt noted in 1939,[4]

> Arab immigration into Palestine since 1921 has *vastly* exceeded the total Jewish immigration during this whole period. . . .*

*Emphasis added.

It is startling to realize that, if all those Jews and all those Arabs who arrived in Western Palestine between 1893 and 1948 had remained, and if they were forced to leave now, a dual exodus of at least equal proportion would in all probability take place. "Palestine" would be depopulated once again.

Young Israelis and young Arabs don't know the realities of their own and each other's histories. The older Israelis remember; they say they knew, but never thought of proving it—or that any of it was calculable. A prominent Palestinian, born in Jerusalem and specializing in the Arab world, described, as we sat in his office, the "scandal" in the "thirties," when British officials were caught giving "thousands of genuine Palestine citizenship papers" to illegal Arab immigrants. He also recalled that in his "mother's house the servants changed every week— and every week the Arab helpers came from someplace else outside of 'Palestine.' "

By itself, no recollection has weight as an overall indicator. However, with the substantiated evidence supplied by the preceding documentation, the professor's memories and other recollections do serve to flesh out the picture of the conditions that prevailed. It is perhaps for political reasons that no Arab social scientist has elected to trace the multi-ethnic backgrounds of the "Palestinian" Arabs. To do so would give many cruelly manipulated "refugees" back their actual histories, their identities, and would allow them to focus on their real rights to citizenship in the lands where they live today.

Today's twelve- or twenty-year-old "Arab Palestinian people" were not yet born when the Arab exodus from Israel occurred. Most have no notion themselves of the prior history of in-migration and immigration to the Jewish enclaves of settlement within Western Palestine. They do, however, know that to verbalize out loud the thought that it was their Arab "brothers" who kept them in a suspended state of animation called "refugeehood" would bring ostracism and perhaps worse. The Arab Palestine "Liberation" Organization "eliminates traitors," as the PLO's United Nations "observer" Terzi declared in 1978.

The injustices done to the "Arab Palestinian refugees" have been perpetuated by the Arab world, which has also masked and denied the "Palestinian state" that exists. By fanning intolerance toward Jews as "infidels" into violence against Israel as "the enemy," the PLO, or "Palestinian revolutionaries," have taught the twelve-year-old Arab born in a refugee camp that his oppressor is Israel.[5] He knows not about the Arab *effendi* or sheikh who may have stolen his grandfather's or his father's land, through graft or usury; he knows nothing of the thousands of his Arab brothers who had, in the years before 1948, been "landless" peasants, streaming into the newly reclaimed wastelands of the Jewish-settled areas from the very countries where some are still in camps; he has not learned that the Arab world's oil wealth has been used to keep his hatred directed against Israel, by keeping him and his family from the dignity of citizenship in the "brother" country where he is encamped. Moreover, he does not know what many Arabs have admitted: that the Arab world which has rejected its responsibility for his plight must eventually undertake it.

The violent opposition by PLO strongmen and the Arab world in general toward rehabilitation and resettlement of the Arab refugees has brought confusion, frustration, and a state of suspended animation to the lives of some younger Arab "refugees." While a number of the Arab refugees by now actually possess citizenship in countries such as Kuwait, some families have been absorbed in one or another of the Arab countries *except* for the formal identity of citizenship, which is still withheld; there are also others whose families belong to the hard-core nucleus of militant "revolutionaries." In that small fanatical group which has become the main source and the conduit for Arab propaganda, to assume any role other than the sacrificial one slotted for them by their leaders would be interpreted as "treachery" by his or her peers. Among the Arab refugees interviewed, many of the youths expressed sentiments similar to those of Muhammad (he asked that his real name be withheld):

Muhammad:	I come from Palestine—some say Israel, but the Jews came only 30 years ago . . . Jews came from Europe . . . from Russia—it's not our fault . . . Dayan came from England . . . Begin from, I don't know, Switzerland. . . . Why they leave the United States? Why they leave England? The East is for Arabs.
Q:	Isn't Jordan also Palestine?
Muhammad:	No, Jordan is Jordan . . . it used to be Palestine but when English finished up, they gave it to Hussein. . . . A million, maybe a million and half Palestinians, all the merchants live in Jordan. Bedouins live way outside on the desert. . . .
Q:	If Jordan has a majority of Palestinians, and is "Palestine," then isn't Jordan a Palestinian country?
Muhammad:	No, because we can't get rid of Hussein—he's in CIA. The United States protects him—he's killed 10,000 Palestinians in '69, '70. . . . We refuse citizenship.
Q:	In Israel or in Jordan?
Muhammad:	Both of them.
Q:	Why?
Muhammad:	If we took citizenship we wouldn't get back our land—we'd forget.
Q:	But Israel is only a small part of Palestine—what will you do with the Jews in Israel?
Muhammad:	It takes time, twenty, thirty, forty years, but we try to get our land —we get rid of them. We have to believe in *something,* you know?

Israelis too are confused and troubled. The older Jewish population can remember the violence, the Arab in-migration, and the influx of Arabs from surrounding borders. But many young Israeli "Palestinian" Jews react with anxiety, empathy, and concern about their alleged culpability, in response to widespread perceptions about the Israeli "occupation" of the West Bank, and the myth of the "three-or-four million Arab Palestinians excluded from their home-land inhabited by them since time immemorial." For so long the propaganda has reiterated that "Jews displaced Arab natives" in "Palestine," without even any factual framework for evaluating such allegations, that many Jews feel they must bear that guilt. It is not a new syndrome. Arthur Miller caught it well in his play *Incident at Vichy,* a treatment of the Nazi-collaborationist Vichy regime in France and its mass arrests of Jews during World War II.[6] In an exchange between two Jewish prisoners, Leduc, a psychiatrist, and Lebeau, a painter:

Leduc: You feel guilty, then?
Lebeau: A little, I guess. Not for anything I've done but . . . I don't know why.
Leduc: For being a Jew, perhaps?
Lebeau: I'm not ashamed of being a Jew.
Leduc: Then why feel guilty?
Lebeau: I don't know. Maybe it's that they keep saying such terrible things about us, and you can't answer. After years and years of it, you . . . I wouldn't say you believe it, but . . . you do, a little.

Goebbels, Nazi exponent of Hitler's "Big Lie," averred that if a lie were repeated often enough and long enough, it would come to be perceived as truth. What he did not add was that the *victim* of the lie may also grow to believe it.

Arab propaganda has attempted to sell several other false ideas. The numbers of Arab refugees have been distorted, just as the numbers of "settled existing Arab natives since time immemorial" were twisted and misrepresented. Even by the Arabs' own refugee count in 1948, higher than the highest United Nations calculations by 150,000, the number of Arab refugees was, by remarkable coincidence, almost identical to the number of Jews—600,000 to 800,000—fleeing or expelled from Arab countries into Israel in 1948.

The Arabs who fled Israel in 1948 came mainly from the coastal areas where the Jews' settlement was heavy—the same areas into which so many Arabs had recently arrived. This might explain why the United Nations was moved to describe, as eligible for refugee status, any Arab who had lived in Israel for the minimal two years.

There were in 1982 about 1,500,000 Jewish citizens in Israel who either themselves fled from or were the offspring of parents who fled from Arab countries.[7] That figure is almost equivalent to even the swollen 1982 total of Arab refugees and descendants—1,900,000—as reported by the largely Arab-staffed UNRWA camps.[8] The Israeli figure did *not* include those Jewish refugees and descendants who fled from the Arab world to countries other than Israel (300,000 in 1982–1983). If those persons were included, the total of Jewish refugees would match even the total UNRWA figure for Arab refugees and their descendants, living both in and away from camps.

In fact, UNRWA reported that, as of June 1982, out of their 1.9 million total figure, 1,249,599 Arab "refugees" registered with UNRWA—and thus presumably receiving refugee benefits—were *not* living in camps! Of the total UNRWA figure of 1,900,000, there were only 676,127 "in camps." That is the *maximum* figure. It should also be noted that most of the Arabs in camps work close by and obtain the rent-free attribute of "camp" residence, which in very many cases is in an urban setting far superior to the refugee's pre-Israel or other possible habitat. Nevertheless, camp life, however physically endurable, can only be debilitating, given the politicization and enmity existing there. In Israel, where encampments of hundreds of thousand of Jewish refugees were almost all replaced, many problems still plagued former refugees.

There should be sufficient compassion among the Arab states at last to bestow well-earned citizenship upon those living "out of camps" who long ago were absorbed in all other respects into their various countries. Further, the Arabs must be encouraged to discriminate no longer against those still registered as living in camps.[9]

UNRWA's report through June 1982, which is generally acknowledged to be inflated for political exploitation, listed: 65,425 Arab refugees "in camps" in Syria (many of the refugees took over the properties of Syrian Jews who managed to flee the country); in Lebanon 123,442 "in camps"; in Gaza 208,662 "in camps"; and in Jordan (what UNRWA calls "East Jordan") 192,392 "in camps." A total of only roughly 676,000 souls altogether were living—or were *reported* by a politically motivated Arab-run organ to be living—in camps throughout the Arab Middle East. In other words, those camps that were commonly believed to be holding as many as "four million" Palestinian Arabs were inhabited by 676,000 Arabs, including the refugees and their descendants (and probably a large number of "others"), according to the Arabs' own traditionally inflated numbers. Included in that figure are those in the West Bank, that is, the area of *Western* Palestine that was purged of Jews around 1929, and where afterward Jews were restricted by the British from buying land; it was both an integral part of the "Jewish National Home" and later regarded as the "purely-Arab" area, from which Arab in-migrants poured into the Jewish-settled area throughout the Mandatory period. The number of West Bank "refugees" reported by UNRWA to be "in camps" there was 86,206.[10]

Syria has been stating an earnest need for new population; the need presumably still exists. Egypt, with or without the restraints of the peace program, might be given incentive to absorb the 208,662 refugees in Gaza. For the relatively small number who either have not or could not presently be accepted and rehabilitated in their host countries, surely there is room for welcome in the multimillion-mile expanse of the Arab world, particularly for those in Lebanese "camps."

In Lebanon, the number of refugees reported by UNRWA through June 1982 totaled 238,667 altogether, both *in* and *out* of camps. That figure covered the period *before* many Arabs who were registered as refugees had left the area that became embattled in mid-1982. Thus UNRWA's total figure undoubtedly would be the *maximum* number, a number that must have diminished with the height, and the tragic aftermath, of the 1982 fighting. Yet somehow that number shot up from about 230,000 to "300,000" by early 1983.[11] Further, according to UNRWA's figures, reported *before* the height of the hostilities in Lebanon, 123,442, a majority of the refugees, lived *in* camps. Yet, according to *New York Times'* correspondent Thomas Friedman, "the majority of Palestinians in Lebanon" in March 1983 were "living *outside* the camps in rental apartments.*"[12]

It's little wonder that, to escape from the tedium of tracing such constant and confusing discrepancies, one would be likely to give up wearily and accept whatever the latest figure quoted might be. As a consequence, however, over 61,000 had been added, against all logic and feasibility, to the UNRWA overall totals: in that one brief moment, in that one place, the figure was swelled more than twenty-five percent—with hundreds of top-notch reporters looking on, and nobody but the Arab UNRWA staff allowed to verify. That was an apt modern example of the continuing escalation, resulting in ever-larger "Palestinian diaspora" figures, and the somewhat helpless attempts to explain the "incredible" or "unprecedented" numbers.

The Arab refugees-plus-descendants who do *live in* refugee camps totaled 676,000 in 1982, throughout the Middle East; that aggregate Arab refugee group was about equal, *including offspring* of Arab parents who were refugees, to just the *original* number of *Jewish refugees* who fled from the Arab world in 1948— *not* including the offspring of Jewish refugees, which by 1980 would bring the total of Jewish refugees to about 1.5 million.

By way of further contrast, the number of refugees throughout the world in 1982 totaled more than 10 million, including well over 2 million African refugee souls, 1 million Asians, and the 2.6 million Afghans who fled to Pakistan.[13] Yet that world figure, while enormous, was significantly reduced from the number reported two years earlier: in 1980, more than 12.6 million, including 6 million Africans and 2 million Asians, had been reported. In 1980 alone, "two million men, women and children fled their home countries, pushed out by war or oppression . . . [and] joined millions" of others in seeking resettlement.[14] As the United Nations High Commissioner for Refugees observed, ". . . communities, institutions, cities and nations have generously opened their doors to refugees and —a fact which should be stressed—many refugees have, in their turn, been valuable assets. . . ."[15]

Most of those refugees had fled within the period of a few years before the report. A great number of those who fled two years ago are already removed from the lists, and other unfortunate refugees have taken their places. The United States Committee for Refugees *Survey* noted that more than a million Indochinese refugees were resettled between 1975 and 1981. That report also made special mention of the fact that among those African refugees recorded, "substantial number of the refugees . . . are 'settled in place.' " To be "settled in place" or "resettled in a third country" is considered by the United Nations as a "durable solution" for Indochinese, Africans, and in fact all the world's refugees.[16]

In the case of the Palestinian Arab refugees, perhaps even more than elsewhere, recognition of a "durable solution" in their present lands had been strongly indicated, for those still reported "in camps." Many of them might be in fact returning to the Arab homeland they had abandoned to seek the benefits

*Emphasis added.

of the Jewish-settled areas in Western Palestine. Unlike the Afghans, or the Ethiopians, or the Vietnamese, or the Cambodians, the Arabs were largely *returning* to areas nearby—in many cases only a few miles from the places they left. Most of the Arab "refugees" who fled still remained within "Palestine." Yet it is the *Arab* refugees and Israel upon whom the United Nations, the media, and consequently the public focus the most attention.

Politicizing of refugee statistics, no new phenomenon in this situation, has further stimulated that attention. One lopsided presentation exhibits a double-standard reminiscent of British Mandatory reports: in an exceptional treatment of its reported statistics, the United States Committee for Refugees presented the Palestinian Arabs' total Arab UNRWA figure for refugees and descendants among the roster of current refugees, without qualification. Though considered by that report for many years to be lower on the list of significant refugee situations, the "Palestinians" were in 1982 raised to second on the list after the Afghans, and deemed more "significant" than the destitute Ethiopians, Vietnamese, Cambodians, Laotians, or Salvadorans.

Although the pertinent facts are well known in the refugee-concerned community, no mention is made of the "durable solutions" found by that vast majority of Arabs who have long been living "away from camps," or of the village-like comfortable surroundings within most of today's Arab refugee "camps" themselves. Unlike the squalid quarters established for refugees in other parts of the world, many are permanent urban units, far from the wretched image immediately triggered by the term "refugee camp." Moreover, the United States Committee for Refugees has included in its calculations as "refugees" the Jordanian/-Palestinians in Jordan ("733,000"), overlooking the fact that Jordan's nationality code offered immediate citizenship—a law of return—to "Palestine."

On the strange other hand, *because* "Israel" offers the "right to citizenship in the Jewish homeland" to Jewish immigrants "under the law of return," the United States Committee for Refugees suddenly declared in 1982 for the first time the politicized judgment that the hundreds of thousands of Jewish refugees whom the Committee had listed as refugees in the preceding annual report "can no longer be considered refugee(s) by Israel."[17]

The Arab refugees have been used as a weapon by the Soviets as well as the Arabs; several Arab countries have their own Soviet-trained, Soviet-equipped Palestinian "guerrilla" forces.[18] Some of those forces had originally in fact been living *outside* Israel's 1949–1967 lines, in territory *excluded* from Israel when they "fled." What those "refugees" were "escaping" from may have been the Jordanian Army, since they were leaving territory seized by Jordan in 1948. But that group could not have been fleeing from Israel, since the towns they left had already been purged of Jews well before 1948, and the districts of their towns had been excluded from Israel's territory. Abu Daoud, the PLO mastermind of the Munich massacre, was one such case. Another is Bassam Abu Sharif, a strong-man of the Palestine Front for the Liberation of Palestine (PFLP), an offshoot of the PLO–al-Fatah combine.[19] Yasser Arafat, who, according to one biography, may not have been born in "Palestine" at all,[20] has claimed to be from East Jerusalem, an area that was excluded from Israel between 1948 and 1967. His training by the Soviets reportedly was completed during that time.

The "Palestinian Problem," no new phenomenon, is but the pan-Arab enmity by another name. The Arab refugees' manipulation at the cruel whim of leaders in the Arab world is traditional; in earlier days, too, Arabs were periodically whipped into fanatically anti-Jewish onslaughts. What is new is the sophisticated use of Middle-East turnspeak,* twisted rhetoric artfully aimed at the hearts and minds of the West, originated by the Arabs, and rivaling the Soviets, who are veterans of "semantic infiltration" and the word war. Just as, in their lexicon, totalitarianism translates into "democracy," and degradation becomes "freedom," so has the flawed but democratic Israel been branded "Zionist imperialist" and "racist." So has the carving of Jordan out of the internationally Mandated "Jewish National Home" during the Mandatory period been transformed into the notion that "Israel is all of Palestine"—the "homeland" of all the Arab refugees. It is *1984*, where as George Orwell wrote,[21]

War is peace; freedom is slavery; ignorance is strength.

According to *turnspeak*, those Arab migrants and immigrants who, in Sir John Hope Simpson's words, committed the "injustice" of "taking the places" of Jews in the "Jewish National Home" are today's "displaced" Arab Palestinian people, "excluded" from the Jewish-settled area of Western Palestine, their "homeland since time immemorial." The free world is targeted for deception by the twisted speech of Arab propaganda.

From past history it is apparent that the Arab-Muslim world would not, without prodding and pressure, perhaps, from the rest of the world, accept an infidel or non-Muslim minority community as equals; as Arabs say, the land is forever Arab. Arab writers frankly recognize that the world, however cynical, would not take kindly to an abrupt or "quick" destruction of Israel. By promoting "Palestinian nationalism" through the publicized and orchestrated violence of "guerrilla attacks," as the Arab writer al-Ayubi wrote in the early 1970's that they should, the Arabs had *changed the perception* of reality *from the xenophobic and powerful Arab world pitted against the tiny Jewish state* into the image of *one tiny nation of Israel against an equally tiny nation of "Palestine."* Israel is portrayed, then, as *all* of "Palestine," the giant "aggressor."

The question is often posed, "What difference does it make whether or not the Palestinians' historical claim is justified?" As one Middle East scholar put it, "Granted, most of the 'Palestinian' claim is specious, but they feel as they do now, and isn't that what is important?" However, the "Palestinians'" claim is avowedly based upon "history" and their goal is the dissolution of another state. Their alleged right of "self-determination" is based upon the erroneous alleged "90% majority of Arabs" in 1917 on the Jewish-settled area that became Israel

*See definition in Chapter 9.

in 1948. If they invoke "historical rights" and base their claims upon historical justifications, then those historical rights must be examined and verified. Assuming that the real "rights" of the Palestinian peoples to their "homeland" are what the justice-seeking free world is after—whatever those rights may prove to be— then to prevent injustice, the documented truths must be weighed and considered.

In discussing the question of an independent West Bank "mini-state," the PLO and its sponsor, the United Nations, have relied upon and alleged the existence of "inalienable rights" of self-determination of the Palestinian people.[22] Putting aside the fallacy of the "90%-Arabs, 9%-Jews" premise of the Arab claim, and the dubiousness of the assertion that any rights are "inalienable," it is helpful to consider the question of the existence of such a principle as an unqualified right of self-determination.

In the historical instances where a national group has been reorganized as a separate sovereign state, the peoples have been distinct from their neighbors in race, language, religion, culture, and tradition, or at least in a majority of such characteristics. With respect to the PLO and the Palestinian Arabs, that is not the case and it is doubtful, therefore, whether the principle of self-determination had even a *prima facie* application at all.

The concept of self-determination was largely a product of the Treaty of Versailles at the conclusion of World War I and of the League of Nations, which grew out of that peace process. President Beneš of Czechoslovakia, who was one of the chief proponents of the principle of self-determination, wrote that "the principle of self-determination itself would need very detailed and precise explanation. It was misused and continues to be misused in an incredible degree. Everybody gives to it the interpretation that serves his political interests and aims. Post-war political experiences will force political science as well as practical politicians to proceed to a real and complete revision on this matter."[23]

Alfred Cobban, in his book on the subject, states:

> We may begin by asking, since self-determination is assumed by this theory to be a right, what kind of right is understood? Is it a right to self-determination where and insofar as circumstances permit, and subject to limitation by the *competing claims of other rights?* Or is it an absolute right, knowing no qualification? In practice, there can be no doubt which is the most appropriate description of the methods of the treatymakers at Paris. Practically every one, including Wilson himself, recognized that self-determination could only be applied with due regard to circumstances.*[24]

If there is a right of self-determination, as the Arabs seem to contend, for everyone at all times and under all conditions, can the individual prevail over the group always, can the minority overrule the majority? Can the withdrawing unit be minuscule? Can those who secede disregard the rights and conditions of others who are affected by their secession? To be consistent with "Palestinian Arab"

*Emphasis added.

claims—were they not distorted—should the United Nations, for example, recognize the right of self-determination of the Ibos in Nigeria, of the Kurds in Iraq and Iran, of the Katangans in Zaire or of the Ulstermen in Ireland? Did the United States recognize the rights of the southern states to secede? Have the oil-rich states of Texas and Oklahoma a similar right to self-determination if they proclaim it? As Cobban says,[25]

> If self-determination means this kind of thing, where, and with what unit, can the process possibly stop?

If there is an absolute right to self-determination, should not Lithuania, Latvia, and Estonia be permitted to withdraw from the Soviet Union? May the Uzbeks, who were incorporated by conquest around 1875 into tsarist-ruled Central Asia, not insist on an independent country of their own? Could the Volga Germans or the Soviet Jews not demand self-determination in the form of a separate country and government with a part of the land of the Soviet Union? May the Christian Copts in Egypt not claim self-determination, since they find problems living in the midst of a Muslim population?

In short, are there not geographical, historical, economic, and political considerations that rule out national self-determination in the form of the sovereign state for many of the smaller nationalities of the world? Even if the majority of the members of a nation desire political independence, circumstances may prohibit it, and the mere desire of however many people will not alter them. As Cobban wrote, "In the words of Burke, 'If we cry, like children, for the moon, like children, we must cry on.'"

According to Cobban,[26] the "right of self-determination, therefore, if it means anything at all, cannot mean an absolute right to complete national sovereignty . . . and such political independence may be objectively possible, or it may not. *Circumstances, in the end, are the determining factor.*"*

The principle of self-determination is alleged by representatives of the Soviet Union to be a basic doctrine of Soviet policy and a fundamental principle essential to a valid and justifiable international relationship. One comprehensive and authoritative Moscow-published volume by G. Starushenko, entitled *The Principle of National Self-Determination in Soviet Foreign Policy,* sets forth "the Soviet Union's decisive role in formulating the principle of self-determination and having it recognized as a principle of international law." The author claims that,

> Unlike the Imperialist states, the Soviet Union strictly abides by the principle of national self-determination.[27]

> The recognition of the principle of self-determination in international law is a revolutionary development.[28]

*Emphasis added.

In 1961, Soviet Foreign Minister Andrei Gromyko declared that the "unconditional recognition" of self-determination is "one prerequisite for peaceful coexistence"; he then asserted that self-determination was an "inalienable right," using the same question-begging rhetoric now utilized by Arab clients of the Soviet Union in connection with any and all claims of Arab "Palestinians."[29]

It is difficult to accept this Soviet doctrine as a matter of principle, as distinct from tactical political maneuver, when one considers the Russian handling of the Baltic states of Latvia, Lithuania, and Estonia; they each would undoubtedly opt for separate nationhood if Russian guns did not forbid their self-determination; consider also Soviet intervention and repression by force in Hungary and Czechoslovakia.

The Arab advocacy of a "secular democratic state" is profoundly unconvincing. Democracy as an Arab concept has been singularly absent from Arab tradition, as demonstrated by historical and modern references to institutionalized anti-Semitism, as well as systematic discrimination against other non-Muslim minorities, non-Muslim "Arabs," and even certain fellow-Muslim sects. The concept of "racial purity"—apartheid—evidenced by current Arab rejection of any Jewish settlements among Arabs in the West Bank and the Sinai, is a graphic case in point.

The "moderate" Arab proposal for a "mini-state" on the West Bank and in Gaza, and the strategy behind additional vague Arab demands, have been set forth in Arab writings frequently. The fact that a "mini-state" was not created in the nineteen years when the area was under Arab domination, has been pointed out; the candid comments of "moderates" and the PLO regarding the mini-state —as a "first step" to the destruction of the enemy—must be seen in context, not as bluster but as threat.

When the Arab claim based on fraudulent "historical" devices is exposed and thus discarded, another popular argument surfaces. "After all," it is said, "it doesn't matter when the 'nationalism' evolved. The important thing is that it exists; it's a violent nationalism now and the refugees—the 'Palestinians'—exist." Yet, a violence born of unworthy incitation, aggravated by unnatural camp conditions and deliberate indoctrination to that violence, ought not necessarily command credence or respect because it calls itself "nationalism." The movement, whatever its label—terrorism or nationalism—is no more a legitimate excuse for the attempt to destroy one small Jewish state than the "repatriation" of other refugees around the world would be seen as a reason for the destruction of any other state.

The world has treated both Arab and Jewish "refugees" cruelly—the Jewish refugees' hardships, their cruel history and difficulties in Israel have been shunted aside as an unwelcome "complication," after having been omitted from consideration for decades. Theodore Draper wrote,[30]

There is something suspicious and ominous about a world which permits one rule for refugees from a Jewish state and another rule for refugees from all other kinds of states.

There is, too, a sad implication in the world's failure to give any consideration at all to the hundreds of thousands of Jewish refugees terrorized and expelled from Arab lands in 1948 and after.

In the name of humanitarianism, the Arab refugees have been bred to believe that the fraudulent history they learn by rote is true: their "dream" of "identity" can only materialize, they believe, at the cost of the destruction of a people. The young "Palestinian refugee" of twelve or thirteen or even twenty has no choice. All persons must dream, and the only dream that has been drilled into the Arab refugee child—in or out of the camps—is "to return to the Palestinian home- land." That they and their families may have little desire to "return" themselves, that a legitimate Palestinian homeland in Jordan already exists, which has been open to them, or that many of them can claim origins and legitimate rights to citizenship in Syria, or Egypt, or Algeria, or wherever their families came from —none of these options for identity has even the slightest chance of gaining credence among them under present conditions of thought control. Merely to verbalize such an idea would bring rejection, if not violence.

In June 1977, during interviews in Damascus, Syrian officials expressed the wish that Syria might get American technological assistance to develop the arable Syrian land, which requires implementation of the Euphrates Dam irrigation potential. The Syrian Minister of Trade and Economy asked that a message be given to the American government. Syria hadn't the population to develop that land, he said, because there was virtually 100 percent employment in Syria, so that they needed people as well as technology. They would give plots of valuable land in Syria to anyone who would come to work it.[31]

Since it was known that in the late 1940s and 1950s the Arab refugees had been in the process of accepting just such an offer until the Arab League and other factors acted against it, I asked various Syrian officials, "Why not give the land to those Palestinian Arabs who would choose to accept your offer?" The answer was always the same. As one of the Syrians responded angrily,

> We will give the land to anyone—the Ibos, the Koreans, Americans . . . anyone who comes—anyone but the Palestinians! We must keep their hatred directed against Israel.

The Palestinian Arabs and the Palestinian Jews have become the sacrificial goats in a world power game. After reviewing the results of this making of a myth, it is difficult to find an easy answer: "justice" would be served by a long-overdue recognition, out loud, that there are indeed two states in Palestine today—one Arab and one Jewish. Yet, as Yasser Arafat boasted in 1977,[32] "Our people in the occupied areas are carrying out brilliant operations. Our children have turned stones into bombs. . . . These people cannot be defeated."

There is no glib or ready solution to the present confrontation. Enmity bred over decades cannot be easily defused. The Palestinian Arab "refugees" have found their "myth," as Musa Alami prescribed. They found an identity in that myth. And a dream. But surely a dream of destruction and bloodshed, of "injustice" masquerading as justice, of "rights" based upon falsehoods, cannot continue to capture the sympathy and imagination of the outside world at the expense of the Jews, whose identity the Palestinian Arabs would usurp.

If Egypt and the late President Anwar Sadat could make peace with Israel, however tenuous, after the saber rattling and the religiously inspired anti-Jewish sentiments that created a warm bond between Egypt and Nazism, then so might the other "moderates" and "rejectionists" in the Arab world today. Once, during Solomon's reign (965–928 B.C.), "united Israel" was so "highly honored as the leading state between Egypt and Asia Minor," that Egypt's pharaoh had "given his daughter in marriage" to Solomon, for "good diplomatic and political reasons."[33]

As the Minister of Agriculture of Syria, an avowed supporter and supportee of the Soviet Union, had illustrated, it was "American" technological assistance that Syria wanted. But might it have been the irrigation expertise of Israel that he really needed? The result of the peace-making process depends greatly on the international community's continued adherence to the truth as it is sometimes tacitly acknowledged, and not the totalitarian-sponsored pan-Arab inversion of truth. To achieve their short-sighted ends—a "peaceful" piece of the Arab oil action—some nations among the free world community appear to be buying the turnspeak.

For thirty-five years, while the real nature of the Arab "refugee problem" has often been identified, the affluent Arab world has paid only a relative pittance to the care of the "refugees"; on the other hand, prodigious Arab funds have supported terror. The Arabs have, in addition, rejected every genuine humanitarian attempt to solve the "problem" of their brethren, whose right to the dignity of citizenship is their legitimate human right.

The world community has made the mistake of unwittingly creating a breeding ground of violence. Through perpetuation of the "humanitarian" conditions of the "temporary" camps, it hoped perhaps to avoid having to exact from the Arab world an attitude toward its refugees that conformed to the customary humanitarian requirements expected from other nations; the penalty for such demand was perceived to be the possible loss of substantial Arab oil benefits. The wound was allowed to fester until it began to burst into the terrorism of the PLO and other offspring of the earlier terror tactics in Western Palestine organized by the Mufti, in consultation with his Nazi soulmates. Now, the world community is being faced with the pan-Arab suggestion for another blunder, this one even more difficult to retrieve. The new "moral" claim is presently offered, to take the place of justice. Through the revisionist history of the Arab propaganda, it is asserted that Israel must bear the guilt for the Arab "refugees," since the Jews "in 1948 excluded the Arabs from their homeland since time immemorial."

Unfortunately, and perhaps not surprisingly to those sophisticated in the art of politics, the case as it has been distorted by propaganda does not benefit the "Palestinian" Arab refugees themselves. As the Arab Palestinian writer Fawaz Turki summed it up, although it was "Arab governments" who "continued to oppose . . . integration,"

> the price for this intransigence and inflexibility was paid by the Palestinians alone and not by the Arabs. . . . Pawn politics and indifference were the two foci of a problem of tragic and human dimensions.[34]

The Arab-Soviet distortion has prolonged the refugee's frustration, and supports —indeed justifies—Arab terrorist activities, even against Arab Palestinians. The very political process by which the refugee's plight has been highlighted has condemned many Arab "refugees" to encampment psychologically if not physically. However, hundreds of thousands of other Arab "refugees" are already living and working in the critically labor-needy Arab states, in some instances running those countries, and they feel that citizenship is "owed" to them. Indeed, unpublicized and largely unknown, many are in fact already bona fide citizens.

The present propaganda argument is based on the "historical claims" of the "native Arab Palestinian on his land"—now called Israel. According to the propaganda claim, it is from that Jewish-settled area of Western Palestine that the "Arabs were excluded from their homeland since time immemorial." That claim cannot be sustained. If the "historical" claim is *measured* against documented history, which *contradicts* that claim, the Arab propagandists and their supporters often shift to an argument based on pragmatics: the "Palestinian [Arab] people" exist, therefore they must have a "homeland." That argument must run head-on into the realities of justice, of Jordan, and of the Arab-Jewish exchange of refugee populations in 1948.

The Arabs' recognition of how vulnerable was their "return of the Arab refugees" argument inspired the transformation of the "refugee" claim into an "historical" claim. "Palestinian self-determination" was the "new tool"; and its claim is based on the specious and misconceived comparison of the "90%-Arab-native and 9%-Jewish population," in all "Palestine"—what we now know should properly be limited, for comparison, to the *Jewish-settled areas* of *Western* Palestine. As a few Arab strategists have admitted, the real "refugee" rights could too easily become evident. The "consequences" of the obvious Arab-Jewish refugee exchange of populations were frankly assessed by the Arab writer Sabri Jiryis: "Jews have absorbed the Jews who were expelled or forced from Arab states and the Arab states must, in their turn, settle the Palestinians [Arabs] within their borders and solve their problem."*

Although that Arab-born segment of the Jewish population has finally been recognized, inevitably, as the bulk of the "Sephardic" majority within an "Orientalized" Israel, Western observers are seldom reminded that the Sephardic Israeli

---

*See Chapter 2.

majority is in fact mainly composed either of descendants or of those who were themselves the Jewish refugees who fled or were expelled from Muslim-Arab countries. Thus the accompanying social problems, the Arab-born Jews' distrust of the Arab world and their support of a "hardline" government position toward the Arabs—all conditions that are predictable and logical when seen in context —are not evaluated in context. That the social problems are the result of Israel's attempt to absorb a refugee population at least equal to the number of Arabs who purportedly left Israel in 1948—a massive Jewish refugee population that matched the number of Jews already in Israel in 1948—and that all the Arab-born Jewish refugees converged on the Jewish state at the same time that the Arabs left, while Israel was improvising its urgent defense against Arab warfare—the connection is rarely if ever made. What was an obvious, literal exchange of Jewish and Arab refugee populations, remarkably equal in numbers even if one accepts the inflated Arab counts, goes unrecognized or is shrugged aside as an unwelcome complication.

Moreover, to judge the attitudes and viewpoints of Sephardic Jewish refugees from oppression in Arab lands *apart* from the critically significant historical circumstance that made them that way is as faulty and incomplete as it would be for an observer to try to judge the reactions and activities of American blacks toward civil rights without ever having heard of slavery or the history of the blacks in America and the genesis of the Civil Rights movement. Yet the Sephardic Jews' attitudes toward their former masters—attitudes born of harsh experience and the Arabs' continued avowed hostility toward the *dhimmi* Jewish State —are scarcely ever related to the bitter history and the circumstances surrounding that pivotal Jewish exodus from the Arab world.

Meanwhile the Arab émigré-refugees remain exploited by Arab leaders in that Arab world, their own milieu. Most are actually already absorbed: a small percentage are still in their camps. All remain without moderate leadership and many fear for their lives; were they to take a truly moderate stance, they might well be murdered, as others have been.

One must care about the "Palestinian" peoples, whatever their heritage. They are Arabs and Jews and "others" who have been long abused in a world misled by its torturous misconceptions. Instead of permitting those Arab "refugees" who are outside of Jordanian Palestine to suffer the planned discrimination of adamant Arab governments in lands where many "refugees" have lived for a generation or more, the free world might begin a fair and realistic effort to solve the problem.

The possibility of solution is there. An Arab Palestinian state already exists in Jordan. The other Arab states can be encouraged to make room for those among the Arab refugees who have not yet been absorbed, and to give citizenship in their respective states of asylum to those outside Jordan. There is no bromide here for a facile solution, or one that would not be fraught with bitterness and antagonism. Before the India-Pakistan exchange of refugee populations was resolved, years of rancor and violence elapsed.

What must not continue, what cannot be allowed to continue, is the cynical scapegoating of the Jewish state and the Jewish refugees therein, or the sacrifice of the Arab refugees who are, in the name of "humanitarianism," being employed inhumanely as a war weapon against Israel by the Arab world. In the face of these major problems, too many politicians and persons of influence choose to shut their eyes to the facts. Too many refrain from critical analysis of propaganda in order to preserve their illusions about the price of oil. And far too many, the overwhelming bulk of us, had never been furnished with enough data to understand what the problem really was.

A program calculated to furnish incentives to the Arab states and others— a "Marshall-type" plan to cooperate for peace—has been proposed by many eminent bipartisan political figures. Such a program would[35]

> convert that bilateral peace into a truly regional peace, by demonstrating that the fruits of peace exceed the spoils of war. The plan could be financed by all the countries which have a great interest in peace and stability in the Middle East because of their dependency upon the oil in that region. It would be based on the knowledge that there is also an Arab dependency upon the free world to continue its present relationship with Arab states. Such a plan ought to create an incentive to solve the problems that stand in the way of regional space.
>
> To the extent that we render aid, it would necessarily be linked with "the settlement of the refugees" or, if they are already settled, then citizenship for the Arab refugees within these various Arab lands.

The United States has provided most of the over-a-billion dollars in UNRWA funds over the last thirty-plus years, for what was to have been "temporary relief before resettlement." Is is not possible that the fund which has prolonged the refugee status of the "Arab refugees" could be replaced by aid in conjunction with development, and that permanent Arab refugee resettlement in the Arab regions could follow? The Arab world wants the benefits of co-existence with the "West" and therefore a major role can be played by the United States in helping to resolve the Arab refugee-émigré problem.

All the necessary ingredients exist: recent reports of migrant labor in the Arab states have shown that the Arabs are urgently in need of labor, skilled and unskilled. Within the Arab world there is now an abundance of capital to pay the costs of integrating the refugees. Foreign funds, once freed from no-longer-necessary UNRWA camps, could assist the rehabilitation of the Arab refugees. The Jewish refugees from Arab lands have already been absorbed by the Israelis, but those of their properties that were confiscated would match or exceed whatever the Arab refugees left behind. The de facto exchange of Arab and Jewish refugee populations is undeniable, a *fait accompli.* Its recognition by the Arabs should be facilitated with the West's endorsement. Recall the Syrian official's offer to "give land away to workers who come—except the Palestinians," whose "hatred must be directed at Israel." Syria's request for "American technology," along with United States and other Western assistance now in effect or projected in many Arab "rejectionist" states, ought to be reciprocal; cooperation should be enlisted and required from nations that are aided by the United States and the West.

If the Arab world's political and unjustified discrimination against its refugee-émigré brothers were to cease, and if the camp indoctrination could no longer act as a catalyst to the rejection of peace with Israel, if the Jordanian-Palestinian state, the Arabs' "displacement" of Jews, and the exchange of populations that took place between Jews and Arabs are all finally understood and recognized by the free world, then the Arab "rejectionist" front dedicated to the *jihad* (holy war) against Israel may finally realize that the program of propaganda deception cannot succeed. They may then accede to a policy of genuine moderation, of a kind which in the Western sense means toleration and peace.

At long last the Arab refugees would then be allowed the right to live in a more normal environment, to the refugees' optimal benefit, and to the ultimate advantage of the Arab host nations. This possibly peaceful and ultimately most humane course of action would entail only a relatively minor financial transaction for the Arab nations. It would dignify the refugees and enable the Arab countries of asylum to observe the universal laws of hospitality and decency toward their refugees. It will also, if done, demonstrate that the Arabs are genuinely concerned for the welfare of their brethren, that they have finally observed the humanitarian requirements expected of any government that wishes to benefit from mutual relationships in the free world, and that they are not primarily interested in utilizing the refugees, human beings, flesh and blood, as their weapon in their war.

Thus far, merely mouthing the deceptive words of turnspeak has achieved an amazing measure of success for the revisionist history and the propaganda of the "Arab-Israeli conflict."[36] As the late PLO-Saiqa (Syrian PLO) leader Zuheir Muhsein observed in a PLO strategy discussion in 1974, many nations had already accepted the calculated interchange of images: the Arabs had managed "to juxtapose the Israeli existence with a 'Palestinian' one."[37] Muhsein went on to explain the proposed "Independent Palestinian State" on the West Bank:

> Our purpose is a democratic State in the whole of Palestine. . . . A State in the occupied areas will not constitute an obstacle. The contrary is true—it will be a point of departure. . . . This State will be the backbone of our struggle against Israel.[38]

The Arabs, through terror and the enticement of oil-power, actually manipulated the prevention of the Jewish majority that should, as mandated, have become in turn the Jewish State of Palestine *before World War II.* Had the Arabs not succeeded, the "final solution to the Jewish problem" might have been haven, not Holocaust.

The cruelest instance of willful blindness to the nature of one's actions is attributable to British immigration policy. It is horrifying to learn that the British —a "civilized people"—were willing to see Jews in Europe put to death by the Nazis; for "fear" of "Arab comment," the British claimed that "Palestine" had "no more places" for Jews, while at the very same moment the British were importing "illegal" Arab immigrants by tens of thousands into Palestine to do "necessary" work—work and place that they denied to Jews.

In the end, Britain's systematic policy of virtual exclusion of Jews had resulted in utter disaster. It was disaster in the eyes of the British because they left Palestine defeated; for the Arabs, who had won a battle against the entry of perhaps six million prospective Palestinian/Israeli Jews, it was disaster then to be faced, ironically, with the anathema of a *dhimmi* nation that the Jews achieved ultimately *because* of the world's horror at the senseless slaughter of those six million; for the Jews, there was disaster in the tragic timing of Israel's independence: had it been unrepressed it would have culminated in time to preclude the Holocaust. As it turned out, Israel emerged just in time to gather in not only the survivors of Hitler's savagery, but that great swell of Arab-born Zionists who fled seeking refuge. The probable fate of those refugees from Arab lands, had the Jewish state been voted down, became, mercifully, only a matter for abstract speculation.

Today, the explicitly stated Arab goals appear to be gaining credence once again through the medium of propaganda and twisted rhetoric, unquestioned by those of us who haven't known the questions to ask, and unhindered by many who have guessed. Those who understand the reality ought to demand more.

Throughout the Mandate, the British attempted to gain peace by appeasing intimidation and terror. It was a self-imposed intimidation to a perception of oil-power and force that the Western powers by themselves in fact evoked. Yet, others are considering a similar course. But the lesson ought to be clear by now that the West's continuation of the protracted British policy of submission has not brought a peaceful life. As Winston Churchill cautioned in 1939, the acts that we engage in for appeasement today we will have to remedy at far greater cost and remorse tomorrow.

APPENDIXES

413

ANCIENT "PALESTINE"

Sidon

Mt. Lebanon

Litani River

Damascus

Mt. Hermon

PHOENICIA

Tyre

Dan

BASHAN

Hazor

Lake Huleh

Accho

Capernaum

GALILEE

Cana

Sepphoris

Tiberias

Sea of Galilee

Yarmuk River

Mediterranean Sea

Mt. Carmel

Nazareth

Kishon River

Gadara

Dor

Megiddo

Beth-Shan
(Scythopolis)

GILEAD

Ramoth-Gilead

Caesarea

PLAIN OF SHARON

Taanach

Pella

Samaria

Gerasa

Shechem

Apollonia

Jabbok River

Antipatris

SAMARIA

Joppa

Bethel

Jericho

Jordan River

Rabbath Ammon

Lydda

Ekron

Gezer

AMMON

Emmaus

Jerusalem

Eltekeh

Mt. Nebo

Ashdod

Libnah

Bethlehem

Beth-Shemesh

Dead Sea Scrolls
found here

TRANSJORDAN

Ascalon

Gath

Dead

Lachish

PHILISTIA

Eglon

Hebron

Sea

Arnon River

Gaza

Raphia

JUDAH

Gerar

Sharuhen

Beer-Sheba

WILDERNESS OF ZIN

MOAB

Zered River

Petra

EDOM

APPENDIX II
Official British Police Report Regarding Jews' Appeal to Arabs

C o p y

10/PS.

District Police Headquarters,
(C.I.D.)
P.O.B. 700.
Haifa.

26th April, 1948.

S E C R E T

A/A.I.G., C.I.D.

Subject:-   General Situation - Haifa District.

Haifa remains quiet.   Yesterday produced a noticeable change
in the general atmosphere and businesses and shops in the lower
town were open for the first time in many days.   Traffic started
to move normally around the town and people returning to their
places of business filled the streets.   In fact, Haifa presented
a more normal appearance than it had done for a long while.
Some Arabs were seen moving among the Jews in the lower town and
German Colony area and these were allowed free and unmolested
passage.   An appeal has been made to the Arabs by the Jews to re-
open their shops and businesses in order to relieve the difficulties
of feeding the Arab population.   Evacuation was still going on
yesterday and several trips were made by 'Z' craft to Acre. Roads,
too, were crowded with people leaving Haifa with their belongings.
At a meeting yesterday afternoon Arab leaders reiterated their
determination to evacuate the entire Arab population and they have
been given the loan of ten 3-ton military trucks as from this
morning to assist the evacuation.

Yesterday morning a Jew attempted to pass the drop barrier of
Police H.Q. facing Palmers Gate wheeling a barrow.   He was shot
and killed by a Police sentry.

At 0640 hrs. yesterday Tireh village was again attacked with
mortar fire.   Casualties and damage not known.

A report has been received from Military to the effect that
at 23.50 hrs. yesterday Jews attacked Acre from the direction of
Ein Hamifratz and Tall al Fukhkhar.   An advance party succeeded in
demolishing three houses in the Manshiya Quarter and then heavy
mortar fire was directed at the town.   Several mortar bombs landed
in Acre Prison and all the inmates have escaped.   The British warder
staff are safe.   Military proceeded to the scene and opened fire
with artillery on Ein Hamifratz.   The Jews thereupon withdrew and
a convoy of 11 vehicles was seen proceeding in the direction of
Haifa.   Casualties to both sides are not known.

(A.J. Bidmead.)
for SUPERINTENDENT OF POLICE.

Copy:-   District Commissioner, Haifa.
Superintendent of Police, Haifa.
File.

Source: Carl Hermann Voss, *The Palestine Problem Today* (Boston, 1953).

APPENDIX III. The Palestinian National Charter

(Palestine Liberation Organization)*

1. Palestine is the homeland of the Palestinian Arab people; it is an indivisible part of the Arab homeland, and the Palestinian people are an integral part of the Arab nation.

2. Palestine, with the boundaries it had during the British mandate, is an indivisible territorial unit.

3. The Palestinian Arab people possess the legal right to their homeland and have the right to determine their destiny after achieving the liberation of their country in accordance with their wishes and entirely of their own accord and will.

4. The Palestinian identity is a genuine, essential and inherent characteristic; it is transmitted from parents to children. The Zionist occupation and the dispersal of the Palestinian Arab people, through the disasters which befell them, do not make them lose their Palestinian identity and their membership of the Palestinian community, nor do they negate them.

5. The Palestinians are those Arab nationals who, until 1947, normally resided in Palestine regardless of whether they were evicted from it or have stayed there. Anyone born, after that date, of a Palestinian father—whether inside Palestine or outside it—is also a Palestinian.

6. The Jews who had normally resided in Palestine until the beginning of the Zionist invasion will be considered Palestinians.

7. That there is a Palestinian community and that it has material, spiritual and historical connection with Palestine are indisputable facts. It is a national duty to bring up individual Palestinians in an Arab revolutionary manner. All means of information and education must be adopted in order to acquaint the Palestinian with his country in the most profound manner, both spiritual and material, that is possible. He must be prepared for the armed struggle and ready to sacrifice his wealth and his life in order to win back his homeland and bring about its liberation.

8. The phase in their history, through which the Palestinian people are now living, is that of national struggle for the liberation of Palestine. Thus the conflicts among the Palestinian national forces are secondary, and should be ended for the sake of the basic conflict that exists between the forces of Zionism and of imperialism on the one hand, and the Palestinian Arab people on the other. On this basis the Palestinian masses, regardless of whether they are residing in the national homeland or in diaspora, constitute—both their organizations and the individuals—one national front working for the retrieval of Palestine and its liberation through armed struggle.

9. Armed struggle is the only way to liberate Palestine. Thus it is the overall strategy, not merely a tactical phase. The Palestinian Arab people assert their absolute determination and firm resolution to continue their armed struggle and to work for an armed popular revolution for the liberation of their country and their return to it. They also assert their right to normal life in Palestine and to exercise their right to self-determination and sovereignty over it.

---

*Decisions of the National Congress of the Palestine Liberation Organization held in Cairo July 1st–17th, 1968.

10. Commando action constitutes the nucleus of the Palestinian popular liberation war. This requires its escalation, comprehensiveness and the mobilization of all the Palestinian popular and educational efforts and their organization and involvement in the armed Palestinian revolution. It also requires the achieving of unity for the national struggle among the different groupings of the Palestinian people, and between the Palestinian people and the Arab masses so as to secure the continuation of the revolution, its escalation and victory.

11. The Palestinians will have three mottoes: national unity, national mobilization and liberation.

12. The Palestinian people believe in Arab unity. In order to contribute their share towards the attainment of that objective, however, they must, at the present stage of their struggle, safeguard their Palestinian identity and develop their consciousness of that identity, and oppose any plan that may dissolve or impair it.

13. Arab unity and the liberation of Palestine are two complementary objectives, the attainment of either of which facilitates the attainment of the other. Thus, Arab unity leads to the liberation of Palestine; the liberation of Palestine leads to Arab unity; and work towards the realization of one objective proceeds side by side with work towards the realization of the other.

14. The destiny of the Arab nation, and indeed Arab existence itself, depends upon the destiny of the Palestine cause. From this interdependence springs the Arab nation's pursuit of, and striving for, the liberation of Palestine. The people of Palestine play the role of the vanguard in the realization of this sacred national goal.

15. The liberation of Palestine, from an Arab viewpoint, is a national duty and it attempts to repel the Zionist and imperialist aggression against the Arab homeland, and aims at the elimination of Zionism in Palestine. Absolute responsibility for this falls upon the Arab nation—peoples and governments—with the Arab people of Palestine in the vanguard. Accordingly the Arab nation must mobilize all its military, human, moral and spiritual capabilities to participate actively with the Palestinian people in the liberation of Palestine. It must, particularly in the phase of the armed Palestinian revolution, offer and furnish the Palestinian people with all possible help, and material and human support, and make available to them the means and opportunities that will enable them to continue to carry out their leading role in the armed revolution, until they liberate their homeland.

16. The liberation of Palestine, from a spiritual point of view, will provide the Holy Land with an atmosphere of safety and tranquillity, which in turn will safeguard the country's religious sanctuaries and guarantee freedom of worship and of visit to all, without discrimination of race, color, language, or religion. Accordingly, the people of Palestine look to all spiritual forces in the world for support.

17. The liberation of Palestine, from a human point of view, will restore to the Palestinian individual his dignity, pride and freedom. Accordingly the Palestinian Arab people look forward to the support of all those who believe in the dignity of man and his freedom in the world.

18. The liberation of Palestine, from an international point of view, is a defensive action necessitated by the demands of self-defence. Accordingly, the Palestinian people, desirous as they are of the friendship of all people, look to freedom-loving, justice-loving and peace-loving states for support in order to restore their legitimate rights in Palestine, to re-establish peace and security in the country, and to enable its people to exercise national sovereignty and freedom.

19. The partition of Palestine in 1947 and the establishment of the state of Israel are entirely illegal, regardless of the passage of time, because they were contrary to the will of the Palestinian people and to their natural right in their homeland, and inconsistent with the principles embodied in the Charter of the United Nations, particularly the right to self-determination.

20. The Balfour Declaration, the mandate for Palestine and everything that has been based upon them, are deemed null and void. Claims of historical or religious ties of Jews with Palestine are incompatible with the facts of history and the true conception of what constitutes statehood. Judaism, being a religion, is not an independent nationality. Nor do Jews constitute a single nation with an identity of its own; they are citizens of the states to which they belong.

21. The Palestinian Arab people, expressing themselves by the armed Palestinian revolution, reject all solutions which are substitutes for the total liberation of Palestine and reject all proposals aiming at the liquidation of the Palestinian problem, or its internationalization.

22. Zionism is a political movement organically associated with international imperialism and antagonistic to all action for liberation and to progressive movements in the world. It is racist and fanatic in its nature, aggressive, expansionist and colonial in its aims, and fascist in its methods. Israel is the instrument of the Zionist movement, and a geographical base for world imperialism placed strategically in the midst of the Arab homeland to combat the hopes of the Arab nation for liberation, unity and progress. Israel is a constant source of threat *vis-à-vis* peace in the Middle East and the whole world. Since the liberation of Palestine will destroy the Zionist and imperialist presence and will contribute to the establishment of peace in the Middle East, the Palestinian people look for the support of all the progressive and peaceful forces and urge them all, irrespective of their affiliations and beliefs, to offer the Palestinian people all aid and support in their just struggle for the liberation of their homeland.

23. The demands of security and peace, as well as the demands of right and justice, require all states to consider Zionism an illegitimate movement, to outlaw its existence, and to ban its operations, in order that friendly relations among peoples may be preserved, and the loyalty of citizens to their respective homelands safeguarded.

24. The Palestinian people believe in the principles of justice, freedom, sovereignty, self-determination, human dignity, and in the right of all peoples to exercise them.

25. For the realization of the goals of this Charter and its principles, the Palestine Liberation Organization will perform its role in the liberation of Palestine in accordance with the Constitution of this Organization.

26. The Palestine Liberation Organization, representative of the Palestinian revolutionary forces, is responsible for the Palestinian Arab people's movement in its struggle—to retrieve its homeland, liberate and return to it and exercise the right to self-determination in it—in all military, political and financial fields and also for whatever may be required by the Palestine case on the inter-Arab and international levels.

27. The Palestine Liberation Organization shall cooperate with all Arab states, each according to its potentialities; and will adopt a neutral policy among them in the light of the requirements of the war of liberation; and on this basis it shall not interfere in the internal affairs of any Arab state.

28. The Palestinian Arab people assert the genuineness and independence of their

national revolution and reject all forms of intervention, trusteeship and subordination.

29. The Palestinian people possess the fundamental and genuine legal right to liberate and retrieve their homeland. The Palestinian people determine their attitude towards all states and forces on the basis of the stands they adopt *vis-à-vis* the Palestinian case and the extent of the support they offer to the Palestinian revolution to fulfill the aims of the Palestinian people.

30. Fighters and carriers of arms in the war of liberation are the nucleus of the popular army which will be the protective force for the gains of the Palestinian Arab people.

31. The Organization shall have a flag, an oath of allegiance and an anthem. All this shall be decided upon in accordance with a special regulation.

32. Regulations, which shall be known as the Constitution of the Palestine Liberation Organization, shall be annexed to this Charter. It shall lay down the manner in which the Organization, and its organs and institutions, shall be constituted; the respective competence of each; and the requirements of its obligations under the Charter.

33. This Charter shall not be amended save by (vote of) a majority of two-thirds of the total membership of the National Congress of the Palestine Liberation Organization (taken) at a special session convened for that purpose.

APPENDIX IV:
Feisal-Weizmann Agreement Regarding "The Arab State and Palestine"

His Royal Highness the Emir FEISAL, representing and acting on behalf of the Arab Kingdom of Hedjaz, and Dr. CHAIM WEIZMANN, representing and acting on behalf of the Zionist Organisation,

mindful of the racial kinship and ancient bonds existing between the Arabs and the Jewish people, and realising that the surest means of working out the consummation of their national aspirations, is through the closest possible collaboration in the development of the Arab State and Palestine, and being desirous further of confirming the good understanding which exists between them,

have agreed upon the following Articles:-

ARTICLE I.

The Arab State and Palestine in all their relations and undertakings shall be controlled by the most cordial goodwill and understanding and to this end Arab and Jewish duly accredited agents shall be established and maintained in the respective territories.

ARTICLE II.

Immediately following the completion of the deliberations of the Peace Conference, the definite boundaries between the Arab State and Palestine shall be determined by a Commission to be agreed upon by the parties hereto.

ARTICLE III.

In the establishment of the Constitution and Administration of Palestine all such measures shall be adopted as will afford the fullest guarantees for carrying into effect the British Government's Declaration of the 2nd of November, 1917.

ARTICLE IV.

All necessary measures shall be taken to encourage and stimulate immigration of Jews into Palestine on a large scale, and as quickly as possible to settle Jewish immigrants upon the land through closer settlement and intensive cultivation of the soil. In taking such measures the Arab peasant and tenant farmers shall be protected in their rights, and shall be assisted in forwarding their economic development.

ARTICLE V.

No regulation nor law shall be made prohibiting or interfering in any way with the free exercise of religion; and further the free exercise and enjoyment of religious profession and worship without discrimination or preference shall forever be allowed. No religious test shall ever be required for the exercise of civil or political rights.

ARTICLE VI.

The Mohammedan Holy Places shall be under Mohammedan control.

ARTICLE VII.

The Zionist Organisation proposes to send to Palestine a Commission of experts to make a survey of the economic possibilities of the country, and to report upon the best means for its development. The Zionist Organisation will place the aforementioned Commission

at the disposal of the Arab State for the purpose of a survey of the economic possibilities of the Arab State and to report upon the best means for its development. The Zionist Organisation will use its best efforts to assist the Arab State in providing the means for developing the natural resources and economic possibilities thereof.

ARTICLE VIII.

The parties hereto agree to act in complete accord and harmony on all matters embraced herein before the Peace Congress.

ARTICLE IX.

Any matters of dispute which may arise between the contracting parties shall be referred to the British Government for arbitration.

Given under our hand at LONDON, ENGLAND, the THIRD day of JANUARY, ONE THOUSAND NINE HUNDRED AND NINETEEN.

If the Arabs are established as I have asked in my manifesto of January referendum to the British Secretary of State in Foreign Affairs, I will carry out what is written in this agreement. ~~If any documents are changed to~~.

If changes are made, I can not be answerable for failing to carry out this agreement

Feisal ibn
Hussein

Legend for Appendix V

DEFINITIONS:

I. Main areas of Jewish settlement — Incl. in Israel 1949–1967

II. Intermediate areas } Contain most of Jewish population
- Safed
- Tiberias
- Beisan
- Nazareth (excl. Nazar. town)
- Haifa
- Tulkarem
- Ramleh
- Jaffa
- Jerusalem town

III. Intermediate areas } Excl. from Israel 1949–1967

IV. Intermediate areas } Incl. in Israel 1949–1967 — Contain very little Jewish population
- Acre
- Nazareth town
- Jenin
- Nablus
- Ramallah
- Jerusalem (excl. Jeru. town)
- Hebron
- Gaza
- Beersheba

V. Main area of Arab settlement — Excl. from Israel 1949–1967

[Names of 1944 Subdistricts—very roughly equivalent to Ottoman Cazas.]

Note: The Ottoman Census apparently registered only known Ottoman subjects; since most Jews had failed to obtain Ottoman citizenship (see Chapter 10), a representative figure of the Palestinian Jewish population could not be extrapolated from the 1893 Census.

A. Arab settled population (1893 population and descendants)
B. Arab nomads
C. Arab "legal immigrants"
D. Arab "illegal immigrants"
E. Arab migrants (from main area of Arab settlement and intermediate areas) and descendants (since modern Jewish settlement began)
+ incoming
– outgoing
(Statistics *prior* to 1944 give categories A–E as single figure since no detailed breakdown was available.)
F. Jewish population

1. "Mixed" towns:
- Jerusalem
- Haifa
- Jaffa
- Tiberias
- Safed

2. "Jewish" towns
3. "Non-Jewish" towns
4. Rural areas

APPENDIX V. Population Movement within and into Western Palestine (Officially Recorded) 1893–1948

All Demographic Statistics in Thousands

Legend for symbols given above chart

1893

ABCDE		%	F
I	92,3		
II	38,9 } 145,5	31.2	
III	14,3		
IV	87,4 } 320,9	68.8	
V	233,5		
Total	**466,4**	**100.0**	

	%
I, II, III	100.0
IV, V	100.0
Total	100.0

1915

ABCDE		%	F	%
I				
II	} 195,2	32.3	83,5	98.2
III				
IV	} 409,1	67.7	1,5	1.8
V				
Total	**604,3**	**100.0**	**85,0**	**100.0**

	%
	134.2
	127.5
	129.6

1922

ABCDE		%	F	%
I				
II	} 255,5	37.9	82,2	98.1
III				
IV	} 417,9	62.1	1,6	1.9
V				
Total	**673,4**	**100.0**	**83,8**	**100.0**

	%
	175.6
	130.2
	144.4

1922—detailed geographical breakdown

	ABCDE	F
1	82,7	52,7
2	0,1	15,1
3	22,9	0,1 [110]
4	149,9	14,4
3	89,9	0,7 [746]
4	327,7	0,8

1944

ABCDE		%	F	%
I	429,9			
II	103,0 } 570,0	47.1	544,3	98.3
III	37,1			
IV	160,8 } 640,9	52.9	6,0 } 3,4	1.7
V	480,1			
Total	**1,210,9**	**100.0**	**553,7**	**100.0**

	%
	391.8
	199.7
	259.6

Population Movement, 1893–1948 (continued)

1944—detailed geographical breakdown

	ABCDE	F
1	204,0	199,4
2	0,9	215,9
3	48,8	...... [30]
4	316,4	129,0
3	156,8	0,1 [70]
4	484,2	9,2

1944/1922—expressed as a percentage

	ABCDE	F
1	247.5	612.5
2	213.1	
3	211.1	27.3
4		895.8
3	174.4	9.4
4	147.8	1,150.0

1947

ABCDE		%	A	B	C	D	E	F	%
I	462,9		249,2	8,8	27.3	9,5	+168,1		
II	110,9 } 613,7	47.1	108,7	—	—	—	+2,2	596,4	98.1
III	39,9		39,9	—	—	—	—		
IV	173,1 } 690,1	52.9	125,1	48,0	—	—	−71,2	5,3 }	1.9
V	517,0		507,2	9,8	—	—	−135,6	6,5	
Total	**1,303,8**	**100.0**						**608,2**	**100.0**

	%
	421.8
	215.1
	279.5

425

Non-Jewish Population by Subdistricts (Cazas) and Relevant Towns: 1893, 1922, 1944

	1922		1944		1944/1922%		Subdist.	1944	
	Rur.	Tot.	Rur.	Tot.	Rur.	Tot.		N-J Pop.	%†
Ga.	47,1	73,6	79,0	134,3	167,7	182,5	Jaffa	104,7	100.0
Beis.	71,1	73,4	48,0	53,6	67,5	73,0	Jer. Ur.	60,1	100.0
He.	37,0	53,1	65,0	89,6	175,7	168,7	Beis.	16,6	100.0
J (R).	45,0	83,4	75,1	147,8	166,9	177,2	Tiber.	26,1	100.0
Ra.	26,9	30,0	42,2	47,3	156,9	157,7	Haifa	115,9	96.5
Nb.	40,7	56,7	68,9	92,1	169,3	162,4	Safed	37,5	79.9
Jn.	30,9	33,5	52,9	56,9	171,2	169,9	Tuck.	31,2	45.7
Ac.	29,0	35,4	53,1	65,4	183,1	184,7	Raml.	24,7	26.2
N (U).		7,4		14,2		191,9	Naz. Ru.	4,3	17.5
N (R).	14,6	22,0	24,3	38,5	166,4	175,0	Nomads	8,8	—
Beer.	8,1	10,0	11,4	16,6	140,7	166,0		429,9	
Ti.	12,0	14,5	20,8	26,1	173,3	180,0		1893	
Sa.	13,2	13,9	37,4	46,9	283,3	243,1	Jaffa	51,4	
Ha.	27,0	47,7	53,7	120,1	198,9	251,8	Jer Ur.	27,0	
Tu.	31,6	34,9	65,3	73,3	206,6	210,0	Tiber.	5,4	
Ja.	13,6	41,2	37,6	104,7	276,5	254,1	Haifa	15,9	
Re.	29,8	45,1	65,9	97,9	221,1	217,1	Safed	14,2	
J (U)		28,6		60,1		210,1	Benisap	31,3	
							Naz. Ru.	0,3	
Total	477,7	673,4	800,5	1,211,0	167,6	179,8		145,5	

Jewish Population in "Arab" Towns	
1912	1,350
1922	856
1931	621
1944	100
1947	—

†Approximate percentage of non-Jews in focal Jewish areas: according to 1947 Partition Plan plus Jerusalem area.

Israel 1948

Land ownership as percentage of area in Western Palestine	%
Jewish-owned land	8.6
Arab-owned land	3.3
Arab-owned abandoned land	16.9
State domains	71.2

	Arabs in areas included in Israel, 1948					
	areas	A	B	CD	E	ABCDE
present 1947		483,0	56,8	36,8	170,3	746,9
remained 1948	I, II, IV	140,2	19,8	—	—	160,0
refugees		342,8	37,0	36,8	170,3	586,9

APPENDIX VI. Methodology

Description of Methodology, Population Study

The population figures used for the study were extracted, first, from Turkish census data, which were compiled according to Turkish subdistricts, and later, from British censuses and reports of British sub-districts that correspond closely to the earlier Turkish geographical divisions. The figures concerning the "Arab" (non-Jewish) population were then applied to those subdistricts that were 1) largely, 2) partially, 3) negligibly, and 4) not settled by Jews. Five geographic areas were examined, comprising the land that was included within the Armistice agreement. Three of the areas (see map on p. 246 for more specific borders) were included within the established pre-1967 borders of Israel. For the years 1893 and 1915, the Turkish census figures were used; for the years 1922, 1944, and 1947, the British census data corresponding to the same geographic areas were used. The Arab population in these areas was then divided into five categories: A) the Arab settled population (1893 inhabitants and their descendants), B) Arab nomads, C) Arab "legal immigrants," D) Arab "illegal immigrants," and E) Arab migrants. The rate of natural increase of the Arab population in the non-Jewish areas of Western Palestine was applied to the Arabs in the Jewish area. That rate was applied to the original settled Arab population. This figure was then subtracted from the total registered population in order to get a reliable estimate of the in-migration that occurred in each area between 1893 and 1947. Afterward, the number of *legally* registered Arab immigrants (Source: Anglo-American *Survey of Palestine,* 1946–1947) was subtracted from the total in-migrant population figure, as were the token number of *illegal* non-Jewish immigrants that the British government records officially reported. After all these variables were figured in for each area, the remainders are those who in-migrated from the Arab hill country. These absolute figures were also converted to percentages (see Appendix V). In this way, the ratio of Arab to Jew, particularly in the Jewish areas, could be presented for each year (1893, 1915, 1922, 1944, 1947).

The areas that actually came under Israeli rule were the areas that were included in the calculations regarding 1) the amount of out-migration around 1948 and 2) the number of refugees resulting from the establishment of the state. The number of those who stayed behind, subtracted from the total "original settled population" in 1947–1948 leaves a remainder of those who are the possible refugees. The 1947 population figures are used as a base, due to the fact that, by the end of 1947, people had already begun to flee.

Demographer's Note on Population Study

Two procedures have been used to estimate the volume of net in-migration of Arabs into areas of Jewish settlement between 1893 and 1947.

The first procedure involved using the Turkish census population figures, and applying the rate of Arabs' natural increase in Arab (no-Jewish settlement) areas: applying the percentages of actual births and deaths as obtained from the British Government censuses and reports. Natural increase was calculated from birth and death data, and then that figure and the Arab immigration total which had been reported were subtracted from the total population increase to give an estimate of net in-migration.

The second procedure involved the following: A) using data for Arab births and deaths available from the *Statistical Abstract of Palestine—1941* for the period of 1922 to 1927; B) calculating the percentage of the total population increase resulting from natural increase and assuming that the remainder of the total population growth provided an estimate of net Arab in-migration, and C) applying these percentages of total growth attributable to natural increase and net in-migration respectively to the total increase in Arab population in Jewish-settled Area I between 1893 and 1947.

The rationale for this second procedure was that fertility and mortality of the Arabs in Palestine between 1922 and 1927—and therefore also natural increase—were reasonably recorded in the *Statistical Abstract of Palestine—1941,* and in general consistent with expectations for a developing area.

It was surprising to discover that these two independent procedures produced the same estimate of minimum Arab net in-migration into Area I between 1893 and 1947. Both procedures resulted in an estimate of minimum net in-migration for that period, of roughly 168,000. Needless to say, the fact that both procedures resulted in the same figure lends credibility.

Philip M. Hauser, *Director Emeritus,*
Population Research Center,
The University of Chicago

December 30, 1980

APPENDIX VII. Examples of Private Official Correspondence and Documents Regarding Arab Immigrants to Western Palestine and Jewish-Settled Areas

Ref. No. _____ 9491

DISTRICT COMMISSIONER'S OFFICES,
SOUTHERN DISTRICT,
JAFFA.

I/ 398/36

14 May, 1936.

Chief Secretary.

Subject:- Relief of distressed
British Subjects.

Reference:- Telephone conversations-
Mr.Jacobs - Mr. Farley.

    I forward, in accordance with your verbal request, particulars concerning 50 British subjects who have applied to me for relief. While many of them owe their present unemployment to the strike which followed upon the recent disturbances, others became unemployed some time before the strike. It is clear that in the majority of cases, their mode of living in Palestine has been precarious; in many cases, moreover, they entered Palestine without permission.

2.   My recommendation is, therefore, that these persons should be repatriated with the least possible delay, since, in present circumstances, they are likely to become a not inconsiderable burden on Government.

3.   In virtue of the authority given to me by telephone, I have expended the sum of LP. 31 from a fund which, at your direction, has been described as "Advances". In view of the indefinite continuance of the strike, and of the period which is likely to elapse before repatriation may be effected, I made payments to each person of LP 1; subsequently at your suggestion, I have restricted the payments to amounts of 250 mils. In the case of persons who have been unable to produce documents in authentication of their right to British Protection, I have endeavoured to obtain the testimony of a prominent citizen of Jaffa that the person concerned is, in fact, a native of British Protected Territory.

4.   I am transmitting a copy of this letter with its enclosures to the Commissioner for Migration and Statistics whom you may find it necessary to consult.

G J Farley
District Commissioner,
Southern District.

H/AH.

Copy to: Commissioner for Migration and Statistics,
Jerusalem.

Example of Enclosures, May 14, 1936

- 3 -

Name.	Entrance to Palestine.	Papers.	Occupation	Average wage per month. LP.	Why Unemployed and remarks.
Mohamed Yusef, 12) of Hergeisa, Habarawat tribe, Sultan Derir-Sheikh.	On foot from Hejaz, 1929.	No passport. Certificate No. 2685 of 3.12.31 (out of date) of registration as British protected person from British Consul, Beirut.	Labourer.	4½	Work ceased owing to strike, but will resume. Money saved sent to parents.
13) Ali Mohamed of Berbera, Dulbahanta tribe, Hersi Kal.	On foot from Hejaz, 1926.	No passport. No papers.	Labourer.	4½	Work ceased owing to strike, may resume. No money saved.
14) Mursalni Juma Khan, of Peshawar District, Spinsang Village, India.	With Army of occupation from Egypt.	No passport. Discharge certificate from Indian Army dated 2.11.1931.	Ghaffir.	3½	Work ceased owing to strike, will resume. No money saved.
15) Mohamed Farah, Somali of Aden.	Entered on passport No.894 of 1.6.35, as pilgrim, January 1936.	Entered as a pilgrim on British Indian Passport No.894 of 1.6.35 (Visa expired on 10.4.36).	None.	None.	Says money awaits him in Egypt.
16) Yuha Ighabieh Bamba, of Khartoum, Soudan.	Entered to Palestine in 1935, by train.	Sudan passport, No.2079 of 9.8.35.	Mechanic.	6 - 7	Out of work since strike.
17) Mohamed Rashad Dardiri, Kasala, Soudan.	On foot from Egypt, 1933.	No documents.	Garage-hand.	5	Work ceased owing to strike. No money saved.
18) Abdo Ibrahim Issa -Warde, Doubaira, near Halfa, Soudan.	On foot from Egypt.	No documents.	Waiter.	3	Resigned from last post owing to small pay. No money saved.
19) Hasaan Mahmoud Abu-Harbi.	On foot from Hejaz, 1931.	No documents.	Mason.	4	Work ceased owing to strike. Money saved sent to parents.
20) Azab Mabrouk Sodani, of Khartoum, Soudan.	With British Army, 1919.	No documents.	Cook.	4½	Discharged from last position.

Number of Immigrants Annually by Race: Total Number of Persons Registered as Immigrants

(Including persons who entered as travellers and subsequently registered as immigrants)

Year	Total	Jews	Christians	Moslems
1920 (Sept.–Dec.)	5,716	5,514	202	
1921	9,339	9,149	190	
1922	8,128	7,844	284	
1923	7,991	7,421	402	168
1924	13,553	12,856	510	187
1925	34,641	33,801	741	99
1926	13,910	13,081	611	218
1927	3,595	2,713	758	124
1928	3,086	2,178	710	198
1929	6,566	5,249	1,117	200
1930	6,433	4,944	1,296	193
1931	5,533	4,075	1,245	213
1932	11,289	9,553	1,524	212
1933	31,977	30,327	1,307	343
1934*	44,143	42,359	1,494	290
1935	64,147	61,854	903	1,390
1936	31,671	29,727	675	1,269
1937	12,475	10,536	743	1,196
1938	15,263	12,868	473	1,922
1939	18,433	16,405	376	1,652
1940	5,611	4,547	390	674
1941	4,270	3,674	280	343
1942	3,052	2,194	423	435
1943	9,867	8,507	503	857
1944	16,476	14,464	680	1,332
1945 (Jan.–Nov.)	13,984	12,032	714	1,238
Total	401,149	367,845	33,304	

*In this "comprehensive" British Report, for the year 1934, only 1,784 non-Jews were recorded as immigrants; the "30,000–35,000 Houranis" who immigrated to Western Palestine were not included in British calculations.

Source: Anglo-American Committee of Inquiry, *A Survey of Palestine,* vol. 1, p. 185.

APPENDIX VIII. Evidence of Haj Amin al-Husseini Before the Royal Commission, January 12, 1937 (excerpt)

LORD PEEL: . . . Just one question, then. You want completely to stop Jewish immigration. What do you want to do with the 400,000 Jews here at present?

MUFTI: They will live as they always did live previously in Arab countries, with complete freedom and liberty, as natives of the country. In fact Moslem rule has always been known for its tolerance, and as a matter of fact Jews used to come to Eastern countries under Arab rule to escape persecution in Europe. According to history, Jews had a most quiet and peaceful residence under Arab rule. . . .

MUFTI: But I can say that the Jews, many thousands, are actually living in Iraq and Syria under Arab rule and have the same rights and the same position as the other inhabitants of the countries.

SIR L. HAMMOND: Would you give me the figures again for the land. I want to know how much land was held by the Jews before the Occupation.

MUFTI: First of all I would like to say that one of the members of our Committee will deal later with the land question, but nevertheless I will give you the figures. At the time of the Occupation the Jews held about 100,000 dunams.

SIR L. HAMMOND: What year?

MUFTI: At the date of the British Occupation.

SIR L. HAMMOND: And now they hold how much?

MUFTI: About 1,500,000 dunams: 1,200,000 dunams already registered in the name of the Jewish holders, but there are 300,000 dunams which are the subject of written agreements, and which have not yet been registered in the Land Registry. That does not, of course, include the land which was assigned, about 100,000 dunams.

SIR L. HAMMOND: What 100,000 dunams was assigned. Is that not included in the 1,200,000 dunams? The point is this. He says that in 1920 at the time of the Occupation, the Jews only held 100,000 dunams, is that so? I asked the figures from the Land Registry, how much land the Jews owned at the time of the Occupation. Would he be surprised to hear that the figure is not 100,000 but 650,000 dunams?

MUFTI: It may be that the difference was due to the fact that many lands were bought by contract which were not registered.

SIR L. HAMMOND: There is a lot of difference between 100,000 and 650,000.

MUFTI: In one case they sold about 400,000 dunams in one lot.

SIR L. HAMMOND: Who? An Arab?

MUFTI: Sarsuk. An Arab of Beyrouth.

SIR L. HAMMOND: His Eminence gave us a picture of the Arabs being evicted from their land and villages being wiped out. What I want to know is, did the Government of Palestine, the Administration, acquire the land and then hand it over to the Jews?

MUFTI: In most cases the lands were acquired.

SIR L. HAMMOND: I mean forcibly acquired—compulsory acquisition as land would be acquired for public purposes?

MUFTI: No, it wasn't.

SIR L. HAMMOND: Not taken by compulsory acquisition?

MUFTI: No.

SIR L. HAMMOND: But these lands amounting to some 700,000 dunams were actually sold?

MUFTI: Yes, they were sold, but the country was placed in such conditions as would facilitate such purchases.

SIR L. HAMMOND: I don't quite understand what you mean by that. They were sold. Who sold them?

MUFTI: Land owners.

SIR L. HAMMOND: Arabs?

MUFTI: In most cases they were Arabs.

SIR L. HAMMOND: Was any compulsion put on them to sell? If so, by whom?

MUFTI: As in other countries, there are people who by force of circumstances, economic forces, sell their land.

SIR L. HAMMOND: Is that all he said?

MUFTI: They were not prevented from selling the land, and mostly the country was in such economic condition as facilitated the sale. If the Government had the interest of these poor people at heart they should have prevented sales and these people would not have been evicted from their land. A large part of these lands belong to absentee landlords who sold the land over the heads of their tenants, who were forcibly evicted. The majority of these landlords were absentees who sold their land over the heads of their tenants. Not Palestinians but Lebanese.

SIR L. HAMMOND: Is His Eminence in a position to give the Commission a list of the people, the Arabs who have sold lands, apart from those absentee landlords?

MUFTI: I am sure the Department of Lands can supply such a list.

SIR L. HAMMOND: I didn't ask him to tell me where I could get the information from. I asked was he in a position to give it to me.

MUFTI: It is possible for me to supply such a list.

SIR L. HAMMOND: I ask him now this: does he think that as compared with the standard of life under the Turkish rule the position of the fellahin in the villages has improved or deteriorated?

MUFTI: Generally speaking I think their situation has got worse.

SIR L. HAMMOND: Is taxation heavier or lighter?

MUFTI: Taxation was much heavier then, but now there are additional burdens.

SIR L. HAMMOND: I am asking him if it is now, the present day, as we are sitting together here, is it a fact that the fellahin has a much lighter tax than he had under the Turkish rule? Or is he taxed more heavily?

MUFTI: The present taxation is lighter, but the Arabs nevertheless have now other taxation, for instance, customs. On this very point a member of the Arab Committee will deal.

LORD PEEL: On the burden of taxation?

MUFTI: Yes.

LORD PEEL: And the condition of the fellahin as regards, for example, education. Are there more schools or fewer schools now?

MUFTI: They may have more schools, comparatively, but at the same time there has been an increase in their numbers.

SIR L. HAMMOND: Is there any conscription for the army now?

MUFTI: No.

SIR L. HAMMOND: Would the people like to have that back?

MUFTI: Yes. Provided we have our own Government.

SIR L. HAMMOND: Then am I to take it from his evidence that he thinks the Arab portion of the population would be more happy if they reverted to a Turkish rule than under the present Mandatory rule?

MUFTI: That is a fact.

APPENDIX IX. Muftism and Nazism: World War II Collaboration.
Documents (examples of original correspondence)

U.S. Confirms Role of Mufti as Nazi Middle East Leader

OFFICE OF U.S. CHIEF OF COUNSEL
FOR PROSECUTION OF AXIS CRIMINALITY

No. 792—PS   17 September 1945

Source of Original OKW Files, Flensburg

[*Excerpt*]

LEADS: CANARIS, IBN SAUD, GRAND MUFTI.

SUMMARY OF RELEVANT POINTS (with page references):

1. Only through the funds made available by Germany to the Grand Mufti of
Jerusalem was it possible to carry out the revolt in Palestine. (Page 1).
2. Germany will keep up the connection with the Grand Mufti. Weapons will be
stored for the Mufti with Ibn Saud in Arabia. (Page 2).
3. Ibn Saud himself has close connections with the Grand Mufti and the revolting
circles in TransJordan. (Page 2).
4. To be able to carry out our work one of Germany's agents will be placed in
Cairo (Page 3).
5. The document is undated but obviously written before the outbreak of the war
in 1939. It is not signed.

Analyst Landmann   Doc. No. 792-PS

Source: *The Arab Higher Committee, Its Origins, Personnel and Purposes.* The Documentary Record
Submitted to The United Nations, May 1947, by Nations Associates.

Summons to a Holy War Against Britain
*A "Fatwa" Issued by Haj Amin al-Husseini, May, 1941**

In the name of Merciful and Almighty God.
I invite all my Moslem brothers throughout the whole world to join in the Holy
War for God, for the defense of Islam and her lands against her enemy. O Faithful,
obey and respond to my call.
O Moslems!
Proud 'Iraq has placed herself in the vanguard of this Holy Struggle, and has
thrown herself against the strongest enemy of Islam certain that God will grant her
Victory.
The English have tried to seize this Arab-Moslem land, but she has risen, full of

*Translated from:—"Oriente Moderno," 1941, pp. 552–553; broadcast over the 'Iraqi and Axis
radios.

dignity and pride to defend her safety, to fight for her honor and to safeguard her integrity. 'Iraq fights the tyranny which has always had as its aim the destruction of Islam in every land. It is the duty of all Moslems to aid 'Iraq in her struggle and to seek every means to fight the enemy, the traditional traitor in every age and every situation.

Whoever knows the history of the East has everywhere seen the hand of the English working to destroy the Ottoman Empire and to divide the Arab countries. British politics toward the Arab people is masked under a veil of Hypocrisy. The minute she sees her chance, England squeezes the prostrate country in her Imperialist grasp, adding futile justifications. She creates discord and division within a country and while feeding it in secret openly she assumes the role of advisor and trusted friend. The time when England could deceive the peoples of the East is passed. The Arab Nation and the Moslem people have awakened to fight British domination. The English have overthrown the Ottoman Empire, have destroyed Moslem rule in India, inciting one community against another; they stifled the Egyptian awakening, the dream of Mohammed Ali, colonizing Egypt for half a century. They took advantage of the weakening of the Ottoman Empire to stretch out their hands and use every sort of trick to take possession of many Arab countries as happened to Aden, the 9 Districts, the Hadramut, Oman, Masqat and the Emirates of the Persian Gulf and Transjordania. The vivid proof of the imperialistic designs of the British is to be found in Moslem Palestine which, although promised by England to Sheriff Hussein has had to submit to the outrageous infiltration of Jews, shameful politics designed to divide Arab-Moslem countries of Asia from those of Africa. In Palestine the English have committed unheard of barbarisms; among others, they have profaned the el-Aqsa Mosque and have declared the most unyielding war against Islam, both in deed and in word. The Prime Minister at that time told Parliament that the world would never see peace as long as the Koran existed. What hatred against Islam is stronger than that which publicly declares the Sacred Koran an enemy of human kind? Should such sacrilege go unpunished? After the dissolution of the Moslem Empire in India and of the Ottoman Caliphate, England, adhering to the policy of Gladstone, pursued her work of destruction to Islam depriving many Islamic States both in the East and in the West of their freedom and independence. The number of Moslems who today live under the rule of England and invoke liberation from their terrible yoke exceeds 220,000,000.

Therefore I invite you, O Brothers, to join in the War for God to preserve Islam, your independence and your lands from English aggression. I invite you to bring all your weight to bear in helping 'Iraq that she may throw off the shame that torments her.

O Heroic 'Iraq, God is with Thee, the Arab Nation and the Moslem World are solidly with Thee in Thy Holy Struggle!

Source: *The Arab War Effort—A Documentary Account.* The American Christian Palestine Committee (New York, n.d.).

The Mufti's Diary on His Meeting with Hitler

Haj Amin al Husseini, recording in his own handwriting his meeting with Hitler in his diary, says:

The words of the Fuehrer on the 6th of Zul Qaada 1360 of the Hejira (which falls on the 21st of November 1941) Berlin, Friday, from 4:30 P.M. till a few minutes after 6.

The objectives of my fight are clear. Primarily, I am fighting the Jews without respite, and this fight includes the fight against the so-called Jewish National Home in Palestine because the Jews want to establish there a central government for their own pernicious purposes, and to undertake a devastating and ruinous expansion at the expense of the governments of the world and of other peoples.

It is clear that the Jews have accomplished nothing in Palestine and their claims are lies. All the accomplishments in Palestine are due to the Arabs and not to the Jews. I am resolved to find a solution for the Jewish problem, progressing step by step without cessation. With regard to this I am making the necessary and right appeal, first to all the European countries and then to countries outside of Europe.

It is true that our common enemies are Great Britain and the Soviets whose principles are opposed to ours. But behind them stands hidden Jewry which drives them both. Jewry has but one aim in both these countries. We are now in the midst of a life and death struggle against both these nations. This fight will not only determine the outcome of the struggle between National Socialism and Jewry, but the whole conduct of this successful war will be of great and positive help to the Arabs who are engaged in the same struggle.

This is not only an abstract assurance.* A mere promise would be of no value whatsoever. But assurance which rests upon a conquering force is the only one which has real value. In the Iraqi campaign, for instance, the sympathy of the whole German people was for Iraq. It was our aim to help Iraq, but circumstances prevented us from furnishing actual help. The German people saw in them (in the Iraqis—Ed.) comrades in suffering because the German people too have suffered as they have. All the help we gave Iraq was not sufficient to save Iraq from the British forces. For this reason it is necessary to underscore one thing: in this struggle which will decide the fate of the Arabs I can now speak as a man dedicated to an ideal and as a military leader and a soldier. Everyone united in this great struggle who helps to bring about its successful outcome, serves the common cause and thus serves the Arab cause. Any other view means weakening the military situation and thus offers no help to the Arab cause. Therefore it is necessary for us to decide the steps which can help us against world Jewry, against Communist Russia and England, and which among them can be most useful. Only if we win the war will the hour of deliverance also be the hour of fulfillment of Arab aspirations.

The situation is as follows: We are conducting the great struggle to open the way to the North of the Caucasus. The difficulties involved are more than transportation because of the demolished railways and roads and because of winter weather. And if I venture in these circumstances to issue a declaration with regard to Syria, then the pro-de Gaulle elements in France will be strengthened and this might cause a revolt in France. These men (the French) will be convinced then that joining Britain is more advantageous and the detachment of Syria is a pattern to be followed in the remainder of the French Empire. This will strengthen de Gaulle's stand in the colonies. If the declaration is issued now, difficulties will arise in Western Europe which will cause the diversion of some (German—Ed.) forces for defensive purposes, thus preventing us from sending all our forces to the East.

---

*This is a reply to the insistent request of the Mufti for an Axis declaration to the Arabs.

Now I am going to tell you something I would like you to keep secret.

First, I will keep up my fight until the complete destruction of the Judeo-Bolshevik rule has been accomplished.

Second, during the struggle (and we don't know when victory will come, but probably not in the far future) we will reach the Southern Caucasus.

Third, then I would like to issue a declaration; for then the hour of the liberation of the Arabs will have arrived. Germany has no ambitions in this area but cares only to annihilate the power which produces the Jews.

Fourth, I am happy that you have escaped and that you are now with the Axis powers. The hour will strike when you will be the lord of the supreme word and not only the conveyer of our declarations. You will be the man to direct the Arab force and at that moment I cannot imagine what would happen to the Western peoples.

Fifth, I think that with this Arab advance begins the dismemberment of the British world. The road from Rostov to Iran and Iraq is shorter than the distance from Berlin to Rostov. We hope next year to smash this barrier. It is better then and not now that a declaration should be issued as (now) we cannot help in anything.

I understand the Arab desire for this (declaration—Ed.), but His Excellency the Mufti must understand that only five years after I became President of the German government and Fuehrer of the German people, was I able to get such a declaration (the Austrian Union—Ed.), and this because military forces prevented me from issuing such a declaration. But when the German Panzer tanks and the German air squadrons reach the Southern Caucasus, then will be the time to issue the declaration.

He said (in reply to a request that a secret declaration or a treaty be made) that a declaration known to a number of persons cannot remain secret but will become public. I (Hitler) have made very few declarations in my life, unlike the British who have made many declarations. If I issue a declaration, I will uphold it. Once I promised the Finnish Marshal that I would help his country if the enemy attacks again. This word of mine made a stronger impression than any written declaration.

Recapitulating, I want to state the following to you: When we shall have arrived in the Southern Caucasus, then the time of the liberation of the Arabs will have arrived. And you can rely on my word.

We were troubled about you. I know your life history. I followed with interest your long and dangerous journey. I was very concerned about you. I am happy that you are with us now and that you are now in a position to add your strength to the common cause.

Source: *The Arab Higher Committee* . . . , The Documentary Record.

Auswärtiges Amt   Berlin, den 28. April 1942.

Eminenz!

In Beantwortung Ihres mir heute gemeinsam mit Seiner Exzellenz dem Ministerpräsidenten Raschid Ali El
Gailani übersandten Briefes und in Bestätigung meiner

Heimstätte in Palästina zuzustimmen.

Es testeht Einverstandnis daruber, das der Wort-
laut und der Inhalt dieses bri _ s unbeufngt geheim
gehalten werden, bis im gegenseitigen Einverhehmen et-
was anderes bestimmt wird.

Genehmigen Euere Eminenz die Versicherung meiner
ausgezeichnetsten Hochachtun .

Ribbentrop Promises Mufti to Destroy Jewish National Home

Ministry of Foreign Affairs

Berlin, April 28, 1942
Your Eminence:

In response to your letter and to the accompanying communication of His Excellency, Prime Minister Raschid Ali El Gailani, and confirming the terms of our
conversation, I have the honour to inform you:

The German Government appreciates fully the confidence of the Arab peoples in
the Axis Powers in their aims and in their determination to conduct the fight against
the common enemy until victory is achieved. The German Government has the
greatest understanding for the national aspirations of the Arab countries as have been
expressed by you both and the greatest sympathy for the sufferings of your peoples

under British oppression.

I have therefore the honour to assure you, in complete agreement with the Italian Government, that the independence and freedom of the suffering Arab countries presently subjected to British oppression, is also one of the aims of the German Government.

Germany is consequently ready to give all her support to the oppressed Arab countries in their fight against British domination, for the fulfillment of their national aim to independence and sovereignty and for the destruction of the Jewish National Home in Palestine.

As previously agreed, the content of this letter should be maintained absolutely secret until we decide otherwise.

I beg your Eminence to be assured of my highest esteem and consideration.

(Signed)   Ribbentrop

To His Eminence
the Grossmufti of Palestine
Amin El Husseini.

Source: *The Arab Higher Committee . . .* , The Documentary Record. Original German, p. 439.

The Mufti Asks Arab Americans Not to Support FDR

ADDRESS TO AMERICAN ARABS

*Excerpts from a Radio Speech by Haj Amin al-Husseini
March 19, 1943, in Rome*

The Arabs and Moslems will not be deceived by Britain once again because not only have they known its true intentions but they have also known those of Britain's allies —America—and I want to draw the attention of the Arab emigrants in America to this fact, reminding them of their glorious past when they supported the National movement. I would also like to remind them that their efforts will be wasted if, God forbid, America and her Allies may be victorious in this War because at such a time the Arabs will never rise again. I therefore know that those Arab emigrants in America will refrain from helping Roosevelt or taking part in a war which he brought on to his country.

If those Allies win this war the Jewish influence will be the arbiter in the world resources and one can thus imagine the future of the Arabs and Moslems, and the dangers which they are exposed to in their fatherlands and beliefs if the Jews and their Allies dominate them and spread the latent hatred on to them.

Then the world will become Hell—God forbid: But Allah is too just and merciful to grant such murderous violators any victory. We are sure that victory will be ours and that of our friends. We have not the slightest doubt about that, we shall not slacken our struggle nor will we be deterred or quietened. Do not be deceived by the allegations of your enemies, because you know full well about their intrigues, and be sure that the nation which fights, sacrifices and awaits will be the victorious one in the end.

Source: *The Arab War Effort, A Documented Account.*

Himmler to The Mufti

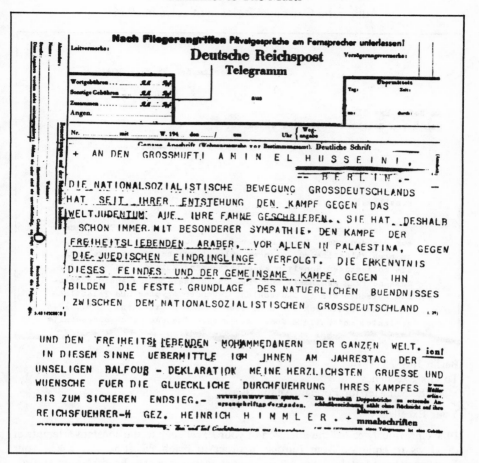

November 2, 1943, message from Heinrich Himmler to an anti-Balfour Declaration meeting:

"To the Grand Mufti:

"The National Socialist Movement of Greater Germany has, since its beginning, inscribed upon its flag the fight against world Jewry. It has, therefore, followed with particular sympathy the struggle of the freedom-loving Arabians, especially in Palestine, against the Jewish interlopers. It is in the recognition of this enemy and of the common struggle against him that lies the firm foundation of the natural alliance that exists between National-Socialist-Greater Germany and the freedom-loving Moslems of the whole world. In this spirit I am sending you on the anniversary of the infamous Balfour Declaration my hearty greetings and wishes for the successful pursuit of your struggle until the certain final victory.

Signed: Reichsfuehrer–S.S. Heinrich Himmler

Source: *The Arab Higher Committee* . . . , The Documentary Record.

The Mufti Communicates Anger to Ribbentrop
upon the Germans' Release of Jews in 1944

Berlin, den 25. Juli 1944

An Seine Exzellenz
den Herrn Reichsminister des Ausseren.

                                        B e r l i n.
                                        ================

Exzellenz!

     Schon früher hatte ich die Aufmerksamkeit Luer Exzellenz
auf die dauernden Versuche der Juden aus Europa auszuwandern,
um nach Palästina zu gelangen gelenkt, und bat Euere Exzellenz
die notwenidgen Schritte zu unternehmen, Lamit die Juden an der
Auswanderung gehindert werden. Auch anlässlich des Austauschpla-
nes zwischen den in Deutschland lebenden Agypter und Palästina-
Deutschen, hatte ich ein Schreiben an Euere Exzellenz am 5.6.1944
gerichtet und bat, die Juden aus diesem Austauschplan auszuschlie.
          ber erf........ die J...en am .... abge-

Berlin July 25, 1944
To His Excellency
    The Minister for Foreign Affairs, Berlin

Your Excellency:

I have previously called the attention of your Excellency to the constant attempts of
the Jews to emigrate from Europe in order to reach Palestine, and asked your
Excellency to undertake the necessary steps so as to prevent the Jews from emigrating.
I had also sent you a letter, under date of June 5, 1944, in regard to the plan for an
exchange of Egyptians living in Germany with Palestinian Germans, in which I asked
you to exclude the Jews from this plan of exchange. I have, however, learned that the
Jews did depart on July 2, 1944, and I am afraid that further groups of Jews will leave
for Palestine from Germany and France to be exchanged for Palestinian Germans.

     This exchange on the part of the Germans would encourage the Balkan countries
likewise to send their Jews to Palestine. This step would be incomprehensible to the
Arabs and Moslems after your Excellency's declaration of November 2, 1943 that
"the destruction of the so-called Jewish national home in Palestine is an immutable
part of the policy of the greater German Reich" and it would create in them a feeling
of keen disappointment.

     It is for this reason that I ask your Excellency to do all that is necessary to prohibit
the emigration of Jews to Palestine, and in this way your Excellency would give a new
practical example of the policy of the naturally allied and friendly Germany towards
the Arab Nation.

                                        Yours, etc.

Source: *The Arab Committee* . . . , The Documentary Record.

Notes

2. The Invitation

1. November 24, 1975, Beirut.
2. Revolutionary Command, Radio Baghdad, November 25, 1975.
3. *New York Times, Le Monde, Toronto Star,* December 11, 1975.
4. *New York Times,* December 11, 1975. The Iraqi Minister of Justice in 1941 stated that "Judaism"—not Zionism—was "a threat to mankind." He did not attempt to disguise the Iraqis' anti-Jewish sentiments, which exploded that year into an old-fashioned Cossack-style pogrom, long before Israel's statehood. Further, the killing of the Jewish Dutch citizen, whom the Iraqis hanged as a "Zionist spy" the same year they extended their "welcome," gave lie to Iraq's extensive promises of "full rights" to its Jews. See Sylvia Haim, "Arabic Anti-Semitic Literature," in *Jewish Social Studies,* vol. 17 (1955), pp. 307–12.
5. *Toronto Star,* February 3, 1976.
6. Libya's Major Abdul-Huni, Council Commanding the Revolution, to ex-Libyan Jewish refugees then in Italy, May 29, 1970. Libyan leader Qadaffy invited former Libyan Jews living in Israel to return, November 24, 1973; see Chapter 7. Also, Sudanese President Numeiry, in a speech at a rally celebrating Independence Day, E-Damar, January 1, 1975. Also Egyptian President Sadat to Jews who fled or were expelled since 1948, filing the caveat that Egyptians "are against the racial policies of the Zionists." The invitation and its qualification occurred in September 1977, interestingly, just weeks before President Sadat's Jerusalem peace pilgrimage. See *Chicago Daily News,* September 10–11; also see *The Oregonian* (Portland), July 18, 1977.
7. *Newsweek,* November 17, 1975, interview; also see *Chicago Daily News,* December 30, 1975; see also *Newsweek,* March 14, 1977.
8. Sir Geoffrey Furlonge, *Palestine Is My Country: The Story of Musa Alami* (New York and London: Praeger Press, 1969), p. 152.
9. Muhamed Nimer Al Hawari described the Arab leaders' ruthless incitement of the Arabs in Jaffa in December 1947: ". . . Jaffa was boiling: every second that passed you heard a new rumour, and after every minute the imaginary tales and lies became bigger, finally, they were accepted as definite truth by the public. When the sun was setting down, many of the Mufti henchmen patrolled the streets in private and lorry cars, calling upon the people: oh! people, oh! men, oh! heros; Help . . . Help . . . , stop the Jewish attack! They have attacked your brothers in the Manshiya; they pillaged their properties; burned their holdings and raped their women and girls. They have committed awful acts of horror and brutality against your brothers!! In

but a few minutes Jaffa's inhabitants were incited and agitated shouted and fired in the air:—On Them! On Them! On Tel-Aviv, the town of the wicked . . . Groups and individuals, they marched on and among them, behind them or in front of them, went the Mufti henchmen belittling the Jewish strength . . ." *The Secret of the Catastrophe* [Arabic] (Nazareth, 1955), pp. 34–37, cited in translation by Rony E. Gabbay, *A Political Study of the Arab-Jewish Conflict: The Arab Refugee Problem (A Case Study)* (Geneva: Librairie E. Droz; Paris: Librairie Minard, 1959), pp. 82–83.

10. United Nations General Assembly, 2nd session 1947, Resolution 181 (II), November 29, 1947. For earlier partition proposals and Arab reaction, see Chapter 14.

11. In March 1948, according to a study, these outside forces included 2,500 Syrians, 2,500 Iraqis, "several hundred" Lebanese and Egyptians, and Yugoslav Muslims as well. Harry Sacher, *Israel: The Establishment of a State* (London, 1951), p. 235, cited by Gabbay, *Political Study,* p. 81. General Isma'il Safwat reported to the League Palestine Committee the total number of Arab volunteers as "7,700 persons," March 23, 1948, Iraq Parliamentary Investigating Commission, cited in Gabbay, p. 81.

12. Nicholas Bethell, *The Palestine Triangle: The Struggle for the Holy Land, 1935–48* (New York: G. Putnam's Sons, 1979), p. 351; Azzam Pasha, Secretary General of the Arab League, described "three characteristics of the future war: the belief in glorious death as a road to paradise, the opportunities of lust and the Bedouin love of slaughter for its own sake." Interview in *Akhbar al-Yom,* October 11, 1947, cited by Gabbay, *Political Study,* p. 83, n. 103.

13. In September 1947, the Political Committee of the Arab League, at its meeting in Sofer, Lebanon, advised the Arab governments to accept and care for the evacuees from Palestine. *Iraq Parliamentary Investigation Commission on the Causes of the Failure in Palestine,* submitted to Iraq Parliament on September 4, 1949, Appendix 8, pp. 43–50, cited in Gabbay, *Political Study,* p. 92; see also "The Arab Refugee Problem and How It Can Be Solved," proposals submitted to the United Nations General Assembly, December 1951, by Dewey Anderson, Executive Director, Public Affairs Institute; Archibald MacLeish, Harvard University; Henry Atkinson, Church Peace Union; Ivan Lee Holt, Methodist Bishop of Missouri; Kenneth Scott Latourette, President, American Baptist Convention; Daniel Marsh, Chancellor, Boston University; James T. Shotwell, Carnegie Endowment; James G. Patton, President, Farmers International and Cooperative Union; Norman B. Nash, Episcopal Bishop of Massachusetts; and others.

14. "This will be a war of extermination and a momentous massacre . . . like the Mongolian massacres and the Crusades." Azzam Pasha, Secretary General of the Arab League, at Cairo press conference, May 15, 1948, *New York Times,* May 16, 1948.

15. Habib Issa, ed., *Al-Hoda,* Arabic daily, June 8, 1951, New York; see *Economist* (London), May 15, 1948, regarding "panic flight"; also see *Economist,* October 2, 1948, for British eyewitness report of Arab Higher Committee radio "announcements" that were "urging all Arabs in Haifa to quit."

16. Near East Arabic Radio, April 3, 1948: "It must not be forgotten that the Arab Higher Committee encouraged the refugees to flee from their homes in Jaffa, Haifa and Jerusalem, and that certain leaders . . . make political capital out of their miserable situation . . ." Cited by Anderson et al., "The Arab Refugee Problem and How It Can Be Solved," p. 22; for more regarding Arab responsibility, see Sir Alexander Cadogan, Ambassador of Great Britain to the United Nations, speech to

the Security Council, S.C., O.R., 287th meeting, April 23, 1948; also see Harry Stebbens, British Port Officer stationed in Haifa, letter in *Evening Standard* (London), January 10, 1969.

17. April 28, 1948; according to the *Economist* (London), October 1, 1948, only "4000 to 6000" of the "62,000 Arabs who formerly lived in Haifa" remained there until the time of the war; also see Kenneth Bilby, *New Star in the Near East* (New York: Doubleday, 1950), pp. 30–31; Lt. Col. Moshe Pearlman, *The Army of Israel* (New York: Philosophical Library, 1950), pp. 116–17; and Major E. O'Ballance, *The Arab-Israeli War of 1948* (London, 1956), p. 52.

18. David Shipler, *New York Times,* October 23, 1979, p. A3. Shipler cites Larry Collins and Dominique Lapierre, *O Jerusalem,* and Dan Kurzman, *Genesis 1948.*

19. *New York Times,* October 23, 1979.

20. Yitzhak Rabin, *The Rabin Memoirs* (Boston and Toronto: Little, Brown, 1979), p. 23, pp. 22–44.

21. Peter Dodd and Halim Barakat, *River Without Bridges: A Study of the Exodus of the 1967 Arab Palestinian Refugees* (Beirut: Institute for Palestine Studies, 1969), p. 43; on April 27, 1950, the Arab National Committee of Haifa stated in a memorandum to the Arab States: "The removal of the Arab inhabitants . . . was voluntary and was carried out at our request . . . The Arab delegation proudly asked for the evacuation of the Arabs and their removal to the neighboring Arab countries. . . . We are very glad to state that the Arabs guarded their honour and traditions with pride and greatness." Cited by J.B. Schechtman, *The Arab Refugee Problem* (New York: Philosophical Library, 1952), pp. 8–9; also see *Al-Zaman,* Baghdad journal, April 27, 1950.

22. Musa Alami, "The Lesson of Palestine," *The Middle East Journal,* October 1949.

23. Lord Caradon, "Cyprus and Palestine," lecture at the University of Chicago, Center for Middle Eastern Studies, February 17, 1976. Similar statement by Folke Bernadotte, *To Jerusalem,* p. 113.

24. P.J. Vatikiotis, *Nasser and His Generation* (London: Croom Helm, 1978), pp. 256–57.

25. Ibid. p. 234, quoting a speech by Nasser at Suez, July 26, 1956; in 1952, Sheikh Pierre Gemayel, then leader of the Lebanese National Youth Organization "Al Kataeb," wrote: "Why should the refugees stay in Lebanon, and not in Egypt, Iraq and Jordan which claim that they are all Arab and beyond that, Moslem? . . . Isn't it for that alone that these so-called nationalist elements are demanding to resettle the refugees in Lebanon because they are themselves Arab and Moslems?" *Al-Hoda,* Lebanese journal, January 3, 1952, cited in Schechtman, *Arab Refugee Problem,* p. 84; also see Ibrahim Abu-Lughod, "Quest for an Arab Future," in *Arab Journal,* 1966–67, vol. 4, nos. 2–4, pp. 23–29.

26. "Mohammed Hassanein Heykal Discusses War and Peace in the Middle East," *Journal of Palestine Studies,* Autumn 1971. Heykal thus joined the Arab chorus heard after the 1967 war.

27. Vatikiotis, *Nasser,* p. 257; also see Mohamed Heikal, *The Road to Ramadan* (New York: Ballantine Books, 1975), p. 56.

28. Interview with Nasser, *Le Monde* (Paris: February 1970), cited in Vatikiotis, *Nasser,* p. 259.

29. Charles Foltz, interview with Nasser, *U.S. News and World Report,* May 1970, cited in Vatikiotis, *Nasser,* p. 259; see also *Le Monde* interview, February 1970.

30. "... contrary to the popular view ... in the West," a "great many refugees" were living out of camps "in comfortable housing outside," in the beginning of the 1960s, according to Fawaz Turki, *The Disinherited: Journal of a Palestinian Exile* (New York and London: Monthly Review Press, 1972), p. 41.

31. Al-Haytham Al-Ayubi, "Future Arab Strategy in the Light of the Fourth War," *Shuun Filastiniyya* (Beirut), October 1974. Al-Ayubi, also called Abu-Hammam, has been military head of Popular Front for the Liberation of Palestine, Lieutenant Colonel in the Syrian army, and highly respected strategist on Israel. He perceived the "guerrilla" war against Israel as the ultimately successful one.

32. Rosemary Sayigh, "Sources of Palestinian Nationalism: A Study of a Palestinian Camp in Lebanon," *Journal of Palestinian Studies,* vol. 6, no. 4, 1977, p. 21; see also Sayigh, "The Palestinian Identity Among Camp Residents," *Journal of Palestinian Studies,* vol. 6, no. 3, 1977, pp. 3–22.

33. In 1981, the Organization of African Unity's executive secretary, Ambassador Oumarou Garba Youssoupou from Niger, reflected upon why the millions of displaced souls in Africa were not as visible: "We're not getting the publicity because of our culture. No refugee is turned away from the host countries, so we're not dramatic enough for television. We have no drownings, no piratings. . . . We don't make the news." "Aiding Africa's Refugees," by Gertrude Samuels, *The New Leader,* May 4, 1981.

34. Al-Ayubi, "Future Arab Strategy in the Light of the Fourth War."

35. Musa Alami, "The Lesson of Palestine," *The Middle East Journal,* October 1949.

36. Khaled Al-Azm, *Memoirs* [Arabic], 3 vols. (Al-Dar al Muttahida lil-Nashr, 1972), vol. 1, pp. 386–87, cited by Maurice Roumani, *The Case of the Jews from Arab Countries: A Neglected Issue,* preliminary edition (Jerusalem: World Organization of Jews from Arab Countries [WOJAC], 1975), p. 61.

37. Jordanian National Law, Official Gazette, No. 1171, February 16, 1954, p. 105, Article 3(3). Between 1948 and 1967, 200,000 to 300,000 Arabs moved from the West Bank to the "East Bank," according to Eliyahu Kanovsky, in *Jordan, People and Politics in the Middle East,* Michael Curtis, ed. (New Brunswick, N.J.: Transaction Books, 1971), p. 111.

38. Walter Pinner, *How Many Arab Refugees?* (London: MacGibbon and Kee, 1959).

39. In 1967, an additional 250,000 Arab refugees from the Israel-occupied territories were reported; added to the number who left in 1948, they brought the total to 789,000 Arab refugees.

40. This estimate was made by officers of the Disaster Relief Organization and confirmed by statistical calculation of the potential number of refugees who might have left after the second truce. Gabbay, *Political Study,* p. 166.

41. Marguerite Cartwright, "Plain Speech on the Arab Refugee Problem," in *Land Reborn,* American Christian Palestine Committee, November–December 1958; according to a United Nations Interim Report, 1951, A/145/Rev. 1, p. 17: "... the figures for Lebanon (128,000) are confused, due to the fact that many Lebanese nationals . . . claimed status as refugees"; UNRWA was "forbidden" by Jordan, Syria, and Gaza from counting newborn children among refugees, according to *Falastin,* Jordanian daily, January 25, 1956; see Joseph Schectman, *The Refugee in the World* (New York: A.S. Barnes & Co., 1963), pp. 201–207.

42. W. de St. Aubin, Director of Field Operations for the UN Disaster Relief Project,

"Peace and Refugees in the Middle East," *The Middle East Journal,* vol. iii, no. 3, July 1949.

43. Report of the Director, Special Report of Director and Advisory Commission, UNRWA to Sixth Session, General Assembly, UN Document A/1905; compare, for example, with OAU (Organization of African Unity) definition at 1969 Convention: "Any person . . . compelled to leave his place of *habitual* residence. . . ." Quoted in "Africa and Refugees," by Neville Rubin, *African Affairs,* July 1974, Journal of Royal African Society, University of London.

44. UNRWA, Annual Report of the Director, July 1, 1951, to June 30, 1952, General Assembly, Seventh Session, Supp. No. 13 (A/2171). See also October 1950, UNRWA Interim Report of Director, A/1451: "there is reason to believe that births are always registered for ration purposes, but deaths are often, if not usually, concealed so that the family may continue to collect rations for the deceased." Cited by Schechtman, *Refugee in the World,* p. 206.

45. *Assistance to Palestine Refugees,* Report on UN Relief to Palestine Refugees (UNPRP) from December 1948 to September 1949; the UNRWA staff was largely "Palestinian" and "nationals of the countries" concerned, "increasingly assuming larger duties" regarding "UNRWA's responsibility." UNRWA, Annual Report of the Director, July 1951–June, 1952, G.A. 7th Session, Supp. No. 13 (A/2171), p. 8.

46. Cartwright, "Plain Speech," cited by Schechtman, *Refugee in the World,* pp. 200–201.

47. UN General Assembly, Official Record, 5th session, Ad Hoc Political Committee 31st Meeting, November 11, 1950, p. 194, and Anderson et al, "Arab Refugee Problem and How It Can Be Solved," p. 26.

48. Special Report of the Director, UNRWA, 1954–55, UN Document A/2717.

49. Schechtman, *Refugee in the World,* p. 248, citing *Al-Hayat* (Lebanon), June 25, 1959.

50. Ibid., p. 249, citing *Al-Hayat,* August 14, 1959.

51. UNRWA, Annual Report of the Director, July 1951–June 1952, General Assembly, 7th Session, Supp. No. 13 (A/2171), pp. 3, 10.

52. Cable by McGee and Gore from Amman, Jordan, to President Eisenhower, Secretary of State Christian Herter, and the United Nations, October 1959, while traveling in the Mideast for the Senate Foreign Relations Committee and Senate Appropriations Committee.

53. Dr. John H. Davis, October 1959, cited in Schechtman, *Refugee in the World,* pp. 207–208.

54. Ibid., quoting George B. Vinson, UNRWA eligibility officer stationed in Jerusalem.

55. Dr. Harry Howard, from the United States *Congressional Record,* April 20, 1960.

56. UNRWA, Annual Report of the Director. Under the auspices of the Arab Information Center in New York, by 1970 Davis was reporting the figures he himself had proved erroneous and grossly inflated, as the bona fide refugee count. "Why Are There Still Arab Refugees?", *The Arab World,* Arab Information Center, New York, December 1969–January 1970, p. 3.

57. See *New York Times,* May 15, 1949; *Life* magazine, September 29, 1958; *Time* magazine, December 2, 1957.

58. See, for example, Dr. Ali Ghalib, *Malaria in Iraq* (Jerusalem, 1944), pp. 39, 49; Hashim Jawad, *The Social Structure of Iraq* (Jerusalem, 1945), pp. 17–18; Sir George Buchanan, *The Tragedy of Mesopotamia* (Edinburgh, 1938), p. 247.

59. International Development Advisory Board, *Report,* March 7, 1951.

60. F. T. Witcamp, *The Refugee Problem in the Middle East* (The Hague: Research Group for European Migration Problems, 1959), pp. 39–41.
61. S.G. Thicknesse, *Arab Refugees: A Survey of Resettlement Possibilities* (London: Royal Institute of International Affairs, 1949), p. 51.
62. Herbert Hoover, reported in the *New York World Telegram,* November 19, 1945.
63. *El-Balad,* September 13, 19, 1951, cited in Joseph Schechtman, *The Arab Refugee Problem* (New York: Philosophical Library, 1952), p. 91.
64. Dewey Anderson et al., "Arab Refugee Problem and How It Can Be Solved," p. 39, citing *El-Balad* (Jerusalem), September 18, 1951.
65. Schechtman, *Arab Refugee Problem,* p. 91; p. 94, n. 41.
66. Anderson et al., "Arab Refugee Problem and How It Can Be Solved," citing a report by Alexander Gibbs Co., "The Economic Development of Syria" (London, 1949).
67. Fawaz Turki, *The Disinherited: Journal of a Palestinian Exile* (New York and London: Monthly Review Press, 1972), p. 37.
68. Anderson et al., "Arab Refugee Problem," p. 50, citing a report by a study group composed of members and associates of Chatham House and members of the Royal Asian Society under the chairmanship of Sir Harold MacMichael on Arab refugee settlement possibilities. Arnold Toynbee was also a participant.
69. Editorial in *al-Qubs* (The Torch), Damascus, January 1949. Quoted on March 28, 1949, in *az-Sameer,* an Arabic paper published in New York. Cited in Schechtman, *Arab Refugee Problem,* p. 80.
70. *al-Qubs,* quoted in *az-Sameer,* March 28, 1949, cited in Anderson et al., "Arab Refugee Problem," p. 52.
71. *Musamaret El Geib* (Cairo), June 3, 1951, cited in Anderson et al., "Arab Refugee Problem," p. 50. See Chapter 18 for interview with Syrian official who expressed similar needs in 1977.
72. Near East Arabic radio, May 12, 1949, cited in Anderson et al., p. 51.
73. W. de St. Aubin, "Peace and Refugees in the Middle East," *Middle East Journal,* Washington, July 1949, pp. 359–60. According to Schechtman, *Arab Refugee Problem,* p. 81, "In March 1951, premier Khaled el-Azam stated in connection with the visit to Damascus of UN Secretary General Trygve Lie, Syria would be *willing to accept* refugees provided they were paid compensation for their property in Israel." (Emphasis added.)
74. From 1949 until 1951 Egyptians were receptive to resettlement proposals. In September 1949, Egypt was planning to hire the refugees to dig wells in Gaza, conditional upon Israel's cooperation with irrigation methods, *New York Times,* October 1, 1949; in 1951, Egypt and UNRWA negotiated to resettle 50,000 refugees in the Sinai at one point, *New York Times,* August 18, 23, 1950, and March 23, 1951; an additional 20,000 refugees were agreed upon for resettling in the same period, *New York Times,* December 26, 1950, *Times,* London, January 23, 1951.
75. John Davis, "Why Are There Still Arab Refugees?", *Arab World,* December 1969–January 1970. Also see data on Syria and on Libya, etc., in UNRWA Annual Report of the Director, July 1952 to June 1953, General Assembly, 8th Session, Supp. No. 12 (A/2470), pp. 10–11; in UN Resolution 513 (VI) the General Assembly adopted the Authorization to *"transfer"* UNRWA funds "allocated for relief" into funds for *"reintegration,"* dated January 26, 1952, item no. 10. An American representative

in Lebanon, Ambassador Ira Hirschmann, submitted a comprehensive report to the Assistant Secretary of State re: "Arab Refugee Situation," April 6, 1968, Hirschmann to William B. Macomber, Jr.

76. Dewey Anderson et al., "Arab Refugee Problem and How It Can Be Solved," p. 77, citing *Al-Misri,* October 11, 1949.

77. Ibid., citing *Al-Ziyyad,* April 6, 1950.

78. "General Progress Report of the United Nations Conciliation Commission for Palestine," covering the period from December 11, 1949, to October 23, 1950 (pamphlet), General Assembly Official Records, 5th Session, Supp. No. 18 (A/1367/Rev. 1).

79. See UN Ad Hoc Committee Sessions, November 11, 29, 30, December 1, 1950, for positions of Denmark, Canada, Britain, Australia, Bolivia, Belgium, and Holland. Although giving perfunctory acknowledgment to the Arab position, a substantial bloc among the UN Ad Hoc Committee concluded that "the Arab refugees would have a happier and more stable future if the bulk of them were resettled in Arab countries."

80. League Resolution No. 389, October 10, 1951.

81. Mohammad Iqbal Ansari, *The Arab League 1945–1955* (Aligarh: Aligarh Muslim University, 1968), pp. 71–74.

82. *Revue du Liban* (French), May 12, 1951, cited by Anderson et al., "Arab Refugee Problem," p. 38.

83. For additional support of resettlement see Thicknesse, *Arab Refugees,* pp. 38–58; Vahe Sevian, "Economic Utilization and Development of the Water Resources of the Euphrates and Tigris," E/Conf. 7/Sec/W.397, August 1, 1949, p. 16; Doreen Warriner, *Land and Poverty in the Middle East* (London and New York: Royal Institute of International Affairs, 1948), pp. 26–33, 75–80, 95.

84. *Berlut al Massa* (Lebanese daily), July 11–12, 1957, cited by Terence Prittie and Bernard Dineen, *The Double Exodus: A Study of Arab and Jewish Refugees in the Middle East* (pamphlet), (London: Goodhart Press, n.d.), p. 13.

85. Prittie, "Middle East Refugees," in Michael Curtis et al., eds., *The Palestinians: People, History, Politics* (New Brunswick, N.J.: Transaction Books, 1975), p. 71.

86. Ibid., citing Associated Press interview, January 1960.

87. See Robert MacDonald, *The League of Arab States* (Princeton: Princeton University Press, 1965); also see Mohammad Khalil, *The Arab States and the Arab League: A Documentary Record* (Beirut: Khayat's, 1962), vol. 2, pp. 517–22, 935ff.

88. "Biggest Little Superpower in the World," *Forbes,* August 1, 1975; author's interview with Jim Cook, January 5, 1979.

89. Abbas Kelidar, "Iraq: The Search for Stability," *Conflict Studies,* No. 59, The Institute for the Study of Conflict, London, July 1975, p. 21.

90. Pablo de Azcarate, *Mission in Palestine 1948–1952* (Washington, D.C.: Middle East Institute, 1966), p. 191. Resolution 194 (III) of the United Nations General Assembly, which de Azcarate dates December 14, 1948, is generally recorded as December 11, 1948. The UN "proclamation" referred to by de Azcarate includes the following: "Resolves that the refugees willing to return to their homes and live at peace with their neighbors should be permitted to do so at the earliest practicable date, and that compensation should be paid for the property of those choosing not to return, and for loss of or damage to property which, under principles of international law or in

equity, should be made good by the Governments or authorities responsible;

"Instructs the Conciliation Committee to facilitate the repatriation, resettlement and economic and social rehabilitation of the refugees and the payment of compensation, and to maintain close relations with the Director of the United Nations Relief for Palestine Refugees and, through him, with the appropriate organs and agencies of the United Nations."

91. Maurice Roumani, *The Case of the Jews from Arab Countries: A Neglected Issue,* with Deborah Goldman and Helene Korn, vol. I, World Organization of Jews from Arab Countries (WOJAC), Jerusalem, 1975, p. 82.

92. Transmission from Damascus, political agent, Political Department of the Jewish Agency, to Eliahu Sasson, Political Department, Palestine, May 16, 1939 (from the English translation), CZA-525/5630 (Central Zionist Archives).

93. For example, see Permanent Mandates Commission, Minutes of the 32nd Session, pp. 111–118; particularly August 13, 1937: Lord William Ormsby Gore advocated the transfer of the Arab population of Palestine, who "had not hitherto regarded themselves as 'Palestinians' but as part of Syria as a whole, as part of the Arab world. . . . They would be going only a comparatively few miles away to a people with the same language, the same civilisation, the same religion . . . ," cited by Martin Gilbert, *Exile and Return: The Struggle for a Jewish Homeland* (Philadelphia and New York: J.B. Lippincott, 1978), p. 185. Also see reactions to Ormsby Gore, PRO FO 371/E71 34/976/31, minute, E.W. Rendel, December 8, 1937: According to British Foreign Office official Rendel, the transfer of "the Arab population from the Jewish state . . . seems clearly to have been regarded as a matter of enforcement by his Majesty's Government," judging from Lord Ormsby Gore's statements in the cabinet and his interview in the *Jewish Chronicle* of August 13, 1937. Rendel feared it would "be very difficult to answer the Saudi Minister's inquiry." In 1944, the British Labor Party officially endorsed the proposed transfer of Palestinian Arabs to Arab countries, and a year later the British Commonwealth passed a similar resolution. Schectman, *European Population Transfers 1939–1945* (New York: Oxford University Press, 1946), p. 457.

94. Interview, *New York World Telegram,* November 19, 1945.

95. Carl Hermann Voss, *The Palestine Problem Today: Israel and Its Neighbors* (Boston: Beacon Press, 1953), p. 36.

96. See United States Committee for Refugees, *Biennial Reports;* C.G. Paikert, *The German Exodus* (The Hague: Nijhoff, 1962); G. Frumkin, *Population Changes in Europe Since 1939* (New York: A.M. Kelley, 1951).

97. YMCA World Alliance, "World Communiqué," no. 4, July–August 1957.

98. See speech by Charles S. Rhyne, past president of the American Bar Association, "Fundamental Human Rights of Refugees," August 1972, *Vital Speeches,* September 15, 1972.

99. United States Committee for Refugees, 1969 *Report.*

100. April 16, 1961.

101. August 28, 1947.

102. *New York Times,* November 12, 1960.

103. Schechtman, *European Population Transfers,* p. 12; Schechtman, *Refugee in the World,* p. 156; for Bulgarian-Turkish Convention of 1913, see Mark Vishniak, *Transfer of Populations as a Means of Solving Problems of Minorities* (New York: Yiddish Scientific Institute, 1942), p. 15.

104. See surveys of the United States Committee for Refugees, particularly 1975–76 Biennial Report.
105. United States Committee for Refugees, 1982 *World Refugee Survey.*
106. United States Committee for Refugees, 1981 *World Refugee Survey.* Contrary to the UN, the United States Committee for Refugees until recently excluded other de facto "resettled" peoples who had "not," as yet, "acquired a new nationality," but its *Survey* still included the *total* UN estimate of "1.8 million *Palestinian* refugees in the Near East," despite the fact that so many, as the *Survey* noted, were living "out of camps" throughout the Middle East and the world, p. 37. Also see Chapter 18.
107. United States Committee for Refugees, 1975–76 *Report;* Iraq, Jordan, Egypt, Lebanon, and Syria.
108. Matthew Mitchell, then director of the United States Committee for Refugees, to the author, March 1976.
109. Author's interview with John McCarthy, December 19, 1978, New York.
110. For examples of statements reiterating this policy, see an address by Under Secretary of State for Political Affairs David D. Newsom at the Consultations on Indochinese Refugees convened by the United Nations High Commissioner for Refugees, December 11, 1978, Geneva; remarks by Assistant Secretary of State for Human Rights and Humanitarian Affairs, Patricia Derian, on ABC, "The Boat People: No Port in the Storm?", February 5, 1978; "Refugees are Pawns of Natural and Man-Made Disasters . . ." (pamphlet), United States Committee for Refugees, Washington; Richard F. Jannsen, "The Uprooted," *Wall Street Journal,* July 18, 1975; Ronald Yates, "Asian refugees: 'Mother of Jesus have pity on us,' " *Chicago Tribune,* October 21, 1979.
111. "A solution will be further complicated by the property claims against Arab States of the many Jews from those States who moved to Israel in its early years after achieving statehood." Deputy Assistant Secretary Harold Saunders, testifying before House of Representatives Committee on International Relations, Subcommittee on Investigations, November 12, 1975, Department of State Bulletin, December 1, 1975, p. 798.
112. *Al-Muharrir,* January 25, 1966.
113. Interview by Yitzhak Ben Gad, *Philadelphia Inquirer,* December 1, 1974.
114. Interview, *Jeune Afrique,* July 4, 1975.
115. *Al Nahar* (Beirut), May 15, 1975.
116. *Chicago Sun-Times,* January 24, 1977, issued after a "secret conclave;" later the same year, a similar statement was issued by Lebanese Christian leaders' joint "manifesto," including Camille Chamoun, a former President of Lebanon, Suleiman Franjieh, President "during the recent civil war," Pierre Gemayel, then Christian Phalangist leader, and others, *New York Times,* August 27, 1977.
117. Interview with author, November 25, 1978; March 15, 1981. Professor Philip M. Hauser, Director Emeritus, Population Research Center, University of Chicago, was, beginning in 1938: Assistant Chief Statistician for Population, then Deputy Director (until 1947), then Acting Director (1949–50), U.S. Bureau of the Census; U.S. Representative to UN Population Commission, 1947–51.
118. Statement of the organizing conference, World Organization of Jews from Arab Countries (WOJAC), Paris, November 24, 1975. In an Israeli Parliament debate in 1975, Mordechai Ben Porath (later a Cabinet Minister in charge of the rights of Jews from Arab lands) reproached the government: "The State of Israel, regrettably, has

discriminated in this case, and has played down the rights of the Jews from the Arab States." Translation from transcript of Knesset Debate, January 1, 1975.

119. United States Committee for Refugees, 1981 *World Refugee Survey,* New York, p. 27.
120. United States Committee for Refugees, 1982 *World Refugee Survey,* p. 18.
121. See Article 20 of the PLO Covenant in Appendix III.

3. The Arab Jew

1. Bernard Lewis, *The Arabs in History,* 4th rev. ed. (New York, Evanston, San Francisco, London: Harper-Colophon Books, 1966), pp. 31–32; S.D. Goitein, *A Mediterranean Society,* vols. I and II (Berkeley, Los Angeles, London: 1971), p. 28; see also H.Z. Hirschberg, *The Jews in Islamic Lands,* 2nd rev. ed. (Leiden, 1974).
2. S.D. Goitein, *Jews and Arabs, Their Contacts Through the Ages,* 3rd ed. (New York: Schocken Books, 1974), p. 49.
3. Ibid., p. 50.
4. Lewis, *Arabs in History,* p. 42; also see Norman A. Stillman, *The Jews of Arab Lands: A History and Source Book* (Philadelphia: The Jewish Publication Society of America, 1979), pp. 113–114. For further information and fascinating reading, the Stillman work provides new and in-depth insights into the "Jewish social history in the Arab world, spanning 1500 years," with original translations from Arabic and other languages.
5. Lewis, *Arabs in History,* p. 45, pp. 38–48. See Chapter 8.
6. See examples in Chapter 4; also see Stillman, *The Jews,* "Some Koranic Pronouncements on the Jews," pp. 150–151.
7. André Chouraqui, *Between East and West, A History of the Jews of North Africa,* trans. from French by Michael M. Bernet (Philadelphia: The Jewish Publication Society of America, 1968), pp. 45–46; D.G. Littman, *Jews Under Muslim Rule in the Late Nineteenth Century,* reprinted from the Weiner Library Bulletin, 1975, vol. XXVIII, New Series Nos. 35/36 (London, 1975), p. 65.
8. *The Meaning of the Glorious Koran,* Surah IX, v. 29, Mohammed Marmaduke Pickthall, ed. (New York: Mentor Books, 1953).
9. Chouraqui, *Between East and West,* p. 46. Also see Hayyim Cohen, *The Jews of the Middle East 1860–1972* (New York, 1973); S.D. Goitein, *Jews and Arabs.*
10. World Jewish Congress, *The Jews of French Morocco and Tunisia* (New York, 1952).
11. Saul Friedman, "The Myth of Arab Toleration," *Midstream,* January 1970; Goitein, *Jews and Arabs,* p. 67ff.
12. Ibn Battuta, *Ibn Battuta Travels in Asia and Africa 1325–1354,* trans. and selected with introduction and notes by H.A.R. Gibb (London, 1929), p. 125.
13. Edward William Lane, *Manners and Customs of the Modern Egyptians 1833–1835* (London, New York, Melbourne: 1890), p. 512.
14. The visit to Harat al-Yahud, Cairo's Jewish Quarter, was recorded in letters from a journalist in Arabic dated June 11 and June 18, 1920, cited by Jacob M. Landau, *Jews in Nineteenth Century Egypt* (New York, 1969), pp. 30–31.
15. Hayyim J. Cohen, *The Jews of the Middle East 1860–1972* (Jerusalem, 1973), pp. 1–3.
16. See interviews in Chapter 6.
17. Goitein, *Jews and Arabs,* pp. 6–7, 87, 88, for examples.
18. Heinrich Graetz, *History of the Jews,* 5 vols. (New York, 1927), vol. 5, pp. 634–639.

19. By Habib Faris, 1890, original title in newspaper, 1890: "The Cry of the Innocent with the Trumpet of Freedom," originally published in Egyptian newspaper *al-Mahrusa,* then as 1890 book, *Human Sacrifices in the Talmud.* Book republished in 1962 as one of a series of information pamphlets, "National Books," no. 184, 1962, 164 pages, listed as one of the publications by UAR Ministry of Education, #3931, edited by Abd al-Ati Jalal, introduction dated June 16, 1962. Cited by Y. Harkabi, *Arab Attitudes to Israel* (Jerusalem, 1971), pp. 270–271.
20. Ibid., cited in Harkabi, *Arab Attitudes,* p. 271.
21. Abd al-Karim Gharayiba, *Suriyya fi al-Qarn al-Tasi Ashar 1840–1876* (Cairo, 1961–62), p. 47, cited by Moshe Ma'oz, *The Image of the Jew in Official Arab Literature and Communications Media* (Jerusalem, 1976), p. 21.
22. 'Abdallah al-Tall, *The Danger of World Jewry to Islam and Christianity* (in Arabic) (Cairo, 1964), p. 104, cited by Harkabi, *Arab Attitudes,* pp. 273–274.
23. Mustafa Sa'adani, "The Tragedy of Good Father Thomas," *Akhir Sa'ah,* November 28, 1973, cited by Ma'oz, *The Image of the Jew,* p. 22.
24. *Al-Sayyad,* November 29, 1973, as cited by Ma'oz, *The Image of the Jew,* p. 23.
25. "Sanctifying War and Hating Peace," by Salem al-Yamani, *Al-Gumhuriya,* June 22, 1982.
26. "The Arabs and the Jews—Who Will Destroy Whom?" by Dr. Lutfi Abd Al-Azim, *Al-Ahram Iktisadi,* September 27, 1982.
27. Official Records of the Second Session of the General Assembly of the United Nations. Summary Record of Meetings 25 September–25 November, 1947, p. 185. During the proposed partition of Palestine, in November, 1947, Egyptian Representative in the United Nations General Assembly, Haykal Pasha, declared that "The Arab governments will do all in their power to defend the Jewish citizens in their countries, but we all know that an excited crowd is sometimes stronger than the police. Unintentionally, you are about to spark an anti-Semitic fire in the Middle East which will be more difficult to extinguish than it was in Germany."

The Egyptian spokesman's threat made clear that the Arab world has interpreted the term "anti-Semitism" correctly—in the only sense it has been used historically —as a definition of anti-Jewish attitude and action. Arabs do not, as Egypt's President Sadat and others have occasionally claimed, use it themselves as a term connoting both Arabs and Jews.
28. Goitein, *Mediterranean Society,* vol. II, p. 283.
29. Bernard Lewis, *Islam in History: Ideas, Men and Events in the Middle East* (New York: The Library Press, 1973), p. 136.
30. Fritz Grobba, *Männer und Mächte im Orient* (Zurich, Berlin, Frankfurt, 1967), p. 194–197, 207–208. Bernard Lewis notes that "this draft was an Arab request to the Germans, not a German offer to the Arabs." Also see: Jon Kimche, *The Second Arab Awakening* (London, 1970); L. Hirszowicz, *The Third Reich and the Arab East* (London, 1966), particularly regarding Mufti's 1937 contact with the Nazis: p. 34.
31. Sadat's letter, *Al Musawwar,* No. 1510, September 18, 1953, cited in D.F. Green, ed., *Arab Theologians on Jews and Israel* (Geneva, 1976 ed.), p. 87. Quoted also by Gideon Hausner, November 16, 1971, at New York. Also see Harkabi, *Arab Attitudes,* pp. 276–277, for other examples.
32. *Al-Akhbar,* August 19, 1973.
33. *Akhar Sa'ah,* Cairo, April 10, 1974, cited by Ma'oz, *The Image of the Jew,* p. 22.
34. *Akhar Sa'ah,* Cairo, December 3, 1975.

35. Goitein, *Jews and Arabs,* p. 47. "That Jews were present in *Northern* Arabia is proved by the existence of Jewish tombstones on ancient sites halfway between al-Medina and Palestine. These date to an even earlier period, the years before and after the destruction of the Second Temple."

36. Ibid., pp. 77–79.

37. Ibid., p. 76.

38. The Hedjaz (or Hejaz).

39. "When all the states of the region, except Turkey, came under the domination of Islam in the 7th century, the political status of the Jews underwent a change." Cohen, *The Jews of the Middle East,* p. 1.

40. Joseph Schechtman, *On Wings of Eagles, The Plight, Exodus and Homecoming of Oriental Jewry* (New York: Thomas Yoseloff, 1961), p. 35. Cohen, *The Jews of the Middle East,* p. 3. Cohen adds that "In the two Shi-ite [Muslim] countries, Yemen and Iran, the status of the non-Muslims was more difficult than in all the other Muslim lands. . . . They were not only deprived of rights, but were also defenseless and considered unclean."

41. In 1172. Cohen, *The Jews of the Middle East,* p. 3. See also Goitein, *Jews and Arabs,* p. 170; Isadore Twersky, ed., *A Maimonides Reader* (New York, 1972), pp. 437–462; Jacob S. Minkin, *The World of Moses Maimonides* (New York, London: Thomas Yoseloff, 1957), pp. 67–78.

42. Schechtman, *On Wings of Eagles,* p. 36.

43. Cohen, *Jews of the Middle East,* p. 4.

44. Garsten Niebuhr, *Reisebeschreibungen,* vol. I, p. 422ff. Translated into English by Robert Herson, *Travels Through Arabia and Other Countries in the East, Performed by M. Niebuhr* (Edinburgh, 1792).

45. Jacob Sappir, *Even Sappir* (Lyck, 1866), p. 52, cited by Schechtman, *Eagles,* p. 37; see also A. Ya'ari, *Sefer Massa Teyman* (A Book of a Journey to Yemen) (Jerusalem, 1951), with intro. and notes by A. Ya'ari.

46. Goitein, *Jews and Arabs,* pp. 76–77.

47. Cohen, *Jews of the Middle East,* p. 5.

48. Yoshua Feldman, *The Yemenite Jews* (London, 1913), p. 17.

49. Reported by Yomtov Zemach, *Bulletin de l'Alliance Israelite Universelle,* 1910, Beirut.

50. Schechtman, *Eagles,* pp. 48–49. The story of the Yemenite Jews' detainment in the desert, and British threats to deport them, is fascinatingly related by Schechtman on pp. 49–52. See Chapters 5 and 10.

51. United States Intelligence Report, May 29, 1946, cited in Schechtman, *Eagles,* p. 41.

52. Schechtman, *Eagles,* p. 31, pp. 49–52.

53. Goitein, *Jews and Arabs,* pp. 46–47.

54. Ibid., p. 47.

55. Cohen, *Jews of the Middle East,* p. 6. Cohen deals very little with the Jews of Aden because, as he explains, "their history is less known."

56. Goitein, *Jews and Arabs,* p. 102.

57. Ibid., p. 115.

58. Ibid., p. 162.

59. Cohen, *Jews of the Middle East,* p. 6.

60. Ibid.
61. "The Disaster of Jews of Aden," December 13, 1947, Aden. Cited by Schechtman, *Eagles*, p. 76.
62. This is in a sense a distillation of the whole Arab propaganda effort, successfully perpetuated by the British authorities while at the same time there was existing evidence, by other more fair-minded British authorities, to contradict that evidence used in the propaganda.
63. Sir Tom Hickinbotham, *Aden* (London, 1958), pp. 82–83.
64. Colonel A.H. Sigrist, Colonial Office, *Report of the Commission of Inquiry into Disturbances in Aden in December 1947,* Colonial Paper N233 (London, 1948), pp. 6–7.
65. Martin Gilbert, *The Jews of Arab Lands, Their History in Maps* (Oxford, 1975), p. 8.
66. Cohen, *Jews of the Middle East,* p. 67.
67. Gilbert, *The Jews of Arab Lands,* p. 8; *Report of the Commission of Inquiry into Disturbances in Aden in December 1947,* pp. 24–25; also Goitein, *Jews and Arabs,* p. 236.
68. Norman Bentwich, "Aden After the Riots," *Commentary,* May 1948.
69. Reported by Rabbi Kopel Rosen, President of the Mizrachi Foundation of Great Britain and Ireland, in the *Jewish Chronicle,* London, January 14, 1949.
70. In 1946, the community of Jews in Aden had been almost 8,000. *British Colonial Office Annual Report on Aden for the Year 1946* (London, 1948), p. 12.
71. There was also a very small community of Jews in Bahrein, traceable "at least from the middle of the 19th century," where anti-Jewish riots exploded in 1947, in the capital city of Manama. Unlike Aden, there are still Jews—"some scores of them" —living in Bahrein, or were in 1973—perhaps the only Jews in Arabia. Cited by Cohen, *Jews of the Middle East,* p. 66.
72. A.J. Mack, "Jewish Life in Aden," *Jewish Chronicle,* February 12, 1959.
73. Hickinbotham, *Aden,* p. 87; Cohen, *Jews of the Middle East,* p. 67. Other sources for information on the Jews of Aden include unpublished studies by B.J. Yaish, entitled *History of the Jews of Aden* and *Modern History of the Jews of Aden;* cited by Schechtman in *Eagles,* p. 401, n. 1.
74. 123,371. Israel Government Statistical Abstracts.
75. See Stillman, *The Jews,* pp. 29–32, for influence of Babylonia (Jewish Bavel), and "authority of Jewish exilarch" when the Arabs "invaded Iraq . . . ," p. 29; S.D. Goitein, *Jews and Arabs,* p. 105; also see S. Baron, *Ancient and Medieval Jewish History* (New Brunswick, N.J., 1972); David Sassoon, *History of the Jews in Baghdad* (Letchworth, 1949).
76. Martin Gilbert, *The Jews of Arab Lands, Their History in Maps,* p. 2.
77. Lewis, *Islam in History,* p. 319, n. 9. Lewis gives an illustration of the "traditional relationship" between Muslim and Jew from a report by H.E. Wilkie Young, the British Vice-Consul in Mosul, written January 1909, *Middle Eastern Studies,* vii (1971), p. 232.
78. Cohen, *Jews of the Middle East,* pp. 24–25.
79. Schechtman, *Eagles,* p. 89; also see David Sassoon, *History of the Jews in Baghdad,* pp. 178, 213.

80. Ibid., p. 92.
81. On August 29, 1933.
82. *New York Times,* July 18, 1937; Cohen, *Jews of the Middle East,* pp. 27–28.
83. Ibid.
84. Cohen, *Jews of the Middle East,* pp. 29–31.
85. Sylvia Haim, "Arabic Anti-Semitic Literature," *Jewish Social Studies,* pp. 307–312. Judaism, not Zionism, was a "threat"; moreover, it was not Zionism but friendship with the British that combined with traditional attitudes toward *dhimmi* Jews to accelerate anti-Jewish attacks. Elie Kedourie, *The Sack of Basra and the Farhud of Baghdad,* International Conference on Jewish Communities in Muslim Lands, Institute of Asian and African Studies, The Hebrew University of Jerusalem, pp. 33–34.
86. Abd al-Razzaq al-Hasani, *al-Asrar al-Khafiyya fi hawadith al-sana 1941 al-taharur-riyya* (Hidden Secrets of the Events of the Liberatory Year 1941) (Sidon, 1958), pp. 226–236. "The point about the police and the army is made on p. 231." Cited by Kedourie, *The Sack of Basra,* p. 21.
87. Terence Prittie and Bernard Dineen, *The Double Exodus, A Study of Arab and Jewish Refugees in the Middle East* (London, n.d.), p. 25; Schechtman, *Eagles,* p. 98.
88. Abd al-Razzaq al-Hasani, *Tarikh al-wizarat al-iraqiyya* (History of the Ministries of Iraq), vol. 5, new ed. (Sidon, 1967), p. 268, n. 1. Hasani's informants were Abdullah al-Qassab, a member of the investigation committee, and Ali Khalid al-Hijazi, Baghdad Chief of Police. Cited by Kedourie, *The Sack of Basra,* p. 22.
89. Schechtman, *Eagles,* pp. 87–125. Also see S.H. Longrigg and Frank Stoakes, *Iraq, 1900–1950* (New York, 1958), p. 350.
90. George Lenczowski, *The Middle East in World Affairs,* 2nd ed. (Ithaca, N.Y., 1956), p. 253.
91. Sir Alec Kirkbride, *From the Wings, Amman Memoirs 1947–1951* (London, 1976), p. 115.
92. Ibid.
93. "Law for the Control and Administration of Property of Jews who have Forfeited Iraqi Nationality," no. 5, 1951, *Iraqi Official Gazette No. 2938,* March 10, 1951.
94. As of 1948, fines levied against Jews amounted to $80,000,000, reported by *Al-Amal,* Beirut, October 31, 1948. Cited by Schechtman, *Eagles,* p. 106.
95. *Al-Zaman,* Cairo, August 10, 1948. Cited by Schechtman, *Eagles,* p. 107.
96. Law No. 1, 1950, "Supplement to Ordinance of Cancelling the Iraqi Nationality No. 62 of 1933," *Iraqi Official Gazette No. 2816,* March 9, 1950.
97. Shlomo Hillel, *Derekh Ba Midbar* (A Way in the Desert) (Jerusalem, 1965), p. 70ff. Hillel was one interviewee contacted for this book.
98. Arif al-'Arif, *Al-Nakba, Nakbat Beit al-Maqdis Walfirdaus al-Mafqud, 1947–1955,* vol. IV (Al-Maktaba Asriyya Littiba: Wal-Nashr, 1960), p. 893. An eminent Palestinian historian, Arif al'Arif, reproached Nuri Said for allowing the Iraqi Jews to flee.

    "This is what the Iraqi Prime Minister Nuri al-Said Pasha told me when we met in Jerusalem on January 13, 1951. I asked him about the limitations imposed on the Iraqi Jews as to their leaving Iraq. He said: 'Nothing, only their relinquishing their Iraqi nationality.'

    "I said: 'Was it not possible to defer it until the Palestinian and refugee problems are settled?'

    "He said: 'Not at all. The Jews have always been and will forever be a source of evil and mischief for Iraq. They are spies. They sold their properties. They do not possess land which they sow. So how will they live? What would they do if they remained in Iraq? No, my friend. We had better get rid of them, as long as the opportunity for getting rid of them is open.' "

99. American Committee for Rescue and Resettlement of Iraqi Jews, Inc., by Dr. Heskel Haddad, President.

100. Schechtman, *Eagles,* pp. 184–185; Terence Prittie and Bernard Dineen, *The Double Exodus,* p. 23.

101. R. Nissim, *Ha-Mafteah,* ed. by J. Goldenthal (1847), chapter I, p. 2, intro., p. 75. Cited by H.Z. Hirschberg, *A History of the Jews in North Africa,* vol. I (Leiden: E.J. Brill, 1974), p. 198.

102. A.D. 638.

103. Friedman, "The Myth of Arab Toleration," p. 58.

104. Stillman, *Jews,* p. 68.

105. Cohen, *Jews of the Middle East,* p. 3.

106. L.A. Mayer, *Mamluk Costume: A Survey* (Geneva, 1952), p. 65.

107. Stillman, *Jews,* p. 70.

108. Hirschberg, *History,* p. 402.

109. From 1517.

110. Lane, *Manners and Customs,* p. 512.

111. Ibid., pp. 512–517.

112. The Alexandria blood libel described was recorded on June 3, 1869; J. Landau, *Jews in Nineteenth-Century Egypt,* pp. 30–32. The Cairo blood libel was recorded October 18, 1844; ibid., p. 30. Landau's book contains multilingual documented evidence of many libels; Landau refers the reader to a more exhaustive work of his on the subject, "Blood Libels and the Persecution of the Jews in Egypt at the End of the Nineteenth Century," *Sefunot,* V, 1961 (Jerusalem, Hebrew). Also see article by H.Z. Hirschberg, "Turkey and Religious Slanders, the Attitudes of the Authorities of the Ottoman Empire to Blood Libels," *Mahanayim,* no. 110, 1966 (Israel Defense Forces, Chief Military Rabbinate, Tel Aviv); Bezalel Landau, "The Blood Libel in Jewish History," *Mahanayim* no. 80, 1963.

113. 1888 British report of fellahin hatred of Jews: FO. 78/4145. "This is E.W.P. Foster's report, dated March 21, 1888, from Alexandria, enclosed in Baring's Report No. 138 to the Marquis of Salisbury (British Foreign Secretary) dated March 24, 1888. Foster's account seems trustworthy if one remembers his long connection with the *fallahin* [sic] during his employment in the Egyptian Department of Irrigation. Baring (better known, later, as Lord Cromer) notes here that this refers to Riyad Pasha, a well-known official and minister during the earlier years of the British Occupation." Cited by Landau, *Jews in Nineteenth-Century Egypt,* p. 228, including notes 2 and 3.

114. Habib Faris, *Surakh al-Bari fi Buq al-Hurriyya* (The Cry of the Innocent with the Trumpet of Freedom), cited by Harkabi, *Arab Attitudes,* p. 271.

115. Landau cites a report of "a regrettable incident" dated April 30, 1883, from Port Said French Consul to French Foreign Minister in *Jews in Nineteenth-Century Egypt,* p. 225; and a letter reporting persecution dated March 29, 1903, from S. Somekh in Port Said to President of the AIU, ibid., p. 298.

116. Article 10 (4) of Egyptian Nationality Code cited by Maurice de Wee, *La Nationalité Egyptienne, Commentaire de la Loi du 26 Mai, 1926,* p. 35.

117. Cohen, *The Jews of the Middle East,* pp. 48–49.

118. 1945. Schechtman, *Eagles,* p. 187.
119. Jewish Agency for Palestine, *Memorandum on the Position of the Jewish Communities in the Oriental Countries,* submitted to the Anglo-American Committee of Inquiry, Jerusalem, March 1946.
120. Prittie, *Double Exodus,* p. 23. Schechtman, *Eagles,* pp. 187–189. Called the Egyptian Company Law, July 29, 1947, the act introduced prohibitive quotas for non-Egyptian workers and brought into use the 1926 Nationality Code (see note 116 above), which militated against the Jews. See also Cohen, *The Jews of the Middle East,* pp. 49–88.
121. Martin Gilbert, *Exile and Return, the Struggle for a Jewish Homeland* (Philadelphia and New York, 1978), pp. 306–307. "For the Arabs outside Palestine a similar wave of anti-Jewish hatred led to violence against Jews in almost every Arab city: in British-ruled Aden, scene of a savage attack on Jewish life and property, 82 Jews were killed on December 9. In Beirut, Cairo, Alexandria and Aleppo Jewish houses were looted, and synagogues attacked."
122. *Basler National Zeitung,* August 10, 1948. Cited by Schechtman, *Eagles,* p. 190.
123. Egyptian newspaper *Akhar Saa,* letter reprinted in Press Review of *Bourse Egyptienne,* July 22, 1948. Cited by Yahudiya Masriya, *Les Juifs en Egypte* (The Jews of Egypt) (Geneva, 1971), p. 54.
124. Immigration Department, Jewish Agency, Jerusalem.
125. The trials of twelve Jews were begun on the heels of a purge of the Muslim Brotherhood, to distract from the executions of those anti-government forces by forcing attention to the "Zionists," according to the *Washington Post* and *Times Herald,* December 22, 1954; 77 were tried in another case, and 7 in yet another in the same period. Schechtman, *Eagles,* pp. 194–195.
126. *New York Times,* Osgood Caruthers, November 24, 1956.
127. Charles Issawi, ed., *The Economic History of the Middle East, 1800–1914* (Chicago, 1966), p. 507. "The Arab-Israeli war led to an exodus of Jews and the loss of much of their property. And the nationalization of the Suez Canal and the war that followed resulted in the taking over of a huge amount of British, French, and Jewish property, the expulsion of thousands of foreigners, and the passing of legislation Egyptianizing all foreign banks and insurance companies."
128. *Alliance Review,* April 1957, cited by Schechtman, *Eagles,* p. 199.
129. Law No. 391 of 1956. See *Revue Egyptienne de Droit International,* vol. 12, 1956, pp. 80–90, Arabic Section, Article 1 (1) (a) on page 80. Cited by Dr. Ya'akov Meron, *The "Complicating" Element of the Arab-Israeli Conflict* (Jerusalem, 1977), p. 11.
130. April 15, 1978, Official Gazette, cited by Meron, *"Complicating" Element,* p. 11.
131. Interviewed by correspondent of the *Deutsche National Zeitung,* April 1, 1964. Cited by Dafna Alon, *Arab Racialism,* p. 14.
132. Cohen, *Jews of the Middle East,* pp. 51–52.
133. Prittie, *Double Exodus,* p. 24.
134. *New York Post,* January 8, 1957.
135. Total of refugees from Tunisia, Morocco, and Algeria, 1975, Israel Statistical Abstract.
136. Chouraqui, *Between East and West,* pp. 46–47.
137. Hirschberg, *History,* pp. 19, 197; also see J. Mann, *Texts and Studies in Jewish History and Literature,* vol. I (Cincinnati, 1931), p. 246.
138. Littman, *Jews Under Muslim Rule,* p. 65; Chouraqui, *Between East and West,* p. 48.
139. Hirschberg, *History,* pp. 96–97. According to Hirschberg, "The victories of Hasan

ibn Nu'man and Musa ibn Nusayr in the late 7th and early 8th centuries, through which the whole of North Africa fell into Arab hands, mark the beginning of a new era for Jews. . . . The Jews are mostly described as *dhimmi* (protected persons), an expression which in Maghreb refers only to them, and not the Christians . . ." Arab writers of the period of Arab conquest have affirmed that the Jews were virtually North Africa's only *dhimmi:* "Ibn 'Abd al-Hakam reports that Hasan, the conqueror of North Africa, imposed the *kharaj* on the *'ajam* (the strangers, i.e., Byzantines) and the (native) Berbers who adhered to Christianity. He subsequently says that after a time the Rum (Byzantines) reconquered Antablus (the Pentapolis) and staged riots against the *dhimmi.* . . .

"Ibn Hawqal (middle of 10th century) notes the *jawali* (poll-tax) imposed on the Jews in Qabes. Immediately afterwards, he relates that the Bedouin attacked the *dhimmi,* i.e. Jews, who had entered into a protective covenant by paying the *jawali.*

"A poem describing the rough climate of Tahert, where winter was jokingly said to last thirteen months, contains the following verse:
'We rejoice at the sun when it shines
as the *dhimmi* rejoice on the Sabbath.' "
See also E.F. Gautier, *Le Passe de l'Afrique du Nord* (Paris, 1952), p. 324.

140. Chouraqui, *Between East and West,* p. 48. Khalifa ben Ragasa and his family were "massacred" in 1302.

141. Ibid., p. 49. Chouraqui tells of "the rich Jew of the Dar ben Meshal family [who] was stripped and killed by Mulay Rashid in the seventeenth century." The "lawlessness" of the wanton murder was cloaked in terms of heroics, and celebrated thereafter at Fez, Morocco.

142. Ibid., p. 51. Littman's *Jews Under Muslim Rule* has reprinted documents containing eyewitness reports from North Africa of the "endless complaints . . . about acts which were iniquitous even according to Islamic law . . . a glimpse into the harsh reality of life under Muslim rule," p. 67.

143. Hirschberg, *History,* p. 108.

144. Ibid., pp. 127–128. Hirschberg writes: "A detailed account of developments is given in the letter of Solomon Cohen, a resident of Fustat, who heard of the events from eye-witnesses, Jewish and Muslim refugees in Egypt, and reported them to his father, then in South Arabia (probably in Aden). The father was eager for news of the Maghreb, since he was a native of Sijilmasa and still had relatives in Moroccan cities. The letter, written in Judeo-Arabic, is dated of the month of Shebat in the year 1459 of the Seleucid Era, i.e. January 1148 C.E." The following is the text of the account:

"Here is the story of the persecutions, as told by Solomon Cohen: 'Abd al-Mu'min the Susi (i.e. the one of the Sus Valley), leader of the Almohads after the death of Muhammad ibn Tumart the Mahdi, marched against the Emir Tashfin, who was in Oran, besieged and captured the city, killed Tashfin and crucified his body. Thereafter he captured Tlemcen and killed all those who were in it (i.e. including the Jews), except those who embraced Islam. At the news of these events, the Berbers in Sijilmasa rose against the Almoravid governor and expelled him and his garrison force from the city. Some 200 Jews, sensing the impending trouble, fled Sijilmasa at this juncture. They included two brothers of his father Yehuda, as well as Yehuda ben Farhon, whom Solomon mentions specially, probably because he was a local notable and rabbinical scholar or a relative. They escaped to Dar'a, but it was not known what had happened to them afterwards. Following the expulsion of the

Almoravid governor from Sijilmasa, the inhabitants of the latter sent a surrender delegation to 'Abd al Mu'min. On entering the city, the Almohads tried to convert the Jews to Islam by debate and persuasion, but after seven months of religious disputations, a new commander arrived in the city, who solved the problem by a more efficient method. One hundred and fifty persons were killed for clinging to their faith; the remainder converted. The first to adopt Islam was the *dayyan* (religious judge) of Sijilmasa, Joseph ben 'Amaran. All the cities in the Almoravid state were conquered by the Almohads. One hundred thousand persons were killed in Fez on that occasion, and 120,000 in Marrakesh. Only Dar'a and Meknes had not been captured by the time of reporting. The Jews in all the localities from Bajaya (Bougie) westward groaned under the heavy yoke of the Almohads; many had been killed, many others converted, none were able to appear in public as Jews. The news of the capture of Bajaya reached Fustat on the day the letter was written. Large areas between Seville and Tortosa had likewise fallen into Almohad hands."

According to Hirschberg, "This account tallies with the sequence of events as given by Arab historians and in particular by Ibn Baydhaq, the biographer of Ibn Tumart and 'Abd al-Mu'min, who was their contemporary and comrade-in-arms. This permits us to date the events as follows: Oran, 1145 or 1146; Tlemcen, Sijilmasa, 1146; Fez, 1146/7; Marrakesh area, 1147; Bajaya, end of 1147 or beginning of 1148.

"It should be noted that with regard to certain details Solomon's account clarifies some obscure passages in the Arab sources.

"It was published by J.M. Toledano, *HUCA,* 4 (1927), pp. 449–458, and a second time, with an introduction and translation into Hebrew, by the present writer, in *Y.F. Baer Jubilee Volume,* 1960, pp. 134–153. We therefore content ourselves with a summary of the historical parts."

145. Ibid., pp. 138–139.
146. Minkin, *The World of Moses Maimonides* (New York, 1957), pp. 428–429ff.
147. Ibid., p. 29. Also see Hirschberg, *History,* p. 137: ". . . in the opening lines of that *Epistle,* Maimonides most strongly deprecates the condemnation of the forced converts by 'the self-styled sage who had never experienced what so many Jewish communities experienced in the way of persecution,' his conclusion is that a Jew must leave the country where he is forced to transgress the divine law: 'He should not remain in the realm of that king; he should sit in his house until he emigrates, and if he must pursue any occupation he should do so secretly, until he emigrates.' And once more, with greater insistence: 'He should on no account remain in a place of forced conversion; whoever remains in such a place desecrates the divine name and is nearly as bad as a wilful sinner; as for those who beguile themselves, saying that they will remain until the Messiah comes to the Maghreb and leads them to Jerusalem, I do not know how he is to cleanse them of the stigma of conversion.' "
148. Ibid., p. 30.
149. R. Dozy, ed., *The History of the Almohades by . . . al-Marrakoshi* (Leyden, 1881), p. 223. Second ed., Amsterdam, 1978. Cited by Hirschberg, *History,* p. 201.
150. Hirschberg, *History,* p. 371.
151. Ibid., p. 202.
152. Sabbateans and Marranos, for example. See H.H. Ben-Sasson, ed., *A History of the Jewish People* (Cambridge, Mass.: Harvard University Press, 1976), passim; Cecil Roth, *A History of the Marranos* (Philadelphia: The Jewish Publication Society of America, 1932); H.Z. (J.W.) Hirschberg, *A History of the Jews in North Africa,* vol.

1, pp. 191–196; Heinrich Graetz, *History of the Jews*, vol. 4, passim; Gershom Sholem, *Sabbetai Zvi* (Tel Aviv, 1957); Joachim Prinz, *The Secret Jews* (New York: Random House, 1973). Also see Chapter 5.

153. D.F. Green, ed., *Arab Theologians on Jews and Israel: Extracts from the Proceedings of the Fourth Conference of the Academy of Islamic Research* (Geneva: Editions de l'Avenir, 1971), p. 24. "Jews' Attitude Towards Islam and Muslims in the First Islamic Era" by Sheikh Abd Allah Al Meshad. Al Meshad quotes from the Holy Quran: "When they meet those who believe, they say: 'we believe' " (Baqara, 44); "Saying with their lips what was not in their hearts" (Al-Imran 167).

154. Hirschberg, *History*, p. 359.

155. *Shebet Yehuda*, ed. Shohet, 1947, Chapter 27. Cited by Hirschberg, *History*, p. 385.

156. Leo l'Africain, *Description de l'Afrique* (Paris, 1956), cited by Hirschberg, *History*, p. 390; see also Leo Africanus, *The History and Description of Africa and of the Notable Things Therein Contained*, ed. Dr. Robert Brown (London, 1896); *A Geographical Historie of Africa (by) Johannes Leo* (New York: Da Capo Press, 1969). Leo Africanus: al-Hassan ibn-Mohammed al-Wezaz al-Fasi, a Moor, baptized as Giovanni Leone, but better known as Leo Africanus.

157. Hirschberg, *History*, pp. 390, 399.

158. Stillman, *Jews*, pp. 78–79.

159. Arab term for North African region comprising mainly Morocco, Algeria, and Tunisia.

160. Chouraqui, *Between East and West*, p. 49.

161. Ibid., pp. 52–53.

162. Text published by J. Bennaim, *Malkhey Rabbanan* (Jerusalem, 1931), 96c-d. Also see Ben-Zvi Institute MS. No. 2651. Cited by Hirschberg, *History*, pp. 400–401.

163. Chouraqui, *Between East and West*, p. 39.

164. The years 1883–1884, Charles de Foucauld, *Reconnaissance au Maroc*, cited in ibid., pp. 118–119.

165. Gilbert, *Exile*, p. 27. "The European and American concern over the Damascus persecutions did not alleviate for long the plight of the Jews . . . under Muslim rule elsewhere."

166. Ibid., pp. 41–42. In May 1885. In addition to the furor in the Jewish press, the British Jewish leader, Sir Moses Montefiore, "mounted a solemn protest."

167. Prittie, *Double Exodus*, p. 20.

168. Schechtman, *Eagles*, p. 272; Prittie, *Double Exodus*, p. 21.

169. May 23, 1948. Chouraqui, *Between East and West*, p. 181.

170. Hirschberg, *History*, p. 369.

171. Africanus, *The History and Description of Africa*, p. 431, cited by Hirschberg, *History*, p. 402.

172. Hirschberg, *History*, p. 444. Hirschberg gives the following account of one of many violent moments of history for Tlemcen's Jews: "At the . . . reign of Charles V, who in 1555 renounced his crowns and retired to a monastery, the Turks took Tripoli and later expelled the troops of the sherif Muhammad al-Mahdi from Tlemcen. The latter city changed hands several times between the Spaniards, the Turks and the sherif's Berber soldiers. The Jews suffered from these changes more than the rest of the population. Joseph ha-Kohen reports: 'It was in the year 5203, i.e. 1543, that Mansur plotted against his master, the king of Tlemcen in Barbary. He called the Spaniards who were in Oran and they came to the city in force and pillaged it, and the Jews,

too, of whom there were many there, were led captive by the enemy, and they were sold as slaves in the month of Adar. Some were redeemed in Oran and some in Fez, and some were led to Spain and estranged from the Lord, the God of Israel.' Armed intervention did not end here. About a year later, Khayr al-Din's son, Hasan Pasha, set out to take revenge upon Mansur and the Spaniards, and then it was the other way again—and each retaliatory action brought trouble for the Jews. The sons of the nagid and some Jews who were with them, who were fleeing for their lives, were seized on the road to Debdou, thrown into prison and forced to redeem themselves with a heavy ransom."

173. Almanac of the Bey's secretary Titteri, *Revue Africaine,* trans. Feraud (1874), p. 316, cited by Chouraqui, *Between East and West,* p. 115.
174. William Shaler, *Sketches of Algiers* (Boston, 1826), cited by Chouraqui, *Between East and West,* pp. 114–115.
175. Chouraqui, *Between East and West,* p. 117.
176. Hirschberg, *History,* p. 6.
177. Ibid., pp. 17–18.
178. Ibid., p. 7. In fact, the Berber language, "despite its cultural backwardness, survives in . . . Algeria with 33 [per cent of the population]." Forty percent of Moroccans and 23 percent of "Tripolitania"—Libyans—still employed the Berber language at the time Hirschberg revised his introduction, 1974. Tunisia was the only North African state in which the Berber tongue was practically extinct—"1 per cent." However, Hirschberg noted that ". . . no doubt . . . Arab consciousness will make further progress in the sovereign states which Libya, Tunisia, Morocco and Algeria have become in the past twenty years" (p. 9).
179. Prittie, *Double Exodus,* p. 21.
180. Chouraqui, *Between East and West,* p. 152.
181. Ibid., p. 153.
182. Prittie, *Double Exodus,* p. 21; Chouraqui, *Between East and West,* p. 153.
183. Chouraqui, *Between East and West,* p. 153.
184. Ibid.; Leon Blum was appointed premier of France in June 1936, and again in March 1938.
185. Ibid., p. 154. Chouraqui cited Michel Ansky, *Les Juifs Algeriens, du Décret Cremieux à la Liberation* (Paris, 1950), pp. 75–76. See also Maurice Eisenbeth, *Pages Vécues,* 1940–1943 (Algiers, 1945).
186. October 2, 1940.
187. Schechtman, *Eagles,* p. 328.
188. Prittie, *Double Exodus,* p. 22.
189. Ibid.
190. Chouraqui, *Between East and West,* p. xvi.
191. Algerian Nationality Code, Article 34 (Law No. 63–69, March 27, 1963, published in the *J.O.R.A.,* April 2, 1963, p. 306), as cited in Annuaire de l'Afrique du Nord, pp. 806–814. On December 15, 1970, an updated ordinance, No. 70–86, Article 32, pertaining to the Algerian Nationality Code repeats the limitation of 1963, published in *J.O.R.A.,* December 18, 1970. All cited in Meron, *The "Complicating" Element,* p. 12.
192. Hirschberg, *History,* pp. 8–11.

193. Anselm Adorne, a Flemish nobleman, visited Tunis in 1470. R. Brunschvig, *Deux Récits de Voyage Inédits en Afrique du Nord* (Paris, 1936), p. 29b/158, p. 192; cited by Hirschberg, *History,* pp. 475–476.

194. Hirschberg, *History,* p. 478.

195. Foreign Jewish traders wore the "round cape, a distinctive mark of Jews from Christian countries"; "wearers of the round cape" is a frequent designation in contemporary literature for Jews of Spanish origin. The term originated with the royal decree that the Jews of thirteenth-century Aragon must wear "distinctive cloaks known as *cape ronde,* whence . . . 'wearers of the capos or caperon[de].' " The *capos* —originally "marks of shame"—evolved over the centuries into "robes of honor" among the Spanish rabbis exiled in Turkey. Cited by Hirschberg, *History,* pp. 462–463. See also A. Neumann, *The Jews in Spain* (Philadelphia, 1942), vol. II, pp. 201–202; 205–206; 327, n. 135; and 345. Also H.Z. Hirschberg, "The Oriental Jewish Communities" in A.J. Arberry, ed., *Religion in the Middle East* (Cambridge, 1969), vol. I, p. 186.

196. Ibid., p. 477.

197. Jews were expelled from Hammamet at the same time, for the same reason. D. Cazes, *Essai sur l'histoire des Israelites de Tunisie depuis les temps les plus recules* (Paris, 1888), pp. 83–84, cited by Hirschberg, *History,* p. 116.

198. Hirschberg, *History,* p. 403.

199. Al-Jannabi's account of Muhammed al-Qa'im in E. Fagnan, *Extraits inédits relatifs au Maghreb* (Algeria, 1924), p. 340, cited by Hirschberg, *History,* p. 479.

200. Cazes, *Essai sur l'histoire des Israelites de Tunisie,* p. 92ff; Chouraqui, *Between East and West,* p. 53.

201. Chouraqui, *Between East and West,* p. 223.

202. Simon Schwartzfuchs, "Persecution of Jews in the Land of Islam," *L'Arche,* December 1973.

203. Chouraqui, *Between East and West,* p. 159.

204. Ibid., p. 160.

205. Dated letters from Tunisian Jews to the Alliance Israelite Universelle, in Paris in 1860s, cited by Littman, *Jews Under Muslim Rule,* pp. 67–68.

206. From a letter (28.10.1864) by Salomon Garsin in Tunis to the President of the AIU Paris (AIU Tunis I.C.3). Cited by Littman, *Muslim Rule,* p. 67.

207. From a letter (23.3.1866) by Salomon Garsin, President of the Tunis AIU Committee, to the President of the AIU Paris (AIU Tunis I.C.3.), cited in ibid.

208. Letter (14.2.1869) by all the members of the Tunis AIU Committee to Adolphe Cremieux, President of the AIU, Paris (AIU Tunis I.C.3), cited in ibid., p. 68.

209. From a letter (22.9.1880) by A. Daninos, Vice-President of the Tunis Regional AIU Committee, to the President of the AIU, Paris (AIU Tunis I.C.3), cited in ibid.

210. Prittie, *Double Exodus,* p. 22.

211. "Tunisia Faces the Future," *World's Documents,* 1956, published by *Le Monde Economique,* cited by Schechtman, *Eagles,* p. 316.

212. Albert Hourani, *Syria and Lebanon, A Political Essay* (London, New York, Toronto, 1947), pp. 20, 62–63.

213. Hirschberg, *History,* p. 359.

214. Moshe Ma'oz, "Changes in the Position of the Jewish Communities of Palestine and

Syria in Mid-Nineteenth Century," in Moshe Ma'oz, ed., *Studies on Palestine During the Ottoman Period* (Jerusalem: The Magnes Press, The Hebrew University, Yad Izhak Ben-Zvi, 1975), pp. 142–143.

215. 'Abd al-Rahim al-Jawbari, quoted by C.E. Bosworth, "Jewish Elements in the Banu Sasan," in Moshe Ma'oz, ed., *Studies in the History of the Jewish Communities in Muslim Lands* (in preparation), cited by Ma'oz in *The Image of the Jew in Official Arab Literature and Communications Media* (Shazar Library, University of Jerusalem, 1976), p. 12; also see Stillman, *The Jews,* pp. 61, 75–77.

216. Ma'oz, "Changes," in Ma'oz, *Studies on Palestine,* p. 142.

217. J.L. Burkhardt, *Travels in Syria and the Holy Land* (London, 1822), p. 180, cited by Ma'oz, "Changes," in Ma'oz, ed., *Studies on Palestine,* p. 144.

218. Ibrahim Al-Awra, *Tarikh Wilayat Sulayman Basha-al-'Adil* (Sidon, 1936), p. 477, cited by Ma'oz, "Changes," p. 144.

219. Burkhardt, *Travels in Syria,* p. 180.

220. As'ad Mansur, *Ta'rikh al-Nasira* (Egypt, 1924), p. 59, cited in Ma'oz, "Changes," p. 144. See Chapter 9.

221. See E.B.B. Barker, *Syria and Egypt Under the Last Five Sultans of Turkey* (London, 1876), vol. I, p. 306; H.L. Bodman, *Political Factions in Aleppo, 1760–1826* (North Carolina, 1963), pp. 45, 48, 102; Ma'oz, "Changes in the Position," *Studies on Palestine,* pp. 145–146.

222. M.M. Raysher, *Sha'arei Yerushalayim* (Lemberg, 1866), p. 29. On extortion, see Ma'oz, "Changes in the Position," in *Studies on Palestine,* pp. 145–156.

223. Ma'oz, "Changes in the Position," *Studies on Palestine,* p. 147.

224. Letter from Jews in Tiberias to Sir Moses Montefiore, dated 5599 (1839), in Montefiore's collection, Ben-Zvi Institute, The Hebrew University, Jerusalem; Abd al-Karim Gharayiba, *Surriyya fi al-Qarn al-Tasi Ashar,* pp. 124–125, cited by Ma'oz, "Changes in the Position," *Studies on Palestine,* p. 147.

225. Cohen, *Jews of the Middle East,* p. 12; Ma'oz, "Changes in the Position," in *Studies on Palestine,* p. 148.

226. See "A Report on the Treatment of Jewish Prisoners in the Damascus Affair," in Stillman, *The Jews,* p. 396ff; Cohen, *Jews of the Middle East,* pp. 15, 45.

227. Graetz, *History of the Jews,* vol. V, pp. 660–661; see also pages 634–661.

228. "A Translation of the Firman Hatti-Sherif . . . of 12 Ramazan 1256," in M. Montefiore, *Diaries,* L. Loewe, ed. (London, 1890), pp. 278–279.

229. Moshe Ma'oz, *Ottoman Reform in Syria and Palestine 1840–1861* (Oxford, 1968), p. 186ff, pp. 189–194.

230. Schechtman, *Eagles,* p. 150; Elizabeth P. MacCallum, *The Nationalist Crusade in Syria* (New York, 1928), p. 63.

231. Cohen, *Jews of the Middle East,* pp. 45–46; Schechtman, *Eagles,* pp. 150–51.

232. Schechtman, *Eagles,* p. 150.

233. October 10, 1938, to Dr. Chaim Weizmann, cited by Schechtman, *Eagles,* pp. 150–151.

234. *Al-Alam al-Isra'ili* (The Jewish World), Beirut weekly in Arabic, January 14, 1944, and May 31, 1945, cited by Cohen, *Jews of the Middle East,* p. 46.

235. Cohen, *Jews of the Middle East,* p. 69, also p. 46. According to Cohen, "Unfortunately, there is no reliable material on this subject [concerning their number] with

the exception of Egypt, where a population census was conducted in 1882, in no country of the Middle East was such a census taken prior to the last few decades . . . ," p. 68. According to the *New York Herald-Tribune,* the remaining number in 1943 was 30,000: April 14, 1947.

236. October 1945, cited by Schechtman, *Eagles,* p. 154.
237. Jewish Agency for Palestine, *Memorandum on the Position of the Jewish Communities in the Oriental Countries,* submitted to the Anglo-American Committee of Inquiry, Jerusalem, March 1946.
238. Schechtman, *Eagles,* p. 157.
239. Description of Syrian Jews' testimony before Anglo-American Committee of Inquiry, reported by Committee under Bartley C. Crum in *Behind the Silken Curtain, a Personal Account of Anglo-American Diplomacy in Palestine and the Middle East* (New York, 1947), p. 239.
240. April 14, 1947.
241. Letter to American Jewish Organizations, dated December 21, 1947.
242. *New York Herald Tribune,* April 14, 1947.
243. Cohen, *Jews of the Middle East,* p. 46.
244. *Jewish Agency Digest of Press and Events,* December 28, 1947.
245. Cohen, *Jews of the Middle East,* p. 46.
246. *Al-Salam,* Arabic weekly, Beirut, January 16, 1948, pp. 6, 9, cited in ibid.
247. April 28, 1948, letter to Mogen David Congregation, Brooklyn, New York.
248. *Al Hayat,* Beirut, December 20, 1947; Schechtman, *Eagles,* p. 162.
249. January 1948; Schechtman, *Eagles,* p. 163.
250. See H. Cohen, "Jews in Arab and Moslem Countries," *American Jewish Yearbook 1971* (New York, 1971), pp. 443–449.
251. *New York Times,* August 7 and 10, 1949.
252. Yehezkel Hameiri, *Prisoners of Hate* (Jerusalem, 1969), pp. 61–62.
253. *New York Times,* December 30, 1949.
254. In 1954 and 1958. "Since 1947 Jews were not allowed to leave Syria, except for short periods: in 1954 by Hashim al-Atasi, and in 1958 after the proclaiming of the United Arab Republic." Cohen, *The Jews of the Middle East,* p. 47.
255. Evidence and counterclaims—concerning the persecution of Syria's Jews in the past several years—are treated in Chapters 6 and 7.
256. Gilbert, *Exile,* p. 11.
257. Abbas Kelidar and Michael Burrell, *Lebanon: The Collapse of a State, Conflict Studies,* no. 74, (London: Institute for the Study of Conflict), p. 1.
258. Abraham Galante, *Histoire des Juifs d'Istanbul,* 2 vols. (Istanbul, 1941–1942), vol. 2, pp. 3–10, cited by Cohen, *Jews of the Middle East,* p. 8.
259. In 1826, fifteen Jewish families in Beirut, fifteen in (Lebanese) Tripoli and twenty-five in Sidon, according to A. Massa'ot Ya'Ari, "(Travels of) Rabbi David d'Beth Hillel," *Sinai,* IV, publ. 1939, pp. 48–50, cited by Cohen, *Jews of the Middle East,* p. 13.
260. Harkabi, *Arab Attitudes to Israel,* p. 272. Harkabi cited the Egyptian edition of a blood libel published officially in 1962 by the UAR, the reprint of an 1890 Egyptian book; the editor also "surveys other blood libel cases in the Middle East. . . ." Also see pp. 270–276.
261. Cohen, *Jews of the Middle East,* p. 13.

262. Gilbert, *Exile,* p. 307.
263. Schechtman, *Eagles,* pp. 170–175; Cohen, *Jews of the Middle East,* p. 44; *Alliance Review* (monthly, New York, 1946–1965), June 1951, p. 1; *al-Alam al-Israeli* (The Jewish World), Beirut weekly in Arabic (1929–1934, 1938–1946), July 31, 1939; August 8, 1939, p. 26.
264. Cohen, *Jews of the Middle East,* p. 44.
265. Carl Hermann Voss, *The Palestine Problem Today, Israel and Its Neighbors* (Boston, 1953), p. 49.
266. *Al-Hayat,* Arabic daily, Beirut, November 2, 3, 1957.
267. See Arnold Bruner, "Beirut's Jews of Silence," *Jerusalem Post Magazine,* January 12, 1973.
268. Hirschberg, *History,* p. 24.
269. Flavius Josephus, *The Complete Works of Flavius Josephus, the Celebrated Jewish Historian,* trans. W. Whiston (Philadelphia, 1895); *The Famous and Memorable Works by Josephus . . . Faithfully Translated out of the Latin and French by Thos. Lodge* (London, 1602), both containing the essay "Against Apion." Cited by Hirschberg, *History,* p. 24.
270. Saint Augustine wrote of Hebrew-speaking rabbis in fourth-century Tripoli. Some evidence exists to establish continued Jewish existence despite the rebellion in A.D. 73. H.Z. Hirschberg states that "the few Geniza documents, hints in Arab literature and the literature of the Gaonic period, and some contemporary epitaphs . . . suffice . . . to evoke a continuous chain of Jewish communities in Tripolitania and Tunisia, continuous both in space and time." Hirschberg, *History,* p. 129. Also see N. Slouschz, *Travels in North Africa* (Philadelphia, 1927); Philo, *In Flaccum 43* (trad. Pelletier, Paris, 1967), p. 75. Philo reported that Egypt and Libya contained about a million Jews before the destruction of the Second Temple, cited in Hirschberg, *History,* p. 25–26.
271. Gilbert, *The Jews of Arab Lands,* p. 1; also see Hirschberg, *History,* Ch. 2.
272. Hirschberg, *History,* pp. 119, 124.
273. Ibid., pp. 130–131; Chouraqui, *Between East and West,* p. 52.
274. Hirschberg, *History,* p. 126; Chouraqui, *Between East and West,* p. 52.
275. Hirschberg, *History,* pp. 133–134; also see Chouraqui, *Between East and West,* p. 51. Cited is a portion of the lament of Abraham Ibn Ezra, whose records provided a "main source" of information about which areas were conquered by the Almohads, and when. The lament, Hirschberg reports, shows "striking faithfulness" to the conditions "as known from Arab sources," such as D. Cazes, *Revue des Etudes Juives* 20 (Paris, 1890), p. 85.
276. Hirschberg, *History,* p. 125, quoting Abraham ben David, *Sefer Ha-Qabbalah—The Book of Tradition,* edited by Gerson D. Cohen (Philadelphia, 1967), pp. 66–88; see Stillman, *The Jews,* Geniza documents on "calamity," pp. 186–189ff.
277. Some of the Jewish Spaniards, however, had suffered their own *dhimmi* "protection"; an African-born writer "living in Spain at the end of the Middle Ages" described the "duties" of the judicially empowered official—*muhtasib*—"in charge of markets, morals and protected persons" *(ahl al-dhimma)*: the official "must prevent protected persons from looking down upon Muslims in their houses . . . from wielding authority (over Muslims); from . . . riding saddled and decorated horses in Muslim streets, and other acts of ostentation. He must prescribe signs for them . . . to be distinguished from Muslims, such as the *shikla* for men and bells for women. [According to

Hirschberg, the *shikla* or *shakla* differed from one Maghreb to another—"the exact form is not known."] He must prevent Muslims being asked to do anything degrading and offensive to them, such as removing refuse, . . . tending pigs, or anything expressive of unbelief or superiority over Islam." Levi-Provençal, *Documents Arabes inédits sur la vie sociale et économique* (Paris, 1955), p. 122; cited by Hirschberg, *History,* p. 203.

278. Ibid., p. 204.
279. Chouraqui, *Between East and West,* pp. 90–92.
280. In 1588. Gilbert, *The Jews of Arab Lands,* p. 4.
281. In 1785. Ibid.
282. Littman, *Jews Under Muslim Rule,* p. 67.
283. Ibid., p. 69. Extracts from a letter (21.7.1867) in Italian by Saul Labi, President of the Tripoli AIU Committee to Adolphe Cremieux, President of the AIU, Paris (AIU Libya [Tripoli] I.C.4).
284. Ibid. From a letter (10.7.1879) by Saul Labi, President of the Tripoli Regional Committee, to Adolphe Cremieux, President of the AIU, Paris (AIU Libya [Tripoli] I.C.7).
285. Ibid., pp. 69–70. From a letter (21.2.1897) by the "Comunita Israelitica di Tripoli di Barbaria" (Saul Labi, Mesoud Nahum, Mos. J. Hassan, Abr. Nahum, Aug. Arbib, Clemente Tajar, I. Hassan) to the President, AIU, Paris (AIU Libya I.C.11).
286. Ibid., p. 71. From a letter (16.5.1900) by J. Hoefler, teacher at the Tripoli Boys' School to the President of the AIU, Paris (AIU Libya I.C.12).
287. Schechtman, *Eagles,* p. 130.
288. Prittie, *Double Exodus,* p. 22–23.
289. Schechtman, *Eagles,* p. 132; Prittie, *Double Exodus,* p. 23.
290. Schechtman, *Eagles,* p. 133. See Chapters 16 and 17.
291. *New York Times,* November 7, 1945.
292. *New York Times,* November 14, 1945.
293. Mustafa Bey Misran, member of Arab Advisory Council to the British Military Administration, *New York Times,* November 16, 1945.
294. Gilbert, *Exile,* p. 307.
295. Maurice Roumani, *The Case of the Jews from Arab Countries: A Neglected Issue* (Jerusalem: Alpha Press, 1975), p. 21.
296. Here, as in Syria and Iraq, the practical advantage of the population exchange was clearly employed.
297. Roumani, *Case of the Jews,* p. 21; according to Prittie, *Double Exodus,* p. 23, "17 Jews were murdered and many arrested."
298. *London Daily Telegraph,* June 14, 1967, reported sixteen Jews thrown from roofs to their deaths. See also *New York Post,* July 15, 1967.
299. *New York Times,* July 22, 1970.
300. Major Abd ul-Huni, Council Commanding the Revolution, addressed a letter to ex-Libyan Jewish refugees then in Italy that once the Jews from Libya returned, "Then will be abolished the law of sequestration as far as everyone who returns to this country is concerned." May 29, 1970, cited by Y. Meron, *The "Complicating" Element,* p. 20, n. 51.
301. K. Bilby, *New Star in the Near East* (New York, 1950), p. 30. Bilby "never found the slightest evidence" of "ruthless slaughter" of Arabs by Jews; *Palestine Royal Commission Report,* p. 121; *Palestine Partition Commission Report,* p. 261; *Anglo-*

American Survey of Palestine, p. 45; Leopold Amery in House of Commons speech, 1939, quoted in Gilbert, *Exile,* p. 229; M. Begin, *The Revolt,* pp. 162–163. "The success of Arab terrorism," as the *Anglo-American Committee Report* called it in 1946, had, in the months before Deir Yaseen, been unrestrained. Between late 1947 and March, 1948, 875 Jews were murdered and nearly 2,000 wounded in Arab attacks." Gabbay, *Political Study,* pp. 61–62.

302. From a statement to the President of Libya in Paris, November 1973, included in Albert Memmi, *Jews and Arabs* (Chicago, 1975), pp. 30–37. According to Memmi, "On Saturday, November 24, 1973, four major European newspapers *(Le Monde, The Times, La Stampa,* and *Die Welt)* organized a discussion with Libya's Colonel Kadhafi. I was invited to attend by *Le Monde,* and my questions to the colonel were reported in the press the next day."

4. Ideology of the East, Rhetoric of the West

1. *New York Times,* March 6, 1976, report on conversation in November 1973, as quoted by *Foreign Policy Magazine,* Spring 1976.

2. King Hussein of Jordan, *Uneasy Lies the Head* (New York: Bernard Geis, 1962), p. 91.

3. Article 3(3) of Law No. 6 of 1954, Jordanian Nationality Law, *Official Gazette* No. 1171 of February 16, 1954, p. 105.

4. *Ha-Aretz,* Tel Aviv, January 29, 1974.

5. CBS Radio, May 28, 1972, cited by Gil Carl Alroy, *Behind the Middle East Conflict* (New York: Capricorn Books, G.P. Putnam's Sons, 1975), p. 178.

6. "The Jihad is the Way to Gain Victory," by Sheikh Abdallah Goshah, quoted in *Arab Theologians on Jews and Israel, The Fourth Conference of the Academy of Islamic Research* (Al Azhar), D.F. Green, ed. (Geneva, 1971), p. 61.

7. Phillip K. Hitti, *The Arabs, A Short History* (Princeton, 1943), p. 126; also see Bernard Lewis, *The Arabs in History*, p. 36.

8. Professor Yehoshafat Harkabi, *The Arab Position in the Arab-Israeli Conflict (Emadat Ha'aravim besikhsukh Israel-Arav)* (Tel Aviv, 1968), p. 250. Cited in Moshe Ma'oz, *The Image of the Jew in Official Arab Literature and Communications Media* (The Institute of Contemporary Jewry: Hebrew University of Jerusalem, 1976), p. 14.

His Eminence Sheikh Nadim Al-Jisr, Member of the Islamic Research Academy, cited several more versions of this *hadith* in his presentation at the Fourth Conference of the Academy, "Good Tidings about the Decisive Battle Between Muslims and Israel, in the Light of the Holy Quran, the Prophetic Traditions, and the Fundamental Laws of Nature and History."

"In Muslim's Sahih, is reported on the authority of Ibn'Umar that the Prophet (P.B.U.H.) had said, 'Verily, you will combat against the Jews, so carry through the fight, until a stone would say: O Muslim This is a Jew; come along and smite him down.'

"In another version of this Hadith, reported also on the authority of Ibn'Umar, the Prophet—P.B.U.H.—had said, 'The Jews will combat against you. But you will be given power over them, until the stone would say: "O Muslim! This is a Jew lying behind me; come and do away with him." '

"In a third version . . . on the authority of Abu Huraira . . . 'The Hour would never rise until Muslims fight against the Jews. Muslims would despatch them. The Jews would hide themselves behind stones and trees which would say: "O Muslim Servant of God! There are Jews behind me; come and kill them." '

"In Bukhari's Sahih . . . on the authority of Abdullah Ibn'Umar . . . you will take up arms against the Jews, until one of them would lie concealed behind a stone which would say, 'O Muslim, Servant of God! This is a Jew lying behind me; come and kill him.' "

"It is reported on the authority of Abu Huraira that the Prophet . . . has said, 'The Hour would not come, until you fight against the Jews; and the stone would say, "O Muslim! There is a Jew behind me; come and kill him." '

D.F. Green notes: " 'The Hour' is the resurrection i.e. the final salvation. Its arrival is made conditional upon the battle against the Jews that has to precede it." Green, *Arab Theologians,* p. 45.

9. Surah III, v. 112, *The Meaning of the Glorious Koran,* an explanatory translation by Mohammed Marmaduke Pickthall (New York: Mentor Books, 1953). Also see The Koran, trans. with notes by N.J. Dawood (England: Penguin Books, rev. ed, 1981), in which the translations are listed chronologically rather than by *surah* number, clearly illustrating that the anti-Jewish and anti-Christian implorations were introduced after Jews and Christians had refused to embrace Islam above their own religion. The themes illustrated in the text also are frequently reiterated with slight variations.

10. Surah II, v. 96, ibid.
11. Surah II, v. 90, ibid.
12. Surah III, v. 181, ibid., referring to the Jews of Medina. Two examples of the frequent variation on this theme in the Koran:

    Surah IX, v. 35: "Proclaim a woeful punishment to those that hoard up gold and silver. . . . Their treasures shall be heated in the fires of Hell, and their foreheads, sides and backs branded with them. . . . 'Taste then the punishment which is your due.' "

    Surah III, v. 117–120: "They [the Jews] are the heirs of Hell. . . . They will spare no pains to corrupt you. They desire nothing but your ruin. Their hatred is clear from what they say . . . When evil befalls you they rejoice." Ibid.

13. Surah IV, v. 56, ibid.
14. Surah IV, v. 160, 161, ibid.
15. Surah IV, v. 46, ibid.
16. Surah III, v. 117–120, Dawood trans.
17. Surah IV, v. 101, Pickthall trans.
18. Surah V, v. 62, 63, ibid.
19. Surah V, v. 51, ibid.
20. Surah V, v. 82, ibid.
21. Surah IX, v. 29, ibid.
22. Surah IX, v. 30, ibid.
23. Surah IX, v. 26–34, Dawood trans.
24. Surah V, v. 62–66, ibid.
25. Surah II, v. 71–85, ibid.
26. The Fourth Conference of the Academy of Islamic Research, Cairo, September 1968.
27. Quoted from Dr. Mahmud Hubballah, Secretary General of the Islamic Research Academy, speech delivered on the inauguration of the Academy's Fourth Confer-

ence, in Green, *Arab Theologians*, p. 11. According to Green, "Seventy-seven Muslims, Ulemas and invited guests participated in the Conference. I gather that some of the proceedings were reproduced immediately after the conference in *Majallat al-Azhar*, the University's monthly. The complete transactions of this conference were then published in 1970 in Arabic (3 volumes) [*Al-Azhar, Majma' al-Buhut al-Islamiyya, Kitab al-Mu'tamar al-Rabi' li-majma al-Buhuth al-Islamiyya*. The original volume has no copyright], and in English (1 volume, 935 pp.) In the latter, it is stated on the front page that the book was printed by the U.A.R. Government Printing Office, which signifies government support. The efforts involved by the authorities to have these transactions translated into English indicate . . . their decision to propagate to the world the views contained in this volume." Green explains that the order of "extracts" has been "modified in order to group together similar subjects. Repetitions by the authors have been retained in a few cases. The reader will thus be in a better position to decide whether the views are mere eccentricities of one sage, or more common conceptions." (Introduction, p. 1.)

28. Quoted from Sheikh Abd Allah Al Meshad, "Jews' Attitude Toward Islam and Muslims in the First Islamic Era," in Green, *Arab Theologians*, p. 21.

29. Quoted from Mohammed Taha Yahia, "The Attitude of the Jews Toward Islam and Muslims in the Early Days of Islam" in ibid., p. 19.

30. Quoted from Kamal Ahmad Own, Vice-Principal, Tanta Institute, "The Jews are the Enemies of Human Life as Evident from their Holy Book," in ibid., p. 16–17.

31. Israel-Benjamin (II), *Cinq Années de Voyage en Orient 1846–1851* (Algeria, 1855), p. XXVIII, cited by David Littman, *Protected Peoples Under Islam* (Geneva, 1975), pp. 2–3.

32. Young, British Consul in Jerusalem, 1839. F.O. 78/368, Young to Palmerston, No. 13, May 25, 1839, cited by A.M. Hyamson, *The British Consulate in Jerusalem (In Relation to the Jews of Palestine, 1838–1914)*, 2 vols. (London, 1939–1942), vol. 1, p. 6.

33. Léon Godard, *Le Maroc, Notes d'un Voyageur: 1858–59* (Algeria, 1859), cited by Littman, *Jews Under Muslim Rule in the Late Nineteenth Century* (The Weiner Library Bulletin, 1975), vol. XXVIII, p. 66.

34. Chouraqui, *Between East and West*, p. 51.

35. Ibid., p. 52.

36. Robert Brunschvig, *La Berberie orientale sous les Hafsides*, vol. 1 (Paris, 1940), p. 404, cited by Littman, *Protected Peoples*, p. 2. According to S.D. Goitein, "The yellow badge for Jews was known in Muslim countries many centuries before it was introduced into Christian Europe." *Jews and Arabs* (New York: Schocken Books, 1974), p. 67.

37. Bernard Lewis, *Islam in History* (New York, 1973), p. 135.

38. Arminius Vambery, *The Story of My Struggles* (London, n.d.), p. 395, quoted in Lewis, *Islam in History* (New York, 1973), p. 135. Lewis describes Vambery (1832–1918) as: ". . . one of the leading authorities in Europe on Turkish studies, and one of the founders of the new science of Turkology" (p. 133).

39. *Middle Eastern Affairs*, March 1950, "Facts and Figures," vol. 1, no. 3, p. 90.

40. Excerpted from conversation on January 13, 1951, as reported by Arif al-Arif, from his series "Al-Nakba, Nakbat Beit Al-Maqdis Walfirdaus Al Mafqud," 1947–1955, vol. IV (Al-Maktaba Al-Asriyya Littiba Wal-Nashr, n.d., intro. dated 12/1/59), p. 893.

41. Amman radio, September 22, 1967, cited by Y. Harkabi, *Arab Attitudes to Israel* (Jerusalem, 1971), pp. 295–296.
42. Except where otherwise indicated, the excerpts are from *"Hatred is Sacred,"* *Extracts from Arab School Texts,* E. Hess, comp. (Jerusalem: Ministry for Foreign Affairs, n.d.).
43. Dafna Alon, Arab Racialism (Jerusalem: The Israel Economist, 1969), p. 94.
44. *Indictments Expressed in the Textbooks Used in the Educational System in Egypt and the Gaza Strip* (Jerusalem: Ministry of Education and Culture, Department of Arab Education and Culture, 1967), p. 33; also see pp. 37–38. Also see Alon, *Arab Racialism;* Ma'oz, *Image of the Jew.*

5. Last Year and Next Year in Jerusalem: Zionism in the Arab World and the Holy Land

1. Walter Laqueur, *A History of Zionism* (New York: Schocken Books, 1976), p. 592.
2. Of the diminished post-war Jewish population of 56,000 in Jerusalem, more than 22,000 were non-European "Palestinians." *Statistical Abstract of Palestine,* 1929, David Gurevich, ed. (Jerusalem, 1930).
3. See *Palestine Royal Commission Report* (London, 1937), pp. 2–5, 7, 9, particularly p. 11, para. 23.
4. James Parkes, *Whose Land?, A History of the Peoples of Palestine* (Harmondsworth, Middlesex, Great Britain: Penguin Books, 1970), p. 266.
5. Ibid., pp. 31, 26.
6. Samuel Katz, *Battleground: Fact and Fantasy in Palestine* (New York, 1973), p. 88.
7. Avraham Yaari, *Igrot Eretz Yisrael* (Tel Aviv, 1943), p. 46; see F. Nau, "Sur la synagogue de Rabbat Moab (422), et un mouvement sioniste favorisé par l'imperatrice Eudocie (438), d'après la vie de Barsauma le Syrien," *Journal Asiatique,* LIX (1927), pp. 189–192.
8. A. Malamat, H. Tadmor, M. Stern, S. Safrai, *Toledot Am Yisrael Bi'mei Kedem* (Tel Aviv, 1969), p. 348, cited by Katz, *Battleground,* p. 88.
9. Parkes, *Whose Land?,* p. 72.
10. Ibid.; also see S.D. Goitein, *A Mediterranean Society,* 3 vols. (Berkeley, Los Angeles, London, 1971), vol. 2, p. 6ff. ". . . the main synagogue [in Ramle] was the Palestinian."
11. Al-Waqidy, ninth-century Arab historian, recorded a Jewish-settled area in Jericho in the seventh century and "there are other references to Jewish communal life in Jericho as late as the ninth century." Cited by Itzhak Ben-Zvi, *The Exiled and the Redeemed* (Philadelphia, 1961), p. 146.
12. Ben-Zvi, *The Exiled,* pp. 144–145. The Nadhir and Kainuka Arabian-Jewish tribes' "battles for their survival . . . is found in Dr. Israel Ben-Zeev's remarkable book, *Jews in Arabia,"* Ben-Zvi states.
13. Israel Ben Zeev, *Jews in Arabia,* cited by Ben-Zvi, *The Exiled,* p. 145.
14. Ben-Zvi, *The Exiled,* p. 145. Ben-Zvi cites Arabian historian Al-Waqidy, as reported in Ben-Zeev, *Jews in Arabia.*
15. Ibid., p. 146. Ben-Zvi states that some Jews who could "produce letters of protection and treaties signed by or on behalf of the Prophet" were permitted to remain. ". . . there is reason to believe that these surviving Jewish communities were maintained intact until the twelfth century."

16. Quoted from Sheikh Abd Allah Al Meshad, "Jews' Attitudes Towards Islam and Muslims in the First Islamic Era," in D.F. Green, ed., *Arab Theologians on Jews and Israel* (Geneva, 1971), p. 22.

17. Quoted from Muhammad Azzah Darwaza, "The Attitude of the Jews Towards Islam, Muslims and the Prophet of Islam—P.B.U.H. [Peace Be Unto Him]—at the Time of His Honourable Prophethood," in ibid., pp. 29–30.

18. Ben-Zvi, *The Exiled*, pp. 146–147. ". . . the existence of which we have records."

19. Parkes, *Whose Land?*, pp. 97–99.

20. Ibid., p. 110.

21. Martin Gilbert, *Exile and Return, The Struggle for a Jewish Homeland* (Philadelphia and New York, 1978), p. 17. "In 1322 Jewish geographer from Florence, Ashtory Ha-Parhi, had settled in the Jezreel Valley where he wrote a book on the topography of Palestine. . . ."

22. Ibid., pp. 17–19. Elijah of Ferrara.

23. Parkes, *Whose Land?*, p. 111.

24. Gilbert, *Exile*, p. 17.

25. Ibid., p. 21.

26. Ibid. For a more detailed account, see Joachim Prinz, *The Secret Jews* (New York, 1973), p. 147ff.

27. One writer claims all the Messianic movements in Jewish history were led by Sephardic Jews: ". . . not a single one was led by an East European Jew." Prinz, *Secret Jews*, p. 101.

28. Simon Dubnow, *Précis d'Histoire Juivre* (A Concise Jewish History) (Educational Service of the Federation of Jewish Societies in France, Paris, 1963); also see Dubnow's more comprehensive *History of the Jews*, 5 vols. (New York, 1967–73); also see Parkes, *Whose Land?*, pp. 140–141.

29. H.H. Ben-Sasson, ed., *A History of the Jewish People* (Cambridge, Mass.: Harvard University Press, 1976), p. 701.

30. Gershom Scholem, *Sabbatai Sevi, the Mystical Messiah* (Princeton, 1973) p. 95.

31. Ben-Sasson, *History*, p. 706.

32. Ibid. "The paradox of a traitorous Messiah is far greater than that of an executed Messiah." Scholem, *Sabbatai Sevi*, pp. 683–684.

33. Ben-Sasson, *History*, pp. 704–706.

34. J. Sasportas, *Zizat Novel Zvi*, J. Tishby, ed. (Jerusalem, 1954), p. 267, cited by Ben Sasson, *History*, p. 704.

35. Heinrich Graetz, *History of the Jews*, 5 vols. (New York, 1927), vol. V, pp. 32–49.

36. H.Z. Hirschberg, *A History of the Jews in North Africa* (Leiden, Netherlands: E.J. Brill, 1974), vol. 1, p. 70.

37. Ibid. At that time, according to Hirschberg, "the Cyrenians complained to the Emperor Augustus of attempts to prevent the sending of the half-shekel to the Temple, won their case and obtained the discontinuance of restrictive practices."

38. Acts of the Apostles (2:10), cited by Hirschberg, *History*, p. 70.

39. Acts of the Apostles (6:9), cited in ibid.

40. Matthew (27:32); Mark (15:21); Luke (23:26); cited in ibid.

41. David de Sola Pool, "Centrality of the Holy Land in Jewish Life," from *The Folk*, vol. II of the Jewish Library, Leo Jung, ed. (London and New York: Soncino Press, 1968).

42. See Nina Salaman, trans., *Selected Poems of Jehudah Halevi* (Philadelphia, 1946);

also see Goitein, *Jews and Arabs, Their Contacts Through the Ages,* 3rd ed. (New York, 1974).

43. Rudolf Kayser, *The Life and Time of Jehudah Halevi,* Frank Gaynor, trans. (New York: Philosophical Library, 1949), pp. 117–119. According to Kayser, Halevi was inspired to "his greatest poem, the deepest, most heartfelt hymn of the Jewish race, cast out of its homeland, and longing to return to it. Like Moses, he saw the Promised Land, but like Moses, it was not to be his to live in it." Kayser records a different moment of death than the more popular "kissing of stones" legend: "The details . . . are unknown to us, but the legend has it that Jehudah Halevi was singing his hymn of Zion . . . when he was run through by the sword of an Arab assassin." (p. 118).

44. Goitein, *Mediterranean Society,* vol. 2, pp. 156–157.

45. Ibid., p. 157.

46. André Chouraqui, *Between East and West, A History of the Jews of North Africa,* trans. Michael M. Bernet (Philadelphia, 1968), p. 126.

47. According to Jewish tradition.

48. Daily Prayer Book *Ha-Siddur Ha-Shalem,* intro. by Philip Birnbaum (New York, 1949).

49. Chouraqui, *East and West,* pp. 16, 59.

50. See, for example, Bernard Lewis, *The Arabs in History,* rev. ed. (New York, Evanston, San Francisco, London: Harper-Colophon Books, 1966); Goitein, *Jews and Arabs;* Philip K. Hitti, *The Arabs* (Princeton, 1943).

51. Goitein, *Mediterranean Society,* vol. 2, p. 21.

52. Ibid., p. 20.

53. Ibid., p. 9.

54. Ibid., p. 51.

55. Rabbi Isaac ben Jacob Alfassi (1013–1103), Chouraqui, *East and West,* p. 83.

56. Goitein, *Mediterranean Society,* vol. 1, p. 67.

57. Laqueur, *History of Zionism,* p. 55.

58. Laqueur was discussing the German-born rabbi Hirsch Kalisher, author of *Drishat Zion* (Seeking Zion), published 1862.

59. W.T. Young to Viscount Palmerston, Jerusalem, June 26, 1839, F.O. 78/368 (No. 15), cited in A.H. Hyamson, ed., *The British Consulate in Jerusalem in Relation to the Jews in Palestine, 1838–1914,* 2 vols. (London: Edward Goldston Ltd., 1939–1941), vol. 1, p. 11.

60. Gilbert, *Exile,* p. 27.

61. Hyamson, *Consulate,* vol. 1, p. lvii.

62. W.T. Young to Colonel P. Campbell, Jerusalem, July 19, 1839. (Enclosure 2 to No. 9) (No. 27), cited in ibid., p. 16; see also Young to Palmerston, May 1839, ibid., pp. 4–7.

63. Ibid., p. lviii.

64. James Finn to Sir Stratford Canning, Jerusalem, April 6, 1850, F.O. 195/292 (No. 3), ibid., p. 163.

65. Ibid., p. lviii.

66. James Finn, *Stirring Times or Record from Jerusalem Consular Chronicles* from 1835–56, 2 vols. (London: C. Kegan, Paul & Co., 1878), vol. 1, pp. 127–128. For other references to the subject see vol. 1, p. 117 n., vol. 2, pp. 67, 103, 104, 360.

67. Elizabeth Finn, *Reminiscences of Elizabeth Anne Finn* (Edinburgh and London,

1929), p. 56; also see p. 160, cited by Hyamson, *Consulate,* p. lviii.

68. Charles Churchill to Sir Moses Montefiore, June 11, 1842, quoted in Gilbert, *Exile,* p. 28.

69. Katz, *Battleground,* p. 101.

70. Ibid.

71. George Gawler, *Tranquillisation of Syria and the East* (London, 1845), pp. 6–8.

72. A.W.C. Crawford, Lord Lindsay, *Letters of Egypt, Edom and the Holy Land* (London, 1847), vol. 2, p. 71, cited in Katz, *Battleground,* p. 101.

73. Gilbert, in *Exile,* p. 34, says that in 1874 "a British explorer, Charles Warren, published a book entitled, boldly, *The Land of Promise.* In his book he envisaged a Palestine with as many as fifteen million inhabitants. In order to reach this goal Warren advocated widespread Jewish rural settlement. In a second book, *Underground Jerusalem,* published a year later, in 1875, Warren wrote that for the time being Palestine would have to be governed on behalf of the Jews by someone else, 'allowing the Jew gradually to find his way into its army, its law, and its diplomatic services, and gradually to superintend the farming operations, and work himself on the farms.' But after only twenty years of such activity, Warren believed, the Jewish principality 'might stand by itself, as a separate kingdom guaranteed by the Great Powers.' "

74. *Spectator,* May 10, 1879.

75. Moshe Aumann, *Land Ownership in Palestine 1880–1948* (Jerusalem, 1976), pp. 11–12. The first European settlement, Rishon l'Tsion, was established by Russian Jewish pioneers.

76. Judah ben Solomon Hai Alkalay, *Destiny of the Lord* (Vienna, 1857).

77. Howard Sachar, *A History of Israel, From the Rise of Zionism to Our Time* (New York: Alfred A. Knopf, 1976), pp. 6–7. Alex Bein, *Theodore Herzl,* trans. Maurice Samuel (Philadelphia, 1940), pp. 5, 15.

78. *Encyclopaedia Judaica,* vol. 2, pp. 638–639; Alkalay's 1840 work concerning the Damascus blood libel, and "hints" of Zionism, *Shelom Yerushalayim,* led to his first Hebrew publication, *Minhat Yehudah,* in 1843.

79. Ibid. Before Alkalay died in 1878, he had "managed to organize a small group of followers." Sachar, *History,* p. 6.

80. Among other works citing Yehudah Alkalay: Arthur Hertzberg, *The Zionist Idea* (New York: Doubleday, 1959).

81. Mordecai Soussan, *L'éveil politique Sepharade* (Political Awakening of the Sephardim, doctoral thesis) (Faculté de droit et de Science Politique d'Aix-Marseilles, 1975), p. 62.

82. Isadore Twersky, ed., *A Maimonides Reader* (New York, 1972), pp. 456–57.

83. Goitein, *Jews and Arabs,* p. 75.

84. Ibid., p. 75ff.

85. Paula Stern, "Obituary for a People: The Jews of Tunisia," Alicia Patterson Fund Award Winner, May 1971. Unpublished study.

86. Hayyim Cohen, *The Jews of the Middle East: 1860–1972* (New York, 1973), p. 160.

87. Cohen, *Jews,* p. 160.

88. Raphael Patai, *Israel Between East and West* (Westport, Conn.: Greenwood Publishing Corp., 1970), pp. 207–208.

89. According to the Jewish Agency, *Report of the Executive Submitted to the 24th Zionist Congress,* 1951–1955 (Jerusalem: Zionist Organization, 1955), p. 147, cited

in Maurice Roumani, Deborah Goldman, Helene Korn, *The Case of the Jews from Arab Countries: A Neglected Issue* (Jerusalem, 1975), p. 27.

90. Excerpted from UN General Assembly (32nd G.A.), December 1977, by Mordechai Ben Porath, member, Israel UN delegation, speech on General Assembly Resolution 194 (III) of 1948.

91. Hayyim J. Cohen, *Absorption Problems of Jews from Asia and Africa in Israel* (Jerusalem, 1974), p. 1.

92. Carl Hermann Voss, *The Palestine Problem Today, Israel and Its Neighbors* (Boston, 1953), p. 31.

93. Ibid., pp. XIV–XV, preface.

94. Goitein, *Jews and Arabs,* pp. 13–14.

6. Invitation Declined

1. The interviews, recorded on tape, were conducted between 1976 and 1982, in New York, Chicago, Washington, D.C., Paris, London, Tel Aviv, and Jerusalem; the Jewish refugees' professional backgrounds varied, and their ages ranged from 18 to 68, but they shared one goal, to a remarkable extent: they all sought freedom to live proudly within their traditions, as Jews, as Zionists, and as first-class citizens.

7. Remnant of a Tradition: The Arab-Jewish Diaspora

1. Current population estimates compiled from the *American Jewish Yearbook,* 1983 edition, George Gruen, editor, published in New York by the American Jewish Committee; Government of Israel, Ministry of Foreign Affairs, Jerusalem, 1983 figures. Figures for 1948 compiled from the World Organization of Jews from Arab Countries (WOJAC); Anglo-American Committee of Inquiry, "The Position of the Jewish Communities in Oriental Countries," a memorandum submitted by the Jewish Agency; Hayyim Cohen, *The Jews of the Middle East,* 1973, Halsted Press, New York.

2. Medina, Khaibar, Qaraiza; see Chapter 8.

3. March 6, 1975, Rashad Nowilaty, Saudi Arabian Ambassador to The Hague.

4. America established its own precedent in 1885. President Grover Cleveland's choice for United States representative in Vienna, Anthony Keiley of Virginia, was turned down because, "the position of a foreign envoy wedded to a Jewess by civil marriage would be untenable and even impossible in Vienna," May 1885, *Foreign Relations,* p. 48. When the Secretary of State objected to "infraction" of an "essential principle" —never to "inquire into" or "even hear testimony . . . upon the religious belief of any official," the Austrian government found a different reason for its objection: an ostensible "want of political tact" exhibited by appointee Keiley on an earlier visit to Vienna. Ibid, p. 55.

President Cleveland resolved the matter in his address to the United States Congress on December 8, 1885: ". . . The Government of Austria-Hungary invited this Government to take cognizance of certain exceptions, based upon allegations against the personal acceptability of Mr. Keiley, the appointed envoy, asking that in view thereof, the appointment should be withdrawn. The reasons advanced were such as could not be acquiesced in, without violation of my oath of office and the precepts of the Constitution since they necessarily involved a limitation in favor of a foreign government upon the right of selection by the Executive, and required such an application of a religious test as a qualification for office under the United States as would have resulted in the practical disfranchisement of a large class of our citizens and the abandonment of a vital principle in our Government. . . . I have made no new nomination, and the interests of this Government in Vienna are now in the care of the secretary of legation, acting as chargé d'affaires ad interim."

5. Statement by Max Van Der Stoel, Dutch Foreign Minister to the Dutch Parliament, The Hague, March 12, 1975, regarding cancellation of official visit to Saudi Arabia.

6. Reported by Anthony Sampson, *Observer Review,* "Desert Diary," March 9, 1975, London.

7. Jordanian Nationality Law, Article 3(3) of Law No. 6 of 1954, *Official Gazette* No. 1171, February 16, 1954.

8. George E. Gruen, "Morocco: Plotting for Peace," in *Reform Judaism,* June 1981, New York, pp. 10–11.

9. The first group of four rabbis visited in May 1976; George Gruen, ibid.

10. Ibid.

11. Jonathan Tumin, "Letter to the Editor," *Commentary,* December 1976.

12. *New York Times,* April 18, 1979.

13. Gruen, "Morocco," pp. 10–11. This also applies to Tunisia's Jewry.

14. Estimates vary from 4,500 in 1980, according to the *American Jewish Yearbook,* 1983, p. 278, to 5,500, as reported by the American Syrian Jewish Community's Steven Shalom, February 7, 1979, New York, to 5,000 estimated in 1980 by the American Jewish Committee, and 4,300 as estimated by the Israeli government, Ministry of Foreign Affairs, Jerusalem, 1983.

15. For example, in the Italian journal *Epoca,* April 28, 1974, "Drama in the Ghetto of Damascus," by Livio Caputo; Copenhagen, *Politiken,* December 21, 1974, "Jews in Syria Holed up in Nameless Street," by Ole Roessell; Stockholm, *Espressen,* June 17, 1972, "Concern When Being Faced with the Reports from Syria," by Per Ahlmark.

16. See Chapter 6.

17. George E. Gruen, "Assad's Syria," in *Worldview,* June 1981, pp. 11–12.

18. Stanley F. Reed III, quoted in George E. Gruen, ibid., p. 11.

19. *London Observer,* April 21, 1974.

20. *Le Figaro,* May 1974.

21. Then UN Secretary General U Thant, June 15, 1970.

22. Letter to Secretary General Dr. Kurt Waldheim, Paris, July 10, 1974.

23. On "60 Minutes" they were benignly referred to initially as "Information" officers.

24. As a member of the Anglo-American Committee had noted in 1945 while investigating conditions for Jews in Arab states. Bartley C. Crum, *Behind the Silken Curtain. A Personal Account of Anglo-American Diplomacy in Palestine and the Middle East* (New York: Simon and Schuster, 1947), p. 239. Tactics of intimidation had changed little in thirty years.

25. Robert Azzi, "Damascus, Syria's Uneasy Eden," *National Geographic,* April 1974.

26. *National Geographic,* editorial, November 1974, p. 587.

27. "Syria: Israel's Toughest Enemy," CBS, February 16, 1975, rebroadcast June 1975, with addendum re: criticism of report.

28. During a hearing Wallace agreed with those who attacked the accuracy of the program; he admitted that escapees "leave for the reasons that you [the complainant] suggest." He went on to say that many left purely for "economic reasons" and that,

although he had not yet returned to Syria to do the update, "there is not the slightest doubt in my mind that the report [the first] was 100% on target." Mike Wallace to H. William Shore, at televised CBS "Town Meeting," October 21, 1975, in Hartford, Conn.

29. Sequel "60 Minutes" segment televised March 21, 1976.
30. Memorandum, March 21, 1976, "CBS Syrian Jewry" by George E. Gruen, Director, Israel and Middle East Affairs, American Jewish Committee.
31. Ibid.
32. "The International Convention on Civil and Political Rights of 1966 to which Syria adhered on 21st April, 1969, . . . particularly . . . Article 12(2) of the Convention which stipulates that: 'Every person has the right to leave any State, including his own.' "

    Letter to Senator Claiborne Pell from Council for Jews in Arab Lands, November 24, 1978.
33. March 17, 1976.
34. *Evening News,* October 25, 1978, London, "The Forgotten Jews Who Live in Prison City." According to Murphy, in addition to 3,000 Jews in Damascus, 1,500 lived in Aleppo to the north and 300 in Kamishli near the Turkish border.
35. Gruen, "Assad's Syria," p. 12.
36. Henry Tanner, *New York Times,* August 30, 1982.
37. Elenore Lester, *The Jewish Week,* September 24, 1982.
38. Stephen Shalom, interview, February 7, 1979.
39. *Chicago Sun-Times,* April 2–3, 1979; *New York Times,* April 3, 1979.
40. *New York Times,* December 30, 1974.
41. Henry Tanner, *New York Times,* February 28, 1974.
42. Jesse Zel Lurie, *New Leader,* October 28, 1974, p. 11.
43. *Commentary,* "In Search of Moderate Egyptians," May 1975.
44. June 1977, interview in Alexandria.
45. *Chicago Sun-Times,* report by Jay Bushinsky, April 3, 1979.
46. *New York Times,* report by Jonathan Kandell, April 3, 1979.
47. *Chicago Sun-Times,* April 2, 1979.
48. Leo Szilard, *The Voice of the Dolphins* (New York, 1961), p. 78.
49. Joachim Prinz, *The Secret Jews* (New York, 1973), pp. 52–53. The *New York Times,* on August 18, 1934, reported, on page 2, a story headed "Berlin Jewish Group for a Unified Reich." The news item under the boldface heading related that The League of National German Jews, a "small Jewish organization in Berlin, issued a summons to all German Jews to vote for Chancellor Hitler in the plebiscite Sunday. . . . The statement reads:

    " 'We members of the League of National German Jews, founded in 1921, have always in war or peace placed the good of the German people and the German Fatherland above our own good. Accordingly, we greeted the national uprising of January, 1933 [when Hitler came to power], although it brought rigors for us. . . .

    " 'We agree fully with the political testament of Reich President and Field Marshall von Hindenburg, who called the accomplishment of Reich Chancellor Hitler and his movement a decisive step of major historical importance. . . .

    " 'To the German fatherland belongs body and soul that portion of the Jews who, like ourselves, know no other fatherland than Germany. In the spirit of the dead

Notes for pages 137–140

Reich President's testament, we support the unification of the offices of Reich leader and Reich Chancellor.

" 'We urge all Jews who feel themselves German to vote "Yes" on August 19.' "

Hitler's *Mein Kampf* had been published a decade earlier.

8. "Palestina": A Precedent of Prey

1. P.J. Vatikiotis, *Nasser and His Generation* (London, 1978), p. 254.
2. Thames Television Series, London, "Palestine," aired in the United States January–February, 1979.
3. Minutes of the Supreme Council, in D.H. Miller, *My Diary at the Conference of Paris,* 22 vols. (New York, 1924), vol. 14, p. 405.
4. *Palestine Royal Commission Report,* Command Paper #5479, 1937, p. 120, para. 14.
5. James Parkes, *Whose Land?* (Middlesex, England: Penguin Books, 1970), p. 31.
6. Ibid., p. 17.
7. Bernard Lewis, "The Palestinians and the PLO, a Historical Approach," *Commentary,* January 1975, p. 32–48.
8. Yehoshua Porath, "Social Aspects of the Emergence of the Palestinian National Movement," in *Society and Political Structure in the Arab World,* M. Milson, ed. (New York, 1973), pp. 101, 107, 119.
9. Marie Syrkin, "Palestinian Nationalism: Its Development and Goal," in Michael Curtis et al., eds., *The Palestinians: People, History, Politics* (New Brunswick, N.J.: Transaction Books, 1975), p. 200. Syrkin found that Haj Amin al-Husseini—the notorious Mufti of Jerusalem himself—"originally opposed the Palestine Mandate because it separated Palestine from Syria." Ibid.
10. Ibid. According to Neville Mandel, *Arabs and Zionism Before World War I* (Berkeley, 1976), p. 152, n. 49:

    "After World War I, when the nature of an independent Arab state and its component parts were being discussed, the term 'Greater Syria' was advanced to embrace the Fertile Crescent and its desert hinterland. Palestine, as an integral part of that area, was dubbed 'Southern Syria.' But these terms were not in use in 1913 and 1914, when very few nationalists contemplated complete Arab independence."
11. George Antonius, *The Arab Awakening: The Story of the Arab National Movement* (Philadelphia, New York, Toronto: J.B. Lippincott, 1939), p. 15, n.1; also see Mandel, *Arabs and Zionism,* pp. 151–153.
12. The Ba'ath Party "describes itself as a 'national, popular revolutionary movement fighting for Arab unity, Freedom and Socialism,' " in 1951. Syrkin, "Nationalism," in Curtis et al., *Palestinians,* p. 200; also see Menahem Milson, "Medieval and Modern Intellectual Traditions in the Arab World," in *Daedalus,* Summer 1972, particularly pp. 24–26; Michel Aflaq, prominent Ba'athist and Christian, on Arab Nationalism, cited in Milson, above; also see Aflaq, *Fi Sabil al Ba'ath* (Arabic) Beirut, 1962 (3rd printing), cited in Milson, p. 26; also see Albert Hourani, *Arabic Thought in the Liberal Age 1798–1939* (London: Oxford, 1962), particularly p. 301.
13. Ahmed Shukeiry, as head of the PLO, to Security Council on May 31, 1956, cited by Syrkin in "Nationalism," in Curtis et al., *Palestinians,* p. 201.
14. President Hafez Assad of Syria, Radio Damascus, March 8, 1974.
15. *Palestine Royal Commission Report,* Chapter 1, p. 6, para. 11.

16. Psalm 137:5, quoted by British M.P. Alfred Duff Cooper, July 30, 1939. Members of British Parliament Cooper, Josiah Wedgewood and Leopold Amery "spoke bitterly against . . . the policy of not accepting . . . Jews" in Palestine, in Martin Gilbert, *Exile and Return: The Struggle for a Jewish Homeland* (Philadelphia and New York: J.B. Lippincott, 1978), pp. 239–40.

17. Parkes, *Whose Land?*, p. 26.

18. Ibid., p. 10.

19. J.B. Pritchard, *Ancient Near Eastern Texts Relating to the Old Testament* (Princeton, N.J.: Princeton University Press, 1955), p. 378.

20. M. Stern, "The Political and Social History of Judea Under Roman Rule," in *A History of the Jewish People,* H.H. Ben-Sasson, ed. (Cambridge, Mass.: Harvard University Press, 1976), p. 266.

21. *Encyclopaedia Britannica,* 11th ed. (1911), vol. XX, p. 622.

22. Ibid., pp. 621–622.

23. Yigael Yadin, *Masada* (New York: Random House, 1966), p. 11.

24. Ibid.

25. *Encyclopaedia Britannica,* vol. XX, p. 622.

26. Alfred Guillaume, *Islam* (Baltimore: Penguin Books, 1954), pp. 10–11.

27. Bernard Lewis, *The Arabs in History,* rev. ed. (New York, Evanston, San Francisco, London: Harper-Colophon Books, 1966), pp. 31–32.

28. Salo W. Baron, *A Social and Religious History of the Jews,* 3 vols. (New York: Columbia University Press, 1937), I, pp. 308ff.

29. Lewis, *Arabs in History,* p. 40.

30. S. Safrai, "The Lands of the Diaspora," in *A History of the Jewish People,* Ben-Sasson, ed., p. 380.

31. S. Safrai, "From the Abolition of the Patriarchate to the Arab Conquest (425–640)," in *History of the Jewish People,* Ben-Sasson, ed., pp. 358–359. Of this little-known history Safrai writes: "Twice the Jews of Himyar succeeded in throwing off Ethiopian domination; even in the eyes of Byzantium it was a Jewish kingdom, small but occupying a strategic position. The king of Himyar prevented Byzantine traders from passing through to India on the grounds that Jews were being persecuted in Roman lands. Byzantium was reluctant to risk a war so far away in South Arabia, but was able to persuade Ethiopia to take up its quarrel. The king of Himyar hoped for Persian aid, but there was a lull in the fighting between Rome and Persia at the time, and the Persians did not appreciate the importance of this outlet from the Red Sea being controlled by an ally of Byzantium. Du Noas fell in a battle against an invading Ethiopian army, and the Jewish Kingdom came to an end."

32. Guillaume, *Islam,* pp. 11–12.

33. Ibid., p. 12.

34. Ibid. See examples in Chapter 4.

35. For details of the Prophet Muhammad—Abū al-Qasim Muhammad ibn 'Abd Allāh ibn 'Abd al-Muttal-ib ibn Hashim—see Guillaume, *Islam,* pp. 20–54; the "traditional" biography of Muhammad (Arabic) is Ibn Hisham's recension of Ibn Ishaq's *al-Sira al-Nabawiyya,* 2 vols. (Cairo, 1955); *The Life of Muhammad,* abridged English trans. by A. Guillaume (Karachi, 1955). Cited by Norman A. Stillman, *Jews of Arab Lands, A History and Source Book* (Philadelphia, 1979), p. 6, n. 9. See also Lewis, *Arabs in History.*

36. Guillaume, *Islam,* p. 43.

37. Ibid., pp. 43–44.

38. Ibid., p. 44.

39. The Nadir tribe. Ibid., p. 46. Also see Stillman, *Jews of Arab Lands,* pp. 8–10, for a study of "exclusively Muslim" sources, tracing Muhammad's "face-to-face contact with a large, organized Jewish Community," an "encounter" that "did not prove to be an auspicious one." The Nadir tribe in Medina went to Khaibar in "exile," Stillman, *Jews,* p. 14.

40. Salo W. Baron, *Social and Religious History,* vol. 1, p. 311. He cites Muwatta, in Al-Zurkani's commentary IV, p. 71.

41. Lewis, *The Arabs in History,* p. 45.

42. Al-Bukhari, *al-Jami al-Sahih,* bk. 56 (Kitab al-Jihad, Bab 157), ed. M. Ludolf Krehl (Leiden, 1864), vol. 2, p. 254, cited by Stillman, *Jews,* p. 17. According to Stillman, "This *hadith* appears in several other canonical collections."

43. Stillman, *Jews,* p. 17, citing Ibd Sa'd, *Kitab al-Tabaqat al-Kabir,* ed. by Edvard Sachau et al. (Leiden, 1909), vol. 2, pt. 1, pp. 66–67; al-Waqidi, *Kitab al-Maghazi,* vol. 2, pp. 566–68; Ibn Hisham, *al-Sira al-Nabawiyya,* vol. 2, pp. 618–619.

44. Itzhak Ben-Zvi, *The Exiled and the Redeemed* (Philadelphia, 1961), p. 144. Also see Stillman, *Jews,* p. 14ff.

45. The Koran, Surah 33, v. 26–32, Dawood translation.

46. Guillaume, *Islam,* p. 49.

47. Lewis, *Arabs,* p. 45.

48. Guillaume, *Islam,* p. 49.

49. Ibid., pp. 49–50. The appellation Bedouin derives from the word *badia* (steppe), which connotes the Arabian desert territories native to the wanderers. Also see C.M. Doughty, *Travels in Arabia Deserta* (London, 1888), since then in many editions; H. St. Philby, *Arabia* (1930); *Heart of Arabia* (1922); *Arabia of the Wahhabis* (1928); T.E. Lawrence, *Revolt in the Desert* (1927) and *The Seven Pillars of Wisdom* (1935); In Arabic, A'rif al-A'rif, *Al Kada' Bein Al Badou* (1937), *Ta'arikh Beir Al Sab'* (1932). In German see G.H. Dalman, *Arbeit und Sitte in Palestina* (1928), 5 vols.

50. Quoted in Philip K. Hitti, *The Arabs, A Short History* (Princeton, N.J.: Princeton University Press, 1943), p. 57.

51. Jacob de Haas, *History of Palestine* (New York: The Macmillan Co., 1934), p. 145. According to de Haas, "It was more than usually futile, and evidently had no great popular support, for Syrene was captured and, when brought before the Caliph, was shrewdly ridiculed by the monarch for his pretensions, and handed over to the Jews to be punished for claiming to be the Messiah."

52. M.A. Beek, *A Short History of Israel from Abraham to Bar Cochba* (London, 1963), p. 212.

53. "Josephus," quoted in Samuel Katz, *Battleground: Fact and Fantasy in Palestine* (New York: Bantam Books, 1973), p. 106.

54. Dio Cassius, *History of the Romans,* lxix, 12–14, cited by de Haas, *History,* p. 55; see also pp. 52–56; also Theodor Mommsen, *Provinces of the Roman Empire,* I, p. 243.

55. Parkes, *Whose Land?,* pp. 44–45; *Encyclopaedia Britannica,* 11th ed., vol. XX, pp. 622–623.

56. S. Safrai, "The Characteristics of the Era," in *A History of the Jewish People,* Ben-Sasson, ed., p. 310.

57. *Palestine Royal Commission Report,* p. 11, para. 23.

58. "The discovery of ossuary and synagogue inscriptions in all parts of Palestine throw welcome light on the position of the Jews from the century prior to the fall of Jerusalem, to about the end of the third century. The notable inscription on a synagogue in Jerusalem and the massive remains of buildings in Galilee are all most probably of dates prior to 70 C.E., for Robinson well says (Researches, 1858, p. 71) 'the splendor of these edifices . . . suggest a condition of prosperity, and wealth, and influence' of which there is not evidence in the centuries following the Roman conquest. On the other hand, a number of the finds indicate by their longing for peace that the humbler structures were erected in the second and third centuries. Dr. Samuel Klein, 'Corpus Inscriptionum,' the first attempt to catalogue the Jewish material discovered to 1920, lists building or synagogue inscriptions of Emmaus ('Amwas) Ashdod, Chorazin, Umm Al-'Amad, Edditike, Ummel Kanatir, Chirbet Semmaka (Carmel), 'Ain ed Dok (north of Jericho), Gaza, Kefar Kenna, 'Alma (north of Safed), Gischala (ed-Dschis), Kasjun (Kesun), Meron, Capernaum, Kefar Birim, Irbid, Tel Hum, Kedes, and, in Trans-Jordan, at Chirbet Kanef, in the Jaulan, Nawe (Naua), Jakuk (north of Irbid), and at Beisan (p. 63 et seq.). The information has been increased since this compilation. All the facts indicate close settlement of the land, and justify Josephus' descriptions of contemporary conditions." A footnote by J. de Haas, *History of Palestine*, p. 29.
59. Ibid., p. 67.
60. Lewis, *Arabs*, p. 49.
61. Parkes, *Whose Land?*, pp. 60–61.
62. Ibid., p. 61.
63. David George Hogarth, "Arabs and Turks," *The Arab Bulletin*, April 21, 1917, no. 48.
64. Antonius, *Arab Awakening*, p. 267. Antonius was a prominent Arabist authority and a negotiator for the Arabs in the 1920–1930 period, and his book was influential in propagating Arab "nationalism."
65. Parkes, *Whose Land?*, p. 74.
66. Hitti, *The Arabs*, p. 81.
67. Ibid., p. 83.
68. Ibid., p. 89.
69. Ibid.
70. Hogarth, "Arabs and Turks," *The Arab Bulletin*, #48.
71. Ibid.
72. Ibid. According to Hogarth, "They themselves, even when Baghdad was filled with Semites, were patently anti-Arab and obscurely Shiah, though later they would parade conformity to the Sunna, which Baghdad itself had laid down and if Abbasid rule in Iraq will not satisfy our formula, neither will it nor will that of the Omayyads satisfy it in Egypt, North Africa, Spain or Iran. For there the subjects were non-Arab, and soon many governors would not be Arabs either, but Turks like the Tulunids of Egypt, or Berbers like the dynasties which were to detach the Mediterranean shores of Africa from the distant inland Caliphate, which knew nothing about the sea."
73. Hitti, *The Arabs*, pp. 59–60.
74. Ibid., p. 2.
75. Hogarth, "Arabs and Turks," *The Arab Bulletin*, #48.
76. Lewis, *Arabs*, p. 12.

77. Ibid., p. 13.
78. Ibid., p. 14.
79. Parkes, *Whose Land?*, p. 63.
80. Hitti, *The Arabs*, pp. 48–49. See Hitti's conclusion that the tribute or collection, allotted to followers by the Koran's edict, was most important: See Sarah 9, verse 29ff, in Chapter 4 herein.
81. Parkes, *Whose Land?*, p. 65; also see Hitti, *The Arabs*, pp. 59–60; Daniel Pipes, *In the Path of God: Islam and Political Power* (New York: Basic Books, 1983).
82. Parkes, *Whose Land?*, p. 65.
83. Ibid., p. 66.
84. Ibid.
85. Hitti, *The Arabs*, p. 50.
86. Lewis, *Arabs*, pp. 14–15.
87. Steven Runciman, *A History of the Crusades*, 3 vols. (Middlesex, England: A Peregrine Book published by Penguin Books, 1965, first pub. Cambridge, 1951), vol. 2, p. 295. Runciman added, "Benjamin of Tudela was distressed to see how small their colonies were when he visited the country in about 1170." See Benjamin of Tudela, *Voyages*, ed. Adler (London, 1907), Hebrew text, pp. 26–47.
88. Runciman, *Crusades*, 2, pp. 294–295, has found that "In the kingdom of Jerusalem these (Christians) were of mixed origin, most Arabic-speaking ... almost all members of the Orthodox Church. In the County of Tripoli some of the inhabitants were members of the Monothelete sect called the Maronites. Farther north the indigenous inhabitants were mostly Monophysites of the Jacobite Church, but there were very large colonies of Armenians, almost all of the Separated Armenian Church, and in Antioch, Lattakieh and Cilicia, considerable groups of Greek-speaking Orthodox. In addition there were in the Holy Land religious colonies of every Christian denomination. The monasteries were mainly Orthodox and Greek-speaking; but there were also Orthodox Georgian establishments, and, especially in Jerusalem itself, colonies of Monophysites, both Egyptian and Ethiopian Copts and Syrian Jacobites, and a few Latin groups who had settled there before the Crusades. Many Moslem communities had emigrated when the Christian kingdom was set up." Also see Runciman, pp. 319–323; E. G. Rey, *Les Colonies Franques de Syrie* (Paris, 1883), pp. 75–94; E. Geruli, *Etiopi in Palestina* (Rome, 1943), pp. 8ff, about Abyssinians and Copts.
89. As documented by Hogarth and other authoritative historians, Saladin, often considered an Arab, was really a Kurd. Hogarth, "Arabs and Turks," *The Arab Bulletin*.
90. De Haas, *History*, p. 300, citing Gaudefroy-Demombynes, *La Syrie au debut du Quinzième Siècle d'après Qal Qachandi* (Paris, 1923), p. xxxii. Also see Ernest Frankenstein, *Justice for My People* (New York, 1944), p. 121.
91. Philip Graves, *Palestine, The Land of Three Faiths* (London, 1923), p. 55, n.1.
92. De Haas, *History*, p. 300. Also see Frankenstein, *Justice*, pp. 121–122.
93. Ibid., p. 259.
94. Makrizi, *Histoire des Sultans Mamlouks de L'Egypte*, trans. M. Quartremere (Paris, 1937–1945), vol. II, part II, pp. 29–30. Cited by Frankenstein, *Justice*, p. 122.
95. Compiled from data of Hogarth, Hitti, Leish, Frankenstein, Katz, Guillaume, Parkes, Ben-Sasson, Anglo-American *Survey* (1946), pp. 1–86, particularly pp. 1, 4, 5, 13, 14. For a more comprehensive chronology of entire Arab world, see Lewis, *Arabs*, pp. 179–183.
96. Lewis, *Arabs*, p. 15; also see Marshall G.S. Hodgson, *The Venture of Islam* (Chicago:

University of Chicago Press, 1974), 3 vols., particularly 1, p. 57ff.
97. Ibid., p. 17.
98. According to de Haas, "The Turkish officials in Palestine, at all times, had declined to speak Arabic officially. In fact most of them did not know it. This resistance went back to Mamluk days, for the Arab historians noted with pride, or pleasure, when a Mamluk sovereign knew Arabic passably well." *History,* p. 446.
99. Hogarth, "Arabs and Turks," *The Arab Bulletin.*
100. Mark Twain, *The Innocents Abroad* (London, 1881; cited here, New York, 1966), pp. 367–369. "It was in this distressing and poverty-stricken period that Palestine was visited by writers who saw the glow of the orient, who were enamoured by its romantic coloring, and who revelled in its bizarre presentation of life. Disraeli, who visited Palestine in 1831, standing before the Tombs of the Kings, visualized the historic pageant of the people from whom he was descended. He saw Jerusalem in a blaze of emotion that left its mark on all his subsequent writings, and even on his policy as British statesman. The Frenchman Lamartine was moved to an ecstasy of another kind. To him all the bizarre characters, their pompousness, the barbaric splendor, made a great appeal." De Haas, *History,* p. 387.
101. Had only the information of Muslim-Arab writers been available, "we would not know much about the Jews . . . during the first centuries of the Arab conquest," according to H.Z. Hirschberg, *A History of the Jews in North Africa* (Leiden: E.J. Brill, 1974), vol. 1, p. 87. Hirschberg writes: "We are accustomed to the historical accounts of Arab writers, who almost completely ignore the existence of Jews and Christians, mentioning them and their affairs only incidentally" (p. 369). And then, often with distortion: according to Hirschberg, the woman who at one point led the Berber fight against Muslim Arabs was purported to be Jewish, and "a brutal sorceress" whose sons were "saved . . . from destruction by guiding . . . into the haven of Islam." In fact, a historian of Tunisian Jewry discovered "proof that the woman was not a Jew," and the story is judged to have been "intended as a propaganda among the Berbers for wholehearted conversion to Islam." Yet after thirteen or fourteen hundred years, it was left to scholars to devote years of painstaking research to piece together a puzzle of fragmented historical Jewish materials buried under the reams of "concentrated data from Arab authors of the 8th to 14th centuries." The notion of the "Jewish" military leader was still preserved as such in Algerian and Tunisian Jewish folklore until the nineteenth century, when the "propaganda" was finally disputed. See Hirschberg, *History,* especially pp. 87–96.
102. Richard Hartmann, *Palestina unter den Araben, 632–1516* (Leipzig, 1915), cited by de Haas, *History,* p. 147.
103. De Haas, *History,* p. 258. John of Wurzburg list from Reinhold Rohricht edition, pp. 41, 69.
104. F. Eugene Roger, *La Terre Sainte* (Paris, 1637), p. 331, cited by de Haas, *History,* p. 342.
105. Frederich Hasselquist, *Reise nach Palastina, etc., 1749–52* (Rostock, 1762), p. 598, cited by de Haas, *History,* p. 355.
106. Parkes, *Whose Land?,* p. 212. See Chapters 13 and 14.
107. *Encyclopaedia Britannica,* 11th ed., vol. XX, p. 604.
108. Ibid.
109. In a handbook, prepared under the direction of the historical section of the Foreign Office, no. 60, entitled "Syria and Palestine" (London, 1920), p. 56.

110. Dio Cassius, *History of the Romans,* lxix, 12–14, cited by de Haas, *History,* pp. 55–56. De Haas adds: "In the third of the Schweich Lectures of 1922 the late Israel Abrahams ('Campaigns in Palestine from Alexander the Great,' London, 1927) belittles Dio Cassius' record of this war, and repeats the suggestion that the Jews were influenced by Hadrian's 'consent to the rebuilding of the Temple.' This rebuilding myth, depending upon the alleged visit of Hadrian to Palestine on the death of Trajan, has been fully dealt with by Henderson in his biography of Hadrian. All the dimensions of the war, its gravity, and its duration, are fully attested by the inscriptions relating to the legions and by the honors distributed at the end of the campaign. The archeological records, carefully analyzed, support Dio Cassius and not his would-be corrector."

111. Carl Hermann Voss, *The Palestine Problem Today, Israel and Its Neighbors* (Boston, 1953), p. 13.

112. Gunner Edward Webbe, *Palestine Exploration Fund, Quarterly Statement,* p. 86, cited in de Haas, *History,* p. 338.

113. De Haas, *History,* p. 337, citing *Palestine Exploration Fund, Quarterly Statement,* 1925, p. 197, translation of Latin manuscript by a Franciscan pilgrim.

114. Henry Maundrell, *The Journal of Henry Maundrell from Aleppo to Jerusalem, 1697,* Bohn's edition (London, 1848), respectively pp. 477, 428, 450.

115. Thomas Shaw, *Travels and Observations Relating to Several Parts of Barbary and the Levant* (London, 1767), p. 331ff. De Haas notes: "Hasselquist, the Swedish botanist, munching some roasted ears of green wheat which a shepherd generously shared with him, in the plain of Acre, reflected that the white bread of his northern homeland and the roasted wheat ears symbolized the difference between the two civilizations. Had he known that Mukaddasi boasted in the tenth century of the excellence of Palestine's white bread he might have been still more impressed by the low estate to which the country had fallen in seven hundred years. . . . Hasselquist joined a party of four thousand pilgrims who went to Jericho under an escort of three hundred soldiers. He estimated that four thousand Christians, mostly of the eastern rites, entered Jaffa each year, and as many Jews. The Armenian Convent in Jerusalem alone could accommodate a thousand persons. The botanist viewed *the pilgrim tolls as the best resource of an uncultivated and uninhabited country.* . . . Ramleh was a ruin." (Emphasis added.) De Haas, *History,* pp. 349, 358, 360, citing Frederich Hasselquist, *Reise nach Palastina,* etc., 1749–1752, pp. 139, 145–146, 190.

116. Norman Lewis, "The Frontier of Settlement in Syria, 1800–1950," in Charles Issawi, ed., *The Economic History of the Middle East* (Chicago, 1966), p. 260.

117. Count Constantine F. Volney, *Travels Through Syria and Egypt in the Years 1783, 1784, 1785* (London, 1788), vol. 2, p. 147. According to Volney, ". . . we with difficulty recognize Jerusalem. . . . remote from every road, it seems neither to have been calculated for a considerable mart of commerce, nor the centre of a great consumption. . . . [the population] is supposed to amount to twelve to fourteen thousand. . . . The second place deserving notice, is Bait-el-labm, or Bethlehem, . . . The soil is the best in all these districts . . . but as is the case everywhere else, cultivation is wanting. They reckon about six hundred men in this village capable of bearing arms. . . . The third and last place of note is Habroun, or Hebron, the most powerful village in all this quarter, and . . . able to arm eight or nine hundred men . . ." (pp. 303–325).

118. Volney, *Travels,* vol. 2, p. 431.

119. A. Keith, *The Land of Israel* (Edinburgh, 1843), p. 465. "The population (viz., of the whole of Syria), rated by Volney at two million and a half, is now estimated at half that amount."

120. J.S. Buckingham, *Travels in Palestine* (London, 1821), p. 146.

121. Ibid., p. 162.

122. James Mangles and the Honorable C.L. Irby, *Travels in Egypt and Nubia* (London, 1823), p. 295.

123. Brockhaus, *Allg. deutsch Real-Encyklopaedie*, 7th ed. (Leipzig, 1827), vol. VIII, p. 206.

124. S. Olin, *Travels in Egypt, Arabia Petraea and the Holy Land* (New York, 1843), vol. 2, pp. 438–439.

125. Ibid., pp. 77–78.

126. No. 238, "Report of the Commerce of Jerusalem During the Year 1863," F.O. 195/808, May 1864. ". . . The population of the City of Jerusalem is computed at 15,000, of whom about 4,500 Moslem, 8,000 Jews, and the rest Christians of various denominations . . ." From A.H. Hyamson, ed., *The British Consulate in Jerusalem*, 2 vols. (London, 1939–1941), vol. 2, p. 331.

127. James Finn to the Earl of Clarendon, Jerusalem, September 15, 1857, F.O. 78/1294 (Pol. No. 36). Finn wrote further that "The result of my observations is, that we have here Jews, who have been to the United States, but have returned to their Holy Land —Jews of Jerusalem do go to Australia and instead of remaining there, do return hither, even without the allurements of agriculture and its concomitants." Ibid., 1, pp. 249–52.

128. J.B. Forsyth, *A Few Months in the East* (Quebec, 1861), p. 188.

129. H.B. Tristram, *The Land of Israel: A Journal of Travels in Palestine* (London, 1865), p. 490.

130. Mark Twain, *The Innocents Abroad*, pp. 349, 366, 367.

131. Ibid., p. 349.

132. Ibid., p. 429.

133. Ibid., p. 366, 375.

134. Ibid., pp. 441–442.

135. Ibid.

136. Jules Hoche, *Les Pays des croisades* (Paris, n.d.), p. 10, cited by David Landes, "Palestine Before the Zionists," *Commentary*, Feb., 1976, p. 49.

137. Brother Lievin de Hamme, *Guide indicateur*, vol. III, pp. 163, 190.

138. The Reverend Samuel Manning, *Those Holy Fields* (London, 1874), pp. 14–17. W.M. Thomson reiterated the Reverend Manning's observations: "How melancholy is this utter desolation! Not a house, not a trace of inhabitants, not even shepherds, seen everywhere else, appear to relieve the dull monotony. . . . Isaiah says that Sharon shall be wilderness, and the prediction has become a sad and impressive reality." Thomson, *The Land and the Book* (London: T. Nelsons & Sons, 1866), p. 506ff.

139. W.C. Prime, *Tent Life in the Holy Land* (New York, 1857), p. 240, cited by Fred Gottheil, "The Population of Palestine, Circa 1875," *Middle Eastern Studies*, vol. 15, no. 3, October 1979.

140. S.C. Bartlett, *From Egypt to Palestine* (New York, 1879), p. 409, cited in ibid.

141. Ibid., p. 410.

142. W. Allen, *The Dead Sea: A New Route to India* (London, 1855), p. 113, cited in ibid.

143. W.M. Thomson, *The Land and the Book* (New York: Harper Bros., 1862), p. 466, cited in ibid.

144. E.L. Wilson, *In Scripture Lands* (New York, n.d.), p. 316, cited in ibid.

145. Colonel C.R. Conder, *Heth and Moab* (London, 1883), pp. 380, 376.

146. Ibid., p. 366.

147. Pierre Loti, *La Galilee* (Paris, 1895), pp. 37–41, 69, 85–86, 69, cited by David Landes, "Palestine Before the Zionists," *Commentary,* February 1976, pp. 48–49.

148. Landes, "Palestine," p. 49.

149. *Palestine Royal Commission Report,* p. 6, para. 12.

150. *The Koran,* Surah 8, "The Spoils," v. 41.

151. "In the book, *Kitab al-Kharaj* (Book of Offerings) by Abu-Yussuf, a disciple of Abu-Hanifa, in the chapter on 'The Division of the Spoils,' it is deduced from that chapter of the Koran, that *ganima,* the spoils, after a fifth has been set aside from it to God, belong to the victorious Moslems, not individually, but to all together, the collective body." See the translation of this chapter in the periodical *Der Islam,* vol. I, pp. 347–353, appendix to the article by F.F. Schmidt, 'Die Occupato im islamischen Recht,' ibid; p. 300ff., cited by A. Granott, *The Land System in Palestine* (London, 1952), p. 327, n. 8.

152. Belin, 'Du Régime des fiefs militaires dans l'Islamisme, et principalement en Turquie,' *Journal Asiatique,* 1870, Sixième série, tome XV, pp. 196–197. Cited in A. Granott, *The Land System in Palestine* (London: Eyre & Spottiswoode, 1952), p. 18.

153. "During the seventeenth century some of the more permanently established leaseholders began to coalesce with the landowners into a new landed aristocracy—the *ayan-i memleket* or country notables, whose appearance and usurpation of some of the functions and authority of government were already noted at the time." Bernard Lewis, *The Emergence of Modern Turkey* (London, 1961), p. 33. Lewis notes the following: cf. the remarks of Huseyin Hezarfen, writing in 1669 (R. Anhegger, "Hezarfen Huseyin Efendi'nin Osmanli devlet teskilatina dair mulahazalari," *TM,* x(1951–3), 372, 387. The *ayan-i vilayet* already appear occasionally in *Kanuns* of the sixteenth century (Barkan, *XV ve XVI inci asirlarda . . . Kaunular,* i (1943, index).

154. A. Granott, *The Land System in Palestine,* pp. 31–32. According to de Haas: "The sultans regarded Palestine as their personal domain, acquired by the law of arms and war. The inhabitants, except a few tribes like the Druzes who were never conquered, *could not pretend to real or personal property. Even private inheritance reverted to the sultan.* Though the peasants were not serfs as under the feudal system, and under no obligation of service, all the country was crown land. When this system of crown land was compromised by grants to nobles, the peasants did not go with the land. The census when it was introduced, was employed for imperial military purposes. The individual could not be imprisoned for debt though the village, as a unit, could be made to suffer for its collective obligation. The struggle, therefore, was between the land and the tax collector. If the assessor arrived at the right moment he seized what he claimed, and satisfied his demand. The peasant had no interest in thorough cultivation, or in the fertilization of the soil. His primitive tools were evidence of his poverty and indifference. The like picture was presented in Greece to the middle of the nineteenth century." From de Haas, *History,* pp. 361–362; also see Volney, *Travels,* vol. 2, pp. 370, 406, 408. (Emphasis added.)

155. Granott, *System,* p. 31.
"They were abolished by the well-known edict of Tanzimat ('the new regime') . . . of

Gulhane in 1839. This proclamation declared that, in spite of its deplorable consequences, there was still to be found in the Ottoman Empire the 'destructive principle' of *iltizam*—a principle which produced the unlimited rule of the governors in the provinces and a crushing exploitation of the inhabitants. The object of the reforms was to enable the State to recover for itself all its rights of ownership of the landed properties" (p. 32).

156. Volney, *Travels*, vol. 2, pp. 406–431.
157. Volney, *Travels*, vol. 2, p. 411. He also said, "When the peasants are in want of money to purchase grain, cattle, etc. they can find none but by mortgaging the whole, or part of their future crop, greatly under its value. The danger of letting money appear closes the hands of all by whom it is possessed; and if it is parted with it must be from the hope of a rapid and exorbitant gain; the most moderate interest is twelve per cent, the usual rate is twenty, and it frequently rises as high even as thirty."
158. Issawi, *Economic History*, p. 72. *"Their extortion was usually proportionate to the shortness of their tenure;* this led the government to introduce in the 18th century a system of life farming of taxes, *malikane*, in the hope of checking abuses but its application was not universal." (Emphasis added.)
159. Ibid.
160. Granott, *System*, p. 57.
161. I.M. Smilianskaya, "The Disintegration of Feudal Relations in Syria and Lebanon in the Middle of the Nineteenth Century," from Issawi, *Economic History*, p. 234.
162. Olin, *Travels in Egypt*, p. 138.
163. Hope Simpson, *Report*, p. 146.
164. W.G.A. Ormsby-Gore, Secretary of State for the Colonies, testimony at 32nd session of Permanent Mandates Commission, August 1937.
165. See C.F. Volney, *Travels*, vol. 2, pp. 406–431; Bernard Lewis, *Emergence of Modern Turkey*, p. 33, text and n. 21.
166. John Lewis Burckhardt, *Travels in Syria and the Holy Land* (London, 1882), p. 299; according to Smilianskaya, "Reports from Volney, Petkovich and Uspenskii of peasants migrating in search of a living were substantiated by Urquehart." "Disintegration," in Issawi, *Economic History*, p. 235.
167. Burkhardt, *Travels*, p. 299.
168. Ibid., cited by Norman Lewis, "The Frontier of Settlement in Syria, 1800–1950," *International Affairs*, XXXI (January 1955), pp. 48–60; reprinted in Issawi, *Economic History*, p. 261.
169. N. Lewis, "Frontiers," p. 261.
170. Writer P. Uspenskii, Russian Foreign Policy Archives (Embassy in Constantinople Fund), case 915, 1. 174, cited by Smilianskaya in "Disintegration," in Issawi, *Economic History*, p. 235.
171. Ibid., pp. 234–235, n. 46.
172. N. Lewis, "Frontier," Issawi, *Economic History*, p. 265. He cites C. Doughty, *Travels in Arabia Deserta* (New York, n.d.).
173. "When the mandatory powers took over the territories of these four countries [Palestine, Trans-Jordan, Syria, Lebanon, and Iraq] [sic] after the last war, the system of land tenure was based on the Ottoman Land Code. This was a body of civil law . . . on the statute books during the nineteenth century. Its *weakness was that it was never generally enforced* . . . [emphasis added] . . . the main legal categories into which land was divided by the Ottoman Land Code (promulgated in 1858) . . . are:

"1. *Mulk land:* This is the land held in absolute freehold ownership. It is governed by the provisions of sacred law and not by those of the Civil Statute Law. Landownership comprises two rights: the *raqaba,* or right of absolute ownership, and the *tasarruf,* or right of the *usufruct* of land. In *mulk* tenure both rights belong to the individual.

"2. *Miri land:*. . . the *raqaba* or absolute ownership belongs to the state but the *usufruct* to the individual. It is a form of heritable leasehold ownership in which the state leases land to the individual.

"3. *Waqf land:*. . . dedicated to some pious purpose and is not very important in this region.

"4. *Matruka:* Land reserved for some public purpose as for example village threshing floors.

"5. *Mawat land:* Dead or unreclaimed land.

". . . these different divisions do not cover the leasehold tenancies between landlord and cultivator. . . . The Ottoman Land Code apparently does none of the things that a land-tenure code ought to do."

[The purpose of these categories of land, then, was really] "the collection of revenue. The real purpose of the code was to tax every piece of land, and therefore to establish clearly the title to it by registering its legal owner as a *miri* owner. The state's claim to ownership really meant only that the state did not recognize ownership unless the titles were registered and the land therefore taxable." Doreen Warriner, "Land Tenure in the Fertile Crescent," in Issawi, *Economic History,* pp. 72–73.

174. Elie Kedourie, "Islam Today," in Bernard Lewis, ed., *Islam and the Arab World* (New York: Alfred A. Knopf, 1976), p. 331. According to Kedourie, the new state law "resulted in the transformation of customary tenures and of land in common or tribal ownership or use into state-registered, individually owned free-holds. This reform rode rough-shod over customary rights which, though not set down in official documents, yet had immemorially regulated agrarian relationships in large parts of the empire."

175. Thomson, *Land and Book,* 1868 edition (New York: Harper & Bros.), vol. I, pp. 497–498.

176. Roderique H. Davison, *Reform in the Ottoman Empire* (Princeton, 1963), p. 63. Davison refers to "forceful" evidence of such conditions in Mustafa Fazil Pasa's *Lettre adresse a S.M. le Sultan* (n.p., n.d., "but Paris, either late 1866 or early 1867").

177. Ibid., p. 65.

178. Fatima Aliye, *Ahmed Cevdet Pasa and His Time* (Istanbul, 1332), pp. 33–34, cited by Davison, *Reform,* p. 67.

179. Davison, *Reform,* p. 69, citing Ziya Bey from *Hurriyet* #5, as quoted in *Tanzimat,* I, p. 841 (The Tanzimat, on the Occasion of its Hundredth Anniversary) (Istanbul, 1940).

180. Ahmed Midhat, who wrote, "in exile, for Turkey and against Russia," quoted by Davison, *Reform,* p. 69.

181. Suleyman Pasa zade Sami, ed., *Suleyman Pasa muhakemesi* (Suleyman Pasha's Trial) (Istanbul, 1328). "A biography and defense of his constitutionalist father by the son, with large portions on his interrogation and trial arising from his generalship in the Russo-Turkish War of 1877," cited by Davison, *Reform,* p. 69.

182. Granott, *Land,* p. 58.

183. Thomson, *Land and Book,* pp. 497–498; C.T. Wilson, *Peasant Life in the Holyland*

(London, 1906), pp. 288–297; also see Issawi, *Economic History;* Davison, *Reform;* Granott, *Land.*

184. C.T. Wilson, *Peasant Life in the Holy Land* (London: John Murray, 1906), pp. 288, 290, cited by Granott, *Land System,* p. 64.
185. Issawi, *Economic History,* p. 258. He adds: "This process had been described and analyzed, with unrivalled depth and vividness, by the fourteenth century historian and sociologist, Ibn Khaldun."
186. Issawi, *Economic History,* p. 258.
187. Volney, *Travels,* vol. 2 (1787 ed.), pp. 196–197.
188. Issawi, *Economic History,* p. 258. A "vivid account" by the British consul in Aleppo: Skene to Bulwer, May 12, 1860, FO 78 No. 1538.
189. N. Lewis, "Frontier," in Issawi, *Economic History,* pp. 258–260.
190. J.L. Burckhardt, *Travels,* pp. 301–302. At one spot, ". . . the whole neighborhood of Aleppo is infested by obscure tribes of Arab and Kurdine robbers, who through the negligence of the Janissaries, acquire every day more insolence and more confidence in the success of their enterprises. Caravans of forty or fifty camels have in the course of last winter been several times attacked and plundered at five hundred yards from the city gate; not a week passes without somebody being ill-treated and stripped in the gardens near the town; and the robbers have been sometimes taken their night's rest in one of the suburbs of the city, and there sold their cheaply acquired booty" (pp. 654–655).
191. H.B. Tristram, *The Land of Israel: A Journal of Travels in Palestine* (London, 1865), p. 490. According to de Haas, "To 1900 Beersheba had no permanent inhabitants, but about that year the government obtained control of the Negeb, and in order to exercise police power over the Bedouins established a station at the site of the Biblical wells." *History,* p. 445. Thus Beersheba in 1909 became "a straggling little town with government buildings, a few stores . . . and dwelling houses for eight hundred people." Ellsworth Huntington, *Palestine and its Transformation* (Boston, 1911), p. 115. Across the fifteen miles between Debir and Beersheba, Huntington found "no sign of any village, merely three ruins, and the tents of some Bedouins." The land was so impoverished that the government rented 7,500 acres in the Negev for an annual rental of $2,000. Huntington, *Palestine,* p. 117.
192. Lortet, *La Syrie d'aujourd'hui: Voyages dans la Phénicie, le Liban et la Judée, 1875–80* (Paris, 1881), p. 137.
193. Smilianskaya, "Disintegration," in Issawi, *Economic History,* p. 234. Also see account in 1841 by K.M. Bazilli, Russian Consul General in Beirut, Arkhiv vneshnei politiki Rossii, fond "Posolstvo v Konstantinopole" (Russian Foreign Policy Archives, "Embassy in Constatinople" Fund), case 718, 1.112, cited by Smilianskaya, "Disintegration."
194. Ibid. ". . . representatives of the feudal class used the capital they accumulated by the exploitation of peasants. This capital was not invested in agriculture as a rule, but in trade and usurious operations. . . . One branch of the ancient feudal family of Dahdah, owners of a *muqata'a* in northern Lebanon, had commercial offices in Marseilles, Paris and London" (p. 239).
195. "The Jews in Jerusalem are in general very poor. . . . the whole Jewish people are suffering the greatest distress—and if some relief be not afforded . . . whole families must, during this next winter, perish from want. . . . In the midst of their wretched condition they look upon 500 as acknowledged paupers. . . ." Young to Palmerston,

Jerusalem, May 25, 1839, FO 78/368 (No. 13), cited in Hyamson, *British Consulate,* vol. I, p. 5.

196. Exact population statistics for the mid-nineteenth century are unlikely, and estimates of the period varied broadly. One source, *Murray's Handbook for Travellers in Syria and Palestine* (1858), was reprinted in the *Encyclopaedia Britannica,* 8th ed., vol. XVII, pp. 180–198 (1860). According to that set of statistics, covering a wider area than historic Palestine—the whole Turkish Pashalic of Sedon—coupled with the 1895 figures of Vital Cuinet, *Syrie, Liban,* the number of Jews in Palestine in 1858 is roughly estimated at about 15,000.

197. In 1839 the British Consul wrote from Jerusalem: "I commenced with the intention of numbering the whole Jewish population. . . . I found the religious prejudice so strong against their being numbered at all—for by their law it is not allowed—that at present I am only able to give your Lordship the aggregate number, which I think may be considered as pretty accurate—but certainly, *rather under, than overstated, as the Jews will ever be considered less in number than they really are."* (Emphasis added.) Young to Palmerston, Jerusalem, May 25, 1839, FO 78/368 (No. 13), from Hyamson, *British Consulate,* pp. 4–7.

198. James Finn, *Stirring Times or Record from Jerusalem Consular Chronicles* from 1853–1856 (London, 1878), vol. I, pp. 180–181.

199. Mandel, *Arabs and Zionism,* p. xxii. The office of Mufti of Jerusalem belonged to the Husseini family from the "mid-19th century on," Porath, "Social Aspects," in *Society,* Milson, ed., p. 98.

200. D. Warriner, "Land Tenure," in Issawi, *Economic History,* p. 77. One factor that "influences the land system is the existence of a parasitic landlord class, a result of the Turkish system in which grants of land were made to political supporters of the sultan or in which powerful chiefs seized in the rights to farm taxes. But the more general cause for the rise of the city-notable type of landlord is the perpetual indebtedness of the peasants, which results from the uncertainty of grain yields. One or two years of bad harvests impoverish cultivators, force them to borrow even to buy seed, and after borrowing at high rates of interest, they are eventually forced to sell their holdings to wealthy merchants in the town and to continue to exist as tenants of the big landowners. . . .

"The landlords who have acquired land in this way are rarely farmers and may not even visit the villages they own. . . . Landownership is a credit operation and nothing more. . . . In this case the large landowner . . . appears simply in the role of a money lender without responsibility to the land. This type of ownership is injurious, since it prevents constructive investment in the land."

201. G. Schumacher, "Der arabische Pflug," *Zeitschrift des deutschen Palaestina-Vereins,* 1889, Bd. XII, p. 165. According to Granott, *Land System,* pp. 335–336, n. 13: "There was no need to flee to a distance in order to escape the pursuers, since there were places of refuge within the country itself. Among the swamps of Nahr ez Zerqa in Samaria, between Caesarea and Tantura, there are several lonely stretches without a footpath and without any connection with the outer world, so that it is almost impossible to find anyone hiding there. These marshes were used as places of refuge by the Arabs who ran away to escape confiscation of their property, and other oppressive requirements of the Turkish Government. See G.A. Smith, *The Historical Geography of the Holy Land* (London: Hodder and Stoughton, 1931, 25th ed.), p. 145."

202. Hermann Guthe, *Palaestina* (Bielefeld und Leipzig: Verlag von Velhagen und Klasing, 1908), p. 47; cited by Granott, *Land System,* p. 61.

203. Granott, *Land System,* p. 61.

204. Charles M. Doughty, *Travels in Arabia Deserta* (New York: Random House, n.d.), p. 56.

205. N. Lewis, "Frontier," in Issawi, *Economic History,* p. 261.

206. Ibid., p. 263.

207. Makrizi, *Histoire des Sultans Mamlouks,* II, pp. 29–30, cited in Frankenstein, *Justice,* p. 122.

208. Parkes, *Whose Land?,* pp. 210, 212. See Parkes' map of various ethnic settlements in Palestine, and their locations, p. 211.

209. N. Lewis, "Frontier," in Issawi, *Economic History,* p. 266, 263.

210. De Haas, *History,* p. 419.

211. Ibid., p. 425; 3,000 Albanians were brought into Acre, according to Sir Sidney Smith's dispatch of May 9, 1799, in de Haas, *History,* p. 355.

212. N. Lewis, "Frontier," p. 266. According to Davis Trietsch, "In the last decades, several Turkish provinces have been lost to Christian neighbors because the Christian population was recognized as independent by the State (Ottomans). *Many Muslims had to leave.*" (Emphasis added.) *Jüdische Emigration und Kolonisation* (Berlin, 1923), p. 31.

213. Abdel Razak Kader, *The Jerusalem Post,* January 8, 1969.

214. Sherif Hussein, *Al-Qibla,* Mecca, March 23, 1918.

215. Ameen Rihani, *Around the Coasts of Arabia* (London, 1930), pp. 101, 109, 96–109.

9. *Dhimmi* in the Holy Land

1. "Still, the Jew in Jerusalem is not estimated in value much above a dog. . . . What the Jew has to endure, at all hands, is not to be told. Like the miserable dog without an owner he is kicked by one because he crosses his path, and cuffed by another because he cries out." British Consul Wm. T. Young to Viscount Palmerston, Jerusalem, 25 May 1839, F.O.78/363 (No. 13), in Albert M. Hyamson, ed., *The British Consulate in Jerusalem,* 2 vols. (London, 1939), 1, p.6. Christians, too, were the occasional scapegoat as infidels, though they were usually less vulnerable, because of their protection by a powerful European base: In 1860, for example, a consul in Damascus reported of "an awful day of slaughter . . ." when "the cry was got up that the Christians had murdered some Mahometans; and . . . not a Christian found was spared." British Consul Jas. Brant, July 12, 1860, Enclosure 4 in No. 23, in *Despatches from Her Majesty's Consuls in the Levant, Respecting Past or Apprehended Disturbances in Syria, 1858–1860* (London: Harrison and Sons, 1860), p. 53.

2. James Finn to the Earl of Malmesbury, Jerusalem, July 8, 1858, F.O. 78/1383 (Pol. No. 12), in Hyamson, *Consulate,* 1, p. 260.

3. *Palestine Royal Commission Report* (Peel Report) (London, 1937), p. 7, para. 14. For example, immediately upon the end of the Crusaders' reign, some 300 rabbis made a pilgrimage from Provence and Flanders to rebuild the Jewish communities that the Crusaders had unsuccessfully attempted to eradicate. Martin Gilbert, *Exile and Return* (Philadelphia, 1978), p. 12. At the time of the Crusaders, "a full thousand years after the fall of the Jewish state, there were Jewish communities all over the country. Fifty of them are known to us; they include Jerusalem, Tiberias, Ramleh,

Ashkalon, Caesarea, and Gaza." Samuel Katz, *Battleground, Fact and Fantasy in Palestine* (New York, 1973), p. 89. In the eleventh–twelfth centuries, the time of the Crusaders' conquest, although the vast majority of the Holy Land's inhabitants were "native Christians"—most of them were "of mixed origin, most Arabic-speaking, and carelessly known as Christian Arabs." Steven Runciman, *A History of the Crusades,* 3 vols. (London, 1965), vol. 2, pp. 294–295; Jewish communities were plentiful enough to fight as a group and "were among the most vigorous defenders of Jerusalem against the Crusaders." Katz, *Battleground,* p. 89. In Haifa "The Jews almost single-handedly defended . . . against the Crusaders, holding out in the besieged town for a whole month (June–July, 1099)." Katz, *Battleground,* p. 89. The fact is that it was at the time the Jews were prohibited by law from becoming citizens of the Holy Land that Jehudah Halevi, the famous Jewish writer and poet (whose travails were discussed in earlier pages) immigrated to Judah-cum-Palestine and commanded his fellow Jews to follow. See Chapter 5.

4. Yasser Arafat, *New York Times,* December 3, 1968, p. 6.

5. In fact, the 1946 *Anglo-American Committee Report* remarked that, "An immediate result of the *success of Arab terrorism* was the *beginning* of Jewish terrorism and, even more significant, a closing of the ranks, a tightening of the discipline, and a general militarization of Jewish life in Palestine. . . . a citizen army which felt that at any moment it might have to fight for its very existence." *Anglo-American Committee of Inquiry Report,* April 20, 1946, Lausanne, Switzerland, p. 32. (Emphasis added.) This seems to contradict the mournful plaints that the "old" Israel of the '50s and '60s has been "abandoned" to "militarism."

6. For example, during the speeches before an audience of 90 to 100, at the organizing meeting of the Chicago Chapter of the Palestine Human Rights Committee, activist David Dellinger and Professor Ibrahim Abu-Lughod discussed, from the dais, the "parallel between Israel and Nazi Germany." November 1980.

7. See Chapter 7.

8. Gérard Chaliand, *The Palestine Resistance* (London, 1972), p. 10, cited by Lewis, *Islam in History,* p. 320, n. 11.

9. Abd Al-Monem Al-Sawi, *Al-Gumhuriya,* August 8, 1982.

10. Anis Mansour, "What if the PLO Leaves Lebanon?" *October* magazine, August 8, 1982.

11. In *Palaestina Handbuch,* in addition to the large Jewish populations in Jaffa (10,000), Safed (8,000–10,000) and Haifa (1,600–2,000), Davis Trietsch found a Jewish population in the following towns as of 1910: Gaza (160), Ramle (100), Beersheba (20), Acre (50—twenty years earlier there were nearly 1,000, but most went to Haifa), Sh'fa Amr (20), and Hebron (1,000—according to Nawratski, 1,500—5.5 to 8 percent of the total population). Davis Trietsch, *Palaestina Handbuch,* 2nd ed. (Berlin-Schmargedorf: Orient-Verlag, 1910), pp. 34–40, 41–44. Compare another scholar's figures for 1913, which are higher: Curt Nawratski, *Die jüdische Kolonisation Palastinas* (Munich: Verlag Ernst Reinhardt, 1914), p. 394ff. In 1922, the Jewish populations were: Gaza (54), Khan Yunis (1), Beersheba (98), Ramle (35), Lydda (11), Hebron (430), Bethlehem (2), Ramallah (7), Tulkarem (23), Nablus (16), Jenin (7), Nazareth (53), Beisan [Beit Shean] (41), Acre (78). Anglo-American Committee of Inquiry, *A Survey of Palestine* (1946), vol. 1, p. 148.

12. By 1944, in all of the towns listed above—except Acre (50) and Lydda (20)—the Anglo-American Committee's *Survey,* p. 151, reports the number of Jews to be zero.

13. As one of many examples of Arabs victimized by Arab terrorism, in March of 1970 the *New York Times* reported that grenade attacks had killed 27 in the Gaza Strip, wounding 132. According to the report, "Although Arab guerrillas are acknowledged to be responsible for the terrorism, most of the victims are Arabs. Only four of last month's fatalities and 16 of the wounded were Israelis."

According to prominent Palestinian Arabs in the United States, the "secular democratic state" would be the only free state in the Middle East. Professor Ibrahim Abu Lughod, Northwestern University, stated in 1980 that "The PLO has the consensus of its population. There is no coercive policy." November 1980 address to Palestine Human Rights Committee, Chicago.

Yet after the murder of a Palestinian Arab from Ramallah, the PLO United Nations observer Zehdi Labib Terzi told an incredulous NBC interviewer that "Those who collaborate with the enemy should be executed." December 26, 1977. For earlier examples, see Chapter 14.

14. James Parkes, *Whose Land?* (Great Britain, 1970), pp. 70–71.

15. Ibid.

16. Martin Kabtanik, *Journey to Jerusalem* (1491), from Gilbert, *Exile and Return,* p. 19.

17. Arnold van Harff, *The Pilgrimage of Arnold van Harff* (London, 1946), p. 217.

18. Felix Fabri, *The Wanderings of Felix Fabri* (London, 1897), p. 130, cited by Katz, *Battleground,* p. 92.

19. David Landes, "Palestine Before the Zionists," *Commentary,* February 1976, p. 52.

20. Jacob de Haas, *History of Palestine* (New York, 1934), p. 334.

21. Ibid., p. 338; also see Katz, *Battleground,* p. 93. For additional information on Murad III see C. Brockelmann, *History of the Islamic Peoples* (New York, 1960), pp. 302, 328; Bernard Lewis, *The Emergence of Modern Turkey* (London, 1961), p. 27.

22. Ibid. According to de Haas, "Solomon Ashkenazi, [Murad's] confidential agent, prevented the execution of this decree. . . . Sandys, however, [George Sandys, *A Relation of a Journey Begun in 1610* (London, 1627)] infers that the Jews were saved by Esther Kiera, who was the confidant of the Sultan's chief wife, and a great power in Constantinople till 1600, when she was butchered by the Janizaries."

23. Ibid. De Haas cites an illustrative description of Jerusalem in 1590 by Gunner Edward Webbe, a British traveler, in the *Palestine Exploration Fund, Quarterly Statement,* p. 86.

24. Katz, *Battleground,* pp. 96–98. "Among the *immigrants* who began arriving when the Crusaders' grip on Palestine had been broken by Saladin was an organized group of three hundred rabbis who came from France [Provence] and England [Flanders] in the year 1210 to strengthen especially the Jewish communities of Jerusalem, Acre and Ramleh. Their work proved in vain. A generation later came the destruction by the Mongol invaders. Yet no sooner had they passed than a new immigrant, Moses Nachmanides, came to Jerusalem, finding only two Jews, a dyer and his son; but he and the disciples who answered his call reestablished the community.

"Though Yehuda Halevi and Nachmanides were the most famous medieval preachers of *aliyah,* they were not the only ones. From the twelfth century onward, the surviving writings of a long series of Jewish travelers described their experiences in Palestine. Some of them remained to settle; all propagated the national duty. . . .

"There were periods, moreover, when the Popes ordered their adherents to prevent Jewish travel to Palestine. For most of the fifteenth century the Italian

maritime states denied Jews the use of ships for getting to Palestine, thus forcing them
to abandon their project or to make the whole journey by a roundabout land route,
adding . . . the dangers of movement through Germany, Poland, and Southern Russia
or through the inhospitable Balkans and a Black Sea crossing before reaching the
comparative safety of Turkey. In 1433, shortly after the ban was imposed, there came
a vigorous call by Yitzhak Tsarefati, urging the Jews to come by way of then tolerant
Turkey. Immigration of the bolder spirits continued."

25. Ibid., pp. 96–97.
26. Siebald Rieter and Johann Tucker, cited by Katz, *Battleground,* pp. 97–98.
27. Katz, *Battleground,* p. 93.
28. *Palestine Royal Commission Report,* pp. 11–12.
29. John Hayman and Joseph von Egmont, *Travels* (London, 1759), cited by Katz,
    Battleground, p. 93.
30. H.H. Ben-Sasson, *Toledot Hayehudim Bi-Mei Habeinayim* (Tel Aviv, 1969), pp.
    239–240.
31. Y. Ben-Zvi, *The Land of Israel and Its Settlements During the Turkish Regime,* pp.
    205–206, cited by David Ben-Gurion, *Israel, A Personal History* (Tel Aviv, 1971),
    p. 15.
32. Ben-Gurion, *Israel,* p. 15.
33. See Katz, *Battleground,* p. 94.
34. Ibid.
35. Ibn Barouk bought the rule under the reign of Murad IV (1623–1640). De Haas,
    History, p. 342.
36. Ibid. De Haas notes that "In 1630, owing to the renewal of the Red and White feuds,
    Bethlehem was almost destroyed. In 1644–45 Nazareth, which contained some sixty
    ruined houses, was captured by the Pasha of Safed, and the population fled." Until
    1658 in the holy Christian town of Nazareth, *"none but Muslims were permitted to
    settle* there. Later a few Greek Christians were admitted to the town, which became
    a center for the Turkish cavalry and by the end of the century numbered eighty-one
    houses." (Emphasis added.)
37. A.Y. Brawer, *Haaretz* (Tel Aviv, 1929), p. 169, from *Palestine, A Study of Jewish,
    Arab and British Policies,* published for the Esco Foundation for Palestine, Inc. (New
    Haven: Yale University Press, 1947), pp. 519–520.
38. De Haas, *History,* p. 345, citing M. Franco, *Essai sur l'Histoire des Israelites de
    l'Empire Ottoman* (Paris, 1897), p. 88.
39. R.P. Michael, *Voyage Nouveau de la Terre-Sainte* (Paris, 1702), pp. 58, 563.
40. Ben-Gurion, *Israel,* p. 15. Sheikh Daher invited Rabbi Chaim Aboulafia, who com-
    menced "renewing the tradition of Don Joseph Nasi in settling Jews in the villages
    and establishing an agricultural community in nearby Shfaram."
41. Ibid.
42. Katz, *Battleground,* p. 94.
43. John Lewis Burckhardt, *Travels in Syria and the Holy Land* (London, 1822), p. 317.
44. De Haas, *History,* p. 360.
45. E.D. Clarke, *Travels* (1812), pp. 364–365. According to Clarke the "Butcher's" real
    name of Ahmed was obscured by his acts. Ahmed had sold himself into slavery as
    a boy in Constantinople and was eventually taken by Ali Bey into Egypt, where
    Ahmed bragged of his achievement of the rank of governor; see also Moshe Ma'oz,
    "Changes in the Position of the Jewish Communities of Palestine and Syria in

Mid-Nineteenth Century," in *Studies on Palestine During the Ottoman Period,* Ma'oz, ed.(Jerusalem, 1975), p. 145.

46. Baron Geramb, monk of the Order of La Trappe, *Pilgrimage to Jerusalem and Mount Sinai* (Philadelphia, 1840), vol. 1, p. 288.

47. De Haas, *History,* p. 368. Also see an interesting account in R.A. Stewart Macalister and E.W.G Masterman, "A History of the Doings of the Fellahin during the First Half of the Nineteenth Century from Native Sources," *Palestine Exploration Fund, Quarterly Statement,* 1906 (London), pp. 221–225.

48. Salomon Munk, *La Palestine, description géographique, etc.* (Paris, 1845), p. 648, as cited by de Haas, *History,* p. 367.

49. William Jowett, "Christian Researches," 1823–1824, quoted by James Aikken Wylie, *Modern Judea* (London, 1850), pp. 293–294.

50. De Haas, *History,* p. 368; also see Ma'oz, "Changes," in *Studies,* pp. 143–145; in Arabic, Abd al'Qadir al Maghribi, "Yahud al-Sham mundhu Mi'at Am," *Majallat al-Majama' al-'Ilmi al'Arabi,* vol. IX (1929), p. 642, cited by Ma'oz, "Changes," p. 143; in Hebrew, see S. Lulqo, *Aliyatah Shel Mishpahat Farhi ri-Yridatah,* M.A. seminar paper, Hebrew University, Jerusalem, 1966, cited by Ma'oz, "Changes," p. 144.

51. Ibid.

52. Ibid.

53. According de Haas: "Scores of . . . fiendish acts are reported of him. His spirit of cruelty spread. The Nablusians, in 1785, began a persecution of the Samaritans which lasted twenty-five years. Djezzar for his part fiercely persecuted the Metawalis, and their small representation in the present population is probably due to his having beheaded most of those he took prisoner." *History,* p. 369.

54. Burckhardt, *Travels,* p. 340. For more detailed observations of El Djezzar, see Count C.F. Volney, *Travels Through Syria and Egypt in the Years 1783, 1784, 1785* (London, 1787), II. Sir Sidney Smith assisted Djezzar in 1799 against Napoleon: Conder, *Tent Work,* vol. 1, p. 195.

55. Volney, *Travels,* II, p. 449; Brown's *Travels,* pp. 366–370, as cited by de Haas, *History,* pp. 369–370.

56. Heinrich Graetz, *History of the Jews,* 5 vols. (New York, 1927), vol. V, pp. 459–460.

57. Ibid.

58. See Chapter 3; also see André Chouraqui, *Between East and West, A History of the Jews of North Africa,* trans. Michael M. Bernet (Philadelphia, 1968), pp. 45–46; David Littman, *Jews Under Muslim Rule in the Late Nineteenth Century,* reprinted from the Wiener Library Bulletin, 1975, vol. XXVIII, New Series Nos. 35/36 (London, 1975) p. 65; Ismar Elbogen, *A Century of Jewish Life* (Philadelphia, 1944), p. 76. According to the Esco Foundation for Palestine, *Palestine,* p. 520: "To the Arabs, the Jews as a group were *kuffar* (infidels) and often *frangi* (Europeans). Some hostility to them was always latent, as it was to all foreigners."

59. Moshe Ma'oz, *Ottoman Reform in Syria and Palestine* (Oxford, 1968), p. 10.

60. Dr. John Martin Augustus Scholz, *Travels* (London, 1821), p. 103, cited by de Haas, *History,* pp. 380–381.

61. Landes, "Palestine Before the Zionists," p. 50.

62. Ibid., p. 52.

63. James Finn, *Stirring Times or Record from Jerusalem Consular Chronicles from 1853–56* (London, 1878), pp. 118–119.

64. Landes, "Palestine," p. 52.

65. Viscount Palmerston to Viscount Ponsonby, F.O. 195/165 (No. 251), Foreign Office, 25 November 1840 (Enclosure 1), extract from a letter from Mr. Calman to Lord Ashley, dated 3 August 1840. Cited in Hyamson, *Consulate,* 2, pp. lxvii–lxx.
66. Burckhardt, *Travels,* pp. 317, 327.
67. Ibid., p. 328.
68. From disciples of the Vilna Gaon, from Abraham Yaari, *Irgot Eretz Yisrael* (Tel Aviv, 1943), p. 330, cited by Katz, *Battleground,* p. 99.

    According to Katz, "Surviving letters tell about the adventures of groups who came from Italy, Morocco, and Turkey. Other letters report on the steady stream of Hasidim, disciples of the Baal Shem-Tov, from Galicia and Lithuania, proceeding during the whole of the second half of the eighteenth century.

    "It is clear that by now the state of the country was exacting a higher toll in lives than could be replaced by immigrants."
69. Finn, *Stirring Times,* vol. 1, p. 127; see also *Despatches from Her Majesty's Consuls in the Levant,* p. 53.
70. Graetz, *History,* vol. V, pp. 633–634.
71. Ibid., p. 633.
72. De Haas, *History,* p. 393, citing Baron Geramb, *Pilgrimage to Jerusalem,* vol. 1, pp. 181–182, quoting a letter dated Jerusalem, July 16, 1834.
73. Ma'oz, "Changes," in *Studies,* pp. 147–148; also see K. Schulman, *Sefer Ariel* (Vilna, 1856), p. 76; S.N. Spyridon, ed., *Annals of Palestine* (1821–1841), p. 100.
74. Y. Ben-Zvi, "Me'ora'ot Tzfat," *Sefunot,* Jerusalem, 5723, vol. VII, pp. 277ff; see also Yusuf al-Dibs, *Ta'rikh Suriyya* (Beirut, 1893–1905), vol. VIII, p. 649. Cited by Ma'oz, ibid., pp. 147–148.
75. Viscount Palmerston to Viscount Ponsonby, F.O. 195/165 (No. 251), Foreign Office, 25 November 1840 (Enclosure 1 to No. 23b.), extract of a letter from Mr. Calman to Lord Ashley, dated August 3, 1840. In Hyamson, *Consulate,* 2. pp. lxix–lxx.
76. Albert Hourani, *Arabic Thought in the Liberal Age 1798–1939* (London, 1962), p. 40; also see Ma'oz, "Changes," in *Studies,* p. 147, and *Ottoman Reform.*
77. Ma'oz, *Ottoman Reform,* pp. 189–190.
78. See Ma'oz, "Changes," in *Studies,* pp. 148–150.
79. Katz, *Battleground,* p. 94.
80. Joseph Amzalek to W.T. Young, Jerusalem, 25 March 1839, F.O. 78/368, in Hyamson, *Consulate,* 1, p. 20.
81. Colonel Campbell to W.T. Young, Alexandria, 22 June 1839, F.O. 78/368, (Enclosure 7 to No. 10), in ibid., p. 22.
82. Wm. T. Young to Colonel Patrick Campbell, Jerusalem, 25 May 1839, F.O. 78/368, in ibid., p. 8.
83. A.W. Kinglake, *Eothen* (London: T. Nelson & Sons, Ltd., 1844), pp. 261–265.
84. For more detailed information about the blood libel see Chapters 3 and 4.
85. Wm. T. Young to Viscount Palmerston, Jerusalem, 25 May 1839, F.O. 78/368 (No. 13), abstract, in Hyamson, *Consulate,* 1, pp. 6–7.
86. Michaud and Poujoulat, *Correspondence d'Orient, 1830–1831* (Brussels, 1841), vol. VI, pp. 73–74.
87. Ma'oz, "Changes," in *Studies,* pp. 147–148.
88. Neville Mandel, *Arabs and Zionism Before World War I* (Berkeley, 1976), p. 33. Mandel reports that the Christians as *dhimmi,* along with Jews, were competing in Palestine as in other Muslim countries (see Chapter 3 above, especially in Syria) for

the "goodwill and favours of the dominant Muslim majority." In addition, the Arab Christians were united in their "deep religious prejudice against Jews."

Also see information about the slanders in 1849 and 1870 in Jerusalem: H.Z. Hirschberg, "Blood Libels . . . at the end of the Nineteenth Century," in *Mahanayim* No. 110, IDF, Tel Aviv (Hebrew).

89. Ismar Elbogen, *A Century of Jewish Life,* p. 76.

90. W.T. Young to Viscount Canning, Highbury Grange, Nr. London, 13 January 1842, F.O. 78/501, (Enclosure 2 to No. 29), cited in Hyamson, *Consulate,* 1, p. 44.

91. Report submitted to British Consul, Viscount Palmerston to Viscount Ponsonby Foreign Office, 25 November 1840, F.O. 195/165 (No. 251), (Enclosure 1 to No. 23b), extract of a letter from Mr. Calman to Lord Ashley, dated August 3, 1940, ibid., 2, p. lxvii.

92. Viscount Palmerston to Viscount Ponsonby, APPd. Victoria R. F.O. 78/427 (No. 33), Foreign Office, 17 February 1841, in ibid., 1, p. 38.

93. W.T. Young to Col. Hugh Rose, Beirout, dated Jerusalem, 24 May 1841, F.O. 78/444 (abstract), ibid., 1, pp. 40–41.

94. Viscount Palmerston to Viscount Posonby, Foreign Office, 17 February 1841, F.O. 78/427 (No. 33), ibid., 1, pp. 37–38.

95. Palmerston to Chekib Pasha, of 9 August 1841, F.O. 78/463, F.S. Rodkey, "Lord Palmerston's Policy for the Regeneration of Turkey, 1839–41," *Royal Historical Society Transactions,* Fourth Series, vol. XII, p. 179.

96. Palmerston to Ponsonby, 17 February 1841, F.O. 78/427 (No. 33), Hyamson, *Consulate,* vol. 1, p. 38.

97. Hyamson, *Consulate,* 1, p. 134, n.1.

98. James Finn to Lord Palmerston, Jerusalem, 13 March 1847, F.O. 78/705 (No. 12), ibid., 1, p. 96. Responding to Consul Finn's memo: "Viscount Palmerston has had under his consideration your Despatch No. 12 of the 13th of March last detailing the circumstances of an attempt recently made at Jerusalem, to revive the calumnious accusation against the Jewish people, that they use Christian blood in their Paschal Rites; —And I am directed by His Lordship to express to you his entire approval of your conduct as reported in that Despatch.

"I am further directed by His Lordship to instruct you to take an opportunity to convey to Mehemed Pacha the thanks of Her Majesty's Government for the decisive and liberal manner in which His Excellency executed the commands of the Sultan in putting down this fanatical attempt to revive such unjust accusations against the Jewish People." John Bidwell to James Finn, Foreign Office, 19 May 1847, F.O. 78/705 (No. 2), ibid., 1, p. 103.

99. Israel Ben Yosef Binyamin, *Sefer Masa'ei Israel* (Lyck, 1859), pp. 8–9. Cited by Ma'oz, *Studies,* p. 154.

100. W.T. Young to Viscount Palmerston, Jerusalem, 25 May 1839, F.O. 78/368 (No. 13), in *Consulate,* 1, pp. 6–7.

101. Ma'oz, *Ottoman Reform,* p. 120, quoting Consul James Finn; F.O. 78/705, Finn to Palmerston, No. 7, Jerusalem, 5 February 1847; F.O. 78/755, Finn to Palmerston, No. 22, Jerusalem, 17 July 1848.

102. James Finn to Viscount Palmerston, Jerusalem, 2 May 1848, F.O. 78/755 (No. 19), *Consulate,* 1, p. 106.

103. James Finn to Sir Stratford Canning, Jerusalem, 1 March 1849, F.O. 78/803 (No. 8), abstract, ibid., 1, p. 110.

104. James Finn to Viscount Palmerston, Jerusalem, 27 September 1850, F.O. 78/839 (No. 20), abstract, ibid., 1, 168–169. Hyamson adds: "Abderrahhman el Amer, a chief of the neighbouring village of Dura, for many years terrorized the inhabitants of Hebron, Jews as well as others, of which town he was for periods *de facto* ruler at times, despite the Government. He first appeared there on the expulsion of the Egyptians in 1840 when, murdering the local Egyptian governor in the street, he proclaimed the Sultan of Turkey, and appointed himself governor of the town." Also see James Finn, *Stirring Times,* 1, pp. 236 et seq., 250 et seq., and 392 et seq.; and vol. 2, pp. 33 et seq.

105. James Finn to Sir Stratford Canning, Jerusalem, 15 July 1851, F.O. 78/874 (No. 10), ibid., 1, pp. 171–172.

106. James Finn to Viscount Palmerston, Jerusalem, 29 December 1851, F.O. 78/874 (Consular No. 21), ibid., 1, pp. 183–184.

107. James Finn to Viscount Palmerston, Jerusalem, 29 December 1851, F.O. 78/874 (Political No. 10), ibid., 1, p. 185.

108. James Finn to the Earl of Malmesbury, Jerusalem, 29 May 1852, F.O. 195/369 (Political No. 2), ibid., 1, p. 198–202.

109. James Finn to the Earl of Malmesbury, Jerusalem, 18 November 1852, F.O. 78/913 (Political No. 13), abstract, ibid., 1, p. 211.

110. James Finn to the Earl of Clarendon, Jerusalem, 19 July 1853, F.O. 78/962 (No. 9), ibid., 1, p. 215.

111. James Finn to Lord Stratford de Redcliffe, Jerusalem, 13 October 1853, F.O. 195/369 (No. 32), ibid., 1, p. 216.

112. James Finn to the Earl of Clarendon, 28 December 1853, F.O. 78/963 (Political No. 33), ibid., 1, pp. 218–219.

113. James Finn to the Earl of Malmesbury, Jerusalem, 8 July 1858, F.O. 78/1383 (Political No. 12), ibid., 1, p. 260.

114. James Finn to the Earl of Malmesbury, Jerusalem, 11 November 1858, F.O. 78/1383 (Political No. 34), ibid., 1, p. 261.

115. Thomas B. Sandwith, Vice Consul, Caiffa, to Noel Temple Moore, Caiffa, 20 May 1863, F.O. 78/1775 (No. 18), ibid., 2, pp. 311–312.

116. Noel Temple Moore to the Honorable E.M. Erskine, Jerusalem, 3 March 1864, F.O. 195/808 (No. 6), ibid., 2, pp. 330–331.

117. Earl Russell to Noel Temple Moore, Foreign Office, 11 June 1864, F.O. 78/1816 (No. 1), ibid., 2, p. 332.

118. Ibrahim Abu Lughod, address at Palestine Human Rights Committee Meeting, November 1980, Chicago.

119. *Palestine Royal Commission Report,* p. 144.

120. Ibid., p. 131.

10. The Population Under the Turks: Mid-Nineteenth Century to 1918

1. "The process of disintegration of the feudal mode of production in Syria evolved under the conditions of a growing influx of foreign capital and of the subjection of the country's economic development to the interests of foreign capital. The legacy of this process was the ruin of industry and the impoverishment of the peasant economy.

   "The growing feudal oppression, along with exploitation by foreign capital, delayed the development of new relations of production. Feudal forms of exploitation were preserved under these conditions and this led to an even greater aggravation of economic and political contradictions and to an intensification of the class struggle." I.M. Smilianskaya, "The Disintegration of Feudal Relations in Syria and Lebanon in the Middle of the Nineteenth Century" *Peredneaziatskii Etnograficheskii Sbornik* (Moscow), I (1958), 156–179, from Charles Issawii, ed., *The Economic History of the Middle East 1800–1914* (Chicago: The University of Chicago Press, 1966), p. 247; also see Hope Simpson, *Report on Immigration, Land Settlement and Development,* Command Paper #3686, London, 1930, p. 90; also see Chapter 8.

2. "Palestine in the early 19th century . . . did not appear as a well-defined geographical or administrative unit. Only the area around Jerusalem, including some of the adjacent biblical places, was defined as Palestine or Filistin . . ." Kemal Karpat, *Research Prospectus on the Demographic History of Palestine,* submitted to the Institute for Mediterranean Affairs (New York, 1972), p. 2; in the United States recommendation at the 1919 Peace Conference, it was stated "(1) That there be established a separate State of Palestine." Outline of Tentative Report and Recommendations prepared by the Intelligence Section for President Wilson and the Plenipotentiaries, January 21, 1919.

3. Ernst Frankenstein, *Justice for My People* (London: Nicholson and Watson, 1943), p. 127.

4. Viscount Palmerston to Viscount Ponsonby, Foreign Office, 25 November 1840, FO 195/165 (No. 251), (Enclosure 2), extract of a letter from Lord Ashley to Palmerston, dated 25 September 1840, cited in Albert Hyamson, ed., *The British Consulate in Jerusalem 1838–1914,* 2 vols. (London, 1939–1941), 2, p. lxxii, Introduction.

5. Jacob de Haas, *History of Palestine, The Last Two Thousand Years* (New York, The MacMillan Co., 1934), p. 419.

6. Frankenstein, *Justice,* p. 127.

7. W.F. Lynch, *Narrative of the United States Expedition to the River Jordan and the Dead Sea* (London, 1849), p. 446.

8. James Finn to the Earl of Clarendon, 16 September 1857, FO 78/1294 (Political No. 37), (Enclosure 1), from Elizabeth A. Finn, wife of the British Consul, Jerusalem, July 1857, cited in Hyamson, *Consulate,* 1, p. 254.

9. James Finn to the Earl of Clarendon, Jerusalem, 1 January 1858, FO 78/1383 (Political No. 1), cited in Hyamson, *Consulate,* 1, p. 257.

10. The Algerians had been settled in Damascus by the Moor leader Abd-el-Kader in 1852 after his efforts at Arab independence in Morocco against the Moroccans and then the French were defeated. De Haas, *History,* p. 425.

11. From James Finn to Sir Bulwer, Jerusalem, 19 June 1860, in *Papers Relating to the Disturbances in Syria,* no. 2, June 1860, p. 35.

12. From Consul James Finn to the Earl of Malmesbury, Jerusalem, 1 January 1859, in *Despatches from Her Majesty's Consuls in the Levant, Respecting Past or Apprehended Disturbances in Syria: 1858–1860,* p. 64.

13. From letter sent by Peter Meshulam to Consul James Finn, Haifa, 29 June 1860, *Further Papers Relating to Disturbances in Syria, June 1960,* presented to the House of Commons . . . July 30, 1860, p. 52.

14. See Chapter 8 chronology.

15. From Consul James Finn to Lord J. Russell, Jerusalem, 2 July 1860, *Further Papers,* p. 18.

16. Norman N. Lewis, "The Frontier of Settlement, 1800–1950," in Issawi, ed., *Economic History*, p. 266.

17. See complete study of observations by C.G. Smith, "The Geography and Natural Resources of Palestine as Seen by British Writers in the Nineteenth and Early Twentieth Centuries," in Moshe Ma'oz, ed., *Studies on Palestine During the Ottoman Period* (Jerusalem, 1975), pp. 87–100.

18. George Adam Smith, *The Historical Geography of the Holy Land* (London: Hodder and Stoughton, 1894), pp. 84–85.

19. C. Conder, *Palestine* (London, 1889), pp. 212–213. See also Conder, *Tent Work in Palestine*, 2 vols. (London, 1878), vol. 2, especially Chapter XII, "The Fertility of Palestine."

20. De Haas, *History*, p. 407.

21. "As late as 1877 Colonel C.R. Conder declared the population insufficient, and suggested the land could support ten times the total of its then population." Ibid., citing Conder, *Tent Work in Palestine*, p. 368.

22. Outside the gates of Jerusalem "we saw, indeed, no living object, heard no living sound, we found the same void, the same silence . . . as we should have expected before the entombed gates of Pompeii or Herculaneum." Alphonse de Lamartine, *A Pilgrimage to the Holy Land*, trans. from French (New York, 1948), I, p. 268; "a complete eternal silence reigns in the town, on the highways, in the country . . . the tomb of a whole people," Lamartine, I, pp. 308–309, as cited by de Haas, *History*, p. 407.

23. According to Dean Stanley, "Palestine . . . is an island in a desert waste . . . also an island in the midst of pirates. The Bedouins are the corsairs of the wilderness." And Jerusalem: "A city of ruins. Here and there a regular street, or a well-built European house emerges from the general chaos, but the general appearance is that of a city which has been burnt down in some great conflagration." Dean Stanley, "Sinai and Palestine," as cited by de Haas, *History*, p. 407.

24. De Haas, *History*, p. 407, citing C. Conder, *Tent Work*, p. 327.

25. "There was . . . no interest in the contemporary inhabitants. Not a kind word was written about them." De Haas, *History*, p. 407.

    "Conder was one of the few, if not the solitary exception. He called attention to the fact that the native Muslim population was generally considered 'fit for the fate of the Red Indian and the Australian, as savages who must disappear before the advance of a superior race.' " De Haas, *History*, p. 407.

26. Consul James Finn to the Earl of Malmesbury, Jerusalem, 1 January 1859, *Past or Apprehended Disturbances*, p. 61.

27. British Consul James Finn to Earl of Clarendon, Jerusalem, 1 January 1858, FO 78/1383 (Political No. 1), in Hyamson, *Consulate*, 1, p. 257.

28. British Consul James Finn to Lord John Russell, Jerusalem, 4 January 1860, F.O. 78/1521 (Political No. 1), in *Past or Apprehended Disturbances*, p. 89; also extract in Hyamson, *Consulate*, 1, p. 268.

29. British Consul James Finn to Earl of Clarendon, Jerusalem, 15 September 1857, F.O. 78/1294 (Political No. 36), in Hyamson, 1, *Consulate*, p. 249.

30. From letter of March 19, 1933, by the Department of Development, Public Record Office, PRO FO 371/17204/33.

31. British Consul James Finn to Viscount Palmerston, Jerusalem, 7 November 1851, FO 78/874 (No. 20), in Hyamson, *Consulate*, 1, p. 179.

". . . in Safed and Tiberias, if not in Jerusalem, they form the majority of the inhabitants . . . in them lies a germ of development for future time, and a character different from that of the ordinary population of Palestine.

"The Jews are almost the only artisans—and it is remarkable that the glaziers, blacksmiths, watchmakers, tailors, shoemakers, bookbinders, &c are almost exclusively Jews."

32. British Consul James Finn to Earl of Clarendon, Jerusalem, 1 January 1858, FO 78/1383 (Political No. 1), in Hyamson, *Consulate,* 1, p. 257. "Their number amounts to 8,000, almost half of the city, and the majority of them are of the Spanish-speaking class, called Sephardem, and are generally Turkish subjects."

    Also see Moshe Ma'oz, *Ottoman Reform in Syria and Palestine* (Oxford, 1968), p. 208; see comparative figures compiled by Itzhak Ben-Zvi, *Israel Under Ottoman Rule—Four Centuries of History* (Jerusalem: Yad Itzhak Ben-Zvi, 1955), p. 365ff.

33. British Consul James Finn to the Earl of Clarendon, Jerusalem, 17 January 1856, FO 78/1217 (Political No. 1), in Hyamson, *Consulate,* 1, p. 239.

34. Letter to Jas. Graham, Esq., Jerusalem, July 1857, FO 78/1294, in Hyamson, *Consulate,* 1, p. 255. "I would particularly draw attention to the fact that the Sultan of Turkey by the Laws of the Empire gives every encouragement to the cultivation of land and the planting of trees."

35. Martin Gilbert, *Exile and Return: The Struggle for a Jewish Homeland* (Philadelphia and New York: J.B. Lippincott, 1978), pp. 28–30. "Montefiore [bought] agricultural land both at Jaffa and Jerusalem, and later extend[ed] his land-purchases to the Galilee, at Tiberias and Safed." Also see Ma'oz, *Ottoman Reform,* pp. 207–208.

36. Ma'oz, *Reform,* p. 207; also see Finn to Clarendon, Jerusalem, December 28, 1853, FO 78/963 (No. 33); Finn to Malmesbury, Jerusalem, January 1, 1859, FO 78/1454 (No. 1); Finn to Russell, Jerusalem, January 4, 1869, FO 78/1521 (No. 1); also see Braver in *Zion,* v (1939–1940), p. 169; Vinreb in *Zion,* iii (1938), p. 76. Cited in Ma'oz, *Reform,* p. 207.

37. Hyamson, *Consulate,* 1, p. xlvii, Introduction.

"Young, in his report on the condition of the Jews in his district which was called for on his appointment, estimated the Jewish population, Sephardim and Ashkenazim, in 1839 at 9690 souls, of whom 5500 were to be found in Jerusalem and 1500 in Safed. There were already then about 400 Jews living in the villages of Palestine."

    By 1864, "The population of the City of Jerusalem is computed at 18,000 of whom about 5000 are Moslems, 8000 to 9000 Jews, and the rest Christians of various denominations." From "Report on the Trade and Commerce of Jerusalem in the Year 1864," March, 1865, FO 195/808, in Hyamson, *Consulate,* 2, p. 336.

38. Sir George Gawler, *Jewish Chronicle,* August 16, 1860, cited in Gilbert, *Exile,* p. 28; see Chapter 9.

39. Ma'oz, *Reform,* p. 207.

40. Finn to Canning, FO 78/874 (No. 10), Enclosure in Finn to Palmerston, Jerusalem, 24 July 1851 (No. 6); *Jewish Intelligence,* xxii, No. 260, cited in FO 78/1217 (No. 1), Finn to Clarendon, Jerusalem, January 7, 1856; see also FO 78/2068, Moore to Palmerston, Beirut, 1 December 1849, FO 78/2068 (No. 45), in Hyamson, *Consulate,* 1, p. 156; H.H. Jessup, *Fifty-Three Years in Syria,* 2 vols. (New York, 1910), 1, p. 269; M. Raysher, *Sefer sh'arey Yerushalayim* (Lemberg, 1866), p. 18, 28; G. Williams, *The Holy City* (London, 1845), p. 432. All cited in Ma'oz, *Reform,* p. 207, n. 3.

41. Itzhak Ben-Zvi, *Eretz-Israel* (Poalei Tsion Palestine, 1918), p. 195.

42. A.J. Sussnitzki, "Zur Gliederung wirtschaftslicher Arbeit nach Nationalitäten in der Turkei," *Archiv für Wirtschaftsforschung im Orient*, II, 1917, pp. 382–407, in Issawi, *Economic History*, p. 116. According to Sussnitzki, "The Jews formerly played a very different part in agriculture. On the ancient significance of the Jews as the most important factors in Mesopotamia, see Krauss, 'Die Juden Mesopotamiens in Handel und Wandel,' Oe. M.O., 1916, nos. 1–6, pp. 71, 84; on the decline of Jewish agriculture, ibid., p. 87." From Issawi, ed., *Economic History*, p. 117.

43. "You are aware that I have for some years had at heart the distressed and degraded condition of the Jewish people in this country who are generally speaking without employment and in the bondage of pauperism," British Consul James Finn to the Earl of Clarendon, Jerusalem, July 1857, FO 78/1294, in Hyamson, *Consulate*, 1, p. 253.

44. See Ben Zion Gat, *Jewish Community in Palestine Between 1840–1881* (Jerusalem: Ben Zvi Institute, 1964); Mordechai Eliav, *Love of Zion and the Men of Hod; German Jewry and the Settlement of Eretz-Israel in the 19th Century* (Tel Aviv: Hakibbutz Hameuchad, 1970).

45. Consul Finn to the Earl of Malmesbury, Jerusalem, 1 January 1859, in *Past or Apprehended Disturbances*, p. 63.

46. Simon Schama, *Two Rothschilds and the Land of Israel* (New York: Alfred A. Knopf, 1978), pp. 161, 162–165.

47. Ibid., p. 167.

48. Ibid., p. 61ff.

49. Ibid., p. 133.

50. C.G. Smith, "Geography and Natural Resources in Palestine," in Ma'oz, ed., *Studies*, p. 93.

51. Schama, *Two Rothschilds*, p. 158.

52. Ibid., pp. 133–134, citing PICA 11/59.

53. *Ketavim*, vol. III, December 18, 1889, p. 66. From letter written by Y. Grazavsky to Y. Eisenstadt.

54. Simon Schama, *Two Rothschilds*, p. 117.

55. Ibid., p. 156, quoting Emile Meyerson report, *La Colonisation Juivre en Palestine*, December 13, 1914, p. 4.

56. Sir John Hope Simpson, *Palestine: Report on Immigration, Land Settlement and Development*, Command Paper 3686 of 1930, London, pp. 146–147.

57. *Palestine Royal Commission Report*, Command #5479, London, 1937, p. 125.

58. Mordechai Abir, "Local Leadership and Early Reform in Palestine, 1800–1834," published in Ma'oz, ed., *Studies*, pp. 304–305.

59. Roderique H. Davison, *Reform in the Ottoman Empire, 1856–1876* (Princeton, 1963), pp. 99, 141; see Elie Kedourie, "Islam Today," in Bernard Lewis, ed., *Islam and the Arab World*, pp. 321–336, particularly pp. 330–331; also see Albert Hourani, *Syria and Lebanon: A Political Essay* (London: Oxford University Press, 1946), pp. 29–32; A. Granott, *The Land System in Palestine, History and Stucture* (London, 1952), p. 81; Neville Mandel, *Arabs and Zionism Before World War I* (Berkeley, 1976), pp. xxi, xxii, introduction; Abir, "Local Leadership and Early Reforms in Palestine, 1800–1834," in Ma'oz, ed., *Studies*, pp. 284–310.

60. Abd-el-Hadi family of Nablus and Jenin, 60,000 dunams; El-Husseini family of Jerusalem and Jericho, 50,000 dunams; Taji (al Farouki) family of Ramle, 50,000 dunams (4 dunams = 1 acre). Granott, *Land System*, p. 81.

61. Ibid., p. 83; see also Mandel, *Arabs and Zionism,* p. xxii; *Palestine, A Study of Jewish, Arab and British Policies,* Esco Foundation for Palestine, 2 vols. (New Haven: Yale University Press, 1947), 1, p. 466.

62. Granott, *Land System,* p. 83.

63. Moshe Aumann, "Land Ownership in Palestine 1880–1948," from Michael Curtis et al., eds., *The Palestinians, People, History, Politics* (New Brunswick, N.J.: Transaction Books, 1975), p. 24.

64. Granott, *Land System,* p. 40.

65. Mandel, *Arabs and Zionism,* p. xxiii.

66. Ma'oz, *Reform,* pp. 79–80, 145, 160–161; also see Mandel, *Arabs and Zionism,* p. 2.

67. According to Neville Mandel, *Arabs and Zionism,* p. 18, and reports of the period, Mehmed Sherif Rauf Pasa, who governed in 1877–1889, "tried earnestly to enforce the entry restrictions against Jews, and he made difficulties for foreign Jews already residing in his Mutasarriflik [district of Jerusalem, where most Jewish development was taking place] who wished to become Ottoman subjects"; see also David Farhi, "Documents on the Attitude of the Ottoman Government Towards the Jewish Settlement in Palestine After the Revolution of the Young Turks, 1908–1909" in Ma'oz, ed., *Studies,* pp. 190–210.

68. De Haas, *History,* pp. 439–443.

69. *U.S. Consular Reports 1880,* II, pp. 67–68, cited by de Haas, *History,* p. 437.

70. "Exports fell off 50% and the imports 15% at Jaffa . . . influenza so serious that business was suspended for a time." De Haas, History, p. 437.

71. *U.S. Consular Reports,* October 1890, IV, p. 683, cited in ibid.

72. *U.S. Consular Reports,* October 1881, IV, p. 513, cited in ibid.

73. Moza, near Jerusalem, marked the beginning of Jewish agricultural endeavor in Palestine in 1873. In 1878, Petach Tikvah was founded northwest of Jaffa, and Rishon l'Tsion was established in 1882 in the same general area. Because the other two earlier ventures proved to be premature, they foundered; hence, "Jewish agricultural colonization" is considered to have begun with Rishon l'Tsion in 1882, although Petach Tikvah also began anew in the same year. De Haas, *History,* p. 439.

74. For detailed data on Ottoman restrictions against Jewish immigration and related factors, see David Farhi, "Documents," in Ma'oz, *Studies,* pp. 190–210; Mandel, *Arabs and Zionism;* Schama, *Two Rothschilds;* de Haas, *History;* Alter Druyanow, *Ketavim,* vol. III, 1889; Esco, *Palestine.*

75. De Haas, *History,* p. 440. See also Farhi, "Documents," in *Studies,* pp. 190–191.

76. Mandel, *Arabs and Zionism,* pp. 2–3.

77. Ibid. When foreign governments attempted to investigate the restrictions, the Turkish ruling powers gave as one reason that "Jewish immigrants were a threat to public order and hygiene in the city." Mandel, *Arabs and Zionism,* p. 3; PRO FO 195/1581 (No. 9), March 5, 1887, N.T. Moore (Jerusalem) to Sir W.A. White (Constantinople); cf. State Department, *Papers,* 1888, ii, 1559–60, no. 57 (28.1.1888), O.S. Straus (Constantinople) to Secretary of State Bayard; and ISA (T) no. 47 (15.12.1887), Ministry of Internal Affairs (SP) to Mutasarrif (Jerusalem).

78. Mandel, *Arabs and Zionism,* pp. 3–4ff. Mandel attributes more "nationalism" to the Arabs than does T.E. Lawrence; compare with Lawrence, *Seven Pillars of Wisdom* (London: Jonathan Cape, Ltd., 1934); David Lloyd George, *The Truth About the Peace Treaties* (London: Victor Gallancz, Ltd., 1938).

79. De Haas, *History,* p. 441.
80. David Vital, *Origins of Zionism* (Oxford: Clarendon Press, 1975), p. 182; also see Mandel, "Turks, Arabs, and Jewish Immigration into Palestine, 1882–1914," in A. Hourani, ed., *St. Antony's Papers,* no. XXVII, Middle Eastern Affairs, Number IV (Oxford, 1965), p. 49.
81. From *Palestine Exploration Fund, Quarterly,* January 1888, C. Schick, October 26, 1887, entry, "Jerusalem"; see FO 195/1581 (No. 9), Moore to White, Jerusalem, March 5, 1887; also see *Ketavim,* vol. III, 1889, Druyanow, ed.; Schama, *Two Rothschilds.*
82. *U.S. Consular Reports,* November 1892, XXXI, p. 307.
83. Farhi, "Documents," in Ma'oz, *Studies,* p. 191. Farhi cites Mandel, "Turks, Arabs and Jewish Immigration into Palestine, 1882–1914," in A. Hourani (ed.), *Middle Eastern Affairs,* no. IV, *St. Antony's Papers,* no. XXVII, Oxford, 1965, pp. 77–108; Y. Ro'i, "Ha-'Emda ha-Tziyonit Klapei ha-'Aravim, 1898–1914" [The Zionist Attitude towards the Arabs], *Keshet,* XLII (Winter 1969), pp. 153–159; Porath, "The Political Awakening of the Palestinian Arabs and Their Leadership Towards the End of the Ottoman Period," in Ma'oz, *Studies;* Y. Yehoshua, "Tel-Aviv as Seen by the Arabic Press During the First Years of its Existence (1909–1914)," *Hamizrah Hehadash,* vol. XIX, no. 3 (1969), pp. 218–222 (in Hebrew). Farhi dates the first decree "prohibiting Jews from Russia, Rumania and Bulgaria from settling in Palestine" at 1882. Neville Mandel traces the Ottoman government's "ostensible response to the Anglo German group"—a group of "solid gentlemen . . . who in 1881" proposed to the Porte that Jews be settled "along a railroad which they wanted to build from Smyrna to Baghdad." According to Mandel, the Turkish restrictions were announced in 1881. *Arabs and Zionism,* p. 2.
84. *Havazzelet* (The Rose), XII, 41 (September 1, 1882); cf. *Levant Herald,* iii, 444 (November 24, 1881), cited in Mandel, *Arabs and Zionism,* p. 2.
85. Schama, *Two Rothschilds,* p. 160.
86. E.C. Blech to Sir Nicholas O'Conor, Jerusalem, 16 November 1907, FO 371/356 No. 40321 (No. 62), cited by Farhi, "Documents," in Ma'oz, *Studies,* p. 190. According to Farhi, "This quotation appears in a detailed report on the Zionist movement, in which Blech tries to prove that only the 'fanatics' believe in the feasibility of building a Jewish state. It is interesting to note that a copy of the report was forwarded to Lord Rothschild, but the above quoted words were omitted." See entire correspondence in Hyamson, *Consulate,* 2, pp. 569–571.
87. Vital, *The Origins of Zionism,* p. 196.
88. The other four "Biluim" stayed in Constantinople, where "they constituted themselves as the Central Bilu Constantinople Bureau and continued the efforts towards obtaining free land from the Government." Shulamit Laskov, *Biluim* (Hebrew with English abstract, p. viff) (Jerusalem: Publishing House of the World Zionist Organizations, 1979) p. vi. See Laskov's study for detailed history of the pioneer movement, an example which may mirror in microcosm the struggles of the Jewish developments in Jewish-settled Palestine.
89. See S. Laskov, *Biluim,* p. vi; Gilbert, *Exile,* p. 39.
90. Laskov, *Biluim,* pp. vi, vii.
91. Mandel, *Arabs and Zionism,* p. 5.
92. Ibid.
93. Laskov, *Biluim,* p. vii.

94. Ibid.
95. Ibid., pp. vii, viii.
96. Ibid., p. vii.
97. ". . . as many as one in two of them departed again in view of the difficult local conditions (besides the efforts of the authorities)." Mandel, *Arabs and Zionism,* p. 29.
98. Ibid., p. 7; see *Havazzelet,* xiv, 23 (2.5.1884).
99. Vital, *Origins,* p. 182; Lilienblum to Ussiskin, June 1882, *Mi-yamim rishonim,* ii, pp. 136–137; also see Greenberg to Mohilever, October 16, 1891 (O.S.), CZA, A9/63/1.
100. *Encyclopaedia Judaica,* Cecil Roth, Geoffrey Wigoder, eds. (Jerusalem: Macmillan and Co., 1972), vol. 8, col. 1248.
101. Vital, *Origins,* p. 183. According to Vital, Jewish development was, however, "moderately reinforced: two major, and several minor settlements had been established. In 1890 30,000 dunams (7,500 acres) of land were bought half-way between Haifa and Jaffa, the biggest single acquisition yet. A further 10,000 dunams were brought the same year just south of Rishon le-Zion. Hadera was built on the first tract, Rehovot on the second. Smaller points of settlement followed: Mishmar ha-Yarden (1890), Ein Zeitim (1891), Benei Yehuda (1891), Meir Shefeya (1891), Moza (1894), Hartuv (1895), Be'er Tuvia (1896), Metula (1896), Mahanayim (1899), and the Sejera training farm (1899). Most of these were offshoots of existing settlements, two were backed by Hibbat Zion, two by Baron Edmond de Rothschild, one was established independently by Jews from Bulgaria" (pp. 182–183).
102. In southern Transjordan, for example, the populations had diminished. Kerak, which had 8,000 inhabitants in 1872, had only 2,000 in 1895. Christian Ginsburg, *Report on Exploration of Moab* (Brighton, England, 1872); Vital Cuinet, *Syrie, Liban et Palestine, Géographie administrative, statistique, descriptive et raisonée* (Paris, 1896); de Haas, *History,* p. 431; also the 15,000 inhabitant Circassian (Persian) settlement that had arrived after the Russo-Turkish War had shrunk, to 5,000.
103. John Dickson to Edmund Fane, Jerusalem, 16 July 1891, FO 195/1727 (No. 25), in Hyamson, *Consulate,* 2, p. 461.
104. Ibrahim Hakki, The Governor of Jerusalem to Mr. Consul Dickson, June 24/July 6, 1891, FO 195/1727, in Hyamson, *Consulate,* p. 462.
105. "That much of the land was held by the Crown merely added to the confusion and difficulty. In 1892 Jaffa landowners [Jewish], on whose property orange plantations had been established, were notified by Constantinople they would have to surrender all their freehold deeds, and in exchange receive documents showing that they were tenants of crown lands. Someone had discovered that this area was made part of the imperial domain in 1517. The case was not fought in any court, but wholesale bribery was employed to prevent the imperial order being carried out." De Haas, *History,* pp. 441–442; also see United States Consular Reports, November 1892, XLI, p. 309.
106. Vital, *Origins,* p. 88; according to Vital, "Yemenite Jews" worked their way to "Erez-Israel" from the end of the fifteenth century, "at least."
107. De Haas, *History,* p. 448.
108. See Chapters 3 and 5.
109. Extract of letter from the Reverend A. Ben Oliel of the "Presbyterian Alliance Mission," Jerusalem, February 11, 1892, FO 195/1765, in Hyamson, *Consulate,* 2, pp. 478–480.
110. Esco, *Palestine,* p. 520ff; see also David Landes, "Palestine Before the Zionists,"

Commentary, February 1976; Great Britain Foreign Office, *Syria and Palestine, Peace Handbook,* No. 60 (London, 1920).

111. According to British Consul Dickson, the Turkish authorities were given instructions "to apply the restrictions to all Jews without distinction of nationality." Dickson to Clare-Ford, Jerusalem, April 29, 1893, FO 195/1806 (No. 19), in Hyamson, *Consulate,* 2, p. 485.

112. Enclosure to FO 195/1806, Jerusalem, March 22, 1893. Petition to "Her Brittanic Majesty's Consul, Jerusalem" from Simeon S.E. Judah, in ibid.

113. Pierre Loti, *Jerusalem* (Paris, 1895), pp. 128, 183–184, cited by Landes, "Palestine."

114. Despatch No. 56 from Consular Agent Amzalak, Jaffa, August 27. Enclosure to Dickson to Currie, Jerusalem, September 16, 1895, FO 195/1895, Hyamson, *Consulate,* 2, p. 501.

115. John Dickson to Sir Philip Currie, Jerusalem, September 16, 1895, FO 195/1895; for additional Consular Reports, see Hyamson, *Consulate.*

116. Esco, *Palestine,* pp. 521–522.

117. Mandel, *Arabs and Zionism,* p. 22.

118. Theodor Herzl, *Der Judenstaat* (Vienna, 1896).

119. See Chapter 5.

120. See Albert Hyamson, *Consulate,* 1, p. liii, introduction; de Haas, *History,* p. 442; Farhi, "Documents," in Ma'oz, ed., *Studies,* pp. 190–210.

121. Vital Cuinet, *Syrie, Liban et Palestine, Géographie administrative, statistique, descriptive et raisonnée* (Paris, 1896), pp. 583–584. Cuinet estimated the area as roughly 22,000 square kilometers.

122. Hyamson, *Consulate,* 1, p. liii.

123. *U.S. Consular Reports,* 1898, LVIII, p. 476.

124. Hyamson, *Consulate,* for more detailed reports.

125. Mandel, *Arabs and Zionism,* p. 8; also see Granott, *Land System,* Ch. V.

126. See John Dickson to Sir Francis Clare-Ford, Jerusalem, December 30, 1892, FO 195/1765 (No. 35) and Enclosure to same dated December 22, 1892, in Hyamson, *Consulate,* 2, p. 481; also see Mandel, *Arabs and Zionism,* p. 8.

127. Mandel, *Arabs and Zionism,* p. 25; see Central Zionist Archives, W/125/1 (May, 1905), Levontin to Wolffsohn. Mandel traces Ottoman restrictions and their inconsistencies in execution; see Chapter 1, "Ottoman Policy and Practice: 1881–1908," pp. 1–31.

128. De Haas, *History,* p. 442.

129. Israel State Archives (T), No. 34, September 8, 1904, Minister of the Interior to Mutasarrif of Jerusalem Resid Bey, cited by Mandel, *Arabs and Zionism,* p. 26.

130. The late historian David Farhi recalled: "In an interview which I had in Istanbul (21.1.1965) with Dr. Sami Gunzberg, the Sultan's dentist, who seems to have played a certain role in introducing Herzl to the Sultan, he maintained that, 'The Sultan was inclined to help Herzl, but Herzl associated with "undesirable people." The Sultan passed on a message through me, to the effect that he had to reject Herzl's request, since he feared that the masses would be aroused.' Gunzberg would not explain who the 'undesirable people' were." David Farhi, "Documents," in Ma'oz, ed., *Studies,* p. 193; also see Vital, *Origins,* pp. 280–308.

131. Abraham Galanté, "Abdul Hamid II et le Sionisme," *Haménora* (Jan.–March 1933, Stambul), p. 9, "quoting a private file kept by the grandson of the Chief Rabbi," cited by Farhi, "Documents," in Ma'oz, ed., *Studies,* p. 194. According to Mandel, Herzl

tried until his death in 1904 to convince Abdulhamid, "to no avail." Mandel, *Arabs and Zionism,* p. 16.

132. Galanté, "Abdul Hamid", p. 13, cited by Farhi, "Documents," p. 194.

133. E.Z. Karal, *Birinci Mesrutiyet ve Istibdad Devirleri (1896–1907)* (Ankara, 1962), p. 486, "quoting a manuscript by Dr. Atif Huseyin, kept in the library of the T.T.K."; cited by Farhi, "Documents," in Ma'oz, *Studies,* pp. 194–195; for another interpretation, see Mandel, *Arabs and Zionism,* pp. 9ff.

134. Ma'oz, *Reform,* p. 194; Esco, *Palestine,* p. 521.

135. Esco, *Palestine,* p. 521.

136. *Anglo-American Committee Survey,* vol. 2, p. 582; *Palestine Royal Commission Report,* p. 368; "It may be that there was a growth in apprehension, particularly in light of the fact that there was much propaganda among the *fellahin,* but in the first decade expressions of opposition to the Jews because of *fear of displacement* were not in evidence." Esco, *Palestine,* p. 528.

137. Ernest Main, *Palestine at the Crossroads* (London: George Allen and Unwin, 1937), p. 267.

138. Elija Sapir, "ha-Sin'a le-yisra'el ba-sifrut ha-'aravit," *ha-Shilo'ah,* vol. vi (1899), pp. 228–231, cited in Mandel, *Arabs and Zionism,* p. 53. A Palestinian Jew, Antebi, reported to Paris that in 1900 "Jerusalem already possesses its German anti-Semitic club," JCA 263/No. 37, January 8, 1900, Antebi to President, JCA, in Mandel, p. 54.

   The Russian Imperial Society's clinics "were open to all sections of the local population—save the Jews." Ibid.; see *Otchet,* vol. 1 (1896), p. 39.

139. Central Zionist Archives (Austro-Hungarian material) Z3/114 May 17, 1913, Hochberg, Constantinople, "Le mouvement arabe," cited in Mandel, *Arabs and Zionism,* p. 155.

140. F. Kassab, *Le nouvel Empire Arabe: La Curie Romaine et le Pretendu Peril Juif Universel—Response a M.M. Azoury bey* (Paris, 1906), pp. 28–38ff. Kassab was a Greek Orthodox Arab from Beirut, of whom "little is known," according to Neville Mandel; another pamphlet, "Palestine Hellenisme et Clericalisme" (Constantinople, 1909), which Mandel reports has "a staunchly Ottomanist point of view . . ." Mandel, *Arabs and Zionism,* pp. 50–51.

141. The price paid for land skyrocketed when that transaction was deemed "illegal," and forced underground, it must be noted.

142. Mandel, *Arabs and Zionism,* p. 77, citing *Ha-Zevi* (Jerusalem), xxvi, no. 28, 1 November 1909.

143. Ibid., citing *Ha-Zevi,* xxvi, no. 29, 2 November 1909.

144. Ibid., p. 121, citing *Ha-Or* (Jerusalem), ii xxvii, 204/379, 9 July 1911.

145. Central Zionist Archives Z2/7, December 5, 1908, Jacobson to Wolffsohn; Mandel, *Arabs and Zionism,* p. 66.

146. Alliance Israelite Universelle Archive IX E27 (October 18, 1909), Antebi to Frank; according to Mandel, the "function" of the group is "doubtful" and if it operated, it "confined itself to direct approaches" to Jerusalem officials. Mandel, *Arabs and Zionism,* p. 78.

147. Alliance Israelite Universelle Archive X E29 (January 4, 1910), Antebi to S. Loupo, cited in Mandel, *Arabs and Zionism,* p. 78.

148. Mandel, *Arabs and Zionism,* p. 55; *Ha-Zevi,* xxv, 129 (March 15, 1909), from *al-Asma'i,* Jaffa.

149. Ibid.
150. Ibid. For many examples: The governor of the Jerusalem district between 1906 and 1908 reported that "There are here influential people and notables who have attained wealth and fame through injuring the rights of the people . . . on account of the ascendancy of the Arab inhabitants. . . ." Letter from Ali Akram to Ministry of the Interior, Doc. no. 11, ISA, Ali Akram Bey Archive, cited in Porath, "Social Aspects," in Milson, ed., *Society,* p. 99. Also see Hope Simpson *Report;* Granott, *Land System.*
151. De Haas, *History,* p. 442.
152. Vital, *Origins,* p. 179. "The simple, stated prohibition on Jews taking up *new* residence in rural areas came to serve as the grounds for their being barred from returning home after a journey to town for the High Holidays in one province, from renewing leases on their homes in a second province, from moving from one village to another in a third. In all cases, the consequence was accelerated pauperization and general social misery in the overcrowded towns in which residence was free."
153. Farhi, "Documents," in Ma'oz, ed., *Studies,* p. 193. According to the British Consul in Jerusalem, the Jews numbered 100,000 in a total Palestine population of 400,-000–450,000. FO 371/356, Blech to O'Conor, November 16, 1901, cited in ibid., pp. 195–196.
154. Vital, *Origins,* p. 196; among "numerous" examples of "officials taking bribes," see Chaim Chissim, *Miyyoman ahad habiluyim,* trans. S. Herberg (Tel Aviv, 1925), p. 77, December 9, 1885; Druyanow, Ketavim, i, 847, September 21, 1886; and Alliance Israelite Universelle Archive I C 3., October 4, 1887, Hirsch to Pres. AIU; cited in Mandel, *Arabs and Zionism,* p. 19, n. 84.
155. Gilbert, *Exile,* p.74.
156. E. Yellin, *Le-ze-eza-ai* (Jerusalem, 1938), pp. 31–33, 171–172; Zalman David Levontin, L-erez Avontenu (Tel Aviv, 1924), p. 56, as cited in Mandel, *Arabs and Zionism,* p. 19.
157. Chaim Chissim, *Miyyoman,* p. 75, cited in Mandel, *Arabs,* p. 19.
158. PRO FO 78/3506, enc. to no. 48 (January 22, 1883), Wyndham to Granville, "Notification officielle" (n.d.); cf. FO 195/1447 no. 3, January 16, 1883, Elderidge to Dufferin; *Times* (London), no. 30,730, January 30, 1883, letter from Oliphant (Haifa), enclosing order (26.12.1882) Vali (Sam) to Kay. (Haifa); and *Havazzelet,* xiii, 9, (16.2.1883), as cited by Mandel, *Arabs,* p. 6.
159. *Havazzelet,* xxxi, 9, February 16, 1883; cf. 15, April 6, 1883, and 16, April 15, 1883, cited by Mandel, *Arabs,* p. 6.
160. PRO FO 195/2097, enclosure to No. 33 (April 26, 1901), Drummond-Hay to O'Conor, cited by Mandel, *Arabs,* p. 22.
161. PRO FO 195/2097, No. 19 (March 7, 1901), Monahan to Drummond-Hay; Jewish Colonization Association 258/no. 57, March 7, 1901, S.I. Pariente (Beirut) to President, JCA; and Jewish Colonization Association 259/no. 85 (August 30, 1901), C. Dreyfuss (Beirut) to same; cited by Mandel, *Arabs,* p. 22.
162. Mandel, *Arabs,* p. 121.
163. Alliance Israelite Universelle, Archive X E 29 (June 21, 1911), Antebi to Haham Basi (Constantinople), cited in Mandel, *Arabs,* p. 121.
164. Ruhi Bey al-Khalidi, reported in *Ha-Zevi,* xxvi, 29 (November 2, 1909), as cited by Mandel, *Arabs,* p. 77. Professor Farhi agreed that Arab active reaction to Jews "both on village and city level" in the 1907 period was not political. As Farhi noted, Mandel

and Porath have "somewhat different interpretations." Farhi, "Documents," in Ma'oz, ed., *Studies,* pp. 195–196.

165. Mandel, *Arabs,* p. 106; Central Zionist Archives, L18/275, January 22, 1911.

166. Ibid., p. 88; Shukri al-'Asali, open letter to Sami Pasa, *al Karmil,* December 8, 1910; *Ha-Herut,* iii, 26, December 21, 1910. Original published in *al-Muqtabas,* Damascus, vi, 2, 1911, pp. 121–122.

167. *Ha-Or,* ii [xxvii], 91/266 (5.2.1911), cited by Mandel, *Arabs,* p. 107.

168. Central Zionist Archives (CZA), Z2/11 (May 16, 1911), Jacobson to Wolffsohn, cited by Mandel, *Arabs,* p. 112.

169. "When Ruhi Bey pointed out that the Arabs were opposed only to foreign Jews, Vartkis Efendi retorted that the masses were incapable of making the distinction." Mandel, *Arabs,* p. 113.

170. Najib Nassar; Nassar was an "Ottomanist," who believed in "forming societies for Ottomans which will strive for Ottomanism . . . ." Among Ottomans were surely many Herzls who must display "their own worth and moral courage." When the so-called "Ottomanism" was rendered null and void by the British defeat of the Turks in 1918, some among the British imbued anti-Jewish hostility among the Arabs in Palestine with the purpose of "nationalism"; Mandel, *Arabs,* pp. 107–112. Mandel calls Nassar's book, *Zionism: Its History, Object and Importance* (Haifa, 1911), "the first book in Arabic about Zionism."

171. Alliance Israelite Universelle, Archive IX E 28 (June 3, 1910), Antebi to President, AIU, ibid., p. 78.

172. *Falastin,* iii, 84, November 8, 1913, cited by Mandel, *Arabs,* p. 175.

173. Gilbert, *Exile,* p. 74; also see Gilbert's map, p. 75, illustrating the Jewish villages attacked by Arab gangs.

174. For example, William B. Quandt, Fuad Jabber, Ann Mosley Lesch, *The Politics of Palestinian Nationalism* (Berkeley, University of California Press, 1973); Y. Porath, "Palestinian Arab National Movement," in *Society and Political Structure in the Arab World,* Menahem Milson, ed. (New York: Humanities Press, 1973), pp. 93–144. For contradictory observations see Lloyd George, *Truth about the Peace Treaties,* vol. 1, pp. 118–119; Furlonge, *Palestine Is My Country, The Story of Musa Alami,* p. 151; also see report by T.E. Lawrence, *Arab Bulletin,* March 1917: "There is no national feeling." Elie Kedourie, *England and the Middle East,* p. 102ff.

175. Malcolm MacDonald's report of talks with Sir Harold MacMichael, High Commissioner and Commander-in-Chief General Haining. Memorandum, "Talks in Jerusalem," Cabinet Papers, 24/278, August 6 and 7, 1938, cited in Gilbert, *Exile,* p. 205.

176. CZA Z3/48 (January 23, 1914), Lichtheim to ZAC; Order no. 1845/2217 (January 31, 1914), Minister of the Interior (SP) to Governors (Beirut and Jerusalem) enclosed in CZA Z3/48, February 11, 1914, Lichtheim to ZAC, cited in Mandel, p. 171.

177. Ibid.

178. P.J.C. McGregor to Sir I. Mallet, Jerusalem, 15 March 1914, No. 16140 (No. 16 Conf.), Hyamson, *Consulate,* 2, p. 583.

179. Alex Bein, ed., *Arthur Ruppin: Memoirs, Diaries, Letters* (New York: Herzl Press, 1971), p. 149.

180. Schama, *Two Rothschilds,* pp. 211–212; also see Aaron Cohen, *Israel and the Arab World* (London, 1970), p. 113ff; Alex Bein, *The Return to the Soil* (Jerusalem: Department of Publishing, Jewish Agency, 1952), p. 155ff.

181. Ibid., p. 212; also see Ruppin, *Memoirs,* p. 153.

182. *Ha Lebanon,* the first Hebrew weekly, was founded in Jerusalem in 1864, and in 1877 *Habazeleth* ("The Rose") became the "only publication approximating a weekly newspaper printed in Palestine" for many years. De Haas, *History,* p. 438; also see Reports of British Consuls in Jerusalem in the nineteenth century, Hyamson, *Consulate,* pp. lvii, lviii; James Finn, *Stirring Times;* Samuel Katz, *Battleground: Fact and Fantasy in Palestine* (New York: Bantam Books, 1973); also see Chapter 9.

183. Schama, *Two Rothschilds,* p. 212.

184. Ibid.

185. Ibid., p. 213, citing Bein, *The Return,* p. 155ff.

186. Ibid.

187. Ibid. At the end of 1915, "11,277 were recorded as having *emigrated* (i.e. excluding conscript)": also see Bein, *The Return,* p. 155ff; Aaron Cohen, *Israel and the Arab World* (London, 1970), pp. 113ff.

188. PICA (Palestine Jewish Colonization Association) 13/439, Jaffe-Kohn, March 22, 1915, cited in Schama, *Rothschilds,* pp. 213–214.

189. Schama, *Rothschilds,* pp. 214–215.

190. Nili, the initial letters of the Hebrew biblical verse, from the book of Samuel, "The Strength of Israel will not lie," Gilbert, *Exile,* p. 89, also pp. 95–96, 102–103, 111; Katz, *Battleground,* pp. 190–191; Schama, *Two Rothschilds,* p. 217.

191. May 11, sent through Sir Reginald Wingate in Cairo, received by Ronald Graham, British Foreign Office. Gilbert, *Exile,* p. 97.

192. *London Times,* March 30, 1917.

193. *London Daily Chronicle,* March 30, 1917; see also *Sunday Chronicle,* April 15, 1917.

194. *New Europe,* April 19, 1917. While the war was still on, the Russian government had already been contacted by Britain's Ambassador, who asked what the Russian reaction would be to the "Zionist homeland." March 13, 1916, aide-memoire from Sir George Buchanan, Great Britain's Ambassador at Petrograd to Sazanov, Esco, *Palestine,* p. 83; see also Gilbert, *Exile,* p. 95.

195. Lloyd George–Sir Mark Sykes discussion, April 3, 1917. Cabinet Papers 24/9, cited by Gilbert, *Exile,* p. 95.

196. For relatively favorable Arab reaction to the Balfour Declaration, see D.H. Miller, *My Diary at the Conference of Paris,* vol. 14; at the Paris Peace Conference in 1919, Syrian delegation stated that the "doors of Palestine" should "open wide" to the Jews. "Will not a Palestine enjoying wide internal autonomy be for them a sufficient guarantee? If they form the majority there, they will be the rulers . . ." February 13, 1919 entry, p. 399ff, p. 414ff. For the Arab perspective, see George Antonius, *The Arab Awakening,* pp. 390–392, regarding "promises" made to the Arabs prior to the Balfour Declaration. On the "McMahon Pledge" the purported promise to the Arabs, see letter from Sir Henry McMahon in *The Times,* London, July 23, 1937, in which he wrote: "I feel it my duty to state, and I do so definitely and emphatically, that it was not intended by me . . . to include Palestine in the area in which Arab independence was promised. I also had every reason to believe at the time [Oct. 24, 1915] that the fact that Palestine was not included in my pledge was well understood by King Hussein." Cited in Esco, *Palestine,* pp. 186–187.

For adverse reactions see Gilbert, *Exile,* Chapters 9 and 10; Nicholas Bethell, *The Palestine Triangle* (New York, 1979), pp. 21–22; according to the Esco study "no objection to the Balfour Declaration was registered by the Arabs at the time of its announcement." *Palestine,* p. 110ff. For favorable reactions of T.E. Lawrence, see interview with *Jewish Guardian,* November 28, 1918; also see Lloyd George, *The Truth About the Peace Treaties,* pp. 1141–1151; London *Times,* May 28, 1917, article by Lord Rothschild; *Palestine Royal Commission Report,* 1937; Antonius, *Arab Awakening,* pp. 390–392.

197. *Palestine Royal Commission Report,* pp. 23–24.

198. Ibid.

199. PICA 137/439. According to Schama, *Two Rothschilds,* p. 369, n. 67, the locust plague began in 1915, a year before "usually thought."

200. Schama, *Two Rothschilds,* p. 216, citing PICA, Doc. 7/433, December 22, 1916.

201. The Syrian delegation to the Paris Peace Conference stated that 400,000–500,000 "Syrians" "died of famine and want." D. H. Miller, *My Diary,* vol. 14, p. 404; according to Ernst Frankenstein, *Justice for my People,* p. 129, if the figures given by the Syrian delegation included Palestine, "they mean 13%–16% of the population" was lost, "otherwise 17%–21%." The non-Jewish population of Palestine in 1914 was 595,000, according to Roberto Bachi, *The Population of Israel,* Committee for International Coordination of National Research in Demography (Jerusalem, 1974), p. 36; in 1919, 582,550, according to the *Palestine Royal Commission Report,* p. 156; and in 1922, 668,258 according to the 1922 census as reported in *Report . . . for the Year 1937,* Colonial No. 146, p. 221.

202. September 1917, Schama, *Two Rothschilds,* p. 217.

203. Gilbert, *Exile,* p. 111; Katz, *Battleground,* pp. 120–121.

204. Sarah Aaronson, sister of Aaron, Katz, *Battleground,* pp. 120–121. Also see Anita Engle, *The Nili Spies* (London, 1959); Hebrew works cited in Katz, *Battleground,* n. 3, p. 121; Chaim Weizmann, *Trial and Error;* Vladimir Jabotinsky, *Story of the Jewish Legion* (New York, 1945).

205. Twenty of those condemned to hanging "were kept alive, though under lock and key, until the liberation at the end of the year." Schama, *Two Rothschilds,* p. 217, also n. 73, p. 370.

206. "End of October, 1917," *Palestine Royal Commission Report,* pp. 22–23.

207. Ibid. According to the report, "On the 14th February and the 9th May, 1918, the French and Italian Governments publicly endorsed it." For an inclusive description of the political events preceding and resulting from the Balfour Declaration, see Gilbert, *Exile.*

208. The policy statement "took the form of a letter from Secretary of State for Foreign Affairs," Lord Arthur James Balfour, "to Lord Rothschild." *Palestine Royal Commission Report,* pp. 22–23. It began, "I have much pleasure in conveying to you on behalf of His Majesty's Government the following declaration of sympathy with Jewish Zionist aspirations, which had been submitted to and approved by the Cabinet": The body of the statement was followed by: "I should be grateful if you would bring the Declaration to the knowledge of the Zionist Federation."

The Balfour Declaration would form the base for the international adoption by the League of Nations for a Jewish National Home in Palestine. The Jews' acceptance of a home "in Palestine," rather than Palestine as the "Jewish nation" or Jewish state, was a "compromise." The Jews, the British, and the Americans all stated the recognition that a Jewish independent state would indeed exist when Jews were the majority of the country and had set up their governing apparatus. The British took over the administration of the Palestine Mandate of the League of Nations in 1922, and England pledged to "facilitate" the "immigration" and "close settlement" by Jews in their Jewish National Home—without prejudicing the civil and religious rights of the existing population. Esco, *Palestine,* pp. 68–70; see Chapters 13–15.

The general expectations at the time were that ". . . the effort to establish a Jewish state in Palestine, has certainly entered 'the realm of practical politics,' and events of the year 1918 have proved that the British cabinet has an understanding with the Zionist leaders which most assuredly goes far beyond the declaration of November 2, 1917." Herbert Adams Gibbons, "Zionism and the World Peace," *Century* (New York), January 1919, vol. 97, no. 3.

11. Popular Misconceptions About the Population of "Palestine"

1. *New York Times,* from Associated Press, October 6, 1980, p. 3; *Chicago Tribune,* from United Press International, October 7, 1980, p. 6.

2. A.J. Sussnitzki, "Zur Gliederung wirtschaftlicher Arbeit nach Nationalitäten in der Turkei," *Archiv für Wirtschaftsforschung im Orient,* II, 1917, 382–407, in Charles Issawi, ed., *Economic History of the Middle East 1800–1914* (Chicago and London: University of Chicago Press, 1966), p. 116. According to Sussnitzki, "The Jews formerly played a very different part in agriculture. On the ancient significance of the Jews as the most important factors in Mesopotamia, see Krauss, 'Die Juden Mesopotamiens in Handel und Wandel,' Oe. M. O., 1916, no. 1–6, pp. 71, 84; on the decline of Jewish agriculture, ibid., p. 87." Issawi, p. 117.

3. Lewis French, *Reports on Agricultural Development and Land Settlement in Palestine,* Jerusalem, 1931–1932.

4. Sir John Hope Simpson, *Palestine: Report on Immigration, Land Settlement and Development,* 1930, Command Paper #3686, London; Sir John Hope Simpson's findings were preceded and inspired by the Shaw Commission Report of 1930, *Commission on the Palestine Disturbances of August 1929,* Command Paper 3530, 1930, London, the first official British Administration document in support of Arab contentions that Jewish settlement was "displacing" Arabs in Palestine. The Hope Simpson report formed the basis for the 1930 White Paper of Lord Passfield, Command Paper #3692, which restricted Jewish immigration to guard against what was termed "landless Arabs."

5. Hope Simpson, *Report,* p. 26.

6. A.M. Carr-Saunders, *World Population* (Oxford: Clarendon Press, 1936), p. 313. Carr-Saunders' findings were incorporated into the important *Palestine Partition Commission Report,* Command #5854, London, 1938, pp. 23, 25–26, which played a large role in determining the continuance of immigration restrictions against Jews in Palestine during and after World War II.

7. According to the census, "In the settled population of 969, 268 persons, 132, 692 are immigrants having been born abroad. Thus, 14 per cent of the population are foreign-born. The proportions in the communities are, of course, very different. Not quite 2 per cent of the Moslem population are immigrants, while 58 per cent of the Jewish population are foreign-born. Of the Christians, nearly 20 per cent are from abroad. Thus the actual population of Moslems is very nearly equal to that part of the natural population of Moslems which is to be found in Palestine, while Jewish population is predominantly immigrant in character." *Census of Palestine,* vol. I, part I, report by E. Mills, B.A., O.B.E., Assistant Chief Secretary Superintendent of Census, 1933, Alexandria, p. 59.

8. Anglo-American Committee of Inquiry, *Report to the United States Government and His Majesty's Government in the United Kingdom,* Lausanne, Switzerland, April 20, 1946, p. 23; also see *Palestine Royal Commission Report,* Command Paper #5479 of 1937, p. 125.

9. Anglo-American Committee, *Survey,* vol. 3 (unpublished), p. 1151.

10. *Palestine Royal Commission Report,* pp. 128–129.

11. *Statistical Abstract of Palestine,* 1936, cited by Moshe Braver, "Immigration as a Factor in the Growth of the Arab Village in Eretz-Israel," *Economic Review* (Jerusalem), vol. 28, nos. 7–9, July–September, 1975, pp. 12–13.

12. Philip Hauser, Gladys Epting, demographers: author's interviews, November 1980.

13. *Palestine Partition Commission Report,* p. 22; see n. 18, Ch. 14 herein.

14. "While it is undoubted that the difference reflects a greater expectation of life, particularly in infancy, among Jews than Moslems, it must be noted that the Jewish population is made up largely of young adult immigrants who are in those years of life when the risk of dying is at its lowest and the smaller proportion of infants and old people which this immigration has produced is itself a cause of a low crude death-rate." *Report . . . for the Year 1937,* Colonial No. 146, p. 224.

15. *Palestine Royal Commission Report,* p. 282.

16. As the figures in Chapter 12 determine, there was not a consistent "600,000," as prevalent authorities stated.

17. Malcolm MacDonald, British Secretary for the Colonies, statement before the House of Commons, November 24, 1938; Carr-Saunders, *World Population,* pp. 310–311; Anglo-American Committee, *Survey,* vol. 3, p. 1150.

18. "The very high birth-rate of Palestine is established by the preponderance of the Moslems, who show the highest birth-rate of all the religions. The Moslem settled population rose by natural increase at an average rate of 18,000 per annum, or about 2½ per cent per annum in the five years 1931–5. The Jewish birth-rate is considerably lower than the Moslem." *Report . . . for the Year 1937,* Colonial No. 146, pp. 223–224; also see *United Nations Special Committee on Palestine Report to the General Assembly,* vol. I, pp. 11–12, New York, 1947.

19. "The increase in the Moslem and Christian populations is to be attributed mostly to their higher rate of natural increase, due not only to the very high birth rate, but also to the fall in the death rate of infants, as well as a considerable increase in the life span of life while the increase in the Jewish population (more than seven fold) is to be credited mostly to immigration." Rony Gabbay, *A Political Study of the Arab-Jewish Conflict* (Paris: Librairie Minard, 1959), p. 7; A. Granovsky, *The Land Issue in Palestine* (Jerusalem: Keren Kayemeth Le Israel, 1936), pp. 66–67, stated that "The rate of natural increase of the Arab population of Palestine is . . . among the highest in the world, in fact" (pp. 66–67).

20. Anglo-American Committee, *Survey,* 1945–1956, vol. I, p. 144.

21. Carr-Saunders, *World Population,* p. 310.

22. *Palestine Partition Commission Report,* p. 27.

23. "Comparable with the mass immigration movements into Australia and New Zealand in the latter half of the nineteenth century." *Partition Commission Report,* p. 22.

24. Ibid.

25. The Report went on: "Official statistics show that in the four years 1933–36 there was an increase of 164,267 persons in the Jewish section of the population. This

shows that the Jewish population as it stood in 1932 has very nearly doubled in the last four years. The average Jewish immigration for the period 1933–36 has been at the rate of rather over 40,000 persons a year." *Palestine Royal Commission Report,* p. 280.

26. Ibid., p. 125.
27. Carr-Saunders, *World Population,* p. 307.
28. *Department of Migration Annual Report,* 1936, p. 20.
29. *Report . . . for the Year 1934,* Colonial No. 104, p. 35.
30. *Palestine Royal Commission Report,* p. 125.
31. See the table "Number of Immigrants Annually by Race. Total Number of Persons Registered as Immigrants," in Appendix VII. "The table indicates that *all three main religious communities have gained by migration, the smallest proportional gain being that of the Moslems.* It is of interest that the Jewish increase by migration in the fourteen year period is very nearly the same as the Moslem natural increase in the same period, about 237,000." Memoranda by the Government of Palestine, Memo No. 1, "Growth of Population," p. 2. (Emphasis added.)
    ". . . Meanwhile, the Arabs, though their proportion of the total population was falling, had increased by an even greater number—the Moslems alone from 589,000 to 1,061,000. Of this Moslem growth by 472,000 *only 19,000 was accounted for by immigration.* This expansion of the Arab community by natural increase has been in fact one of the most striking features of Palestine's social history under the Mandate." Anglo-American Committee, *Report to the United States Government and His Majesty's Government . . . ,* p. 23. (Emphasis added.)
    "Although different considerations from those relevant to Jewish immigration apply to Arab immigration, special consideration need not be given to the latter as, out of a total number of 360,822 immigrants who entered Palestine between 1920 and 1942 only 27,981 or 7.8% were Arabs." Anglo-American Committee, *Survey,* vol. 2, p. 795.
32. ". . . In a less important degree the records may be held to be defective in respect of the inhabitants of the limitrophic districts of Palestine on the one side and Syria and the Lebanons on the other along the northern frontier, for these people have the right of freedom of unrestricted passage across the frontier so long as they remain within the limitrophic districts. But these defects are of no great consequence in the *consideration* of the records of migration as revelatory of the execution of the mandatory policy of conducting Jewish immigration into Palestine according to the capacity of the country to absorb immigrants and it is in that aspect of the matter that the statistics may be held to have a high degree of accuracy." *Department of Migration Annual Report,* 1936, p. 20. Emphasis added.
33. *Census of Palestine—1931,* vol. I, part I, Report by E. Mills, pp. 148–151.
34. Ibid., p. 170–171.
35. Anglo-American Committee, *Survey,* vol. 1, p. 216.
36. Hope Simpson, *Report,* p. 126.
37. For example, Anglo-American Committee, *Survey; Report . . . for the Year 1934,* Colonial No. 104; *Report . . . for the Year 1937,* Colonial No. 146; Memoranda by the Government of Palestine, Memo No. 1, "Growth of Population," 1937.
38. *Report . . . for the Year 1934,* Colonial No. 104, p. 34.
39. *Palestine Royal Commission Report,* pp. 280–282, 291–292; Hope Simpson, *Report,* p. 138.

40. For example: "There has been unrecorded illegal immigration both of Jews and of Arabs in the period since the census of 1931, but no estimate of its volume will be possible until the next census is taken." *Report . . . for the Year 1937,* Colonial No. 146, p. 221.

    "There has been unrecorded illegal immigration both of Jews and of Arabs in the period since the census of 1931, but it is clear that, since it cannot be recorded, no estimate of its volume is possible." Memoranda by the Government of Palestine, Memo No. 1, "Growth of Population," 1937, p. 2.

    ". . . It was pointed out in the Blue Book of the Palestine Government for 1928 that there was an under-estimation of the population of Palestine for that year by about 20,000–25,000, owing to unrecorded immigration. This immigration consists in part of Arabs who enter from adjoining countries, in part of Jews who come into the country in various ways without the ordinary formalities of regular immigrations." Hope Simpson, *Report,* p. 157.

    "In addition to this increase by recorded immigration, a number of persons are known to enter Palestine illegally from both adjacent and European countries and to remain there permanently." *Report . . . for the Year 1934,* Colonial No. 104, p. 34.

    ". . . the smuggling of immigrants into Palestine by land and sea. This has been checked in large part by the recruitment of additional police for patrol along the coastal and inland frontiers, by assistance from the Trans-Jordan Frontier Force, by the establishment of a small preventive force for service in the port areas of Jaffa and Haifa, and by the prosecution of all persons arrested, in addition to their deportation. The preventive force consists of a British Police Inspector and twenty-five N.C.O.'s and other ranks who board all ships, check crews, search for stowaways, and prevent persons refused admission from landing." *Report . . . for the Year 1934,* Colonial No. 104, p. 44.

    "Not all the migratory movements are recorded. It is well known that a considerable movement of illegal immigration occurs across the borders of Palestine. Since 1939 records are kept of illegal immigrants enumerated in ships, arrested or interred from reliable evidence and are included in the population estimates." Anglo-American Committee, *Survey,* vol. 1, p. 162.

    ". . . Within the country . . . the discovery of a source of wealth and prosperity in the south would be followed by a permanent migration from the central and northern parts of Palestine. In this type is, of course, included immigration of settlers into Palestine from other countries.

    "The problem of illegal immigration into Palestine is that concerned with permanent settlement in the country whether by Jew or Arab, contrary to the provisions of the immigration legislation in force from time to time." Anglo-American Committee, *Survey,* vol. 1, p. 209.

41. For example: "At the Twenty-Seventh Session of the Permanent Mandates Commission a question was asked as to the number of Trans-Jordanians who enter Palestine and leave after the seasonal work is done. No reliable statistics are available, but it is believed that few remain in Palestine permanently. Most seek to make a little capital in Palestine with which to return to Trans-Jordan and to assist their livelihood there." *Report . . . for the Year 1935,* Colonial No. 112, p. 50.

    ". . . there has been some immigration from the surrounding territories, which, since it avoids the frontier controls, is not recorded." *Palestine Royal Commission Report,* p. 291.

"The dimensions of the volume of illegal immigration from neighboring territories are not known. . . . It is probable that seasonal immigration leaves a residue in Palestine of people who have decided to settle permanently in the country." *Palestine Royal Commission Report*, p. 292.

"The conclusion is that Arab illegal immigration for the purposes of permanent settlement is insignificant." Anglo-American Committee, *Survey*, vol. 1, p. 212.

"These records are not complete and similar data for previous years are not known. No allowance has therefore been made for illegal immigration in the years previous to 1939." Anglo-American Committee, *Survey*, vol. 1, p. 162.

42. "Arab illegal immigration is mainly casual, temporary and seasonal. It is effected chiefly by illegal entry across the land frontiers of Palestine. Owing to the fact that the bulk of illegal immigration is unrecorded on entry and departure, since the Arabs do not pass through the frontier controls, evidence as to the character of the immigration of Arabs is not easily found in Palestine." *Palestine Royal Commission Report*, p. 291.

"Arab illegal immigration is mainly of the types described . . . as casual, temporary and seasonal. It is illegal in the sense that the entry and the mode of entry do not conform with the provisions of the Immigration Ordinance and it is therefore not susceptible of statistical record. On the other hand it is not illegal in the sense that the immigrants settle permanently in Palestine." Anglo-American Committee, *Survey*, vol. 1, p. 210.

"The length of the land-frontiers of Palestine . . . makes effective frontier-control difficult. . . ." Ibid., p. 216.

"In the case of Moslems, uncertainty in the definition of 'settled' population, incompleteness of records of natural increase and a certain amount of illegal immigration (mainly from neighboring countries) are the factors most capable of introducing a margin of error in the compilation of population estimates." Ibid., p. 162.

43. Martin Gilbert, *Winston S. Churchill*, 5 vols., *The Prophet of Truth: 1922–1939*, vol. 5 (Boston: Houghton-Mifflin, 1977), particularly pp. 847–849, 867, 1069–1072.

44. "The increase in Jewish immigration was accompanied by . . . large-scale dispossession of Arabs. Thousands of Arab farm families, driven from the land on which they and their ancestors had lived, were forced to go to the towns." Mahmoud Rousan, *Palestine and the Internationalization of Jerusalem* (Baghdad: Ministry of Culture and Guidance, 1965), p. 31, cited by Fred Gottheil, "Arab Immigration into Pre-State Israel: 1922–1931," in Curtis et al., *The Palestinians*, p. 30.

45. Martin Gilbert, *Churchill*, vol. 5, p. 1072.

46. 27th Session, June 3 to June 18, 1935, Geneva, p. 47, League of Nations Publication VI.A. Mandates 1935.

47. From Mandatory records left by the British in May 1948: Israel State Archives (hereafter ISA), Group 11, File 1180/37, Imm. 35, January 3, 1926. To Palestine Gendarmerie, Samakh, from Controller (of Permits) Memo, "Entry of refugees into Palestine." Those who "appear to be Syrian, Lebanese or Palestinian by nationality may be admitted into Palestine without passport or visa."

48. See, for example, "urgent" memo, "Refugees from Syria," giving orders to "furnish blank passes as speedily as possible." ISA Group 11, File 1180/37 to District Commissioner from Controller of Permits, November 18, 1925; Arabs from "Damascus without a proper permit . . . scattered all over Palestine."; ISA Group 11, File 1180/37 No. 180/7. To Controller of Permits, Jerusalem from District Office, Na-

blus, October 25, 1926; also see ISA Group 11, File 1180/37 memo March 9, 1926, "Refugees from Syria," J. Broadhurst to Controller of Permits; ISA Group 11, File 1180/37 IMM/35, November 26, 1931, "Syrian Affairs"; ISA Group 11, File 11578/36, May 2, 1936, "Hauranis"; minutes to preceding document, May 2, 1936, signed (High Commissioner) A. Wauchope and P.T.O.

49. *Palestine Royal Commission Report,* pp. 291–292: ". . . it is certain that many of the inhabitants of Syria and the Lebanon enter Palestine without formality although they are not inhabitants of the adjoining districts of Syria. Such entry is illegal.

"A large proportion of Arab immigrants into Palestine come from the Hauran. These people go in considerable numbers to Haifa, where they work in the port. . . . Most persons in this category probably remain permanently in Palestine, wages there being considerably higher than in Syria.

"The Deputy Inspector-General of the Criminal Investigation Department has recently estimated that the number of Hauranis illegally in the country at the present time is roughly 2,500."

Under the heading "Arab Illegal Immigration," a 1945–1946 report noted that ". . . the 'boom' conditions in Palestine in the years 1934–1936 led to an inward movement into Palestine particularly from Syria." Anglo-American Committee, *Survey,* vol. 1, p. 211.

50. Palestine Royal Commission, *Minutes of Evidence Heard at Public Session,* Colonial Nos. 134, 135, 137: Wednesday, December 2, 1936, pp. 80–92, and Tuesday, December 8, 1936, pp. 93–101.

51. *Palestine Royal Commission Report,* p. 292.

52. In fact, the total number of Jews approved for immigration for the entire year of 1934 was 42,359, according to the *Report . . . for the Year 1934,* Colonial No. 104, p. 35.

53. *Report . . . for the Year 1935,* Colonial No. 112, p. 49, 214.

54. According to the *Report . . . for the Year 1934,* Colonial No. 104, p. 44, 772 Jews and 1,635 non-Jews were deported.

55. *Report . . . for the Year 1934,* Colonial No. 104, p. 11.

56. According to the *Report for the Year 1937,* Colonial No. 146, p. 68: The numbers of persons deported in 1935 for immigration offenses is as follows: Total 2,445; Jews 293; Non-Jews 2,152. It is interesting to note that for the year 1933, almost three times as many non-Jews as Jews were reported as "travellers entering" Palestine, while almost three times as many Jews as non-Jews were reported as "travellers remaining illegally." No reasons were given for such a surprising disparity in the reporting; figures for 1934 and 1935 are similarly skewed.

57. C.S. Jarvis, *United Empire,* vol. 28, p. 633, cited by Gottheil, "Immigration," in Curtis et al., *The Palestinians,* p. 31; see also *Palestine Royal Commission Report,* p. 291.

58. Hope Simpson, *Report,* p. 138: ". . . Egyptian labour is being employed in certain individual cases, and its ingress has been the subject of adverse comment in the Press. . . . It may be a difficult matter to ensure against this illicit immigration, but steps to this end must be taken if the suggested policy is adopted, as also to prevent unemployment lists being swollen by immigrants from Trans-Jordania."

59. Ibid.

60. Ibid., p. 126.

61. Palestine Royal Commission, *Minutes of Evidence,* November 24, 1936.

62. September 26, 1937.

63. *Report . . . for the Year 1937,* Colonial No. 146, p. 221.
64. For example, Hope Simpson, *Report; Palestine Royal Commission Report.*

12. A Hidden Factor in Western Palestine: Arab In-Migration

1. The Old Testament indicates that historic Palestine included land on both sides of the Jordan River, east bank as well as west bank, including the territory now known as Jordan. The portion of historic Palestine east of the Jordan River equaled or exceeded in area the portion west of Palestine. In biblical times the tribe of Manasseh occupied more territory to the east of the Jordan River than to the west, the entire tribe of Reuben dwelled east of the Jordan, and the land called Gad was east of the Jordan. Mount Gilead and Ramoudh Gilead all were east of the Jordan, as were other biblical places and people. (See map, page 12, *Literary and Historical Atlas of Asia,* prepared by J. G. Bartholomew for the Everyman Library.) Even in the time of the New Testament (as shown by the map in Appendix I). the land included territory on the east side of the Jordan River as well as the west. The New Testament city of Philadelphia was well east of the Jordan River, as was the city of Golan, which was part of Palestine, according to the Old Testament as well as the New. For an additional example, see *Rand McNally Atlas of World History*, ed. R.R. Palmer, Chicago, 1957, p. 25.
2. For map of Palestine, east, see O. R. Conder, *The Survey of Eastern Palestine,* Committee of the Palestine Exploration Fund, London, 1889; also see J. Stoyanovsky, *The Mandate for Palestine* (London, New York, Toronto, 1928), pp. 66, 204–210. Arthur Balfour's memorandum of August 11, 1919, stated: "Palestine should extend into the lands lying east of the Jordan." Balfour, who led the British delegation to the Paris Peace conference (in 1919) "determined the frontiers" of Palestine in a memorandum to Prime Minister Lloyd George, June 26, 1919: "In determining the Palestinian frontiers, the main thing to keep in mind is to make a Zionist policy possible by giving the fullest scope to economic development in Palestine. Thus, the Northern frontier should give to Palestine a full command of the water power which geographically belongs to Palestine and not to Syria; while the Eastern frontier should be so drawn as to give the widest scope to agricultural development on the left bank of the Jordan, consistent with leaving the Hedjaz Railway completely in Arab possession."
3. December 2, 1918—Toynbee minute: Foreign Office Papers; 371/3398—Arnold Toynbee agreed with the Mandate: "It might be equitable [to include in Palestine] that part . . . which lies east of the Jordan stream . . . at present desolate, but capable of supporting a large population if irrigated and cultivated scientifically . . . The Zionists have as much right to this no-man's land as the Arabs, or more," cited in Martin Gilbert, *Exile and Return,* p. 115. See also David Lloyd George, *The Truth About the Peace Treaties* (vol. I), pp. 1144–1145.
4. United States recommendation at the Paris Peace Conference, January 21, 1919. See also U.S. Congressional Resolution, June 30, 1922, in *Survey of Palestine,* p. 21.
5. In Arabia itself, largely equivalent to present Saudi Arabia, Jews had been present and had developed towns such as Medina and Khaibar, where they thrived from Roman days and before, until the conquest by Muhammad and subsequent directions from Omar. Then the Jews were slaughtered or their land expropriated and Jews were forced to flee for their lives if they did not convert to Islam. Many of those Jews

in the seventh century fled as refugees back to "Palestine," where Jewish inhabitants could even then be found in most towns referred to today as purely Arab areas.

Into the twentieth century, between 3,000 and 5,000 Jews lived in "purely Arab towns," such as Jenin, Tyre, Sidon, and Nablus during the Turkish domination; roughly 1,500 held on under the British Mandate; and in 1944–1947, zero. Those towns had been rendered *judenrein* by Arab pogroms; see Chapter 9.

6. Lord Balfour speech, July 12, 1920, cited in *Palestine Royal Commission Report,* para. 27, p. 27, 1937; see maps in this chapter and Appendix I. See n. 15 here.

7. High Commissioner Harold MacMichael to the Secretary of State for the Colonies, regarding Transjordan, cipher telegram, private, personal and most secret, 1941, PRO CO733/27137.

8. David Lloyd George, *The Truth About the Peace Treaties,* pp. 1119, 1140. Also see Esco, *Palestine,* vol. 1, pp. 64ff.

9. Gilbert, *Exile,* p. 132; see T.E. Lawrence, *Revolt in the Desert,* about Abdullah, particularly pp. 1–7. Feisal's role is woven throughout Lawrence's account. Also see King Abdullah of Jordan, *My Memoirs Completed* (Washington, D.C., 1954).

10. August 1, 1921, Secret dispatch #2301/pol., CO733/41683, Enclosure "A," Report No. 6.

11. PRO FO 371/6342, March 23, 1921.

12. July 4, 1921, telegram to Secretary of State for the Colonies, CO733/35186; response to "Very Confidential" memo "from the Civil Secretary after his recent tour in Trans-Jordania," Churchill to Samuel, July 2, 1921, CO733/36252.

13. Churchill Papers 17/14, January 17, 1921; cited in Gilbert, *Exile and Return,* p. 132; the British chose Feisal to be King in March 1921, at the Cairo Conference. See Esco, *Palestine,* pp. 121–126.

14. MacMichael hoped in 1941 to offer Abdullah a "consolation prize" of "Trans Jordan" when the country gained independence of the Mandate, and *after* Abdullah "has realized that his hopes . . . for Syria . . . are vain. We simply cannot have recrimination of these pledges to the Arabs until we are absolutely clear how and when they are to be converted into practice. The smaller the time gap between any promise and its implementation, the better. . . ." MacMichael to the Secretary of State for the Colonies, PRO CO733/27137.

15. According to the 1937 *Palestine Royal Commission Report*, "Trans-Jordan was cut away from that field [in which the Jewish National Home was understood to be established at the time of the Balfour Declaration, . . . the whole of historic Palestine]." The reason given was the later claim of the Arabs that a letter, called the McMahon pledge, from Sir Henry McMahon on October 24, 1915, had included Palestine in the territory that Britain promised to the Arabs. A formal Arab protest, called "The Holyland. The Muslim-Christian Case Against Zionist Aggression," was not declared until November 1921, six years after the date of the McMahon letter and four years after the Balfour Declaration. The fact that McMahon had *excluded* Palestine from his promise—as had the Emir Feisal excluded it from his request at the Paris Peace Conference in 1919, ignoring the McMahon letter—was conspicuously absent. The British government's failure to publish the complete correspondence gave credence to what otherwise would have been a quickly squelched, rather obvious ploy, until 1939, when a committee of British and Arab delegates scrutinized the correspondence; the British then determined that, in the words of one delegate, the Lord High Chancellor, Lord Maugham, "The correspondence as a whole, and

particularly . . . Sir Henry McMahon's letter of the 24th October, 1915, not only did exclude Palestine but should have been understood to do so. . . ." Similar testimony came from many eminent British government officials. Most notably, from Sir Henry McMahon himself: in *The Times* of London, July 23, 1937, McMahon wrote, "I feel it my duty to state, and I do so definitely and emphatically, that it was not intended by me in giving this pledge to King Hussein to include Palestine in the area in which Arab independence was promised. I also had every reason to believe at the time that the fact that Palestine was not included in my pledge was well understood by King Hussein." The British case supporting McMahon was strengthened even further by the fact that Feisal waited until January 29, 1921—nearly six years later—to bring up the subject, and then he was quoted by Winston Churchill as being "prepared to accept" the exclusion of Palestine.

The logical deduction to be made from the plethora of evidence seems clear: Palestine was indeed excluded—and in any case, the Balfour Declaration was incorporated by the Council of the League of Nations and was thus binding upon its trustee, England as Mandatory power, while no British letter of pledge could have been binding even if one had been given. Nevertheless, Arabs and their supporters have continued to attempt to cast doubt, as though the written documents didn't exist. Significantly, however, the 1937 *Palestine Royal Commission Report,* which was issued the same year that McMahon published his *Times* rejoinder, made the recommendation that "Transjordan should be opened to Jewish immigration." It never was. *Palestine Royal Commission Report,* pp. 22–38; for texts of several British witnesses and full McMahon text: Esco, *Palestine,* vol. 1, p. 181ff. Great Britain, *Correspondence,* Cmd. #5957; Churchill White Paper, June 3, 1922, Statement of British policy in Palestine, Cmd. #1700, p. 20; Lloyd George, *The Truth About the Peace Treaties,* vol. II, pp. 1042, 1140–1155; D.H. Miller, *Diary,* vol. XIV, pp. 227–234 and 414, vol. II, pp. 188–189, vol. XVII, p. 456; H.F. Frischwasser-Ra'anan, *The Frontiers of a Nation* (London: Batchworth Press, 1955), pp. 104–107. Frischwasser-Ra'anan writes of the statement by British Foreign Office expert on the Near East, Lord Robert Cecil: " 'Our wish is that the Arab country shall be for the Arabs, Armenia for the Armenians and Judea for the Jews,' " pp. 104–105; Antonius, *Arab Awakening,* pp. 390–392; *The Letters of T.E. Lawrence,* David Garnett, ed. (Doubleday, Doran, 1939), pp. 281–282; for international legal interpretation, see J. Stoyanovsky, *The Mandate for Palestine* (London, New York, Toronto: Longmans, Green & Co., 1928), pp. 66, 205–223; Parliamentary Debates, Commons, vol. 113, col. 115–116, May 23, 1939, for the views of the Archbishop of Canterbury; for examples of discussion of the McMahon-Hussein matter that omit available evidence described or referred to above, and suggest support of the Arab protestations, see William B. Quandt, Fuad Jabber, Ann Mosely Lesch, *The Politics of Palestinian Nationalism* (Berkeley, Los Angeles, London: University of California Press, 1973), pp. 8–11; John S. Badeau, *East and West of Suez* (New York: The Foreign Policy Association, 1943), p. 45.

16. In the Anglo-American Committee's "Historical Summary of Principal Political Events in Palestine Since the British Occupation in 1917," a chronological summary beginning in 1917, no mention at all is made of the gift of Transjordan to the Arabs by the British—neither in the 1922 summary nor in 1928, when an "organic Law" was enforced, nor in 1929 when the ratification of the "Agreement" took place. See Summary in *Survey of Palestine,* vol. 1, pp. 15–25.

Yet that act, which severed roughly seventy-five percent of the Mandate of Palestine, is ignored as a "principal political event"—the de facto creation of an Arab state on seventy-five percent of what had been deemed the "Jewish National Home," and which had been specifically set aside by the British and Arabs alike as an area "not purely Arab," as compared to Iraq and Syria. In the chapter preceding the "Summary," the Arabs' acquisition of an Arab-Palestinian state—a Palestinian state surely no less than Israel became—is presented as a *fait accompli:* "Prior to the 12th August, 1927, the High Commissioners for Palestine included within their jurisdiction the entire Mandatory area *without separate mention of Transjordan.* Since that date, however, the High Commissioners have received separate commissions for Palestine and Trans-Jordan respectively." See *Survey of Palestine,* p. 14. (Emphasis added.)

In the Summary, however, exhaustive attention is drawn to the Balfour Declaration and its ramifications upon the Arab community in Palestine; on the rioting:— "The hostility shown towards the Jews [which was] . . . shared by Arabs of all classes; Moslem and Christian Arabs, whose relations had hitherto been uneasy, were for once united. Intense excitement was aroused by the wild anti-Jewish rumors which were spread during the course of the riots." See Haycraft Inquiry, October 1921, in *Survey of Palestine,* pp. 18, 19.

17. The only proposal Britain as Mandatory power submitted to the League of Nations "during the lifetime of the League . . ." was a 1922 memorandum citing Article 25 of the Mandate; Article 25 allowed the Mandatory power "with the consent of the Council of the League of Nations, to postpone or withhold application of such provisions of the mandate as he may consider suitable to those conditions, provided that no action . . . is inconsistent with . . . Article 15, 16 and 18." The article referred to "the territories *lying between the Jordan and the Eastern boundary of Palestine . . . ,*" the eastern boundary being the Hejaz (Saudi Arabia). In Dr. Paul S. Riebenfeld, "Israel, Jordan and Palestine," (unpublished manuscript), pp. 10–18ff, exhaustive study of documentation concerning Transjordan and the Mandate.

In fact it appears that, to humor Emir Abdullah, the British gave the appearance of a severance, with the real consequences of a severance from Palestine upon the Jewish National Home, and the de facto creation of the Palestinian Arab state, while the British never *attempted* to legalize their actions, only to record them; "the only legal action ever taken by the British Government" was taken under Article 25: the Resolution of September 16, 1922. *League of Nations Official Journal,* November 1922, pp. 1390–1391; Riebenfeld, ibid., p. 18.

For an absorbing account of "what exactly happened on September 16, 1922" see Dr. Riebenfeld's "Integrity of Palestine," *Midstream,* August/September, 1975, p. 12ff; also see Ernest Frankenstein, *Justice for My People.*

18. Alec Kirkbride, *A Crackle of Thorns* (1956), pp. 19–20. Kirkbride goes on to say, however, that "There was no intention" in 1920 "of forming the territory east of the river Jordan into an independent Arab state." Also see *Palestine Royal Commission Report,* suggesting that Transjordan—Eastern Palestine—"if fully developed could hold a much larger population than it does at present," p. 308.

19. When Britain entered into an agreement to transfer the exercise of administration on February 20, 1928, the League of Nations Permanent Mandates Commission challenged the agreement as a "conflict with the Mandate for Palestine." Quincy Wright, *Mandates Under the League of Nations* (Chicago: University of Chicago Press, 1930), p. 458. The statement of the Commission (in part) was: "Since the

Commission is charged with the duty of seeing that the mandate is fully and literally carried out, it considers it necessary to point out . . . , in particular, Article 2 of the Agreement, which reads as follows:

" 'The powers of legislation and administration entrusted to His Britannic Majesty as mandatory for Palestine shall be exercised in that part of the area under Mandate known as Transjordan by His Highness the Amir . . .' does not seem compatible with the stipulation of the Mandate of which Article 1 provides that: 'The mandatory shall have full powers of legislation and of administration, save as they may be limited by the terms of this mandate.' "

League of Nations, *Official Journal,* Oct. 1928, p. 1574; also see pp. 1451–1453; also in Riebenfeld, *Israel, Jordan and Palestine,* pp. 24–25; . . . At that point Britain's Council member "explained that Great Britain still regarded itself as responsible for the . . . mandate in Transjordan and the Council was satisfied." Quincy Wright, *Mandates Under the League of Nations* (Chicago: University of Chicago Press, 1930), p. 458; as another example, in 1937 the Permanent Mandates Commission, at the 32nd Session, insisted that no obstacle should "prevent that Jewish National Home being established." Minutes of the 32nd Session, p. 90.

20. May 1946. See Chapter 17.
21. April 12, 1948, Arab League Resolution: No partition would be acceptable, and all Palestine must be liberated from the Zionists; on April 16, 1948, Abdullah abolished the Jordan Senate and appointed 20 new Senators: 7 Senators were Palestinian Arabs; on April 24, 1948, Jordan's House of Delegates and House of Notables, in joint session of Parliament, adopted a resolution: ". . . basing itself on the right of self-determination and on the existing de facto position between Jordan and Palestine and their national, natural and geographic unity and their common interests and living space. . . ." The parliament supported the "unity between the two sides of the Jordan. . . ." Cited in "Jordan Annexes Arab Palestine," by Benjamin Schwadran, *Middle Eastern Affairs,* vol. 1, no. 4, April 1950.
22. April 12, 1948, cited in Paul Riebenfeld, "The Integrity of Palestine," in *Midstream,* August–September 1975, p. 22.
23. Ibid.
24. Jordanian Nationality Law, *Official Gazette,* No. 1171, Article 3 (3) of Law No. 6, 1954, February 16, 1954, p. 105.
25. Ahmed Shukeiry to the Council of the Arab League, November 1966, cited in Riebenfeld, "The Integrity," *Midstream,* p. 23.
26. Mohamed Heikal, *Road to Ramadan* (New York: Ballantine Books, 1975), p. 96. See Heikal's account of a meeting between Arab heads of state, including King Faisal, Ghadaffi, and President Nasser; according to Heikal, King Hussein's war ended September 27, 1970, with the signed agreement between Hussein and Yasser Arafat, and the "withdrawal of all . . . forces from every city in the country" (p. 99). According to another source, the ceasefire took place September 25, but fighting continued well into 1971. *Political Terrorism,* edited by Lester Sobel (New York: Facts on File, Inc., 1975), cited in *Hashemite Kingdom of Jordan and the West Bank,* edited by Anne Sinai and Allen Pollack (New York: American Academic Association for Peace in the Middle East, 1977), p. 60.
27. June 2, 1971: Hussein's orders to Jordanian Premier Wasfi Tel, cited in *Hashemite Kingdom,* p. 61.
28. Description in documentary film of Golda Meir's life, originally broadcast on PBS,

New York, December 1978, after her death on December 8, 1978.
29. The area of Israel within Armistice Demarcation lines contained roughly this area plus the previously barren southern half of Western Palestine called Negev. The Negev was fifty percent of the seventy percent of land in Western Palestine that was included in Israel in 1948.
30. Jews had remained in the "holy cities" of the "Land" throughout their "exile." The actual agricultural redevelopment was begun by Jewish pioneers much earlier, but the "first wave" of Jewish settlers from abroad is said by some to have begun in 1872; by others, to have begun in 1878–1882. See Chapters 5 and 10.
31. United States Recommendation, by Delegation to the Peace Conference on January 21, 1919.
32. Erich W. Bethman, ed., *Decisive Years in Palestine 1918–1948* (New York: American Friends of the Middle East, Inc., 1957), p. 19.
33. Martin Gilbert, *Sir Horace Rumbold—Portrait of a Diplomat* (London: Heinemann, 1973), p. 398.
34. Carl Hermann Voss, *Answers on the Palestine Question* (Boston: 1949), p. 17.
35. Stephen H. Longrigg, *Syria and Lebanon Under French Mandate* (London: Oxford University Press, 1958), p. 60. Longrigg laments the loss of the Arab character, attributing it to the Balfour Declaration.
36. See Chapter 8.
37. Colonel Conder, *Heth and Moab* (London, 1883), p. 366. In Colonel Conder's repeat visit in 1881–1882 after the Turk's war with Russia, he found Palestine a "ruined land." In the ten years between his visits the population had "diminished most sadly in numbers and wealth."
38. According to Arthur Ruppin, the 1882 population for "Palestine"—Western Palestine—was 300,000. Arthur Ruppin, *The Jews in the Modern World* (London, 1934), pp. 367–368. Professor Fred M. Gottheil estimates, through painstaking examination of Palestine Exploration Quarterly reports of 1875 and 1887, and the other most reliable partial data published before the 1893 Ottoman census, that the settled population of (Western) Palestine was about 475,000 (474,085) in 1875: See "The Population of Palestine" in *Middle Eastern Studies*, vol. 15, no. 3, October 1979, Table 7; since Colonel Conder noted that the population of 1872 had "diminished sadly" by 1882, the above figures are not incompatible; also see Luke and Keith-Roach, *Handbook of Palestine and Transjordan* (London: Macmillan and Co., 1934).
39. Ruppin, *The Jews*, p. 368; Luke and Keith-Roach, *Handbook*, p. 59, estimates 35,000 Jews.
40. According to projection of the statistics of Vital Cuinet for 1895, and the earlier source, *Murray's Handbook for Travellers in Syria and Palestine*, 1858, which was reprinted in the *Encyclopaedia Britannica*, 8th edition, 1860, vol. XX, p. 905, the "settled" Muslims—not wandering Bedouin tribes—numbered approximately 141,-000; Bedouin Muslims, 65,000; Christians, 55,000; Jews, 34,000; Druses and foreigners, 5,000.
41. Vital Cuinet in his *Syrie, Liban et Palestine, Géographie administrative, statistique, descriptive et raisonnée* (Paris, 1896), assesses the total Palestine population in 1895 at 457,592: 341,638 in Sandjak of Jerusalem and 115,954 in Sandjaks of Nablus and Acre (the area approximating "Western" Palestine).
42. As Ernst Frankenstein, in his demographic breakdown based on statistics of Cuinet and others, *Justice For My People* (London, 1943), pp. 127ff.

43. Carl H. Voss, *The Palestine Problem Today, Israel and Its Neighbors* (Boston: Beacon Press, 1953), p. 13.
44. Ibid.; see also James Parkes, *A History of Palestine from 135 A.D. to Modern Times* (New York, 1949), pp. 320–321; also see Franklin Delano Roosevelt, memorandum to United States Secretary of State, May 17, 1939.
45. Kemal H. Karpat, *Research Prospectus in the Demographic History of Palestine,* submitted to the Institute of Mediterranean Affairs, New York, 1972 (unpublished).
46. See Winston Churchill, debate on 1935 White Paper, May 22, 1939, in Gilbert, *Churchill,* vol. 5, p. 1072 (quoted in Chapter 11).
47. *Palestine Royal Commission Report,* July 1937, p. 71, noting the earlier Hope Simpson Report, *Report on Immigration, Land Settlement and Development,* 1930.
48. For the Turkish period, the "Ottoman Population Records and the Census of 1881/82–1893" in English, complete, compiled and analyzed by Professor Kemal Karpat, History Department, University of Wisconsin, in *International Journal of Middle East Studies,* vol. 9, no. 2, 1978, Great Britain, pp. 237–72. According to Professor Karpat, "The validity of the census results obtained in 1893 can be tested against some other reliable estimates." On the other hand, Karpat noted that in the service of vested interest, ". . . the Armenian Catholic Patriarch Hassoun IX in a letter to the British showed the Armenian Catholics of [the vilayet—a Turkish geographical division—of] Sivas as numbering 10,000. The Ottoman census of 1893 showed the number of Catholic Armenians in Sivas province as 3,052 people . . . Other vilayets show more or less the same pattern," pp. 256–257; For "Patriarch Hassoun's inflated estimates" see Great Britain, House of Commons, *Accounts and Papers,* vol. 100 (1881), no. 6, p. 99, cited in Karpat, p. 257. Professor Karpat also cites Vital Cuinet, *Syrie, Liban,* which was used by this study as a comparative source for the period (noted above).

    According to Karpat, ". . . despite all these shortcomings, the official Ottoman censuses still supply useful data because their margin of error was far less than the figures given by observers, travellers, and biased informants, as shown by various comparative tables. There are several arguments that sustain the value of these censuses. As indicated later, they had to be accurate and complete since they provided the only factual basis available to the government for levying taxes and conscripting men into the army. The government itself constantly tried to improve its census results by introducing new methods, seeking the advice of outside experts, and using European models." Karpat, *Ottoman,* p. 240.

    Professor Karpat's citations include Engin Akarli, "The Ottoman Population in the Nineteenth Century," M.A. thesis, University of Wisconsin (Madison, 1970). See also Marc Pinson, "Demographic Warfare: An Aspect of Ottoman and Russian Policy, 1854–1866," Ph.D. diss. (Harvard, 1970). Nineteenth-century population data are included in the Ottoman Government Yearbooks, Devleti Aliye Salnameleri (Salname), 68 vols., 1847–1918. Also see Karpat, *The Gecekondu, Rural Migration and Urbanization* (New York, 1976), and "Ottoman Immigration Policies and Settlement in Palestine," *Settler Regimes in Africa and the Arab World,* I. Abu-Lughod and B. Abu-Laban, eds. (Wilmette, 1974), pp. 57–72; George Sabagh, "The Demography of the Middle East," *Middle East Studies Association Bulletin, 4,* 2 (15 May, 1970), 1–19.

    A comment on the reliability of the Ottoman census, from demographer Stanford Shaw: "There is no evidence to substantiate accusations that the records were falsified for political purposes. Indeed, Ottoman reluctance to publish their figures as well as procedures, if anything, seems to indicate the reverse. There was a conscious effort to make the count as complete and up to date as possible throughout the period under discussion, and the figures seem to reflect this ideal. Not perfect, then, by any means, but *probably as good as contemporary efforts in the other nations of Europe, and far more accurate than the rough estimates left by foreign visitors, the Ottoman census reports stand as a vital indication of the state of Ottoman society at the time and an important source for all those who seek to understand its history,"* Shaw, "The Ottoman Census System and Population, 1831–1914" in *International Journal of Middle East Studies,* vol. 9, no. 3, August 1978, p. 337. (Emphasis added.)

Additional sources on the Turkish period for the study: Davis Trietsch, *Palaestina Handbuch* (Berlin-Schmargendorf, 1907 [1st ed.], 1910 [2nd ed.]); Arthur Ruppin, *Syria: An Economic Survey* (New York, 1918); Curt Nawratzki, *Die Jüdische Kolonisation Palästinas* (Munich, 1914).

A map of the Jewish settled areas of Western Palestine fitted over a comparable map used for Turkish census purposes readily enables a translation of Turkish census figures to be made; also see *Woodhead Commission Map,* for proposal no. 2.

49. For the British Mandatory period, 1922 and 1944 census figures, in Anglo-American Committee, *A Survey of Palestine,* vol. 1, pp. 144–146, 214; for the 1947 population figures, in UN Series, *Official Records of the Second Session, General Assembly,* Ad Hoc Committee on the Palestine Question, Summary Record of Meetings September 25–November 25, 1947, Lake Success, N.Y. (Annex 25 Report of Subcommittee II to Ad Hoc Committee on the Palestine Question, Afghanistan, Egypt, Iraq, Lebanon, Colombia, Pakistan, Saudi Arabia, Syria and Yemen, pp. 291–308, Appendix IV, V, VI (the study chart's Arab population in 1947—747,000—total was not clarified in 1947 because of the 1947–1948 Arab-Israeli War). The UN annex data do not contain certain figures for areas within Israel which were in addition to the 1947 partition plan. *Israel's Struggle for Peace* (New York: Israel Information Office, 1960) provided January 1, 1948, population in Israel under armistice agreement of 1949, p. 89; for land percentages, p. 20; the UN annex data (Arab–UN figures) were the 1947 basis of the study's calculations; for reported Arab immigration, Anglo-American Committee, *Survey,* p. 795.

50. "The difference between births and deaths gives one the natural increase, which, when compared with the total increase, yields the presumed net movement into or out of the area." William Peterson, *Population* (London, 1969), p. 43.

Natural increase equals births minus deaths. Net immigration or in-migration equals total population minus natural increase.

Until now, natural increase according to Jewish and non-Jewish areas has not been calculated. Thus the actual difference between natural and increase by immigration in those breakdowns has not been properly considered.

51. See E. Mills, *Census of Palestine, 1931* (Alexandria, 1933), list of non-Arab peoples by nationality and native language, Table X, Language, Table XI, Birthplaces (see lists in Chapter 11); see *Encyclopaedia Britannica,* 11th ed., 1911, vol. XX, p. 604; see Bernard Lewis, *The Arabs in History* (London, 1966), p. 9.

52. Also, the use of the categories is inconsistent. Whereas the 1937 *Report . . . for the Year 1937,* Colonial No. 146, primarily used the categories, "Jews, Arabs and Others," or "Jews, Non-Jews," the Department of Migration was able to delineate their figures into the categories "Jews, Moslems, Christians." The 1936 Department

of Migration *Annual Report 1936,* Jerusalem, 1935–[1939], acknowledges this inconsistency with its statement, "The statistics for the year are not strictly comparable with those given in the annual report . . . unless adjustments are made for tables concerned with immigrants arriving, travellers subsequently registered as immigrants and all persons registered as immigrants whether they arrived as immigrants or travellers," p. 20.

Does this mean that some of those listed as Jewish immigrants were actually travelers? Does it mean that those listed as Muslim travelers were actually immigrants? It is difficult to know for sure. This is all of interest, because different categories used in reporting appear to have depended upon what exactly was being reported, whether it was immigration or travel, and what was being described of the immigrants or travelers. For example, within each year, the *Official Mandatory Reports* used the following categories:

1920–21	"Jews, Non-Jews" for immigrants
1922	"Jews, Non-Jews" for immigrants but "Jews, Christians, Moslems" for returning immigrants
1923	"Jews, Christians, Moslems" for "Provenance of Immigrants," yet "Jews, Non-Jews" for immigration summary
1925	"Jews, Christians, Moslems" for "Provenance of Immigrants"; however, "Jews, Non-Jews" for labor and immigration statistics
1926	"Jews, Christians, Moslems" for "Provenance of Immigration" and general immigration data, but "Jews, Non-Jews" for labor categories of immigrants
1928	"Jews, Non-Jews" for Labor Schedules but "Jews, Christians, Moslems" for "Provenance of Immigrants"
1930	"Jews, Christians, Moslems" for "Provenance of Immigrants" but other classifications according to "Jews, Non-Jews"
1931	"Jews, Christians, Moslems" for "Provenance of Immigrants" but the classification of labor and occupation of immigrants according to "Jews, Non-Jews"
1933	"Jews, Christians, Moslems" for occupation of immigrants, "Provenance of Immigrants," and other classifications
1934	"Jews, Christians, Moslems" for "Provenance of Immigrants" and labor/occupation, but "Non-Jews, Jews" for general immigration data
1935	"Jews, Non-Jews, Other" for arrivals/departures in Palestine and travelers, yet "Jews, Non-Jews" for recording immigration and emigration
1936	"Jews, Non-Jews" for travelers, immigration and emigration, but "Jews, Arabs, Others" for labor/occupation, and "Provenance of Immigrants"
1937	"Jews, Arabs, Others" for arrivals/departures and "Provenance of Immigrants" while "Jews, Non-Jews" for travelers, immigration, and emigration data

During this year, the categories "Jews, Moslems, Christians" were used in the Department of Migration Report to describe arrivals/departures.

53. In the *Palestine Royal Commission Report*, July, 1937, the figures for population are broken down into (a) "Jews, Moslems, Christians and Others," as well as (b) "Jews, and Non-Jews," p. 279.

The *Palestine Partition Commission Report*, London, 1938, changes categories arbitrarily: the category "Jews and Moslems including Non-Arab Christians" appears on the same page with another listing that notes the qualification: " 'Arab' in this section is used in its strict sense and not an equivalent [*sic*] to 'non-Jews,' " p. 23. At still another point, the same official report vacillates between a "Jews-and-non-Jews" listing and a "Jews-and-non-Jews-and-Arabs" listing—the last two contradictory listings used in the same chart! Ibid.

54. Bethman, ed., *The Decisive Years*, pp. 19–20.

55. Department of Migration, *Annual Report*, 1936, p. 20; similar observations in *Annual Reports*, 1935, 1937, 1938.

56. Anglo-American Committee, *Survey*, p. 795.

57. For example, the *Report* by the Government of the United Kingdom to the Council of League of Nations on Administration of Palestine and Transjordan—1937 stated that: "It was recognized at the census of 1931 that classification by 'race' or 'nationality' into the broad groups, Arabs, Jews and Others, is a political necessity. Statistics of migration were put on a 'racial' basis in 1935, and in 1938 the classification of vital occurrences will be two-fold, namely, by religious confession and by 'race' or 'nationality.' The re-introduction of a classification of migration by religious confession will enable population records to be kept *in future* [emphasis added] both by religion and by 'race,' " p. 219; also, from the *Palestine Partition Commission Report*, London, 1938: "For the purpose of our report, except where it is expressly otherwise stated, we have treated the population as falling into two categories, Arabs and Jews. The Arab section includes persons who are not Arabs, but as nearly 98 percent of the non-Jewish population are Arabs, the use of the term Arab, which we prefer to that of non-Jew, generally causes no distortion of the picture," p. 33.

58. The source, Vital Cuinet, *Syrie,* corroborates our 1893 calculations almost exactly, although Cuinet did not have the benefit of the Turkish census figures. Re: Population of Western Palestine, pp. 93, 100, 178, 183–184, 520, 627, 628.

59. Jews, 1895—59,000–60,000; Muslims—58,000; Christians—37,800 according to Cuinet, ibid.

60. See chart in Appendix V.

61. Vital Cuinet's estimate of the total non-Jewish population in Western Palestine is remarkably close to the Ottoman census—in 1895, Palestine (*Sandjaks* of Jerusalem, Nablus, and Acre) contained 252,784 settled Muslims, 64,820 Bedouin Muslims (nomads), 70,802 Christians, 60,800 Jews, 1,175 Druses, and 7,211 foreigners, totaling 457,592.

62. J.L. Burckhardt, *Travels,* p. 299; also see note 165, Chapter 8 footnotes.

63. Others had informally begun even earlier. See Chapter 10.

64. A. Druyanow, *Ketavim letoldot hibbat ziyyon ve-yishshuv erez yisra'el* (Odessa, Tel Aviv, 1919, 1925, 1932) vol. 3, pp. 66–67 (December 18, 1889), from Y. Grazowski (Rishon l'Tsion) to Y. Eisenstadt (Barzelei). See Chapters 10, 11. Also see N. Mandel, *Arabs and Zionism,* p. 38, for his citation in another context.

65. According to another source, twenty-one Jewish settlements had been established by

1893: see *Palestine News,* November 1, 1918; also see David Vital, *Origins of Zionism* (Oxford, 1975), p. 100; Gurevich and Gertz, *Jewish Agricultural Settlement in Israel* (Jerusalem, 1938), p. 34.

66. Gideon Kressel, "Agnatic Endogamy as a Cultural Mode of Social Stratification: FBD and FBS Marriage in Jawarish," *Asian and African Studies*, vol. 14, no. 3 (1980), p. 255ff.

67. If we assumed each family equaled 5 souls, then 40 Jewish families = 200 Jews, followed by 400 Arab families = 2,000 Arabs; we would find the hypothetical ratio which applied was 10 Arabs following 1 Jew. There were 15 other Jewish settlements with roughly an overall total of over 900 Jews in 1889 (which estimated total was computed by factoring the 1914 total for Rishon l'Tsion back to its 1889 total, which equals a 7.5-times increase; dividing by 7.5 the 1914 total for the other 15 Jewish settlements' population—6,860—we arrive at 914.6—roughly 915 Jews in the 15 settlements in 1889 (1893) according to Arthur Ruppin, *Syria,* pp. 29–31.

68. Areas I and II on map in this chapter.

69. Areas III, IV, and V, ibid.

70. John Hope Simpson, *Palestine: Report on Immigration, Land Settlement and Development,* Command Paper #3686, 1930, pp. 145–147.

71. For example, according to an early British census report, after 1914 Arab "tribes from the Hedjaz and Southern Transjordan" were coming into Western Palestine, not only into the Jewish-settled areas, but to other places in the country as well, for reasons of "adequate rainfalls" and "pressure exerted by other tribes east of the River Jordan." J. B. Barren, comp., *Palestine Report and General Abstracts of the Census of 1922* (Jerusalem: Greek Convent Press, 1922), p. 4.

72. *"Egypt's modern rate,* in time of both 'population explosion' and modern medicine, *is only 25 per thousand per year.* Surely the Egypt of the 1890s could not have equalled it. Such a rate would be considerably higher than *present-day* India's (19/1000/year), almost equal to Turkey's (28/1000/year)—both countries at their highest growth rates in history." Justin A. McCarthy, "Nineteenth Century Egyptian Population," *Middle Eastern Studies,* vol. 12, no. 3, October, 1976, p. 25. McCarthy's observation of Egyptian demographics undoubtedly applies similarly to the nearby population in Western Palestine.

73. *The Statistical Abstract of Palestine 1944–45* reported that 570,800 Arabs were living in the Jewish-settled area of (Western) Palestine; by October 1948, the United Nations had announced two figures, the higher estimating that the number would "shortly increase to 500,000" according to Disaster Relief Organization figures, confirmed by statistical calculation of the potential number of refugees who might have left after the second truce. The Arab League total, unverifiable, was 150,000 greater than the higher of the UN totals. The total number of possible "settled" refugees, according to the results of this book's calculations, after subtracting Arab immigrant figures, is: 343,-000 "Arab settled population and descendants" from the Jewish-settled area and included in Israel in 1949; 37,000 Arab nomads; 36,800 Arab "legal" immigrants; and 170,000 in-migrants—a total of 586,900 "refugees" including in-migrants, immigrants, and nomads. The U.S. State Department reported 472,000 Arab refugees, distributed as follows: 61,000, Lebanon; 86,000, Transjordan; 9,000, Egypt; 4,000, Iraq; 73,000, Syria; and 237,000 in "Palestine." *New York Times,* February 2, 1949.

74. See demographic expert's comment on the population study, in Appendix VI following description of methodology.

75. In fact, some of those places were needed for the Jews who were expelled from the so-called "purely Arab towns" in non-Jewish areas of Western Palestine, particularly during the British Mandate. See Chapter 9.
76. A.M. Carr-Saunders, *World Population* (Oxford: Clarendon Press, 1936), p. 310, as cited in *Palestine Partition Commission Report*, London, 1938, p. 23.
77. Interviews with author, November 25, 1978; March 15, 1981. Professor Philip Hauser, Director Emeritus, Population Research Center, University of Chicago. Beginning in 1938: Assistant Chief Statistician for Population, then Deputy Director (until 1947), then Acting Director (1949–1950), U.S. Bureau of the Census; U.S. Representative to UN Population Commission, 1947–1951.
78. Even after averaging the Arab population increase of Jewish-settled areas and non-Jewish areas in Western Palestine, the resulting artificially lowered rate was inordinately high. According to the *Palestine Post* in December 1945: "Palestine's net rate of increase is high compared even with other near-eastern countries: 1944:

	Birth rate (per 1000)	Death rate	Natural increase
Cyprus	295	124	171
Lebanon	170	65	105
Syria	220	90	130
Egypt	381	286	95
Transjordan	425	188	237
Palestine Moslems	524	190	334

"The fertility even of Egypt, which is among the highest in the whole world, is surpassed by that of the Palestinian Moslems—according to the statistics. As in most other countries, a downward trend is observed in Egypt: while in 1927 it had in the age group up to five years 100,000 persons more than the five to nine group, only ten years later, it had 171,000 fewer in the former than in the latter group. There is no such trend to be seen among the Palestinian Moslems, however. Their birthrate, according to the statistics, has varied between 45 and 53 since the year 1922, actually reaching a peak in 1943 and 1944." M. Lefebre, "Palestine's High Birthrate—A Doubtful Miracle," *The Palestine Post*, December 14, 1945, p. 6.
79. Justin A. McCarthy, "Nineteenth Century Egypt Population," *Middle Eastern Studies*, vol. 12, no. 1, October 1976, pp. 31–33. "The rate of natural increase between 1966 and 1970 had risen to 27.6, one of the highest in the world, but this is a purely modern phenomenon. In the period studied in this work [19th Century], 18 per thousand per year is the highest to be expected.

"These figures must be kept in mind for comparisons. Birth rates may not have changed drastically for the nineteenth century, but death rates have. With the differences between the health standards of the two, the nineteenth-century rate of increase must necessarily have been lower than the modern figure. Any population estimate that demands a growth rate of perhaps 20 per thousand for the nineteenth century cannot be correct. Yet estimates that demand rates well above this have repeatedly been made. Comparisons to the above make it possible to judge their accuracy.

"Russell, in *Late Ancient and Medieval Population*, has demonstrated that the

natural rate of increase (i.e. without migration) can never be more than 6.2 percent."
[McCarthy notes here that: "Russell calculates that approximately one-third of
women in a given population are of marriageable age and that 10% of all marriages
are sterile. He quotes studies which show a woman can (statistically) have one child
every 29 months, if no restraints exist. That is, there is a 41% chance of a woman
being able to bear a child in any one year. Taking the one-third who are married,
dividing out the men, he arrives at 16.7% rate of child-bearing women. 41% of these
can have a child in a year, or 6.9%, considering the 10% sterility rate, 6.2%."] Since,
however, this figure assumes that in one year no one will die and everyone who can
will have children, it is never even closely reached. With medicine allowing developing countries tremendously high birth and low death rates, the *modern* area of
greatest increase, Latin America, *has not even reached 30 per thousand.* (Emphasis
added.) McCarthy, p. 31; see also Riad Tabbarah, Chief Population Division, UN
Economic Commission for Western Asia, *Population and Human Resources in Arab
Development,* Beijing (Peking) International Roundtable Conference on Demography, Beijing, October 20–27, 1980, conference organized jointly by the United Nations and the Government of the People's Republic of China, pp. 3–4.

80. Moshe Aumann, *Land Ownership in Palestine, 1880–1948* (Jerusalem: Israel Academic Committee on the Middle East, 1976); also see L. Shimony, *The Arabs of
Palestine* (Tel Aviv, 1947), pp. 422–423.

81. *New York Times,* December 17, 1980, letter dated December 8, 1980, from Bruce
J. Chasan, Bala Cynwyd, Pa.

82. In the area where ninety-eight percent of all Jews would live between 1893 and 1948,
the Jewish population was over 596,000 in 1947.

83. The data available for this study accounted for all the population in Western Palestine; we could trace that population's whereabouts in the prescribed area, but we
cannot tell where the population came from because the British did not quantify Arab
immigration.

84. Kemal Karpat, *Research Prospectus,* pp. 2–7.

85. Fred M. Gottheil, "Arab Immigration into Pre-State Israel: 1922–1931," from Curtis
et al., eds., *The Palestinians,* p. 38; also see ibid., p. 3; Carl Hermann Voss, *The
Palestine Problem Today,* p. 13; James Parkes, *A History of Palestine from 135 A.D.
to Modern Times* (New York: Oxford University Press, 1949), pp. 320–331.

86. Riad Tabbarah, *Population,* p. 5.

87. Ibid., p. 5ff.

88. Prof. Moshe Braver, "Immigration as a Factor in the Growth of the Arab Village
in Eretz-Israel" from *Economic Review—Problems of Aliyah and Absorption,* vol. 28,
nos. 7–9, July–September 1975, p. 20. According to Professor Braver, "Obviously full
credibility cannot be attached to the 'investigation' of elders and savants in the
villages. We used several methods of verification, comparing various testimonies
obtained in each village about itself and information about it obtained in others. We
ignored any information which seemed to be unreliable. We took into account the
fact that, in the atmosphere of political distrust toward the Israeli researchers in
Judea and Samaria, questions about population movements in the past would necessarily draw answers of faulty veracity. Nevertheless, we believe that we have in our
possession sufficient factual material on which to base our conclusion *that the proportion of internal migration in the settlement of Arab migrants in the coastal plain,*
during the period under review *is small—smaller in the southern section* of the coastal

plain and somewhat larger in the central and northern part of the area. *This means that the major increase in the population of the Arab villages in the coastal plain, during the British period, had come largely from immigrants from the neighboring countries,"* p. 20; on this subject, also see Ruth Kark, *"Land Purchase in Emek Hefer"* in A. Schmueli and D. Grossman, eds., *The Sharon,* Tel Aviv.

89. See the population study chart in Appendix V.
90. Interview with Professor M. Braver, July 1979, Tel Aviv University.
91. Moshe Braver, "Immigration as a Factor in the Growth of the Arab Village in Eretz-Israel," *Economic Review,* vol. 28, nos. 7–9, Jerusalem, 1975, p. 16.
92. Braver, "Immigration," p. 16.
93. Richard T. Antoun, *Arab Village—A Social Study of a TransJordanian Peasant Community,* Indiana University Press, (Bloomington, 1972), p. 33.
94. Ibid., p. 30.
95. According to Antoun, most of the Kufr al-Ma households were, by Sir John Hope Simpson's rule of measure, "landless" Arabs—yet no blame was placed in that area of Eastern Palestine as it was in Western Palestine, where all "landless Arabs" were judged to be the victims of Jewish development and thus counted against the Jewish immigration and labor quota.
96. Gideon Kressel, "Agnatic Endogamy," pp. 255–56ff.
97. According to Kressel's study the Jawarish ("the collective name of the descendants of one A'merel Abani Jarushi, of the children—*awlad*—of Musalam of the Tarhunah Bedouin Tribe of Tripolitania, Libya") had "fled to Hebron" during the 1948 war, but were "persecuted by the Egyptians for their previous ties with Jews," and so in 1949 had "smuggled themselves back" into Israel, finally settling in homes near Ramle provided and erected by the Israeli government in 1952; p. 5, "Realization of Agnatic Endogamy: Diachronic Perspectives." *Mediterranean Marriage Strategies and Marriage Prestations*, John Peristiany, ed. (Paris, 1984).
98. Kressel, "Realization," n.2.
99. One of U'kashah's brothers, an agricultural worker, "in his own words." Kressel, *Realization,* pp. 13–14. The U'Kashahs are "now living in Ramla, Lod and Jaffa," as well as Jawarish, p. 15. According to Kressel, the commonality of Egyptian origin is not unifying as "the name of Libya united the M'arabat." The "concealment" of Egyptian origins thus resulted, 1) because "most of the settlers and like them the Arab inhabitants of Ramla of today could claim this pedigree" so that the "Egyptian pedigree loses its strength as an exclusive social distinction"; there is no "occupational unity" to the claim of Egyptian origin "like the Maghrabite descent"; 3) to admit Egyptian identity in Israel would refute the "Palestinian-since-time-immemorial claim" and "cause difficulties" for the Egyptian-descended Arabs in Israel "as a result of the extreme enmity toward Israel from Egypt and in the resultant atmosphere of hostility since 1948." Kressel, *Individuality Versus Tribality* (Tel Aviv: 1975), p. 43.
100. Kressel, "Agnatic Endogamy," p. 267. Kressel concludes that "allegiances to former cultural-ethnic groups in most cases survived radical changes of environmental milieu . . ." and that "one of the most salient expressions of this fact pertained to the pattern of marriage." Ibid., pp. 266–68.
101. Also see Richard Oestermann, "Who are the Palestinians?" *Jerusalem Post,* January 12, 1975.
102. Another study, conducted in the years 1943 to 1947, and 1949 to 1963, surveyed

more than 800 villages in Western Palestine and found that the Arab residents were predominantly of foreign origin. Dr. Shlomo A. Ben-Elkanah, historian and Orientalist, cited as an example the village of Um el-Fahan, which he investigated in 1943: of a total population of 2,800, approximately 900 came from Egypt, 1,400 from the Hejaz, and 500 from Transjordan–Eastern Palestine. Exhaustive data, now in preparation for publication, were seen by this writer during interview, May 1983.

13. A Hidden Movement: Illegal Arab Immigration

1. The records reproduced in this book that have been taken from the files of various archives containing British government and other Mandatory period documents are by no means all-inclusive; as previously stated, the data relevant to *Arab* immigration were difficult to locate. Among the massive volume of material on immigration and stacks of files on visas, passport control, etc., there was virtually no such category or reference to the data. The author has included recorded evidence of illegal Arab immigration sufficient to indicate decisively that the phenomenon indeed existed. However, an exhaustive and extended investigation of the remaining unpublished documentation on the subject could well become the subject for a dissertation or another book.

2. ISA Record Group 11, File 1180/37. November 18, 1925, Urgent—District Commissioner, Northern District from Controller, "Copy to Chief Secretary (Interview with Acting Chief Secretary of November 18, 1925)"; see also ISA 11 1180/37, March 16, 1926, "Subject: Refugees from Syria."

3. ISA Record Group 11, File 1180/37, Imm/35, January 3, 1926, O.C. Palestine Gendarmerie, Samakh. Subject: Entry of Refugees into Palestine. From: Controller.

4. ISA Record Group 11, File 1180/37, No. 180/7. From District Offices, Nablus, 25 October 1926. To Controller of Permits, Jerusalem. Subject: Damascene Refugees; see also Nov. 8, 1926, "Damascene Refugees."

5. ISA Imm/35-126, November 8, 1931.

6. ISA Imm/35-13 or HA/274 December 22, 1931. From Immigration Officer to A.D.S.P. i/c Acre Sub-District; see also ISA Record Group 11, File Imm/35, November 26, 1931. From N.I. Mindel to Deputy Commandant of Police, C.I.D., Subject: Syrian Affairs; ISA Record Group 11, File 1180/57, Imm/35, December 30, 1931, From Chief Immigration Officer to Deputy Commandant of Police, C.I.D., Jerusalem, Subject: Syrian Affairs; ISA Record Group 11, File 1180/37, AP/174 Acre, 25th January, 1932, From Asst. Supt. of Police, Acre Division to District Superintendent of Police, Northern District, Subject: Syrian Affairs; ISA Record Group 11, File 1180/37, Imm/35, June, 1932. From Inspector of Immigration, Subject: Mukhtar's certificate; ISA Record Group 11, File 1180/37, Imm/35, January 15, 1932. From Immigration Officer to A.S.D.P., Acre, Subject: Druzes who are in Palestine without permission.

7. ISA I/398/36 Ref. 9491 to Chief Secretary from G. Farley, District Commissioner, Southern District, copy to Commissioner for Migration and Statistics, Jerusalem. May 14, 1936.

8. ISA Record Group 2, File I/588/33, No. 1a. Memorandum from Albert M. Hyamson, 6-28-33.

9. Ibid. Still another case cited: A beggar of Syrian origin would bring "great difficulty" because of the "delay."

10. ISA Record Group 2, File I/578/36, Doc. #1, May 2, 1936.
11. Ibid., Doc. #1–5, May 2, 1936.
12. Handwritten Minute, A. Wauchope, May 2, 1936, Doc. #2, ibid., followed by ISA Record Group 2, File I/578/36, CR/246/365, May 2, 1936, to Southern District Commissioner from Chief Secretary Hall, implementing High Commissioner Wauchope's instructions.
13. ISA Record Group 2, File I/578/36, May 2, 1936, R 4, Minutes signed PTO and AGW. See also "Prevalence of Countrymen in the Southern District" memo from Palestine Police Deputy Inspector-General, ibid., May 4, 1936, Doc. #6.
14. See Chapter 17.
15. ISA I/578/35, May 11, 1936.
16. ISA Record Group 2, File I/578/36, Minute 19, May 30, 1936.
17. ISA Record Group 2, File I/478/36, Minute 15, May 23, 1936.
18. ISA Record Group 2, I/578/36, No. 9A, May 6, 1936, to POLSEC from AMN-KHAS; also see ISA 2, I/578/36, No. 7, CF/246/36, May 7, 1936, Subject: "Prevalence of Countrymen in Southern District"; ISA 2, I/578/36 Telegram No. 337, May 26, 1936 from Wauchope, High Commissioner for Palestine, Transjordan to Commissioner, Berbera Somaliland; ISA 2, I/578/36, No. 11, minutes, May 19, 20, 1936 regarding Egyptian, Somali and Sudanese wishing to repatriate.
19. ISA 2, I/578/36, No. 436, June 5, 1936, #23. Another example: High Commissioner Wauchope to Governor General of Sudan, ISA 2, I/578/36. "Confidential" No. 38, Ref. #CF/246/36, July 18, 1936.
20. ISA I/578/36, No. 19, Enclosure to letter, May 14, 1936 (Ref. # 9491). See letter and enclosure in Appendix VII.
21. Ernest Main, *Palestine at the Crossroads* (London: George Allen and Unwin Ltd., 1937), p. 56; also see Esco, *Palestine,* pp. 493–494.
22. Ibid., p. 37.
23. Nation Associates, *The Arab Higher Committee,* The Documentary Record Submitted to United Nations, May 1947, New York, pp. 4–7.
24. Anglo-American Committee, *Survey,* vol. I, according to the later official historical chronology, p. 17. Winston Churchill at that time estimated that "about 250 casualties occurred, of which nine-tenths were Jewish." Gilbert, *Exile,* p. 129.
25. Esco Foundation for Palestine, *Palestine,* vol. I, pp. 132–133; "The Government was finally forced to disarm the Arab police, proclaim martial law and hand over the control to the military. Order was not restored until two days after the outbreak.

    "The Jews accused the Military Administration, headed by Sir Louis J. Bols, of complicity. The Zionist authorities blamed the Government particularly for allowing the Moslem-Christian Associations to agitate against the Balfour Declaration. The actions of the military authorities after the riots confirmed the feeling that they were motivated by an anti-Jewish attitude. Severe penalties were inflicted on Jewish defense organizations which had armed the Jews for self-protection. Vladimir Jabotinsky who had been an officer in the British army—one of the initiators of the Zion Mule Corps and the Jewish Legion, and the godfather of the Haganah (Jewish secret defense force)—and other members of the Jewish defense were sentenced to fifteen years' imprisonment for the possession of firearms and ammunition. The Jews were incensed at this, particularly because at the same time an exactly similar penalty was meted out to an Arab rioter convicted of rape. The Administration on its part made accusations against the Zionist Commission. Sir Louis Bols in a long memorandum charged the Commission with attempting to create a political fait accompli in the country before the Mandate had been determined. He implied that the Christians and Moslems were justified in feeling that the status quo was not being maintained, in view of the fact that Hebrew had been recognized as an official language, Jewish courts had been established, a quasi-governmental structure of the Zionist Commission had been introduced, etc. A local Committee of Inquiry was appointed to investigate the causes of the disturbances but the results of its inquiry were not revealed on the grounds that 'their publication could serve no useful purpose' " (pp. 133–134).

26. See Chapters 9 and 10.
27. Colonel R. Meinertzhagen, *Middle East Diary, 1917–1956* (London, 1959), pp. 81–82.
28. *The Times,* London, February 7, 1938.
29. Esco Foundation for Palestine, *Palestine,* vol. 1, p. 134; "A little over a month after the decision on the Mandate at San Remo (April 24, 1920), the Military Administration under Sir Louis Bols came to an end and the Civil Administration was initiated on July 1, 1920, under Sir Herbert Samuel as High Commissioner."
30. *Arab Higher Committee,* p. 9.
31. League of Nations, Mandate for Palestine, Command #1785, Article 6, 1922.
32. Ibid.
33. August 26, 1920. "The first Immigration Ordinance was enacted and a quota of 16,500 immigrant Jews fixed for the first year." Chronology, Anglo-American Committee, *Survey,* vol. I, p. 18.
34. As the *Survey of Palestine* stated, "Different considerations from those relevant to Jewish immigration apply to Arab immigration . . ." (p. 795).
35. Statistics from the *Report . . . for the Year 1935,* Colonial No. 112, p. 13, cited by Count de Penha Garcia, League of Nations Permanent Mandates Commission, Minutes of the 29th Session, Annex 13.
36. League of Nations Permanent Mandates Commission, Minutes of the 29th Session, pp. 139–141.
37. *Report . . . for the Year 1935,* p. 14.
38. League of Nations Permanent Mandates Commission, Minutes of the 29th Session, p. 140.
39. *Report . . . for the Year 1935,* Colonial No. 112, p. 50, para. 21.
40. Permanent Mandates Commission, Minutes of the 29th Session, p. 141.
41. Report by M. Palacios, September 3, 1935, Minutes of the 29th Session, Permanent Mandates Commission, Annex 6, p. 187.
42. Report by Count de Penha Garcia, Minutes of the 29th Session, Permanent Mandates Commission of the League of Nations, Annex 13, p. 194.
43. See Chapters 14 and 15.
44. PRO CO 733/287 1936, signed O.G.R. Williams, November 2, 1936.
45. PRO FO 371/E1203, January 23, 1937, to Lord Ormsby-Gore, Secretary of State for the Colonies, *Secret.*
46. PRO FO 371/E1203/976/31, Minute written by L. Baggallay, Feb. 27, 1937.
47. PRO FO 371/E1330, Telegram from Sir R. Bullard, Jeddah.
48. PRO FO 371/20819; see MacKereth letter, October 23, 1937, particularly pp. 19–20.

49. PRO FO 371/20819.
50. PRO FO 371/20819; see also interview between the officer administering the Government (OAG) and Shertok, October 16, 1937.
51. "Confidential letter," PRO FO 371/20819.
52. PRO FO 371/20818.
53. PRO FO 371/20817.
54. PRO FO 371/20818.
55. PRO FO 371/20817, "Immediate Secret" *"Expulsion of Palestinian Terrorists from Syria."*
56. PRO FO 371/20818.
57. PRO FO 371/20817.
58. PRO FO 371/20818.
59. PRO FO 371/20818.
60. PRO FO 371/20818, cited in Gilbert, *Exile,* pp. 189–190.
61. PRO FO 371/20818.
62. PRO FO 371/20819.
63. PRO FO 371/20819.
64. PRO FO 371/20819, RE: MacKereth Transfer to Jerusalem.
65. PRO FO 371/20819.
66. PRO FO 371/20819, "Palestine: Further Proposals for Strong Action."
67. PRO FO 371/20818, cited in Gilbert, *Exile,* p. 191.
68. PRO FO 371/20819.
69. PRO FO 371/20821.
70. PRO FO 371/20818. Cited in Gilbert, *Exile,* p. 190.
71. PRO FO 271/20819.
72. PRO FO 371/20819.
73. PRO FO 371/20821.
74. PRO FO 371/20821.
75. Foreign Office Memorandum, November 19, 1937; Cabinet Papers 24/273. Cited in Gilbert, *Exile,* p. 193.
76. MacKereth, 1893–1962; additional correspondence, Middle East Centre, St. Antony's College, Oxford, re: Arab terrorist activities, etc., from *Britain and Palestine 1914–1948*, compiled by Philip Jones (Oxford: Oxford University, 1979), p.83.

14. Official Disregard of Arab Immigration

1. See, for example, C. F. Strickland, *Report on the Possibility of Introducing a System of Agricultural Cooperation in Palestine* (Jerusalem, 1930), pp. 1–3, cited by Esco Foundation for Palestine, *Palestine: A Study of Jewish, Arab and British Policies,* 2 vols. (New Haven: Yale University Press, 1947), vol. 2, pp. 708–712, 810; also see Government of Palestine, *Census of Palestine 1931,* 2 vols. (Alexandria, 1933), vol. 1, pt. 1, E. Mills, *Report;* also see Permanent Mandates Commission, *Report of 17th Session,* 1930, particularly p. 142; also see Permanent Mandates Commission, *Minutes, June 1930,* for rejection of Hope Simpson findings; also see *Palestine Royal Commission Report,* p. 74, paras. 61, 62; also see statement in House of Commons, November 17, 1930, in *Report of the Experts of the Joint Palestine Survey Commission* (Boston, 1928), p. 404; also see Government of Palestine, *Report of a Committee on*

the *Economic Conditions of Agriculturists in Palestine and the Fiscal Measures of Government in Relation thereto,* 1930, pp. 17–18, 22, para. 42, especially Tables XIX, XX (Points 32, 35–36), XXII; also see testimony of Lewis Andrews, November 24, 1936, in *Palestine Royal Commission: Minutes of Evidence Heard at Public Sessions,* Colonial 134; also see League of Nations Mandate for Palestine, Article 9; also see William M. Thompson, *The Land and the Book* (New York: Harper Brothers, 1873), vol. 1, pp. 497–498; also see Lewis French, *Reports on Agricultural Development and Land Settlement in Palestine,* 1931, particularly p. 79, para. 77; p. 37, para. 9; pp. 23–26, paras. 93, 96; also see *Report . . . for the Year 1934,* Colonial No. 104, p. 78, para. 20; p. 58, para. 36; also see A. Granowsky, *Land and the Jewish Reconstruction of Palestine* (Jerusalem, 1931), pp. 17–128.

2. John Hope Simpson, *Report on Immigration, Land Settlement and Development,* 1930, Command Paper #3686, p. 126.

3. "Importation of other than Jewish labour. —Further, it is clear that if unemployment is a valid reason for preventing Jewish immigration, it is also a reason for preventing importation of labour of other nationalities. At the time of writing, even with marked unemployment among Arabs, Egyptian labour is being employed in certain individual cases, and its ingress has been the subject of adverse comment in the Press." Hope Simpson, ibid., p. 138.

4. Ibid.

5. Ibid.

6. Ibid., p. 126.

7. Memorandum on Deportation—Arabs, April 9, 1942, ISA Record Group 2, File I/588/33.

8. "Seasonal and occasional labour.—There are two obvious dangers against which provision must be made in the execution of any measures dealing with the registration of unemployment. The first lies in the large amount of casual and temporary unemployment of the agricultural labourer and indeed of the small Arab cultivator. Of this class many individuals flock to the towns in order to earn something in addition to what is yielded by the land. The agricultural labourer is paid entirely in kind, while, in the case of the small cultivator, unless he can eke out his income during the agricultural off-season, he is frequently unable to obtain the cash necessary to pay his taxes or his moneylender, and for the year's purchases which are essential for his household. There can be no valid reason for refusal to register as unemployed temporary labourers of this kind, if they are in fact in the labour market, and in fact unemployed. The regulations of the employment exchanges should, however, be so framed as to ensure that the names of persons of this class seeking employment should be removed when seasonal activity causes them to return from the towns to the villages." Hope Simpson, *Report,* pp. 137–138.

9. Ibid., pp. 138–139.

10. *A Survey of Palestine,* prepared for the Anglo-American Committee of Inquiry, 1945–1946, vol. I, p. 28.

11. Statement of Policy, 1930, Command #3692.

12. *A Survey of Palestine,* vol. I, p. 28.

13. Ibid., p. 27.

14. Hope Simpson, *Report,* p. 142.

15. *A Survey of Palestine,* vol. I, p. 23.

16. Rhodes House, File 7, Box 15, March 15, 1937, extract of letter from Hope Simpson to J. R. Chancellor.

17. "Great Britain and Palestine, 1915–1945," published by the Royal Institute of International Affairs (London and New York, 1946), Paper #20, p. 56.

18. October 29, 1930, *A Survey of Palestine,* vol. 1, pp. 27–28. Weizmann's indignation was apparently at times tempered by obsequious support of the British "system of immigration": see one 1934 report from Sir Eric Drummond, British envoy in Rome, regarding Weizmann's concern at "the large influx of German Jews into Palestine." Daniel Carpi, *Zionism: Studies in the History of the Zionist Movement and the Jewish Community of Palestine* (Tel Aviv: Masada, 1975), p. 242; earlier, Sir Herbert Samuel provoked outrage in the Palestinian Jewish community with his "redefinition" of the Balfour Declaration, in 1921. Neil Caplan, *Palestine Jewry and the Arab Question 1917–1925* (London: Frank Cass, 1978), pp. 88ff; also see Moshe Mossek, *Palestine Immigration Policy Under Sir Herbert Samuel: British Zionist and Arab Attitudes* (London: Cass, 1978).

19. February 14, 1931, ibid., pp. 28–29. According to Martin Gilbert, MacDonald "read out" the letter in the House of Commons on February 13. *Exile,* p. 156.

20. *Report . . . for the Year 1935,* Colonial #112, pp. 62ff.

21. Ibid., p. 315.

22. Hope Simpson, *Report,* p. 26.

23. See, for example, Ernest Main, *Iraq* (London, 1935), p. 182; "Notes on Syria," in *Great Britain of the East,* August 6, 1936.

24. *Report . . . for the Year 1935,* Colonial #112, p. 315; also see Minutes of League of Nations Permanent Mandates Comm.: "Lord Lugard: there was apparently a growing recognition that Transjordan contrasted unfavourably with Palestine . . ."; XXIII (23rd Session), p. 98.

25. Main, *Palestine at the Crossroads,* p. 116. See n. 1 above.

26. PRO FO 371/17204/33, *Comments of Department of Development on the Memorandum of the Jewish Agency on the 1st and supplementary Reports on Agricultural Developments and Land Settlement in Palestine,* c.i.e., c.b.e., p. 2.

27. A. Granovsky, *The Land Issue in Palestine* (Jerusalem: Keren Kayemeth LeIsrael Ltd., 1936), p. 39.

28. *Report . . . for the Year 1934,* Colonial #104, p. 58.

29. *Report . . . for the Year 1935,* Colonial #112, p. 63. According to Granovsky, "All but a few of the tenants of tracts acquired by Jews have remained on the land, either as independent farmers or tenants. Of the 688 (the figure given by the Jews) tenants who formerly lived in the Plain of Jezreel, 526, or 76%, remained in agricultural occupations, and their position was made anything but worse by the transfer of the land to Jewish owners." Granovsky, *The Land Issue in Palestine,* pp. 40–41.

30. Protection of Cultivators Ordinance, 1929, see Laws of 1929, vol. I, p. 299; cited in Anglo-American Committee, *Survey,* vol. I, p. 290.

31. Cultivator's Protection Ordinance of 1933, see *Survey of Palestine*, vol. I, pp. 290–291, citing Drayton, vol. I, p. 506. By this ordinance, any Arab who claimed (vis-à-vis claimants to be "Arab refugees" in '48 in camps, who were in part itinerants from elsewhere) to be grazing or a "statutory tenant" . . . not "grossly neglected" his

"holding"—in other words, if he proved he'd wandered over the area, it was declared he must be given subsistence area, remuneration based on landlord's earnings.

32. A total of 3,271 applications for resettlement had been received; "2,607 being disallowed." *Palestine Royal Commission Report,* p. 240.

33. From the letter to Chancellor from John Hope Simpson, August 4, 1936, File 7 in Box 15 MSS British Empire s. 284 at Rhodes House (extract).

34. PRO FO 371/4882, letter to Duff Cooper (Right Honorable) from Sir Ormsby-Gore, May 6, 1937.

35. Evidence of Arab illegal immigration taken from Palestine Royal Commission Notes of Evidence, Wednesday, December 2, 1936, 14th Meeting (Public), testimony of M. Shertok and Dr. David Werner Senator, pp. 90–92, Tuesday, December 8, 1936, 17th Meeting (Public), testimony of M. Shertok and Eliahu Epstein, representing Jewish Agency for Palestine; pp. 93–101.

36. Ibid.
   Question: "Are you giving any suggestions in regard to a remedy?"
   Answer: "The first remedy is an effective control of the frontiers, with some system of check in the country itself."
   Question: "It means a very big system. No doubt you have thought that out. It means practically that every man in Palestine would have to have a card of identity. Then the police can go and say to him: 'Let me see your card,' and if he has not got one you can get at him?"
   Answer: "If the control of the frontiers, after an experimental period, did not prove effective, such a measure as you indicate might have to be resorted to, but in our submission the control of the frontiers has never been effective, and if it was it might deter these people from coming into Palestine. . . . I submit that if these people knew there were the Police after them who would not let them across, a large number of them would be deferred from even attempting to cross."

37. Hammond to Weizmann, Palestine Royal Comission, *"Secret"* Notes of Evidence taken on Friday, December 18, 1936, twenty-sixth meeting (private), testimony of Dr. Chaim Weizmann, pp. 33–35; see also Ninth Meeting testimony of Thursday, November 26, 1936, particularly pp. 9, 14, 23, 36; see also testimony of Thirty First meeting (Private), Wednesday, December 23, 1936, particularly pp. 7, 31, 39–40, 53, 63, 68.

38. Chaim Weizmann, born in Motol, near Pinsk, Russia; Zionist leader who explained Zionism to Arthur Balfour and was critically involved in the events of Palestine throughout the Mandatory period.

39. George Antonius, *The Arab Awakening—the Story of the Arab National Movement* (Philadelphia: Lippincott, 1939).

40. Palestine Royal Commission, Notes of Evidence (Public), testimony of George Antonius, January 18, 1937.

41. Palestine Royal Commission, Notes of Evidence, taken on January 12, 1937, testimony of Haj Amin al-Husseini. See excerpt of Mufti testimony in Appendix VIII.

42. Abdul Hadi, former Arab Secretary of the Strike Committee, in testimony before Palestine Royal Commission, January 13, 1937. See *Palestine,* January 20, 1937.

43. *Palestine Royal Commission Report,* June 1937, London, Command #5479. (Also known as Peel Commission Report.)

44. Foreign Office Official Ronald Campbell, Egyptian Department, cautioned against

implementing a policy "which would be hateful to the Arabs." October 15, 1937, Minute, FO 371/20816. In Gilbert, *Exile,* p. 188.
45. *The Palestine Royal Commission Report,* pp. 291–292.
"A large proportion of Arab immigrants into Palestine come from the Hauran. These people go in considerable numbers to Haifa, where they work in the port. It is, however, important to realize that the extent of the yearly exodus from the Hauran depends mainly on the state of the crops there. In a good year the amount of illegal immigration into Palestine is negligible and confined to the younger members of large families whose presence is not required in the fields. Most persons in this category probably remain permanently in Palestine, wages there being considerably higher than in Syria. According to an authoritative estimate as many as ten or eleven thousand Hauranis may go to Palestine temporarily in search of work in a really bad year. The Deputy Inspector-General of the Criminal Investigation Department has recently estimated that the number of Hauranis illegally in the country at the present time is roughly 2,500."
46. Ibid.
47. Ibid., pp. 292–293.
48. Ibid., p. 39.
49. Palestine Royal Commission, Notes of Evidence, November 24, 1936, pp. 22–29.
50. From *The Palestine Royal Commission Report,* p. 300:
"76. The heavy immigration in the years 1933–6 would seem to show that the Jews have been able to *enlarge the economic absorptive capacity of the country for Jews.* The process can be continued for some time to come and it would appear that its expansion need only be limited by the amount of the funds which Jewish philanthropy and enterprise are prepared to pour into the country. But such an expansion of the economic absorptive capacity is calculated to lead to a development of the Jewish National Home which is not organic but is unnatural, *since it ignores one of the conditions of the Home, namely the hostile attitude of the Arab inhabitants of Palestine.*" (Emphasis added.)
51. Ibid., p. 394.
52. July 16, 1937: cited in Martin Gilbert, *Exile and Return,* p. 182.
53. Esco Foundation for Palestine, *Palestine, A Study of Jewish, Arab and British Policies.* Published for the Esco Foundation for Palestine, Inc., vol. II (New Haven: Yale University Press, 1947), pp. 852–853; Chaim Weizmann was the partition plan's "leading spokesman."
54. *Palestine Partition Commission Report,* printed and published by His Majesty's Stationery Office, London, 1938, Command #5854, p. 18.
55. Esco, *Palestine,* vol. II, p. 854. For text of 20th Zionist Congress' resolution, see pp. 18–19, *Palestine Partition Commission Report.*
56. *Palestine,* published for British Palestine Committee at Letchworth, England, January 27 issue, article dated January 20, 1937.
57. *Palestine Partition Commission Report,* p. 17.
58. *Palestine Royal Commission Report,* p. 366.
59. Ibid., p. 135.
60. "Japheth in the Tents of Shem," *Asia and the Americans,* December 1942, pp. 692–694.

61. *Arab vs. Arab,* pamphlet (Wadsworth and Co., Rydal Press, Keighley, England, 1939), p. 3. Rhodes House Doc. 905 17.75 (22).
62. James Parkes, *A History of Palestine from 135 A.D. to Modern Times* (N.Y: Oxford University Press, 1949), pp. 321–322.
63. Ibid., p. 321.
64. Ernest Main, *Palestine at the Crossroads* (London: George Allen and Unwin, 1937), p. 107.
65. Stuart Emeny, *News Chronicle,* London, December 10, 1938.
66. Martin Gilbert, *Exile and Return, The Struggle for a Jewish Homeland* (Philadelphia, 1978), p. 204.
67. Lieutenant Colonel H.J. Simson, *British Rule and Rebellion* (London: Blackwood, 1937), p. 315.

    Simson pointed out that "The label on the money box had been altered from 'strike fund' to 'distressed Palestine,' but otherwise there was no change," p. 290.
68. On October 15, 1937, Esco Foundation for Palestine, *Palestine, A Study of Jewish, Arab and British Policies,* vol. II, p. 879; the Mufti's "figurehead," Jamal Husseini, President of the Arab Party, had escaped earlier.
69. November 21, 1938; also see Esco, ibid., p. 878 ff.
70. "The murdered were as follows—

Feb. 1937	Mukhtar of	Arab Birket Caesarea
Sept. 1937	"	Balad Esh Sheikh
Dec. 1937	"	Shahmata
April 1938	"	Migdal. He was a Christian Arab. His wife was also murdered.
April 1938	"	Mafaleen
Aug. 1938	"	Ejn Razal
Aug. 1938	"	Beth Mahsir
Sept. 1938		Wife and three sons of the Mukhtar of Deir Es Sheikh. Mukhtar was absent at the time.
Oct. 1938		Mukhtar of Ard-el-Yehud, near Haifa. He was a Christian Arab.
Oct. 1938	"	Beth Hema
Nov. 1938	"	Akaba Quarter, Nablus

    "During the same period, attempts were made on the life of the Mukhtar of Lifta village (July 1937), and the Mukhtar of Seir (October, 1938)"; cited in *Arab v. Arab,* pamphlet, Wadsworth and Co., Rydal Press, Keighley, England, 1939, p. 13; also see *Palestine,* October 6, 1937, vol. XII, no. 40, for list of Arab "notables" "murdered between April and September, 1937."
71. Ibid.
72. Letter to James Malcolm, February 22, 1937, transmitted to Former High Commissioner of Palestine, John Chancellor, RH File 7/Box 15. From "an English correspondent in Palestine whose name for obvious reasons it is undesirable to disclose but for whose impartiality and veracity I can thoroughly vouch." J. Malcolm.
73. RH File No. 7 of Box 15, letter to John Chancellor from Peake, June 20, 1937, extract, p. 3.
74. PRO FO 371/20817, Havard to Foreign Office, No. 15, "important, repeated to Jerusalem, Paris, Baghdad, and Damascus saving."

75. Ormsby-Gore Cabinet Papers 24/272, November 9, 1937; cited in Gilbert, *Exile*, p. 191.
76. August 21, 1938, Cabinet Papers, 24/278, cited in Gilbert, ibid., p. 206.
77. August 12, conversation with Dr. Izzet Tannous, Arab Christian head of the Arab Centre, London; cited in Gilbert, ibid., p. 206.
78. *Palestine Partition Commission Report,* 1938, Command #5458, p. 246; Esco Foundation for Palestine, *Palestine, A Study of Jewish, Arab and British Policies,* pp. 874–875, 1146, 1156ff.
79. Esco Foundation for Palestine, ibid., p. 1156.
80. October 24, 1938, Cabinet Committee Minutes: Cabinet Papers 27/651, cited in Gilbert, *Exile and Return,* p. 210.
81. League of Nations Permanent Mandates Commission, 1937, Minutes of the 32nd Session, pp. 73–74.
82. Ibid.
83. Colonel Wedgewood, June 1938, *Survey of International Affairs,* 1938, vol. I, p. 417, n. 1.
84. *Palestine Partition (Woodhead) Commission Report,* 1938, from Martin Gilbert, *The Arab-Israeli Conflict, Its History in Maps* (London: Weidenfield and Nicolson, 1974), p. 28
85. *Palestine Partition Commission Report,* pp. 144–45.
86. *Report . . . for the Year 1937, Colonial #146,* p. 80.
87. *A Survey of Palestine,* vol. I, p. 297.
88. PRO FO371/17204/33, High Commission Despatch #247 (REF. ADM. 305), July 23, 1921, in Dept. of Development Response to Jewish Agency, (See n. 26 above), p. 5.
89. Granovsky, *The Land Issue in Palestine,* p. 40.
90. *Palestine Royal Commission Report,* p. 240.
91. *Palestine Partition Commission Report,* Note of Reservations by Sir Alison Russell, p. 257.
92. Sir Geoffrey Furlonge, *Palestine is My Country, The Story of Musa Alami* (New York: Praeger Press, 1969), p. 136.
93. Main, *Palestine at the Crossroads,* pp. 193–194. Main reported that "It is shown in Chapter 6 how greatly the Shaw Commission and the Hope-Simpson Inquiry went astray in their estimates of the displacement of Arab tenants and agricultural workers, although it must be noted that both made it clear that in any event no blame attached to the actual Jewish purchasers. The Shaw Report (Command #3530, 1930, p. 62) says of the land sales between 1921 and 1929 'no criticism can be levied against the Jewish land companies in respect to these transactions.' The Hope Simpson Report (Command #3686, 1930, p. 51) says of the Jewish purchases in Jezreel, the scene of most of the alleged displacements, 'the Jewish authorities have nothing with which to reproach themselves.' "
94. *Report . . . for the Year 1936,* Colonial #112, p. 62ff.
95. Main, *Palestine at the Crossroads,* pp. 193–194.
96. Granovsky, *Land and the Jewish Reconstruction in Palestine,* Palestine's Near East Publications, Jerusalem, 1931, pp. 155–156.
97. Parkes, *A History of Palestine from 135 A.D. to Modern Times,* p. 321; also see Doreen Warriner, "Land Tenure in the Fertile Crescent" from Issawi (ed.), *The Economic History of the Middle East* (Chicago: University of Chicago Press, 1966), p. 5.

98. Government of Palestine, *Report by C. F. Strickland of the Indian Civil Service on the Possibility of Introducing a System of Agricultural Co-operation in Palestine* (Jerusalem, 1930), pp. 1–2: In 1930 C. F. Strickland concluded that in (Western) Palestine "His [the fellah's] trouble is his debt; so long as a small cultivator sees the burden of his debt to be so great and the rate of accruing interest so high . . . he will make no sincere attempt to alter his plan of cultivation. If his present crops allow him to pay only one half of the interest upon his debt, there is little inducement to make such improvements as will enable him to pay three-quarters of the amount. The benefit will fall entirely into the hands of his creditors, while he will only labour the harder without hope of reaching freedom."

    Also see Furlonge, *Palestine is My Country, The Story of Musa Alami,* p. 135ff.

99. Main, *Palestine at the Crossroads,* p. 40.

100. Enclosure: re: Arab Executive Committee rejection of French's Arab aid and development proposal and regarding: landless Arabs; signed O.G.R. Williams of Colonial Office on Downing Street (handwritten note) January 1, 1934, PRO CO 733/17249.

101. *Palestine Royal Commission Report,* p. 263, quoting Lewis French Report. According to the French Report, "In one Sub-District in the hilly tracts it is reported that in a decade no less than 30 percent of the land has passed from Arab peasants to Arab capitalists."

102. Parkes, *A History of Palestine from 135 A.D. to Modern Times,* p. 321.

103. ". . . for the employed the rate of wages has steadily gone up. The daily wage paid to an Arab for skilled labour is now from 250 to 600 mils, and for unskilled labour from 100 to 180 mils. In Syria the wage ranges from 67 mils in older industries to 124 mils in newer ones. Factory labour in Iraq is paid from 40 to 60 mils." *Palestine Royal Commission Report,* 1938, Command #5479, p. 127. (100 mils equals 2 shillings.)

104. Main, *Palestine at the Crossroads,* p. 124. According to the *Palestine Royal Commission Report,* in the three-year period of 1933–1935, Arab estate holders received over $20 million for land sales, with Jewish purchases paying several times more than the land value. *Palestine Royal Commission Report,* p. 126.

105. November 24, 1936, Palestine Royal Commission, Minutes of Evidence, pp. 22–23.

106. Ibid., p. 27.

107. Ibid., pp. 27–29.

108. Ibid., p. 29.

109. Andrews was murdered on September 26, 1937, by Arab terrorists, identified in Chapter 13 as "probably" led by Sheikh Kassab, as per correspondence from W.D. Battershill, October 12, 1937.

110. Cited in Gilbert, *Exile and Return,* p. 186.

111. ". . . though in the immediate neighborhood of Jerusalem dairy and fruit farms might eventually prove self-supporting." *Palestine Royal Commission Report,* p. 268.

15. Britain's Double Standard

1. King Hussein of Jordan, *Uneasy Lies the Head* (New York, 1962); Dr. Paul Riebenfeld, "The Integrity of Palestine—Jews and Arabs, Israel and Jordan," *Midstream,* August/September 1975, p. 22; also see Hussein of Jordan, *My "War" with Israel* (London, 1969), p. 15.

2. The total population was over 1,200,000, excepting nomads. A. Granovsky, *The*

Land Issue in Palestine, Keren Kayemeth LeIsrael, Ltd. (Jerusalem, 1936), p. 46.

3. Martin Gilbert, *Exile and Return,* p. 226.

4. Speech, June 27, 1923, cited in Esco Foundation, p. 288.

5. John Gunther, *Inside Asia* (New York: Harper and Brothers, 1939), pp. 600–601.

6. According to this German source, "Von Falkenhayn decided to move to Nablus. On being ordered to evacuate, the Jews shed bitter tears, but the native population was stolidly indifferent, 'they knew no fatherland.' " Schlachten des Weltkrieges, Reichsarchivs, IV, "Jildirim" (Berlin, 1926), pp. 122–123. Cited in de Haas, *History,* p. 459.

7. Sir Geoffrey Furlonge, *Palestine Is My Country, The Story of Musa Alami* (New York: Praeger Press, 1969), pp. 114–129.

8. Colonel R. Meinertzhagen, Letter, *The Times,* London, February 7, 1938. Cited in Martin Gilbert, *Exile,* p. 196.

9. David Lloyd George, *The Truth About the Peace Treaties* (London: Victor Gollancz, Ltd., 1938), vol. I, pp. 1118–1119.

10. Cited by Bernard Lewis, "The Return of Islam," *Commentary,* January 1976, p. 41.

11. Ibid., pp. 40–41.

12. T.E. Lawrence, *Secret Despatches from Arabia* (London, n.d.), p. 39, *Arab Bulletin,* November 26, 1916.

13. Lawrence, *Secret,* p. 70; *Arab Bulletin,* March 12, 1917.

14. T.E. Lawrence, *Seven Pillars of Wisdom* (London: Jonathan Cape, Ltd., 1935), p. 100.

15. B. H. Liddell Hart, *T.E. Lawrence to His Biographer* (1938), p. 101; cited by Elie Kedourie, *England and the Middle East,* p. 103.

16. T.E. Lawrence, *Seven,* p. 23 (1940 ed.), as cited in Kedourie, *England,* p. 103.

17. T.E. Lawrence, *Seven,* p. 101.

18. *Haycraft Commission of Inquiry Report,* July 1, 1921, p. 19. Command #1540.

19. August 22, 1921. Cited in Martin Gilbert, *Exile,* p. 139.

20. Anglo-American Committee of Inquiry, *A Survey of Palestine* (Palestine, 1945–1946), vol. I, p. 31.

21. Protokoll der Verhandlungen des XVIII. Zionistenkongress, Vienna, 1934, p. 83. Cited in Esco Foundation for Palestine, *Palestine,* vol. II, p. 770.

22. November 1, 1933, "Secret Report on the Political Situation" from Amman, C.H.F. Cox, British Resident. Doc. #2, vol. E, p. 2, 7177/169/31 in vol. 16927, Colonial Office No. 7754/33.

23. For example, Permanent Mandates Commission, *Minutes* of 27th Session, 1935, p. 47; also see Christopher Sykes, *Crossroads to Israel* (London: Collins, 1965), pp. 60–61ff, 239.

24. Weizmann to Churchill, March 1, 1921. Dr. Paul S. Riebenfeld, *Israel, Jordan and Palestine* (unpub.), App. E.

25. On the "critical" issue of "frontiers," after the "agreement reached with France" had "cut Palestine off" from "access to" and "possession of" the Northern territories. "Most promising" for "Jewish settlement on a large scale." Weizmann, ibid.

26. Permanent Mandates Commission, *Minutes* of 27th Session, 1935, p. 48.

27. Ibid.

28. Major J.B. Glubb, "The Economic Situation of the Trans-Jordan Tribes," *Royal Central Asian Society Journal,* 1938, vol. 25, pp. 458–459. Glubb's response to April 1938 article by E. Epstein, "The Bedouin of Transjordan," *Royal Central Asian Society Journal,* vol. 25, 1938.

29. Ibid., p. 459.

30. From Mr. Williams (Colonial Office) to Mr. Rendel (Foreign Office): Attitude of His Majesty's Representatives abroad regarding Zionist functions, PRO FO 371 E 779/257/31, February 6, 1933; also see PRO FO 371 E 7177/16927 signed J.C. Sterndale Bennet (extract).

31. Matiel Mogannam, *The Arab Women and the Palestine Problem* (London: Herbert Joseph, Ltd., 1937), pp. 217–218, cited in Esco, p. 528.

32. Esco, *Palestine,* pp. 771–772.

33. *Palestine Royal Commission Report* (London, 1938), p. 82.

34. August 14, 1937, Permanent Mandates Commission of the League of Nations, Geneva. Cited in Gilbert, *Exile,* p. 186.

35. Martin Gilbert, *Exile,* p. 198.

36. Bernard Wasserstein, *Britain and the Jews of Europe—1939–1945* (Oxford: Clarendon Press, 1979), pp. 5–6. The Nuremberg laws, intricately defining qualifications of "non-Aryans" and harshly restricting Jewish existence, were enacted in 1935.

37. Bernard Wasserstein, *Britain,* pp. 6–7.

38. Ehud Avriel, *Open the Gates,* p. 15.

39. Ibid.

40. Martin Gilbert, *Exile,* p. 198.

41. Avriel, *Open,* p. 15.

42. July 6, 1938. For background prior to the Evian Conference see Henry Feingold, *Politics of Rescue,* p. 22ff; also see Dorothy Thompson, "Refugees, A World Problem," in *Foreign Affairs,* April 1938, pp. 375–378; for British view, see Wasserstein, *Britain,* pp. 8–9, 189.

43. "Undersecretary of State, Sumner Welles, had devised the idea of an international conference," believing that the calling of the conference and its related commotion "would in themselves act as an indicator of the American Government's stand and perhaps influence the Nazis." Ehud Avriel, *Open,* pp. 20–21; also see Arthur Morse, *While Six Million Died* (New York: Hart Publishing Co., 1967), p. 60; also see Joint Hearings before a Subcommittee of the Committee on Immigration, United States Senate, and a Subcommittee of the Committee on Immigration and Naturalization, House of Representatives, 16th Congress, 1st Session, April 20, 21, and 24, 1939, p. 160ff.

44. Speech at Konigsberg, April 1938. Cited in Avriel, *Open,* p. 21.

45. *New York Times,* July 4, 1938.

46. June 19, 1938.

47. Morse, *While,* pp. 203–215, particularly 207–211; also see Feingold, *Politics,* p. 23.

48. Avriel, *Open,* p. 24. For German Foreign Office reaction, see *Deutsche Diplomatische Korrespondenz,* July 12, 1938, quoted in *New York Times,* July 13, 1938, p. 13; also see Feingold, *Politics of Rescue,* pp. 36–37.

49. Avriel, *Open,* p. 19.

50. Morse, *While,* p. 213.

51. Avriel, *Open,* p. 25; also see Morse, *While,* p. 212.

52. Morse documented the votes:

"Australia, with vast, unpopulated areas announced: 'As we have no real racial problem, we are not desirous of importing one.' New Zealand was unwilling to lift its restrictions. The British colonial empire, reported Sir John Shuckburgh, contained no territory suitable to the large-scale settlement of Jewish refugees. Canada wanted agricultural migrants and none others. The same was true of Colombia, Uruguay and Venezuela.

"France, whose population already included two hundred thousand refugees and three million aliens, stressed that it had reached its saturation point.

"Nicaragua, Honduras, Costa Rica and Panama issued a joint statement saying that they could accept no 'traders or intellectuals.' Argentina, with a population one-tenth that of the United States reported that it had welcomed almost as many refugees as the United States hence could not be counted on for large-scale immigration.

"The Netherlands and Denmark reflected their traditional humanitarianism. Though Holland had already accepted twenty-five thousand Jewish refugees, it offered itself as a country of temporary sojourn. Denmark, so densely populated that its own citizens were forced to emigrate, had already taken in a disproportionately large number of German exiles. Within its narrow limits, it would continue to do so."

Morse, *While,* pp. 212–213.
53. Avriel, *Open,* p. 26.
54. Gilbert, *Exile,* p. 203.
55. Ibid.
56. In 1938, the total population of all Western Palestine was estimated at less than 1.5 million. Anglo-American Committee, *Survey,* vol. I, p. 141; in 1951, when the population of Israel—not all of Western Palestine—was roughly 1.3 million, "population density in Israel was only 200 per sq. mile, compared with 280 in Lebanon and 1,400 in the inhabited areas of Egypt." *UN Yearbook,* 1951, p. 303.
57. PRO FO 371/20821; Nov. 26, 1937, Eden to Lindsay, British Ambassador to the United States. Cited in Gilbert, *Exile,* pp. 193–194.
58. Eden to Harvey, 7 September 1951, BL 56402. Cited in Wasserstein, *Britain,* p. 34.
59. Diary of Oliver Harvey, entry dated 25 April 1943, BL 56399. Cited in Wasserstein, *Britain,* p. 34.
60. Cabinet Committee Minutes: Cabinet Papers 24/285, April 20, 1939. Cited in Gilbert, *Exile,* p. 226; also see correspondence to Winston Churchill reporting of British officials who were "strongly anti-Semite" in Bucharest and Prague, despite the "persecution" of Jews there. Cited in Gilbert, *Exile,* p. 226.
61. January 18, 1939. PRO FO 371/23221, cited in Gilbert, *Exile,* p. 218.
62. Anglo-American Committee, *Survey,* vol. I, pp. 52–53.
63. Ibid., p. 52.
64. Cabinet Minutes: Cabinet Papers 23/97, March 8, 1939. Cited in Gilbert, *Exile,* p. 225.
65. Anglo-American Committee, *Survey,* vol. I, p. 53. The *White Paper,* Statement of Policy, Command #6019, May 1939, full text in ibid., pp. 90–99.
66. Cabinet Minutes: May 1, 1939, Cabinet Papers 23/99. Cited in Gilbert, *Exile,* p. 228. Also see Bethell, *Palestine Triangle,* for interesting observations by MacDonald many years afterward, pp. 72–75.
67. June 24, 1891. Cited in Gilbert, *Exile,* p. 43.

68. Cabinet Papers 24/282, January 1939. Cited in Nicholas Bethell, *The Palestine Triangle, The Struggle for the Holy Land, 1935–1948* (New York: G.P. Putnam's Sons, 1979), p. 19.

69. *Report of the Commission on the Palestine Disturbances of August, 1929* (The Shaw Report), Command Paper #3530, London, 1930.

70. Hope Simpson, *Report*, p. 136.

71. According to Sir Christopher Sykes, the Zionists' "indignation" at appointment of the Mufti Haj-Amin, an "avowed enemy" of the Jews, was subordinated by "the threatening developments in the Eastern part of the British mandated territory" of Palestine. Sykes, *Crossroads to Israel*, p. 60ff.

72. In August 1939, the four opposing members insisted that the White Paper was in violation of the Mandate in its stand on Jewish immigration restrictions, on land restrictions, and its acquiescence in a probable rule by the Arabs. *Manchester Guardian*, August 18, 1939. Cited in Bethell, *The Palestine Triangle*, p. 70; see also Sykes, *Crossroads*, p. 259.

73. July 30, 1939, in correspondence with a sister. Cited in Gilbert, *Exile*, p. 239.

74. The United States added the word "Property" to the rights that must be safeguarded in the American delegation's recommendation to the Paris Peace Conference two years later.

75. The 1938 *Palestine Partition Commission Report* (p. 22) is a clear example of the British use of the term "existing" to describe Palestine's non-Jewish population increase: "an abnormally high (and possibly unprecedented) rate of natural increase in the *existing* indigenous population" was, according to the report, responsible for the growth of population aside from the Jews' immigration.

    According to a report on world population, published in 1936, "there is no evidence that the population increased or diminished during the last two centuries." Carr-Saunders, *World Population*, p. 310. The Palestine Partition Commission stated, "If the numbers fluctuated, the fluctuations cancelled out." From 1919 until 1938, the "Arab population" ("the word 'Arab' in this section is used in its strictest sense and not a [*sic*] equivalent to 'non-Jew.' ") increased "nearly 56 percent."

    "It is worthwhile to study the vital statistics for some explanation of this astonishing change in the Arab population since the war, which it is very unlikely that the authors of the Balfour Declaration or of the Mandate foresaw." *Palestine Partition Commission Report*, p. 23.

76. Professor Braver, in his geographical study, found that the so-called "landless peasants were new immigrants." "Immigration as a Factor in the Growth of the Arab Village in Eretz-Israel," *Economic Review—Problems of Aliyah and Absorption*, vol. 28, nos. 7–9, July–September 1975, p. 15.

77. "On the Arab side the number of landless Arabs has, no doubt been exaggerated and no account has been taken of the sources of employment opened to displaced tenant cultivators by the development of the larger towns or the increase of the area under citrus, *but in my view, the real basis of the outcry was not the existing state of affairs, as apprehension for the future."* Response entitled "Comments of the Department of Development on the Memorandum of the Jewish Agency," from the Department of Development. Document Number 17204/33 FO 371, Reply to the Jewish Agency

regarding the letter sent by the former to the High Commissioner on March 19, 1933, pp. 3–4.

78. *Palestine Royal Commission Report; Palestine Partition Commission Report* (The Woodhead Report), 1938.

79. "Great Britain and Palestine, 1915–1945," published by the Royal Institute of International Affairs (London and New York, 1946), Paper #20, p. 58.

16. Jews in Palestine as "Illegals" and as War Allies

1. From Germany alone the number of immigrant Jews to the Jewish-settled area of Western Palestine had risen from only 353 in 1932 to 5,392 in 1933; overall Jewish immigration in 1935 reached a "peak" of 61,844, the year the Nuremberg laws were enacted against Jews. Nicholas Bethell, *The Palestine Triangle, The Struggle for the Holy Land, 1935–48* (New York: G.P. Putnam's Sons, 1979), p. 25.

2. *Report . . . for the Year 1934,* Colonial No. 104, p. 28; *Report . . . for the Year 1935,* Colonial No. 112, p. 13; *Annual Report of the Dept. of Migration,* 1935, p. 19.

3. ISA 2 I/588/33 R2 July 1, 1933, Memorandum from AGW (Wauchope).

4. "Only 90 immigrants, all of whom were Jews, entered Palestine during the month. A large number of immigrants were *refused admission* to Palestine during the *temporary suspension of Immigration,* and on the 9th of June, officers of the department left for Trieste and Constantinople where these persons had collected, to examine their cases. The examination is not yet concluded, but about 700, all of whom had already started on their journey to Palestine, have been granted permission to proceed." Public Record Extract, Doc. No. CO 7033, #42315. The administrative report of July 1921, under Immigration & Travel, p. 7. Sent by Sir W.H. Deedes, August 2, 1921. (Emphasis added.)

5. Memorandum On the Control of Immigration to Palestine 1920–30, July 16, 1930. ISA Group 2, File No. Imm/40/2.

6. Ibid., para. 7.

7. Ibid., para. 22.

8. PRO CO 537/848 (Doc. 36560). Handwritten, Personal July 11, 1921, from Sir Wyndham Deedes to Major H. Young, from Martin Gilbert's files.

9. PRO CO 537/854/22, December 13, 1921, from Chaim Weizmann to Sir Wyndham Deedes.

10. In 1921, Civil Secretary Winston Churchill intended Transjordan as "a moderately efficient administration" with "at its head some Arab official . . ." utilizing "Palestinians of experience. . . ." July 2, 1921, Churchill to Herbert Samuel, High Commissioner, PRO CO 733/36252; also see PRO CO 733/35186, July 4, 1921, Samuel to Churchill.

11. For interesting insights during the period into the boundaries of the country that would be "Palestine," see David Lloyd George, *The Truth About the Peace Treaties,* pp. 1144–1145; also see C.R. Conder and H.H. Kitchener, *The Survey of Western Palestine,* ed. by E.H. Palmer and Walter Besant (London: Comm. of Palestine Exploration Fund, 1881), particularly map of Palestine (east and west).

12. PRO CO 537/854/22, December 13, 1921. From Chaim Weizmann to Sir Wyndham Deedes.

13. PRO CO 537/854/22, December 22, 1921.

14. Statement of British Policy in Palestine, Command #1700, London, 1922.
15. Anglo-American Committee, *Survey*, vol. I, p. 165: "Immigrants had to satisfy two sets of conditions. First they must qualify as immigrants in the several categories; and secondly they (and travellers also) must not be disqualified for admission to Palestine in virtue of certain statutory disabilities," p. 166.
16. Memorandum on the Control of Immigration to Palestine 1920–30, July 16, 1930. ISA Group 2, Imm/40/2, paragraphs 24, 25, 30.
17. Ibid., para. 33.
18. Ibid., para. 34.
19. Ibid., para. 36.
20. PRO FO 18615/26, "Instructions to His Majesty's Consuls and Passport Control Officers regarding the Grant of Visas For Palestine," regarding office circular of July 12, 1926; FO 372/3171 Doc. No. 7291/95, June 15, 1928: ". . . Deputations from the Zionist Executive and Vaad Leumi are asking for removal of restriction on immigration."
21. PRO CO 733/152, Memorandum from the Palestine Zionist Executive, F.H. Kisch to the Chief Secretary Government Offices, Jerusalem, August 30, 1928.
22. Phillip Jones, *Britain and Palestine 1914–1948* (Oxford: Oxford University Press, 1979), p. 80.
23. PRO CO 733/152 Doc. No. 57198/28 November 9, 1928.
24. Memorandum on the Control of Immigration to Palestine 1920–30, July 16, 1930, para. 40.
25. "Among these immigrants were 1,580 persons who were in Palestine illegally (Jews 939, Christians 502, Moslems 137, Druzes 2) but received permission to remain permanently in the country." *Report . . . for the Year 1931,* Colonial No. 75, p. 22. On p. 21, the report noted that "Steps were taken to regularize the position of a large number of persons in Palestine . . . without permission" who were now "absorbed." "This action was considered to be desirable on general grounds, and also in view of the possibility that the persons concerned would otherwise be deterred from registering at the Census by fear of prosecution for the offence of *illegal presence* in the country." The "great majority" who "took advantage of it were Jews." (Emphasis added.)
26. The 1933 Annual Report stated: "There was, however, an unexpectedly large number of illegal Jewish settlers as well." *Report . . . for the Year 1933,* Colonial No. 94, p. 36. On page 35: "There was a considerable increase of *illicit* immigration, *mostly of Jews,* entering as transit travellers or tourists. . . ." And on page 180, separated from the "immigration" material by 145 pages, was the report that "The extent of illicit and unrecorded immigration into Palestine from or through Syria and Trans-Jordan has been estimated at about 2,000 and Jewish as to fifty percent." From "mostly Jews," the estimate had dropped to fifty percent. *Report . . . for the Year 1933,* Colonial No. 94, pp. 35–36, 180.
27. Conference of Protestant and Catholic Leaders, New York, December 1936, reported in *Palestine,* January 13, 1937, vol. XII, no. 2.
28. United States Senators' statement, reported in *Palestine,* January 13, 1937, vol. XII, no. 2.
29. *Manchester Guardian,* August 18, 1939. Cited in Bethell, *The Palestine Triangle,* p. 70.
30. May 17, 1939, 867N. 01/1556 1/2. Cited in Bethell, *The Palestine Triangle,* p. 69.

31. For detailed documentation of the United States actions and reactions, see Morse, *While;* Wasserstein, *Britain;* Feingold, *Politics,* Laqueur, *Terrible.* William Polk describes many British attempts at "compromise," against what Britain deemed "American irresponsibility"—after the war, in 1946 unlimited immigration into "Palestine" was recommended by both the Democrats and the GOP, an entirely political maneuver according to Polk, motivated only to gain Jewish votes. *The United States and the Arab World* (Cambridge, Mass.: Harvard University Press, 1975), p. 201.

32. Colonial Office note; FO 371/24091, July 22, 1939. Cited in Gilbert, *Exile,* pp. 238–239.

33. March 2, 1939, Foreign Office to Sir Neville Henderson: Treasury Papers, 188/226. Cited in Gilbert, *Exile,* p. 223. The text of the cable was: "There is a large irregular movement from Germany of Jewish refugees who as a rule, set out without visas or any arrangements for their reception, and their attempt to land in any territory that seems to them to present the slightest possibility of receiving them. This is a cause of great embarrassment to His Majesty's Government and also, it appears, to the American Government, and the latter have expressed a wish that you should join American Chargé d'Affaires in Berlin in bringing situation to the attention of appropriate German Authorities and requesting them to discourage such travel on German ships."

34. Gilbert, *Winston S. Churchill, The Prophet,* vol. V, pp. 1970–1971.

35. See examples of documents in Appendix IX; also see Chapter 17.

36. Parliamentary Debates, House of Commons, Col. 2144, May 23, 1939. Cited in Esco, *Palestine,* pp. 916–917.

37. July 30, 1939. Cited in Gilbert, *Exile,* p. 239.

38. Signed October 1, 1938, by Chamberlain, Hitler, Mussolini, and Daladier. As Martin Gilbert writes, "at the Munich Conference, from which the Czechs themselves were excluded, the Czechoslovak State—after twenty years of independence—was made to cede the Sudetenland to Germany." Gilbert, *Exile,* p. 209.

39. Jewish Agency, FO 371/23239. Cited in Bethell, *Palestine Triangle,* p. 71.

40. Esco Foundation, *Palestine,* vol. II, p. 908; also see *Oriente Moderno,* July 1939, pp. 379–380.

41. Bethell, *Palestine Triangle,* pp. 69–71.

42. Chaim Weizmann told British Secretary of State for Foreign Affairs Anthony Eden's Principal private secretary, Oliver Harvey, that the Jews of Eastern Europe would swim to Palestine if necessary, no matter what the British did. Diary of Oliver Harvey, BL 56398 dated entry January 29, 1942; for a detailed account of several instances when the Jews tried literally to do just that, see Wasserstein, *Britain,* p. 141ff.

43. Anglo-American Committee, *Survey of Palestine,* p. 53; also see Wasserstein, *Britain,* pp. 51–52, 348–349; also see Gilbert, *Winston S. Churchill,* vol. V (Boston: Houghton-Mifflin Co., 1977), p. 1069; Gilbert, *Exile,* pp. 225–226; Wasserstein, *The Diplomatic Diaries of Oliver Harvey.*

44. Department of Migration Report, 1938, p. 24.

45. Bethell, *Palestine Triangle,* pp. 56–57.

46. United States Recommendation by Delegation to the Paris Peace Conference, January 21, 1919.

47. Wasserstein, *Britain,* p. 109. Latham minute, R.T.E. Latham, 24 December 1940, PRO FO 371/2524/487 (W 12667/12667/48).

48. Palestine Statement of Policy, Command #6019, The White Paper of May 1939, para. 14.
49. Anglo-American Committee, *Survey,* vol. I, pp. 212–213. See Chapter 17.
50. High Commissioner to Colonial Office, July 10, 1940, PRO CO 733/431 (76039). Cited in Wasserstein, *Britain,* p. 353.
51. Anglo-American Committee, *Survey,* vol. I, p. 56.
52. Ibid. See Menachem Begin's account of the broadcasting network in *The Revolt* (New York: Nash Publishing, 1977), pp. 82–84.
53. Ibid.
54. Lord Halifax report to the Cabinet of conversation with Kennedy, April 20, 1939. Cabinet Committee Minutes, Cabinet Papers, 24/285. Cited in Gilbert, *Exile,* p. 226.
55. August 30, 1938. Charles Bateman, afterward British Ambassador to Poland and Mexico. Cited in Bethell, *Palestine Triangle,* p. 44.
56. Bethell, *Palestine Triangle,* p. 45. Lacy Baggallay, Foreign Office.
57. See Weizmann's letter of May 31, 1939, to the High Commissioner of Palestine "with the request that its representations be forwarded to the Permanent Mandates Commission," in Esco, *Palestine,* pp. 911–912.
58. Viscount Halifax to Weizmann, December 19, 1939. PRO FO 371/24563/273 (E97/31/31). Cited in Wasserstein, *Britain,* p. 352.
59. Sloan, editor, *Ringleblum Journal,* p. 125. Cited in Wasserstein, *Britain,* p. 344. Wasserstein's work is one of the most comprehensive of the documented studies of the subject of Britain's attitude and its role in the crisis of European Jewry.
60. The American Christian Palestine Committee, *The Arab War Effort, A Documented Account* (New York: American Christian Palestine Committee, 1947), p. 13.
61. Anglo-American Committee, *Survey,* vol. I, p. 57.
62. The American Christian Palestine Committee, *The Arab War Effort,* p. 12.
63. *Palestine Partition Commission Report,* London, 1938, p. 261.
64. *Palestine Royal Commission Report* (The Peel Report), 1937, p. 121.
65. *Palestine Royal Commission Report,* p. 200.
66. The Palestine Royal Commission presented a plan for 3 zones in Palestine: "a Jewish state, including coastal region from South of Tel Aviv to North of Acre, the Valley of Esdraelon and Galilee; an Arab state, including the rest of Palestine as well as Transjordan; and a British enclave under permanent mandate, including Jerusalem, Bethlehem and a narrow corridor to Mediterranean including Lydda & Ramle." Laqueur, *A History of Zionism,"* pp. 514–518.
67. June 29, 1937, Cabinet Papers, 24/166. Cited in Gilbert, *Exile,* p. 180.
68. Baxter, FO 371/21868. Cited in Bethell, *Palestine Triangle,* p. 56.
69. May 22, 1939. Cited in Gilbert, *Exile,* p. 229.
70. I.F. Stone, *PM,* April 15, 1944, cited in Esco Foundation, *Palestine,* p. 1044.
71. Parkes, *Whose Land?,* p. 305; see Anglo-American Report for the 1946 observation that the "success of Arab terrorism" had only begun to provoke Jews to self-defense, p. 32. Just before the attack of Deir Yaseen, during January to March 1948, 875 Jews "had fallen victims" and more than 1850 "were wounded in Arab attacks . . . throughout the country." Gabbay, *Political Study,* pp. 61–62.
72. Albert Memmi, *Jews and Arabs,* p. 33.
73. According to Philip J. Baram and the Zionist Archives of Bierbrier, "The American oil interests did not feel unduly threatened by Zionism," *The Department of State in the Middle East, 1919–1945* (Philadelphia: University of Pennsylvania Press,

1978), p. 309, n. 8. Baram adds, however, that no definitive research has as yet been presented.

74. "The first of ARAMCO's four parent companies, Standard Oil of California," got a sixty-year concession in 1933, resulting in that company's becoming a "pillar of the Saudi state," second only to its religion in influence, and "at the service" of the Saudis to a greater extent even than the East India Company of Britain, according to J.B. Kelly, *Arabia, the Gulf and the West* (New York: Basic Books, 1980), p. 252.

75. Baram, *Department,* p. 277; also pp. 77, 78, 85, 91, n. 15. First posited in 1941, the proposal was renewed in December 1942.

76. Ibid., pp. 277–278. Wallace Murray, Near East head, was eager to discourage any "British-Saudi" ties. In the United States State Department, according to Baram's exhaustive study of the subject, "The Jews, more than the Russians or the Germans or anyone else . . . while not in any official sense the enemy, . . . were regarded as Unofficial Adversary Number One in the Middle East, obstructing America's natural inheritance of hegemony." *Department,* p. 307.

77. Elie Kedourie, "Misreading the Middle East," *Commentary,* July 1979, p. 35.

78. Baram, *Department,* p. 279, 308, n. 6.

79. Letter, President Roosevelt to Ibn Saud, as drafted May 14, 1943, by Murray and Lieutenant Harold Hoskins; Roosevelt signed the draft after amending the wording, but not the meaning of the key assurance, to wit: " . . . without full consultation with both Arabs and Jews." Roosevelt to Ibn Saud, in Hull to Kirk, May 26, 1943, FR 4 (1943):787, cited in Baram, *Department,* p. 242, n. 23.

80. According to Philip Baram, the State Department had shown a "passivity," in the 1930s, toward Saudi Arabia and Ibn Saud, stemming from the facts that 1) the California Arabian Standard Oil Company—later ARAMCO—was "doing satisfactorily on its own, unlike American companies in Iraq, or Kuwait . . . which got State Department assistance around 1930." 2) King Ibn Saud of Saudi Arabia "was more independent of direct British influence" than other heads of state in the region. *Department,* pp. 204–222; also see J.B. Kelly, *Arabia,* pp. 65–70, 252ff.

81. Kedourie, "Misreading . . . ," *Commentary,* July 1979, p. 34.

82. Michael Widlanski, "How Britain Worked Against Mideast Peace," *Los Angeles Herald Examiner,* January 30, 1983; Columbia University Fellow Dore Gold recently came upon the secret documents while conducting unrelated research for a dissertation, he explained in a conversation with the author, March 17, 1983.

83. Cabinet Middle East Policy Note by Secretary of State for Foreign Affairs Ernest Bevin, on Israel: Bevin's report reviewing meetings with England's representatives in the Middle East, to Cabinet, August 25, 1949, PRO CAB 129/2 (CP/49 183).

84. The seeking of Arab "agreement" may in some measure have been, may yet be, in reality, a modern rendition on the theme of "divide and conquer." That might explain the initial extreme perturbation of the Carter administration when Egypt's foundering economy brought Anwar Sadat to his surprise peace pilgrimage to Menachem Begin in Jerusalem in 1977. In that speculative vein, according to the account of a highly placed unofficial Saudi spokesman, King Fahd of *Saudi Arabia* was *following* "misguided *American* dictates," not the reverse, in asserting a Saudi position against bilateral Lebanese-Israeli peace in 1983 and ramifications following therefrom. Therein, however, lies the topic for another book. (Emphasis added.)

85. For additional information on the subject, see Chaim Weizmann, *Trial and Error* (New York: Harper and Bros., 1949), pp. 427, 432–433; Yehuda Bauer, *From Diplo-*

macy to Resistance: A History of Jewish Palestine 1939–1945, pp. 224–227, 250–252; H. St. John B. Philby, *Arabian Jubilee,* pp. 213–217.

86. R. Niebuhr, "Jews After the War," *The Nation,* February 28, 1942, p. 254. Niebuhr wrote in 1942, before the enormity of Nazi extermination camps' efficiency was fully effected.
87. *Survey of International Affairs,* 1938, vol. I, p. 417, n. 1, in Esco, *Palestine,* p. 878.
88. Esco, *Palestine,* p. 878.
89. *Jewish Frontier,* May 1939, p. 54ff; Esco, *Palestine,* p. 910.
90. James Parkes, *A History of Palestine from 135 A.D. to Modern Times,* p. 331.
91. Moshe Aumann, "Land Ownership in Palestine, 1880–1948," in *The Palestinians,* by Curtis et al., p. 26. "Iowa land prices according to the U.S. Dept. of Agriculture."
92. July 21, 1939, WO 216 46. Cited in Bethell, *Palestine Triangle,* p. 71.
93. August 6, 1942, Parliamentary Debates, House of Commons, vol. 382, cols. 1251–1253. Captain de Chair. Cited in Esco, *Palestine,* p. 1031.

17. "Muftism" and Britain's Contribution to the "Final Solution"

1. In Munich, on August 13, 1920, Hitler gave a two-hour speech about "Why we are Against the Jews"; there he instituted the motto "Anti-Semites of the World, Unite! People of Europe, Free Yourselves." Quoted by Martin Gilbert, *Exile and Return,* pp. 131–132.
2. The four days of "massacring, burning, pillaging" in Jerusalem's Jewish quarters began April 4, 1920, on the Muslim holiday of Nebi Musa, which corresponds to the Christian Easter and the Jewish Passover. Maurice Pearlman, *Mufti of Jerusalem* (London: Victor Gollancz, Ltd., 1947), pp. 11–12; also see Esco, *Palestine,* pp. 132–134, 474. The conviction was decided by British Military courts; see Sir Ronald Storrs, *The Memoirs of Sir Ronald Storrs* (New York, 1937) for an account of the period. Storrs was Governor of Jerusalem in 1920. Also see Gilbert, *Exile,* p. 132; for contemporary description of Nebi Musa festivals, see Sir Harry Luke and Edward Keith-Roach, *Handbook of Palestine and Trans-Jordan* (London: MacMillan and Co., Ltd., 1934), pp. 206–207.
3. The post of Mufti "had been in the hands of the [*effendi*] Husaini family for a number of generations." Esco, *Palestine,* p. 467; according to the Esco Foundation study, Haj Amin got "his real power" from his Supreme Muslim Council (established 1921) appointment, particularly after his election as President in 1922, an election preordained by the tradition from Turkish-held times, when "the Mufti of Jerusalem was generally recognized as the head" of the Muslims. Esco, *Palestine,* pp. 467–468. Haj Amin died in the Beirut area in 1972.
4. Ernest Main, *Palestine at the Crossroads,* p. 267; James Parkes, *A History of Palestine from 135 A.D. to Modern Times,* pp. 315, 321–322. *Palestine Royal Commission Report,* Command #5479, 1938, pp. 130–131.

    Also see David Landes, "Palestine Before the Zionists," *Commentary,* February 1976; Sir John Glubb Pasha, article regarding peasants in Transjordan—"The Economic Situation of the Trans-Jordan Tribes," *Royal Central Asian Society Journal,* 1938, vol. 25, pp. 458–459.
5. The American Christian Palestine Committee, *The Arab War Effort, A Documented Account* (New York, 1947), p. 5. This documented series contradicts Arab historian Philip Hitti, who doubted that Islamic ideology might find practical agreement with

Nazi thought. Hitti's *The Arabs* was written at the same time that in Baghdad the anti-Jewish *farhud*, a bloody pogrom, resulted in the massacre of Iraqi Jews and at the time when the foreign minister of Iraq declared that Jews were an offense against mankind. Philip Hitti, *The Arabs, A Short History*, p. viii, introduction.

6. American Christian Palestine Committee, *Arab War Effort*, p. 3.

7. Somerset DeChair, *The Golden Carpet* (New York, 1945), appendix, p. 243.

8. *Oriente Moderno*, 1941, pp. 552–553, broadcast over Iraqi and Axis radio. Cited in The American Christian Palestine Committee, *Arab War Effort*, p. 41.

9. Bernard Wasserstein, *Britain*, p. 79; also see Chapter 3; In the Mufti's call to holy war, among the crimes against Iraq that had been committed by Britain—for which "in the name of merciful and almighty God I invite all my Muslim brothers throughout the whole world to join in the holy war for God, for the defense of Islam and her lands against her enemy . . . Oh faithful, obey and respond to my call, Oh Muslims!"—the Mufti cited an example of the "vivid proof of the imperialistic designs of the British is to be found in Muslim Palestine, which, although promised by England to Sherif Hussein has had to submit to the outrageous infiltration of Jews. . . ." American Christian Palestine Committee, *Arab War Effort*, p. 41.

10. *Manchester Guardian*, February 26, 1942; March 2, 1942.

11. Ibid.

12. Minute by J.S. Bennett: "The present serious state . . . justifies strong measures," May 4, 1941, PRO CO 733/449/PI/O/20. Cited in Wasserstein, *Britain*, pp. 79–80.

13. Memorandum by J.E.M. Carvell, February 5, 1940, PRO FO 371/25239/150 ff W 2500/38/48. Cited in Wasserstein, *Britain*, p. 49.

14. In 1941, Lord Moyne cited the "threat" of enemy fugitives being smuggled into Palestine as the motivation for sending away the *Struma*, which subsequently sank in mysterious circumstances off the coast of Turkey. Wasserstein, *Britain*, p. 144ff; also compare Wasserstein's documented account with an official account, which reports a "loss of 760 Jewish passengers" based on "security reasons." Anglo-American Committee, *Survey*, vol. I, pp. 63–64.

15. Wasserstein, *Britain*, p. 49; Wasserstein observed that in one correspondence from the Foreign Office to the Colonial Office, both the Colonial Office and the High Commissioner were criticized for "invoking the threat of enemy agents, without being able, when invited to do so, to produce any evidence" of a single Axis agent entering the "Middle East in the guise of illegal Jewish immigrants." Snow to Downie, January 14, 1941, PRO CO 733/445/Part II/76 021.

16. *Arab Higher Committee: Its Origins, Personnel and Purposes: The Documentary Record submitted to the United Nations, May 1947, by Nation Associates of New York*, p. 5; a documentary record of the Mufti's and other Arab notables' pro-Nazi activities.

17. Captured files of German High Command in Flensburg, cited in ibid.

18. *Arab Higher Committee*, p. 7; Diary of Major General Erwin LaHousen, of German Abwehr, September 3, 1941: ". . . Mufti . . . is currently in connection with Abwehr II [Sabotage division of Nazi intelligence]"; June 2, 1942: ". . . utilization of the connections with the Grand Mufti for the purpose of Abwehr II . . . to demonstrate the solidarity of the Axis powers"; July 13, 1942: "I took part in discussion" with the Mufti and Hitler's representative—"chief of the Abwehr" Canaris concerning "Arabian Freedom Movement." "The Mufti made an offer . . . that followers of the . . . movement led by him, as well as the followers of former Iraq Prime Minister,

Kailani [leader of Iraqi revolt against Britain] were to be used for purposes of sabotage and sedition in the Near East in accordance with purposes of the Abwehr II." Secret Diary, cited in *The Arab Higher Committee.*

Among many documents included are photocopies of originals and translations of Hitler's "secret pledges to the Mufti for Revolt against British"; of Italy's "promise" to the Mufti to "aid in revolt against British"; "of Mufti's handwritten diary entries recording Hitler's "words of the Fuehrer on Nov. 21, 1941, Berlin, Friday from 4:30 P.M. till a few minutes after 6." The following is an extract of the November 1941 meeting between Hitler and the Mufti, with the Mufti quoting Hitler: ". . . It is clear that the Jews have accomplished nothing in Palestine and their claims are lies. All the accomplishments in Palestine are due to the Arabs and not to the Jews. *I am resolved to find a solution for the Jewish problem, progressing step by step without cessation.* "

In reply to the Mufti's demand for an "Axis declaration to the Arabs," Hitler assured that, "Only if we win the war will the hour of deliverance also be the hour of fulfillment of Arab aspirations. . . . If the declaration is issued now, difficulties will arise. . . . Now I am going to tell you something I would like you to keep secret. First, I will . . . fight until the complete destruction of the Judeo-Bolshevik rule has been accomplished. Second . . . we will reach the Southern Caucasus. Third, then I would like to issue a declaration; for then the hour of liberation of the Arabs will have arrived. Germany has no ambitions in this area but cares only to annihilate the power which produces the Jews. Fourth, I am happy that you have escaped and that you are now with the Axis powers . . . You will be the man to direct the Arab force. . . . I understand the Arab desire for this (declaration—Ed.) but his Excellency the Mufti must understand that only five years after I became President of the German Government and Fuehrer of the German people, was I able to get such a declaration (the Austrian Union—Ed.) . . . you can rely on my word.

"We were troubled about you. I know your life history . . . I am happy that you are with us now . . . to add your strength to the common cause." The full text of Mufti's diary entries paraphasing Hitler are found in *Arab Higher Committee.*

19. See original letters from the Mufti, in ibid., Documentary Record, submitted to the United Nations, May 1947; example in text and in Appendix IX.
20. The Mufti to "His Excellency, the Minister of Foreign Affairs for Hungary," June 28, 1943. Ibid; see p. 16a.
21. American Palestine Christian Committee, *The Arab War Effort,* p. 6.
22. Ibid.
23. "Decode of Telegram," Bucharest to Foreign Office, December 10, 1940, PRO FO 371/25242/400 (W 12451/38/48). Cited in Wasserstein, *Britain,* p. 74.
24. Wasserstein, *Britain,* p. 74.
25. "Evidence of an eyewitness" (translated from Hebrew), PRO CO 733/445/76021/31. Cited in ibid., pp. 74–75.
26. Wasserstein, *Britain,* p. 74.
27. "Evidence of an eyewitness," PRO CO 733/445/76021/32, cited in ibid.
28. Wasserstein, *Britain,* p. 75.
29. Foreign Office to Swiss Legation, August 15, 1941. PRO CO 733/499/P5/1/63. Cited in Wasserstein, *Britain,* p. 76.
30. Wasserstein, *Britain,* pp. 74–76.
31. Wavell to Eden, November 30, 1940. PRO PREM 4/51/2/116. Ibid., p. 71. For

Mufti's probable first official contact with the Third Reich, July 16, 1937, see L. Hirszowicz, *Third Reich and the Arab East* (London, 1966), p. 34.

32. Anglo-American Committee, *Survey,* vol. I, pp. 63–64.

33. Sir Hughe Knatchbull-Hugessen, in reply to Assistant Secretary to Turkish Ministry of Foreign Affairs, December 20, 1941: Angora to Foreign Office, PRO CO 733/449 (P3/4/30). Cited in Wasserstein, *Britain,* p. 145.

34. S.E.V. Luke minute, December 23, 1941. PRO CO 733/449/P3/4/30. Cited in Wasserstein, *Britain,* p. 145; also see Bethell, *Palestine Triangle,* p. 133ff.

35. Moyne to Law, December 24, 1941. PRO CO 733/449/P3/4/30. Cited in Wasserstein, *Britain,* pp. 145–146; also see High Commissioner, Jerusalem, to Colonial Office, December 22, 1941.

36. *Foreign Relations of the U.S.,* 1941, vol. II, p. 860. Cited in Bethell, *Palestine Triangle,* p. 112.

37. Shertok to Macpherson, February 13, 1942. PRO CO 733/446/76021/42/55. Cited in Wasserstein, *Britain,* p. 147.

38. CO 722 455, 1941; from Thomas Snow; Richard Catling, "senior Palestine policemen specializing in Jewish Affairs," in Bethell, *Palestine Triangle,* p. 114.

39. To Colonial Office, telegram, February 17, 1942. PRO FO 371/32661/56 W2483/652/48. Cited in Wasserstein, *Britain,* p. 151.

40. Randall to Boyd, February 19, 1942. PRO FO 371/32661/57 W 2483/652/48. Cited in Wasserstein, *Britain,* p. 151; also see Bethell, *Palestine Triangle,* pp. 116–117; also see account of Menachem Begin, *The Revolt* (New York: Nash Publishing, 1951, 1952, 1977), p. 35, in which the *Struma* was reported to have "arrived off the coast of Eretz Israel," when it was ordered back to Rumania and "sank" when it was "half-way there."

41. Wasserstein, *Britain,* p. 156.

42. David Stoliar to Jaffa C.I.D., May 3, 1942. PRO CO 733/446 76021/42/26–7. Cited in Wasserstein, *Britain,* pp. 152–153.

43. Wasserstein, *Britain,* pp. 152–153.

44. Ibid., p. 156; High Commissioner Jerusalem to Colonial Office, March 19, 1942. PRO CO 733/466/76021/42 (1942)/62; Beyoglu to Admiralty, February 27, 1942. PRO CO 733/466 76021/42/105. Cited in Wasserstein, *Britain,* p. 153.

45. SSP file 15, 26. "Translation of report from the Polish 'working-class party,' " the *Bund,* based on Yehuda Bauer, "When Did They Know?" in *Midstream,* April 1968, p. 57. Cited in Walter Laqueur, *The Terrible Secret, Suppression of the Truth about Hitler's "Final Solution,"* (Boston: Little, Brown, 1980), pp. 136–137.

The "mass killings" of Jews "began in June 1941 and continued with mounting ferocity for the next three years," according to an exhaustive study by Nora Levin, *The Holocaust. The Destruction of European Jewry 1933–1945* (New York: Schocken Books, 1973), pp. 287–289.

46. Laqueur, *Terrible Secret,* p. 137.

47. In 1941 only 47.7 percent of the refugee quota had been filled. David S. Wyman, *Paper Walls: America and the Refugee Crisis 1938–1941* (Amherst, 1968), pp. 220–222; also see Arthur Morse, *While Six Million Died;* Henry Feingold, *The Politics of Rescue.*

48. Wasserstein, *Britain,* p. 161.

49. Harold MacMichael, extract from note of discussion, 23 April 1942. PRO CO 733/445 (76021/41), cited in Wasserstein, *Britain,* p. 160–161.

50. Bethell, *Palestine Triangle,* p. 119.
51. Martin Gilbert, *Exile,* p. 261; Esco, *Palestine,* vol. II, pp. 1080–1081.
52. Lucy Dawidowicz, in her authoritative tracing of *The War Against the Jews, 1933–1945* (New York: Holt, Rinehart, Winston, 1975) includes a recounting of "The Fate of the Jews in Hitler's Europe," country by country (New York, 1975). Appendix A, pp. 357–401.
53. Extracts from Cabinet Conclusions, 5 March 1942. PRO CO 733/445 (76021/41), cited in Wasserstein, *Britain,* p. 158–159.
54. *Arab Higher Committee:* Letter to "Reichsführer S.S. and Minister of the Interior H. Himmler" from Mufti, July 27, 1944, reproduced in this chapter; letter from Ribbentrop to "Grossmufti of Palestine Amin El Husseini," from Berlin, April 28, 1942; letter to Minister of Foreign Affairs of Rumania, June 28, 1943; letter to Bulgaria, May 6, 1943; letter to Italy, June 10, 1943; letter to Berlin, July 25, 1944.
55. October 3, 1944, letter from the Mufti to Himmler; photocopy of letter and translation in *Arab Higher Committee.*
56. High Commissioner Wauchope's "secret" letter to Ormsby-Gore in 1937 confirmed that the government was aware of Arab immigration from as far afield as "Iraq." Wauchope assured that "migrating tribes" from Iraq would continue to be permitted. PRO FO 371/E1203, January 23, 1937.
57. *Palestine Royal Commission Report,* pp. 198–202.
58. See Chapter 13.
59. *Palestine Partition Commission Report,* pp. 144–145.
60. Hope Simpson, *Report,* pp. 126, 138.
61. Anglo-American Committee, *Survey,* vol. III, p. 1331.
62. Ibid.
63. Anglo-American Committee, *Survey,* vol. III, pp. 1330–1334.
64. Sir John Schuckburgh, Deputy Under-Secretary in the British Colonial Office in 1940, Minute, April 27, 1940. PRO CO 733/426/75872/16. Cited in Wasserstein, *Britain,* p. 50.
65. See, for example, ISA M/91/4 January 28, 1941, Box 1190/N; ISA M/91/41 Box 1190, Doc. No. 7/91/41; "Transjordanians living in Jaffa," memo from D.S.P. Tulkarem, ISA March 3, 1941, TKC/125/S.
66. ISA Record Group 2, File I/588/33 No. 14, April 15, 1942.
67. ISA Record Group 2, File I/588/33, 14a, A.I.G. "C," Memorandum on Deportation —Arabs, April 9, 1942.
68. The Polish government in exile published the facts in London, September 28, 1942, cited in Gilbert, *Exile,* p. 262.
69. ISA Record Group 2, File I/558/33, 14a, A.I.G. "C," Memorandum on Deportation —Arabs, April 9, 1942.
70. Ibid.
71. ISA Record Group 2, File I/588/33/15, April 21, 1942, from Acting Chief Secretary D. Thompson to Inspector General of Police.
72. Anglo-American Committee, *Survey,* vol. I, pp. 212–213.
73. Ibid.
74. "Of this number it is known that 713 deserted; 828 were officially repatriated; and 178 remained in employment at 31st December, 1945. The balance (2081) must be presumed to have been discharged in Palestine and either returned to their countries

of origin of their own volition or remained in Palestine illegally." Anglo-American Committee, *Survey,* vol. I, p. 212.
75. See Chapters 11–14.
76. "No precise figures of their number are available but a recent police estimate is as follows:

a) Haifa and Jaffa ports	400
b) Haifa District (excluding Haifa port)	6,580
c) Galilee District	990
d) Lydda District (excluding Jaffa port)	1,100
e) Samaria District	472
f) Gaza District	140
g) Jerusalem District	5
	9,687

It is thought that nearly 7,000 of these are Syrians or Lebanese (including over 1000 Hauranis) and that the balance of about 2,700 are mainly Egyptians and Sudanese." Anglo-American Committee, *Survey,* vol. I, p. 214.
77. Ibid., p. 213.
78. Ibid.
79. Ibid., p. 220.
80. Wasserstein, *Britain,* p. 348.
81. Henry Feingold, *The Politics of Rescue* (New York, 1970), pp. 208–247; also see Wasserstein, *Britain,* particularly pp. 188–205.
82. Stephen Wise, *Challenging Year* (London, 1951), p. 193; Morgenthau to Roosevelt, January 16, 1944, in Michael Mashberg, "Documents Concerning the American State Department and the Stateless European Jews, 1942–1944," *Jewish Social Studies,* vol. XXXIX, nos. 102, Winter–Spring 1977, pp. 174–176. Cited in Wasserstein, *Britain,* pp. 246–248.
83. Quoted in Winant (London) to State Department, Washington, December 15, 1943, USNA 840.51 Frozen Credits 12144; also see "Memorandum on telegram from Bern dated October 6, 1943" from United States Embassy (London) Economic Warfare Division, Black List Section, 4 November 1943, PRO FO 371/36747 W 15684/48; Halifax to M.E.W., 24 November 1943, PRO FO 371/36747 W 15684/48; Bliss (M.E.W.) to Walker (Foreign Office), 1 December 1943, PRO FO 371/36747 W 16460/15684/48; Walker to Bliss, 10 December 1943, PRO FO 371/36747 W 16460/15684/48; Ministry of Economic Warfare to British Embassy, Washington, 11 December 1943, PRO FO 371/36747 W 17176/15684/48. Cited in Wasserstein, *Britain,* p. 247.
84. Halifax to Foreign Office, December 22, 1943, PRO FO 371/36747 W 17686/15684/48. Cited in Wasserstein, *Britain,* p. 248.
85. December 23, 1943, minute, Ian Henderson, PRO FO 371/36747 W 17686/15684/48. Cited in Wasserstein, *Britain,* p. 248.
86. Wasserstein, *Britain,* p. 248; AGW Randall minute, December 24, 1943, PRO FO 371/36747/47 W 17686/15684/48.
87. Morgenthau to Roosevelt, January 16, 1944, in Michael Mashberg, "Documents," cited in Wasserstein, *Britain,* p. 248.
88. Anglo-American Committee of Inquiry, *Report to the U.S. Government and His Majesty's Government in the United Kingdom,* Lausanne, Switzerland, April 20,

1946, Department of State, U.S. Government Printing Office, Washington, 1946, Appendix IV, p. 76.

89. Ibid.

90. Ibid., Appendix IV, p. 74.

91. Ibid., Appendix V, pp. 84–85.

92. Anglo-American Committee, United States *Survey,* p. 70. The United States and Britain abandoned proposals in 1944 to save what remained of Europe's Jewish community; one British official asked, "What should we do with a million Jews? Where should we put them?" Another remarked, in September 1944, and with full knowledge of the "final solution," that too much "time" was "wasted on dealing with these wailing Jews." Cited in Bethell, *Palestine,* p. 168ff., particularly p. 171; also see Morse, *While Six Million Died,* pp. 353–374, particularly for roles in rescue efforts played by Amb. Ira Hirschman, Joel Brand, Raoul Wallenberg, and others.

93. Ibid., pp. 70–71.

94. Eichmann was quoted as saying, "We accepted the obligation toward Hungarians that not a single deported Jew should return alive." However, he offered a Hungarian Jewish leader the deal that, for money, he "would not carry out the deportation." But before the grim bargain could be negotiated, 475,000 (Hungarian) Jews had been deported to Nazi concentration camps. According to the Hungarian leader, Maurizio Kostner, Eichmann said, "I will transport them to Auschwitz and keep them on ice. If my generous offer is accepted I will release them. If not, they will be gassed." But the "negotiations apparently broke down." *Palestine Post,* December 14, 1945, p. 1.

95. The "total entries" of Jews from 1939, including "20,304 illegal" immigrants deducted from quota, was still under 75,000 as of January 1, 1946, seven months after the war's end. PRO CO 537/1703, "inward telegram" from Lieutenant General Sir A. Cunningham to Secretary of State for the Colonies, January 7, 1946.

96. PRO CO 537/1768 No. 8589, "Most immediate secret" telegram to Foreign Office, London, from Earl of Halifax, December 27, 1945.

97. PRO FO 371/14500 within E1767 January 1, 1946.

98. Feingold, *Politics,* p. 326. Feingold traces the state of public awareness of the systematic extermination of Jews, pp. 326–327; also see Laqueur, *The Terrible Secret.*

99. PRO CO 537/1768. Personal and Secret-Telegram No. 40 from Foreign Office to Washington; "This telegram is of particular secrecy and should be retained by the author and its recipient and not passed on." January 2, 1946.

100. PRO CO 537/1768 No. 308. Prime Minister's personal telegram no. 24, January 4, 1946.

101. The British government had "good reason at the end of 1945 to fear a re-examination of the status of Transjordan that would invalidate their contention that Palestine was too small a country to accommodate the number of Jewish survivors in Europe. . . ." The Anglo-American Committee of Inquiry proposed to "examine" the situation deeply enough as Harold Laski, Chairman of the Labor Party Executive, said on January 25, 1946, to the *Jewish Chronicle:* "to make possible the abandonment of that administrative separation between Palestine and Transjordan. . . ." Paul Riebenfeld, "The Integrity of Palestine," *Midstream,* August–September 1975, pp. 18–19. According to Riebenfeld, Foreign Secretary Bevin "decided to avoid any risks; he took the bold step of announcing the forthcoming grant of independence to Transjordan

even while the Committee was about to begin its hearings in London . . ." (p. 18). Transjordan became an independent Arab state in Palestine in May 1946.

102. PRO CO 537/1703. Extract of Colonial Office note regarding "conversation with Mr. Locker and Mr. Ettinghausen of the Jewish Agency," January 4, 1946.

103. PRO CO 537/1703, inward telegram, Sir A. Cunningham to Secretary of State for the Colonies, January 7, 1946; see also CO 537/1703 Telegram No. 475 "Secret," March 24, 1946, from Cunningham to Secretary of State for the Colonies, regarding "deduction of Jewish enlistees from quota."

104. PRO CO 537/1768 January 21, 1946.

105. PRO CO 537/1768, note of Enclosure, from Sir Douglas Harris to Sir George Gater, January 22, 1946.

106. See Sir Alan Cunningham, "Palestine—The Last Days of the Mandate," in *International Affairs,* October 1948, p. 488; UN Palestine Commission, *First Special Report,* Doc. No. S/676, February 16, 1948, para. 8, 9; Jewish Agency, Doc. No. S/721, pp. 10–14. Cited in Gabbay, *A Political Study of the Arab-Israeli Conflict,* p. 60; also see Bethell, *Palestine Triangle,* particularly p. 350ff.

107. February 11, 1948, Cairo, cited in Gabbay, *A Political Study,* pp. 60–61.

108. December 17, 1947. Cited in Bethell, *Palestine Triangle,* p. 352.

109. Gilbert, *Exile,* p. 307.

110. Kenneth Bilby, *New Star in the Near East* (New York, 1950), p. 30; also see R.M. Graves, *Experience in Anarchy* (London, 1949), p. 133; Edgar O'Ballance, *The Arab-Israeli War of 1948* (London, 1956), pp. 38–44, particularly p. 103ff; Gabbay, *A Political Study,* p. 89.

111. See the following Arab accounts: *Al Nida* (Arabic), Egyptian daily, February 14, 19, 24, 29; March 3, 8, 16, 30, 1948. *Al Tahrir* (Arabic), Syrian daily, January 5, 12, 16, 22, 31; Feb. 3, 8, 14, 22, 29, March 3, 4, 7, 13, 21, 1948 (published only until 1952).

112. Gilbert, *Exile,* p. 307.

113. PRO CO 537/1703, February 1, 1946. From R.J.M. Wilson, Undersecretary of State for the Colonies, to A.E. Judge, Esq., Home Office, Aliens' Department.

114. PRO CO 537/1703 "Secret" Telegram, February 1, 1946; see also PRO CO 537/1703, Telegram, March 18, 1946, from High Commissioner for Palestine/Transjordan to the Secretary of State, regarding one-month interim immigration allowance of "1600 persons . . . commencing 15th March and ending 14th April, 1946. . . . 1,500 will be for Jews and remainder for Arab and other immigrants."

115. Anglo-American Committee, *Report,* p. 7.

116. Chaim Weizmann to Winston Churchill, June 13, 1945. Cited in Gilbert, *Exile,* p. 272.

117. PRO CO 537/1703, April 2, 1946, from High Commissioner of Palestine to Secretary of State for the Colonies, regarding telegram no. 474 from Secretary of State for the Colonies—"Jewish Immigration."

118. PRO CO 537/1703, June 24, 1946, extract from interview between the Secretary of State for the Colonies and the Chief Rabbi of Palestine regarding 100,000 quota as one of "ten recommendations."

119. PRO FO 371/57597, July 5, 1946, Foreign Office "Confidential note." Cited by Gilbert, *Exile,* p. 294.

120. PRO FO 371/57529, British officials Nuremberg to Foreign Office. Cited by Gilbert, *Exile,* pp. 291–292.

121. Bevin to Weizmann, Foreign Office meeting, October 1, 1946. Cited by Gilbert, *Exile,* p. 294; see Gilbert's study for detailed tracing of British postwar attitudes through primary source material, especially pp. 282–309; see also Richard Crossman, *Palestine Mission* (London, 1946), particularly pp. 21, 43; also see Bethell, *Palestine Triangle,* pp. 214 ff.

122. The International Military Tribunal at Nuremberg (first session October 18, 1945, subsequent sessions November 20, 1945–October 1, 1946), tried 24 Nazi leaders, while others escaped; 12 of the accused were given the death penalty by hanging, 3 were acquitted, 3 were sentenced to life imprisonment, and the remaining defendants received lesser sentences. In twelve trials (called Subsequent Nuremberg Proceedings) between 1946 and 1949, 177 Nazi war criminals were convicted of "crimes against humanity"; 12 received a death sentence, while the rest received long prison terms; most were liberated earlier by the Clemency Act of January 1951, passed by United States High Commissioner in Germany, John J. McCloy. *Encyclopaedia Britannica,* 15th ed. (Chicago, 1979), vol. 19, pp. 554–557; *Encyclopaedia Judaica* (Jerusalem, 1972), vol. 16, pp. 287–302. The search for and discovery of countless other war criminals has continued until the present. The proceedings, affidavits, and documents are included in *Trial of the Major War Criminals,* official publication of the International Military Tribunal, 42 vols., between 1947 and 1949 ("Blue Series").

123. PRO FO 371/57583 O'Neill minute, January 8, 1946. Cited by Gilbert, *Exile,* p. 291.

124. PRO CO 537/1811 "Illegal Immigration: Reaction to His Majesty's Government Statement," Cabinet distribution from Washington to Foreign Office, extract, August 14, 1946.

125. It was, however, American Jews who nevertheless "rescued" the endangered crucial United States loan of $370 million for Britain. See Bethell, *Palestine Triangle,* pp. 255–256.

126. Cabinet distribution from Washington to Foreign Office, extract, "Illegal Immigration: Reaction to His Majesty's Government Statement," August 14, 1946, PRO CO 537/1811.

127. For details of Palestine from the end of World War II until 1948, see: Government of Palestine, *Supplementary Memoranda by the Government of Palestine, Including Notes of Evidence to the United Nations' Special Committee on Palestine up to July 12, 1947* (Jerusalem, July 1947); The Jewish Agency Observations on Above Government Memorandum (Jerusalem, 1947); United Nations Special Committee on Palestine, *Report to the General Assembly,* vol. III, Annex A: Oral Evidence Presented at Public Meetings, Lake Success. Also see this book, Chapter 2; Nicholas Bethell, *The Palestine Triangle;* Martin Gilbert, *Exile and Return;* Arthur Koestler, *Promise and Fulfillment, Palestine 1917–1949* (New York, London: Macmillan, 1949); Samuel Katz, *Battleground: Fact and Fantasy in Palestine* (New York: Bantam Books, 1973); Geoffrey Furlonge, *Palestine Is My Country, The Story of Musa Alami* (New York: Praeger Press, 1969); Bernard Lewis, "The Palestinians and the PLO," *Commentary,* January 1975; Rony Gabbay, *A Political Study of the Arab-Jewish Conflict* (Geneva, Paris: Librairie E. Droz, Librairie Minard, 1959); James Parkes, *The Story of Jerusalem* (London: Crescent Press, 1950); J. Bowyer Bell, *The Long War: Israel and the Arabs Since 1946* (Englewood Cliffs, N.J., 1969); Christopher Sykes, *Crossroads to*

Israel (London: Collins, 1965); Kenneth Bilby, *New Star in the Middle* East (New York, 1950).

18. The Flight from Fact

1. Terence Prittie, "The British Media and the Arab-Israeli Dispute," in *Middle East Review,* Summer/Fall 1980, p. 67. See also *New York Times,* February 23, 1981, p. 19.
2. An ILO report described the "natural migration" between Syria and Jordan as late as 1977: "These movements of labour are difficult to quantify as they are often informal in nature and go unrecorded." J.S. Birks and C.A. Sinclair, "Migration for Employment Project—A Preliminary Assessment of Labour Movement in the Arab Region: Background, Perspectives and Prospects," *World Employment Programme Working Paper* (Geneva: International Labour Organization, 1977), p. 43.
3. The constitutions of Algeria, Egypt, Iraq, Jordan, Kuwait, Libya, Morocco, Qatar, Sudan, Syria, Tunisia, and the United Arab Emirates contain articles providing that Islam is the state religion. Bernard Lewis, "Palestinians and the PLO," *Commentary,* January 1975.
4. Franklin Delano Roosevelt, to United States Secretary of State, May 17, 1939, memorandum, *U.S. Foreign Relations,* 1939, vol. 4, p. 757.
5. Tawfic E. Farah, "Political Socialization of Palestinian Children in Kuwait," presented at Arab-American University Graduates Convention, October 1–3, 1976, New York. *Journal of Palestine Studies,* vol. 6, no. 4, Summer 1977.
6. Arthur Miller, *Incident at Vichy,* opened December 31, 1964; in *The Portable Arthur Miller* (Middlesex, England: Penguin Books, 1977), p. 326.
7. American Sephardic Federation, New York, estimated between 1.4 million and 1.7 million; Foreign Ministry of Israel estimated between 1.4 and 1.5 million. However, the Sephardic Jews are a majority in Israel's *Jewish* population, which in 1982 was 3.5 million.
8. UNRWA Chart and Report, June 30, 1982, Vienna, 1982.
9. For information regarding refugee discrimination in Gaza, see A. Plascov, *Palestinian Refugees in Jordan, 1948–1957* (London and Totowa, N.J.: Frank Cass, 1981), p. 8. According to Dr. Don Peretz, after a study trip to the area more than twenty years ago, the camps' "refugee" employees, in the thousands, "constituted a great political pressure group, especially in Jordan. No politician in any . . . host countries dares to recommend abolition of their [refugee's] livelihood." *Arab Refugee Report,* 1962, in Schechtman, *Refugee in the World,* p. 207. Also see Chapter 1.
10. UNRWA Report, June 1982.
11. Thomas Friedman, *New York Times,* March 12, 1983.
12. Ibid.
13. U.S. Committee for Refugees, *1982 World Refugee Survey,* New York, 1982, p. 40.
14. U.S. Committee for Refugees, *1981 World Survey,* New York, 1981, p. 39.
15. Poul Hartling, Nobel Peace Prize acceptance speech, 1981, in *World Refugee Survey 1982,* U.S. Committee for Refugees.
16. Ibid., pp. 40–41.
17. Ibid., p. 18.
18. The historian-Orientalist Daniel Pipes reports: "In recent years, the organization

received about $250 million yearly from Saudi Arabia and . . . $60 million a year from Kuwait" as well as "generous" aid from the "Soviet Bloc." Pipes tells of the PLO request for "help from the Arab states last summer [1982, when] the Algerian foreign minister called in the Soviet ambassador in Algiers at four in the morning and gave him a check for $20 million: the weapons reportedly arrived in Beirut several days later by air." From "How Important is the PLO?" *Commentary,* April 1983, p. 19.

Zehdi Labib Terzi, the PLO's UN "observer," with inimitable candor confirmed the Soviet role in a TV interview in 1979; according to Terzi, "the Soviet Union, and all the socialist countries, they give us full support—diplomatic, moral, educational, and also open their military academies to some of our freedom fighters. . . . I mean our boys go to the Soviet Union. . . . There's no secret about that. . . ." PBS, September 25, 1979.

19. Bassam abu-Sharif is reportedly from Kafr 'Aqab. Abu Daoud was reported to come originally from the same district, excluded from Israel 1948–1967; abu-Sharif was noted, in an ABC program on the Palestinians, to have been "expelled in 1948." Yet no Jews remained in his village at the time, and no Israeli military force entered there before 1967. ABC, "Terror in the Promised Land," 1979. See Karl Meyer, *Saturday Review,* February 3, 1979, for a critique of ABC broadcast.

20. Thomas Kiernan traces Arafat's birth to Egypt, in *Yassir Arafat* (London, 1976); *Time,* April 14, 1980, states, however, that Arafat's brother, Fathi, was "Born in the Old City of Jerusalem."

21. George Orwell, *1984* (New York, 1949), p. 87.

22. *The Committee on the Exercise of the Inalienable Rights of the Palestinian People,* Office of Public Information, UN, New York, 1978.

23. E. Benes, *Democracy To-day and To-morrow* (1939), p. 21, cited in Alfred Cobban, *National Self-Determination* (London, New York, Toronto: Oxford University Press, 1945), p. 45.

24. Ibid., p. 46.

25. Ibid., p. 69.

26. Ibid., p. 74.

27. G. Starushenko, *The Principle of National Self-Determination in Soviet Foreign Policy* (Moscow: Foreign Languages Publishing, n.d.), p. 9.

28. Ibid., p. 235.

29. U.S.S.R. Foreign Minister Andrei Gromyko, *Izvestia,* September 27, 1961, quoted in Starushenko, *Principle,* p. 11.

30. Theodore Draper, "The United States and Israel," *Commentary,* April 1975, p. 32.

31. Damascus, June 1977, interviews with Syrian Minister of Trade and Economy, Dr. Muhammad Imadi; Deputy Foreign Minister Abdallah al-Khani; Dr. Daoudy, "Political Advisor to President Al Assad." Daoudy informed me that Syria intervened in Lebanon because "the Palestinians were going to partition Lebanon, and Syria wanted them to keep all their hostility directed at Israel, not to settle in Lebanon." June 26, 1977, under auspices of NCAFP fact-finding mission led by Ambassador Angier Biddle Duke.

32. Interview with Yasser Arafat, Cairo Voice of Palestine (Arabic), March 12, 1977, rebroadcast from Egyptian Television, March 11, 1977.

33. Hayim Tadmor, "The Period of the First Temple, the Babylonian Exile and the

Restoration," in Ben Sasson, *History,* Part 1, p. 102.

34. Fawaz Turki, *Journal of a Palestinian Exile* (New York: Monthly Review Press, 1972), pp. 37–38.

35. Senator Frank Church, interview with author, February 24, 1979; Senator Joseph Biden, speech at Israel Bond dinner, Chicago, November 21, 1978. In report by Ambassador Ira Hirschmann, in Lebanon, to William Macomber, Jr., U.S. Assistant Secretary of State, such a plan was proposed, April 6, 1968.

36. As the official daily of the Syrian government suggested in 1978, while the "Arab strategy for liberation continues to have as its ultimate aim the eradication of Zionism, . . . Arab leaders who deal in foreign diplomacy should . . . adapt their language, and properly so, to the style accepted in international diplomacy." *Al Ba'ath,* Damascus, April 23, 1978.

   Thus in 1981, Sheikh Yamani of Saudi Arabia asked for a more "Pro-Arab" stance in the United States in regard to giving friendly Saudis arms "only for defense." Then with his next breath, Sheikh Yamani called for a *jihad*—holy war —against Israel. "ABC Evening News," January 27, 1981.

37. From *Palestinian Leaders Discuss the New Challenges for the Resistance,* Palestine Research Center, Beirut, April 1974, reprinted in "The Positions of the Palestinian Organizations on Establishment of a Palestinian State and on Peace" in *The Palestinians,* Michael Curtis et al., eds. (New Brunswick: Transaction Books, 1975), pp. 166–172; see p. 167.

38. Ibid., p. 171.

Bibliography

Abbreviations:

PRO—Public Record Office, Kew Gardens (London)
CO—Colonial Office, Great Britain
FO—Foreign Office, Great Britain
ISA—Israel State Archives (former Palestine Mandatory Government records), Jerusalem
Survey—Anglo-American Committee of Inquiry, *A Survey of Palestine*
Report . . . for the Year 19xx—*Report by His Britannic Majesty's Government to the Council of the League of Nations on the Administration of Palestine and Trans-Jordan for the Year 19xx*, Colonial No. xx.
RH—Rhodes House, Oxford, England
Hope Simpson, *Report*—Sir John Hope Simpson, *Palestine: Report on Immigration, Land Settlement and Development*, Command #3686, 1930.
UNRWA—United Nations Relief and Works Agency
USCR—United States Committee for Refugees

I

The unpublished archival sources, periodicals, official publications, and reports drawn upon for this book have been cited fully in the reference notes. The following are only the official data referred to most frequently, which were often abbreviated after the initial citation in the reference notes.

Despatches from Her Majesty's Consuls in the Levant, Respecting Past or Apprehended Disturbances in Syria: 1858 to 1860; Further Papers Relating to the Disturbances in Syria: June 1860. London, 1860.
Reports of the Commission of Inquiry, Palestine, Disturbances in May, 1921, Command #1540, London, 1921 (the Haycraft Report).
Statement of British Policy in Palestine, Command #1700, London, 1922 (the Churchill White Paper).
Report of the Commission on the Disturbances of August, 1929, Command #3530, London, 1930 (the Shaw Report).
John Hope Simpson. *Palestine: Report on Immigration, Land Settlement and Development,* Command #3686, London, 1930.
Palestine. Statement of Policy by His Majesty's Government in the United Kingdom, Command #3692, 1930 (the Passfield White Paper).

Census of Palestine, 1931. Vol. I, *Palestine,* Part I, *Report* by E. Mills, B.A., O.B.E., Assistant Chief Secretary of Census, Alexandria, 1933.

Palestine Royal Commission Report, Command #5479, London, 1937 (the Peel Report).

Palestine Partition Commission Report, Command #5854, London, 1938 (the Woodhead Report).

Palestine: Statement by His Majesty's Government in the United Kingdom, Command #5893, London, 1938.

Palestine: A Statement of Policy, Command #6019, London, 1939 (the MacDonald White Paper).

Report by His Britannic Majesty's Government to the Council of the League of Nations on the Administration of Palestine and Trans-Jordan for the Year 1925, Colonial No. 20.

Report . . . for the Year 1926, Colonial No. 26.

Report . . . for the Year 1927, Colonial No. 31.

Report . . . for the Year 1928, Colonial No. 40.

Report . . . for the Year 1929, Colonial No. 47.

Report . . . for the Year 1930, Colonial No. 59.

Report . . . for the Year 1931, Colonial No. 75.

Report . . . for the Year 1932, Colonial No. 82.

Report . . . for the Year 1933, Colonial No. 94.

Report . . . for the Year 1934, Colonial No. 104.

Report . . . for the Year 1935, Colonial No. 112.

Report . . . for the Year 1936, Colonial No. 129.

Report . . . for the Year 1937, Colonial No. 146.

Report . . . for the Year 1938, Colonial No. 166.

Anglo-American Committee of Inquiry, *A Survey of Palestine,* 3 vols., Palestine, Government Printer, 1945–1946.

Anglo-American Committee of Inquiry, *Report to the United States Government and His Majesty's Government in the United Kingdom.* Lausanne, Switzerland, April 20, 1946. Department of State, United States Government Printing Office, Washington, 1946.

Supplementary Memorandum by the Government of Palestine, including Notes on Evidence given to the United Nations' Special Committee on Palestine up to the 12th July, 1947, Government of Palestine, Jerusalem, 1947.

League of Nations Permanent Mandates Commission:

Minutes of the First Session, Geneva, 1921. Doc. No. C. 416. M. 296. 1921. VI. Mandate for Palestine C. 259. M. 314. 1922. VI.

Mandate for Palestine C.P.M. 466. C. 667. M. 396. 1922. VI. (same as Cmd. 1785, 1922).

Minutes of the Thirteenth Session, 1928. Doc. No. C. 341. M. 99. 1928. VI.

Minutes of the Twenty Seventh Session, 1935. C. 251. M. 123. 1935. VI.

Minutes of the Twenty Ninth Session, 1936. C. 259. M. 153. 1936. VI.

Minutes of the Thirty Second (Extraordinary) Session, 1937. C. 330. M. 222. 1937, VI.

Minutes of the Thirty Ninth Session, Geneva, 1939.

II Books, Pamphlets, and Articles

Every source drawn upon for this book is fully cited in the reference notes and each had a role in the development of the research. The list that follows is neither a repetitious account of every single source used nor an exhaustive compilation of the infinite number of publications on the subjects of this book. It is, rather, a partial listing of those works principally called upon and thus abbreviated in some of the reference notes. In a few instances, I have noted works that contain related information not directly discussed here, but of value to those interested in further reading.

Africanus, Leo. *The History and Description of Africa and of the Notable Things Therein Contained.* Ed. Dr. Robert Brown. London, 1896.

Alami, Musa. "The Lesson of Palestine." *The Middle East Journal,* October 1949.

Al-Ayubi, Al-Haytham. "Future Arab Strategy in the Light of the Fourth War." *Shuun Filastiniyya,* Beirut, October 1974.

Al-Azm, Khaled. Memoirs, 3 vols. Al-Dar al Muttahida lil-Nashr, 1972.

Alkalay, Judah ben Solomon Hai. *Destiny of the Lord.* Vienna, 1857.

Alon, Dafna. *Arab Radicalism.* Jerusalem, 1969.

Alroy, Gil Carl. *Behind the Middle East Conflict, The Real Impasse Between Arab and Jew.* New York, 1975.

———. "Do the Arabs Want Peace?" *Commentary,* February 1974.

Al-Tall, 'Abdallah. *The Danger of World Jewry to Islam and Christianity* (Arabic). Cairo, 1964.

American Christian Palestine Committee. *The Arab War Effort, A Documented Account.* New York, 1947.

Ansari, Mohammed Iqbal. *The Arab League 1945–55.* Calcutta, 1968.

Antonius, George. *The Arab Awakening: The Story of the Arab National Movement.* Philadelphia, New York, Toronto, 1939.

Antoun, Richard. *Arab Village—A Social Study of a TransJordanian Peasant Community.* Bloomington, 1972.

Arab Higher Committee: Its Origins, Personnel and Purposes. The Documentary Records submitted to the United Nations by Nation Associates, New York, May 1947.

The Arab Refugee Problem: How It Can Be Solved. Proposals submitted to the General Assembly of the United Nations, December 1951, by Dr. Dewey Anderson, Dr. Henry A. Atkinson, Dr. Donald B. Cloward, Dr. Frederick May Eliot, The Rt. Rev. Charles K. Gilbert, Earl G. Harrison, The Very Rev. Ivan Lee Holt, Freda Kirchway, Dr. Kenneth Scott Lautourette, Archibald MacLeish, Dr. Daniel L. Marsh, The Rt. Rev. Norman B. Nash, Dr. Reinhold Niebuhr, James G. Patton, Paul Porter, Jacob S. Potofsky, Prof. James T. Shotwell, Dr. Russell H. Stafford, Sumner Welles.

Arab vs. Arab, pamphlet. Keighley, England, 1939.

Atiyah, Edward. *The Arabs.* Edinburgh, 1955.

Atlas of Israel. Jerusalem, 1970.

Aumann, Moshe. *Land Ownership in Palestine 1880–1948.* Jerusalem: Israel Academic Committee on the Middle East, 1976.

Avriel, Ehud. *Open the Gates.* New York, 1975.

Azcarate, Pablo. *Mission in Palestine 1948–1952.* Washington, 1966.

Bachi, Roberto. *The Population of Israel.* Jerusalem, 1974.

Baer, Gabriel. *Population and Society in the Arab East.* London, 1964.

Baldensperger, Philip G. "The Immovable East," *Palestine Exploration Fund Quarterly.* London, 1917.

Barker, E.B.B. *Syria and Egypt Under the Last Five Sultans of Turkey.* London, 1876.

Baron, Salo Wittmayer. *Ancient and Medieval Jewish History.* New Brunswick, N.J., 1972.

———. *A Social and Religious History of the Jews,* 3 vols. New York, 1937.

Barron, J.B. *Report and General Abstracts of the Census of Palestine, 1922.* Jerusalem, n.d.

Battuta, Ibn. *Travels in Asia and Africa 1325–1354.* Trans. H.A.R. Gibb. London, 1957.

Bauer, Yehuda. *Flight and Rescue, the Organized Escape of the Jewish Survivors of Eastern Europe 1944–1948.* New York, 1970.

Beek, M.A. *A Short History of Israel From Abraham to Bar Cochba.* London, 1963.

Begin, Menachem. *The Revolt.* New York, 1977.

Bein, Alex. *Theodore Herzl, A Biography.* Trans. Maurice Samuel. Philadelphia, 1940.

Bein, Alex, ed. *Arthur Ruppin: Memoirs, Diaries, Letters.* New York, 1971.

Belkind, Israel. *The First Steps of the Colonization of Eretz Israel.* New York, 1917.

Ben-Sasson, H.H., ed. *A History of the Jewish People.* Cambridge, Mass., 1976.

Bentwich, Norman. "Aden After the Riots." *Commentary,* May 1948.

Ben-Zvi, Yitzchak. *The Exiled and the Redeemed.* Philadelphia, 1961.

———*Israel Under Ottoman Rule—Four Centuries of History.* Jerusalem, 1955.

Bernadotte, Folke. *To Jerusalem.* London, 1951.

Bethell, Nicholas. *The Palestine Triangle: The Struggle for the Holy Land, 1935–48.* New York, 1979.

Bethman, Erich W. *Decisive Years in Palestine 1918–48.* New York, 1957.

Bilby, Kenneth. *New Star in the Near East.* New York, 1950.

Birks, J.S., and Sinclair, C.A. *Migration for Employment Project—A Preliminary Assessment of Labour Movement in the Arab Region: Background, Perspectives and Prospects.* World Employment Programme Working Paper. International Labour Organisation, Geneva, 1977.

Bodman, H.L. *Political Factions in Aleppo, 1760–1826.* Raleigh, N.C., 1963.

Brant, Jas. *Despatches from Her Majesty's Consuls in the Levant, Respecting Past or Apprehended Disturbances in Syria, 1858–1860.* London, 1860.

Braver, Moshe. "Immigration as a Factor in the Growth of the Arab Village in Eretz-Israel." *Economic Review—Problems of Aliyah and Absorption,* vol. 28, nos. 7–9, July–September 1975.

Brockelmann, C. *History of the Islamic Peoples.* New York, 1960.

Brunschvig, Robert. *Deux Récis de Voyage Inédits en Afrique du Nord.* Paris, 1936.

———. *La Berberie orientale sous les Hafsides,* vol. I. Paris, 1940.

Buckingham, J.S. *Travels in Palestine.* London, 1821.

Burckhardt, J.L. *Travels in Syria and the Holy Land.* London, 1822.

Caplan, Neil. *Palestine Jewry and the Arab Question 1917–1925.* London, 1978.

Carr-Saunders, A.M. *World Population.* Oxford, 1936.

Cartwright, Marguerite. "Plain Speech on the Arab Refugee Problem." *Land Reborn,* November–December 1958.

Cazes, D. *Essai sur l'histoire des Israelites de Tunisie depuis les temps les plus recules.* Paris, 1888.

————. *Revue des Etudes Juives 20.* Paris, 1890.

Choucri, Nazli. *Migration Processes Among Developing Countries: The Middle East.* Center for International Studies, Massachusetts Institute of Technology. Cambridge, Mass., May 1978.

————. *The New Migration in the Middle East: A Problem for Whom?* Center for International Studies, Massachusetts Institute of Technology. Cambridge, Mass., January 1977.

Chouraqui, André. *Between East and West, A History of the Jews of North Africa.* Trans. from French by Michael M. Bernet. Philadelphia, 1968.

Cobban, Alfred. *National Self-Determination.* London, New York, Toronto, 1945.

Cohen, Aaron. *Israel and the Arab World.* London, 1970.

Cohen, Hayyim J. *Absorption Problems of Jews from Asia and Africa in Israel.* Jerusalem, 1974.

————. *The Jews of the Middle East 1860—1972.* New York, 1973.

Conder, Colonel C.R. *Heth and Moab.* London, 1883.

————. *The Survey of Eastern Palestine.* London, 1889.

————. *Tent Work in Palestine,* 2 vols. London, 1878.

Conder, C.R., and Kitchener, H.H. *The Survey of Western Palestine.* Ed. E.H. Palmer and Walter Besant. London, 1881.

Crawford, A.W.C., Lord Lindsay. *Letters of Egypt, Edom and the Holy Land.* London, 1847.

Crossman, Richard. *Palestine Mission.* London, 1946.

Crowfoot, J.W., and Hamilton, R.W. "The Discovery of a Synagogue at Jerash." *Palestine Exploration Fund Quarterly LXI,* 1929.

Crum, Bartley C. *Behind the Silken Curtain, a Personal Account of Anglo-American Diplomacy in Palestine and the Middle East.* New York, 1947.

Cuinet, Vital. *Syrie, Liban et Palestine, Géographie Administrative, Statistique, Descriptive et Raisonée.* Paris, 1896.

Cunningham, Sir Alan. "Palestine—The Last Days of the Mandate." *International Affairs,* October 1948.

Curtis, Michael, ed. *Jordan, People and Politics in the Middle East.* New Brunswick, N.J.: Transaction Books, 1971.

Curtis, Michael, Joseph Neyer, Chaim Waxman, and Allen Pollack, eds. *The Palestinians.* New Brunswick, N.J., 1975.

Davison, Roderique. *Reform in the Ottoman Empire 1856–1876.* Princeton, 1963.

Dawidowicz, Lucy. *The War Against the Jews, 1933–1945.* New York, 1975.

Dawood, N.J., trans. *The Koran.* Harmondsworth, Middlesex, England, 1981.

DeChair, Somerset. *The Golden Carpet.* New York, 1945.

De Haas, Jacob. *History of Palestine, the Last Two Thousand Years.* New York, 1934.

De Lamartine, Alphonse. *A Pilgrimage to the Holy Land.* Trans. from French. New York, 1948.

De St. Aubin, W. "Peace and Refugees in the Middle East." *The Middle East Journal,* vol. III, no. 3, July 1949.

Dodd, Peter, and Barakat, Halim. *River Without Bridges: A Study of the Exodus of the 1967 Arab Palestinian Refugees.* Beirut, 1969.

Doughty, C.M. *Travels in Arabia Deserta.* London, 1888.

Draper, Theodore. "The United States and Israel." *Commentary,* April 1975.

Dubnow, Simon. *History of the Jews.* New York, 1967–1973.

Encyclopaedia Britannica, 8th edition, 1860; 11th edition, 1911.

Encyclopedia Judaica. Eds. C. Roth, G. Wigoder. Jerusalem, 1972.

Epstein, E. "The Bedouin of Transjordan." *Royal Central Asian Society Journal,* vol. 25, 1938.

Esco Foundation for Palestine. *Palestine, A Study of Jewish, Arab, and British Policies.* 2 vols. New Haven, Yale University Press, 1947.

Farah, Tawfic E. "Political Socialization of Palestinian Children in Kuwait." *Journal of Palestine Studies,* vol. 6, no. 4, Summer, 1977.

Farhi, David. "Ottoman Attitude Towards Jewish Settlement." In Ma'oz, ed. *Studies on Palestine During the Ottoman Period.* Jerusalem, 1975.

Feingold, Henry. *The Politics of Rescue.* New York, 1970.

Finn, Elizabeth. "Fellaheen of Palestine." *Palestine Exploration Fund Quarterly,* 1879.

Finn, James. *Stirring Times or Record from Jerusalem Consular Chronicles from 1835–56,* 2 vols. London, 1878.

Frankenstein, Ernst. *Justice for My People.* London, 1943.

Friedman, Saul. "The Myth of Arab Toleration." *Midstream,* January 1970.

Frischwasser, Ra'anan H.F. *Frontiers of a Nation.* London, 1955.

Frumkin, G. *Population Changes in Europe Since 1939.* New York, 1951.

Furlonge, Sir Geoffrey. *Palestine Is My Country: The Story of Musa Alami.* New York and London, 1969.

Gabbay, Rony E. *A Political Study of the Arab-Jewish Conflict: The Arab Refugee Problem (A Case Study).* Paris, 1959.

Galante, Abraham. *Histoire des Juifs d'Istanbul,* 2 vols. Istanbul, 1941–1942.

Gawler, George. *Tranquillisation of Syria and the East.* London, 1845.

Geffner, Edward. *Sephardi Problems in Israel.* Jerusalem, n.d.

George, David Lloyd. *The Truth About the Peace Treaties.* London, 1938.

Gilbert, Martin. *Exile and Return: The Struggle for a Jewish Homeland.* Philadelphia and New York, 1978.

———. *The Arab-Israeli Conflict. Its History in Maps.* London, 1974.

———. *The Jews of Arab Lands, Their History in Maps.* Oxford, 1975.

———. *Sir Horace Rumbold—Portrait of a Diplomat.* London, 1973.

———. *Winston S. Churchill, The Prophet of Truth: 1922–1939,* 5 vols. Boston, 1977.

Glubb, John Bagot. "The Economic Situation of the Trans-Jordan Tribes." *Royal Central Asian Society Journal,* vol. 25, 1938.

———. *The Empire of the Arabs.* London, 1963.

Goitein, S.D. *Letters of Medieval Jewish Traders.* Princeton, 1973.

———. *Jews and Arabs, Their Contacts Through the Ages.* New York, 1974.

———. *A Mediterranean Society,* 4 vols. Berkeley, Los Angeles, London, 1983.

Gottheil, Fred M. "The Population of Palestine, circa 1875." *Middle Eastern Studies,* vol. 15, no. 3, October 1979.

———. "Arab Immigration into Pre-state Israel: 1922–1931." In Curtis et al., eds. *The Palestinians,* New Brunswick, N.J., 1975.

Gottheil, Richard J.H. *Zionism.* Philadelphia, 1914.

Graetz, Heinrich. *History of the Jews,* 5 vols. New York, 1927.

Granott, A. *The Land System in Palestine, History and Structure.* London, 1952.

Granovsky, A. *Land and the Jewish Reconstruction of Palestine.* Jerusalem, 1931.

Granzow, Brigitte. *A Mirror of Nazism. British Opinion and the Emergence of Hitler 1929–1933.* London, 1964.

Graves, Philip. *Palestine, The Land of Three Faiths.* London, 1923.

Graves, R.M. *Experiment in Anarchy.* London, 1949.

Green, D.F., ed. *Arab Theologians on Jews and Israel, Al-Azhar, The Fourth Conference of the Academy of Islamic Research.* Geneva, 1971.

Grobba, Fritz. *Männer und Mächte im Orient.* Zurich, Berlin, Frankfurt, 1967.

Gruen, George, ed. *American Jewish Yearbook 1983.* New York, 1983.

Guillaume, Alfred. *Islam.* Baltimore, 1954.

Gunther, John. *Inside Asia.* New York, 1939.

Gurevich, David, and Gertz, Aaron. *Jewish Agricultural Settlement in Israel.* Jerusalem, 1938.

Ha Am, Ahad. *Selected Essays.* Philadelphia, 1948.

———. *Ten Essays on Zionism and Judaism.* London, 1922.

Haim, Sylvia. "Arabic Anti-Semitic Literature." *Jewish Social Studies,* vol. 17, 1955.

Haim, Sylvia, ed. *Arab Nationalism.* Berkeley, 1962.

Hameiri, Yehezkel. *Prisoners of Hate.* Jerusalem, 1969.

Harkabi, Yehoshafat. *Arab Attitudes to Israel.* Jerusalem, 1971.

Hart, B.H. Liddell. *T.E. Lawrence to His Biographer.* 1938.

Hertzberg, Arthur. *The Zionist Ideal.* 1960.

Herzl, Theodor. *Der Judenstaat.* Vienna, 1896.

Heykal, Mohammed Hassanein. *The Cairo Documents.* New York, 1973.

———. "Mohammed Hassanein Heykal Discusses War and Peace in the Middle East." *Journal of Palestine Studies,* Autumn 1971.

———. *The Road to Ramadan.* New York, 1975.

Hickinbotham, Sir Tom. *Aden.* London, 1958.

Hilberg, Raul. *The Destruction of the European Jews.* Chicago, 1967.

Hirschberg, H.Z. *A History of the Jews in North Africa.* Leiden, Netherlands, 1974.

———. *The Jews in Islamic Lands,* 2nd rev. ed. Leiden, 1974.

———. "The Oriental Jewish Communities," A. J. Arberry, ed. *Religion in the Middle East.* Cambridge, England, 1969.

———. "Turkey and Religious Slanders, the Attitudes of the Authorities of the Ottoman Empire to Blood Libels." *Mahanayim,* no. 110, Israel Defense Forces, Chief Military Rabbinate, Tel Aviv, 1966.

Hirszowicz, L. *The Third Reich and the Arab East.* London, 1966.

Hitti, Philip K. *The Arabs, A Short History.* Princeton, 1943.

Hodgson, Marshall G.S. *The Venture of Islam.* Chicago, 1974.

Hogarth, David George. "Arabs and Turks." *The Arab Bulletin,* no. 48, April 21, 1917.

Hourani, Albert. *Arabic Thought in the Liberal Age 1798–1939.* London, 1962.

———. *Minorities in the Arab World.* London, 1947.

———. *Syria and Lebanon: A Political Essay.* London, 1946.

Huntington, Ellsworth. *Palestine and its Transformation.* Boston, 1911.

Hussein, King of Jordan. *My "War" with Israel.* London, 1969.

———. *Uneasy Lies the Head.* New York, 1962.

Hyamson, A.M. *The British Consulate in Jerusalem (In Relation to the Jews of Palestine, 1838–1914),* 2 vols. London, 1939–1942.

Ishaq, Ibn. *The Life of Muhammed,* abridged English trans. by A. Guillaume. Karachi, 1955. (*Al-Sira al-Nabawiyya,* 2 vols. Cairo, 1955.)

Issawi, Charles, ed. *The Economic History of the Middle East, 1800–1914.* Chicago and London, 1966.

Jones, Phillip. *Britain and Palestine 1914–1948.* Oxford, 1979.

Josephus, Flavius. *The Complete Works of Flavius Josephus, the Celebrated Jewish Historian.* Trans. W. Whiston. Philadelphia, 1895.

Kark, Ruth. "Jerusalem and Jaffa in the 19th Century as an Example of Traditional Near East Cities." In *Studies in the Geography of Israel,* no. 10, 1978.

———. "Land Purchase in Emek Hefer." In Schmueli, A., and Grosman, D., eds. *The Sharon.* Tel Aviv, n.d.

Karpat, Kemal. *The Gecekondu, Rural Migration and Urbanization.* New York, 1976.

———. "Ottoman Population Records and the Census of 1881/82–1893." *International Journal of Middle East Studies,* vol. 9, no. 2, 1978.

———. *Research Prospectus on the Demographic History of Palestine.* Submitted to Institute for Mediterranean Affairs. New York, 1972.

Katz, Samuel. *Battleground: Fact and Fantasy in Palestine.* New York, 1973.

Kayser, Rudolphe. *The Life and Time of Judah Halevi.* Trans. Frank Gaynor. New York, 1949.

Kedourie, Elie. *Arabic Political Memoirs and Other Studies.* London, 1974.

———. *The Chatham House Version and Other Middle-Eastern Studies.* London, 1970.

———. *England and the Middle East, the Destruction of the Ottoman Empire 1914–1921.* London, 1956.

———. "How to (and How Not To) Seek Peace in the Middle East." *Encounter,* May 1978.

———. "Islam Today." In Lewis, ed., *Islam and the Arab World.* New York, 1976.

———. "Misreading the Middle East." *Commentary,* July 1979.

———. *The Sack of Basra and the Farhud of Baghdad.* Jerusalem: Hebrew University International Conference on Jewish Communities in Muslim Lands; later included in Kedourie, *Arabic Political Memoirs:* See above.

Keith, A. *The Land of Israel.* Edinburgh, 1843.

Kelidar, Abbas. "Iraq: The Search for Stability." *Conflict Studies,* no. 59, Institute for the Study of Conflict, July 1975.

Kelidar, Abbas, and Burrell, Michael. "Lebanon: The Collapse of a State." *Conflict Studies,* no. 74, Institute for the Study of Conflict, August 1976.

Kelly, J.B. *Arabia, the Gulf and the West.* New York, 1980.

Khalil, Mohammed. *The Arab States and the Arab League: A Documentary Record.* Beirut, 1962.

Kiernan, Thomas. *Yassir Arafat.* London, 1976.

Kimche, Jon. *The Second Arab Awakening.* London, 1970.

Kinglake, A.W. *Eothen.* London, 1844.

Kirkbride, Sir Alec. *From the Wings, Amman Memoirs 1947–1951.* London, 1976.

Konikoff, A. *Transjordan—An Economic Survey.* Jerusalem, 1946.

Kressel, Gideon. "Agnatic Endogamy as a Cultural Mode of Social Stratification: FBD and FBS Marriage in Jawarish." *Asian and African Studies,* vol. 14, no. 3, 1980.

———. *Individuality Against Tribality.* Tel Aviv, 1975.

———. "Realization of Agnatic Endogamy: Diachronic Perspectives." *Mediterranean Marriage Strategies and Marriage Prestations.* Ed. John Peristiany. Paris, 1984.

Landau, Bezalel. "The Blood Libel in Jewish History." *Mahanayim,* no. 80, Israel Defense Forces, Chief Military Rabbinate, Tel Aviv, 1963.

Landau, Jacob. "Blood Libels and the Persecution of the Jews in Egypt at the End of the Nineteenth Century." *Sefunot,* V, 1961, Jerusalem. (Hebrew.)

—. *Jews in Nineteenth Century Egypt.* New York, 1969.

Landes, David. "Palestine Before the Zionists." *Commentary,* February 1976.

Lane, Edward William. *Manners and Customs of the Modern Egyptians 1833–1835.* London, New York, Melbourne, 1890.

Laqueur, Walter. *A History of Zionism.* New York, 1976.

—. *The Terrible Secret, Suppression of the Truth about Hitler's "Final Solution."* Boston and Toronto, 1980.

Laskov, Shulamit. *Biluim.* Hebrew with English abstract. Jerusalem, 1979.

Lawrence, T.E. *Revolt in the Desert.* New York, 1927.

—. *Secret Dispatches from Arabia.* London, n.d.

—. *Seven Pillars of Wisdom.* London, 1935.

Lefebre, M. "Palestine's High Birthrate—A Doubtful Miracle." *Palestine Post,* December 14, 1945.

Lenczowski, George. *The Middle East in World Affairs,* 2nd ed. Ithaca, N.Y. 1956.

Levin, Nora. *The Holocaust.* New York, 1973.

Lewis, Bernard. *The Arabs in History,* 4th rev. ed. New York, Evanston, San Francisco, London, 1966.

—. *The Emergence of Modern Turkey.* London, 1961.

—. *Islam in History, Ideas, Men and Events in the Middle East.* New York, 1973.

—. "The Palestinians and the PLO, a Historical Approach." *Commentary,* January 1975.

—. *Race and Color in Islam.* New York, 1971.

—. "Studies in Ottoman Archives." *Bulletin of the School of Asian and African Studies,* XVI, 3, 1954, London.

Lewis, Bernard, ed. *Islam and the Arab World.* New York, 1976.

Lewis, Norman. "The Frontier of Settlement in Syria, 1800–1950." In Issawi, ed., *Economic History.* Chicago, 1966.

Lie, Trygve. *In the Cause of Peace.* New York, 1954.

Littman, David G. *Jews Under Muslim Rule in the Late Nineteenth Century.* London: Weiner Library Bulletin, vol. XXVIII, New Series nos. 35/36, 1975.

—. *Jews Under Muslim Rule, II, Morocco 1903–1917.* London: Weiner Library Bulletin, vol. XXVIII, New Series nos. 37/38, 1976.

—. *Protected Peoples Under Islam.* Geneva, 1975.

Longrigg, Stephen H. *Syria and Lebanon Under French Mandate.* London, 1958.

Loti, Pierre. *La Galilee.* Paris, 1895.

Luke, Sir Harry, and Keith-Roach, Edward. *Handbook of Palestine and Trans-Jordan.* London, 1934.

Lynch, W.F. *Narrative of the United States Expedition to the River Jordan and the Dead Sea.* London, 1849.

MacDonald, Robert. *The League of Arab States.* Princeton, 1965.

Main, Ernest. *Iraq.* London, 1935.

—. "Notes on Syria." In *Great Britain of the East,* August 6, 1936.

—. *Palestine at the Crossroads.* London, 1937.

Makrizi. *Histoire des Sultans Mamlouks de L'Egypte.* Trans. M. Quartremere. Paris, 1937–1945.

Mandel, Neville. *Arabs and Zionism Before World War I.* Berkeley, 1976.

Manning, the Reverend Samuel. *Those Holy Fields.* London, 1874.

Ma'oz, Moshe. "Homogeneity and Pluralism in the Middle East." In *Case Studies on Human Rights and Fundamental Freedoms, A World Survey,* The Hague, 1976.
———. *The Image of the Jew in Official Arab Literature and Communications Media.* Institute of Contemporary Jewry, Jerusalem, 1976.
———. *Ottoman Reform in Syria and Palestine 1840–1861.* Oxford, 1968.
Ma'oz, Moshe, ed. *Studies on Palestine During the Ottoman Period.* Jerusalem, 1975.
Mashbert, Michael. "Documents Concerning the American State Department and the Stateless European Jews, 1942–1944." *Jewish Social Studies,* nos. 1–2, Winter–Spring 1977.
Masriya, Yahudiya. *Les Juifs en Egypte (The Jews of Egypt).* Geneva, 1971.
Maundrell, Henry. *The Journal of Henry Maundrell from Aleppo to Jerusalem, 1697.* London, 1848.
Mayer, L.A. *Mamluk Costume: A Survey.* Geneva, 1952.
McCallum, Elizabeth P. *The Nationalist Crusade in Syria.* New York, 1928.
McCarthy, Justin A. "Nineteenth Century Egyptian Population." *Middle Eastern Studies,* vol. 12, October 1976.
Meinertzhagen, Colonel R. *Middle East Diary, 1917–1956.* London, 1959.
Memmi, Albert. *Jews and Arabs.* Chicago, 1975.
Meron, Dr. Ya'akov. *The "Complicating" Element of the Arab-Israeli Conflict.* Jerusalem, 1977.
Miller, David Hunt. *My Diary at the Conference of Paris,* 22 vols. New York, 1924.
Mills, E. *Census of Palestine, 1931.* Alexandria, 1933.
Milson, Menahem. "Medieval and Modern Intellectual Traditions in the Arab World." *Daedalus,* Summer 1972.
———. *Society and Political Structure in the Arab World.* New York, 1973.
Minkin, Jacob S. *The World of Moses Maimonides.* New York, 1957.
Mogannam, Matiel. *The Arab Women and the Palestine Problem.* London, 1937.
Montefiore, M. *Diaries,* ed. L. Loewe. London, 1890.
Morse, Arthur. *While Six Million Died.* New York, 1967.
Mossek, M. *Palestine Immigration Policy Under Sir Herbert Samuel.* London, 1978.
Murray. *Murray's Handbook for Travellers in Syria and Palestine.* 1858. (Reprinted in *Encyclopaedia Britannica,* 8th ed., 1860.)
Nawratzki, Curt. *Die Jüdische Kolonisation Palestinas.* Munich, 1914.
Niebuhr, Reinhold. "Jews After the War." *The Nation,* February 28, 1942.
Neumann, A. *The Jews in Spain.* Philadelphia, 1942.
Olin, S. *Travels in Egypt, Arabia Petraea and the Holy Land.* New York, 1843.
Oliphant, Lawrence. *Haifa or Life in Modern Palestine.* London, 1887.
Paikert, C.G. *The German Exodus.* U.S. Committee for Refugees, Biennial Reports. The Hague, Netherlands, 1962.
Palestine Research Center. *Palestinian Leaders Discuss the New Challenges for the Resistance.* Beirut, 1974.
Parkes, James William. *A History of Palestine from 135 A.D. to Modern Times.* New York, 1949.
———. *Whose Land? History of the Peoples of Palestine.* Harmondsworth, Great Britain, 1970.
Patai, Raphael. *Israel Between East and West.* Westport, Conn., 1970.
Pearlman, Maurice. *Mufti of Jerusalem.* London, 1947.
Pearlman, Moshe. *The Army of Israel.* New York, 1950.

Peters, Joan. "A Conversation with Dayan." *Harper's,* November 1976.
———. "An Exchange of Populations." *Commentary,* August 1976.
———. "In Search of Moderate Egyptians." *Commentary,* May 1975.
Peterson, William. *Population.* London, 1969.
Pickthall, Mohammed Marmaduke, trans. *The Meaning of the Glorious Koran.* New York, 1953.
Pinner, Walter. *How Many Arab Refugees?* London, 1959.
———. *The Legend of the Arab Refugees.* Tel Aviv, 1967.
Pinson, Marc. "Demographic Warfare: An Aspect of Ottoman and Russian Policy, 1854–1866." Ph.D. Dissertation, Harvard University, 1970.
Pipes, Daniel. "How Important is the PLO?" *Commentary, April 1983.*
———. *In the Path of God: Islam and Political Power.* New York, 1983.
Plascov, A. *Palestinian Refugees in Jordan, 1948–1957.* London, 1981.
Polk, William. *The United States and the Arab World.* Cambridge, Mass., 1975.
Pool, David de Sola. "Centrality of the Holy Land in Jewish Life." From *The Folk,* vol. II of the Jewish Library, ed. Leo Jung (New York: 1968).
Porath, Y. *The Emergence of the Palestinian Arab National Movement 1918–1929.* London, 1974.
Prinz, Joachim. *The Secret Jews.* New York, 1973.
Prittie, Terence. "Middle East Refugees." In Curtis et al., eds., *Palestinians.* New Brunswick, N.J., 1975.
———. *Miracle in the Desert.* New York, 1967.
Prittie, Terence, and Dineen, Bernard. *The Double Exodus: A Study of Arab and Jewish Refugees in the Middle East* (pamphlet). London, n.d.
Quandt, William B., Jabber, Fuad, and Lesch, Ann Mosley. *The Politics of Palestinian Nationalism.* Berkeley, 1973.
Rabin, Yitzhak. *The Rabin Memoirs.* Boston, Toronto, 1979.
Riebenfeld, Paul. "The Integrity of Palestine." *Midstream,* August–September, 1975.
———. "Israel, Jordan and Palestine." Unpublished manuscript.
Rihani, Ameen. *Around the Coasts of Arabia.* London, 1930.
Roth, Cecil. *A History of the Marranos.* Philadelphia, 1932.
Roumani, Maurice. *The Case of the Jews from Arab Countries: A Neglected Issue.* Jerusalem, 1975.
Royal Institute of International Affairs. *Great Britain and Palestine, 1915–1945.* London and New York, 1946.
Rubin, Neville. "Africa and Refugees." *African Affairs* (Journal of Royal African Society, University of London), July 1974.
Runciman, Steven. *A History of the Crusades,* 3 vols. Harmondsworth, Middlesex, England, 1965.
Ruppin, Arthur. *The Jews in the Modern World.* London, 1934.
———. *Memoirs, Diaries, Letters.* New York, 1971.
———. *Syria: An Economic Survey.* New York, 1918.
Sabagh, George. "The Demography of the Middle East." *Middle East Studies Association Bulletin 4,* May 15, 1970.
Sachar, Howard. *History of Israel.* New York, 1976.
Sasson, David. *History of the Jews in Baghdad.* Letchworth, 1949.
Sayigh, Rosemary. "Sources of Palestinian Nationalism: A Study of a Palestinian Camp in Lebanon." *Journal of Palestinian Studies,* vol. 6, no. 3, 1977.

Schama, Simon. *Two Rothschilds and the Land of Israel.* New York, 1978.
Schechtman, Joseph B. *The Arab Refugee Problem.* New York, 1952.
————. *European Population Transfers 1939–45.* New York, 1946.
————. *On Wings of Eagles, The Plight, Exodus and Homecoming of Oriental Jewry.* New York, 1961.
Schwartzfuchs, Simon. "Persecution of Jews in the Land of Islam." *L'Arche,* December 1973.
Shaler, William. *Sketches of Algiers.* Boston, 1826.
Sharf, Andrew. *The British Press and Jews Under Nazi Rule.* London, 1964.
Shaw, Stanford. "The Ottoman Census System and Population, 1831–1914." *International Journal of Middle East Studies,* vol. 9, no. 3, August 1978.
Shaw, Thomas. *Travels and Observations Relating to Several Parts of Barbary and the Levant.* London, 1767.
Scholem, Gershom. *Sabbatai Sevi, the Mystical Messiah.* Princeton, 1973.
Sinai, Anne, and Pollack, Allen, eds. *Hashemite Kingdom of Jordan and the West Bank.* New York, 1977.
————. *The Syrian Arab Republic.* New York, 1976.
Smilianskaya, I.M. "The Disintegration of Feudal Relations in Syria and Lebanon in the Middle of the Nineteenth Century." In Charles Issawi, ed. *The Economic History of the Middle East.* Chicago and London, 1966.
Smith, George Adam. *The Historical Geography of the Holy Land.* London, 1931.
Sobel, Lester, ed. *Political Terrorism.* New York, 1975.
Soussan, Mordecai. "L'éveil Politique Sepharade" (Political Awakening of the Sephardim). Doctoral thesis, Faculté de Droit et de Science Politique d'Aix-Marseilles, 1975.
Starushenko, G. *The Principle of National Self-Determination in Soviet Foreign Policy.* Moscow, n.d.
Stillman, Norman A. *The Jews of Arab Lands: A History and Source Book.* Philadelphia, 1979.
Stoyanovsky, J. *The Mandate for Palestine.* London, New York, Toronto, 1928.
Sussnitzki, A.J. "Zur Gliederung wirtschaftlicher Arbeit nach Nationalitäten in der Turkei." *Archiv für Wirtschaftsforschung im Orient,* II, 1917. In Issawi, ed., *Economic History.*
Sykes, Christopher. *Crossroads to Israel.* London, 1965.
Tabbarah, Riad. *Population and Human Resources in Arab Development.* Peking: International Roundtable Conference on Demography, October 20–27, 1980.
Thicknesse, S.G. *Arab Refugees: A Survey of Resettlement Possibilities.* London, 1949.
Thompson, Dorothy. "Refugees, A World Problem." *Foreign Affairs,* April 1938.
Thomson, William M. *The Land and the Book.* London, 1873.
Trietsch, David. *Jüdische Emigration und Kolonisation.* Berlin, 1923.
————. *Palaestina Handbuch,* 2nd ed. Berlin-Schmargedorf, 1910.
Tristram, H.B. *The Land of Israel: A Journal of Travels in Palestine.* London, 1865.
Turki, Fawaz. *The Disinherited: Journal of a Palestinian Exile.* New York and London, 1972.
Twain, Mark. *The Innocents Abroad.* London, 1881.
Twersky, Isadore, ed. *A Maimonides Reader.* New York, 1972.
Vambery, Arminius. *Arminius Vambery, His Life and Adventures Written by Himself.* London, 1884.

————. *Travels in Central Asia.* London, 1864.

Vatikiotis, P.J. *Nasser and His Generation.* London, 1978.

Vilnay, Zev. *Palestine Guide.* Jerusalem, 1942.

Vishniak, Mark. *Transfer of Populations as a Means of Solving Problems of Minorities.* New York, 1942.

Vital, David. *Origins of Zionism.* Oxford, 1975.

Volney, Count Constantine F. *Travels Through Syria and Egypt in the Years 1783, 1784, 1785.* London, 1787 (2nd edition, 1788).

Voss, Carl Hermann. *Answers on the Palestine Question.* 1949.

————. *The Palestine Problem Today: Israel and Its Neighbors.* Boston, 1953.

Warriner, Doreen. *Land and Poverty in the Middle East.* London and New York, 1948.

————. *Land Reforms and Development in the Middle East, Study of Egypt, Syria and Iraq.* London, 1957.

————. "Land Tenure in the Fertile Crescent." In Issawi, ed., *The Economic History of the Middle East,* Chicago and London, 1966.

Wasserstein, Bernard. *Britain and the Jews of Europe—1939–1945.* Oxford, 1979.

Weizmann, Chaim. *Trial and Error.* New York, 1949.

Wilson, C.T. *Peasant Life in the Holyland.* London, 1906.

Wise, Stephen. *Challenging Years.* London, 1951.

Witcamp, F. T. *The Refugee Problem in the Middle East.* The Hague, 1959.

World Jewish Congress. *The Jews of French Morocco and Tunisia.* New York, 1952.

Wright, Quincy. *Mandates Under the League of Nations.* Chicago, 1930.

Ye'or, Bat. *Oriental Jewry.* Geneva, 1979.

Index

Jewish immigration (*cont.*)
Palestine's "absorptive capacity" in,
304–305, 311, 317–318, 323, 330, 334,
336–338, 344, 350, 377, 380–381
post-World War II, 384–390
quotas in, 275–276, 296–297, 318–320,
336–337, 341–350, 359, 370–371, 385–388
refugee ships repulsed in, 362, 365–370
state land in, 275, 318–319
Turkish restrictions vs., 273, 275
"uncultivable" land in, 323, 381
violent reprisals against, 351, 353, 358–359
see also White Paper (1939)
Jewish immigration, Turkish restrictions on,
202–215, 217, 251, 259, 326
British restrictions vs., 273, 275
effendi encouragement of, 201, 204–206,
209–211
enforcement of, 204–209, 212, 214–215, 275
Jewish circumvention of, 212
reasons for, 203–204
"red tickets" in, 208–209, 214
Jewish refugees, Sephardic, 4–5, 10, 25–33, 63,
93–115, 155
Arab "invitations" to, 11–12, 29–31, 60*n*,
70–71, 98, 127–128
Arab refugees exchanged for, *see* exchange
of populations
Arab terrorism against, 29, 355
"hard-line" attitudes of, 98–99, 409
hardships of, 94–96
Israeli society strained by, 31, 95, 409
as majority population, 79, 408–409
nostalgia of, 96–97, 100, 103–104
number of, 11, 20, 31, 33, 38, 43, 50, 54, 57,
60, 116–118, 400
obscurity of, 4, 25–26, 28, 31, 71, 117–118,
406
old vs. new, 95–96, 98
organization of, 30–31
propaganda value of, 12, 28–31
property left by, 20, 25, 29, 40, 43, 45, 65,
70, 78*n*, 103, 107
refugee status denied to, 401
religiosity of, 41, 93–94, 101, 103–104
temporary housing of, 94–96, 104
see also Arab Jews; Holocaust, refugees
from
Jewish settlement, British restrictions on, 241,
318–320, 324–325, 327, 393
on behalf of "landless Arab cultivators,"
299–302, 318–319, 321, 323–325, 340
creation of Transjordan and, 239, 241, 300,
318
Land Transfer Regulations and, 320
Mandate violated by, 275, 299–300, 337
state land in, 299, 321, 324–325
Jewish settlement, Turkish restrictions on,
202–203, 208, 211–212, 337

Jewish State, The (Der Judenstaat) (Herzl),
208
Jews:
early dominance and settlement in Saudi
Arabia, 38–40, 46, 50–51, 67–68, 84, 89,
92, 94, 143–144, 146
Holocaust in self-image of, 7
Jerusalem as spiritual center for, 88–90, 176
Nazis compared to, 37, 174–175, 347, 353
occupations of, 39, 41, 151, 167, 173,
200–201, 203, 345, 368, 383
"Palestinian Arabs'" propaganda believed
by, 174, 397–398
racial theories invoked against, 37
see also "Palestine," continuous Jewish
presence in; "Palestinian Jews"
Jews, Arab, *see* Arab Jews
Jews, European:
Arab Jews compared to, 75–76, 81, 87, 94,
101, 133–134
assimilation of, 133
Nazi persecution of, *see* Holocaust
pilgrimages of, 85–88, 90, 140–141, 177,
179, 182
"shtetl" living of, 81, 101
Jews in Arab Lands, The (Stillman), 52–53
Jezreel Valley, 159, 202, 301
Jiryis, Sabri, 29–30, 79
John of Wurzburg, 156
John Paul II, Pope, 5, 221
Johnson, Lyndon B., 115
Joint Distribution Committee, American
Jewish, 118
Jordan:
Arab emigration from, 264–265, 401
Eastern Palestine as, 235–241, 330–331
historical Jewish presence in, 117–118
as Palestinian-Arab state, 240–241, 267–268,
393, 397, 409
"Palestinian law of return" excludes Jews
in, 240
PLO attacked by, 240, 397
refugee population in, 18–19, 399
refugees granted citizenship in, 16, 240, 393,
401
territory seized by (1948), 401
West Bank claimed by, 13–14
see also Transjordan
Jordan Valley, historical Jewish presence in,
82
"Joseph," testimony of, 112–113
Josephus Flavius, 67, 147
Journal of Palestine Studies, 15*n*
Judah Halevy, 80, 87–88, 90
Julia Mammae, 147

Kaddoumi, Farouk, 11–12
Kader, Abdel Razak, 196
Kairouan, Jews expelled from, 58
Kamal, Wasef, 363

596   *Index*